THE BARGAIN HUNTER'S BIBLE

THE GOOD DEAL DIRECTORY 2003

NOELLE WALSH

CARLTON BOOKS

THIS IS A CARLTON BOOK

First published in 1993 by
Macmillan Reference, a division of
Pan Macmillan Publishers Limited

This edition published by Carlton Books Limited 2002
20 Mortimer Street
London W1T 3JW

ISBN 1 84222 650 9

A CIP catalogue record for this book is available from the British Library

Research team: particular thanks to Tracy Campbell and Micola Nevile

Editorial Manager: Judith More
Executive Editor: Zia Mattocks
Jacket Design: Barbara Zuñiga
Editors: Sarah Townsend and Sian Parkhouse
Typeset by: E-Type, Liverpool
Production Manager: Sarah Corteel

Printed and bound in Great Britain

Dear Reader

We hope you enjoy reading this book, the definitive guide to value-for-money shopping in Britain.

We also run Discount Designer Fashion Sales at the elegant Pavilion at Ascot Racecourse in Berkshire every late October/early November and May and at Ripley Castle, North Yorkshire in mid-October. These sales feature up to 100 top fashion and accessory companies selling ends of lines, last season's stock and overruns at fantastically reduced prices.

If you'd like to know more about how to apply for a ticket, send us a card with your name and address to the address below and we will send you the information you require.

Contents

Welcome to the tenth edition of The Good Deal Directory, packed with more bargain outlets than ever before, a massive 3,300 value-for-money businesses.

The book goes from strength to strength, reflecting the marketplace that it features. As retailers learn to respond more quickly to consumer tastes and trends, they also seek ways to clear stock that didn't take off sufficiently quickly to merit any more time in their high-rental shops. By clearing unsold stock quickly, they have more money to buy new items and more space to feature them

Factory shopping villages continue to evolve and grow. Each of the major operators has put their own stamp on their outlet centres, changing tenants as other, better-known brand names appear, or as their customer base changes and new brands appeal more.

Multi-brand companies, or those that don't spend sufficient on advertising to merit top brand-name status, are not fêted by the factory shopping villages. Instead, they quite happily set up their own individual factory shop. With lower overheads, they can offer a better deal than in the villages – except perhaps at sale time, when prices may converge.

The latter tends to happen much more in the home sector. Not so much for the small goods – cutlery, china, tableware, glassware – which are all features of most shopping villages, but for the larger items such as sofas, tables, chairs, office furniture, kitchens, carpets, fabric and curtains, which are hardly seen in factory outlet centres. And when they have been seen, they tend to disappear quickly. Great bargains can be found in all of these product areas if you know where to look (go to the chapter for Furniture and Soft Furnishings and you'll find everything from Habitat to Wesley Barrell, Slumberdown to Silent Night.)

Keep the book handy in your car and use the website of the same name to check up on showroom and factory shop sales taking place on a day-to-day basis, as well as to look up where favourite brand names can be found at discount prices. The website is easy to use and has a special members' section, where you can access information on outlets that had not yet opened when this edition of the book went to press. That way, you can keep up to date on all the new shops. Anyone who buys a book can become a member of The Good Deal Directory Club. It doesn't cost anything. You will, however, need a membership card and password to obtain entry to the special members' area of the website. To apply, simply write to The Good Deal Directory, PO Box 4, Lechlade, Gloucestershire GL7 3YB with your name and address, stating that you have recently bought a copy of *The Good Deal Directory 2003*.

While factory shops and factory shopping villages thrive as we all learn to mix and match full-price and discounted items, what I call the permanent discount outlet sector is also increasing at a massive rate. Matalan and TK Maxx – offshoot of the well-known TJ Maxx in the USA – are both adding new branches month by month. Both offer a mix of fashion for all the family, homewares and an ever-changing selection of merchandise, from perfumes and tights to gifts and beauty products, luggage and handbags.

TK Maxx operate by buying huge quantities of unsold stock from well-known brand names and famous designers. Although they may only pay the supplier a small amount per item, because they have well over 100 branches, they can buy huge amounts, clearing all one company's unsold stock in one fell swoop. They never advertise the brands they sell but they often feature the top designer names in fashion, shoes and homewares. However, their outlets are fairly basic and you do need to be a bargain hunter and have some time to spare to make great finds.

This book also covers dress agencies, those places where gently worn designer clothes and shoes go when you're tired of them or realise they were a mistake, and salvage outlets. Once, salvage outlets were the place to find that authentic wooden floor for your Victorian cottage. Now, many of the best finds have been found and prices are higher than they were ten years ago. However, they are still a great place to go if you are keen to renovate your home in the correct period, and if they can't find what you want, many of them now offer very realistic reproductions.

Fabrics

Some companies, such as Osborne & Little, Colefax and Fowler and Designers Guild, hold their own 'warehouse' sales, reducing stock significantly to clear it to existing customers whom they mail. If you want to find out about these clearance sales, write to the company and ask for your name to be put on the mailing list (the addresses are in the book under Furniture & Soft Furnishings, London, Designer Sales).

There are hundreds of fabric discount shops countrywide, such as Knickerbean, which has four outlets selling famous-name bargains as well as fabrics sourced directly from the same mills and manufacturers as the 'top names', both here and abroad. They offer the same top quality, in the latest colours and designs, at relatively lower prices, because they are buying and selling directly and cutting out the middlemen.

If you're looking for curtain fabric, try one of the many second-hand curtains businesses countrywide first. They stock a wide range of curtains, many of which are from show houses or are interior designers' mistakes, or simply bought by people who didn't like them once they hung them. Others are made from incredibly expensive fabric, lined, interlined and weighted, are in almost-perfect condition and are sold at between one-third and one-half of the as-new price. Most second-hand curtains shops let you take the curtains home and try them out against your windows before they cash your cheque so that you, too, won't make a costly mistake.

Kitchen and Dining Room

Brand names such as Remington, Pifco, Moulinex and Swan are all available in factory shops, where you can also buy Oneida cutlery, Swan fryers, Kenwood food mixers, kitchen knives, Russell Hobbs kettles, Tower and Le Creuset pans and Krups kitchen appliances at discounts of at least 25%. If a new food processor comes out, shops no longer want to sell the old one, so it goes back to the factory for selling in the factory shop. Occasionally, items are returned because of damaged packaging (at which time they are rechecked by factory technicians) and then sold at discount prices.

The result of all this is that for you, the customer, there is greater choice than ever before. As long as you are prepared to wait, and don't buy when an item is first on the market, you can get some great bargains.

Factory Shopping Centres

Factory shopping centres – the smallest has 12 shops, the largest more than 140 – are for a different type of bargain shopper than the traditional stand-alone factory outlet. The latter attracts those who take pleasure in the hunt: in finding an out-of-the-way, sometimes unattractive shed on an industrial estate miles off the beaten track. The level of attractiveness of the site is usually directly related to the price of the goods on sale – the more unattractive the actual factory outlet is, the lower the prices. However, you can't go shopping with a list at these individual outlets. Factory shopping centres, on the other hand, offer a higher level of certainty. If there are 140-plus shops – as at the McArthurGlen Designer Outlet in Cheshire Oaks, South Wirral – you'd have to be pretty picky not to find something you like and can afford. The choice is usually enormous – most of the shops are fashion oriented although they now offer a growing selection of children's goods, luggage, jewellery, shoes, cookware, toys, glassware and electrical goods. But the choice comes at a price. On the whole, prices are higher at factory shopping centres than at stand-alone factory shops – except at traditional sale times when the village shops also slash prices in order to clear stock.

Factory shopping centres in this country began with the Freeport Leisure Village in Hornsea on the East Yorkshire coast in the late Eighties. This was followed by the first purpose-built factory shopping centre, Clarks Village in Street, Somerset, built around an already-existing shoe museum and shoe discount town. In the early Nineties, the American developers came over here, factory shopping centres in the USA having reached a plateau. Many of them tied up with an existing British company in joint ventures. Being American, they thought BIG. Their centres tended to be much, much bigger than the traditional British ones, with twice the number of shops. Now that they have reached a plateau here, too, they have moved onto the Continent.

Outlet Villages

Atlantic Village Outlet Centre, Clovelly Road, off A39, west of Bideford, North Devon; 01237 422544 (30 shops, interactive maze)

Bicester Outlet Shopping Village, junction 9 of M40, Pingle Drive, Bicester, Oxfordshire OX6 7WD; 01869 323200 (approx. 90 shops)

Brighton Marina Village, Brighton, East Sussex BN2 5WB; 01273 818504 (11 shops)

Clacton Factory Outlet Village, Stephenson Road West, Clacton, Essex; 01255 479595 (approx. 48 shops)

Clarks Village, Farm Road, Street, Somerset BA16 OBB (junction 23 of M5); 01458 840064 (approx. 57 shops)

Evesham Country Park, Country Park Management, Evesham, at northern end of the Evesham by-pass at its junction with Stratford Road, Worcestershire WR11 4TP; 01386 41661 (factory shops, garden centre, leisure facilities)

Festival Park Factory Outlet Shopping, Festival Park, Victoria, Ebbw Vale, South Wales NP23 8FP; 01495 350010 (40 shops)

Freeport Braintree Outlet Village, Charter Way, Chapel Hill, Braintree, Essex CM77 8YH; 01376 348168 (80 shops)

Freeport Castleford, Carrwood Road, Glasshoughton, Castleford, off Junction 32 of M52, West Yorkshire WF10 4SB; 01977 520153 (75 shops)

Freeport Scotland Outlet Village, Five Sisters, Westwood, West Calder, West Lothian EH55 8QB; 01501 763488 (25 shops)

Freeport Shopping Village, Anchorage Road, Fleetwood, junction 3 of M55, Lancashire FY7 6AE; 01253 877377 (approx. 40 shops)

Freeport Talke Outlet Mall, Pit Lane, Talke Pits, Stoke-on-Trent, Staffordshire ST7 1XD; 01782 774113 (approx. 30 factory shops)

Galleria Outlet Centre, Comet Way, Hatfield, Herts AL10 0XR; 01707 278301 (80 shops)

Gretna Gateway Outlet Village, Glasgow Road, Gretna DG16 6GG; 01461 339028 (30 factory shops with 50 planned)

Gunwharf Quays, Portsmouth Harbour, Hampshire PO1 3TZ; 023 9283 6700 (65 factory shops, cinema, bowling, comedy club)

Hornsea Freeport Shopping Village, Rolston Road, Hornsea, East Yorkshire HU18 1UT; 01964 534211 (more than 40 shops)

K Village, Lound Road, Kendal, junction 36 of M6, Cumbria LA9 7DA; 01539 732363 (12 shops)

Loch Lomond Factory Outlets, Main Street, Alexandria, on the A82, Loch Lomond, Scotland G83 0UG; 01389 710077 (approx. 18 shops)

Lowry Designer Outlet Centre, The Quays, Salford Quays, Manchester M5 2WZ; 0161 848 1800 (factory shopping centre with 80 shops in a site next to the Manchester Ship Canal and across the bridge from the Imperial War Museum North)

Massons Mill Shopping Village, Derby Road, Matlock Bath, Matlock, Derbyshire DE4 3PY; 01629 760208 (anchored by Edinburgh Woollen Mills and set on four floors, this shopping village is set in a regenerated eighteenth-century mill building with a working textile museum and conference facilities)

McArthurGlen Designer Outlet Ashford, Kimberley Way, Ashford, Kent TN24 0SD; 01233 895900 (70 shops)

McArthurGlen Cheshire Oaks Designer Outlet Village, junction 10 of M53, Kinsey Road, near Ellesmere Port, South Wirral CH65 9JJ; 0800 316 4352 (approx. 140 shops)

McArthurGlen Designer Outlet Derbyshire, Mansfield Road, South Normanton, Alfreton, junction 28 of M1, Derbyshire DE55 2ER; 01773 545000 (up to 74 different stores but not in traditional shop format)

McArthurGlen Designer Outlet Livingston, Almondvale Avenue, Livingston, junction 3 of M8, West Lothian EH54 6QX; 01506 423600 (80 factory shops)

McArthurGlen Designer Outlet Village Great Western, Kemble Drive, Churchward Village, junction 16 of M4, Swindon, Wilts SN2 2DY; 0800 316 4352 (more than 100 shops)

McArthurGlen Designer Outlet Wales, The Derwen, Bridgend, junction 36 of M4, South Wales CF32 9SU; 01656 665700 (approx. 80 shops)

McArthurGlen Designer Outlet York, St Nicholas Avenue, Fulford, Junction A19 and A64, York, North Yorkshire YO19 4TA; 01904 682700 (120 shops)

Peak Village, Chatsworth Road, Rowsley, on the A6 between Bakewell and Matlock, Derbyshire DE4 2JE; 01629 735326 (20 factory shops and leisure facilities)

Pendle Village Shopping Outlet, Hollin Bank, Brierfield, Nelson, junction 12 of M65, Lancashire; 01282 605004 HOMEWARES/01282 605023 FASHION (a huge mill shop with different areas selling fashion for men and women, home furnishings, bedding, towels, pine and cane furniture, dining sets, three-piece suites, carpets and rugs)

Royal Quays Factory Outlet Centre, Coble Dene, North Shields, Newcastle-upon-Tyne, Tyne & Wear NE29 6DW; 0191 296 3743 (42 shops)

Sterling Mills Designer Outlet Village, Tillicoultry, near Stirling, midway between M9 and M90, Clackmananshire, Scotland FK13 6HQ; 01259 752100 (22 outlets with more planned)

Whiteley Village, off M27 between Southampton and Portsmouth, junction 9 of M27, Hampshire PO15 7LJ; 01489 886886 (50 factory shops)

Wilton Factory Shopping Village, Minster Street, Wilton, near Salisbury, Wiltshire SP2 0RS; 01722 741 211 (approx. 10 factory shops)
The Yorkshire Outlet, White Rose Way, junction 3 of M18, Doncaster Lakeside, South Yorks DN4 5JH; 01302 366444 (more than 30 shops)

Factory Shops

Run by the manufacturer or a representative of the manufacturer (who may also be a retailer), factory shops sell manufacturer's surplus stock – cancelled orders, returned merchandise from the store, slow-selling or over-produced items, seconds, last season's stock or discontinued lines – at prices much lower than those in the high street shops that the factory supplies. A few global manufacturers bring in stock from other countries, which may not have been on sale here before. A few others make up clothes from the same fabric that was used to make the clothes originally on sale in high street shops. Thus, if they have hundreds of a particular skirt left over but only a few dozen of its matching jackets, but plenty of the fabric, they will make up jackets to match. They will then not be able to give two prices – an original and a discounted price – for these items.

Discounts vary but in general they are higher in the fashion sector where an outfit can be out of date very quickly and where mark-ups can be as high as 280%, and lower in ceramics and glassware. There are far fewer homeware factory shops than fashion ones because for a housewares retailer whose mark-up is not very high, half-price is not profitable, whereas if you're a fashion manufacturer with a high mark-up, half-price still leaves a significant profit margin. The older the item, the cheaper the price. As a general rule, you can expect at least 30% off, and up to 80%.

Getting the best out of factory shopping

1 The vast majority of customers visit factory shopping village at weekends, resulting in queues at the tills, parking problems and less chance of getting a table at the centre's restaurants. If you can, shop at villages during the week when they are usually quiet.
2 Although they don't advertise the fact, most factory shopping villages discount their products even further at traditional high street sale times (January and June). So, if you only visit the villages twice a year, phone and check the sale times before you go. The disadvantage, however, is that you will be getting the last of the line in stock, so colour and size choices will be limited. This is offset by the really good bargains.
3 Keep your eyes and ears open all the time. On a day trip, look out for signs for out-of-the-way factory shops; scour the small ads of your local papers for one-day factory shop sales.
4 Put your name down on the mailing list of factory shops you visit. Fabric factory shops, for instance, often hold twice-yearly sales at their warehouses to which they invite customers and sell last year's stock at greatly reduced prices. Many fashion factory shops have one- or two-day sales when even the reductions are reduced.
5 Tourist information centres are useful sources of free information on factory shops in their area.
6 If it's a particular brand name you're after, such as Jaeger, Burberry or Aquascutum, and you want a specific item (a raincoat or blazer) ring first and check their stock. There are certain times of year when it is very low. The staff are usually very helpful.
7 Check if the item is a second – usually there is a label on the garment stating why this is so. For example, Aquascutum label their seconds 'Slightly Imperfect' and mark

on an illustration of the garment where the imperfection lies. You cannot return a second if it says what's wrong with it – although all your statutory rights are in place at factory shops.

8 Never travel a long way without phoning first to check opening hours and stock levels. It's also a good idea to phone for directions, as many of the individual factory shops are in out-of-the-way, hard-to-find places.
9 If you're looking to be the height of fashion, factory shopping isn't for you – unless you're a natural stylist and can mix looks to modernise. Fashion factory shopping is great for children's clothes, jeans, leisurewear, sweaters, underwear and classic items such as blazers, coats and raincoats.
10 If you see something you like, buy it. You won't find it again.
11 If you want to pay by credit card, check first, as some of the smaller, individual factory shops don't accept them.
12 If you're looking for small electrical appliances for the kitchen, it's unlikely that you will find the latest gadget, but there will be good end-of-line bargains.
13 Whatever the condition of the outlet, your rights are just the same as if you were shopping in the mainstream. You are covered by the Sale of Goods Act and the Consumer Protection Act.
14 Factory outlets sell limited ranges, colours and sizes, so don't expect co-ordinated ranges or to be able to exchange an item for the same thing but bigger/smaller a few days later.
15 Some of the major high street stores insist on the manufacturer cutting out their label before selling in the factory outlet, so some of the goods may be unbranded. This applies even to the washing instructions in some cases.
16 If there isn't a double price on the price tag (the original selling price crossed out and replaced with the reduced one), it may be that this item has been specially made for the factory shop from leftover fabric used in the manufacture of the original garment. Sometimes, factories are left with hundreds of a particular skirt but very few of the matching blouses, so they make up more blouses from the same fabric. Watch out that the colours match exactly. Or it may be that the item was originally made for export and has never been on sale in the UK.
17 Don't always believe what the size tag tells you – some items are seconds because they are incorrectly marked up.
18 Before you travel, sit down with a map and plot your journey. Often, there are three or four factory shops within a few miles of each other or on your route, so you can make the most of your trip.
19 Carry room and window measurements with you if visiting carpet or fabric factory shops, and children's ages and sizes with you if visiting toy or clothing outlets. What you see when you visit is all there usually is of that item.
20 In the more traditional factory shops, you may not find items as flatteringly presented as they are in department and high street stores. Be prepared to rummage.

Permanent discount outlets

These are run by entrepreneurs who buy in stock from a variety of sources: overseas manufacturers' clearance lines; bankrupt stock; fortuitous purchasing (perhaps from a designer who needs cash quickly); other full-price shops' slower-selling lines; returns from department stores; overstocks from the chain stores (although these usually have the labels removed). Those outlets selling clothes from Marks & Spencer usually have to agree to remove the St Michael label and any other identifying label such as the care label. Although now, Marks & Spencer has their own factory shops within a small number of factory shopping villages.

Permanent discount outlets also include all the shops run by mail order companies clearing their old catalogue stock. These are often very good value for large electrical equipment, although these items sell out so quickly that you almost have to visit the shop every day in order to buy one. Many mail order companies now also sell designer-led merchandise and some of this makes its way into these clearance shops, but you have to be willing to scour the rails. Remember that half price in these shops isn't necessarily half price, in that in the major companies up to 11% is added to the cost of items to cover direct marketing costs and mailing of catalogues, so half price is actually a discount of 39%.

Dress Agencies

Have you ever wondered how some women always manage to look smartly dressed? Have they just got lashings of natural style, a family member who owns a dress shop or simply money to burn? It's just as likely that they have discovered the secret of second-hand clothes shopping.

Now called dress agencies by those anxious to dispel visions of jumble sale leftovers, these recession-spawned shops are a boon both to those wishing to spend money and those wanting to earn some. As a customer, you have the opportunity to buy good-quality clothes at very reasonable prices, and you can also clear out your own 'mistakes' and make a bit of money.

Dress agency owners are very particular about which clothes they choose to sell. They have to be – the quality of their merchandise reflects how successful they – and, ultimately, you if you're a seller – will be. If you're looking for designer labels, choose the best areas of town to shop in. For example if the dress agency is in London's Beauchamp Place or Hampstead, the labels will be the best: Armani, DKNY, Valentino, Bruce Oldfield. If it's in the high street, Suburbia, there will probably be a good mix of labels such as Jaeger and Country Casuals as well as a sprinkling of high street favourites: Next, Principles, Marks & Spencer. But dress agency owners rely on the clients who bring in clothes to sell, so one visit may yield a goldmine of covetable clothes; another just fool's gold.

Dress agencies only accept cleaned, pressed clothes in mint condition. A price is agreed, of which most agencies take 40%–50% as their commission. The clothes are put on the rails for a set period of time – usually 6–12 weeks. If, after that time, an item hasn't sold, some proprietors will talk to the owner about reducing the price. If it still doesn't sell, it will be returned to the owner. Uncollected items are usually sent to charity shops.

Dress agencies are usually friendly places – many offer coffee or tea and some even have small coffee rooms where you can relax and read a paper. The best ones build up a rapport with their regular customers, letting them know if something comes in which might be of interest.

Getting the best out of dress agencies

1 If you're looking for top designer labels, choose a dress agency in an expensive neighbourhood. They're most likely to have the sort of clientele who dress in the best and then sell it on.

2 If your child is about to start a new school and requires an expensive uniform, find out if there is a dress agency dealing in childrenswear in the vicinity of the school – there are bound to be some second-hand uniforms there.
3 Clearing out your own wardrobe is a good way to find out if a dress agency is right for you. If they sift carefully through your clothes, insisting on a certain quality and on the garments being dry-cleaned, then you know they're good enough to buy from. It's also a way of making money for yourself from clothes which you no longer wear or which were mistakes.
4 Instead of spending money hiring an evening outfit for that once-a-year special occasion, buy your evening gown/cocktail dress from a dress agency. Whether you hire or buy, you'll still be wearing a garment that's already been worn, and you might as well have use of it for another occasion.
5 Dress agencies are great places to buy almost brand-new ski wear and horse-riding gear, which are sold there by people who tried skiing and didn't like it or who had a short-lived passion for horses.
6 If the garment or accessory you're buying is a top designer label and that's the main reason you're buying it, insist on that fact being written on your receipt. If it turns out to be a fake, you will then have evidence that you bought what you were told was the real thing.

Architectural salvage

Someone else's rubbish could be your treasure. Architectural salvage businesses deal in reclaimed items from homes and gardens. Some specialise in, say, garden statuary, fireplaces or floorboards. They tend to be vast caverns and you need to have a keen eye. Many now offer reproduction facilities.

Showroom sales

Like any business, the fashion trade has surplus stock and, precisely because it is a fashion business, it can't hang on to it for too long before it becomes unsellable. Showroom sales are held by a variety of different people: wholesalers who haven't sold in to shops all the stock they bought; agents who have lots of last season's samples which they use to show buyers (remember, 'last season' in fashion language is usually 'this season' in yours – thus, by May, summer stock may be last season's, just as the weather is hotting up sufficiently for you to buy it for this); designers who control the design, manufacture and wholesaling of their clothes who may have a mixture of samples, unsold items, returned goods and overstock; and individuals who gather together surplus stock from a variety of different sources, hire a venue and sell it to the general public, taking a cut of the total sales.

The majority of these sales take place in London and many are advertised in the days preceding the sale in the *Evening Standard* newspaper. (There is also a list of Designer Showroom Sales in this book in the Womenswear chapter under Designer Sales.) They're well worth visiting – if you don't mind a scrum and aren't over-modest (most don't boast changing rooms). Showroom sales at venues usually charge a small fee to cover their mailing costs. They keep a list of everyone who has visited their Sales and mail them with the date of the next one.

Some Sale organisers also run sales outside London, including The Good Deal Directory, which runs the Really Good Deal Fashion Sale every late October/early November and late May at the elegant Pavilion at Ascot Racecourses and in 2003 for the first time at Ripley Castle, North Yorkshire on 10th and 11th October. These Sales were inspired by the book, *The Good Deal Directory*, and offer a huge range of designer and top brand-name fashion and accessories at end-of-line prices. (For more information, see Womenswear & Menswear, Berkshire and Womenswear Only, Yorkshire.)

More Bargain-Hunting Tips

1 Discount shopping isn't all about factory shops. There are lots of permanent discount shops all over the country, run by people who know how to find a bargain. Many of these are selling items left over from the big catalogue companies – anything from babygros to television sets, jewellery to hi-fis. Others sell Continental designers obtained direct from the manufacturers abroad.

2 Don't ignore dress agencies as a way of saving – and making – money. You can buy clothes you couldn't otherwise afford in these nearly-new shops which are springing up all over the country. Or sell off your mistakes or items you no longer like wearing and make a bit of cash yourself.

3 Someone else's rubbish may be your treasure. If you're doing up your house and want, for example, to put floorboards down instead of carpets, check out the architectural salvage experts first. They may have floors that have been taken out of old school rooms or manor houses at very reasonable prices.

4 Visit large exhibitions such as Gardener's World or The Clothes Show Live on the afternoon of the last day. Exhibitors don't always want to take the stock on their stand home, so will often sell it off at rock-bottom prices, making the ticket price well worthwhile.

5 If you buy women's magazines, always check out the small ads at the back where lots of companies advertise end-of-line fabrics, direct-from-the-factory spiral staircases, factory-shop sofas, architectural reclamation services and the like.

6 Free information – and sometimes even samples – is widely available from supermarkets (recipe suggestions for a new vegetable they're stocking), large food companies, and perfume and cosmetic companies launching new products.

7 If you're trying to buy curtain fabric to match sofa upholstery, bring a cushion from the sofa with you if you can. If you're trying to match curtains with your walls, paint a piece of wood with your wall colour and bring that with you.

8 The best buys at discount shops are always the most expensive items. Thus, large items such as sofas, beds and carpets offer the best bargains.

9 White goods, such as fridges, washing machines and vacuum cleaners have quite small mark-ups anyway – 20–28% compared with 110% for furniture and up to 280% for clothes – so don't expect huge discounts on these items.

10 Anything that shouts out the season will always be the better bargain: dates on T-shirts, for example. Bear in mind, though, that everyone will know what year you bought it.

11 The advice for clever bargain home buys is the same as for fashion: buy classics. The classic tin of white or cream paint; cream fabric; white tiles … you can always introduce some splashes of colour later to add interest and excitement.

12 Buy items such as eveningwear. Because they're expensive to start with, you will save more. Even if you have no particular event in mind, it's much better to have that half-price bargain in your wardrobe in six months time when an unexpected invitation arrives than rush out the Saturday before and buy something expensive just to have something different to wear.

13 If you're buying shoes, trade up – buy top-brand shoes at the sort of price you would normally pay for your full-price cheaper brands. Good shoes do last much longer

than cheap ones. Invest in shoe trees and shoe brushes and vow to maintain them.

14 If you're trying to create a designer wardrobe from scratch, start with an anchor piece. If you've got a good coat or jacket, you will always look well dressed. Or buy a classic suit that can also be worn as separates. Go for classic colours that will stand the test of time and inject the 'now' colours from the full-price high street.

15 If you need a flat pair of shoes, a handbag or a scarf in order to eke out your wardrobe and wear things you haven't been able to, look out for one buy that will give you a totally new look when added to what you already have in your wardrobe.

16 Remember, the price of something can be divided by the number of times you wear it, so if you can see yourself getting a lot of wear out of something that's still a bit more than you would normally pay for an item, it's probably worth it.

17 Don't buy something that looks wonderful but just doesn't go with your lifestyle.

18 Your home is as much a victim of fashion trends as your wardrobe. Homes shops make it their business to sell the newest fabrics, the latest sofa shape, the most technologically advanced piece of kitchen equipment, so the following season, when the next new designs are ready to take their place on the shop floor, the only-just arriveds have to depart. Some of the unsold stock is held over in the shop's limited storage space until the twice-yearly sale; the remainder makes it way to a wide variety of disposal channels ranging from warehouse sales to factory shops. If you don't mind buying last year's trend-setting fabric to cover your Ottoman, you can pick up some exciting bargains. The same is true for almost everything you find in the home from carpets to curtains, fridges to furniture, bedlinen to breadmakers and cutlery to ceramics.

19 Buy baby equipment such as prams, pushchairs and car seats in late October. These are all fashion items. That means the fabric cover gets replaced with a new design every year. The big trade baby show with the new designs and colours happens at the beginning of October – after that, shops drop their prices on last year's ranges.

20 Sign on with mail order companies whose clothes you like and wait for their end-of-season sale catalogues and buy everything at reduced prices.

21 Don't go food shopping every week on the same day. Delay it by one day each week so that you're extending your shopping cycle; instead of making 52 trips to the supermarket a year, you'll make 44.

22 Volunteers can often have a haircut for a small fee, and more sophisticated treatments, such as perms or colour, for the price of the products used. There are always trained staff on hand to watch over the trainees. Ask at your local hairdresser or the hair and beauty department of the nearest further education college. There, you may also be able to enjoy a wide range of free beauty treatments from the students, from foot massages and aromatherapy to waxing and manicures.

23 Don't leave gift-buying until the last minute, when you're tempted to pay anything just to turn up with something. Keep a list of everyone on your birthday/Christmas/wedding anniversary list and take it with you whenever you go shopping. Look over it quickly before you shop in case you find something that suits someone on your list. The right gift at the right price may not be around the week before a birthday, but it might be there six months before. Remember to keep a note of what you've bought and when it has been given.

24 Re-examine your regular expenses. For example, if you have your hair cut every six weeks, lengthening the time to six and a half or even seven weeks will cut one visit to the hairdressers a year.

25 When factory shopping for clothes, if you haven't got a definite must-buy in mind, find replacements for your old favourites which are beginning to look a bit shoddy. If you've got a jacket or a pair of trousers that you wear almost every day, look out for something that fulfils the same purpose. Or, if you've got a jacket in your wardrobe that you haven't worn this season because you never had the right thing to go with it, now is the time to fill in that gap.
26 Avoid outrageous outfits that people will remember you in, as you won't be able to wear them more than once.

The Good Deal Directory isn't about where to find items cheaply. If it was, the book would be full of details of markets and car boot sales. What it is about is buying quality goods at prices that are lower than they were originally. Most of the information has been gathered by myself and my team of researchers over the past ten or more years; now, a lot of it is also supplied by readers of *The Good Deal Directory*. My readers tell me what they bought, what else was for sale there, what the discounts were and what the service was like. I couldn't ask for a better team of researchers, and all those who contributed to this book are thanked overleaf. I pay £10 for tips that I subsequently publish: places that readers have visited and believe are good value and which I don't already know about, so if you know of somewhere that isn't in this book, you could end up receiving £10 – the price of this book. There are pages at the back of the book which you can fill in and send to me; if you don't want to tear pages out, simply photocopy a page and send it to me or write a letter to PO Box 4, Lechlade, Gloucestershire GL7 3YB.

Happy bargain hunting!

Noelle Walsh

THANKS
TO GOOD DEAL DIRECTORY
READERS

My grateful thanks to the following readers who all contributed information about discount shops they have visited, which has helped to make this edition of the book the definitive guide to bargain shopping.

Maria Addison . . . . *Northampton*
Melody Alloebrook . . . . *Swindon*
Christine Barker . . . . *Yorkshire*
Kathleen Bean . . . . *Yorkshire*
Rita Berger . . . . *Leeds*
Jane Cooper . . . . *Walsall*
Trevor Copestake . . . . *Stoke-on-Trent*
Jane Dale . . . . *Gloucestershire*
Gerald Della-Porta . . . . *Edinburgh*
Jane Demmen . . . . *Swindon*
Barbara Farthing . . . . *Nairobi*
Alison Ford . . . . *Torquay*
Barbara Harwood . . . . *Northern Ireland*
Mrs D Healey . . . . *Keighley*
Hazel Lakey . . . . *Newcastle-upon-Tyne*
Patricia Lesley-Jones . . . . *Hampshire*
Gary Lovell . . . . *Northamptonshire*
George McKain . . . . *Argyll*
Denise McLaughlin . . . . *Halifax*
Mrs R Morton . . . . *Lincolnshire*
Lesley Palmer-Jones . . . . *Peterborough*
Helen Pillinger . . . . *Bristol*
Martin Rickman . . . . *Peterborough*
Denise Strang . . . . *Glasgow*
P A Webber . . . . *Nottingham*

Womenswear Only

BEDFORDSHIRE

GOSSARD FACTORY SHOP

GROVEBURY ROAD, LEIGHTON BUZZARD, BEDFORDSHIRE, LU7 4SN, ☎ 01525 859749, FAX: 01525 850038, 9.30–5.30 MON–SAT. **FACTORY SHOP**

Factory shop sells seconds and discontinued ranges of Gossard and Berlei underwear including bras, briefs, suspender belts and bodies at discounted prices (no nightwear or long-line slips). Most of the stock is last year's trade catalogue styles at discounts of between 25% and 75%. Large car park at rear of building; wheelchair ramp.

NIGHTINGALES FACTORY SHOP

26 HIGH STREET, TODDINGTON, NEAR DUNSTABLE, BEDFORDSHIRE LU5 6BY, ☎ 01525 873888, 10–5 MON–SAT. **FACTORY SHOP**

The mail order company which sells smart but casual clothes for women – button-through dresses, pinafore dresses, shirtwaisters, pure cotton blouses, lined short-sleeved jackets, blouses, trousers, skirts and cotton nightdresses – sells samples, ends-of-lines, seconds and material lengths here at discounted prices. There are regular one-day clearance sales throughout the year. Please phone for details.

SALLY HAIR & BEAUTY SUPPLIES

UNIT 1, SERGEANTS WAY, OFF CAXTON ROAD, ELMS INDUSTRIAL ESTATE, BEDFORD, BEDFORDSHIRE MK41 0EH, ☎ 01234 346544, 8.30–8 MON, 8.30–6 TUE–FRI, 10–3 SAT, 10–4 SUN. **PERMANENT DISCOUNT OUTLET**

Sally Hair & Beauty sells a large range of hair and beauty items used by the professionals throughout the UK. You can find many of the items you see in salons, including those by Wella, L'Oreal, Schwarzkopf and Goldwell. Products range from low-priced nail polishes to top quality salon equipment. You will also find many exclusive products which compare to well-known brands but are a fraction of the price, such as the Aura hair care range and Beyond Belief professional skin care products. There are 120 stores throughout the UK. Telephone 0800 525118 for details of your nearest store.

SIZE-UP

17 MARKET SQUARE, BIGGLESWADE, BEDFORDSHIRE SG18 8AS, ☎ 01767 314321/ Customer Service. Freephone 0800 856540, **e-mail:** cs@sizeup.co.uk, www.sizeup.co.uk, 9.30–5.30 MON–SAT. **PERMANENT DISCOUNT OUTLET**

45 HIGH STREET, LEIGHTON BUZZARD, BEDFORDSHIRE LU7 3DN, ☎ 01525 379866/Customer Service. Freephone 0800 856540, **e-mail:** cs@sizeup.co.uk, www.sizeup.co.uk, 9–5.30 MON–SAT. **PERMANENT DISCOUNT OUTLET**

A store that offers an extensive range of top quality, affordable and fashionable women's clothing in sizes 14 to 32. With new trends, contemporary fabrics and fresh new colours there is always something to suit everyone. Visit their web site at www.sizeup.co.uk, or **e-mail** cs@sizeup.co.uk. Alternatively, telephone their Customer Service department on Freephone 0800 856540 for further information.

THE VANITY BOX

16 CHURCH STREET, DUNSTABLE, BEDFORDSHIRE LU5 4RU, ☎ 01582 600969, 10–4.30 MON–SAT. **DRESS AGENCY**

Large shop on two levels which has been in operation for 26 years selling good as new seasonal womenswear. Only items up to two years old accepted and 50% of stock is designer wear, all in sizes 10 to 26. Both day and evening wear, hats, shoes, jewellery and bags are also stocked. Twice yearly sales are usually held in July and January.

WALTER WRIGHT FACTORY SHOP

29 ALBION ROAD, LUTON, BEDFORDSHIRE LU2 0DS, ☎ 01582 721616, **e-mail:** enquiries@walterwright.com, www.walterwright.com, 10–6 MON–FRI BY APPOINTMENT. **FACTORY SHOP**

Walter Wright, family hat manufacturer since 1889, makes headwear for a variety of national and international couture milliners and dress houses, as well as one high quality partnership department store. If you are lucky, you may be able to purchase a hat from stock at a fraction of the retail price. The factory also serves the public with its own one-off couture service, normally reserved for the trade, at far less cost than normal designer outlets.

BERKSHIRE

SECONDS OUT DESIGNER COLLECTION

HIGH STREET, COOKHAM, BERKSHIRE SL6 9SQ, ☎ 01628 850371, FAX: 01628 850371, www.secondsout.org.uk, 9.30–5 TUE–SAT, 9.30–9 THUR. **DRESS AGENCY**

This shop, situated in a large, timbered building in the riverside village of Cookham, has been in operation for 17 years, offering middle to upper range designer labels, including Armani, Gucci, Prada, Versace and Chanel. There's casual wear and smart Ascot and wedding outfits, as well as evening wear displayed in spacious surroundings. All the clothes are colour coded by hangers. There is also a selection of brand new clearance stock and never-worn outfits and accessories including up to 80 hats at any one time, shoes, and new stock handbags at unbelievable prices. Recently voted the best nearly-new in the Thames Valley and the number two dress agency in the UK. Opening hours change seasonally so please phone first.

SWITCHGEAR

20 ST LEONARD'S ROAD, WINDSOR, BERKSHIRE SL4 3BU, ☎ 01753 867438, 9–5 MON–SAT. **DRESS AGENCY**

Established in 1970, this dress agency offers many labels including Frank Usher, Nicole Farhi, Karen Millen, Betty Jackson, Gerry Weber, Paul Costelloe, Armani, Cerutti, Moschino, Versace, Patsy Seddon, Viyella, Jaeger, Mulberry and French Connection. Clothes for day, evening, Ascot, wedding outfits and leisurewear are in stock, including designer jeans. There is also a good selection of hats, handbags, shoes, jewellery, scarves, belts and sunglasses, with as much as two-thirds off original prices. All garments are arranged in sizes from 8 to 20.

WALTON DESIGN LTD

129 HIGH STREET, HUNGERFORD, BERKSHIRE RG17 0DL, ☎ 01488 686838, 9–6 MON–SAT, 10–4 SUN, 10–5 BANK HOLIDAYS. **PERMANENT DISCOUNT OUTLET**

A chain of 17 stores across the south of England selling well-known labels for women at greatly reduced prices. Current stock from high street stores might include Liz Claiborne, DKNY, Nougat, Ralph Lauren, Banana Republic, Calvin Klein and Tommy Hilfiger. New lines come in each week and are often one-offs, so regular customers know to buy things when they see them or risk missing out.

BRISTOL

GRACEFUL GOWNS

69 BELL HILL ROAD, ST GEORGE, BRISTOL BS5 7LY, ☎ 0117 955 7166, SHOP OPEN BY APPOINTMENT SEVEN DAYS A WEEK. **PERMANENT DISCOUNT OUTLET**

Wedding dresses, shoes, veils, headdresses – dresses from £50 to £1,000; bridesmaids' dresses from £20 to £200. Labels include Alfred Angelo, Dreammaker and Sincerity by Sweetheart. Large selection of bridal headdresses and veils including Trudy Lee. Nicholas House handmade veils made to order and alterations by hand.

JACQUES VERT SALE SHOP

78 QUEENS ROAD, CLIFTON, BRISTOL BS8 1QU, ☎ 0117 925 4546, 10–5 MON–SAT.
PERMANENT DISCOUNT OUTLET

Sale shop for Jacques Vert merchandise at very reasonable prices with large discounts. Occasion wear, workwear, hats, suits, dresses and Lotus shoes.

SALLY HAIR & BEAUTY SUPPLIES

UNIT 3, EAST COURT, SOUTH BRISTOL TRADE PARK, WINTERSTOKE ROAD, BRISTOL BS3 2LD, ☎ 0117 963 6247, 8.30–8 MON, 8.30–6 TUE–FRI, 10–3 SAT, 10–4 SUN. **PERMANENT DISCOUNT OUTLET**

See page 18 (BEDS)

BUCKINGHAMSHIRE

ECHOES

NIGHTINGALES CORNER, LITTLE CHALFONT, BUCKINGHAMSHIRE HP7 9PY, ☎ 01494 764174, FAX: 01494 764174, 10–5.30 TUE–SAT. **DRESS AGENCY**

A relaxed, friendly shop with a rapid turnover of stock. A familiar cry is "I wish I'd bought it when I saw it!". It stocks stylish, exciting names at sensible prices. New and as-new designer names such as Escada, Valentino, Betty Barclay, Basler, and many more, mingle together, surrounded by an eclectic mix of handbags, hats and jewellery.

HANG-UPS

1A THE SQUARE, LONG CRENDON, AYLESBURY, BUCKINGHAMSHIRE HP18 9AA, ☎ 01844 201237, 9.30–5 TUE, THUR, FRI, SAT. **DRESS AGENCY**

New and nearly-new top designer labels offered at a fraction of their original price in sizes 8 to 22. Free parking.

KINGSHILL DESIGNER COLLECTION

THE STUDIO, LITTLE KINGSHILL GRANGE, GREAT MISSENDEN, BUCKINGHAMSHIRE HP16 0DZ, ☎ 01494 890555, www.kingshilldirect.com. **DESIGNER SALE**

Designer fashion mail order company which holds regular discount sales in different parts of the country. Designers on sale can include Paul Costelloe, Paddy Campbell and Amanda Wakeley. Phone to be put on the mailing list.

NUMBER TWENTY

20 HIGH STREET, OLD AMERSHAM, BUCKINGHAMSHIRE HP7 0DJ, ☎ 01494 432043, 9.30–5.30 MON–SAT. **DRESS AGENCY**

Spacious shop in historic market town of Old Amersham which works in partnership with a Knightsbridge dress agency. Labels stocked include Chanel, Caroline Charles, Cerruti, Mondi, MaxMara, Mulberry, Joseph, Jaeger, Jasper Conran, Betty Barclay, Burberry, Episode, Escada, Armani and many more. Also stocks a fabulous range of handbags from designer names such as Chanel, Gucci, Chloe and Prada, as well as brand new shoes including Gina, LK Bennett, Prada and more Italian names. Extremely friendly, helpful staff are on hand to help coordinate a wardrobe.

SALLY HAIR & BEAUTY SUPPLIES

UNIT A, WESSEX ROAD, BOURNE END, BUCKINGHAMSHIRE SL8 5EZ, ☎ 01628 525913, 8.30–8 MON, 8.30–6 TUE–FRI, 10–3 SAT, 10–4 SUN. **PERMANENT DISCOUNT OUTLET**

See page 18 (BEDS)

SCENT TO YOU

THE DESIGNER ROOM, SCENT TO YOU COUNTER, UNIT 4A, XSCAPE SHOPPING CENTRE, AVEBURY BOULEVARD, 602 MARLBOROUGH GATE, CENTRAL MILTON KEYNES, BUCKINGHAMSHIRE MK9 3XF, ☎ 01908 232164, FAX: 01908 233150, 10–6 MON–WED, 10–8 THUR–SAT, 12–6 SUN. **PERMANENT DISCOUNT OUTLET**

Discounted perfume, cosmetics, skincare and accessories, including body lotions, shower gels and gift sets. The company, which has more than 45 branches, buys in bulk and sells more cheaply, relying on a high turnover for profit. Discounts range from 5% to 60%, with greater savings during their twice-yearly sales (phone for details). Most of the leading brand names in perfume are stocked, including Armani, Dolce & Gabbana, Chanel, Diesel, Christian Dior, Issey Miyake, Nino Cerutti and many more. Also stocks cosmetics from Elizabeth Arden, Lentheric and Spectacular, skincare from Clarins, Elizabeth Arden and Lancôme as well as Scent To You's own range of contemporary accessories, including bags, watches, hairbrushes and brush kits, sold under the name of STY Designs. Stock varies greatly due to fast turnover and varying supplies, so more than one visit may be necessary to obtain the scent of your choice. Or phone first to avoid disappointment.

THE DRESSING ROOM

50 HIGH STREET, CHALFONT ST GILES, BUCKINGHAMSHIRE HP8 4QQ, ☎ 01494 876100, 10–4 TUE–SAT.

Set in the pretty, historical village of Chalfont St Giles, just 10 minutes from junction 18 of the M25, and near Milton's cottage, the Dressing Room offers a wide selection of as-new designer fashion labels including Escada, Basler, Gerry Weber, Paul Costelloe, Jaeger and Cerruti at very affordable prices. Dresses, suits, separates, shoes, hats, handbags and other accessories are available at a fraction of the original price. If you're looking for a bargain, the Dressing Room is not to be missed.

THE GO BETWEEN

34B THE MARKET PLACE, OLNEY, BUCKINGHAMSHIRE MK46 4AJ, ☎ 01234 241193, 10.30–4.30 MON–SAT. **DRESS AGENCY**

Designer labels from Escada and Mondi to Nicole Farhi, Betty Barclay, Jaeger and many more. Also stocks good quality, modern, high street labels. There is a full range of accessories, shoes, hats, jewellery, handbags, maternity wear and perfume. Stock is constantly changing, so if you are after something special, please phone first.

THE MATERNITYWEAR EXCHANGE LTD

WYEVERN, CORES END ROAD, BOURNE END, BUCKINGHAMSHIRE SL8 5HR, ☎ 01628 851187, **e-mail:** miriam@maternityexchange.co.uk, www.maternityexchange.co.uk, 9–8 SEVEN DAYS A WEEK BY APPOINTMENT ONLY. **PERMANENT DISCOUNT OUTLET**

Stocking more than 1,000 new and nearly-new items with new merchandise coming in every week, they sell either from their Bourne End outlet or via the secure website. All the items are listed on the website, most accompanied by a photograph. Brand names stocked include Mothercare, Marks & Spencer, Dorothy Perkins, Next, JoJo Maman Bebe, Blooming Marvellous, Vida Vita, Two Plus One, Valja, Blooming and Formes. Prices are 30% to 75% of the recommended list price. Items are current to the weather season but out of season items are always available. They also hire maternity wear, including evening wear, business suits and even bride-to-be outfits! Open by appointment for complete privacy, small children can be supervised while customers shop and there is always tea, coffee and biscuits available. Bourne End is between junctions 3 and 4 of the M40 and about 20 minutes from junction 8/9 of the M4.

WALTON DESIGN LTD

45 SYCAMORE ROAD, AMERSHAM, BUCKINGHAMSHIRE HP6 5EQ, ☎ 01494 723493, 9–6 MON–SAT, 10–4 SUN, 10–5 BANK HOLIDAYS. **PERMANENT DISCOUNT OUTLET**

186 HIGH STREET, BERKHAMSTED, BUCKINGHAMSHIRE HP4 3AP, ☎ 01442 866426, 9–6 MON–SAT, 10–5 BANK HOLIDAYS. **PERMANENT DISCOUNT OUTLET**

77A HIGH STREET, CHESHAM, BUCKINGHAMSHIRE HP5 1BZ, ☎ 01494 774959, 9–6 MON–SAT, 10–5 BANK HOLIDAYS. **PERMANENT DISCOUNT OUTLET**

See page 19 (BERKS)

LA PERLA FASHION GROUP

HORNVALE LTD, UNIT 1, THE HOWARD ESTATE, CHILTON ROAD, CHESHAM, BUCKINGHAMSHIRE HP5 2AU, ☎ 01494 798100. **DESIGNER SALE**

Samples and discontinued lines of lingerie, beachwear and outerwear from the La Perla Fashion Group with up to 90% discounts. Sizes are usually limited. Write or phone to join the mailing list for the sales which are held three times a year.

CAMBRIDGESHIRE

CIRCLES OF YAXLEY

CHAPEL STUDIO, CHAPEL STREET, YAXLEY, PETERBOROUGH, CAMBRIDGESHIRE PE7 3LN, ☎ 01733 242539, 10–4 MON–SAT. **DRESS AGENCY**

Circles sells womenswear and childrenswear. Evening wear is stocked all year round, as are accessories such as hats, handbags and belts. Sizes range from 8 to 24. For children, labels include Marks & Spencer, Laura Ashley and Next. There are sales in January and July, during which everything except evening wear is reduced by 25%, with 40% off promotions for adult clothes during February and August.

OUNDLE DRESS AGENCY

2 WEST STREET, OUNDLE, PETERBOROUGH, CAMBRIDGESHIRE PE8 4EG, ☎ 01832 275556, 9.30–5 MON–SAT, CLOSED WED. **DRESS AGENCY**

Dress agency selling top quality nearly-new clothes for women including Planet, Windsmoor, Patsy Seddon, Gardeur, Versace etc. Downstairs, they sell evening wear, handbags, shoes, coats, jackets, unusual costume jewellery and maternity wear, as well as new Sloggi underwear and wax jackets and raincoats. Also runs a hat hire service with 60 hats in stock at any one time. For ski enthusiasts, from December to March, runs a ski wear operation for men, women and children.

PRETTY BRIDES

TOWN STREET, UPWELL, WISBECH, CAMBRIDGESHIRE PE14 9DA, ☎ 01945 772592, **e-mail:** prettybrides@yahoo.com, www.prettybrides.co.uk, 10–8 MON AND THUR, 10–5 TUE, FRI, SAT **PERMANENT DISCOUNT OUTLET**

Wedding dress shop which offers discounts on styles which have been discontinued by the manufacturer and therefore cannot be ordered in again. Also offers a limited range for hire, and very competitive prices on all brand new stock.

SIZE-UP

5 MARKET PLACE, ELY, CAMBRIDGESHIRE CB7 4NU, ☎ 01353 669143

117-118 HIGH STREET, HUNTINGDON, CAMBRIDGESHIRE PE29 3LG, ☎ 01480 437135

39 BROAD STREET, MARCH, CAMBRIDGESHIRE PE15 8TP, ☎ 01354 658656

8A THE PAVEMENT, ST IVES, CAMBRIDGESHIRE PE17 4AD, ☎ 01480 493204

2 HIGH STREET, ST NEOTS, HUNTINGDON, CAMBRIDGESHIRE PE19 1JA, ☎ 01480 403963

13 MARKET PLACE, WISBECH, CAMBRIDGESHIRE PE13 1DT, ☎ 01945 584869/Customer Service Freephone 0800 856540, **e-mail:** cs@sizeup.co.uk, www.sizeup.co.uk, 9–5.30 MON–SAT. **PERMANENT DISCOUNT OUTLET**

See page 18 (BEDS)

THE FROCK EXCHANGE

22 EAST STREET, KIMBOLTON, HUNTINGDON, CAMBRIDGESHIRE PE18 0HJ, ☎ 01480 860920, 10–5 TUE–FRI, 10–4 SAT. **DRESS AGENCY**

Located in the charming Cambridgeshire village of Kimbolton, they stock very good quality womenswear and accessories. Mostly German designer labels such as Bianca, Ara Fink but also includes Nicole Farhi and Paul Costelloe.

CHANNEL ISLANDS

CINDERELLA'S WARDROBE

10 CONWAY STREET, ST HELIER, JERSEY, CHANNEL ISLANDS JE2 3NT, ☎ 01534 618545, FAX: 01534 618545, 10–5.30 MON–SAT. **DRESS AGENCY**

Sells nearly-new and new designer outfits, shoes, hats and accessories. Labels are top quality: MaxMara, Ralph Lauren, Louis Feraud, Escada, Chanel, Byblos and Krizia.

STONELAKE LTD

5 SMITH STREET, ST PETER PORT, GUERNSEY, CHANNEL ISLANDS GY1 2JN, ☎ 01481 720053, FAX: 01481 713808, **e-mail:** hersch@guernsey.net, 9–5.15 MON–SAT. MAIL ORDER AVAILABLE. **PERMANENT DISCOUNT OUTLET**

Family-run business which has operated in Guernsey for more than 80 years serving both locals and tourists alike. In recent years, they have added a mail order service. They have two shops – one a pharmacy and perfumery, the other selling perfume and cosmetics – and specialise in fragrance bargains from UK and French companies, in aftershaves, cosmetics, perfumes, toilet waters, soaps, and talcs. Being duty-free, and with no VAT, they have competitive prices on standard ranges and by buying excess stocks and ends of lines, they have a large list of extra special offers including ranges no longer sold in the UK. Brand names stocked include Yves Saint Laurent, Paloma Picasso, Cacharel, Boss, Georgio, Paco Rabanne, Gucci, Safari, Elizabeth Arden, Givenchy, Oscar de la Renta, Nina Ricci, Rochas, Davidoff, Ghost, Armani, Royal Secret, Apple Blossom and lots of other old favourites. Free postage and packaging on orders of over £40.

CHESHIRE

DELIA METCALFE

15A BRIDGE STREET, CONGLETON, CHESHIRE CW12 1AS, ☎ 01260 297521, 9.30–5 MON–THUR, 9–5.30 FRI, SAT. **PERMANENT DISCOUNT OUTLET**

Chainstore and designer surplus stock are sold in this small, town centre shop. The children's clothes range from six months to 12 years; women's sizes from 8 to 30. Marks & Spencer merchandise is discounted by 50%, and there are many German designer labels such as Verse and Bianca. They also sell shoes, handbags and accessories.

HOME AND BEAUTY DISCOUNTS

29 MILL STREET, CONGLETON, CHESHIRE CW12 1AG, ☎ 01260 273009, 9–5 MON–SAT, 9–1.15 WED. **PERMANENT DISCOUNT OUTLET**

Three-storey shop with a picture gallery also selling mirrors downstairs, café upstairs and in the middle a floor full of competitively-priced items for the kitchen and household. These include cleaning materials, make-up, toys, ornaments, pottery, aromatherapy oils, shampoo, toothpaste, soaps, lipsticks. They claim prices here are cheaper than in supermarkets and high street shops. Some of the brands are well-known: Flex shampoo, for instance, and Colgate toothpaste.

JANE SHILTON

DESIGNER OUTLET CHESHIRE OAKS, KINSEY ROAD, NEAR ELLESMERE PORT, JUNCTION 10 OF M53, CHESHIRE CH65 9JJ, ☎ 0151 355 8266, FAX: 0151 355 3951, **e-mail:** info@janeshilton.co.uk, www.janeshilton.co.uk, 10–8 MON–FRI, 9–6 SAT, 11–5 SUN. **FACTORY SHOP IN A FACTORY SHOPPING VILLAGE**

Merchandise from past seasons' collections or factory seconds at discounts of at least 30% and up to 70% off the original price. There is a wide range of handbags, small leather goods, shoes, luggage, umbrellas and travel bags. Example of price reduction: handbags at £24.99 originally £37.

JUMPER

MCARTHURGLEN DESIGNER OUTLET CHESHIRE OAKS, KINSEY ROAD, NEAR ELLESMERE PORT, JUNCTION 10 OF M53, CHESHIRE CH65 9JJ, ☎ 0151 356 7414, 10–8 MON–FRI, 9–6 SAT, 11–5 SUN. **FACTORY SHOP IN A FACTORY SHOPPING VILLAGE**

A wide range of Jumper label sweaters, gloves, scarves, shirts and cardigans for women all at discount prices of up to 50% off. Prices start at £2.

LIZ CLAIBORNE

UNIT 21A, CHESHIRE OAKS, KINSEY ROAD, NEAR ELLESMERE PORT, JUNCTION 10 OF M53, CHESHIRE CH65 9JJ, ☎ 0151 355 9183, FAX: 0151 355 9182, 10–8 MON–FRI, 9–6 SAT, 11–5 SUN. **FACTORY SHOP IN A FACTORY SHOPPING VILLAGE**

American designer Liz Claiborne's factory shops offer mid-range, mid-priced smart clothes for work and casual wear. All are end of lines or styles which are at least one year old. Stock quantities and sizes vary, depending on whether there has recently been a delivery, so it's worth making frequent visits. A range is available in petite sizing, and, under the Elizabeth label, for sizes 18 and over. There is a good selection of discounted accessories, including belts and bags. Most items are reduced by from 30% to 70% with further reductions always on offer.

ONE-NIGHT AFFAIR

1 MARKET STREET, ALTRINCHAM, CHESHIRE WA14 1QE, ☎ 0161 928 8477, 10–5 MON–SAT. **HIRE SHOP**

Situated within the Elite Dress Agency (see page 95), you can choose from more than 350 dresses, including cocktail wear, ballgowns, party gear, prom dresses and accessories (including jewellery, evening bags and masks) to hire or to buy. Stock changes frequently. Hire costs £75 to £95. No appointment necessary.

PILOT OUTLET LTD

MCARTHURGLEN DESIGNER OUTLET CHESHIRE OAKS, KINSEY ROAD, NEAR ELLESMERE PORT, JUNCTION 10 OF M53, CHESHIRE CH65 9JJ, ☎ 0151 355 8082, 10–8 MON–FRI, 9–6 SAT, 11–5 SUN. **FACTORY SHOP IN A FACTORY SHOPPING VILLAGE**

Contemporary women's fashionwear. Most of the clothing stocked here is end of season and end of line. Stock is mostly new and similar to the high street stores at reductions of about 30%. For example, in the summer of 2001, T-shirts cost from £3 and jeans from £17.

SCENT TO YOU

MCARTHURGLEN DESIGNER OUTLET CHESHIRE OAKS, KINSEY ROAD, NEAR ELLESMERE PORT, JUNCTION 10 OF M53, CHESHIRE CH65 9LA, ☎ 0151 356 2796, FAX: 0151 356 1478, 10–8 MON–FRI, 9–6 SAT, 11–5 SUN. **FACTORY SHOP IN A FACTORY SHOPPING VILLAGE**

See page 20 (BUCKS)

TOP NOTCH

54 HOSPITAL STREET, NANTWICH, CHESHIRE CW5 5RP, ☎ 01270 623334, 10–4.30 MON–SAT, CLOSED WED. **DRESS AGENCY**

Dress agency selling names such as Betty Barclay, Louis Feraud and Paul Costelloe, as well as shoes, accessories and handbags. Specialises upstairs in a new Danish range of women's smart–casual wear in sizes up to 30.

VELMORE LTD

UNIT 6, APPIN WAY, ARGYLE INDUSTRIAL ESTATE, BIRKENHEAD, CHESHIRE CH65 9JJ, ☎ 0151 666 1579, 10.30–3 MON–THUR.

UNIT 14, THORNTON ROAD INDUSTRIAL ESTATE, ELLESMERE PORT, CHESHIRE CH65 5EP, ☎ 0151 357 1212, 10.30–3 TUE, WED, THUR, 10.30–2 FRI, 9–1 SAT. **FACTORY SHOP**

Leading chainstore seconds of women's jackets, skirts, trousers, dresses and suits, all at reduced prices.

VOGUE ELEVEN

11 PARK LANE, MACCLESFIELD, CHESHIRE SK11 6TJ, ☎ 01625 427031, **e-mail:** vogue.eleven@virgin.net, 10–4 MON–SAT, 10–1 WED. **DRESS AGENCY**

Small shop in a 200-year-old building run by the irrepressible Marjorie Potts, who dispenses advice cheerfully and knowledgeably. Marjorie wouldn't have been running the business so successfully for more than 20 years without being extremely good at it and the quality of the clothes and the labels prove that. There's Shiren Guild, Mani, Prada, Emporio Armani, Caroline Charles, Margaret Howell, Donna Karan, Katharine Hamnett, Workers for Freedom, Jasper Conran, Diane Fres, Jaeger, Escada, Basler, Louis Feraud and Ralph Lauren. There are also some brand new samples. Prices range from £5 to £200 in sizes from 8 to 18.

WALLIS

MCARTHURGLEN DESIGNER OUTLET CHESHIRE OAKS, KINSEY ROAD, NEAR ELLESMERE PORT,

JUNCTION 10 OF M53, CHESHIRE CH65 9JJ, ☎ 0151 356 9297, 10–8 MON–FRI, 9–6 SAT, 11–5 SUN. **FACTORY SHOP IN A FACTORY SHOPPING VILLAGE**

Wide range of clothes from summerwear to coats, all at discount prices of up to 30%.

WAREHOUSE

UNIT 18, MCARTHURGLEN DESIGNER OUTLET CHESHIRE OAKS, KINSEY ROAD, NEAR ELLESMERE PORT, JUNCTION 10 OF M53, CHESHIRE CH65 9JJ, ☎ 0151 357 3168, 10–8 MON–FRI, 9–6 SAT, 11–5 SUN. **FACTORY SHOP IN A FACTORY SHOPPING VILLAGE**

Warehouse fashions are aimed at young women in their late teens and twenties. Here you'll find the hottest looks on the high street at up to 30% off the recommended retail price.

WINDSMOOR GROUP

MCARTHURGLEN DESIGNER OUTLET CHESHIRE OAKS, KINSEY ROAD, NEAR ELLESMERE PORT, JUNCTION 10 OF M53, CHESHIRE CH65 9JJ, ☎ 0151 357 2728, FAX: 0151 357 3744, 10–8 MON–FRI, 9–6 SAT, 11–5 SUN. **FACTORY SHOP IN A FACTORY SHOPPING VILLAGE**

Previous season's stock as well as any returned merchandise and overmakes from the Windsmoor, Planet and Precis Petite ranges at discounts averaging about 50% off the original price. Also stocks Danimac womenswear and menswear at discounted prices of around 50%.

CORNWALL

SCENT TO YOU

6 CATHEDRAL LANE, TRURO, CORNWALL TR1 2QS, ☎ 01872 263663, FAX: 01872 263773, 9–5.30 MON–SAT. HOURS MAY BE EXTENDED AT CHRISTMAS, PLEASE PHONE FOR DETAILS. **PERMANENT DISCOUNT OUTLET**

See page 20 (BUCKS)

COUNTY DURHAM

CLASSY CLOTHES

USWORTH ROAD, HARTLEPOOL, CO DURHAM TS25 1PD, ☎ 01429 868553, 9–5 MON–FRI, 9–5.30 SAT. **PERMANENT DISCOUNT OUTLET**

Deals mostly in brand new, well-known high street names such as Wallis, Principles, BhS and Ann Harvey. All are on sale at savings of at least 40% in sizes 8 to 24. For example, trousers reduced from £28.99 to £15; jackets £29.99 from £59.99; dresses, £15 from £49.99.

COCO

11 GRANGE ROAD, DARLINGTON, CO DURHAM DL1 5NA, ☎ 01325 383720, 10–5 MON–SAT. **DRESS AGENCY**

Small shop packed with day wear, evening wear and accessories from designer labels – from Armani and Moschino to Basler, Escada and Nicole Farhi. Clothes are immaculate and often mistaken for new by window shoppers. Sizes are mostly 8 to 20, and prices range from £5 to £200. Also stocks a really good selection of shoes from Moschino, Patrick Cox and Nicholas Deakin.

NEXT ENCOUNTER

3B HOUNDGATE, DARLINGTON, CO DURHAM DL1 1RL, ☎ 01325 255033, 11–4 MON, 10–5 TUE–SAT. **DRESS AGENCY**

Women's clothing in a wide range of sizes, mostly high street labels such as Next, Principles, Oasis, Miss Selfridge, Laura Ashley and Marks & Spencer. Also sells shoes, handbags and other accessories.

SCENT TO YOU

JACKSONS LANDING FACTORY OUTLETS, THE HIGHLIGHT, HARTLEPOOL MARINA, HARTLEPOOL, CO DURHAM TS24 0XN, ☎ 01429 275308, FAX: 01429 265506, 10–6 MON–SAT, 11–5 SUN. **FACTORY SHOP IN A FACTORY SHOPPING VILLAGE**

See page 20 (BUCKS)

CUMBRIA

FINE FEATHERS

6 LIBRARY ROAD, KENDAL, CUMBRIA LA9 4QB, ☎ 01539 727241, 10–5 MON–SAT. **DRESS AGENCY**

Wide range of mid-market names such as Country Casuals and Lakelands, with mix of in-season styles. Also Jacques Vert, Principles, Next, and Jaeger. More than 7,000 clients sell their as-new clothes here.

LINTON TWEEDS LTD

SHADDON MILLS, CARLISLE, CUMBRIA CA2 5TZ, ☎ 01228 527569, FAX: 01228 512062, www.lintontweeds.co.uk, 9.30–5 MON–SAT. MAIL ORDER. **FACTORY SHOP**

Eighty per cent of Linton Tweeds' business is for the couture trade for export and includes exclusive fabrics for Chanel, Escada, MaxMara, Christian Lacroix and Brioni. British designers to whom it supplies fabrics include Burberry, Wallis, Jigsaw, Aquascutum and Jaeger, and ranges from fancy yarns to silk and wool crepes. The mill shop has a large selection of ends of lines and remnants at prices ranging from £15 to £25 per metre. You have to buy the fabric when you see it as there are no repeat orders. Also offer an exclusive designer knitwear section sold at discounted prices. There is an exhibition section, small museum and restaurant on site with hands-on display for adults and children. The site also has its own car park and coffee shop selling homemade cakes etc.

NEW TO YOU

1 BOUNDARY ROAD, CURROCK, CARLISLE, CUMBRIA CA2 4RS, ☎ 01228 592669, 10–5 TUE–FRI, 10–4 SAT. **DRESS AGENCY**

Classic clothing, shoes and bags from Louis Feraud, Mansfield, Frank Usher and Mondi to Kanga, Next and Laura Ashley at anything from one half to one quarter of the original price. Sizes range from 10 to 24. Also sells and hires hats from a range of about 40 for £12 with a refundable £2.

DERBYSHIRE

ALEXON SALE SHOP

DE BRADELEI HOUSE, CHAPEL STREET, BELPER, DERBYSHIRE DE56 1AR, ☎ 01773 829309/829830, 9.30–5.30 MON–FRI, 9.30–6 SAT, 10.30–4.30 SUN. **PERMANENT DISCOUNT OUTLET**

Alexon, Eastex, Kaliko and Minuet from last season at 40% less than the original price. During sale time in January and June, reductions are 70%. Stock includes skirts, blouses and jackets.

DAVID NIEPER

ORANGE STREET, OFF NOTTINGHAM ROAD, ALFRETON, DERBYSHIRE DE55 7LE, ☎ 01773 833335, 9–5 MON–SAT AND BANK HOLIDAYS. **FACTORY SHOP**

Classic women's clothing and specialists in nightwear/lingerie. David Nieper is an internationally acclaimed designer and private customers from all over the world order directly from this factory shop in Alfreton. The factory shop has design room samples including beautiful silk fabrics and laces; pure cotton nightdresses; luxury velvet housegowns; Liberty blouses and skirts. There is also an amazing range of lingerie from well-known designers. Free car park.

JANE SHILTON

MCARTHURGLEN DESIGNER OUTLET MANSFIELD, MANSFIELD ROAD, SOUTH NORMANTON, ALFRETON, JUNCTION 28 OF M1, DERBYSHIRE DE55 2ER, ☎ 01773 545183, FAX: 01773 545184, **e-mail:** info@janeshilton.co.uk, www.janeshilton.co.uk, 10–6 MON–FRI, 8 ON THUR, 9–6 SAT, 11–5 SUN. **FACTORY SHOP IN A FACTORY SHOPPING VILLAGE**

See page 23 (CHESH)

JUMPER

MCARTHURGLEN DESIGNER OUTLET MANSFIELD, MANSFIELD ROAD, SOUTH NORMANTON,

ALFRETON, JUNCTION 28 OF M1, DERBYSHIRE DE55 2EF, ☎ 01773 545251, 9.30–5.30 MON–SAT, 11–5 SUN. **FACTORY SHOP IN A FACTORY SHOPPING VILLAGE**

See page 23 (CHESH)

LABELS OF BASLOW

CHURCH STREET, BASLOW, BAKEWELL, DERBYSHIRE DE4 1RY, ☎ 01246 582971 10–5.30 MON–SAT. **DRESS AGENCY**

Friendly and accommodating shop, selling women's upmarket and designer labels in immaculate condition. Business terms are 60 to 40% and only quality items less than two years old are accepted for sale. The range includes everything from beachwear to designer evening wear and includes a huge stock of accessories to complement any outfit.

LIZ CLAIBORNE

DE BRADELEI HOUSE, CHAPEL STREET, BELPER, DERBYSHIRE DE56 1AR, ☎ 01773 882442, FAX: 01773 828190, 9.30–5.30 MON–FRI, 9.30–6 SAT, 10.30–4.30 SUN. **FACTORY SHOP IN A FACTORY SHOPPING VILLAGE**

See page 23 (CHESH)

MORE POSH THAN DOSH

2 HIGH STREET, DRONFIELD, CHESTERFIELD, DERBYSHIRE, ☎ 01246 418316, 10–5 TUE–SAT. **PERMANENT DISCOUNT OUTLET**

Amazing savings on high street and designer fashion, mainly for women. Stocks the main high street labels' current stock at, typically, a 50% discount, as well as designer day and evening wear. These are not seconds or imperfects. For example a silk designer evening dress costs £65 (£180 on the high street), sweater £18 (£38 on the high street). Ask for a 'personal shopping assistant' who will select a wardrobe for you free of charge. Alteration service available. New stock arrives four times a week. Sizes 8 to 20.

PILOT OUTLET LTD

MCARTHURGLEN DESIGNER OUTLET VILLAGE, MANSFIELD ROAD, SOUTH NORMANTON, ALFRETON, DERBYSHIRE DE55 2JW, ☎ 01773 545173, 10–6 MON–FRI, 8 ON THUR, 9–6 SAT, 11–5 SUN. **FACTORY SHOP IN A FACTORY SHOPPING VILLAGE**

See page 24 (CHESH)

PRETTY PERFECTS

5B ST JOHNS STREET, ASHBOURNE, DERBYSHIRE DE6 1GP, ☎ 01335 344497, 9–4.30 MON, TUE, THUR, 9–3 WED, 9–5 FRI, SAT. **FACTORY SHOP**

Playtex and Pretty Polly lingerie, hosiery, socks and branded toiletries. All stock is discontinued lines sold at greatly reduced prices. Stock is constantly changing so come with an open mind.

TOG 24

DERBYSHIRE DESIGNER OUTLET VILLAGE, MANSFIELD ROAD, SOUTH NORMANTON, DERBYSHIRE DE55 2JW, ☎ 01773 545206, **e-mail:** mail-order@tog24.com, www.tog24.com, 10–6 MON–FRI, 8 ON THUR, 9–6 SAT, 11–5 SUN. **FACTORY SHOP IN A FACTORY SHOPPING VILLAGE**

Tog 24 is the UK's fastest-growing brand name in outdoor clothing and leisurewear. The company utilises the world's finest performance fabrics, including GoreTex and Polartec, to produce merchandise which caters for all the family for all seasons. Their range includes fleeces and waterproofs for the winter, and trekking ranges, shorts and T-shirts for the summer. They also stock accessories, including sunglasses, toiletries and swimwear. All merchandise is available by mail order: phone 01924 236507 for a brochure or to order. All prices here are at least 30% below RRP. This branch stocks womenswear and childrenswear only, but nearby within the village is another branch selling menswear.

WINDSMOOR GROUP

DE BRADELEI MILL SHOP, CHAPEL STREET, BELPER, DERBYSHIRE DE56 1AR, ☎ 01773 882442 EXT 206, 9.30–5.30 MON–FRI, 9.30–6 SAT, 10.30–4.30 SUN. **FACTORY SHOP IN A FACTORY SHOPPING VILLAGE**

MCARTHURGLEN DESIGNER OUTLET MANSFIELD, MANSFIELD ROAD, SOUTH NORMANTON,

ALFRETON, JUNCTION 28 OF M1, DERBYSHIRE DE55 2ER, ☎ 01773 545068, 10–6 MON–FRI, 8 ON THUR, 9–6 SAT, 11–5 SUN. **FACTORY SHOP IN A FACTORY SHOPPING VILLAGE**

See page 25 (CHESH)

DEVON

JANE SHILTON

ATLANTIC VILLAGE, CLOVELLY ROAD, OFF A39, BIDEFORD, NORTH DEVON EX39 3QU, ☎ 01237 424413, FAX: 01237 473126, **e-mail:** info@janeshilton.co.uk www.janeshilton.co.uk, 10–6 MON–FRI, 8 ON THUR, 9–6 SAT, 11–5 SUN. **FACTORY SHOP IN A FACTORY SHOPPING VILLAGE**

See page 23 (CHESH)

ORIGIN

STATION ROAD INDUSTRIAL ESTATE, BAMPTON, NEAR TIVERTON, DEVON EX16 9NG, ☎ 01398 331704, www.origin-uk.com, 9–5 MON–FRI, 9–1 SAT. **FACTORY SHOP**

The Origin factory shop offers a large range of womenswear (dresses, soft suits and separates) suitable for casual and special occasions at approximately 50% less than the recommended retail price. The fabrics used are of a high quality, predominantly natural fibres, including Liberty of London. Situated in the attractive town of Bampton on the edge of Exmoor, the factory offers parking, wheelchair access and a friendly, relaxed atmosphere. Dresses and skirts can be shortened free of charge.

PILOT OUTLET LTD

ATLANTIC VILLAGE, BIDEFORD, NORTH DEVON EX39 3QU, ☎ 01237 475025, 10–6 MON–SAT, 10.30–4.30 SUN. **FACTORY SHOP IN A FACTORY SHOPPING VILLAGE**

See page 24 (CHESH)

SCENT TO YOU

THE DESIGNER ROOM, ATLANTIC VILLAGE OUTLET CENTRE, CLOVELLY ROAD, BIDEFORD, NORTH DEVON EX39 3QU, ☎ 01237 422550, FAX: 01237 422548, 10–6 MON–SAT, 8 ON THUR, 10.30–4.30 SUN. **FACTORY SHOP IN A FACTORY SHOPPING VILLAGE**

See page 20 (BUCKS)

WINDSMOOR GROUP

ATLANTIC VILLAGE, CLOVELLY ROAD, BIDEFORD, NORTH DEVON EX39 3QU, ☎ 01237 475104, 10–6 MON–SAT, 8 ON THUR, 10.30–4.30 SUN. **PERMANENT DISCOUNT OUTLET**

34 FLEET STREET, TORQUAY, DEVON TQ2 5DY, ☎ 01803 201081, 9–5.30 MON–SAT. **FACTORY SHOP IN A FACTORY SHOPPING VILLAGE**

See page 25 (CHESH)

DORSET

ANCORA DRESS AGENCY

275 CHARMINSTER ROAD, BOURNEMOUTH, DORSET BH8 9QJ, ☎ 01202 523848, 10–5 MON–SAT. **DRESS AGENCY**

Top designer labels including Armani, Escada, Caroline Charles, Christian Dior, Versace, Christian Le Croix, Jaeger, Country Casuals, Viyella, Louis Feraud. Clothes to suit all ages, sizes 8 to 24.

BROWSERS

35 CHEAP STREET, SHERBORNE, DORSET DT9 3PU, ☎ 01935 813326, FAX: 01935 813326, 10–5 MON–SAT. **DRESS AGENCY**

An upmarket dress agency selling nearly-new labels from Jaeger to Mondi, Viyella to Valentino. While most of their range consists of designer labels, some better quality high street names are also available. The shop has a large stock with a high turnover. They also stock belts, hats, handbags, jewellery and other accessories.

IRENE

3 STATION APPROACH, BROADSTONE, POOLE, DORSET BH18 8AX, ☎ 01202 659700, 10–5 MON–SAT. **DRESS AGENCY**

Dress agency on two floors with the ground floor devoted to nearly-new and a selection of new sale lines from the first floor department which stocks new clothing, particularly mother-of-the-bride wear.

LORI'S BOUTIQUE

MILLSTREAM CLOSE, EAST STREET, WIMBORNE, DORSET BH21 1DX, ☎ 01202 889575, 10–5 MON–FRI, 10–4 SAT. **DRESS AGENCY**

Quality high street names such as Country Casuals, Windsmoor, Jaeger as well as designer names, mostly German, such as Gerry Weber and Bianca. Also sell hats from £10 to £60 and competitively priced shoes, handbags and accessories.

SALLY HAIR & BEAUTY SUPPLIES

254–256 OLD CHRISTCHURCH ROAD, BOURNEMOUTH, DORSET BH1 1PF, ☎ 01202 298550, 8.30–8 MON, 8.30–6 TUE–FRI, 10–3 SAT, 10–4 SUN. **PERMANENT DISCOUNT OUTLET**

See page 18 (BEDS)

SCENT TO YOU

POOLE POTTERY LTD, SCENT TO YOU COUNTER, SOPERS LANE, POOLE, DORSET BH17 7PP, ☎ 01202 668681, FAX: 01202 682894, 9–5.30 MON–SAT, 10.30–4.30 SUN. **FACTORY SHOP IN A FACTORY SHOPPING VILLAGE**

See page 20 (BUCKS)

THE WARDROBE

422 LYMINGTON ROAD, HIGHCLIFFE, CHRISTCHURCH, DORSET BH23 5HE, ☎ 01425 276928, 10 -5 MON–SAT, 10–1 WED. **DRESS AGENCY**

Stocks anything from Marks & Spencer to Ralph Lauren in sizes 8 to 20, with a wide range of shoes available. Bargain rail of older stock sold at half-price; sales in the summer and after Christmas. Large range of hats, handbags, scarves and jewellery.

TRIO

179 NEW ROAD, WEST PARLEY, DORSET BH22 8ED, ☎ 01202 594242, 10–5 MON, TUE, THUR, FRI, 10–1 WED AND SAT. **DRESS AGENCY**

Good high street and designer labels such as Frank Usher, Condici, Gina Bacconi, Gerry Weber, Country Casuals, Jaeger, Viyella and Betty Barclay in a selection that includes day and evening wear, beachwear, handbags, belts, scarves, shoes and jewellery. Free parking outside.

WALTON DESIGN LTD

16A HIGH STREET, SHAFTESBURY, DORSET SP7 8JG, ☎ 01747 858462, 9–6 MON–SAT, 10–4 SUN, 10–5 BANK HOLIDAYS. **PERMANENT DISCOUNT OUTLET**

See page 19 (BERKS)

ESSEX

JANE SHILTON

FREEPORT ESSEX VILLAGE, CHARTER WAY, CHAPEL HILL, BRAINTREE, ESSEX CM7 8YH, ☎ 01376 341696, FAX: 01376 344739, **e-mail:** info@janeshilton.co.uk, www.janeshilton.co.uk, 10–6 MON–SAT, 8 ON THUR, 11–5 SUN. **FACTORY SHOP IN A FACTORY SHOPPING VILLAGE**

UNIT 49, CLACTON COMMON FACTORY OUTLET VILLAGE, STEPHENSON ROAD WEST, CLACTON-ON-SEA, ESSEX CO15 4TZ, ☎ 01255 436651, FAX: 01255 424650, **e-mail:** info@janeshilton.co.uk, www.janeshilton.co.uk, 10–6 MON–FRI, 8 ON THUR, 9–6 SAT, 11–5 SUN. **FACTORY SHOP IN A FACTORY SHOPPING VILLAGE**

See page 23 (CHESH)

PILOT OUTLET LTD

CLACTON SHOPPING VILLAGE, STEPHENSON ROAD WEST, CLACTON-ON-SEA, ESSEX CO15 4TL, ☎ 01255 479979, 10–6 MON–SAT, 11–5 SUN. **FACTORY SHOP IN A FACTORY SHOPPING VILLAGE**

See page 24 (CHESH)

SALLY HAIR & BEAUTY SUPPLIES

UNIT 24, BAKERS COURT, PAYCOCKS ROAD, CRANES INDUSTRIAL ESTATE, BASILDON, ESSEX SS14 3DR, ☎ 01268 286302, 8.30–8 MON, 8.30–6 TUE–FRI, 10–3 SAT, 10–4 SUN. **PERMANENT DISCOUNT OUTLET**

See page 18 (BEDS)

SCENT TO YOU

THE DESIGNER ROOM, FREEPORT ESSEX VILLAGE, CHARTER WAY, CHAPEL HILL, BRAINTREE, ESSEX CM7 8YH, ☎ 01376 554642, FAX: 01376 554643, 10–6 MON–SAT, 8 ON THUR, 11–5 SUN. **FACTORY SHOP IN A FACTORY SHOPPING VILLAGE**

CLACTON COMMON FACTORY OUTLET VILLAGE, STEPHENSON ROAD WEST, CLACTON-ON-SEA, ESSEX CO15 4ZO, ☎ 01255 479779, FAX: 01255 479588, 10–6 MON–SAT, 11–5 SUN. **FACTORY SHOP IN A FACTORY SHOPPING VILLAGE**

See page 20 (BUCKS)

SIZE-UP

54–56 HIGH STREET, BILLERICAY, ESSEX CM12 9BS, ☎ 01277 636337

12 GEORGE YARD, BRAINTREE, ESSEX CM7 1RB, ☎ 01376 554728

3 MARKET HILL, SAFFRON WALDEN, ESSEX CB10 1HQ, ☎ 01799 516536/Customer Service Freephone 0800 856540, **e-mail:** cs@sizeup.co.uk, www.sizeup.co.uk, 9–5.30 MON–SAT. **PERMANENT DISCOUNT OUTLET**

See page 18 (BEDS)

TSAR SOLUTIONS LTD

1195–1197 LONDON ROAD, LEIGH-ON-SEA, ESSEX SS9 3JB, ☎ 01702 480505, FAX: 01702 480707, 9.30–2 TUE–SAT OR BY APPOINTMENT. **FACTORY SHOP**

As manufacturers of top quality women's clothes, which are sold only in this retail showroom, prices are extremely competitive as there is no wholesaler to add his margin. Wide range of womenswear from dresses, jackets and tops to skirts, shorts and blouses – everything except swimwear, nightwear and coats. The range covers casual and dressy – in particular for mother-of-the-bride and groom outfits.

VALROSE

610 CHIGWELL ROAD, WOODFORD BRIDGE, ESSEX 1G8 8AA, ☎ 020 8506 1667, 9.30–5 TUE–SAT. **DRESS AGENCY**

Valrose is a well-established dress agency dealing mostly in designer label womenswear for the past 16 years. A range of childrenswear is also stocked, from quality high street names to Moschino. There is always plenty of stock available and friendly, helpful staff. Clothing is sectioned into skirts, trousers, blouses, jumpers, coats, swimwear, suits, bags, hats and shoes and then divided into sizes and seasons.

WINDSMOOR GROUP

CLACTON FACTORY SHOPPING VILLAGE, STEPHENSON ROAD, CLACTON, ESSEX CO15 4TL, ☎ 01255 224131, FAX: 01255 225123, 10–6 MON–SAT, 11–5 SUN. **FACTORY SHOP IN A FACTORY SHOPPING VILLAGE**

See page 25 (CHESH)

GLOUCESTERSHIRE

ANCILLA DRESS AGENCY

15 LECKHAMPTON ROAD, CHELTENHAM, GLOUCESTERSHIRE GL53 0AZ, ☎ 01242 242799, 10–5 TUE, THUR, FRI, 10–1 WED, SAT. **DRESS AGENCY**

Wide selection of womenswear from casual to occasion wear; good range of separates and accessories. Caters for ages 18 to 80 in sizes 8 to 20. Examples of labels sold include Windsmoor, Planet, Basler, Paul Costelloe, Louis Feraud, Armani and Jaeger.

BECKFORD SILK

BECKFORD, NEAR TEWKESBURY, GLOUCESTERSHIRE GL20 7AD, ☎ 01386 881507, FAX: 01386 882019, **e-mail:** sales@beckfordsilk.co.uk, www.beckfordsilk.co.uk, 9–5.30 MON–SAT. **FACTORY SHOP**

Silk printing centre for making scarves, ties, blouses, etc, currently printing for major museums. Customers can watch the printing process and visit the retail shop which also has a seconds division.

ENCORE

19 WEST MARKET PLACE, CIRENCESTER, GLOUCESTERSHIRE GL7 5AE, ☎ 01285 885223, 10–4 MON–FRI, 10–5 SAT. **DRESS AGENCY**

Using their celebrity contacts, the owners of this relatively new dress agency sell top-name, up-to-date, hardly worn clothes at very reasonable prices. Stock usually includes Armani, Escada, MaxMara, Planet, Valentino, Amanda Wakeley as well as items from smaller fashion chains such as Karen Millen, Jigsaw, Kookai, Hobbs, Warehouse, etc. Designer samples are also available.

JUST THOUGHTS

56 CHURCH STREET, TEWKESBURY, GLOUCESTERSHIRE GL20 5RZ, ☎ 01684 293037, 10–5 TUE–SAT, CLOSED 1.30–2.30 DAILY AND ALL DAY MONDAYS. **DRESS AGENCY**

Wide selection of labels, mostly middle to upmarket including many designer names. For example, MaxMara, Marella, Escada, Paul Costelloe, Frank Usher, Versace and Betty Barclay usually selling at a third of the original retail price. Sales are held twice yearly, at the end of summer and at the end of winter. Situated opposite Tewkesbury Abbey.

SEQUELS

DIGBETH STREET, STOW-ON-THE-WOLD, GLOUCESTERSHIRE GL54 1BN, ☎ 01451 870041, 10–5 TUE–SAT, CLOSED 1–2 DAILY. **DRESS AGENCY**

One of the best dress agencies in central England. They always have an excellent range of labels at competitive prices from MaxMara, August Silk and Jaeger to plenty of good high street brands. Also sell new samples and designer discount lines for day and evening, as well as full price German designer wear. Stocks a limited range of accessories, such as shoes, handbags and scarves.

STOCK EXCHANGE

14 CHURCH STREET, NEWENT, GLOUCESTER, GLOUCESTERSHIRE GL18 1PP, ☎ 01531 821681, 9–1 AND 2–5 MON, TUE, THUR, FRI, SAT, 9–1 WED. **DRESS AGENCY**

Dress agency stocking labels from Mondi to Marks & Spencer, Laura Ashley, Next, Wallis and Principles. Also childrenswear from babygros to clothes for 14-year-olds, family videos and books, curtains, jewellery, children's and women's shoes and hats.

THE NATIONAL STAR STORE

10 MARKET PLACE, TETBURY, GLOUCESTERSHIRE GL8 8JG, ☎ 01666 502297, 9.30–4.30 TUE–SAT. **DRESS AGENCY**

A shop set up to support a charity, The National Star College (charity no 220239), a specialist residential college for students with a physical disability. It sells nearly new womenswear, shoes, handbags and accessories, as well as childrenswear, books, toys and bric-a-brac, as donated.

TOAD HALL: THE DRESS AGENCY

7 ROTUNDA TERRACE, MONTPELLIER, CHELTENHAM, GLOUCESTERSHIRE GL50 1SW, ☎ 01242 255214, 9.30–5 MON–SAT. **DRESS AGENCY**

Toad Hall is situated in the fashionable Montpellier area in a large shop with two floors where they hold an extensive range of clothing, shoes, bags and accessories. This is a top quality shop with labels such as Louis Vuitton, Hermes, Chanel, Armani, Caroline Charles, Jean Muir, Givenchy, Escada, MaxMara, Moschino, Gucci, Fendi, Nicole Farhi, Loewe, Burberry and Prada.

WALTON DESIGN LTD

20 MARKET PLACE, CIRENCESTER, GLOUCESTERSHIRE GL7 2NW, ☎ 01285 655400, 9–6 MON–SAT, 10–4 SUN, 10–5 BANK HOLIDAYS. **PERMANENT DISCOUNT OUTLET**

7 LONG STREET, TETBURY, GLOUCESTERSHIRE GL8 8AA, ☎ 01666 505671, 9–6 MON–SAT, 10–4 SUN, 10–5 BANK HOLIDAYS. **PERMANENT DISCOUNT OUTLET**

See page 19 (BERKS)

HAMPSHIRE

ALEXON SALE SHOP

HART SHOPPING CENTRE, FLEET, HAMPSHIRE GU51 3LA, ☎ 01252 815055, 9–5.30 MON–SAT. **PERMANENT DISCOUNT OUTLET**

See page 26 (DERBY)

ARTIGIANO

49 HIGH STREET, COWES, ISLE OF WIGHT PO31 7RR, ☎ 01983 297773, FAX: 01983 297773, **e-mail:** info@arigiano.com, www.artigiano.com, 10–5 MON–SAT IN SUMMER, 10–4 IN WINTER. PHONE TO CHECK. **PERMANENT DISCOUNT OUTLET**

Artigiano, the mail order company, has a shop which sells overstocks from the previous catalogues at discounted prices. Artigiano is known for its women's fashion exclusively made in Italy, from cool wool suits to angora sweaters and silk scarves. Available in sizes 10 to 30.

GHOST

WHITELEY VILLAGE DESIGNER OUTLET CENTRE, WHITELEY WAY, FAREHAM, JUNCTION 9 OF M27, HAMPSHIRE PO15 7LJ, ☎ 01489 565620, 10–6 MON–SAT, 11–5 SUN. **FACTORY SHOP IN A FACTORY SHOPPING VILLAGE**

Garments will be on sale at up to 70% discount. This will be the company's only outlet store so worth making a trip if you're a Ghost fan at least twice a year to save yourself the elbow-grappling experience of their showroom sale in early December at their Kensal Rise, London, warehouse (see page 45).

JANE SHILTON

WHITELEY VILLAGE DESIGNER OUTLET CENTRE, WHITELEY WAY, FAREHAM, JUNCTION 9 OF M27, HAMPSHIRE PO15 7LJ, ☎ 01489 565069, FAX: 01489 565071, **e-mail:** info@janeshilton.co.uk, www.janeshilton.co.uk, 10–6 MON–SAT, 11–5 SUN. **FACTORY SHOP IN A FACTORY SHOPPING VILLAGE**

See page 23 (CHESH)

PILOT OUTLET LTD

WHITELEY VILLAGE, WHITELEY WAY, FAREHAM, HAMPSHIRE PO15 7BS, ☎ 01489 565554, 11–6 MON–SAT, 11–5 SUN. **FACTORY SHOP IN A FACTORY SHOPPING VILLAGE**

See page 24 (CHESH)

PRIVATE COLLECTION

SHOEMAKERS COTTAGE, 7 UNION STREET, FAREHAM, HAMPSHIRE PO16 7XX, ☎ 01329 826123, 10–5 MON–SAT
DRESS AGENCY

Exclusive dress agency with no chainstore items. Sells mother-of-the-bride/groom and special occasion outfits, evening dresses, day wear, casual wear, hats and bags. Labels include MaxMara, Gerry Weber and Jaeger.

SCENT TO YOU

ALDERSHOT GALLERIES, THE WELLINGTON CENTRE, ALDERSHOT, HAMPSHIRE GU11 1DB, ☎ 01252 328894, FAX: 01252 328873, 9–6 MON–SAT, 10–4 SUN. **FACTORY SHOP IN A FACTORY SHOPPING VILLAGE**

THE DESIGNER ROOM, WHITELEY VILLAGE DESIGNER OUTLET CENTRE, WHITELEY WAY, FAREHAM, JUNCTION 9 OF M27, HAMPSHIRE PO15 7BS, ☎ 01489 580509, FAX: 01489 580502, 10–6 MON–SAT, 11–5 SUN. **FACTORY SHOP IN A FACTORY SHOPPING VILLAGE**

UNIT 3–6, THE BROOKS SHOPPING CENTRE, WINCHESTER, HAMPSHIRE SO23 8QY, ☎ 01962 827752, FAX: 01962 827751, 9–6 MON–SAT, 10.30–4.30 SUN. **FACTORY SHOP IN A FACTORY SHOPPING VILLAGE**

See page 20 (BUCKS)

THE CLOTHES LINE

171 HIGH STREET, WINCHESTER, HAMPSHIRE SO23 9BQ, ☎ 01962 868892, 10–4 MON–SAT, CLOSED WED. **DRESS AGENCY**

Designer and high street labels from Next and Laura Ashley to Frank Usher, Laurel, Yves Saint Laurent, Marella and Jacques Vert, Ramsay of Dublin, Yarell, Paul Costelloe, Nicole Farhi, Moschino and MaxMara, plus accessories: hats, costume jewellery and shoes. The shop is situated below King Alfred's statue before Chesil Bridge.

THE DESIGNER ROOM

THE BROOKS CENTRE, WINCHESTER, HAMPSHIRE SO23 8QY, ☎ 01962 827752, 9–6 MON–SAT, 10.30–4.30 SUN. **FACTORY SHOP IN A FACTORY SHOPPING VILLAGE**

See page 92 (BUCKS)

HEREFORDSHIRE

DESIGNER DISCOUNT CLUB

UNIT E, ASHBURTON ESTATE, ROSS-ON-WYE, HEREFORDSHIRE HR9 7BW, ☎ 01989 564357, 9.30–5 MON–FRI, 10–5 SAT. **PERMANENT DISCOUNT OUTLET**

This designer discount business has a retail outlet in Ross-on-Wye where members can come and purchase top quality German clothes at wholesale prices. Provides classic, smart clothes for work or day wear and plenty of special occasion wear and evening clothes. Members are kept informed of special offers by post. You can join during your first visit when you will be issued with your own card and membership number at a cost of £5.

HERTFORDSHIRE

CENTRAL PARK

88A HIGH STREET, BARNET, HERTFORDSHIRE EN5 5SN, ☎ 020 8440 9950, 10–5.30 MON–SAT. **PERMANENT DISCOUNT OUTLET**

Large multiple group stocking cancelled orders and overruns for women, although most of the clothes are delabelled before they come here. There are dresses, suits, skirts, trousers and tops. Prices are very cheap. Formerly called The Outlet, the shops are now changed to Central Park.

DISCOUNT DRESSING

UPPER LEVEL, GALLERIA OUTLET CENTRE, COMET WAY, HATFIELD, HERTFORDSHIRE AL10 0XR, ☎ 01707 259925, 10–8 MON–FRI, 10–6 SAT, 11–5 SUN. **FACTORY SHOP IN A FACTORY SHOPPING VILLAGE**

Discount Dressing specialises in Italian, German and French designer brands. The stock on offer ranges from casual knitwear and separates to special occasion and evening wear. They also sell raincoats, coats and jackets. Sizes range from 6 to 24 and sometimes larger. All merchandise is brand new but offered at less than the original wholesale price (in other words, more than 50% off normal retail prices). These prices are so much lower than the high street that they have promised not to advertise the manufacturer's names, but you will recognise them when you see them. Discount Dressing is so confident of the excellent value for money that it offers that they guarantee to give you any outfit free of charge if you find it cheaper elsewhere. Good Deal Directory readers will be given an additional 10% discount on presentation of a copy of this book. There are five Discount Dressing outlets.

GLASERS FACTORY SHOP

ENTRANCE C, REMBRANDT HOUSE, KING GEORGE'S AVENUE, WHIPPENDELL ROAD, WATFORD, HERTFORDSHIRE WD18 7PW, ☎ 01923 234067, 9.30–4.30 MON–FRI.
DESIGNER SALES

End of season sales of well-made women's smart knitted suits, dresses and dress and jacket sets. Skirts tend to be knee-length, although some suits also have long skirts.

JANE SHILTON

GALLERIA OUTLET CENTRE, COMET WAY, HATFIELD, HERTFORDSHIRE AL10 0XR, ☎ 01707 276611, FAX: 01707 266662, **e-mail:** info@janeshilton.co.uk www.janeshilton.co.uk, 10–8 MON–FRI, 10–6 SAT, 11–5 SUN. **FACTORY SHOP IN A FACTORY SHOPPING VILLAGE**

See page 23 (CHESH)

JUST BETWEEN US

29 HILLSIDE ROAD, ST ALBANS, HERTFORDSHIRE AL1 3QW, ☎ 01727 811172, BY APPOINTMENT ONLY. **HIRE SHOP**

Offers an enormous selection of evening wear from 150 long and zappy party dresses to formal ballgowns and cocktail dresses in sizes 8 to 26, wraps, coats and boleros. Hire fee £72 plus £50 deposit for a flexible number of days. By appointment only, including evenings. The entire stock is changed every season and brand new stock is introduced. The old stock is then put into twice-yearly sales. Phone for dates. The sales are exceedingly popular as dresses can go for less than £50. Also sells dresses from new at wholesale prices.

MARVELLOUS SECONDS

3 MOUNT PARADE, MOUNT PLEASANT, COCKFOSTERS, HERTFORDSHIRE EN4 9DD, ☎ 020 8441 5582, 10–5 MON–SAT. **FACTORY SHOP**

This tiny shop sells previous catalogue and end of season plus imperfects from this popular catalogue label. Small baby and childrenswear section, from birth to three years, as well as a comprehensive maternity range including tights, trousers, dresses, skirts and tops. Prices are 50% less than shop or catalogue prices.

PILOT OUTLET LTD

GALLERIA OUTLET CENTRE, COMET WAY, HATFIELD, HERTFORDSHIRE AL10 0XR, ☎ 01707 258144, 10–8 MON–FRI, 10–6 SAT, 11–5 SUN. **FACTORY SHOP IN A FACTORY SHOPPING VILLAGE**

See page 24 (CHESH)

SCENT TO YOU

HATFIELD GALLERIA SHOPPING CENTRE, COMET WAY, HATFIELD, HERTFORDSHIRE AL10 0XR, ☎ 01707 258714, FAX: 01707 275027, 10–8 MON–FRI, 10–6 SAT, 11–5 SUN. **FACTORY SHOP IN A FACTORY SHOPPING VILLAGE**

UNIT 142A, HARLEQUIN CENTRE, WATFORD, HERTFORDSHIRE WD1 2TL, ☎ 01923 225712, FAX: 01923 225712, 9–6 MON–WED AND SAT, 8 ON THUR, FRI, 11–5 SUN. **PERMANENT DISCOUNT OUTLET**

See page 20 (BUCKS)

SIZE-UP

13 HIGH STREET, ROYSTON, HERTFORDSHIRE SG8 9AA, ☎ 01763 245436/Customer Service Freephone 0800 856540, **e-mail:** cs@sizeup.co.uk www.sizeup.co.uk, 9–5.30 MON–SAT.
PERMANENT DISCOUNT OUTLET

See page 18 (BEDS)

KENT

ALEXON AND EASTEX SALE SHOP

64 HIGH STREET, RAMSGATE, KENT CT11 9RS, ☎ 01843 589860, 9–5.30 MON–SAT.
PERMANENT DISCOUNT OUTLET

Eastex, Dash and Alexon clothing at reduced prices. Savings are between 20% and 75% and there are short term offers such as jackets for £19.99 reduced from £139. Stock is mostly last year's and at least half the original price.

ALEXON SALE SHOP

DE BRADELEI WHARF, CAMBRIDGE ROAD, DOVER, KENT CT17 9BY, ☎ 01304 226616, FAX: 01304 226617, 9.30–5.30 MON–FRI, 9.30–6 SAT, 11–5 SUN. **PERMANENT DISCOUNT OUTLET**

See page 26 (DERBY)

BE-WISE

5 GLOUCESTER PARADE, BLACKFEN ROAD, SIDCUP, KENT DA15 8PS, ☎ 020 8859 2658, 10–5 MON–SAT, CLOSED THUR. **DRESS AGENCY**

Middle market names including Principles, Marks & Spencer, Next and Warehouse as well as the occasional designer label. The shop works on a sale or return basis, so it offers a fast turnover of stock.

BON MARCHE

47 NORTHGATE, CANTERBURY, KENT CT1 1BE, ☎ 01227 764823, 9.30–5.30 MON–SAT.
DRESS AGENCY

A large, well-established dress agency which offers across-the-board labels, including Marks & Spencer, Jaeger, MaxMara, Jigsaw, French Connection, In-Wear and Karen Millen. Current season samples from J Taylor, Conran at Debenhams and House of Fraser are also available. Prices range from £10 for a Marks & Spencer top-quality outfit to £189, though most items are in the £20 to £69 price range. Day and evening wear as well as shoes, bags, scarves and hats are stocked. The owner says that style is more important than the label and is as likely to stock Dorothy Perkins as Dior. After one month in the shop, stock is reduced by one third.

CLOTHESLINE

58 UNION STREET, MAIDSTONE, KENT ME14 1ED, ☎ 01622 758439, 10–5 TUE–SAT.
DRESS AGENCY

Designer women's clothes at non-designer prices. Everything is half price or less, making Clothesline well worth a visit. There is a stunning range of occasion wear from names such as Gina, Simon Ellis, Condici and Frank Usher, and day wear from Episode, Bianca, Linea and Marella for formal and business needs. Separates and leisurewear are also stocked, as well as shoes and bags from Gabor, Bally, Roland Cartier and Carvela. New stock arrives daily and car parking is available close by.

DEJA VU

OLD SEAL HOUSE, 19 CHURCH STREET, SEAL, NEAR SEVENOAKS, KENT TN15 0DA,
☎ 01732 762155, 10–4 TUE–FRI, 10–1 SAT. **DRESS AGENCY**

In this small, friendly shop, established in 1977, you will find British and European designers such as Paul Costelloe, Gerry Weber, Betty Barclay, Liz Claiborne, Patsy Seddon and Ouiset as well as old favourites such as Jaeger, Marks & Spencer and Laura Ashley. The price range is from £10 to £200. There is also a small range of children's dresses. After six to eight weeks, clothes which haven't sold or been collected are sent to charity. An alteration service is also offered.

EUROBE

STATION APPROACH, ST MARY CRAY STATION, KENT BR5 2NB, ☎ 01689 822722, FAX: 01869 876517. **e-mail:** sales@eurobe.co.uk, www.eurobe.co.uk, 10–4.30 FRI–SAT.
PERMANENT DISCOUNT OUTLET

Wholesale warehouse open to the public. Customers are provided with a free Privilege Trade Card which must be produced on each visit. Labels on offer include Gerry Weber (including Taifun, Court One, sizes 16/18 in Samoon) Apriori (Escada Group) Michele trousers, Delores knitwear, Apanage coordinates, Cavita coordinates, Lebek coordinates and outerwear, Gardeur trousers and skirts, Rondissimo (size 18) and many more. Stock varies from current and future season showroom samples, late deliveries, and some items of second quality. All merchandise is sold at the wholesale/trade price plus VAT. Prices represent a saving of around 55% to 60% on normal retail prices.

FROCK FOLLIES

49 HIGH STREET, BECKENHAM, KENT BR3 1DA, ☎ 020 8650 9283, 9.30–5.30 MON–SAT.
DRESS AGENCY

Middle market labels from Marks & Spencer to Armani with some new samples. Specialises in hats, with more than 100 to choose from, as well as swimwear, shoes, hat pins, belts and scarves. The hats and jewellery are new. Plenty of evening wear, particularly ballgowns, especially from September to Christmas.

JANE SHILTON

MCARTHURGLEN DESIGNER OUTLET ASHFORD, ROMNEY MARSH ROAD, ASHFORD, JUNCTION 10 OF M20, KENT TN23 1EZ, ☎ 01233 625030, FAX: 01233 625033, **e-mail:** info@janeshilton.co.uk, www.janeshilton.co.uk, 10–6 MON–FRI, 8 ON THUR, 9–6 SAT, 11–5 SUN.
FACTORY SHOP IN A FACTORY SHOPPING VILLAGE

See page 23 (CHESH)

LIZ CLAIBORNE

DE BRADELEI WHARF, CAMBRIDGE, DOVER, KENT CT17 9BY, ☎ 01304 226616, FAX: 01304 226636, 9.30–5.30 MON–FRI, 9.30–6 SAT, 11–5 SUN. **FACTORY SHOP IN A FACTORY SHOPPING VILLAGE**

See page 23 (CHESH)

PANACHE

90–92 HIGH STREET, ROYAL TUNBRIDGE WELLS, KENT TN1 1YF, ☎ 01892 522883, 10–5 MON–SAT. **DRESS AGENCY**

On two floors, Panache sells women's nearly-new at savings of up to 50% on high street prices. The agency stocks a wide range of labels from Marella and Viyella to Paul Smith, LK Bennett, MaxMara and Escada. They also sell hats, a large selection of evening wear, coats, shoes, jackets, handbags and belts.

PILOT OUTLET LTD

MCARTHURGLEN DESIGNER OUTLET CENTRE, KIMBERLEY WAY, ASHFORD, KENT TN24 0SD, ☎ 01233 647369, 10–6 MON–FRI, 8 ON THUR, 9–6 SAT, 11–5 SUN. **FACTORY SHOP IN A FACTORY SHOPPING VILLAGE**

See page 24 (CHESH)

SCENT TO YOU

UNIT U073B, UPPER THAMES WALK, BLUE WATER, GREEN HIVE, KENT DA9 9ST, ☎ 01322 387373, FAX: 01322 387373, 10–9 MON–FRI, 10–8 SAT, 11–5 SUN. **FACTORY SHOP IN A FACTORY SHOPPING VILLAGE**

See page 20 (BUCKS)

THE DRESS AGENCY

5 BOURNE ROAD, BEXLEY, KENT DA5 1LG, ☎ 01322 523451, 10.30–5 TUE–SAT. **DRESS AGENCY**

Mixed selection of chainstore clothes and nearly-new designer wear in sizes 6 to 24 plus a large selection of shoes, hats and other accessories. Labels include Rodier and Betty Barclay.

THE FROCK EXCHANGE

7 WALDEN PARADE, WALDEN ROAD, CHISLEHURST, KENT BR7 5DW, 9–4 MON–SAT, CLOSED WED. **DRESS AGENCY**

Under new ownership since March 2001, this shop has undergone refurbishment. Located less than one mile from Chislehurst high street, with easy free parking, the Frock Exchange sells an extensive range of nearly-new clothes from the high street chains, plus names such as Karen

Millen, Giorgio Armani, Episode, Versace, Moschino, Gucci, Nicole Farhi, Joseph and Jacques Vert. There are also wonderful outifts from top houses such as Jean Muir, Bruce Oldfield, Escada and Valentino. Apart from dresses and separates, the shop also has a wide selection of bags, belts, jewellery (real diamonds as well as fakes), hats, scarves and footwear. Most clothing is not more than two years old and there is a rapid turnover with new stock constantly arriving each day. They also stock children's designer clothes such as Polo Ralph Lauren, Donna Karan and Moschino. All the women's fashions and accessories in the basement are discounted by a further 25%. The basement also sells bric a brac and household linens.

WAREHOUSE

UNIT 59, MCARTHURGLEN DESIGNER OUTLET, ASHFORD, KENT TN24 0SD, ☎ 01233 633817, 10–6 MON–SAT, 8 ON THUR, 11–5 SUN. **FACTORY SHOP IN A FACTORY SHOPPING VILLAGE**

See page 25 (CHESH)

WINDSMOOR GROUP

MCARTHURGLEN DESIGNER OUTLET ASHFORD, KIMBERLEY WAY, ASHFORD, JUNCTION 10 OF M20, KENT TN24 0SD, ☎ 01233 625846, FAX: 01233 895902, 10–6 MON–FRI, 8 ON THUR, 9–6 SAT, 11–5 SUN. **FACTORY SHOP IN A FACTORY SHOPPING VILLAGE**

DE BRADELEI WHARF (DOVER) LTD, CAMBRIDGE ROAD, DOVER, KENT CT17 9BY, ☎ 01304 226616, FAX: 01304 226636, 9.30–5.30 MON–FRI, 9.30–6 SAT, 11–5 SUN. **FACTORY SHOP IN A FACTORY SHOPPING VILLAGE**

See page 25 (CHESH)

LANCASHIRE

ALEXON

BOUNDARY MILL, BURNLEY ROAD, COLNE, LANCASHIRE BB8 8LS, ☎ 01282 865229, FAX: 01282 763153, 10–6 MON–FRI, 9 ON THUR, 9–6 SAT, 10–5 SUN. **PERMANENT DISCOUNT OUTLET**

469 LORD STREET, SOUTHPORT, LANCASHIRE PR9 0AQ, ☎ 01704 531281, 9–5.30 MON–SAT. **PERMANENT DISCOUNT OUTLET**

See page 26 (DERBY)

CROFT MILL

LOWTHER LANE, FOULRIDGE, COLNE, LANCASHIRE BB8 7NG, ☎ 01282 869625, FAX: 01282 870038, **e-mail:** info@croftmill.co.uk www.croftmill.co.uk, 10–4 SEVEN DAYS A WEEK. ALSO MAIL ORDER. **FACTORY SHOP**

Sells fabrics, dress and furnishing, haberdashery and sheeting material, both in the shop and by mail order. Also stocks high quality upholstery fabrics and chenilles and offers a home make up service. Most of the fabrics are overruns, samples, ends of lines, bankrupt stock and some seconds. Nearly all, including the dress fabrics, are 60in (150cm) wide and range in price from £1 to £30 or so a metre. They include cottons, jerseys, sweatshirting, drills, linings, anorak fabric, coatings, and suitings. They send out a catalogue describing their current stock every two months or so and will supply samples up to ten items for £1; up to 30 items for £2; up to 50 items for £5, all of which is refundable if you make a purchase. Most have been manufactured for high street store clothes for shops such as Marks & Spencer, BhS, Laura Ashley and for Dorma. There are also pillows, cushion pads, tea towels and quilts, all at factory shop prices.

DESIGN R FINE FRAGRANCES

PO BOX 231, BOLTON, LANCASHIRE BL3 4FF, ☎ 01204 650132, **e-mail:** info@designr.co.uk www.design-r.freeserve.co.uk, MAIL ORDER. **PERMANENT DISCOUNT OUTLET**

Up to 75% off well-known fragrances. Specialises in the newer lines from Calvin Klein, Dolce & Gabbana, Armani, Versace and Polo Sport.

FOUR SEASONS

154 COLLEGE ROAD, CROSBY, LIVERPOOL, LANCASHIRE L23 3DP, ☎ 0151 924 2863, 9.30–5.30 MON–SAT. **HIRE SHOP**

Specialists in hiring and selling hats, Four Seasons has been in business for 17 years and has more than 450 hats from which to choose. The main business is in hiring hats for all occasions – customers can bring their outfit to find the perfect match, and trimmings can be added from as little as £2.50. Hire fees start from £10 up to £30 for a period of four days or longer by arrangement. There are also accessories for sale, particularly jewellery, scarves, gloves and handbags. Ex-hire hats are sold off at reasonable prices.

JANE SHILTON

FREEPORT SHOPPING VILLAGE, ANCHORAGE ROAD, FLEETWOOD, LANCASHIRE FY7 6AE, ☎ 01253 773875, FAX: 01253 878945, **e-mail:** info@janeshilton.co.uk www.janeshilton.co.uk, 10–6 SEVEN DAYS A WEEK, 8 ON THUR, FRI. **FACTORY SHOP IN A FACTORY SHOPPING VILLAGE**

See page 23 (CHESH)

JUMPER

BRIDGE MILL, COWAN BRIDGE, CARNFORTH, LANCASHIRE LA6 2HS, ☎ 0845 130 9595, 10–4 SEVEN DAYS A WEEK IN WINTER, 10–5 SUMMER. **FACTORY SHOP**

BOUNDARY MILL STORES, BURNLEY ROAD, COLNE, LANCASHIRE BB8 8LS, ☎ 01282 865229, 9–6 MON–SAT, 11–5 SUN. **FACTORY SHOP**

See page 23 (CHESH)

LIZ CLAIBORNE

BOUNDARY MILL, BURNLEY ROAD, COLNE, LANCASHIRE BB8 8LS, ☎ 01282 865229, FAX: 01282 863153, 10–6 MON–FRI, 9 ON THUR, 9–6 SAT, 10–5 SUN. **FACTORY SHOP IN A FACTORY SHOPPING VILLAGE**

See page 23 (CHESH)

OAK MOUNT MILL SHOP

WISEMAN STREET, BURNLEY, LANCASHIRE BB11 1RU, ☎ 01282 414950, 9.15–5 MON–SAT. **FACTORY SHOP**

Factory shop selling a small range of dress fabrics and a wide range of curtain fabrics.

PILOT OUTLET LTD

FREEPORT VILLAGE, ANCHORAGE ROAD, FLEETWOOD, LANCASHIRE FY7 6AE, ☎ 01253 877575, 10–6 MON–WED, 10–8 THUR, FRI, 10–6 SAT, SUN. **FACTORY SHOP IN A FACTORY SHOPPING VILLAGE**

THE DESIGNER OUTLET AT THE LOWRY, QUAYS ROAD, SALFORD QUAYS, MANCHESTER, LANCASHIRE M5 2WZ, ☎ 0161 848 1850, 10–8 MON–FRI, 9–7 SAT, 11–5 SUN. **FACTORY SHOP IN A FACTORY SHOPPING VILLAGE**

See page 24 (CHESH)

SCENT TO YOU

BOUNDARY MILLS, BURNLEY ROAD, COLNE, LANCASHIRE BB8 8LS, ☎ 01282 865229, FAX: 01282 863153, 10–6 MON–FRI, 9 ON THUR, 9–6 SAT, 10–5 SUN. **PERMANENT DISCOUNT OUTLET**

UNIT 5, WEST ONE FASHION PARK, ECCLES, MANCHESTER, LANCASHIRE M30 0DY, ☎ 0161 789 4227, 10–6 MON–FRI (8 IN SUMMER), 9–6 SAT, 11–5 SUN. **FACTORY SHOP IN A FACTORY SHOPPING VILLAGE**

THE DESIGNER ROOM, FREEPORT FLEETWOOD OUTLET VILLAGE, ANCHORAGE ROAD, FLEETWOOD, 12 MILES FROM JUNCTION 3 OF M55, LANCASHIRE FY7 6AE, ☎ 01253 770080, 10–6 SEVEN DAYS A WEEK, 8 ON THUR, FRI. **FACTORY SHOP IN A FACTORY SHOPPING VILLAGE**

THE MANCHESTER OUTLET MALL AT THE LOWRY, THE QUAYS, SALFORD QUAYS, NEAR

MANCHESTER, LANCASHIRE M52 2WZ, ☎ 0161 873 8970, 10–8 MON–FRI, 9–7 SAT, 11–5 SUN. **FACTORY SHOP IN A FACTORY SHOPPING VILLAGE**

See page 20 (BUCKS)

THE DESIGNER ROOM

WEST ONE RETAIL PARK, ECCLES, MANCHESTER, LANCASHIRE M30 0DX, ☎ 0161 789 4227, 10–6 MON–FRI, 9–6 SAT, 11–5 SUN. **FACTORY SHOP IN A FACTORY SHOPPING VILLAGE**

CENTRAL 12 RETAIL PARK, OFF DERBY ROAD, SOUTHPORT, LANCASHIRE PR9 0TY, ☎ 01704 546105, 10–6 MON–SAT, 11–4 SUN. **FACTORY SHOP IN A FACTORY SHOPPING VILLAGE**

See page 92 (BUCKS)

THE FASHION AGENCY

FIRST FLOOR, 21 QUEEN STREET, BLACKPOOL LANCASHIRE FY1 1LN, ☎ 01253 628679, 10.30–4.30 TUE–FRI, 10.30–4 SAT. **DRESS AGENCY**

A spacious showroom above a fashion shop called Elizabeth Todd. In business for more than 25 years, it offers top end of the market nearly-new outfits and Continental separates. A large and constantly-changing selection of labels such as Yves Saint Laurent, Escada, Chanel, Morgan, Versace and Moschino make this a very popular shop. It caters for all ages and from casual to cocktail wear. It also sells shoes, handbags and jewellery; there is a permanent half-price sale rail.

WINDSMOOR SALE SHOP

BOUNDARY MILL, BURNLEY ROAD, COLNE, LANCASHIRE BB8 8LF, ☎ 01282 865229, FAX: 01282 870263, 10–6 MON–FRI, 8 ON THUR, 9–6 SAT, 10–5 SUN. **FACTORY SHOP**

Previous season's stock as well as any returned merchandise and overmakes from the Windsmoor, Planet and Precis Petite ranges at discounts averaging about 50% off the original price. Also stocks Danimac womenswear and menswear at discounted prices of around 50%.

LEICESTERSHIRE

BRAND NAMES FOR LESS

45 CASTLE STREET, HINCKLEY, LEICESTERSHIRE LE10 1DA, ☎ 01455 611558, 9–5 MON–SAT. **PERMANENT DISCOUNT OUTLET**

Sells quality brand names for less, this shop sells perfect stock sourced from throughout Europe. Sells women's clothing, cotton knitwear, separates and jackets at factory direct prices, which can be as much as 70% off the normal retail prices. The shop is small but well stocked and organised to make the maximum use of the space. The stock includes dresses, jackets, rainwear, shoes, underwear, tights, suits, blouses, sweaters, nightwear, trousers, jeans and anoraks, with dressing gowns and evening wear at Christmas only. There is another branch at Hinckley, Leicestershire.

DIRECT COSMETICS LTD

LONG ROW, OAKHAM, LEICESTERSHIRE LE15 6LN, ☎ 0870 746 0040, FAX: 0870 746 0042, **e-mail:** customercare@directcosmetics.com www.directcosmetics.com, MAIL ORDER. **PERMANENT DISCOUNT OUTLET**

This mail order and now internet business has been supplying international brands of cosmetics, perfumes, skincare and beauty products direct to the public since 1977. Brands available include Max Factor, Revlon, Elizabeth Arden, Estee Lauder, Clinique, Clarins, Coppertone, Cacharel, Givenchy, Yves Saint Laurent and Crown Perfumery, to name just a few, at prices up to 90% off the UK retail price. Phone for a price list with more than 400 offers to be sent direct to you free of charge. Alternatively, look at the website which features more than 2,200 product lines. Direct Cosmetics is a Which? Web Trader authorised site and has been featured in the Daily Mail, Essentials magazine, Shop@Home and The Sunday Times.

EVEDEN FACTORY SHOP

NORTH STREET, WHITWICK, COALVILLE, LEICESTERSHIRE, ☎ 01530 837647, 10–4 TUE–FRI, 9–1 SAT. **FACTORY SHOP**

This factory shop sells designer lingerie and women's swimwear. Many bargains are available in large cup sizes and a fitting service is available if required. The shop has a car park and level access for wheelchairs and pushchairs.

JAEGER/VIYELLA

C/O MITCHELL GRIEVE LTD, WOLSLEY ROAD, COALVILLE, LEICESTERSHIRE LE7 3TR, ☎ 01530 835506, 10–5 MON–SAT. **FACTORY SHOP**

Contemporary classics from Jaeger at excellent prices. Most of the merchandise is previous seasons' stock, but you might also find some special makes.

JILLY'S DRESS AGENCY

THE SONDES BARN, MAIN STREET, ROCKINGHAM, NEAR MARKET HARBOROUGH, LEICESTERSHIRE LE16 8TG, ☎ 01536 770352, 10.30–4 MON–SAT. **DRESS AGENCY AND HIRE SHOP**

Designer dress agency and evening wear hire. Labels tend to be designer oriented – the high street names stocked regularly include Windsmoor, Wallis, Monsoon and Marks & Spencer. Hire costs from £35 to £75 for designer ballgowns. Also sells shoes, bags and jewellery and hat hire is now available from £20 to £55.

RIGBY & PELLER & FANTASIE FACTORY SHOP

EVEDEN LTD, NORTH STREET, WHITWICK, COALVILLE, LEICESTERSHIRE LE67 5HA, ☎ 01530 510330, www.eveden.com, 10–4 TUE–FRI, 9–1 SAT. **FACTORY SHOP**

Range of Fantasie lingerie and swimwear, as well as Rigby & Peller and Freya underwear including bras, pants, thongs and suspender belts at discounted prices. Specialises in larger cup sizes up to J-cup fitting. Some of the stock is seconds but most is perfect, redundant stock. The bra sized swimwear goes up to a G fitting.

SIZE-UP

16 NOTTINGHAM STREET, MELTON MOWBRAY, LEICESTERSHIRE LE13 1NN, ☎ 01664 562408 **e-mail:** cs@sizeup.co.uk www.sizeup.co.uk, 9–5.30 MON–SAT. **PERMANENT DISCOUNT OUTLET**

See page 18 (BEDS)

THE DRESS AGENCY

THE CROSS, ENDERBY, LEICESTERSHIRE LE9 5NJ, ☎ 0116 275 0501, www.thedressagency.co.uk, 10–4 MON–SAT. **DRESS AGENCY**

Described as 'Leicester's best-kept secret', The Dress Agency is an Aladdin's cave of fantastic bargains in womenswear. They stock up-to-the-minute nearly-new fashions ranging from Next to Nicole Farhi, with new stock arriving daily. Clothes range from business suits to leisure wear, and from evening wear to outfits for special occasions. Also stocks a popular selection of accessories and cosmetics, and has a size 16+ department and sale room.

WINDSMOOR GROUP

DE BRADELEI MILL SHOP, LOWER LEICESTER ROAD, LUTTERWORTH, LEICESTER, LEICESTERSHIRE LE17 4NF, ☎ 01455 557571, 9.30–5.30 MON–FRI, 9.30–6 SAT, 10.30–4.30 SUN. **FACTORY SHOP IN A FACTORY SHOPPING VILLAGE**

See page 25 (CHESH)

LINCOLNSHIRE

ALEXON SALE SHOP

BOUNDARY MILL, GONERBY MOOR, GRANTHAM, LINCOLNSHIRE NG32 2AB, ☎ 01476 591001, FAX: 01476 591184, 9.30–5.30 MON–SAT, 11–5 SUN. **PERMANENT DISCOUNT OUTLET**

4 ST BENEDICTS SQUARE, LINCOLN, LINCOLNSHIRE LN5 7AR, ☎ 01522 545220, 9–5.30 MON–SAT. **PERMANENT DISCOUNT OUTLET**

See page 26 (DERBY)

DISCOUNT DRESSING

45 STEEP HILL, LINCOLN, LINCOLNSHIRE LN2 1LU, ☎ 01522 532239, 10–6 MON–SAT.
PERMANENT DISCOUNT OUTLET

See page 33 (HERTS)

JAEGER/VIYELLA FACTORY OUTLET

BOUNDARY MILLS STORES, GONERBY MOORE, OFF THE A1, GRANTHAM, LINCOLNSHIRE NG32 2AB, ☎ 01476 591001, 9.30–5.30 MON–SAT. **FACTORY SHOP**

Contemporary classics from Jaeger at excellent prices. Most of the merchandise is previous seasons' stock, but you might also find some special makes. This branch stocks tailoring and knitwear for women only.

JUMPER

BOUNDARY MILL STORES, GONERBY MOOR, GRANTHAM, LINCOLNSHIRE NG32 2AB, ☎ 01476 591001, 9–6 MON–SAT, 11–5 SUN. **FACTORY SHOP**

See page 23 (CHESH)

LIZ CLAIBORNE

GRANTHAM MILL, DOWNTOWN, GONERBY MOOR, GRANTHAM, LINCOLNSHIRE NG32 2AB, ☎ 01476 591001, FAX: 01476 591184, 9.30–5.30 MON–SAT, 11–5 SUN. **FACTORY SHOP IN A FACTORY SHOPPING VILLAGE**

See page 23 (CHESH)

SIZE-UP

72 LUMLEY ROAD, SKEGNESS, LINCOLNSHIRE PE25 3NG, ☎ 01754 766777/Customer Service Freephone 0800 856540 **e-mail:** cs@sizeup.co.uk www.sizeup.co.uk, 9–5.30 MON–SAT, 10–4 SUN. **PERMANENT DISCOUNT OUTLET**

See page 18 (BEDS)

WINDSMOOR GROUP

BOUNDARY MILL STORES, DOWNTOWN SUPERSTORE, GONERBY MOOR, GRANTHAM, LINCOLNSHIRE NG32 2AB, ☎ 01476 591001, FAX: 01476 591184, 9.30–5.30 MON–SAT, 11–5 SUN. **FACTORY SHOP IN A FACTORY SHOPPING VILLAGE**

See page 25 (CHESH)

LONDON

ANNIES VINTAGE COSTUME AND TEXTILES

12 CAMDEN PASSAGE, ISLINGTON, LONDON N1 8ED, ☎ 020 7359 0796, 11- 6 MON–SAT.
SECONDHAND AND VINTAGE CLOTHES

Mainly women's clothes from late Victorian times to the Fifties, specialising in Twenties beaded garments, as well as ballgowns, silk lingerie, Forties suits and blouses, table linen, cushions, curtains, textiles and bed linen.

ARTWORK

GOTTELIER LTD, 103 BERMONDSEY STREET, LONDON SE1 3XB, ☎ 020 7403 6332, PHONE TO BE ADDED TO MAILING LIST. **DESIGNER SALES**

Twice-yearly showroom sales of distinctive chunky knitwear and clothing made mostly from natural fibres. Sales are usually held in June and November when stock is offered at half price or less. Limited parking outside. Phone to put your name on the mailing list.

BERTIE GOLIGHTLY (UK) LTD

48 BEAUCHAMP PLACE, NEAR HARRODS, LONDON SW3 1NX, ☎ 020 7584 7270, FAX: 020 7584 7270, www.bertiego.co.uk, 10–6 MON–SAT, 7 ON WED, 12–5 SUN. **DRESS AGENCY**

Former stunt girl, Roberta Gibbs, celebrates 21 years of Bertie Golightly and is selling a richly diverse selection of the world's most famous labels including Chanel, Valentino, Armani, Yves

Saint Laurent. To complete your outfit, there are also hats, scarves, costume jewellery and shoes from Hermes, Philip Somerville and Gucci, etc. Ballgowns and evening wear are Bertie's speciality – a whole floor full awaits you. Many samples are 50% off the normal price. All items are immaculate and in season. Come to Bertie's and put the fun back into shopping, says Roberta.

BODIE & GIBBS

16 MOTCOMB STREET, LONDON SW1X 8LB, ☎ 020 7259 6620, **e-mail:** bodieandgibbs@yahoo.co.uk www.bodie&gibbs.co.uk, 10–6 MON–FRI, 7 ON WED, 11–5 SAT. **HIRE SHOP**

Designer and couture dresses to hire. Long evening dresses from Bruce Oldfield, Calvin Klein, Tomasz Starzewski and Amanda Wakeley are just some of the 300 dresses from which to choose in sizes up to 16. Also a selection of evening bags and jewellery to buy or to hire.

BUTTERFLY

3 LOWER RICHMOND ROAD, PUTNEY BRIDGE, LONDON SW15 1EJ, ☎ 020 8788 8304, 10.30–6 MON–FRI, 10–5 SAT. **DRESS AGENCY**

New and nearly-new designer clothes, new samples and end of ranges, this shop has been established since 1981. Selection includes Armani, Nicole Farhi, French Connection, Jigsaw and Ghost. Lots of linen, silks, cashmere, wool and natural fibres. Also some samples and clothes used for modelling, handbags, scarves and accessories. Mainly young designers.

BUTTERFLY

28 OLD BAILEY, LONDON EC4M 7HS, ☎ 020 7489 8288, 12–6.30 MON, TUE, 12–4.30 WED, THUR, FRI. **PERMANENT DISCOUNT OUTLET**

28A PONSONBY PLACE, LONDON SW1P 4PR, ☎ 020 7821 1983, 12–6.30 TUE–FRI. **PERMANENT DISCOUNT OUTLET**

Sells fashion samples obtained through extensive contacts in the industry at wholesale price or less. Stock is from the current season and the following season so that you can be ahead of the fashion – but only if you are a size 10 or 12 as samples are mostly model-sizes with a few sizes 14 and 16. As well as some British designers, the shop has a lot of German, French and Italian labels, many of which can be seen in Harrods designer department. There's Dusk, Caroline Roumer, Character, Frank Usher, Tuzzi, Fenn Wright & Manson, raincoats and rain jackets from Savannah at less than half price and hats, jewellery and handbags.

CAROLINE CHARLES

9 ST JOHN'S WOOD HIGH STREET, LONDON NW8 7NG, ☎ 020 7483 0080, FAX: 020 7483 0090, 10–6 MON–SAT. **PERMANENT DISCOUNT OUTLET**

This shop has stock at full price and a sale basement, selling merchandise at reductions of up to 75%, for Caroline Charles clothing. Here, end of season outfits, samples and one-offs which never made it into production are sold at discounts of at least 30%. Day wear to evening wear is covered as well as handbags, belts, jewellery, scarves, hats and knitwear at up to 50% off.

CATHERINE GROSVENOR DESIGNS

3 ELYSTAN STREET, CHELSEA GREEN, LONDON SW3 3NT, ☎ 020 7584 2112, FAX: 020 7591 0905, www.catherinegrosvenor.co.uk, 10–5.30 MON–FRI, 10–4 SAT. **PERMANENT DISCOUNT OUTLET**

Own designer knitwear at competitive prices. There are pashminas, cottons, cashmere and merino wools, and linens, jumpers, cardigans, jackets, skirts, designer jewellery and accessories. Offers made-to-measure service.

CATWALK NEARLY-NEW DESIGNER CLOTHES

52 BLANDFORD STREET, LONDON W1U 7HY, ☎ 020 7935 1052, 12.30–6 MON, 11.15–6 TUE, WED, THUR, FRI, 11.15–5 SAT. **DRESS AGENCY**

Nearly-new designer clothes from Chanel to Ghost, Gucci to Whistles and including Prada, Armani and Jil Sander. Has a good range of young funky designer gear such as Dolce & Gabbana, Joseph, Mui Mui, DKNY and Katherine Hamnett. Always has a wide variety of suits, tops, skirts, trousers etc. Lots of accessories including shoes especially good quality handbags such as Prada, Gucci and Anya Hindmarch. For example, Emporio Armani suit, £129; Prada trousers, £50; MaxMara jumper, £30; and Mui Mui dress, £69.

CENTRAL PARK

152 MUSWELL HILL BROADWAY, MUSWELL HILL, LONDON N10, ☎ 020 8883 9122, 9.30–6 MON–SAT, 1–5 SUN. **PERMANENT DISCOUNT OUTLET**

UNIT B AND C, BAKER STREET STATION, BAKERLOO TICKET HALL, LONDON NW1, ☎ 020 7935 2820, 10–8 MON–SAT, 12–6 SUN. **PERMANENT DISCOUNT OUTLET**

WEST 1 SHOPPING CENTRE, LOWER GROUND FLOOR, BOND STREET STATION, LONDON W1, ☎ 020 7495 5097, 10 -7 MON–SAT, 1–5 SUN. **PERMANENT DISCOUNT OUTLET**

67 MALL, EALING, LONDON W5 5LS, ☎ 020 8567 2250, 10–7 MON–SAT, 11–5 SUN. **PERMANENT DISCOUNT OUTLET**

9 EALING BROADWAY, EALING, LONDON W5 2NH, ☎ 020 8567 0503, 10–7 MON–SAT, 11–5 SUN. **PERMANENT DISCOUNT OUTLET**

HAMMERSMITH BROADWAY STATION, LONDON W6 9YE, ☎ 020 8563 1700, 10–7 MON–SAT, 1–6 SUN. **PERMANENT DISCOUNT OUTLET**

See page 33 (HERTS)

CERRUTI 1881

BATTERSEA, LONDON, ☎ 020 7720 6262. **DESIGNER SALES**

Put your name down on the mailing list for an automatic invitation to the showroom sales at which prices are considerably reduced. As we went to press, the showroom was relocating. Phone the above telephone number for new details.

CHANGE OF HABIT

65 ABBEVILLE ROAD, CLAPHAM, LONDON SW4 9JW, ☎ 020 8675 9475, 11–6 MON–FRI, 10–6 SAT. **DRESS AGENCY**

Day and evening wear as good as new from high street to designer label. Described by the owner as 'everyday clothes for everyday people at realistic prices'. Very high turnover. Also brand new clothes and accessories and recently added antiques and furnishing for the garden and conservatory.

CHLOE BROMLEY FASHIONS LTD

21 MONTPELIER VALE, BLACKHEATH VILLAGE, LONDON SE3 0TJ, ☎ 020 8318 4300, 9.30–6 MON–SAT, 11–5 SUN. **PERMANENT DISCOUNT OUTLET**

Chloe has been trading in top quality fashion for more than 30 years, specialising in special occasion outfits in sizes 8 to 22. Chloe 2, on the lower ground floor, stocks thousands of samples and seconds from Chloe's usual suppliers, specialising in factory rejects and seconds from Frank Usher and Joseph Ribkoff. This enables customers to buy top quality clothes at prices which range from 25% to 75% off the usual retail price. There is always a batch clearance rail for under £40; hats at half price; jewellery from £6; but no shoes.

CORNUCOPIA

12 UPPER TACHBROOK STREET, LONDON SW1V 1SH, ☎ 020 7828 5752, FAX: 020 7828 5752, 11–6 SEVEN DAYS A WEEK. **SECONDHAND AND VINTAGE CLOTHES**

This marvellous vintage clothes shop has been established for more than 34 years. Glamorous evening wear for women from the Twenties to modern day. Huge selection of evening wear, some designer samples, silk suits and hats, shoes, accessories, handbags, jewellery.

DELLA FINCH DESIGNER SALE

LONDON, ☎ 020 7834 9161, FAX: 020 7233 6385, PHONE FOR INFORMATION ABOUT TWICE YEARLY SALES. **DESIGNER SALE**

If you are in search of retail therapy, instant gratification is promised at Della's twice-yearly designer sales. Selling top designer labels at wholesale prices, often months before they arrive in the shops, and current season clothing at greatly reduced prices. Sizes range from 10 to 26. Membership is free: phone 020 7834 9161 to add your name to the mailing list to receive details of the next sale. Sales are always held in the London area.

DENNER CASHMERE

BEMCO BUILDING, JEWS ROW, LONDON SW18 1TB, ☎ 0870 120 0055, FAX: 020 8874 5053, **e-mail:** dennercashmere@bizonline.co.uk www.dennercashmere.co.uk, 24-HOUR MAIL ORDER LINE. WAREHOUSE SHOP THURSDAYS 10–5, EXCEPT AUGUST. ALSO OPEN BY APPOINTMENT AND HOLD SPECIAL SALES FROM TIME TO TIME. **PERMANENT DISCOUNT OUTLET**

Finest quality designer cashmere and silk/cashmere knitwear from as little as one third of shop prices. Because they only sell through mail order and their warehouse shop, overheads are low and profit margins can be kept to a minimum. Only the best quality yarns are used and the finishing is impeccable. They produce two collections a year: the spring/summer consists of garments made from silk/cashmere; the autumn/winter features items made of 100% cashmere. Styles include long cardigans, dresses, twinsets, cable knits, wraps, scarves, skinny ribs, tunics, classic V, round and polo neck sweaters. Each collection is designed so that pieces can be worn together to create a whole outfit or bought separately to mix and match with basics from a typical wardrobe. Prices from £39.90. Phone for the list of forthcoming sales, special offers and an up-to-date brochure.

DESIGNER BARGAINS

29 KENSINGTON CHURCH STREET, LONDON W8 4LL, ☎ 020 7795 6777, 10–6.30 MON–SAT. **DRESS AGENCY**

There are lots of top labels on sale here, as befits the catchment area, with hundreds of garments. Labels on sale include Thierry Mugler, Armani, Escada, Chanel, Dolce & Gabbana, Gucci, Moschino, Prada and Versace.

DESIGNER SALE

3 CLARENDON TERRACE, LONDON W9 1BZ, ☎ 020 7286 5573, FAX: 07958 945557. **e-mail:** lelsbells@amserve.com, 11–6 TUE–SAT. **PERMANENT DISCOUNT OUTLET**

A large and eclectic range of ex-sale designer labels including Vintage Voyage, Kyri, Viva Maria and Nina Morris. Evening wear, casual outfits, separates and accessories are all stocked. Also stocks Gharani Strok, Alice Temperley and a new range of young designers. Typical examples would be Voyage coats, originally retailing at £3.000, are sold for £300; Voyage jeans, £2.500, reduced to £250; Gharani Strok dresses, originally £700, now £250. Kyri bustiers are down from £250 to £80. All merchandise is brand new.

DESIGNS

60 ROSSLYN HILL, LONDON NW3 1ND, ☎ 020 7435 0100, 10–5.45 MON–SAT, 6.30 ON THUR. **DRESS AGENCY**

Designs has been established for more than 18 years, and sells women's designer clothes and accessories. Their most sought-after labels include Hermes, Chanel, Donna Karan, Ralph Lauren, Giorgio Armani, Prada, Gucci, Joseph, Issey Miyake and Jil Sander and they have a constant supply of covetable Gucci and Prada handbags and shoes. They only accept perfect merchandise under two years old and have a rapid turnover with the most exciting pieces coming their way. Regular customers talk about the spacious, relaxed atmosphere and prices remain keenly competitive: ranging from £5 to £500. They have more than 6,000 clients and take in stock from the UK, America and Italy. They also keep a range of girls' clothes from birth to seven years.

DISCOUNT DRESSING

16 SUSSEX RING, WOODSIDE PARK, LONDON N12, ☎ 020 8343 8343, 10–6 SEVEN DAYS A WEEK. **PERMANENT DISCOUNT OUTLET**

58 BAKER STREET, LONDON W1, ☎ 020 7486 7230, 10–6 SEVEN DAYS A WEEK. **PERMANENT DISCOUNT OUTLET**

See page 33 (HERTS)

DYNASTY

12A TURNHAM GREEN TERRACE, CHISWICK, LONDON W4 1QP, ☎ 020 8995 3846, 10.30–5 MON–SAT. **DRESS AGENCY**

Sells good quality secondhand clothes. Labels include Gucci, Prada, Joseph, Moschino, as well as occasionally La Perla swimwear. Examples of outfits for sale include a Gucci suit, £175; Christian Lacroix dress, £99; Paul Costelloe Dress, £49; La Perla swimsuits from £25 to £39; and Valentino three-piece, £220, originally £1,000.

EXCLUSIVO

24 HAMPSTEAD HIGH STREET, HAMPSTEAD, LONDON NW3 1QA, ☎ 020 7431 8618, **e-mail:** www.info@exclusivo.com, 11.30–6 SEVEN DAYS A WEEK. **DRESS AGENCY**

A small shop stocked high with every kind of label from Yves Saint Laurent, Prada, Gucci, Dior, Chanel, Donna Karan and Nicole Farhi. Prices vary according to age and condition of the garment, but can be up to 70% off the normal retail price. For example, French suits from £69.99, Prada and Gucci handbags from £80. There are usually about 1,500 outfits to choose from.

FACTORY DIRECT

17 STRUTTON GROUND, VICTORIA, LONDON SW1P 2HY, ☎ 020 7799 2651, 10.30–6 MON–FRI, 10–4 SAT. **PERMANENT DISCOUNT OUTLET**

Fashion for women which mostly consists of day and work wear: coats, suits, dresses, tops, skirts. Buying direct from a variety of different factories enables Factory Direct to offer current stock at discounts of up to 50% off normal retail prices. Clubwear is available occasionally.

FELICITY HAT HIRE

226 MUNSTER ROAD, LONDON SW6 6AZ, ☎ 020 7381 5128, **e-mail:** bubs@cheerful.com, 10–7 MON, THUR, FRI, 10–5 TUE, 10–1 SAT, BY APPOINTMENT ONLY ON WED. **HIRE SHOP**

113B NORTHCOTE ROAD, CLAPHAM, LONDON SW11 6PW, ☎ 020 7738 0838, **e-mail:** bubs@cheerful.com, 10–7 MON, THUR–FRI, 10–5 TUE, WED AND SAT. **HIRE SHOP**

The alternative to spending a fortune on a hat for a formal occasion. Choose from more than 400 hats, many of which are new, bought directly from milliners each season. Styles vary from Sir Frederick Fox straw hats to more contemporary styles from Caroline Hickman. To hire a hat for four days costs from £20 to £60.

FROCK FOLLIES

18 THE GRANGEWAY, GRANGE PARK, LONDON N21 2HG, ☎ 020 8360 3447, 9.30–5 TUE–SAT. **DRESS AGENCY**

Recommended by one of our readers who says that the owner is so helpful that shopping here is a pleasure. Double-fronted shop with more than 2,000 items in stock including costume jewellery, handbags, swimwear and shoes. Labels include Escada, Frank Usher, Karen Millen, Jacques Vert, Basler, Betty Barclay, Betty Jackson, Principles, Next and Monsoon – in other words, across the fashion spectrum. Also has hats for hire from £5 to £25, as well as smart maternity wear for hire. One of the cheapest secondhand clothes shops you will find.

GHOST LTD

263 KENSAL ROAD, LONDON W10 5DB, ☎ 020 8960 3121, **e-mail:** info@ghost.co.uk www.ghost.co.uk, **DESIGNER SALES**

Annual warehouse sale of famous Ghost label which consists of old stock, current season damaged stock, show pieces and one-off samples usually takes place in first or second week of December. Write to put your name down on the mailing list. Be prepared to spend a reasonable amount of time here as it gets very busy and queueing to pay can take a while.

JOEL & SON FABRICS

75–83 CHURCH STREET, LONDON NW8 8EU, ☎ 020 7724 6895, **e-mail:** info@JoelandSonfabrics.com www.joelandsonfabric.com, 8.30–5 MON–SAT. **PERMANENT DISCOUNT OUTLET**

London's foremost designer fabric store sells up-to-date fabrics used by the top catwalk designers and couturiers from Yves St Laurent and Cerruti to Versace and Gianfranco Ferre. Prices are very competitive, though not cheap, and the fabric is exceptional. Also carries a wide range of supplies for bridal wear including embroidered laces, beaded fabrics, Jacquards, Duchess satins, as well as veils in silk and silk mixes. Good range of designer lookalike buttons. Mr Joel & Son have been in the business for 45 years and at the same premises for more than 20 years. Staff are always on hand to advise and are proud of their personal service.

JOSEPH CLEARANCE SHOP

53 KING'S ROAD, LONDON SW3 1QN, ☎ 020 7730 7562, 10.30–6.30 MON–SAT, 7 ON WED, 1–6 SUN (12–5 IN WINTER). **PERMANENT DISCOUNT OUTLET**

End of season and clearance lines from the Joseph label at reductions of 60% and over. Several concessions include Gucci, Paul and Joe, Marni, Cacherel, Veronique Branquinho, Helmut Lang, Prada, Miu Miu, Michael Kors, Elspeth Gibson. Faulty stock from the current season is reduced by 30% upwards.

LAUREL HERMAN

18A LAMBOLLE PLACE, LONDON NW3 4PG, ☎ 020 7586 7925, FAX: 020 7586 7926, **e-mail:** info@pospres.co.uk www.pospres.co.uk, 10–7 MON–SAT BY APPOINTMENT ONLY. **PERMANENT DISCOUNT OUTLET**

Established for over 25 years, and with 2,000 regular clients, this is London's best-kept secret in order to maintain its exclusivity. Housed in a spacious, airy 'concealed' Hampstead showroom is an ever-changing melange of 6,000 upmarket designer items (Armani, Escada, MaxMara, Donna Karan, Chanel, Gucci, Valentino, etc) at a fraction of their original price. Both brand new and 'gently-worn' but sourced only from Laurel's own personal contacts who shop the world over to answer all requirements for day or evening, casual or formal, business or leisure. This unique concept is ideal for those who normally hate shopping, need a new look, have figure problems, or are simply clothesaholics. Many clients work towards the ultimate wardrobe solution – Laurel Herman's Wardrobe That Works – but all advice is totally objective, free of charge, and based on personal lifestyle, shape, personality and budget. (There is a brochure to explain the concept in more detail.) In order to maintain the peaceful, relaxed ambience, appointments are necessary. Open from 10am until 7pm Monday to Saturday, but twice weekly until 11pm for working women. Be warned, customers usually stay three or four hours! The collection is taken twice yearly to Southampton in May and November. Laurel Herman is also the MD of Positive Presence which offers a wide range of consultancy for men, women and organisations on improving personal or business wardrobe, style and/or image. This includes real life makeovers that last, image consultations, metamorphosis, workshops, seminars and talks. Positive Presence – another Laurel Herman creation – is an independent image consultancy and specialises in helping men and women to make the best of themselves in the most appropriate way. Laurel also creates women's events for the corporate market, professional organisations, fundraising, networks and social groups such as golf clubs and often appears on television and radio, as well as being regularly featured in the press (including The Times, Telegraph, Financial Mail on Sunday, The Finishing Touch, New Woman, Independent on Sunday) and both businesses are recommended by numerous clients.

LEVY AND FRIEND

9 EBURY BRIDGE ROAD, LONDON SW1W 8QX, ☎ 020 7730 5695, 11–6 MON–SAT, CLOSED WED. **DRESS AGENCY**

Well presented garments in pristine condition are sold in a relaxed atmosphere in this ground floor shop. Specialising in day wear, the shop offers fashionable, functional, affordable modern clothing from labels such as Prada, Joseph, Dolce & Gabbana, Ralph Lauren, Gucci, Gina and Karen Millen, as well as lots of accessories, designer bags, belts, shoes and boots. Established for 15 years, the shop has a clientele from around the world and the owner is ready with advice, if needed. Prices range from £10 to £200. Payment can be made by Switch, American Express, MasterCard, Visa and Electron.

OAKVILLE

GROUND FLOOR, 43 PORTLAND PLACE, LONDON W1B 1QH, ☎ 020 7580 3686, FAX: 020 7255 2050, **e-mail:** info@oakville.co.uk www.oakville.co.uk, **DESIGNER SALES**

Phone or write to put your name down on the mailing list for an automatic invitation to the showroom sales at which prices are considerably reduced. Designers include Ungaro and evening wear by Tadashi and other designer labels.

ONE NIGHT STAND

8 CHELSEA MANOR STUDIOS, FLOOD STREET, LONDON SW3 5SR, ☎ 020 7352 4848, FAX: 020 7376 8866, **e-mail:** joanna@onenightstand.co.uk www.onenightstand.co.uk, 10–6.30 MON–FRI, 10–4 SAT BY APPOINTMENT ONLY. **HIRE SHOP**

More than 500 designer dresses in stock, sizes 8 to 18, comprising mainly long evening wear. Also hires jewellery, evening bags, capes and jackets. Cost £130 to £180 for four days with a small number of more expensive items. Retail section with lingerie to complement clothes.

PANDORA

16–22 CHEVAL PLACE, LONDON SW7 1ES, ☎ 020 7589 5289, FAX: 020 7581 9256, 9–6 MON-SAT AND MOST BANK HOLIDAYS. **DRESS AGENCY**

Based around the corner from Harrods, this large shop with more than 5,000 items in stock sells only the top, well-known designer names: Anna Molinari, Boyd, Issey Miyake, JP Tods, Louis Vuitton, Voyage and Prada. They sell everything to do with a woman's wardrobe but it has to be in good condition and sport a top label. Also stocks a range of size 16 plus, as well as handbags, belts, hats and shoes. Shoes have to be mistakes (in other words, new or very gently worn) though bags can be older and can include crocodile, Hermes and Gucci. Everything is categorised into day wear, evening wear, trousers, skirts, etc so it is easy to browse. Clear-out sales are held in December/January and July/August, when all stock is reduced by 30%. Previous seasons' items are reduced by a further 20% in February and September.

RELLIK

8 GOLBORNE ROAD, LONDON W10, ☎ 020 8962 0089, OPEN 10–6 TUE–SAT.
SECONDHAND AND VINTAGE CLOTHES

Vintage clothes shop selling items from the Twenties including lots of well-known names of the Sixties and Seventies. Offers a customisation service. Also sells shoes, jewellery and accessories.

SALLY HAIR & BEAUTY SUPPLIES

81 SHAFTESBURY AVENUE, LONDON W1V 7AD, ☎ 020 7434 0064, 8–8 MON–SAT, 11–5 SUN. **PERMANENT DISCOUNT OUTLET**

See page 18 (BEDS)

SALOU

6 CHEVAL PLACE, LONDON SW7 1ES, ☎ 020 7581 2380, 10–5 MON–SAT. **DRESS AGENCY**

Two-storey shop which sells evening wear and separates downstairs, suits upstairs, as well as jewellery, hats and accessories. Labels include Giorgio Armani, Valentino, Gucci, Prada, Christian Lacroix, Chanel and Jean Paul Gaultier. Prices from £10 to £600 for a Chanel suit. The average price for a suit is between £60 and £120; the top end of the market averages £200 to £400. Loads of shoes from £30 including Gucci, Prada, Christian Dior and Chanel.

SCENT TO YOU

STY PERFUMES AND ACCESSORIES, UNIT 19, THE EXCHANGE SHOPPING CENTER, PUTNEY, LONDON SW15 1TW, ☎ 020 8780 0336, FAX: 020 8780 0343, 9–6 MON–SAT, 11–5 SUN. **PERMANENT DISCOUNT OUTLET**

UNIT 205B, CENTRE COURT SHOPPING CENTRE, 4 QUEENS ROAD, WIMBLEDON, LONDON SW19 8YA, ☎ 020 8944 0122, FAX: 0208 944 0133, 9.30–7 MON–FRI, 8 ON THUR, 9.30–6 SAT, 11–5 SUN. **PERMANENT DISCOUNT OUTLET**

See page 20 (BUCKS)

SCREENFACE LTD

20 AND 24 POWIS TERRACE, LONDON W11 1JH, ☎ 020 7221 8289, FAX: 020 7792 9357, **e-mail:** info@screenface.co.uk www.screenface.com, 9–6 MON–SAT. MAIL ORDER. **PERMANENT DISCOUNT OUTLET**

48 MONMOUTH STREET, LONDON WC2 9EP, ☎ 020 7836 3955, FAX: 0207 792 9357, **e-mail:** info@screenface.co.uk www.screenface.com, 10–7 MON–SAT, 12–5 SUN. **PERMANENT DISCOUNT OUTLET**

Stocks the largest selection of make-up in the UK and is open to individuals as well as professionals. The shop has collected together the very best from all over the world. In addition to everyday make-up, they stock body paints, eyelashes, temporary tattoos, camouflage products, shaders, highlighters, eye colours, glittering powders and a vast selection of accessory items. Their huge selection of brushes include retractable lip, eyeline and mascara brushes, perfect for the handbag. They make bags from UV proof PVC that will not crack or split and stock a huge range of powder puffs and sponges. Now stock airbursh systems which you can use to apply body paint or fake tan. All the products are available by mail order using a credit card. Or you could have a make-up lesson, £45 for one hour. Screenface also runs a business renting out mirrors and make-up chairs for location shoots.

SHEILA WARREN-HILL

THE GARDEN FLAT, 63 SHEPHERDS HILL, HIGHGATE, LONDON N6 5RE, ☎ 020 8348 8282 OR 078731 715981, **e-mail:** craig.connar@btinternet.com, BY APPOINTMENT ONLY. **DRESS AGENCY**

Sheila is a lovely, lively character who operates from her garden flat in London's Highgate, offering open house on Sundays when lunch and drinks are served while customers try on couture outfits. Many of her outfits were originally owned by rich and famous personalities. Having worn a dress to a special event, they can't be seen wearing the same outfit twice and so pass it on to Sheila to dispose of discreetly and enable them to recoup some of the costs and buy another dazzling creation for the next outing. The labels are top range – Jasper Conran, Giorgio Armani, Yves Saint Laurent, Chanel, Place Vendome, Gianfranco Ferre, Escada. The atmosphere is relaxed, with Sheila on hand to dispense advice if wanted. She also sells day wear, designer shoes, swimwear and jewellery. Sheila also has an arrangement with other nearly-new businesses around the country, who take some of her stock, which means that she always has a very good supply. Customers can also have clothes delivered to their home by chauffeur-driven Bentley. Phone her for details of her regular sales and for details of other shops taking her stock.

SIGN OF THE TIMES

17 ELYSTAN STREET, LONDON SW3 3NT, ☎ 020 7589 4774, 10–6 MON–FRI, 7.30 ON WED, 10–5.30 SAT. **DRESS AGENCY**

A broad range of clothes from casual to evening wear which includes Prada, Gucci, Donna Karan, Voyage, Fendi, Louis Vuitton, Chanel and Armani among its range of nearly-new bargains. Also lots of hats (Frederick Fox, Gilly Forge), handbags and shoes (Manolo Blahnik, Christian Laubourton, Gucci, J P Todds, Joseph Azurgary – in sizes 3 to 8).

SIZE PLUS

168 MUSWELL HILL BROADWAY, MUSWELL HILL, LONDON N10, ☎ 020 8444 5748, 9.30–6 MON–SAT, 12–5 SUN. **PERMANENT DISCOUNT OUTLET**

An offshoot of the Central Park group, this store caters especially for more mature women and larger sizes from 16 to 28. Stock is mostly cancelled orders and overruns with very good prices.

SOUTH MOLTON STREET DRUG STORE

583 ROMAN ROAD, LONDON E3 5EL, ☎ 020 8981 5040, FAX: 020 8981 7524, 10–5 MON, WED, FRI, 9.30–5 TUE, THUR, 9.30–6 SAT. MAIL ORDER. **PERMANENT DISCOUNT OUTLET**

1B HIGH STREET, WANSTEAD, LONDON E11 2AA, ☎ 020 8989 7372, 10–6 MON–SAT. MAIL ORDER. **PERMANENT DISCOUNT OUTLET**

Formerly situated in South Molton Street, now relocated, this permanent discount shop sells a wide range of cosmetics, some of which is current season, at discount prices. They usually stock Elizabeth Arden, Revlon, Ultima 11 and Max Factor as well as some of the more trendy brands. Also sells hair accessories, make-up brushes, mirrors, nail equipment toiletries and special purchases such as make-up cases, £9.99.

SURPRISE SURPRISE FOR WOMEN

51 GOLDERS GREEN ROAD, LONDON NW11 8EL, ☎ 020 8209 0042, 9–6.30 MON–SAT, 10–6 SUN. **PERMANENT DISCOUNT OUTLET**

A very good selection of women's clothing a very competitive prices.

THE CHANGING ROOM

148 ARTHUR ROAD, WIMBLEDON PARK, LONDON SW19 8AQ, ☎ 020 8947 1258, 1–6 MON, 11–6 TUE–FRI, 10–6 SAT. **DRESS AGENCY**

Fast-moving stock of designer samples, end of line and secondhand labels including: Ghost, Whistles, Jigsaw, Kenzo, Moschino, Armani, Resource, Marina Avaran, Mr Cat, Romeo Gigli. Also shoes and accessories. Sample and secondhand childrenswear: Gap, Parsisal, Kenzo, Monsoon, Jigsaw, Petit Bateau, Armani.

THE CORRIDOR

309A KING'S ROAD, CHELSEA, LONDON SW3 5EP, ☎ 020 7351 0772, 10.30–6.30 MON–SAT. **DRESS AGENCY**

Small, personalised boutique providing women's nearly-new and sample high quality designer clothing, handbags and jewellery. Names include Chanel, Prada, Valentino, Ralph Lauren, Alberta Ferretti and MaxMara, sold seasonally. Clothing is taken in on a sale or return basis. An alteration service is also available. Costume jewellery and accessories are also available.

THE MAKE-UP CENTRE

52A WALHAM GROVE, FULHAM, LONDON SW6 1QR, ☎ 020 7381 0213, **e-mail:** info@themake-upcentre.co.uk www.themake-upcentre.co.uk, 10–4 MON–FRI. **PERMANENT DISCOUNT OUTLET**

Sells own brands of matt eyeshadow, foundation, and blusher which are twice the size of those you can buy in department stores, as well as good sable brushes which are cheaper than those found in artists' shops. Also do makeovers and offer make-up lessons for £125 for one and a half hours. With more than 30 years' experience in the business, they have not only trained the best makeup artists, but made up prime ministers, film stars and television presenters. Full wedding makeovers from £125.

TWENTIETH CENTURY FROX

614 FULHAM ROAD, LONDON SW6 5RP, ☎ 020 7731 3242, 10–7 MON, WED, THUR, 10–6 TUE, FRI, SAT. **HIRE SHOP**

Two hundred dresses, mainly ballgowns and cocktail dresses, to hire or to buy. Costs £75 to £95 for three days' hire. No appointment necessary. Also new and ex-hire stock available to buy.

UPSTAIRS DOWNSTAIRS

8 MALCOLM COURT, MALCOLM CRESCENT, HENDON, LONDON NW4 4PJ, ☎ 020 8202 7720, BY APPOINTMENT ONLY. **DRESS AGENCY**

Now established for 20 years, Upstairs Downstairs features top designer makes in perfect condition on uncluttered rails which makes for unhurried browsing. Accessories are for sale as well as day clothes. Customers come from all over the country and clothes from all over the world, where they both enjoy personal attention. Designers include Louis Feraud, Valentino, Jobis, Yarell, MaxMara and Cerruti. There is also an alterations service.

USA FASHION

111 FONTHILL ROAD, LONDON N4 3JH, ☎ 020 7272 3992, 9.30–5.30 MON–FRI, 9–4 SAT. **PERMANENT DISCOUNT OUTLET**

Specialists in special occasion wear: bridalwear, bridesmaid dresses and evening wear (more than 300 different styles) in sizes 8 to 26. They also stock women's casual wear from familiar high street and American designers, all at discounted prices. For example, a garment which would retail at £170 costs only £60 here. All the stock is brand new. There is also childrenswear from age 12 upwards.

VIRGINIA

98 PORTLAND ROAD, HOLLAND PARK, LONDON W11 4LQ, ☎ 020 7727 9908, FAX: 020 7229 2198, **e-mail:** virginia@dircon.co.uk, 11–6 MON–SAT. **SECONDHAND AND VINTAGE CLOTHES**

Antique clothing from the 1900s to the Forties. There are nightgowns, beaded dresses, chiffon, hats and accessories. Everything is a one-off and top quality.

MIDDLESEX

OCEAN

ST ANN'S ROAD, HARROW, MIDDLESEX HA1 11G, ☎ 020 8861 3554, **e-mail:** info@claudiainternational.co.uk, 9–6 MON–SAT, 7 ON THUR, 11–5 SUN, 10–5 BANK HOLIDAYS. **PERMANENT DISCOUNT OUTLET**

Manufacturers of women's fashion, they sell everyday wear at very cheap prices: tops, £2.50; dresses, £10; suits, £20; evening wear from £20; skirts and trousers, £10 each, all in sizes ranging from 10–26.

SESSION

GARDEN ROOM, SYON PARK, BRENTFORD, MIDDLESEX, ☎ 020 8994 4983, **DESIGNER SALES**

Designer sales run by fashion trade insider and featuring big-name British and international labels, all at discounted prices. There are usually about eight sales each year, each one featuring a variety of different names which can't be mentioned here as the designers are very sensitive about their names being used in promoting discount sales. Membership costs £29.50 a year which also entitles you to other concessions, which were being put together as we went to press. Phone for more details. Also offers exclusive one-day showroom sales for members.

THE CLOTHES HORSE

166 HIGH STREET, TEDDINGTON, MIDDLESEX TW11, ☎ 020 8977 1887, 11–6 TUE–SAT. **DRESS AGENCY**

Nearly-new outfits from dresses, jackets, suits, coats to shoes, handbags, belts and jewellery. Labels include Whistles, Ghost, Gap, Hobbs and Next.

NORFOLK

ALEXON SALE SHOP

THEATRE PLAIN, GREAT YARMOUTH, NORFOLK NR30 2BE, ☎ 01493 332146, 9–5 MON–SAT. **PERMANENT DISCOUNT OUTLET**

See page 26 (DERBY)

ESSENTIAL COLLECTION

63 SUSSEX STREET, NORWICH, NORFOLK NR3 3BP, ☎ 01603 219266, 10–4 MON–SAT.
DRESS AGENCY

Two-storey shop on the limits of the city centre with a marble entrance and staircase. It specialises in bridal wear, mother-of-the-bride, evening wear and ballgowns, plus a good selection of casual day wear. Labels range from high street to designer: Frank Usher, Jacques Vert, Mark Angelo, Bianca, Wallis, Next, Marks & Spencer, Monsoon as well as some one-off samples and large sizes. There is a large selection of shoes, bags, belts, scarves and jewellery. A special room is set aside with hundreds of fancy dress costumes. There is a hat, ballgown and men's dinner suit hire service. A seamstress service is available, too.

SIZE-UP

1 HIGH STREET, EAST DEREHAM, NORFOLK NR19 1DZ, ☎ 01362 853214

5 HIGH STREET, EAST DEREHAM, NORFOLK NR19 1DZ, ☎ 01362 699641

34 MARKET PLACE, GREAT YARMOUTH, NORFOLK NR30 1LX, ☎ 01493 332187

83 HIGH STREET, KINGS LYNN, NORFOLK PE30 1BL, ☎ 01553 763425

47 MARKET PLACE, SWAFFHAM, NORFOLK PE37 7LE, ☎ 01760 725035

19–23 KING STREET, THETFORD, NORFOLK IP24 2AN, ☎ 01842 754821/Customer Service Freephone 0800 856540, **e-mail:** cs@sizeup.co.uk www.sizeup.co.uk, 9–5.30 MON–SAT.
PERMANENT DISCOUNT OUTLET

See page 18 (BEDS)

NORTHAMPTONSHIRE

ORCHIDS BOUTIQUE

3 PARK STREET, TOWCESTER, NORTHAMPTON NN12 6DQ, ☎ 01327 358455/☎ 01327 353961, 9.30–5 MON–SAT. **PERMANENT DISCOUNT OUTLET**

Sells womenswear and childrenswear casual clothing including end of ranges from the high street multiples at a fraction of the recommended retail price. Ladies sizes range from 8–24 and children's from birth to twelve years.

BELLE OF THE BALL

42 LONDON ROAD, KETTERING, NORTHAMPTONSHIRE NN15 7QA, ☎ 01536 484949, 11–5 TUE–SAT, CLOSES AT 2 ON THUR. **DRESS AGENCY**

Sells both new and secondhand clothes for women, as well as wedding dresses, mother-of-the-bride outfits and hats. High street names as well as designer labels: wedding dresses by well-known designers with headdresses, veils and shoes. Now also stocks hand-painted silk shoes.

ELEGANZ

66 BIRCHFIELD ROAD, CORNER OF COLLINGWOOD ROAD, NORTHAMPTON, NORTHAMPTONSHIRE NN1 4RE, ☎ 01604 712820, 9.30–5 MON–FRI, 10–4 SAT. **FACTORY SHOP**

Women's designer shoes and boots at greatly reduced prices, plus the Shoe Boutique, showing high quality, latest fashion German and Italian footwear.

FINEDON DRESS AGENCY

23 HIGH STREET, FINEDON, (OFF A14 JCT 10 TO A6), NORTHAMPTONSHIRE NN9 5JN, ☎ 01933 680080, FAX: 01933 680714, 9.30–5 TUE–FRI, 9.30–4.30 SAT. CLOSED MON.
DRESS AGENCY

Located in the delightful village of Finedon, this lovely shop specialises in secondhand bridal and occasion wear, mother-of-the-bride outfits with matching hats, smart guestwear and evening wear, all at amazing prices. Stunning wedding outfits with a range of favourite labels range in size from 8 to 24, and an enormous selection of hats, perfect for Ascot, are all beautifully presented along with casual wear and samples. The dress agency also stocks lots of larger sizes, all at good prices. Fairytale wedding wear for formal weddings in church, registry office, hotels or abroad, are all available in the chandelier-lit showrooms, along with veils, tiaras, shoes and all accessories. If you are planning a wedding, treat yourself to a visit. Twenty years' experience in fashion and bridal await you, with friendly service, in air-conditioned comfort. Wheelchair access and free, easy parking.

JANE'S DESIGNER EVENING WEAR

69 ST LEONARD'S ROAD, NORTHAMPTON, NORTHAMPTONSHIRE NN4 8DL, ☎ 01604 705256, 11–2 MON–SAT OR BY APPOINTMENT. **PERMANENT DISCOUNT OUTLET**

Evening wear from names such as House of Nicholas, Roots, Gina Bacconi and Consortium to buy, or to hire at a cost of £50 to £60 for up to six days. There are usually rails of ex-hire for sale at bargain prices as well as brand new merchandise at competitive prices.

LITTLESTONE & GOODWIN

VICTORIA STREET, DESBOROUGH, NORTHAMPTONSHIRE NN14 2LX, ☎ 01536 760084, FAX: 01536 762550, 1.30–5 FRI, 9–1 SAT. **PERMANENT DISCOUNT OUTLET**

First class women's handbags, accessories and a large range of evening bags at reasonable prices.

RIGBY & PELLER & FANTASIE FACTORY SHOP

ROTHWELL ROAD, DESBOROUGH, NORTHAMPTONSHIRE NN14 2PG, ☎ 01536 761252, www.eveden.com, 10–4 TUE–FRI, 9–1 SAT. **FACTORY SHOP**

See page 40 (LEICS)

SIZE-UP

8 THE MALL, NEWLANDS CENTRE, KETTERING, NORTHAMPTONSHIRE NN16 8JL, ☎ 01536 412770, 9–5.30 SAT, 10–4 SUN.

87–89 BROOK STREET, RAUNDS, NORTHAMPTONSHIRE NN9 6LL, ☎ 01933 461433, 9–5 MON–FRI, 9–5.30 SAT.

67 HIGH STREET, RUSHDEN, NORTHAMPTONSHIRE NN10 0QE, ☎ 01933 356832, 9–5.30 MON–SAT. **PERMANENT DISCOUNT OUTLET**

57 HIGH STREET, RUSHDEN, NORTHAMPTONSHIRE NN10 8HQ, ☎ 01933 411990/Customer Service. Freephone 0800 856540, **e-mail:** cs@sizeup.co.uk www.sizeup.co.uk, 9–5.30 MON–SAT. **PERMANENT DISCOUNT OUTLET**

See page 18 (BEDS)

SPECIAL OCCASIONS

9A HIGH STREET, HIGHAM FERRERS, NORTHAMPTONSHIRE NN10 8BW, ☎ 01933 314970, www.specialoccasionsuk.co.uk, PHONE FOR OPENING HOURS. **DRESS AGENCY**

Formerly Occasions dress agency, now Special Occasions following a complete refit. Small, friendly shop specialising in wedding and evening wear. Large range of bridal gowns (many samples), as well as once-worn outfits and hats for guests and mother-of-the-bride or groom. Names on sale include Jacques Vert and Condici. New bridesmaid dresses are available to order from just £69. Also sells veils, shoes and a huge range of tiaras and jewellery.

NORTHUMBERLAND

A M S FABRICS

UNIT 7, MAURICE ROAD INDUSTRIAL ESTATE, WALLSEND, NORTHUMBERLAND NE28 6BY, ☎ 0191 263 4095, 10–4 TUE, WED, SAT. **FACTORY SHOP**

Factory shop selling mainly dress and suiting fabric and linings and also plain curtain fabrics such as organzas, voiles and jacquards. Large range of accessories such as header tape, thread, needles, curtain tape, hooks, zips, buttons, elastic.

GLADRAGS

51 BONDGATE WITHIN, ALNWICK, NORTHUMBERLAND NE66 1HZ, ☎ 01665 602396, 10–4 MON–SAT, CLOSED WED. **DRESS AGENCY**

High quality nearly-new women's clothing with labels such as Alexon, Planet, Armani, Basler, Jacques Vert and Donna Karan.

JANE SHILTON

ROYAL QUAYS FACTORY OUTLET CENTRE, COBLE DENE, MAYHOLE ROAD, NORTH SHIELDS, NEWCASTLE UPON TYNE, NEAR A19, TYNE & WEAR NE29 6DW, ☎ 0191 257 3672, FAX: 0191 296 3871, **e-mail:** info@janeshilton.co.uk www.janeshilton.co.uk, 10–6 MON–SAT, 11–5 SUN. **FACTORY SHOP IN A FACTORY SHOPPING VILLAGE**

See page 23 (CHESH)

MARGARET WILLIAMS DRESS AGENCY

19 EAST STREET, WHITBURN, TYNE & WEAR SR6 7BY, ☎ 0191 529 2247, www.reprotique.co.uk, 10–5 MON–SAT. **DRESS AGENCY**

Large shop selling mainly designer labels, varying from Frank Usher, Louis Feraud and Betty Barclay to the occasional selection of Marks & Spencer, Laura Ashley and Next. Stocks both day wear and special occasion outfits, including hats, costume jewellery and shoes. Also holds seasonal stock such as shorts and T-shirts, as well as antiques, prints, paintings, porcelain and a large selection of reproduction furniture.

PENNY PLAIN

10 MARLBOROUGH CRESCENT, NEWCASTLE UPON TYNE, TYNE & WEAR NE1 4EE, ☎ 0191 232 1124, FAX: 0191 222 0316, **e-mail:** info@pennyplain.co.uk www.pennyplain.co.uk, 10–4 THUR, FRI, SAT. **FACTORY SHOP**

Overstocks and ends of lines from exclusive Penny Plain mail order collections; also designer samples and slight seconds. High quality, extremely well made clothes. Superb savings on original prices, with discounts of up to 75%. Women's separates and knitwear in smart and casual, summer and winter styles. Garments are made in colourful, luxurious fabrics, especially natural fibres: pure cotton, linen, silk, wool and velvet. Sizes 8 to 24. Also stocks jewellery, shoes and accessories.

PILOT OUTLET LTD

ROYAL QUAYS OUTLET SHOPPING CENTRE, NORTH SHIELDS, TYNE & WEAR NE29 6DW, ☎ 0191 296 4745, FAX: 0191 270 8552, 10–6 MON–SAT, 11–5 SUN. **FACTORY SHOP IN A FACTORY SHOPPING VILLAGE**

See page 24 (CHESH)

SCENT TO YOU

ROYAL QUAYS SHOPPING CENTRE, COBLE DENE, NORTH SHIELDS, NEWCASTLE UPON TYNE, TYNE & WEAR NE29 6WD, ☎ 0191 272 8382, FAX: 0191 272 8378, 10–6 MON–SAT, 8 ON THUR, 11–5 SUN. **FACTORY SHOP IN A FACTORY SHOPPING VILLAGE**

See page 20 (BUCKS)

THE DRESSING ROOM

7 ASHBURTON ROAD, OFF SALTERS ROAD, GOSFORTH, NEWCASTLE UPON TYNE, TYNE & WEAR NE3 4XN, ☎ 0191 285 9000, OPEN 10–5 TUE–SAT. **DRESS AGENCY**

Dress agency catering for the middle to upper end of the market. They also hire out evening dresses and hats.

WINDSMOOR GROUP

ROBBS, TYNEDALE PARK, ALEMOUTH ROAD, HEXHAM, NORTHUMBERLAND NE46 3PJ, ☎ 01434 607788, FAX: 01434 608164, 10–6 MON–FRI, 9.30–6 SAT, 11–5 SUN. **FACTORY SHOP IN A FACTORY SHOPPING VILLAGE**

ROYAL QUAYS OUTLET CENTRE, COBLE DENE, NORTH SHIELDS, TYNE & WEAR NE29 6DW, ☎ 0191 270 8683, FAX: 0191 258 3810, 9.30–6 MON–FRI, 8 ON THUR, 11–5 SUN. **FACTORY SHOP IN A FACTORY SHOPPING VILLAGE**

See page 25 (CHESH)

NOTTINGHAMSHIRE

CHANGE OF A DRESS

294 BROXTOWE LANE, NOTTINGHAM NG8 5NB, ☎ 0115 929 1531, FAX: 0115 929 6688, **e-mail:** angela@coaddress.com www.coaddress.com, 9.30–5 TUE–SAT. **DRESS AGENCY**

This must be the country's most glamorous dress agency, as its appearance on television can testify. Where else could you find Chanel, Armani, Moschino and Escada modelled by the agency's 'in house' mannequin, while accompanied by their resident pianist at a grand piano? The owner imports clothing from Hollywood and has sold garments from Joan Collins, Priscilla Presley and Zsa Zsa Gabor. The extensive salon is decorated with 15 chandeliers and ornate gilded mirrors, with a coffee lounge for customers' comfort; alterations can be undertaken on site. Clients travel far and wide to this mecca for the fashion-conscious and penny-wise.

LABELS OF EDWINSTOWE

25 HIGH STREET, EDWINSTOWE, NOTTINGHAMSHIRE NG21 9QP, ☎ 01623 825479, 10–5.30 MON–SAT. **DRESS AGENCY**

Friendly and accommodating shop, concentrating on barely worn upmarket and designer labels, stocking garments, accessories and jewellery in immaculate condition. The emporium at Edwinstone is set on two floors and also incorporates gifts, beauty salon and sought after pieces for the home such as Persian rugs, old olive jars and other decorative items. In addition, a range of imported Indonesian and Asian furniture is also displayed, although the main part of the business is still women's clothes from beachwear to designer evening and day wear. (Business terms are 50:50%.)

PRETTY POLLY FACTORY SHOP

UNWIN ROAD, SUTTON-IN-ASHFIELD, NOTTINGHAMSHIRE NG14 4JJ, ☎ 01623 557724, 10-4 MON–FRI, 9–1 SAT. **FACTORY SHOP**

Playtex and Pretty Polly lingerie, hosiery, socks and branded toiletries. All stock is discontinued lines sold at greatly reduced prices. Stock is constantly changing so come with an open mind.

SIZE-UP

34 CAROLGATE, RETFORD, NOTTINGHAMSHIRE DN22 6DY, ☎ 01777 860090/Customer Service, Freephone 0800 856540, **e-mail:** cs@sizeup.co.uk www.sizeup.co.uk, 9–5.30 MON–SAT, 10–4 SUN. **PERMANENT DISCOUNT OUTLET**

See page 18 (BEDS)

OXFORDSHIRE

CERRUTI 1881 – FEMME LTD

BICESTER OUTLET SHOPPING VILLAGE, PINGLE DRIVE, BICESTER, JUNCTION 9 OF M40, OXFORDSHIRE OX6 7WD, ☎ 01869 325519, FAX: 01869 246165, 10–6 SEVEN DAYS A WEEK. **FACTORY SHOP IN A FACTORY SHOPPING VILLAGE**

Cerruti has a very stylish shop in this designer village, offering a range of their women's clothes at discounts of up to 60%. Examples of prices include jackets reduced from £499 to £299; silk blouses reduced from £159 to £89; linen dresses reduced from £229 to £115; trousers suits reduced from £625 to £339; trousers reduced from £199 to £99.

HILARY'S HAT HIRE

THE OVEN, 1 HIGH STREET, BODICOTE, OXFORDSHIRE OX15 4BZ, ☎ 01295 263880, 9.30–7 MON–FRI, BY APPOINTMENT ONLY. **HIRE SHOP**

Home-based business in a converted barn with more than 500 hats from which to choose. Hire a hat for the weekend for £20 or £25. Whether you're looking for something for a wedding, funeral or graduation, regattas or race events, you'll find something suitable here.

HOBBS

BICESTER OUTLET SHOPPING VILLAGE, PINGLE DRIVE, BICESTER, JUNCTION 9 OF M40, OXFORDSHIRE OX6 7WD, ☎ 01869 325660, 10–6 SEVEN DAYS A WEEK. **FACTORY SHOP IN A FACTORY SHOPPING VILLAGE**

A range of clothes for women and a large shoe selection. All carry reductions of between 30% and 70%. Styles include business suits, evening wear and fashionable high street designs.

JANE SHILTON

BICESTER OUTLET SHOPPING VILLAGE, PINGLE DRIVE, BICESTER, JUNCTION 9 OF M40, OXFORDSHIRE OX6 7WD, ☎ 01869 325387, FAX: 01869 325389, **e-mail:** info@janeshilton.co.uk www.janeshilton.co.uk, 10–6 SEVEN DAYS A WEEK. **FACTORY SHOP IN A FACTORY SHOPPING VILLAGE**

See page 23 (CHESH)

MONSOON

UNIT 3, BICESTER OUTLET SHOPPING VILLAGE, PINGLE DRIVE, BICESTER, JUNCTION 9 OF M40, OXFORDSHIRE OX26 6WD, ☎ 01869 323286, 10–6 SEVEN DAYS A WEEK. **FACTORY SHOP IN A FACTORY SHOPPING VILLAGE**

Medium-sized outlet selling marked down current stock for some of the year as well as last year's stock and discontinued lines, including jewellery. There is another outlet at Clarks Village in Street, Somerset.

SCENT TO YOU

BICESTER OUTLET SHOPPING VILLAGE, PINGLE DRIVE, BICESTER, JUNCTION 9 OF M40, OXFORDSHIRE OX6 7LD, ☎ 01869 320052, FAX: 01869 252057, 10–6 MON–SAT, 11–5 SUN. **FACTORY SHOP IN A FACTORY SHOPPING VILLAGE**

See page 20 (BUCKS)

SCOOP

77 BELL STREET, HENLEY-ON-THAMES, OXFORDSHIRE RG9 2BD, ☎ 01491 572962, 10–5 MON–SAT. **DRESS AGENCY**

Nearly-new womenswear from designers at the top end of the market, including MaxMara, Gucci, Escada, Betty Barclay, Valentino, Armani, Emanuel, Louis Feraud. Often stocks seasonal wear for Ascot, Henley Regatta and Derby Day, as well as cocktail and wedding outfits. Also has a supply of holiday wear, shoes, hats, jewellery and other accessories. Holds twice yearly sales: phone for details.

THE DESIGNER ROOM

BICESTER OUTLET SHOPPING VILLAGE, PINGLE DRIVE, BICESTER, JUNCTION 9 OF M40, OXFORDSHIRE OX6 7WD, ☎ 01869 320052, 10–6 SEVEN DAYS A WEEK. **FACTORY SHOP IN A FACTORY SHOPPING VILLAGE**

See page 92 (BUCKS)

THE PAMELA HOWARD FASHION CONSULTANCY

WOODLAND, BEDWELLS HEATH, BOARS HILL, OXFORDSHIRE OX1 5JE, ☎ 01865 735735, BY APPOINTMENT ONLY. **DRESS AGENCY**

Pamela Howard holds successful open days of new and nearly-new designer clothes, shoes and accessories including Armani, Valentino, Joseph, Chanel, Moschino, Nicole Farhi etc. Prices range from £25 to £400. The open days have become extremely popular over a number of years, and have been described as fun and a totally different concept of shopping in a relaxed and friendly atmosphere. For shopaholics it is an Aladdin's cave, but women who hate clothes shopping also save time and gain confidence by trying different colours and styles that are not just in the current season's fashion. The hire service – Prelude – for designer evening wear, ballgowns and outfits for Ascot and Henley, is available by appointment. Write or phone to be added to the mailing list or, if you are visiting Oxford, phone and arrange to view the wide selection of clothes.

TOGS

13 HIGH STREET, THAME, OXFORDSHIRE OX9 2BZ, ☎ 01844 215002, 9.30–5 MON–SAT. **PERMANENT DISCOUNT OUTLET**

Togs elegant shop front on Thame High Street has been established for more than 17 years and suggests something of the quality fashions you will find inside. What may not be apparent is the value-for-money women's separates on offer, most of which are priced beween £5 and £50. This policy extends to Togs' other outlet in Monmouth. Catering for all ages, they introduce new lines frequently, and regulars drop in often to see what's new or just for a chat. Staff are friendly and helpful and will always advise honestly on what suits each customer. Each of the three shops is situated in a building full of character with dark green paintwork and a distinctive oval signboard. Wide range of casual wear for women at competitive prices, including labels such as Viz-A-Viz, Adini and Poppy. Sizes range from 10 to 18. All items are perfects and current fashion.

WALTON DESIGN LTD

9 MARKET PLACE, CHIPPING NORTON, OXFORDSHIRE OX7 5NA, ☎ 01608 642153, 9–6 MON–SAT, 10–5 BANK HOLIDAYS. **PERMANENT DISCOUNT OUTLET**

3 DUKE STREET, HENLEY-ON-THAMES, OXFORDSHIRE RG9 1UR, ☎ 01491 412636, 9–6 MON–SAT, 10–4 SUN, 10–5 BANK HOLIDAYS. **PERMANENT DISCOUNT OUTLET**

14 MARKET PLACE, WALLINGFORD, OXFORDSHIRE OX10 0AD, ☎ 01491 832797, 9–6 MON–SAT, 10–5 BANK HOLIDAYS. **PERMANENT DISCOUNT OUTLET**

6 MARKET PLACE, WANTAGE, OXFORDSHIRE OX12 8AB, ☎ 01235 771115, 9–6 MON–SAT, 10–4 SUN, 10–5 BANK HOLIDAYS. **PERMANENT DISCOUNT OUTLET**

See page 19 (BERKS)

SHROPSHIRE

NIGHTINGALES FACTORY SHOP

NIGHTINGALES HOUSE, LONG LANE, CRAVEN ARMS, SHROPSHIRE SY7 8DU, ☎ 01588 674108, 9.30–4.30 MON–FRI. **FACTORY SHOP**

See page 18 (BEDS)

SCENT TO YOU

TELFORD FORGE RETAIL PARK, COLLIERS WAY, OLD PARK, TELFORD, SHROPSHIRE TF3 4AZ, ☎ 01952 292674, 10–6 MON–FRI, 9–6 SAT, 11–5 SUN. **FACTORY SHOP IN A FACTORY SHOPPING VILLAGE**

See page 20 (BUCKS)

THE DESIGNER ROOM

TELFORD FORGE RETAIL PARK, COLLIERS WAY, TELFORD, SHROPSHIRE TF3 4AZ, ☎ 01952 292674, 10–6 MON–FRI, 9–6 SAT, 11–5 SUN. **PERMANENT DISCOUNT OUTLET**

See page 92 (BUCKS)

SOMERSET

ALEXON AND EASTEX SALE SHOP

CLARKS VILLAGE, STREET, SOMERSET BA16 0BB, ☎ 01458 841831, FAX: 01458 841132, 9–6 MON–SAT, 10–5 SUN (9–5.30 IN WINTER). **PERMANENT DISCOUNT OUTLET**
See page 26 (KENT)

BROWSERS

THE BOROUGH, WEDMORE, SOMERSET BS28 4EB, ☎ 01934 713663, FAX: 01934 713663, 10–5 MON–SAT. **DRESS AGENCY**
Stocks a good selection of smart-casual clothes for women who like luxurious natural fibres, including silk and linen, at realistic prices. Labels include Adini, Fragile and Danishware companies Norandra and Part Two. For the real bargain hunter there is end-of-line merchandise from top German mail-order company Madeleine. For example, cashmere sweaters, £45.

GEAR CHANGE

8 CLAVERTON BUILDINGS, WIDCOMBE, BATH, SOMERSET BA2 4LD, ☎ 01225 442188, 10.30–4.30 MON–SAT. **DRESS AGENCY**
High quality womenswear and accessories including good shoes, leather bags and costume jewellery. Labels range from Marks & Spencer to Versace, depending on what is available.

JANE SHILTON

CLARKS VILLAGE FACTORY SHOPPING CENTRE, FARM ROAD, STREET, JUNCTION 23 OF M5 SOMERSET BA16 0BB, ☎ 01458 440162, FAX: 01458 840504, **e-mail:** info@janeshilton.co.uk www.janeshilton.co.uk, 9–6 MON–SAT, 11–5 SUN. **FACTORY SHOP IN A FACTORY SHOPPING VILLAGE**

See page 23 (CHESH)

JANE'S DRESS AGENCY

THE TRIANGLE, SOMERTON, SOMERSET TA11 6QJ, ☎ 01458 273711, 9.30–5 MON–FRI, 9.30–4.30 SAT. **DRESS AGENCY**

Small, well-stocked shop selling high street and designer labels,Viyella, Bianca Country Casuals, and German labels such as Escada and Betty Barclay. Also sells belts, secondhand jewellery, shoes, scarves, handbags and lots of hats. Evening wear and cruise wear stocked. Will gladly help put together outfits for weddings and special occasions.

LIZ CLAIBORNE

UNIT 34 CLARKS VILLAGE FACTORY SHOPPING CENTRE, FARM ROAD, STREET, JUNCTION 23 OF M5 SOMERSET BA16 0YL, ☎ 01458 840912, FAX: 01458 841132, 9–6 MON–SAT, 10–5 SUN. **FACTORY SHOP**

See page 23 (CHESH)

MONSOON

UNIT 6, CLARKS VILLAGE FACTORY SHOPPING CENTRE, FARM ROAD, STREET, JUNCTION 23 OF M5 SOMERSET BA16 0BB, ☎ 01458 840890, 9–6 MON–SAT, 11–5 SUN. **FACTORY SHOP IN A FACTORY SHOPPING VILLAGE**

See page 54 (OXON)

SCENT TO YOU

CLARKS VILLAGE, FARM ROAD, STREET, JUNCTION 23 OF M5 SOMERSET BA16 0BB, ☎ 01458 440626, FAX: 01458 440623, 9–6 MON–SAT, 10–5 SUN. **FACTORY SHOP IN A FACTORY SHOPPING VILLAGE**

See page 20 (BUCKS)

WALTON DESIGN LTD

46 HIGH STREET, WELLS, SOMERSET BA5 2SN, ☎ 01749 671946, 9–6 MON–SAT, 10–4 SUN, 10–5 BANK HOLIDAYS. **PERMANENT DISCOUNT OUTLET**

See page 19 (BERKS)

WINDSMOOR GROUP

CLARKS VILLAGE FACTORY SHOPPING CENTRE, FARM ROAD, STREET, JUNCTION 23 OF M5 SOMERSET BA16 0BB, ☎ 01458 840888, 9–6 MON–SAT, 10–5 SUN. **FACTORY SHOP IN A FACTORY SHOPPING VILLAGE**

See page 25 (CHESH)

STAFFORDSHIRE

ALEXON SALE SHOP

34 GEORGE STREET, TAMWORTH, STAFFORDSHIRE B79 7LT, ☎ 01827 310041, FAX: 01827 310041, 9–5.30 MON–SAT. **PERMANENT DISCOUNT OUTLET**

See page 26 (DERBY)

BEVERLEY'S DRESS AGENCY

211 TRYSULL ROAD, WOLVERHAMPTON, WEST MIDLANDS WV3 7JP, ☎ 01902 839111, **e-mail:** petbevsal@yahoo.com, 10–5 TUE–SAT. **DRESS AGENCY**

Good quality designer clothes at realistic prices including Moschino jeans, Jacques Vert, Alexon,

Jaeger, Versace jeans and high street labels such as Wallis and Windsmoor. Now sells mother-of-the-bride outfits, as well as shoes, hats, bags and jewellery. Hat hire is also available.

FIVE STAR DRESS AGENCY

7–8 BRIDGTOWN BUSINESS CENTRE, NORTH STREET, BRIDGTOWN, CANNOCK, STAFFORDSHIRE WS11 3AZ, ☎ 01543 571397, 10–4 MON–SAT. **DRESS AGENCY**

Good range of designer wear as well as high street names. For example, Planet, Laura Ashley, Next, Wallis and Windsmoor to Frank Usher, Betty Barclay, Klass and Louis Feraud. Offers a small selection of evening wear, mother-of-the-bride and groom outfits, as well as a large selection of day wear, shoes and handbags. All occasions catered for.

JANE SHILTON

FREEPORT OUTLET MALL, JAMAGE ROAD, TALKE PITS, STOKE-ON-TRENT, STAFFORDSHIRE ST17 1QE, ☎ 01782 787340, FAX: 01782 787318, **e-mail:** info@janeshilton.co.uk www.janeshilton.co.uk, 9.30–8 MON–FRI, 9.30–6 SAT, 11–5 SUN. **FACTORY SHOP IN A FACTORY SHOPPING VILLAGE**

See page 23 (CHESH)

PILOT OUTLET LTD

FREEPORT OUTLET MALL, JAMAGE ROAD, TALKE PITS, STOKE-ON-TRENT, STAFFORDSHIRE ST7 1QE, ☎ 01782 785914, 9.30–8 MON–FRI, 9.30–6 SAT, 11–5 SUN. **FACTORY SHOP IN A FACTORY SHOPPING VILLAGE**

See page 24 (CHESH)

REVUE DRESS AGENCY

12 FORSTER STREET, TUNSTALL, STOKE-ON-TRENT, STAFFORDSHIRE ST6 5AQ, ☎ 01782 813939, 10.30–4 MON, TUE, WED, CLOSED THUR, 10.30–4.30 FRI–SAT. **DRESS AGENCY**

A wide selection of nearly-new women's clothes. The labels are middle of the market and more inclined to the high street – names such as Laura Ashley, Morgan and Wallis – and there are also shoes, bags, jewellery and perfume.

SCENT TO YOU

THE DESIGNER ROOM, FREEPORT TALKE OUTLET MALL, PIT LANE, TALKE PITS, STOKE-ON-TRENT, STAFFORDSHIRE ST7 1QE, ☎ 01782 784997, FAX: 01782 782978, 9.30–8 MON–FRI, 9.30–6 SAT, 11–5 SUN. **FACTORY SHOP IN A FACTORY SHOPPING VILLAGE**

See page 20 (BUCKS)

SLIMMA

7 CROSS STREET, CHEADLE, STAFFORDSHIRE ST10 1NP, ☎ 01538 751455, www.slimma.com, 9–5 MON, TUE, THUR, FRI, 9–1 WED, 9–4 SAT. **FACTORY SHOP**

JAMES STREET, LEEK, STAFFORDSHIRE ST13 8BQ, ☎ 01538 388096, www.slimma.com, 9–5 MON–FRI, 9–3 SAT. **FACTORY SHOP**

Manufacturers for 600 independent retailers countrywide of smart, tailored clothing, the factory shops stock overruns and seconds from the Slimma ranges as well as chainstore seconds. Examples of prices include, skirts from £4, trousers from £5. Coordinated ranges available.

THE DRESS AGENCY

6 SANDFORD STREET, LICHFIELD, STAFFORDSHIRE WS13 6QA, ☎ 0797 427 7891, OPEN 10–4 TUE–SAT. **DRESS AGENCY**

Three rooms packed with day and evening wear, blouses, skirts, suits, jackets, coats, shoes, boots, handbags, scarves, some swimwear, jewellery, hats and belts in sizes 10-20. Labels include Gucci, Versace, Dolce & Gabbana, Wallis, Next.

THE STOCK EXCHANGE

49 MAIN STREET, BARTON-UNDER-NEEDWOOD, STAFFORDSHIRE D13 8AA, ☎ 01283 713177, 10–4 TUE–SAT. **DRESS AGENCY**

Situated in the main street of this olde worlde village, you can park outside this shop selling designer and good quality womenswear. Labels on sale include Country Casuals, Laurel and Bianca. There are also nearly-new accessories including shoes, bags, hats and jewellery.

SUFFOLK

GREENS CLOTHING COMPANY

GAOL LANE, SUDBURY, SUFFOLK CO10 1JL, ☎ 01787 881500, 9–5 MON–SAT, 9–1 WED.
PERMANENT DISCOUNT OUTLET

Women's clothes made by Frank Green, all brand new and at very cheap prices. For example, 100% cotton dresses, £12, jackets, £6, skirts, £6. Some in flowery prints, some plain. The shop also stocks good quality school clothing from nursery age to secondary school.

SHUFFLES

16 OXFORD STREET, EXNING, NEWMARKET, SUFFOLK CB8 7EW, ☎ 01638 578297, 10–4 TUE–SAT. **DRESS AGENCY**

Friendly little shop in village location selling day dresses, suits, separates and evening gowns and a small selection of accessories. Labels include Gerry Weber, Escada, Betty Barclay, Mondi, Jaeger, Paul Costelloe and Windsmoor.

SIZE-UP

35 BUTTER MARKET, BURY ST EDMUNDS, SUFFOLK IP133 1DN, ☎ 01284 769090

87 HAMILTON ROAD, FELIXSTOWE, SUFFOLK IP11 7BQ, ☎ 01394 279846

8 THE CHAUNTRY CENTRE, HAVERHILL, SUFFOLK CB9 8BE, ☎ 01440 762738

4 TOWER RAMPARTS CENTRE, IPSWICH, SUFFOLK IP1 3BB, ☎ 01473 230421

UNIT 7, THE BRITTEN CENTRE, LOWESTOFT, SUFFOLK NR32 1LR, ☎ 01502 511409

6 THE ROOKERY CENTRE, NEWMARKET SUFFOLK CB8 8EQ, ☎ 01638 560790

10 IPSWICH STREET, STOWMARKET SUFFOLK IP14 1AQ, ☎ 01449 674777/Customer Service Freephone 0800 856540, **e-mail:** cs@sizeup.co.uk www.sizeup.co.uk, 9–5.30 MON–SAT.
PERMANENT DISCOUNT OUTLET

See page 18 (BEDS)

THE DRESS CIRCLE

64 UPPER ORWELL STREET, IPSWICH, SUFFOLK IP4 1HR, ☎ 01473 258513, 10–5 MON–SAT. **DRESS AGENCY**

Sells nearly-new top high street and designer labels in sizes 8 to 20, including evening wear. Hats, shoes and other accessories are stocked all year round.

TOP DRAWER

21A THORO'FARE, WOODBRIDGE, SUFFOLK 1P12 1AA, ☎ 01394 388775, 9.30–5 MON–SAT.
DRESS AGENCY

Women's clothing with a mixture of labels from high street names to Armani, Escada, Paul Costelloe and Jaeger. There are also shoes, hats and accessories. Recently under new ownership, there is a new mother-of-the-bride section welling beautiful outfits and accessories.

SURREY

ANCORA DRESS AGENCY

74 CHURCH STREET, WEYBRIDGE, SURREY KT13 8DL, ☎ 01932 855267, 9.30–5.30 MON, TUE, THUR, FRI, 9.30–5 SAT. **DRESS AGENCY**

Middle to upper range designer outfits from Morgan, Monsoon and Wallis to Betty Barclay, Mondi and Whistles and many more.

ANGELA MARBER'S PRIVATE BUY

TRANQUILLITY HOUSE, COOMBE PARK, KINGSTON, SURREY KT2 7JA, ☎ 020 8549 8453, FAX: 020 8541 5049, **e-mail:** angelamarber@hotmail.com www.privatebuy.co.uk, DESIGNER SALES

Private Buy arranges for its club members to purchase current and next season's top label European and American samples and stock in the agents' intimate and friendly London showrooms nine months ahead of the season at half the cost. Also available at trade prices are household linens, fabrics and wallpapers. Usually a recommendation-only club; due to this exclusivity, some personal references may be required. Membership costs £70 a year and £40 for size 14 and over and includes a regular newsletter informing you of future showroom visits, restaurant reviews and member-to-member recommendations.

BROWSERS OF RICHMOND

36 FRIARS STILE ROAD, RICHMOND, SURREY TW10 6QN, ☎ 020 8332 0875, 10.30–5.30 MON–SAT. **DRESS AGENCY**

The largest dress agency in Surrey, Browsers carries a wide range of top designer labels at realistic and irresistible prices. The owners keep up to date with fashion trends and are experienced at both pricing and merchandising their stock at a realistic level. They have a large volume of stock and a fast turnover and are therefore constantly looking for new stock.

CHANTERELLE

95–99 STATION ROAD EAST, OXTED, SURREY RH8 OAX, ☎ 01883 714389, FAX: 01883 716800, **e-mail:** chanterelle@saqnet.co.uk, 9.30–5.30 MON–SAT, 11–5 SUN AND BANK HOLIDAYS. **PERMANENT DISCOUNT OUTLET**

Probably one of the largest women's fashion discounters in the south east, Chanterelle is based in a stylish building in the main shopping centre in Oxted, Surrey. Customers come from miles around because it's packed with a huge range of current season's ranges, including well-known high street brands, all at massive discounts. With new, exciting collections arriving daily there are ranges to suit everyone. All are fully coordinated and cover everything from casual wear and daytime wear to executive suits, special occasion wear and evening wear. Sizes range from 10 to 20. Chanterelle contracts to buy surplus stock from exactly the same top UK and European fashion houses that supply many of the major store groups. Their buyers visit Europe, especially Germany, every three to four weeks, to purchase leading German designer ranges at huge discounts. At Chanterelle you can restock your entire wardrobe at can't-go-wrong prices. Only minutes by car from junction 6 on the M25, and there is free parking nearby.

CLOTHES LINE

KILNHANGER, FARLEY HEATH, ALBURY, NEAR GUILDFORD, SURREY GU5 9EW, ☎ 01483 898855, BY APPOINTMENT ONLY. **DRESS AGENCY**

Beautifully cut jackets, infinitely wearable skirts and trousers, modern tailoring from business suits to special occasion wear. Designers include Jasper Conran, Edina Ronay, Ghost, Betty Jackson and Nicole Farhi. Most are nearly-new, although some are one-off samples from designer ranges. There is also an evening wear hire service from designers such as Belville Sassoon, David Fielden and Roland Klein at prices ranging from £25 to £45.

DESIGNER NEARLY NEW

109 SANDERSTEAD ROAD, SOUTH CROYDON, SURREY CR2 OPJ, ☎ 020 8680 5734, 10–5.30 MON–SAT. **DRESS AGENCY**

Upmarket women's designer wear such as Joseph, Prada, Gucci, Chanel, Armani, Nicole Farhi and Jaeger. This branch also offers ballgown and hat hire.

ENCORE

22–23 VICTORIA STREET, ENGLEFIELD GREEN, SURREY TW20 OQY, ☎ 01784 439475, **e-mail:** info@encore-uk.co.uk www.encore-uk.co.uk, 10–5.30 TUE, FRI, SAT, 10–4 WED, 10–7 THUR. **DRESS AGENCY**

The service is friendly and the shop is bright, giving you the impression of being in a high class dress shop. The prices are reasonable as the owner is prepared to negotiate on commission rates for more expensive items. There is a large range of end of lines and designer samples as well as nearly-new and an evening wear section. Labels include Moschino, Mondi, Betty Barclay, Armani, Versace and many more. Encore also offer colour analysis, image consultancy and a range of beauty treatments and alternative therapies. Carries 350 dresses to choose from.

FLAIR OF ASHTEAD

11 CRADDOCKS PARADE, CRADDOCKS AVENUE, LOWER ASHTEAD, SURREY KT21 1QL, ☎ 01372 277207, 10–5 MON–SAT. **DRESS AGENCY**

A popular, well established dress agency selling casual wear and outfits for special occasions and offering a wide variety of good labels. Strong on seasonal event clothing as well as wedding outfits. Friendly and well informed, they will alter garments and assist in wardrobe selection, and even keep an eye out for suitable outfits for regular customers. Some costume jewellery, as well as shoes, handbags and belts. Hat hire service offering a variety of more than 150 hats at £10 to £30 a hiring. Ex-hire hats also sold at bargain prices.

FUSSPOTS NEARLY NEW

121 STATION ROAD EAST, OXTED, SURREY RH8 0QE, ☎ 01883 717604, 10–5.30 MON–SAT, 11–4 SUN. **DRESS AGENCY**

Upmarket designer wear such as Joseph, Prada, Gucci, Chanel, Armani, Nicole Farhi and Jaeger.

LINDA AMARNANI

21 STANLEY GARDENS, WALTON-ON-THAMES, SURREY KT12 4HB, ☎ 01932 241649, PHONE FOR APPOINTMENT. **PERMANENT DISCOUNT OUTLET**

Made-to-measure cashmere knitwear in a variety of colours to Linda's own designs.

MUMS2BE

3 MORTLAKE TERRACE, MORTLAKE ROAD, KEW, RICHMOND, SURREY TW9 3DT, ☎ 020 8332 6506, **e-mail:** mums2be@dial.pipex.com, 10–5.30 MON–SAT. **HIRE SHOP**

Independent shop offering stylish maternity wear. Whether you're looking for business or leisurewear, there is a comprehensive selection from around Europe. Evening wear hire department available at £60. They also offer a bra fitting service and a petite collection. For a small fee, you can use their unique re-tailoring system after the birth.

PHOENIX

5 CHURCH STREET, COBHAM, SURREY KT11 3EG, ☎ 01932 862147, 9.30–5 MON–SAT. **DRESS AGENCY**

Established now for more than 20 years, Phoenix, housed in a black and pink cottage devotes two floors and four rooms to middle to upmarket labels, usually no more than two years old, from Marks & Spencer to Escada, Laurel, Mondi, Simon Ellis and Parigi. Sizes range from 8 to 18. There are plenty of accessories from jewellery and hats to handbags, belts and shoes, as well as a bargain rail.

PILOT OUTLET LTD

ALDERSHOT GALLERIES, WELLINGTON CENTRE, LITTLE WELLINGTON STREET, ALDERSHOT, SURREY GU11 1DB, ☎ 01252 328859, 9–6 MON–SAT, 10–4 SUN. **FACTORY SHOP IN A FACTORY SHOPPING VILLAGE**

See page 24 (CHESH)

RICHE

87 HIGH STREET, EWELL, SURREY KT17 1RX, ☎ 020 8393 2256, 9.30–5 MON–SAT. **DRESS AGENCY**

Riche has made its name selling current top quality designer wear at much reduced prices. The owner is a former model and fashion buyer and has brought a wealth of experience to this small high street shop, making it more than just another nearly-new agency. Escada, Yves Saint Laurent, Mondi, Gucci, Chanel and Krizia are just a few of the regular labels. While most of the stock is nearly-new, some is ex-fashion show samples and ends of lines and stock is constantly changing. There's an extensive range of new accessories such as jewellery and hats at reasonable prices, as well as a range of new clothing for all occasions, all competitively priced.

SCENT TO YOU

UNIT 151, THE WHITGIFT CENTRE, CROYDON, SURREY, ☎ 020 8680 5238, FAX: 020 8680 9231, 9.30–6 MON–SAT, 8 ON THUR, 11–5 SUN. **FACTORY SHOP IN A FACTORY SHOPPING VILLAGE**

UNIT 48, THE FRIARY SHOPPING CENTRE, GUILDFORD, SURREY GU1 4YW, ☎ 01483 459440, FAX: 01483 459440, 9–5.30 MON–SAT, 11–5 SUN. **FACTORY SHOP IN A FACTORY SHOPPING VILLAGE**

See page 20 (BUCKS)

SEQUEL

181 CHESSINGTON ROAD, WEST EWELL, SURREY KT19 9XE, ☎ 020 8786 7552, 10–5 MON–SAT, CLOSED WED. **DRESS AGENCY**

Sells new and nearly-new womenswear including ends of lines and samples in sizes 8 to 18. There is always a good cross-section of garments to be found on the rails with labels such as Armani, Moschino, Whistles, Tuzzi, Betty Barclay, Gerry Weber, Jaeger, Jigsaw, DKNY and Karen Millen, complemented by a wide range of hats, handbags, new scarves and jewellery. Nothing is more than two seasons old.

THE DRESS AGENCY

5B RECTORY LANE, ASHTEAD, SURREY KT21 2BA, ☎ 01372 271677, http://business.virgin.net/d.agency, 9.30–5 MON–FRI, 3 ON WEDS, 9–4 SAT. **DRESS AGENCY**

Double-fronted shop, half of which is devoted to nearly-new day wear, the other of which has nearly-new bridal dresses. The day wear includes good quality names such as Planet, Basler, Jaeger, Jigsaw, Mondi, Frank Usher, Betty Barclay, Karen Millen, Monsoon and Episode. Their speciality is the bridal section which has about 60 wedding dresses at any one time from £100 to £700, plus veils, tiaras, shoes and jewellery. They also have a large range of ballgowns, in sizes 8 to 22, for hire from £40 upwards, as well as a good selection of accessories including shoes, bags, jewellery and hats.

WALTON DESIGN LTD

24-25 DOWNING STREET, FARNHAM, SURREY GU9 7PD, ☎ 01252 717557, 9–6 MON–SAT, 10–5 BANK HOLS. **PERMANENT DISCOUNT OUTLET**

108 HIGH STREET, GODALMING, SURREY GU7 1DW, ☎ 01483 423855, 9–6 MON–SAT, 10–5 BANK HOLIDAYS. **PERMANENT DISCOUNT OUTLET**

See page 19 (BERKS)

SUSSEX

ALWAYS IN VOGUE

1 THE OLD MILL, RIVER ROAD, ARUNDEL, SUSSEX BN18 9JR, ☎ 01903 883192, 10–4.30 MON–SAT. **DRESS AGENCY**

Established in 1993 but now under new ownership, this charming shop has a stunning collection of good-as-new designer fashions, with realistic and irresistible prices, with sizes to suit everyone. This spacious shop is in the heart of historic Arundel, just yards from the river and the magnificent castle and within 200 yards of a car park. Clothes are accepted every day so you can always be sure of something special to choose from when you visit ranging from Frank Usher, MaxMara, Armani, Prada and Yves St Laurent to Burberry, Mondi, Jacques Vert, Gerry Weber and Aquascutum, to name just a few. The new proprietor, Veronica Tooley, is happy to make a personal home visit for customers unable to visit the shop. A 10% discount is offered to all customers who come via The Good Deal Directory so do mention our name!

BROWNS

32 EAST STREET, HORSHAM, SUSSEX RH12 1HL, ☎ 01403 259711, 10–4.30 MON–SAT. **DRESS AGENCY**

Sell everything from T-shirts to ballgowns from high street names to designer labels. Sizes range from 8 to 20+. Designs by Jaeger, Country Casuals, Betty Barclay, Yarell and Gerry Weber. Also stocks accessories, including shoes, bags and scarves.

COBWEB CLOTHING AGENCY

12 STATION PARADE, EASTBOURNE, SUSSEX BN21 1BE, ☎ 01323 737449, 9.30–5 MON–SAT. **DRESS AGENCY**

Designer nearly-new from Valentino, Betty Jackson, Nicole Farhi, Yves St Laurent, Chanel and Versace to Mondi, Jaeger, Betty Barclay, Jacques Vert, Viyella, Monsoon, Asascutum, Marks & Spencer and Laura Ashley. The emphasis is on good quality and choice and stock includes new samples from Sweden plus new linens and cheongsams. Near to Eastbourne railway station, there is a car park situated behind the shop.

DIAMONDS DRESS AGENCY

4 SCHOOL HILL, STORRINGTON, SUSSEX RH20 4NB, ☎ 01903 746824, 10–4 MON–SAT. **DRESS AGENCY**

Large ground floor shop in the centre of the town, selling many designer labels such as MaxMara, Gerry Weber, Betty Barclay, Marilyn Moore, Anne Storey, Amazing Woman, LeComte and Duo. Diamonds also stocks quality high street names and accessories, such as belts, shoes and bags, as well as offering a hat hire service.

ELIZABETH'S EXCHANGE

THE MARKET, BURWASH ROAD, HEATHFIELD, SUSSEX TN21 8RA, ☎ 01435 866400, FAX: 01435 866400, 9.30–5 WED AND FRI, 9.30–1 SAT, BY APPOINTMENT MON AND THUR. **PERMANENT DISCOUNT OUTLET AND DRESS AGENCY**

New and as new women's clothes, including Country Casuals, Gerry Weber, Hanber, Mamot, Jaegar and Austin Reed. Prices range from £8 to £80. Sizes 8 to 26. Hats, bags, belts and scarves are available, too. Elizabeth's Exchange started in 1993 to raise funds for Breakthrough Breast Cancer Research and has donated more than £11,000 to date. Several fashion houses give samples and items used for photographic shoots to be sold for Breakthrough. Spacious surroundings in which to browse and try on clothes, and to enjoy a complimentary tea or coffee. Good parking and easy access.

NAPIER FACTORY SHOP

3 COURTLANDS ROAD, EASTBOURNE, SUSSEX BN22 8SW, ☎ 01323 644511, 9.30–5.30 MON–SAT. **PERMANENT DISCOUNT OUTLET**

Ends of lines and limited edition designer fashion jewellery in classic and contemporary styles direct from US manufacturers. Stock includes classic chains, necklaces, brooches, earrings, rings, chokers and bracelets at up to 50% discount. Prices range from £2.50 to £100. Parking available.

PANACHE

5 STANFORD SQUARE, WARWICK ST, WORTHING, SUSSEX BN11 3EZ, ☎ 01903 212503, 10–5 MON–SAT. **DRESS AGENCY**

Two shops in one: Panache sells women's nearly-new at savings of up to 75% on high street prices; Smarties sells childrenswear up to the age of nine. The children's selection ranges from Petite Bateau, Laura Ashley and Oilily to Marese and OshKosh. They do not stock children's sleepwear or underwear. The adult dress agency stocks a wide range of labels from Marella and Viyella to Paul Smith, LK Bennett, MaxMara and Escada. They also sell hats, evening wear, coats, shoes, jackets, handbags and belts.

QUONTUM

3, NILE PAVILIONS, 10 NILE STREET, BRIGHTON SUSSEX BN1 1HW, ☎ 01273 321509, **e-mail:** info@quontom.com, www.quontum.com, 11–5.30 MON–FRI, 10–5.30 SAT, 12–5 SUN AND BANK HOLIDAYS. **DRESS AGENCY**

Original own-label designs sold at high street prices, with the emphasis on a directional look. Prices are very reasonable.

REVIVAL DRESS AGENCY

24 GROVE ROAD, EASTBOURNE, SUSSEX BN21 4TR, ☎ 01323 649552, 9.30–4.30 MON–SAT. **DRESS AGENCY**

Excellent selection of good chainstore labels such as Principles, Monsoon, Wallis, Jaeger, Country Casuals and some designer stock such as Giorgio Armani, Calvin Klein and Nicole Farhi. The majority of items are less than two years old. Shoes and accessories are also available. A relaxed and comfortable environment with friendly staff. Browsers are more than welcome.

ROUNDABOUT

31 CLIFFE HIGH STREET, LEWES, SUSSEX BN7 2AN, ☎ 01273 471325, 9.30–4.30 TUE, THUR, FRI, SAT. **DRESS AGENCY**

Good quality women's clothes. Also small selection of hats, some jewellery, shoes and handbags.

SOMETHING SPECIAL

15 ARDSHEAL ROAD, BROADWATER GREEN, WORTHING, SUSSEX BN14 7RN, ☎ 01903 217317, 9.30–5 MON–SAT. **DRESS AGENCY**

Sells good-as-new clothes for women at discount prices from Marks & Spencer to designer labels, as well as manufacturers' samples, once-worn bridal gowns, hats and accessories. The shop also hires out bridesmaids dresses and evening wear.

WARWICKSHIRE

BRAND NAMES FOR LESS

144 THE PARADE, LEAMINGTON SPA, WARWICKSHIRE CB32 0AG, ☎ 01926 430407, 9–5.30 MON–SAT. **PERMANENT DISCOUNT OUTLET**

See page 39 (LEICS)

THE CHANGING ROOM AT FOUR OAKS

11 MERE GREEN ROAD, FOUR OAKS, SUTTON COLDFIELD, WARWICKSHIRE B75 5BL, ☎ 0121 308 1848, 10–5 MON–SAT. **DRESS AGENCY**

A very exclusive dress agency selling such labels as Versace, Moschino, Armani, Prada, George Rech, Louis Feraud and Christian Dior. The shop itself occupies three floors and is full to the brim with constantly changing stock including accessories such as jewellery, belts, shoes, hats and handbags. Hats are also available to hire. Due to the expansion of the shop there is now a wide range of beautiful, one off, accessories for the home, both indoor and out, including lamps, cushions, pictures, rugs, plant pots etc. Because the items on sale are constantly changing, more than one visit may be necessary to find that special something for you or your home.

THE CUCKOO'S NEST

70 SMITH STREET, WARWICK, WARWICKSHIRE CV34 4HU, ☎ 01926 496804, 9.30–5 TUE–SAT. **DRESS AGENCY**

Wide range of women's clothing from Marks & Spencer to Margaret Howell and John Rocha. Prices equally variable, anything from £8 to £250. For example, a Margaret Howell suit retailing at £600 was sold for £210. Limited stock of evening wear, although there are usually some special occasion outfits including once-worn mother-of-the-bride outfits as well as designer sample wedding dresses, bridesmaid dresses and bridal accessories. A lot of casual wear, suits and jackets, as well as classical tailored wear. The varied contents of the shop is reflected in the rapid turnover and age range – between 14 and 95 – of those who visit. No garment is more than two years old, and there are plenty of accessories, ranging from hats to jewellery.

TOP DRAWER AS NEW

19–20 WOOD STREET, STRATFORD-UPON-AVON, WARWICKSHIRE CV37 6JF, ☎ 01789 269766, 10–4.30 TUE–SAT. **DRESS AGENCY**

Described as selling 'clothes and acccesories for the discerning woman', Top Drawer, established in 1978, has hundreds of 'gently used' top quality items and designer womenswear. Proprietor Joanne Hastie carefully selects her collection which boasts, among others, labels such as Valentino and Escada. It's an adventure in itself setting out to find this pretty shop with its Tudor beams and friendly atmosphere, discreetly tucked away above Bottoms Up.

WEST MIDLANDS (Birmingham)

CHRYSALIS FABRICS

WEST MIDLANDS, ☎ 0121 247 7276, FAX: 0121 247 7276, **e-mail:** chrsyalisfabrics@cjls.fsnet.co.uk, MAIL ORDER ONLY. **PERMANENT DISCOUNT OUTLET**

Designer and high quality dress fabrics from well-known British manufacturers, all sold by the metre from £6. Many natural fibre fabrics. No minimum purchase. The Fabric Club allows you to receive six collections of outstanding quality dressmaking fabrics throughout the year for £16 (£21 overseas), enabling you to purchase top quality fabrics at reasonable prices. Customers will receive over 200 samples during the year. Most of the fabrics are suited to smart day wear, although there are some evening wear fabrics at Christmas.

DEJA VU

5 BOLDMERE ROAD, SUTTON COLDFIELD, BIRMINGHAM, WEST MIDLANDS B73 5UY, ☎ 0121 321 3110, 10–5 MON–SAT. CLOSED WEDNESDAY. **DRESS AGENCY**

Stock anything from Marks & Spencer to top designer labels, all at very reasonable prices. Names include Mondi, Escada, Windsmoor and Country Casuals. All sizes from 10 to 22. Also sells shoes, belts, handbags, hats and costume jewellery.

DJ GOLD DEPOT LTD

37 VYSE STREET, BIRMINGHAM, WEST MIDLANDS B18 6JY, ☎ 0121 554 6165, FAX: 0121 554 2438, 9–4 MON–SAT, SUN BEFORE CHRISTMAS ONLY. **PERMANENT DISCOUNT OUTLET**

Manufacturers of wedding rings, engagement rings, bracelets, necklaces, earrings and pendants, with the emphasis on diamond jewellery. As you are dealing directly with the manufacturer, you benefit from savings of at least 30% off the high street equivalent. Gold jewellery can be made to customer's own design with any gem stones. Also sells glassware and pewter items.

DRESS EXCHANGE

1003 ALCESTER ROAD (ABOVE THREE COOKS), THE MAYPOLE, BIRMINGHAM, WEST MIDLANDS B14 5JA, ☎ 0121 474 5707, 10–5 MON–SAT. **DRESS AGENCY**

Middle to upmarket designer wear, with accessories to match, at prices ranging from £10 to £200. Designers range from Marks & Spencer upwards and include MaxMara, Escada, Ghost, Jasper Conran, Moschino, Armani and Valentino. Occasionally stocks wedding outfits, as well as seasonal event wear. Casual wear is stocked.

GOWNS GALORE

1 OLD WARWICK ROAD, HOCKLEY HEATH, SOLIHULL, WEST MIDLANDS B94 6HH, ☎ 01564 783003, www.gownsgalore.com, 9–5 MON–SAT, 8 ON TUE. **HIRE SHOP**

Specialises in the hire of designer ballgowns, cocktail wear and accessories. A three-day hire, including alterations and VAT, costs from £65.

PRIMA

5 FINCHFIELD ROAD WEST, WOLVERHAMPTON, WEST MIDLANDS WV3 8AY, ☎ 01902 380398, 9.30–5 MON–SAT. **DRESS AGENCY**

Elegant shop with friendly owner selling a good selection of nearly-new designer clothes, with a small selection for children. Accessories include shoes, handbags, hats and some jewellery.

SCENT TO YOU

UNIT 1–3, TRIDENT RETAIL PARK, 6 WESTLEY STREET, BIRMINGHAM, WEST MIDLANDS B9 4EH, ☎ 0121 773 6375, FAX: 0121 773 8463, 10–6 MON–SAT, 11–5 SUN. **FACTORY SHOP IN A FACTORY SHOPPING VILLAGE**

See page 20 (BUCKS)

THE DESIGNER ROOM

TRIDENT RETAIL PARK, 6 WESTLEY STREET, BIRMINGHAM, WEST MIDLANDS B9 4EH, ☎ 01233 639498, FAX: 01233 623332, 10–6 MON–SAT, 11–5 SUN. **PERMANENT DISCOUNT OUTLET**

See page 92 (BUCKS)

V & F PARKER LTD

(ARDEN JEWELLERY), 51 VYSE STREET, OFF GREAT HAMPTON STREET, BIRMINGHAM, WEST MIDLANDS B18 6HS, ☎ 0121 554 3587, FAX: 0121 523 2232, 9–4.30 WED–FRI, 9.30–2 SAT. MAIL ORDER. ALSO BY APPOINTMENT. **FACTORY SHOP**

Part of Birmingham's famous jewellery quarter, V & F Parker specialise in making rings, pendants, bangles and earrings. They are suppliers to jewellers, stocking more than 3,000 lines and hold stocks of major patterns enabling them to make or remake old rings. As manufacturers with a small showroom, personal customers obviously save on the middleman's cut. They have a range of lockets, silver and gold chains which are not made on the premises. They claim to be able to sell at 'best prices available'. Repairs carried out. They also sell or mount loose stones including diamond, ruby, sapphire, emerald and 'healing' gemstones. The designer on sale is Ashton Bradford.

WILTSHIRE

ALEXON SALE SHOP

MCARTHURGLEN DESIGNER OUTLET GREAT WESTERN, KEMBLE DRIVE, SWINDON, JUNCTION 16 OF M4, WILTSHIRE SN2 2DY, ☎ 01793 431854, 10–6 MON–FRI, 8 ON THUR, 9–6 SAT, 11–5 SUN. **PERMANENT DISCOUNT OUTLET**

See page 26 (DERBY)

CHANGE GEAR

2 RIVER STREET, PEWSEY, WILTSHIRE SN9 59H, ☎ 01672 563304, OPEN 9.30–1 AND 2–4 MON, TUE, THUR, FRI, 9.30–1 WED, SAT. **DRESS AGENCY**

Dress agency selling designer labels and shoes, handbags and belts.

DOROTHY PERKINS

MCARTHURGLEN DESIGNER OUTLET GREAT WESTERN, KEMBLE DRIVE, SWINDON, JUNCTION 16 OF M4, WILTSHIRE SN2 2DY, ☎ 01793 512220, 10–6 MON–FRI, 8 ON THUR, 9–6 SAT, 11–5 SUN. **FACTORY SHOP IN A FACTORY SHOPPING VILLAGE**

End of season lines with the normal Dorothy Perkins refund guarantee. The range includes knickers, scarves, suits, blouses, sweaters, coats, jackets, dresses and jewellery.

ENCORE

42 GEORGE STREET, WARMINSTER, WILTSHIRE BA12 8QB, ☎ 01985 846022, 9.30–5 MON–SAT. **DRESS AGENCY**

Sells nearly-new ballgowns, handbags, shoes, hats, accessories and many Italian designer labels. Labels on sale include Liz Claiborne, Country Casuals, Mondi, Windsmoor, Jacques Vert and Jaeger. At Christmas, there is evening wear and for the New Year and summer ball season, ball-gowns and cocktail wear. Examples of prices include Laura Ashley two-piece £30, evening wear from £20 to £200. Sizes range from 8 to 26.

FROCK FOLLIES

34 HIGH STREET, CORSHAM, WILTSHIRE SN13 0HB, ☎ 01249 713981, OPEN 10–4 MON, TUE, THUR–SAT, CLOSED 1–1.30 DAILY, 10–1 WED. **DRESS AGENCY AND SECONDHAND SHOP**

Dress agency on two floors with womenswear on one floor and secondhand curtains on another. Labels include Frank Usher, Mondi, Agnes B, Betty Barclay, Calvin Klein, Mexx, Morgan, Kaliko, Karen Millen and MaxMara.

HANRO OF SWITZERLAND

MCARTHURGLEN DESIGNER OUTLET GREAT WESTERN, KEMBLE DRIVE, SWINDON, JUNCTION 16 OF M4 WILTSHIRE SN2 2DY, ☎ 01793 480118, 10–6 MON–FRI, 8 ON THUR, 9–6 SAT, 11–5 SUN. **FACTORY SHOP IN A FACTORY SHOPPING VILLAGE**

Luxury lingerie for women which is normally sold through Harvey Nichols, Harrods and Selfridges is available here at reduced prices. For example, a bra which normally retails for £100 would be reduced by 35% to 50%. Sizes range from extra small to extra large and the company specialises in garments for smaller busts, although some D-cups are stocked. Very well known for their mercerised cottons which never fade or shrink.

JANE SHILTON

MCARTHURGLEN DESIGNER OUTLET GREAT WESTERN, KEMBLE DRIVE, SWINDON, JUNCTION 16 OF M4 WILTSHIRE SN2 2DY, ☎ 01793 430356, FAX: 01793 529846, **e-mail:** info@janeshilton.co.uk www.janeshilton.co.uk, 10–6 MON–FRI, 8 ON THUR, 9–6 SAT, 11–5 SUN. **FACTORY SHOP IN A FACTORY SHOPPING VILLAGE**

See page 23 (CHESH)

LIZ CLAIBORNE

MCARTHURGLEN DESIGNER OUTLET GREAT WESTERN, KEMBLE DRIVE, SWINDON, JUNCTION 16 OF M4 WILTSHIRE SN2 2DY, ☎ 01793 694370, FAX: 01793 507610, 10–6 MON–FRI, 8 ON THUR, 9–6 SAT, 11–5 SUN. **FACTORY SHOP IN A FACTORY SHOPPING VILLAGE**

See page 23 (CHESH)

LONG TALL SALLY

MCARTHURGLEN DESIGNER OUTLET GREAT WESTERN, KEMBLE DRIVE, SWINDON, JUNCTION 16 OF M4 WILTSHIRE SN2 2DY, ☎ 01793 527228, www.longtallsally.co.uk, 10–6 MON–FRI, 8 ON THUR, 9–6 SAT, 11–5 SUN. **FACTORY SHOP IN A FACTORY SHOPPING VILLAGE**

Targeted at women from 5ft 9 inches to 6ft 2 inches between sizes 8 and 20, this shop offers discounts of at least 30% over high street stores.

PILOT OUTLET LTD

MCARTHURGLEN DESIGNER OUTLET VILLAGE, CHURCHWARD VILLAGE, SWINDON, WILTSHIRE SN2 2DY, ☎ 01793 538913, 10–6 MON–FRI, 8 ON THUR, 9–6 SAT, 11–5 SUN. **FACTORY SHOP IN A FACTORY SHOPPING VILLAGE**

See page 24 (CHESH)

SCENT TO YOU

MCARTHURGLEN DESIGNER OUTLET GREAT WESTERN, KEMBLE DRIVE, SWINDON, JUNCTION 16 OF M4 WILTSHIRE SN2 7AA, ☎ 01793 436941, FAX: 01793 436899, 10–6 MON, WED, FRI, 10–8 ON THUR, 9–6 SAT, 11–5 SUN. **FACTORY SHOP IN A FACTORY SHOPPING VILLAGE**

See page 20 (BUCKS)

SMART CHOICE

32–34 GLOUCESTER STREET, MALMESBURY, WILTSHIRE SN16 0AA, ☎ 01666 822327, 10–5 MON–SAT, CLOSED THUR. **DRESS AGENCY AND HIRE SHOP**

Dress agency selling designer womenswear, shoes and accessories, including some larger sizes. Labels on sale vary from Jigsaw, Planet and Escada to Cerruti, Valentino, Pirigi and Armani. They also sell new Gossard and Playtex underwear and Levantie tights. There is a large selection of designer hats for hire, at prices ranging from £10 to £35.

THE CHANGING ROOM

38 CHURCH STREET, CALNE, WILTSHIRE SN11 0HZ, ☎ 01294 814660, OPEN 10–4 TUE–FRI, 10–1 SAT (PHONE FIRST). **DRESS AGENCY**

Dress agency selling good quality outfits for women, most of which are high street labels. Also shoes, handbags, hats, accessories and some glass and china.

THE DESIGNER ROOM

MCARTHURGLEN DESIGNER OUTLET GREAT WESTERN, KEMBLE DRIVE, SWINDON, JUNCTION 16 OF M4 WILTSHIRE SN2 7AA, ☎ 01793 436941, 10–6 MON–FRI, 8 ON THUR, 9–6 SAT, 11–5 SUN. **FACTORY SHOP IN A FACTORY SHOPPING VILLAGE**

See page 92 (BUCKS)

THE SHOESTRING

5 APSLEY HOUSE ARCADE, WOOTTON BASSETT, SWINDON, WILTSHIRE SN4 7AQ, ☎ 01793 850106, 10–4 MON–SAT, CLOSED THUR. **DRESS AGENCY**

Small shop full of fahionable clothes from casual to evening wear which are a mixture of high street and designer labels, Frank Usher, Jaeger, Windsmoor etc. Also sells hats, bags, belts and shoes. There is also a sales rail with clothes reduced even further for clearance items.

WALTON DESIGN LTD

1 BEECH TERRACE, CALNE, WILTSHIRE SM11 ORD, ☎ 01249 824992, 9–6 MON–SAT, 10–5 BANK HOLIDAYS. **PERMANENT DISCOUNT OUTLET**

22A HIGH STREET, MALMESBURY, WILTSHIRE SN16 9AA, ☎ 01666 825994, 9–6 MON–SAT, 10–4 SUN, 10–5 BANK HOLIDAYS. **PERMANENT DISCOUNT OUTLET**

119 HIGH STREET, MARLBOROUGH, WILTSHIRE SN8 1LZ, ☎ 01672 516954, 9–6 MON–SAT, 10–4 SUN, 10–5 BANK HOLIDAYS. **PERMANENT DISCOUNT OUTLET**

See page 19 (BERKS)

WEAR IT WELL

59 NORTH STREET, OFF EASTCOTT HILL, OLD TOWN, SWINDON, WILTSHIRE SN1 3JY, ☎ 01793 695223, 10–4.30 TUE, THUR, FRI, SAT. **DRESS AGENCY**

Two-storey shop, established for nine years, selling many high street labels in 'as new' condition, including Wallis, Principles, Precis, Windsmoor, Alexon, Louis Feraud, Betty Barclay and Rodier. This is the perfect shop for the creative individual who wants to look her best for less. There is also a selection of bridal wear, £900 down to £300, often ex-exhibition, maternity wear, evening wear, hats, bags, shoes, mother-of-the-bride outfits and groom outfits. New stock arrives daily. Also caters for the younger, trendier market with outfits from Oasis, Morgan and some high street labels. The atmosphere is friendly and relaxed, and staff are always on hand to help if needed in this Aladdin's cave of clothing.

WINDSMOOR GROUP

MCARTHURGLEN DESIGNER OUTLET GREAT WESTERN, KEMBLE DRIVE, SWINDON, JUNCTION 16 OF M4 WILTSHIRE SN2 2DY, ☎ 01793 693615, 10–6 MON–FRI, 8 ON THUR, 9–6 SAT, 11–5 SUN. **FACTORY SHOP IN A FACTORY SHOPPING VILLAGE**

See page 25 (CHESH)

WORCESTERSHIRE

CONTINENTAL COLLEXTION

48 HEWELL ROAD, BARNT GREEN, WORCESTERSHIRE B45 8NF, ☎ 0121 447 7544, 10–5 TUE–FRI, 10–4 SAT. **DRESS AGENCY**

Stock includes some designer samples, evening wear, wedding outfits, ballgowns, hats and accessories, though the shop specialises in cocktail wear, ballgowns, hats and wedding outfits. Examples of recent prices include a Simon Ellis wedding outfit, £180 original price, £350. Ballgowns and hats are also available for hire. Stockist of Frank Usher, John Charles, and Della hats.

DESIGNER DEPOT

UNIT 5, CHARLES HOUSE, CHARLES STREET, WORCESTER, WORCESTERSHIRE WR1 2AQ, ☎ 01905 611568, 9.30–5.30 MON–SAT. **PERMANENT DISCOUNT OUTLET**

At Designer Depot, you'll find one of the best selections of top quality branded fashions for women anywhere with amazing discounts of up to 50% off the normal retail price. With new stock arriving weekly, you'll always find something special here.

EXCHANGE & SMART

45 NEW STREET, WORCESTER, WORCESTERSHIRE WR1 2DL, ☎ 01905 611522, 10–4.30 MON–FRI, 10–5 SAT. **DRESS AGENCY**

Lovely, relaxed shopping with a huge amount of stock on two floors of excellent quality clothing, bags and shoes. The stock includes designer labels such as Nicole Farhi, MaxMara, Armani, and high street labels such as Marks & Spencer, Jaeger and Principles.

STUDIO

11 ABBEY ROAD, MALVERN, WORCESTERSHIRE WR14 3ES, ☎ 01684 576253, 9.30–5.30 MON–SAT. **PERMANENT DISCOUNT OUTLET**

Finest designer clothes from the Continent (mostly Germany) at 50% discount. The company's team of buyers search out and secure considerable discounts on top-name European ranges which include both this season's stock and next. The names are well-known but they cannot be divulged here – suffice it to say that they are excellent labels. All stock is perfect, and the vast range covers everything from casual wear to special occasion outfits.

TOP DRAWER

THE OLD MALT HOUSE, CHADDESLEY CORBETT, WORCESTERSHIRE DY10 4FD, ☎ 01562 777808, 10–4 TUE–FRI, 10–1 SAT. **DRESS AGENCY**

Upmarket dress agency whose labels include Workers for Freedom, Armani, Paul Smith, Ben de Lisi, MaxMara, Betty Jackson, Paul Costelloe and Nicole Farhi. Situated in a very pretty village in a delightful old building. Also sell accessories, such as shoes, hats and scarves.

YORKSHIRE

ALEXON SALE SHOP

FREEPORT HORNSEA OUTLET VILLAGE, ROLSTON ROAD, HORNSEA, EAST YORKSHIRE HU18 1UT, ☎ 01964 535441, 9.30–6 SEVEN DAYS A WEEK. **PERMANENT DISCOUNT OUTLET**

10–14 BRIDGEGATE, ROTHERHAM, SOUTH YORKSHIRE S60 1PQ, ☎ 01709 382491, 9–5.30 MON–SAT. **PERMANENT DISCOUNT OUTLET**

See page 26 (DERBY)

BOMBAY STORES

SHEARBRIDGE ROAD, BRADFORD, WEST YORKSHIRE BD7 1NX, ☎ 01274 729993, 10–5.30 SEVEN DAYS A WEEK.

PERMANENT DISCOUNT OUTLET

Large shop selling a huge selection of fabrics: bridal fabric, theatrical costume fabrics, crepe de chine, chiffon, satin, as well as sari fabrics and a huge craft centre. Buy in bulk and sell at low margins so prices very competitive.

BRIGGS SHOES

DRESS FOR LESS, THE OLD SUNDAY SCHOOL, LIDGET STREET, LINDLEY, HUDDERSFIELD, WEST YORKSHIRE HD3 3JF, ☎ 01484 640498/01484 640658, www.briggsshoes.co.uk, 10–5 MON–SAT. **PERMANENT DISCOUNT OUTLET**

Vast selection of well-known brands of shoes for women including Hotter, Gabor, Equity, Hush Puppy, Van-Dal, Servas, and the wider-fitting Elmdale range.

COLDSPRING MILL

HAWORTH ROAD, CULLINGWORTH, BRADFORD, WEST YORKSHIRE BD13 5EE, ☎ 01535 275646, FAX: 01535 271541, **e-mail:** coldspringmill@aol.com, 10–5 SEVEN DAYS A WEEK. CLOSED CHRISTMAS DAY AND BOXING DAY. **FACTORY SHOP**

Coldspring Mill is set in beautiful Yorkshire countryside, 1.5 miles from Haworth. Originally a soap mill, the building has been recently converted to create a unique local attraction. The country mill shop sells Bronte outdoor clothing at direct-from-the-manufacturer prices. There are loads of other bargains with a country theme, most sourced direct from UK manufacturers. The Wool Cellar is a knitter's paradise, selling knitting yarn from top spinners at vastly discounted prices: many at one third off RRP. There is always literally tons of yarn to choose from. Patterns and accessories are also available at bargain prices. After browsing the range of offers, you can take a break in the tea room where you can enjoy a home cooked meal or afternoon tea with fresh schones and cakes. Parking is free, and payment by credit and debit card is accepted.

DENHOLME VELVETS MILL SHOP

HALIFAX ROAD, DENHOLME, BRADFORD, WEST YORKSHIRE BD13 4EZ, ☎ 01274 839108, www.denholme-velvets.co.uk, 1–5 MON–FRI, 9.30–4.30 SAT. **FACTORY SHOP**

Claims to be the only factory producing dress velvet in Britain, most of which is for export. Lots of remnants as well as slight seconds. They also sell rayon and cotton, all at huge savings, and a range of velvet cushions. Opening hours may vary during the summer holidays. Free parking.

EAST END

5 VICTORIA SQUARE, SKIPTON, NEAR YORK, NORTH YORKSHIRE BD23 1JF, ☎ 01756 791670, 10–5.30 MON–SAT, 12–5.30 SUN. **PERMANENT DISCOUNT OUTLET**

Specialises in ethnic garments and accessories sold at very reasonable prices, some of which are seconds, some end of season stock and some current lines. Velvet jackets, embroidered suits, dresses and coats, hats, devore scarves, blouses.

HIGH SOCIETY

THE MARKET PLACE, EASINGWOLD, YORK, NORTH YORKSHIRE YO61 3AD, ☎ 01347 822668, www.highsociety.uk.com, 10–5 MON–SAT, OR BY APPOINTMENT OUT OF HOURS. **DRESS AGENCY**

Up to 300 new evening dresses to buy or to hire by Mon Cheri, John Charles, Serenade, Simon Ellis, among others. Sale rail with new and ex-hire frocks from £20. Clearance sales take place in January and August to make way for new stock. The dress agency sells secondhand day wear and accessories, from Marks & Spencer to top designers, all in perfect condition, freshly laundered and less than three years old.

JANE SHILTON

FREEPORT CASTLEFORD DESIGNER OUTLET VILLAGE, CARRWOOD ROAD, GLASSHOUGHTON, CASTLEFORD, JUNCTION 32 OF M52, WEST YORKSHIRE WF10 4BS, ☎ 01977 517710, FAX: 01977 517762, **e-mail:** info@janeshilton.co.uk, www.janeshilton.co.uk, 10–8 MON–FRI, 10–6 SAT, 11–5 SUN. **FACTORY SHOP IN A FACTORY SHOPPING VILLAGE**

THE YORKSHIRE OUTLET, WHITE ROSE WAY, DONCASTER, SOUTH YORKSHIRE DN4 5JH, ☎ 01302 320035, FAX: 01302 322116, **e-mail:** info@janeshilton.co.uk, www.janeshilton.co.uk, 10–6 MON–SAT, 11–5 SUN. **FACTORY SHOP IN A FACTORY SHOPPING VILLAGE**

See page 23 (CHESH)

LABELS

1 MARKET ROW, BARKERS ARCADE, NORTHALLERTON, NORTH YORKSHIRE DL7 8LN, ☎ 01609 779483, 9.30–5 TUE–SAT. **DRESS AGENCY**

Two-storey shop selling designer nearly-new clothing from the top end of the high street, such as Next, to Viyella, Country Casuals, Jaeger and many more, all at about half the initial shop price. Sizes range from 10 to 20. Two-piece suits, wedding outfits, holiday wear, blazers, evening wear, cocktail dresses and hats.

LIZ CLAIBORNE

YORKSHIRE MILL VILLAGE, BRADFORD ROAD, BATLEY, WEST YORKSHIRE WF17 5LZ, ☎ 01924 426602, FAX: 01924 446096, 9.30–5.30 MON–SAT, 11–5 SUN. **FACTORY SHOP IN A FACTORY SHOPPING VILLAGE**

BROOKS MILL, SOUTH LANE, ELLAND, WEST YORKSHIRE HX5 0XQ, ☎ 01422 377337/01422 374095, 9.30–5.30 MON–SAT, 8 ON THUR, 10.30–5 SUN. **FACTORY SHOP IN A FACTORY SHOPPING VILLAGE**

See page 23 (CHESH)

MIDAS CLOTHES

10 LITTLE STONEGATE, YORK, NORTH YORKSHIRE YO1 8AX, ☎ 01904 625870 10–4 TUE–SAT. **DRESS AGENCY**

Clothes exchange shop selling designer labels and high street names, shoes, hats, handbags and a small selection of jewellery. The shop is all on one level.

MORE POSH THAN DOSH

768 ECCLESALL ROAD, SHEFFIELD, SOUTH YORKSHIRE S11 4TB, ☎ 0114 267 6060, 10–5 TUE–SAT. **PERMANENT DISCOUNT OUTLET**

17 SANDYGATE ROAD, SHEFFIELD, SOUTH YORKSHIRE, ☎ 0114 268 4556, 10–5 TUE–SAT. **PERMANENT DISCOUNT OUTLET**

See page 27 (DERBY)

NIGHTINGALES

13 CHESTERFIELD ROAD, SHEFFIELD, SOUTH YORKSHIRE S8 0RL, ☎ 0114 255 4623, 10–5 MON–SAT, 10–4.30 WED. **FACTORY SHOP**

See page 18 (BEDS)

OPPORTUNITIES

13 PROVIDENCE STREET, WAKEFIELD, WEST YORKSHIRE WF1 3BG, ☎ 01924 290310, 10–5.30 MON–SAT, EVENINGS BY APPOINTMENT. **DRESS AGENCY**

Two floors of nearly-new outfits, from wedding outfits, evening wear and cruise wear to suits and separates for day wear. Larger sizes always in stock. Anything from Louis Feraud and Calvin Klein to Next and Principles. Childrenswear includes OshKosh, Oilily, Gap and Mothercare. New and gently-worn jewellery. A large selection of designer shoes, handbags and belts. Free parking, comfy sofas, and coffee and tea available.

PILOT OUTLET LTD

THE MILL DISCOUNT DEPARTMENT STORE, BRADFORD ROAD, BATLEY, WEST YORKSHIRE WF17 5LZ, ☎ 01924 443474, 9.30–5.30 MON–SAT, 11–5 SUN. **FACTORY SHOP IN A FACTORY SHOPPING VILLAGE**

FREEPORT DESIGNER OUTLET VILLAGE, GLASSHOUGHTON, NEAR CASTLEFORD, WEST YORKSHIRE WF10 4SB, ☎ 01977 553508, 10–8 MON–FRI, 10–6 SAT, 11–5 SUN. **FACTORY SHOP IN A FACTORY SHOPPING VILLAGE**

THE YORKSHIRE OUTLET, WHITE ROSE WAY, DONCASTER, SOUTH YORKSHIRE DN4 5JH, ☎ 01302 366196, 10–6 MON–SAT, 11–5 SUN. **FACTORY SHOP IN A FACTORY SHOPPING VILLAGE**

MCARTHURGLEN DESIGNER OUTLET VILLAGE, SELBY ROAD, NABURN, YORK, NORTH YORKSHIRE YO19 4TA, ☎ 01904 679011, 10–6 MON–SAT, 8 ON THUR, 11–5 SUN. **FACTORY SHOP IN A FACTORY SHOPPING VILLAGE**

See page 24 (CHESH)

SCENT TO YOU

YORKSHIRE MILL VILLAGE, BRADFORD ROAD, BATLEY, WEST YORKSHIRE WF17 5LZ, ☎ 01924 423172, FAX: 01924 446096, 9.30–5.30 MON–SAT, 11–5 SUN. **FACTORY SHOP IN A FACTORY SHOPPING VILLAGE**

THE DESIGNER ROOM, FREEPORT CASTLEFORD DESIGNER OUTLET VILLAGE, CARRWOOD ROAD, GLASSHOUGHTON, CASTLEFORD, JUNCTION 32 OF M52, WEST YORKSHIRE WF10 4SB, ☎ 01977 519243, FAX: 01977 519256, 10–8 MON–FRI, 10–6 SAT, 11–5 SUN. **FACTORY SHOP IN A FACTORY SHOPPING VILLAGE**

THE YORKSHIRE OUTLET, WHITE ROSE WAY, DONCASTER, SOUTH YORKSHIRE DN4 5JH, ☎ 01302 739190, FAX: 01302 364554, 10–6 MON–SAT, 11–5 SUN. **FACTORY SHOP IN A FACTORY SHOPPING VILLAGE**

FREEPORT HORNSEA OUTLET VILLAGE, ROLSTON ROAD, HORNSEA, EAST YORKSHIRE HU18 1UT, ☎ 01964 537480, FAX: 01964 537481, 9.30–6 SEVEN DAYS A WEEK. **FACTORY SHOP IN A FACTORY SHOPPING VILLAGE**

SCENT TO YOU COUNTER, ATKINSONS STORE, 78–82 THE MOOR, SHEFFIELD, SOUTH YORKSHIRE S1 3LT, ☎ 0114 276 8811 (EXT 362), FAX: 0114 272 2673, 9–5.30 MON–SAT, 9.30–5.30 TUE. **FACTORY SHOP IN A FACTORY SHOPPING VILLAGE**

MCARTHURGLEN DESIGNER OUTLET YORK, ST NICHOLAS AVENUE, FULFORD, JUNCTION OF A19 AND A64, YORK, NORTH YORKSHIRE YO19 4TA, ☎ 01904 629884, 10–6 MON–SAT, 8 ON THUR, 11–5 SUN. **FACTORY SHOP IN A FACTORY SHOPPING VILLAGE**

See page 20 (BUCKS)

SOPHIE'S CHOICE

159 NEW ROADSIDE, HORSFORTH, LEEDS, WEST YORKSHIRE LS18 4DR, ☎ 0113 2743913, 10–5 MON–SAT. **DRESS AGENCY**

Nearly-new women's and children's clothes which caters for middle to upmarket labels. Also sells shoes, handbags, hats and children's accessories. Examples of prices include Dolce & Gabbana trouser suits, originally £800, now £95, and Joseph designer dresses, originally £200, now £35.

TEXERE YARNS

COLLEGE MILL, BARKEREND ROAD, BRADFORD, WEST YORKSHIRE BD1 4AU, ☎ 01274 722191, 9–5 MON–FRI. **FACTORY SHOP**

Factory shop selling every type of yarn you can imagine: wool, cotton, silk, linen, viscose, acrylic, alpaca, fine metallics, Lurex yarns, braid making yarns for rugs, textured colours for creative embroidery, but no mohair or cashmere. A must visit for the hand or machine knitter, the embroiderer, weaver or rug maker.

THE BOSTON DRESSER

154 HIGH STREET, BOSTON SPA, WETHERBY, EAST YORKSHIRE LS23 6BW, ☎ 01937 844944, 10–5 TUE–FRI, 10–4 SAT. **DRESS AGENCY**

New and nearly-new top quality womenswear in sizes 8 to 24 including names such as MaxMara, Viyella, Yarell, Ischiko and Cerutti. Hats, belts, handbags and shoes are also available in sizes from 3 to 8.

THE DESIGNER ROOM

VICTORIA SHOPPING CENTRE, HARROGATE, NORTH YORKSHIRE HG1 1AE. **FACTORY SHOP IN A FACTORY SHOPPING VILLAGE**

See page 92 (BUCKS)

THE ILKLEY DRESS AGENCY

VICTORIAN ARCADE, HAWKSWORTH STREET, ILKLEY, WEST YORKSHIRE, ☎ 01943 600732, 10–4.30 MON–FRI, 10–5.30 SAT. **DRESS AGENCY**

Ever-changing stock of womenswear from names including MaxMara, Paul Costelloe, Monsoon, and Marks & Spencer on sale in stylish premises. Also has costume jewellery, handbags, shoes, hats and accessories for sale.

THE REALLY GOOD DEAL FASHION SALE

RIPLEY CASTLE, RIPLEY, Nr. HARROGATE, NORTH YORKSHIRE, ☎ 01367 860017, FAX: 01367 860177, **e-mail:** nheslam@aol.com www.gooddealdirectory.co.uk, 10–6 FRI, SAT. **DESIGNER SALES**

(see page 90)

WINDSMOOR GROUP

THE YORKSHIRE OUTLET, WHITE ROSE WAY, DONCASTER, SOUTH YORKSHIRE DN4 5JH, ☎ 01302 320531, FAX: 01302 325990, 10–6 MON–SAT, 11–5 SUN. **FACTORY SHOP IN A FACTORY SHOPPING VILLAGE**

FREEPORT OUTLET VILLAGE, CARRWOOD ROAD, GLASSHOUGHTON, JUNCTION 32 OF M52, CASTLEFORD, WEST YORKSHIRE WF10 4SB, ☎ 01977 519206, FAX: 01977 520156, 10–8 MON–FRI, 10–6 SAT, 11–5 SUN. **FACTORY SHOP IN A FACTORY SHOPPING VILLAGE**

ALDERS IN FASHION, KIRKSHALL, LEEDS, WEST YORKSHIRE LS5 3HR, ☎ 0113 274 8428/0113 305 8888, 10–5.30 MON–WED, 10–8 THUR, FRI, 9.30–5.30 SAT, 10.30–4.30 SUN. **FACTORY SHOP IN A FACTORY SHOPPING VILLAGE**

MCARTHURGLEN DESIGNER OUTLET YORK, ST NICHOLAS AVENUE, FULFORD, JUNCTION OF A19 AND A64, YORK, NORTH YORKSHIRE YO19 4TA, ☎ 01904 654879, FAX: 01904 682715, 10–6 MON–SAT, 8 ON THUR, 11–5 SUN. **FACTORY SHOP IN A FACTORY SHOPPING VILLAGE**

See page 25 (CHESH)

YORKSHIRE MOHAIR MILL

GIBSON STREET, BRADFORD, WEST YORKSHIRE BD3 9TS, ☎ 01274 668686, 9.30–4.30 MON–FRI. **FACTORY SHOP**

Factory shop with a huge range of good quality wool, mohair, acrylic, alpaca and cotton for hand and machine knitting. They don't stock silks or knitting equipment.

SOUTH WALES

ALEXON SALE SHOP

C/O MEAD, CARDIFF ROAD, HAWTHORN, PONTYPRIDD, MID GLAMORGAN, SOUTH WALES CF37 5AB, ☎ 01443 480673, FAX: 01443 480845, 10–5 MON–SAT. **PERMANENT DISCOUNT OUTLET**

See page 26 (DERBY)

BEULAH DRESS AGENCY

3B BEULAH ROAD, RHIWBINA, CARDIFF, SOUTH WALES CF14 6LT, ☎ 02920 691039, FAX: 02920 691039, www.rhiwbinavillage.netbda, 10–5 MON–SAT. **SECONDHAND AND VINTAGE CLOTHES**

Top quality, nearly-new women's clothing: high street labels and some designer wear. Also stocks accessories, shoes, hats and jewellery.

CHANGES DRESS AGENCY

27A HIGH STREET, COWBRIDGE, VALE OF GLAMORGAN, SOUTH WALES CF71 7HE, ☎ 01446 772184, 10–5 TUE–SAT, CLOSED MON. **DRESS AGENCY**

Designer and high quality labels such as MaxMara, Cerruti, Mani, Jaeger, Frank Usher, Nicole Farhi, Karen Millen, Jobis and Basler. All the outfits are bought and sold on a commission basis at a fraction of the original price. Also stocks a large selection of accessories.

GAINSBOROUGH

12 SWANSEA ROAD, LLANGYFELACH, SOUTH WALES SA5 7JD, ☎ 01792 799409, 10–5 SAT, BY APPOINTMENT MON–FRI. **PERMANENT DISCOUNT OUTLET**

Formerly a dress agency, this shop now sells perfect brand new unworn clothing from top labels such as Lacroix, Versace, Frank Usher, Jacques Vert, Betty Barclay and Louis Feraud with the emphasis on German brands. Substantial discounts are offered on the original retail price. For example, suits normally selling at £250-£350 are sold for £90. A vast selection of day, evening and special occasion wear, and hats and in sizes 8-26. They also offer a first class alteration service.

JOJO MAMAN BEBE

WAREHOUSE SALES SHOP, OXWICH ROAD, REEVESLAND PARK, NEWPORT, SOUTH WALES NP19 4PU, ☎ 01633 294465, www.jojomamonbebe.co.uk, 10–3 WED AND FRI. **FACTORY SHOP**

Maternity wear, children's and baby clothes as well as some gifts, toys and nursery equipment. There is no current season stock, only ends of ranges, seconds and samples from the company's catalogue. Many items discounted by more than 50%. The type and amount of stock varies from week to week so more than one visit may be necessary.

LIZ CLAIBORNE

MCARTHURGLEN DESIGNER OUTLET WALES, THE DERWEN, BRIDGEND, JUNCTION 36 OF M4, SOUTH WALES CF32 9SU, ☎ 01656 665650, 10–8 MON–FRI, 10–6 SAT, 11–5 SUN. **FACTORY SHOP IN A FACTORY SHOPPING VILLAGE**

See page 23 (CHESH)

PEGGY SUE DRESS AGENCY

28 BRIDGE STREET, USK, MONMOUTHSHIRE, SOUTH WALES NP15 1BG, ☎ 01291 673309 10–5 MON–SAT, CLOSED 1 WED. **DRESS AGENCY**

Popular labels here include Armani, Jacques Vert and Windsmoor, although they also stock Marks & Spencer, Next and Gap, as well as ballgowns, jewellery and hats to buy or to hire, or hats that are designed to order. There is a large, new bridal department selling Sally B, Dizzy Lizzy, Joanna Hall and Sincerity. New lingerie is also available, including Triumph, Lepel, Charnos, Lejaby and Rigby & Peller, all at very competitive prices.

PILOT OUTLET LTD

MCARTHURGLEN DESIGNER OUTLET VILLAGE, THE DERWEN, BRIDGEND, SOUTH WALES CF32 9SU, ☎ 01656 647711, 10–8 MON–FRI, 10–6 SAT, 11–6 SUN. **FACTORY SHOP IN A FACTORY SHOPPING VILLAGE**

FESTIVAL PARK SHOPPING VILLAGE, VICTORIA ROAD, EBBW VALE, SOUTH WALES NP3 6FP, ☎ 01495 350383, 9.30–5.30 MON–SAT, 7 ON THUR, 11–5 SUN. **FACTORY SHOP IN A FACTORY SHOPPING VILLAGE**

See page 24 (CHESH)

SCENT TO YOU

MCARTHURGLEN DESIGNER OUTLET WALES, THE DERWEN, BRIDGEND, JUNCTION 36 OF M4, SOUTH WALES CF32 9SU, ☎ 01656 668 044, FAX: 01656 668045, 10–8 MON–FRI, 10–6 SAT, 11–5 SUN. **FACTORY SHOP IN A FACTORY SHOPPING VILLAGE**

THE DESIGNER ROOM, MERMAID QUAYS, CARDIFF, SOUTH WALES CF10 5BZ, ☎ 02920 485626, FAX: 0292 046 1443, 10–6 MON–SAT, 8 ON FRI, 10–5 SUN. **FACTORY SHOP**

THE DESIGNER ROOM, FESTIVAL PARK FACTORY OUTLET CENTRE, VICTORIA, EBBW VALE, SOUTH WALES NP3 6FP, ☎ 01495 301399, FAX: 01495 352002, 9.30–5.30 MON–SAT, 7 ON THUR, 11–5 SUN. **FACTORY SHOP IN A FACTORY SHOPPING VILLAGE**

UNIT 14, CWMBRAN RETAIL CENTRE, NEWPORT, SOUTH WALES, ☎ 01633 256321, FAX: 01633 256323, 9–6 MON–SAT, 7 ON THUR. **FACTORY SHOP IN A FACTORY SHOPPING VILLAGE**

See page 20 (BUCKS)

THE DESIGNER ROOM

MERMAID QUAY, CARDIFF BAY, CARDIFF, SOUTH WALES CF10 5BZ, ☎ 02920 485626, FAX: 02920 461443, 10–6 MON–WED, 10–8 THUR–SAT, 10–5 SUN. **PERMANENT DISCOUNT OUTLET**

THE CAMBRIAN CENTRE, CAMBRIAN ROAD, NEWPORT, SOUTH WALES NP20 4AH, ☎ 01633 256321, 9–6 MON–SAT, 7 ON THUR. **PERMANENT DISCOUNT OUTLET**

See page 92 (BUCKS)

TOGS

6 MONNOW STREET, MONMOUTH, SOUTH WALES NP25 3EE, ☎ 01600 772629, 9.30–5 MON–SAT. **PERMANENT DISCOUNT OUTLET**

See page 54 (OXON)

WINDSMOOR GROUP

MCARTHURGLEN DESIGNER OUTLET WALES, THE DERWEN, BRIDGEND, JUNCTION 36 OF M4, SOUTH WALES CF32 9SU, ☎ 01656 663562, FAX: 01656 665711, 10–8 MON–FRI, 10–6 SAT, 11–5 SUN.

FESTIVAL PARK FACTORY OUTLET, EBBW VALE, GWENT, SOUTH WALES NP23 8FP, ☎ 01495 352545, 9.30–5.30 MON–SAT, 7 ON THUR, 11–5 SUN. **FACTORY SHOP IN A FACTORY SHOPPING VILLAGE**

See page 25 (CHESH)

NORTH WALES

PHOEBE'S NEARLY NEW

45 HIGH STREET, MENAI BRIDGE, NORTH WALES LL59 5EF, ☎ 01248 717454
10–5 TUE, THUR, FRI, 10–2 WED, SAT. **DRESS AGENCY**

New and nearly-new shop selling high quality designer labels such as Basler, Armani, Alexon, Louis Feraud, Jaeger, Jobis, Vyella, Sandwich, Jacques Vert and many more. Now also sells a large stock of quality secondhand curtains. Car park at rear of shop.

SCENT TO YOU

THE TWEED MILL FACTORY OUTLET, LLANNERCH PARK, ST ASAPH, NORTH WALES LL17 OUY, ☎ 01745 730072, FAX: 01745 731008, 9.30–6 MON–SAT, 8 ON THUR, 11–5 SUN. **FACTORY SHOP IN A FACTORY SHOPPING VILLAGE**

See page 20 (BUCKS)

VELMORE LTD

1–2 JAEGER HOUSE, 141 HOLT ROAD, WREXHAM, CLWYD, NORTH WALES LL13 9DY, ☎ 01978 363456, 10.30–3 MON, WED, FRI. **FACTORY SHOP**

See page 24 (CHESH)

SOUTHERN SCOTLAND

JANE SHILTON

GRETNA GATEWAY OUTLET VILLAGE, GLASGOW ROAD, GRETNA, DUMFRIESSHIRE, SCOTLAND DG16 5DT, ☎ 01461 339062, FAX: 01461 339061, **e-mail:** info@janeshilton.co.uk, www.janeshilton.co.uk, 10–6 SEVEN DAYS A WEEK. **FACTORY SHOP IN A FACTORY SHOPPING VILLAGE**

See page 23 (CHESH)

SCENT TO YOU

THE DESIGNER ROOM, GRETNA GATEWAY OUTLET VILLAGE, GLASGOW ROAD, GRETNA, DUMFRIES, SCOTLAND DG16 5GE, ☎ 01461 339075, FAX: 01461 339074, 10–6 SEVEN DAYS A WEEK EXCEPT CHRISTMAS AND NEW YEAR'S DAY. **FACTORY SHOP IN A FACTORY SHOPPING VILLAGE**

See page 20 (BUCKS)

CENTRAL SCOTLAND

ENCORE

48 WATERSIDE STREET, STRATHAVEN, LANARKSHIRE, SCOTLAND ML10 6AW, ☎ 01357 529779, 10–5.15 TUE, THUR, FRI AND SAT, CLOSED 1–2 DAILY. **DRESS AGENCY**

Encore has a large stock of nearly-new outfits from designers such as Frank Usher, Condici, Basler, Jacques Vert, Escada, Mondi, Tom Bowker, Mansfield and Alexon. Clothes range from day wear and suits to coats and evening wear and there is a large number to choose from. Good place to find mother-of-the-bride outfits as well as accessories such as hats, bags and shoes.

HERMIONE SPENCER

UNIT 15, LOMOND TRADE CENTRE, ALEXANDRIA, DUMBARTONSHIRE, SCOTLAND G83 0TL, ☎ 01389 721542, FAX: 01389 721534, 9–4 MON–FRI. **FACTORY SHOP**

Knitwear, mostly cashmere, as well as wool for knitting in this factory which manufactures for all the top designers. Everything on sale here has been designed on site, mostly for export to the United States. Phone first to check stock levels.

JANE SHILTON

MCARTHURGLEN DESIGNER OUTLET LIVINGSTON, ALMONDVALE AVENUE, LIVINGSTON, SCOTLAND EH54 6QX, ☎ 01506 429861, FAX: 01506 429862, **e-mail:** info@janeshilton.co.uk, www.janeshilton.co.uk, 10–8 MON–FRI, 10–6 SAT, 11–5 SUN. **FACTORY SHOP IN A FACTORY SHOPPING VILLAGE**

See page 23 (CHESH)

ORCHID

110 ST CLAIR'S STREET, KIRKCALDY, FIFE, SCOTLAND KY1 2BZ, ☎ 01592 655364, 10–5 TUE–SAT. **PERMANENT DISCOUNT OUTLET**

Samples and cancelled orders of a wide range of German, Italian, French, Irish and British designers at reduced prices. Names cannot be mentioned here as confidentiality is demanded by the suppliers to this shop. Day and evening wear is stocked in sizes 10 to 22.

PILOT OUTLET LTD

STERLING MILLS, MOSS ROAD, TILLICOULTRY, CLACKMANNANSHIRE FK13 6NS, ☎ 01259 753359, 10–6 SEVEN DAYS A WEEK. **FACTORY SHOP IN A FACTORY SHOPPING VILLAGE**

FREEPORT VILLAGE, WESTWOOD, WEST CALDER, WEST LOTHIAN, SCOTLAND EH55 8QB, ☎ 01501 763554, 10–6 SEVEN DAYS A WEEK. **FACTORY SHOP IN A FACTORY SHOPPING VILLAGE**

See page 24 (CHESH)

REDRESS

ARDGOWAN PLACE, KILMACOLM, SCOTLAND PA13 3AJ, ☎ 01505 874343, FAX: 01505 874343, 9–5.30 MON–SAT. **DRESS AGENCY**

Under new ownership and set in newly-refurbished premises, Redress sells both new and nearly-new fashion items at bargain prices. The designers range from high street to top designers, and often feature Parigi, Armani, Versace, Betty Barclay, Puccini, and Jacques Vert. Sells everything from blouses, shirts, suits and dresses to beads, shoes, hats, bags, belts and jewellery. Prices range from £10 upwards and sizes from 8 to 20. There is also a hairdressing salon, Combs, on site.

REDRESS

71 HIGH STREET, NORTH BERWICK, EAST LOTHIAN, SCOTLAND EH39 4HG, ☎ 01620 895633, 10–4.30 MON–SAT. **DRESS AGENCY**

Established for over nine years, this shop has a friendly atmosphere, with clothes arriving daily from all over the country. Names include Escada, Nicole Farhi, MaxMara, Tomasz Starzewski, Moschino, Sisley, Yves Saint Laurent, Betty Barclay, Jaeger, Geiger, Monsoon, Gucci, Ferragamo and lots more from casual wear to special occasions, sizes 8 to 28 when available. They also have a large selection of hats, bags, shoes and jewellery.

REDRESS

51 EASTWOODMAINS ROAD, GIFFNOCK, GLASGOW, SCOTLAND G46 6PW, ☎ 0141 638 5090 9.30–5.30 MON -SAT. **DRESS AGENCY**

Designer labels on sale here include Escada, Armani, Mondi and Betty Barclay as well as good quality high street brands. New and nearly-new day and evening wear is sold, as well as handbags, shoes, hats, and costume jewellery. Hats are also available to hire.

RUMMAGE

5 STEWART STREET, MILNGAVIE, SCOTLAND G62 6BW, ☎ 0141 956 2333, 10–5 MON–SAT. **DRESS AGENCY**

New and nearly-new designer clothes from Lagerfeld and Dior to Givenchy as well as items from high street chainstores. There are usually at least 200 special occasion outfits available as well as handbags, shoes and costume jewellery. There's also evening wear, ballgowns, bric-a-brac, china, ornaments, glassware, hat boxes and hat hire.

SARATOGA TRUNK

THIRD FLOOR, 61 HYDE PARK STREET, GLASGOW, SCOTLAND G3 8BW, ☎ 0141 221 4433, 10.30–5 MON–FRI. **SECONDHAND AND VINTAGE CLOTHES**

Old-fashioned and antique clothing, Paisley shawls, embroidered shawls, wedding dresses from the Forties and Fifties, and Christening robes. Victorian to Fifties day wear, evening wear and underwear. Accessories including costume jewellery. Patchwork, lace curtains, bedlinen, table covers and collectables including dolls and teddy bears. The business was relocating as we went to press. Please phone for new address.

SCENT TO YOU

LOCH LOMOND FACTORY OUTLETS, MAIN STREET, ALEXANDRIA, SCOTLAND G83 0UG, ☎ 01389 607777, FAX: 01389 607774, 9.30–5.30 SEVEN DAYS A WEEK.

THE GLASS HOUSE, GLASSFORD STREET, GLASGOW, SCOTLAND G1 1UL, ☎ 0141 553 1788, FAX: 0141 553 1165, 10–6 MON–SAT, 8 ON THUR, 7 ON FRI. **FACTORY SHOP IN A FACTORY SHOPPING VILLAGE**

See page 20 (BUCKS)

SHELAGH BUCHANAN

65 BATH STREET, GLASGOW, SCOTLAND G2 2BX, ☎ 0141 331 1862, 9–5 MON–FRI, 9–12 SAT. **DRESS AGENCY**

Situated in the centre of Glasgow, this shop sells anything from shoes to ballgowns, including cocktail dresses, evening wear, suits and outfits, bags and accessories. Designer labels in this outlet can be found on the second floor and include Armani, Versace, Country Casuals, Jaeger, Mondi, Escada, Jean Muir, Jobis and Basler. There is a tailoring alterations service on the premises. Situated near to the bus and train station as well as Buchanan Galleries Shopping Mall.

THE DESIGNER ROOM

THE GLASSHOUSE, GLASSFORD STREET, GLASGOW, SCOTLAND G1 1UG, ☎ 0141 553 1607, 10–6 MON–WED, SAT, 10–8 THUR, 10–7 FRI, 11–5 SUN. **FACTORY SHOP IN A FACTORY SHOPPING VILLAGE**

See page 92 (BUCKS)

THE MAD HATTER

5 STEWART STREET, MILNGAVIE, SCOTLAND G62 6BW, ☎ 0141 956 3146, 10–5 MON–SAT. **HIRE SHOPS**

Hats hired out from a superb selection. There are top-name designer hats for Ascot, garden parties and other special occasions. Hire charges from £15 to £75.

WHAT'S THE LABEL

UNIT 16, THE OLYMPIA ARCADE, TOWN CENTRE, EAST KILBRIDE, SCOTLAND G74 1LX, ☎ 01355 230863, 9–5.30 MON–SAT, 11.30–4.30 SUN.

UNIT 34, MITCHELL ARCADE, RUTHERGLEN, GLASGOW, SCOTLAND G73 2LS, ☎ 0141 647 8605, 9.15–5.15 MON–SAT.

UNIT 40, THE PAISLEY CENTRE, PAISLEY, SCOTLAND PA1 2AQ, ☎ 0141 848 9696, 9–5.30 MON–SAT.

KINGSGATE RETAIL PARK, GLASGOW ROAD, EAST KILBRIDE, SOUTH LANARK, SCOTLAND G74 4UN, ☎ 01355 224470, 9.30–5.30 MON–WED, SAT, 9–8 THUR, 9.30–6 FRI, 10.30–5.30 SUN. **PERMANENT DISCOUNT OUTLET**

What's the Label is a clearance outlet for high street stores including Marks & Spencer, Woolworths, Principles, Next and Debenhams. Prices are discounted by up to 70%.

WINDSMOOR GROUP

MCARTHURGLEN DESIGNER OUTLET LIVINGSTON, ALMONDVALE AVENUE, LIVINGSTON, WEST LOTHIAN, JUNCTION 3 OFF THE M8, BETWEEN EDINBURGH AND GLASGOW, SCOTLAND EH54 6QX, ☎ 01506 417638, FAX: 01506 423622, 10–6 SEVEN DAYS A WEEK, 8 ON THUR. **FACTORY SHOP IN A FACTORY SHOPPING VILLAGE**

See page 25 (CHESH)

SCOTTISH HIGHLANDS AND ISLANDS

ELYSEES DRESS AGENCY

129 HOLBURN STREET, ABERDEEN, SCOTLAND AB10 6BP, ☎ 01224 582257, 10.30–4.30 MON–WED, FRI, 10.30–6.30 THUR, 10.30–5 SAT. **DRESS AGENCY**

Now moved to much larger premises with more stock available. New and nearly-new clothes including ends of ranges and designer samples as well as a few high street names. Day wear, evening wear and accessories, as well as a very extensive mother-of-the-bride and hat selection. Labels stocked include Escada, Moschino, Fendi, Christian Dior, Yves Saint Laurent and Versace.

INNOVATIONS

5 ABBOT STREET, PERTH, SCOTLAND PH2 0EB, ☎ 01738 638568, 10–4 MON–SAT. **DRESS AGENCY**

Small, friendly shop where customers speak to each other over countless cups of coffee sipped by women who come from afar to snap up some of the wonderful clothes which come and go on a daily basis. Prices are kept low to maintain a high turnover. Stocks ballgowns, wedding outfits, business suits and casual/holiday wear, all at less than one third of the original price. Examples of prices include Armani jeans, £26, originally £95; Escada suit, £250, originally £900; Gina two-piece, £100, originally £439; Louis Vuitton bag, £80, originally £450; Burberry sunglasses, £50, originally £140. There are usually hundreds of different outfits in stock in sizes 8 to 24, plus lots of costume jewellery, scarves, handbags, and some shoes. Half-price sales take place in January and July.

LABELS FOR LESS

78 HIGH STREET, AUCHTERARDER, PERTHSHIRE, SCOTLAND PH3 1BJ, ☎ 01764 664482, 10–5 MON–SAT, WED 10–4.30, CLOSED 1–1.30. **DRESS AGENCY**

The agency with a touch of class and top quality designers in abundance. Attention to layout and display is second to none and prices for gently worn garments very competitive. Lynne Francis, the owner accepts new garments in pristine condition daily. Well worth a visit.

RE-DRESS

43 NEW ROW, OFF GLASGOW ROAD, PERTH, SCOTLAND PH1 5QA, ☎ 01738 444447, 10–4.30 MON–SAT. **DRESS AGENCY**

Situated in a discreet area in the town of Perth, Re-dress stocks a range of middle to top name nearly-new designer labels and some new clothes. There are wedding outfits and matching accessories at about one third of the original price, as well as evening wear, and a large selection of day wear, shoes and hats. You can choose from labels such as Laurel, Marella, Louis Feraud, Escada, MaxMara, Paul Costelloe, Caroline Charles, Basler, Geiger, OuiSet, Betty Barclay and Austin Reed. Clearance sales are usually held twice a year. Stock changes constantly.

SCENT TO YOU

UNIT 12A, BON ACCORD CENTRE, GEORGE STREET, ABERDEEN, SCOTLAND AB15 1HZ, ☎ 01224 625340, FAX: 01224 625346, 9–5.30 MON–FRI, 8 ON THUR, 9–6 SAT, 12–5 SUN.

UNIT 23, CITY QUAY FACTORY SHOPPING OUTLET, DUNDEE, SCOTLAND DD1 3WU, ☎ 01382 227675, FAX: 01224 625346, 9.30–5.30 MON–SAT, 11–5 SUN.

THE DESIGNER ROOM, STERLING MILLS DESIGNER OUTLET VILLAGE, TILLICOULTRY, NEAR STIRLING, MIDWAY BETWEEN M9 AND M90, SCOTLAND FK13 6HN, ☎ 01259 753895, FAX: 01259 753896, 10–6 SEVEN DAYS A WEEK. **PERMANENT DISCOUNT OUTLET**

See page 20 (BUCKS)

NORTHERN IRELAND

ANNE STOREY OUTLET STORE

THE LINEN GREEN, 17 WEAVING SHEDS, MAIN ROAD, MOYGASHEL, DUNGANNON, NORTHERN IRELAND BT71 7HB, ☎ 028 8772 9770, FAX: 028 8772 9771, **e-mail:** sylvia@annestorey.com, www.limegreen.com, 9.30–5.30 MON–SAT. **FACTORY SHOP**

Modern designer collection of easy clothes for women of today. Currently there is no other outlet store in Northern Ireland or the UK for Anne Storey. Reductions from 30% upwards.

CANCER RESEARCH CAMPAIGN

50 HIGH STREET, NEWTOWNARDS, COUNTY DOWN, NORTHERN IRELAND, BT23 3HZ, ☎ 028 9182 0268, 9–5 MON–SAT. **DRESS AGENCY**

Charity shop with a difference. Ground floor sells everything that you would expect to find in such a shop. The first floor caters specifically for the bridal market and sells wedding dresses, bridesmaids dresses and pageboy outfits, with accessories. All of the stock is donated by the public or the manufacturers.

DISCOUNT DRESSING

70 BLOOMFIELD AVENUE, BELFAST, NORTHERN IRELAND BT5 5AE, ☎ 028 9073 8853, 9.30–5.30 MON–SAT. **PERMANENT DISCOUNT OUTLET**

See page 33 (HERTS)

THE ELLIOTT DESIGNER SALE STORE

10 MAIN STREET, HILLSBOROUGH, COUNTY DOWN, NORTHERN IRELAND BT26 6AE, ☎ 028 9268 9992, 10–5 MON–SAT. **PERMANENT DISCOUNT OUTLET**

Sells brand new designer clothes from some of the best known names at very competitive prices.

Labels include Gerard Darel, Philippe Adec, Caractere, as well as other designers from time to time. There are skirts, blouses, dresses, sweaters, waistcoats, coats and jackets, and traditional knitwear, including Arran and some jewellery. Recently extended to include separates from the Continent also with accessories and shoes. Sizes range from 8 to 18.

Menswear Only

CHESHIRE

FAIRWAY MENSWEAR

BEAM HEATH WAY, MIDDLEWICH ROAD, NANTWICH, CHESHIRE CW5 6PQ, ☎ 01270 625900, 9–5 MON–SAT. OPEN BANK HOLIDAYS 10–4. **FACTORY SHOP**

Men's suits, jackets, trousers and coats which are either own brand or made for chainstores, but sold here under the Fairway name. Good selection in most sizes with larger sizes up to 52in now available. Suits from £89.95. Changing rooms. Car park.

JAMES BARRY MENSWEAR

MCARTHURGLEN DESIGNER OUTLET CHESHIRE OAKS, KINSEY ROAD, NEAR ELLESMERE PORT, JUNCTION 10 OF M53, CHESHIRE CH65 9JJ, ☎ 0151 357 1416, 10–8 MON–FRI, 9–6 SAT, 11–5 SUN. **FACTORY SHOP IN A FACTORY SHOPPING VILLAGE**

Range of men's suits, jackets, trousers, socks, belts, briefs, shirts and casual wear from James Barry and Wolsey. Some of the factory shops also stock the Double Two range of brand names. Suits from £120; casual shirts, £11.95 or two for £20; trousers reduced from £44.95 to £29.95.

SLATER MENSWEAR

44 BRIDGE STREET, CHESTER, CHESHIRE CH1 1NQ, ☎ 01244 329555, www.slatermenswear.com, 8.30–5.30 MON–SAT, 7.30 ON THUR, 11.30–4.30 SUN. **PERMANENT DISCOUNT OUTLET**

Full range of men's clothes from underwear and shoes to casual wear, suits and dresswear and including labels such as Odermark, Bulmer, Valentino, Charlie's Co and Charlton Gray. Men's suits from £69.

SUITS YOU

UNIT 58, MCARTHURGLEN DESIGNER OUTLET CHESHIRE OAKS, KINSEY ROAD, NEAR ELLESMERE PORT, JUNCTION 10 OF M53, CHESHIRE CH65 9JJ, ☎ 0151 355 6701, 10–8 MON–FRI, 9–6 SAT, 11–5 SUN. **FACTORY SHOP IN A FACTORY SHOPPING VILLAGE**

Suits You offers a large selection of formal and casual wear – suits, jackets, overcoats, formal and casual shirts, trousers and accessories, including shoes – across a variety of brands that include the following: Pierre Cardin, Daniel Hechter, Tom English, Cezan, Van Kollem, Scott and Taylor, Cerruti and Pierre Balmain. All merchandise is discounted: for example, buy two £100 suits for £180, or two £150 suits for £270; two shirts for £26; two pairs of trousers for £45 and so on. This is one of over 40 branches around the UK. Phone 020 8327 3000 for details of your nearest branch. A selection of womenswear and designer products can be found in the company's Autonomy and Woodhouse stores (see pages 80 and 93).

THE SUIT COMPANY

MCARTHURGLEN DESIGNER OUTLET CHESHIRE OAKS, KINSEY ROAD, NEAR ELLESMERE PORT, JUNCTION 10 OF M53, CHESHIRE CH65 9JJ, ☎ 0151 355 7473, www.mossbros.com, 10–8 MON–FRI, 9–6 SAT, 11–5 SUN. **FACTORY SHOP IN A FACTORY SHOPPING VILLAGE**

This shop is part of the Moss Bros group and includes labels such as Yves Saint Laurent, Pierre Cardin, Wolsey and Jockey underwear, as well as gloves, belts, ties, work shirts, suits and jackets.

TIE RACK

MCARTHURGLEN DESIGNER OUTLET CHESHIRE OAKS, KINSEY ROAD, NEAR ELLESMERE PORT, JUNCTION 10 OF M53, CHESHIRE CH65 9JJ, ☎ 0151 355 6166, 0208 230 2333, **e-mail:** customerservices@tie-rack.co.uk, 10–8 MON–FRI, 9–6 SAT, 11–5 SUN. **FACTORY SHOP IN A**

FACTORY SHOPPING VILLAGE
An extensive array of accessories including woven/printed silk ties, silk scarves, pashminas, stoles, beachwear, silk and cotton boxer shorts, and socks, all at massive reductions.

WOODHOUSE

UNIT 80, CHESHIRE OAKS DESIGNER OUTLET VILLAGE, ELLESMERE PORT, SOUTH WIRRAL, CHESHIRE CH65 9JJ, ☎ 0151 355 2424, 10–8 MON–FRI, 10–6 SAT, 11–5 SUN. **FACTORY SHOP IN A FACTORY SHOPPING VILLAGE**
Woodhouse caters for the design-conscious man, offering a large selection of Woodhouse own-brand formal and casual wear, plus branded merchandise from designer labels including Boss, Armani, Stone Island and Burberry at exceptional discounts.

DERBYSHIRE

SUITS YOU

UNIT 39, DERBYSHIRE DESIGNER OUTLET VILLAGE, MANSFIELD ROAD, SOUTH NORMANTON, ALFRETON, DERBYSHIRE DE55 2JH, ☎ 01773 545296, 10–6 MON–FRI, 8 ON THUR, 9–6 SAT, 11–5 SUN. **FACTORY SHOP IN A FACTORY SHOPPING VILLAGE**

See page 79 (CHESH)

ESSEX

SUITS YOU

CLACTON FACTORY SHOPPING VILLAGE, STEPHENSON ROAD WEST, CLACTON-ON -SEA, ESSEX CO15 4TL, ☎ 01255 223437, 10–6 MON–SAT, 11–5 SUN. **FACTORY SHOP IN A FACTORY SHOPPING VILLAGE**

See page 79 (CHESH)

HAMPSHIRE

SUITS YOU

THE GALLERIES, HIGH STREET, ALDERSHOT, HAMPSHIRE GU11 1PE, ☎ 01252 329466, 9–6 MON–SAT, 10–4 SUN. **FACTORY SHOP IN A FACTORY SHOPPING VILLAGE**

See page 79 (CHESH)

HERTFORDSHIRE

SUITS YOU

UNIT 6A, THE GALLERIA, HATFIELD, HERTFORDSHIRE AL10 0XR, ☎ 01707 260009, 10–8 MON–FRI, 10–6 SAT, 11–5 SUN. **FACTORY SHOP IN A FACTORY SHOPPING VILLAGE**

See page 79 (CHESH)

KENT

SLATER MENSWEAR

10 LONGMARKET, CANTERBURY, KENT CT1 2JS, ☎ 01227 765599, www.slatermenswear.com, 8.30–5.30 MON–SAT, 7 ON THUR, 11–4 SUN. **PERMANENT DISCOUNT OUTLET**

See page 79 (CHESH)

SUITS YOU

UNIT 88–90, MCARTHURGLEN DESIGNER OUTLET, KIMBERLEY WAY, ASHFORD, KENT TN24 0SD, ☎ 01233 646730, 10–6 MON–FRI, 8 ON THUR, 9–6 SAT, 11–5 SUN. **FACTORY SHOP IN A FACTORY SHOPPING VILLAGE**

See page 79 (CHESH)

LANCASHIRE

CHATLEYS

14 CHATLEY STREET, MANCHESTER, LANCASHIRE M3 1HX, ☎ 0161 833 3230/0161 819 1122, **e-mail:** sales@chatleys.co.uk, www.chatleys.co.uk, 10–6 MON–FRI, 7 ON THUR, 10–5 SAT, SUN AND BANK HOLIDAYS. **PERMANENT DISCOUNT OUTLET**

Classic clothes for men from Gabicci, Oakman and Peter England. Shirts, trousers, ties, coats and shoes are all discounted by 20%. Specialists in big size menswear.

SLATER MENSWEAR

14 WILLIAMSON STREET, LIVERPOOL, LANCASHIRE L1 1EB, ☎ 0151 707 1600, www.slatermenswear.com, 8.30–5.30 MON–SAT, 7.30 ON THUR, 11.30–4.30 SUN. **PERMANENT DISCOUNT OUTLET**

7 DALE STREET, MANCHESTER, LANCASHIRE M1 1JA, ☎ 0161 228 6482, FAX: 0161 236 7457, www.slatermenswear.com, 8.30–5.30 MON–SAT, 7.30 ON THUR, 11–4 SUN. **PERMANENT DISCOUNT OUTLET**

See page 79 (CHESH)

THE SUIT COMPANY

FREEPORT SHOPPING VILLAGE, ANCHORAGE ROAD, FLEETWOOD, LANCASHIRE FY7 6AE, ☎ 01253 773998, www.mossbros.com, 10–6 SEVEN DAYS A WEEK, 8 ON THUR, FRI. **FACTORY SHOP IN A FACTORY SHOPPING VILLAGE**

See page 79 (CHESH)

LONDON

BERTIE WOOSTER

284 FULHAM ROAD, LONDON SW10 9EW, ☎ 020 7352 5662, FAX: 020 7351 6785, www.bertie-wooster.co.uk, 10–6 MON, WED, FRI, 10–7 TUE, THUR, 10–5 SAT. **DRESS AGENCY**

52 WEBBS ROAD, LONDON SW11 6SD, ☎ 020 7924 3030/020 7924 3300, www.bertie-wooster.co.uk, 10–5 MON–SAT. **DRESS AGENCY**

Finest quality secondhand and new clothes and good luggage. New clothes are excellent quality at low prices – suits cost £420 made to measure. Secondhand clothes are of the quality rarely seen outside bespoke tailoring and include suits, ties, blazers, waistcoats and hankies at extremely attractive prices. The new and made-to-measure clothing includes morning coats, morning coat trousers, full backed waistcoats, city suits, dinner, smoking and sports jackets. The Webbs Road branch specialises in formal wear.

CHARLES TYRWHITT SHIRTS

UNIT 13, SILVER ROAD, LONDON W12 7RR, ☎ 020 8735 1000/0870 777 0444, **e-mail:** service@ctshirts.co.uk, www.ctshirts.co.uk, 9–11 MON–FRI, 9–6 SAT, 10–5 SUN. MAIL ORDER ONLY. **PERMANENT DISCOUNT OUTLET**

Traditional, top quality Jermyn-Street shirts at high street prices. Selling through mail order, overheads are low and the price is kept down by a policy of high volume and low margins. The comparison with Jermyn Street comes not just from the cut of the shirts, but also from the fabric: longstaple Egyptian cotton, which produces a soft, silky finish which washes well and is hardwearing. All shirts come with brass collar stiffeners. The mail order catalogue also includes cufflinks, £5 to £60; a range of silk ties; felt; and many other accessories. Phone for details of their introductory offer.

CLOTHES DIRECT

48B HENDON LANE, FINCHLEY, LONDON N3 1TT, ☎ 020 8343 4072, 10–6 TUE–SAT, 10–2 SUN. **PERMANENT DISCOUNT OUTLET**

Warehouse selling Italian brand name clothes for men at discount prices.

DESIGNERS FOR LESS

203 UXBRIDGE ROAD, WEST EALING, LONDON W13 9AA, ☎ 020 8579 5954, FAX: 020 8579 4463, **e-mail:** designersforless@villaroma.freeserve.co.uk, 9.30–6 MON–SAT. **PERMANENT DISCOUNT OUTLET**

High street shop, established in 1973, which sells 'top quality designer menswear at rock bottom prices': factory seconds, ends of ranges, samples and previous season's stock in a range of men's clothes. Their main attractions are suits from Germany, although the labels have to be removed from their best contacts' merchandise. Suits that normally retail for £350 sell here for as little as £135, Danish knitwear from Belika usually £65, sells at £27.50; fashion suits from Masterhand generally retail at £275 but sell here at £125. Variety of modern suits by Gino Madelli of Paris from £99 includes 4/5 button style jackets and Mayor collars. Sportswear by Bison Club of Denmark typically retails at less than half the general retail price. There are a large selection of trousers by Hoal of Germany which sell for £27.50 and are normally found at £65. Cotton shirts by Kings Road sell at £17.50 instead of £35. Jockey or giant, they promise to kit you out with a king-size department up to size 60. There are two clearance sales a year; phone or email Roy or Malcolm at the shop for details and to be added to the mailing list to receive details of latest offers. There is also an extensive dresswear hire department.

DYNASTY MAN

12 TURNHAM GREEN TERRACE, CHISWICK, LONDON W4 1QP, ☎ 020 8994 4450, 10.30–5 MON–SAT. **DRESS AGENCY**

Small dress agency which sells only labels from Jaeger upwards and including Boss suits and jackets, Yves St Laurent and Armani suits, Jean Paul Gaultier, business shirts, pure silk ties, jumpers, leathers, Burberry raincoats and wool and cashmere coats. Alteration service available.

GEORGIANA GRIMSTON

18 EDNA STREET, LONDON SW11 3DP, ☎ 020 7978 6161, BY APPOINTMENT ONLY. **PERMANENT DISCOUNT OUTLET**

Georgiana Grimston bespoke tailoring service is perfectly suited to workaholic men and women who barely have time to go home, let alone to the tailor. She and her team of Savile Row cutters produce high quality clothes at prices considerably lower than Savile Row (starting at £695) and conduct fittings almost anywhere: at the office, at home or in Savile Row. All patterns are individually designed, cut in the traditional method and are 100% handmade and hand-stitched.

GIOTTO LTD

3–4 LITTLE PORTLAND STREET, LONDON W1 7JB, ☎ 020 7580 2185, FAX: 020 7323 1439, 10.30–5.30 MON–FRI, 11.30–3.30 SUN. **PERMANENT DISCOUNT OUTLET**

Men's suits and trousers, coats, jackets, shirts, ties, casual wear, designer menswear by names such as Armani, Versace, and more, all costing substantially less (up to 60%) off normal retail prices. Stocks a huge range: over 3,000 suits, 4,000 pairs of trousers, 2,000 jackets, and 5,000 shirts at any time, all heavily discounted.

L'HOMME DESIGNER EXCHANGE

50 BLANDFORD STREET, LONDON W1U 7HX, ☎ 020 7224 3266, 11–6 MON–THUR, 11.30–6 FRI, 11–5 SAT. **DRESS AGENCY**

This shop sells designer menswear from the outrageous to the classic for the beach, the office, the nightclub and special evenings out. Designers in stock vary, but usually include Versace (couture jackets from £180) and Armani (suits from £180), Boss (suits and coats from £140) and Prada, Gucci and Gaultier. All stock is less than two years old. Sales in July and December see the sell-off of hire stock.

LIPMANS HIRE DEPARTMENT

22 CHARING CROSS RD, LONDON WC2, ☎ 020 7240 2310, FAX: 020 7497 8733, 9–6 MON–FRI, 8 ON THUR, 9–6 SAT. **SECONDHAND AND VINTAGE CLOTHES AND HIRE SHOP**

Menswear outfitters which also hires ex-rental clothing in immaculate condition. For example, dinner suits which would normally cost £160 to buy are £110 while those which have seen more wear cost from £50. New business suits in pure wool cost from £159. They also hire out dinner suits and top and tails from £27.95 TO £43. Separates, dinner jackets and trousers can be hired from £22.95. They hold twice-yearly sales in summer and winter when business suits in pure wool can cost as little as £99. Other branches can be found at 156 Fenchurch Street, EC3 (nearest tube Monument), 83 Old Broad Street, EC3 (nearest tube Liverpool Street), 4 Staples Inn, WC1 (nearest tube Chancery Lane) and at 3 The Broadway, SW1 (nearest tube St James' Park). These branches do not open on Saturdays, or late on Thursdays.

MOSS BROS

27–28 KING STREET, COVENT GARDEN, LONDON WC2E 8JD, ☎ 020 7632 9700, 9–6 MON–SAT, 7 ON THUR AND SAT. **PERMANENT DISCOUNT OUTLET**

This Moss Bros London store has a permanent own-label ex-hire department. Morning suits from £205, black morning coats from £165, top hats from £40, dinner jackets from £79, trousers £30, kilts from £199, white tuxedos £79: prices depend on condition of garments.

NORTON & TOWNSEND

71 BONDWAY, LONDON SW8 1SQ, ☎ 020 7735 4701, FAX: 020 7735 4702, **e-mail:** enquiries@nortonandtownsend.co.uk, www.tailorslondon.com, 8–8 MON–FRI. **FACTORY SHOP**

Norton & Townsend offer bespoke tailoring at off-the-peg prices with all the traditional hand-finishing and attention to detail that you expect from a quality tailor. You can buy a hand cut and finished, perfectly fitting, 100% wool/worsted suit in four to six weeks for as little as £375 (some geographic limitations may apply). The tailor will visit you at home or at work to help you choose from a range of hundreds of cloths. They carry a range of cloths that are bought straight from mills as well as well known merchants such as Dormeuil and Holland & Sherry. They will also tailor suits or jackets using customer's own fabric. Phone for their regional offices.

SURPRISE SURPRISE

57 HIGH STREET, WALTHAMSTOW, LONDON E17 7AD, ☎ 020 8223 0386, 9–6.30 MON–SAT, 10–6 SUN.

414 MARE STREET, LONDON E8 1HP, ☎ 020 8533 4453, 9–6 MON–SAT, 10–6 SUN.

52 CHAPEL MARKET, LONDON N1 9EW, ☎ 020 7833 3171, 9–6 MON–SAT, 9–5 SUN.

13 CHEAPSIDE, WOOD GREEN, LONDON N22 6HH, ☎ 020 8888 5189, 9–7 MON–SAT, 10–6.30 SUN.

61 HARLESDEN HIGH STREET, LONDON NW10 4NJ, ☎ 020 8838 3331, 9–6.30 SEVEN DAYS A WEEK.

18 GOLDERS GREEN ROAD, LONDON NW11 9PU, ☎ 020 8209 0003, 9–6.30 MON–SAT, 10–6.30 SUN.

167 FINCHLEY ROAD, LONDON NW3 6LB, ☎ 020 7624 9988, 9–7 MON–SAT, 10–6 SUN.

98 LEWISHAM HIGH STREET, LONDON SE13 5JH, ☎ 020 8297 2444, 9–6.30 MON–SAT, 10–6 SUN.

3 RYE LANE, PECKHAM, LONDON SE15 5EW, ☎ 020 7639 0434, 9–6 MON–SAT, 10–5 SUN.

299 WALWORTH ROAD, LONDON SE17 2TG, ☎ 020 7703 5164, 9–6.30 MON–SAT, 9–5 SUN.

146 OXFORD STREET, LONDON W1N 9DL, ☎ 020 7323 1124, 9–8 MON–SAT, 10–7.30 SUN. **PERMANENT DISCOUNT OUTLET**

Men's shirts, ties and socks at very reasonable prices. For example, polo shirts, £4.99 each or three for £12; silk ties, £4.99 or three for £12; socks from £3.99 to £6.99 for a pack of six.

THE SHIRT PRESS

65 KINGSWAY, LONDON WC2B 6TD, ☎ 020 7430 1433, FAX: 020 7430 1436, www.shirt-press.co.uk, MAIL ORDER. **PERMANENT DISCOUNT OUTLET**

Specialises in pure cotton, non-iron Eton shirts which are all guaranteed to be wrinkle-free throughout their lifetime. Frequent travellers find them a godsend but they are also bought by anyone who wants to chuck out the iron but still look immaculate. As you can imagine, these shirts are not cheap but The Shirt Press and its online business sell them much cheaper than other stockists and they always have special offers both on the website and in the store.

TIMOTHY EVEREST

32 ELDER STREET, LONDON E1 6BT, ☎ 020 7377 5770, 9–5.30 MON–FRI, 9–4 SAT. PHONE FOR AN APPOINTMENT. **FACTORY SHOP**

Having trained at Tommy Nutter in Savile Row, Timothy Everest has now been offering bespoke tailoring under his own name for 10 years. Prices are accessible, with suits starting from £900. Located in Spitalfields, the business operates from a unique Georgian building where you can experience the relaxed and intimate atmosphere of this exquisite environment while experiencing what they claim to be another dimension in the art of bespoke tailoring.

WOODHOUSE

97 KINGS ROAD, LONDON SW3 9AD, ☎ 020 7823 3014, 10–6 MON–SAT, 7 ON WED, 12–6 SUN.

28–32 CHRISTOPHERS PLACE, LONDON W1M 5HB, ☎ 020 7486 1099, 10–6.30 MON–SAT, 7 ON THUR, 12–5.30 SUN.

141 HIGH STREET, KENSINGTON, LONDON W8 6SU, ☎ 020 7937 2420, 10–6.30 MON–SAT, 7.30 ON THUR, 12–6 SUN.

138 LONG ACRE, LONDON WC2E 9AD, ☎ 020 7240 2008, 10–7 MON–SAT, 8 ON THUR, 12–6 SUN. **PERMANENT DISCOUNT OUTLET**

See page 80 (CHESH)

XEN

11 HARROW PLACE, MIDDLESEX STREET, LONDON E1 7DB, ☎ 020 7247 2634, FAX: 020 7377 0292, **e-mail:** mail@suits2boots.com, www.suits2boots.com, 10–6 MON–FRI, 9–2 SUN. **PERMANENT DISCOUNT OUTLET**

Goldsmith & Company have moved from Clerkenwell to their new shop called Xen, near Liverpool Street Station. They specialise in discounted menswear: Christian Dior shirts, £35; pure cotton business shirts with extra long sleeves and up to size 21 by Laine & Taylor, £25; Loakes all-leather shoes, £49.95 for grade A seconds, £59.95 for perfects, and just £65 for Chelsea boots. Even when not having a sale, Good Deal Directory readers are offered £50 off marked prices on European business suits.

MIDDLESEX

SURPRISE SURPRISE

3 WEALDSTONE HIGH STREET, HARROW, MIDDLESEX HA3 5BY, ☎ 020 8863 6018, 9–6.30 MON–SAT, 10–6 SUN. **PERMANENT DISCOUNT OUTLET**

See page 83 (LOND)

NORTHAMPTONSHIRE

CHURCH'S SHOES FACTORY SHOP

SPENCER STREET, OFF ST JAMES ROAD, NORTHAMPTON, NORTHAMPTONSHIRE NN5 5JB, ☎ 01604 751251, 9.30–4.30 MON–FRI, 9.30–2 SAT. **FACTORY SHOP**

Now owned by Prada this shop now sells only men's shoes and slippers which are made locally.

JOSEPH CHEANEY FACTORY SHOP

2 RUSHTON ROAD, DESBOROUGH, NORTHAMPTONSHIRE NN14 2RZ, ☎ 01536 763760, OPEN 10–5 TUE–FRI, 10–4 SAT. **FACTORY SHOP**

Shop opposite the factory which, since 1886, has been making men's top quality shoes and boots, all of which are Goodyear-welted. Styles vary from traditional classics such as Oxford brogues to contemporary styles and prices from £35-£100 for shoes which would normally retail from £100-£200. Wide variety of sizes and half sizes and width fittings available.

NORTHUMBERLAND

SLATER MENSWEAR

10 GRAINGER STREET, NEWCASTLE UPON TYNE, TYNE & WEAR, NORTHUMBERLAND NE1 5EW, ☎ 0191 232 5557, FAX: 0191 232 5557, www.slatermenswear.com, 8.30–5.30 MON–SAT, 7.30 ON THUR, 11–4 SUN. **PERMANENT DISCOUNT OUTLET**

See page 79 (CHESH)

SUITS YOU

UNIT 49, ROYAL QUAYS, COBLE DENE ROAD, NORTH SHIELDS, NEWCASTLE UPON TYNE, NORTHUMBERLAND NE29 6DL, ☎ 0191 296 2995, 10–6 MON–SAT, 8 ON THUR, 11–5 SUN. **FACTORY SHOP IN A FACTORY SHOPPING VILLAGE**

See page 79 (CHESH)

OXFORDSHIRE

THE SUIT COMPANY

BICESTER OUTLET SHOPPING VILLAGE, PINGLE DRIVE, BICESTER, JUNCTION 9 OF M40, OXFORDSHIRE OX6 7WD, ☎ 01869 321127, www.mossbros.com, 10–6 SEVEN DAYS A WEEK. **FACTORY SHOP IN A FACTORY SHOPPING VILLAGE**

See page 79 (CHESH)

SOMERSET

JAMES BARRY MENSWEAR

71 HIGH STREET, STREET, SOMERSET, 10–8 MON–FRI, 9–6 SAT, 11–5 SUN. **FACTORY SHOP IN A FACTORY SHOPPING VILLAGE**

See page 79 (CHESH)

SURREY

O H HEWETT LTD

21 FARNCOMBE STREET, FARNCOMBE, GODALMING, SURREY GU7 3AY, ☎ 01483 426917, FAX: 01483 424810, **e-mail:** enquiries@ohhewett.co.uk, www.ohhewell.co.uk, 10–5 TUE–SAT. **PERMANENT DISCOUNT OUTLET**

Sells high quality menswear – shirts, ties, jackets, suits, blazers and sportswear including golfwear. Samples and ends of ranges are priced at one third to one half of the London shop prices. Suits from £150, normally £400; cotton shirts from £29, usually £60; pure silk ties from £5; and pique shirts from £15, normally £40.

SUIT CITY

15 HOLMETHORPE AVENUE, HOLMETHORPE INDUSTRIAL ESTATE, REDHILL, SURREY RH1 2NB, ☎ 01737 789963, 11–3 WED, FRI, 10–4 SAT, SUN. **PERMANENT DISCOUNT OUTLET**

Quality menswear: suits, blazers, jackets, trousers and overcoats at discounts of up to 65% in sizes from 36 inch to 60 inch chests.

WEST MIDLANDS (BIRMINGHAM)

SLATER MENSWEAR

3 CANNON STREET, BIRMINGHAM, WEST MIDLANDS B2 5EP, ☎ 0121 633 3855, FAX: 0121 633 3874, www.slatermenswear.com, 8.30–5.30 MON–SAT, 7.30 ON THUR, 11–4 SUN.
PERMANENT DISCOUNT OUTLET

See page 79 (CHESH)

WILTSHIRE

TIE RACK

MCARTHURGLEN DESIGNER OUTLET GREAT WESTERN, KEMBLE DRIVE, SWINDON, JUNCTION 16 OF M4, WILTSHIRE SN2 2DY, ☎ 01793 531070, 10–6 MON–FRI, 8 ON THUR, 9–6 SAT, 11–5 SUN. **FACTORY SHOP IN A FACTORY SHOPPING VILLAGE**

See page 79 (CHESH)

YORKSHIRE

DUNSFORD WELSEY MENSWEAR

OXFORD STREET, CASTLEFORD, WEST YORKSHIRE WF10 5SZ, ☎ 01977 710200, 9–5 MON–SAT. **FACTORY SHOP**

Dunsford Welsey sells good quality menswear at affordable prices. Suits from £50 to £120, trousers from £4.99, T-shirts from £2.99, shirts from £2.99 to £20, jackets from £10, leather belts from £6.99 to £9.99, and casual tops.

SLATER MENSWEAR

83 ALBION STREET, LEEDS, WEST YORKSHIRE LS1 5AP, ☎ 0113 234 9933, www.slatermenswear.com, 8.30–5.30 MON–SAT, 7.30 ON THUR, 11–4 SUN. **PERMANENT DISCOUNT OUTLET**

See page 79 (CHESH)

SPENCER'S TROUSERS

FRIENDLY WORKS, BURNLEY ROAD, SOWERBY BRIDGE, WEST YORKSHIRE HX6 2TL, ☎ 01422 833020, FAX: 01422 839777, **e-mail:** sales@spencerstrousers.com, www.spencers-trousers.com, 9–5 MON–SAT. **FACTORY SHOP**

Spencer's Trousers manufactures better quality trousers and plus twos in traditional fabrics (cords, moleskin, worsteds) and sells overstocks, returns and ends of lines at marvellous savings. The shop is situated on the A646 between Halifax and Hebden Bridge in West Yorkshire and is a traditional factory shop. It also offers a made-to-measure service with next-day delivery on some materials.

SUITS YOU

UNITS 52–53, MCARTHURGLEN, ST NICHOLAS AVENUE, FULFORD, NORTH YORKSHIRE YO19 4TA, ☎ 01904 678676, 10–6 MON–SAT, 8 ON THUR, 11–5 SUN. **FACTORY SHOP IN A FACTORY SHOPPING VILLAGE**

See page 79 (CHESH)

TIE RACK

MCARTHURGLEN DESIGNER OUTLET YORK, ST NICHOLAS AVENUE, FULFORD, JUNCTION OF A19 AND A64, YORK, NORTH YORKSHIRE YO19 4TA, ☎ 01904 624431, 10–6 MON–SAT, 8 ON THUR, 11–5 SUN. **FACTORY SHOP IN A FACTORY SHOPPING VILLAGE**

See page 79 (CHESH)

SOUTH WALES

SLATER MENSWEAR

116 ST MARY'S STREET, CARDIFF, SOUTH WALES CF1 1DY, ☎ 02920 384186/02920 384196, www.slatermenswear.com, 8.30–5.30 MON–SAT, 7.30 ON THUR, 11–4 SUN.
PERMANENT DISCOUNT OUTLET

See page 79 (CHESH)

SUITS YOU

UNIT 84-85, WELSH DESIGNER VILLAGE, BRIDGEND, SOUTH WALES CF32 9SU, ☎ 01656 648890, 10–8 MON–FRI, 10–6 SAT, 11–5 SUN. **FACTORY SHOP IN A FACTORY SHOPPING VILLAGE**

See page 79 (CHESH)

TIE RACK

MCARTHURGLEN DESIGNER OUTLET WALES, THE DERWEN, BRIDGEND, JUNCTION 36 OF M4, SOUTH WALES CF32 9SU, ☎ 01656 658913, 10–8 MON–FRI, 10–6 SAT, 11–5 SUN.
FACTORY SHOP IN A FACTORY SHOPPING VILLAGE

See page 79 (CHESH)

SOUTHERN SCOTLAND

SLATER MENSWEAR

184 HIGH STREET, AYR, AYRSHIRE, SCOTLAND KA7 1RQ, ☎ 01292 261730, FAX: 01292 610559, www.slatermenswear.com, 8.30–5.30 MON–SAT, 7.30 ON THUR, 12–5 SUN.
PERMANENT DISCOUNT OUTLET

See page 79 (CHESH)

CENTRAL SCOTLAND

CORSTON SINCLAIR LTD

INDUSTRIAL PROTECTIVE CLOTHING, 36 GLENBURN ROAD, COLLEGE MILTON NORTH, EAST KILBRIDE, SCOTLAND G74 5BA, ☎ 01355 238161, FAX: 01355 263682, **e-mail:** sales@corstonsinclair.com, www.corstonsinclair.com, 8.30–4.30 MON–THUR, 8.30–4 FRI.
PERMANENT DISCOUNT OUTLET

Designer trainers from Reebok, Nike, Dunlop and Inter trainers as well as protective clothing (safety helmets, safety footwear, overalls), sports and leisure items: jeans, shorts, sweatshirts, socks and underwear at discounts of between 20% and 30% off normal retail prices.

McCALLS OF THE ROYAL MILE

11 THE HIGH STREET, EDINBURGH EH1 1SR, ☎ 0131 557 3979, 9–5.30 MON–SAT, 7.30 ON THUR, 12–4 SUN. **HIRE SHOP**

Hire and sell men's formal wear, whether a dinner suit or the full regalia. Kilt, shoes, bow tie, sporran costs £32.50 plus £5 for the shirt, socks £5.50; men's formal dinner suit, £22.50. Also hires morning suits, jackets, waistcoats, trousers, shirts and cravat or tie, £40; boys outfits, £29.50. No discounted womenswear or girls' clothes are available, although the shop does sell women's outfits at full retail price.

SLATER MENSWEAR

100 GEORGE STREET, EDINBURGH, SCOTLAND EH2 3DF, ☎ 0131 220 4343, FAX: 0131 220 4747, www.slatermenswear.com, 8.30–5.30 MON–SAT, 7.30 ON THUR, 12–5 SUN.

165 HOWARD STREET, GLASGOW, SCOTLAND G1 4HF, ☎ 0141 552 7171, FAX: 0141 553 1720, www.slatermenswear.com, 8.30–5.30 MON–SAT, 7.30 ON THUR, 12–5 SUN.
PERMANENT DISCOUNT OUTLET

See page 79 (CHESH)

SUITS YOU

UNIT 39–41, MCARTHUR GLEN DESIGNER OUTLET VILLAGE, ALMONDVALE AVENUE, LIVINGSTON, WEST LOTHIAN, SCOTLAND EH54 6QX, ☎ 01506 416212, 10–6 MON–FRI, 8 ON THUR, 9–6 SAT, 10–6 SUN. **FACTORY SHOP IN A FACTORY SHOPPING VILLAGE**

See page 79 (CHESH)

SCOTTISH HIGHLANDS AND ISLANDS

SLATER MENSWEAR

10 BON ACCORD STREET, ABERDEEN, SCOTLAND AB11 6EL, ☎ 01224 212334, FAX: 01224 212914, www.slatermenswear.com, 8.30–5.30 MON–SAT, 7.30 ON THUR, 12–5 SUN. **PERMANENT DISCOUNT OUTLET**

See page 79 (CHESH)

NORTHERN IRELAND

ALBION

MALDON STREET, DONEGAL ROAD, WEST BELFAST, NORTHERN IRELAND, ☎ 028 9032 5411 9.30–5 MON–SAT. **FACTORY SHOP**

Albion has been a major producer of quality menswear for more than 100 years. Their products can be found in the top high street shops in the UK. The factory outlet sells overruns, samples, surplus stock and seconds of men's suits, trousers and jackets at bargain prices.

Womenswear & Menswear

BEDFORDSHIRE

MATALAN

RACE MEADOWS WAY, AMPTHILL ROAD, BEDFORD, BEDFORDSHIRE MK42 7AZ, ☎ 01234 365077, FAX: 01234 360671, www.matalan.co.uk, 10–8 MON–FRI, 9–6 SAT, 11–5 SUN.

UNIT 2, LONDON ROAD INDUSTRIAL ESTATE, BIGGLESWADE, BEDFORDSHIRE SG18 8PW, ☎ 01767 310810, FAX: 01767 601876, www.matalan.co.uk, 10–8 MON–FRI, 9–6 SAT, 11–5 SUN. **PERMANENT DISCOUNT OUTLET**

Matalan is a fashion and homewares value retailer giving customers what they claim to be unbeatable value for money with huge savings on a wide range of products including high quality fashionable clothing for men, women and children at up to 50% off high street prices. Matalan is situated out of town and stores are open seven days a week all year round. The Matalan website contains maps of how to get to any of the 145 stores.

QD STORES

22–30 GREYFRIARS, BEDFORD, BEDFORDSHIRE MK40 1HP, ☎ 01234 345204, 9–5.30 MON–SAT. **PERMANENT DISCOUNT OUTLET**

Discount shop selling a mixture of clothes, household textiles, ceramics, kitchenware, knitting wool, garden tools, curtains, toys, stationery, dusters, Christmas decorations, masking tape, lingerie and a host of other items. Stock changes regularly because the low prices mean a quick turnover. Some items are seconds or end of season stock from the major chain stores.

TK MAXX

UNIT 14, THE HOWARD CENTRE, BEDFORD, BEDFORDSHIRE MK40 1UH, ☎ 01234 270787, www.tkmaxx.com, 9–5.30 MON–FRI, 8.30–6 SAT, 10–4 SUN.

BEACON RETAIL PARK, WATLING STREET, BLETCHLEY, BEDFORDSHIRE MK1 1BN, ☎ 01908 644406, www.tkmaxx.com, 10–8 MON–FRI, 9–6 SAT, 11–5 SUN. **PERMANENT DISCOUNT OUTLET**

TK Maxx is a unique shopping experience, based on an American concept, offering an ever-changing range of famous names, high street brands and designer labels at up to 60% off normal retail prices. The majority of the stock is current season which makes the savings even more amazing. With 50,000 items in store and 10,000 new pieces arriving each week there is always something fresh and exciting to be found in every department: womenswear, menswear, childrenswear, sports and leisurewear, shoes, accessories and homewares. The stores are spacious and functional, with wide aisles enabling easy disabled and pushchair access. There are individual changing rooms, the stores accept all major credit and debit cards, and there is a return and refund policy. There are now over 120 easily accessible stores, often situated in main shopping centres or retail parks. All stores are open seven days a week and late in the evenings, though times vary from store to store. For details of your nearest store and opening hours, visit the website at www.tkmaxx.com.

BERKSHIRE

LANDS' END DIRECT MERCHANTS

UNIT 11, THE BISHOP CENTRE, BATH ROAD, TAPLOW, MAIDENHEAD, BERKSHIRE SL6 0NX, ☎ 01628 602804, **FACTORY SHOP**

Genuine overstocks of jumpers and leggings to turtlenecks, trouser and leggings are priced at 25% to 40% below normal catalogue prices; catalogue returns and near-perfect seconds are reduced by between 40% and 85%. All overstock items are guaranteed, first quality Lands' End label products, all of which have been offered previously in their catalogues at regular prices. You cannot buy current catalogue merchandise from the clearance outlet.

MATALAN

ROSE KILN LANE, READING, BERKSHIRE RG2 0SN, ☎ 0118 939 1958, FAX: 0118 939 4605, www.matalan.co.uk, 10–8 MON–FRI, 9–6 SAT, 11–5 SUN.

217A BATH ROAD, SLOUGH, BERKSHIRE SL1 4AA, ☎ 01753 487900, FAX: 01753 523353, www.matalan.co.uk, 10–8 MON–FRI, 9–6 SAT, 11–5 SUN. **PERMANENT DISCOUNT OUTLET**

See page 89 (BEDS)

THE REALLY GOOD DEAL FASHION SALE

THE PAVILION, ASCOT RACECOURSE, ASCOT, BERKSHIRE SL5 7JN, ☎ 01367 860017, FAX: 01367 860177, **e-mail:** nheslam@aol.com www.gooddealdirectory.co.uk, 10–6 FRI, SAT. **DESIGNER SALES**

The Really Good Deal Fashion Sale takes place twice a year in the elegant Pavilion building at Ascot Racecourse. The summer sale, which is usually the last, or second to last, Friday and Saturday in May, features about 70 different companies; the winter sale, which is usually the first Friday and Saturday of November, or the last Friday and Saturday of Ocobter, features 95 different companies. The range of businesses taking part is firmly middle to upper middle end of the market, with well-known names like Mulberry, N Peal Cashmere, Dents, and Paddy Campbell usually taking stands to sell their ends of lines and overstocks to the public at reduced prices. Almost anything you can think of is on sale here: coats, dresses, smart suits, wedding suits, evening wear, hats, shoes, boots, a variety of fabulous jewellery, stretch jeans, designer jeans, ties, men's shirts and sweaters, scarves, shawls, pashmina shawls, wraps, handbags, briefcases, gloves, wallets, swimwear, nightwear and there are usually one or two childrenswear companies. Tickets to the event cost £5 and are only available in advance. To join the mailing list, phone the above telephone number or write to PO Box 4, Lechlade, Glos GL7 3YB and you will receive advance notification of each sale and a ticket order form. The sale is organised by the team behind this book, The Good Deal Directory. They also run a sale in Yorkshire in October (see page 71).

THE STOCK EXCHANGE

1 HIGH STREET, SUNNINGHILL, ASCOT, BERKSHIRE SL5 9NQ, ☎ 01344 625420, 9–5.30 MON–FRI, 8 ON THUR, 9–4.30 SAT. DRESS AGENCY

Excellent selection of nearly-new designer and high street labels for women, men and children including Calvin Klein, Boss and Yves Saint Laurent. Rapid turnover of clothes, all very well presented, in this very busy shop with cheerful, helpful staff. Clothes are sold in season and all items are clean and up-to-date. Garments are displayed for four weeks at full price and then one week at half price. Also sell shoes, hats, handbags and belts.

TK MAXX

6 THE MALL, THE KENNETT CENTRE, NEWBURY, BERKSHIRE RG14 5EN, ☎ 01635 522323, www.tkmaxx.com, 9–5.30 MON–FRI, 7 ON THUR, 9–6 SAT, 11–5 SUN.

UNIT A39, BROAD STREET MALL, BROAD STREET, READING, BERKSHIRE RG1 7QE, ☎ 0118 951 1117, www.tkmaxx.com, 9–5.30 MON–FRI, 9–6 SAT, 11–5 SUN.

UNIT 30–40, OBSERVATORY CENTRE, HIGH STREET, SLOUGH, BERKSHIRE SL1 1LL, ☎ 01753 572550, www.tkmaxx.com, 9–5.30 MON–FRI, 8 ON THUR, 9–6 SAT, 11–5 SUN. **PERMANENT DISCOUNT OUTLET**

See page 89 (BEDS)

BRISTOL

BLUNTS

127 EAST STREET, BEDMINSTER, BRISTOL BS3 4ER, ☎ 0117 963 3816, 9–5.30 MON–SAT. **PERMANENT DISCOUNT OUTLET**

This shoe retailer, established for over 135 years, sells well-known brand name shoes for women and men at big discounts for discontinued stock, second and ends-of-ranges. Names on sale include Clarks, K, Lotus, Grenson, Loakes, Adidas, Nike, Reebok, HiTec and Truka. Men's shoes range from £10 to £79.99, women's from £5 to £45, children's from £5 to £15.

MATALAN

ALDERMOOR WAY, LONGWELL GREEN, BRISTOL BS15 7AD, ☎ 0117 935 2828, FAX: 0117 935 3035, www.matalan.co.uk, 10–8 MON–FRI, 9–6 SAT, 11–5 SUN.

ABBEY RETAIL PARK, STATION ROAD, FILTON, BRISTOL BS2 7JW, ☎ 0117 974 8000, FAX: 0117 969 5904, www.matalan.co.uk, 10–8 MON–FRI, 9–6 SAT, 11–5 SUN. **PERMANENT DISCOUNT OUTLET**

See page 89 (BEDS)

SUITS YOU

UNIT 045, LOWER LEVEL, THE MALL, CRIBBS CAUSEWAY, BRISTOL BS34 5GG, ☎ 0117 950 2266, 10–8 MON–FRI, 9–7 SAT, 11–5 SUN. **FACTORY SHOP IN A FACTORY SHOPPING VILLAGE**

Suits You offers a large selection of formal and casual wear – suits, jackets, overcoats, formal and casual shirts, trousers and accessories, including shoes – across a variety of brands that include the following: Pierre Cardin, Daniel Hechter, Tom English, Cezan, Van Kollem, Scott and Taylor, Cerruti and Pierre Balmain. All merchandise is discounted: for example, buy two £100 suits for £180, or two £150 suits for £270; two shirts for £26; two pairs of trousers for £45 and so on. This is one of over 40 branches around the UK. Phone 020 8327 3000 for details of your nearest branch. A selection of womenswear and designer products can be found in the company's Autonomy and Woodhouse stores (see pages 80 and 93), both of which also offer exceptional discounts.

TK MAXX

THE GALLERIES CENTRE, 31–32 CASTLE GALLERY, BROADMEAD, BRISTOL BS1 3XE, ☎ 0117 930 4404, www.tkmaxx.com, 9–5.30 MON–SAT, 7 ON THUR, 11–5 SUN. **PERMANENT DISCOUNT OUTLET**

See page 89 (BEDS)

BUCKINGHAMSHIRE

MATALAN

103 WATLING STREET, BLETCHLEY, MILTON KEYNES, BUCKINGHAMSHIRE MK1 1HS, ☎ 01908 625400, FAX: 01908 641935, www.matalan.co.uk, 10–8 MON–FRI, 9–6 SAT, 11–4 SUN. **PERMANENT DISCOUNT OUTLET**

See page 89 (BEDS)

QD STORES

HAMPDEN HOUSE, HIGH STREET AYLESBURY, BUCKINGHAMSHIRE HP20 1RE, ☎ 01296 428231, 9–5.30 MON–SAT. **PERMANENT DISCOUNT OUTLET**

See page 89 (BEDS)

ROHAN DESIGNS PLC

1–3 KNEBWORTH GATE, GIFFORD PARK, MILTON KEYNES, BUCKINGHAMSHIRE MK14 5QD, ☎ 01908 615407, FAX: 01908 616624, www.rohan.co.uk, 9.30–5.30 MON–SAT. **FACTORY SHOP**

High performance fabrics with unique design features ranging from waterproof jackets to the famous Rohan 'bags'. Seconds and discontinued items available at discount prices. Also sells shirts, trousers, T-shirts and fleeces.

THE DESIGNER ROOM

XSCAPE, AVEBURY BOULVARD, MILTON KEYNES, BUCKINGHAMSHIRE MK9 3XS, ☎ 01908 232164, FAX: 01908 233150, 10–6 MON–WED, 10–8 THUR–SAT, 12–6 SUN. **PERMANENT DISCOUNT OUTLET**

The Designer Room chain specialises in branded designer clothes and accessories. Stores sell clothing for men and women, lingerie/underwear plus discounted perfumes. Brands that are regularly stocked include: Boxfresh, Elle, Kangol, French Connection, Tommy Hilfiger, Jasper Conran, Ghost, Klass, Roman Originals, Betty Jackson, Yves St Laurent shirts and ties for men, Carlisle, Full Circle, Le Pel and Calvin Klein lingerie, Elizabeth Emmanuel nightwear.

CAMBRIDGESHIRE

CATALOGUE BARGAIN SHOP

51 WEST STREET, WISBECH, CAMBRIDGESHIRE PE13 2LY, ☎ 01945 584327, www.bargaincrazy.com, 9–4.30 MON–SAT, 10–4 SUN. **PERMANENT DISCOUNT OUTLET**

Catalogue Bargain Shop is a growing national chain of stores which obtains the majority of its goods from mail order giants Great Universal and Kays, and offers a range of clothing for all the family, a wide selection of shoes, bed linen, household goods, electrical equipment and hundreds of other catalogue items at very competitive prices. The merchandise consists of ends of ranges and previous season's stock for which there is no longer storage space when the catalogues change.

CHOICE DISCOUNT STORES LIMITED

UNITS 5–6 VIKING WAY, BARHILL, CAMBRIDGESHIRE CB3 8EL
10–6 MON–WED, 10–7 THUR, FRI, 9–6 SAT, 11–5 SUN. **PERMANENT DISCOUNT OUTLET**

Surplus stock including women's, men's and children's fashions from Next plc, Next Directory, other high street fashion houses, Next Interiors and footwear. You can save up to 50% off normal retail prices for first quality; up to two thirds for seconds. There are special sales each January and September. Easy access for wheelchairs and pushchairs.

COBBLERS

9 CHURCH STREET, PETERBOROUGH, CAMBRIDGESHIRE PE1 1XB, ☎ 01733 558783, 9–5.30 MON–SAT. **FACTORY SHOP**

Full price and discounted shoes for men and women. For women, the brand names include Rapisardi, Eseno, Nickles and Gabor in sizes 2 to 11. A typical example of the reduction is Eseno flatties, normally retailing at £69.99, are sold here for £49.99. For men, the brand names include Eseno, Loakes and Prestige with a typical reduction from £87.99 to £57.99. There are half price sample shoes on sale as well as leather handbags.

MATALAN

EAST STATION ROAD, PETERBOROUGH, CAMBRIDGESHIRE PE2 8AA, ☎ 01733 341229, FAX: 01733 341246, www.matalan.co.uk, 10–8 MON–FRI, 9–6 SAT, 11–5 SUN. **PERMANENT DISCOUNT OUTLET**

See page 89 (BEDS)

QD STORES

ORTON CENTRE, PETERBOROUGH, CAMBRIDGESHIRE PE2 OUD, ☎ 01733 237311
9–5.30 MON–SAT, 10–4 SUN. **PERMANENT DISCOUNT OUTLET**

62 BURLEIGH STREET, CAMBRIDGE, CAMBRIDGESHIRE CB1 1DG, ☎ 01223 323174, 9–5.30 MON–SAT, 10–4 SUN. **PERMANENT DISCOUNT OUTLET**

16–17 MARKET PLACE, WISBECH, CAMBRIDGESHIRE PE13 1DY, ☎ 01945 466756, 9–5.30 MON–SAT. **PERMANENT DISCOUNT OUTLET**

See page 89 (BEDS)

STAGE 2

SAVILLE ROAD, PETERBOROUGH, CAMBRIDGESHIRE PE3 7RP, ☎ 01733 263308, 10–8 MON–FRI, 9–6 SAT, 10–4 SUN, BANK HOLIDAYS. **PERMANENT DISCOUNT OUTLET**

Sells surplus stock from both Grattan and Freemans catalogues. Womenswear, childrenswear, menswear and household items, at up to 50% off catalogue prices. Includes a wide range of brands from both designer and high street on a regularly changing basis. Electrical goods are sold at discounts of up to 30% off catalogue prices, and include big-name brands. 14-day refund policy.

SUITS YOU

UNIT 12, PETTY GUY, LION YARD SHOPPING CENTRE, CAMBRIDGE, CAMBRIDGESHIRE CB2 3NE, ☎ 01223 355979, 9–5.30 MON–FRI, 9–6 SAT, 10.30–4.30 SUN. **FACTORY SHOP IN A FACTORY SHOPPING VILLAGE**

See page 91 (BRIS)

THE DRESS AGENCY

1 THE BROADWAY, ST IVES, HUNTINGDON, CAMBRIDGESHIRE PE28 4BX, ☎ 01480 464 952, 10–5 MON-SAT. **DRESS AGENCY**

Designer clothes and contemporary fashions. There are women's evening wear, prom dresses, ball gowns and special occasion hats. New handbags, and Italian shoes, including Prada and Miu Miu, are also on sale at discounted prices. There is also a new range of Italian lingerie sold at very competitive prices.

THE FROCK EXCHANGE

7 HIGH STREET, FENSTANTON, CAMBRIDGESHIRE PE28 9LQ, ☎ 01480 461187, FAX: 01480 461187, 9–5 TUE–SAT. **DRESS AGENCY**

The Frock Exchange opened its doors in 1981, the first dress agency in East Anglia. 1983 saw the introduction of ballgown hire, again a first for the area. Esquire, a men's formal occasion wear business to buy or to hire, was opened in 1984. Originally in premises facing the women's shop, Esquire has now moved above the Frock Exchange and complements the evening and special occasion wear which is such a feature of this popular and busy shop. Hat hire completes the services on offer. The Frock Exchange has been featured on The Clothes Show, Look East and About Anglia television. Designer labels are always in stock.

CHESHIRE

ADIDAS

MCARTHURGLEN DESIGNER OUTLET CHESHIRE OAKS, KINSEY ROAD, NEAR ELLESMERE PORT, JUNCTION 10 OF M53, CHESHIRE CH65 9JJ, ☎ 0151 355 6893, FAX: 0151 355 0816, 10–8 MON–FRI, 9–6 SAT, 11–5 SUN. **FACTORY SHOP IN A FACTORY SHOPPING VILLAGE**

Specialising in a wide range of sports apparel for men, women and children, this store sells end of season products at 30% to 70% off RRP. Footwear and accessories such as sports bags, shinpads etc. Saloman outdoor wear and the Adidas golf range are also stocked. Regular promotions run throughout the year.

AUTONOMY

UNIT 159, CHESHIRE OAKS DESIGNER OUTLET VILLAGE, ELLESMERE PORT, SOUTH WIRRAL, CHESHIRE CH65 9JJ, ☎ 0151 355 6701, 10–8 MON–FRI, 9–6 SAT, 11–5 SUN. **FACTORY SHOP IN A FACTORY SHOPPING VILLAGE**

Autonomy offers a selection of women's suits and accessories including blouses, knitwear, casual tops and handbags. Autonomy offers a 'three for' offer where you can buy jacket, skirt and trousers or a dress from as little as £60.

BIG L FACTORY OUTLET

UNIT 6, MCARTHURGLEN DESIGNER OUTLET CHESHIRE OAKS, KINSEY ROAD, NEAR ELLESMERE PORT, JUNCTION 10 OF M53, CHESHIRE CH65 9HN, ☎ 0151 356 8484, FAX: 0151 356 8484, 10–8 MON–FRI, 9–6 SAT, 11–5 SUN. **FACTORY SHOP IN A FACTORY SHOPPING VILLAGE**

Men's and women's Levi's jeans, jackets, cord and Sherpa fleece jackets, T-shirts and shirts but no children's, all at discount prices.

BURBERRY

MCARTHURGLEN DESIGNER OUTLET CHESHIRE OAKS, KINSEY ROAD, NEAR ELLESMERE PORT, JUNCTION 10 OF M53, CHESHIRE CH65 9JJ, ☎ 0151 357 3203, 10–8 MON–FRI, 9–6 SAT, 11–5 SUN. **FACTORY SHOP IN A FACTORY SHOPPING VILLAGE**

The Burberry factory shops sell surplus stock from the famous Burberry London men's and women's collections as well as accessories such as the distinctive umbrellas, scarves and handbags. It also sells children's clothing, though different factory shops stock different amounts. Stock is not current season but all carry the Burberry label and discounts are about one third off the normal price.

CATALOGUE BARGAIN SHOP

ROYAL AVENUE, WIDNES, CHESHIRE WA8 7BR, ☎ 0151 424 6161, www.bargaincrazy.com, 10–6 MON–FRI, 9–5 SAT. **PERMANENT DISCOUNT OUTLET**

See page 92 (CAMBS)

CHESTER BARRIE

WESTON ROAD, CREWE, CHESHIRE CW1 6BA, ☎ 01270 508900, FAX: 01270 584049, **e-mail:** handtailoring@chesterbarrie.co.uk, www.chesterbarrie.co.uk, 9.30–5.30 MON–SAT. **FACTORY SHOP**

Busy and friendly shopping environment located just a quarter of a mile from Crewe railway station and four miles from junction 16 on the M6. The factory shop has continued to grow in popularity with almost 8,000 people now on its mailing database. Customers who visit recognise and enjoy the value of top quality, British made products; men's and women's tailored clothing being the speciality. The shop includes large fitting and changing areas, free parking and excellent access from the road network. A tailoring alteration service, and men's and women's bespoke tailoring are available. Core offerings include an extensive range and selection of Chester Barrie men's ready-to-wear garments, Chester Barrie women's tailored clothing, top quality coats, formal shirts and women's blouses and knitwear. Regular special offers and sales are held in the factory shop as well as factory sales, held three times a year within the factory itself, which dispose of stock overruns at reasonable prices. Details of these events can be obtained from the shop staff on the above telephone number. Chester Barrie also manufactures product for other famous brand names such as Austin Reed, Burberry, Hackett, Moss Bross, Turnbull & Asser and Harrods, to name but a few. The shop also focuses on the accessory market with products such as belts, caps, cashmere, knitwear, cufflinks and women's and men's footwear. Bladen country wear is available all year round. All items on display are of perfect quality, not seconds as in many outlets. The shop concentrates on the old-fashioned virtue of customer service, in particular the bespoke tailoring service which offers clients an opportunity to select their own cloth and style of suit, to have a bespoke fitting and a final fitting upon completion of the garment, thus guaranteeing quality and fit.

CIRO

MCARTHURGLEN DESIGNER OUTLET CHESHIRE OAKS, KINSEY ROAD, NEAR ELLESMERE PORT, JUNCTION 10 OF M53, CHESHIRE CH65 9JJ, ☎ 0151 355 4037, 10–8 MON–FRI, 9–6 SAT, 11–5 SUN. **FACTORY SHOP IN A FACTORY SHOPPING VILLAGE**

One of more than 120 outlets, all selling brand name merchandise at discounted prices, with more outlets in the pipeline. Internationally famous jewellers Ciro sell a range of jewellery. There is a children's play area, a Garfunkels restaurant and free car parking. Another branch is situated in Bridgend, south Wales. Phone 01656 655916.

CLARKS FACTORY SHOP

CHESHIRE OAKS OUTLET, KINSEY ROAD, NEAR ELLESMERE PORT, JUNCTION 10 OF M53, SOUTH WIRRAL CH65 9JJ, ☎ 0151 356 7492, 10–8 MON–FRI, 9–6 SAT, 11–5 SUN. **FACTORY SHOP IN A FACTORY SHOPPING VILLAGE**

Clarks International operate a chain of factory shops nationally which specialise in selling discontinued lines and slight sub-standards for men, women and children from Clarks, K Shoes and other famous brands. These shops trade under the name of K Shoes Factory Shop or Clarks Factory Shop and while not all are physically attached to a shoe factory, they are treated as factory shops by the company. Customers can expect to find an extensive range of quality shoes, sandals, walking boots, slippers, trainers, handbags, accessories and gifts, while their major outlets also offer luggage, sports clothing, sports equipment and outdoor clothing. Brands stocked include Clarks, K Shoes, Springer, CICA, Hi-Tec, Caterpillar, Kickers, Timberland, Regatta, Craghoppers, Kangol, Kangaroo Poo, Diadora, Mercury, Antler, Eminent, Travelon, Hudson and Carlton, although not all are sold in every outlet. Phone first to find out what your particular store is offering. Discounts are from 30% to 60% off normal high street price for perfect stock.

DIESEL

MCARTHURGLEN DESIGNER OUTLET CHESHIRE OAKS, KINSEY ROAD, NEAR ELLESMERE PORT, JUNCTION 10 OF M53, CHESHIRE CH65 9JJ, ☎ 0151 355 1478, 10–8 MON–FRI, 9–6 SAT, 11–5 SUN. **FACTORY SHOP IN A FACTORY SHOPPING VILLAGE**

Diesel, which claims to be the fastest growing jeans label in the world, sells Modern Basic in addition to Diesel Spare Part accessories. Based in Molvena, Italy, Diesel now distributes to 72 countries worldwide, though this is its only outlet store in the UK as we went to press. First-quality jeans cost from £35 a pair.

DIRECT SPECS LTD

1 ST WERBURGHS SQUARE, BIRKENHEAD, CHESHIRE CH41 2XZ, ☎ 0151 647 6800, www.directspecs.co.uk, 9–5.30 MON–SAT. **PERMANENT DISCOUNT OUTLET**

62 FRODSHAM STREET, CHESTER, CHESHIRE CH1 3JL, ☎ 01244 400395, www.directspecs.co.uk, 9–5 MON–SAT. **PERMANENT DISCOUNT OUTLET**

UNIT 4, CECIL HOUSE, HIGHTOWN, CREWE, CHESHIRE CW1 3B2, ☎ 01270 585392, www.directspecs.co.uk, 9–5 MON–SAT. **PERMANENT DISCOUNT OUTLET**

Spectacles and sunglasses at prices which the owner claims beat any competitor's. Most designer names are stocked at one time or another, though if you have a favourite, check first. Bring along your prescription and glasses will be found to suit. No eye tests conducted.

ECCO

MCARTHURGLEN DESIGNER OUTLET CHESHIRE OAKS, KINSEY ROAD, NEAR ELLESMERE PORT, JUNCTION 10 OF M53, CHESHIRE CH65 9JJ, ☎ 0151 356 3045, www.ecco.com, 10–8 MON–FRI, 9–6 SAT, 11–5 SUN. **FACTORY SHOP IN A FACTORY SHOPPING VILLAGE**

Women's, men's and children's shoes, all discounted by at least 25% and sometimes by as much as 60%. Other outlets in Wiltshire, Somerset, South Wales and Hertfordshire.

ELITE DRESS AGENCY

1 MARKET STREET, ALTRINCHAM, CHESHIRE WA14 1QE, ☎ 0161 928 5424, 10–5 MON–SAT. **DRESS AGENCY**

Established in 1964, this shop sells mainly womenswear which is less than two years old, with a small but comprehensive selection of menswear. Wide range of clothing includes some sportswear. Labels range from high street to designer and include names such as Prada, DKNY, Yves St Laurent, Dior, Valentino, Ungaro, Thierry Mugler, Marks & Spencer, Kookai, Morgan and Ralph Lauren for women, and Boss, Versace, Armani, Yves Saint Laurent, Cerruti and Ralph Lauren for men. Twice yearly sales at the end of June and December. A dress hire section stocks a wide selection of brand new dresses, updated twice a year (see One-Night Affair, page 24). They have recently expanded to include a childrenswear department.

FAMOUS FOOTWEAR

MCARTHURGLEN DESIGNER OUTLET CHESHIRE OAKS, KINSEY ROAD, NEAR ELLESMERE PORT, JUNCTION 10 OF M53, CHESHIRE CH65 9JJ, ☎ 0151 357 1512, 10–8 MON–FRI, 9–6 SAT, 11–5 SUN. **FACTORY SHOP IN A FACTORY SHOPPING VILLAGE**

Wide range of brands including Lilley & Skinner, Hush Puppies, Lotus, Wrangler, Frank Wright, Red Tape, Rohde, Brevitt, Padders, Rombah Wallace and Rieker, all at discount prices of up to 50%.

GAP

MCARTHURGLEN DESIGNER OUTLET CHESHIRE OAKS, KINSEY ROAD, NEAR ELLESMERE PORT, JUNCTION 10 OF M53, CHESHIRE CH65 9JJ, ☎ 0151 355 2488, 10–8 MON–FRI, 9–6 SAT, 11–5 SUN. **FACTORY SHOP IN A FACTORY SHOPPING VILLAGE**

Gap has two shops in this outlet, one selling casual clothes for men and women and another opposite catering for children of all ages. The minimum discount is 30% with many items at 50% off and some reduced by as much as 90%.

JAEGER FACTORY OUTLET

MCARTHURGLEN DESIGNER OUTLET CHESHIRE OAKS, KINSEY ROAD, NEAR ELLESMERE PORT, JUNCTION 10 OF M53, CHESHIRE CH65 9JJ, ☎ 0151 355 0022, 10–6 MON–SAT, 8 ON THUR, 11–5 SUN. **FACTORY SHOP IN A FACTORY SHOPPING VILLAGE**

See page 158 (NORF)

KANGOL FACTORY SHOPS

MCARTHURGLEN DESIGNER OUTLET CHESHIRE OAKS, KINSEY ROAD, NEAR ELLESMERE PORT, JUNCTION 10 OF M53, CHESHIRE CH65 9JJ, ☎ 0151 356 4968, **e-mail:** kangol_uk@hotmail.com, 10–8 MON–THUR, 10–6 FRI–SAT, 11–5 SUN. PLEASE PHONE FOR CHRISTMAS AND BANK HOLIDAY OPENING HOURS. **FACTORY SHOP**

Sells Kangol-branded accessories at a minimum of 30% off normal retail prices.

LEE COOPER

MCARTHURGLEN DESIGNER OUTLET CHESHIRE OAKS, KINSEY ROAD, NEAR ELLESMERE PORT, JUNCTION 10 OF M53, CHESHIRE CH65 9JJ, ☎ 0151 355 8808, 10–8 MON–FRI, 9–6 SAT, 11–5 SUN. **FACTORY SHOP IN A FACTORY SHOPPING VILLAGE**

Denim jeans, jackets and shirts, each ranked by size and gender at discounts from 30%. Casual shirts from £10, jeans from £15, T-shirts and womenswear. Lee Cooper was founded in 1908 as a workwear manufacturer before becoming a supplier to the armed forces. Most of the stock here is current, discontinued, overstocks and irregular merchandise, all of which comes straight from Lee Cooper's factories in Europe.

LITTLEWOODS CATALOGUE DISCOUNT STORE

MCARTHURGLEN DESIGNER OUTLET CHESHIRE OAKS, KINSEY ROAD, NEAR ELLESMERE PORT, JUNCTION 10 OF M53, CHESHIRE CH65 9JJ, ☎ 0151 356 0501
10–8 MON–FRI, 9–6 SAT, 11–5 SUN. **FACTORY SHOP**

Littlewoods clearance shops offer up to 70% off the catalogue price for clothing and offer big discounts off electrical goods. Stock changes constantly and varies from day to day but can include well-known brand names such as Berlei and Gossard lingerie, Vivienne Westwood, Pamplemousse leisurewear, Nike and Adidas sports shoes, and Timberland and Caterpillar footwear. Stock depends on the size and location of the shop: larger shops get the longer discontinued runs, while smaller shops get overruns with only a small amount of colour and size variations left. Littlewoods also runs a mobile shop which operates in cities which don't have a sale shop. For details of venues for the sales, which usually take place once a month, write to Melanie Lamb, c/o Crosby DC Kershaw Avenue, Endbutt Lane, Crosby, Merseyside L70 1AH.

MARKS & SPENCER

MCARTHURGLEN DESIGNER OUTLET VILLAGE CHESHIRE OAKS, ELLESMERE PORT, SOUTH WIRRAL CH65 9JJ, ☎ 0151 356 0985, 10–8 MON–FRI, 9–6 SAT, 11–5 SUN. **FACTORY SHOP IN A FACTORY SHOPPING VILLAGE**

Fashion and footwear – no homewares – which are mostly last season's stock for families at least 30% below usual retail prices.

MATALAN

UNITS 3, 4 & 5A, THE ROCK RETAIL PARK, GREEN LANE, BIRKENHEAD, CHESHIRE CH41 9AG, ☎ 0151 650 6820, FAX: 0151 650 0487, www.matalan.co.uk, 10–8 MON–FRI, 9.30–6 SAT, 11–5 SUN.

NEW CHESTER ROAD, BROMBOROUGH, SOUTH WIRRAL, CHESHIRE CH62 7EK, ☎ 0151 343 9494, FAX: 0151 343 9321, www.matalan.co.uk, 9.30–8 MON–FRI, 9–6 SAT, 11–5 SUN.

STADIUM WAY, CHESTER, CHESHIRE CH1 4PZ, ☎ 01244 665260, FAX: 01244 665908, www.matalan.co.uk, 9.30–8 MON–FRI, 9–6 SAT, 11–5 SUN.

KERFOOT STREET, OFF WINWICK ROAD, WARRINGTON, CHESHIRE WA2 8NU, ☎ 01925 235365, FAX: 01925 230371, www.matalan.co.uk, 9.30–8 MON–FRI, 9–6 SAT, 11–5 SUN. **PERMANENT DISCOUNT OUTLET**

See page 89 (BEDS)

MCARTHURGLEN DESIGNER OUTLET

KINSEY ROAD, NEAR ELLESMERE PORT, JUNCTION 10 OF M53, CHESHIRE CH65 9JJ, ☎ 0800 316 4352 FREE INFORMATION LINE OR 0151 348 5600, FAX: 0151 357 3744, www.mcarthurglen.com/cheshireoaks, 10–8 MON–FRI, 9–6 SAT, 11–5 SUN. **FACTORY SHOPPING VILLAGE**

The McArthurGlen Designer Outlet Cheshire Oaks is Europe's largest designer outlet with over 140 stores selling top brands and designer names at up to 50% off typical retail prices. Facilities include a food court, a children's play area and free parking. Stores include: Gap Outlet, Big L, Fruit of the Loom, Monsoon, Timberland, Tie Rack, Principles, Petroleum, James Barry, Donnay, Aquascutum, Burberrys, Viyella, Warehouse, Racing Green, Famous Footwear, Jeffrey Rogers, Liz Claiborne, Winning Line, Overland, Ciro Pearls, Diesel, Jokids, Fred Perry, Travel Accessory Outlet, Baron Jon, La Senza, Nike, Next to Nothing, Helly Hansen, Jane Shilton, Joe Bloggs, Birthdays, Thorntons, Toyworld, D2, Pilot, Jumper, Clarks, Villeroy & Boch, Episode, Windsmoor, Jaeger, Daks Simpson, Mexx, Bed & Bath Works, Woods of Windsor, The Suit Company, XS Music & Video, Suits You, Claire's Accessories, Lee Cooper, Tog 24, Fila, Warners, Cecil Gee, Remington, Whittard of Chelsea, Kitchen Store, Denby, Edinburgh Crystal, Price's Candles, Reebok, Hobbs, Kurt Muller, Bookends, Pictureport, Kappa, Easy Jeans, Woodhouse, Designer Room, DKNY, Ponden Mill, U Wear/I Wear, Penn, Le Coq Sportif, Roman Originals, Revlon, Monet, Walker and Hall, Ben Sherman, Van Heusen, Austin Reed, Antler, Ecco, Blazer, Watson/Chillii Pepper, Red/Green, Soled Out, Carphone Warehouse, Cotton Traders, Royal Doulton, Royal Worcester, Oneida, Proibito, Vans, Reiss, Garden Outlet, Proudfoot Leather, Playtime Toys, Wedgwood, Prima Tessuti, Natural World, WHSmith, Littlewoods, Bose, The Body Shop, Samsonite, Adidas, Kangol, Dune, Marks & Spencer Outlet, Daniel Footwear, Polo Jeans Company, The North Face, Elle, Sergio Tacchini, Chapelle, Fiorelli, Julian Graves, Spiegelau, Bose, Kitch N Sync, Early Learning Centre, Tommy Hilfiger, Triumph and Professional Cookware.

MEXX INTERNATIONAL

MCARTHURGLEN DESIGNER OUTLET CHESHIRE OAKS, KINSEY ROAD, NEAR ELLESMERE PORT, JUNCTION 10 OF M53, CHESHIRE CH65 9JJ, ☎ 0151 355 8238, 10–8 MON–FRI, 9–6 SAT, 11–5 SUN. **FACTORY SHOP IN A FACTORY SHOPPING VILLAGE**

High street fashion at factory outlet prices for men, women, babies and children, all of which is discounted by more than 30%.

NEXT TO NOTHING

MCARTHURGLEN DESIGNER OUTLET CHESHIRE OAKS, KINSEY ROAD, NEAR ELLESMERE PORT, JUNCTION 10 OF M53, CHESHIRE CH65 9JJ, ☎ 0151 356 7404, www.next.co.uk, 10–8 MON–FRI, 9–6 SAT, 11–5 SUN. **FACTORY SHOP IN A FACTORY SHOPPING VILLAGE**

Sells perfect surplus stock from Next stores and the Next Directory catalogue – from belts, jewellery and underwear to day and evening wear – at discounts of 50% or more. The ranges are usually last season's and overruns. Stock consists of women's, men's and children's clothing, with some homeware and shoes. Stock is replenished three times a week and there is plenty of it.

PRINCIPLES

MCARTHURGLEN DESIGNER OUTLET CHESHIRE OAKS, KINSEY ROAD, NEAR ELLESMERE PORT, JUNCTION 10 OF M53, CHESHIRE CH65 9JJ, ☎ 0151 357 1033, 10–8 MON–FRI, 9–6 SAT, 11–5 SUN. **FACTORY SHOP IN A FACTORY SHOPPING VILLAGE**

End of season lines with the normal Principles refund guarantee. The range includes, for women, dresses, blouses, coats, outerwear, knitwear, casual wear and a selection of Petite clothing for women who are 5ft 3ins and under.

QS FASHION SALE

1–5 BROAD ROAD, SALE, CHESHIRE M33 2AE, ☎ 0161 976 2747, FAX: 0161 962 9244, 9–8 MON–FRI, 9–5.30 SAT, 11–5 SUN. **PERMANENT DISCOUNT OUTLET**

Fashion for all the family includes brands such as Timberland, Fila, Nike, Reebok, Adidas, Calvin Klein and Ralph Lauren and many more. Homeware products include towels, bedding, plastics, pictures, toys and mirrors. The stock is constantly changing so come with an open mind. QS Fashion has a price promise that if you can purchase the same item at a cheaper price at another store, QS will give you the product free.

RACING GREEN

MCARTHURGLEN DESIGNER OUTLET CHESHIRE OAKS, KINSEY ROAD, NEAR ELLESMERE PORT, JUNCTION 10 OF M53, CHESHIRE CH65 9JJ, ☎ 0151 351 1159, www.racinggreen.co.uk, 10–8 MON–FRI, 9–6 SAT, 11–5 SUN. **FACTORY SHOP IN A FACTORY SHOPPING VILLAGE**

Overstocks and clearance lines from this mail order catalogue are sold here at discount prices.

REDGREEN

MCARTHURGLEN DESIGNER OUTLET CHESHIRE OAKS, KINSEY ROAD, NEAR ELLESMERE PORT, JUNCTION 10 OF M53, CHESHIRE CH65 9JJ, ☎ 0151 356 3660, 10–8 MON–FRI, 9–6 SAT, 11–5 SUN. **FACTORY SHOP IN A FACTORY SHOPPING VILLAGE**

RedGreen is Scandinavian leisurewear for men and women. The high quality and classic design has a nautical heritage and a stylish look. The collection includes outerwear, sweaters, shirts, trousers, skirts, dresses, sweatshirts, T-shirts, tailored jackets, footwear and accessories at discount of between 25% and 70%.

T J HUGHES

BOROUGH PAVEMENT, GRANGE PRECINCT, BIRKENHEAD, CHESHIRE L41 2XX, ☎ 0151 647 5151, FAX: 0151 666 1610, **e-mail:** info@tjhughes.co.uk, www.tjhughes.co.uk, 9–5.30 MON–SAT, 10–4 SUN.

THE FORUM, HAMILTON PLACE, CHESTER, CHESHIRE CH1 2BH, ☎ 01244 316600, FAX: 01244 316646, **e-mail:** info@tjhughes.co.uk, www.tjhughes.co.uk, 9–5.30 MON–SAT, 11–5 SUN.

2 MERCIER WALK, SOUTH WIRRAL, CHESHIRE CH65 0AP, ☎ 0151 357 3151, FAX: 0151 357 3174, **e-mail:** info@tjhughes.co.uk, www.tjhughes.co.uk, 9–5.30 MON–SAT, 10–4 SUN.

EXCHANGE STREET, MACCLESFIELD, CHESHIRE SK11 6UZ, ☎ 01625 611807, FAX: 01625 611859, **e-mail:** info@tjhughes.co.uk, www.tjhughes.co.uk, 9–5.30 MON–SAT, 10–4 SUN.

GREENOAKS SHOPPING CENTRE, WIDNES, CHESHIRE WA8 6UD, ☎ 0151 420 1010, FAX: 0151 423 4570, **e-mail:** info@tjhughes.co.uk, www.tjhughes.co.uk, 9–5.30 MON–SAT, 10–4 SUN. **PERMANENT DISCOUNT OUTLET**

Expanding chain of shops offering, not discounts as such, but very competitively priced goods including clothes for all the family, china, towels, bedlinen, duvets, pots and pans, kettles, vacuum cleaners, television sets, CDs, toasters, many from top brand names.

THE FACTORY SHOP LTD

UNIT 1 EDDISBURY SQUARE, FRODSHAM, CHESHIRE WA6 6QS, ☎ 01928 734624, FAX: 01928 734906, 9–5.30 MON–SAT, 10.30–4 SUN. **FACTORY SHOP**

Wide range on sale includes men's, women's and children's clothing and footwear; household textiles; toiletries; hardware; luggage; lighting; electrical goods; and bedding, most of which are chainstore and high street brands at discounts of approximately 30% to 50%. There are kitchen and furniture displays and on sale is the Cape Country Furniture range with free-standing kitchens, as well as living, bedroom and dining furniture. There are weekly deliveries and brands include famous names such as Adidas, Nike, Joe Bloggs and Brabantia, among others. Lines are continually changing and few factory shops offer such a variety under one roof. Parking is free.

THE FAMOUS BRUNSWICK WAREHOUSE LTD

UNIT 5B, THE ROACK, GREEN LANE, BIRKENHEAD, CHESHIRE CH41 9AG, ☎ 0151 650 1505, **e-mail:** northshoe@mcmail.com, 10–8 MON–FRI, 9–6 SAT, 11–5 SUN.

UNIT 3, ST DAVIDS RETAIL PARK, SALTNEY, CHESTER, CHESHIRE CH4 8SN, ☎ 01244 676431, **e-mail:** northshoe@mcmail.com, 9–6 MON–SAT, 10–4 SUN.

UNIT 1B, 2 GRAND JUNCTION RETAIL PARK, EARLE STREET, CREWE, CHESHIRE CW1 2RP, ☎ 01270 254156, **e-mail:** northshoe@mcmail.com, 10–8 MON–FRI, 9–6 SAT, 11–5 SUN.

UNIT 3, COCKHEDGE CENTRE, COCKHEDGE WAY, WARRINGTON, CHESHIRE WA1 2QQ, ☎ 01925 232306, **e-mail:** northshoe@mcmail.com, 9–6 MON–WED, SAT, 9–7 THUR, FRI, 10.30–4.30 SUN.

49 DEWHIRST ROAD, BIRCHWOOD, WARRINGTON, CHESHIRE WA3 7PG, ☎ 01925 822718, **e-mail:** northshoe@mcmail.com, 9–6 MON–WED, SAT, 9–8 THUR, FRI, 10.30–4.30 SUN.

PERMANENT DISCOUNT OUTLET
Self-service discount store chain with 60 branches selling branded sportswear and sports footwear, such as Nike, Adidas and Reebok, as well as non-branded footwear at discounts of 50%. Also a reasonable selection of clothing and accessories. Phone the number above for details of your nearest branch.

TIMBERLAND

MCARTHURGLEN DESIGNER OUTLET CHESHIRE OAKS, KINSEY ROAD, NEAR ELLESMERE PORT, JUNCTION 10 OF M53, CHESHIRE CH65 9JJ, ☎ 0151 357 1359, FAX: 0151 357 3788, 10–8 MON–FRI, 9–6 SAT, 11–5 SUN. **FACTORY SHOP IN A FACTORY SHOPPING VILLAGE**
Footwear, clothing and outdoor gear from the extensive Timberland range at discounts of 30% or more. Most of the stock is from previous seasons with some limitation on colours and sizes. Occasionally the store will stock discontinued lines, samples and less than perfect items.

TK MAXX

178–182 GRANGE ROAD, BIRKENHEAD, CHESHIRE CH41 2PF, ☎ 0151 647 2837, www.tkmaxx.com, 9–5.30 MON–FRI, 9–6 SAT, 10.30–4.30 SUN.

STANLEY GREEN RETAIL PARK, EARL ROAD, CHEADLE HULME, CHESHIRE, ☎ 0161 485 3734, www.tkmaxx.com, PHONE FOR OPENING HOURS DETAILS.

UNIT 3, CHESTER RETAIL PARK, CHESTER, CHESHIRE, www.tkmaxx.com, VISIT WEBSITE FOR DETAILS.

UNIT B, TRIDENT RETAIL PARK, RUNCORN, CHESHIRE WA7 2FQ, ☎ 01928 714050, www.tkmaxx.com, 9–6 MON, 9–7 TUE–WED, 9–8 THUR–FRI, 9–6 SAT, 11–5 SUN.

UNIT C, THE COCKHEDGE CENTRE, 2 PRINCE HENRY SQUARE, WARRINGTON, CHESHIRE, ☎ 01925 636262, www.tkmaxx.com, 9–6 MON–SAT, 9 ON THUR, 10–4. SUN.

UNIT 12, ISLAND GREEN, WREXHAM, CHESHIRE LL13 7LW, ☎ 01978 261133, www.tkmaxx.com, 9–5.30 MON–FRI, 9–6 SAT, 11–5 SUN. **PERMANENT DISCOUNT OUTLET**

See page 89 (BEDS)

TOG 24

MCARTHURGLEN DESIGNER OUTLET CHESHIRE OAKS, KINSEY ROAD, NEAR ELLESMERE PORT, JUNCTION 10 OF M53, CHESHIRE CH65 9JJ, ☎ 0151 356 7477, **e-mail:** mail-order@tog24.com, www.tog24.com, 10–8 MON–FRI, 9–6 SAT, 11–5 SUN. **FACTORY SHOP IN A FACTORY SHOPPING VILLAGE**
Tog 24 is the UK's fastest-growing brand name in outdoor clothing and leisurewear. The company utilises the world's finest performance fabrics, including GoreTex and Polartec, to produce merchandise which caters for all the family for all seasons. Their range includes fleeces and waterproofs for the winter, and trekking ranges, shorts and T-shirts for the summer. They also stock accessories, including sunglasses, toiletries and swimwear. All merchandise is available by mail order: phone 01924 236507 for a brochure or to order. All prices are at least 30% below RRP.

TOMMY HILFIGER

MCARTHURGLEN DESIGNER OUTLET, CHESHIRE OAKS, KINSEY ROAD, ELLESMERE PORT, CHESHIRE CH65 9JJ, ☎ 0151 355 4501, FAX: 0151 355 2201, www.tommy.com, 10–8 MON–FRI, 9–6 SAT, 11–5 SUN. **FACTORY SHOP IN A FACTORY SHOPPING VILLAGE**
Sells men's and women's sportswear, sweatshirts, polo shirts, jeans, T-shirts, jackets, men's underwear and accessories.

TRIUMPH INTERNATIONAL

MCARTHURGLEN DESIGNER OUTLET CHESHIRE OAKS, KINSEY ROAD, NEAR ELLESMERE PORT, JUNCTION 10 OF M53, CHESHIRE CH65 9JR, ☎ 0151 356 9155, 10–8 MON–FRI, 9–6 SAT, 11–5 SUN. **FACTORY SHOP IN A FACTORY SHOPPING VILLAGE**
Factory shop selling a wide and ever-changing range of Triumph lingerie; a French range, Valisere; Sloggi underwear for men and women; and swimwear, all of which are last season's stock or discontinued lines at discounts of between 30% and 50%.

VIYELLA

MCARTHURGLEN DESIGNER OUTLET CHESHIRE OAKS, KINSEY ROAD, NEAR ELLESMERE PORT,

JUNCTION 10 OF M53, CHESHIRE CH65 9JJ, ☎ 0151 357 2627, 10–6 MON–FRI, 8 ON THUR, 9–6 SAT, 11–5 SUN. **FACTORY SHOP IN A FACTORY SHOPPING VILLAGE**
Wide range of Viyella clothing at discounts from 30% on women's formal and casual wear.

WALKER & HALL

MCARTHURGLEN DESIGNER OUTLET CHESHIRE OAKS, KINSEY ROAD, NEAR ELLESMERE PORT, JUNCTION 10 OF M53, CHESHIRE CH65 9LA, ☎ 0151 356 3706, www.goldsmiths.co.uk, 10–8 MON–FRI, 9–6 SAT, 11–5 SUN. **FACTORY SHOP IN A FACTORY SHOPPING VILLAGE**
Walker & Hall sells Raymond Weil watches, reduced from £550 to £385; Longines, Gucci, Maurice Lacroix and Tag Heuer. Some ranges reduced from 20% up to 50%.

WARNERS

UNIT 64, CHESHIRE OAKS DESIGNER VILLAGE, KINSEY ROAD, ELLESMERE PORT, SOUTH WIRRAL CH65 9LA, ☎ 0151 355 5353, 10–8 MON–FRI, 9–6 SAT, 11–5 SUN. **FACTORY SHOP IN A FACTORY SHOPPING VILLAGE**
This shop sells a wide range of women's lingerie from Lejaby Warners, with bras, slips, thongs, bodies and briefs at discounts from 25% to 70%. Each item is labelled with both the RRP and the discounted prices. For example, bikini briefs £6.99, reduced from £17; underwired bra £14.99, reduced from £33; body £24.99, reduced from £65. Slightly imperfect stock as well as perfect quality, end of season and discontinued merchandise and swimwear are also stocked. Underwear for men, including Calvin Klein briefs, is on offer, too.

WILKINSONS HOME & GARDEN STORES

THE MARKET CENTRE, CREWE, CHESHIRE CW1 2NG, ☎ 01270 250754, www.wilko.co.uk, 8.30–5.30 MON–WED, 8.30–6.30 THUR–SAT, 10–4 SUN. **PERMANENT DISCOUNT OUTLET**
Family-owned business offering value on the high street through its 205 stores, selling 25,000 high quality, low-priced essential everyday products for all the family including kitchenware, household disposables, clothing, DIY decoration, stationery, homewares, bedlinen, picture frames, china, cutlery, toys, pet foot, curtains, mirrors, gardening equipment including outdoor furniture, Christmas decorations, confectionery and seasonal goods. It also caters for the ardent gardener with fertiliser, grass seed – loose or boxed – plants, insecticides, composts – both multi-purpose or tub and basket – garden tools, strimmers, hoses and attachments, watering cans, water butts, wheelbarrows, and reels on wheels. In season, they sell bedding plants, garden lights, coolboxes, paint, paint brushes and rollers, and climbing plants such as honeysuckle, but as the summer progresses these are replaced by barbecues and picnic ranges. Phone 01909 505505 for details of your local outlet or visit their website.

WYNSORS WORLD OF SHOES

WARRINGTON ROAD, PENKETH, NR WARRINGTON, CHESHIRE WA2 7AP, ☎ 01925 727481 9–5.30 MON, TUE, WED, SAT, 9–8 THUR, FRI, 10–4 SUN AND BANK HOLIDAYS.

LONDON ROAD, HAZEL GROVE, STOCKPORT, CHESHIRE SK7 4AX, ☎ 0161 456 2632, 9–5.30 MON, TUE, SAT, 9–8 WED–FRI, 10–4 SUN. **PERMANENT DISCOUNT OUTLET**

Stocks top brand-name shoes at less than half price. Special monthly offers always available. There are shoes, trainers, slippers, sandals and boots for all the family, with a selection of bags, cleaners and polishes available, all at discount prices.

YOU & YOURS

UNIT 42, ORCHARD WALK, HALTON LEAS SHOPPING CENTRE, RUNCORN, CHESHIRE WA7 2GZ, ☎ 01928 795 792, 9–5.30 MON–SAT. **PERMANENT DISCOUNT OUTLET**
Sells surplus stock from both Grattan and Freemans catalogues. Womenswear, childrenswear, menswear and household items, at up to 50% off catalogue prices. Includes a wide range of brands from both designer and high street on a regularly changing basis. Electrical goods are sold at up to 30% off catalogue prices, and include many big-name brands. 14-day refund policy.

COUNTY DURHAM

CATALOGUE DISCOUNT STORES

UNIT 17, IN SHOP CENTRE, 1–2 WRIGHTON HOUSE, TRENCHARD AVENUE, THORNABY ON TEES TS17 9EP, ☎ 01642 751935, 9–5 MON–SAT. **PERMANENT DISCOUNT OUTLET**

Grattan catalogue store, selling a wide selection of items from those featured in the catalogue, including women's, men's, children's, home, electrics and toys. All items are discounted by up to 50% with regular special promotions. All stores offer a 14-day refund policy, and a 12-month guarantee on electrical items. A wide range of brands are in stock on a regularly changing basis. Each store carries a slightly different range, so phone to check that they have what you want.

CHARLES CLINKARD

JACKSONS LANDING, THE HIGHLIGHT, HARTLEPOOL, CO DURHAM TS24 0XN, ☎ 01429 866939, 10–6 MON–SAT, 11–5 SUN. **FACTORY SHOP IN A FACTORY SHOPPING VILLAGE**

Footwear for the family at discounts of between 30% and 50%. Labels on sale here include Rockport, Loake, Barker, Grenson, Base, Ecco, Gabor, Rohde, Van-Dal, Kickers, Clarks, Dr Martens, K Shoes and Lotus. At the time of going to print, the future of Jacksons Landing is uncertain. Please phone before making a special trip.

DEWHIRST IMPRESSIONS

MILL HILL NORTH WEST INDUSTRIAL ESTATE, PETERLEE, CO DURHAM SR8 2HR, ☎ 0191 586 4525, **e-mail:** kim.mcmaster@dewhirst.com, 9–6 MON–WED, FRI, SAT, 9–7 THUR, 10.30–4.30 SUN.

PENNYWELL INDUSTRIAL ESTATE, PENNYWELL, SUNDERLAND, TYNE & WEAR SR4 9EN, ☎ 0191 534 7928, **e-mail:** kim.mcmaster@dewhirst.com, 9–6 MON–SAT, 10.30–4.30 SUN.

WEST COATHAM LANE, DORMANSTOWN, REDCAR, CO DURHAM TS10 5QD, ☎ 01642 474210, kmcmaster@dewhirst.com, 10–8 MON–FRI, 9–6 SAT, 10.30–4.30 SUN. **FACTORY SHOP**

Dewhirst Impressions sells garments from the manufacturing side of the business direct to the public as part of the Dewhirst Group plc which manufactures women's, men's and childrenswear for a leading high street retailer. You can choose from a huge selection of surplus production and slight seconds at bargain prices, making savings of more than 50% of the normal retail cost. For men there is a wide range of suits, formal shirts and casual wear. For example, suits from £60, formal and casual shirts from £7. For women there's a selection of blouses, smart tailoring and casual wear that includes a denim range. You can find women's jackets from £30, skirts, trousers and blouses from £8. There is also a selection of women's and men's underwear. Children's clothes start at £3. High street quality and style at wholesale prices.

DISCOUNT CLOTHING STORE

68 HOPE STREET, CROOK, CO DURHAM DL15 9HT, ☎ 01388 768272, 9.30–5.30 MON–SAT.

UNIT 5A, FOLLINGSBY PARK, WARDLEY, GATESHEAD, TYNE & WEAR NE10 8YA, ☎ 0191 415 4015, 9.30–5.30 MON–SAT. **PERMANENT DISCOUNT OUTLET**

With discounts of up to 50%, DCS offers a wide range of clothes for all the family and some bedlinen and towels, most of which are from high street stores.

JOCKEY UNDERWEAR FACTORY SHOP

EASTERN AVENUE, TEAM VALLEY TRADING ESTATE, GATESHEAD, TYNE & WEAR NE11 0PB, ☎ 0191 491 0088, www.jockeyuk.com, 9–4 MON–FRI, 10–2 SAT. **FACTORY SHOP**

Stocking many different types of men's underwear from Y-fronts and boxers to tangas and hipsters. Also women's underwear: briefs, ribbed vests, cami-tops, bodies, crop tops and thongs. Although well known for underwear, the factory shop also sells golfing clothing, Wolsey socks, towels, bedding, pillows, blankets and a few duvet covers. All merchandise is discounted by at least one third to 50% discount off normal retail prices.

LABELS OF BARNARD CASTLE

8 THE BANK, BARNARD CASTLE, CO DURHAM DL12 8PQ, ☎ 01833 6905481, **e-mail:** cynsillars@aol.com, www.labels-of-barnardcastle.co.uk, 10.30–5 MON–SAT. **DRESS AGENCY**

Located in a historic market town with easy parking, women's clothes here range from top end Chanel and Moschino Couture to Nicole Farhi, Paul Costelloe and Joseph with a good measure of quality Italian designer labels as well. Popular men's ranges include Hugo Boss, Armani and Cerruti suits as well as casual wear. As-new clothes sell for about one third of the brand new price. New end of range clothes are sometimes available – phone for details. Clothes are reduced in price periodically, usually after a couple of months.

LITTLEWOODS CATALOGUE DISCOUNT STORE

19 FAWCETT STREET, SUNDERLAND, TYNE & WEAR SR1 1RH, ☎ 0191 564 0684, 9–5 MON–THUR, 9–5.30 FRI, SAT. **FACTORY SHOP**

See page 96 (CHESH)

LITTLEWOODS DISCOUNT STORE

UNIT 2A, METRO RETAIL PARK, GATESHEAD, TYNE & WEAR NE11 9XU, ☎ 0191 461 1491 10–8 MON–FRI, 9–6 SAT, 11–5 SUN. **PERMANENT DISCOUNT OUTLET**

Brand new, surplus women's, men's and children's clothing from last year's catalogue is on sale at greatly discounted prices. Returned and sometimes slightly damaged televisions and furniture can be found at as much as 70% below the original price. If you see an item you like, buy it there and then as stock is constantly changing and you are unlikely to see it on sale again. The store also has sales when stock is discounted even further.

MATALAN

173 HIGH STREET WEST, GATESHEAD, TYNE & WEAR NE8 1EJ, ☎ 0191 478 8140, FAX: 0191 478 9480, www.matalan.co.uk, 10–8 MON–FRI, 9–6 SAT, 11–5 SUN.

48 CAMERON RETAIL PARK, METRO CENTRE, GATESHEAD, TYNE & WEAR NE11 9XU, ☎ 0191 461 0880, FAX: 0191 460 1340, www.matalan.co.uk, 9.30–8 MON–FRI, 9–6 SAT, 11–6 SUN.

ANCHOR RETAIL PARK, MARINA WAY, HARTLEPOOL, CO DURHAM TS24 0XR, ☎ 01429 855960, FAX: 01429 264028, www.matalan.co.uk, 10–8 MON–FRI, 9–6 SAT, 11–5 SUN.

BRIDGE ROAD RETAIL PARK, PARKFIELD ROAD, STOCKTON-ON-TEES, STOCKTON, CO DURHAM TS18 3AY, ☎ 01642 702410, FAX: 01642 702415, www.matalan.co.uk, 10–8 MON–FRI, 9–6 SAT, 11–5 SUN.

UNIT 1, HYLTON RIVERSIDE RETAIL PARK, SUNDERLAND, TYNE & WEAR SR5 3XG, ☎ 0191 516 0141, FAX: 0191 548 1572, www.matalan.co.uk, 10–8 MON–FRI, 9–6 SAT, 11–5 SUN. **PERMANENT DISCOUNT OUTLET**

See page 89 (BEDS)

SCOOPS CATALOGUE DISCOUNT STORE

15 THE PRECINCT, THE IN CENTRE, JARROW, TYNE & WEAR NE32 3LS, ☎ 0191 483 4318, 9–5 MON–SAT.

8 THE FORUM SHOPPING CENTRE, WALLSEND, TYNE & WEAR NE28 8JR, ☎ 0191 236 9501, 9–5 MON–SAT. **PERMANENT DISCOUNT OUTLET**

Scoops the catalogue discount store sells surplus stock from both Grattan and Freeman's catalogues. Womenswear, menswear and childrenswear are on sale, as well as household items, all at up to 50% off catalogue prices. Stock changes on a regular basis, and includes a wide range of brands from both designer and high street. A 14-day refund policy is offered.

THE FACTORY SHOP

2–4 COMMERCIAL STREET, CROOK, CO DURHAM DL15 9HP, ☎ 01388 763211, 9–5.30 MON–SAT, 10.30–4.30 SUN. **FACTORY SHOP**

See page 98 (CHESH)

THE FAMOUS BRUNSWICK WAREHOUSE LTD

1–2 WEST ROW, DARLINGTON, CO DURHAM DL1 5PL, ☎ 01325 488446, **e-mail:** northshoe@mcmail.com, 9–5 MON–SAT.

25 JACKSON STREET, GATESHEAD, TYNE & WEAR, ☎ 0191 477 2364, **e-mail:** northshoe@mcmail.com, 9–5 MON–SAT.

UNIT 3 ANCHOR RETAIL PARK, MARINA WAY, HARTLEPOOL, CO DURHAM TS24 0XB, ☎ 01429 264519, **e-mail:** northshoe@mcmail.com, 10–7 MON–FRI, 9–6 SAT, 11–5 SUN.

UNIT 2, PETERLEE RETAIL DEVELOPMENT, HOWLETCH LANE, OFF EASTINGTON ROAD, PETERLEE, CO DURHAM SR8 2BL, ☎ 0191 587 0709, **e-mail:** northshoe@mcmail.com, 9–6 MON–SAT, 10–4 SUN.

UNIT 4, PALLION RETAIL PARK, WOODBINE TERRACE, SUNDERLAND, TYNE & WEAR SR4 6TY, ☎ 0191 565 7302, **e-mail:** northshoe@mcmail.com, 9.30–6 MON–WED, 9.30–7 THUR, FRI, 9–6 SAT, 10.30–4.30 SUN.

UNIT 4, OLD FULWELL ROAD, ROKER, SUNDERLAND, TYNE & WEAR SR6 0JD, ☎ 0191 565 0965, **e-mail:** northshoe@mcmail.com, 9–6 MON–SAT, 7 ON THUR, 10–4 SUN.

CHARLOTTE STREET, SOUTH SHIELDS, TYNE & WEAR NE33 1QQ, ☎ 0191 427 6545, **e-mail:** northshoe@mcmail.com, 9–5 MON–SAT, 9–6 THUR, 10–4 SUN.

42 WHITES MARKET, SUNDERLAND, TYNE & WEAR SR1 3DG, ☎ 0191 514 2653, **e-mail:** northshoe@mcmail.com, 9–5 MON–SAT.

UNIT 2A, SANDS INDUSTRIAL ESTATE, SWALWELL, GATESHEAD, TYNE & WEAR NE16 3DG, ☎ 0191 488 1333, **e-mail:** northshoe@mcmail.com, 9–7 MON–FRI, 9–6 SAT, 10–4 SUN.
PERMANENT DISCOUNT OUTLET

See page 98 (CHESH)

TK MAXX

TEAM VALLEY, RETAIL WORLD, GATESHEAD, TYNE & WEAR, ☎ 0191 487 4468, www.tkmaxx.com, PHONE FOR DETAILS.

UNIT 3, THE HIGHLIGHT RETAIL PARK, HARTLEPOOL MARINA, MARINA WAY, HARTLEPOOL, CO DURHAM TS24 0UX, ☎ 01429 222296, www.tkmaxx.com, 10–8 MON–FRI, 9–6 SAT, 11–5 SUN.

THE BRIDGES SHOPPING CENTRE, 34 CROWTREE ROAD, SUNDERLAND TYNE & WEAR SR3 3JU, ☎ 0191 514 4484, www.tkmaxx.com, 9–5.30 MON–FRI, 9–6 SAT, 11–5 SUN.
PERMANENT DISCOUNT OUTLET

See page 89 (BEDS)

WYNSORS WORLD OF SHOES

PARKFIELD ROAD, OFF BRIDGE ROAD, STOCKTON-ON-TEES, CO DURHAM TS18 3DJ, ☎ 01642 672525, 9–5.30 MON, TUE, WED, SAT, 9–8 THUR, FRI, 10–4 SUN AND BANK HOLIDAYS.
PERMANENT DISCOUNT OUTLET

See page 100 (CHESH)

CORNWALL

CORNISH MARKET WORLD

STADIUM RETAIL PARK, PAR, ST AUSTELL, CORNWALL PL25 3RP, ☎ 01726 812544, FAX: 01726 812346, **e-mail:** info@cornishmarketworld.co.uk, www.cornishmarketworld.co.uk, 9–5 SAT, SUN AND BANK HOLIDAYS, AND WED JUNE–SEPT **PERMANENT DISCOUNT OUTLET**
Huge indoor market that sells an enormous range of goods and food at very competitive prices: for example, a good quality breadmaker, £45. Sells clothes, fabrics, phones, bags, tools, electric equipment, motability equipment, jewellery and furniture. There is a good butchers, fish, and fruit and veg stands.

SILKEN LADDER

VICTORIA SQUARE, NEAR ROCHE, CORNWALL PL26 8LX, ☎ 01726 891092, 9.30–5.30 MON–SAT, 10–5 SUN, BANK HOLIDAYS. **FACTORY SHOP**

Silken Ladder originally specialised in the design, manufacture and wholesale of women's blouses and tops in a myriad of options, both pretty and classic. Now their ranges extend to four labels. They still produce two complete new ranges of blouses, one under the Silken Ladder label, while La Scala di Seta is their upmarket label for evening wear and special occasions. The Victoria Roche label designates coordinating jackets, skirts, trousers and dresses in beautiful fabrics, both natural and manmade, printed and plain. Their fast-growing clientele are discerning women with busy lifestyles who need to be practical about easy care, look smart and prefer to buy from other than the multinationals. The factory outlet at Roche sells, at appropriately reduced prices, the prototypes, samples, ends-of-lines, overmakes and less-than-perfect garments that inevitably result from an operation which supplies between 300 and 400 shops and organisations in one season. There is an enormous selection – around 3,500 different options at any one time – of quality garments at very reasonable prices. Bargains range from £3 and sizes from 8 to 30. Current ranges are also available. Exclusive nightwear and underwear, in cotton, polycotton and pure silk, is also available, as is a range of scarves and other accessories. For men, Silken Ladder's own shirt label is Sanderson Hall. Superbly cut shirts now range in size up to 19½ inch collar. Silk ties and boxer shorts are also available. Find Silken Ladder on the A30, six miles west of Bodmin and six miles north of St Austell (six miles from the Eden Project), next to a BP petrol station and opposite the Victoria Inn and business park. Recently refurbished, this highly individual operation is well worth a visit.

THE FACTORY SHOP

OLD STATION YARD, BERRYCOMBE ROAD, BODMIN, CORNWALL PL31 2NF, ☎ 01208 78492, 9–5.30 MON–SAT, 10.30–4.30 SUN.

MOUNT AMBROSE, SCORRIER, REDRUTH, CORNWALL TR15 1QT, ☎ 01209 219116, 9.30–5.30 MON–SAT, 10–4 SUN. **FACTORY SHOP**

See page 98 (CHESH)

TRAGO MILLS

ARWENACK STREET, FALMOUTH, CORNWALL TR11 3LF, ☎ 01326 315738, www.trago.co.uk, 9–5.30 MON–SAT, 10.45–4.45 SUN.

TWOWATERSFOOT, LISKEARD, CORNWALL PL14 6HY, ☎ 01579 348877, www.trago.co.uk, 9–5.30 MON–SAT, 10.45- 4.45 SUN. **PERMANENT DISCOUNT OUTLET**

The historic Trago's original Cornish site is in the Glynn Valley on the A38 between Liskeard and Bodmin. You can bargain hunt here for brand name art materials, bathrooms and bedrooms and ceramics, carpets and rugs, clothing, DIY and home improvement, furniture, garden accessories, gifts, textiles, lighting, pet care, saddlery, stationery, tools, motoring products, toys and sport equipment and much more. There's a restaurant and picnic area by the beautiful Fowey river bank, free parking and disabled access. The Falmouth store is smaller, with only limited free car parking outside, but there is a public car park adjacent.

TRIPLE M FASHION

NEW PORTREATH ROAD, JUST OUTSIDE REDRUTH, CORNWALL TR16 4QL, ☎ 01209 842931, 10–5.30 SEVEN DAYS A WEEK. **PERMANENT DISCOUNT OUTLET**

Large permanent discount shop selling men's and women's clothes, toys, bedding, footwear, bags, children's clothes.

WILLIAMSON'S FACTORY SHOP

NEW PORTREATH ROAD, REDRUTH, CORNWALL TR16 4QL, ☎ 01209 843366, 10–5 SEVEN DAYS A WEEK. **FACTORY SHOP**

Two factory shops in one, the smaller one sells shoes and household goods, mainly textiles, in equal quantities. The shoes are very reasonably priced and include some designer trainers, shoes by Moshulu, Wrangler, R and Ricker, and deck shoes. The household textiles include bedlinen, tea towels, towels, duvets and pillows. The larger shop opposite sells men's and women's middle market clothes including coats, underwear and socks from names such as Regatta, Double TwoWrangler, Outdoor Scene and HJ socks at discounted prices.

CUMBRIA

BRIGGS SHOES

SOUTHEND ROAD, PENRITH, CUMBRIA CA11 8JH, ☎ 01768 899001, FAX: 01768 899001, www.briggsshoes.co.uk, 9.30–5.30 MON–SAT. **PERMANENT DISCOUNT OUTLET**

Vast selection of well-known brands of shoes with permanent clearance lines always on display. Some of the brands stocked include Hotter, Gabor, Equity, Hush Puppy, Van-Dal, Servas and the wider-fitting Elmdale range. Also stocks a large selection of children's clearance and sub-standards, from Start-Rite and Hush Puppy.

CATALOGUE BARGAIN SHOP

UNITS 4–5, SOUTH LAKELANDS RETAIL PARK, KENDAL, CUMBRIA LA9 6DU, ☎ 01539 740734, www.bargaincrazy.com, 9–8 MON–SAT, 11–5 SUN. **PERMANENT DISCOUNT OUTLET**

See page 92 (CAMBS)

EDINBURGH WOOLLEN MILL CLEARANCE SHOP

UNIT 4, PACKHORSE COURT, KESWICK, CUMBRIA CA12 5JB, ☎ 01768 771322, OPEN 10–4 MON–SAT, 12–4 SUN. **PERMANENT DISCOUNT OUTLET**

Clearance outlet for the Edinburgh Woollen Mill stores, the stock here changes constantly so buy when you see. Merchandise includes knitwear, socks, trousers, jackets and men's outerwear and includes labelled brands such as Antartex.

FAMOUS FOOTWEAR

20–30 SANDES AVENUE, KENDAL, CUMBRIA LA9 4SG, ☎ 01539 738403, 9–5.30 MON–FRI, 9–6 SAT, 11–5 SUN. **FACTORY SHOP**

See page 95 (CHESH)

FURNESS FOOTWEAR FACTORY SHOP

LONG LANE, DALTON-IN-FURNESS, CUMBRIA LA15 8PB, ☎ 01229 468837, 9–5.30 MON–SAT, 9–8 ON FRI, 10–4 SUN. **PERMANENT DISCOUNT OUTLET**

Stocks top brand-name shoes at less than half price. Special monthly offers always available. There are shoes, trainers, slippers, sandals and boots for all the family, with a selection of bags, cleaners and polishes available, all at discount prices.

GAYNOR SPORTS

MARKET CROSS, AMBLESIDE, CUMBRIA LA22 9BT, ☎ 015394 33305, **e-mail:** sales@gaynors.co.uk, www.gaynors.co.uk, 9–6 MON–SAT, 10.30–4.30 SUN, SUMMER. 9–5.30 MON–FRI, 9–6 SAT, 10.30–4.30 SUN, WINTER. **FACTORY SHOP**

One of the largest equipment stores in the north-east. Brands offered at competitive prices include Berghaus, Sprayway, The North Face, Craghoppers, Regatta, Lowe Alpine and Karrimor. Gaynor Sports Factory Outlet guarantees a minimum of 30% savings on normal retail prices of the stock offered for sale. Join its email database for up-to-date information on the latest offers.

K SHOES FACTORY SHOP

K VILLAGE, NETHERFIELD, KENDAL, CUMBRIA LA7 7BT, ☎ 01539 721892, 9.30–6 MON–FRI, 9–6 SAT, 11–5 SUN. **FACTORY SHOP**

Clarks International operate a chain of factory shops nationally which specialise in selling discontinued lines and slight sub-standards for men, women and children from Clarks, K Shoes and other famous brands. These shops trade under the name of K Shoes Factory Shop or Clarks Factory Shop and while not all are physically attached to a shoe factory, they are treated as factory shops by the company. Customers can expect to find an extensive range of quality shoes, sandals, walking boots, slippers, trainers, handbags, accessories and gifts, while their major outlets also offer luggage, sports clothing, sports equipment and outdoor clothing. Brands stocked include Clarks, K Shoes, Springer, CICA, Hi-Tec, Caterpillar, Timberland, Regatta, Craghoppers, Kangaroo Poo, Mercury, Antler, Eminent, Travelon, Hudson and Carlton, although not all are sold in every outlet. Phone first to find out what your particular store is offering. Discounts are from 30% to 60% off the normal high street price for perfect stock.

K VILLAGE OUTLET SHOPPING

LOUND ROAD, KENDAL, NEAR JUNCTION 36 OF M6, CUMBRIA LA9 7DA, ☎ 01539 732363, **e-mail:** mdixon@realm-ocm.com, www.kvillage.co.uk, 9.30–6 MON–FRI, 9–6 SAT, 11–5 SUN (9.30–5.30 MON–FRI NOVEMBER TO MARCH). **FACTORY SHOPPING VILLAGE**

Twelve outlets including Cotton Traders, Crabtree & Evelyn, Dartington Crystal selling Cloverleaf as well as glassware, Van Heusen, Denby Pottery, The Food Factory, Ponden Mill, Prices Candles, Tog 24, National Trust Gift Shop and a giant K Shoes factory shop selling a wide range of labels from K Shoes, Clarks, Cica, Delsey and Antler, as well as a full-price K Shop. There is also a heritage centre where you can discover the history of shoemaking, a 150-seater restaurant, a coffee shop, children's play area, baby changing facilities, a riverside picnic area, disabled facilities and free parking. Take the South Kendal exit and follow the signs for K Village.

KANGOL FACTORY SHOP

CLEATOR, ON THE A5086 BETWEEN COCKERMOUTH AND EGREMONT, CUMBRIA CA23 3DJ, ☎ 01946 810312, **e-mail:** kangol_uk@hotmail.com, 9–5 MON–SAT, 11–4 SUN. PLEASE PHONE FOR XMAS, EASTER AND BANK HOLIDAY OPENING HOURS. **FACTORY SHOP**

Referred to locally as 'the largest hat shop in the world', this factory shop has a huge selection of headwear and millinery, all at factory prices, plus branded clothing and accessories. At the rear of the shop is a bespoke millinery service with a huge range of hat shapes, trims and fabrics. Customers can bring in their outfit and the experts will help them to create a hat to go with the outfit. Free car and coach parking available.

LITTLEWOODS CATALOGUE DISCOUNT STORE

RAWLINSON STREET, BARROW-IN-FURNESS, CUMBRIA LA14 1BS, ☎ 01229 870668, 8.45–5.15 MON–SAT, 11–5 SUN. **PERMANENT DISCOUNT OUTLET**

See page 96 (CHESH)

MATALAN

WALNEY ROAD, BARROW-IN-FURNESS, CUMBRIA LA14 5UN, ☎ 01229 430899, FAX: 01229 430948, www.matalan.co.uk, 9.30–8 MON–FRI, 9–6 SAT, 11–5 SUN.

UNIT 2, 3, 4, STATION RETAIL PARK, WATER STREET, CARLISLE CUMBRIA CA2 5AF, ☎ 01228 403510, FAX: 01228 510068, www.matalan.co.uk, 10–8 MON–FRI, 9–6 SAT, 11–5 SUN.

DERWENT HOWE, SOLWAY ROAD, WORKINGTON, CUMBRIA CA14 3YA, ☎ 01900 870966, FAX: 01900 870967, www.matalan.co.uk, 9.30–8 MON–FRI, 9–6 SAT, 11–5 SUN. **PERMANENT DISCOUNT OUTLET**

See page 89 (BEDS)

NEW BALANCE ATHLETIC SHOES UK LTD

15 BANK STREET, KESWICK, CUMBRIA, ☎ 01768 774631, www.newbalance.co.uk, 9.30–5.30 MON–SAT, 10–5 SUN.

ST HELENS LANE, FLIMBY, MARYPORT, CUMBRIA CA15 8RY, ☎ 01900 602850, www.newbalance.co.uk, 9.30–5.30 MON–FRI, 9–5 SAT, 12–4 SUN.

MAIN STREET, SHAP, PENRITH, CUMBRIA CA10 3NL, ☎ 01931 716333, www.newbalance.co.uk, 9.30–5.30 MON–FRI, 9–5 SAT, 12–4 SUN. **FACTORY SHOP**

Factory outlet selling running shoes, walking shoes and boots, fell running shoes, cross trainers, sports bags, sports clothing and children's trainers, all with discounts starting at 30% off.

THE FACTORY SHOP

EMPIRE BUILDINGS, MAIN STREET, EGREMONT, CUMBRIA CA22 2BD, ☎ 01946 820434, 9–5 MON–SAT. 10–4 SUN.

THE GILL, ULVERSTON, CUMBRIA LA12 7BN, ☎ 01229 583360, 9–5.30 MON–SAT, 10.30–4.30 SUN.

5 MARKET PLACE, WIGTON, CUMBRIA CA7 9NW, ☎ 01697 342171, 9–5.30 MON–SAT, 10.30–4.30 SUN. **FACTORY SHOP**

See page 98 (CHESH)

THE FAMOUS BRUNSWICK WAREHOUSE LTD

UNIT 5, THE BRIDGES RETAIL PARK, FLAT WALKS, WHITEHAVEN, CUMBRIA CA28 7RQ, ☎ 01946 694706, **e-mail:** northshoe@mcmail.com, 9–6 MON–SAT, 7 ON THUR, 10.30–4.30 SUN. **PERMANENT DISCOUNT OUTLET**

See page 98 (CHESH)

TK MAXX

THE EDEN CENTRE AND MARKET HALL, FISHER STREET, CARLISLE, CUMBRIA CA3 8JB, ☎ 01228 819292, www.tkmaxx.com, 9–5.30 MON–FRI, 8.30–6 SAT, 11–4 SUN. **PERMANENT DISCOUNT OUTLET**

See page 89 (BEDS)

TOG 24

UNIT 4, MARKET CROSS, AMBLESIDE, CUMBRIA LA22 9BT, ☎ 01539 433913, **e-mail:** mail-order@tog24.com, www.tog24.com, 9.30–6 MON–SAT, 10–5 SUN.

10 CRAG BROW, BOWNESS, CUMBRIA LA23 3BX, ☎ 01539 488656, **e-mail:** mail-order@tog24.com, www.tog24.com, 9.30–5.30 MON–THUR, 9.30–6 FRI, SAT, 10–5.30 SUN.

K VILLAGE, LOUND ROAD, KENDAL, CUMBRIA LA9 7DA, ☎ 01539 721555, **e-mail:** mail-order@tog24.com, www.tog24.com, 9.30–6 MON–FRI, 9–6 SAT, 11–5 SUN.

9 MARKET SQUARE, KESWICK, CUMBRIA CA12 5BJ, ☎ 01768 780876, **e-mail:** mail-order@tog24.com, www.tog24.com, 10–5 MON–FRI, 9.30–5.30 SAT, SUN. **FACTORY SHOP IN A FACTORY SHOPPING VILLAGE**

See page 99 (CHESH)

WYNSORS WORLD OF SHOES

FURNESS FOOTWEAR, DALTON FIELDS LANE, DALTON-IN-FURNESS, CUMBRIA LA15 8PB, ☎ 01229 468837, 9–5.30 MON–SAT, 8 ON FRI, 10–4 SUN. **PERMANENT DISCOUNT OUTLET**

See page 100 (CHESH)

DERBYSHIRE

ADIDAS

MCARTHURGLEN DESIGNER OUTLET MANSFIELD, MANSFIELD ROAD, SOUTH NORMANTON, ALFRETON, JUNCTION 28 OF M1, DERBYSHIRE DE55 2ER, ☎ 01773 545135, FAX: 01773 524720, 10–6 MON–SAT, 8 ON THUR, 11–5 SUN. **FACTORY SHOP IN A FACTORY SHOPPING VILLAGE**

See page 93 (CHESH)

ARMSTRONG'S MILL

MIDDLETON STREET, OFF STATION ROAD, ILKESTON, DERBYSHIRE DE7 5TT, ☎ 0115 932 4913, FAX: 0115 930 0083, **e-mail:** info@armstrongsmill.co.uk, 9.15–5 MON–FRI, 6 ON WED, 9.30–5.30 SAT, 10.30–4.30 SUN. **FACTORY SHOP**

Designer wear, top quality suits and jackets, casual wear, handbags, scarves, lingerie, linen, gifts. Men's suits by James Barry, one of Britain's leading manufacturers of men's suits (in sizes from 34 to 56 inch chest) jackets and trousers for more than 40 years. Trousers by Lancers in sizes 28 to 52 inch waist. Large car park, tea room, alterations service and on-site hairdresser.

AUTONOMY

MCARTHURGLEN DESIGNER OUTLET MANSFIELD, MANSFIELD ROAD, SOUTH NORMANTON, ALFRETON, JUNCTION 28 OF M1, DERBYSHIRE DE55 2JH, ☎ 01904 671502, 10–6 MON–FRI, 8 ON THUR, 9–6 SAT, 11–5 SUN. **FACTORY SHOP IN A FACTORY SHOPPING VILLAGE**

See page 93 (CHESH)

BIG L FACTORY OUTLET

UNITS 28 & 29, MCARTHURGLEN DESIGNER OUTLET MANSFIELD, MANSFIELD ROAD, SOUTH NORMANTON, ALFRETON, JUNCTION 28 OF M1, DERBYSHIRE DE55 2ER, ☎ 01773 545000, FAX: 01773 545000, 10–6 MON, TUE, WED, FRI, 10–8 THUR, 9–6 SAT, 11–5 SUN. **FACTORY SHOP IN A FACTORY SHOPPING VILLAGE**

See page 93 (CHESH)

BROUGHTON SHOE WAREHOUSE

7 CROWN SQUARE, MATLOCK, DERBYSHIRE DE4 3AL, ☎ 01629 55616, 9–5.30 MON–SAT, 10–4 SUN. **PERMANENT DISCOUNT OUTLET**

Sells women's boots, shoes, sandals, handbags and slippers seasonally, as well as men's footwear, at savings of between 20% and 50%. Brands include Trickers and Italian and Spanish designers.

DE BRADELEI MILL SHOPS LTD

DE BRADELEI HOUSE, CHAPEL STREET, BELPER, DERBYSHIRE DE56 1AR, ☎ 01773 882442, FAX: 01773 829830, 9.30–5.30 MON–FRI, 9.30–6 SAT, 10.30–4.30 SUN. **PERMANENT DISCOUNT OUTLET**

A delightful Mill centre with individual shops based round a central courtyard, each one selling top brand names in fashions and footwear for men and women, along with Liberty giftware. The womenswear includes such names as Paul Costelloe, Windsmoor, Planet, Precis Petite, Alexon, Kaliko, Eastex, Minuet Petite, Liz Claiborne, Jaeger Knitwear Shop, French Connection, Elle, Country Casuals, Elvi, top American and German designer labels, plus many more. The menswear range includes underwear, socks, sweaters, trousers, jackets, coats and suits from labels such as Wolsey, French Connection, Jaeger Knitwear Shop and Glenmuir. Robert Leonard's Menswear provides Pierre Cardin, Gabicci, Gurteen, Oakman and many more. There is a large shoe department with an excellent range of shoes and accessories for men and women. A Tenson department sells outerwear for men and women. The giftware department offers a superb collection of Liberty giftware with scented candles, Arran Aromatic toiletires, photo frames, baskets, toilet bags and chocolates from Italo Suisse. Chevin Coffee Shop serves delicious home-cooked food throughout the day. De Bradelei Mill Shop has its own car park with alternative parking nearby; coach parties are always welcome though booking is preferred.

DIRECT SPECS LTD

30 OSMASTON ROAD, DERBY, DERBYSHIRE DE1 2HR, ☎ 01332 295384, www.directspecs.co.uk, 9–5 MON–SAT. **PERMANENT DISCOUNT OUTLET**

See page 95 (CHESH)

GIFTTREE

38 MAIN CENTRE, DERBY, DERBYSHIRE DE1 2PE, ☎ 01332 204078, 9–5 MON–SAT.

36 HIGH STREET, SWADLINCOTE, DERBYSHIRE DE11 8HY, ☎ 01283 226700, 9–5 MON–SAT. **FACTORY SHOP**

Items from the Express Gifts mail order catalogues at reduced prices including cards, giftwrap, gifts, stationery, kitchenware, household products, clothes and toys, including Galt products. Discounts in most departments range from at least 50% off original catalogue selling prices.

GILLIVERS FOOTWEAR AND CLOTHING WAREHOUSE

1–3 ASHBY ROAD, MOIRA, SWADLINCOTE, DERBYSHIRE DE12 6DJ, ☎ 01283 214255, 9–8 MON–FRI, 9–5.30 SAT, 10–5 SUN. **PERMANENT DISCOUNT OUTLET**

Large warehouse in the heart of the National Forest selling high street quality clothing for the whole family at greatly reduced prices. Shoes cost from 99p to £40; clothing is discounted by between 25% and 50%. They also stock bags, accessories and hosiery. Refreshments are available, and there is free parking and disabled access.

JAEGER FACTORY SHOP

VIYELLA HOUSE, NOTTINGHAM ROAD, SOMERCOTES, DERBYSHIRE DE55 4SB, ☎ 01773 541183, 9–5 MON–SAT, 10.30–4.30 SUN. **FACTORY SHOP**

See page 96 (CHESH)

JAMES BARRY

ARMSTRONG'S MILL, MIDDLETON STREET, OFF STATION ROAD, ILKESTON, DERBYSHIRE DE7 5TT, ☎ 0115 932 4913, 9.15–5 MON–FRI, 6 ON WED, 9.30–5.30 SAT, 10.30–4.30 SUN.
FACTORY SHOP

Designer menswear and womenswear available at discount of up to 50% off RRP. Join the mailing list at any of the James Barry outlets which will give you advance notice of any promotions (your details will not be passed on to anyone else). Gift shop, coffee shop, hair salon and luggage also available on site. Also stocks Daks and Aquascutum for men and women, among many other brands.

JOHN SMEDLEY LTD

LEA MILLS, LEA BRIDGE, MATLOCK, DERBYSHIRE DE4 5AG, ☎ 01629 534571
10–4 SEVEN DAYS A WEEK AND MOST BANK HOLIDAYS. **FACTORY SHOP**

Sells John Smedley high quality knitwear, all ends of ranges or seconds, at substantial discounts. There are more than 5,000 garments to choose from in cotton and wool, including cardigans and sweaters for women and men; own range underwear and an assortment of accessories. There is another outlet in Doncaster.

LABEL TRADERS

30 MAIN CENTRE, DERBY, DERBYSHIRE DE1 2PE, ☎ 01332 381439, www.labeltraders.co.uk, 9–5 MON–SAT. **FACTORY SHOP**

Good quality ex-chainstore merchandise from well-known high street shops with all the labels cut out. Stock includes knitwear, dresses, suits, blouses, skirts, sportswear, nightwear, trousers for women, and childrenswear. Also stocks some household goods such as towels. Discounts range up to 50%. There are other branches in Sutton-in-Ashfield and Ruddington.

LEE COOPER

MCARTHURGLEN DESIGNER OUTLET MANSFIELD, MANSFIELD ROAD, SOUTH NORMANTON, ALFRETON, JUNCTION 28 OF M1, FOLLOW SIGNS FOR A38, DERBYSHIRE DE55 2ER, ☎ 01773 545153, 10–6 MON–FRI, 8 ON THUR, 9–6 SAT, 11–5 SUN. **FACTORY SHOP IN A FACTORY SHOPPING VILLAGE**

See page 96 (CHESH)

LILLEY & SKINNER

MCARTHURGLEN DESIGNER OUTLET MANSFIELD, MANSFIELD ROAD, SOUTH NORMANTON, ALFRETON, JUNCTION 28 OF M1, DERBYSHIRE DE55 2JW, ☎ 01773 545000, 10–6 MON–FRI, 8 ON THUR, 9–6 SAT, 11–5 SUN. **FACTORY SHOP IN A FACTORY SHOPPING VILLAGE**

Wide range of brand names including Lilley & Skinner, Hush Puppies, Lotus, Wrangler, Frank Wright, Red Tape, Rohde, Brevitt, Padders, Rombah Wallace and Rieker, all at discount prices of up to 50%.

MARKS & SPENCER

MCARTHURGLEN DESIGNER OUTLET VILLAGE MANSFIELD, MANSFIELD ROAD, ALFRETON, DERBYSHIRE DE55 2ER, ☎ 01773 545342. 10–6 MON–FRI, 8 ON THUR, 9–6 SAT, 11–5 SUN. **FACTORY SHOP IN A FACTORY SHOPPING VILLAGE**

See page 96 (CHESH)

MASSON MILLS SHOPPING VILLAGE

DERBY ROAD, MATLOCK BATH, NEAR MATLOCK, DERBYSHIRE DE4 3PY, ☎ 01629 760208, FAX: 01629 761525, 10–5.30 MON–SAT, 11–5 SUN. **FACTORY SHOPPING VILLAGE**

Anchored by Edinburgh Woollen Mills and set on four floors, this shopping village is set in a regenerated 18th century mill building with a working textile museum and conference facilities. There are shops selling fashion, golfwear and equipment, gifts, speciality foods and country goods and include Julian Graves food items, Woods of Windsor, and Ponden Mill selling bedlinen and towels. The top floor is a designer clothing store stocking labels such as DKNY, Kangol, Ben Sherman, Miss Sixty, Tommy Hilfiger and many others, all with up to 50% off normal retail prices. There is a riverside restaurant on site.

MATALAN

BRADSHAW RETAIL PARK, BRADSHAW WAY, DERBY, DERBYSHIRE DE24 5WA, ☎ 01332 223850, FAX: 01332 298020, www.matalan.co.uk, 9.30–8 MON–FRI, 9–6 SAT, 11–5 SUN. **PERMANENT DISCOUNT OUTLET**

See page 89 (BEDS)

MATLOCK SHOE SALES

SLACK'S FOOTWEAR LTD, PAXTON WAREHOUSE, MATLOCK GREEN, MATLOCK, DERBYSHIRE DE4 3BX, ☎ 01629 583105, FAX: 01629 580457, 9–5.30 MON–SAT, 10–5 SUN. **PERMANENT DISCOUNT OUTLET**

Discounted shoes from all around the world from formal dress shoes to casual for both men and women. Huge range of hiking/leisure wear. They always have a good range of wide fitting shoes as well as everything from sandals to Wellingtons.

MCARTHURGLEN DESIGNER OUTLET

MANSFIELD ROAD, SOUTH NORMANTON, ALFRETON, JUNCTION 28 OF M1, DERBYSHIRE DE55 2ER, ☎ 01773 545000, www.mcarthurglen.com/mansfield, 10–6 MON–FRI, 8 ON THUR, 9–6 SAT, 11–5 SUN. **FACTORY SHOPPING VILLAGE**

The McArthurGlen Designer Outlet Mansfield has recently undergone a year-long development programme, transforming it from an open-plan department store layout to individual shops. The new look outlet is now bigger and better. Find all your favourite brands at discounts of up to 50% off typical retail prices. Facilities include a children's play area, a food court and plenty of free parking. Stores include: Antler, Banana Books, Bed & Bath Works, Big L, Camille Lingerie, Chapelle, Claire's Accessories, Coloroll, Cotton Traders, Donnay, Edinburgh Crystal, Harbi, Jaeger, Jane Shilton, Julian Graves, Kitch N Sync, Leading Labels, Lee Cooper, Mountain Warehouse, Pavers Shoes, Petroleum, Pilot, Price's Candles, Professional Cookware, Remington, Roman Originals, Sky, Soled Out, Speedo, Sportsmill, Suits You, Thorntons, Tog 24, Toyworld, Revlon, Marks & Spencer Outlet, Windsmoor, Sportz, Reebok, Jumper, HKA, Proudfoot Leather, Garden Outlet, Lilley & Skinner, Adidas, Viyella, Whittards, XS Records and many more.

OAKHAM CLOTHING

BULLBRIDGE, AMBERGATE, DERBYSHIRE DE56 2HH, ☎ 01773 853473, 10–5.30 MON–FRI, 10–5 SAT, 10–4 SUN AND BANK HOLIDAYS. **FACTORY SHOP**

Previously Stevenson's of Ambergate, now under new ownership, this factory shop sells a wide range of women's knitwear, blouses, skirts, dresses, underwear, nightdresses, hosiery, men's trousers, outerwear, knitwear and childrenswear, as well as towels, face cloths and shoes for men and women. Women's clothes range from 8 to 22 in size, men's from 28in waist to 44in in season. There is a huge range of underwear, as well as wool coats, macs and anoraks in the outerwear. Childrenswear ranges from babies to teenwear.

PEAK VILLAGE

CHATSWORTH ROAD, ROWSLEY, (ON THE A6 BETWEEN BAKEWELL AND MATLOCK) DERBYSHIRE DE4 2JE, ☎ 01629 735326, www.peakvillage.co.uk, 9.30–5.30 MON–SAT, 10–5 SUN, EXCEPT CHRISTMAS DAY. **FACTORY SHOPPING VILLAGE**

More than 20 factory outlets including Leading Labels, Cotton Traders, Luggage & Bags, The Book Depot, Pavers Shoes, Sports & Mountain Warehouse, Yeoman Outdoors outdoor wear and equipment, Ponden Mill, Mansworld, New Beginnings and Woodlands Fitness Centre, all just 30 minutes from the M1 at the entrance to the Peak District National Park. On-site catering includes Massarella's Restaurant, which offers everything from an ice cream sundae to a traditional Sunday roast. The Wind in the Willows Attraction is a magical journey through the world of Ratty, Badger, Mole and of course the irrepressible Mr Toad. The latest sound and lighting effects bring Kenneth Grahame's classic tale to life in an enchanting recreation that's not just for kids! Free parking for up to 400 cars. Recently opened the Woodlands Fitness Centre.

R S DESIGNER LEISUREWEAR LTD

192–194 NORMAN STREET, COTMANHAY, ILKESTON, DERBYSHIRE DE7 8NR, ☎ 0115 932 3865, FAX: 0115 877 9915, **e-mail:** roger@sweatshirtsdirect.co.uk, www.sweatshirtsdirect.co.uk, 9.30–3.30 MON–FRI. SAT: PHONE FIRST. **PERMANENT DISCOUNT OUTLET**

Sports, leisurewear, sweatshirts and cardigans for schoolwear in sizes from 1 year to XXXXL

(60in waist) at discounts of up to 50%. Women's cardigans, sweatshirts and ski pants plus a variety of clothes, but no shoes, ranging from £1 to £12. All the merchandise is made up of overmakes, slight imperfects and end of season lines. There is a permanent sale rail. There is also a made-to-measure service which caters for all shapes and sizes, as well as an embroidery service.

TDP FACTORY SHOP

TDP HOUSE, RAWDON ROAD, MOIRA, SWADLINCOTE, DERBYSHIRE DE12 6DT, ☎ 01283 550400, www.tdptex-promotions.com, 9.30–5.30 MON–FRI, 10–4 SAT, SUN. **FACTORY SHOP**

In the heart of the National Forest, this factory shop sells clothes for children, mainly nightwear and underwear, at very good discounts. Also women's and menswear at reasonable prices. TDP specialises in womenswear in sizes 16 to 30, and sells branded and ex-chainstore goods at a fraction of normal retail prices.

THE FAMOUS BRUNSWICK WAREHOUSE LTD

UNIT 4, SOUTHGATE RETAIL PARK, NORMANTON ROAD, DERBY, DERBYSHIRE DE23 6UX, ☎ 01332 204532, **e-mail:** northshoe@mcmail.com, 9–6 MON–WED, SAT, 9–8 THUR, FRI, 11–5 SUN. **PERMANENT DISCOUNT OUTLET**

See page 98 (CHESH)

THE SHOE FACTORY SHOP

UNIT 6, TRAFFIC STREET, EAGLE CENTRE, DERBY, DERBYSHIRE DE1 2NL, ☎ 01332 372823, 9–5 MON–SAT, 10.30–4.30 SUN. **FACTORY SHOP**

Men's and women's accessories which are bought in from other manufacturers including Spanish, Portuguese and Italian companies. All are unbranded. The range covers from mocassins to dressy shoes. Women's shoes from £10 to £30. Men's shoes from £20 upwards. They also sell slippers for men, women and children all year round.

TK MAXX

8 EAST STREET, DERBY, ☎ 01332 364225, www.tkmaxx.com, 9–5.30 MON–THUR, 9–6 FRI–SAT, 11–5 SUN. **PERMANENT DISCOUNT OUTLET**

See page 89 (BEDS)

WILKINSON STORES

13 INSTITUTE LANE, ALFRETON, DERBYSHIRE DE55 7BQ, ☎ 01773 836845, www.wilko.co.uk, 9–5.30 MON–THUR, SAT, 9–6 FRI, 10–2 SUN. MAIL ORDER. **PERMANENT DISCOUNT OUTLET**

See page 100 (CHESH)

WIRKSWORTH FACTORY SHOP

BENCO HOSIERY, NORTH END MILLS, WIRKSWORTH, DERBYSHIRE DE4 4FG, ☎ 01629 824731, 9–5 SEVEN DAYS A WEEK, 8 ON THUR. **FACTORY SHOP**

Wide selection of clothes for the family, household goods, giftware and linen. There are T-shirts, shorts, sun vests, skirts, blouses, shirts, sweatshirts, jeans, trousers, dresses, work shirts, swimwear, jog suits, underwear, babywear, socks, tea towels, pillows, duvets and towels. There is a children's play corner and snacks facility. Men's shirts are up to 19-inch collar. For women, the stockings are less than half shop prices and there is cotton, thermal and woollen underwear. Large, free car park. You can see machines making socks on most days.

WYNSORS WORLD OF SHOES

NETTO RETAIL DEVELOPMENT, SHEFFIELD ROAD, CHESTERFIELD, DERBYSHIRE S41 8JT, ☎ 01246 276690, 9–5.30 MON, TUE, WED, SAT, 9–8 THUR, FRI, 10–4 SUN AND BANK HOLIDAYS. **PERMANENT DISCOUNT OUTLET**

See page 100 (CHESH)

DEVON

ATLANTIC VILLAGE OUTLET CENTRE

CLOVELLY ROAD, OFF A39, WEST OF BIDEFORD, NORTH DEVON, ☎ 01237 422544, **e-mail:** rmorris@realm-ocm.com, www.atlanticvillage.co.uk, JULY–MID SEPT, 9.30–7 MON–SAT, 11–5 SUN; MID SEPT–MID OCT AND EASTER TO JULY 9.30–6.30 MON–SAT, 11–5 SUN; MID OCT–EASTER 9.30–5 MON–SAT, 11–5 SUN. **FACTORY SHOPPING VILLAGE**

More than 30 shops with famous names and Devon's largest interactive maze make this village a good family day out. Shops include Banana Books; Claire's Accessories; Colony Candles; Cotton Traders, Designer Room, Ecco; Edinburgh Woollen Mill; Event Jewellery; Jane Shilton; Jean Scene; Julian Graves; Nickelby's; Pavers Shoes; Pilot; Ponden Mill; Puma; Roman Originals; Room, selling home accessories, fabrics and soft furnishings; Sportsmill; Suits You; Tog 24; Toyzone; Triumph; Warners; Windsmoor; XS Sound & Media. Free car parking, disabled and baby changing facilities. Atlantic Village also features an attractive piazza, cafés, a food court, visitor garden, arts and crafts market, open-air amphitheatre, and an adventure park set in an additional three-acre site linked to the shopping area by the piazza and amphitheatre. The Adventure Park features a mystery maze, adventure golf, wrecker's cove and adventure play boat.

BOB LOVELL SPORTS

36 FORE STREET, BRIXHAM, DEVON TQ5 8DZ, ☎ 01803 859115, FAX: 01803 859845, **e-mail:** Sales@Lovell-Rugby.co.uk, www.Lovell-Rugby.co.uk, MAIL ORDER. **PERMANENT DISCOUNT OUTLET**

Discounted rugby gear among other full-price stock.

CLARKS FACTORY SHOP

SHOE VALUE, 22 THE CROSSWAYS, HYDE ROAD, PAIGNTON, DEVON TQ4 5BL, ☎ 01803 553444, 9–5.30 MON–SAT. **FACTORY SHOP**

See page 94 (CHESH)

MATALAN

UNIT 2, HAVEN BANKS, WATER LANE, EXETER, DEVON EX2 8DW, ☎ 01392 413375, FAX: 01392 413376, www.matalan.co.uk, 10–8 MON–FRI, 9–6 SAT, 11–5 SUN.

TRANSIT WAY, HONICKNOWLE, PLYMOUTH, DEVON PL5 3TW, ☎ 01752 237600, FAX: 01752 767216, www.matalan.co.uk, 9–8 MON–FRI, 9–6 SAT, 11–5 SUN. **PERMANENT DISCOUNT OUTLET**

See page 89 (BEDS)

NEXT TO NOTHING

30 EASTLAKE WALK, DRAKE CIRCUS, PLYMOUTH, DEVON PL1 1BL, ☎ 01752 229 487, www.next.co.uk, 9–5.30 MON–SAT, 11–5 SUN. **PERMANENT DISCOUNT OUTLET**

See page 97 (CHESH)

STEWART'S

58–60 FORE STREET, BRIXHAM, DEVON TQ5 8DZ, ☎ 01803 852000, FAX: 01803 852000, 9–5 MON–SAT, 10–4 SUN.

RICHMOND COURT, DAWLISH, DEVON EX7 9PL, ☎ 01626 895022, FAX: 01626 895022, 9–5 MON–SAT, 10.30–4.30 SUN.

24–26 QUEEN STREET, NEWTON ABBOT, DEVON TQ12 2EF, ☎ 01626 362721, FAX: 01626 362721, 9–5.30 MON–SAT.

9–15 STATION ROAD, TEIGNMOUTH, DEVON TQ14 8PE, ☎ 01626 775616, FAX: 01626 775616, 9–5.30 MON–SAT, 10.30–4.30 SUN.

37 FORE STREET, TOTNES, DEVON TG9 5HN, ☎ 01803 865093, FAX: 01803 865093, 9–5 MON–SAT, 10–4 SUN. **FACTORY SHOP**

Branded merchandise from most of the major UK chainstores, all well-known department store names, offered at a discount of 40% to 70% off normal high street prices. The garments are selected with great care by experienced buyers direct from factories worldwide to bring customers top quality merchandise at highly competitive prices.

SUITS YOU

ATLANTIC VILLAGE, CLOVELLY ROAD, BIDEFORD, NORTH DEVON EX39 3QU, ☎ 01237 471222, 10–6 MON–SAT, 8 ON THUR, 9–6 SAT, 10.30–4.30 SUN. **FACTORY SHOP IN A FACTORY SHOPPING VILLAGE**

See page 91 (BRIS)

THE FAMOUS LEE MILL FACTORY OUTLET

PLYMOUTH ROAD, NEAR IVYBRIDGE, DEVON PL21 9EE, ☎ 01752 691100, 9.30–5 MON–SAT, 10–4 SUN. **PERMANENT DISCOUNT OUTLET**

A factory outlet selling fashion for men and women including golf clothes from Glenmuir and Lyle & Scott. There is also a selection of childrenswear from three to 16 years, and kitchenware, including wooden kitchen goods and a wide range of gifts from key rings to mugs. There is a coffee shop on site which serves cream teas, light meals and refreshments. Free parking.

TOG 24

ATLANTIC VILLAGE, CLOVELLY ROAD, BIDEFORD, NORTH DEVON EX39 3QU, ☎ 01237 473799, **e-mail:** mail-order@tog24.com, www.tog24.com, 10–6 MON–SAT, 8 ON THUR, 10.30–4.30 SUN. **FACTORY SHOP IN A FACTORY SHOPPING VILLAGE**

See page 99 (CHESH)

TK MAXX

YEO BUILDING, 28 ROYAL PARADE, NEW GEORGE STREET, PLYMOUTH, DEVON PL1 1SA, ☎ 01752 255081, www.tkmaxx.com, 9–5.30 MON–WED, 9–8 THUR, 9–6 FRI–SAT, 11–5 SUN.

FIRST FLOOR, 56–62 FLEET WALK, FLEET WALK SHOPPING CENTRE, TORQUAY, DEVON TQ2 5EN, ☎ 01803 215682, www.tkmaxx.com, 9–5.30 MON–SAT, 7 ON THUR, 10–7 SAT, 11–5 SUN. **PERMANENT DISCOUNT OUTLET**

See page 89 (BEDS)

TRAGO MILLS SHOPPING AND LEISURE PARKS

LIVERTON, NEWTON ABBOT, DEVON TQ12 6JD, ☎ 01626 821111, www.trago.co.uk, 9–5.30 MON–SAT, 10.45–4.45 SUN. **PERMANENT DISCOUNT OUTLET**

The biggest range of discounted goods in the West Country, with a whole range of activities to keep the family amused on the 100 acre site. Sells virtually everything from men's, women's and childrenswear, gardening equipment and cookware to wallpaper, carpets and fitted kitchens. Most are branded goods and there is a café, pizza bar and petrol station. A reasonable amount of the women's fashion comes from high street multiples. The menswear offers a wide range of clothes, as well as all-leather classic brogues and Oxford shoes, and Doc Martens in the Shoes Yard. For the home, there are Black & Decker Dustbusters, Hotpoint dryers and washing machines with cosmetic blemishes; curtain fabrics from Monkwell, Sekers, Filigree, Laura Ashley as well as Janet Reger for Vantona double quilt covers, with matching sheets, pillow cases and valances. There is a vast range of tiles including Pilkington seconds. A huge gardening section with everything from hose pipes and garden machinery to imported trees and shrubs. An excellent leisure section offers bicycles and accessories, golf gear, keep-fit systems, fishing rods and flies. Comparison prices are not given here, although staff say most items are discounted by up to 50%, so if you're looking for a bargain, make sure you've done your homework on the high street first. The best deals are in fabrics, carpets, tiles and DIY. There is a leisure park with a giant free fall slide, supakart and family go-kart circuit, bumper boats, trawler rides, swan pedalos, pirate ship, aquablasters, orbiters, shooting gallery, remote control cars and cruisers, forklifts and mini-diggers, fun dungeon, animal park, model railway, narrow gauge steam railway, nature reserve, coarse fishing, Edwardian penny arcade and plenty of space to picnic and to park.

TRIUMPH INTERNATIONAL

ATLANTIC VILLAGE, BIDEFORD, NORTH DEVON EX39 3QU, ☎ 01237 422227, 9.30–6 MON–SAT, 10.30–4.30 SUN. SUMMER OPENING HOURS VARY, PLEASE PHONE FIRST. **FACTORY SHOP IN A FACTORY SHOPPING VILLAGE**

See page 99 (CHESH)

WARNERS

UNIT 39, ATLANTIC VILLAGE, CLOVELLY ROAD, BIDEFORD, NORTH DEVON EX39 3DF, ☎ 01237 478200, 10–6 MON–SAT, 8 ON THUR, 10.30–4.30 SUN. **FACTORY SHOP IN A FACTORY SHOPPING VILLAGE**

See page 100 (CHESH)

DORSET

BAILIE HOUSE WAREHOUSE

STURMINSTER MARSHALL, DORSET BH21 4AE, ☎ 01258 857112, www.middleditchsalvage.com, OPEN 10–6 FRI, 10–5 SAT, 10–2 SUN. **PERMANENT DISCOUNT OUTLET**

Wide range of goods which are the result of insurance claims due to fire, flood, burglary or other insurance problems. A salvage warehouse which has been in operation for 38 years, stock includes sports clothing from names such as Nike, Adidas and Reebox; cricket, tennis and keep fit outfits; men's casual clothing including Fred Perry, underwear and socks; women's fashion including jeans, jackets, tops, many from top London boutiqes; records, CDs, books, pine furniture, curtain and upholstery fabrics.

DAMART

ADELINE ROAD, OFF CHRISTCHURCH ROAD, BOSCOMBE, BOURNEMOUTH, DORSET BH5 1EE, ☎ 01202 301627, 9–5 MON–SAT. **FACTORY SHOP**

Damart underwear and merchandise – anything from tights, socks and gloves to dresses, coats, cardigans and jumpers – some of which is current stock sold at full price, some discontinued and ends of lines sold at discount. There are several shops selling some discounted stock from the Damart range, known as Clearmart.

MATALAN

TURBARY RETAIL PARK, RINGWOOD ROAD, BOURNEMOUTH, DORSET BH12 3JJ, ☎ 01202 590686, FAX: 01202 590697, www.matalan.co.uk, 10–8 MON–FRI, 9–6 SAT, 10–4 SUN.

JUBILEE RETAIL PARK, RADIPOLE PARK DRIVE, WEYMOUTH DORSET DT4 7BG, ☎ 01305 831300, FAX: 01305 830472, www.matalan.co.uk, 9–8 MON–FRI, 9–6 SAT, 10.30–4.30 SUN. **PERMANENT DISCOUNT OUTLET**

See page 89 (BEDS)

T J HUGHES

616-622 CHRISTCHURCH ROAD, BOSCOMBE, BOURNEMOUTH, DORSET BH1 4BR, ☎ 01202 300333, FAX: 01202 303515, **e-mail:** info@tjhughes.co.uk, www.tjhughes.co.uk, 9–5.30 MON–FRI, 9–6 SAT, 10–4 SUN. **PERMANENT DISCOUNT OUTLET**

See page 98 (CHESH) .

THE CATALOGUE SHOP

401 LYMINGTON ROAD, HIGHCLIFFE, DORSET BH23 5HE, ☎ 01425 271202, FAX: 01425 278478, **e-mail:** thecatalogueshop@virgin.net www.the catalogueshop.virgin.com, 9–5 MON–SAT, 10–5 SUN. **PERMANENT DISCOUNT OUTLET**

Returns, damaged and worn goods as well as clearance lines and ends of lines of branded merchandise from mail order catalogues. This includes men's, women's and children's wear, footwear, bedding, curtains, furniture, exercise equipment and leather coats. These items are always in stock but the shop also has an ever-changing range of items as well. Turnover is very fast with new deliveries every day. All items are sold at less than 50% of the catalogue price starting at 99p, with branded trainers from £14.99.

THE SHOE SHED

UNIT 9, QUADRANT ARCADE, HINTON ROAD, BOURNEMOUTH, DORSET BH1 2AD, ☎ 01202 292992, 9–5.30 MON–SAT, 10–4 SUN. **FACTORY SHOP**

This shoe retailer, established for over 135 years, has a large factory shop selling a vast range of all types of women's, men's and children's shoes, all of which are perfects, at up to 30% below normal high street prices. Women's sandals cost from £2.99; shoes from £5. Men's shoes cost from £7.99; sports shoes from £5. Famous brands include Grenson, Loakes, Clarks, K Shoes, Elmdale, Caterpillar and Adidas. A large range of casual wear, including T-shirts and tracksuits for women, men and children, plus a selection of women's underwear. Kitchenware, ceramics, household goods and giftware are also stocked at discounted prices.

TK MAXX

QUADRANT ARCADE, OLD CHRISTCHURCH ROAD, BOURNEMOUTH, DORSET BH1 2BX, ☎ 01202 316367, www.tkmaxx.com, 9–5.30 MON–FRI, 8 ON THUR, 9–6 SAT, 11–5 SUN.
PERMANENT DISCOUNT OUTLET

See page 89 (BEDS)

ESSEX

BRANDED STOCKS (UK) LTD

SHARP HOUSE, 1–5 ARTERIAL ROAD, LAINDON, ESSEX SS15 6DR, ☎ 01268 418000, FAX: 01268 418222, **e-mail:** sales@brandedstocks.co.uk, www.brandedstocks.co.uk, 9–4.30 MON–SAT. **PERMANENT DISCOUNT OUTLET**

This shop buys wholesale discounted clothes – some ends-of-lines – in bulk and sells them to the public at competitive prices. Stocks men's and women's casual wear from Thomas Burberry, Burberry, Versace, Armani, Ralph Lauren, Romeo Gigli, Diesel, Aquascutum, Moschino, Gucci, MaxMara Weekend, Jean Paul Gaultier, Iceberg and Calvin Klein.

BURBERRY

FREEPORT RETAIL OUTLET VILLAGE, BRAINTREE, ESSEX CM7 8YH, ☎ 01376 554851 10–6 MON–SAT, 8 ON THUR, 11–5 SUN. **FACTORY SHOP IN A FACTORY SHOPPING VILLAGE**

See page 94 (CHESH)

CATALOGUE BARGAIN SHOP

ST JOHN'S WALK SHOPPING CENTRE, COLCHESTER, ESSEX CO2 7AL, ☎ 01206 563126, www.bargaincrazy.com, 9–5.30 MON–THUR, 9–7 FRI, 9–6 SAT, 10.30–4.30 SUN. **PERMANENT DISCOUNT OUTLET**

See page 92 (CAMBS)

CHARLES CLINKARD

CLACTON FACTORY OUTLET VILLAGE, STEPHENSON ROAD WEST, CLACTON-ON-SEA, ESSEX CO15 4TL, ☎ 01255 220384, FAX: 01255 230384, 10–6 MON–SAT, 8 ON THUR, 11–5 SUN.
FACTORY SHOP IN A FACTORY SHOPPING VILLAGE

See page 101 (CO DURH)

CHOICE DISCOUNT STORES LIMITED

14–20 RECTORY ROAD, HADLEIGH, BENFLEET, ESSEX SS7 2ND, ☎ 01702 555245, 9–5.30 MON–THUR, 9–6 FRI, SAT.

26–28 HIGH STREET, BARKINGSIDE, ILFORD, ESSEX IG6 2DQ, ☎ 020 8551 2125, 9–5.30 MON–FRI, 9–6 SAT, 11–5 SUN.

10–11 LADYGATE CENTRE, HIGH STREET, WICKFORD, ESSEX SS12 9AJ, ☎ 01268 764893, 9–5.30 MON–FRI, 9–6 SAT.

UNIT 6A, MAYFLOWER RETAIL PARK, GARDINERS LINK, BASILDON, ESSEX SS14 3AP, ☎ 01268 288331, 10–6 MON–WED, 10–7 THUR, FRI, 9–6 SAT, 11–5 SUN. 14–16 HIGH STREET, GRAYS, ESSEX RM17 6LU, ☎ 01375 385780, 9–5.30 MON–FRI, 9–6 SAT.

CLACTON FACTORY SHOPPING VILLAGE, STEPHENSON ROAD WEST, CLACTON-ON-SEA, ESSEX CO15 4TL, ☎ 01255 474786, 10–6 MON–SAT, 11–5 SUN. **PERMANENT DISCOUNT OUTLET**

See page 92 (CAMBS)

CLACTON FACTORY SHOPPING VILLAGE

STEPHENSON ROAD WEST, CLACTON-ON-SEA, ESSEX CO15 4TL, ☎ 01255 479595/01255 430777 INFORMATION LINE, 10–6 MON–SAT, 11–5 SUN. **FACTORY SHOPPING VILLAGE**

Forty eight units centred around a Victorian winter garden comprising the following: Banana Bookshop selling books, games and stationery; Because It's There (BIT) for sports and camping equipment; Bed & Bath Works, a homeware outlet with discounted branded linens and housewares from Janet Reger, Sheridan, Christy and Kingsley; Birthdays, stocking mainstream cards and gifts from manufacturers such as Andrew Brownsword, Disney, Parker, Galt and Warner Brothers; Camille for lingerie; Caterpillar selling foorwear from the Cat range; Choice, which sells family clothing from Next; Claire's Accessories; Clinkards family footwear from Church's, Gabor, Bally and Loake; Cook 'N Dine kitchenware, glass and ceramics; Cotton Traders casual wear; Dannimac outdoor wear; Designer Room selling designer fashion for men and women; Event fashion costume jewellery and watches from Accurist, Timberland, Seiko and Timex; Garden Store selling garden furniture, barbecues and equipment and, in season, Christmas decorations; Jacques Vert selling womenswear; JD Sports selling branded sports merchandise from Adidas, Nike, Reebok, Ellesse and Le Coq Sportif; Joanna Hall selling handbags from the Jane Shilton range; Julian Graves foods and nut mixes; Kids Play Factory with toys from ranges such as Fisher-Price and Lego; Leading Labels, with men's and women's fashions; Mobile Phone Shop; MX Active selling branded denim and casual wear for men, women and children; Nickelbys fashion wear for men and women; Olli Moda selling branded jeans and casual wear; Pilot, a young women's fashion outlet; Ponden Mill with a range of bedlinen and bathroom ware; Price's Candles; Roman Originals womenswear; Sasperilla for young women's fashions; Spotlight, a young women's fashion outlet; Suits You men's shirts, suits, and casual separates as well as wedding hire and Autonomy womenswear; Thorntons chocolates; Tog 24 outdoor activity wear; Windsmoor women's fashions; Travel Accessory Shop with travel goods from Delsey and Samsonite; Woods of Windsor toiletries and gift items; XS Music CDs and videos. There are also two restaurants, a tourist information centre, parking for 1,000 cars and a bus service link to Clacton-On-Sea town centre and railway station.

DESIGNER SHADES

FREEPORT ESSEX VILLAGE, CHARTER WAY, CHAPEL HILL, BRAINTREE, ESSEX CM7 8YH, ☎ 01376 334007, **e-mail:** info@sunglass-time.com, 10–6 MON–SAT, 8 ON THUR, 11–5 SUN. **FACTORY SHOP IN A FACTORY SHOPPING VILLAGE**

Designer Shades offer a wide selection of top-notch sunglasses and watches at more than 30% off typical high street prices. The frames are invitingly displayed on back-lit columns – no locked cabinets, messy stickers or hanging labels to contend with. Gucci, Polo Ralph Lauren, Valentino, Police, Christian Dior and Diesel are included in the ever-changing stock of top international brand names. Designer Shades ensure that all their sunglasses have quality lenses which protect against UVA and UVB rays, as well as filtering out damaging reflective blue light. Their range of high fashion unisex watches includes Dolce & Gabbana, Guess and Pulsar. They plan to have 20 shops throughout Europe by the end of 2003. For details of other locations, phone 01423 858007 or email info@sunglass-time.com.

DOUBLE TWO

UNIT K7, FREEPORT BRAINTREE, CHARTER WAY, CHAPEL HILL, BRAINTREE, ESSEX CM7 8YH, ☎ 01376 346502, 10–6 MON–SAT, 8 ON THUR, 11–5 SUN. **FACTORY SHOP IN A FACTORY SHOPPING VILLAGE**

Men's shirts (both casual and formal), belts, ties, jeans and dress shirts and women's blouses, coordinates, dresses, trousers, skirts and waistcoats at discount prices of about 30% to 50%.

FAIRHEADS

60–64 CRANBROOK ROAD, ILFORD, ESSEX IG1 4NQ, ☎ 020 8478 0328, 9–5.30 MON–SAT. **PERMANENT DISCOUNT OUTLET**

There are 13 different departments at Fairheads, including household goods, linen, soft furnishings, lingerie, fashion, hosiery, craft and haberdashery. There are often 'blue ticket' specials: for example, buy three pairs of Sloggi briefs and get a fourth free. Best quality stock at the lowest price possible and always special offers and reduced lines throughout the store. At sale time stock is half price or less. There are two genuine sales a year: after Christmas and at the end of June. Phone for details.

FREEPORT BRAINTREE DESIGNER OUTLET VILLAGE

FREEPORT ESSEX VILLAGE, CHARTER WAY, CHAPEL HILL, BRAINTREE, JUNCTION 8 OF M11, THEN A120, ESSEX CM7 8YH, ☎ 01376 348168, www.freeportbraintree.com, 10–6 MON–SAT, 8 ON THUR, 11–5 SUN. **FACTORY SHOPPING VILLAGE**

Freeport Braintree is a designer outlet village with over 80 shops. Situated in the heart of Essex with easy access from the A120, Freeport Braintree has its own dedicated railyway station and is only a one-hour journey from central London. Womenswear includes Aquascutum, Amazing Jeans, Antonio d'Errico, Box Fresh, Burberry, Christian Lacroix, Cotton Traders, Elle, Gossard, Karen Millen, Ted Baker, Tommy Hilfiger and Versace and The Designer Room with a host of designer labels. Menswear includes Aquascutum, Cecil Gee, Ciro Citterio, Cotton Traders, Kurt Muller, Nickleby's, Proibito, Ted Baker, Tommy Hilfiger, Van Heusen and Versace. For children there's Base 2 Base, Mexx and Toy Dome; there is also plenty to keep children entertained, such as the Cheeky Chimps indoor play area. Sportwear outlets include Brand Fusion, Donnay, Fila, Mountain Warehouse, Nike, Reebok, Regatta and Trespass. Footwear is covered by Ecco Shoes, Franchetti Bond, Hush Puppies, Jane Shilton, Lilley & Skinner, Soled Out and Vans Shoes. Shops selling household goods from kitchenware to pot pourri include Churchills, Denby, Edinburgh Crystal, Glen Eagles, Le Creuset, Professional Cookware, The Design House, Waterford Wedgwood and Villeroy & Boch. Other retail outlets, selling everything from luggage to music, include Body Shop, Carlton, Claire's Accessories, Designer Shades, Mobile Phone Store, Watch Store and XS Music, and there are no less than six cafés and restaurants on site.

HUSH PUPPIES

FREEPORT ESSEX VILLAGE, CHARTER WAY, CHAPEL HILL, BRAINTREE, ESSEX CM7 8YH, ☎ 01376 554682, 10–6 MON–SAT, 8 ON THUR, 11–5 SUN. **FACTORY SHOP**

Hush Puppies footwear sold at least 30% below normal retail prices. Also sells Loakes for men at prices from £59.99.

LABELS

THE COCKPIT, EMSON CLOSE, SAFFRON WALDEN, ESSEX CB10 1HF, ☎ 01799 523533, FAX: 01279 815541, 9.45–5.30 MON–FRI, 10–5.30 SAT. **PERMANENT DISCOUNT OUTLET**

Designer womenswear, menswear and footwear including labels such as Calvin Klein, Ralph Lauren, Moschino, Versace, Yves Saint Laurent, Timberland, Lacoste and Armani.

LEE COOPER

FREEPORT ESSEX VILLAGE, CHARTER WAY, CHAPEL HILL, BRAINTREE, ESSEX CM7 8YH, ☎ 01376 554684, 10–6 MON–SAT, 8 ON THUR, 11–5 SUN. **FACTORY SHOP IN A FACTORY SHOPPING VILLAGE**

See page 96 (CHESH)

LILLEY & SKINNER

FREEPORT ESSEX VILLAGE, CHARTER WAY, CHAPEL HILL, BRAINTREE, ESSEX CM7 8YH, ☎ 01376 327490, 10–6 MON–SAT, 8 ON THUR, 11–5 SUN. **FACTORY SHOP IN A FACTORY SHOPPING VILLAGE**

See page 109 (DERBY)

MATALAN

CRICKETERS RETAIL PARK, CRICKETERS WAY, BASILDON, ESSEX SS13 1SA, ☎ 01268 290260, FAX: 01268 534860, www.matalan.co.uk, 10–8 MON–FRI, 9–6 SAT, 10–4 SUN.

UNIT 4, RIVERSIDE RETAIL PARK, VICTORIA ROAD, CHELMSFORD, ESSEX CM2 6LL, ☎ 01245 348787, FAX: 01245 348989, www.matalan.co.uk, 10–8 MON–FRI, 9–6 SAT, 11–5 SUN.

UNIT E, COLCHESTER RETAIL PARK, SHEEPHEN ROAD, COLCHESTER ESSEX CO3 3LE, ☎ 01206 812400, FAX: 01206 541716, www.matalan.co.uk, 10–8 MON–FRI, 9–6 SAT, 11–5 SUN.

TOWER RETAIL PARK, CRAYFORD ROAD, CRAYFORD, DARTFORD, ESSEX DA1 4LD, ☎ 01322 552140, FAX: 01322 522516, www.matalan.co.uk, 9 -8 MON–FRI, 9 -6 SAT, 10–4 SUN.

117 NORTH STREET, ROMFORD, ESSEX RM1 1EX, ☎ 01708 759780, FAX: 01708 760102, www.matalan.co.uk, 10–8 MON–FRI, 9–6 SAT, 10–4 SUN.

THE GREYHOUND RETAIL PARK, SUTTON ROAD, SOUTHEND ESSEX SS2 5PY, ☎ 01702 466248, FAX: 01702 617571, www.matalan.co.uk, 10 -8 MON–FRI, 9 -6 SAT, 10–4 SUN.

UNIT 4B, THE TUNNEL ESTATE, LAKESIDE, WEST THURROCK, ESSEX RM20 3WZ, ☎ 01708 864350/01708 864334, www.matalan.co.uk, 10–8 MON–FRI, 9–6 SAT, 11–5 SUN. **PERMANENT DISCOUNT OUTLET**

See page 89 (BEDS)

QD STORES

GREAT OAKS HOUSE, GREAT OAKS, BASILDON, ESSEX SS14 1JD, ☎ 01268 522999, 9–5.30 MON–SAT.

72–78 ROSEMARY ROAD, CLACTON-ON-SEA, ESSEX CO15 1TZ, ☎ 01255 479974, 9–5.30 MON–SAT, 10–4 SUN.

45–51 HIGH STREET, GRAYS, ESSEX RM16 5UF, ☎ 01375 385250, 9–5.30 MON–SAT.

UNITS 101–108, VICTORIA PLAZA, SOUTHEND-ON-SEA, ESSEX SS2 5FB, ☎ 01702 618777, 9–5.30 MON–SAT. **PERMANENT DISCOUNT OUTLET**

See page 89 (BEDS)

REGATTA

FREEPORT ESSEX VILLAGE, CHARTER WAY, CHAPEL HILL, BRAINTREE, ESSEX CM7 4YH, ☎ 01376 349755, FAX: 01376 349755, www.regatta.com, 10–6 MON–SAT, 8 ON THUR, 11–5 SUN. **FACTORY SHOP IN A FACTORY SHOPPING VILLAGE**

Regatta is the UK's biggest supplier of outdoor clothing and equipment for the whole family. The ranges comprise wovens, waterproofs, fleece, rucksacks and accessories for men, women and children, and are suitable for a whole range of outdoor activities. Regatta prides itself on offering excellent quality products at very reasonable prices. Craghoppers, the innovator in travel and outdoor wear, is a technical brand that leads with innovation. Its offering of waterproofs, fleece, wovens and rucksacks are intended for travel at home or abroad and suitable for a wide range of climates. All stock is sold here at discounted prices of at least 30%.

T J HUGHES

25–29 MARKET PLACE, ROMFORD, ESSEX RM1 3AB, ☎ 01708 747159, FAX: 01708 721126, **e-mail:** info@tjhughes.co.uk, www.tjhughes.co.uk, 9–5.30 MON–SAT, 10–4 SUN. **PERMANENT DISCOUNT OUTLET**

See page 98 (CHESH) .

THE FACTORY SHOP LTD

THE GLOUCESTERS, LUCKYN LANE, PIPPS HILL INDUSTRIAL ESTATE, BASILDON, ESSEX SS14 3AX, ☎ 01268 520546, www.thefactoryshopsessexltd.co.uk, 9–6 MON–SAT, 10–5 SUN.

PURDEY'S INDUSTRIAL ESTATE, 1 MAGNOLIA WAY, ROCHFORD, ESSEX SS4 1ND, ☎ 01702 531153, www.thefactoryshopsessexltd.co.uk, 9–6 MON–SAT, 10–5 SUN. **FACTORY SHOP**

THE CROSS ROADS, KELVEDON ROAD, TIPTREE, ESSEX CO5 0LJ, ☎ 01621 817662, 9–5.30 MON–SAT, 10–4 SUN. **FACTORY SHOP**

See page 98 (CHESH)

TK MAXX

93 EASTGATE SHOPPING CENTRE, SOUTHERNHAY, BASILDON, ESSEX SS14 1AF, ☎ 01268 273604, PHONE FOR DETAILS OF OPENING HOURS.

THE ROYAL SHOPPING CENTRE, HIGH STREET, SOUTHEND SS1, FAX: 01702 600020, www.tkmaxx.com, 9–5.30 MON–SAT, 11–5 SUN.

26 SIR ISAAC WALK, CULVER SQUARE, COLCHESTER, ESSEX CO1 1JJ, ☎ 01206 368745, www.tkmaxx.com, 9–6 MON, 9–7 TUE–WED, 9–8 THUR–FRI, 9–6 SAT, 11–5 SUN.

THE EXCHANGE, ILFORD, ESSEX IG1 1AS, ☎ 020 8514 1288, www.tkmaxx.com, 9.30–6 MON–FRI, 8 ON WED, 9–6 SAT, 11–5 SUN.

THE BREWERY, ROMFORD, ESSEX, ☎ 01708 761978, PHONE FOR DETAILS OF OPENING HOURS.

UNIT 4, TUNNEL ESTATE RETAIL PARK WEST, LONDON ROAD, THURROCK, ESSEX RM22 3HH, ☎ 01708 860296, www.tkmaxx.com, 10–8 MON–FRI, 10–7 SAT, 11–5 SUN. **PERMANENT DISCOUNT OUTLET**

See page 89 (BEDS)

TOG 24

CLACTON FACTORY OUTLET VILLAGE, STEPHENSON ROAD WEST, CLACTON-ON-SEA ESSEX CO15 4TL, ☎ 01255 435035, **e-mail:** mail-order@tog24.com, www.tog24.com, 10–6 MON–SAT, 8 ON THUR DURING SUMMER AND AT CHRISTMAS, 11–5 SUN. **FACTORY SHOP IN A FACTORY SHOPPING VILLAGE**

See page 99 (CHESH)

TOMMY HILFIGER

UNIT G6, FEEPORT DESIGNER VILLAGE, CHAPEL HILL, BRAINTREE, ESSEX CM7 8YH, ☎ 01376 342985, FAX: 01376 349482, www.tommy.com, 10–6 MON–SAT, 8 ON THUR, 11–5 SUN. **FACTORY SHOP IN A FACTORY SHOPPING VILLAGE**

See page 99 (CHESH)

WARNERS

UNIT F2, FREEPORT DESIGNER VILLAGE, CHARTER WAY, CHAPEL HILL, BRAINTREE, ESSEX CM7 8YH, ☎ 01376 330888, 10–6 MON–SAT, 8 ON THUR, 11–5 SUN. **FACTORY SHOP IN A FACTORY SHOPPING VILLAGE**

See page 100 (CHESH)

GLOUCESTERSHIRE

BRANDMART

WESTWARD ROAD, CAINSCROSS, STROUD, GLOUCESTERSHIRE GL5 4JE, ☎ 01453 756655, 9–5 MON–SAT, 10–4 SUN. **FACTORY SHOP**

The original factory shop in Cainscross, Stroud, has recently relocated next door into a 12,000 square foot premises and is now trading under the name of Brandmart, offering even more savings on branded household and family goods. The range includes men's, women's and children's clothing and footwear, household textiles, toiletries, hardware, luggage, lighting, electrical goods and bedding, most of which are chainstore and high street brands at discounts of between 30% and 50%. There are weekly deliveries and brands include famous names such as Calvin Klein, Adidas, Nike, Fcuk, Cat, Reebok, Ben Sherman, Kangol, Timberland and many more. There are kitchen and furniture displays and a new line in Cape Country furniture on sale. Ranges are continually changing and few factory shops offer such a variety under one roof.

CATALOGUE BARGAIN SHOP

1–6 GROSVENOR HOUSE, STATION ROAD, GLOUCESTER, GLOUCESTERSHIRE GL1 1SZ, ☎ 01452 308779, www.bargaincrazy.com, 9–5.30 MON–SAT, 10.30–4.30 SUN. **PERMANENT DISCOUNT OUTLET**

See page 92 (CAMBS)

DAMART

LISTER BUILDINGS, STATION ROAD, GLOUCESTER, GLOUCESTERSHIRE GL1 1DH, ☎ 01452 526510, 9.30–5 MON–SAT. **FACTORY SHOP**

See page 114 (DORS)

HAWICK CASHMERE COMPANY LTD

2 BREWERY YARD, SHEEP STREET, STOW-ON-THE-WOLD, GLOUCESTERSHIRE GL54 1AA, ☎ 01451 870840, FAX: 01451 870840, 9.30–5.30 MON–SAT. **FACTORY SHOP**

Hawick Cashmere offers you the luxury of Scottish knitwear direct from their own factory in the Scottish borders at competitive retail prices. You can choose from cashmere, merino and lambswool for men and women. Hawick Cashmere also offers a large selection of accessories in cashmere and fine wool.

JUST-IN LIMITED

21 ST JOHNS AVENUE, CHURCHDOWN, GLOUCESTERSHIRE GL3 2DG, ☎ 01452 530530, 10–5 MON–SAT.

2 HAILES STREET, WINCHCOMBE, GLOUCESTERSHIRE GL54 5HU, ☎ 01242 603204, 10–5.30 MON–SAT, 12–5 SUN. **PERMANENT DISCOUNT OUTLET**

Both branches sell quality fashion seconds, Continental designer wear, a range of nearly-new clothes and incorporate Nightingales Ltd. The Churchdown shop, recently enlarged, is well stocked and has a large car park. The Winchcombe branch is made up of three shops and also carries a large stock. The latter consists of anything from Marks & Spencer to designer labels and there is also a new section of designer clothes, mostly German makes, in sizes 8 to 30. Alterations can be carried out on the premises. Wax jackets are sold from the Oxford range from £25 to £85 and there is an evening dress hire service for men and women. Accessories such as handbags, jewellery, scarves and hats are also stocked.

LEGS CLOTHING CO

7 THREADNEEDLE STREET, STROUD, GLOUCESTERSHIRE GL5 1AS, ☎ 01453 764621 9–5 MON–SAT. **FACTORY SHOP**

Exclusive outlet for Europe's leading trouser manufacturer. Sells trousers, jeans and shorts for all ages, at factory-direct prices, plus ancillary lines of casual wear at bargain prices.

MASH

INNSWORTH TECHNOLOGY PARK, INNSWORTH LANE, GLOUCESTER, GLOUCESTERSHIRE GL3 1DL, ☎ 01452 730577, FAX: 01452 731999, **e-mail:** tim@dowco.co.uk, www.mashcamping.com, 8.30–5.30 MON–FRI, 8.30–5 SAT, 10–4 SUN, BANK HOLIDAYS. **SECONDHAND SHOP**

Warehouse/shop carrying an extensive range of backpacking and camping equipment, outdoor clothing, tools, Gelert tents, Sunngas cookers, Victorinox knives, Maglite torches and government surplus stock at discount prices.

MATALAN

27 SWINDON ROAD, CHELTENHAM, GLOUCESTERSHIRE GL50 4DF, ☎ 01242 579840, FAX: 01242 282142, www.matalan.co.uk, 10–8 MON–FRI, 9–6 SAT, 11–5 SUN.

QUEDGELEY DISTRICT CENTRE, GLOUCESTER, GLOUCESTERSHIRE GL2 4PF, ☎ 01452 726040, FAX: 01452 725216, www.matalan.co.uk, 9.30–8 MON–FRI, 9–6 SAT, 10–4 SUN. **PERMANENT DISCOUNT OUTLET**

See page 89 (BEDS)

TK MAXX

REGENT ARCADE SHOPPING CENTRE, CHELTENHAM, GLOUCESTERSHIRE GL50 1J2, ☎ 01242 513848, www.tkmaxx.com, 9–5.30 MON–WED, 9–8 THUR, 9–6 FRI–SAT. **PERMANENT DISCOUNT OUTLET**

See page 89 (BEDS)

TOP MARKS

SWISS COTTAGE, HIGH STREET, BOURTON-ON-THE-WATER, GLOUCESTERSHIRE, ☎ 01451 820369, 10–5 MON–SAT, 11–5 SUN.

23 HIGH STREET, MORETON-IN-MARSH, GLOUCESTERSHIRE GL56 0AF, ☎ 01608 651272, 9–5 MON–SAT. 10–4 SUN. **PERMANENT DISCOUNT OUTLET**

Sells seconds from leading chainstores for all family. Most of the stock is made up of menswear and womenswear, with some childrenswear. The clothes are mainly Marks & Spencer seconds, sold at about one third cheaper than in the high street. Wide range of stock in various sizes with new stock arriving twice a week. They also sell Debenhams' stock when available.

WOOSTERS & CO

2 BATH ROAD, OFF HIGH STREET, CHELTENHAM, GLOUCESTERSHIRE GL53 7HA, ☎ 01242 256855, 10–5 TUE–SAT. **DRESS AGENCY**

Busy shop in town centre location with a brisk turnover so there's always something new to see.

One of the very few in the area which also sells men's nearly-new, which has resulted in Woosters cornering the market in the good quality clothes. Ground level packed with very stylish womenswear, with an excellent selection of designer labels such as Nicole Farhi, Armani, Mulberry etc, plus accessories to complement any outfit. The lower ground floor houses good quality menswear: country tweeds, business and dinner suits from Armani, Boss, Paul Smith and Ralph Lauren, among others, while casual wear includes names such as Tommy Hilfiger, Quiksilver and Chevignon. Prices range from £39 to £139 for business suits. Friendly atmosphere in which to browse with expert advice if needed.

HAMPSHIRE

ADIDAS

GUNWHARF QUAYS, PORTSMOUTH, HAMPSHIRE PO1 3TA, ☎ 02392 779974, FAX: 02392 779975, 10–6 MON, WED, 10–8 TUE, THUR, 10–8 FRI, SAT, 11–5 SUN. **FACTORY SHOP IN A FACTORY SHOPPING VILLAGE**

See page 93 (CHESH)

BALLY OUTLET STORE

UNIT 54, GUNWHARF QUAYS, PORTSMOUTH, HAMPSHIRE PO1 3TX, ☎ 02392 830834, FAX: 02392 830835, **e-mail:** jwright@bally.ch www.bally.com, 10–6 MON–WED, 10–8 THUR–SAT, 11–5 SUN, SOME LATE NIGHTS AND MOST BANK HOLIDAYS. PHONE FOR DETAILS. **FACTORY SHOP IN A FACTORY SHOPPING VILLAGE**

Situated on the Gunwharf Quays Leisure and Outlet Centre, the Bally Outlet sells high quality womens and mens footwear, plus handbags, accessories and a range of Bally clothing. Merchandise is from the company's European stores and is end-of-line or ex-sale. Savings of at least 30% off normal retail prices can be made.

BENETTON

UNIT 8GF, GUNWHARF QUAYS, PORTSMOUTH, HAMPSHIRE PO1 3TA, ☎ 023 928 30099, FAX: 023 928 30066, www.benetton.co.uk, SUMMER: 10–6 MON–WED, 10–8 THUR–SAT, 11–5 SUN. WINTER: 10–6 MON–SAT, 10–5 SUN. **FACTORY SHOP IN A FACTORY SHOPPING VILLAGE**

Benetton stocks a wide range of clothes for women, men and children including colourful T-shirts, sweatshirts, men's button-neck T-shirts, swimwear, jeans, children's jackets, stretch shorts and all-in-one shorts. Some of the stock is marked seconds, but it is often difficult to tell why. Now also stocks luggage.

BURBERRY

GUNWHARF QUAYS, PORTSMOUTH, HAMPSHIRE PO1 3PZ, ☎ 02393 864620, 10–8 SUN–WED, 10–9 THUR–SAT IN SUMMER. 10–6 SEVEN DAYS A WEEK IN WINTER. **FACTORY SHOP IN A FACTORY SHOPPING VILLAGE**

See page 94 (CHESH)

CAMEO OF COWES

16 BATH ROAD, THE PARADE, COWES, ISLE OF WIGHT, HAMPSHIRE PO31 7QN, ☎ 01983 297907, FAX: 01983 281129, 10–5 SEVEN DAYS A WEEK. **SECONDHAND SHOP**

Buy and sell unclaimed lost property from airports, parcels lost in transit, London Transport and police departments. This can include anything from clothes and shoes to umbrellas and jewellery; make-up and perfume to purses and designer items.

CLARKS FACTORY SHOP

UNIT 56 GUNWHARF QUAYS, PORTSMOUTH, HAMPSHIRE PO1 3TZ, ☎ 02392 838578, 10–6 MON–WED, 10–9 THUR–SAT, 10–6 SUN. **FACTORY SHOP**

See page 94 (CHESH)

DESIGNER SHADES

GUNWHARF QUAYS, PORTSMOUTH, HAMPSHIRE PO1 3TA, ☎ 0239 287 2007, **e-mail:** info@sunglass-time.com, 10–6 SEVEN DAYS A WEEK. **FACTORY SHOP IN A FACTORY SHOPPING VILLAGE**

See page 116 (ESSEX)

FRENCH CONNECTION/NICOLE FARHI

GUNWHARF QUAYS, PORTSMOUTH, HAMPSHIRE PO1 4TT, ☎ 02392 837833, 10–6 MON–WED, 10–8 THUR–SAT, 11–5 SUN. **FACTORY SHOP IN A FACTORY SHOPPING VILLAGE**

Previous season's womenswear and menswear, including shoes, but no childrenswear, and seconds, at discounts of between 30% and 50% off normal retail prices.

GAP

GUNWHARF QUAYS, PORTSMOUTH, HAMPSHIRE PO1 3TA, ☎ 023 92 755 493, 10–6 MON–WED, 10–8 THUR–SAT, 11–5 SUN. **FACTORY SHOP IN A FACTORY SHOPPING VILLAGE**

Gap sells casual clothes for men, women and children of all ages. Discounts at this factory outlet village range from 30% upwards. At the time of calling, they had women's trousers which usually retail for £38 on sale for 99p.

GIEVES & HAWKES

GUNWHARF QUAYS, PORTSMOUTH, HAMPSHIRE PO1 3TU, ☎ 0239 282 6648, JAN TO EASTER: 10–6 MON–SAT, 11–5 SUN. REST OF YEAR: 10–6 MON–WED, 10–8 THUR–SAT, 11–5 SUN. **FACTORY SHOP IN A FACTORY SHOPPING VILLAGE**

This Savile Row retailer's clearance shop sells Gieves & Hawkes menswear at exceptional discounts, and provides tailoring and alterations services.

GUNWHARF QUAYS

PORTSMOUTH HARBOUR, HAMPSHIRE PO1 3TZ, ☎ 023 9283 6700, FAX: 023 9283 6701, **e-mail:** info@gunwharf-quays.com, www.gunwharf-quays.com, SUMMER: 10–6 MON–WED, 10–8 THUR–SAT, 11–5 SUN WINTER: 10–6 MON–SAT, 11–5 SUN. **FACTORY SHOPPING VILLAGE**

Designer outlet shopping centre comprising 65 stores on a site next to Portsmouth Harbour station and Portsmouth Historic Dockyard, home to HMS Victory and the Mary Rose. As well as the designer outlets, which include Adidas, Benetton, Ben Sherman, Burberry, cK Calvin Klein, Crabtree & Evelyn, Ecco, Episode, Fenn Wright & Manson, Gap, Gieves & Hawkes, Marks & Spencer, Nicole Farhi, Nike, Tommy Hilfiger, Villeroy & Boch, Waterford Wedgwood and Whittard of Chelsea, there are 20 restaurants, bars and coffee shops, an 11-screen cinema, 26-lane bowling complex, comedy club and a year-round events programme.

HUSH PUPPIES

UNIT 26 NORTH PROMENADE BUILDING, GUNWHARF QUAYS, PORTSMOUTH, HAMPSHIRE PO1 3TR, ☎ 023 9286 4288, 10–6 MON, TUE, WED, SUN, 10–6 THUR, FRI, SAT. **FACTORY SHOP**

See page 117 (ESSEX)

JAMES MEADE LTD

48 CHARLTON ROAD, ANDOVER, HAMPSHIRE SP10 3JL, ☎ 01264 387700, FAX: 01264 363200, **e-mail:** info@jamesmeade.com, www.jamesmeade.com, 9–5.30 MON–FRI, 10–4 SAT. **FACTORY SHOP**

Discontinued lines from the well-known mail order catalogues, James Meade Ltd, Men's and Women's Classics, Jake, Sparklers and Cashmere by James Meade, are available at discounted prices at this factory shop. Classic clothing for men and women including shirts, jackets, skirts, trousers, ties and knitwear. Items in the current catalogues can also be bought at normal prices, including cashmere. Displays are good and there are facilities for trying on clothes.

LILLEY & SKINNER

WHITELEY VILLAGE OUTLET SHOPPING, WHITELEY WAY, WHITELEY, HAMPSHIRE PO15 7LJ, ☎ 01489 589026, 10–6 MON–SAT, 11–5 SUN. **FACTORY SHOP IN A FACTORY SHOPPING VILLAGE**

See page 109 (DERBY)

MATALAN

CHANNON RETAIL PARK, WOODSIDE AVENUE, EASTLEIGH, HAMPSHIRE SO50 9ER, ☎ 02380 626 150, FAX: 02380 650 749, www.matalan.co.uk, 10–8 MON–FRI, 9–6 SAT, 10–4 SUN.

STATION STREET, PORTSMOUTH, HAMPSHIRE PO1 1BE, ☎ 0239 285 1967, FAX: 0239 275 5316, www.matalan.co.uk, 9–8 MON–FRI, 9–6 SAT, 11–5 SUN. **PERMANENT DISCOUNT OUTLET**

See page 89 (BEDS)

PARTRIDGE

WHITELEY VILLAGE DESIGNER OUTLET CENTRE, WHITELEY WAY, FAREHAM, JUNCTION 9 OF M27, HAMPSHIRE PO15 7LJ, ☎ 01489 573804, 10–6 MON–SAT, 11–5 SUN. **FACTORY SHOP IN A FACTORY SHOPPING VILLAGE**

Partridge specialises in fashionable outdoor clothes and accessories. Ranges include waxed jackets, GoreTex jackets, waterproof jackets, tweeds, quilts, fleece jackets and waistcoats, knitwear, shirts, chinos, hats and caps. Discontinued lines are on sale at discounted prices with a minimum of 30% and up to 70% off during promotions.

PEPE JEANS

LEVI'S FACTORY OUTLET, 13 GUNWHARF QUAYS, PORTSMOUTH, HAMPSHIRE PO1 3TZ, ☎ 0239 275 5484, 10–6 MON–SAT, 8 ON THUR, 11–5 SUN. **FACTORY SHOP IN A FACTORY SHOPPING VILLAGE**

All stock at this store is discounted by at least 30% off normal retail prices. World-renowned Levi's clothing is sold here: stock is current and last seasons, including 501s, 507s (bootcut style), 525s and 544s (both flared styles) and the new engineered jeans with twisted seams. Other styles available include vintage look and acid wash jeans, and Dockers cotton twill trousers. Jeans range in size from 8 to 16 for women, and from 28 to 38 for men. Dockers are available in sizes 28 to 42. There are often special offers available if you buy two or more pairs. Students displaying an NUS card save an additional 10% off all purchases.

PRET A PORTER

SHOP ONE, 18–20 HIGH STREET, RINGWOOD, HAMPSHIRE BH24 1AF, ☎ 01425 476090, 10–5 MON–SAT. **DRESS AGENCY**

Dress agency selling top designer fashions including Versace, Dior and Jaeger, as well as wedding outfits from Condici, Jacques Vert, Frank Usher and many more, all at a fraction of their original price. Recently under new ownership and now on two floors. There is a newly-opened department specialising in sizes 20 to 30. Evening wear and clothing for cruises are available all year round. Hats are a passion at Pret à Porter: they have in excess of 100 hats at any time, ideal for weddings and Ascot. Hats can be 'dressed' with flowers, ribbons, feathers and hat pins if required. Day wear comes from quality brand names including Monsoon, Alexon, Principles, Wallis and Next. A range of skiwear, accessories and aprés skiwear is available from October to February. Stock is seasonal and around 200 new items are added to the range every week to ensure a continuous flow of new and exciting items. Accessories, including shoes, bags, scarves, jewellery and belts, are also stocked.

SUITS YOU

UNIT 40, GUNWHARF QUAYS, PORTSMOUTH, HAMPSHIRE PO1 3TT, ☎ 0239 283 2722, 10–6 MON–WED, 10–8 THUR–SAT, 11–5 SUN. JANUARY TO EASTER, 10–6 MON–SAT. **FACTORY SHOP IN A FACTORY SHOPPING VILLAGE**

See page 91 (BRIS)

THE GALLERIES

HIGH STREET, ALDERSHOT, HAMPSHIRE GU11 1PE, ☎ 01252 341111, FAX: 01252 329800, **e-mail:** thegalleries@web-hq.com, www.thegalleriesaldershot.co.uk, 9–6 MON–SAT, 10–4 SUN. **FACTORY SHOPPING VILLAGE**

This town centre shopping mall has 20 discount shops on two levels such as Bed & Bath Works for bedlinen and bathroom ware; Cotton Traders casual wear; Designer Room selling women's and men's designer fashion; Hush Puppies shoes; Kitchen Kiosk with branded kitchen and homeware ranges including barbecues and some electrical goods such as bread making machines;

Leading Labels selling men's, women's and childrenswear; MX Active for men's, women's and children's branded denim and casual wear; Optisave, an optician selling designer branded glasses; Pilot selling young women's fashions; Pocket Phone selling mobile phones and accessories; Roman Originals womenswear; Room for furniture and household accessories; Suits You men's shirts, suits and casual separates as well as Autonomy womenswear; and Young's dress hire; Surf Skate and Snow for branded casual and activity wear; Toyzone for children's toys; and XS Music selling CDs and videos. The centre also has a café, wheelchair access, a lottery kiosk and baby changing facilities.

TK MAXX

173–178 HIGH STREET (BELOW BAR), SOUTHAMPTON, HAMPSHIRE SO14 2BY, ☎ 023 80 631600, www.tkmaxx.com, 9–5.30 MON–FRI, 7 ON THUR, 9–6 SAT, 11–5 SUN.
2 WELLINGTON RETAIL PARK, HAMBLEDON ROAD, WATERLOOVILLE, HAMPSHIRE, ☎ 023 92 267626, www.tkmaxx.com, PHONE FOR DETAILS.
PERMANENT DISCOUNT OUTLET

See page 89 (BEDS)

TOG 24

GUNWHARF QUAYS, PORTSMOUTH, HAMPSHIRE PO1 3TU, ☎ 0239 283 3717, **e-mail:** mail-order@tog24.com, www.tog24.com, 10–6 MON–WED, 10–8 THUR–SAT, 11–5 SUN. **FACTORY SHOP IN A FACTORY SHOPPING VILLAGE**

See page 99 (CHESH)

TOMMY HILFIGER

UNIT 7, GROUND FLOOR, GUNWHARF QUAYS, PORTSMOUTH, HAMPSHIRE PO1 3TA, ☎ 01233 646622, FAX: 01233 645375, www.tommy.com, 10–6 SEVEN DAYS A WEEK.
FACTORY SHOP IN A FACTORY SHOPPING VILLAGE

See page 99 (CHESH)

TRIUMPH INTERNATIONAL

GUNWHARF QUAYS, PORTSMOUTH, HAMPSHIRE PO1 3TR, ☎ 0239 229 8823, 10–6 SUN–WED, 10–8 THUR–SAT, 11–5 SUN. **FACTORY SHOP IN A FACTORY SHOPPING VILLAGE**

See page 99 (CHESH)

UNITED FOOTWEAR

117–125 FRATTON ROAD, PORTSMOUTH, HAMPSHIRE, ☎ 0239 282 6799, 9–5.30 MON–SAT, 10–4 SUN. **PERMANENT DISCOUNT OUTLET**

This shoe retailer, established for over 135 years, sells shoes for all the family as well as clothes, handbags, sports shoes, boots, giftware and household goods, all at discounted prices. Famous brands include Clarks, K Shoes, Elmdale, Grenson, Loakes, Caterpillar and Adidas. Part of a national chain.

WHITELEY VILLAGE OUTLET SHOPPING

OFF THE M27 BETWEEN SOUTHAMPTON AND PORTSMOUTH, JUNCTION 9 OF M27, HAMPSHIRE PO15 7LJ, ☎ 01489 886886, FAX: 01489 886887, www.whiteleyvillage.com, 10–6 MON–SAT, 11- 5 SUN. **FACTORY SHOPPING VILLAGE**

Whiteley Village has more than 50 outlets, all offering shoppers up to 50% savings on high street prices. Top designer names fashion names are here – including Antonio D'Errico, Banana Bookshop, Camille Lingerie, Lilley & Skinner, Roman Originals, Surf, Skate & Snow, Top Table, High & Mighty, Chilli Pepper, Claire's Accessories, Helter Skelter, Cloverleaf, Marzotto, Cotton Traders, D2 Jeans, Elle, Emma Sommerset, Ethos, The Baggage Factory, Ghost, HKA, Jane Shilton, Jasper Conran Jeans, Jigsaw, John Jenkins, John Partridge, Joseph, Julian Graves, Mobile Phone Store, Outdoor Direct, Photo Optix, Pilot, Ponden Mill, Pringle, Proibito, Puma, Rio Jeweller and The Designer Room with a host of designer labels. Refreshments are available from Starbucks Coffee and Boswells Restaurant. There is free parking on site for 1,400 cars, as well as an area for coaches.

WILKINSON STORES

22–30 BRIDGE STREET, ANDOVER, HAMPSHIRE SP10 1BN, ☎ 01332 551241, www.wilko.co.uk, 9–5.30 MON–SAT, 10–4 SUN. MAIL ORDER. **PERMANENT DISCOUNT OUTLET**

See page 100 (CHESH)

HEREFORDSHIRE

M & M SPORTS FACTORY SHOP

LEOMINSTER INDUSTRIAL ESTATE, SOUTHERN AVENUE, LEOMINSTER, HEREFORDSHIRE HR6 0SP, ☎ 01568 616161, FAX: 01568 619555, **e-mail:** sales@mandmsports.com, www.mandmsports.com, 10–8 THUR, 10–5 FRI, SAT, 10–4 SUN. MAIL ORDER. **FACTORY SHOP**

M & M Sports is the UK's largest sports and leisurewear mail order company, offering brand names for all the family at huge discounts including Nike, Adidas, Reebok, Fila, Ellesse, Berghaus and Rockport. Five catalogues a year are packed with all types of sports clothing, footwear and watches. M&M buys up huge quantities of end-of-line ranges direct from the manufacturers and passes on the massive savings to its customers. The Factory Shop sells discontinued catalogue items. A football kit catalogue is available, while the Equipment Catalogue offers products for golf, tennis, cricket, cycling, fishing, snooker, fitness equipment plus a lot more. To order a catalogue, phone or fax the above telephone numbers or visit their website where orders can be placed and there are many internet-only sale offers. Just click on the Exclusive Internet Offers logo.

ROSS LABELS LTD

ROSS PARK, OVERROSS, ROSS-ON-WYE, HEREFORDSHIRE HR9 7QJ, ☎ 01989 769000, www.rosslabels.co.uk, 9.30–6 MON–SAT, 10–4 SUN. **PERMANENT DISCOUNT OUTLET**

Factory outlet centre selling everything from women's and men's underwear and jeans to good, middle-of-the-road brand name outfits and suits bought direct from the manufacturer, as well as homewares. Over 100 leading brands are on sale. Discounts range from 20% to 50%.

STEWART'S SECONDS

33 HIGH STREET, ROSS-ON-WYE, HEREFORDSHIRE HR9 5HD, ☎ 01989 762403, 9.30–5 MON–WED, 9–5 THUR–SAT. **FACTORY SHOP**

See page 112 (DEV)

THE FACTORY SHOP

52 BROAD STREET, LEOMINSTER, HEREFORDSHIRE HR6 8BS, ☎ 01568 613944, 9–5.30 MON–SAT, 10–4 SUN. **FACTORY SHOP**

See page 98 (CHESH)

TK MAXX

5 TRINITY SQUARE, MAYLORD ORCHARD, HEREFORD, HEREFORDSHIRE HR1 2BX, ☎ 01432 355000, www.tkmaxx.com, 9–5.30 MON–FRI, 9–6 SAT, 11–5 SUN. **PERMANENT DISCOUNT OUTLET**

See page 89 (BEDS)

HERTFORDSHIRE

AQUASCUTUM

MAYLANDS WOOD ESTATE, CLEVELAND ROAD, HEMEL HEMPSTEAD, HERTFORDSHIRE HP2 7EY, ☎ 01442 248333, 10–5 MON–SAT. **FACTORY SHOP**

This is the last resting place for previous season's stock and seconds for women and men at greatly reduced prices. For men, blazers, suits and silk ties. New special offers are available monthly. Clearance sales are held here intermittently – phone for details.

AUTONOMY

UNIT 22, THE GALLERIA, HATFIELD, HERTFORDSHIRE AL10 0XR, ☎ 01707 274699, 10–8 MON–FRI, 10–6 SAT, 11–5 SUN. **FACTORY SHOP IN A FACTORY SHOPPING VILLAGE**

See page 93 (CHESH)

BhS FOR LESS

GALLERIA OUTLET CENTRE, COMET WAY, HATFIELD, HERTFORDSHIRE AL10 0XR, ☎ 01707 258351, 10–8 MON–FRI, 10–6 SAT, 11–5 SUN. **FACTORY SHOP IN A FACTORY SHOPPING VILLAGE**

BhS for Less sells the high street chain's men's, women's and childrenswear ranges, plus selections from its home and lighting ranges, at discounts of at least 30% and up to 75%.

BROUGHTON SHOE WAREHOUSE

UNIT 1, OLD TOWN SQUARE, HEMEL HEMPSTEAD, HERTFORDSHIRE HP1 1BB, ☎ 01442 218486, 9–5.30 MON–SAT. **PERMANENT DISCOUNT OUTLET**

See page 108 (DERBY)

CHARLES CLINKARD

GALLERIA OUTLET CENTRE, COMET WAY, HATFIELD, HERTFORDSHIRE AL10 0XS, ☎ 01707 258653, FAX: 01707 258653, 10–8 MON–FRI, 10–6 SAT, 11–5 SUN. **FACTORY SHOP IN A FACTORY SHOPPING VILLAGE**

See page 101 (CO DURH)

CHOICE DISCOUNT STORES LIMITED

GALLERIA OUTLET CENTRE, COMET WAY, HATFIELD, HERTFORDSHIRE AL10 0XR, ☎ 01707 258545, 10–8 MON–FRI, 10–6 SAT, 11–5 SUN. **FACTORY SHOP IN A FACTORY SHOPPING VILLAGE**

46 HIGH STREET, WATFORD, HERTFORDSHIRE WD1 2BS, ☎ 01923 233255, 9–5.30 MON–FRI, 9–6 SAT. **PERMANENT DISCOUNT OUTLET**

See page 92 (CAMBS)

CLARKS FACTORY SHOP

100 THE PARADE, HIGH STREET, WATFORD, HERTFORDSHIRE HD1 2AW, ☎ 01458 843155, 9.30–5.30 MON–FRI, 9–5.30 SAT. **FACTORY SHOP**

See page 94 (CHESH)

ECCO

GALLERIA OUTLET CENTRE, COMET WAY, HATFIELD, HERTFORDSHIRE AL10 0XR, ☎ 01707 258399, www.ecco.com, 10–8 MON–FRI, 10–6 SAT, 11–5 SUN. **FACTORY SHOP IN A FACTORY SHOPPING VILLAGE**

See page 95 (CHESH)

GALLERIA OUTLET CENTRE

COMET WAY, HATFIELD, HERTFORDSHIRE AL10 0XR, ☎ 01707 278301, www.factory-outlets.co.uk, 10–8 MON–FRI, 10–6 SAT, 11–5 SUN. **FACTORY SHOPPING VILLAGE**

The Galleria Outlet Centre, often referred to as the bargain hunter's best-kept secret, based in north London, houses more than 80 retail outlets. It offers a wide choice of shops for the discerning customer, providing up to 60% off designer labels and quality brands. The Designer Room is a must for branded men's and women's fashions at huge discounts, stocking DKNY, Jasper Conran, Ghost and Tommy Hilfiger clothing. Looking for a designer evening dress or smart-casual wear? Then visit Discount Dressing. For the latest in fashionable menswear, pay a visit to any of the leading menswear shops. City Menswear offers new season, discounted Yves Saint Laurent and Ben Sherman clothing; Choice sells ranges from Next; B52 Jeans stocks Levi's, Lee and Wrangler ranges; and Baron Jon sells a selection of international names from Versace to Valentino. Going on holiday or looking for a new set of luggage? Then visit the Baggage Factory which sells top quality brands including Carlton and Samsonite. For all your bathroom and bedroom needs pop in to Ponden Mill or the Bed and Bath Works, selling a selection of bedlinen, towels from Christy, soaps and duvets. BhS For Less sells a range of end-of-season men's women's and children's fashions, as well as homewares and lighting. For all your footwear fancies, take a stroll to Charles Clinkard, Ecco, Soled Out and Pavers, selling great brand names including Timberland, Loake, Grenson, Nike, Reebok and Kickers. For women, D Kaye Cosmetics stocks a host of leading beauty and skincare ranges including Revlon, Max Factor, Lancome and Yardley, all at up to 75% off normal retail prices. Walker & Hall represent the finest in jewellery, stocking Tag, Gucci and Raymond Weil watches all at affordable prices. It also sells gold by weight and guarantees savings of at least 30% per gram. While, for the home, Chinacraft specialises in glass, china and giftware, from Wedgwood to Royal Doulton. If interior soft furnishings are on the agenda, then the Furniture Zone is the largest of its type, selling Oriental, middle eastern and Continental rugs, plus great ranges of sofas and sofa-beds, teak, cherry and oak furniture from Wall Nuts and the Khokhar Collection. To complement any room, the Big Picture and Big Poster sell modern and classical pictures ranging from £5 to £20,000. Visit the Garden Outlet Store for all your outdoor gardening and furniture requirements. Music Surplus, the home entertainment store, is a recent addition to the centre, selling a wide range of imported jazz, pop, chart and classical CDs, as well as the latest DVDs. For the PC enthusiast, UK Software sells CD-Roms at up to 70% off the normal retail price. Tool Ware House sells DeWalt, considered by many to be the Armani of the tool worlds, as well as offering fantastic savings on Black & Decker. The centre also offers three cafés, six restaurants and an abundance of children's activities including Toddler World, a futuristic crazy golf course and bouncing slides as well as a mini go-karting track during weekends and holidays. With over 1,800 free car parking spaces and a nine-screen UCI cinema, the centre offers a complete family day out. The Galleria Outlet Centre is a 20-minute drive from north London, and is signposted from junction 3 and 4 of the A1M.

IMPRESSIONS

48 CHURCH STREET, WARE, HERTFORDSHIRE SG12 9EW, ☎ 01920 461188, FAX: 01920 461188, 10–4 TUE–SAT. CLOSED MON AND THUR. **DRESS AGENCY. HIRE SHOP**

On two floors, this pretty little shop in Ware's town centre specialises in once-worn wedding gowns and holds about 150 gowns at any one time, together with accessories. Labels include Dizzie Lizzie, Amanda Wyatt, Sally B, Ellis, Mon Cherie, with constantly changing stock. Prices from £100. Also sell evening dresses, ballgowns, bridesmaids dresses, shoes, veils, mother-of-the-bride and groom outfits and a selection of christening wear. Also offers formal wear hire for men and boys, as well as wedding dress hire.

MATALAN

MADFORD RETAIL PARK, WARE ROAD, HERTFORD, HERTFORDSHIRE SG13 7EZ, ☎ 01992 512820, FAX: 01992 589515, www.matalan.co.uk, 10–8 MON–FRI, 9–6 SAT, 11–4 SUN.

DANESTRETE, STEVENAGE, HERTFORDSHIRE SG1 1XR, ☎ 01438 312433, FAX: 01438 312377, www.matalan.co.uk, 9–6 MON–SAT, 10–4 SUN. **PERMANENT DISCOUNT OUTLET**

See page 89 (BEDS)

MILLANO

GALLERIA OUTLET CENTRE, COMET WAY, HATFIELD, HERTFORDSHIRE AL10 0XR, ☎ 01707 259199, 10–8 MON–FRI, 10–6 SAT, 11–5 SUN. **FACTORY SHOP IN A FACTORY SHOPPING VILLAGE**

One of more than 70 shops in this glass and steel factory shopping centre straddling the A1. This outlet sells designer suede, leather and sheepskin jackets, coats and trousers for men, women and children at discount prices. Of particular interest are the highly fashionable Toscana lamb's coats. Larger than average sizes can sometimes be made on request. Prices can be up to 60% cheaper than in the high street, with samples, overruns or slight seconds as well as a selection of last and current season's perfects. Also stocked are leather and sheepskin soft furnishings such as beanbags, throws, cushions, etc and a selection of leather handbags and belts.

QD STORES

29 TOWN SQUARE, 38 QUEENSWAY, STEVENAGE, HERTFORDSHIRE SG1 1BP, ☎ 01438 747437, 9–5.30 MON–SAT. **PERMANENT DISCOUNT OUTLET**

See page 89 (BEDS)

R S SHOES

35 BRIDLINGTON ROAD, SOUTH OXHEY, WATFORD, HERTFORDSHIRE WD1 6AE, ☎ 020 8421 2592, 9–5 MON–SAT. **PERMANENT DISCOUNT OUTLET**

Sells men's, women's and children's shoes including Dr Martens, Kickers, Wrangler and CAT.

TK MAXX

UNIT 30–31, A1 GALLERIA, COMET WAY, HATFIELD, HERTFORDSHIRE AL10 0XR, ☎ 01707 260066, www.tkmaxx.com, 10–8 MON–FRI, 8.30 ON THUR, 9–7 SAT, 11–5 SUN.

UNIT 50, 18 THE MALTINGS, ST ALBANS, HERTFORDSHIRE AL1 3HL, ☎ 01727 855999, www.tkmaxx.com, 9.30–6 MON–TUE, 9.30–7 WED–FRI, 9–6 SAT, 11–5 SUN.

UNIT 10, FORUM SHOPPING CENTRE, STEVENAGE, HERTFORDSHIRE SG1 1ES, ☎ 01438 728408, www.tkmaxx.com, 9.30–8 MON–FRI, 9.30–6 SAT, 11–5 SUN. **PERMANENT DISCOUNT OUTLET**

See page 89 (BEDS)

TOG 24

GALLERIA OUTLET CENTRE, COMET WAY, HATFIELD, HERTFORDSHIRE AL10 0XS, ☎ 01707 258088, **e-mail:** mail-order@tog24.com, www.tog24.com, 10–8 MON–FRI, 10–6 SAT, 11–5 SUN. **FACTORY SHOP IN A FACTORY SHOPPING VILLAGE**

See page 99 (CHESH)

WALKER & HALL

GALLERIA OUTLET CENTRE, COMET WAY, HATFIELD, HERTFORDSHIRE AL10 0X5, FAX: 01707 270121, www.goldsmiths.co.uk, 10–8 MON–FRI, 9- 6 SAT, 11–5 SUN. **FACTORY SHOP IN A FACTORY SHOPPING VILLAGE**

See page 100 (CHESH)

KENT

AUTONOMY

MCARTHURGLEN DESIGNER OUTLET ASHFORD, KIMBERLEY WAY, ASHFORD, JUNCTION 10 OF M20, KENT TN24 0SD, ☎ 01233 646730, 10–6 MON–FRI, 8 ON THUR, 9–6 SAT, 11–5 SUN. **FACTORY SHOP IN A FACTORY SHOPPING VILLAGE**

See page 93 (CHESH)

BIG L FACTORY OUTLET

UNITS 70 & 71, MCARTHURGLEN DESIGNER OUTLET ASHFORD, KIMBERLEY WAY, ASHFORD, JUNCTION 10 OF M20, KENT TN24 0SD, ☎ 01233 621149, FAX: 01233 621149, 10–6 MON–FRI, 8 ON THUR, 9–6 SAT, 11–5 SUN. **FACTORY SHOP IN A FACTORY SHOPPING VILLAGE**

See page 93 (CHESH)

CATALOGUE BARGAIN SHOP

19A PRESTON STREET, FAVERSHAM, KENT ME13 8NZ, ☎ 01795 591203, www.bargaincrazy.com, 9–5.30 MON–SAT, 10–4 SUN. **PERMANENT DISCOUNT OUTLET**

See page 92 (CAMBS)

CLARKS FACTORY SHOP

UNITS 44–47 RETAIL OUTLET VILLAGE, ASHFORD, KENT TN24 0SD, ☎ 01233 637562, 10–6 MON–SAT, 8 ON THUR, 11–5 SUN. **FACTORY SHOP**

168 HIGH STREET, CHATHAM, KENT ME4 4AS, ☎ 01634 845215, 9–5.30 MON–SAT. **FACTORY SHOP**

See page 94 (CHESH)

DE BRADELEI WHARF

DE BRADELEI WHARF (DOVER) LTD, CAMBRIDGE ROAD, DOVER, KENT CT17 9BY, ☎ 01304 226616, FAX: 01304 226636, 9.30–5.30 MON–FRI, 9.30–6 SAT, 11–5 SUN. **PERMANENT DISCOUNT OUTLET**

Large outlet in superb maritime setting just off the Dover Seafront, selling top brand names for all the family, including shoes. The womenswear includes such names as Paul Costelloe,

Dannimac, Windsmoor, Planet, Precis Petite, Alexon, Kaliko, Eastex, Minuet Petite, Country Casuals, Elle, French Connection, Tigi Wear, plus top American and German designer labels, handbags and much more including a new accessory department. The menswear range includes underwear, socks, coats, sweaters, jackets, suits and trousers from labels such as Wolsey, Countrywear, French Connection, Virgin and Tog 24. Robert Leonard's Menswear provide Greiff, Pierre Cardin, Gabicci, Gurteen, Oakman, Saville Row, John Slim and many more. For children, there are brands such as OshKosh B'Gosh, Lily by Lily, Smarties, Vitamins, Rebble Pebble, Zip-Zap, O'Neill, MCA and Hickory as well as fluffy toys and melamine tableware with Pokemon and Toy Story 2 designs as well as a new department selling clothing, shoes, books and scientific toys. There is a large shoe department featuring international shoes for all the family and a wonderful Home Furnishings Department. The Interior Design shops sell bedding, towels, top-name furnishing fabric, cushions, throws, furniture and curtains. The Glass and China Department has an amazing selection from Waterford/Wedgwood, Stuart Crystal, Royal Doulton, Arthur Price of England Silverware, Staffordshire Tableware, Churchill, Cloverleaf, Hornsea Pottery, Cristal d'Arques and much more. There is superb Liberty shop in the giftware department and a Cromwell and Morgan Cook Shop. Parking is easy with a large car park behind the store. The Waves Coffee Shop is open all day, serving delicious home-cooked food.

GAP

MCARTHURGLEN DESIGNER OUTLET ASHFORD, KIMBERLEY WAY, ASHFORD, JUNCTION 10 OF M20, KENT TN23 1EZ, ☎ 01233 663951, 10–6 MON–FRI, 8 ON THUR, 9–6 SAT, 11–5 SUN.

FACTORY SHOP IN A FACTORY SHOPPING VILLAGE

Gap sells casual clothes for men, women, children and babies. Deliveries at this factory outlet are only six to eight weeks behind the high street, so this is not old stock. Discounts can be as much as 70%. There is a children's play area, restaurants and free car parking.

HANGERS

53 CROYDON ROAD, BECKENHAM, KENT BR3 4AB, ☎ 020 8658 5386, 9.30–5.30 MON–SAT.

DRESS AGENCY

Mixture of high street and designer labels including Valentino, Boss, Windsmoor, Planet and Country Casuals. For men, there are suits, jackets, coats, shirts, trousers, ties and shoes. For women, day and evening wear, dresses, skirts, tops, hats and shoes. Prices range from £5 to £100.

LEE COOPER

MCARTHURGLEN DESIGNER OUTLET ASHFORD, KIMBERLEY WAY, ASHFORD, JUNCTION 10 OF M20, KENT TN24 0SD, ☎ 01233 611186, 10–6 MON–SAT, 8 ON THUR, 11–5 SUN.

FACTORY SHOP IN A FACTORY SHOPPING VILLAGE

See page 96 (CHESH)

LILLEY & SKINNER

MCARTHURGLEN DESIGNER OUTLET ASHFORD, KIMBERLEY WAY, ASHFORD, JUNCTION 10 OF M20, KENT TN24 0SD, ☎ 01233 623963, 10–6 MON–SAT, 10–8 THUR, 11–5 SUN.

FACTORY SHOP IN A FACTORY SHOPPING VILLAGE

See page 109 (DERBY)

LITTLEWOODS CATALOGUE OUTLET STORE

MCARTHURGLEN DESIGNER OUTLET ASHFORD, KIMBERLEY WAY, ASHFORD, JUNCTION 10 OF M20, KENT TN24 0SD, ☎ 01233 625242, 10–6 MON–FRI, 8 ON THUR, 9–6 SAT, 11–5 SUN. **FACTORY SHOP IN A FACTORY SHOPPING VILLAGE**

Littlewoods clearance shops offer up to 70% off the catalogue price for clothing and offer big discounts off electrical goods. Stock changes constantly and varies from day to day but can include well-known brand names such as Berlei and Gossard lingerie, Vivienne Westwood, Pamplemousse leisurewear, Nike and Adidas sports shoes, and Timberland and Caterpillar footwear. Stock depends on the size and location of the shop: larger shops get the longer discontinued runs, while smaller shops get overruns with only a small amount of colour and size variations left. Littlewoods also runs a mobile shop which operates in cities which don't have a sale shop. For details of venues for the sales, which usually take place once a month, write to Melanie Lamb, c/o Crosby DC Kershaw Avenue, Endbutt Lane, Crosby, Merseyside L70 1AH.

MARKS & SPENCER

MCARTHURGLEN DESIGNER OUTLET VILLAGE, KIMBERLEY WAY, ASHFORD, JUNCTION 10 OF M20, KENT TN24 0SD, ☎ 01233 662418, 9–6 MON–FRI, SAT, 8 ON THUR, 11–5 SUN. **FACTORY SHOP IN A FACTORY SHOPPING VILLAGE**

See page 96 (CHESH)

MATALAN

BROOKFIELD ROAD, ASHFORD, KENT TN24 8ME, ☎ 01233 898460, FAX: 01233 661438, www.matalan.co.uk, 10–8 MON–FRI, 9–6 SAT, 11–5 SUN.

STOUR RETAIL PARK, STURRY ROAD, CANTERBURY, KENT CT1 1AD, ☎ 01227 817910, FAX: 01227 764860, www.matalan.co.uk, 10–8 MON–FRI, 9–7 SAT, 10–4 SUN.

BROADWAY SHOPPING CENTRE, THE BROADWAY, MAIDSTONE, KENT ME16 8PS, ☎ 01622 675153, FAX: 01622 672841, www.matalan.co.uk, 10–8 MON–FRI, 9–6 SAT, 10–4 SUN.

STROOD RETAIL PARK, COMMERCIAL ROAD, STROOD, KENT ME2 2JG, ☎ 01634 731670, FAX: 01634 718048, www.matalan.co.uk, 10–8 MON–FRI, 9–6 SAT, 11–5 SUN.

WESTWOOD RETAIL PARK, WESTWOOD ROAD, BROADSTAIRS, THANET, KENT CT10 2RQ, ☎ 01843 608700, FAX: 01843 871248, www.matalan.co.uk, 10–8 MON–FRI, 9–6 SAT, 11–5 SUN. **PERMANENT DISCOUNT OUTLET**

See page 89 (BEDS)

MCARTHURGLEN DESIGNER OUTLET CENTRE

KIMBERLEY WAY, ASHFORD, JUNCTION 10 OF M20, KENT TN24 0SD, ☎ 01233 895900, www.mcarthurglen.com/ashford, 10–6 MON–FRI, 8 ON THUR, 9–6 SAT, 11–5 SUN. **FACTORY SHOPPING VILLAGE**

Voted 'Retail Destination of the Year' 2001 in the Retail Week awards, the McArthurGlen Designer Outlet Ashford in Kent is one of Europe's most spectacular shopping destinations. The outlet offers over 70 top brands and designer labels at up to 50% off typical retail prices. There is a food court, cafés, a children's play area, and parking for over 1,500 cars. A shuttle bus runs between the town centre, station and the outlet every eight minutes. Shops include: Ben Sherman, Cotton Traders, Designer Room/Classic Room, Daks, Fire Trap, Gap, Lee Cooper, Levi's Littlewoods Catalogue Outlet, Marks and Spencer, Mexx, Miss Sixty, Mountain Warehouse, Pilot, Polo Jeans Co. Factory Store, Proudfoot, Roman Originals, Thomas Pink, Tog 24, Tommy Hilfiger, Warehouse, Warner's, Windsmoor, Baron Jon, Ben Sherman, Cotton Traders, Daks, Fire Trap, Fred Perry, Gap, Lee Cooper, Levi's, Petroleum, Proudfoot, Suits You, The Suit Company, Thomas Pink, Van Heusen, Woodhouse, Donnay, Fila, Gap, JoKids, Mexx, Nike, Reebok, Toyzone, Clarks, Ecco, Jane Shilton Kiplings, Lilley & Skinner, Soled Out, Antler, Kipling, Samsonite Company Stores. Arran Aromatics, Body Shop, Chapelle Jewellery, Claire's Outlet, Gizmo, One 2 One, Picture Port, Revlon, Sekonda, Sunglass Hut International, Watch Station, Walker and Hall, Woods of Windsor, Bed and Bath Works, Bookends, Bose, China Place, Cloverleaf, Design House, Edinburgh Crystal, Le Creuset, Mountain Warehouse, Price's Candles, Professional Cookware Company, Spiegelau, Waterford Wedgwood, Whittard of Chelsea, XS Music and Video.

PJN DISCOUNT

UNIT IB, EDDINGTON BUSINESS PARK, THANET WAY, HERNE BAY, KENT CT6 5TT, ☎ 01227 741112, FAX: 01227 365123, 9–5.30 MON–SAT, 10–4 SUN. **FACTORY SHOP**

Discontinued styles, slight seconds and end of line adult and children's shoes displayed in a 6,000 square foot warehouse with up to 10,000 pairs of shoes at any one time. Clarks, Lee, Pods, Lotus, Equity, Hush Puppies and Hi-Tec sportswear are typical names, available at up to 35% reductions. A GDD reader bought a pair of Clarks children's shoes for £20, usual price £29; and two pairs of sandals for £10 and £12, usual price, £29.95 and £34.95. Also sell bags. Small refreshment area, car parking and wheelchair accessibility. Also have a good range of clothing for men and women at very reasonable prices. For example, two pairs of men's trousers, £25; women's suit, £29.99. Labels include Klass and Elite, among others. Stock is constantly changing, so go with an open mind.

SUITS YOU

LOWER ROSE GALLERY, BLUEWATER, GREENHITHE, KENT DA9 9SN, ☎ 01322 624963, 10–9 MON–FRI, 9–8 SAT, 11–5 SUN. **FACTORY SHOP**

See page 91 (BRIS)

T J HUGHES

THE CHEQUERS SHOPPING CENTRE, PADS HILL, MAIDSTONE, KENT ME15 6AT, ☎ 01622 771600, FAX: 01622 753374, **e-mail:** info@tjhughes.co.uk, www.tjhughes.co.uk, 9–5.30 MON–SAT, 10–4 SUN. **PERMANENT DISCOUNT OUTLET**

See page 98 (CHESH)

THE FACTORY SHOP LTD

THE FOREMAN CENTRE, HIGH STREET, HEADCORN, KENT TN27 9NE, ☎ 01622 891651, 9–5.30 MON–SAT, 10–4 SUN. **FACTORY SHOP**

See page 98 (CHESH)

TK MAXX

BROADWAY SQUARE, BEXLEYHEATH BROADWAY, BEXLEYHEATH, KENT, ☎ 020 8301 0508, www.tkmaxx.com, 9–6 MON–SAT, 9 ON THUR, 10–4 SUN. **PERMANENT DISCOUNT OUTLET**

See page 89 (BEDS)

TOG 24

MCARTHURGLEN DESIGNER OUTLET ASHFORD, KIMBERLEY WAY, ASHFORD, JUNCTION 10 OF M20, KENT TN24 0SD, ☎ 01233 647357, **e-mail:** mail-order@tog24.com, www.tog24.com, 10–6 MON–FRI, 8 ON THUR, 9–6 SAT, 11–5 SUN.

DE BRADLEI WHARF, CAMBRIDGE ROAD, DOVER, KENT CT17 9BY, ☎ 01304 216126, **e-mail:** mail-order@tog24.com, www.tog24.com, 9.30–5.30 MON–FRI, 9.30–6 SAT, 11–5 SUN. **FACTORY SHOP IN A FACTORY SHOPPING VILLAGE**

See page 99 (CHESH)

TOMMY HILFIGER

UNIT 5 MCARTHUR GLEN DESIGNER OUTLET, KIMBERLEY WAY, ASHFORD, KENT TN24 0SD, ☎ 01233 646622, FAX: 01233 645375, www.tommy.com, 10–6 MON–SAT, 8 ON THUR, 11–5 SUN. **FACTORY SHOP IN A FACTORY SHOPPING VILLAGE**

See page 99 (CHESH)

WALKER & HALL

MCARTHURGLEN DESIGNER OUTLET ASHFORD, KIMBERLEY WAY, ASHFORD, JUNCTION 10 OF M20, KENT TN24 0SD, ☎ 01233 612 233, www.goldsmiths.co.uk, 10–6 MON–FRI, 8 ON THUR, 9- 6 SAT, 11–5 SUN. **FACTORY SHOP IN A FACTORY SHOPPING VILLAGE**

See page 100 (CHESH)

WARNERS

UNIT 12, DESIGNER OUTLET VILLAGE, KIMBERLEY WAY, ASHFORD, KENT TN24 0SD, ☎ 01233 636036, 10–6 MON–FRI, 8 ON THUR, 9–6 SAT, 11–5 SUN. **FACTORY SHOP IN A FACTORY SHOPPING VILLAGE**

See page 100 (CHESH)

WOODHOUSE

UNIT 60, MCARTHUR GLEN DESIGNER OUTLET, KIMBERLEY WAY, ASHFORD, KENT TN24 0SD, ☎ 01233 621913, 10–6 MON–SAT, 8 ON THUR, 10.30–5.30 SUN. **FACTORY SHOP IN A FACTORY SHOPPING VILLAGE**

WESTERN MALL, LOWER GUILDHALL, BLUEWATER, GREENHITHE, KENT DA9 9SN, ☎ 01322 624 967, 10–9 MON–FRI, 9–8 SAT, 11–5 SUN. **FACTORY SHOP IN A FACTORY SHOPPING VILLAGE**

See page 80 (CHESH)

LANCASHIRE

AFFLECK'S PALACE

52 CHURCH STREET, MANCHESTER, LANCASHIRE M4 1PW, ☎ 0161 834 2039, FAX: 0161 839 9541, **e-mail:** theboss@affleck'spalace.co.uk, www.affleck's-palace.co.uk, 10–5.30 MON–FRI, 10–6 SAT. **SECONDHAND AND VINTAGE CLOTHES**

Indoor fashion market specialising in street and alternative fashion such as Seventies' fashion including platform shoes, Fifties' and Sixties' nostalgia, outfits from the Twenties' to the present day and new designer clothes. Also jewellery, rubber clothes, body piercing, tattooing (and exclusively black henna tattooing) and hair extensions. Two cafés and two hairdressers, offering hair beading, on site.

BARDEN MILL SHOP

BARDEN LANE, BURNLEY, LANCASHIRE BB12 0DX, ☎ 01282 420333, FAX: 01282 420336, **e-mail:** info@bardenmillshop.co.uk, 10–6 MON–SAT, 11–5 SUN (LATE NIGHTS TILL 8 THUR APRIL–SEPTEMBER). **FACTORY SHOP**

A true working mill full of bargains, most of which are high street brands at discounted prices. Full range of branded and non-branded merchandise includes Ladieswear from Tagg, Ambience, Affinity, Diva Design, Donna Bella, Prima Casamia, plus Solo from Italy and Camille lingerie; BMB Menswear from Jeff Banks, Regatta, Gola, Le Shark, Centaur, Jonathan Adams, Carabou, Umbro, Bentley, Alexandre and Gibson. Plus Musbury Fabrics selling towels, bedding, fabrics, curtains, from Dorma, Fogarty, Whiteheads, SMD Curtains, Zorbit and Swatch Box. Briggs Shoes with shoes for men, women and children from Hotter, Sterling and Hunt, Van Dal, Gabor and Hotter Subs. Plus Hothouse selling gifts, furniture, pictures, mirrors, candles, kitchenware, lighting, dried flowers, Staffordshire pottery, crystal and glassware. There is also a luggage, books and market stall section. A 140-seat tea room, ample frre car and coach parking, disabled access and facilities and weekend boat trips and organised midweek tours.

BARNEYS

JULIA STREET, LANCASHIRE M3 1LN, ☎ 0161 833 0533, FAX: 0161 832 5223, **e-mail:** info@barneys-stores.co.uk, www.barneys-stores.co.uk, 9.30–5.30 MON–FRI, 7 ON THUR, 9.30–6 SAT, 11–5 SUN. **PERMANENT DISCOUNT OUTLET**

Versace, Prada, Paul Smith, Armani, Boss, Diesel, Calvin Klein, Iceberg, Moschino, Gianfranco Ferre and Gucci at around half their normal retail value. Prices range from about £20 for a pair of designer sunglasses up to as much as £500 for a Versace suit.

BOHEMIA PERIOD CLOTHING

11 WARNER STREET, ACCRINGTON, LANCASHIRE BB51HN, ☎ 01254 231119, 10.30–5 TUE, THUR, FRI, SAT, CLOSED MON, WED. **SECONDHAND AND VINTAGE CLOTHES**

Specialises in Fifties, Sixties and Seventies gear, although their clothing and accessories date from the Forties.

BOUNDARY MILL STORES

BURNLEY ROAD, COLNE, LANCASHIRE BB8 8LS, ☎ 01282 865229, www.boundarymill.co.uk, 10–6 MON–FRI, 9 ON THUR, 9–6 SAT, 11–5 SUN, 10–6 BANK HOLIDAYS, OPENS AT 10 ON SUNDAYS FOR BREAKFAST AND BROWSING, PURCHASES CAN BE MADE FROM 11. **PERMANENT DISCOUNT OUTLET**

One of the largest clearance stores in Britain, it covers more than 100,000 square feet with over 300 quality brands, all now under one roof. Many of the top end of the high street designer labels are on sale here for both women and men. Women's labels include: Alexon, Windsmoor, Austin Reed, Eastex, Planet, Jaeger, Jacques Vert, Liz Claiborne and Viyella. Men's labels include: Austin Reed, Centaur, Dannimac, Farah, Pierre Cardin, Lyle & Scott and Yves St Laurent. The women's and men's departments are very extensive – not to mention impressive – and cover the whole range from casual to evening wear with reductions of between 30% and 70%. There are also large leisurewear departments for women and men including Polo Ralph Lauren, Timberland, Wrangler and Tog 24, and a whole floor dedicated to women's lingerie. The new extension building, which links the fashion and home stores, contains a massive shoe department stocking Bally, Nine West and Hush Puppies, among others. On the ground floor, there is a huge new cookshop stocking up-to-the-minute ranges and a greatly extended luggage department including

Globetrotter, Antler and Jane Shilton. The home store sells brand-name home furnishings, glass and china including Dorma, Sanderson, Denby, Edinburgh Crystal, Dartington Crystal, Portmeirion, Royal Worcester, Villeroy & Boch and Wedgwood. Four times a year, there are special sales at which prices are discounted further. Most of the stock is end of lines with the occasional marked seconds. There is a choice of food outlets: a large coffee shop, a restaurant and a pub, and there is extensive free parking.

BRAND CENTRE

1 STANLEY ROAD, WHITEFIELD, BURY, MANCHESTER, LANCASHIRE M45 6GT, ☎ 0161 796 2525, 10–8 MON–FRI, 9.30–6.30 SAT, 11–5 SUN. **PERMANENT DISCOUNT OUTLET**

Not a discount store as such, this department store stocking this season's fashions guarantees lower prices than any other UK competitor in non-sale periods. Stock includes menswear, womenswear, kidswear, lingerie, footwear, accessories and perfumes. Brands sold on a regular basis include Calvin Klein jeans, Calvin Klein underwear, Diesel, DKNY Jeans, DKNY Kids, Kenzo Kids, Kickers, French Connection, Morgan, Moschino Mare, Osh Kosh, Ted Baker, Versace Classic V2 and Yves St Laurent. A membership scheme operates with extra benefits such as big discounts on blue cross days and special sale previews. Membership costs just £3.

BRIGGS SHOES

BARDEN MILL, BARDEN LANE, BURNLEY, LANCASHIRE BB12 0DX, ☎ 01282 420333, FAX: 01282 420336, www.briggsshoes.co.uk, 10–6 MON–SAT, 10–5 SUN.

205 MARINE ROAD, MORECAMBE, LANCASHIRE LA4 4BU, ☎ 01524 419293, FAX: 01524 419293, www.briggsshoes.co.uk, 10–5.30 MON–SAT, 10.30–4.30 SUN. **PERMANENT DISCOUNT OUTLET**

See page 105 (CUMB)

CATALOGUE BARGAIN SHOP

UNIT 1, EASTGATE RETAIL PARK, ACCRINGTON, LANCASHIRE BB5 6PW, ☎ 01254 879195, www.bargaincrazy.com, 9–8 MON–FRI, 9–6 SAT, 10.30–4.30 SUN.

KINGSWAY, BURNLEY, LANCASHIRE BB11 1AB, ☎ 01282 420202, www.bargaincrazy.com, 9–5 MON–SAT, 7 ON THUR, 10.30–4.30 SUN.

40–42 MARKET STREET, CHORLEY, LANCASHIRE PR7 2SE, ☎ 012572 68325, www.bargaincrazy.com, 9–5.30 MON–SAT, 10.30–4.30 SUN.

HALL BANK, WORSLEY RD, PATRICROFT, ECCLES, MANCHESTER, LANCASHIRE M30 8NR, ☎ 0161 787 7726, www.bargaincrazy.com, 9–8 MON–SAT, 9 ON THUR, FRI, 11–5 SUN.

UNIT 3, THE PARSONAGE RETAIL PARK, LEIGH, LANCASHIRE WN7 5SJ, ☎ 01942 671911, www.bargaincrazy.com, 9–8 MON–FRI, 9–6 SAT, 11–5 SUN. 10–5.30 MON–FRI, 8 ON THUR, 9–5 SAT, 10.30–4.30 SUN.

UNITS 1–2, HIGH STREET, HULME, MANCHESTER, LANCASHIRE M15 5AF, ☎ 0161 226 5379, www.bargaincrazy.com, 9–5. MON–SAT. 10.30–4.30 SUN.

1318–1324 ASHTON OLD ROAD, OPENSHAW, MANCHESTER, LANCASHIRE M11 1JG, ☎ 0161 371 8243, www.bargaincrazy.com, 9–5.30 MON–SAT.

2 BURY OLD ROAD, CHEETHAM HILL, MANCHESTER, LANCASHIRE M8 7JN, ☎ 0161 795 9312, FAX: 0161 7407 274, www.bargaincrazy.com, 9–5.30 MON–SAT

UNIT 4, QUEENS RETAIL PARK, QUEENS STREET, PRESTON, LANCASHIRE PR1 4HZ, ☎ 01772 884104, www.bargaincrazy.com, 9–8 MON–FRI, 9–6 SAT, 10.30–4.30 SUN.

82–83 EGARTON WALK, ELLESMERE CENTRE, WALKDEN, MANCHESTER, LANCASHIRE M28 3ZD, ☎ 0161 703 9311, www.bargaincrazy.com, 9–5.30 MON–SAT. **PERMANENT DISCOUNT OUTLET**

See page 92 (CAMBS)

CRAGHOPPERS

FREEPORT SHOPPING VILLAGE, ANCHORAGE ROAD, FLEETWOOD, LANCASHIRE FY7 6AE, ☎ 01253 778372, FAX: 01253 778372, www.regatta.com, 10–6 MON–WED, 10–8 THUR, FRI, 10–6 SAT, SUN. **FACTORY SHOP IN A FACTORY SHOPPING VILLAGE**

Craghoppers, the innovator in travel and outdoor wear, is a technical brand that leads with innovation. Its offering of waterproofs, fleece, wovens and rucksacks are intended for travel at home or abroad and suitable for a wide range of climates. All stock is sold at a discount of at least 30%.

DALE MILL DISCOUNTS

DALE STREET, MILNROW, NEAR ROCHDALE, LANCASHIRE OL16 3NJ, ☎ 01706 359737, 9.30–6 MON–WED, FRI, 9.30–8 THUR, 9.30–5.30 SAT, 10–5.30 SUN. **PERMANENT DISCOUNT OUTLET**

A wide range of items from clothes and shoes for all the family to kitchenware, furniture, tablecloths, beds and bedding, television's and general electrical goods, fridges, cookers, microwaves, kitchen and bedroom fittings and units, all on sale at discounted prices. On site there is also a designer clothes store and sportswear outlet, plus a new conservatory extension selling glassware, pottery, dried flowers, table lamps and other household goods.

DALESWEAR FACTORY OUTLET

LAUNDRY LANE, INGLETON, VIA CARNFORTH, LANCASHIRE LA6 3DF, ☎ 01524 241047, www.daleswear.co.uk, 9–5 MON–SAT, 9.30–5 SUN. **FACTORY SHOP**

Manufacturers and direct retailers of fleeces, waterproofs, caving suits and bags. Also children's fleeces, waterproofs and accessories. Non-standard sizes a speciality. They also stock boots, maps, walking poles etc.

DAMART

85–87 DEANE ROAD, BOLTON, LANCASHIRE BL3 5AG, ☎ 01204 524608, 9.30–5 MON–SAT. **FACTORY SHOP**

See page 114 (DORS)

DIRECT SPECS LTD

60 GREAT MOOR STREET, BOLTON, LANCASHIRE BL1 1SN, ☎ 01204 528555, www.directspecs.co.uk, 9–5 MON–SAT.

30 STANDISHGATE, WIGAN, LANCASHIRE WN1 1QH, ☎ 01942 493949, www.directspecs.co.uk, 9–5 MON–SAT. **PERMANENT DISCOUNT OUTLET**

See page 95 (CHESH)

DOUBLE TWO

FREEPORT SHOPPING VILLAGE, FLEETWOOD, LANCASHIRE, ☎ 01253 777117, 10–6 MON–WED AND SAT–SUN, 10–8 THUR–FRI. **FACTORY SHOP IN A FACTORY SHOPPING VILLAGE**

See page 116 (ESSEX)

ECHOES

650A HALIFAX ROAD, EASTWOOD, TODMORDEN, LANCASHIRE OL14 6DW, ☎ 01706 817505, 11–6 WED–SAT, 12–5 SUN. **SECONDHAND AND VINTAGE CLOTHES**

Stocks period clothing for men and women from the Victorian era to the 1960s, as well as accessories such as hats, bags, scarves, shoes and jewellery. There is also a selection of linen and lace.

FREEPORT FLEETWOOD OUTLET VILLAGE

ANCHORAGE ROAD, FLEETWOOD, 12 MILES FROM JUNCTION 3 OF M55, LANCASHIRE FY7 6AE, ☎ 01253 877377, www.freeportfleetwood.com, 10–6 SEVEN DAYS A WEEK, 8 ON THUR, FRI. **FACTORY SHOPPING VILLAGE**

Large, brightly-coloured New-England-style seaside shopping village. There are more than 40 shops selling at up to 50% off high street prices, as well as restaurants, family attractions and free parking. Women's fashions include Next to Nothing, Spotlight, Easy Jeans, VF Corp, Double Two, Warner's, Edinburgh Woollen Mill, The Designer Room, Giorgio, BhS for Less, Madhouse and Roman Originals. For men, there is Petroleum, Ciro Citterio, Double Two, Giorgio, VF Corp, Madhouse, Easy Jeans and BhS for Less. Sportswear and outdoor wear shops include Sports Mill, Craghoppers, Regatta and VF Corp. Footwear outlets comprise Lilley & Skinner, Jane Shilton, Shoe Sellers, BhS For Less, Next to Nothing and Petroleum. Sweet-toothed visitors can indulge at Thorntons or The Sweet Shop, and there is Julian Graves for nuts and dried fruits. Household outlets include Ponden Mill, Dartington Crystal, Home Zone, Picture Port and China Traders.

Childrenswear stockists include Next to Nothing, BhS for Less, Vecopri, VF Corp and Giorgio. Other stores include Woods of Windsor, Hallmark Cards and Gifts, XS Music & Video, Claire's Accessories, Watch Store and Book Depot.

GIFTTREE

CHURCHBRIDGE WORKS, HENRY STREET, ACCRINGTON, LANCASHIRE BB5 4EU, ☎ 01254 237324, 9–5 MON–SAT

REEDYFORD MILL, WESTFIELD ROAD, NELSON, LANCASHIRE BB9 7YM, ☎ 01282 619540, FAX: 01282 696639, 9–5 MON–SAT
PERMANENT DISCOUNT OUTLET

See page 108 (DERBY)

K SHOES FACTORY SHOP

UNIT 3, CLIFTON RETAIL PARK, BLACKPOOL, LANCASHIRE FY4 4RA, ☎ 01253 699380, 9.30–6 MON–FRI, 7 ON THUR, 9.30–5.30 SAT, 11–5 SUN.

18–19 WILLIAMSON SQUARE, LIVERPOOL, LANCASHIRE L1 LEJ, ☎ 0151 708 7564, 9.30–5.30 MON–SAT, 11–4 SUN. **FACTORY SHOP**

See page 105 (CUMB)

LAMBERT HOWARTH FOOTWEAR

GREENBRIDGE WORKS, FALBARN ROAD, OFF BOCHOLT WAY, RAWTENSTALL, ROSSENDALE, LANCASHIRE BB4 7NX, ☎ 01706 235160, FAX: 01706 235129, 9.30–5 MON–FRI, 9.30–4 SAT, 10–4 SUN. **FACTORY SHOP**
A real mixture of seconds and perfects. They sell clothes, handbags and towels. The seconds in footwear are from shoes made for major high street chainstores and all are at discounted prices. These include slippers, walking boots, flat shoes and sandals for men, women and children. The perfects in clothes, towels and bags are two-thirds of the high street prices. They also stock a large selection of pottery. There is an on-site creche and coffee shop serving drinks and light refreshments, wheelchair access and disabled facilities, plus free car parking.

LAMBERT HOWARTH MILL SHOP

FINSLEY GATE, BURNLEY, LANCASHIRE, ☎ 01282 471283, 9.30–5 MON–FRI, 9–4 SAT.
FACTORY SHOP
A real mixture of seconds from their own factories and perfects from other sources – footwear, clothes, handbags and towels. The seconds in footwear are from shoes made for major high street chainstores and all are at discounted prices. These include slippers, walking boots, flat shoes and sandals for men, women and children. The perfects in clothes, towels and bags are two-thirds of the high street prices. Also sells home furnishings, pottery and curtains, from Marks & Spencer.

LANDS' END DIRECT MERCHANTS

THE LOWRY CENTRE, THE QUAYS, SALFORD, MANCHESTER, LANCASHIRE, ☎ 0161 848 7923, 10–8 MON–FRI, 9–7 SAT, 11 0 5 SUN. **FACTORY SHOP**

See page 90 (BERKS)

LILLEY & SKINNER

FREEPORT VILLAGE, ANCHORAGE ROAD, FLEETWOOD, LANCASHIRE FY7 9AE, ☎ 01253 877377, 10–6 SEVEN DAYS A WEEK, 8 ON THUR, FRI.

THE MANCHESTER OUTLET MALL AT THE LOWRY, THE QUAYS, SALFORD QUAYS, NEAR MANCHESTER LANCASHIRE M5 2SQ, ☎ 0161 848 1800, 10–8 MON–FRI, 9–7 SAT, 11 0 5 SUN. **FACTORY SHOP IN A FACTORY SHOPPING VILLAGE**

See page 109 (DERBY)

LITTLEWOODS CATALOGUE DISCOUNT STORE

185 STAMFORD STREET, ASHTON-UNDER-LYNE, LANCASHIRE OL6 7PY, ☎ 0161 339 0966, 9–5.30 MON–SAT.

UNIT 2, KINGS STREET, FARNWORTH, LANCASHIRE BL4 7AZ, ☎ 01204 861464, 9–5.30 MON–SAT, 10.30–4.30 SUN.

69–74 LORD STREET, FLEETWOOD, LANCASHIRE FY7 6DS, ☎ 01253 773418, 9–5.30 MON–SAT, 10.30–4.30 SUN.

UNIT 3, MONUMENT BUILDINGS, LONDON ROAD, LIVERPOOL L3 8JY, ☎ 0151 708 6118, 9–5 MON–SAT, 9.30–5.30 TUE, 11–5 SUN.

160 MARINE ROAD, CENTRAL MORECAMBE, LANCASHIRE LA4 4BU, ☎ 01524 412074, 9.30–5.30 MON, 9–5.30 TUE–SAT, 10.30–4.30 SUN. **PERMANENT DISCOUNT OUTLET**

See page 96 (CHESH)

LONDON LEATHERS DIRECT

FREEPORT VILLAGE, ANCHORAGE ROAD, FLEETWOOD, LANCASHIRE FY7 6AE, ☎ 01253 779090, FAX: 01253 770687, 10–6 SEVEN DAYS A WEEK, 8 THUR, FRI.

THE MANCHESTER OUTLET MALL AT THE LOWRY, THE QUAYS, SALFORD QUAYS, NEAR MANCHESTER, LANCASHIRE M5 2SQ, ☎ 0161 848 0480, FAX: 0161 848 0880, 10–8 MON–FRI, 9–7 SAT, 11–5 SUN. **FACTORY SHOP IN A FACTORY SHOPPING VILLAGE**

Superb quality leather and suede jackets, coats and trousers, at discounts of at least 30%, with most at 50% off in this village which features lots of restaurants and fun things for the family.

LOWRY DESIGNER OUTLET

THE QUAYS, SALFORD QUAYS, MANCHESTER, LANCASHIRE M5 2WZ, ☎ 0161 848 1800, FAX: 0161 848 1801, **e-mail:** peter.cronin@emerson.co.uk, www.lowrydesigneroutlet.co.uk, 10–8 MON–FRI, 9–7 SAT, 11–5 SUN. **FACTORY SHOPPING VILLAGE**

A new outlet shopping centre with 80 shops in a site next to the Manchester Ship Canal. The site includes a hotel, Warner Village multiplex cinema, 15 cafés/restaurants and a health and fitness club. It is built alongside the £127 million Lowry Millennium Project for the Arts. The newly-opened Imperial War Museum North, is just a bridge away. Names with outlets here include Whistles, Karen Millen, Cotton Traders, Proibito (selling Moschino, Armani, Diesel, Calvin Klein, Gianfranco Ferre, Replay, Guess, Boss, Fendi and Valentino), Marks & Spencer, Donnay International, Carphone Warehouse, Antler, Scotts and Diadora Italian sportswear, among others.

MATALAN

FOUNTAIN RETAIL PARK, HYNDBURN ROAD, ACCRINGTON LANCASHIRE BB5 4AA, ☎ 01254 356100, FAX: 01254 879037, www.matalan.co.uk, 9.30–8 MON–FRI, 9–6 SAT, 11–5 SUN.

207 LOWER AUDLEY STREET, BLACKBURN, LANCASHIRE BB1 1DG, ☎ 01254 507200, www.matalan.co.uk, 10–8 MON–FRI, 9–6 SAT, 11–5 SUN.

UNIT 2, CLIFTON RETAIL PARK, CLIFTON ROAD, BLACKPOOL, LANCASHIRE FY4 4UJ, ☎ 01253 697850, FAX: 01253 697852, www.matalan.co.uk, 10- 8 MON–FRI, 9–6 SAT, 11–5 SUN.

TURNER BRIDGE, TONGE MOOR ROAD, BOLTON, LANCASHIRE BL2 2DJ, ☎ 01204 383733, FAX: 01204 383542, www.matalan.co.uk, 10–8 MON–FRI, 9–6 SAT, 11–5 SUN.

SEFTON RETAIL PARK, DUNNINGS BRIDGE ROAD, BOOTLE, LIVERPOOL, LANCASHIRE L30 6UU, ☎ 0151 525 1190, FAX: 0151 525 3404, www.matalan.co.uk, 9.30–8 MON–FRI, 9–6 SAT, 11–5 SUN.

FOUNDRY STREET/GEORGE STREET, BURY, LANCASHIRE BL9 0BZ, ☎ 0161 705 4520, FAX: 0161 797 5680, www.matalan.co.uk, 9.30–8 MON–FRI, 9–6 SAT, 11–5 SUN.

NORTH VALLEY RETAIL PARK, NORTH VALLEY ROAD, COLNE, LANCASHIRE BB8 8LU, ☎ 01282 857700, FAX: 01282 859692, www.matalan.co.uk, 10–8 MON–FRI, 9–6 SAT, 11–5 SUN.

LANCASTER RETAIL PARK, MELLISHAW LANE, LANCASTER, LANCASHIRE LA1 5JR, ☎ 01524 541960, FAX: 01524 849911, www.matalan.co.uk, 10–8 MON–FRI, 9–6 SAT, 11–5 SUN.

UNITS G & H, THE TRIUMPH CENTRE, HUNTS CROSS, LIVERPOOL, LANCASHIRE L24 9GB, ☎ 0151 486 0325, FAX: 0151 486 2952, www.matalan.co.uk, 9.30–8 MON–FRI, 9–6 SAT, 11–5 SUN.

BROOKWAY RETAIL PARK, 452 ALTRINCHAM ROAD, BAGULEY, MANCHESTER, LANCASHIRE

M23 9BP, ☎ 0161 902 2500, FAX: 0161 945 1582, www.matalan.co.uk, 9.30–8 MON–FRI, 10–6 SAT, 11–5 SUN.

UNIT 3, ALEXANDRA CENTRE, PARK ROAD, OLDHAM LANCASHIRE OL4 1SG, ☎ 0161 620 6686, FAX: 0161 620 6690, www.matalan.co.uk, 10–8 MON–FRI, 9–6 SAT, 11–5 SUN.

HOLME ROAD, BAMBER BRIDGE, PRESTON, LANCASHIRE PR5 6BP, ☎ 01772 627365, FAX: 01772 314856, www.matalan.co.uk, 10–8 MON–FRI, 9–6 SAT, 11–5 SUN.

CENTRAL RETAIL PARK, OLDHAM ROAD, ROCHDALE, LANCASHIRE OL11 1OZ, ☎ 01706 752320, FAX: 01706 527339, www.matalan.co.uk, 10–8 MON–FRI, 9–6 SAT, 11–5 SUN.

2 WATTS CLIFF WAY, TODD ROAD, ST HELENS, LANCASHIRE WA9 1JL, ☎ 01744 766200, FAX: 01744 750904, www.matalan.co.uk, 9.30–8 MON–FRI, 9–6 SAT, 11–5 SUN

WESTOVER STREET, OFF STATION ROAD, SWINTON, LANCASHIRE M27 2AH, ☎ 0161 794 3441, FAX: 0161 794 3461, www.matalan.co.uk, 10–8 MON–FRI, 9–6 SAT, 11–5 SUN.

LOIRE DRIVE, ROBIN RETAIL PARK, WIGAN, LANCASHIRE WN5 0UH, ☎ 01942 629500, FAX: 01942 217625, www.matalan.co.uk, 10–6 MON–FRI, 10–6 SAT, 11–5 SUN. **PERMANENT DISCOUNT OUTLET**

See page 89 (BEDS)

NEWMANS FOOTWEAR FACTORY SHOP

GARDEN STREET WORKS, BLACKBURN, LANCASHIRE BB2 1TZ, ☎ 01254 676198, 10–6 MON–SAT, 10–4 SUN. **FACTORY SHOP**

Not just a shoes shop selling footwear for men, women and children but also a general product outlet with clothes, bedding, bags, belts, candles, glassware, dried flowers, ceramics and textiles.

NEXT TO NOTHING

FREEPORT SHOPPING VILLAGE, FLEETWOOD, LANCASHIRE L65 9JJ, ☎ 01253 779826, www.next.co.uk, 10–6 MON–SAT, 8 ON THUR, FRI, 12–6 SUN. **FACTORY SHOP IN A FACTORY SHOPPING VILLAGE**

See page 97 (CHESH)

PENDLE VILLAGE SHOPPING OUTLET

HOLLIN BANK, BRIERFIELD, NELSON, JUNCTION 12 OF M65, LANCASHIRE, ☎ 01282 605004 HOMEWARES/01282 605023 FASHION, OPEN 10–5.30 MON–SAT, 10.30–4.30 SUN. **PERMANENT DISCOUNT OUTLET**

A huge mill shop with different areas selling fashion for men and women, home furnishings, bedding, towels, pine and cane furniture, dining sets, three-piece suites, carpets and rugs. The fashion department boasts many famous high street names and features lingerie and footwear while the homewares department offers a wide range of bedding with matching accessories, ready-made curtains, cushions, towels in a wide range of colours and sizes and a collection of cookware and gifts. The furniture showroom offers a wide range of upholstery in modern fabrics, chenilles and leathers; traditional dining room furniture; kitchen sets; pine bedroom, dining and occasional furniture; and an extensive selection of different types of beds. The carpet department offers an extensive selection of rolls and roll ends in carpets and vinyls as well as wood flooring and more than 600 traditional Chinese, Indian and Oriental rugs in a variety of sizes and colours.

PUMPKINS DRESS HIRE

14 ST MARY STREET, MANCHESTER M3 2LB, ☎ 0161 831 7610, FAX: 0161 766 3418, 10–6 MON–SAT, 7 ON THUR. **HIRE SHOP**

Pumpkins stocks over 500 items of women's and mens evening wear at any one time. Shop here and you could find yourself mixing with the stars of Granada Television, to whom the shop is well-known. Dresses start from £40 to hire or to buy. A 20% discount is offered to all students, and a corporate rate can also be arranged with any company within the city. There is a comprehensive range of dresses ranging in sizes from 8 to 26, plus a wide range of accessories for both men and women.

QS FASHION

114–116 BOLTON ROAD, ATHERTON, LANCASHIRE M29 9JZ, ☎ 01942 873847, FAX: 01942 897954, 9–5.30 MON–WED, 9–7 THUR, FRI, 9–5 SAT, 11–5 SUN.

GREEN LANE/PRESTON OLD ROAD, CHERRY TREE, BLACKBURN, LANCASHIRE BB2 5LX, ☎ 01254 209800, FAX: 01254 209833, 10–8 MON–FRI, 10–5.30 SAT, 10–5 SUN.

11–14 PALL MALL, CHORLEY, LANCASHIRE PR7 2LA, ☎ 01257 267113, FAX: 01257 263485, 9–8 MON–FRI, 9–5.30 SAT, 10–4 SUN.

148 MARKET STREET, FARNWORTH, LANCASHIRE BL4 9AE, ☎ 01204 862625, FAX: 01204 701855, 9–5.30 MON–WED, SAT, 9–6 THUR, FRI, 10–4 SUN. **PERMANENT DISCOUNT OUTLET**

See page 97 (CHESH)

QUIGGINS CENTRE

12–16 SCHOOL LANE, LIVERPOOL, LANCASHIRE L1 3BT, ☎ 0151 709 2462, www.quiggins@quiggins.com, 10–6 MON–SAT. **SECONDHAND AND VINTAGE CLOTHES**

There are 45 different shops at the Quiggins Centre, the second biggest market in Liverpool, selling a variety of goods including theatrical and period costumes, secondhand clothes, furniture, bric-a-brac, jewellery, antiques, a café, music shop, and a large tattoo and piercing unit.

REGATTA

FREEPORT SHOPPING VILLAGE, ANCHORAGE ROAD, FLEETWOOD, LANCASHIRE FY7 6AE, ☎ 01253 777705, FAX: 01253 777705, www.regatta.com, 10–6 MON, TUE, WED, SAT, SUN, 10–8 THUR, FRI. **FACTORY SHOP IN A FACTORY SHOPPING VILLAGE**

See page 118 (ESSEX)

REVIVAL

34 WARNER STREET, ACCRINGTON, LANCASHIRE BB5 1HN, ☎ 01254 382316, 10.30–5 MON–SAT, CLOSED WED. **SECONDHAND AND VINTAGE CLOTHES**

Vintage clothes from the beginning of the century to the Seventies including men's and women's flares from £8 to £12; tank tops and shirts from £4; cheesecloth tops; Biba trousers; Levi's jeans from £9 up to £18; Levi's jackets, £10 to £35; Adidas and Lacoste T-shirts from £5 to £12; cocktail dresses from £14 to £28; ballgowns from £20 to £75; Fifties-style shirts, £6 to £12; dinner suits, £26 to £28. They also stock accessories, shoes, hats, gloves and costume jewellery. Hire is also available.

SCOOPS CATALOGUE DISCOUNT STORE

UNIT 56, ARNDALE CENTRE, MIDDLETON, MANCHESTER, LANCASHIRE M24 4EL, ☎ 0161 653 5435, FAX: 0161 653 9066, 9–5.30 MON–SAT.

1318–1324 ASHTON OLD ROAD, OPPENSHAW, MANCHESTER, LANCASHIRE M11 1JG, ☎ 0161 371 8243, 9–5.30 MON–SAT.

C/O DISCOUNT GIANT, SISSION STREET, OFF OLDHAM ROAD, FAILSWORTH LANCASHIRE M35 0EJ, ☎ 0161 682 5684, FAX: 0161 684 8991, 9–6 MON, TUE, SAT, 9–7 WED, 9–8 THUR, 9–7 FRI, 10–4 SUN.

THE IN SHOP CENTRE, TELEGRAPH WAY, KIRKBY, MERSEYSIDE LANCASHIRE, L32 8VS, ☎ 0151 545 0226, FAX: 0151 546 2899, 9.30–5.30 MON–SAT.

984 STOCKPORT ROAD, LEVENSHULME, MANCHESTER M19 3NN, ☎ 0161 257 3515, FAX: 0161 225 1390, 9–5.30 MON–SAT.

2 BURY OLD ROAD, CHEETHAM HILL, MANCHESTER M8 7JN, ☎ 0161 795 9312, FAX: 0161 684 8991, 9–5.30 MON–SAT

UNIT 102, CONCOURSE SHOPPING CENTRE, SOUTH WAY, SKELMERSDALE, LANCASHIRE WN8 6LJ, ☎ 01695 50965, FAX: 01695 50759, 9–5.30 MON–SAT. **PERMANENT DISCOUNT OUTLET**

See page 102 (CO DURH)

STAMPER ENTERPRISES & CO LTD

ALMA HOUSE, GRIMSHAW LANE, MIDDLETON, MANCHESTER M24 1GQ, ☎ 0161 655 1000, www.sales@stamper.co.uk, 9–5.30 MON–FRI. **PERMANENT DISCOUNT OUTLET**

Permanent discount outlet selling vast stocks of high street names for men, women and children from shops such as Marks & Spencer, BhS, Debenhams, Gap, Next, Ladybird and Mothercare. All the items are end of season or slight seconds and are sold without labels.

SUNGLASS TIME

THE LOWRY CENTRE, QUAYS ROAD, SALFORD QUAYS, MANCHESTER, LANCASHIRE M5 2WZ, ☎ 0161 848 9007, **e-mail:** info@sunglass-time.com, 10–8 MON–FRI, 9–7 SAT, 11–5 SUN.
PERMANENT DISCOUNT OUTLET

Sunglass Time offers a wide selection of top-notch sunglasses and watches at more than 30% off typical high street prices. The frames are invitingly displayed on back-lit columns – no locked cabinets, messy stickers or hanging labels to contend with. Gucci, Polo Ralph Lauren, Valentino, Police, Christian Dior and Diesel are included in the ever-changing stock of top international brand names. Designer Shades ensure that all their sunglasses have quality lenses which protect against UVA and UVB rays, as well as filtering out damaging reflective blue light. Their range of high fashion unisex watches includes Dolce & Gabbana, Guess and Pulsar. They plan to have 20 shops throughout Europe by the end of 2003. For details of other locations, phone 01423 858007 or email info@sunglass-time.com.

SUTTONS FACTORY SHOP

NEW CHURCH ROAD, BACUP, LANCASHIRE OL13 9DT, ☎ 01706 875578, 10–5.30 MON–FRI, 9–5.30 SAT, 10–4 SUN. **PERMANENT DISCOUNT OUTLET**

Stocks top brand-name shoes at less than half price. Special monthly offers always available. There are shoes, trainers, slippers, sandals and boots for all the family, with a selection of bags, cleaners and polishes available, all at discount prices.

T J HUGHES

59–63 CHURCH STREET, BLACKBURN, LANCASHIRE BB1 5AF, ☎ 01254 693333, FAX: 01254 693232, **e-mail:** info@tjhughes.co.uk, www.tjhughes.co.uk, 9–5.30 MON–SAT, 11–5 SUN.

MONS SQUARE, NEW STRAND, BOOTLE, LANCASHIRE L20 4SY, ☎ 0151 922 4397, FAX: 0151 933 1622, **e-mail:** info@tjhughes.co.uk, www.tjhughes.co.uk, 9–5.30 MON–SAT.

4 CURZON STREET, BURNLEY, LANCASHIRE BB11 1BB, ☎ 01282 838383, FAX: 01282 435400, **e-mail:** info@tjhughes.co.uk, www.tjhughes.co.uk, 9–5.30 MON–SAT, 11–4 SUN.

105 LONDON ROAD, LIVERPOOL, LANCASHIRE L3 8JA, ☎ 0151 207 2600, FAX: 0151 298 1339, **e-mail:** info@tjhughes.co.uk, www.tjhughes.co.uk, 9–5.30 MON–SAT, 11–5 SUN.

UNIT 32, TOWN SQUARE SHOPPING CENTRE, OLDHAM, MANCHESTER, LANCASHIRE OL1 1XF, ☎ 0161 628 3880, FAX: 0161 628 3886, **e-mail:** info@tjhughes.co.uk, www.tjhughes.co.uk, 9–5.30 MON–SAT.

FISHERGATE CENTRE, PRESTON, LANCASHIRE PR1 8HJ, ☎ 01772 887326, FAX: 01772 887328, **e-mail:** info@tjhughes.co.uk, www.tjhughes.co.uk, 9–5.30 MON–SAT, 8 ON WED, 11–5 SUN.

UNIT 6–7, THE WHEATSHEAF CENTRE, ROCHDALE, LANCASHIRE OL16 1NZ, ☎ 01706 750555, FAX: 01706 750666, **e-mail:** info@tjhughes.co.uk, www.tjhughes.co.uk, 9–5.30 MON–SAT, 10.30–4.30 SUN.

86 RAVENS WAY, SALFORD SHOPPING CITY, SALFORD, MANCHESTER M6 5JA, ☎ 0161 736 1472, FAX: 0161 736 0656, **e-mail:** info@tjhughes.co.uk, www.tjhughes.co.uk, 9–5.30 MON–SAT.

UNIT 1, THE HARDSHAW CENTRE, ST HELENS, LANCASHIRE WA10 1EB, ☎ 01744 453221, FAX: 01744 453065, **e-mail:** info@tjhughes.co.uk, www.tjhughes.co.uk, 9–5.30 MON–SAT, 10.30–4.30 SUN.

31–36 ARNDALE CENTRE, CHESTER ROAD, STRETFORD, MANCHESTER M32 9BB, ☎ 0161 866 9733, FAX: 0161 864 4627, **e-mail:** info@tjhughes.co.uk, www.tjhughes.co.uk, 9–5.30 MON–SAT, 10–4 SUN.

27–31 SANKEY STREET, WARRINGTON, LANCASHIRE WA1 1XG, ☎ 01925 634 4321, FAX: 01925 445966, **e-mail:** info@tjhughes.co.uk, www.tjhughes.co.uk, 9–5.30 MON–SAT, 10.30–4.30 SUN. **PERMANENT DISCOUNT OUTLET**

See page 98 (CHESH)

TERRY'S STORES

47 STATION ROAD, URMSTON, MANCHESTER, LANCASHIRE M41 9JG, ☎ 0161 748 6011, 9.30–5 MON–SAT, CLOSED WED. **PERMANENT DISCOUNT OUTLET**

Described as 'the final resting-place for ex-catalogue stock', Terry's sells everything that is normally available by catalogue at half price. This includes leather jackets, jeans, shoes, trainers, dress and curtaining fabric, whatnot stands, nests of tables, dining tables and chairs, bedlinen, curtains, electrical goods, wedding and bridesmaids dresses. The company has been in operation for 46 years and is privately owned.

THE ELITE DRESS AGENCY

35 KINGS STREET WEST, MANCHESTER M3 2PW, ☎ 0161 832 3670, www.elitedressagency.co.uk, 9.30–5.30 MON–SAT, 11–4 SUN. **DRESS AGENCY**

Three floors of good quality men's, women's and children's clothing, many with a Continental flavour. Among the womenswear can be found labels such as Moschino, Escada, Prada, Armani and DKNY among others, with lots of chainstore makes, too. For men, there are Italian designer suits from £50 to £150, including Boss, Paul Smith and Armani. There are lots of hats from £8; also shoes, handbags, accessories and a selection of unwanted gifts for sale.

THE FACTORY SHOP

SHAWBRIDGE STREET, CLITHEROE, LANCASHIRE BB7 1NA, ☎ 01200 428784, 9–5.30 MON–SAT, 10.30–4.30 SUN.

LANCASTER LEISURE PARK, WYRESDALE ROAD, LANCASTER, LANCASHIRE LA1 3LA, ☎ 01524 846079, 10–5 MON–SAT, 11–5 SUN. **FACTORY SHOP**

See page 98 (CHESH)

THE FAMOUS BRUNSWICK WAREHOUSE LTD

UNIT 6, ASHTON RETAIL PARK, 102 WELLINGTON ROAD, ASHTON UNDER LYNE, LANCASHIRE OL6 6DJ, ☎ 0161 330 7400, **e-mail:** northshoe@mcmail.com, 9–5 MON–FRI, 6 ON THUR, SAT, 10.30–4.30 SUN.

UNIT C, 454 BROOKWAY RETAIL PARK, ALTRINCHAM ROAD, BAGULEY, MANCHESTER, LANCASHIRE M23 9BL, ☎ 0161 945 1441, **e-mail:** northshoe@mcmail.com, 10–6 MON–WED, 10–8 THUR, FRI, 9–6 SAT, 11–5 SUN.

UNIT B2, TOWNSMOOR RETAIL PARK, BLACKBURN, LANCASHIRE BB2 3DY, ☎ 01254 278772, **e-mail:** northshoe@mcmail.com, 9.30–6 MON–WED, 9.30–7 THUR, FRI, 9–6 SAT, 11–5 SUN.

CHURCHILL WAY, LEYLAND, LANCASHIRE PR25 2LZ, ☎ 01772 455053, **e-mail:** northshoe@mcmail.com, 9–6 MON–WED, SAT, 9–7 THUR, FRI, 10.30–4.30 SUN.

24 MIDDLETON GARDENS, MIDDLETON, LANCASHIRE M24 4DF, ☎ 0161 653 9905, **e-mail:** northshoe@mcmail.com, 9–6 MON–SAT.

UNIT 4B, CABLES RETAIL PARK, STELEY WAY, RAINHILL, PRESCOT, MERSEYSIDE, LANCASHIRE L34 5NO, ☎ 0151 426 8262, **e-mail:** northshoe@mcmail.com, 9–6 MON–WED, SAT, 9–7 THUR, FRI, 10–4 SUN.

UNIT 2C, QUEENS RETAIL PARK, PRESTON, LANCASHIRE PR1 4HZ, ☎ 01772 253003, **e-mail:** northshoe@mcmail.com, 9–6 MON, TUE, FRI, SAT, 9–7 WED, THUR, 10.30–4.30 SUN.

UNIT E1, REGENTS PARK, ORDSALL LANE, SALFORD, LANCASHIRE M5 3TP, ☎ 0161 833 2173, **e-mail:** northshoe@mcmail.com, 10–6 MON–WED, 10–7 THUR, FRI, 9–6 SAT, 11–5 SUN.

UNIT D, WARRINGTON NEW ROAD, ST HELENS RETAIL PARK, ST HELENS, LANCASHIRE WA9 1JJ, ☎ 01744 754410, **e-mail:** northshoe@mcmail.com, 9–6 MON–WED, SAT, 9–7 THUR, FRI, 10–4 SUN.

UNIT 19, ELLESMERE RETAIL PARK, WALKDEN, WORSLEY, LANCASHIRE M28 3ZD, ☎ 0161 790 330, **e-mail:** northshoe@mcmail.com, 9–6 MON–WED, SAT, 9–7 THUR, FRI, 10.30–4.30 SUN.

25 LOIRE DRIVE, ROBIN PARK, WIGAN, LANCASHIRE WN5 OUH, ☎ 01942 211901 **e-mail:** northshoe@mcmail.com, 10–6 MON, TUE, 10–7 WED, FRI, 10–8 THUR, 9–6 SAT, 11–5 SUN. **PERMANENT DISCOUNT OUTLET**

See page 98 (CHESH)

TIMBERLAND

BOUNDARY MILL STORES, BURNLEY ROAD, COLNE, LANCASHIRE BB8 8LS, ☎ 01282 865229, FAX: 01282 863153, 10–6 MON–FRI, 9–6 SAT, 10–5 SUN. **FACTORY SHOP IN A FACTORY SHOPPING VILLAGE**

See page 99 (CHESH)

TK MAXX

76 BANK HEY STREET, BLACKPOOL, LANCASHIRE B19 0B7, FAX: 01253 752754, www.tkmaxx.com, PHONE FOR DETAILS.

1ST FLOOR, THE GATES SHOPPING CENTRE, MEALHOUSE LANE, BOLTON, LANCASHIRE, ☎ 01204 385527, www.tkmaxx.com, PHONE FOR DETAILS.

UNIT 1 AND 2, ANGOULEME RETAIL PARK, BURY, LANCASHIRE B19 0B7, FAX: 0161 7611700, www.tkmaxx.com, 9–5.30 MON–FRI, 7 ON THUR, 9–6 SAT, 11- 5 SUN.

1ST FLOOR, 15 PARKER ST, OFF CLAYTON SQUARE, LIVERPOOL, LANCASHIRE L1 1DP, ☎ 0151 708 9919, www.tkmaxx.com, 9–6 MON–SAT, 11–5 SUN.

BASEMENT LEVEL, LEWIS'S BUILDING, MARKET STREET, MANCHESTER M60 1TX, ☎ 0161 236 1885, www.tkmaxx.com, 9–6.30 MON–FRI, 8 ON THUR, 9–6 SAT, 11–5 SUN.

FISHERGATE SHOPPING CENTRE, PRESTON, LANCASHIRE PR1 2BT, ☎ 01772 253220, www.tkmaxx.com, 9–5.30 MON–FRI, 8 ON WED, 9–6 SAT, 11–5 SUN.

THE POINT RETAIL PARK, MOLEWORTH STREET, ROCHDALE, LANCASHIRE, ☎ 01706 759187, www.tkmaxx.com, PHONE FOR DETAILS.

UNIT A1, REGENT ROAD RETAIL PARK, ORDSALL LANE, SALFORD, LANCASHIRE M5 3TP, ☎ 0161 833 2200, www.tkmaxx.com, 9.30–8 MON, THUR, FRI, 9.30–6 TUE, WED, 9–6 SAT, 11–5 SUN.

7–9 MARBLE PLACE SHOPPING CENTRE, CHAPEL STREET, SOUTHPORT, LANCASHIRE PR8 1DF, ☎ 01704 501900, www.tkmaxx.com, 9–5.30 MON–FRI, 9–6 SAT, 11–5 SUN.

ST HELEN'S RETAIL PARK, WARRINGTON NEW ROAD, LANCASHIRE, ☎ 01744 615847, www.tkmaxx.com, PHONE FOR DETAILS.

PERMANENT DISCOUNT OUTLET

See page 89 (BEDS)

TOG 24

7 THE LINKWAY, HORWICH, BOLTON, LANCASHIRE BL6 6JA, ☎ 01204 469899, **e-mail:** mail-order@tog24.com, www.tog24.com, 10–6 MON–FRI, SAT, 8 ON WED, THUR, 11–5 SUN.

BOUNDARY MILLS STORE, BURNLEY ROAD, COLNE, LANCASHIRE BB8 8JN, ☎ 01282 870042, **e-mail:** mail-order@tog24.com, www.tog24.com, 10–6 MON–FRI, 9 ON THUR, 9–6 SAT, 10–5 SUN. **PERMANENT DISCOUNT OUTLET**

See page 99 (CHESH)

TOMMY BALLS

HART STREET MILL, BLACKBURN, LANCASHIRE BB11HW, ☎ 01254 261910, 10–5 MON–SAT, 11–5 SUN. **PERMANENT DISCOUNT OUTLET**

A large discount shoe warehouse selling quality shoes from leading British manufacturers for the whole family. Some are seconds, all are brand new. There is also a store at Eanam, which sells reconditioned footwear: phone 01254 261910.

TOP MARKS

149–151 HOLLAND STREET, DENTON, MANCHESTER, LANCASHIRE M34 3GE, ☎ 0161 336 1279, 9.30–5.30 MON–SAT, 8 ON THUR, 11–5 SUN. **PERMANENT DISCOUNT OUTLET**

A two-floor, 7,000-foot warehouse selling famous chainstore clothing (cancelled orders, over-stocks, ends-of-lines and some grade A seconds) at up to 50% off normal retail prices. Shoes and clothing for women are available in sizes 8 to 18; men's clothing ranges from small to XXL, 30 to 42-in waist and 29 to 33-in leg; children's clothing is available from birth up to nine years. Also stocks homeware, giftware and furniture at discounted prices. All major credit cards are accepted and free parking is available.

TRADEX

CARLISLE STREET, RINGWAY, PRESTON, LANCASHIRE PR1 1EH, ☎ 01772 888333, FAX: 01772 880015, 9.30–8.30 MON–FRI, 9–5.30 SAT, 10.30–4.30 SUN. **PERMANENT DISCOUNT OUTLET**

Clothing and shoes for all the family, jewellery, household goods, toiletries, bedding and home furnishings, food and confectionery. Leading and high street brand names can be found in all departments with discounts of up to 60% off recommended retail prices. To shop here, you have to be a member: bring two forms of identity showing your address and you can join instantly for £2. There is a coffee shop serving meals and snacks.

UNITED FOOTWEAR

12 LORD STREET, LEIGH, LANCASHIRE, ☎ 01942 604440, 9–5.30 MON–WED, 9–8 THUR, 9–6 FRI, 9–5.30 SAT.

68–70 OLDHAM STREET, MANCHESTER, ☎ 0161 228 1706, 9–5.30 MON–SAT.

126 FRIARGATE BROW, PRESTON, LANCASHIRE, ☎ 01772 204410, 9–5.30 MON–SAT, 11–4.30 SUN.

CARRMILL ROAD, OFF EAST LANCS ROAD, ST HELENS, LANCASHIRE, ☎ 01744 737777, 9–6 MON–WED, 9–8 THUR, FRI, 9–5.30 SAT, 10–4 SUN. **PERMANENT DISCOUNT OUTLET**

See page 124 (HAMPS)

WARNERS

FREEPORT SHOPPING VILLAGE, ANCHORAGE ROAD, FLEETWOOD, LANCASHIRE FY7 6AE, ☎ 01253 773770, 10–6 SEVEN DAYS A WEEK, 8 ON THUR, FRI. **FACTORY SHOP IN A FACTORY SHOPPING VILLAGE**

See page 100 (CHESH)

WINFIELDS

HAZEL MILL, BLACKBURN ROAD, HASLINGDEN, ROSSENDALE, LANCASHIRE BB4 5DD, ☎ 01706 227916, FAX: 01706 831125, **e-mail:** info@winfields.co.uk, www.winfields.co.uk, 10–5.30 MON–FRI, 8 ON THUR, 9–5.30 SAT, 11–5 SUN. **PERMANENT DISCOUNT OUTLET**

Winfields is a big mill discount store with other outlets in Barrow-in-Furness, Middleton and Hull, offering tremendous savings on shoes (more than 100,000 pairs to choose from, including trainers, boots, dressy shoes and sandals), womenswear (casual wear, sportswear, swimwear, lingerie, suits and dresses and designer fashions), traditional and contemporary menswear (shirts, trousers, jeans, polo shirts, denim jackets, sleepsuits and underwear), and accessories such as leather belts and wallets. There is a young fashion department and a range for women in sizes 18 plus. Winfields is the word on the street for children and teens for footwear, sportswear and clothing in up-to-the-minute styles. In addition, Winfields has a massive selction of outdoor wear, fleeces, waterproofs, wellingtons, hiking boots, socks, hats, scarves and gloves for all the family. There is a wide variety of outdoor and indoor furniture, timber decking, garden tools, pet accessories, cookware, utensils, electrical goods, bath towels, mirrors, picture frames, and gifts such as watches, crystalware and beauty products, with new stock arriving weekly. Luggage can be found in the Winair holiday department. Dine or take a break at Cloggers, the restaurant. Free car parking. Wheelchair friendly.

WRANGLER LEE

BOUNDARY MILLS STORES, OFF BURNLEY ROAD, COLNE, LANCASHIRE BB8 8LS, ☎ 01282 865229, 10–6 MON–SAT, 9 ON THUR, 11–5 SUN.

FREEPORT SHOPPING VILLAGE, ANCHORAGE ROAD, FLEETWOOD, LANCASHIRE FY7 6AE, ☎ 01253 773988, 10–6 MON–WED, SAT, 10–8 THUR, FRI, 11–5 SUN. **FACTORY SHOP**

Previous season's stock as well as overmakes and seconds. Men's, women's and youths' jeans and casual wear, plus Jansport backpacks, at 30% to 70% below high street prices.

WYNSORS WORLD OF SHOES

E SUTTON & SON LTD, NEWCHURCH ROAD, BACUP, LANCASHIRE OL13 9DT, ☎ 01706 875578, 10–5.30 MON–FRI, 9.30–5.30 SAT, 10–4 SUN.

DOCK STREET, FLEETWOOD, NEAR BLACKPOOL, LANCASHIRE FY7 6JW, ☎ 01253 779871, 9–5.30 MON–SAT, 8 ON THUR, FRI, 10–5 SUN.

EAST PRESCOTT ROAD, KNOTTY ASH, LIVERPOOL LANCASHIRE L14 5NA, ☎ 0151 228 6673, 9–5.30 MON, TUE, SAT, 9–8 WED, THUR, FRI, 10–4 SUN, BANK HOLIDAYS.

BOUNDARY ROAD, ST HELENS, LANCASHIRE WA10 2PX, ☎ 01744 454983, 8.30–8 MON, TUE, WED, 8–8 SAT, 8.30–9 THUR, FRI, 10–4 SUN, 9–6 BANK HOLIDAYS.
PERMANENT DISCOUNT OUTLET

See page 100 (CHESH)

LEICESTERSHIRE

BLUNTS

128–132 GRANBY STREET, LEICESTER LE1 1DL, ☎ 0116 255 5959, 8.30–6 MON–SAT, 10–4 SUN. **PERMANENT DISCOUNT OUTLET**

See page 91 (BRIS)

BECK MILL FACTORY SHOP

33 KINGS ROAD, MELTON MOWBRAY, LEICESTERSHIRE LE13 1QF, ☎ 01664 501105, 10–5 MON–SAT, 11–4 SUN. **FACTORY SHOP**

Top high street women's and menswear at discounts of up to 70%. For women, there is Roman Originals, Dannimac, Legs and Co Swimwear, Double Two, Blast, Alexara, Richard Stump, Silken Ladder blouses, Windsmoor, Planet and Precis. For men, there is Double Two, Dannimac, Barracuta, Wolsey, and David Andrews Ratcatcher Moleskins. Excellent selection of giftware. There is easy parking at the side of the shop.

CATALOGUE BARGAIN SHOP

UNIT D, WHITWICK RETAIL PARK, COALVILLE, LEICESTERSHIRE LE67 3FA, ☎ 01530 830294, www.bargaincrazy.com, 9–8 MON–SAT, 9 ON THUR, FRI, 10–4 SUN. **PERMANENT DISCOUNT OUTLET**

See page 92 (CAMBS)

CHARTERHOUSE RETAIL OUTLET

173 CHARNWOOD ROAD, SHEPSHED, LOUGHBOROUGH, LEICESTERSHIRE LE12 9NN, ☎ 01509 505050, FAX: 01509 507373, **e-mail:** factoryshop@charterhouse-holdings.co.uk, www.charterhouseholdings.co.uk, 9.30–6 MON–SAT, 11–4 SUN. **FACTORY SHOP**

The Charterhouse Retail Outlet was established 30 years ago and now enjoys its reputation as probably the largest factory shop of its kind in the UK. With over £2 million worth of stock always available, Charterhouse offers family clothing, fashion, footwear, kitchenware, homeware and more – all ex-chain and branded products at a fraction of high street prices. Womenswear includes casual, evening, swimwear, nightwear and lingerie – all styles and sizes. Childrenswear ranges from babies upwards with a special department for early teen fashions. Men will also find an excellent selection of branded sportswear, smart and casual clothing as well as footwear. The expanded kitchenware and household department stocks a huge selection of home and gift ideas, including luggage and toiletries. There is free parking, a children's play area, parent and baby room, wheelchair access and café area. The outlet is only one mile from Junction 23 of the M1.

DE BRADELEI MILL SHOP LTD

LOWER LEICESTER ROAD, LUTTERWORTH, LEICESTERSHIRE LE17 4NF, ☎ 01455 557571, FAX: 01455 557332, 9.30–5.30 MON–FRI, 9.30–6 SAT, 10.30–4.30 SUN. **PERMANENT DISCOUNT OUTLET**

A light and airy outlet centre, easily accessible from M1 junction 20 and M6 junction 1, selling leading high street and designer labels with up to 70% discount. Brands include Windsmoor, Planet, Precis Petite, Jaegar Knitwear, Jacques Vert, Country Casuals, French Connection, Elle, Elvi, and Studio selling a small selection of designer labels. Lee Cooper has an extensive range of jeans and casuals. Menswear brands include French Connection, Wolsey, Lee Cooper, Farah, and Robert Leonards menswear selling Gabicci, Gurteen and Ben Sherman. The children's section stocks fashions from birth to 12 years plus. A large shoe department stocks well-known brands for all the family. Ponden Mill offers a range of soft furnishings and everything for the home. Liberty giftwear and Arran Aromatics toiletries also available. Car parking. Coaches welcome.

GIFTTREE

BRITANNIA CENTRE, HINCKLEY, LEICESTERSHIRE LE10 1RU, ☎ 01455 891920, 9–5 MON–SAT. **FACTORY SHOP**

See page 108 (DERBY)

GILLIVERS FOOTWEAR AND CLOTHING WAREHOUSE

MARKET STREET, COALVILLE, LEICESTERSHIRE LE67 3DX, ☎ 01530 811452, 9–5 MON–SAT. **PERMANENT DISCOUNT OUTLET**

See page 108 (DERBY)

LANDS' END DIRECT MERCHANTS

LANDS' END WAY, OAKHAM, RUTLAND LE15 6US, ☎ 01572 722553, 10–6 MON–SAT, 10–4 SUN AND BANK HOLIDAYS. **FACTORY SHOP**

See page 90 (BERKS)

MATALAN

100 CHURCHGATE, VAUGHAN WAY, LEICESTER, LEICESTERSHIRE LE1 4AL, ☎ 0116 242 6700, FAX: 0116 253 8398, www.matalan.co.uk, 9–8 MON–FRI, 9–6 SAT, 11–5 SUN. **PERMANENT DISCOUNT OUTLET**

See page 89 (BEDS)

THE DOC SHOP

BRUCE WAY, CAMBRIDGE ROAD INDUSTRIAL ESTATE, WHETSTONE, LEICESTERSHIRE LE8 6HP, ☎ 0116 286 5958, 9–5.30 MON–SAT. **PERMANENT DISCOUNT OUTLET**

Sells Doc Martens shoes and boots, as well as clothing and a vast range of accessories at discounted prices.

THE UPPINGHAM DRESS AGENCY

2–6 ORANGE STREET, UPPINGHAM, RUTLAND LE15 9SQ, ☎ 01572 823276, FAX: 01572 823815, www.dressagency.co.uk, 9–5 MON–SAT, 12–4 SUN AND BANK HOLIDAYS. **DRESS AGENCY**

One of Britain's largest, longest established and most reputable dress agencies packed with over 4,000 quality new, nearly-new and end of line garments from famous high street names to top designer labels. Featured on television and in numerous national newspapers and magazines, this agency, situated in a picturesque market town, has everything from casuals to occasion wear, evening wear, suits and separates, hats, shoes, handbags, scarves and costume jewellery. There are departments for men, women and children, and ten rooms to explore. Further discounts are available with the agency's own loyalty card – ask for details.

TK MAXX

HAYMARKET CENTRE, 10 KEMBLE SQUARE, LEICESTER, LEICESTERSHIRE LE1 3YD, ☎ 0116 251 0155, www.tkmaxx.com, 9–5.30 MON–THUR, 9–6 FRI–SAT, 11–5 SUN. **PERMANENT DISCOUNT OUTLET**

See page 89 (BEDS)

UNITED FOOTWEAR

114 MAIN STREET, NEWBOLD VERDON, LEICESTERSHIRE, ☎ 01455 822407, 9–8 MON–FRI, 9–5.30 SAT, 10–4 SUN. **PERMANENT DISCOUNT OUTLET**

See page 124 (HAMPS)

ROHDE SHOES

FOSSE WAY, SYSTON, LEICESTER, LEICESTESHIRE LE7 1PG, ☎ 0116 260 3443, www.rohdeshoes.co.uk, 10–4 WED–SUN. **FACTORY SHOP**

Factory shop wherer the majority of the stock is Rohde footwear for men and women, as well as some Daniel Hechter and occasionaly other brands such as Ecco and Portland. Rohde haved been making sandals, slippers, shoes and boots in Germany for the past 50 years, using the best craftsmen and materials. Their winter range includes a special selection of waterproof footwear incorporating the Sympatex membrane.

LINCOLNSHIRE

BOUNDARY MILL STORES

AT DOWNTOWN SUPERSTORE, GONERBY MOOR, A1, GRANTHAM, LINCOLNSHIRE NG32 2AB, ☎ 01476 591001, 9.30–5.30 MON–SAT, 11–5 SUN. **PERMANENT DISCOUNT OUTLET**

See page 132 (LANCS)

BROUGHTON SHOE WAREHOUSE

18 ST MARK'S SQUARE, LINCOLN, LINCOLNSHIRE LN5 7EX, ☎ 01522 532300, 9.30–6 MON–SAT, 8 ON THUR, 11–5 SUN. **PERMANENT DISCOUNT OUTLET**

See page 108 (DERBY)

CATALOGUE BARGAIN SHOP

12–14 SILVER STREET, GAINSBOROUGH, LINCOLNSHIRE DN21 2DP, ☎ 01427 810604, www.bargaincrazy.com, 9–5.30 MON, THUR, FRI, 8.30–5 TUE, 9–5 WED, 8.30–5.30 SAT, 10–4 SUN.

29–31 THE STRAIT, LINCOLN, LINCOLNSHIRE LN1 1JD, ☎ 01522 527276, www.bargaincrazy.com, 9–5.30 MON–SAT, 10.30–4.30 SUN. **PERMANENT DISCOUNT OUTLET**

See page 92 (CAMBS)

COSALT INTERNATIONAL LTD

WICKHAM ROAD, GRIMSBY, LINCOLNSHIRE DN31 3SL, ☎ 01472 504300, www.cosalt.co.uk, 8.30–5 MON–FRI. **PERMANENT DISCOUNT OUTLET**

Specialises in workwear, safety clothing and marine wear but some of the merchandise is eminently wearable for everyday and is sold at very reasonable prices. There is plenty of stock on the shelves, but you can also order some lines from the catalogue. There is a wide selection of leisure and outdoor clothes from Doc Martens to padded jackets and denim shirts, dungarees and donkey jackets. VAT has to be added to prices. They also provide marine safety and life-raft servicing.

GYMPHLEX SPORTSWEAR

BOSTON ROAD, HORNCASTLE, LINCOLNSHIRE LN9 6HU, ☎ 01507 523243, **e-mail:** sales@gymphlex.co.uk, **DESIGNER SALES**

Holds a one day factory shop sale just once a year: phone 01507 523243 for details. Your chance to buy a huge range of sportswear for all the family: jogging pants, tracksuits, rugby and football shirts, rugby shorts, T-shirts, polo shirts, Lycra swimwear, leotards, tights, socks. Some of the stock is seconds, some overmakes. The rest is freshly-made stock which is specially reduced for the sale.

MATALAN

JOHN ADAMS WAY, BOSTON, LINCOLNSHIRE PE21 6TY, ☎ 01205 312040, FAX: 01205 352991, www.matalan.co.uk, 10–8 MON–FRI, 9–6 SAT, 11–5 SUN.

UNIT 1, HEWITTS CIRCUS, CLEETHORPES, GRIMSBY, LINCOLNSHIRE DN35 9QH, ☎ 01472 200255, FAX: 01472 200156, www.matalan.co.uk, 9–8 MON–FRI, 9–6 SAT, 11–5 SUN.

LINDIS RETAIL PARK, TRITTON ROAD, LINCOLN, LINCOLNSHIRE LN6 7QY, ☎ 01522 696541, FAX: 01522 684946, www.matalan.co.uk, 10–8 MON–FRI, 9–6 SAT, 11–5 SUN.

DUDLEY ROAD, SCUNTHORPE, LINCOLNSHIRE DN16 1BA, ☎ 01724 270958, FAX: 01724 270856, www.matalan.co.uk, 9.30–8 MON–FRI, 9–6 SAT, 11–5 SUN. **PERMANENT DISCOUNT OUTLET**

See page 89 (BEDS)

STAGE 2

TRITTON RETAIL PARK, TRITTON ROAD, LINCOLN, LINCOLNSHIRE LN6 7YA, ☎ 01522 560303, 10–8 MON–FRI, 9–6 SAT, 11–5 SUN AND BANK HOLIDAYS. **PERMANENT DISCOUNT OUTLET**

See page 92 (CAMBS)

SUNDAES SANDALS

THE CHASE, 18 HIGH STREET, MOULTON, SPALDING, LINCOLNSHIRE PE12 6QB, ☎ 01406 371370, FAX: 01406 371646, **e-mail:** sundaessandals@aol.com, 9–3.30 MON–FRI, SAT BY APPOINTMENT. MAIL ORDER. **FACTORY SHOP**

Handmade sandals in bright summer colours, top quality materials, including leather uppers, insoles and linings. Women's sandals are available up to size 10. Their small, informal factory shop sells the full range of Sundaes made on the premises and usually has a selection of discontinued styles, colours and slight seconds at bargain prices. Visitors are always welcome, but do phone first.

THE FACTORY SHOP

MALT KILN ROAD, BARTON ON HUMBER, NORTH LINCOLNSHIRE DN18 5JT, ☎ 01652 636701, 9–7 MON, TUE, WED, 9–8 THUR, FRI, 8.30–7 SAT, 10–4 SUN.

43 HIGH STREET, MABLETHORPE, LINCOLNSHIRE LN12 1XA, ☎ 01507 473705, 9.30–6 MON–SAT, 10.30–4.30 SUN.

CARRE STREET, SLEAFORD, LINCOLNSHIRE NG34 7TW, ☎ 01529 410155, 9–5.30 MON–SAT, 10–4 SUN.

51 FLEET STREET, HOLBEACH, SPALDING, LINCOLNSHIRE PE12 7AU, ☎ 01406 422180, 9–5 MON–SAT, 10–4 SUN. **FACTORY SHOP**

See page 98 (CHESH)

THE FAMOUS BRUNSWICK WAREHOUSE LTD

UNIT A, VICTORIA RETAIL PARK, VICTORIA STREET NORTH, GRIMSBY, LINCOLNSHIRE DN31 1NX, ☎ 01472 250622, **e-mail:** northshoe@mcmail.com, 9–6 MON–WED, SAT, 9–7 THUR, FRI, 10.30–4.30 SUN.

THE CARLTON CENTRE, OUTER CIRCLE ROAD, LINCOLN, LINCOLNSHIRE LN2 4WA, ☎ 01522 520037, **e-mail:** northshoe@mcmail.com, 9–6 MON–WED, SAT, 9–7 THUR, FRI, 10–4 SUN.

UNIT 2, CARLTON STREET, OFF STATION ROAD, SCUNTHORPE, LINCOLNSHIRE DN15 6TZ, ☎ 01724 857307, **e-mail:** northshoe@mcmail.com, 9–6 MON–WED, SAT, 9–7 THUR, FRI, 10–4 SUN. **PERMANENT DISCOUNT OUTLET**

See page 98 (CHESH)

THE SHOE FACTORY SHOP

21 WELLOWGATE, GRIMSBY, LINCOLNSHIRE DN32 0RA, ☎ 01472 342415, 9–5 MON–SAT, 9–7 THUR. **FACTORY SHOP**

See page 111 (DERBY)

TK MAXX

FRESHNEY PLACE SHOPPING CENTRE, GRIMSBY, LINCOLNSHIRE, ☎ 01472 352842, www.tkmaxx.com, PHONE FOR DETAILS.

UNIT 16, ST MARK'S CENTRE, STATION STREET, LINCOLN, LINCOLNSHIRE LN5 7EY, ☎ 01522 530933, www.tkmaxx.com, 9–6 MON–SAT, 8 ON THUR, 11–5 SUN.

UNIT E, GALLAGHER RETAIL PARK, DONCASTER ROAD, SCUNTHORPE, LINCOLNSHIRE, ☎ 01724 868965, www.tkmaxx.com, PHONE FOR DETAILS. **PERMANENT DISCOUNT OUTLET**

See page 89 (BEDS)

TOG 24

BOUNDARY MILL STORES, GONERBY MOOR, ON THE A1, GRANTHAM, LINCOLNSHIRE NG32 2AB, ☎ 01476 591001, **e-mail:** mail-order@tog24.com, www.tog24.com, 9.30–5.30 MON–SAT, 11–5 SUN. **FACTORY SHOP IN A FACTORY SHOPPING VILLAGE**

See page 99 (CHESH)

TRADEX

MONKS ROAD, LINCOLN, LINCOLNSHIRE LN2 5HN, ☎ 01522 512251, FAX: 01522 513332, 9.30–8.30 MON–FRI, 9–5.30 SAT, 10.30–4.30 SUN. **PERMANENT DISCOUNT OUTLET**

See page 142 (LANCS)

VOGUE CLOTHING AGENCY

94 EASTGATE, LOUTH, LINCOLNSHIRE LN11 9AA, ☎ 01507 604233, 10–5 MON–FRI, 9.30–5.30 SAT. **DRESS AGENCY, HIRE SHOP**

Trading for 27 years, this shop stocks a wide range of middle to high quality designer women's clothing. Consisting of two floors situated next to Curry's on the main street, it offers day wear, wedding and evening outfits with appropriate accessories including shoes and handbags. Labels include Escada, Jaeger, Laurel, Mondi and Wallis. There is a well-stocked hat hire department. Since 1996 a separate men's department has been established within the premises offering designer clothes such as Daks, Aquascutum, Armani and Hugo Boss plus casual wear separates. There is also a range of dinner suits and accessories. The shop has recently introduced a department carrying a range of skiwear and motorcycle clothing, including one piece and two piece suits and boots. A selection of cruise wear, including beaded jackets, embroidered shawls and pashminas, has also been introduced.

WILKINSON STORES

2 THE BROADWAY, ASHBY, SCUNTHORPE, LINCOLNSHIRE NG5 7EL, ☎ 01724 867767, www.wilko.co.uk, 9–5.30 MON–FRI, 8.30–5.30 SAT, 10–4 SUN. MAIL ORDER. **PERMANENT DISCOUNT OUTLET**

See page 100 (CHESH)

WYNSORS WORLD OF SHOES

123 CROMWELL ROAD, GRIMSBY, LINCOLNSHIRE DN31 2BB, ☎ 01472 251627, 9–5.30 MON, TUE, WED, SAT, 9–8 THUR, FRI, 10–4 SUN AND BANK HOLIDAYS. **PERMANENT DISCOUNT OUTLET**

See page 100 (CHESH)

LONDON

AMAZON

1, 3, 7 AND 22 KENSINGTON CHURCH STREET, LONDON W8, ☎ 020 7937 4692, **PERMANENT DISCOUNT OUTLET**

Amazon ranges over five shops at the Kensington High Street end of Kensington Church Street. Numbers 1, 3 and 22 feature much the same merchandise which changes from one week to the next according to what the buyers can get hold of. Number 7 features menswear in the left hand shop, women's shoes and childrenswear on the right. The most common labels seen here are In Wear, French Connection, Great Plains, Fenn, Wright & Manson, Nicole Farhi and Sticky Fingers. There's always plenty of stock in good condition and very reasonable prices.

ANGELS FANCY DRESS

119 SHAFTESBURY AVENUE, LONDON WC2H 8AE, ☎ 020 7836 5678, FAX: 020 7240 9527, **e-mail:** party@fancydress.com, www.fancydress.com, 9–5.30 MON–FRI, LAST COSTUME FITTING 4.30. **HIRE SHOP**

Angels hires the best costumes for parties and sells accessories, wigs, masks, make-up and tiaras. You can party like a star dressed in a Georgian, Victorian, 1970s, Halloween, Christmas, animal or space costume. Angels has been dressing the entertainment industry for 160 years, recently supplying films such as Topsy-Turvy, Shakespeare in Love and Titanic.

BENNY DEE LTD

74–80 MIDDLESEX STREET, LONDON E1 7EZ, ☎ 020 7377 9067, FAX: 020 7247 7728, www.bennydee.com, 9–6 MON–FRI, 10–4 SAT, 9.30–4.30 SUN.

136–138 WALTHAMSTOW HIGH STREET, LONDON E17 7JS, ☎ 020 8520 4637/020 8520 4637, www.bennydee.com, 9–6 MON–SAT.

110–114 KILBURN HIGH ROAD, LONDON NW6 4HY, ☎ 020 7624 2995, FAX: 020 7624 2995, 9–6 MON–SAT, 10–4 SUN.

4–6 HIGH ROAD, WOOD GREEN, LONDON N22 6BX, ☎ 020 8881 8101, FAX: 020 8881 8101

e-mail: info@bennydee.com, www.bennydee.com, 9–6 MON–SAT, 10–4 SUN. **PERMANENT DISCOUNT OUTLET**

Discounted women's, men's and childrenswear, specialising in lingerie. High street brands with at least 50% savings. Some of the brands there include Zorbit, Mothercare, Baby Gap, Baby Togs and Grasshopper. The ground floor contains predominantly women's lingerie with masses of bras, all brand names such as Marks & Spencer, Berlei, Gossard, Triumph and Warner and some clothing. For men there are socks, ties, underwear, shirts, T-shirts, jogging bottoms and occasionally suits.

BLACKOUT 2

51 ENDELL STREET, COVENT GARDEN, LONDON WC2H 9AD, ☎ 020 7240 5006, www.blackout2.com, 11–7 MON–FRI, 11.30–6.30 SAT. **SECONDHAND AND VINTAGE CLOTHES**

Sells Twenties to Eighties gear, plus accessories, for sale and to hire at reasonable prices.

BROWNS LABELS FOR LESS

50 SOUTH MOLTON STREET, LONDON W1K 5RD, ☎ 020 7514 0052, www.brownsfashion.com, 10–6.30 MON–SAT, 7 ON THUR. **PERMANENT DISCOUNT OUTLET**

This designer sale shop supplies rails of clothes which, if you're a keen bargain hunter and don't mind rummaging, offers exciting names for bargain prices. Designers on sale here include most of those sold in the main, full-price shop including Jil Sander, Helmut Lang, Sonia Rykiel, Missoni, Comme Des Garcons, and Browns Focus. Men's rails are at the front of the narrow, winding shop; women's at the back near the six changing rooms. Prices are advertised as representing reductions of 50% to 80%. Assistants are helpful and there's always lots of stock.

BURBERRY

29–53 CHATHAM PLACE, LONDON E9 6LP, ☎ 020 8985 3344, 11–6 MON–FRI, 10–5 SAT, 11–5 SUN. **FACTORY SHOP**

See page 94 (CHESH)

CATALOGUE BARGAIN SHOP

252 GREEN LANES, PALMERS GREEN, LONDON N13 5TU, ☎ 020 8886 9532, www.bargaincrazy.com, 9–5.30 MON–SAT, 10–4 SUN. **PERMANENT DISCOUNT OUTLET**

See page 92 (CAMBS)

CENCI

31 MONMOUTH STREET, LONDON WCH 9DD, ☎ 020 7836 1400, FAX: 020 8766 8564, 11–6 MON–SAT. **SECONDHAND AND VINTAGE CLOTHES**

Small shop selling vintage clothing from the Forties to the Seventies from America and Europe. There are about 10,000 items in the shop at any one time, many of which are bought from a factory in Italy devoted to the recycling of old style, quality clothing. As well as Sixties' sweaters from £16 to £125, Forties' and Sixties' suits from £75 and a large selection of cashmere, there are also accessories such as luggage, watches, rings, hats, cufflinks and glasses from the Twenties to the Sixties and a small selection of shoes.

CHANGE OF HEART

THE OLD SCHOOL, 59C PARK ROAD, LONDON N8 8DP, ☎ 020 8341 1575, 10–6 MON–SAT. **DRESS AGENCY**

Sells a mixture of designer and good high street labels for women including labels such as DKNY, Ghost, Betty Jackson, Armani, Jigsaw, Whistles, MaxMara, Joseph and Paul Smith. Prices vary from £20 for a pair of Armani shorts to £50 for a Nicole Farhi silk two-piece suit.

CHOICE DISCOUNT STORES LIMITED

67 GOLDERS GREEN ROAD, GOLDERS GREEN, LONDON NW11 8EL, ☎ 020 8458 8247, 9–6 MON–SAT, 11–5 SUN.

11 ARCADIA CENTRE, THE BROADWAY, EALING, LONDON W5 2ND, ☎ 020 8567 2747, 9.30–6 MON–SAT, 7 ON THUR, 11–5 SUN. **PERMANENT DISCOUNT OUTLET**

See page 92 (CAMBS)

CLARKS FACTORY SHOP

61-63 RYE LANE, PECKHAM, LONDON SE15 5EX, ☎ 020 7732 2530, 9.30–5 MON–SAT.

UNIT 2, 67-83 SEVEN SISTERS ROAD, LONDON N7 6BU, ☎ 020 7281 9364, 9.30–5.30 MON–SAT, 11–5 SUN.

113-117 POWIS STREET, WOOLWICH, LONDON SE18 6JB, ☎ 020 8854 3163, 9.30–5.15 MON–SAT. **FACTORY SHOP**

See page 94 (CHESH)

DESIGNER SALES UK

OLD TRUMAN BREWERY COMPLEX, BRICK LANE, E1. WRITE TO: STUDIO 6, STAR GALLERY, CASTLE DITCH LANE, LEWES, SUSSEX BN7 1YJ, ☎ 01273 470 880, FAX: 01273 470 881, **e-mail:** sales@designersales.co.uk, www.designersales.co.uk, PHONE FOR DETAILS. **DESIGNER SALES**

During its 13 years in operation, Designer Sale UK has established itself as an increasingly popular way to buy desirable designer gear. Whether you are looking for something really offbeat or that classic item to complement your wardrobe, there are many bargains to be had at prices discounted by 80% to 90% off the normal shop price. Now representing over 50 different fashion companies, they hold sale five times a year – February, March/April, May, September and November – within the Old Truman Brewery Complex in Brick Lane, East London. Each sale runs over four days, from Thursday to Sunday, with an extra day (Wednesday) for mailing list customers. Phone to join the mailing list and for information on venue details and upcoming sales. Labels on sale include Valentino, Armani, Burro, Vivienne Westwood, Duffer of St George, Joe Caseley Hayford, Neisha Crosland, William Hunt, Dolce & Gabbana, Clements Ribeiro, Boyd, Matthew Williamson, Stephen Sprouse, Anthony Symonds, Alberta Ferretti, Helmut Lang, Fake London, Burro, Vexed Generation and Wale Adejemi.

DISPOSAL SERVICES AGENCY (DSA)

ROOM 727, MINISTRY OF DEFENCE, 6 HERCULES ROAD, LONDON SE1 7DJ, ☎ 020 7261 8968, www.disposalservices.agency.mod.uk. **PERMANENT DISCOUNT OUTLET**

The Disposal Services Agency is an agency of the Ministry of Defence set up to dispose of surplus equipment. It runs the largest disposal operation in the UK, organising the sale of both military equipment and commodities in use commercially, such as embassy furniture, government department office furniture, closed-down RAF-base vehicles and housing stock, ex-marine boats, ex-army tents, boots and ski equipment, medical and dental equipment, clothing, ship and aircraft spares, scrap metal and IT equipment. The DSA uses companies throughout the UK, each with their own specialist area, to dispose of stock. These companies also dispose of stock from a host of other, usually public sector, organisations varying from fire brigades and hospitals to health authorities and the police. Equipment from these companies varies from kitchen equipment and fax machines to mobile radios, cars, generators, jewellery and telecommunications equipment to food trolleys, X-ray equipment, telephones, uniforms, dinghies, fishing nets, photocopiers and chair lifts. Visit the website to find out which companies sell which products and how to contact them direct.

EMPORIUM

330–332 CREEK ROAD, GREENWICH, LONDON SE10 9SW, ☎ 020 8305 1670, www.emporiumoriginals.com, 10.30–6 WED–SUN. **SECONDHAND AND VINTAGE CLOTHES**

One of London's finest vintage clothes stores selling high quality vintage wear from the Thirties to the Seventies. Supplies film, theatre and pop promo companies as well as members of the public. Also sells ballgowns and has a large selection of evening wear for men and women.

GOLD'S FACTORY OUTLET

108–114 GOLDERS GREEN ROAD, LONDON NW11 8HB, ☎ 020 8905 5721, 10–6 MON–FRI AND SUN. **PERMANENT DISCOUNT OUTLET**

Famous men's and women's clothing and shoes. Labels on sale include Vandal and Loakes shoes and Hugo James and Austin Reed clothing.

IN WEAR FACTORY OUTLET

100 GARRATT LANE, WANDSWORTH, LONDON SW18 4DJ, ☎ 020 8871 2155, 10–6 MON–SAT, 11–5 SUN. **FACTORY SHOP**

In Wear and Jackpot for women and Matinique and Cottonfield for men as well as Part Two for both men and women at discounts of between 30% and 70% for last season's stock, ends of lines and seconds. All the stock is made up of separates and tends to be stylishly casual urbanwear and includes blazers, jeans, trousers, dresses, knitwear, suits and outerwear. Twice-yearly designer sample sale is held here. Phone for details. There is another factory shop at Bicester Village.

KATE KUBA SALE SHOP

49 CHASE SIDE, SOUTHGATE, LONDON N14 5BU, ☎ 020 8886 1185, www.katekuba.com, 9.30–5.30 MON–THUR, 9.30–6 FRI, SAT. **PERMANENT DISCOUNT OUTLET**

Discounted shoes for men and women from names such as DKNY, Charles Jourdan and Kenzo though, as you would expect from an end of line shop, size availability varies. There is usually an under £10 table. Also now have a new season selection.

LA SCALA

39 ELYSTAN STREET, LONDON SW3 3NT, ☎ 020 7589 2784, 10–5.30 MON–SAT. **DRESS AGENCY**

La Scala sells women's nearly-new clothes, accessories, men's and children's clothes under the same roof. Top designer men's clothes including Armani, Prada and Gucci, and large quantities of women and men's cashmere as well as a range of shoes in immaculate condition. Owner Sandy Reid lived for 14 years in Northern Italy and uses her experience there in her shop behind the Conran Shop in Chelsea. There, she sells end of season Italian designer wear and current top designer nearly-new outfits from DKNY, Dolce & Gabbana, Voyage, MaxMara, Prada and Gucci. Italian is spoken in the shop which has a large Italian clientele. There's an emphasis on younger lines and the price reductions are fantastic.

LAURENCE CORNER

62–64 HAMPSTEAD ROAD, LONDON NW1, FAX: 020 7813 1010, FAX: 020 7813 1413, 9.30–6 MON–SAT. **SECONDHAND AND VINTAGE CLOTHES. HIRE SHOP**

Famous, long-established unique niche retail store specialising in probably the largest selection of genuine Government Surplus clothing and equipment anywhere. Also stocks outdoor and protective clothing and off-beat fashion. Extensive costume hire department. Catalogue on request.

MASSIMO

43A COMMERCIAL STREET, LONDON E1 6BD, ☎ 020 7247 3220, 10.30–5.30 MON–FRI, 11.30–3.30 SUN. **PERMANENT DISCOUNT OUTLET**

There's a vetted entry system to this large, glass fronted warehouse-type shop. Best buys here are jeans from Moschino, Versace and Armani, although they also stock knitwear, T-shirts, jackets, underwear, suits, shirts, ties and shoes for both men and women by Dolce & Gabbana, Valentino, Hugo Boss, Gianfranco Ferre and Zegna. Items aren't priced, which leaves room for a bit of haggling, but they're generally about 30% to 40% cheaper than the high streeet. For example, Iceberg, Armani, Versace and Moschino jeans from £40. Merchandise is 50/50 for men and women. There is also a new casual range including stock from Diesel and Calvin Klein.

MATALAN

ALPINE RETAIL PARK, ALPINE WAY, EAST BECKTON, LONDON E6 6LA, ☎ 020 7473 9780, FAX: 020 7511 5554, www.matalan.co.uk, 10–8 MON–FRI, 9–6 SAT, 10–4 SUN.

HIGH ROAD, LEYTONSTONE, LONDON E11 1HH, ☎ 020 8988 8630, FAX: 020 8558 3048, www.matalan.co.uk, 10–8 MON–FRI, 9–6 SAT, 10–4 SUN.

317 EDGWARE ROAD, CRICKLEWOOD BROADWAY, CRICKLEWOOD, LONDON NW2 6PH, ☎ 020 8450 5667, FAX: 020 8450 8575, www.matalan.co.uk, 10–8 MON–FRI, 9–6 SAT, 11–5 SUN.

THURSTON ROAD, LOAMPIT VALE, LEWISHAM LONDON SE13 7SN, ☎ 020 8463 9830, FAX: 020 8318 1936, www.matalan.co.uk, 10–8 MON–FRI, 9–6 SAT, 10–4 SUN.

59 BUGSBY WAY, CHARLTON, LONDON SE7 7SE, ☎ 020 8269 4290, FAX: 020 8858 6469, www.matalan.co.uk, 10–8 MON–FRI, 9–6 SAT, 11–5 SUN. **PERMANENT DISCOUNT OUTLET**

See page 89 (BEDS)

MODERN AGE VINTAGE CLOTHING

65 CHALK FARM ROAD, LONDON NW1 8AN, ☎ 020 7482 3787, FAX: 020 8459 4157, www.modern-age.co.uk, 10.30–6 MON–FRI, 10–6 SAT, SUN. **SECONDHAND AND VINTAGE CLOTHES**

American and English secondhand clothing, particularly from the Fifties, Sixties and Seventies to buy and to hire. Average price for any garment is £15; men's shirts from £8 to £50, dinner suits for hire at £29. Women's evening wear for hire from £25.

MORRY'S

39-40 THE BROADWAY, EDMONTON, LONDON N9 0TJ, ☎ 020 8807 6747, 8.30–5 MON–SAT, CLOSED 1 ON THUR. **PERMANENT DISCOUNT OUTLET**

Liquidation stock which includes some famous makes and can comprise anything from gardening equipment (shovels, forks and hoses) and household items to electrical equipment (CDs, radios, televisions, radio alarms) and clothing for men, women and children. For example, BhS padded jacket £3.99, normal retail price £30; Etam dress £2, normal retail price £40. Everything is at least half the retail price. Specialises in Philips electrical equipment from CD players and videos, car stereos and radio cassettes to shavers and baby alarms, all with full repair and spares back-up. If you live nearby, drop in frequently as stock is constantly changing.

NICOLE FARHI/FRENCH CONNECTION OUTLET SHOP

3 HANCOCK ROAD, BROMLEY-BY-BOW, LONDON E3 3DA, ☎ 020 7399 7125, 10–3 TUE, WED, SAT, 11–6.30 THUR, 10–5.30 FRI. **FACTORY SHOP**

Nicole Farhi/French Connection's Outlet Shop in Bow, next door to the warehouse, may be small but it's packed with rails of clothes for women and men. Stock is mainly made up of previous seasons' merchandise, samples and seconds from Nicole Farhi and French Connection, with some Great Plains merchandise. There's a selection of blouses, knitwear, trousers, skirts, coats, jackets, bags, leather and suede wear, some shoes and boots, and a small amount of evening wear, although stock varies. Womenswear makes up about 80% of the shop's contents. Great finds include a cream cashmere longline polo neck sweater, £60; chunky grey roll neck fisherman's jumper with a snag in the collar, £99, reduced from £279; grey pinstripe classic suit, £70; Great Plains sample blouse, £15; little black sleeveless dress, £20 reduced from £99 because of a torn seam; long black leather skirt, £150. Seconds are marked and faults are also pointed out at the cash desk as you can't return goods. Discounts vary according to how old the stock is so some outfits may only be reduced from £179 to £150; others are practically given away. There are two changing rooms. There is also a Nicole Farhi/French Connection factory shop at Bicester Village designer outlet centre in Oxfordshire.

NOTTING HILL HOUSING TRUST

33 SOUTH END ROAD, HAMPSTEAD, LONDON NW3 2PY, **e-mail:** charityshop@nhhg.org.uk, www.nottinghillonline.com/supporters, 10–6 MON–SAT, 12–5 SUN.

53 ST JOHN'S WOOD HIGH STREET, LONDON NW8 7NJ, ☎ 020 7586 9493, **e-mail:** charityshop@nhhg.org.uk, www.nottinghillonline.com/supporters, 10–6 MON–SAT, 12–5 SUN.

309 FULHAM ROAD, LONDON SW10 9QH, ☎ 020 7352 7986, FAX: 020 8357 5344, **e-mail:** charityshop@nhhg.org.uk, www.nottinghillonline.com/supporters, 10–6 MON–SAT, 12–4 SUN.

3 BARNES HIGH STREET, LONDON SW13 9LB, ☎ 020 8878 6170, **e-mail:** charityshop@nhhg.org.uk, www.nottinghillonline.com/supporters, 10–6 MON–SAT, 12–5 SUN.

288 UPPER RICHMOND ROAD, LONDON SW15 6TH, ☎ 020 8788 5763, **e-mail:** charityshop@nhhg.org.uk, www.nottinghillonline.com/supporters, 10–6 MON–SAT.

36 HIGH STREET, TOOTING, LONDON SW17 0RG, ☎ 020 8767 3431, **e-mail:** charityshop@nhhg.org.uk, www.nottinghillonline.com/supporters, 10–6 MON–SAT, 12–5 SUN.

211 BROMPTON ROAD, LONDON SW3 2EJ, ☎ 020 7581 7987, **e-mail:** charityshop@nhhg.org.uk, www.nottinghillonline.com/supporters, 10.30–6.30 MON–SAT, 12–5 SUN.

303 KINGS ROAD, LONDON SW3, FAX: 020 7352 8606, **e-mail:** charityshop@nhhg.org.uk, www.nottinghillonline.com/supporters, 10–6 MON–SAT, 12–5 SUN.

654A FULHAM ROAD, LONDON SW6 5RU, **e-mail:** charityshop@nhhg.org.uk, www.nottinghillonline.com/supporters, 10–6 MON–SAT, 12–5 SUN.

3 BUTE STREET, SOUTH KENSINGTON, LONDON SW7 3EY, ☎ 020 7581 9458, **e-mail:** charityshop@nhhg.org.uk, www.nottinghillonline.com/supporters, 10–6 MON–SAT, 12–5 SUN.

24 GOODGE STREET, LONDON W1T 2QF, ☎ 020 7636 4201, **e-mail:** charityshop@nhhg.org.uk, www.nottinghillonline.com/supporters, 10–6 MON–SAT.

59 NOTTING HILL GATE, LONDON W11 3JS, ☎ 020 7229 1476, **e-mail:** charityshop@nhhg.org.uk, www.nottinghillonline.com/supporters, 10–7 MON–SAT, 1–6 SUN.

76 ASKEW ROAD, LONDON W12 9BJ, ☎ 020 8740 4878, **e-mail:** charityshop@nhhg.org.uk, www.nottinghillonline.com/supporters, 10–6 MON–SAT.

178 QUEENSWAY, LONDON W2 6LY, ☎ 020 7221 8582, **e-mail:** charityshop@nhhg.org.uk, www.nottinghillonline.com/supporters, 10–6 MON–SAT, 1–6 SUN.

46 TURNHAM GREEN TERRACE, LONDON W4 1QP, ☎ 020 8995 8864, **e-mail:** charityshop@nhhg.org.uk, www.nottinghillonline.com/supporters, 10–6 MON–SAT, 1–6 SUN.

40 HIGH STREET, EALING, LONDON W5 5DB, ☎ 020 8567 8003, **e-mail:** charityshop@nhhg.org.uk, www.nottinghillonline.com/supporters, 10–6 MON–SAT, 12–5 SUN.

57 KENSINGTON CHURCH STREET, LONDON W8 4BA, ☎ 020 7937 5274, **e-mail:** charityshop@nhhg.org.uk, www.nottinghillonline.com/supporters, 10–6 MON–SAT. **DRESS AGENCY**

Notting Hill Housing Trust has over 20 shops around London, well-known for their unique findings: designer wares including Duffer of St George, Gucci, Valentino, Armani, even Versace can be found, as well as other little gems. The shops also feature a brand new range of home furnishings, glassware, wooden items etc. A delight for bargain-hunters.

OFFICE SALE SHOP

61 ST MARTINS LANE, LONDON WC2, ☎ 020 7497 0390, 10–7 MON–SAT, 12–6 SUN.
PERMANENT DISCOUNT OUTLET

Sale shop for Office own-brand shoes which also sells some brand-name shoes and trainers such as DKNY and Camper.

OXFAM ORIGINAL

26 GANTON STREET, LONDON W1, FAX: 020 7437 7338, 11.30–6 MON–SAT. **SECONDHAND AND VINTAGE CLOTHES**

Secondhand shop famous in the past for its one-off designs made up by fashion students using donated fabric from top designers, this shop sells trendy high-street clothes with a mixture of retro and funky fashion. Motto 'Original clothes for original people'. All stock has been pre-sorted to contain only desirable garments, contemporary designer labels and a few tasteful high street basics. Also stocks accessories including shoes, scarves and belts, as well as clothes donated by film and television production companies.

OXFAM SUPER SAVING SHOP

570 KINGSLAND ROAD, LONDON E8 4AH, ☎ 020 7923 1532, 9.15–5.15 MON–SAT.
SECONDHAND SHOP

Vast secondhand shop selling loads of cheap bric a brac, records and clothes. Stock is made up of unsold items from Oxfam's other shops in London so it's very cheap indeed. For example, bric-a-brac items from 9p; items of clothing from £2.29; electrical items (which have all been tested), such as lamps, from £2.99. Other end-of-line Oxfam shops include Kilburn, Burnt Oak, Tooting and Walthamstow.

PAUL SMITH SALE SHOP

23 AVERY ROW, LONDON W1X 9HB, ☎ 020 7493 1287, www.paulsmith.co.uk, 10–6 MON–SAT, 7 ON THUR. **PERMANENT DISCOUNT OUTLET**

Offers year-round seconds, ends of lines and sample stock in the heart of London's West End. This sale shop sells last season's stock for men, women and children, from the main shop at discounts of 40% to 50%, including R Newbold workwear range, jeans, shirts, knitwear, hats, gloves, suits, trousers and sportswear. There are lots of bargains with reductions of 75% off original retail price, and a wide selection of accessories from belts to cufflinks. As with all permanent sale shops, stock varies, so more than one visit may be necessary. Once a year, usually in June, there is a large clearance sale of all the previous season's clothing for women. Please phone for details.

PENGUIN SOCIETY

144 WEST END LANE, LONDON NW6 1SD, ☎ 020 7625 7778, FAX: 020 7624 9721, 11–7 MON–FRI, 10.30–5.30 SAT, 2–4.30 SUNDAYS IN SUMMER. **DRESS AGENCY**

New and 'gently worn' designer womenswear and menswear. Designers range from Whistles and

Ghost to Jigsaw and Warehouse in the womens' range and from Vivienne Westwood, Jean-Paul Gaultier and Alaia for both women and men. The clothes stocked cover both casual working day and evening wear, and prices range from £10 to £200. Twice yearly sales are held in summer and winter. Also women's and men's accessories: belts, jewellery, sunglasses etc. Quick turnover and deposits accepted on items of clothing. Their buyers now visit Paris on a monthly basis to bring back wonderful French goodies not seen in London. All are sold at very reasonable prices. All 'gently worn' clothing is seasonal and not more than 12 months old.

POSH LABELS

75 WILTON ROAD, NEAR VICTORIA STATION, LONDON SW1V 1DE, ☎ 020 7233 6385, www.poshlabels.co.uk, 10–6 MON–SAT, 12–6 SUN. **PERMANENT DISCOUNT OUTLET**

Posh Labels sells top name clothes direct from the showroom at wholesale prices. Next season's clothes are for sale at least four months before they reach the shops. Some clothes are from the current season. The range includes evening wear, smart suits, blouses and swimwear in sizes 10 to 26 for both men and women. For example, a dress which retails at £1,250 would be priced at £150. New collections arrive at least once a week. Please phone with any enquiries. The shop is a three-minute walk from Victoria Station. Labels seen here regularly include Jenny Packham, Givenchy, Versace, Armani, Dolce & Gabbana, Hunza, Gerry Weber, Moschino and Elizabeth Emanuel. Also stocks leather and suede.

PROIBITO

9 GEES COURT, OFF OXFORD STREET, LONDON W1, ☎ 020 7409 2769, www.proibito.com, 10–6.30 MON–WED, 10–8 THUR, 10–7 FRI, SAT, 12–6 SUN. **PERMANENT DISCOUNT OUTLET**

94 NEW BOND STREET, LONDON W1, ☎ 020 7493 0589, FAX: 020 8743 9026, www.proibito.com, 10–6.30 MON–WED, 10–8 THUR, 10–7 FRI, SAT, 12–6 SUN. **PERMANENT DISCOUNT OUTLET**

42 SOUTH MOLTON STREET, LONDON W1 1HB, ☎ 020 7491 3244, www.proibito.com, 10–6.30 MON–WED, 10–8 THUR, 10–7 FRI, SAT, 12–6 SUN. **PERMANENT DISCOUNT OUTLET**

Labels seen at all the branches include Moschino, Iceberg, Armani Jeans, Gianfranco Ferre, Dolce & Gabbana, Christian Lacroix and Valentino. Good for casual wear – it has racks of designer jeans, jackets and T-shirts – it also caters for the office market. Phone before making a special visit as shop location can change.

ROKIT

101 AND 107 BRICK LANE, LONDON E1 6SE, ☎ 020 7375 3864, 10.30–6.30 SEVEN DAYS A WEEK.

225 CAMDEN HIGH STREET, LONDON NW1 7BU, ☎ 020 7267 3046, 10–6.30 SEVEN DAYS A WEEK. **SECONDHAND AND VINTAGE CLOTHES**

Vintage and original clothing from the Forties to the present day. You can find vintage sportswear, denim and designer accessories.

ROYAL NATIONAL THEATRE

HIRE DEPARTMENT, CHICHESTER HOUSE, 1–3 BRIXTON ROAD, LONDON SW9 6DE, ☎ 020 7735 4774, FAX: 020 7582 8233, www.nationaltheatre.org.uk, 10–6 MON–FRI BY APPOINTMENT ONLY, CLOSED 1-2 DAILY. **HIRE SHOP**

A huge selection of quality theatrical costumes, props, furniture and weaponry available for hire. The collection covers most periods: with an average of 20 new productions each year there are always new discoveries to be made. Hires are available for theatre, film, television, amateur dramatics, opera and education. Fancy dress hire is also available.

SHIPTON & HENEAGE

117 QUEENSTOWN ROAD, LONDON SW8 3RH, ☎ 020 7738 8484, FAX: 020 7498 5638, **e-mail:** sales@shipton.com, www.shipton.com, 9–6 MON–FRI, 10–2 SAT. MAIL ORDER. **PERMANENT DISCOUNT OUTLET**

Traditional men's and women's shoes, loafers, half brogues, Oxfords, and Chelsea boots manufactured and supplied by the very best factories in Northampton, the traditional home of British footwear, and stocked typically by Savile Row outfitters and Jermyn Street tailors but sold here at discounts of up to 30% off shop prices. Their premium range is made from the finest hides from the best tanneries in Europe, while their grade range shoes are from sides of more mature hides. These are priced at £155 and £95 respectively. Additionally, they also sell a comprehensive range of deck shoes, plus a range of slippers equally discounted. Any style can be ordered from the catalogue and because there is no retail outlet, prices are low.

STEINBERG & TOLKIEN

193 KING'S ROAD, LONDON SW3 5EB, ☎ 020 7376 3660, 11–7 MON–SAT, 12–6 SUN.
SECONDHAND AND VINTAGE CLOTHES

London's most famous vintage clothes store is situated on two floors. One floor is devoted totally to jewellery, handbags, scarves, shoes and accessories, the other floor to American vintage and European couture clothing from the Twenties and Thirties to the Seventies. Some of the more interesting items were worn by movie stars of the Thirties and Forties and the garment is often seen on the original wearer in photographs around the shop. Popular with those looking for something unusual for a theme evening or a gala event, it's also frequented by those searching for an individual look in a style and quality unmatched even by couture designers today. Here, you can find Halston suede button-through dresses from the Seventies alongside heavily beaded cardigans from the Fifties, Pucci shirts and Gucci bags, bias-cut slips from the Thirties, shirtwaisters from the Seventies, Fortuny gowns and Ossie Clark outfits. There is also a selection of men's clothes. Many of the clothes are now featured in the book: Vintage: The Art of Dressing Up by Tracy Tolkein, published by Pavilion and sold here in the shop, £19.99.

SURPRISE SURPRISE

175–179 VICTORIA STREET, LONDON SW1E 5NE, ☎ 020 7233 5421, 9–7 MON–SAT, 10–6.30 SUN.

527 OXFORD STREET, LONDON W1R 1DD, ☎ 020 7495 7161, 9–7 MON–SAT, 10–7 SUN.

114 HIGH STREET, BARNET, LONDON EN5 5XQ, ☎ 020 8440 8958, 9–6.30 MON–SAT, 10–6 SUN.

752 HIGH ROAD, NORTH FINCHLEY LONDON N12 9QG, ☎ 020 8445 4766, 9–6.30 MON–SAT, 10–6 SUN.T

357 STRAND, LONDON WC2R, ☎ 020 7240 2812, 9–7 MON–SAT, 10–6.30 SUN.

SWISS CENTRE, 10 WARDOUR STREET, LONDON W1V 3HG, ☎ 020 7434 3688, 9–11 MON–SAT, 9–10 SUN. **PERMANENT DISCOUNT OUTLET**

Men's shirts, ties and socks at very reasonable prices. For example, polo shirts, £4.99 each or three for £12; silk ties, £4.99 or three for £12; socks from £3.99 to £6.99 for a pack of six. Also sells women's mid-range fashion clothing.

SWIMGEAR

11 STATION ROAD, FINCHLEY, LONDON N3 2SB, ☎ 020 8346 6106, FAX: 020 8346 7211, www.swimgear.co.uk, 9.30–5 MON–FRI. MAIL ORDER. **PERMANENT DISCOUNT OUTLET**

A mail order company which also operates via a retail outlet opposite Finchley Central station. As well as selling their swimwear at less than the normal retail price by not putting the full markup on their products, they also sell discontinued and ends of line ranges of swimwear for men, women and children at between 20% to 30% less than normal retail prices. They also stock swimming hats, bubble hats, kickboards, goggles and flippers in adult and children's sizes. Flippers normally cost about £18.50, but can be bought here for about £8 in black rubber; Lycra trunks, plain £7.35 up to £10 for patterned ones. Bikinis are on sale all year round, with women's swimwear ranging up to size 50 with Swimgear's own brand, full colour Mark One brochure or leaflet. Prices are lower than would be offered at swim meets and retail shops. As part of their service, they do not cash your cheque until your full order has been completed. Postage and packaging extra. Orders over £20 are post free, excluding heavy items such as flippers and shampoo on which p&p is charged.

THE COSTUME STUDIO

MONTGOMERY HOUSE, 159–161 BALLS POND ROAD, ISLINGTON, LONDON N1 4BG, ☎ 020 7388 4481, FAX: 020 7837 6576, **e-mail:** costume.studio@easynet.co.uk, www.thecostumestudioltd.co.uk, 9.30–6 MON–FRI, 10 -5 SAT. **HIRE SHOP**

Twenty thousand costumes for adults from ancient to the far future. Clients include television and video companies. Individual hiring costs from £70 upwards plus VAT for one week. There are plenty of accessories, from shoes and hats to bags and gloves, to complete an outfit.

THE DESIGNER WAREHOUSE SALES FOR WOMEN AND MEN

DWS LTD, STUDIO 6, THE IVORIES, 6–8 NORTHAMPTON STREET, LONDON N1 2HY, ☎ 020 7704 1064, FAX: 020 7704 1379, **e-mail:** info@dwslondon.co.uk, www.dwslondon.co.uk, SALES USUALLY OPEN 10–8 FRI, 10–6 SAT, 11–5 SUN. **DESIGNER SALES**

More designer labels can be found at the Designer Warehouse Sales than housed at either Selfridges or Harvey Nichols. With 60% or more off the usual retail prices, these Sales were nominated by Time Out as one of the Top Ten Reasons for living in London. Recognised as 'the biggest and best' designer sales in the country, DWS uniquely boasts items from current collections as well as catwalk one-offs and studio samples. Aspirational designers such as Hussein Chalayan, Boyd, Elspeth Gibson, Orla Kiely and Fake London vie for space downstairs alongside established UK designers such as Paul Smith, Vivienne Westwood and Ghost. Upstairs, a huge studio houses international labels such as Prada, Cerruti, Victor Victoria, Romeo Gigli, Prada, Miu Miu, Donna Karan and Gucci alongside among others. A separate studio boasts shoes and leather goods, meaning the sales offer complete head-to-toe dressing at a fraction of the usual price. As well as enjoying a large presence at the five men's and five women's DWSs, exclusive Nicole Farhi sales are held by DWS mid-season twice a year. These incorporate menswear, womenswear and accessories, all under one roof.

THE DRESS BOX

8–10 CHEVAL PLACE, LONDON SW7 1ES, ☎ 020 7589 2240, 10–6 MON–FRI, 10.30–6 SAT. **DRESS AGENCY**

Operating for more than 50 years, the Dress Box caters for the top end of the market including new and nearly-new couture – Yves Saint Laurent, Chanel, Gucci, Hermes, Valentino, Prada and Pierre Cardin. Those looking for special occasion wear, evening outfits or ballgowns are well catered for. Among the 500 or so outfits in the shop at any one time are Chanel suits from £425 and Valentino and Ungaro suits from £295. Wonderful collection of Yves St Laurent suits, some Chanel jackets and suits. Prices range from £150 to £1,000 for suits though most outfits cost £200 to £400. There is also a collection of hats from £95 (Philip Somerville, Philip Treacy) and shoes from £75. Alterations service available. There are also Chanel handbags, scarves from £95, costume jewellery, as well as a small selection of menswear. You can buy a whole wardrobe here from swimwear to coats. Also offers an in-house couture alteration service.

THE DRESSER

10 PORCHESTER PLACE, LONDON W2 2BS, ☎ 020 7724 7212, **e-mail:** sally.ormsby@virgin.net, 11–6 MON–FRI, 11–5 SAT. **DRESS AGENCY**

The Dresser is a trendy, upmarket dress agency which sells nearly-new couture and contemporary women's and men's clothes including Armani, Donna Karan, Jil Sander, Dolce & Gabbana, Gucci, Prada, Comme des Garcons, at prices ranging from £50 to £400. The men's department has such as Paul Smith, Yohji Yamamoto, Jasper Conran, Armani, Gaultier and Comme des Garcons at prices ranging from £30 to £400. There is more women's merchandise than men's, with lots of separates and some accessories.

THE EXCHANGE DRESS AGENCY

30 ELIZABETH STREET, BELGRAVIA, LONDON SW1, FAX: 020 7730 3334, www.nkrf.org.uk 9.30–5 MON–FRI, 6 ON THUR, 10–4 SAT. **DRESS AGENCY**

Set up in aid of The National Kidney Research Fund, to whom all the profits are donated, it stocks a range of new and nearly-new women's clothing including Paul Costelloe, Valentino, Flyte Ostell, Gucci, Prada, Chanel, Moschino, Guy Laroche, Givenchy, Caroline Charles and Rifat Ozbek. Thirty per cent of stock is new and current season samples. Also stocks accessories including handbags, shoes, jewellery and scarves. Upstairs has now been converted to house an extensive selection of menswear, including merchandise from designers such as Gucci, Valentino, Yves St Laurent and many more top names. Stock includes suits, jackets, shirts, ties, coats and shoes. They also stock a selection of brand new cut glass, silver, china, figurines, candlesticks and some jewellery, all making ideal gifts.

THE GALLERY OF ANTIQUE COSTUME & TEXTILES

2 CHURCH STREET, MARYLEBONE, LONDON NW8 8ED, ☎ 020 7723 9981, FAX: 020 7723 9981, **e-mail:** info@gact.co.uk, www.gact.co.uk, 10–5.30 MON–SAT. **SECONDHAND AND VINTAGE CLOTHES**

Original costumes from the 18th century to the 1940s and waistcoats and fabrics from the early textiles in the 16th century to the early 20th century. Cushions from £65 to £500; table covers from £100; curtains from £400; Edwardian tea dresses from £100; Twenties and Thirties evening wear from £200 upwards.

THE LOFT

35 MONMOUTH STREET, COVENT GARDEN, LONDON WC2H 9DD, ☎ 020 7240 3807, www.the-loft.co.uk, 11–6 MON–SAT, 1–5 SUN. **DRESS AGENCY, HIRE SHOP**

One-offs, ends of lines, nearly-new for men and women from the likes of Vivienne Westwood, Jean-Paul Gaultier, DKNY, Versace, Paul Smith, Gucci, Prada, Armani, Moschino, Nicole Farhi, Voyage, Joseph, Jill Sander, Comme Des Garcon, APC, Helmut Lang, Chanel, Stussy, Ralph Lauren, Antonio Miro, Iceberg, Hugo Boss, Kenzo, Costume National, Costume Homme, John Rocha, Diesel, Romeo Gigli, Stone Island, Clements Ribeiro, Katherine Hamnet, Miu Miu, Evisu, Matsuda and Burberry. A hire service is also available in this two-storey shop which is packed with bargains. Denise Van Outen, Bjork and George Michael have all been kitted out in The Loft's designer outfits at a fraction of their original price. Fed up with some of your own designer outfits? Take them here and turn them into cash.

THE OBSERVATORY

20 GREENWICH CHURCH STREET, GREENWICH, LONDON SE10 9BJ, ☎ 020 8305 1998, 10–6 SEVEN DAYS A WEEK. **SECONDHAND AND VINTAGE CLOTHES**

This retrospective clothing shop (combining retro with new) has been established for over 10 years. It sells turn-of-the-century fashion as well as Fifties, Sixties, Seventies and early Eighties gear. Women's frocks, shoes, hats and jewellery as well as lots of leather, suede and denim garments. Men's suits, jackets, trousers and shoes. Also sell retro gifts and cards to complement the clothing.

THE WEDDING STORE

232 STAMFORD HILL, LONDON N16 6TT, ☎ 020 8800 7466, FAX: 020 8809 6540, www.losners.co.uk, 9–5.30 MON–SAT, 7 ON THUR. **HIRE SHOP**

Specialises in top end of the market wedding outfits to hire and to buy. Basic hire costs anything from £100 to £300; you can choose from a huge range that includes new and nearly-new bridal outfits. Labels include Ronald Joyce, Ellis, Alfred Angelo, Mori Lee. Can also make dresses to order. All the accessories are to buy only and they offer a shoe-dyeing service. There are also morning and dinner suits to hire from £40 to £200. Other branches in Dunstable, Ilford, Winchmore Hill, Edgware, Gants Hill, Hampstead, Ealing and St Albans (winners of the 2002 British Bridal Buyer Retail Menswear awards), however these are all menswear outlets with the exception of St Albans which also carries the bridal range.

TK MAXX

PENINSULA RETAIL PARK, BUGSBY WAY, CHARLTON, LONDON, ☎ 020 8293 1957, www.tkmaxx.com, PHONE FOR DETAILS.

THE ARCADIA CENTRE, THE BROADWAY, EALING, LONDON W5 2ND, ☎ 020 8566 0447, www.tkmaxx.com, 9.30–8 MON–FRI, 7.30 ON THUR, 9–7 SAT, 11–5 SUN.

UNIT B, FIRST FLOOR, WOOD GREEN SHOPPING CENTRE, LONDON N22 6YD, ☎ 020888 88803, www.tkmaxx.com, 9–6 MON–SAT, 10–5 SUN. **PERMANENT DISCOUNT OUTLET**

See page 89 (BEDS)

TOG 24

PUTNEY EXCHANGE SHOPPING CENTRE, PUTNEY HIGH STREET, LONDON SW15 1TW, ☎ 020 8785 3565, **e-mail:** mail-order@tog24.com, www.tog24.com, 9–6 MON–SAT, 11–5 SUN. **FACTORY SHOP IN A FACTORY SHOPPING VILLAGE**

See page 99 (CHESH)

UNIVERSITY VISION

UNIVERSITY OF LONDON UNION BUILDING, MALET STREET, LONDON WC1, ☎ 020 7636 8925, 9–5.30 MON–FRI, 10–2 SAT. PHONE FIRST FOR SATURDAY OPENING HOURS DURING HOLIDAYS. **PERMANENT DISCOUNT OUTLET**

Permanent discount outlet used mostly by students but available for use by the general public selling spectacles and contact lenses and solutions at very competitive prices. On production of a genuine quote they will price match any competitor's price for spectacles or contact lenses.

VIDAL SASSOON

20 GROSVENOR STREET, LONDON W1, FAX: 020 7491 0030, 1.30 APPOINTMENTS TUE TO THUR.

54 KNIGHTSBRIGDGE, LONDON SW1X 7JN, ☎ 020 7318 5205, 10–3 MON–FRI.

56 DAVIES MEWS, LONDON W1Y 1AS, ☎ 020 7318 5205, 10–3 MON–FRI. **PERMANENT DISCOUNT OUTLET**

Cuts and styles undertaken by students at the School of Hairdressing for £9.50, or £6.50 if you are a student, nurse, unemployed or an OAP. Appointments must be made at least one week in advance. At the Staff Training School in Bayswater, you can pay between £15 and £29 – £42 if tinting or colouring – depending on the level of experience of the staff. Again, appointments must be made. The Grosvenor Street school is for hairdressers who have trained for at least seven years so you are assured of a high level of competence.

WALLERS

21–24 NEWPORT COURT, CHARING CROSS ROAD, LONDON WC2H 7JS, ☎ 020 7437 1665, www.wallersclothing.co.uk, 9–5.30 MON–FRI, 10–5 SAT. **PERMANENT DISCOUNT OUTLET**

Wallers is a family firm established at the same address for more than 75 years. They specialise in famous name suits, sports jackets, blazers, trousers, coats and morning and evening dress wear at greatly reduced prices. Well known to television and film designers, who appreciate the value of choice, their Chinatown shop looks small on the outside but inside is a rabbit warren, full to the brim. Wallers clothes have been seen in Inspector Morse, Minder, Yes Minister, The Bill, Between The Lines, Only Fools and Horses and even blockbuster Hollywood films such as Mission Impossible and many James Bond films. There are usually at least 5,000 items in stock at any one time, in all sizes, most of which are ends of ranges, cancelled orders, seconds (clearly marked as such) or bought as a result of liquidations. Examples of prices include suits, £125, usual price £225; jackets, £79.50, usual price £125; trousers, £25, usual price £59.50; raincoats and over-coats from £49.50; dinner suits, from £110; three-piece morning suits, from £175. They also have a smart range of business clothes for women.

WELLINGTONS

1 WELLINGTON PLACE, LONDON NW8 7PE, ☎ 020 7483 0688, 11–5 MON–SAT. **DRESS AGENCY**

Stunning selection of Gucci, Prada, Chanel, MaxMara, Armani and Joseph. Women's suits from £18, jackets from £28. There's also a bargain basement full of high street names such as Marks & Spencer and Karen Millen as well as reduced designer clothing. Also sells a range of children's clothing, from birth to five years, including Timberland and Ralph Lauren, all at fantastic prices. A large range of accessories and also available, including shoes, belts, scarves and handbags.

MIDDLESEX

BRAND CENTRE

12 HAREFIELD ROAD, UXBRIDGE, MIDDLESEX UB8 1JS, ☎ 01895 814888, FAX: 01895 814222, 10–8 MON–FRI, 9.30–6.30 SAT, 11–5 SUN. **PERMANENT DISCOUNT OUTLET**

See page 133 (LANCS)

DAMART

63–67 HIGH STREET, HOUNSLOW, MIDDLESEX TW3 1RB, ☎ 020 8570 6796, 9–5 MON–SAT. **FACTORY SHOP**

See page 114 (DORS)

GORDONS CONNECTIONS

92–100 HIGH STREET, YEWSLEY, WEST DRAYTON, MIDDLESEX UB7 7DU, ☎ 01895 441846, 9–6 TUE, WED, THUR, SAT, 9–7 FRI. SEVEN DAYS A WEEK FROM NOVEMBER TO CHRISTMAS. **PERMANENT DISCOUNT OUTLET**

Well-known high street brands including Marks & Spencer and Principles at discounts of up to 70%. Rapid turnover of stock. There is a men's shop, a lingerie shop, a coffee shop and butcher.

MATALAN

PUMP LANE, HAYES, MIDDLESEX UB3 3NB, ☎ 020 8606 6700, FAX: 020 8573 5268, www.matalan.co.uk, 10–8 MON–FRI, 9–6 SAT, 11–5 SUN.

GREAT WESTERN INDUSTRIAL PARK, WINDMILL LANE, SOUTHALL, MIDDLESEX UB2 4SD, ☎ 020 8574 9660, FAX: 020 8574 4924, www.matalan.co.uk, 10–8 MON–FRI, 9–6 SAT, 11–5 SUN. **PERMANENT DISCOUNT OUTLET**

See page 89 (BEDS)

THE SALVAGE SHOP

34–40 WATLING AVENUE, BURNT OAK, MIDDLESEX HA8 0LR, ☎ 020 8952 4353, **e-mail:** lss@salvage1.co.uk, www.salvage1.co.uk, 9–5.30 MON–SAT, 10–4 SUN. **PERMANENT DISCOUNT OUTLET**

An Aladdin's cave of salvaged stock for the avid bargain hunter, most of which has been the subject of insurance claims for fire or flood, salvage, bankruptcy or is simply clearance stock. Stock changes every two or three days and regular visitors have found anything from half price Kenwood Chefs, televisions and toys to furniture, kitchen items, linens and especially fantastic bargains in designer clothing. Yves Saint Laurent, Armani, Ungaro, Hugo Boss and Valentino, as well as all major high street names, are just some of the names to be found (though the labels are often cut out). Discounts range from 50% to 80%. Phone first to check stock.

TK MAXX

UNIT 31, ST GEORGE'S CENTRE, ST ANNE'S ROAD, HARROW, MIDDLESEX HA1 1HS, ☎ 020 8863 9292, www.tkmaxx.com, 9.30–8 MON–FRI, 9–7 SAT, 11–5 SUN. **PERMANENT DISCOUNT OUTLET**

See page 89 (BEDS)

NORFOLK

BALLY OUTLET STORE

HALL ROAD, NORWICH, NORFOLK NR4 6DP, ☎ 01603 760590, FAX: 01603 616366, **e-mail:** sjackson@bally.ch www.bally.com, 9.30–5.30 MON–FRI, 9–5.30 SAT, 11–5 SUN AND MOST BANK HOLIDAYS. PHONE FIRST. **FACTORY SHOP**

The Bally Outlet is located on the outskirts of Norwich, and sells high quality women's and men's footwear, plus a range of handbags and accessories. The merchandise is from the company's European stores and is end-of-line or ex-sale stock. A saving of at least 30% off the normal retail price can be made. Also on site is a coffee shop serving morning coffee, light lunches and afternoon teas in a pleasant and relaxing atmosphere. There is ample free parking, toilet facilites, and coaches are welcome by prior arrangement.

GLADRAGS

20 THETFORD ROAD, WATTON, NORFOLK IP25 6BB, ☎ 01953 885210, 10–4 TUE–SAT. **DRESS AGENCY**

Sells women's new and nearly-new outfits, including ballgowns from designers such as Gerry Weber, Versace and Escada, as well as quality high street names such as Marks & Spencer. Accessories also on sale range from hats and bags to shoes and belts.

JAEGER/VIYELLA FACTORY SHOP

1 HANSA ROAD, KING'S LYNN, NORFOLK PE30 4HZ, ☎ 01553 732132, 9–5.30 MON–SAT, 11–4 SUN. **FACTORY SHOP**

Contemporary classics from Jaeger at excellent prices. Most of the merchandise is previous seasons' stock, but you might also find some special makes. This branch stocks tailoring and knitwear for women and men.

LATHAMS

BRIDGE STREET, POTTER HEIGHAM, GREAT YARMOUTH, NORFOLK NR29 5JE, ☎ 01692 670080, 9–5.30 MON–SAT, 10–4 SUN. **FACTORY SHOP**

Sell a wide range of fashions, hardware, china, fishing tackle, books, gardening equipment, linen, groceries and Christmas gifts at very reasonable prices. Most of the makes are high street labels and consist of discontinued lines and seconds. Also jewellery concessions, shoes, computer games kiosk, coffee shop and garden centre.

MATALAN

SOUTHTOWN ROAD, GREAT YARMOUTH, NORFOLK NR31 0JB, ☎ 01493 444734, FAX: 01493 445636, www.matalan.co.uk, 9–8 MON–FRI, 9–6, 11–5 SUN.

BLACKFRIARS ROAD, KINGS LYNN, NORFOLK PE301RX, ☎ 01553 765696, FAX: 01553 764518, www.matalan.co.uk, 10–8 MON–FRI, 9–6 SAT, 11–5 SUN. **PERMANENT DISCOUNT OUTLET**

See page 89 (BEDS)

MR SHOE'S FACTORY SHOP

31 YAXHAM ROAD, DEREHAM, NORFOLK NR19 1HD, ☎ 01362 699599, 9–6 MON–SAT, 10.30–4.30 SUN. **PERMANENT DISCOUNT OUTLET**

Shoes for all the family, including well-known brands, at discounted prices.

QD STORES

143 HIGH STREET, GORLESTON, GREAT YARMOUTH, NORFOLK NR31 6RB, ☎ 01493 652735, 9–5.30 MON–SAT.

128–132 NORFOLK STREET, KINGS LYNN, NORFOLK PE30 1AP, ☎ 01553 770068, 9–5.30 MON–SAT.

7–10 ANGLIA SQUARE, NORWICH, NORFOLK NR3 1DY, ☎ 01603 275201

9–5.30 MON–SAT, 10–4 SUN. 48–54 ST STEPHENS STREET, NORWICH, NORFOLK NR1 3SL, ☎ 01603 622562, 9–5.30 MON–SAT. **PERMANENT DISCOUNT OUTLET**

See page 89 (BEDS)

ROMBAH WALLACE FACTORY SHOP

14–17 IRONSIDE WAY, NORWICH ROAD, HINGHAM, NORFOLK NR9 4LF, ☎ 01953 851106, 9–5 MON–SAT, 10–4 SUN. **FACTORY SHOP**

Good selection of shoes for women and men at discounted prices. Sandals, court shoes, smart or casual. Rombah Wallace shoes are on sale at discounts of 30%. Also sells shirts, ties, handbags and jewellery at competitive prices.

ROYS

BOWTHORPE CENTRE, WENDENE, BOWTHORPE, NORWICH NORFOLK NR5 9HA, ☎ 01603 746622, www.roys.co.uk, 8.30–8 MON–THUR, 8.30–9 FRI, 8–6 SAT, 10–4 SUN.

77–87 MAGDALEN STREET, NORWICH, NORFOLK NR3 1AA, ☎ 01603 612934, www.roys.co.uk, 9–5.30 MON–SAT, 10–4 SUN.

WROXHAM, NORWICH, NORFOLK NR12 8DB, ☎ 01603 782131, www.roys.co.uk, 9–5.30 MON, TUE, 9–8 WED, THUR, FRI, 9–6 SAT, 10.30–4.30 SUN. **PERMANENT DISCOUNT OUTLET**

YAXHAM ROAD, DEREHAM NORFOLK NR19 1HD, ☎ 01362 690555, www.roys.co.uk, 9–8 MON–FRI, 9–6 SAT, 11–5 SUN.

10 YARMOUTH ROAD, NORTH WALSHAM, NORFOLK NR28 9BW, ☎ 01692 501058, www.roys.co.uk, 9–5.30 MON, TUE, 9–8 WED, THUR, FRI, 9–6 SAT, 10–4 SUN.

GUILDHALL STREET, THETFORD, NORFOLK IP24 2DP, ☎ 01842 766161, www.roys.co.uk, 9–5.30 MON–SAT, 10–4 SUN. **PERMANENT DISCOUNT OUTLET**

Roys sell branded household goods at what they call 'valued prices'. The Save 'n' Wear department deals with the cheaper end of the clothing market for men, women and children. They also include DIY, gardening, electrical, housewares, gifts, toiletries and some food lines. The Wroxham store also has a pharmacy department that deals with photography, records and toiletries, all at competitive prices. This branch has a coffee shop on site, as well as free parking.

START-RITE

8 HIGH STREET, KING'S LYNN, NORFOLK P30 1BX, ☎ 01553 760786, 9–5.30 MON–SAT.
FACTORY SHOP

The children's shoe experts have a large factory shop selling clearance lines at discounted prices. They don't stock the full range – it's a matter of choosing from what's available. Rejects are sold at at least half price; end of sales stock with not quite such a high discount. There are also some senior sizes up to size 9. Feet are expertly measured by trained staff.

THE FACTORY SHOE SHOP

BARRACK STREET, NORWICH, NORFOLK NR3 1TH, ☎ 01603 493185, 10–4 MON–SAT, 7 ON THUR. **PERMANENT DISCOUNT OUTLET**

Shoes for men and women which are slight seconds and clearance lines from Van Dahl and other English and Continental suppliers. Typical discounts include shoes which would normally retail for £59.95 sold here at £37.

THE FACTORY SHOP LTD

NORWICH STREET, EAST DEREHAM, NORFOLK NR19 1AD, ☎ 01362 691868, 9–5.30 MON–SAT, 10–4 SUN.

52 LONDON ROAD, HARLESTON, NORFOLK IP20 9BZ, ☎ 01379 854860, 9–5.30 MON–SAT, 10.30–4 SUN.

LYNN ROAD, SNETTISHAM, NORFOLK PE31 7QG, ☎ 01485 544441, 9–5.30 MON–SAT, 10–4 SUN. **FACTORY SHOP**

See page 98 (CHESH)

NORTHAMPTONSHIRE

AIRWEAR

NENE PARK, STATION ROAD, NORTHAMPTONSHIRE NN9 5QG, ☎ 01933 653111, FAX: 01933 654506, www.drmartens.com, 9.30–5.30 MON–SAT, 10–4 SUN. **PERMANENT DISCOUNT OUTLET**

Sells Doc Martens shoes and boots, as well as clothing and a vast range of accessories at discounted prices. Nene Park is the only official outlet for Rushden and Diamonds' merchandise.

AQUASCUTUM

PRINCEWOOD ROAD, EARLSTREES INDUSTRIAL ESTATE, CORBY, NORTHAMPTONSHIRE NN17 4AQ, ☎ 01536 205086, 10–5.30 MON–FRI, 10–4 SAT. **FACTORY SHOP**

See page 125 (HERTS)

BARKER SHOES LTD

STATION ROAD, EARLS BARTON, NORTHAMPTON, NORTHAMPTONSHIRE NN6 0NT, ☎ 01604 813117, FAX: 01604 813117, **e-mail:** barker@barkershoes.co.uk, www.barker-shoes.co.uk, 10–5 MON–FRI, 10–4 SAT. PHONE TO CHECK SUNDAY OPENING TIMES. **FACTORY SHOP**

Discontinued lines of shoes at about 30% off the retail price, and slight imperfects at 40% off the normal retail price. Sells shoes manufactured by its own factory, which include brogues and smart day shoes for men and women. Women's shoes are available in double A width fitting. There are men's high grade, traditional shoes which sell to top stores, casual shoes and moccasins.

BARRATT'S SALE SHOP

BARRACK ROAD, KINGSTHORPE HOLLOW, NORTHAMPTON, NORTHAMPTONSHIRE NN2 6EL, ☎ 01604 718632, www.tall-small.com, 9–5.30 MON–SAT. **FACTORY SHOP**

This shop now stocks solely sales stock of trainers and shoes from last season for men, women and children. Children's range from £5 to £10, men's from £20 to £40, and women's from £10 upwards. They also cater for small and large feet.

FAULKENERS

STATION ROAD, WOODFORD HALSE, NORTHAMPTONSHIRE NN11 3RB, ☎ 01327 260306, 9–5.30 MON, FRI, 9–8 TUE, WED, THUR, 10–4 SUN. **PERMANENT DISCOUNT OUTLET**

This shoe retailer, established for over 135 years, has a large factory shop selling a vast range of all types of women's, men's and children's shoes, all of which are perfects, at up to 30% below normal high street prices. Women's sandals cost from £2.99; shoes from £5. Men's shoes cost from £7.99; sports shoes from £5. A large range of casual wear, including T-shirts and tracksuits for women, men and children, plus a selection of women's underwear. Kitchenware, ceramics, household goods and giftware are also stocked at discounted prices. Also sells riding boots, jodhpurs, climbing boots and hiking boots.

GLOVERALL FACTORY SHOP

LONDON ROAD, WELLINGBOROUGH, NORTHAMPTONSHIRE NN8 2QX, ☎ 01933 225666, OPEN 9–5 MON–FRI. **FACTORY SHOP**

Duffle coats, lightweight jackets, knitwear, silk ties and cufflinks. One reader bought a pure wool duffle coat for £90 whose original price was £395 and another made for Galeries Lafayette of Paris for £59, usual price £120.

MATALAN

UNIT 1, PHOENIX RETAIL PARK, PHOENIX PARKWAY, CORBY, NORTHAMPTONSHIRE NN17 5DT, ☎ 01536 408042, FAX: 01536 408750, www.matalan.co.uk, 9–8 MON–FRI, 9–6 SAT, 10–4 SUN.

UNIT 1, WEEDON ROAD INDUSTRIAL ESTATE, TYNE ROAD, NORTHAMPTON, NORTHAMPTONSHIRE NN5 5BE, ☎ 01604 597890, FAX: 01604 588068, www.matalan.co.uk, 9–8 MON–FRI, 9–6 SAT, 10.30–4.30 SUN.

VICTORIA ROAD, WELLINGBOROUGH, NORTHAMPTONSHIRE NN8 2EF, ☎ 01933 233890, FAX: 01933 272658, www.matalan.co.uk, 10–8 MON–FRI, 9–6 SAT, 11–5 SUN. **PERMANENT DISCOUNT OUTLET**

See page 89 (BEDS)

NORTHAMPTON FOOTWEAR DISTRIBUTORS LTD

SUMMERHOUSE ROAD, MOULTON PARK, NORTHAMPTONSHIRE NN3 6WD, ☎ 01604 790 827, 9–12 AND 2–4 MON–FRI. MAIL ORDER. **PERMANENT DISCOUNT OUTLET**

Direct mail clearance brochures featuring a wide range of footwear at incredible prices. There is no minimum order, although postage and packaging is charged on orders under £300. Size ranges are limited, but not overly so. If they don't fit you get your money refunded if returned within 10 days. Spring, summer and autumn catalogues are available.

THE DESIGNER ROOM

JACKSONS LANDING, HARTLEPOOL MARINA, CLEVELAND, TYNE & WEAR TS24 0XN, ☎ 01429 275308, 10–6 MON–SAT, 11–5 SUN. **FACTORY SHOP IN A FACTORY SHOPPING VILLAGE**

Once the site of a shopping mall at Jacksons Landing, it is now 60,000 square feet of designer-branded goods: clothes, accessories, lingerie, perfumes, cosmetics, jewellery and much more. The store, which is on two floors and the first of its kind in the UK for The Designer Room chain, offers huge discounts of between 30% and 70%, as well as a café with a marina view. This is Hartlepool's one-stop shopping experience. Some of the brands that you will find include: Benetton and Cosmopolitan bed linen, Antler, Carlton and Salisbury luggage, Medici cards and posters, Remainders books and stationery, Edinburgh Crystal, Nachtmann Candlesticks, Arthur Price cutlery, Lifestyle tableware, Woods of Windsor and Scent To You, and Charles Clinkard shoes for adults and children. As for clothing, there is Tommy Hilfiger, Kangol, DKNY, Jasper Conran, French Connection, Calvin Klein lingerie, Elle, Versace, Ghost, Boxfresh, Gloverall duffle coats, Klass, Roman Originals, Peter Golding, Trespass and Bon Bleu childrenswear, plus much more

T GROOCOCK & CO LTD, PADDERS FACTORY SHOP

GORDON STREET, ROTHWELL, NORTHAMPTONSHIRE NN14 6BJ, ☎ 01536 714115, 10–5 MON–FRI, 9–1 SAT. **FACTORY SHOP**

A family business that has been in Rothwell for over 80 years manufacturing women's and men's leather walking and leisure shoes, sandals and boots, including wide fittings, discontinued lines and slight seconds at up to 40% off normal retail prices.

T J HUGHES

THE NEWLANDS CENTRE, GOLD STREET, KETTERING, NORTHAMPTONSHIRE NN16 8JA, ☎ 01536 419700, FAX: 01536 523041, **e-mail:** info@tjhughes.co.uk, www.tjhughes.co.uk, 9–5.30 MON–SAT, 10–4 SUN. **PERMANENT DISCOUNT OUTLET**

See page 98 (CHESH)

THE DOC SHOP

RUSHDEN AND DIAMONDS FOOTBALL CLUB, NENE PARK, DIAMOND WAY, IRTHLINGBOROUGH, NORTHAMPTONSHIRE NN9 5QF, ☎ 01933 652000, 9–5.30 MON–FRI, 9–5 SAT, 11–5 BANK HOLIDAYS, 10–6 ON MATCH DAYS.

71 HIGH STREET, WOLLASTON, NORTHAMPTONSHIRE NN9 5QF, ☎ 01933 666144, 9–5.30 MON–SAT, 11–5 BANK HOLIDAYS. **PERMANENT DISCOUNT OUTLET**

See page 144 (LEICS)

UNITED FOOTWEAR

75–79 STAMFORD ROAD, KETTERING, NORTHAMPTONSHIRE, ☎ 01536 481855, 9–5.30 MON–SAT, 10–4 SUN. **PERMANENT DISCOUNT OUTLET**

See page 124 (HAMPS)

NORTHUMBERLAND

ATTICA

2 OLD GEORGE YARD, OFF HIGHBRIDGE, NEWCASTLE UPON TYNE, TYNE & WEAR NE1 1EZ, ☎ 0191 261 4062, 10.30–5.30 MON–SAT. **SECONDHAND AND VINTAGE CLOTHES**
Two floors of vintage clothing for men and women from the Victorian era to the 1960s. Stock includes a vast range of glamorous evening wear, as well as 1960s furniture and decor.

J BARBOUR & SONS LTD

CUSTOMER SERVICE DEPARTMENT, MONKSWAY, JARROW, TYNE & WEAR NE32 3HL, ☎ 0191 428 4707, 9–5 MON–SAT, 10–4 SUN. **FACTORY SHOP**
The famous waterproof waxed jackets and outdoor wear, all of which are seconds or discontinued lines, at discounts of 20% to 25%. Jackets come in 15 different styles from short to full-length and in various colours, but you may not find the style, colour and size you want as quantities vary. There are also shooting jackets, tweed hats and caps, linings for coats, bags, waxed trousers, waders, waxed jackets, breathable jackets for men and women, fleeces, knitwear and quilted jackets. There is also a small selection of children's jackets. Free parking.

BURBERRY

KITTY BREWSTER INDUSTRIAL ESTATE, BLYTH, NORTHUMBERLAND NE24 4RG, ☎ 01670 352524, 10–4 MON, 9.30–4 TUE–FRI, 8.45–3.30 SAT. **FACTORY SHOP**

See page 94 (CHESH)

CATALOGUE BARGAIN SHOP

51 SHIELDS ROAD, BYKER, NEWCASTLE UPON TYNE, TYNE & WEAR NE6 1DJ, ☎ 0191 265 6033, www.bargaincrazy.com, 9–6 MON–SAT, 8 ON THUR, FRI, 10.30–4.30 SUN. **CATALOGUE DISCOUNT STORES**

15 THE PRECINCT, THE IN CENTRE, JARROW, TYNE & WEAR, ☎ 0191 483 4318, 9–5 MON–SAT. 8 THE FORUM SHOPPING CENTRE, WALLSEND, NORTHUMBERLAND NE28 8JR, ☎ 0191 236 9501
9–5 MON–SAT. **PERMANENT DISCOUNT OUTLET**

See page 92 (CAMBS)

DEWHIRST IMPRESSIONS

NORTH SEATON INDUSTRIAL ESTATE, OFF NEWBIGGIN ROAD, ASHINGTON, NORTHUMBERLAND NE63 0YB, ☎ 01670 813493, **e-mail:** kim.mcmaster@dewhirst.com, 10–8 MON–FRI, 9–6 SAT, 10.30–4.30 SUN. **FACTORY SHOP**

See page 101 (CO DURH)

DISCOUNT CLOTHING STORE

UNIT 7, KINGSTON PARK CENTRE, KINGSTON PARK, NORTHUMBERLAND NE3 2FP, ☎ 0191 271 4126, 9.30–5.30 MON–SAT.

UNIT 1, MORPETH ROAD, ASHINGTON, NORTHUMBERLAND NE53 8PX, ☎ 01670 858300, 9.30–5.30 MON–SAT.

UNIT 16-17, DONKIN ROAD, ARMSTRONG INDUSTRIAL ESTATE, WASHINGTON, TYNE & WEAR NE37 1PF, ☎ 0191 417 4910, 9.30–5.30 MON–SAT. **PERMANENT DISCOUNT OUTLET**

See page 101 (CO DURH)

JAMES SHOES

369 WEST ROAD, NEWCASTLE UPON TYNE, TYNE & WEAR NE15 7NL, ☎ 0191 274 3690, FAX: 0191 241 0194, 9–5 MON–SAT. **PERMANENT DISCOUNT OUTLET**

Discontinued perfects and seconds footwear, most of which are English, Italian or Spanish makes. All the women's shoes are perfects, while the men's Loake shoes are slight seconds and cost between £45 and £51 for shoes that would normally cost £105.

MATALAN

THE KILLINGWORTH CENTRE, CITADEL WEST, KILLINGWORTH, NORTHUMBERLAND NE12, ☎ 0191 216 5360, FAX: 0191 216 1336, www.matalan.co.uk, 10–8 MON–FRI, 9–6 SAT, 11–5 SUN.

BELVEDERE RETAIL PARK, BRUNTON LANE, KINGSTON PARK, NEWCASTLE UPON TYNE TYNE & WEAR NE3 2PA, ☎ 0191 214 0352, FAX: 0191 271 0067, www.matalan.co.uk, 10–8 MON–FRI, 9–6 SAT, 11–5 SUN. **PERMANENT DISCOUNT OUTLET**

See page 89 (BEDS)

MEXX INTERNATIONAL

ROYAL QUAYS FACTORY OUTLET CENTRE, NORTH SHIELDS, NEWCASTLE UPON TYNE, NEAR A19, TYNE & WEAR, ☎ 0191 257 5001, 10–6 MON–SAT, 8 ON THUR, 11–5 SUN. **FACTORY SHOP IN A FACTORY SHOPPING VILLAGE**

See page 97 (CHESH)

ROYAL QUAYS OUTLET CENTRE

COBLE DENE, NORTH SHIELDS, NEWCASTLE UPON TYNE, NEAR A19, TYNE & WEAR NE29 6DW, ☎ 0191 296 3743, **e-mail:** outletcentres@realm-ocm.com, www.royalquaysoutletcentre.co.uk, 10–6 MON–SAT, 11–5 SUN. **FACTORY SHOPPING VILLAGE**

Forty-two shops with leisure facilities nearby including a full-scale steam railway, working harbour, Roman ruins and the usual seaside attractions. Adjacent to the Wet and Wild water park which attracts 350,000 visitors a year and next door to an international ferry terminal, the centre has a nautical feel to it. There is a great range of shops, many new, stocking famous name brands, all with up to 50% discounts off normal retail prices. Phone the above number for more details.

SECOND TIME AROUND

1–3 WOOL MARKET, BERWICK-UPON-TWEED, NORTHUMBERLAND TD15 1DH, ☎ 01289 307875, 10–5 MON–SAT. **DRESS AGENCY**

High quality, nearly-new clothes with designers ranging from Jacques Vert to Marks & Spencer and Laura Ashley. Established for more than nine years, this two-storey shop now caters for the whole family with an across the board selection of clothing from casual day wear to wedding outfits, babywear to men's outfits. There is usually a bargain rail with items going for as little as £1, and twice yearly sales in the summer and winter. A varied selection of clothes can be found all year round as the stock is not necessarily seasonal. Accessories include shoes, hats, handbags and a small amount of jewellery. Menswear includes Armani, Hugo Boss and other Continental designers. Childrenswear ranges from babies to teenagers and there is also a selecton of baby equipment such as high chairs and buggies as well as toys, games and books. This friendly, spacious shop has a rest area, and refreshments are always available.

SHARK GROUP

NORDSTROM HOUSE, NORTH BROOMHILL, NEAR AMBLE, MORPETH, NORTHUMBERLAND NE65 9UJ, ☎ 01670 760365, FAX: 01670 761343, **e-mail:** sales@sharkgroup.co.uk, www.sharkgroup.co.uk, 2–4 MON–FRI (ALL YEAR ROUND), 10–12 SAT (APRIL–MID-DEC).
FACTORY SHOP

Manufactures and sells in the factory shop Shark wetsuits, cag tops, sailing suits, boots, gloves and accessories for men, women and children at factory prices. Children's one-piece wetsuits from £45, adults' two-piece wetsuits from £89, adults' one-piece wetsuits from £69. Also sell the Shark Country range of jackets, over trousers, fleeces and accessories in Real Tree camo and loden green. Special sales are held from time to time. The factory shop closes for the factory holidays in late May/early June and late July/early August and late October as well as bank holiday weekends.

SUNGLASS TIME

ROYAL QUAYS, COBLE DENE ROAD, NORTH SHIELDS, TYNE & WEAR NE29 6DW, ☎ 0161 848 9007, **e-mail:** info@sunglass-time.com, 10–6 MON–SAT, 8 ON THUR, 11–5 SUN.
PERMANENT DISCOUNT OUTLET

See page 139 (LANCS)

THE FAMOUS BRUNSWICK WAREHOUSE LTD

UNIT 1A, ALBION RETAIL PARK, COWPEN ROAD, BLYTH, NORTHUMBERLAND NE24 5BS, ☎ 01670 367951, **e-mail:** northshoe@mcmail.com, 9–5.30 MON–SAT, 6 ON THUR, FRI, 9.530 SAT, 10–4.30 SUN.

2–3 GREEN MARKET, ELDON SQUARE, NEWCASTLE UPON TYNE, TYNE & WEAR NE1 6EP, ☎ 0191 261 2976, **e-mail:** northshoe@mcmail.com, 9–5 MON–SAT.

120–122 GRAINGER MARKET, NEWCASTLE UPON TYNE, TYNE & WEAR NE1 5QN, ☎ 0191 261 2903, **e-mail:** northshoe@mcmail.com, 9–5 MON–SAT.

UNIT 3, COAST ROAD RETAIL PARK, NORTHAM ROAD, NORTH SHIELDS, TYNE & WEAR, NE29 7PQ, ☎ 0191 257 2557, **e-mail:** northshoe@mcmail.com, 9–6 MON–WED, SAT, 9–7 THUR, FRI, 10–4.30 SUN.

UNIT 2B, GALLERIES RETAIL PARK, TOWN CENTRE, WASHINGTON, TYNE & WEAR NE38 7RW, ☎ 0191 417 7447, **e-mail:** northshoe@mcmail.com, 9–6 MON–WED, SAT, 9–7 THUR, FRI, 10–4 SUN. **PERMANENT DISCOUNT OUTLET**

See page 98 (CHESH)

TK MAXX

LOWER GROUND FLOOR, MONUMENT MALL SHOPPING CENTRE, NEWCASTLE UPON TYNE, TYNE & WEAR NE1 7AL, ☎ 0191 261 0404, www.tkmaxx.com, 9–5.30 MON–FRI, 8 ON THUR, 9–6 SAT, 11–5 SUN. **PERMANENT DISCOUNT OUTLET**

See page 89 (BEDS)

TOG 24

32 HIGH FRIARS, ELDON SQUARE, NEWCASTLE UPON TYNE, TYNE & WEAR NE1 7XG, ☎ 0191 260 2810, **e-mail:** mail-order@tog24.com, www.tog24.com, 9–5.30 MON–FRI, 8 ON THUR, 9–6 SAT, 11–5 SUN.

ROYAL QUAYS FACTORY OUTLET CENTRE, COBLE DENE, NORTH SHIELDS, NEWCASTLE UPON TYNE, NEAR A19, TYNE & WEAR NE29 6DW, ☎ 0191 258 3754, **e-mail:** mail-order@tog24.com, www.tog24.com, 9.30–6 MON–SAT, 9.30–8 THUR, 11–5 SUN. **FACTORY SHOP IN A FACTORY SHOPPING VILLAGE**

See page 99 (CHESH)

TYNEDALE RETAIL PARK

HEXHAM, NORTHUMBERLAND NE46 3PJ, ☎ 01434 607788, 10–6 MON–FRI, 9.30–6 SAT, 11–5 SUN. **PERMANENT DISCOUNT OUTLET**

With 15,000 square feet of retail selling across a 10 acre site, all at ground level except the restaurant which has access via a lift, the Tynedale Retail Park is accessible to all. Here you will find overstocks and clearance lines at up to 50% off normal retail prices. Quality names such as Windsmoor, Jaegar, French Connection, Timberland, Elle and Edinburgh Woollen Mill are just a few of the brands available. The clothing is just for adults, but there are shoes for adults and children. There is also furniture, linen, electrical items, bath accessories, toys, gifts and DIY equipment. The main section is a garden centre which also has pets, golf, sporting and outdoor wear departments. The child-friendly restaurant has a kids zone, parking is free and there are disabled facilities on site.

WARNERS

ROYAL QUAYS OUTLET CENTRE, NORTH SHIELDS, NEWCASTLE UPON TYNE, TYNE & WEAR NE29 6DW, ☎ 0191 259 6800, 10–6 MON–SAT, 8 ON THUR, 11–5 SUN. **FACTORY SHOP IN A FACTORY SHOPPING VILLAGE**

See page 100 (CHESH)

WRANGLER LEE

ROYAL QUAYS OUTLET CENTRE, COBLE DENE, NORTH SHIELDS, TYNE & WEAR NE29 6DW, ☎ 01253 773988, 10–6 MON–SAT, 11–5 SUN. **FACTORY SHOP**

See page 142 (LANCS)

NOTTINGHAMSHIRE

BROUGHTON SHOE WAREHOUSE

6 QUEENS COURT, LENTON LANE, NOTTINGHAM, NOTTINGHAMSHIRE NG7 2NR, ☎ 0115 986 1945, 9–6 MON, TUE, FRI, 9–8 WED, THUR, 9–6 SAT 10–4 SUN.

32 KING STREET, SOUTHWELL, NOTTINGHAMSHIRE NG25 0EN, ☎ 01636 812078, 9.30–5 MON–SAT. **PERMANENT DISCOUNT OUTLET**

See page 108 (DERBY)

CATALOGUE BARGAIN SHOP

24–29 LEEMING STREET, MANSFIELD, NOTTINGHAMSHIRE NG18 1NE, ☎ 01623 623353, www.bargaincrazy.com, 9–5.30 MON–SAT, 10–4 SUN.

50 MAIN STREET, BULWELL, NOTTINGHAM, NOTTINGHAMSHIRE NG6 8EY, ☎ 0115 927 8373, www.bargaincrazy.com, 9–5.30 MON–SAT, 10–4 SUN. **PERMANENT DISCOUNT OUTLET**

See page 92 (CAMBS)

CLARKS FACTORY SHOP

111 FRONT STREET, ARNOLD, NOTTINGHAMSHIRE NG5 7ED, ☎ 0115 967 4212, 9–6 MON–SAT, 10–4 SUN. **FACTORY SHOP**

See page 94 (CHESH)

DIRECT SPECS LTD

6 VILLA STREET, BEESTON, NOTTINGHAMSHIRE NG9 2NY, ☎ 0115 922 9418, www.directspecs.co.uk, 9–5 MON–SAT.

UNIT 12, ACORN SHOPPING CENTRE, STATION ROAD, LANGLEY MILL, NOTTINGHAMSHIRE NG16 4AF, ☎ 01773 711911, www.directspecs.co.uk, 9–5 MON–SAT. **PERMANENT DISCOUNT OUTLET**

See page 95 (CHESH)

GIFTTREE

34 HIGH STREET, LONG EATON, NOTTINGHAMSHIRE NG10 1LL, ☎ 0115 973 6611 9–5.30 MON–SAT. **FACTORY SHOP**

See page 108 (DERBY)

LABEL TRADERS

PASTURE LANE, RUDDINGTON, NOTTINGHAMSHIRE NG1 6AJ, ☎ 0115 9405205, www.labeltraders.co.uk, 9–5 MON–FRI, 9–4 SAT, 10–4 SUN. **FACTORY SHOP**

3 KIRKBY ROAD, SUTTON-IN-ASHFIELD, NOTTINGHAMSHIRE NG17 1GP, ☎ 01623 554026, www.labeltraders.co.uk, 9–5 MON–FRI, 10–5 SAT, 10–4 SUN. **FACTORY SHOP**

See page 109 (DERBY)

MATALAN

CHILWELL RETAIL PARK, BARTON LANE, BEESTON, NOTTINGHAM, NOTTINGHAMSHIRE NG9 6DS, ☎ 0115 946 9354, FAX: 0115 972 3184, www.matalan.co.uk, 10–8 MON–FRI, 9–6 SAT, 11–4 SUN.

SPRINGFIELD RETAIL PARK, HUCKNALL LANE, BULWELL, NOTTINGHAM, NOTTINGHAMSHIRE NG6 8AJ, ☎ 0115 977 7800, FAX: 0115 976 3572, www.matalan.co.uk, 10–8 MON–FRI, 9–6 SAT, 10–4 SUN.

PORTLAND RETAIL PARK, STATION ROAD, SUTTON IN ASHFIELD, MANSFIELD, NOTTINGHAMSHIRE NG17 5GA, ☎ 01623 528710, FAX: 01623 554974, www.matalan.co.uk, 9.30–8 MON–FRI, 9–6 SAT, 11–5 SUN.

31 WOLLATON ROAD, BEESTON, NOTTINGHAM, NOTTINGHAMSHIRE NG9 2NG, ☎ 0115 9220653, www.renaissancefashionagency.co.uk, 9–5.30 MON–THUR, SAT, 9–7 FRI. **PERMANENT DISCOUNT OUTLET**

See page 89 (BEDS)

THE COURTAULDS FACTORY SHOP

HAYDN ROAD, NOTTINGHAM, NOTTINGHAMSHIRE NG5 1DH, ☎ 0115 924 6154, 9–5.30 MON–SAT, 7.30 ON WED, 10.30–4.30 SUN. **FACTORY SHOP**

Sells a wide range of women's, men's and childrens high street fashions at between 30% and 50% below high street prices. Also stocks a wide range of household textiles, luggage, shoes and accessories. There is now an on-site coffee shopping serving light meals and snacks.

THE DESIGNER WAREHOUSE FIFTH AVENUE INTERNATIONAL

CASTLE BUILDINGS, CASTLE BOULEVARD, NOTTINGHAM, NOTTINGHAMSHIRE NG7 1SA, ☎ 0115 948 0100, **e-mail:** fifthaveueuk@excite.com, 9–6 MON–SAT, 10–5 SUN. **PERMANENT DISCOUNT OUTLET**

Wholesalers who buy surplus stock in a wide variety of sizes and sell it to the public at this clearance shop. The stock is for men and women and features Ralph Lauren, Versace, Armani, Calvin Klein, Cerruti jeans, leather jackets and sweatshirts at about half price.

THE FACTORY SHOP

DONCASTER ROAD, LANGOLD, WORKSOP, NOTTINGHAMSHIRE DN22 7HY, ☎ 01909 731115, 9 -5.30 MON–SAT, 10–4.30 SUN. **FACTORY SHOP**

See page 98 (CHESH)

THE FAMOUS BRUNSWICK WAREHOUSE LTD

SPRINGFIELD RETAIL PARK, BULWELL, NOTTINGHAM, NOTTINGHAMSHIRE NG6 8AJ, ☎ 0115 951 9286, **e-mail:** northshoe@mcmail.com, 10–6 MON–WED, 10–7 THUR, FRI, 9–6 SAT, 10–4 SUN. **PERMANENT DISCOUNT OUTLET**

See page 98 (CHESH)

THE SHOE SHED

COURTAULDS TEXTILES FACTORY SHOP, ELLIS STREET, KIRKBY-IN-ASHFIELD, NOTTINGHAMSHIRE NG17 7AL, ☎ 01627 23083, 9–5.30 MON–SAT, 10.30–4.30 SUN. **FACTORY SHOP**

See page 114 (DORS)

TK MAXX

CHILWELL RETAIL PARK, BARTON LANE, BEESTON, NOTTINGHAM NOTTINGHAMSHIRE, ☎ 0115 946 3684, www.tkmaxx.com, PHONE FOR DETAILS. **PERMANENT DISCOUNT OUTLET**

See page 89 (BEDS)

TRADEX

QUEENS ROAD, BEESTON, NOTTINGHAM, NOTTINGHAMSHIRE NG9 2FE, ☎ 0115 922 0880, FAX: 0115 922 7333, 9.30–8.30 MON–FRI, 9–5.30 SAT, 10.30–4.30 SUN. **PERMANENT DISCOUNT OUTLET**

See page 142 (LANCS)

UNITED FOOTWEAR

BEECH AVENUE, OFF SHERWOOD RISE, OFF A60, NOTTINGHAM, NOTTINGHAMSHIRE, ☎ 0115 979 2799, 9–6.30 MON–FRI, 9–5.30 SAT, 10–4 SUN.

See page 124 (HAMPS)

WILKINSON STORES

2–6 FRONT STREET, ARNOLD, NOTTINGHAM, NOTTINGHAMSHIRE NG5 7EL, ☎ 0115 926 0805, www.wilko.co.uk, 9–5.30 MON–SAT, 10–4 SUN. MAIL ORDER. **PERMANENT DISCOUNT OUTLET**

See page 100 (CHESH)

WRANGLER LEE

PEPPER ROAD, CALVERTON, NOTTINGHAMSHIRE NG14 6LJ, ☎ 0115 965 4043, 9.30–5.30 MON–SAT. **FACTORY SHOP**

See page 142 (LANCS)

OXFORDSHIRE

AQUASCUTUM

BICESTER OUTLET SHOPPING VILLAGE, PINGLE DRIVE, BICESTER, JUNCTION 9 OF M40, OXFORDSHIRE OX26 7WD, ☎ 01869 325943, 10–6 SEVEN DAYS A WEEK. **FACTORY SHOP IN A FACTORY SHOPPING VILLAGE**

See page 125 (HERTS)

BENETTON

BICESTER OUTLET SHOPPING VILLAGE, PINGLE DRIVE, BICESTER, JUNCTION 9 OF M40, OXFORDSHIRE OX26 7WD, ☎ 01869 320030, FAX: 01869 325518, **e-mail:** sstimpson@fibrenetname.co.uk, www.benetton.co.uk, 10–6 SEVEN DAYS A WEEK. **FACTORY SHOP IN A FACTORY SHOPPING VILLAGE**

See page 121 (HAMPS)

BICESTER OUTLET SHOPPING VILLAGE

PINGLE DRIVE, BICESTER, JUNCTION 9 OF M40, OXFORDSHIRE OX26 7WD, ☎ 01869 323200, 10–6 SEVEN DAYS A WEEK. **FACTORY SHOPPING VILLAGE**

Described as 'Bond Street comes to Bicester', Bicester Village has established itself as the UK's leading outlet shopping destination in terms of offering the largest selection of international brand names to choose from. Currently there are 90 outlet shops offering quality merchandise at discounts of up to 60%, sometimes even more. The choice of famous brands at Bicester Village is second to none. International names include a Polo Ralph Lauren store, which now stocks more goods from their women's sport and home collections, Donna Karan, Versace, Christian Lacroix, Escada, Cerruti 1881 and TSE Cashmere. New arrivals from the international fashion scene are La Perla, Nautica, Gieves & Hawkes, Tommy Hilfiger, Tod's, MaxMara, Salvatore Ferragamo, Zegna, Calvin Klein, Charles Tyrwhitt, Sand, Links, Nautica, Musto and Holland & Holland. Both of Britain's leading designers, Nicole Farhi and Paul Smith, have shops with goods from their men's and women's collections.

Karen Millen and Whistles both cater for the younger set with much more women's fashion to be found in The Designer Room, Episode, Hobbs, Jigsaw and Inwear Matinique. Top high street names are also well represented by Benetton, Principles, French Connection, Monsoon and Racing Green. The more classic customer also has an unequalled choice with Burberry, Aquascutum, Jaeger, Mulberry and the Scandinavian company RedGreen, whose nautical style of casual wear is very popular. Rugged outdoor wear can be found at Helly Hansen, Tog 24, the climbing and walking specialist. Active sportswear, represented by Fred Perry and Reebok, has now been joined by one of America's most famous sports shoe brands, Vans. A comprehensive collection of shoes, including many ranges for children, can be found in Clarks, with elegant high fashion styles in Charles Jourdan from Paris. Also, for women's shoes, handbags and accessories, there is Jane Shilton; for luggage, there is the Samsonite shop, plus the exciting addition of the first TAG-Heuer outlet, which stocks end-of-line designer watches, all fully guaranteed, at very attractive prices. Lingerie and underwear is to be found at Warners and Triumph, with HOM, the French brand, for the men; and the finest French childrenswear at Petit Bateau; English fragrances at Penhaligon's; make-up, bath and body therapies at Molton Brown, and soaps and gifts at Woods of Windsor. For the home, there are Price's candles and towels and duvets from another leading French brand, Descamps; cutlery from Oneida; china and crystal from Villeroy & Boch and Waterford Wedgwood and fine linens and accessories for the home from The White Company. The Cosmetic Company stocks well-known skincare products, cosmetics and fragrances for men and women. Bicester Village is something akin to a 'one-floor department store' and menswear, which can often be found in the designer shops, is also well represented in its own right with Dunhill, Blazer, Sand, Savoy Taylors Guild, Oscar Jacobson and Dockers, plus another international touch being provided by Cerruti Menswear, all offering good size ranges in a wide choice from very casual through to traditional business clothes. To complete the day out at Bicester Village, take home some popular titles from Books etc, get to know more about the location for a return visit from the Tourist Information Centre, and regain strength with top quality refreshment at Pret-A-Manger or Starbucks. There are cash machines, a children's play area, free parking and a shuttle bus (which is free from Thursday to Sunday) and taxi connection to Bicester North Station, which is on the Chiltern Railways line, and runs between Marylebone and Birmingham. Bicester Village is about one hour's drive from London, two miles from Junction 9 on the M40. Take the A41 and follow signs for Village Retail Park.

BURBERRY

BICESTER OUTLET SHOPPING VILLAGE, PINGLE DRIVE, BICESTER, JUNCTION 9 OF M40, OXFORDSHIRE OX6 7WD, ☎ 01869 354071, 10–6 SEVEN DAYS A WEEK. **FACTORY SHOP IN A FACTORY SHOPPING VILLAGE**

See page 94 (CHESH)

CLARKS FACTORY SHOP

BICESTER OUTLET SHOPPING VILLAGE, 27 PINGLE DRIVE, BICESTER, JUNCTION 9 OF M40, OXFORDSHIRE OX26 6WD, ☎ 01869 325646, 10–6 SEVEN DAYS A WEEK. **FACTORY SHOP IN A FACTORY SHOPPING VILLAGE**

See page 94 (CHESH)

FRENCH CONNECTION

BICESTER OUTLET SHOPPING VILLAGE, PINGLE DRIVE, BICESTER, JUNCTION 9 OF M40, OXFORDSHIRE OX6 7WD, ☎ 01869 369582, 10–6 SEVEN DAYS A WEEK. **FACTORY SHOP IN A FACTORY SHOPPING VILLAGE**

Previous season's womenswear, menswear and childrenswear, and seconds, at 30% to 80% less than retail prices.

GIEVES & HAWKES

UNIT 77, BICESTER VILLAGE, 50 PINGLE DRIVE, BICESTER, OXFORDSHIRE OX5 7WD, ☎ 01869 243711, 10–6 MON–SUN. **FACTORY SHOP IN A FACTORY SHOPPING VILLAGE**

See page 122 (HAMPS)

IMPS

52 SHEEP STREET, BICESTER, OXFORDSHIRE OX26 7LG, ☎ 01869 243455, 9–5 MON–SAT

40 UPPER HIGH STREET, THAME OXFORDSHIRE OX9 3AG, ☎ 01844 212985, 9–5 MON–SAT.

32 MARKET SQUARE, WITNEY, OXFORDSHIRE OX8 58A, ☎ 01993 779875, 9–5 MON–SAT.
PERMANENT DISCOUNT OUTLET

High street shops selling popular chainstore seconds fashion for all the family as well as towels, china, trays and flower cachepots. Men's women's and childrenswear from designer brands such as Ralph Lauren, Tommy Hilfiger, Timberland and Gap. Sportswear from Umbro, Adidas and Nike all at up to 50% off high street prices.

IN WEAR FACTORY OUTLET

BICESTER OUTLET SHOPPING VILLAGE, PINGLE DRIVE, BICESTER, JUNCTION 9 OF M40, OXFORDSHIRE OX6 7WD, ☎ 01869 369415, 10–6 SEVEN DAYS A WEEK. **FACTORY SHOP IN A FACTORY SHOPPING VILLAGE**

See page 149 (LOND)

JAEGER FACTORY OUTLET

BICESTER VILLAGE, 35 PINGLE DRIVE, BICESTER, OXFORDSHIRE OX6 7WD, ☎ 01869 369220, 10–6 SEVEN DAYS A WEEK.
FACTORY SHOP IN A FACTORY SHOPPING VILLAGE

See page 158 (CHESH)

MATALAN

UNIT 5, THE JOHN ALLEN CENTRE, COWLEY, OXFORDSHIRE OX4 3JP, ☎ 01865 336100, FAX: 01865 336107, www.matalan.co.uk, 10–8 MON–FRI, 9–6 SAT, 10–4 SUN. **PERMANENT DISCOUNT OUTLET**

See page 89 (BEDS)

NAUTICA

BICESTER OUTLET SHOPPING VILLAGE, PINGLE DRIVE, BICESTER, JUNCTION 9 OF M40, OXFORDSHIRE OX6 7WD, ☎ 01869 248770, www.nautica.co.uk, 10–6 SEVEN DAYS A WEEK.
FACTORY SHOP IN A FACTORY SHOPPING VILLAGE

Nautica, the sports and casual wear brand, is now operating from its first factory shop at Bicester Village. It stocks men's sportswear and seasonal denim products.

NICOLE FARHI AND FRENCH CONNECTION

BICESTER OUTLET SHOPPING VILLAGE, PINGLE DRIVE, BICESTER, JUNCTION 9 OF M40, OXFORDSHIRE OX6 7WD, ☎ 01869 252346, 10–6 SEVEN DAYS A WEEK. **FACTORY SHOP IN A FACTORY SHOPPING VILLAGE**

Separate shops selling previous season merchandise, samples and seconds from Nicole Farhi and French Connection at 30% to 80% less than retail price. There is also a Nicole Farhi/French Connection factory shop in London and at Gunwharf Quays, Portsmouth.

PEPE JEANS

UNIT 3, BICESTER OUTLET SHOPPING VILLAGE, PINGLE DRIVE, BICESTER, JUNCTION 9 OF M40, OXFORDSHIRE OX26 6WD, ☎ 01869 325378, 10–6 SEVEN DAYS A WEEK.
FACTORY SHOP IN A FACTORY SHOPPING VILLAGE

See page 123 (HAMPS)

PERUVIAN CONNECTION

28 HART STREET, HENLEY ON THAMES, OXFORDSHIRE RG9 2AU, ☎ 01491 414446, www.peruvianconnection.com, 9.30–5.30 MON–SAT. **PERMANENT DISCOUNT OUTLET**

Previous season's stock from the well-known Peruvian Connection catalogue. Alpaca and pima cotton sweaters, lighter weight polo necks, cardigans and pullovers for men and women at discounted prices.

POLO RALPH LAUREN FACTORY STORE

BICESTER OUTLET SHOPPING VILLAGE, PINGLE DRIVE, BICESTER, JUNCTION 9 OF M40, OXFORDSHIRE OX26 6WD, ☎ 01869 325200, 10–6 SEVEN DAYS A WEEK. **FACTORY SHOP IN A FACTORY SHOPPING VILLAGE**

Polo Ralph Lauren, the largest shop in this factory shopping village with the prime spot, sells items discounted by between 30% and 60% for men, women and boys. For men: wool jackets, jackets, sports jackets, Polo T-shirts, rugby shirts, trousers, jeans and ties, as well as accessories. For women: outerwear, skirts, jackets, dresses, trousers, knits, T-shirts and accessories. Also home collections and fragrances discounted by 15%.

RACING GREEN

BICESTER OUTLET SHOPPING VILLAGE, PINGLE DRIVE, BICESTER, JUNCTION 9 OF M40, OXFORDSHIRE OX6 7WD, ☎ 01869 325484, www.racinggreen.co.uk, 10–6 SEVEN DAYS A WEEK. **FACTORY SHOP IN A FACTORY SHOPPING VILLAGE**

See page 98 (CHESH)

REDGREEN

BICESTER OUTLET SHOPPING VILLAGE, PINGLE DRIVE, BICESTER, JUNCTION 9 OF M40, OXFORDSHIRE OX6 7WD, ☎ 01869 323324, 10–6 SEVEN DAYS A WEEK. **FACTORY SHOP IN A FACTORY SHOPPING VILLAGE**

See page 98 (CHESH)

REVIVAL CLOTHES AGENCY

60 ST CLEMENT'S, OXFORD, OXFORDSHIRE OX4 1AH, ☎ 01865 251005, 10–4 TUE, WED, THUR, 10–5 FRI, SAT. **DRESS AGENCY**

A large shop containing two spacious rooms behind a showroom. All stock is less than two years old. The women's section includes labels from Wallis and Next to Whistles, Nicole Farhi, Jaeger and Karen Millen. There are also accessories such as hats, shoes, handbags and jewellery. All prices are well under half the original price and sizes range from 8 to 24. The evening dresses range from £30 to £100 and include many ballgowns. The menswear is not extensive but includes Armani, Next and Jaeger suits and dinner suits. Childrenswear includes Next, OshKosh and Laura Ashley. Soft furnishings and curtains are also stocked, and there is a small selection of new and nearly-new wedding dresses from £100 to £600.

THE BALLROOM

5–6 THE PLAIN, OXFORD, OXFORDSHIRE OX4 1AS, ☎ 01865 202303 OR 01865 202303 FOR MENSWEAR, ☎ 01865 241054, 9.15–5.45 MON–SAT. **HIRE SHOP**

Hundreds of bridal gowns, including designer names from £50 to £500. Over 2,000 ballgowns and slinky dresses including clearance. Short dresses from £15, long dresses from £35. Extensive accessories and most items to hire or buy. Menswear and mens' clearance formal wear includes dinner jackets from £15 to £200; £29.50 to hire.

THE FAMOUS BRUNSWICK WAREHOUSE LTD

THE CALTHORPE CENTRE, BANBURY, OXFORDSHIRE DX16 5HS, ☎ 01295 266519, **e-mail:** northshoe@mcmail.com, 9–6 MON–SAT, 11–5 SUN. **PERMANENT DISCOUNT OUTLET**

See page 98 (CHESH)

TIMBERLAND

BICESTER VILLAGE, PINGLE DRIVE, BICESTER, OXFORDSHIRE OX26 6YQ, ☎ 01869 320090, FAX: 01869 325990, 10–6 SEVEN DAYS A WEEK. **FACTORY SHOP IN A FACTORY SHOPPING VILLAGE**

See page 98 (CHESH)

TK MAXX

CALTHORPE STREET, OFF HIGH STREET, BANBURY, OXFORDSHIRE OX16 8ES, ☎ 01295 277022, www.tkmaxx.com, 9–5.30 MON–FRI, 7 ON THUR, 9–6 SAT, 11–5 SUN. **PERMANENT DISCOUNT OUTLET**

See page 89 (BEDS)

TOG 24

BICESTER OUTLET SHOPPING VILLAGE, PINGLE DRIVE, BICESTER, JUNCTION 9 OF M40, OXFORDSHIRE OX6 7WD, ☎ 01869 323278, **e-mail:** mail-order@tog24.com, www.tog24.com, 10–6 SEVEN DAYS A WEEK. **FACTORY SHOP IN A FACTORY SHOPPING VILLAGE**

See page 99 (CHESH)

TOMMY HILFIGER

80–81 BICESTER VILLAGE, PINGLE DRIVE, BICESTER, OXFORDSHIRE OX6 7WD, ☎ 01869 247699, FAX: 01869 247355, www.tommy.com, 10–6 MON–SAT, 11–5 SUN. **FACTORY SHOP IN A FACTORY SHOPPING VILLAGE**

See page 99 (CHESH)

TOP MARKS

8 HIGH STREET, CHIPPING NORTON, OXFORDSHIRE OX7 5ND, ☎ 01608 642653, 9–5.30 MON–FRI, 9–5 SAT. **PERMANENT DISCOUNT OUTLET**

See page 124 (GLOS)

TRIUMPH INTERNATIONAL LTD

BICESTER OUTLET SHOPPING VILLAGE, PINGLE DRIVE, BICESTER, JUNCTION 9 OF M40, OXFORDSHIRE OX6 7WD, ☎ 01869 329930, 10–6 SEVEN DAYS A WEEK.
FACTORY SHOP IN A FACTORY SHOPPING VILLAGE

See page 99 (CHESH)

WARNERS

BICESTER OUTLET SHOPPING VILLAGE, PINGLE DRIVE, BICESTER, JUNCTION 9 OF M40, OXFORDSHIRE OX6 7WD, ☎ 01869 324401, 10–6 SEVEN DAYS A WEEK.
FACTORY SHOP IN A FACTORY SHOPPING VILLAGE

See page 100 (CHESH)

SHROPSHIRE

BLUNTS

8–9 WEST CASTLE STREET, BRIDGNORTH, SHROPSHIRE WV16 4AB, ☎ 01746 763452, 9–5.30 MON–SAT, 10–4 SUN. **PERMANENT DISCOUNT OUTLET**

See page 91 (BRIS)

CATALOGUE SURPLUS CENTRE LTD

28–30 ST MARY'S STREET, NEWPORT, SHROPSHIRE TF10 7AB, ☎ 01952 825889, FAX: 01952 825545, 9–5 MON–SAT.

4 CLAREMONT STREET, SHREWSBURY, SHROPSHIRE SY1 1QG, ☎ 01743 243 629, 9–5 MON–SAT.

21 WILLOW STREET, OSWESTRY SHROPSHIRE SY11 1AF, ☎ 01691 658155, 9–5 MON–SAT.

UNIT 3, OXFORD STREET, OAKENGATE, TELFORD SHROPSHIRE TF2 6AA, ☎ 01952 617406, 9–5 MON–SAT. **PERMANENT DISCOUNT OUTLET**

Ex-catalogue clothes for men, women and children, as well as shoes and bedlinen, all sold at a fraction of the catalogue prices.

DIRECT SPECS LTD

38 CASTLE STREET, SHREWSBURY, SHROPSHIRE SY1 2DW, ☎ 01743 247377, www.directspecs.co.uk, 9–5 MON–SAT. **PERMANENT DISCOUNT OUTLET**

See page 95 (CHESH)

E WALTERS FACTORY SHOP

CHAPEL WORKS, OLD STREET, LUDLOW, SHROPSHIRE SY8 1NR, ☎ 01584 875595, 9–5 SAT, 11–5 SUN, SUMMER MONTHS. **FACTORY SHOP**

Europe's leading trouser manufacturer sells ends of lines, cancelled orders and samples of jeans, trousers and shorts for all the family at factory direct prices. Also available ancillary lines of casual wear at bargain prices.

FASHION FACTORY

THE MALTINGS, PARK STREET, WELLINGTON, TELFORD, SHROPSHIRE TF1 3AE, ☎ 01952 260489, www.fashionfactory.uk.com, 9.30–5.30 MON–SAT, 11–5 SUN. **PERMANENT DISCOUNT OUTLET**

At the Fashion Factory stores in Telford and Cannock (see Staffordshire), you'll find a comprehensive selection of quality branded and designer fashions for men and women, all reduced by up to 70% off the normal high street prices. New merchandise arrives daily, resulting in a constantly changing selection from lingerie and basic fashion essentials to dresses, suits and separates, all at a fraction of the prices you'd normally expect to pay. The boutique-style store in Telford features two floors packed with a huge variety of womenswear, while the Cannock superstore has possibly one of the largest selections of discounted designer wear and footwear under one roof in the Midlands, with between 50,000 and 60,000 garments on display in a massive 20,000 square feet of retail space. Sale prices are available all year round, and these prices are further reduced four times a year: in February, June, August and December.

LEGS CLOTHING CO

MARKET HOUSE, LISTLEY STREET, BRIDGNORTH, SHROPSHIRE WV16 4AW, ☎ 01746 769542, 9–5 MON–SAT, 11–5 SUN AND BANK HOLIDAYS, EASTER TO CHRISTMAS. **FACTORY SHOP**

See page 120 (GLOS)

MATALAN

HARLESCOTT RETAIL PARK, BRIXTON WAY, HARLESCOTT, SHREWSBURY SHROPSHIRE SY1 3AZ, ☎ 01743 453040, FAX: 01743 462489, www.matalan.co.uk, 10–8 MON–FRI, 9–6 SAT, 11–5 SUN.

WREKIN RETAIL PARK, WELLINGTON, TELFORD, SHROPSHIRE TF1 2DE, ☎ 01952 641080, FAX: 01952 240155, www.matalan.co.uk, 10–8 MON–FRI, 9–6 SAT, 11–5 SUN. **PERMANENT DISCOUNT OUTLET**

See page 89 (BEDS)

STEWART'S

19–21 CROSS STREET, ELLESMERE, SHROPSHIRE SY12 0AW, ☎ 01691 624478, FAX: 01691 624478, 9.30–5.30 MON–FRI, 9–5.30 SAT, 10–4 SUN. **FACTORY SHOP**

See page 112 (DEV)

T J HUGHES

RIVERSIDE AND PRIDEHILL SHOPPING CENTRE, SHREWSBURY, SHROPSHIRE SY1 1BU, ☎ 01743 358359, FAX: 01743 271222, **e-mail:** info@tjhughes.co.uk, www.tjhughes.co.uk, 9–5.30 MON–SAT, 10.30–4.30 SUN. **PERMANENT DISCOUNT OUTLET**

See page 98 (CHESH)

THE FAMOUS BRUNSWICK WAREHOUSE LTD

UNIT K, WREKIN RETAIL PARK, TELFORD, SHROPSHIRE TF1 2DE, ☎ 01952 222802, **e-mail:** northshoe@mcmail.com, 10–6 MON–WED, 10–7 THUR, FRI, 9–6 SAT, 10–4 SUN. **PERMANENT DISCOUNT OUTLET**

See page 98 (CHESH)

TK MAXX

DARWIN SHOPPING CENTRE, RAVENS MEADOWS, SHREWSBURY, SHROPSHIRE SY1 1BW, ☎ 01743 341370, www.tkmaxx.com, 9–5.30 MON–FRI, 9–6 SAT, 11–5 SUN.

UNIT 16, TELFORD FORGE RETAIL PARK, ORDSALL LANE, TELFORD, SHROPSHIRE TF3 4AG, ☎ 01952 210200, www.tkmaxx.com, 10–8 MON–FRI, 9–6 SAT, 11–5 SUN. **PERMANENT DISCOUNT OUTLET**

See page 89 (BEDS)

WORKWEAR – BUSINESS CASUALS

UNIT 26, SNEDSHILL TRADING ESTATE, TELFORD, SHROPSHIRE TF2 9NH, ☎ 01952 615976, FAX: 01952 614440, **e-mail:** mike@workwearbc.co.uk, www.workwearbc.co.uk, 9–5 MON, TUE, WED, THUR, 9–3.30 FRI. **PERMANENT DISCOUNT OUTLET**

Fleece jackets, workwear trousers and jackets, dust coats, work shirts, dry socks for walkers, waterproofs, Wellingtons, safety footwear, polo shirts, T-shirts, all at discounted prices. For example, polo shirts from £4.75, fleece jackets from £12.50.

SOMERSET

ABSENT LABELS

51B ST JAMES' STREET, TAUNTON, SOMERSET TA1 IJH, ☎ 01823 330242, 9.30–5.30 MON–FRI, 9–5.30. SAT.

CHURCH HOUSE, CHURCH STREET, YEOVIL SOMERSET BA20 1HE, ☎ 01935 478183, 9.30–5 MON–SAT. **PERMANENT DISCOUNT OUTLET**

Good deals direct from the manufacturer of clothes designed for Marks & Spencer, Next, Principles, BhS and Dorothy Perkins etc, for women and men at reduced prices. Discontinued lines and Grade A garments are reduced by about one third. There are skirts, trousers, socks, underwear, nightwear, sweaters, blouses, dressing gowns, shorts, T-shirts and swimwear.

BIG L FACTORY OUTLET

UNITS 56 & 57, CLARKS VILLAGE, FARM ROAD, STREET, SOMERSET BA16 0XY, ☎ 01458 441941, FAX: 01458 441941, 9–6 MON–SAT, 11–5 SUN. **FACTORY SHOP IN A FACTORY SHOPPING VILLAGE**

See page 93 (CHESH)

CHAPLINS SUPERSTORES HOME & GARDEN

BINDON ROAD, TAUNTON, SOMERSET TA2 6AA, ☎ 01823 288017, FAX: 01823 336189, 9–8 MON–FRI, 9–6 SAT, 10.30–4.30 SUN. **PERMANENT DISCOUNT OUTLET**

A wide range of merchandise for the bargain hunter, including garden tools, plants, fertilisers and accessories; toys; adults clothing and shoes; stationery; household textiles; electrical equipment; DIY items; glass and china; bathroom accessories; partyware; candles; food accessories. Spades are available at £4.99, trowels at 99p, shears at £5.99 (while stocks last)

CLARKS FACTORY SHOP

10A HIGH STREET, BURNHAM-ON-SEA, SOMERSET TA8 1NX, ☎ 01278 794668, 9–5.30 MON–SAT, 11–5 SUN.

CLARKS VILLAGE FACTORY SHOPPING CENTRE, FARM ROAD, STREET, JUNCTION 23 OF M5 SOMERSET BA16 0BB, ☎ 01458 843163, 9–6 MON–SAT, 11–5 SUN.

112–114 HIGH STREET, STREET, SOMERSET BA16 0EW, ☎ 01458 442055, 9–5.30 MON–SAT, 10.30–4.30 SUN.

UNIT 2, WORLE DISTRICT SHOPPING CENTRE, WORLE, SOMERSET BS22 6BT, ☎ 01934 521693, 9–5.30 MON–FRI, 9–6 SAT, 10–4 SUN. **FACTORY SHOP**

See page 94 (CHESH)

CLARKS VILLAGE OUTLET SHOPPING

FARM ROAD, STREET, JUNCTION 23 OF M5, THEN A39, SOMERSET BA16 0BB, ☎ 01458 840064, **e-mail:** bgodwin@realm-ocm.com, www.clarksvillage.co.uk, APRIL–OCTOBER 9–5.30 MON–SAT, 11–5 SUN, NOVEMBER–MARCH 10–6, MON–SAT, 11–5 SUN. **FACTORY SHOPPING VILLAGE**

Purpose-built village of brick-built shops with extensive car parking facilities. Restaurant, fast food stands, carousel, indoor and outdoor play areas, and working village pottery and artists' studio. Here, there are 57 shops with more planned. Shops include: Body Shop, Reebok selling the Reebok brand, Rockport and the Greg Norman Collection; Monsoon/Accessorize, Benetton, Wrangler, The Designer Room, Jaeger, Viyella, Alexon, Triumph/Hom, Gossard, Clarks Factory

Shop, Rohan, Windsmoor, Liz Claiborne, Calvin Klein, Van Heusen, Next, Warehouse, Tom Sayers men's sweaters and trousers, Warner's lingerie, Tog 24 outerwear, Jane Shilton handbags, luggage and shoes, The Suit Company and Blazer and Event jewellery. There is also a purpose-built china and glass pavilion and many other stores, all with up to 50% off famous name brands.

DESIGNER SHADES

CLARKS VILLAGE FACTORY SHOPPING CENTRE, FARM ROAD, STREET, JUNCTION 23 OF M5 SOMERSET BA16 0BB, ☎ 01458 443007, **e-mail:** info@sunglass-time.com, 9–6 MON–SAT, 11–5 SUN. **FACTORY SHOP IN A FACTORY SHOPPING VILLAGE**

See page 116 (DORS)

DICKIES UK LTD

SECOND AVENUE, WESTFIELD INDUSTRIAL ESTATE, MIDSOMER NORTON, NEAR BATH, SOMERSET BA3 4BH, ☎ 01761 410732, FAX: 01761 418786, 9–5 MON–SAT, 10–4 SUN. **FACTORY SHOP**
Casual outdoor wear, workwear, footwear and waterproof clothing: many ends of lines at bargain prices from £2.50.

ECCO

82 HIGH STREET, STREET, SOMERSET BA16 0EN, ☎ 01458 443950, www.ecco.com, 9–5.30 MON–SAT, 11–4 SUN AND BANK HOLIDAYS. **FACTORY SHOP**

See page 95 (CHESH)

FINE SHOES

136 HIGH STREET, STREET, SOMERSET BA16 0ER, ☎ 01458 443603, 10–5 MON–SAT.

31–34 HIGH STREET, WELLS, SOMERSET BA5 2SG, ☎ 01749 679090, 9.30–5.30 mon–fri, 9–5.30 SAT, 10.30–4.30 SUN. **PERMANENT DISCOUNT OUTLET**

Men's and women's shoes, boots, plimsolls, sandals and trainers. Most of the shoes are from Bellina, but other brands on sale here include Roder, Hogl, Flexi, Dubarry, Hush Puppy, Barkers, Lec boots for men, Grensons and DB wider shoes for men.

FOX'S MILL SHOP

TONEDALE MILLS, WELLINGTON, SOMERSET TA21 0BA, ☎ 01823 662271, **e-mail:** enquiries@foxflannel.com, www.foxflannel.com, 10–5 FRI AND SAT ONLY. **FACTORY SHOP**
Wool and cashmere fabrics for men and women, including seconds and perfect quality. End of season lines at very low prices starting at £5 a metre for material that would normally retail at £25 to £35. Cloth can be bought and taken away or the in-house tailor will make up garments at a fraction of the London charges. The shop sells woollen and worsted cloth, wool and cashmere seconds and perfect quality and there's a bargain basket with fabric at silly prices. The tailor is on site on both days and will make men's and women's suits. Cashmere jumpers, silk ties, woollen scarves, umbrellas and fashion accessories are also available.

JAEGER FACTORY OUTLET

CLARKS VILLAGE FACTORY SHOPPING CENTRE, FARM ROAD, STREET, JUNCTION 23 OF M5, SOMERSET BA16 0BB, ☎ 01458 447215, 9–6 MON–SAT, 11–5 SUN. **FACTORY SHOP IN A FACTORY SHOPPING VILLAGE**

See page 158 (NORF)

JPS FOOTWEAR LTD

2 HIGH STREET, BURNHAM-ON-SEA, SOMERSET TA8 1NX, ☎ 01278 780141, 9–5.30 MON–SAT, 11–5.30 SUN. **FACTORY SHOP**
Stock more than 10,000 pairs of shoes for men, women and children. The men's sizes range from 6 to 12; and women's from 4 to 9. Most of the stock consists of warehouse clearance lines and ends of lines.

MATALAN

LOCKING CASTLE DISTRICT CENTRE, WORLE, WESTON-SUPER-MARE, SOMERSET BS22 0BE, ☎ 01934 529830, FAX: 01934 521932, www.matalan.co.uk, 10–8 MON–FRI, 9–6 SAT, 10–4 SUN.

THE PEEL CENTRE, BABYLON HILL, YEOVIL, SOMERSET BA21 5BT, ☎ 01935 403110, FAX: 01935 426280, www.matalan.co.uk, 10–8 MON–FRI, 9–6 SAT, 11–5 SUN. **PERMANENT DISCOUNT OUTLET**

See page 89 (BEDS)

MORLANDS

NORTHOVER (BETWEEN GLASTONBURY AND STREET), SOMERSET BA6 9YA, ☎ 01458 446970, 9.30–5 MON–SAT AND MOST BANK HOLIDAYS. **FACTORY SHOP**

Established in 1870, Morlands is the leading brand name in quality sheepskin garments and footwear. The factory shop on the A39 (just north of Clarks Village) offers the opportunity to buy both men's and women's sheepskin coats, slippers and women's boots at attractive prices. Ranges include first quality design samples, ends of runs and overstock, together with slight seconds. There is also a wide range of rugs, hats, mitts, handbags, belts, slippers, leatherwear and gifts. Relocating as we went to press, please phone for new address.

MULBERRY

THE OLD SCHOOL HOUSE, KILVER STREET ON THE A37, SHEPTON MALLET, SOMERSET BA4 5NF, ☎ 01749 340583, www.mulberry.com, 10–6 MON–SAT, 11–5 SUN AND BANK HOLIDAYS. **FACTORY SHOP**

A very popular large, attractive, factory outlet situated in an old school house with parking outside, which sells a wide variety of end of line stock and seconds including men's and women's leather bags, accessories, tech product cases, planners, agendas and stationery. It also sells last season's clothes and home goods which include a selection of furniture, cushions, lamps, china and fabric. Small coffee shop and toilet and disabled facilities. There are other Mulberry factory shops in York and at Bicester Village, Oxfordshire.

NEXT TO NOTHING

CLARKS VILLAGE FACTORY SHOPPING CENTRE, FARM ROAD, STREET, JUNCTION 23 OF M5, SOMERSET BA16 0BB, ☎ 01458 840828, www.next.co.uk, 9–6 MON–SAT, 11–5 SUN. **FACTORY SHOP IN A FACTORY SHOPPING VILLAGE**

See page 97 (CHESH)

PENNYWISE

10A WESTMINSTER STREET, YEOVIL, SOMERSET BA21 3PE, ☎ 01935 423938, 10–5 MON–SAT. **DRESS AGENCY**

Dress agency selling men's and women's day and evening business and casual clothes, shoes and accessories. Good quality and designer labels. Also, new to Pennywise, is a range of new ballgowns, for sale at very reasonable prices. There is no parking available but the shop is near a large Tesco car park.

T J HUGHES

FAIRFAX HOUSE, HIGH STREET, WESTON-SUPER-MARE, SOMERSET BS23 1HA, ☎ 01934 414466, FAX: 01934 419911, **e-mail:** info@tjhughes.co.uk, www.tjhughes.co.uk, 9–5.30 MON–SAT, 11–5 SUN. **PERMANENT DISCOUNT OUTLET**

See page 98 (CHESH)

THE DOC SHOP

TOWNSEND ROAD, SHEPTON MALLET, SOMERSET BA4 5SB, ☎ 01794 347081, 9.30–4.30 MON–SAT. **PERMANENT DISCOUNT OUTLET**

See page 144 (LEICS)

THE FACTORY SHOP LTD

MART ROAD, MINEHEAD, SOMERSET TA24 5BJ, ☎ 01643 705911, 9.30–5.30 MON–SAT, 11–5 SUN. **FACTORY SHOP**

See page 98 (CHESH)

THE SPORTS FACTORY

CLARKS VILLAGE FACTORY SHOPPING CENTRE, FARM ROAD, STREET, JUNCTION 23 OF M5 SOMERSET BA16 0BB, ☎ 01458 843156, 9–6 MON–SAT, 11–5 SUN. **FACTORY SHOP IN A FACTORY SHOPPING VILLAGE**

Wide range of sports clothes and accessories, some of which are only stocked in season (for example, cricket bats and tennis rackets in summer only). There is also cricket gear and leisure clothing (Timberland and Regatta). All are discontinued lines and are between 10% and 40% cheaper than in the high street.

TOG 24

CLARKS VILLAGE FACTORY SHOPPING CENTRE, FARM ROAD, STREET, JUNCTION 23 OF M5 SOMERSET BA16 0ND, ☎ 01458 840468, **e-mail:** mail-order@tog24.com, www.tog24.com, 9–6 MON–SAT, 10–5 SUN. **FACTORY SHOP IN A FACTORY SHOPPING VILLAGE**

See page 99 (CHESH)

TRIUMPH INTERNATIONAL LTD

CLARKS VILLAGE, FARM ROAD, STREET, JUNCTION 23 OF M5 SOMERSET BA16 0BB, ☎ 01458 840700, 9–6 MON–SAT, 11–5 SUN. **FACTORY SHOP IN A FACTORY SHOPPING VILLAGE**

See page 99 (CHESH)

VIYELLA

CLARKS VILLAGE FACTORY SHOPPING CENTRE, FARM ROAD, STREET, JUNCTION 23 OF M5 SOMERSET BA16 0BB, ☎ 01458 448533, 9–6 MON–SAT, 11–5 SUN. **FACTORY SHOP**

See page 100 (CHESH)

WARNERS

UNIT 45 CLARKS VILLAGE, STREET, SOMERSET BA16 0YA, ☎ 01458 840557, 9–6 MON–SAT, 10–5 SUN. **FACTORY SHOP IN A FACTORY SHOPPING VILLAGE**

See page 100 (CHESH)

WRANGLER LEE

CLARKS VILLAGE, STREET, SOMERSET BA16 0BB, ☎ 01458 841799, 9–6 MON–SAT, 11–5 SUN. **FACTORY SHOP IN A FACTORY SHOPPING VILLAGE**

See page 142 (LANCS)

STAFFORDSHIRE

BDF NEWLIFE

MARTINDALE, HAWK'S GREEN, CANNOCK, STAFFORDSHIRE WS11 2XN, ☎ 01543 468888, FAX: 01543 505989, **e-mail:** info@bdfnewlife.co.uk, 9.30–10 MON–SAT, 10–4 SUN, 10–5 BANK HOLIDAYS. **PERMANENT DISCOUNT OUTLET**

8,000 square foot charity superstore which sells both new merchandise donated by most of the top high street stores and nearly-new. This is the sort of shop where you can find anything from a girl's party dress to a two-seater rowing boat, men's shoes to a cooler bag, in between towels, jewellery, family clothes, furniture, mattresses (new with damaged packaging), beds, clocks, golf bags, umbrellas, wallpaper and designer dresses. Stock changes every 45 minutes. All the profits go to charity. Membership is by donation averaging £2. The shop is on one floor so is very accessible and has disabled toilet facilities. As the store also takes counterfeit goods from national Trading Standards departments' seizures, stress is put on not believing any labelling or assuring authenticity. There are also branches in Kirkby-in-Ashfield, Nottinghamshire and Stoke Aldermoor, Coventry.

BLUNTS

578 BARWOOD ROAD, SMETHWICK, STAFFORDSHIRE B66 4BW, ☎ 0121 429 1794, 9–5.30 MON–SAT. **PERMANENT DISCOUNT OUTLET**

39–43 BROAD STREET, HANLEY, STOKE-ON-TRENT, STAFFORDSHIRE ST1 4HS, ☎ 01782 273686, 9–5.30 MON–SAT. **PERMANENT DISCOUNT OUTLET**

30 MARKET PLACE, WILLENHALL, STAFFORDSHIRE WV13 2AA, ☎ 01902 606781, 9–5.30 MON–SAT. **PERMANENT DISCOUNT OUTLET**

See page 91 (BRIS)

CATALOGUE BARGAIN SHOP

95 CHURCH STREET, BILSTON, STAFFORDSHIRE WV14 0BJ, ☎ 01902 353624, www.bargaincrazy.com, 9–5.30 MON–SAT, 9.30–3.30 SUN.

UNIT 2, CHASE CENTRE, CHURCH STREET, CANNOCK, STAFFORDSHIRE WS11 1AP, ☎ 01543 468614, www.bargaincrazy.com, 9–8 MON–FRI, 9–6 SAT, 10.30–4.30 SUN.

FREEPORT TALKE OUTLET MALL, PIT LANE, TALKE PITS, STOKE-ON-TRENT, STAFFORDSHIRE ST7 1XD, ☎ 01782 775740, www.bargaincrazy.com, 9.30–8 MON–FRI, 9.30–6 SAT, 11–5 SUN.

63 HIGH STREET, BROWNHILLS, STAFFORDSHIRE WS8 6HH, ☎ 01543 372933, 9–5.30 MON–SAT. **PERMANENT DISCOUNT OUTLET**

See page 92 (CAMBS)

CATALOGUE SURPLUS CENTRE LTD

5 HIDE STREET, STOKE-ON-TRENT, STAFFORDSHIRE ST4 1NF, ☎ 01782 744445, 9–5 MON–SAT. **PERMANENT DISCOUNT OUTLET**

See page 171 (SHROP)

CHARLES CLINKARD

FREEPORT TALKE OUTLET MALL, PIT LANE, TALKE PITS, STOKE-ON-TRENT, STAFFORDSHIRE ST7 1QE, ☎ 01782 787016, FAX: 01782 787016, 10–8 MON–SAT, 11–5 SUN. **FACTORY SHOP IN A FACTORY SHOPPING VILLAGE**

See page 101 (CO DURH)

COLOURS

3 PEPPER STREET, NEWCASTLE UNDER LYME, STAFFORDSHIRE ST5 1PR, ☎ 01782 714164, 9.30–5 MON–SAT. **DRESS AGENCY**

Dress agency catering for men and women. Men's labels include Armani, Boss, Joseph, Calvin Klein, Thomas Burberry and Ralph Lauren. Women's labels: Armani, Betty Barclay, Paul Costelloe, Nicole Farhi, Wallis and Next. There is always a marvellous selection of shoes in sizes 3 to 8.

DIRECT SPECS LTD

UNIT 9, NORTHSIDE BUSINESS PARK, HAWKINS LANE, BURTON-ON-TRENT, STAFFORDSHIRE D14 1DB, ☎ 01283 563 782, www.directspecs.co.uk, 9–5 MON–SAT.

8 BERKELEY COURT, BOROUGH ROAD, NEWCASTLE UNDER LYME, STAFFORDSHIRE ST5 1TT, ☎ 01782 620 663, www.directspecs.co.uk, 9–5 MON–SAT.

1 SALTER STREET, STAFFORD, STAFFORDSHIRE ST16 2JU, ☎ 01785 212 001, www.directspecs.co.uk, 9–5 MON–SAT.

DIRECT SPECS LTD STOKE-ON-TRENT, 1 CHURCH HOUSE, OLD HALL STREET, HANLEY, STOKE-ON-TRENT, STAFFORDSHIRE ST1 3AU, ☎ 01782 263038, www.directspecs.co.uk, 9–5 MON–SAT.

39 LOWER GUNGATE, TAMWORTH, STAFFORDSHIRE B79 7AS, ☎ 01827 50233, www.directspecs.co.uk, 9–5 MON–SAT. **PERMANENT DISCOUNT OUTLET**

See page 95 (CHESH)

DOUBLE TWO

UNIT 46, FREEPORT TALKE, JAMAGE ROAD, STOKE-ON-TRENT, STAFFORDSHIRE ST7 1XD, ☎ 01782 787460, 9.30–8 MON–FRI, 9.30–6 SAT, 11–5 SUN. **FACTORY SHOP IN A FACTORY SHOPPING VILLAGE**

See page 116 (ESSEX)

FASHION FACTORY

VINE LANE, BRIDGTOWN, CANNOCK, STAFFORDSHIRE WS11 3XF, ☎ 01543 466000., www.fashionfactory.uk.com, 9.30–5.30 MON–SAT, 11–5 SUN. **PERMANENT DISCOUNT OUTLET**

See page 172 (SHROP)

FREEPORT TALKE OUTLET MALL

FREEPORT TALKE OUTLET MALL, PIT LANE, TALKE PITS, STOKE-ON-TRENT, OFF JUNCTION 16 OF M6 THEN TAKE THE A500 AND THE A34, FOLLOWING SIGNS TO TALKE, STAFFORDSHIRE ST7 1XD, ☎ 01782 774113, www.freeporttalke.com, 9.30–8 MON–FRI, 9.30–6 SAT, 11–5 SUN. **FACTORY SHOPPING VILLAGE**

Fully covered indoor outlet mall with a range of restaurants, including Burger King and Café Ritazza, and an indoor soft play area for children. Womenswear includes The Designer Room, Edinburgh Woollen Mill, Nickelby's, Pilot, Spotlight, Roman Originals and Leading Labels. Menswear includes The Suit Company, Double Two, Petroleum, Nickelby's, Madhouse and Tog 24. Childrenswear can be found at Used Co Kids. Other shops on site include: Claire's Accessories, Charles Clinkard, Jane Shilton, Bags Etc, Trespass, Streetwise Sports, The Golf Company, Catalogue Bargain Shop, Julian Graves, Kitchen and Table, Toy World, Thorntons, Birthdays, Room, Mobile Phone Store, Book Depot, Picture Port, Ponden Mill and XS Music.

GIFTTREE

2 QUADRANT ROAD, POTTERIES SHOPPING CENTRE, HANLEY, STOKE-ON-TRENT, STAFFORDSHIRE ST1 1PP, ☎ 01782 202570, 9–5.30 MON–SAT, 8 ON THUR.
6 MARKET STREET, TAMWORTH, STAFFORDSHIRE B79 7LU, ☎ 01827 60266, 9–5 MON–SAT.
FACTORY SHOP

See page 108 (DERBY)

LILLEY & SKINNER

FREEPORT TALKE OUTLET MALL, PIT LANE, TALKE PITS, STOKE-ON-TRENT, STAFFORDSHIRE ST7 1XD, ☎ 01782 774113, 10–8 MON–SAT, 11–5 SUN. **FACTORY SHOP IN A FACTORY SHOPPING VILLAGE**

See page 109 (DERBY)

MATALAN

UNIT A, LICHFIELD STREET, BURTON-ON-TRENT, STAFFORDSHIRE DE14 3QZ, ☎ 01283 540856, FAX: 01283 540873, www.matalan.co.uk, 10–8 MON–FRI, 9–6 SAT, 11–5 SUN.

QUEENSDALE RETAIL PARK, SILKMORE LANE, STAFFORD STAFFORDSHIRE ST17 4SU, ☎ 01785 226211, FAX: 01785 226279, www.matalan.co.uk, 10–8 MON–FRI, 9–6 SAT, 11–5 SUN.

WOLSTANTON RETAIL PARK, WOLSTANTON, NEWCASTLE, STOKE-ON-TRENT, STAFFORDSHIRE ST5 1DY, ☎ 01782 711731, FAX: 01782 714201, www.matalan.co.uk, 9.30–8 MON–FRI, 9–6 SAT, 11–5 SUN.

VENTURA RETAIL PARK, BONE HILL DRIVE, TAMWORTH, STAFFORDSHIRE B78 3HB, ☎ 01827 50900, FAX: 01827 509151, www.matalan.co.uk, 10–8 MON–FRI, 9–6 SAT, 11–5 SUN. **PERMANENT DISCOUNT OUTLET**

See page 89 (BEDS)

PARTRIDGE ENGLAND LTD

POWER STATION ROAD, TRENT MEADOWS, RUGELEY, STAFFORDSHIRE WS15 2HS, ☎ 01889 584438, 9–5 MON–FRI, 9–4 SAT. **FACTORY SHOP**

See page 123 (HAMPS)

SCOOPS CATALOGUE DISCOUNT STORES

UNIT 3, 567–569 BEARWOOD SHOPPING CENTRE, SMETHWICK, STAFFORDSHIRE B66 4BH, ☎ 0121 434 3086, FAX: 0121 429 8488, 9–5.30 MON–SAT, 11–3 SUN. **PERMANENT DISCOUNT OUTLET**

See page 102 (CO DURH)

T J HUGHES

THREE SPIRES SHOPPING CENTRE, 46 BAKERS LANE, LICHFIELD, STAFFORDSHIRE WS13 6JF, ☎ 01543 418181, FAX: 01543 418185, **e-mail:** info@tjhughes.co.uk, www.tjhughes.co.uk, 9–5.30 MON–SAT, 10.30–4.30 SUN. **PERMANENT DISCOUNT OUTLET**

See page 98 (CHESH)

THE FACTORY SHOP

QUEEN STREET CAR PARK, QUEEN STREET, MARKET DRAYTON, STAFFORDSHIRE TF9 1EQ, ☎ 01630 655673, 9–5 MON–SAT, 10–4 SUN. **FACTORY SHOP**

See page 98 (CHESH)

THE SHOE SHED

CASTLEFIELDS, NEWPORT ROAD, STAFFORD, STAFFORDSHIRE ST16 1BQ, ☎ 01785 211311 9–5.30 MON–SAT, 10–4 SUN. **FACTORY SHOP**

See page 114 (DORS)

TK MAXX

THE OCTAGON SHOPPING CENTRE, BURTON-ON-TRENT, STAFFORDSHIRE DE14 3TN, ☎ 01283 569891, www.tkmaxx.com, 9–5.30 MON–SAT, 10–4 SUN.

THE POTTERIES CENTRE, HANLEY, STOKE-ON-TRENT, STAFFORDSHIRE ST1 1PP, ☎ 01782 207509, www.tkmaxx.com, 9–5.30 MON–FRI, 9–6 SAT, 11–5 SUN, 8 ON THUR. **PERMANENT DISCOUNT OUTLET**

See page 89 (BEDS)

TOG 24

FREEPORT TALKE OUTLET MALL, PIT LANE, TALKE PITS, STOKE-ON-TRENT, STAFFORDSHIRE ST7 1QE, ☎ 01782 787558, **e-mail:** mail-order@tog24.com, www.tog24.com, 9.30–8 MON–FRI, 9.30–6 SAT, 11–5 SUN. **FACTORY SHOP IN A FACTORY SHOPPING VILLAGE**

See page 99 (CHESH)

WEBB IVORY

QUEENSBRIDGE WORKS, QUEEN STREET, BURTON-ON-TRENT, STAFFORDSHIRE DE14 3LP, ☎ 01283 506371, 9–5 MON–FRI, 9–2 SAT. **FACTORY SHOP**

Items from charity catalogues at reduced prices including cards, gifts, soft toys, books, pens, lamps, kitchenware and clothes. Stock is constantly changing, and discounts start from at least 50%.

WILKINSON STORES

OLD HALL STREET, HANLEY, STOKE-ON-TRENT, STAFFORDSHIRE, ☎ 01782 279225, www.wilko.co.uk, 8.30–6 MON–FRI, 8 ON THUR, 11–5 SUN. MAIL ORDER.

CASTLE HOUSE, 47–48 IRONMARKET, NEWCASTLE UNDER LYME, STAFFORDSHIRE ST5 1PD., ☎ 01782 714334, www.wilko.co.uk, 8.30–5.30 MON–SAT
PERMANENT DISCOUNT OUTLET

See page 100 (CHESH)

WYNSOR SHOES

151–153 MARSH STREET NORTH, HANLEY, STOKE-ON-TRENT, STAFFORDSHIRE ST1 5HR, ☎ 01782 266660, 9–5.30 MON, TUE, WED, SAT, 9–8 THUR, 9–6 FRI, 11–5 SUN.
PERMANENT DISCOUNT OUTLET

Stocks top brand-name shoes at less than half price. Special monthly offers always available. There are shoes, trainers, slippers, sandals and boots for all the family, with a selection of bags, cleaners and polishes available, all at discount prices.

SUFFOLK

BUYRIGHT OF HADLEIGH

CALAIS STREET, HADLEIGH, IPSWICH, SUFFOLK IP7 5EW, ☎ 01473 822626, 9–5.30 MON–SAT, 10.30–4.30 SUN. **PERMANENT DISCOUNT OUTLET**

Discount shop selling a mixture of clothes, household textiles, ceramics, kitchenware, knitting yarn, garden tools, curtains, toys, stationery, dusters, Christmas decorations, masking tape, lingerie and a host of other items. Stock changes regularly because the low prices mean a quick turnover. Some items are seconds or end of season stock from the major chain stores.

LAMBOURNE CLOTHING

15 CHRISTCHURCH STREET, IPSWICH, SUFFOLK IP4 2DP, ☎ 01473 250404, FAX: 01473 222282, 10–3 MON–THUR, 10–2 FRI. **FACTORY SHOP**

Family-run business, established for 10 years, which manufactures and sells own brand skirts, trousers, and jackets. The clothes, for men and for women, are overmakes and seconds and are usually discounted by about 50%. At the time of going to press they were considering moving premises. Please phone the number above before visiting.

MATALAN

EASLEA ROAD, BURY ST EDMUNDS, SUFFOLK IP32 7BY, ☎ 01284 748300, FAX: 01284 749146, www.matalan.co.uk, 9–8 MON–FRI, 9–6 SAT, 10–4 SUN.

See page 89 (BEDS)

PUFFA LIMITED FACTORY SHOP

UNIT 2, BRICETT BUSINESS PARK, GREAT BRICETT, IPSWICH, SUFFOLK IP7 7DZ, ☎ 01473 657338, FAX: 01473 658940, **e-mail:** pr@puffa.co.uk, www.puffa.com, 10–4 TUE–THUR, 10–1 FRI. **FACTORY SHOP**

Puffa original and genuine clothing is quality outdoor wear offering style, warmth and unbeatable value. The factory shop sells samples, production overruns, discontinued lines and seconds. It also has a bargain rail with garments at 50% off RRP.

QD STORES

47–51 CARR STREET, THE EASTGATE CENTRE, IPSWICH, SUFFOLK IP4 1HB, ☎ 01473 284220, 9–5.30 MON–SAT.

UNIT 21–25, BRITTEN CENTRE, LOWESTOFT, SUFFOLK NR32 1LR, ☎ 01502 565222, 9–5.30 MON–SAT.

9 IPSWICH STREET, STOWMARKET, SUFFOLK IP14 1AH, ☎ 01449 770438, 9–5.30 MON–SAT. **PERMANENT DISCOUNT OUTLET**

See page 89 (BEDS)

ROYS OF BURY VARIETY STORE

88–89 RISBYGATE STREET, BURY ST EDMUNDS, SUFFOLK IP33 3AQ, ☎ 01284 753535, www.roys.co.uk, 9–5.30 mon–sat, 8 on thur, 10.30–5.30 Sun.

GREAT EASTERN ROAD, SUDBURY, SUFFOLK CO10 6TJ, ☎ 01787 882800, www.roys.co.uk, 9–6 MON, TUE, WED, 8.30–8 THUR, FRI, 8.30–6 SAT, 10–4 SUN. **PERMANENT DISCOUNT OUTLET**

Roys sell branded household goods at what they call 'valued prices'. The Save 'n' Wear department deals with the cheaper end of the clothing market for men, women and children. They also include DIY, gardening, electrical, housewares, gifts, toiletries and some food lines.

THE FACTORY SHOP

BARTON BUSINESS CENTRE, BARTON ROAD, BURY ST EDMUNDS, SUFFOLK IP32 7BQ, ☎ 01284 701578, 9.30–5 MON–FRI, 10–6 SAT, 10–4 SUN.

LONDON ROAD, WRENTHAM, NR BECCLES, SUFFOLK NR34 7HJ, ☎ 01502 676100, 9–5.30 MON–SAT, 10.30–4.30 SUN. **FACTORY SHOP**

See page 89 (CHESH)

TK MAXX

1ST FLOOR, BUTTERMARKET SHOPPING CENTRE, IPSWICH, SUFFOLK IP1 1DT, ☎ 01473 226800, www.tkmaxx.com, 9–5.30 MON–FRI, 9–6 SAT, 11–5 SUN. **PERMANENT DISCOUNT OUTLET**

See page 89 (BEDS)

SURREY

ALAN PAINE KNITWEAR LTD

SCATS COUNTRY STORE COURTYARD, BRIGHTON ROAD, GODALMING, SURREY GU7 1NS, ☎ 01483 419962, FAX: 01483 419962, 9–5 MON–FRI, 9.30–4 SAT. **FACTORY SHOP**

Knitwear, made in Derbyshire, mostly for export and for sale to some of the top London stores, and sold here at factory shop prices. Although the majority of the jumpers and cardigans are made for men and start at size 38-inch chest, they are just as likely to be bought by women. In fact, their recently-expanded women's section also has a selection of styles exclusively for women. Choose from cotton, cashmere, lambswool, camel hair, merino and merino and silk mix.

AMAZON

3 AND 7 THE QUADRANT, RICHMOND, SURREY. **PERMANENT DISCOUNT OUTLET**

The most common labels seen here are In Wear, French Connection, Great Plains, Fenn Wright & Manson, Nicole Farhi and Sticky Fingers. There's always plenty of stock in good condition and at very reasonable prices. For example, Fenn Wright & Manson long dress, £29.99, reduced from £105; James Lakeland shirt, £22, reduced from £80; cashmere blend sweater, £19.99, was £180; French Connection boat neck striped jersey, £20, instead of £65. Caters for office, weekend and party wear. Shoes at number 7 are very cheap: velcro dolly shoe, £19.99 reduced from £50; wedge boot, £42.95 reduced from £78.95; evening shoes, £14.99 was £49.99.

CHOICE DISCOUNT STORES LIMITED

1 WARWICK QUADRANT, LONDON ROAD, REDHILL, SURREY RH1 1NN, ☎ 01737 772777, 9–6 MON–WED, 9–7 THUR, 9–6 FRI–SAT. **PERMANENT DISCOUNT OUTLET**

See page 92 (CAMBS)

MATALAN

268–278 HIGH STREET, SUTTON, SURREY SM1 1PG, ☎ 020 8652 9600, FAX: 020 8770 3581, www.matalan.co.uk, 9–8 MON–FRI, 9–6 SAT, 11–5 SUN. **PERMANENT DISCOUNT OUTLET**

See page 89 (BEDS)

NOTTING HILL HOUSING TRUST

394 RICHMOND ROAD, SURREY TW1 2DY, ☎ 020 8891 6819, **e-mail:** charityshop@nhhg.org.uk, www.nottinghillonline.com/supporters, 10–6 MON–SAT, 12.30–5.30 SUN. **DRESS AGENCY**

See page 151 (LOND)

OPTILABS

109 STAFFORD ROAD, CROYDON, SURREY CRO 4BB, ☎ 020 8686 5708, FAX: 020 8760 9706, **e-mail:** sales@optilabs.com, www.optilabs.com, 8–5.30 MON–FRI, 8–12.30 SAT. MAIL ORDER. **PERMANENT DISCOUNT OUTLET**

Spectacle frames and lenses, sunglasses, prescription sunglasses and sports frames, including designer frames, at factory prices, making them about half the high street price. Designers on sale include Calvin Klein, Giorgio Armani, Jaguar, Paco Rabanne and Dolce & Gabbana. Sports frames are used by professional sportsmen and women worldwide. The showroom is on the first floor at which sight tests are available, or you can take your own prescription. They stock a wide range of lenses which are made on the premises and are often available while you wait. They also offer a mail order service to your prescription.

SUITS YOU

UNIT 67, THE FRIARY, GUILDFORD, SURREY GU1 4YW, ☎ 01483 569446, 9–5.30 MON–SAT, 11–5 SUN. **FACTORY SHOP**

See page 91 (BRIS)

THE FACTORY SHOP LTD

THE ENGINE SHED, CONSORT WAY EAST, HORLEY, SURREY RH6 7AU, ☎ 01293 823883, 9–5.30 MON–SAT, 10–4 SUN. **FACTORY SHOP**

See page 98 (CHESH)

TK MAXX

THE DRUMMOND CENTRE, CROYDON, SURREY CR0 1TY, ☎ 020 8686 9753, www.tkmaxx.com, 9–6 MON–SAT, 9 ON THUR, 11–5 SUN.

102 HIGH STREET, EPSOM, SURREY, ☎ 01372 729060, www.tkmaxx.com, PHONE FOR DETAILS.

BISHOPS PALACE HOUSE, 2 CLARENCE STREET, KINGSTON, SURREY KT1 1PB, ☎ 020 8974 6296, www.tkmaxx.com, 9–6 MON–WED, 9–9 THUR–FRI, 8–7 SAT, 11–5. SUN.

TIMES SQUARE SHOPPING CENTRE, HIGH STREET, SUTTON, SURREY SM1 1LF, ☎ 020 8770 7786, www.tkmaxx.com, 9–5.30 MON–FRI, 8 ON THUR, 9–6 SAT, 11–5 SUN.

THE PEACOCKS CENTRE, WOKING, SURREY GU21 1GA, ☎ 01483 771660, www.tkmaxx.com, 9.30–6 MON–FRI, 8 ON THUR, 9–6 SAT, 11–5 SUN. **PERMANENT DISCOUNT OUTLET**

See page 89 (BEDS)

TOG 24

WHITGIFT CENTRE, CROYDON, SURREY CR0 1LP, ☎ 020 8680 7902, **e-mail:** mail-order@tog24.com, www.tog24.com, 10–6 MON–FRI, 8 ON THUR, 9–6 SAT, 10–5 SUN. **FACTORY SHOP**

See page 99 (CHESH)

SUSSEX

ALFOLD COUNTRY STORE

ALFOLD BARS, NR BILLINGSHURST, SUSSEX RH14 0QS, ☎ 01403 751777, FAX: 01403 751888, 9–6 MON–SAT, 10–4 SUN. **PERMANENT DISCOUNT OUTLET**

Good discounts on country and equestrian clothing including coats, jackets and waterproofs from Barbour, Aigle, Champion and Regatta, among other manufacturers. Pet supplies also.

BRIGHTON MARINA

CITY OF BRIGHTON AND HOVE EAST SUSSEX BN2 5WB, ☎ 01273 818504, FAX: 01273 818701, 10–LATE SEVEN DAYS A WEEK. **FACTORY SHOPPING VILLAGE**

The UK and Europe's largest marina. Boasts an exciting range of outlet shops combined with excellent bars, restaurants and leisure facilities. Currently hosts 11 outlet stores, such as PULSE skating solutions, The Factory Shop, Leading Labels and many more. The marina is currently investing millions into additional facilities, planned to open at the end of 2002, which will include a further 16 outlet stores including some household names.

IMPULSE

LONDON ROAD, HICKSTEAD, SUSSEX RH17 5NA, ☎ 01444 881255, 10–5 MON–SAT. **PERMANENT DISCOUNT OUTLET**

Men's shoes in sizes 6 to 13, as well as a large selection of women's shoes in sizes 35 to 41, and handbags – all at up to 50% discount. Next door to the women's designer fashion warehouse, M & G Designer Fashions.

IN WEAR FACTORY OUTLET

31–32 EAST STREET, BRIGHTON, EAST SUSSEX BN1 1HL, ☎ 01273 722914, 10–5.30 MON–SAT, 12–5 SUN, 11–4 BANK HOLIDAYS. **FACTORY SHOP**

See page 149 (LOND)

JAEGER FACTORY OUTLET

UNIT B, 208–216 LONDON ROAD, BURGESS HILL, SUSSEX RH15 9RD, ☎ 01444 333100, 10–6 MON–FRI, 9–6 SAT, 11–5 SUN. **FACTORY SHOP**

See page 158 (NORF)

M & G DESIGNER FASHIONS

OLD LONDON ROAD (OLD A23), NEAR HICKSTEAD VILLAGE, SUSSEX RH17 5NA, ☎ 01444 881511, FAX: 01444 881511, 10–5 MON–SAT. **PERMANENT DISCOUNT OUTLET**

A large fashion warehouse selling designer and famous brand-name clothes at discounted prices from 20% to 80% less than the normal retail price. Many of the clothes are the current season's fashions, discontinued lines, late deliveries, bankrupt stock and cancelled orders. Twice a year, they hold 'silly' sales where no garment is over £50. They also hold winter and summer clearance sales. Their range covers everything from T-shirts to ballgowns in sizes 10 to 24. An additional 10% discount is available to GDD readers. This discount cannot be used in conjunction with any other offer. There is ample parking, free coffee or tea, easy access for wheelchairs and individual changing rooms. They have recently started selling millinery, women's shoes and handbags in the shop next door. (Follow the signs to Ricebridge and Hickstead Village.) Please phone for Christmas and bank holiday hours. American Express, MasterCard, Visa and Switch cards accepted.

MATALAN

CARDEN AVENUE, HOLLINGBURY INDUSTRIAL ESTATE, BRIGHTON, EAST SUSSEX BN1 8AR, ☎ 01273 543800, FAX: 01273 502608, www.matalan.co.uk, 10–8 MON–FRI, 9–6 SAT, 10.30–4.30 SUN.

SOVEREIGN HARBOUR RETAIL PARK, PEVENSEY BAY ROAD, EASTBOURNE, EAST SUSSEX BN23 6JH, ☎ 01323 470347, FAX: 01323 470601, www.matalan.co.uk, 10–8 MON–FRI, 9–6 SAT, 10.30–4.30 SUN. **PERMANENT DISCOUNT OUTLET**

See page 89 (BEDS)

RICARA

1 OLD MARKET AVENUE, CHICHESTER, SUSSEX PO19 1DR, ☎ 01243 778850, FAX: 01243 778850, www.ricara.co.uk, 9–5 MON–SAT.

12 SURREY STREET, LITTLEHAMPTON, SUSSEX BN17 5BG, ☎ 01903 723843, FAX: 01903 718401, www.ricara.co.uk, 9–5 MON–SAT, 10–4 SUN.

22 HIGH STREET, LITTLEHAMPTON, SUSSEX

BN17, FAX: 01903 723843, FAX: 01903 718401, www.ricara.co.uk, 9–5 MON–SAT. **FACTORY SHOP**

Sells schoolwear for schools in the area from four years upwards. Savings can be made on certain items such as budget polo shirts £3.50 each or two for £6. They also sell martial arts clothing and equipment.

STOCKLEY TRADING

UNIT N10–11, BRIDGE ROAD, RIVERSIDE INDUSTRIAL ESTATE, LITTLEHAMPTON, SUSSEX BN17 5DF, ☎ 01903 732392, FAX: 01903 732754, **e-mail:** sales@stockleytrading.co.uk, www.stockleytrading.co.uk, 9–6 MON–FRI, 9.30–5 SAT, 10–4 SUN. **PERMANENT DISCOUNT OUTLET**

Warehouse shop which sells a range of outdoor wear and sportswear at wholesale prices. There is a good selection of branded leisurewear from Adidas, Umbro, Nike, Reebok, Fila, CAT, Fred Perry, Ben Sherman and Timberland among others. Stock varies, so phone to check stock before visiting if you are after something in particular. The outdoor wear department sells everything from underwear to hats and coats from names such as Regatta, Champion and Opentrack, and the equestrian department offers value for money on leading brands such as Weatherbeeta, Dublin, Stylo and Harry Hall.

T J HUGHES

14–26 THE BROADWAY, CRAWLEY, SUSSEX RH10 1DT, ☎ 01293 537373, FAX: 01293 611676, **e-mail:** info@tjhughes.co.uk, www.tjhughes.co.uk, 9–5.30 MON–FRI, 8 ON THUR, 9–6 SAT, 11–5 SUN.

177–178 TERMINUS ROAD, EASTBOURNE, SUSSEX BN21 3NX, ☎ 01323 732222, FAX: 01323 730110, **e-mail:** info@tjhughes.co.uk, www.tjhughes.co.uk, 9–5.30 MON–FRI, 9–6 SAT, 10.30–4.30 SUN. **PERMANENT DISCOUNT OUTLET**

See page 98 (CHESH)

THE FACTORY SHOP LTD

BRIGHTON MARINA, THE VILLAGE SQUARE, BRIGHTON, SUSSEX BN2 5WA, ☎ 01273 818590, 10–6 MON–FRI, 10–6 SAT, 10.30–4.30 SUN. **FACTORY SHOP IN A FACTORY SHOPPING VILLAGE**

See page 98 (CHESH)

THE SHOE SHED

3 THE ARCADE, BOGNOR REGIS, SUSSEX PO21 1LH, ☎ 01243 829600, 9–5.30 MON–SAT, 10–4 SUN. **FACTORY SHOP**

See page 114 (DORS)

TK MAXX

36–37 NORTH STREET, BRIGHTON, SUSSEX BN1 1EB, ☎ 01273 727483, www.tkmaxx.com, 9–6 MON–SAT, 7 ON THUR, 11–5 SUN.

13 THE MONTAGUE CENTRE, WORTHING, SUSSEX BN11 1YJ, ☎ 01903 234141, www.tkmaxx.com, 9–6 MON–SAT, 11–5 SUN. **PERMANENT DISCOUNT OUTLET**

See page 89 (BEDS)

TOG 24

THE VILLAGE SQUARE SHOPS, BRIGHTON MARINA VILLAGE, BRIGHTON, SUSSEX BN2 5WA, ☎ 01273 818759, **e-mail:** mail-order@tog24.com, www.tog24.com, 10–6 MON–SAT, 10–5 SUN. **FACTORY SHOP IN A FACTORY SHOPPING VILLAGE**

See page 99 (CHESH)

TOM SAYERS II

UNITS 6B & 6C, VILLAGE SQUARE, BRIGHTON MARINA VILLAGE, BRIGHTON, SUSSEX BN2 5UA, ☎ 01273 818705, 10–5.30 MON–FRI, 10–6 SAT, SUN. **FACTORY SHOP IN A FACTORY SHOPPING VILLAGE**

Tom Sayers II, now under new ownership, sells garments at unbeatable prices: at least 25% below high street prices. They stock smart and casual clothing for men, with brands including Cabco, Duke for Men, Vellero and many others. Casual clothing brands for women include Chilli Pepper, Coca Cola and Duke for Ladies.

WARWICKSHIRE AND THE WEST MIDLANDS

BLUNTS

164 HALESOWEN STREET, OWLEY REGIS, BLACKHEATH, WEST MIDLANDS B65 0EF, ☎ 0121 559 9347, 9–5.30 MON–SAT.

THE CIRCLE, KINGSTANDING, BIRMINGHAM, WEST MIDLANDS B44 9RG, ☎ 0121 354 7592, 9–5.30 MON–SAT.

65–67 MARKET STREET, STOURBRIDGE, WEST MIDLANDS DY8 1AQ, ☎ 01384 394324, 9–5.30 MON–SAT.

5–15 BROAD STREET, WOLVERHAMPTON, WEST MIDLANDS WV1 1DA, ☎ 01902 771701, 9–5.30 MON–SAT, 11–3.30 SUN. **PERMANENT DISCOUNT OUTLET**

See page 91 (BRIS)

CATALOGUE BARGAIN SHOP

ROCK BOTTOM CLEARANCE, 24–28 KING STREET, DUDLEY, WEST MIDLANDS DY2 8NY, ☎ 01384 458112, www.bargaincrazy.com, 9.30–5.30 MON–SAT, 10–4 SUN.

78 HIGH STREET, STOURBRIDGE, WEST MIDLANDS DY8 1DX, ☎ 01384 374544, www.bargaincrazy.com, 9–5.30 MON–SAT, 10–4 SUN.

17 BRADFORD STREET, WALSALL, WEST MIDLANDS WS1 1PB, ☎ 01922 722286, www.bargaincrazy.com, 9–5.30 MON–SAT, 10.30–4.30 SUN. **PERMANENT DISCOUNT OUTLET**

See page 92 (CAMBS)

CATALOGUE DISCOUNT STORE

SWAN CENTRE, COVENTRY ROAD, YARDLEY, BIRMINGHAM, WEST MIDLANDS B26 1AJ, ☎ 0121 707 6585, 9–5.30 MON–SAT.

UNIT 67, THE MOOR CENTRE, BRIERLEY HILL, DUDLEY, WEST MIDLANDS DY5 3AH, ☎ 01384 262537, 9–5.30 MON–SAT. **PERMANENT DISCOUNT OUTLET**

See page 101 (CO DURH)

DIRECT SPECS LTD

312 WALSGRAVE ROAD, COVENTRY, WARWICKSHIRE CV2 4PL, ☎ 024 7645 5555, www.directspecs.co.uk, 9–5 MON–SAT.

2288 COVENTRY ROAD, SHELDON, WARWICKSHIRE B26 3JR, ☎ 0121 742 3861, www.directspecs.co.uk, 9–5 MON–SAT.

UNIT 5, TEMPLE COURT, THE MINORIES, BIRMINGHAM, WEST MIDLANDS B4 6AG, ☎ 0121 236 4334, www.directspecs.co.uk, 9–5 MON–SAT.

245 WALSALL ROAD, PERRY BARR, WEST MIDLANDS B42 1TY, ☎ 0121 356 3396, www.directspecs.co.uk, 9–5 MON–SAT.

111 STRATFORD ROAD, SHIRLEY, BIRMINGHAM, WEST MIDLANDS B90 3ND, ☎ 0121 744 9372, www.directspecs.co.uk, 9–5 MON–SAT.

429 BIRMINGHAM ROAD, SUTTON COLDFIELD, WEST MIDLANDS B72 1AX, ☎ 0121 382 5535, www.directspecs.co.uk, 9–5 MON–SAT.

UNIT 3, 179 QUEEN STREET, WALSALL, WEST MIDLANDS WS2 9NX, ☎ 01922 635 301, www.directspecs.co.uk, 9–5 MON–SAT.

UNIT 12, WULFRUN TRADING ESTATE, STAFFORD ROAD, WOLVERHAMPTON, WEST MIDLANDS WV10 6HH, ☎ 01902 717744, www.directspecs.co.uk, 9–5 MON–SAT. **PERMANENT DISCOUNT OUTLET**

See page 95 (CHESH)

ENCORE

48–52A ST MARY'S ROW, MOSELEY, BIRMINGHAM, WEST MIDLANDS B13 8JG, ☎ 0121 442 4888, 9.30–5 MON–FRI, 9.30–4.45 SAT. **DRESS AGENCY**

Established in 1991, Encore sells middle to upmarket designer nearly-new wear and accessories for both men and women with formal and casual clothing for all occasions. Labels include Armani, MaxMara, Frank Usher, Hugo Boss, Moschino, Calvin Klein, alongside High Street names like Mondi, Betty Barclay, Windsmoor, Principles and Next. New stock arrives daily. Prices range from £5 to £200. The shop welcomes customers wishing to sell their own quality clothing.

FORGET-ME-NOT DESIGNER BRIDAL WEAR

THE WEDDING CENTRE, 5–7 LUTTERWORTH ROAD, ATTLEBOROUGH GREEN, NUNEATON, THREE MILES EAST OF JUNCTION 3 ON THE M6, WARWICKSHIRE CV11 4LD, ☎ 02476 375555 BRIDAL OR 02476 374444 SUIT HIRE, 9.30–5 MON–TUE, THUR–FRI, 9.30–5 SAT, CLOSED WED. **DRESS AGENCY HIRE SHOP**

The complete wedding shop. Forget-Me-Not Designer Bridalwear operates from a dedicated Wedding Centre where you can choose from a stunning collection of both new and sample wedding dresses. There is a men's formal wear hire service – with a massive selection of frock coats in brocade velvets and silks, highland wear and a choice of 100 waistcoats. You can find wedding stationers and a wedding cake business, tiaras, balloons and a bridal register of caterers, musicians, pipers, vocalists and video specialists. There are more than 200 dresses on display at any one time, with 600 more on computer. Designers on sale here include Donna Salado, Ian Stewart, Alfred Angelo, Paloma Blanca, Mon Cheri, Sincerity and others. Bridesmaids dresses and separates are available from the JLM occasion range. Accessories including shoes and hats.

INTERNATIONAL STOCK LTD

95–100 REA STREET, DIGBETH, BIRMINGHAM, WEST MIDLANDS B5 6HA, ☎ 0121 622 3232, **e-mail:** mail@international-stock.co.uk, www.international-stock.co.uk, 9–5 MON–SAT, 10–4 SUN, CLOSED 1 ON WED.

1–17 SILVER STREET, KINGS HEATH, BIRMINGHAM, WEST MIDLANDS B14 7QX, ☎ 0121 443 3232, FAX: 0121 444 1792, **e-mail:** mail@international-stock.co.uk, www.international-stock.co.uk, 9–6 MON–SAT, CLOSED 1 ON WED. **PERMANENT DISCOUNT OUTLET**

Bankrupt, fire and flood damaged articles from CDs and videos, household goods and clothes to DIY tools and television sets, carpets and cookers. The King's Heath branch is a two-storey warehouse with ever-changing stock. The upper floor is devoted to electrical goods, some marked down to 30% of their normal retail cost. The Digbeth branch sells bigger items such as kitchens, flooring, tiles, dining room and lounge furniture, central heating radiators and a large clothing section for all the family, all of which is sold below wholesale price and in some cases below manufacturers' cost price. Top brand name kitchens, when in stock, are discounted by 75%.

JEWELLERY QUARTER

NORTH-WEST BIRMINGHAM, WEST MIDLANDS, ☎ 0121 233 3468, **PERMANENT DISCOUNT OUTLET**

The Jewellery Quarter consists of 3,000 small businesses, mostly involved with the manufacture of jewellery. There are 100 retail shops selling direct to the public, cutting out the middleman so that jewellery costs much less than it would on the high street. There is an award-winning museum of jewellery on site. The area is well served by buses and trains and there is a large car park in the centre with some limited street meter parking.

LEGS CLOTHING CO

42 HIGH STREET, BLACKHEATH, ROWLEY REGIS, WEST MIDLANDS B65 0DR, ☎ 0121 559 0774, 9–5 MON–SAT. **FACTORY SHOP**

See page 120 (GLOS)

LITTLEWOODS CATALOGUE DISCOUNT STORE

14–16 NORTH STREET, RUGBY, WARWICKSHIRE CV21 2AF, ☎ 01788 565116, 9.30–5.45 MON–WED, 9–5.45 THUR–SAT.

236 HAWTHORN ROAD, KINGSTANDING, BIRMINGHAM, WEST MIDLANDS B44 8PP, ☎ 0121 373 1276, 9.30–5.30 MON–FRI, 9–5 SAT.

299–303 COVENTRY ROAD, SMALLHEATH, BIRMINGHAM, WEST MIDLANDS B10 0RA, ☎ 0121 772 1637, 9.30–5 MON–SAT, 10–5 WED, 11–4 SUN. **PERMANENT DISCOUNT OUTLET**

See page 96 (CHESH)

M LATIF & SONS

NEW CANAL STREET, DIGBETH, BIRMINGHAM, WEST MIDLANDS B5 5PL, ☎ 0121 643 2822, 9.30–5.30 MON–SAT, 8 ON THUR, 10–2.30 SUN. **PERMANENT DISCOUNT OUTLET**

Household and electrical goods, bedding, linens, ready-made curtains, clothes for all the family, pictures, garden equipment, toys, gifts and silk flowers, all of which are discounted as they are ex-catalogue and department store surplus from high street stores.

MATALAN

SPRING VALE RETAIL PARK, BILSTON, WEST MIDLANDS WV14 0QL, ☎ 01902 406160, FAX: 01902 409534, www.matalan.co.uk, 10–8 MON–FRI, 9–6 SAT, 10–4 SUN.

DARTMOUTH CIRCUS, MIDDLEWAY, BIRMINGHAM, WEST MIDLANDS B6 4BA, ☎ 0121 503 4700, FAX: 0121 333 3870, www.matalan.co.uk, 9–8 MON–FRI, 9–6 SAT, 11–5 SUN.

PORTWAY ROAD, PORTWAY GREEN, OLDBURY, BIRMINGHAM, WEST MIDLANDS B69 2BZ, ☎ 0121 544 4899, FAX: 0121 544 4394, www.matalan.co.uk, 10–8 MON–FRI, 9–6 SAT, 11–5 SUN.

2 FLAXLEY PARKWAY, STECHFORD RETAIL PARK, BIRMINGHAM, WEST MIDLANDS B33 9AN, ☎ 0121 789 5950, FAX: 0121 783 2170, www.matalan.co.uk, 10–8 MON–FRI, 9–6 SAT, 11–5 SUN.

GALLAGHER RETAIL PARK, STONEY STANTON ROAD, COVENTRY, WARWICKSHIRE CV6 5QQ, ☎ 0247 663 7320, FAX: 0247 663 8732, www.matalan.co.uk, 10–8 MON–FRI, 9–6 SAT, 11–5 SUN.

WHEELER ROAD, SEVEN STARS TRADING ESTATE, WHITELEY, COVENTRY SOUTH, WARWICKSHIRE CV3 2LB, ☎ 0247 621 7320, FAX: 0247 621 7321, www.matalan.co.uk, 9.30–8 MON–FRI, 9–6 SAT, 11–5 SUN.

MAYBIRD CENTRE, BIRMINGHAM ROAD, STRATFORD-UPON-AVON, WARWICKSHIRE CV37 0HZ, ☎ 01789 262223, FAX: 01789 262230, www.matalan.co.uk, 10–8 MON–FRI, 9–6 SAT, 11–5 SUN.

UNIT 9, BROADWAY RETAIL PARK, BESCOT CRESCENT, WALSALL, WEST MIDLANDS WS1 4DK, ☎ 01922 615188, FAX: 01922 611984, www.matalan.co.uk, 10–8 MON–FRI, 9–6 SAT, 11–5 SUN.

WALSALL RETAIL PARK, REEDSWOODS WAY, WALSALL, WEST MIDLANDS WS2 8XA, ☎ 01922 619830, FAX: 01922 746898, www.matalan.co.uk, 10–8 MON–FRI, 9–6 SAT, 10.30–4.30 SUN.

HOWARD STREET, BIRMINGHAM ROAD, WOLVERHAMPTON, WEST MIDLANDS WV2 3LQ, ☎ 01902 352813, FAX: 01902 352908, www.matalan.co.uk, 10–8 MON–FRI, 9–6 SAT, 11–5 SUN. **PERMANENT DISCOUNT OUTLET**

See page 89 (BEDS)

NEXT TO NOTHING

104 CORPORATION STREET, BIRMINGHAM, WEST MIDLANDS B2 6SZ, ☎ 0121 233 0022, www.next.co.uk, 9–5.30 MON–SAT, 11–5 SUN. **PERMANENT DISCOUNT OUTLET**

See page 97 (CHESH)

SCOOPS CATALOGUE DISCOUNT STORE

63 HIGH STREET, BROWNHILLS, WEST MIDLANDS WS8 6HH, ☎ 01543 372933, 9–5.30 MON–SAT.

UNIT 6–7 MOOR CENTRE, BRIERLEY HILL, DUDLEY, WEST MIDLANDS DY5 3AH, ☎ 01384 262537, 9–5.30 MON–SAT.

SWAN MARKET CENTRE, YARDLEY, BIRMINGHAM, WEST MIDLANDS, ☎ 0121 707 6585, 9–5.30 MON–SAT. **PERMANENT DISCOUNT OUTLET**

See page 102 (CO DURH)

SCOTTS CLOTHING EXCHANGE

43 PARK STREET, LEAMINGTON SPA, WARWICKSHIRE CV32 4QN, ☎ 01926 337868, 11.30–6 MON–SAT. **DRESS AGENCY**

Good quality women's and men's clothes and shoes with original and reduced prices marked. Merchandise comes from both the top end of the market and the high street end with labels from Top Shop to MaxMara, Marella and Armani for women and Zegna, Boss, Hilton and Yves Saint Laurent for men. There is also a selection of designer jeans such as Calvin Klein, as well as shoes, handbags and jewellery.

STAGE 2

AUSTIN DRIVE, COURTHOUSE GREEN, COVENTRY, WARWICKSHIRE CV6 7NS, ☎ 024 76 681520, 10–8 MON–FRI, 10–5 SAT, 11–5 SUN. **PERMANENT DISCOUNT OUTLET**

See page 92 (CAMBS)

T J HUGHES

98–100 LOWER PRECINCT, COVENTRY, WARWICKSHIRE CV1 1DX, ☎ 0247 662 7450, FAX: 0247 663 3627, **e-mail:** info@tjhughes.co.uk, www.tjhughes.co.uk, 9–5.30 MON–SAT, 10.30–4.30 SUN. **PERMANENT DISCOUNT OUTLET**

See page 98 (CHESH)

THE FAMOUS BRUNSWICK WAREHOUSE LTD

UNIT 12, ONE STOP SHOPPING CENTRE, 2 WALSALL ROAD, PERRY BARR, BIRMINGHAM, WEST MIDLANDS BA2 1AA, ☎ 0121 356 4107, **e-mail:** northshoe@mcmail.com, 9–6 MON–WED, SAT, 9–7.30 THUR, FRI, 11–5 SUN.

UNIT 2, TOWN WHARF, SHAW STREET, WALSALL, WEST MIDLANDS WA2 8PQ, ☎ 0192 616361, **e-mail:** northshoe@mcmail.com, 10–6 MON–WED, 10–8 THUR, FRI, 9–6 SAT, 11–5 SUN. **PERMANENT DISCOUNT OUTLET**

See page 98 (CHESH)

THE OUTLET

HATTON COUNTRY WORLD, DARK LANE, HATTON, NEAR WARWICK, WARWICKSHIRE CV35 8XA, ☎ 01926 842761, **e-mail:** hatton@hattonworld.com, www.hattonworld.com, 10–5 SEVEN DAYS A WEEK. **PERMANENT DISCOUNT OUTLET**

Hatton Country World consists of a Shopping Village with 25 craft and specialist shops and an antiques centre and, for bargain hunters, The Outlet, a department-style store selling discounted brand names in women and men's clothes, kitchenware and gifts. All are housed in a charming cluster of converted Victorian farm buildings. There is a farm park and outdoor activity centre.

T J HUGHES

27 BELL STREET, MANDER CENTRE, WOLVERHAMPTON, WEST MIDLANDS WV1 3PT, ☎ 01902 428011, FAX: 01902 420248, **e-mail:** info@tjhughes.co.uk, www.tjhughes.co.uk, 9–5.30 MON–FRI, 8.30–5.30 SAT, 10.30–4.30 SUN. **PERMANENT DISCOUNT OUTLET**

See page 98 (CHESH)

TK MAXX

UNITS 3-4 CASTLE VALE RETAIL PARK, BIRMINGHAM, WEST MIDLANDS, ☎ 0121 7496122, www.tkmaxx.com, 9–8 MON–FRI, 9–6 SAT, 11–5 SUN.

ONE STOP SHOPPING CENTRE, WALSALL ROAD, PERRY BARR, BIRMINGHAM, WEST MIDLANDS, ☎ 0121 356 5807, www.tkmaxx.com, PHONE FOR DETAILS.

THE GALLAGHER RETAIL PARK, STONEY STANTON ROAD, COVENTRY, WARWICKSHIRE CV6 5QG, ☎ 02476 664158, www.tkmaxx.com, 10–8 MON–FRI, 9–6 SAT, 11–5 SUN.

7–8 CROWN WHARF RETAIL PARK, WOLVERHAMPTON STREET, WALSALL, WEST MIDLANDS, ☎ 01922 649742, www.tkmaxx.com, PHONE FOR DETAILS.

2 WULFRUN SQUARE, WOLVERHAMPTON, WEST MIDLANDS WV1 3HB, ☎ 01902 421004, www.tkmaxx.com, 9–5.30 MON–FRI, 9–6 SAT, 11–5 SUN. **PERMANENT DISCOUNT OUTLET**

See page 89 (BEDS)

UNITED FOOTWEAR

926–928 STRATFORD ROAD, BIRMINGHAM, WEST MIDLANDS, ☎ 0121 778 1978, 9–5.30 MON–SAT, 10–4 SUN.
112–124 HOLBROOK LANE, COVENTRY WARWICKSHIRE, ☎ 024 76 581838, 9–8 MON–FRI, 9–5.30 SAT, 10–4 SUN.
74 BRADFORD STREET, WALSALL, WEST MIDLANDS, ☎ 01922 641577, 9–5.30 MON–SAT, 10–4 SUN. **PERMANENT DISCOUNT OUTLET**

See page 124 (HAMPS)

WEST MIDLANDS OUTLET CENTRE

SHANNON MILLS, WALSALL, WEST MIDLANDS
OPENING EASTER 2003.

WILTSHIRE

ADIDAS

MCARTHURGLEN DESIGNER OUTLET GREAT WESTERN, KEMBLE DRIVE, SWINDON, JUNCTION 16 OF M4, WILTSHIRE SN2 2DY, ☎ 01793 651854, FAX: 01793 651856, 10–6 MON–FRI, 8 ON THUR, 9–6 SAT, 11–5 SUN. **FACTORY SHOP IN A FACTORY SHOPPING VILLAGE**

See page 93 (CHESH)

AQUASCUTUM

MCARTHURGLEN DESIGNER OUTLET GREAT WESTERN, KEMBLE DRIVE, SWINDON, JUNCTION 16 OF M4, WILTSHIRE SN2 2DY, ☎ 01793 693073, 10–6 MON–FRI, 8 ON THUR, 10–6 SAT, 11–5 SUN. **FACTORY SHOP IN A FACTORY SHOPPING VILLAGE**

See page 125 (HERTS)

AUTONOMY

MCARTHURGLEN DESIGNER OUTLET GREAT WESTERN, KEMBLE DRIVE, SWINDON, JUNCTION 16 OF M4, WILTSHIRE SN2 2DY, ☎ 01793 490214, 10–6 MON–FRI, 8 ON THUR, 9–6 SAT, 11–5 SUN. **FACTORY SHOP IN A FACTORY SHOPPING VILLAGE**

See page 93 (CHESH)

BIG L FACTORY OUTLET

MCARTHURGLEN DESIGNER OUTLET GREAT WESTERN, KEMBLE DRIVE, SWINDON, JUNCTION 16 OF M4, WILTSHIRE SN2 2DZ, ☎ 01793 693339, FAX: 01793 693339, 10–6 MON–FRI, 8 ON THUR, 9–6 SAT, 11–5 SUN. **FACTORY SHOP IN A FACTORY SHOPPING VILLAGE**

See page 93 (CHESH)

BURBERRY

MCARTHURGLEN DESIGNER OUTLET GREAT WESTERN, KEMBLE DRIVE, SWINDON, JUNCTION 16 OF M4, WILTSHIRE SN2 2DY, ☎ 01793 486861, 10–6 MON–FRI, 8 ON THUR, 9–6 SAT, 11–5 SUN. **FACTORY SHOP IN A FACTORY SHOPPING VILLAGE**

See page 94 (CHESH)

CHAIN REACTION

15 FISHERTON STREET, SALISBURY, WILTSHIRE SP2 7SU, ☎ 01722 326201
OPEN 9.30–5 MON–SAT. **DRESS AGENCY**

Dress agency on two floors selling men's and women clothes, some of which are designer labels, as well as a selection of soft furnishings. Selection of evening and wedding wear, including hats.

CLARKS FACTORY SHOP

GREAT WESTERN VILLAGE, KEMBLE DRIVE, SWINDON, WILTSHIRE SN2 7AA, ☎ 01793 523723, 10–6 MON–FRI, 10–8 SAT, 9–6 SUN. **FACTORY SHOP IN A FACTORY SHOPPING VILLAGE**

See page 94 (CHESH)

DENTS ACCESSORIES

FAIRFIELD ROAD, WARMINSTER, WILTSHIRE BA12 9DL, ☎ 01985 212291, FAX: 01985 216435, **e-mail:** retail@dents.co.uk, www.dents.co.uk, 9.30–5 TUE–SAT. **FACTORY SHOP**

The accessories company which produces covetable gloves, belts, handbags, leather wallets and purses for most of the world's leading department stores has a factory outlet near Salisbury. Most of the stock in this reasonably-sized warehouse shop are sold at at least 50% discount, and there is also a wonderful selection of gloves, leather briefcases, handbags, silk ties, leather belts and small leather goods. The range of handbags come from three sources: ends of ranges from last season and discontinued ranges; returned sample stock for the current season from their sales agents; and prototypes for next season. Some of the briefcases are in English bridle leather, full hide or split hide. Stock from the discontinued and end of ranges changes constantly.

DOUBLE TWO

UNIT 8, WILTON SHOPPING VILLAGE, KING STREET, SALISBURY, WILTSHIRE SP2 0AY, ☎ 01722 741370, 9.30–5.30 MON–SAT, 11–5 SUN. **FACTORY SHOP IN A FACTORY SHOPPING VILLAGE**

See page 116 (ESSEX)

ECCO

MCARTHURGLEN DESIGNER OUTLET GREAT WESTERN, KEMBLE DRIVE, SWINDON, JUNCTION 16 OF M4, WILTSHIRE SN2 2DY, ☎ 01793 422240, www.ecco.com, 10–6 MON–FRI, 8 ON THUR, 9–6 SAT, 11–5 SUN. **FACTORY SHOP IN A FACTORY SHOPPING VILLAGE**

See page 95 (CHESH)

GAP

MCARTHURGLEN DESIGNER OUTLET GREAT WESTERN, KEMBLE DRIVE, SWINDON, JUNCTION 16 OF M4, WILTSHIRE SN2 2DY, ☎ 01793 486696, 10–6 MON–FRI, 8 ON THUR, 9–6 SAT, 11–5 SUN. **FACTORY SHOP IN A FACTORY SHOPPING VILLAGE**

Gap sells casual clothes for men, women, babies and children, discounted at this factory outlet by a minimum of 30% up to as much as 80% off. There is a children's play area, restaurants and a large car park.

GEORGINA VON ETZDORF

ODSTOCK ROAD, SALISBURY, WILTSHIRE SP5 4NZ, ☎ 01722 326625, FAX: 01722 338541 **e-mail:** sales@gve.co.uk, www.gve.co.uk, 10–5 MON–SAT, 12–5 SUN AND BANK HOLIDAYS. **FACTORY SHOP**

Based on the edge of the village of Odstock lies the Georgina von Etzdorf factory shop, a purpose designed building which itself has won eight design awards, overlooking the beautiful Chalke Valley. Here you will find an extensive range of scarves and accessories at considerably reduced prices from their London flagship shop. Fabric by the metre is also available: velvets, silks, wools, linens and jacquards, printed, woven, knitted, embroidered, embellished and adorned. From classic chiffons to futuristic fibre optics, the collection will have a broad appeal to both men and women. The shop has been recently expanded to accommodate a selection of the following internationally acclaimed designer merchandise: Bill Amberg's bags, purses and wallets; Duchamp's shirts, ties and cufflinks; Cutler and Gross sunglasses; Dinny Hall jewellery; Margaret Howell clothing and accessories; Gabriella Ligenza coats, shoes and hats; Nick Munro tableware and gift items; Fred Bare hats; Matthew Williamson evening wear and Emma Hope shoes.

GOLDSMITHS OUTLET

MCARTHURGLEN DESIGNER OUTLET GREAT WESTERN, KEMBLE DRIVE, SWINDON, JUNCTION 16 OF M4, WILTSHIRE SN2 2DY, ☎ 01793 693369, www.goldsmiths.co.uk, 10–6 MON–FRI, 8 ON THUR, 9–6 SAT, 11–5 SUN. **FACTORY SHOP IN A FACTORY SHOPPING VILLAGE**

Goldsmiths sells Raymond Weil watches, reduced from £550 to £385; Longines, Gucci, Maurice Lacroix and Tag Heuer. Some ranges reduced from 20% up to 50%.

JAEGER

MCARTHURGLEN DESIGNER OUTLET GREAT WESTERN, KEMBLE DRIVE, SWINDON, JUNCTION 16 OF M4, WILTSHIRE SN2 7AA, ☎ 01793 484660, 10–6 MON–FRI, 8 ON THUR, 9–6 SAT, 11–5 SUN. **FACTORY SHOP IN A FACTORY SHOPPING VILLAGE**

See page 158 (NORF)

MATALAN

SOUTHAMPTON ROAD, SALISBURY, WILTSHIRE SP1 2LE, ☎ 01722 342360, FAX: 01722 413721, www.matalan.co.uk, 10–8 MON–FRI, 9–6 SAT, 10–4 SUN.

MANNINGTON RETAIL PARK, WOOTTON BASSETT ROAD, SWINDON, WILTSHIRE SN5 9NP, ☎ 01793 649500, FAX: 01793 431895, www.matalan.co.uk, 10–8 MON–FRI, 9–6 SAT, 10–4 SUN. **PERMANENT DISCOUNT OUTLET**

See page 89 (BEDS)

MCARTHURGLEN DESIGNER OUTLET GREAT WESTERN

KEMBLE DRIVE, SWINDON, JUNCTION 16 OF M4, WILTSHIRE SN2 2DY, ☎ 0800 316 4352 FREE INFORMATION LINE OR 01793 507600, www.mcarthurglen.com, 10–6 MON–FRI, 8 ON THUR, 9–6 SAT, 11–5 SUN. **FACTORY SHOPPING VILLAGE**

The McArthurGlen Designer Outlet Great Western offers over 100 stores selling top names and designer brands at up to 50% off typical retail prices. Housed in the restored Great Western Railway buildings, everything is conveniently located under one roof. A large open plan area dedicated to homewares has everything for the house and home. Facilities include a food court, children's play area, licensed creche and ample parking. Stores include: U Wear/I Wear, Warner UK Ltd, Antler, Ecco Shoes, Walker & Hall, Liz Claiborne, Viyella, Austin Reed, Suits You, Alexon, Jaeger, Windsmoor, Aquascutum, Olsen, Jacques Vert, Overland/Caterpillar, Episode, Long Tall Sally, Pilot, Triumph, Cotton Traders, Villeroy & Boch, Baron Jon, Clarks, HKA, Burberry, Remington, Regatta, Just Sweets, Easy Jeans, Ben Sherman, JoKids, Donnay, Le Creuset, Puma, Tog 24, XS, Gap, Big L, Soled Out, Ted Baker, Nike, Timberland, Quiksilver, Whittard, Marks and Spencer, Polo Jeans Company, Gant, Calp, The Design House, Dartington Crystal, Duvet and Pillow Shop, Henri Lloyd, Mexx, Ravel, The Luxury Beauty Store, Thomas Pink, Thorntons, Tie Rack, Julian Graves, Hanro, Jane Shilton, Birthday, Toy Zone, Bookends, Sofa Works, Designer Room, Petroleum, Next, Daks Simpson, Suit Company, Price's Candles, Claire's Accessories, Samsonite, Van Heusen, Cloverleaf, Poole Pottery, Spiegelau, Edinburgh Crystal, Woods of Windsor, Staffordshire Pottery, Waterford Wedgewood, Stuart Crystal, Gleneagles, The Garden Outlet, Ponden Mill, Jane Heath, Sheridan Australia, Tefal, Professional Cookware, and Oneida.

MEXX INTERNATIONAL

MCARTHURGLEN DESIGNER OUTLET GREAT WESTERN, KEMBLE DRIVE, SWINDON, JUNCTION 16 OF M4, WILTSHIRE SN2 2DY, ☎ 01793 692205, 10–6 MON–FRI, 8 ON THUR, 9–6 SAT, 11–5 SUN. **FACTORY SHOP IN A FACTORY SHOPPING VILLAGE**

See page 97 (CHESH)

NEXT TO NOTHING

MCARTHURGLEN DESIGNER OUTLET GREAT WESTERN, KEMBLE DRIVE, SWINDON, JUNCTION 16 OF M4, WILTSHIRE SN2 2DY, ☎ 01793 525555, www.next.co.uk, 10–6 MON–FRI, 8 ON THUR, 9–6 SAT, 11–5 SUN. **FACTORY SHOP IN A FACTORY SHOPPING VILLAGE**

See page 97 (CHESH)

NIKE FACTORY STORE

MCARTHURGLEN DESIGNER OUTLET GREAT WESTERN, KEMBLE DRIVE, SWINDON, JUNCTION 16 OF M4, WILTSHIRE SN2 2DY, ☎ 01793 484440, FAX: 01793 430092, 10–6 MON–FRI, 8 ON THUR, 9–6 SAT, 11–5 SUN. **FACTORY SHOP IN A FACTORY SHOPPING VILLAGE**

Men's, women's, children's and infants sports clothing and footwear including T-shirts, jumpers, trainers, jackets, T-shirts, sports shirts, shorts, sleeveless T-shirts and tracksuits. Caters for all sporting needs ranging from golf to running, rugby to football. Nike has been making clothes for people who live and play outdoors since 1971. This factory shop sells unsold items from previous seasons. The selection represents their worldwide collection, which means that some garments may not have been offered for sale in the UK. As ranges tend to be incomplete, they are offered at a minimum of 30% off the recommended retail price or the price they would have commanded in the UK. Occasionally, there are some slight seconds on sale, which are always marked as such. Sometimes clearance line items are reduced by up to 70%, and additional savings can be made at sale times. Phone for details of when these take place. There is another factory shop at Cheshire Oaks in Ellesmere Port.

OLD DAIRY SADDLERY LTD

GREENWAY FARM, TOCKENHAM, SWINDON, WILTSHIRE SN4 7PP, ☎ 01793 849284, **e-mail:** odsaddlery@talk21.com, www.olddairysaddlery.co.uk, 10–5 MON–FRI, 9.30–5 SAT, 10–1 SUN.
PERMANENT DISCOUNT OUTLET

A large shop on a farm, selling outdoor wear, a wide range of horse rugs, saddlery, equipment and country clothing etc at competitive prices. Also stocks Cliff Barnsby, Maintain Horse and Kyra K saddlewear.

OXFAM BRIDAL BOUTIQUE

FIRST FLOOR, 5 THE BRIDGE, CHIPPENHAM, WILTSHIRE SN15 1HA, ☎ 01249 447061
BY APPOINTMENT ONLY. **PERMANENT DISCOUNT OUTLET**

Bridal clothes and accessories including up to 300 gowns for brides, as well as bridesmaids; artificial flowers, shoes, headdresses, veils, foundation garments, petticoats. Many of these items have been donated by manufacturers after being used in catwalk shows so have only been worn by a model. Prices from £35 upwards. Make an appointment by telephone on the number above.

PRINCIPLES

MCARTHURGLEN DESIGNER OUTLET GREAT WESTERN, KEMBLE DRIVE, SWINDON, JUNCTION 16 OF M4, WILTSHIRE SN2 2DY, ☎ 01793 693890, 10–6 MON–FRI, 8 ON THUR, 9–6 SAT, 11–5 SUN. **FACTORY SHOP IN A FACTORY SHOPPING VILLAGE**

See page 97 (CHESH)

REGATTA

MCARTHURGLEN DESIGNER OUTLET GREAT WESTERN, KEMBLE DRIVE, SWINDON, JUNCTION 16 OF M4, WILTSHIRE SN2 2DY, ☎ 01793 520900, FAX: 01793 520900, www.regatta.com, 10–6 MON–FRI, 8 ON THUR, 9–6 SAT, 11–5 SUN. **FACTORY SHOP IN A FACTORY SHOPPING VILLAGE**

See page 118 (ESSEX)

SUITS YOU

UNITS 10–11, GREAT WEATERN DESIGNER OUTLET VILLAGE, KEMBLE DRIVE, SWINDON, WILTSHIRE SN2 2DY, ☎ 01793 480511

10–6 MON–FRI, 8 ON THUR, 9–6 SAT, 11–5 SUN. **FACTORY SHOP IN A FACTORY SHOPPING VILLAGE**

See page 91 (BRIS)

THE FACTORY SHOP LTD

23–25 NEW PLACE, CORSHAM, WILTSHIRE SN13 OHL, ☎ 01249 712160, 9–5.30 MON–SAT, 10–4 SUN.

36–37 ROUNDSTONE STREET, TROWBRIDGE, WILTSHIRE BA14 8DE, ☎ 01225 751399, 9–5 MON–SAT.

24 MARKET PLACE, WARMINSTER, WILTSHIRE BA12 9AN, ☎ 01985 217532, 9–5 MON–SAT.
FACTORY SHOP

See page 98 (CHESH)

TIMBERLAND

MCARTHURGLEN DESIGNER OUTLET GREAT WESTERN, KEMBLE DRIVE, SWINDON, JUNCTION 16 OF M4, WILTSHIRE SN2 2DZ, ☎ 01793 480156, FAX: 01793 480394, 10–6 MON–FRI, 8 ON THUR, 9–6 SAT, 11–5 SUN. **FACTORY SHOP IN A FACTORY SHOPPING VILLAGE**

See page 98 (CHESH)

TK MAXX

CROSS KEYS SHOPPING CENTRE, SALISBURY, WILTSHIRE, ☎ 01722 320644, www.tkmaxx.com, 9–5.30 MON–FRI, 8 ON THUR, 9–6 SAT, 10–4 SUN.

THE ARCADE, BRUNEL SHOPPING CENTRE, SWINDON, WILTSHIRE, ☎ 01793 532896, www.tkmaxx.com, PHONE FOR DETAILS. **PERMANENT DISCOUNT OUTLET**

See page 89 (BEDS)

TOG 24

MCARTHURGLEN DESIGNER OUTLET GREAT WESTERN, KEMBLE DRIVE, SWINDON, JUNCTION 16 OF M4, WILTSHIRE SN2 2DY, ☎ 01793 695966, **e-mail:** mail-order@tog24.com, www.tog24.com, 10–6 MON–FRI, 8 ON THUR, 9–6 SAT, 11–5 SUN. **FACTORY SHOP IN A FACTORY SHOPPING VILLAGE**

See page 99 (CHESH)

TRIUMPH INTERNATIONAL LTD

MCARTHURGLEN DESIGNER OUTLET GREAT WESTERN, KEMBLE DRIVE, SWINDON, JUNCTION 16 OF M4, WILTSHIRE SN2 2DY, ☎ 01793 480892, 10–6 MON–FRI, 8 ON THUR, 9–6 SAT, 11–5 SUN. **FACTORY SHOP IN A FACTORY SHOPPING VILLAGE**

See page 99 (CHESH)

UNITED FOOTWEAR

HORHAM CRESCENT, PARK SOUTH, SWINDON, WILTSHIRE SN3 2LX, ☎ 01793 435238, 9–5.30 MON–SAT, 10–4 SUN. **PERMANENT DISCOUNT OUTLET**

See page 124 (HAMPS)

VIYELLA

MCARTHURGLEN DESIGNER OUTLET GREAT WESTERN, KEMBLE DRIVE, SWINDON, JUNCTION 16 OF M4, WILTSHIRE SN2 7AR, ☎ 01793 484450, 10–6 MON–FRI, 8 ON THUR, 9–6 SAT, 11–5 SUN. **FACTORY SHOP IN A FACTORY SHOPPING VILLAGE**

See page 99 (CHESH)

WARNERS

GREAT WESTERN DESIGNER OUTLET VILLAGE, KEMBLE DRIVE, SWINDON, WILTSHIRE SN2 2DY, ☎ 01793 430126, 10–6 MON–FRI, 8 ON THUR, 9–6 SAT, 11–5 SUN. **FACTORY SHOP IN A FACTORY SHOPPING VILLAGE**

See page 100 (CHESH)

WILTON SHOPPING VILLAGE

MINSTER STREET, WILTON, SALISBURY, WILTSHIRE SP2 0RS, ☎ 01722 741 211, www.thewsv@eagleone.co.uk, 9.30–5.30 MON–SAT, 11–5 SUN. **FACTORY SHOPPING VILLAGE**

On the former site of the Royal Wilton Carpet Factory, this village uses the refurbished original factory dye houses and 300-year-old, listed, historic courtyard buildings to house factory shops selling fashion and homewares at discounted prices. It includes shops such as Cotton Traders, Double Two, Edinburgh Woollen Mill, Julian Graves, Old Traditions, Ponden Mill, Remainders Books, Roman Originals, Scotts of Stow and the Wilton Carpet Factory Shop. Free parking, coffee shop, children's play area and disabled facilities. A riverside café is also open during the summer, serving homemade food and refreshments.

WORCESTERSHIRE

BLUNTS

65 LOAD STREET, BEWDLEY, WORCESTERSHIRE DY12 2AW, ☎ 01299 403227, 9–5.30 MON–SAT, 10–4 SUN.

75 HIGH STREET, BROMSGROVE, WORCESTERSHIRE B61 8AQ, ☎ 01527 874063, 9–5.30 MON–SAT.

8–9 BULLRING, KIDDERMINSTER, WORCESTERSHIRE, ☎ 01562 745277, 9–5.30 MON–SAT.

51 UPPER TYTHING, WORCESTER, WORCESTERSHIRE WR1 1DT, ☎ 01905 27738, 9–5.30 MON–SAT.

46–48 LOWESMOOR, WORCESTER, WORCESTERSHIRE WR1 2SG, ☎ 01905 21331, 9–5.30 MON–SAT. **PERMANENT DISCOUNT OUTLET**

See page 91 (BRIS)

CATALOGUE BARGAIN SHOP

233 WORCESTER ROAD, MALVERN LINK, MALVERN WORCESTERSHIRE WR14 1SY, ☎ 01684 893062, www.bargaincrazy.com, 9–5.30 MON–SAT, 10.30–4.30 SUN. **PERMANENT DISCOUNT OUTLET**

See page 92 (CAMBS)

D & C REYNOLDS

EDWIN AVENUE, HOO FARM TRADING ESTATE, WORCESTER ROAD, KIDDERMINSTER, WORCESTERSHIRE DY11 7RA, ☎ 01562 67187, www.reynoldsclothing.co.uk, 9–5 MON–SAT, 11–4 BANK HOLIDAYS. **PERMANENT DISCOUNT OUTLET**

Well-established trade shop offering a huge selection of high quality European clothing and some lingerie at incredible prices. The women's clothes are the German brand, Madeleine, and include raincoats, suits, jackets, trousers, dresses and skirts in a range of sizes, with lots of larger sizes.

DIRECT SPECS LTD

23 ANGEL PLACE, WORCESTER, WORCESTERSHIRE WR1 3QN, ☎ 01905 729313, FAX: 01543 573251, www.directspecs.co.uk, 9–5 MON–SAT. **PERMANENT DISCOUNT OUTLET**

See page 95 (CHESH)

EVESHAM COUNTRY PARK

SHOPPING AND GARDENING CENTRE, COUNTRY PARK MANAGEMENT, EVESHAM, AT THE NORTHERN END OF THE EVESHAM BYPASS, AT ITS JUNCTION WITH THE STRATFORD ROAD WORCESTERSHIRE WR11 4TP, ENQUIRIES: 01386 41661; GARDEN CENTRE: 01386 761888; APPLE BARN RESTAURANT: 01386 761333; VALE WILDLIFE VISITOR CENTRE: 01386 443348; COARSE FISHING/GOTTFRIED: 07973 147323, 9–6 MON–SAT (WINTER 5.30), 10.30–4.30 SUN. **FACTORY SHOPPING VILLAGE**

Courtyard shops and garden centre providing a wide variety of goods at bargain prices. Designer and brand name men's and women's fashions from Leading Labels, leisurewear from Cotton Traders, coordinated soft furnishings, bedlinen and duvets from Ponden Mill, household goods from Lifestyles, dried fuits, nuts and packaged herbs from Julian Graves, an extensive range of books from The Book Depot, plus quality plants, colourful pots and garden equipment. Luggage & Bags sells a range of quality branded luggage and travel goods at great prices. There is also a restaurant, wildlife centre, coarse fishing on the River Avon, and a miniature railway for a real country day out.

LEGS CLOTHING CO

29 HIGH STREET, PERSHORE, WORCESTERSHIRE WR10 1AA, ☎ 01386 550328, 9–5 MON–SAT. **FACTORY SHOP**

See page 120 (GLOS)

MATALAN

FORMER HOMEBASE, PARKER BUTTS, RINGWAY, KIDDERMINSTER WORCESTERSHIRE DY11 6TQ, ☎ 01562 756880, FAX: 01562 753573, www.matalan.co.uk, 9–8 MON–FRI, 9–6 SAT, 10–4 SUN.

UNIT 10, MALVERN RETAIL PARK, ROMAN WAY, MALVERN, WORCESTERSHIRE WR14 1JQ, ☎ 01684 584800, FAX: 01684 584802, www.matalan.co.uk, 10–8 MON–FRI, 9–6 SAT, 11–4 SUN. **PERMANENT DISCOUNT OUTLET**

See page 89 (BEDS)

T J HUGHES

1 HIGH STREET, KIDDERMINSTER, WORCESTERSHIRE DY10 2DS, ☎ 01562 745687, FAX: 01562 744025, **e-mail:** info@tjhughes.co.uk, www.tjhughes.co.uk, 9–5.30 MON–SAT, 10–4 SUN. **PERMANENT DISCOUNT OUTLET**

See page 98 (CHESH)

THE FACTORY SHOP LTD
NEW ROAD, PERSHORE, WORCESTERSHIRE WR10 1BY, ☎ 01386 556467, 9–5 MON–FRI, 9–5.30 SAT, 10.30–4.30 SUN. **FACTORY SHOP**

See page 98 (CHESH)

TK MAXX
UNIT 100, UPPER MALL, MERRYHILL CENTRE, DUDLEY, WORCESTERSHIRE DY5 1QX, ☎ 01384 77878, www.tkmaxx.com, 10–8 MON–FRI, 10–9 THUR, 9–7 SAT, 11–5 SUN.

EVESHAM WALK, KINGFISHER SHOPPING CENTRE, REDDITCH, WORCESTERSHIRE, ☎ 01527 598837, www.tkmaxx.com, PHONE FOR DETAILS.

PERMANENT DISCOUNT OUTLET

See page 89 (BEDS)

UNITED FOOTWEAR
80–81 HIGH STREET, DUDLEY, WORCESTERSHIRE, ☎ 01384 238492, 9–5.30 MON–SAT, 10–4 SUN. NEW ROAD, KIDDERMINSTER, WORCESTERSHIRE, ☎ 01562 744022, 9–6 MON–SAT, 8 ON THUR, 9–1 SUN. **PERMANENT DISCOUNT OUTLET**

See page 124 (HAMPS)

YORKSHIRE

ADIDAS
MCARTHURGLEN DESIGNER OUTLET YORK, ST NICHOLAS AVENUE, FULFORD, JUNCTION OF A19 AND A64, YORK, NORTH YORKSHIRE YO19 4TA, ☎ 01904 655 811, FAX: 01904 628509, 10–6 MON–SAT, 8 ON THUR, 11–5 SUN. **FACTORY SHOP IN A FACTORY SHOPPING VILLAGE**

See page 93 (CHESH)

ALLDERS AT HOME
2 BRIDGE ROAD, KIRKSTALL, LEEDS, WEST YORKSHIRE LS5 3BL, ☎ 0113 230 5800, FAX: 0113 230 5888, 10–5.30 MON–WED, 10–8 THUR, FRI, 9.30–5.30 SAT, 10.30–4.30 SUN.
PERMANENT DISCOUNT OUTLET
The fashion centre within the Allders department store is a clearance outlet for Allders stores selling men's, women's and children's reduced stock. Famous names include Morgan, Benetton, Planet, Precis, Windsmoor, Frank Usher, Jumper, Dannimac, Fenn Wright & Manson, French Connection, Gabicci, O'Neil, Matinique, Yves Saint Laurent, Shoe Studio. Samples are also available at competitive prices twice a year from Gerry Weber, Taifun, She, Ravens, Sigrid Olsen, Erfo and Samoon. The sports department sells a mix of reduced and full price stock.

ALT-BERG BOOTMAKERS
GALLOWFIELDS INDUSTRIAL ESTATE, RACECOURSE ROAD, RICHMOND, NORTH YORKSHIRE DL10 4XB, ☎ 01748 850615, **e-mail:** sales@altberg.co.uk, www.altberg.co.uk, **FACTORY SHOP**
Top quality, British craftsmen made walking, hiking, motor bike and military boots for men and women in a wide range of sizes. Nearby shop in Finkle Street, Richmond, sells outdoor clothes, some of which are at reduced prices.

ARKWRIGHTS MILL
FREEPORT HORNSEA OUTLET VILLAGE, ROLSTON ROAD, HORNSEA, EAST YORKSHIRE HU18 1UT, ☎ 01964 535040, 9.30–6 SEVEN DAYS A WEEK. **FACTORY SHOP IN A FACTORY SHOPPING VILLAGE**
Factory discount outlet selling a wide range of brand names in men's and women's clothing.

AUTONOMY
MCARTHURGLEN DESIGNER OUTLET YORK, ST NICHOLAS AVENUE, FULFORD, JUNCTION OF A19 AND A64, YORK, NORTH YORKSHIRE YO19 4TA, ☎ 01904 671502, 10–6 MON–SAT, 8 ON THUR, 11–5 SUN. **FACTORY SHOP IN A FACTORY SHOPPING VILLAGE**

See page 93 (CHESH)

BIG L FACTORY OUTLET

UNIT 19, THE YORKSHIRE OUTLET, WHITE ROSE WAY, DONCASTER, SOUTH YORKSHIRE DN4 5JH, ☎ 01302 367043, FAX: 01302 367043, 10–6 MON–SAT, 11–5 SUN. **FACTORY SHOP IN A FACTORY SHOPPING VILLAGE**

See page 93 (CHESH)

BRANDMART

5 NORTH STREET, RIPON, NORTH YORKSHIRE HG4 1JY, ☎ 01765 601156, 9–5 MON–SAT. **FACTORY SHOP**

See page 119 (GLOS)

BROOKS FACTORY OUTLET STORES

SOUTH LANE, ELLAND, NEAR HALIFAX, WEST YORKSHIRE HX5 0HQ, ☎ 01422 377337, 9.30–5.30 MON–SAT, 8 ON THUR, 11–5 SUN.

BUYWELL RETAIL PARK, THORP ARCH, WETHERBY, NORTH YORKSHIRE LS23 7BJ, ☎ 01937 541895, 9.30–5.30 MON–SAT, 11–5 SUN. **PERMANENT DISCOUNT OUTLET**

Walk through the store and you can't fail to find a bargain. New stock arrives daily from well-known names such as Nike, French Connection, Gabicci, Klass, Camille and Ben Sherman. Apart from mens and women's clothes, they sell sportswear, linens, lingerie, shoes, accessories, luggage, towels, coordinated bed linen, household textiles, duvets, pillows and lots more from names such as Monogram and Ponden Mill. Everything under one roof at up to 50% off high street prices. The Elland store has a coffee shop.

BROUGHTON SHOE WAREHOUSE

44 NORTH BAR WITHIN, BEVERLEY, NORTH YORKSHIRE HU7 8DG, ☎ 01482 863045, 9.30–5.30 MON–SAT.

17 CLEVELAND STREET, DONCASTER, SOUTH YORKSHIRE DN1 3EH, ☎ 01302 342627, 9–5.30 MON–SAT.

23 COOKRIDGE STREET, LEEDS, WEST YORKSHIRE LS2 3AG, ☎ 0113 243 4550, 9.30–5 MON–SAT.

12 GATEWAY COURT, PARKGATE, ROTHERHAM, SOUTH YORKSHIRE S62 5LH, ☎ 01709 719192, 10–6 MON–SAT, 10–4 SUN.

156–158 SHOREHAM STREET, SHEFFIELD, SOUTH YORKSHIRE S1 4SS, ☎ 0114 279 6037, 9–6 MON–SAT, 10–4 SUN.

10 CRAVEN COURT, OFF HIGH STREET, SKIPTON, WEST YORKSHIRE BD23 1DE, ☎ 01756 700415, 9.30–5.30 MON–SAT, 11–5 SUN. **PERMANENT DISCOUNT OUTLET**

See page 108 (DERBY)

BURBERRY

CORONATION MILLS, ALBION STREET, CASTLEFORD, WEST YORKSHIRE WS10 1QX, ☎ 01977 554411, 10–4.30 MON–FRI, 9.30–3 SAT. **FACTORY SHOP**

WOODROW UNIVERSAL, JUNCTION MILLS, CROSS HILLS, NEAR KEIGHLEY, WEST YORKSHIRE BD20 7SE, ☎ 01535 631991. **FACTORY SHOP**

10–4 MON–SAT. 141 MIDLAND ROAD, ROYSTON SOUTH YORKSHIRE S71 4BP, ☎ 01226 728030, 10–4.30 MON–FRI, 9.30–3.30 SAT, ONCE A MONTH ON SUNS.

OLD MARKET TAVERN, MARKET PLACE, WHITBY, NORTH YORKSHIRE YO22 4DD, ☎ 01947 606161, 9.30–4.30 MON–SAT, 11–4 SUN. **FACTORY SHOP**

MCARTHURGLEN DESIGNER OUTLET CENTRE, ST NICHOLAS AVENUE, FULFORD, YORK, NORTH YORKSHIRE YO19 4TA, ☎ 01904 679190, 10–6 MON–SAT, 8 ON THUR, 11–5 SUN. **FACTORY SHOP IN A FACTORY SHOPPING VILLAGE**

See page 94 (CHESH)

C & R BARNETT LTD

136 HALL LANE, BRADFORD, WEST YORKSHIRE BD4 7DG, ☎ 01274 737046, 9.30–5 MON–FRI. **FACTORY SHOP**

Small room off the mill which sells top quality fabrics in wool and cashmere for coats and suits, all manufactured in Yorkshire.

CATALOGUE BARGAIN SHOP

FREEPORT DESIGNER OUTLET VILLAGE, CARRWOOD ROAD, GLASSHOUGHTON, CASTLEFORD, WEST YORKSHIRE WF10 4SB, ☎ 01977 519112, www.bargaincrazy.com, 10–8 MON–FRI, 10–6 SAT, 11–5 SUN. **FACTORY SHOP IN A FACTORY SHOPPING VILLAGE**

KAYS SHOP, HOLME LANE, OFF TONG STREET, BRADFORD, WEST YORKSHIRE BD4 6NA, ☎ 01274 681711, www.bargaincrazy.com, 9.30–5.30 MON–SAT, 7 ON THUR, 10.30–4.30 SUN.

UNITS 2–3, LEGER CENTRE, THORNE ROAD, DONCASTER, SOUTH YORKSHIRE DN2 4GB, ☎ 01302 341506, www.bargaincrazy.com, 9–8 MON–FRI, 10–6 SAT, 11–5 SUN.

57–59 MARKET PLACE, HECKMONDWIKE, WEST YORKSHIRE WF16 0EZ, ☎ 01924 402674, www.bargaincrazy.com, 9–5.30 MON–SAT, 10–4 SUN.

42 JOHN WILLIAM STREET, HUDDERSFIELD, WEST YORKSHIRE HD1 1ER, ☎ 01484 535112, www.bargaincrazy.com, 9–5.30 MON–SAT, 10.30–4.30 SUN.

28 NEW BRIGGATE, BRIGGATE, LEEDS, WEST YORKSHIRE LS1 6NU, ☎ 0113 243 6425, www.bargaincrazy.com, 9–5.30 MON–SAT, 11–5 SUN.

MARSHALL STREET, LEEDS, WEST YORKSHIRE LS1 1UL, ☎ 0113 254 2350, www.bargaincrazy.com, 10–5 MON–FRI, 7 ON THUR, 9–5.30 SAT, 10.30–4.30 SUN.

51 ACKLAM ROAD, MIDDLESBROUGH, NORTH YORKSHIRE TS5 5HA, ☎ 01642 825925, www.bargaincrazy.com, 9–5.30 MON–SAT, 10.30–4.30 SUN. **PERMANENT DISCOUNT OUTLET**

See page 92 (CAMBS)

CATALOGUE DISCOUNT STORES

UNIT 6, HILLSBOROUGH BARRACKS SHOPPING MALL, SHEFFIELD, SOUTH YORKSHIRE S6 2GY, ☎ 0114 234 5726, FAX: 0114 234 5006, 9–5.30 MON–SAT, 11–5 SUN. **PERMANENT DISCOUNT OUTLET**

See page 101 (CO DURH)

CHARLES CLINKARD

FREEPORT CASTLEFORD DESIGNER OUTLET VILLAGE, CARRWOOD ROAD, GLASSHOUGHTON, CASTLEFORD, JUNCTION 32 OF M52, WEST YORKSHIRE WF10 4SB, ☎ 01977 515391, FAX: 01255 515391, 10–8 MON–FRI, 10–6 SAT, 11–5 SUN. **FACTORY SHOP IN A FACTORY SHOPPING VILLAGE**

See page 101 (CO DURH)

CLARKS FACTORY SHOP

RAILWAY STREET RETAIL PARK, DEWSBURY, WEST YORKSHIRE WF12 8EQ, ☎ 01924 430444, 9.30–6 MON–FRI, 9–6 SAT, 10.30–4.30 SUN. **FACTORY SHOP**

FREEPORT DESIGNER OUTLET VILLAGE, CARRWOOD ROAD, GLASSHOUGHTON, CASTLEFORD, WEST YORKSHIRE WF10 4SB, ☎ 01977 522368, 10–8 MON–FRI, 10–6 SAT, 11–5 SUN.

THE YORKSHIRE OUTLET, WHITE ROSE WAY, DONCASTER, SOUTH YORKSHIRE DN4 5JH, ☎ 01302 322663, 10–6 MON–SAT, 11–5 SUN. **FACTORY SHOP IN A FACTORY SHOPPING VILLAGE**

See page 94 (CHESH)

CONNOISSEUR CASHMERE

THE OLD POST OFFICE, 59 HUDDERSFIELD ROAD, MIRFIELD, WEST YORKSHIRE WF14 8AA, ☎ 01924 490044, FAX: 01904 492637, **e-mail:** sales@cashmere.uk.com, www.cashmerebargains.com, 10–4 MON–SAT. MAIL ORDER ALSO. **FACTORY SHOP**

Connoisseur Cashmere produces a wide range of fashionable, classic cashmere knitwear and accessories for both men and women, all hand finished in the Scottish Borders. They are renowned for their ability to produce soft, sensual cashmere which is sold wholesale to a wide variety of brand-name customers in London, Paris, New York and Japan. Their factory outlet in the heart of Yorkshire includes 100% cashmere gloves at £12 as well as men's and women's socks at £18; scarves in a wide range of colours from £20 and twenty colours of pashminas from only £29. The outlet also sells a range of end of line knitwear in 100% cashmere from £49. Alternatively, visit their London retail shop at Just Cashmere, 23 Filmer Road, Fulham, London SW6. Most of their items are available by mail order; phone the telephone number above for their current catalogue. Or visit their website wwwconnoisseurcashmere.com for Christmas Specials, available from 1st November.

COTTON TRADERS

MCARTHURGLEN DESIGNER OUTLET YORK, ST NICHOLAS AVENUE, FULFORD, JUNCTION OF A19 AND A64, YORK, NORTH YORKSHIRE YO19 4TA, ☎ 01904 625490, FAX: 01904 672171, www.cottontraders.co.uk, 10–6 MON–SAT, 8 ON THUR, 11–5 SUN. **FACTORY SHOP IN A FACTORY SHOPPING VILLAGE**

Sells own label leisurewear for men, women and children.

CRAGHOPPERS

FREEPORT CASTLEFORD DESIGNER OUTLET VILLAGE, CARRWOOD ROAD, GLASSHOUGHTON, CASTLEFORD, JUNCTION 32 OF M52, WEST YORKSHIRE Wf10 4SB, ☎ 01977 667111, FAX: 01977 557771, www.craghoppers.com, 10–8 MON–FRI, 10–6 SAT, 11–5 SUN. **FACTORY SHOP IN A FACTORY SHOPPING VILLAGE**

See page 133 (LANCS)

CREAM DRESS AGENCY OF YORKSHIRE

27 HALIFAX ROAD, HIPPERHOLME, HALIFAX, WEST YORKSHIRE HX3 8HQ, ☎ 01422 205080, 9–5.30 WED–SAT. **DRESS AGENCY**

Three-storey shop established for 19 years and selling a large selection of constantly changing stock: women's day wear, evening wear, accessories. Labels on sale include Gucci, Prada, Lindka Cierach, Fero, Escada, Dolce & Gabbana and Donna Karan. Prices range from £5 to £500. Customer toilet and coffee always available.

DALESOX

6 SWADFORD STREET, SKIPTON, WEST YORKSHIRE BD23 1RD, ☎ 01756 796509, 9–5 MON–SAT, 11–5 SUN. **FACTORY SHOP**

Based in Skipton's main shopping area, Dalesox sells quality hosiery and accessories. Most are perfect women's, men's and children's socks made for the best high street chainstores selling at very competitive discounts. For example, three-pair packs of men's cotton/Lycra socks, £2.50, recommended retail price, £9.99. There is lots of design choice from Disney character socks to Christmas character socks. There are also ties, ski socks made for famous department stores, unusual design Swedish polyester ties, knickers, boxer shorts, pyjamas and nightshirts. Most of the stock is bought in from other manufacturers, cutting out the middleman.

DAMART

BOWLING GREEN MILLS, BINGLEY, WEST YORKSHIRE BD16 4BH, ☎ 01274 567152, 9.30–5 MON–SAT. **FACTORY SHOP**

FREEPORT HORNSEA OUTLET VILLAGE, ROLSTON ROAD, HORNSEA, EAST YORKSHIRE HU18 1UT, ☎ 01964 536581, 9.30–6 SEVEN DAYS A WEEK. **FACTORY SHOP, FACTORY SHOP IN A FACTORY SHOPPING VILLAGE**

See page 114 (DORS)

DESIGNER SHADES

MCARTHURGLEN DESIGNER OUTLET YORK, FULFORD, JUNCTION OF A19 AND A64 SLEBY JUNCTION, YORK, NORTH YORKSHIRE YO19 4TA, ☎ 01904 679007, **e-mail:** info@sunglass-time.com, 10–6 MON–SAT, 8 ON THUR, 11–5 SUN. **FACTORY SHOP IN A FACTORY SHOPPING VILLAGE**

See page 116 (DORS)

DEWHIRST IMPRESSIONS

42 MIDDLE STREET NORTH, DRIFFIELD, EAST YORKSHIRE YO25 6SS, ☎ 01377 256209, **e-mail:** kim.mcmaster@dewhirst.com, 9–5.30 MON–SAT, 10.30–4.30 SUN. **FACTORY SHOP**

See page 101 (CO DURH)

DOUBLE TWO

THE YORKSHIRE OUTLET, WHITE ROSE WAY, DONCASTER, SOUTH YORKSHIRE DN4 5JH, ☎ 01302 367156, 10–6 MON–SAT, 11–5 SUN.

FREEPORT CASTLEFORD DESIGNER OUTLET VILLAGE, CARRWOOD ROAD, GLASSHOUGHTON, CASTLEFORD, JUNCTION 32 OF M52, WEST YORKSHIRE WF10 4SB, ☎ 01977 519122, 10–8 MON–FRI, 10–6 SAT, 11–5 SUN.

FREEPORT HORNSEA OUTLET VILLAGE, ROLSTON ROAD, HORNSEA, EAST YORKSHIRE HU18 1UT, ☎ 01964 533339, 9.30–6 SEVEN DAYS A WEEK. **FACTORY SHOP IN A FACTORY SHOPPING VILLAGE**

THORNES LANE WHARF, WAKEFIELD WEST YORKSHIRE WF1 5RQ, ☎ 01924 291845, 10–6 MON–FRI, 9–5.30 SAT, 11–5 SUN. **FACTORY SHOP**

See page 116 (ESSEX)

DRESS FOR LESS FASHIONS

THE OLD SUNDAY SCHOOL, LIDGET STREET, LINDLEY, HUDDERSFIELD, WEST YORKSHIRE HD3 3JF, ☎ 01484 640498, 10–5 MON–SAT. **PERMANENT DISCOUNT OUTLET**

Enviable classic labels at a discount of up to 75%. They specialise in German and other European manufacturers in sizes 10 to 24 with a choice of up to 15,000 garments. Now based in a beautifully restored old school room with fresh filter coffee offered free of charge. They have just added a large gifts and accessories section offering excellent value for money.

FAMOUS FOOTWEAR

FREEPORT HORNSEA OUTLET VILLAGE, ROLSTON ROAD, HORNSEA, EAST YORKSHIRE HU18 1UT, ☎ 01964 536503, 9.30–6 SEVEN DAYS A WEEK.

MCARTHURGLEN DESIGNER OUTLET YORK, ST NICHOLAS AVENUE, FULFORD, JUNCTION OF A19 AND A64, YORK, NORTH YORKSHIRE YO19 4TA, ☎ 01904 678997, 10–6 MON–SAT, 8 ON THUR, 11–5 SUN. **FACTORY SHOP IN A FACTORY SHOPPING VILLAGE**

See page 95 (CHESH)

FEELGOOD FACTORY FOOTWEAR

27 WEST END, HEBDEN BRIDGE, WEST YORKSHIRE HX7 8UQ, ☎ 01422 846800, 10–5.30 MON–SAT, 12–5 SUN. **FACTORY SHOP**

A factory shop for many factories selling a wide selection of quality footwear for all the family. They offer a range of branded leather shoes, wide fittings, cushioned footbeds, ex-high street store shoes and many one-off bargains. New stock arrives weekly. Find them near the main traffic lights in Hebden Bridge.

FREEPORT CASTLEFORD DESIGNER OUTLET VILLAGE

CARRWOOD ROAD, GLASSHOUGHTON, CASTLEFORD, JUNCTION 32 OF M52, WEST YORKSHIRE WF10 4SB, ☎ 01977 520153, www.freeportcastleford.com, 10–8 MON–FRI, 10–6 SAT, 11–5 SUN. **FACTORY SHOPPING VILLAGE**

Designer outlet village with over 75 shops, indoor and outdoor children's play areas and a wide range of restaurants with easy access from the M52 and 3,500 free car parking spaces. Shops include Amazing Jeans, Baron Jon, BhS For Less, Charles Clinkard, Clarks, Cromwells, Churchill, Ciro Citterio, Craghoppers, CBS, Claire's Accessories, Cotton Traders, Damart, Edinburgh Crystal, Donnay, Double Two, Event Jewellery, Easy Jeans, Edinburgh Woollen Mill, Elle, Fila, Giorgio, Gossard, XS Music, Jane Shilton, John Partridge, Kappa, Kitchen and Table, Kurt Muller, Leading Labels, Lee Cooper, Littlewoods, London Leathers, Mexx, Mobile Phone Store, Nike, Nickleby's, Next to Nothing, Outrage, Petroleum, Picture Port, Pilot, Ponden Mill, Proibito, Rio Jewellery, Roman Originals, Regatta, Room, Ice Jeans, Sergio Tacchini, Sportsmill, Spotlight, Startrite Shoes, Remainders Book Depot, Designer Room, Garden Outlet, Shoe Collection, Toy Factory, Time, X Catalogue Store, Thorntons, Trespass, Waterford Wedgwood, Windsmoor.

FREEPORT HORNSEA OUTLET VILLAGE

ROLSTON ROAD, HORNSEA, JUNCTION 38 OFF THE M62, EAST YORKSHIRE HU18 1UT, ☎ 01964 534211, www.freeporthornsea.com, 9.30–6 SEVEN DAYS A WEEK. **FACTORY SHOPPING VILLAGE**

The original British factory shopping village with over 40 shops offering discounts of up to 50% off high street prices. The village also boasts leisure attractions for all ages, ranging from an adventure playground to a themed soft play area and exciting rides for children. Womenswear labels include Alexon, Designer Room, Roman Originals, Arkwright's Mill, Select, Damart, Edinburgh Woollen Mill, Double Two, Mexx and London Leathers. Sportwear and outdoor clothing are available from Tog 24, Regatta and Sports Mill. Footwear is sold by Famous Footwear, Lilley & Skinner and Charles Clinkard. Menswear stores include The Suit Company, Double Two, Nickleby's, London Leathers and Giorgio. Other shops include Woods of Windsor, Thorntons, Masters Jewellery, Edinburgh Crystal, Waterford Wedgewood, Hallmark, Laura Ashley, The Book Depot, Claire's Accessories, Churchill China and Ponden Mill.

GAP

MCARTHURGLEN OUTLET VILLAGE, ST NICHOLAS AVENUE, YORK, NORTH YORKSHIRE YO19 4TA, ☎ 01904 634670, 10–6 MON–FRI, 8 ON THUR, 10–6 SAT, 11–4 SUN. **FACTORY SHOP IN A FACTORY SHOPPING VILLAGE**

Gap sells casual clothes for men, women, babies and children, discounted at this factory outlet village by a minimum of 30%.

HARRIETS

11 CAVENDISH STREET, KEIGHLEY, WEST YORKSHIRE BD21 3RB, ☎ 01535 611198, 9–5.30 MON–SAT, 10–4 SUN.

11 MARKET PLACE, KNARESBOROUGH, NORTH YORKSHIRE HG5 8AL, ☎ 01423 863375, 9–5 MON, TUE, WED, THUR, 9–5.30 FRI, SAT, 1–5 SUN.

75B NEW ROAD SIDE, HORSFORTH, LEEDS, WEST YORKSHIRE LS18 4QD, ☎ 0113 239 0399, 9–5.30 MON–SAT, 10–4 SUN.

16 WESTGATE, OTLEY, WEST YORKSHIRE LS29 3AS, ☎ 01943 465258, 9–5 MON–THUR, 9–5.30 FRI–SAT, 10–4 SUN. 14 SWADFORD STREET, SKIPTON, NORTH YORKSHIRE, ☎ 01756 795111, 9–5.30 MON–SAT, 10–4 SUN.

2 KIRKGATE, THIRSK NORTH YORKSHIRE YO7 1PQ, ☎ 01845 522079, 9–5 MON–THUR, 9–5.30 FRI, SAT, 12–4 SUN. **PERMANENT DISCOUNT OUTLET**

Many high street chainstore over-productions at discounted prices. Clothes which are mostly Marks & Spencer seconds and discontinued lines, but also some from Next, Dorothy Perkins and Littlewoods. For example, a Marks & Spencer jacket which would normally cost £85, for sale at £40; skirts less than £20; and coats and jackets to suit everyone from teenagers upwards in sizes 8 to 20.

HAWICK CASHMERE CO LTD

20 MONTPELLIER PARADE, HARROGATE, NORTH YORKSHIRE HG1 2TG, ☎ 01423 502519, FAX: 01423 502519, 10–5.30 MON–SAT. **FACTORY SHOP**

See page 119 (GLOS)

HOLMSPUN CLOTHING

262 HUDDERSFIELD ROAD, HOLMFIRTH, HUDDERSFIELD, WEST YORKSHIRE HD9 2TT, ☎ 01484 687911, FAX: 01484 688754, 10–5 WED–SAT, 11–5 SUN. **FACTORY SHOP**

Sources and supplies retail outlets throughout the country. This outlet sells end-of-lines and quality discounted branded items at factory shop prices. Stock includes quality branded clothing, ex-high street brands, plus imported, branded electrical items such as televisions, DVD players, CD players etc. Also sells designer ranges from Armani, Moschino, Versace, Iceberg, Burberry and Valentino at discounts of 50%. If you have a particular electrical item in mind, phone first to see if they can source and supply it at discounted prices.

HUSH PUPPIES

FREEPORT HORNSEA OUTLET VILLAGE, ROLSTON ROAD, HORNSEA, EAST YORKSHIRE HU18 1UT, ☎ 01964 534211, 9.30–6 SEVEN DAYS A WEEK. **FACTORY SHOP IN A FACTORY SHOPPING VILLAGE**

See page 117 (ESSEX)

JAEGER FACTORY SHOP

MCARTHURGLEN DESIGNER OUTLET YORK, ST NICHOLAS AVENUE, FULFORD, JUNCTION OF A19 AND A64, YORK, NORTH YORKSHIRE YO1 4RE, ☎ 01904 678680, 10–6 MON–FRI, 8 ON THUR, 9–6 SAT, 11–5 SUN. **FACTORY SHOP IN A FACTORY SHOPPING VILLAGE**

See page 158 (NORF)

JAMES BARRY

ALEXANDRA MILL, ALEXANDRA ROAD, BATLEY, WEST YORKSHIRE WF17 6IA, ☎ 01924 423913, 10–6 MON–SAT, 11–5 SUN. **FACTORY SHOP IN A FACTORY SHOPPING VILLAGE**

THE YORKSHIRE OUTLET, WHITE ROSE WAY, DONCASTER, SOUTH YORKSHIRE DN4 5JH, ☎ 01302 361127, 10–6 MON–SAT, 11–5 SUN. **FACTORY SHOP IN A FACTORY SHOPPING VILLAGE**

See page 109 (DERBY)

JOHN SMEDLEY LTD

RANDS LANE, ARMTHORPE, DONCASTER, SOUTH YORKSHIRE DN3 3DY, ☎ 01302 832346, 10–3.30 MON–FRI, 10–3 SAT. **FACTORY SHOP**

See page 109 (DERBY)

KANGOL FACTORY SHOP

MCARTHURGLEN DESIGNER OUTLET YORK, ST NICHOLAS AVENUE, FULFORD, JUNCTION OF A19 AND A64, YORK, NORTH YORKSHIRE YO19 4TA, ☎ 01904 673632, **e-mail:** kangol_uk@hotmail.com, 10–6 MON–SAT, 8 ON THUR, 11–5 SUN. PLEASE PHONE FOR CHRISTMAS AND BANK HOLIDAY OPENING HOURS. **FACTORY SHOP IN A FACTORY SHOPPING VILLAGE**

See page 96 (CHESH)

LABELS FOR LESS

141–147 ALLERTON ROAD, BRADFORD, WEST YORKSHIRE BD15 7AB, ☎ 01274 491311, FAX: 01274 480225, **e-mail:** bradford@hoopers.ltd.uk, 9–5.30 MON–SAT. **PERMANENT DISCOUNT OUTLET**

Designer shopping outlet within the elegant department store surroundings of the former Hoopers store. Stocks a wide selection of well-known contemporary designer and classic fashion labels for men and women at prices at least 50% below the original selling price. Seen here in the past have been Betty Barclay, Hugo Boss and Morgan. There is a hair and beauty salon on site, plus a large gift, accessories and fragrance department, and easy parking.

LEE COOPER

FREEPORT CASTLEFORD DESIGNER OUTLET VILLAGE, CARRWOOD ROAD, GLASSHOUGHTON, CASTLEFORD, JUNCTION 32 OF M52, WEST YORKSHIRE WF10 4SB, ☎ 01977 557011 10–8 MON–FRI, 10–6 SAT, 11–5 SUN. **FACTORY SHOP IN A FACTORY SHOPPING VILLAGE**

See page 96 (CHESH)

LIGHTWATER VILLAGE AND FACTORY SHOPPING

NORTH STAINLEY, RIPON, NORTH YORKSHIRE HG4 3HT, ☎ 01765 634508, FAX: 01765 635359, www.lightwatervalley.co.uk, 10–5.30 MON–SUN. **FACTORY SHOPPING VILLAGE**

Large complex of retail and factory outlets with a wide range of branded womenswear including blouses, skirts, suits, dresses, lingerie, outerwear, shoes and accessories as well as menswear from jeans and outdoor wear to formal wear. Shoes, jewellery, home furnishings, crystal and glass, a large range of pottery, garden products, toys, cheese and confectionery. There is a restaurant and coffee shop serving snacks and refreshments, free parking and disabled facilities. A family theme park on site boasts the Ultimate Rollercoaster, the longest in Europe.

LILLEY & SKINNER

FREEPORT CASTLEFORD DESIGNER OUTLET VILLAGE, CARRWOOD ROAD, GLASSHOUGHTON, CASTLEFORD, JUNCTION 32 OF M52, WEST YORKSHIRE WF10 4SB, ☎ 01977 510910, 10–8 MON–FRI, 10–6 SAT, 11–5 SUN. **FACTORY SHOP IN A FACTORY SHOPPING VILLAGE**

See page 109 (DERBY)

LITTLEWOODS CATALOGUE DISCOUNT STORE

FREEPORT CASTLEFORD DESIGNER OUTLET VILLAGE, CARRWOOD ROAD, GLASSHOUGHTON, CASTLEFORD, JUNCTION 32 OF M52, WEST YORKSHIRE WF10 4SB, ☎ 01977 517899, 10–8 MON–FRI, 10–6 SAT, 11–5 SUN. **FACTORY SHOP IN A FACTORY SHOPPING VILLAGE**

602–608 ATTERCLIFFE ROAD, SHEFFIELD, SOUTH YORKSHIRE S9 3QS, ☎ 0114 244 1611, 9.30–5 MON–WED, 9–5.30 THUR–SAT. **PERMANENT DISCOUNT OUTLET**

See page 96 (CHESH)

LONDON LEATHERS DIRECT

FREEPORT CASTLEFORD DESIGNER OUTLET VILLAGE, CARRWOOD ROAD, GLASSHOUGHTON, CASTLEFORD, JUNCTION 32 OF M52, WEST YORKSHIRE WF10 4SB, ☎ 01977 517550, FAX: 01977 517510, 10–8 MON–FRI, 10–6 SAT, 11–5 SUN.

FREEPORT HORNSEA OUTLET VILLAGE, ROLSTON ROAD, HORNSEA, EAST YORKSHIRE HU18 1UT, ☎ 01964 535432, 9.30–6 SEVEN DAYS A WEEK. **FACTORY SHOP IN A FACTORY SHOPPING VILLAGE**

See page 136 (LANCS)

MARKS & SPENCER

MCARTHURGLEN DESIGNER OUTLET VILLAGE, ST NICHOLAS WAY, FULFORD, YORK, NORTH YORKSHIRE YO19 4TA, ☎ 01904 677091, 10–6 MON–SAT, 8 ON THUR, 11–5 SUN. **FACTORY SHOP IN A FACTORY SHOPPING VILLAGE**

See page 96 (CHESH)

MARY COOPER

GINNEL ANTIQUES CENTRE, OFF PARLIAMENT STREET, HARROGATE, NORTH YORKSHIRE HG1 1DH, ☎ 01765 677483, **e-mail:** marycooper@aol.com, www.theginnel.co.uk, 9.30–5.30 MON–SAT. **SECONDHAND AND VINTAGE CLOTHES**
Mainly sells fans and lace but also stocks vintage clothes up to 1935, with Twenties underwear, beaded dresses, accessories and shawls. Also quilts, samplers, sheets, pillowcases, tablecloths, hats, men's hats, waistcoats and shirts. For men, there are only hats and waistcoats; for children, christening gowns. Beaded dresses, £200 to £300. Discounts for cash purchases. Phone before visiting if you have a specific request and Mary will try to get it for you.

MATALAN

1 WOMBWELL LANE, STAIRFOOT, BARNSLEY, SOUTH YORKSHIRE S70 3NS, ☎ 01226 733372, FAX: 01226 733368, www.matalan.co.uk, 9.30–8 MON–FRI, 9–6 SAT, 11–5 SUN.

FORSTER SQUARE RETAIL PARK, VALLEY ROAD, BRADFORD, WEST YORKSHIRE BD1 4RN, ☎ 01274 381000, FAX: 01274 306314, www.matalan.co.uk, 10–8 MON–FRI, 9–6 SAT, 11–5 SUN.

THE RISHWORTH CENTRE, RAILWAY STREET, DEWSBURY, WEST YORKSHIRE WF12 8EQ, ☎ 01924 868180, FAX: 01924 461623, www.matalan.co.uk, 9.30–8 MON–FRI, 9–6 SAT, 11–5 SUN.

THE WHEATLEY CENTRE, WHEATLEY HALL ROAD, DONCASTER SOUTH YORKSHIRE DN2 4PE, ☎ 01302 760444, FAX: 01302 554520, www.matalan.co.uk, 10–8 MON–FRI, 9–6 SAT, 11–5 SUN.

GREENMOUNT RETAIL PARK, PELLON ROAD, HALIFAX, WEST YORKSHIRE HX1 5QN, ☎ 01422 383051, FAX: 01422 383053, www.matalan.co.uk, 10–8 MON–FRI, 9–6 SAT, 11–5 SUN.

RINGWAY INDUSTRIAL ESTATE, HUDDERSFIELD, WEST YORKSHIRE HD1 5DG, ☎ 01484

448800, FAX: 01484 452359, www.matalan.co.uk, 9.30–8 MON–FRI, 9–6 SAT, 11–5 SUN.

KINGSWOOD RETAIL PARK, BUDE ROAD, KINGSTON-UPON-HULL, EAST YORKSHIRE HU7 4AF, ☎ 01482 832880, FAX: 01482 587750, www.matalan.co.uk, 9–9 MON–FRI, 9–6 SAT, 11–5 SUN.

LOWER WORTLEY RING ROAD, LEEDS, WEST YORKSHIRE LS12 4SL, ☎ 0113 290 7400, FAX: 0113 279 5389, www.matalan.co.uk, 9.30–8 MON–FRI, 9–6 SAT, 11–5 SUN.

HALTON DISTRICT CENTRE, SELBY ROAD, LEEDS, WEST YORKSHIRE LS12 4SL, ☎ 0113 284 0110, FAX: 0113 264 1662, www.matalan.co.uk, 9.30–8 MON–FRI, 9–6 SAT, 11–5 SUN.

SKIPPERS LANE RETAIL PARK, SKIPPERS LANE, MIDDLESBROUGH, NORTH YORKSHIRE TS6 6UB, ☎ 01642 443930, FAX: 01642 430559, www.matalan.co.uk, 10–8 MON–FRI, 9–6 SAT, 11–5 SUN.

UNIT 4B, STADIUM WAY, PARKGATE RETAIL PARK, ROTHERHAM SOUTH YORKSHIRE S60 1TG, ☎ 01709 780173, FAX: 01709 780772, www.matalan.co.uk, 10–8 MON–FRI, 9–6 SAT, 11–5 SUN.

HEELEY RETAIL PARK, CHESTERFIELD ROAD, SHEFFIELD SOUTH YORKSHIRE S8 0RG, ☎ 0114 262 9400, FAX: 0114 255 4193, www.matalan.co.uk, 10–8 MON–FRI, 9–6 SAT, 11–5 SUN.

INGS ROAD RETAIL PARK, INGS ROAD, WAKEFIELD, WEST YORKSHIRE WF1 1RN, ☎ 01924 367395, FAX: 01924 298164, www.matalan.co.uk, 10–8 MON–FRI, 9–6 SAT, 11–5 SUN.

UNITS 10 & 11, CLIFTON MOORE RETAIL PARK, YORK, NORTH YORKSHIRE YO3 4XZ, ☎ 01904 693080, FAX: 01904 693797, www.matalan.co.uk, 9.30–8 MON–FRI, 9–6 SAT, 11–5 SUN. **PERMANENT DISCOUNT OUTLET**

See page 89 (BEDS)

MCARTHURGLEN DESIGNER OUTLET

ST NICHOLAS AVENUE, FULFORD, JUNCTION OF A19 AND A64, YORK, NORTH YORKSHIRE YO19 4TA, ☎ 01904 682720, www.mcarthurglen.com/york, 10–6 MON–SAT, 8 ON THUR, 11–5 SUN. **FACTORY SHOPPING VILLAGE**

The McArthurGlen Designer Outlet York is one of Europe's largest covered designer outlets with over 120 stores offering top brands and designer labels with discounts of up to 50% off typical retail prices. Find everything from men's, women's and children's clothing to accessories, shoes, sportswear, luggage, homewares, toys, books, and gifts. Facilities include a food court, a children's play area and free parking. Stores include: Armani, Autonomy, Ben Sherman, Burberry, Calvin Klein Jeans, Cerruti 1881, Chilli Pepper, Cotton Traders, Daks Simpson, Episode, Escada Sport, Gap Outlet, Guess, Hugo Boss, Jacques Vert, Jaeger/Viyella, Jesire/Esensual, Kabuki, Klass, Levi's, Margaret Howell, Marks & Spencer Outlet, Mergler, Mountain Warehouse, Nitya, Olsen, Pilot, Polo Ralph Lauren, Pringle, Proibito, Proudfoot Leather, Roman Originals, Ronit Zilkha, Ted Baker, The Designer Room, Thomas Pink, Tog 24, Tommy Hilfiger, Windsmoor, Alfred Dunhill, Baronjon, Ben Sherman, Haggar, HKA, Marlboro Classics, Paul Smith, Petroleum, Pour Homme, Rockport, Suit Company, Suits You, Timberland, Adidas, Diadora, Donnay, Reebok, Toyworld, Birthdays, Bodum, The Body Shop Depot, Bookends, Franchetti Bond, Le Creuset, Oneida, Paper Mill, Price's Candles, Remington, Scent To You, Whittard Kitchen, Woods of Windsor, XS Music & Video, Bed & Bath Works, China China, Coloroll, Descamps, Garden Outlet, Jane Heath, La Casa del Christallo, Lights 4 Less, Pictureport, Room, Slipperbox, Spiegelau, Professional Cookware, Daniel Footwear, Famous Footwear, Pavers, Rockport, Shoe Studio, Soled Out, Julian Graves, Thorntons, Antler, Kangol, Liberty, Travel Accessory, Chapelle Jewellery, Claire's Accessories, Designer Shades, Monet, Tie Rack, and The Watch Store.

MEXX INTERNATIONAL

FREEPORT CASTLEFORD DESIGNER OUTLET VILLAGE, CARRWOOD ROAD, GLASSHOUGHTON, JUNCTION 32 OF M62, WEST YORKSHIRE WF10 4SB, ☎ 01977 550886, 10–8 MON–FRI, 10–6 SAT, 11–5 SUN.

FREEPORT HORNSEA OUTLET VILLAGE, ROLSTON ROAD, HORNSEA, EAST YORKSHIRE HU18 1UT, ☎ 01964 537401, 9.30–6 SEVEN DAYS A WEEK. **FACTORY SHOP IN A FACTORY SHOPPING VILLAGE**

See page 97 (CHESH)

MR VALUE

KILLINGHALL ROAD, BRADFORD, WEST YORKSHIRE BD3 8DN, ☎ 01274 669674, 9–7 MON–FRI, 9–5.30 SAT, 10–4 SUN. **PERMANENT DISCOUNT OUTLET**

A discount store offering a wide selection of goods which are catalogue returns, factory rejects, seconds and ends of lines – everything from clothes with the labels cut out to tapes, kettles, televisions, microwaves, irons, toasters, bedlinen, towels, sweets, artificial flowers, batteries, toiletries, crockery, glass, stationery, pots and pans, toys and bins. Kitchen equipment brand names include Russell Hobbs and Morphy Richards. There is also a department for mobility, selling wheelchairs, scooters etc.

NEXT TO NOTHING

38 BROADWAY, BRADFORD, WEST YORKSHIRE BD1 1EY, ☎ 01274 301460, www.next.co.uk, 9–5.30 MON–SAT, 11–5 SUN. **PERMANENT DISCOUNT OUTLET**

FREEPORT CASTLEFORD DESIGNER OUTLET VILLAGE, CARRWOOD ROAD, GLASSHOUGHTON, CASTLEFORD, JUNCTION 32 OF M52, WEST YORKSHIRE WF10 4SB, ☎ 01997 522500, www.next.co.uk, 10–8 MON–FRI, 10–6 SAT, 11–5 SUN. **FACTORY SHOP IN A FACTORY SHOPPING VILLAGE**

See page 97 (CHESH)

PARTRIDGE

FREEPORT CASTLEFORD DESIGNER OUTLET VILLAGE, CARRWOOD ROAD, GLASSHOUGHTON, CASTLEFORD, JUNCTION 32 OF M52, WEST YORKSHIRE WF10 4SB, ☎ 01977 555341 10–8 MON–FRI, 9–6 SAT, 11–5 SUN. **FACTORY SHOP IN A FACTORY SHOPPING VILLAGE**

See page 123 (HAMPS)

POSTOPTICS

FREEPOST, YORK, NORTH YORKSHIRE YO26 6ZZ, ☎ 0800 038 3333 MAIL ORDER, ☎ 0800 035 3060, **e-mail:** enquiries@postoptics.co.uk, www.postoptics.co.uk, **PERMANENT DISCOUNT OUTLET**

PostOptics is a division of Viewpoint, one of the largest contact lens practices in the UK. Using their massive purchasing power, they are able to offer dramatic savings of up to 33% on contact lenses and contact lens solutions. Their products are supplied by post in three-month packs which are significantly cheaper than the smaller sizes normally found on sale. £2.50 postage and packaging is added to single orders of solutions and lenses, six month packs are supplied post free.

PREMIER & CAROUSEL

78 STREET LANE, LEEDS, WEST YORKSHIRE LS8 2AL, ☎ 0113 266 6680, 11–5 TUE–FRI, 10–5 SAT. **DRESS AGENCY**

Premier & Carousel has an extensive range of nearly-new designer and high street fashion for all seasons and occasions at a fraction of the original cost. They stock evening wear, day wear, smart casual wear, special occasion outfits, costume jewellery, and accessories for men and women. Phone for more details if looking for that special something.

PRIESTLEY'S

1 NORMAN COURT, 11 GRAPE LANE, YORK, NORTH YORKSHIRE YO1 2HU, ☎ 01904 631565, 11–5 MON–FRI, 9.30–5 SAT. **SECONDHAND AND VINTAGE CLOTHES**

Period clothing from the Thirties to the Seventies, pretty and interesting, vintage wearable evening wear and collectables for men and women. For example, Fifties model dress for £50.

QLM LTD

IDLE ROAD, IDLE, BRADFORD, WEST YORKSHIRE BD2 2AL, ☎ 01274 642222, 9.30–6 MON–SAT, 5.30 ON WED, 11–5 SUN. **PERMANENT DISCOUNT OUTLET**

Toys, household goods, clothes, food, electrical equipment, garden implements, kitchenware and furniture, all sold at discounted prices. For example, reject garden forks £6.99, spades £4.99, pruning tools £2.99 to £19.99.

READMANS LTD

ALFRED HOUSE, SPENCE LANE, HOLBECK, LEEDS, WEST YORKSHIRE LS12 1EF, ☎ 0113 243 6355, FAX: 0113 242 3192, www.readmans.co.uk, CASH AND CARRY OPEN 9–9 MON–FRI,

8.30–6 SAT, 10–4 SUN.

HEALEY RETAIL PARK, CHESTERFIELD ROAD, SHEFFIELD, SOUTH YORKSHIRE, ☎ 0114 258 0077, FAX: 0113 242 3192, www.readmans.co.uk, 9–8 MON–FRI, 9–6 SAT, 11–5 SUN.

PARKGATE RETAIL WORLD, ROTHERHAM, SOUTH YORKSHIRE, ☎ 01709 781020, www.readmans.co.uk, 9–9 MON–FRI, 9–6 SAT, 10–5 SUN.

THE MILL DISCOUNT DEPARTMENT STORE, BATLEY, WEST YORKSHIRE, ☎ 01924 426634, www.readmans.co.uk, 9–5 MON–SAT, 9.30–8 THUR, 11–5 SUN. **PERMANENT DISCOUNT OUTLET**

Mainly women's, men's and children's clothing as well as bedding, textiles, toiletries, footwear, toys, children's books, shoes and towels at prices which are cheaper than the high street. Most of the stock is from well-known labels but they cannot be mentioned here as they are de-labelled before putting in the shop. A proportion of the stock is manufacturers' cancelled contracts and seconds; the rest is designed by the in-house team and is unbranded. The aim, however, is to sell products at 50% or less than the equivalent goods sold on the high street.

REGATTA

FREEPORT CASTLEFORD DESIGNER OUTLET VILLAGE, CARRWOOD ROAD, GLASSHOUGHTON, CASTLEFORD, JUNCTION 32 OF M52, WEST YORKSHIRE WS10 4SB, ☎ 01977 557771, FAX: 01977 557771, www.regatta.com, 10–8 MON–FRI, 10–6 SAT, 11–5 SUN.

FREEPORT SHOPPING VILLAGE, ROLSTON ROAD, HORNSEA, EAST YORKSHIRE HU18 1UT, ☎ 01964 536610, FAX: 01964 536610, www.regatta.com, 9.30–6 SEVEN DAYS A WEEK. **FACTORY SHOP IN A FACTORY SHOPPING VILLAGE**

See page 118 (ESSEX)

RIPON REVIVALS

6 KIRKGATE, RIPON, NORTH YORKSHIRE HG4 1PA, ☎ 01765 604007, 10–5 MON–SAT. **DRESS AGENCY**

Sells nearly-new clothes for men and women for special occasions such as weddings and graduations, as well as evening wear, including Betty Barclay, Betty Jackson, Grace, Olsen, Morgan, Jackpot, MaxMara, Basler, Penny Black, Armani, Escada, Jaeger and Aquascutum. There is a mix of high street and designer wear as well as shoes, bags, jewellery, hats and accessories. Sizes 8 to 24, when available.

SCOOPS CATALOGUE DISCOUNT STORE

ENTERPRISE 5, 5 LANE ENDS, IDLE, BRADFORD, WEST YORKSHIRE BD10 8EG, ☎ 01274 622300, 9–8 MON–FRI, 9–6 SAT, 10–4 SUN.

SCOOPS, SHIRETHORNE CENTRE, 34–43 PROSPECT STREET, HULL, EAST YORKSHIRE HU2 8PX, ☎ 01482 224354, FAX: 01482 221729, 9–5.30 MON–SAT.

25 TOWN STREET, ARMLEY, LEEDS, WEST YORKSHIRE LS12 1UX, ☎ 0113 263 1825, FAX: 0113 231 9885, 9–5.30 MON–SAT.

41 BARNSLEY ROAD, SOUTH ELMSHALL, PONTEFRACT, WEST YORKSHIRE WF9 2RN, ☎ 01977 642256, FAX: 01977 650 629, 9–5.30 MON–SAT.

UNIT 6, SHOPPING MALL, HILLSBOROUGH BARRACKS, SHEFFIELD, SOUTH YORKSHIRE S6 2LR, ☎ 0114 234 5726, 9–7 MON, TUE, SAT, 9–8 WED, FRI, 9–9 THUR, 10–4 SUN.

UNIT 17, THE IN SHOP CENTRE, 1–2 WRIGHTON HOUSE, TRENCHARD AVENUE, THORNABY TS17 9EP, ☎ 01642 751935, 9–5 MON–SAT. **PERMANENT DISCOUNT OUTLET**

See page 102 (CO DURH)

SHIRTS TO SUIT LTD

3A MAIN STREET, FULFORD, YORK, NORTH YORKSHIRE YO10 4HJ, ☎ 01904 634508, FAX: 01904 931624, **e-mail:** info@shirtstosuit.com, www.shirtstosuit.com, 8.30–5 MON–THUR, 8.30–4.30 FRI, 9–4 SAT. **FACTORY SHOP**

Factory shop selling made-to-measure shirts and blouses as well as perfect stock at discounts of 30%. Also sells extra-long-sleeved shirts for the taller man.

SPRINGFIELD CLOTHING

THE MILL SHOP, NORMAN ROAD, DENBY DALE, HUDDERSFIELD, WEST YORKSHIRE HD8 8TH, ☎ 01484 865082, 9–5 MON–SAT, 10–5 SUN. **PERMANENT DISCOUNT OUTLET**

Springfield Clothing sells clothes for all the family at up to 50% discount on high street prices such as Marks & Spencer, Principles, Next, Monsoon and Dorothy Perkins. Also stocks men's and women's underwear, a selection of basic bedding, duvets, sheets, pillows, pillowcases as well as tea towels, tablecloths, rugs, small carpets and Sheffield cutlery, all at discounted prices. They now also sell an exclusive range of handmade lingerie, swimwear and sportswear by EnVie. Also now incorporating instore boutique by Gasp at discounted prices.

START-RITE

FREEPORT CASTLEFORD DESIGNER OUTLET VILLAGE, CARRWOOD ROAD, GLASSHOUGHTON, CASTLEFORD, JUNCTION 32 OF M52, WEST YORKSHIRE WF10 4SB, ☎ 01977 555064, 10–6 MON–SAT, 11–5 SUN. **FACTORY SHOP IN A FACTORY SHOPPING VILLAGE**

See page 160 (NORF)

SUIT LENGTH & FABRIC CENTRE

918 WAKEFIELD ROAD, DUDLEY HILL, BRADFORD, WEST YORKSHIRE BD4 7QQ, ☎ 01274 729103, 8.30–5 MON–SAT. **FACTORY SHOP**

Cloth merchants that specialise in pure wool and cashmere with suit and coat fabrics for men and women.

THE DARLEY MILL CENTRE

DARLEY, NEAR HARROGATE, NORTH YORKSHIRE HG3 2QQ, ☎ 01423 780857, 9.30–5.30 MON–SAT, 11–5 SUN. **PERMANENT DISCOUNT OUTLET**

The centre offers a great day out for the whole family, combining great bargain shopping in clothing, crockery, linens, crafts and exclusive gifts, with lots for children to see and do. This 17th-century corn mill has one of the largest water wheels in Yorkshire and there's a licensed restaurant with an outdoor dining terrace.

THE FACTORY SHOP

PARK ROSE POTTERY, CARNABY COVERT LANE, CARNABY, BRIDLINGTON, NORTH YORKSHIRE YO15 3QF, ☎ 01262 603518, 10–5 MON–SAT, 10.30–4.30 SUN.

WHEATLEY LANE, LEEDS ROAD, ILKLEY, WEST YORKSHIRE LS29 8BS, ☎ 01943 604514, 9–5.30 MON–SAT, 10.30–4.30 SUN. **FACTORY SHOP**

LIGHTWATER VALLEY SHOPPING VILLAGE, NORTH STAINLEY, RIPON, NORTH YORKSHIRE HG4 3HT, ☎ 01765 635438, 10–6 MON–SAT, 11–5 SUN. **FACTORY SHOP IN A FACTORY SHOPPING VILLAGE**

See page 98 (CHESH)

THE FACTORY VALUE SHOP

LAWKHOLME LANE, KEIGHLEY, WEST YORKSHIRE BD21 3JQ, ☎ 01535 611703, 9.30–5 MON–SAT, 10.30–4.30 SUN. **FACTORY SHOP**

Wide range on sale includes men's, women's and children's clothing and footwear; household textiles; toiletries; hardware; luggage; lighting, electrical goods and bedding, most of which are chainstore and high street brands at discounts of approximately 30% to 50%. There are kitchen and furniture displays. The Cape Country Furniture range is on sale with free-standing kitchens, as well as living, bedroom and dining furniture. There are weekly deliveries and brands include famous names such as Adidas, Nike, Joe Bloggs and Brabantia, among others. Lines are continually changing. Few factory shops offer such a variety under one roof. To round off your visit, there are excellent tea rooms offering homemade foods and home baking.

THE FAMOUS BRUNSWICK WAREHOUSE LTD

UNIT 7, KINGSTON SHOPPING CENTRE, HOLDERNESS ROAD, HULL, EAST YORKSHIRE HU9 2AA, ☎ 01482 211157, **e-mail:** northshoe@mcmail.com, 9–5.30 MON–WED, THUR, FRI, 9–6 SAT, 10–4 SUN.

UNIT 5A, HESSLE ROAD, HULL, EAST YORKSHIRE HU3 2AA, ☎ 01482 620519, **e-mail:** northshoe@mcmail.com, 9–5.30 MON–WED, 9–6 THUR–SAT, 10–4 SUN.

UNIT 16, PHASE 2, FORSTER SQUARE RETAIL PARK, BRADFORD, WEST YORKSHIRE BD1 4BA, ☎ 01274 394699, **e-mail:** northshoe@mcmail.com, 9.30–6 MON, 9.30–8 TUE–FRI, 9–6 SAT, 11–5 SUN.

UNIT 2, THE WHEATLEY CENTRE, WHEATLEY HALL ROAD, DONCASTER, SOUTH YORKSHIRE DN2 4PE, ☎ 01302 343866, **e-mail:** northshoe@mcmail.com, 10–8 MON–FRI, 9–6 SAT, 10.30–4.30 SUN.

UNIT 1B, WESLEY SQUARE, GOOLE, SOUTH YORKSHIRE DN14 5EZ, ☎ 01405 768358, **e-mail:** northshoe@mcmail.com, 9–6 MON–SAT, 10–4 SUN.

UNIT 3, WESTSIDE RETAIL PARK, GUISELEY, LEEDS, WEST YORKSHIRE LS20 9NE, ☎ 01943 870565, **e-mail:** northshoe@mcmail.com, 10–6 MON–WED, SAT, 10–7 THUR, FRI, 10.30–4.30 SUN.

NORTHGATE RETAIL PARK, ALBION STREET, HECKMONDWIKE, WEST YORKSHIRE WF16 9LQ, ☎ 01924 408942, **e-mail:** northshoe@mcmail.com, 9–6 MON–WED, SAT, 9–7 THUR, FRI, 10–4 SUN.

UNIT 16, KEIGHLEY RETAIL PARK, HARDINGS ROAD, KEIGHLEY, WEST YORKSHIRE BD21 3NJ, ☎ 01535 600793, **e-mail:** northshoe@mcmail.com, 10–6 MON–WED, SAT, 10–8 THUR, FRI, 11–5 SUN.

SEACROFT GREEN LEEDS, WEST YORKSHIRE LS14 6JD, ☎ 0113 265 1071, **e-mail:** northshoe@mcmail.com, 9–6 MON–SAT, 7 ON THUR, FRI, 11–5 SUN.

UNIT 2A, HEELEY RETAIL PARK, CHESTERFIELD ROAD, SHEFFIELD, SOUTH YORKSHIRE S8 0RG, ☎ 0114 258 3100, **e-mail:** northshoe@mcmail.com, 10–8 MON–FRI, 9–6 SAT, 11–5 SUN.

UNIT 20B, TEESIDE RETAIL PARK, TEESIDE, NORTH YORKSHIRE TS17 7BW, ☎ 01642 634163, **e-mail:** northshoe@mcmail.com, 10–8 MON–FRI, 9–6 SAT, 11–5 SUN.

UNIT 6, CLIFTON MOOR RETAIL PARK, CLIFTON MOOR, YORK, NORTH YORKSHIRE YO3 4WZ, ☎ 01904 690399, **e-mail:** northshoe@mcmail.com, 9–6 MON–WED, SAT, 9–7 THUR, FRI, 10.30–4.30 SUN. **PERMANENT DISCOUNT OUTLET**

See page 98 (CHESH)

THE GREAT CLOTHES FASHION STORE

84 YORK ROAD, LEEDS, WEST YORKSHIRE LS9 9AA, ☎ 0113 2350303, www.greatclothes.co.uk, 9.30–9 MON–FRI, 9.30–6 SAT, 11–5 SUN. **PERMANENT DISCOUNT OUTLET**

50,000 square feet of space with clothes for men, women and children from French Connection, Adidas, Berghaus, Pringle, Wolsey, Puma, Nike, Firetrap and Sonnetti, and including all brands of jeans. There are also accessories such as socks, shoes for adults, hats, scarves and underwear. Formal men's and boyswear includes hire of morning suits and kilts for weddings and a comprehensive 'big man's department' with sizes up to 54in chest. All stock is current season and is discounted by 20%. Free alterations carried out on site and there is a coffee shop and free parking.

THE HARROGATE DRESS AGENCY

3 JOHN STREET, OFF JAMES STREET, HARROGATE, NORTH YORKSHIRE HG1 1JZ, ☎ 01423 521344, 9.30–5 MON–FRI, 10–5 SAT. **DRESS AGENCY**

Two-storey shop with men's and women's top quality labels such as Jean Muir, Moschino, Georges Rech, Pallant, Issey Miyake, Escada, Basler, Daks, Boss and Armani as well as some high street names. Sizes range from 8 to 18. Also stocks jewellery, shoes, handbags and any other accessory you might need.

THE MILL DISCOUNT DEPARTMENT STORE

BRADFORD ROAD, BATLEY, WEST YORKSHIRE WF17 5LZ, ☎ 01924 423172, FAX: 01924 446096, www.themillbatley.com, 9.30–5.30 MON–SAT, 10–4 SUN. **PERMANENT DISCOUNT OUTLET**

The Mill Discount Department Store is the largest Mill retail outlet in the UK, attracting more than one million visitors every year. Situated in a restored Victorian Mill in the heart of West Yorkshire, The Mill offers massive savings in a department-store format. This all-weather centre consists of four floors together with an external parade selling heavily discounted branded men's, women's and children's fashions, sportswear, homewares, accessories, music, videos, sunglasses, books, toys, perfumes, luggage, gifts, shoes, fabrics and lighting. Readmans, whose name is synonymous with unbeatable value, has opened there recently. This is the company's second major store, offering good quality women's, men's and children's wear, lingerie, shoes, homewares and linens at remarkably low prices. Among over 300 brand names sold at The Mill are Puma, Pilot, HKA, Leeds United, Liz Claiborne, Elle, Jumper, Kasper, Amazing Jeans, Spicy, Urban Turban, Chilli Pepper, Tigi Wear, Ponden Mill, Woods of Windsor, Gleneagles Crystal, Dartington, Arthur Price, Skopos home furnishings, Jane Shilton, Book Depot, Toy Factory, Eye Zone, Famous Footwear, Hush Puppies, Lee Cooper, MX Active, Berghaus, Craghopper, Julian Graves, Fox's Biscuits, John Bull and Lion Confectionery. The complex can be reached by car, coach and train. Junction 40 of the M1 and junctions 27 and 28 of the M62 are within five and six miles of the site respectively. Batley Station on the Trans-Pennine railway is just five minutes walk from The Mill, providing easy access to Leeds and Manchester. There are more than 500 car parking spaces and coach parking is available. Amenities include children's creche, self-service licensed restaurant serving hot and cold food and drinks, Yorkshire Board Information Centre and access for the disabled.

THE SHOE SHELTER

UNIT 16A SPRINGFIELD MILLS, DENBY-DALE, HUDDERSFIELD, WEST YORKSHIRE HD8 9TH, ☎ 01484 866221, 9.30–5 MON–FRI, 9–5 SAT, 10–5 SUN AND BANK HOLIDAYS.
PERMANENT DISCOUNT OUTLET

Wide range of men's, women's and children's shoes with labels such as Ecco, Loake, Gabor, Start-Rite and Elefanten. Many of the shoes are discounted by up to 50%.

THE SPORTS FACTORY

THE YORKSHIRE OUTLET, WHITE ROSE WAY, DONCASTER, SOUTH YORKSHIRE DN4 5JH, ☎ 01302 322 663, 10–6 MON–SAT, 11–5 SUN. **FACTORY SHOP IN A FACTORY SHOPPING VILLAGE**

See page 176 (SOM)

THE SUIT LENGTH AND FABRIC CENTRE

BATEMAN OGDEN & CO LTD, ARGYLL HOUSE, 918 WAKEFIELD ROAD, BRADFORD, WEST YORKSHIRE BD4 7QQ, ☎ 01274 729103, FAX: 01274 720818, 8.30–5 MON–SAT. MAIL ORDER. **FACTORY SHOP**

Bateman Ogden & Co Ltd have been leading Yorkshire cloth merchants in Bradford since 1881, providing a top quality service to the bespoke tailoring profession from local businesses to Savile Row. They specialise in finest quality Huddersfield and Scottish worsted suitings and jacketings in pure new wool and wool/cashmere blends, all marketed in individual lengths to customers' requirements. Their women's department has recently expanded to stock a wide range of coatings in pure new wool and wool cashmere blends, tweeds, crepes in all wool and poly/wool, twill suitings in pure new wool, skirt lengths, satin linings, tartans and printed dress weight fabrics. They can recommend bespoke tailors in any part of the country. A mail order service is offered on some of their ranges.

THE YORKSHIRE OUTLET

WHITE ROSE WAY, JUNCTION 3 OF M18, DONCASTER LAKESIDE, SOUTH YORKSHIRE DN4 5JH, ☎ 01302 366444, **e-mail:** cprimrose@realm-ocm.com, www.theyorkshireoutletcentre.co.uk, 10–6 MON–SAT, 11–5 SUN. **FACTORY SHOPPING VILLAGE**

The Yorkshire Outlet, Doncaster, has a great range of stores offering up to 50% off recommended retail prices, with new products and bargains arriving daily. The centre has a range of restaurants, a children's play area, wheelchair hire, and free parking.

TIMBERLAND

MCARTHURGLEN DESIGNER OUTLET, ST NICHOLAS AVENUE, NABURN, YORK, NORTH YORKSHIRE YO19 4TA, ☎ 01904 620333, FAX: 01904 653334, 10–6 MON–FRI, 8 ON THUR, 9–6 SAT, 11–5 SUN. **FACTORY SHOP IN A FACTORY SHOPPING VILLAGE**

See page 99 (CHESH)

T J HUGHES

51–57 ST SEPULCHRE GATE, DONCASTER, SOUTH YORKSHIRE DN1 1UB, ☎ 01302 363119,

FAX: 01302 363126, **e-mail:** info@tjhughes.co.uk, www.tjhughes.co.uk, 9–5.30 MON–SAT, 10–4 SUN.

121 FERENSWAY, HULL, EAST YORKSHIRE HU1 3UW, ☎ 01482 326174, FAX: 01482 329767, **e-mail:** info@tjhughes.co.uk, www.tjhughes.co.uk, 9–5.30 MON–SAT, 10.30–4.30 SUN.

18-19 CAPTAIN COOK SQUARE, MIDDLESBROUGH, NORTH YORKSHIRE TS1 5UB, ☎ 01642 220902, FAX: 01642 220903, **e-mail:** info@tjhughes.co.uk, www.tjhughes.co.uk, 9–5.30 MON–SAT, 11–5 SUN.

50 HIGH STREET, SHEFFIELD, SOUTH YORKSHIRE S1 1QH, ☎ 0114 272 8121, FAX: 0114 272 3146, **e-mail:** info@tjhughes.co.uk, www.tjhughes.co.uk, 9–5.30 MON–SAT, 11–5 SUN.
PERMANENT DISCOUNT OUTLET

See page 98 (CHESH)

TK MAXX

THE ALHAMBRA CENTRE, CHEAPSIDE, UPPER NEW STREET, BARNSLEY, SOUTH YORKSHIRE S70 1SB, ☎ 01226 770078, www.tkmaxx.com, 9–5.30 MON–SAT, 10.30–4.30 SUN.

UNITS 11 AND 12, FORSTER SQUARE RETAIL PARK, 53 VALLEY ROAD, BRADFORD, WEST YORKSHIRE BD1 4RN, ☎ 01274 738600, www.tkmaxx.com, 9.30–8 MON–FRI, 9–6 SAT, 11–5 SUN.

8 THE WHEATLEY CENTRE, WHEATLEY HALL ROAD, DONCASTER, SOUTH YORKSHIRE, ☎ 01302 327 707, www.tkmaxx.com, PHONE FOR DETAILS.

2ND FLOOR, THE VICTORIA SHOPPING CENTRE, HARROGATE, NORTH YORKSHIRE HG1 1AG, ☎ 01423 536636, www.tkmaxx.com, 9–5.30 MON–SAT, 11–4 SUN.

2 KINGSGATE, KING STREET, HUDDERSFIELD, WEST YORKSHIRE, ☎ 01484 519095, www.tkmaxx.com, PHONE FOR DETAILS.

PRINCES QUAY SHOPPING CENTRE, HULL, EAST YORKSHIRE HU1 2PQ, ☎ 01482 223202, www.tkmaxx.com, 9–5.30 MON–FRI, 9–6 SAT, 11–5 SUN.

LEEDS SHOPPING PLAZA, 27 ALBION ARCADE, LEEDS, WEST YORKSHIRE LS1 5ER, ☎ 0113 246 7990, www.tkmaxx.com, 9–5.30 MON–FRI, 9–6 SAT, 11–5 SUN.

12 CAPTAIN COOK SQUARE, MIDDLESBROUGH, NORTH YORKSHIRE TS1 5UB, ☎ 01642 222220, www.tkmaxx.com, 9–5.30 MON–FRI, 9–6 SAT, 11–5 SUN.

ORCHARD SQUARE SHOPPING CENTRE, FARGATE, SHEFFIELD, SOUTH YORKSHIRE S1 2FB, ☎ 0114 275 0755, www.tkmaxx.com, 9–6 MON–SAT, 11–5 SUN.

90–93 CATHEDRAL WALK, WAKEFIELD, WEST YORKSHIRE WF1 1YD, ☎ 01924 382828, www.tkmaxx.com, 9–5.30 MON–WED, 9–7.30 THUR, 9–5.30 FRI–SAT.

UNIT 2 MONKS CROSS RETAIL PARK, MONKS CROSS DRIVE, YORK, SOUTH YORKSHIRE YO32 9GX, ☎ 01904 659996, www.tkmaxx.com, 9–8 MON–FRI, 9–6 SAT, 10.30–5 SUN.
PERMANENT DISCOUNT OUTLET

See page 89 (BEDS)

TOG 24

THE YORKSHIRE OUTLET, WHITE ROSE WAY, DONCASTER, SOUTH YORKSHIRE DN4 5PH, ☎ 01302 364123, **e-mail:** mail-order@tog24.com, www.tog24.com, 10–6 MON–SAT, 11–5 SUN.

SPEN VALE MILLS, STATION LANE, HECKMONDWIKE, WEST YORKSHIRE WF16 0NQ, ☎ 01924 409314, **e-mail:** mail-order@tog24.com, www.tog24.com, 10–5 MON–SAT, 11–5 SUN.

FREEPORT HORNSEA OUTLET VILLAGE, ROLSTON ROAD, HORNSEA, EAST YORKSHIRE HU18 1UT, ☎ 01964 535308, **e-mail:** mail-order@tog24.com, www.tog24.com, 9.30–6 SEVEN DAYS A WEEK.

UNIT 23, BRUNSWICK PAVILION, SCARBOROUGH, NORTH YORKSHIRE YO11 2PA, ☎ 01723 377760, **e-mail:** mail-order@tog24.com, www.tog24.com, 9.30–5 MON–SAT, 11–5 SUN.

93–94 CHURCH STREET, WHITBY, NORTH YORKSHIRE YO22 4BH, ☎ 01947 820456, **e-mail:** mail-order@tog24.com, www.tog24.com, 10–5 EVERY DAY.

MCARTHURGLEN DESIGNER OUTLET YORK, ST NICHOLAS AVENUE, FULFORD, JUNCTION OF A19 AND A64, YORK, NORTH YORKSHIRE YO19 4TA, ☎ 01904 677814, **e-mail:** mail-order@tog24.com, www.tog24.com, 10–6 MON–SAT, 8 ON THUR, 11–5 SUN. **FACTORY SHOP IN A FACTORY SHOPPING VILLAGE**

See page 99 (CHESH)

TOMMY HILFIGER

MCARTHURGLEN DESIGNER OUTLET YORK, ST NICHOLAS AVENUE, FULFORD, JUNCTION OF A19 AND A64, YORK, NORTH YORKSHIRE YO1 4RE, ☎ 01904 627247, FAX: 01904 679268, www.tommy.com, 10–6 MON–SAT, 8 ON THUR, 11–5 SUN. **FACTORY SHOP IN A FACTORY SHOPPING VILLAGE**

See page 99 (CHESH)

TRADEX

RINGWAY INDUSTRIAL ESTATE, BECK WAY, HUDDERSFIELD, WEST YORKSHIRE HD1 5ND, ☎ 01484 448000, FAX: 01484 448001, 9.30–8.30 MON–FRI, 9–5.30 SAT, 10.30–4.30 SUN.

CHATSWORTH ROAD, LEEDS, WEST YORKSHIRE LS8 3QE, ☎ 0113 240 7407, FAX: 0113 200 9819, 9.30–8.30 MON–FRI, 9–5.30 SAT, 10.30–4.30 SUN.

BRADFORD ROAD, PUDSEY, WEST YORKSHIRE LS28 5AS, ☎ 0113 239 3377, 9.30–8.30 MON–FRI, 9–5.30 SAT, 10.30–4.30 SUN. **PERMANENT DISCOUNT OUTLET**

See page 142 (LANCS)

UNITED FOOTWEAR

ROOLEY LANE, DUDLEY HILL, (A6036 RING ROAD), BRADFORD, WEST YORKSHIRE, ☎ 01274 680322, 9–8 MON–FRI, 9–5.30 SAT, 10–4 SUN.

178 EASTERLY ROAD, LEEDS, WEST YORKSHIRE, ☎ 0113 249 3244, 9–5.30 MON–SAT, 10–4 SUN. **PERMANENT DISCOUNT OUTLET**

See page 124 (HAMPS)

VIYELLA

MCARTHURGLEN DESIGNER OUTLET YORK, ST NICHOLAS AVENUE, FULFORD, JUNCTION OF A19 AND A64, YORK, NORTH YORKSHIRE YO19 4TA, ☎ 01904 678680, 10–6 MON–FRI, 8 ON THUR, 9–6 SAT, 11–5 SUN. **FACTORY SHOP IN A FACTORY SHOPPING VILLAGE**

See page 99 (CHESH)

WALKLEYS CANALSIDE MILL SHOPPING

BURNLEY ROAD, HEBDEN BRIDGE, WEST YORKSHIRE HX7 7NH, ☎ 01422 842061 10–5 MON–FRI, 10–5.30 SAT, SUN. **PERMANENT DISCOUNT OUTLET**

Three-storey shop selling a wide selection of goods at discount prices: linen, textiles, footwear, clothes, gifts, crafts, china, fine art and collectables. The ground floor houses the clearance stock or merchandise which is bought in bulk and sold at very competitive prices. Also situated on the ground floor is a comprehensive nursery section sellings prams, buggies, cots etc. The first floor houses clothes for men and women at 30% to 50% discounts, the second floor houses the china and art shop as well as craft stalls.

WARNERS UK LTD

UNIT 23, THE YORKSHIRE OUTLET, WHITE ROSE WAY, DONCASTER SOUTH YORKSHIRE DN4 5JH, ☎ 01302 739650, 10–6 MON–SAT, 11–5 SUN.

FREEPORT HORNSEA OUTLET VILLAGE, ROLSTON ROAD, HORNSEA, EAST YORKSHIRE HU18 1UT, ☎ 01964 536996, 9.30–6 SEVEN DAYS A WEEK. **FACTORY SHOP IN A FACTORY SHOPPING VILLAGE**

See page 100 (CHESH)

WRANGLER LEE

YORKSHIRE OUTLET, WHITE ROSE WAY, DONCASTER, SOUTH YORKSHIRE DN4 5JA, ☎ 01302 325593, 10–6 MON–SAT, 11–5 SUN.

FREEPORT HORNSEA OUTLET VILLAGE, ROLSTON ROAD, HORNSEA, EAST YORKSHIRE HU18 1UT, ☎ 01964 532979, 9.30–6 MON–SAT, 11–5 SUN, IN SUMMER; 10–5.30 MON–SAT, 11–5 SUN, IN WINTER. **FACTORY SHOP IN A FACTORY SHOPPING VILLAGE**

See page 142 (LANCS)

WYNSORS WORLD OF SHOES

90 DONCASTER ROAD, BARNSLEY, SOUTH YORKSHIRE S70 1TW
9–5.30 MON, TUE, WED, SAT, 9–8 THUR, 9–6 FRI, 10–4 SUN.

339 THORNTON ROAD, BRADFORD, WEST YORKSHIRE BD8 9ER, ☎ 01274 495016, 9–5.30 MON, TUE, WED, SAT, 9–8 THUR, FRI, 10–4 SUN AND BANK HOLIDAYS.

ENTERPRISE WAY, CASTLEFORD, WEST YORKSHIRE WF10 1EQ, ☎ 01977 514774, 9–5.30 MON, TUE, WED, SAT, 9–8 THUR, FRI, 10–4 SUN AND BANK HOLIDAYS.

CASTLE MILLS, HORNCASTLE STREET, CLECKHEATON, WEST YORKSHIRE BD19 3HJ, ☎ 01274 851366, 9–5.30 MON, TUE, WED, SAT, 9–8 THUR, FRI.

438 HESSEL ROAD, KINGSTON UPON HULL, EAST YORKSHIRE HU3 3SE, ☎ 01482 223585, 9–5.30 MON, TUE, WED, SAT, 9–8 THUR, FRI, 10–4 SUN AND BANK HOLIDAYS.

MIDDLETON SHOPPING CENTRE, LEEDS, WEST YORKSHIRE LS10 4AX, ☎ 0113 2710849, 9–5.30 MON, TUE, WED, SAT, 9–8 THUR, FRI, 10–4 SUN AND BANK HOLIDAYS.

WOODHOUSE GREEN, THURCROFT, NEAR ROTHERHAM, SOUTH YORKSHIRE S66 9AN, ☎ 01709 540876, 9–5.30 MON, TUE, WED, SAT, 9–8 THUR, FRI, 10–4 SUN AND BANK HOLIDAYS.

INFIRMARY ROAD, SHEFFIELD, SOUTH YORKSHIRE S6 3DG, ☎ 0114 273 7903, 9–5.30 MON, TUE, WED, SAT, 9–8 THUR, FRI, 10–4 SUN AND BANK HOLIDAYS.

12 THE STONEBOW, YORK, NORTH YORKSHIRE YO1 7NY, ☎ 01904 637611, 9–5.30 MON, TUE, WED, SAT, 9–8 THUR, FRI, 11–5 SUN AND BANK HOLIDAYS.
PERMANENT DISCOUNT OUTLET

See page 100 (CHESH)

YOU & YOURS

UNIT 9, CROWN POINT RETAIL PARK, HUNSLET ROAD, LEEDS, WEST YORKSHIRE LS10 1ET, ☎ 0113 234 1924, 10–5 MON, 10–7 TUE–FRI, 9.30–6 SAT, 11–5 SUN.

98–100 NEW STREET, HUDDERSFIELD, WEST YORKSHIRE HD1 2UD, ☎ 01484 543301, 9–5.30 MON–SAT.

WESTFIELD, INGLEBY ROAD (OPPOSITE GRATTAN), BRADFORD WEST YORKSHIRE BD99 2XE, ☎ 01274 624611, 10–5.30 MON, 10–8 TUE–FRI, 9–5.30 SAT, 11–5 SUN. **PERMANENT DISCOUNT OUTLET**

See page 100 (CHESH)

SOUTH WALES

AUTONOMY

MCARTHURGLEN DESIGNER OUTLET WALES, THE DERWEN, BRIDGEND, JUNCTION 36 OF M4, SOUTH WALES CF32 9SU, ☎ 01656 669200, 10–8 MON–FRI, 10–6 SAT, 11–5 SUN.
FACTORY SHOP IN A FACTORY SHOPPING VILLAGE

See page 93 (CHESH)

BIG L FACTORY OUTLET

UNIT 96, MCARTHURGLEN DESIGNER OUTLET WALES, THE DERWEN, BRIDGEND, JUNCTION 36 OF M4, SOUTH WALES CF32 9SU, ☎ 01656 767335, FAX: 01656 767335, 10–8 MON–FRI, 10–6 SAT, 11–5 SUN. **FACTORY SHOP IN A FACTORY SHOPPING VILLAGE**

See page 93 (CHESH)

BURBERRY

YNYSWEN ROAD, TREORCHY, RHONDDA, MID GLAMORGAN, SOUTH WALES, ☎ 01443 772020, 9–4 TUE–THUR, 9–2 FRI, 9–1.30 SAT. **FACTORY SHOP**

See page 94 (CHESH)

CATALOGUE BARGAIN SHOP

FFALDS ROAD SHOPPING CENTRE, PYLE CROSS, PYLE, BRIDGEND, SOUTH WALES CF33 6BH, ☎ 01656 746426, www.bargaincrazy.com, 9–8 MON–FRI, 9–6 SAT, 10.30–4.30 SUN.

PIONEER SUPERSTORE, BRYN-SERTH ROAD, RHD-Y-BLEW, EBBW VALE, GWENT, SOUTH WALES NP3 5YD, ☎ 01495 309297, www.bargaincrazy.com, 9–8 MON–THUR, 9–9 FRI, 9–6 SAT, 10–4 SUN.

61 HIGH STREET, MERTHYR TYDFIL, MID GLAMORGAN, SOUTH WALES CF47 8DE, ☎ 01685 385653, www.bargaincrazy.com, 9–5.30 MON–SAT.

MIDWAY RETAIL PARK, PONTYPRIDD, SOUTH WALES CF37 5NX, ☎ 01443 843718, www.bargaincrazy.com, 9–8 MON–FRI, 9–6 SAT, 11–5 SUN.

UNIT 1A, HAVENS HEAD RETAIL CENTRE, MILFORD HAVEN, PEMBROKESHIRE, SOUTH WALES SA73 3AU, ☎ 01646 697407, www.bargaincrazy.com, 9–8 MON–FRI, 9–6 SAT, 10.30–4.30 SUN.

31 STATION ROAD, PORT TALBOT, WEST GLAMORGAN, SOUTH WALES SA13 1NN, ☎ 01639 899419, www.bargaincrazy.com, 9–5.30 MON–SAT.

229–230 HIGH STREET, SWANSEA, WEST GLAMORGAN, SOUTH WALES SA1 1NY, ☎ 01792 456748, www.bargaincrazy.com, 9–5.30 MON–SAT, 10–4 SUN. **PERMANENT DISCOUNT OUTLET**

See page 92 (CAMBS)

CIRO

MCARTHURGLEN DESIGNER OUTLET WALES, THE DERWEN, BRIDGEND, JUNCTION 36 OF M4, SOUTH WALES CF32 9SU, ☎ 01656 655916, 10–8 MON–FRI, 10–6 SAT, 11–5 SUN. **FACTORY SHOP IN A FACTORY SHOPPING VILLAGE**

See page 94 (CHESH)

CLARKS FACTORY SHOP

42–43 MACARTHUR GLEN OUTLET CENTRE, THE DERWEN, BRIDGEND, SOUTH WALES CF32 9SU, ☎ 01656 651151, 10–8 MON– FRI, 10–6 SAT, 11–5 SUN. **FACTORY SHOP IN A FACTORY SHOPPING VILLAGE**

See page 94 (CHESH)

COSALT INTERNATIONAL LTD

THE DOCKS, MILFORD HAVEN, PEMBROKESHIRE, SOUTH WALES SA73 3AF, ☎ 01646 692032, www.cosalt.co.uk, 8–5 MON–FRI, 9–12 SAT. **PERMANENT DISCOUNT OUTLET**

See page 145 (LINCS)

CRAZY MAC'S

PONTARDULAIS ROAD, FFORESTFACH, SWANSEA, SOUTH WALES SA5 4BA, ☎ 01792 585828, FAX: 01792 585566, **e-mail:** lss@salvage1.co.uk, www.salvage1.co.uk, 9.30–6 MON–THUR, 9.30–8 FRI, 9–6 SAT, 11–5 SUN. **PERMANENT DISCOUNT OUTLET**

An Aladdin's cave of salvaged stock for the avid bargain hunter, most of which has been the subject of insurance claims for fire or flood, salvage, bankruptcy or is simply clearance stock. Stock changes every two or three days and regular visitors have found anything from half price Kenwood Chefs, televisions and toys to furniture, kitchen items, linens and especially fantastic bargains in designer clothing. Yves Saint Laurent, Armani, Ungaro, Hugo Boss and Valentino, as well as all major high street names, are just some of the names to be found (though the labels are often cut out). Discounts range from 50% to 80%. Phone first to check stock.

DEWHIRST IMPRESSIONS

UNIT 22, KINGSWAY, FFORESTFACH INDUSTRIAL ESTATE, FFORESTFACH, SWANSEA, SOUTH WALES SA5 4DL, ☎ 01792 584621, **e-mail:** kim.mcmaster@dewhirst.com, 9–5.30 MON–SAT, 11–5 SUN. **FACTORY SHOP**

See page 101 (CO DURH)

DOUBLE TWO

UNIT 46, FESTIVAL PARK SHOPPING CENTRE, VICTORIA ROAD, EBBW VALE, SOUTH WALES NP3 6UF, ☎ 01495 301414, 9.30–5.30 MON–SAT, 7 ON THUR, 11–5 SUN. **FACTORY SHOP IN A FACTORY SHOPPING VILLAGE**

See page 116 (ESSEX)

ECCO

MCARTHURGLEN DESIGNER OUTLET WALES, THE DERWEN, BRIDGEND, JUNCTION 36 OF M4, SOUTH WALES CF32 9SU, ☎ 01656 767202, www.ecco.com, 10–8 MON–FRI, 10–6 SAT, 11–5 SUN. **FACTORY SHOP IN A FACTORY SHOPPING VILLAGE**

See page 95 (CHESH)

FAMOUS FOOTWEAR

MCARTHURGLEN DESIGNER OUTLET WALES, THE DERWEN, BRIDGEND, JUNCTION 36 OF M4, SOUTH WALES CF32 9SU, ☎ 01656 657779, 10–8 MON–FRI, 10–6 SAT, 11–5 SUN. **FACTORY SHOP IN A FACTORY SHOPPING VILLAGE**

See page 95 (CHESH)

FESTIVAL PARK FACTORY SHOPPING VILLAGE

FESTIVAL PARK, VICTORIA, EBBW VALE, GWENT, SOUTH WALES NP23 8FP, ☎ 01495 350010, FAX: 01495 307363, 9.30–5.30 MON–SAT, 7 ON THUR, 11–5 SUN. **FACTORY SHOPPING VILLAGE**

Factory shopping village with over 40 shops offering a wide range of top brand goods and designer labels, many at half the recommended retail price. Factory shops include: fashion from Windsmoor, Designer Room, Leading Labels, Double Two, Pilot and Roman Originals; shoes from Pavers; china and crystal from Wedgwood and Stuart Crystal; golfing and sports equipment from Edinburgh Woollen Mill and Sportz; chocolates from Thorntons; leisurewear from Cotton Traders; luggage and bags from Antler; accessories from Claire's and lots more to choose from. Built on the former site of the National Garden Festival of Wales, there are over 70 acres of woodland and parkland to explore either on foot or on the land train which operates from Easter to September on weekends and during school holidays, weather permitting. Within the park you can visit the woodland craft centre, owl sanctuary and lakes. There is a 200-seat restaurant, with panoramic views over the valley, serving both snacks and cooked meals. The free car park has dedicated spaces for both the disabled and parent and toddler. There is free wheelchair hire and baby changing facilities.

JAEGER FACTORY SHOP

MCARTHURGLEN DESIGNER OUTLET WALES, THE DERWEN, BRIDGEND, JUNCTION 36 OF M4, SOUTH WALES CF32 9ST, ☎ 01656 648660, 10–6 MON–FRI, 8 ON THUR, 9–6 SAT, 11–5 SUN. **FACTORY SHOP IN A FACTORY SHOPPING VILLAGE**

See page 158 (NORF)

LEE COOPER

MCARTHURGLEN DESIGNER OUTLET WALES, THE DERWEN, BRIDGEND, JUNCTION 36 OFF THE M4, SOUTH WALES CF32 9SU, ☎ 01656 645992, 10–8 MON–FRI, 10–6 SAT, 11–5 SUN. **FACTORY SHOP IN A FACTORY SHOPPING VILLAGE**

See page 96 (CHESH)

LITTLEWOODS CATALOGUE DISCOUNT STORE

MCARTHURGLEN DESIGNER OUTLET WALES, THE DERWEN, BRIDGEND, JUNCTION 36 OF M4, SOUTH WALES CF32 9SU, ☎ 01656 665700, 10–8 MON–FRI, 10–6 SAT, 11–5 SUN. **FACTORY SHOP IN A FACTORY SHOPPING VILLAGE**

See page 96 (CHESH)

MARKS & SPENCER

MCARTHURGLEN DESIGNER OUTLET VILLAGE, THE DERWEN, BRIDGEND, SOUTH WALES CF32 9SU, ☎ 01656 662063, 10–8 MON–FRI, 10–6 SAT, 11–5 SUN. **FACTORY SHOP IN A FACTORY SHOPPING VILLAGE**

See page 96 (CHESH)

MATALAN

UNIT 2, 383–384 NEWPORT ROAD, CARDIFF, SOUTH WALES CF3 7AE, ☎ 02920 491781, FAX: 02920 491782, www.matalan.co.uk, 10–8 MON–FRI, 9–6 SAT, 11–5 SUN.

UNIT 4B, CWMBRAN RETAIL PARK, CWMBRAN DRIVE, CWMBRAN, GWENT, SOUTH WALES NP44 3JQ, ☎ 01633 866944, FAX: 01633 868400, www.matalan.co.uk, 9.30–8 MON–FRI, 9–6 SAT, 11–5 SUN.

UNIT 8, GLAMORGAN VALE RETAIL PARK, LLANTRISANT, MID-GLAMORGAN, SOUTH WALES CF72 8RP, ☎ 01443 224854, FAX: 01443 227138, www.matalan.co.uk, 10–8 MON–FRI, 9–8 SAT, 11–5 SUN.

NEWPORT RETAIL PARK, 7 STILES AVENUE, NEWPORT, SOUTH WALES NP19 4TX, ☎ 01633 636030, FAX: 01633 281271, www.matalan.co.uk, 10–8 MON–FRI, 9–6 SAT, 11–5 SUN.

FOUNDRY ROAD, MORRISTON, SWANSEA, SOUTH WALES SA6 8DU, ☎ 01792 792229, FAX: 01792 702455, www.matalan.co.uk, 10–8 MON–FRI, 9–6 SAT, 11–5 SUN.

CARMARTHEN ROAD, SWANSEA, CARMARTHEN, SOUTH WALES SA5 8LL, ☎ 01792 560010, FAX: 01792 582979, www.matalan.co.uk, 10–8 MON–FRI, 9–6 SAT, 11–5 SUN. **PERMANENT DISCOUNT OUTLET**

See page 89 (BEDS)

MCARTHURGLEN DESIGNER OUTLET WALES

THE DERWEN, BRIDGEND, JUNCTION 36 OF M4, SOUTH WALES CF32 9SU, ☎ 01656 665700, www.mcarthurglen.com/bridgend, 10–8 MON–FRI, 10–6 SAT, 11–5 SUN. **FACTORY SHOPPING VILLAGE**

The McArthurGlen Designer Outlet in Bridgend is Wales' premier designer outlet. Set out in a friendly village street style the outlet has over 80 stores with everything from men's, women's and children's clothing to accessories, shoes, sportswear, luggage, homewares, toys, books, and gifts. All stock is excess stock sold by the retailers themselves at 30% to 50% off typical retail prices. The outlet also has over 1,800 free parking spaces, a food court, two children's play areas and a nine-screen Odeon cinema. Stores include: Reebok, Calvin Klein, Tie Rack, Ciro Pearls, Monet, Picture Port, Ciro Citterio, Bookends, Bed & Bath, Clover House, Overland, Pepe, Famous Footwear, Nickelbys, The Suit Company, Birthdays, Toyzone, Vans, Red/Green, Whittards, Travel Accessories, Ecco, Jacques Vert, Warners, Next, Windsmoor, Pilot, Petroleum, Roman Originals, Antler, Julian Graves, The Watch Shop, Knickerbox, Wedgewood, The Garden Outlet, Claire's Accessories, Clarks, Donnay, JoKids, Ben Sherman, Smiths Signature, Spiegelau, Royal Worcester/Edinburgh Crystal, Littlewoods, Helly Hansen, Woodies, Lee Cooper, Van Heusen/Viyella/Jaeger, Ted Baker, Cotton Traders, Royal Doulton, Walker and Hall, Professional Cookware Co, Thorntons, Price's Candles, Mountain Warehouse, John Partridge, Remington, U Wear/I Wear, Nike, The Body Shop, Mexx, Suits You, Designer Rooms, Winning Line, Tog 24, Elle, Chilli Pepper/Watsons, HKA, XS, Soled Out, Timberland, Carphone Warehouse, Levi's, and The Craft Outlet.

MEXX INTERNATIONAL

MCARTHURGLEN DESIGNER OUTLET WALES, THE DERWEN, BRIDGEND, JUNCTION 36 OF M4, SOUTH WALES CF32 9SU, ☎ 01656 766870, 10–8 MON–FRI, 10–6 SAT, 11–5 SUN. **FACTORY SHOP IN A FACTORY SHOPPING VILLAGE**

See page 97 (CHESH)

NEXT TO NOTHING

MCARTHURGLEN DESIGNER OUTLET WALES, THE DERWEN, BRIDGEND, JUNCTION 36 OF M4, SOUTH WALES CF32 9SU, ☎ 01656 641950, www.next.co.uk, 10–8 MON–FRI, 10–6 SAT, 11–5 SUN. **FACTORY SHOP IN A FACTORY SHOPPING VILLAGE**

See page 97 (CHESH)

REDGREEN

MCARTHURGLEN DESIGNER OUTLET WALES, THE DERWEN, BRIDGEND, JUNCTION 36 OF M4, SOUTH WALES CF32 9SU, ☎ 01656 645464, 10–8 MON–FRI, 10–6 SAT, 11–5 SUN.
FACTORY SHOP IN A FACTORY SHOPPING VILLAGE

See page 98 (CHESH)

START-RITE

FESTIVAL PARK SHOPPING VILLAGE, VICTORIA ROAD, EBBW VALE, SOUTH WALES NP23 6UF, ☎ 01495 305700, 9.30–5.30 MON–FRI, SAT, 7 ON THUR, 11–5 SUN. **FACTORY SHOP**

See page 160 (NORF)

STEWART'S

12 PIER STREET, ABERYSTWYTH, CEREDIGION, SOUTH WALES SY23 2LJ, ☎ 01970 611437, FAX: 01970 611437, 9–5. MON–SAT.

UNIT 4, BETHEL SQUARE SHOPPING CENTRE, BRECON, POWYS, SOUTH WALES LD3 7HU, ☎ 01874 610260, FAX: 01874 610260, 9–5.30 MON–SAT, 11–4 SUN.

MARLAS ROAD, PYLE CROSS, NR BRIDGEND, MID GLAMORGAN, SOUTH WALES CF33 6AY, ☎ 01656 744988, FAX: 01656 744988, 9.30–5.30 MON–SAT, 12–4 SUN.

2–4 CARDIFF ROAD, Y TWYN, CAERPHILLY, MID GLAMORGAN, SOUTH WALES CF83 1JN, ☎ 02920 888054, FAX: 02920 888054, 9–5.30 MON–SAT.

21–22 GREYFRIARS, CARMARTHEN, CARMARTHENSHIRE, SOUTH WALES SA31 3NB, ☎ 01267 232208, FAX: 01267 232021, 9–5.30 MON–SAT, 11–4 SUN.

LONDON HOUSE, HARFORD SQUARE, LAMPETER, CEREDIGION, SOUTH WALES SA48 7HD, ☎ 01570 422205, 9.30–5.30 MON–SAT, 5 ON WED.

52 STEPNEY STREET, LLANELLI, CARMARTHENSHIRE, SOUTH WALES SA15 3TR, ☎ 01554 776957, FAX: 01554 776957, 9–5 MON–SAT.

7–11 MONNOW STREET, MONMOUTH, MONMOUTHSHIRE, SOUTH WALES NP5 3EF, ☎ 01600 716926, FAX: 01600 716926, 9.30–5.30 MON–SAT.

GLAMORE TERRACE, NEW QUAY, CEREDIGION, SOUTH WALES SA45 9PL, ☎ 01545 560740, FAX: 01545 560740, 9.30–5.30 MON–SAT, 11–5 SUN.

THE STRAND, SAUNDERSFOOT, PEMBROKESHIRE, SOUTH WALES SA69 9GE, ☎ 01834 812579, FAX: 01834 812579, 9–5.30 MON–SAT, 10–5.30 SUN.

BREWERY TERRACE, SAUNDERSFOOT, PEMBROKESHIRE, SOUTH WALES SA69 9HG, ☎ 01834 813169, FAX: 01834 813169, 9.30–5.30 MON–SAT, 10–5.30 SUN.

HIGH STREET, TENBY, PEMBROKESHIRE, SOUTH WALES SA70 7EW, ☎ 01834 844621, FAX: 01834 844621, 9.30–5.30 MON–SAT, 10–5.30 SUN. **FACTORY SHOP**

See page 112 (DEV)

THE FACTORY SHOP

SNOWDROP LANE, HAVERFORDWEST, PEMBROKESHIRE, SOUTH WALES SA61 1ET, ☎ 01437 766000, 9–5.30 MON–SAT, 10.30–4.30 SUN. **FACTORY SHOP**

See page 98 (CHESH)

TK MAXX

UNIT 11, QUEENS WEST CENTRE, QUEEN STREET, CARDIFF, SOUTH WALES CF10 2AQ, ☎ 0292 0341290, www.tkmaxx.com, 9–5.30 MON–WED, 9–7 THUR, 9–6 FRI–SAT, 11–5 SUN.

UNIT 25, GREYFRIARS SHOPPING CENTRE, CARMARTHEN, SOUTH WALES SA31 3BN, ☎ 01267 220934, www.tkmaxx.com, 9–5.30 MON–TUE, 9–6 WED– SAT, 9–8 THUR, 10–4 SUN.

2–3 OXFORD STREET, SWANSEA, SOUTH WALES SA1 3AE, ☎ 01792 642055, www.tkmaxx.com, 9–5.30 MON–THUR, 9– 6 FRI–SAT, 11–5 SUN. **PERMANENT DISCOUNT OUTLET**

See page 89 (BEDS)

TOG 24

MCARTHURGLEN DESIGNER OUTLET WALES, THE DERWEN, BRIDGEND, JUNCTION 36 OF M4, SOUTH WALES CF32 9SU, ☎ 01656 767033, **e-mail:** mail-order@tog24.com, www.tog24.com, 10–8 MON–FRI, 10–6 SAT, 11–5 SUN.

FESTIVAL PARK OUTLET CENTRE, VICTORIA, EBBW VALE, GWENT, SOUTH WALES NP23 8FP, ☎ 01495 301902, **e-mail:** mail-order@tog24.com, www.tog24.com, 9.30–5.30 MON–SAT, 7 ON THUR, 11–5 SUN. **FACTORY SHOP IN A FACTORY SHOPPING VILLAGE**

See page 99 (CHESH)

VIYELLA

MCARTHURGLEN DESIGNER OUTLET WALES, THE DERWEN, BRIDGEND, JUNCTION 36 OF M4, SOUTH WALES CF32 9ST, ☎ 01656 648660, 10–6 MON–SAT, 8 ON THUR, 11–5 SUN. **FACTORY SHOP IN A FACTORY SHOPPING VILLAGE**

See page 99 (CHESH)

WALKER & HALL

MCARTHURGLEN DESIGNER OUTLET WALES, THE DERWEN, BRIDGEND, JUNCTION 36 OF M4, SOUTH WALES CF32 9SU, ☎ 01656 767148, www.goldsmiths.co.uk, 10–8 MON–FRI, 10–6 SAT, 11–5 SUN. **FACTORY SHOP IN A FACTORY SHOPPING VILLAGE**

See page 100 (CHESH)

WARNERS

UNIT 26, WELSH DESIGNER VILLAGE, PEN-Y-CAE, BRIDGEND, SOUTH WALES CF32 9ST, ☎ 01656 650888, 10–8 MON– FRI, 10–6 SAT, 11–5 SUN. **FACTORY SHOP IN A FACTORY SHOPPING VILLAGE**

See page 100 (CHESH)

WILKINSON STORES

10-13 CARDIFF STREET, ABERDARE, MID-GLAMORGAN, SOUTH WALES CF44 7DP, ☎ 01685 870393, www.wilko.co.uk, 9–5.30 MON–THUR, 9–6 FRI, SAT, 10–4 SUN. MAIL ORDER.

CIBI WALK SHOPPING CENTRE, FOGMORE STREET, ABERGAVENNY SOUTH WALES NP7 5AJ, ☎ 01685 870393, www.wilko.co.uk, 8.30–5.30 MON–THUR, 8.30–6 FRI, SAT, 10–4 SUN. MAIL ORDER. **PERMANENT DISCOUNT OUTLET**

See page 100 (CHESH)

NORTH WALES

CATALOGUE BARGAIN SHOP

UNITS F1–F2, FLINTSHIRE RETAIL CENTRE, FLINT, NORTH WALES CH6 5RR, ☎ 01352 732460, www.bargaincrazy.com, 9–8 MON–FRI, 9–6 SAT, 10.30–4.30 SUN.

6–8 MADOC STREET, LLANDUDNO, GWYNEDD, NORTH WALES LL30 2TP, ☎ 01492 877561, www.bargaincrazy.com, 9–5 MON–SAT, 10.30–4.30 SUN.

OLD KERRY ROAD, NEWTOWN, POWYS, NORTH WALES SY16 1BJ, ☎ 01686 628283, www.bargaincrazy.com, 9–5.30 MON–SAT, 10–4 SUN. **PERMANENT DISCOUNT OUTLET**

See page 92 (CAMBS)

LEGS CLOTHING CO

25A HIGH STREET, BRECON, POWYS, MID WALES LD3 7LA, ☎ 01874 611432, 9–5 MON–SAT, 11–5 BANK HOLIDAYS, EASTER TO CHRISTMAS.

39 HIGH STREET, BUILTH WELLS, POWYS, NORTH WALES LD2 3AB, ☎ 01982 551043, 9–5 MON–SAT, 11–5 BANK HOLIDAYS.

21 BROAD STREET, NEWTOWN, POWYS, MID WALES SY16 2NE, ☎ 01686 624388, 9–5 MON–SAT. **FACTORY SHOP**

See page 120 (GLOS)

MATALAN

UNIT 1A AND 1B, CAERNARFON ROAD, BANGOR, GWYNEDD, NORTH WALES LL57 4SU, ☎ 01248 362778, FAX: 01248 362779, www.matalan.co.uk, 9.30–8 MON–FRI, 9–6 SAT, 11–5 SUN.

UNIT 1, MOUNT STREET RETAIL, MOUNT STREET, WREXHAM, NORTH WALES LL1 2BN, ☎ 01978 346850, FAX: 01978 262933, www.matalan.co.uk, 10–8 MON–FRI, 9–6 SAT, 11–5 SUN. **PERMANENT DISCOUNT OUTLET**

See page 89 (BEDS)

SCOOPS

FORYD ROAD, KIMMEL BAY, RHYL, NORTH WALES LL18 5EQ, ☎ 01745 353947, 9–5.30 MON–SAT, 10–4 SUN. **PERMANENT DISCOUNT OUTLET**

See page 102 (CO DURH)

STEWART'S

23 MOSTYN STREET, LLANDUDNO, GWYNEDD, NORTH WALES LL30 2NL, ☎ 01492 870733, FAX: 01492 870733, 9–5.30 MON–SAT, 10 – 4 SUN.

Y MAES, PWLLHELI, GWYNEDD, NORTH WALES LL53 5HG, ☎ 01758 701130, FAX: 01758 701130, 9.30–5 MON–SAT. **FACTORY SHOP**

144 HIGH STREET, PORTHMADOG, GWYNEDD, NORTH WALES LL49 9NU, ☎ 01766 514166, FAX: 01766 514166, 9–5.30 MON–SAT, 12–4 SUN.

See page 112 (DEV)

T J HUGHES

UNIT B, HENBLAS SQUARE, CHESTER STREET, WREXHAM, CLWYD, NORTH WALES LL13 8BA, ☎ 01978 359555, FAX: 01978 359500, **e-mail:** info@tjhughes.co.uk, www.tjhughes.co.uk, 9–5.30 MON–SAT, 11–5 SUN. **PERMANENT DISCOUNT OUTLET**

See page 98 (CHESH)

THE FACTORY SHOP

BRUNSWICK ROAD, BUCKLEY, CLYWD, NORTH WALES CH7 2EF, ☎ 01555 759017, FAX: 01555 759018, 9.30–5.30 MON–SAT, 10.30–4.30 SUN. **FACTORY SHOP**

See page 98 (CHESH)

THE FAMOUS BRUNSWICK WAREHOUSE LTD

UNIT H, FLINTSHIRE RETAIL PARK, HOLYWELL ROAD, FLINTSHIRE, NORTH WALES CH6 5GB, ☎ 01352 731942, **e-mail:** northshoe@mcmail.com, 9–6 MON–WED, SAT, 9–7 THUR, FRI, 10–4 SUN.

UNIT 4, ISLAND GREEN RETAIL PARK, WREXHAM, CLWYD, NORTH WALES LL13 7NB, ☎ 01978 310999, **e-mail:** northshoe@mcmail.com, 9–6 MON–SAT, 11–5 SUN. **PERMANENT DISCOUNT OUTLET**

See page 98 (CHESH)

THE TWEEDMILL FACTORY OUTLETS

LLANNERCH PARK, ST ASAPH, DENBIGHSHIRE (OFF A55), NORTH WALES LL17 0UY, ☎ 01745 730072, FAX: 01745 731008, **e-mail:** enquiries@tweedmill.co.uk, www.tweedmill.co.uk, 9.30–6 MON–SAT, 8 ON THUR, 11–5 SUN. **FACTORY SHOP**
Stocks a wide range of clothes for both men and women, luggage, giftware, handbags and home accessories with savings of up to 50% off normal high street prices. Selling directly to the public from the manufacturers, there are always at least 50,000 garments in stock and 5,000 pairs of shoes as well as 100,000 homeware items, all of which are perfects. Labels on sale include Regatta, Klass, Roman, Wolsey, French Connection, Easy Jeans, Glenmuir, James Barry, Double Two, Lotus, Salisbury's and Farah for clothes and shoes; Coloroll, Ponden Mill, Price's Candles, Cloverleaf and Dartington Crystal for homewares. Everything is labelled with the original retail price, so you can see the discounts of up to 50%.

TK MAXX

UNIT 12, ISLAND GREEN, WREXHAM, CLWYD LL13 7LW, ☎ 01978 261133, www.tkmaxx.com, 9–5.30 MON–FRI, 9–6 SAT, 11–5 SUN. **PERMANENT DISCOUNT OUTLETS**

See page 89 (BEDS)

SOUTHERN SCOTLAND

ANDREW ELLIOT LTD

FOREST MILL, DUNSDALE ROAD, SELKIRK, SCOTLAND TD7 5EA, ☎ 01750 720412, FAX: 01750 723160, **e-mail:** enquiries@elliot-weave.co.uk, www.elliot-weave.co.uk, 9–5 MON–THUR, 9–4 FRI, SAT MORN BY ARRANGEMENT. **FACTORY SHOP**

Manufactures short cloth runs for UK clients and sells tweed fabric by the metre here. The factory shop comprises two rooms above the working mill, one set out with lengths of cloth, the other with finished rugs, pashminas and shawls. They also make their own range of rugs, fabric and scarves. This is the place to come if you're handy with a sewing machine as their shooting jacket material and fine lightweight suiting are excellent quality. Commission weaving can also be undertaken.

BALMORAL MILL SHOP

16 CHURCH LANE, GALSTON, AYRSHIRE, SCOTLAND KA4 8HF, ☎ 01563 820213, FAX: 01563 821740, **e-mail:** millshop@balmoralknitwear.co.uk, www.balmoralmill.com, 9–5 MON–SAT, 12–5 SUN, ALSO BANK HOLIDAYS. **FACTORY SHOP**

Sells cashmere and lambswool knitwear, embroidered knitwear, sweatshirts, polo shirts, bowling and golf attire and schoolwear, some of which is brand name and some own label, but all sold at factory direct prices. Women's, men's, children's and babywear are all stocked. Popular ranges are Alice Collins, Emreco, Lyle and Scott, Gabicci, Farah, Hodgsons and Poppy. Examples of prices include embroidered sweatshirts £14.95, polo shirts from £4.95, lambswool jumpers £22.95, seconds from £1.95. Telephone, mail and email orders welcome.

D C DAGLEISH LTD

DUNSDALE MILL, SELKIRK, SCOTLAND TD7 5EB, ☎ 01750 20781, 9–12 AND 1–4 MON–FRI. **FACTORY SHOP**

Small shop to the side of the factory which specialises in tartan manufacture. Pure wool headsquares; tartan braces; tartan dolls; tartan scarves; Celtic brooches; tartan kilts and waistcoasts; knee rugs and woollen rugs.

GRETNA GATEWAY OUTLET VILLAGE

GLASGOW ROAD, GRETNA, SCOTLAND DG16 6GG, ☎ 01461 339028, FAX: 01461 339100 INFORMATION LINE, **e-mail:** info@gretnagateway.com, www.gretnagateway.com, 10–6 SEVEN DAYS A WEEK. **FACTORY SHOPPING VILLAGE**

Thirty trading outlets with a planned second phase of 20 shops. Includes Episode, Bags Etc, Designer Room, Directions Design Studio, Design House, DKNY, Edinburgh Woollen Mill, Jane Shilton, John Partridge, Price's Candles, Polo Ralph Lauren (stocking clothes for men, women and children as well as homewares), Reebok, Rockport, Tag Heuer, The Golf Company, Tog 24, Tommy Hilfiger, La Casa del Cristallo, Book Depot, Mexx, Claire's Accessories, Pavers Shoes, Chapelle Jewellery, Thorntons, Van Heusen and Whittards. There is a children's play area, disabled access, free parking and restaurants.

HAWICK

ROXBURGHSHIRE, SCOTLAND. **PERMANENT DISCOUNT OUTLET**

Renowned for knitwear, Hawick is a cashmere buyer's dream town, with four or five shops selling a wide variety of knits at bargain prices. Walk around the town and you'll find other knitwear treasures.

HAWICK CASHMERE CO LTD

71–81 GRASSMARKET, EDINBURGH SCOTLAND EH1 2HJ, ☎ 0131 225 8634, FAX: 0131 225 8634, 10–5.30 MON–SAT. **FACTORY SHOP**

TRINITY MILLS, DUKE STREET, HAWICK, SCOTLAND TD9 9QA, ☎ 01450 371221, FAX: 01450 377298, 9.30–5 MON–SAT, 11–4 SUN (MAY TO OCTOBER).

20 BRIDGE STREET, KELSO, SCOTTISH BORDERS, SCOTLAND TD5 7JD, ☎ 01573 226776, FAX: 01573 226776, 9.30–5.30 MON– FRI, 9.30–5 SAT. **FACTORY SHOP**

See page 119 (GLOS)

INTERFLOOR LTD

HUNTER OUTLET, EDINBURGH ROAD, HEATHHALL, DUMFRIES, SCOTLAND DG1 1QA, ☎ 01387 240736, 9–5.15 MON–SAT. **FACTORY SHOP**

Hunter boots factory shop which also sells outdoor clothing for the hunting, shooting and fishing enthusiast: waders, raincoats, outdoor jackets, trousers, shirts and socks.

JOHN MOODY

38 THE SQUARE, KELSO, SCOTLAND TD5 7HL, ☎ 01573 224400, 10–5 MON–SAT, CLOSED 1.30–2 DAILY. **PERMANENT DISCOUNT OUTLET**

Cashmere and lambswool sweaters and cardigans for men and women at factory shop prices.

PARTRIDGE

GRETNA GATEWAY OUTLET VILLAGE, GLASGOW ROAD, GRETNA, SCOTLAND DG16 5GG, ☎ 01461 338959, 10–6 SEVEN DAYS A WEEK. **FACTORY SHOP IN A FACTORY SHOPPING VILLAGE**

See page 123 (HAMPS)

PETER SCOTT FACTORY SHOP

11 BUCCLEUCH STREET, HAWICK, SCOTLAND TD9 0HJ, ☎ 01450 372311, 10–5 MON–FRI, 10–4 SAT IN SUMMER; 10–4 MON–SAT DURING WINTER (USUALLY JANUARY TO APRIL). **FACTORY SHOP**

Peter Scott is one of the oldest woollen factories in the country. It stocks sweaters for women and men in mainly lambswool, cashmere and lamora. Some of the stock is current season, some discontinued, but there are no seconds. Visit on a weekday and if they haven't got what you want in stock, they can phone up to the factory for it. Opening times are shorter in the winter time so phone first.

THE FACTORY SHOP LTD

DRAKEMYRE, DALRY, AYRSHIRE, SCOTLAND KA24 5JD, ☎ 01294 832791, 10–5 MON–SAT, 11–5 SUN.

54–60 HIGH STREET, ANNAN, DUMFRIES SCOTLAND DG12 6AJ, ☎ 01461 207687, 9–5 MON–SAT, 10.30–4.30 SUN. **FACTORY SHOP**

See page 98 (CHESH)

THE FAMOUS BRUNSWICK WAREHOUSE LTD

UNIT 14, THE LOREBURN CENTRE, HIGH STREET, DUMFRIES, SCOTLAND DG1 2BD, ☎ 01387 268758, **e-mail:** northshoe@mcmail.com, 9–5.30 MON–SAT, 12–4 SUN. **PERMANENT DISCOUNT OUTLET**

See page 98 (CHESH)

TOG 24

GRETNA GATEWAY OUTLET VILLAGE, GLASGOW ROAD, GRETNA, AYRSHIRE, SCOTLAND DG16 5GG, ☎ 01461 339080, **e-mail:** mail-order@tog24.com, www.tog24.com, 10–6 SEVEN DAYS A WEEK. **FACTORY SHOP IN A FACTORY SHOPPING VILLAGE**

See page 99 (CHESH)

TOMMY HILFIGER

UNIT 36-37, GRETNA GATEWAY OUTLET VILLAGE, GRETNA, SCOTLAND DG16 5GG, ☎ 01461 339162, FAX: 01461 339017, www.tommy.com, 10–6 MON– SUN. **FACTORY SHOP IN A FACTORY SHOPPING VILLAGE**

See page 99 (CHESH)

WHITE OF HAWICK

VICTORIA ROAD, HAWICK, SCOTLAND TD9 7AH, ☎ 01450 373206, FAX: 01450 371900, **e-mail:** sales@whiteofhawick.com, www.whiteofhawick.com, 9–5.15 MON–FRI, 9.30–5 SAT. MAIL ORDER ALSO. **PERMANENT DISCOUNT OUTLET**

White of Hawick is a privately owned family-run business selling the highest quality cashmere and lambswool at the keenest prices in the UK, including garments manufactured by top names such as Lyle & Scott, Peter Scott, Johnstons, and White of Hawick. While their shop is not a discount shop as such, everything there is very competitively priced with many items sold at up to one third of the price of the same merchandise in top London department stores. For example, women's round-neck, long-sleeved jumper in 100% single cashmere, from £79; women's high button, long-sleeved cashmere cardigan with contrast trimming, £99; classic long-sleeved turtle neck jumper in 100% single cashmere, from £79; men's long-sleeved, V-neck pullover with saddle shoulders in 100% double cashmere, from £89. Round neck, long-sleeved women's jumper in 100% shrink resistant single geelong lambswool, £39.95; men's long-sleeved V-neck cardigan with two pockets and saddle shoulders in 100% double lambswool from £39.95. Women's fringed cape in 100% woven double lambswool, £26.95. The shop also sells cashmere scarves from £15.95 and lambswool scarves from £2, cashmere and lambswool gloves and all-wool rugs. Also available are four-ply chunky cashmere and factory seconds at unbeatable prices. Mail order brochure available.

CENTRAL SCOTLAND

ANTARTEX VILLAGE VISITOR CENTRE

LOMOND INDUSTRIAL ESTATE, ALEXANDRIA, DUMBARTONSHIRE G83 0TP, ☎ 01389 752393, FAX: 01389 750656, 10–6 SEVEN DAYS A WEEK. **FACTORY SHOP**

Large, rambling building with a coffee shop, well signposted off the A82, which has a vast retail area and additional manufacturing workshops where you can watch sheepskin jackets being made, or enjoy whisky tasting. It's difficult to tell how good the prices are as most are not double ticketed to show the original and sale price, but there are bargain sections. Edinburgh Woollen Mill has a large area, and other labels on sale include Pitlochry, Country Rose and Regatta. As well as clothes and shoes for men (new One Valley range of waterproof jackets, Hippo and PG Fields) and women and children, there are tea towels, toys, books, food, gifts, blankets, mugs, candles, CDs and tapes, table mats, sports equipment and countrywear. There is a big golf department selling Wilson, Spalding and Arnold Palmer equipment at discounts of 20% to 30% and lots of different workshops. Close to the Loch Lomond outlet village.

AQUASCUTUM

ALMONDALE ROAD, MCARTHURGLEN DESIGNER OUTLET VILLAGE, LIVINGSTON, SCOTLAND EH54 6QX, ☎ 01506 400184, 10–6 SEVEN DAYS A WEEK, 8 ON THUR. **FACTORY SHOP**

See page 125 (HERTS)

AUTONOMY

MCARTHURGLEN DESIGNER OUTLET LIVINGSTON, ALMONDVALE AVENUE, LIVINGSTON, WEST LOTHIAN, JUNCTION 3 OFF THE M8, BETWEEN EDINBURGH AND GLASGOW, SCOTLAND EH54 6QX, ☎ 01506 400800, 10–6 MON–SUN, 8 ON THUR. **FACTORY SHOP IN A FACTORY SHOPPING VILLAGE**

See page 93 (CHESH)

BABYGRO LTD

HAYFIELD INDUSTRIAL ESTATE, KIRKCALDY, FIFE, SCOTLAND KY2 5DN, ☎ 01592 647859, FAX: 01592 205284, 10.30–4.30 MON, 9.30–4.30 TUE–SAT (CLOSED FOR LUNCH BETWEEN 1.30 AND 2, MON–SAT), 12.30–4.30 SUN. **FACTORY SHOP**

Sells baby and childrenswear from birth to 16 years, all Marks & Spencer, at discounts of up to 50%. Also womenswear and menswear from Marks & Spencer, Dorothy Perkins, Principles, Next and many other high street stores, all at 50% discount.

BELINDA ROBERTSON LTD

22 PALMERSTON PLACE, EDINBURGH, SCOTLAND EH12 5AL, ☎ 0131 225 1057, FAX: 0131 226 2148, **e-mail:** admin@belindarobertson.co.uk, www.belindarobertson.co.uk, 9–5.30 MON–FRI, 10–4 SAT, OR BY APPOINTMENT. **FACTORY SHOP**

Belinda Robertson's beautiful designer cashmere knitwear is sought after throughout the world, selling in exclusive stores in the USA, Japan and Germany as well as her own flagship store in London, frequented by celebrities and fashion editors. Belinda Robertson was one of the pioneers of the move from traditional, classic cashmere knitwear into contemporary design, fit and colour. Garments are designed and produced in Scotland using the best cashmere yarns and the most skilled workforce available, with the emphasis on producing high quality, fashion garments. The New Town Studio in Edinburgh boasts a light and spacious showroom where customers can buy from a huge variety of samples and stock, discounted by up to 75% less then retail – a real fashion find.

BETHANY

60 HAMILTON PLACE, STOCKBRIDGE, EDINBURGH, SCOTLAND EH3 9ZA, ☎ 0131 220 5656, OPEN 10–5 MON–SAT. **SECONDHAND SHOP**

Charity shop for the Bethany Christian Trust which one reader recommends as selling excellent condition and restored antique furniture, paintings, books, games, clothes and bric a brac.

BIG L FACTORY OUTLET

UNIT 11, MCARTHURGLEN DESIGNER OUTLET LIVINGSTON, ALMONDVALE AVENUE, LIVINGSTON, WEST LOTHIAN, JUNCTION 3 OFF THE M8, BETWEEN EDINBURGH AND GLASGOW, SCOTLAND EH54 6MB, ☎ 01506 461657, FAX: 01506 461657, 10–6 MON–SUN, 8 ON THUR. **FACTORY SHOP IN A FACTORY SHOPPING VILLAGE**

See page 93 (CHESH)

BROUGHTON SHOE WAREHOUSE

62 CRAIGENTINNEY AVENUE, EDINBURGH, SCOTLAND EH6 7LW, 9.30–6 MON–SAT, 8 ON THUR, 11–5 SUN. **PERMANENT DISCOUNT OUTLET**

See page 108 (DERBY)

CASHMERE AT LOCHLEVEN

LOCHLEVEN MILLS, KINROSS, SCOTLAND KY13 8DH, ☎ 01577 861999, 9–5.30 MON–SAT. **FACTORY SHOP**

For over 100 years Todd and Duncan have been spinning finest cashmere yarn by the side of picturesque Loch Leven in Kinross. Their adjacent factory shop acts as an ideal focal point for those eager to purchase sophisticated cashmere lines at affordable prices. Visitors will be captivated by The Cashmere Story, a visually stimulating pictorial history of the journey taken by cashmere from the barren plains of Mongolia, through the traditional Scottish yarn spinning processes, and on to its final destination – the catwalks of the world's leading fashion designers. The shop provides a terrific selection of clothing of perfect quality, with no damaged goods or seconds. Labels stocked include their own popular Kinross Cashmere label, as well as complementary classics from famed collections such as Daks, Henri White, and Barrie, and the full Pringle range of both men's and women's fashion sportswear. The shop and visitors' centre are located about half an hour's drive from Edinburgh and just five minutes from the M90 motorway.

CATALOGUE BARGAIN SHOP

315–317 HIGH STREET, COWDENBEATH, FIFE, SCOTLAND KY4 9QJ, ☎ 01383 611054, www.bargaincrazy.com, 9–5.30 MON–SAT, 11–4 SUN.

12–16 CADZOW STREET, HAMILTON, LANARKSHIRE, SCOTLAND ML3 6DG, ☎ 01698 421112, www.bargaincrazy.com, 9–5.30 MON–SAT, 12–4 SUN.

THE FORGE SHOPPING CENTRE, PARKHEAD, GLASGOW, SCOTLAND G31 4EB, ☎ 0141 556 5352, www.bargaincrazy.com, 9–6 MON–SAT, 11–5 SUN. **PERMANENT DISCOUNT OUTLET**

See page 92 (CAMBS)

CHARLES CLINKARD

STERLING MILLS DESIGNER OUTLET VILLAGE, DEVONVALE, TILLICOULTRY, CLACKMANNANSHIRE FK13 6HQ, ☎ 01259 753001, FAX: 01259 753001 10–6 MON–SAT, 10–5 SUN.

FREEPORT LEISURE SCOTLAND, FIVE SISTERS, WEST WOOD, WEST CALDER, WEST LOTHIAN SCOTLAND EH55 8BQ, ☎ 01501 763650, FAX: 01501 763650, 10–6 MON–SAT, 8 ON THUR, 11–5 SUN. **FACTORY SHOP IN A FACTORY SHOPPING VILLAGE**

See page 101 (CO DURH)

CLARKS FACTORY SHOP

UNIT 26, PARKHEAD FORGE SHOPPING CENTRE, PARKHEAD, GLASGOW, LANARKSHIRE SCOTLAND G31 4EB, ☎ 0141 556 5290, 9.30–5.30 MON–SAT, 12–4.30 SUN.

UNITS 31–35, ALMONDVALE AVENUE, LIVINGSTON, WEST LOTHIAN, SCOTLAND EH54 6HR, ☎ 01506 461376, 10–6 MON–SAT, 8 ON THUR, 10–6 SUN. **FACTORY SHOP**

See page 94 (CHESH)

CLEARMART

32–33 NEW KIRKGATE, LEITH, EDINBURGH, SCOTLAND EH6 6AB, ☎ 0131 553 3073, 9–5 MON–SAT. **FACTORY SHOP**

Damart underwear and merchandise – anything from tights, socks and gloves to dresses, coats, cardigans and jumpers – discontinued and ends of lines sold at discount.

COSALT INTERNATIONAL LTD

UNIT 7, WEST SHORE TRADING ESTATE, WEST SHORE ROAD, GRANTON, EDINBURGH SCOTLAND EH5 1QF, ☎ 0131 552 0011, www.cosalt.co.uk, 8–5 MON–FRI. **PERMANENT DISCOUNT OUTLET**

See page 145 (LINCS)

DESIGNER EXCHANGE – THE ADDRESS

3 ROYAL EXCHANGE COURT, OFF 17 ROYAL EXCHANGE SQUARE, GLASGOW, SCOTLAND G1 3DB, ☎ 0141 221 6898, **e-mail:** designerexchange@hotmail.com, 10–5 TUE–SAT. CLOSED MONDAYS. **DRESS AGENCY**

A warm, inviting shop tucked away, yet in the heart of the city centre, has just celebrated 11 years in business. Sharp-eyed lovers of style travel from afar to this exciting shop which is full of new and nearly-new designer clothes and accessories ranging from Chanel, Armani, Versace and Moschino to high-fashion high street names such as Whistles, Jigsaw, Kookai and Morgan. Stock turns around quickly with new items arriving daily, all of which are personally selected by the owners. Items come from all over the UK, many from well-known celebrities. Customers can browse in a relaxed, fun and low-pressure environment, where an honest opinion is always given. Examples of prices Armani trouser suit £149 from £700, Escada jacket, £99 from £500, Prada bag £120 from £380, Moschino dress £85 from £360, Hermes scarf £45 from £180.

DESIGNER SHADES

MCARTHURGLEN DESIGNER OUTLET LIVINGSTON, ALMONDVALE AVENUE, LIVINGSTON, WEST LOTHIAN, JUNCTION 3 OFF THE M8, BETWEEN EDINBURGH AND GLASGOW, SCOTLAND EH54 6QX, ☎ 01506 461177, **e-mail:** info@sunglass-time.com, 10–6 MON–WED, SAT, SUN. 10–8 THUR, FRI. **PERMANENT DISCOUNT OUTLET**

See page 116 (DORS)

DOUBLE TWO

UNIT 38, STIRLING MILLS DESIGNER OUTLET VILLAGE, MOSS ROAD, TILLICOULTRY, CLACKMANNANSHIRE, SCOTLAND FK13 6HN, ☎ 01259 753727, 10–6 MON– SUN.
UNIT G4, FREEPORT SCOTLAND, WESTWOOD, WEST CALDER, WEST LOTHIAN, SCOTLAND EH55 8QB, ☎ 01501 762809, 10–6 SEVEN DAYS A WEEK, 8 ON THUR. **FACTORY SHOP**

See page 116 (ESSEX)

FREEPORT SCOTLAND OUTLET VILLAGE

FIVE SISTERS, WESTWOOD, WEST CALDER, NEAR JUNCTION 4 OF THE M8, WEST LOTHIAN, SCOTLAND EH55 8QB, ☎ 01501 763488, www.freeportscotland.com, 10–6 SEVEN DAYS A WEEK. **FACTORY SHOPPING VILLAGE**

Designer outlet village with more than 25 shops offering up to 50% off high street prices, as well as a café and free parking. Outlets for women include The Designer Room, Mexx, London Leathers, Versace, Klass, Select, Iceberg and Jean Scene. Menswear is available from Ciro Citterio, Versace, Double Two, Madhouse, Leading Labels, Iceberg, Mexx, Nickleby's and Proibito. Sweet-toothed visitors can savour the chocolates at Thorntons. Other shops include Tog 24, Bags Etc, Charles Clinkard, Outdoor Adventure, Book Depot, Churchill China and Ponden Mill.

GAP

MCARTHURGLEN OUTLET VILLAGE, ALMONDVALE AVENUE, LIVINGSTON, WEST LOTHIAN, JUNCTION 3 OFF THE M8, BETWEEN EDINBURGH AND GLASGOW, SCOTLAND EH54 6QX, ☎ 01506 419899, 10–6 MON, TUE, 10–8 WED, THUR, FRI, 10–6 SAT, SUN. **FACTORY SHOP IN A FACTORY SHOPPING VILLAGE**

Gap sells casual clothes for men, women, babies and children, discounted at this factory outlet village by a minimum of 30% and as much as 80% to 90%.

GLADRAGS

17 HENDERSON ROW, EDINBURGH SCOTLAND EH3 5DH, ☎ 0131 557 1916, 10.30–6 TUE–SAT. SECONDHAND AND VINTAGE CLOTHES. **SECONDHAND SHOP**

Gladrags has a selection of exquisite vintage clothes, accessories and costume jewellery, lace-edged table and bed linen and paisley shawls. Next door, Wild Rose is a distinctive shop selling decorative/functional silver, women's and men's jewellery, porcelain, pottery, glass and metalware.

HAVEN

473 HILLINGTON ROAD, HILLINGTON INDUSTRIAL ESTATE, GLASGOW, DUMBARTONSHIRE G52 4QX, ☎ 0141 883 4801, 7.50–4 MON–THUR, 7.50–2.50 FRI. **PERMANENT DISCOUNT OUTLET**

A sheltered workshop owned by the Haven Products Trust to whom all the profits go. It sells women's, men's and children's knitwear. Many of the products are high street and brand names at reduced prices.

JAEGER/VIYELLA FACTORY SHOP

ALMONDVALE AVENUE, LIVINGSTON, MCARTHURGLEN DESIGNER OUTLET LIVINGSTON, WEST LOTHIAN, JUNCTION 3 OFF THE M8, BETWEEN EDINBURGH AND GLASGOW, SCOTLAND EH54 6QX, ☎ 01506 460673, 10–6 MON–FRI, 8 ON THUR, 9–6 SAT, 10–6 SUN. **FACTORY SHOP**

See page 158 (NORF)

LEITH MILLS

70–74 BANGOR ROAD, OFF GREAT JUNCTION STREET, LEITH, EDINBURGH, SCOTLAND EH6 5JU, ☎ 0131 553 5161, FAX: 0131 553 4415, SUMMER: 9–5.30 MON–SAT, 10–5 SUN, WINTER 10–5 MON–SAT, 10–5 SUN. **PERMANENT DISCOUNT OUTLET**

Leith Mills is one of those places I find hard to place among discounters and factory shops. It's not really a factory shop as the stock is not made on site but bought in from all over Scotland, but it does claim to be very competitively priced. The only time prices may be equal with those in the high street is when the latter is on sale. As I'm not familiar with prices in Edinburgh, I couldn't tell how much of a good deal they were. Leith Mills is a very big outlet with plenty of car parking. It houses the Edinburgh Woollen Mill, James Pringle and the Clan Tartan Centre where you can trace your clan history and print a scroll. The men's department houses Antartex sweaters, Harris Tweed, One Valley, Clan Royal sweaters, Tulchan knitwear, T-shirts and trousers. The women's department has Country Rose knitwear, blouses, shawls, pleated tartan skirts, Arran knits, gloves, scarves, hats, a shoe department, Ponden Mills, a golf shop and a cashmere shop. There is a very small children's clothing section and also a department selling tapes, teddies, cushions, books, silver spoons, Edinburgh and Stuart Crystal, Portmeirion china and Caithness giftware but at the normal shop prices. A new additions is a whisky shop boasting over 100 malts. There is a coffee shop on site and a small food gift area.

LILLEY & SKINNER

ALMONDVALE AVENUE, LIVINGSTON, MCARTHURGLEN DESIGNER OUTLET LIVINGSTON, WEST LOTHIAN, JUNCTION 3 OFF THE M8, BETWEEN EDINBURGH AND GLASGOW, SCOTLAND EH54 6QX, ☎ 0800 3164352 FREE INFORMATION LINE, www.mcarthurglen.com, 10 -8 MON–FRI, 10–7 SAT, 10–6 SUN. **FACTORY SHOP IN A FACTORY SHOPPING VILLAGE**

See page 109 (DERBY)

LOCH LOMOND FACTORY OUTLETS

MAIN STREET, ALEXANDRIA, JUNCTION 17 OF M8 THEN A82, LOCH LOMOND, SCOTLAND G83 0UG, ☎ 01389 710077, FAX: 01389 605500 INFORMATION LINE, ☎ 01389 607259, **e-mail:** info@lochlomondoutlets.co.uk, www.lochlomondoutletcentre.co.uk, 9.30–5.30 SEVEN DAYS A WEEK. **FACTORY SHOPPING VILLAGE**

Just off the A82, the main route between Glasgow and the West Highlands and Islands, and only one mile from Loch Lomond, this factory outlet centre combines history, heritage, adventure and shopping under one roof. Shops include Bags Etc selling luggage items; Book Depot, Designer Room (Klass, DKNY, Elle), Global Emporium for gifts, Jean Scene for branded denim wear; Julian Graves foods and nut mixes; Leading Labels, Nickleby's, Pavers Shoes, Ponden Mill for bed-linen and bathroom ware; Ramseys womenswear; Room offering homes accessories and furniture; Stuart Crystal; Sportz selling sportswear from Adidas, Nike, etc; Tog 24 for outdoor wear; Trespass; Card & Party Place (greetings cards and posters). There is also Ceramic Experience (a unique opportunity to decorate your own ceramics and pottery merchandise plus a children's soft play area), a Motoring Heritage Centre telling the history of the Scottish motor car industry with a collection of vintage cars, and The Gallery Cafe selling meals, snacks and sandwiches.

LONDON LEATHERS DIRECT WEST

FREEPORT VILLAGE, WEST CALDER, WEST LOTHIAN, SCOTLAND EH55 8QB, ☎ 01501 762405, FAX: 01501 763427, 10–6 SEVEN DAYS A WEEK, 8 ON THUR. **FACTORY SHOP IN A FACTORY SHOPPING VILLAGE**

See page 136 (LANCS)

MACKINNON MILLS

KIRKSHAW ROAD, COATBRIDGE, SCOTLAND ML5 4SL, ☎ 01236 440702, 10–5.30 MON–FRI, 10–6 SAT–SUN. **FACTORY SHOP**

Working woollen mill that sells some seconds and perfect woollens with labels such as Lyle & Scott, Antartex and Edinburgh Woollen Mill. They also sell golf equipment, Scottish music tapes, dress jewellery, books, shoes, bags and bedding. Meals are served in the coffee shop.

MARKS & SPENCER

MCARTHURGLEN DESIGNER OUTLET VILLAGE LIVINGSTON, ALMONDVALE AVENUE, WEST LOTHIAN, SCOTLAND EH54 6QX, ☎ 01506 418206, 10–6 MON, TUE, SAT, SUN, 10–8 WED–FRI. **FACTORY SHOP IN A FACTORY SHOPPING VILLAGE**

See page 96 (CHESH)

MATALAN

UNIT 13A, WEST LODGE ROAD, RENFREW, BLYTHSWOOD SCOTLAND PA4 9EN, ☎ 0141 886 8050, FAX: 0141 886 2447, www.matalan.co.uk, 9.30–8 MON–FRI, 9.30–5.30 SAT, 10–6 SUN.

CLYDE RETAIL PARK, LIVINGSTONE STREET, CLYDEBANK, GLASGOW, SCOTLAND G81 2XA, ☎ 0141 435 7450, FAX: 0141 952 0415, www.matalan.co.uk, 10–8 MON–FRI, 8–5.30 SAT, 10–6 SUN.

UNIT 2, FARADAY RETAIL PARK, WHIFFLET STREET/COATBANK STREET, COATBRIDGE, LANARKSHIRE ML5 3SP, ☎ 01244 665260, FAX: 01236 423950, www.matalan.co.uk, 10–8 MON–FRI, 10–6 SAT, 10–6 SUN.

NITSHILL ROAD, DARNLEY, GLASGOW SCOTLAND G53 7BW, ☎ 0141 880 3900, FAX: 0141 880 4958, www.matalan.co.uk, 10–8 MON–FRI, 9.30–6 SAT, 10–6 SUN.

155 SLATEFORD ROAD, EDINBURGH SCOTLAND EH14 1NZ, ☎ 0131 455 7224, FAX: 0131 443 2570, www.matalan.co.uk, 10–8 MON–FRI, 8.30–5.30 SAT, 10–6 SUN.

CARRON ROAD, BAINESFORD, FALKIRK, SCOTLAND FK1, FAX: 01324 614130, FAX: 01324 627149, www.matalan.co.uk, 10–8 MON–FRI, 10–6 SAT, SUN.

SALTAIRE RETAIL PARK, PENTLAND PARK, GLENROTHES, SCOTLAND KY6 2AL, ☎ 01592 776860, FAX: 01592 773354, www.matalan.co.uk, 10–8 MON–FRI, 9.30–5.30 SAT, 10–6 SUN.

LORENY INDUSTRIAL ESTATE, UMBERLEY ROAD, KILMARNOCK SCOTLAND KA1 5LB, ☎ 01563 555040, FAX: 01563 549832, www.matalan.co.uk, 10–8 MON–FRI, 9.30–5.30 SAT, 10–6 SUN.

3–4 SEAFIELD WAY, SEAFIELD ROAD, LEITH, EDINBURGH, SCOTLAND EH15 1TB, ☎ 0131 657 5045, FAX: 0131 657 5046, www.matalan.co.uk, 10–8 MON–FRI, 9.30–5.30 SAT, 10–6 SUN.

PHOENIX RETAIL PARK, LINWOOD ROAD, PAISLEY, SCOTLAND PA1 2AB, ☎ 0141 840 5120, FAX: 0141 849 7109, www.matalan.co.uk, 10–8 MON–FRI, 9–6 SAT, 10–6 SUN.

UNIT 5, CALEDONIAN CENTRE, NEW ASHTREE INDUSTRIAL ESTATE, WISHAW, LANARKSHIRE ML2 7UR, ☎ 01698 357075, FAX: 01698 357072, www.matalan.co.uk, 10–9 MON–FRI, 9.30–6.30 SAT, 10–6 SUN. **PERMANENT DISCOUNT OUTLET**

See page 89 (BEDS)

MCARTHURGLEN DESIGNER OUTLET LIVINGSTON

ALMONDVALE AVENUE, LIVINGSTON, WEST LOTHIAN, JUNCTION 3 OFF THE M8, BETWEEN EDINBURGH AND GLASGOW, SCOTLAND EH54 6QX, ☎ 01506 423600, FAX: 01506 423602, www.mcarthurglen.com/livingston, 10–6 SEVEN DAYS A WEEK, 8 ON THUR. **FACTORY SHOPPING VILLAGE**

The McArthurGlen Designer Outlet Livingston offers over 80 stores full of top brands and designer labels at up to 50% off typical retail prices. There is a food court, cafés and restaurants as well as an eight-screen licensed cinema, health and fitness club and free parking for 1,800 cars. Stores include: Gap Outlet, XS, Designer Shades, Marks & Spencer Outlet, The Body Shop Outlet, Van Heusen/Jaeger/Viyella, One to One, Antler, Clarks, Suits You, Chappelle, Banana Books, Toyworld, Donnay, Whittard, Price's Candles, Aquascutum, Revlon, The Paper Mill Shop, Regatta, Jane Shilton, Brand Fushion, Early Learning Centre, CK Jeans, Jockey, Autonomy, Cotton Traders, Black and Decker, Room, Surf, Skate and Snow, Ronit Zilkha, Ted Baker, Proudfoot, Thornton's, Arran Aromatics, Bon Bleu, Jokids, Soled Out, Windsmoor, Suit Co, Easy Jeans, Roman Originals, Julian Graves, Directions, Sportz, Lilley & Skinner, Armani, Ben Sherman, Petroleum, Samsonite, Tog 24, Outdoor Scene, Trespass, Logo, Levi's, Professional Cookware, Coloroll, Jane Heath, Bed & Bath, Denby, Pictureport, Waterford/Wedgewood, Poole Pottery, Lights 4 Less, Cloverhouse, Gleneagles, Edinburgh Crystal, and Speigelau.

MEXX INTERNATIONAL WEST

FREEPORT VILLAGE FIVE SISTERS, WESTWOOD, WEST CALDER, NEAR JUNCTION 4 OF THE M8, WEST LOTHIAN, SCOTLAND EH55 8QB, ☎ 01501 763320, 10–6 SEVEN DAYS A WEEK, 8 ON THUR. **FACTORY SHOP**

See page 97 (CHESH)

NEXT TO NOTHING

49–53 UNION STREET, GLASGOW, SCOTLAND G1 3RB, ☎ 0141 221 7100, www.next.co.uk, 10–6 MON–FRI, 7 ON THUR, 9–6 SAT, 11–5 SUN. **PERMANENT DISCOUNT OUTLET**

See page 97 (CHESH)

NIKE FACTORY STORE

UNIT 28, STERLING MILLS DESIGNER OUTLET VILLAGE, TILLICOULTRY, CLACKMANNANSHIRE, SCOTLAND FK13 6HN, ☎ 01259 750148, FAX: 01259 753867, www.nike.com, 10–6 SEVEN DAYS A WEEK. **FACTORY SHOP IN A FACTORY SHOPPING VILLAGE**

See page 191 (WILTS)

PUTTING ON THE RITZ

THE VICTORIAN VILLAGE, 93 WEST REGENT STREET, GLASGOW, SCOTLAND G2 2BA, ☎ 0141 332 9808, **e-mail:** vikkivillage@hotmail.com, 10–5 MON–SAT. **SECONDHAND AND VINTAGE CLOTHES**

Retro jewellery, marcasite and Fifties silver, nightwear, Paisley shawls, vintage dinner suits and tuxedos, Thirties and Forties sportswear, riding boots, stetsons, Thirties USA football outfits. Jewellery from £5, dinner suits from £15. Unusual gifts, exciting decorative items, interior furnishings, small pieces of furniture, also stocked, as well as Victorian jewellery and original Scottish agate jewellery.

REGATTA

MCARTHURGLEN DESIGNER OUTLET VILLAGE, ALMONDALE AVENUE, LIVINGSTON, SCOTLAND EH54 6QX, ☎ 01506 429813, FAX: 01506 429813, www.regatta.com, 10–6 SEVEN DAYS A WEEK, 8 ON THUR. **FACTORY SHOP IN A FACTORY SHOPPING VILLAGE**

See page 118 (ESSEX)

STARRY STARRY NIGHT

19–21 DOWANSIDE LANE, GLASGOW, SCOTLAND G12 9BZ, ☎ 0141 337 1837, 10–5.30 MON–SAT. **SECONDHAND AND VINTAGE CLOTHES**

Retro gear, especially evening gowns, menswear, including morning coats, tails and striped blazers from Victorian through the Twenties and Thirties to Sixties and Seventies gear. Morning suits, £35; dinner suits, £30; leather jackets, £15 to £25; evening gowns, £10 upwards; waistcoats, collarless shirts, bow ties and costume jewellery. Hire service available. They are constantly looking for Seventies stock, in particular Biba, Pucci, Jeff Banks, Ozzie Clark. Also sells white table linen and lace.

STERLING MILLS DESIGNER OUTLET VILLAGE

TILLICOULTRY, NEAR STIRLING, CLACKMANNANSHIRE, MIDWAY BETWEEN M9 AND M90, SCOTLAND FK13 6HQ, ☎ 01259 752100, www.sterlingmills.com, 10–6 SEVEN DAYS A WEEK.

FACTORY SHOPPING VILLAGE

This factory shopping centre guarantees prices of at least 30% off typical high street prices and sometimes as much as 70%. Outlets so far include Mountain Warehouse, Adidas, Penny Plain, Enigma Candles, Jacques Vert, The Officers' Club, Bed & Bath Works, Book Depot, Claire's Accessories, Cotton Traders, Denby Pottery, Designer Room, Double Two, Julian Graves, Nike, Nickelby's, Pavers Shoes, Proibito, Roman Originals, Thorntons, Tog 24, Bags Etc, USA Golf Wear House, VF Corporation Factory Store, Winning Line, XS Music, Charles Clinkard, Naf Naf Chevignon, The Toy Factory, Pilot, Real Jewellery, The Sweet Factory, The Design House, Watson Chilli Pepper, Regatta, Blue Ridge, Playtex and more. There's a restaurant on site, and the very large Sterling Furniture Centre is situated opposite.

T J HUGHES

127–135 TRONGATE, GLASGOW, SCOTLAND G1 5HG, ☎ 0141 548 8400, FAX: 0141 552 6297, **e-mail:** info@tjhughes.co.uk, www.tjhughes.co.uk, 9–5.30 MON– FRI, 8 ON THUR, 9–6 SAT, 11–5 SUN. **PERMANENT DISCOUNT OUTLET**

See page 98 (CHESH)

THE FACTORY SHOP LTD

56 CHAPEL STREET, CARLUKE, SOUTH LANARKSHIRE, SCOTLAND ML8 4BA, ☎ 01555 759017, FAX: 01555 759018, 9–5 MON–FRI, 9–5.30 SAT, 10–5 SUN.

BURNSIDE MILL, CUPAR, FIFE SCOTLAND KY15 4DQ, ☎ 01334 650661, FAX: 01334 656772, 9.30–5.30 MON–SAT, 10–5 SUN. **FACTORY SHOP**

See page 98 (CHESH)

THE FAMOUS BRUNSWICK WAREHOUSE LTD

UNIT 1, KILBOWIE RETAIL PARK, CLYDEBANK, SCOTLAND G81 4QH, ☎ 0141 952 4914, **e-mail:** northshoe@mcmail.com, 10–6 MON–SAT, 7 ON THUR, 10–5 SUN.

UNIT 3, FARADAY RETAIL PARK, COATBRIDGE, SCOTLAND ML5 3SQ, ☎ 01236 449095, **e-mail:** northshoe@mcmail.com, 10–6 MON–WED, 10–8 THUR, FRI, 9–6 SAT, 10–6 SUN.

ST JAMES RETAIL PARK, DUMBARTON, SCOTLAND G82 1RB, ☎ 01389 762897, **e-mail:** northshoe@mcmail.com, 10–6 MON–WED, SAT, SUN, 10–7 THUR, 9–6 FRI.

UNIT 8, MEADOWBANK RETAIL PARK, MARIONVILLE ROAD, EDINBURGH, SCOTLAND EH7, FAX: 0131 652 2885, **e-mail:** northshoe@mcmail.com, 10–6 MON–WED, 10–8 THUR, 10–7 FRI, 9–6 SAT, 11–5 SUN.

11 GRAHAMS ROAD, CENTRAL RETAIL PARK, FALKIRK, SCOTLAND FK1 1LD, ☎ 01324 671177, **e-mail:** northshoe@mcmail.com, 10–6 MON–WED, 10–7 THUR, FRI, 9–6 SAT, 10–5 SUN.

UNIT 9, HAMILTON RETAIL PARK, DOUGLAS STREET, HAMILTON, SCOTLAND ML3 0DF, ☎ 01698 286120, **e-mail:** northshoe@mcmail.com, 10–7 MON–FRI, 8 ON THUR, 9–6 SAT, 10–6 SUN.

UNIT 4, PHASE 2, RIVERWAY RETAIL PARK, IRVINE, SCOTLAND KA12 8AG, ☎ 01294 204042, **e-mail:** northshoe@mcmail.com, 9–6 MON–WED, SAT, 9–7 THUR, FRI, 10–6 SUN.

PORTLAND GATE, KILMARNOCK, SCOTLAND KA1 1HZ, ☎ 01563 537145, **e-mail:** northshoe@mcmail.com, 9–5.30 MON–WED, 9–6 THUR–SAT, 11–5 SUN.

8–20 HIGH STREET, KIRKCALDY, SCOTLAND KY1 1LU, ☎ 01592 205257, **e-mail:** northshoe@mcmail.com, 9–6 MON–SAT, 11–5 SUN.

UNITS 55A AND 25, THE PLAZA SHOPPING CENTRE, PAISLEY, SCOTLAND PA1 1EL, ☎ 0141 848 9127, **e-mail:** northshoe@mcmail.com, 9–6 MON–SAT, 11–5 SUN.

UNIT 3A, WEST END RETAIL PARK, CROW ROAD, PARTICK, GLASGOW, SCOTLAND G11 7SA, ☎ 0141 337 3822, **e-mail:** northshoe@mcmail.com, 10–6 MON–WED, 10–8 THUR, 10–7 FRI, 9–6 SAT, 10–6 SUN.

181 NETHERAULD HOUSE ROAD, POLLOCKSHAWS, GLASGOW, SCOTLAND G43 2YP, ☎ 0141 632 5841, **e-mail:** northshoe@mcmail.com, 10–6 MON–WED, 10–7 THUR, FRI, 9–6 SAT, 10–5.30 SUN.

UNIT 10, THE CALEDONIAN CENTRE, NEW ASHTREE STREET, WISHAW, SCOTLAND ML2 7UR, ☎ 01698 350055, **e-mail:** northshoe@mcmail.com, 10–6 MON–WED, 10–8 THUR, FRI, 9–6 SAT, 10–6 SUN. **PERMANENT DISCOUNT OUTLET**

See page 98 (CHESH)

THE MILL TRAIL

THE MILL TRAIL VISITOR CENTRE, ALVA, CLACKMANNANSHIRE, SCOTLAND FK12 5EN, ☎ 01259 769696, **e-mail:** info@scottish.heartlands.org www.visitscottishheartlands.org, 10–5 SEVEN DAYS A WEEK, 9–5 DURING JULY TO SEPTEMBER. **FACTORY SHOP**

Follow the mill trail and you're guaranteed a great shopping experience. A visit to Scotland's Mill Trail Visitor Centre takes you back 150 years to discover what life was like in the mill factories of the time. Relax in the Ochil View Coffee Shop, before discovering a variety of shops – some factory shops, some not – offering a wide range of products, including cashmere, jewellery, art and chocolate. Admission is free.

TK MAXX

UNIT 10 MEADOW BANK RETAIL PARK, EDINBURGH, SCOTLAND EH7 5TS, ☎ 0131 661 6611, www.tkmaxx.com, 10–8 MON–FRI, 9–6 SAT, 11–5 SUN.

UNIT C1261, CALLENDER SQUARE SHOPPING CENTRE, HIGH STREET, FALKIRK, SCOTLAND FK1 1UU, ☎ 01324 619881, www.tkmaxx.com, 9–5.30 MON–WED, 7.30 ON THUR, 9–6 FRI–SAT, 12–5 SUN.

THE SAUCHIEHALL CENTRE, GLASGOW, SCOTLAND G2 3ER, ☎ 0141 331 0411, www.tkmaxx.com, 9–5.30 MON–FRI, 7 ON THUR, 9–6 SAT, 12–5 SUN.

UNIT 5, ST ENOCH'S CENTRE, 55 ST ENOCH'S SQUARE, GLASGOW, SCOTLAND G1 4BW, ☎ 0141 221 9393, www.tkmaxx.com, 9–6 MON–FRI, 8 ON THUR, 9.30–6 SAT, 11–5 SUN.

GLENCAIRN RETAIL PARK, KILMARNOCK, SCOTLAND, ☎ 01563 532486, www.tkmaxx.com, PHONE FOR DETAILS.

UNIT 25–26 MERCAT CENTRE, KIRKCALDY, FIFE, SCOTLAND KY1 1N1, FAX: 01592 644488, www.tkmaxx.com, 9–5.30 MON– SAT, 11–5 SUN.

UNIT 5, ALMONDVALE WEST RETAIL PARK, ALMONDVALE ROAD, LIVINGSTON, SCOTLAND EH54 6QX, ☎ 01506 462060, www.tkmaxx.com, 10–8 MON–FRI, 9–6 SAT, 11–5 SUN.

THE PHOENIX RETAIL PARK, LINWOOD ROAD, PAISLEY, SCOTLAND, ☎ 0141 849 6796, www.tkmaxx.com, PHONE FOR DETAILS.

ST CATHERINE'S RETAIL PARK, SCOTLAND, ☎ 01738 636751, www.tkmaxx.com, PHONE FOR DETAILS. **PERMANENT DISCOUNT OUTLET**

See page 89 (BEDS)

TOG 24

LOCH LOMOND FACTORY OUTLETS, MAIN STREET, ALEXANDRIA, STRATHCLYDE, SCOTLAND G83 0UG, ☎ 01389 607175, **e-mail:** mail-order@tog24.com, www.tog24.com, 9.30–5.30 SEVEN DAYS A WEEK.

MCARTHURGLEN DESIGNER OUTLET LIVINGSTON, ALMONDVALE AVENUE, LIVINGSTON, SCOTLAND EH54 6QX, ☎ 01506 413630, **e-mail:** mail-order@tog24.com, www.tog24.com, 10–6 SEVEN DAYS A WEEK, 8 ON THUR.

STERLING MILLS DESIGNER OUTLET VILLAGE, TILLICOULTRY, CLACKMANNANSHIRE, SCOTLAND FK13 6HN, ☎ 01259 753911, **e-mail:** mail-order@tog24.com, www.tog24.com, 10–6 SEVEN DAYS A WEEK.

FREEPORT VILLAGE FIVE SISTERS, WEST CALDER, JUNCTION 4 OF M8, WEST LOTHIAN, SCOTLAND EH55 8QB, ☎ 01501 762823, **e-mail:** mail-order@tog24.com, www.tog24.com, 10–6 SEVEN DAYS A WEEK. **FACTORY SHOP IN A FACTORY SHOPPING VILLAGE**

See page 99 (CHESH)

WARNERS WEST

UNIT B6–7, FREEPORT LEISURE (SCOTLAND), FIVE SISTERS, WESTWOOD, WEST CALDER, WEST LOTHIAN, SCOTLAND EH55 8QB, ☎ 01501 762804, 10–6 SEVEN DAYS A WEEK, 8 ON THUR. **FACTORY SHOP IN A FACTORY SHOPPING VILLAGE**

See page 100 (CHESH)

WRANGLER LEE

STERLING MILLS DESIGNER OUTLET, MOSS ROAD, TILLYCOULTRY, CLACKMANNANSHIRE FK13 6NH, ☎ 01259 753735, 10–6 SEVEN DAYS A WEEK. **FACTORY SHOP IN A FACTORY SHOPPING VILLAGE**

See page 142 (LANCS)

SCOTTISH HIGHLANDS AND ISLANDS

DAMART

36–40 MARKET STREET, ABERDEEN, SCOTLAND AB1 2PL, ☎ 01224 571146, 9.30–5 MON–SAT. **FACTORY SHOP**

See page 114 (DORS)

FOOTWEAR DISCOUNT CENTRE

JOHN STREET, OBAN, SCOTLAND PA34 5NS, ☎ 01631 563633, **e-mail:** billyt@eggconnect.net 9–5.30 MON–SAT, 11–4 SUN. **PERMANENT DISCOUNT OUTLET**

Two floors of more than 10,000 pairs of quality branded footwear such as Ecco, Lotus, Nil Simile and Equity, some of which are seconds, discontinued lines, factory directs and Italian imports. Women's shoes, fashion courts to leather walking shoes, from size 2 to 9. Men's leather shoes in sizes 5 to 13, including walking boots, trainers, work boots and safety boots. Children's shoes and Wellingtons.

GLENEAGLES KNITWEAR COMPANY

ABBEY ROAD, AUCHTERARDER, TAYSIDE, SCOTLAND PH3 1DP, ☎ 01764 662112, 9–5 MON–SAT. **FACTORY SHOP**

Perfect knitwear for women and men including cardigans, jumpers and socks. Also stocks coats and jackets, jumpers by Johnstons of Elgin and cashmere made to order.

JOHNSTONS OF ELGIN

CASHMERE VISITORS CENTRE, NEW MILL, ELGIN, SCOTLAND 1V30 4AF, ☎ 01343 554099, FAX: 01343 554080, www.johnstonscashmere.com, 9–5.30 MON–SAT, 11–5 SUN APRIL–DECEMBER. **FACTORY SHOP**

A genuine factory shop where visitors can be guided around the only mill to convert cashmere from fibre to garment. The fibres are dyed, spun, woven/knitted and finished into luxury clothing, scarves, rugs and sweaters. Cashmere scarves from £20, cashmere sweaters from £70 and many more bargains throughout the shop. There is a coffee shop on site, disabled access and ample parking (coaches by appointment).

K SHOES FACTORY SHOP

UNIT 26A, WELLGATE, DUNDEE, ANGUS, SCOTLAND DD1 1DB, ☎ 01382 322048, 9.30–5.30 MON– SAT, 12–4 SUN. **FACTORY SHOP**

See page 105 (CUMB)

MACGILLIVRAY & CO

BALIVANICH, BENBECULA, WESTERN ISLES, SCOTLAND HS7 5LA, ☎ 01870 602525, FAX: 01870 602981, 9.30–5 MON–FRI, CLOSED 1–2, 9.30–4 SAT. MAIL ORDER. **FACTORY SHOP**

The MacGillivray Company has been selling handwoven Harris tweed and hand-knitted sweaters all over the world since 1941. Usually hand-knitted sweaters in pure new wool cost from £60 and 72cm (28in) wide Harris tweed costs £14.25 a metre (£12.95 a yard). They sometimes hold a stock of special offer fabrics, which they obtain from various mills throughout Britain. Because these are surplus stock, cancelled export orders or out-of-season fabrics, they can be sold at less than half the original selling price. These can range from Scottish tweeds, Shetlands, Donegals, dress and fancy fabrics, suitings and coatings. Send for a brochure and sample swatches. Worldwide mail order service.

MATALAN

CONSTITUTION STREET, ABERDEEN SCOTLAND AB24 5ET, ☎ 01224 650690, FAX: 01224 624235, www.matalan.co.uk, 10–8 MON–FRI, 9.30–5.30 SAT, 10–6 SUN.

UNIT1, INCHES RETAIL PARK, INVERNESS, SCOTLAND IV2 3TW, ☎ 01463 227250, FAX: 01463 224772, www.matalan.co.uk, 10–8 MON–FRI, 9.30–5.30 SAT, 10–6 SUN.

VICTORIA ROAD, PERTH, SCOTLAND PH8 9LW, ☎ 01738 587020, FAX: 01738 443883, www.matalan.co.uk, 10–8 MON–FRI, 9.30–5.30 SAT, 10–6 SUN. **PERMANENT DISCOUNT OUTLET**

See page 89 (BEDS)

TK MAXX

KITTY BREWSTER RETAIL PARK, BEDFORD ROAD, ABERDEEN, SCOTLAND, ☎ 01224 497810, www.tkmaxx.com, PHONE FOR DETAILS.

WELLGATE SHOPPING CENTRE, DUNDEE SCOTLAND DD1 2DB, ☎ 01382 322288, www.tkmaxx.com, 9–5.30 MON–WED, FRI, SAT, 9–8 THUR, 12–5 SUN.

UNIT 2, ACADEMY RETAIL PARK, STROTHERS LANE, INVERNESS, SCOTLAND, ☎ 01463 729729, www.tkmaxx.com, 9–5.30 MON–FRI, 7 ON THUR, 9–6 SAT. **PERMANENT DISCOUNT OUTLET**

See page 89 (BEDS)

TOG 24

CITY QUAY, CAMPERDOWN STREET, DUNDEE, SCOTLAND DD1 3ND, ☎ 01382 223883, **e-mail:** mail-order@tog24.com, www.tog24.com, 9.30–5.30 MON–SAT, 11–5 SUN. **FACTORY SHOP**

See page 99 (CHESH)

NORTHERN IRELAND

ADRIA LTD

BEECHMOUNT AVENUE, MELMONT ROAD, STRABANE, COUNTY TYRONE, NORTHERN IRELAND BT82 9BG, ☎ 028 7138 2568, FAX: 028 7138 2910, 9–5 MON–FRI, 10–4 SAT. **FACTORY SHOP**

Manufacturer of tights and socks for Marks & Spencer, this shop sells hosiery which consists of Marks & Spencer seconds, Charnos lingerie, seconds in menswear, children's and women's clothes. Seconds in tights cost 45p.

CRAIGAVON OUTLET CENTRE

CRAIGAVON, NORTHERN IRELAND. **FACTORY SHOPPING VILLAGE**

Still working its way through the planning process, watch out in the local papers for more details.

CV HOME FURNISHINGS/DORMA

MAGHERALANE ROAD, RANDLESTOWN, ANTRIM BT14, ☎ 028 944 444100 BEDDING, FAX: 028 94 444102 CLOTHING, 9–5 MON–SAT, 8 ON THUR. **FACTORY SHOP**

Bedding from Dorma, Laura Ashley and Marks & Spencer, as well as curtains and towels. Clothing for men, women and children, mostly from M&S but de-labelled. Also Cloverleaf tablemats, trays and coasters.

DESMOND & SONS LTD

THE MAIN STREET, CLAUDY, LONDONDERRY, NORTHERN IRELAND BT47 3SD, ☎ 02871 388441, FAX: 08271 295005, 10–5 MON–SAT.

BALLYQUIN ROAD, DUNGWEN, CO LONDONDERRY, NORTHERN IRELAND BT47 4NQ, ☎ 028 7774 2068, 10–5 MON–SAT.

KEVLIN ROAD, OMAGH, NORTHERN IRELAND, ☎ 028 8224 1560, 10–5 MON–SAT.

31 GARVAGH ROAD, SWATRAGH, NORTHERN IRELAND, ☎ 028 7940 1639, 10–5 MON–SAT. **FACTORY SHOP**

Desmonds manufacture high quality clothing. Their factory shops at Claudy, Dungiven, Swatragh and Omagh stock men's, women's and childrenswear, including trousers, jeans, shorts, T-shirts, sweatshirts, fleece jackets, skirts, blouses, pyjamas, nightshirts, dressing gowns, knitwear, underwear and household items. Both perfect and slightly imperfect garments are sold at factory prices.

GILFORD MILL

45 MINUTES SOUTH OF BELFAST, NEAR BANBRIDGE, NORTHERN IRELAND. **FACTORY SHOPPING VILLAGE**

Due to open in autumn 2003, these were the only details we had as we went to press.

LINIAN KNITWEAR

SPAMOUNT MILLS, CASTLEDERG, CO TYRONE NORTHERN IRELAND BT81 7NB, ☎ 028 8167 1181, FAX: 028 816 70492, 10–5 MON–SAT. **FACTORY SHOP**

Irish woollens, knitted on the premises, seconds of which are sold in the factory shop. Ends of lines and last season's garments are sold at up to 50% discounts against normal prices.

LOTUS SHOES

34 BRIDGE STREET, BANBRIDGE, COUNTY DOWN, NORTHERN IRELAND BT32 3JL, ☎ 028 4062 2480, 9–5.30 MON–FRI, 9–5.15 SAT. **FACTORY SHOP**

This manufacturer for well-known chainstores sells all sizes and styles of Lotus shoes – from smart fashion shoes to walking shoes – at discounted prices for discontinued lines and rejects. Prices from £20 to £50 for men's shoes and from £12 to £35 for women's shoes. They also have a bridal shoe department with prices from £25 and a range of matching handbags.

PANACHE SHOES WEAVING SHED

12 LINEN GREEN, MOYGASHEL, DUNGANNON, COUNTY TYRONE BT71 7HB, ☎ 028 8772 5381, OPEN 10–5 MON–SAT. **FACTORY SHOP**

Part of an outlet complex, this shop has a full price area and a discounted, end of season section selling good quality brand name and Continental footwear at reduced prices. Small selection of children's shoes, sandals and slippers.

PAUL COSTELLOE FACTORY STORE

THE WORKSHOP, 9 LINEN GREEN, MAIN ROAD, MOYGASHEL, DUNGANNON, COUNTY TYRONE, NORTHERN IRELAND BT71 7HB, ☎ 028 8775 3867, 9.30–5.30 MON–SAT. **FACTORY SHOP**

A wide range of 1,500 garments, consisting of special purchases, seconds, samples and past seasons' stocks at substantial savings on original prices. The comprehensive selection encompasses business and special occasion designs and menswear as well as a more casual range for relaxed weekend wear. Now the sole stockist of Paul Costelloe womens' footwear in Ireland. Current season stock is sold at around 30% less than normal retail prices.

TK MAXX

UNIT 70, FIRST FLOOR, CASTLE COURT SHOPPING CENTRE, ROYAL AVENUE, BELFAST, NORTHERN IRELAND BT1 1DD, ☎ 028 9033 1151, www.tkmaxx.com, 9–6 MON–SAT, 9 ON THUR, 1–6 SUN.

1 MILL ROAD, SHORE ROAD, NEWTON ABBEY, BELFAST, NORTHERN IRELAND, www.tkmaxx.com, VISIT WEBSITE FOR DETAILS OF OPENING TIMES.

UNIT 31, RUSHMERE SHOPPING CENTRE, CRAIGAVON, NORTHERN IRELAND NORTHERN IRELAND BT64 1AA, ☎ 028 3834 4544, www.tkmaxx.com, 9–5.30 MON–TUE, 9–9 WED–FRI, 9–6 SAT, 1–6 SUN.

MERCHANTS QUAY, NEWRY, NORTHERN IRELAND, ☎ 028 3025 2465, www.tkmaxx.com, PHONE FOR DETAILS OF OPENING TIMES. **PERMANENT DISCOUNT OUTLET**

See page 89 (BEDS)

Childrenswear & Equipment

BEDFORDSHIRE

MATALAN

RACE MEADOWS WAY, AMPTHILL ROAD, BEDFORD, BEDFORDSHIRE MK42 7AZ, ☎ 01234 365077, FAX: 01234 360671, www.matalan.co.uk, 10–8 MON–FRI, 9–6 SAT, 11–5 SUN.

UNIT 2, LONDON ROAD INDUSTRIAL ESTATE, BIGGLESWADE, BEDFORDSHIRE SG18 8PW, ☎ 01767 310810, FAX: 01767 601876, www.matalan.co.uk, 10–8 MON–FRI, 9–6 SAT, 11–5 SUN. **PERMANENT DISCOUNT OUTLET**

Matalan is a fashion and homewares value retailer giving customers what they claim to be unbeatable value for money with huge savings on a wide range of products including high quality fashionable clothing for men, women and children at up to 50% off high street prices. Matalan is situated out of town and stores are open seven days a week all year round. There are 145 stores nationwide. The Matalan website contains maps of how to get to any of the stores.

QD STORES

22–30 GREYFRIARS, BEDFORD, BEDFORDSHIRE MK40 1HP, ☎ 01234 345204, 9–5.30 MON–SAT. **PERMANENT DISCOUNT OUTLET**

Discount shop selling a mixture of clothes, household textiles, ceramics, kitchenware, knitting wool, garden tools, curtains, toys, stationery, dusters, Christmas decorations, masking tape, lingerie and a host of other items. Stock changes regularly because the low prices mean a quick turnover. Some items are seconds or end of season stock from the major chain stores.

TK MAXX

UNIT 14, THE HOWARD CENTRE, BEDFORD, BEDFORDSHIRE MK40 1UH, ☎ 01234 270787, www.tkmaxx.com, 9–5.30 MON–FRI, 8.30–6 SAT, 10–4 SUN.

BEACON RETAIL PARK, WATLING STREET, BLETCHLEY, BEDFORDSHIRE MK1 1BN, ☎ 01908 644406, www.tkmaxx.com, 10–8 MON–FRI, 9–6 SAT, 11–5 SUN. **PERMANENT DISCOUNT OUTLET**

TK Maxx is a unique shopping experience, based on an American concept, offering an ever-changing range of famous names, high street brands and designer labels at up to 60% off normal retail prices. The majority of the stock is current season which makes the savings even more amazing. With 50,000 items in store and 10,000 new pieces arriving each week there is always something fresh and exciting to be found in every department: womenswear, menswear, childrenswear, sports and leisurewear, shoes, accessories and homewares. The stores are spacious and functional, with wide aisles enabling easy disabled and pushchair access. There are individual changing rooms, the stores accept all major credit and debit cards, and there is a return and refund policy. There are now over 120 easily accessible stores, often situated in main shopping centres or retail parks. All stores are open seven days a week and late in the evenings, though times vary from store to store. For details of your nearest store and opening hours, visit the website at www.tkmaxx.com.

BERKSHIRE

KID2KID

HIGH STREET, COOKHAM, BERKSHIRE SL6 9SH, ☎ 01628 531804, FAX: 01628 531804, **e-mail:** cookhamkid@aol.com, www.kid2kid.co.uk, 10–5.30 MON–SAT. **DRESS AGENCY**

Nearly-new designer clothes for children aged from birth to 16 years. Some of the most popular designer labels include La Redoute, Floriane, Bombleu, Jean Bourget, Poivre Blanc and OshKosh, although quality items from Next, Marks & Spencer and Laura Ashley are also on sale. For babies, brands include Alibama and Celebrity Kids. Prices range from £3 to £30, normally at least one-third of the original price. A range of new children's clothes, including Celebrity Kids, Mini Tribu and Quiksilver, are also available, as well as made-to-order bridesmaids dresses, Lucy Locket fairy dresses for girls. They also sell nearly-new baby equipment. There is a large children's play area.

MATALAN

ROSE KILN LANE, READING, BERKSHIRE RG2 0SN, ☎ 0118 939 1958, FAX: 0118 939 4605, www.matalan.co.uk, 10–8 MON–FRI, 9–6 SAT, 11–5SUN.

217A BATH ROAD, SLOUGH, BERKSHIRE SL1 4AA, ☎ 01753 487900, FAX: 01753 523353, www.matalan.co.uk, 10–8 MON–FRI, 9–6 SAT, 11–5 SUN. **PERMANENT DISCOUNT OUTLET**

See page 232 (BEDS)

THE REALLY GOOD DEAL FASHION SALE

THE PAVILION, ASCOT RACECOURSE, ASCOT, BERKSHIRE, ☎ 01367 860017, FAX: 01367 860177, **e-mail:** nheslam@aol.com, www.gooddealdirectory.co.uk, 10–6 FRI, SAT. **DESIGNER SALES**

The Really Good Deal Fashion Sale takes place twice a year in the elegant Pavilion building at Ascot Racecourse. The summer sale, which is usually the last, or second to last, Friday and Saturday in May, features about 70 different companies; the winter sale, which is usually the first Friday and Saturday of November, or the last Friday and Saturday of Ocobter, features 95 different companies. The range of businesses taking part is firmly middle to upper middle end of the market, with well-known names like Mulberry, N Peal Cashmere, Dents, and Paddy Campbell usually taking stands to sell their ends of lines and overstocks to the public at reduced prices. Almost anything you can think of is on sale here: coats, dresses, smart suits, wedding suits, evening wear, hats, shoes, boots, a variety of fabulous jewellery, stretch jeans, designer jeans, ties, men's shirts and sweaters, scarves, shawls, pashmina shawls, wraps, handbags, briefcases, gloves, wallets, swimwear, nightwear and there are usually one or two childrenswear companies. Tickets to the event cost £5 and are only available in advance. To join the mailing list, phone the above telephone number or write to PO Box 4, Lechlade, Glos GL7 3YB and you will receive advance notification of each sale and a ticket order form. The sale is organised by the team behind this book, The Good Deal Directory.

THE STOCK EXCHANGE

1 HIGH STREET, SUNNINGHILL, ASCOT, BERKSHIRE SL5 9NQ, ☎ 01344 625420, 9–5.30 MON–FRI, 8 ON THUR, 9–4.30 SAT. **DRESS AGENCY**

Excellent selection of nearly-new designer and high street labels for women, men and children including Calvin Klein, Boss and Yves Saint Laurent. Rapid turnover of clothes, all very well presented, in this very busy shop with cheerful, helpful staff. Clothes are sold in season and all items are clean and up-to-date. Garments are displayed for four weeks at full price and then one week at half price. Also sell shoes, hats, handbags and belts.

TK MAXX

6 THE MALL, THE KENNETT CENTRE, NEWBURY, BERKSHIRE RG14 5EN, ☎ 01635 522323, www.tkmaxx.com, 9–5.30 MON–FRI, 7 ON THUR, 9–6 SAT, 11–5 SUN.

UNIT A39, BROAD STREET MALL, BROAD STREET, READING, BERKSHIRE RG1 7QE, ☎ 0118 951 1117, www.tkmaxx.com, 9–5.30 MON–FRI, 9–6 SAT, 11–5 SUN.

UNIT 30–40, OBSERVATORY CENTRE, HIGH STREET, SLOUGH, BERKSHIRE SL1 1LL, ☎ 01753 572550, www.tkmaxx.com, 9–5.30 MON–FRI, 8 ON THUR, 9–6 SAT, 11–5 SUN. **PERMANENT DISCOUNT OUTLET**

See page 232 (BEDS)

BRISTOL

MATALAN

ALDERMOOR WAY, LONGWELL GREEN, BRISTOL BS15 7AD, ☎ 0117 935 2828, FAX: 0117 935 3035, www.matalan.co.uk, 10–8 MON–FRI, 9–6 SAT, 11–5 SUN.

ABBEY RETAIL PARK, STATION ROAD, FILTON, BRISTOL BS2 7JW, ☎ 0117 974 8000, FAX: 0117 969 5904, www.matalan.co.uk, 10–8 MON–FRI, 9–6 SAT, 11–5 SUN. **PERMANENT DISCOUNT OUTLET**

See page 232 (BEDS)

TK MAXX

THE GALLERIES CENTRE, 31–32 CASTLE GALLERY, BROADMEAD, BRISTOL BS1 3XE, ☎ 0117 930 4404, www.tkmaxx.com, 9–5.30 MON–SAT, 7 ON THUR, 11–5 SUN. **PERMANENT DISCOUNT OUTLET**

See page 232 (BEDS)

BUCKINGHAMSHIRE

MATALAN

103 WATLING STREET, BLETCHLEY, MILTON KEYNES, BUCKINGHAMSHIRE MK1 1HS, ☎ 01908 625400, FAX: 01908 641935, www.matalan.co.uk, 10–8 MON–FRI, 9–6 SAT, 11–4 SUN. **PERMANENT DISCOUNT OUTLET**

See page 232 (BEDS)

NIPPERS

CODDIMOOR FARM, WHADDON, MILTON KEYNES, BUCKINGHAMSHIRE MK17 OIR, ☎ 01908 504506, FAX: 01908 505636, **e-mail:** hickman@nippers.fsnet.co.uk, www.nippers.co.uk, OPENING HOURS VARY SO PHONE FIRST.

PERMANENT DISCOUNT OUTLET

Nippers, the nursery equipment and toy specialists, operate from previously redundant buildings in rural areas around the country. They offer easy parking, no queues and personal service. This is on top of competitive prices on prams, cots, pushchairs, car seats, outdoor play equipment and toys, some of which are new, some seconds or secondhand and some ends of lines. Prices are low because they avoid the high overheads of traditional retail outlets and also because the successful growth of a number of branches means they can now buy in bulk and negotiate good deals. Customers are invited to try out the merchandise while the children look at the animals, mostly sheep, chickens and pigs. Also offers many brand leaders at discount, including Mamas & Papas, Cosatto, Britax, Maclaren and Bebe Confort, plus Fisher-Price and Little Tikes. You can try out the car seats in your car and there is usually a pram/pushchair repair service on site.

QD STORES

HAMPDEN HOUSE, HIGH STREET AYLESBURY, BUCKINGHAMSHIRE HP20 1RE, ☎ 01296 428231. 9–5.30 MON–SAT. **PERMANENT DISCOUNT OUTLET**

See page 232 (BEDS)

CAMBRIDGESHIRE

CATALOGUE BARGAIN SHOP

51 WEST STREET, WISBECH, CAMBRIDGESHIRE PE13 2LY, ☎ 01945 584327, www.bargaincrazy.com, 9–4.30 MON–SAT, 10–4 SUN. **PERMANENT DISCOUNT OUTLET**

Catalogue Bargain Shop is a growing national chain of stores which obtains the majority of its goods from mail order giants Great Universal and Kays, and offers a range of clothing for all the family, a wide selection of shoes, bed linen, household goods, electrical equipment and hundreds of other catalogue items at very competitive prices. The merchandise consists of ends of ranges and previous season's stock for which there is no longer space when the catalogues change.

CHOICE DISCOUNT STORES LIMITED

UNITS 5–6 VIKING WAY, BARHILL, CAMBRIDGESHIRE CB3 8EL, 10–6 MON–WED, 10–7 THUR, FRI, 9–6 SAT, 11–5 SUN. **PERMANENT DISCOUNT OUTLET**

This new branch of Choice Discount Stores sells surplus stock including women's, men's and children's fashions from Next plc, Next Directory and other high street fashion houses, Next Interiors and footwear. You can save up to 50% off normal retail prices for first quality; up to two thirds for seconds. Special sales are held each January and September.

CIRCLES OF YAXLEY

CHAPEL STUDIO, CHAPEL STREET, YAXLEY, PETERBOROUGH, CAMBRIDGESHIRE PE7 3LN, ☎ 01733 242539, 10–4 MON–SAT. **DRESS AGENCY**

Circles sells womenswear and childrenswear. Evening wear is stocked all year round, as are accessories such as hats, handbags and belts. Sizes range from 8 to 24. For children, labels include Marks & Spencer, Laura Ashley and Next. There are sales in January and July, during which everything except evening wear is reduced by 25%, with 40% off promotions for adult clothes during February and August.

KIDDICARE

1184 LINCOLN ROAD, WERRINGTON, PETERBOROUGH, CAMBRIDGESHIRE PE4 6QF, ☎ 01733 579175, FAX: 01733 321519, **e-mail:** enquiries@kiddicare.com, www.kiddicare.com, **PERMANENT DISCOUNT OUTLET**

10,000 square foot superstore, now in its 26th year, acting as a permanent discount shop for new mothers with a wide range of top brand name baby equipment at lower prices than normal. Most are last season's models. Items on sale include prams, pushchairs, swings, high chairs, baby walkers, cots, three-wheelers, car seats, prams. Brands include Silver Cross, Britax, Aventi, MacLaren, Mamas & Papas. You can order over the internet or by phone and delivery takes about seven working days. Large car park.

MATALAN

EAST STATION ROAD, PETERBOROUGH, CAMBRIDGESHIRE PE2 8AA, ☎ 01733 341229, FAX: 01733 341246, www.matalan.co.uk, 10–8 MON–FRI, 9–6 SAT, 11–5 SUN. **PERMANENT DISCOUNT OUTLET**

See page 232 (BEDS)

QD STORES

ORTON CENTRE, PETERBOROUGH, CAMBRIDGESHIRE PE2 0UD, ☎ 01733 237311 9–5.30 MON–SAT, 10–4SUN.

62 BURLEIGH STREET, CAMBRIDGE, CAMBRIDGESHIRE CB1 1DG, ☎ 01223 323174, 9–5.30 MON–SAT, 10–4SUN.

16–17 MARKET PLACE, WISBECH, CAMBRIDGESHIRE PE13 1DY, ☎ 01945 466756, 9–5.30 MON–SAT. **PERMANENT DISCOUNT OUTLET**

See page 232 (BEDS)

STAGE 2

SAVILLE ROAD, PETERBOROUGH, CAMBRIDGESHIRE PE3 7RP, ☎ 01733 263308, 10–8 MON–FRI, 9–6 SAT, 10–4 SUN, BANK HOLIDAYS. **PERMANENT DISCOUNT OUTLET**

Sells surplus stock from both Grattan and Freemans catalogues. Womenswear, childrenswear, menswear and household items, at up to 50% off catalogue prices. Includes a wide range of brands from both designer and high street on a regularly changing basis. Electrical goods are sold at discounts of up to 30% off catalogue prices, and include many big-name brands. 14-day refund policy.

THE DRESS AGENCY

1 THE BROADWAY, ST IVES, HUNTINGDON, CAMBRIDGESHIRE PE28 4BX, ☎ 01480 464 952, 10–5 MON-SAT. **DRESS AGENCY**

Designer clothes and contemporary fashions. There are women's evening wear, prom dresses, ball gowns and special occasion hats. New handbags, and Italian shoes, including Prada and Miu Miu, are also on sale at discounted prices. There is also a new range of Italian lingerie which is sold at very competitive prices.

CHESHIRE

BURBERRY

MCARTHURGLEN DESIGNER OUTLET CHESHIRE OAKS, KINSEY ROAD, NEAR ELLESMERE PORT, JUNCTION 10 OF M53, CHESHIRE CH65 9JJ, ☎ 0151 357 3203, 10–8 MON–FRI, 9–6 SAT, 11–5 SUN. **FACTORY SHOP IN A FACTORY SHOPPING VILLAGE**

The Burberry factory shops sell surplus stock from the famous Burberry London men's and women's collections as well as accessories such as the distinctive umbrellas, scarves and handbags. It also sells children's clothing, though different factory shops stock different amounts. Stock is not current season but all carry the Burberry label and discounts are about one third off normal.

CATALOGUE BARGAIN SHOP

ROYAL AVENUE, WIDNES, CHESHIRE WA8 7BR, ☎ 0151 424 6161, www.bargaincrazy.com, 10–6 MON–FRI, 9–5 SAT. **PERMANENT DISCOUNT OUTLET**

See page 234 (CHESH)

CHRISTY, THE MILL SHOP

NEWTON STREET, HYDE, CHESHIRE SK14 4NR, ☎ 0161 368 1961 EXT 4603, 9–5 MON–WED, 9–6.30 THUR, 9–5 FRI, 9–4 SAT. **FACTORY SHOP**

Top quality seconds and discontinued lines from the UK's brand leader in towels. The finest quality Christy towels are available, plus well-known high street names as well as Prettywise bedding, Zorbit baby goods and a range of other goods including flannelette sheets and tea towels.

CLARKS FACTORY SHOP

CHESHIRE OAKS OUTLET, KINSEY ROAD, NEAR ELLESMERE PORT, JUNCTION 10 OF M53, SOUTH WIRRAL CH65 9JJ, ☎ 0151 356 7492, 10–8 MON–FRI, 9–6 SAT, 11–5 SUN. **FACTORY SHOP IN A FACTORY SHOPPING VILLAGE**

Clarks International operate a chain of factory shops nationally which specialise in selling discontinued lines and slight sub-standards for men, women and children from Clarks, K Shoes and other famous brands. These shops trade under the name of K Shoes Factory Shop or Clarks Factory Shop and while not all are physically attached to a shoe factory, they are treated as factory shops by the company. Customers can expect to find an extensive range of quality shoes, sandals, walking boots, slippers, trainers, handbags, accessories and gifts, while their major outlets also offer luggage, sports clothing, sports equipment and outdoor clothing. Brands stocked include Clarks, K Shoes, Springer, CICA, Hi-Tec, Caterpillar, Kickers, Timberland, Regatta, Craghoppers, Kangol, Kangaroo Poo, Diadora, Mercury, Antler, Eminent, Travelon, Hudson and Carlton, although not all are sold in every outlet. Phone first to find out what your particular store is offering. Discounts are from 30% to 60% off the normal high street price for perfect stock.

DELIA METCALFE

15A BRIDGE STREET, CONGLETON, CHESHIRE CW12 1AS, ☎ 01260 297521, 9.30–5 MON–THUR, 9–5.30 FRI, SAT. **PERMANENT DISCOUNT OUTLET**

Chainstore and designer surplus stock are sold in this small, town centre shop. The children's clothes range from six months to 12 years; women's sizes from 8 to 30. Marks & Spencer merchandise is discounted by 50%, and there are many German designer labels such as Verse and Bianca. They also sell shoes, handbags and accessories.

ECCO

MCARTHURGLEN DESIGNER OUTLET CHESHIRE OAKS, KINSEY ROAD, NEAR ELLESMERE PORT, JUNCTION 10 OF M53, CHESHIRE CH65 9JJ, ☎ 0151 356 3045, www.ecco.com, 10–8 MON–FRI, 9–6 SAT, 11–5 SUN. **FACTORY SHOP IN A FACTORY SHOPPING VILLAGE**

Women's, men's and children's shoes, all discounted by at least 25% and sometimes by as much as 60%. Other outlets in Wiltshire, Somerset, South Wales and Hertfordshire.

ELITE DRESS AGENCY

1 MARKET STREET, ALTRINCHAM, CHESHIRE WA14 1QE, ☎ 0161 928 5424, 10–5 MON–SAT. **DRESS AGENCY**

Established in 1964, this shop sells mainly womenswear which is less than two years old, with a small but comprehensive selection of menswear. Wide range of clothing includes some sportswear. Labels range from high street to designer and include names such as Prada, DKNY, Yves St Laurent, Dior, Valentino, Ungaro, Thierry Mugler, Marks & Spencer, Kookai, Morgan and Ralph Lauren for women, and Boss, Versace, Armani, Yves Saint Laurent, Cerruti and Ralph Lauren for men. Twice yearly sales at the end of June and December. A dress hire section stocks a wide selection of brand new dresses, updated twice a year (see One-Night Affair). They have recently expanded to include a childrenswear department.

GAP

MCARTHURGLEN DESIGNER OUTLET CHESHIRE OAKS, KINSEY ROAD, NEAR ELLESMERE PORT, JUNCTION 10 OF M53, CHESHIRE CH65 9JJ, ☎ 0151 355 2488, 10–8 MON–FRI, 9–6 SAT, 11–5 SUN. **FACTORY SHOP IN A FACTORY SHOPPING VILLAGE**

Gap has two shops in this outlet, one selling casual clothes for men and women and another opposite catering for children of all ages. The minimum discount is 30% with many items at 50% off and some reduced by as much as 90%.

JOKIDS LTD

MCARTHURGLEN DESIGNER OUTLET CHESHIRE OAKS, KINSEY ROAD, NEAR ELLESMERE PORT, JUNCTION 10 OF M53, CHESHIRE CH65 9JJ, ☎ 0151 357 1404, FAX: 0151 357 1404, www.jokids.com, 10–8 MON–FRI, 9–6 SAT, 11–5 SUN. **FACTORY SHOP IN A FACTORY SHOPPING VILLAGE**

Jokids is an English designer brand for babies and children from birth to 10 years. The shops sell good quality clothing and accessories for babies, boys and girls. The range includes basic lines at very competitive prices as well as easy-to-coordinate fashion lines. They also offer the exclusive Jeffrey Ohrenstein Collection of hand-smocked and embroidered dresses and babywear. Clothing includes snowsuits, rompers, sleepsuits, nightwear, T-shirts, swimwear, dungarees, trousers and dresses for babies; jackets, T-shirts, sweatshirts, trousers, shirts, tops, skirts, swimwear and nightwear for kids; while the range of accessories includes: bags, hats, caps and jewellery.

LEE COOPER

MCARTHURGLEN DESIGNER OUTLET CHESHIRE OAKS, KINSEY ROAD, NEAR ELLESMERE PORT, JUNCTION 10 OF M53, CHESHIRE CH65 9JJ, ☎ 0151 355 8808, 10–8 MON–FRI, 9–6 SAT, 11–5 SUN. **FACTORY SHOP IN A FACTORY SHOPPING VILLAGE**

Denim jeans, jackets and shirts, each ranked by size and gender at discounts from 30%. Casual shirts from £10, jeans from £15, T-shirts and womenswear. Lee Cooper was founded in 1908 as a workwear manufacturer before becoming a supplier to the armed forces. Most of the stock here is current, discontinued, overstocks and irregular merchandise, all of which comes straight from Lee Cooper's factories in Europe.

LITTLEWOODS CATALOGUE DISCOUNT STORE

MCARTHURGLEN DESIGNER OUTLET CHESHIRE OAKS, KINSEY ROAD, NEAR ELLESMERE PORT, JUNCTION 10 OF M53, CHESHIRE CH65 9JJ, ☎ 0151 356 0501, 10–8 MON–FRI, 9–6 SAT, 11–5 SUN. **FACTORY SHOP IN A FACTORY SHOPPING VILLAGE**

Littlewoods clearance shops offer up to 70% off the catalogue price for clothing and offer big discounts off electrical goods. stock changes constantly and varies from day to day but can include well-known brand names such as Berlei and Gossard lingerie, Vivienne Westwood, Pamplemousse leisurewear, Nike and Adidas sports shoes, and Timberland and Caterpillar footwear. Stock depends on the size and location of the shop: larger shops get the longer discontinued runs, while smaller shops get overruns with only a small amount of colour and size variations left. Littlewoods also runs a mobile shop which operates in cities which don't have a sale shop. For details of venues for the sales, which usually take place once a month, write to Melanie Lamb, c/o Crosby DC, Kershaw Avenue, Endbutt Lane, Crosby, Merseyside L70 1AH.

MARKS & SPENCER

MCARTHURGLEN DESIGNER OUTLET VILLAGE CHESHIRE OAKS, ELLESMERE PORT, SOUTH WIRRAL, CHESHIRE CH65 9JJ, ☎ 0151 356 0985, 10–8 MON–FRI, 9–6 SAT, 11–5 SUN.
FACTORY SHOP IN A FACTORY SHOPPING VILLAGE

Fashion and footwear – no homewares – which are mostly last season's stock for families at least 30% below usual retail prices.

MATALAN

UNITS 3, 4 & 5A, THE ROCK RETAIL PARK, GREEN LANE, BIRKENHEAD CHESHIRE CH41 9AG, ☎ 0151 650 6820, FAX: 0151 650 0487, www.matalan.co.uk, 10–8 MON–FRI, 9.30–6 SAT, 11–5 SUN.

NEW CHESTER ROAD, BROMBOROUGH, SOUTH WIRRAL, CHESHIRE CH62 7EK, ☎ 0151 343 9494, FAX: 0151 343 9321, www.matalan.co.uk, 9.30–8 MON–FRI, 9–6 SAT, 11–5 SUN.

STADIUM WAY, CHESTER, CHESHIRE CH1 4PZ, ☎ 01244 665260, FAX: 01244 665908, www.matalan.co.uk, 9.30–8 MON–FRI, 9–6 SAT, 11–5 SUN.

STADIUM WAY, CHESTER, CHESHIRE CH1 4PZ, ☎ 01244 665260, www.matalan.co.uk, 9.30–8 MON–FRI, 9–6 SAT, 11–5 SUN.

KERFOOT STREET, OFF WINWICK ROAD, WARRINGTON, CHESHIRE WA2 8NU, ☎ 01925 235365, FAX: 01925 230371, www.matalan.co.uk, 9.30–8 MON–FRI, 9–6 SAT, 11–5 SUN.
PERMANENT DISCOUNT OUTLET

See page 232 (BEDS)

MCARTHURGLEN DESIGNER OUTLET

KINSEY ROAD, NEAR ELLESMERE PORT, JUNCTION 10 OF M53, CHESHIRE CH65 9JJ, ☎ 0800 316 4352 FREE INFORMATION LINE OR 0151 348 5600, FAX: 0151 357 3744, www.mcarthurglen.com/cheshireoaks, 10–8 MON–FRI, 9–6 SAT, 11–5 SUN. **FACTORY SHOPPING VILLAGE**

The McArthurGlen Designer Outlet Cheshire Oaks is Europe's largest designer outlet with over 140 stores selling top brands and designer names at up to 50% off typical retail prices. Facilities include a food court, a children's play area and free parking. Stores include: Gap Outlet, Big L, Fruit of the Loom, Monsoon, Timberland, Tie Rack, Principles, Petroleum, James Barry, Donnay, Aquascutum, Burberrys, Viyella, Warehouse, Racing Green, Famous Footwear, Jeffrey Rogers, Liz Claiborne, Winning Line, Overland, Ciro Pearls, Diesel, Jokids, Fred Perry, Travel Accessory Outlet, Baron Jon, La Senza, Nike, Next to Nothing, Helly Hansen, Jane Shilton, Joe Bloggs, Birthdays, Thorntons, Toyworld, D2, Pilot, Jumper, Clarks, Villeroy & Boch, Episode, Windsmoor, Jaeger, Daks Simpson, Mexx, Bed & Bath Works, Woods of Windsor, The Suit Company, XS Music & Video, Suits You, Claire's Accessories, Lee Cooper, Tog 24, Fila, Warners, Cecil Gee, Remington, Whittard of Chelsea, Kitchen Store, Denby, Edinburgh Crystal, Price's Candles, Reebok, Hobbs, Kurt Muller, Bookends, Pictureport, Kappa, Easy Jeans, Woodhouse, Designer Room, DKNY, Ponden Mill, U Wear/I Wear, Penn, Le Coq Sportif, Roman Originals, Revlon, Monet, Walker and Hall, Ben Sherman, Van Heusen, Austin Reed, Antler, Ecco, Blazer, Watson/Chillii Pepper, Red/Green, Soled Out, Carphone Warehouse, Cotton Traders, Royal Doulton, Royal Worcester, Oneida, Proibito, Vans, Reiss, Garden Outlet, Proudfoot Leather, Playtime Toys, Wedgwood, Prima Tessuti, Natural World, WHSmith, Littlewoods, Bose, The Body Shop, Samsonite, Adidas, Kangol, Dune, Marks & Spencer Outlet, Daniel Footwear, Polo Jeans Company, The North Face, Elle, Sergio Tacchini, Autonomy, Chapelle, Fiorelli, Julian Graves, Spiegelau, Bose, Kitch N Sync, Early Learning Centre, Tommy Hilfiger, Triumph and Professional Cookware.

MEXX INTERNATIONAL

MCARTHURGLEN DESIGNER OUTLET CHESHIRE OAKS, KINSEY ROAD, NEAR ELLESMERE PORT, JUNCTION 10 OF M53, CHESHIRE CH65 9JJ, ☎ 0151 355 8238, 10–8 MON–FRI, 9–6 SAT, 11–5 SUN. **FACTORY SHOP IN A FACTORY SHOPPING VILLAGE**

High street fashion at factory outlet prices for men, women, babies and children, all of which is discounted by more than 30%.

MOLLY MUMBLES/BABYEQUIP

I BOOTHBED LANE, BOOSTREY, NEAR HOLMES CHAPEL, CHESHIRE CH4 8JP, ☎ 01477 532234, 9.30–3 MON–SAT. **SECONDHAND SHOPS**

Huge selection of top quality secondhand childrenswear and equipment at bargain prices. Labels include Mothercare, Miniman, Gap, OshKosh, Jean Bourget, Oilily, Mamas & Papas, Fisher-Price, Maclaren, Playmobil and Duplo and many more. Also hires out buggies, high chairs, prams, travel cots, car seats by the day, week or month.

NEXT TO NOTHING

MCARTHURGLEN DESIGNER OUTLET CHESHIRE OAKS, KINSEY ROAD, NEAR ELLESMERE PORT, JUNCTION 10 OF M53, CHESHIRE CH65 9JJ, ☎ 0151 356 7404, www.next.co.uk, 10–8 MON–FRI, 9–6 SAT, 11–5 SUN. **FACTORY SHOP IN A FACTORY SHOPPING VILLAGE**

Sells perfect surplus stock from Next stores and the Next Directory catalogue – from belts, jewellery and underwear to day and evening wear – at discounts of 50% or more. The ranges are usually last season's and overruns. Stock consists of women's, men's and children's clothing, with some homeware and shoes. Stock is replenished three times a week and there is plenty of it.

NIKE FACTORY STORE

MCARTHURGLEN DESIGNER OUTLET CHESHIRE OAKS, KINSEY ROAD, NEAR ELLESMERE PORT, JUNCTION 10 OF M53, CHESHIRE CH65 9JJ, ☎ 0151 357 1252, FAX: 0151 355 6724, www.nike.com, 10–8 MON–FRI, 9–6 SAT, 11–5 SUN. **FACTORY SHOP IN A FACTORY SHOPPING VILLAGE**

Men's, women's and children's footwear, clothing and equipment. Trainers, jackets, T-shirts, polo shirts, sweatshirts, shorts, pants, tracksuits, golf balls, footballs, golf bags, gloves, socks and caps. Nike has been making clothes for people who are inspired by sports since 1972. This factory store sells garments only one season behind the high street. The selection is from their European product line, and there are approximately 10,000 pairs of shoes and 20,000 items of clothing to choose from, all at a minimum of 30% off normal retail prices. You will also find slight seconds on sale (marked and signed in store as B grades). The store has four clearance sales throughout the year (phone for details). There are a further 10 factory stores throughout the UK and Ireland.

QS FASHION SALE

1–5 BROAD ROAD, SALE, CHESHIRE M33 2AE, ☎ 0161 976 2747, FAX: 0161 962 9244, 9–8 MON–FRI, 9–5.30 SAT, 11–5 SUN. **PERMANENT DISCOUNT OUTLET**

Fashion for all the family includes brands such as Timberland, Fila, Nike, Reebok, Adidas, Calvin Klein and Ralph Lauren and many more. Homeware products include towels, bedding, plastics, pictures, toys and mirrors. The stock is constantly changing so come with an open mind. QS Fashion has a price promise that if you can purchase the same item at a cheaper price at another store, QS will give you the product free.

T J HUGHES

BOROUGH PAVEMENT, GRANGE PRECINCT, BIRKENHEAD, CHESHIRE L41 2XX, ☎ 0151 647 5151, FAX: 0151 666 1610, **e-mail:** info@tjhughes.co.uk, www.tjhughes.co.uk, 9–5.30 MON–SAT, 10–4 SUN.

THE FORUM, HAMILTON PLACE, CHESTER, CHESHIRE CH1 2BH, ☎ 01244 316600, FAX: 01244 316646, **e-mail:** info@tjhughes.co.uk, www.tjhughes.co.uk, 9–5.30 MON–SAT, 11–5 SUN.

2 MERCIER WALK, SOUTH WIRRAL CHESHIRE CH65 0AP, ☎ 0151 357 3151, FAX: 0151 357 3174, **e-mail:** info@tjhughes.co.uk, www.tjhughes.co.uk, 9–5.30 MON–SAT, 10–4 SUN.

EXCHANGE STREET, MACCLESFIELD, CHESHIRE SK11 6UZ, ☎ 01625 611807, FAX: 01625 611859, **e-mail:** info@tjhughes.co.uk, www.tjhughes.co.uk, 9–5.30 MON–SAT, 10–4 SUN.

GREENOAKS SHOPPING CENTRE, WIDNES, CHESHIRE WA8 6UD, ☎ 0151 420 1010, FAX: 0151 423 4570, **e-mail:** info@tjhughes.co.uk, www.tjhughes.co.uk, 9–5.30 MON–SAT, 10–4 SUN. **PERMANENT DISCOUNT OUTLET**

Expanding chain of shops offering, not discounts as such, but very competitively priced goods including clothes for all the family, china, towels, bedlinen, duvets, pots and pans, kettles, vacuum cleaners, television sets, CDs, toasters, many top brand names. There are branches around the country.

THE FACTORY SHOP LTD

UNIT 1 EDDISBURY SQUARE, FRODSHAM, CHESHIRE WA6 6QS, ☎ 01928 734624, FAX: 01928 734906, 9–5.30 MON–SAT, 10.30–4 SUN. **FACTORY SHOP**

Wide range on sale includes men's, women's and children's clothing and footwear; household textiles; hardware; luggage; lighting; electrical goods; and bedding, most of which are chainstore and high street brands at discounts of approximately 30% to 50%. There are kitchen and furniture displays and on sale is the Cape Country Furniture range with free-standing kitchens, as well as living, bedroom and dining furniture. There are weekly deliveries and brands include famous names such as Adidas, Nike, Joe Bloggs and Brabantia, among others. Lines are continually changing and few factory shops offer such a variety under one roof. Parking is free.

THE FAMOUS BRUNSWICK WAREHOUSE LTD

UNIT 5B, THE ROACK, GREEN LANE, BIRKENHEAD, CHESHIRE CH41 9AG, ☎ 0151 650 1505, **e-mail:** northshoe@mcmail.com, 10–8 MON–FRI, 9–6 SAT, 11–5 SUN.

UNIT 3, ST DAVIDS RETAIL PARK, SALTNEY, CHESTER, CHESHIRE CH4 8SN, ☎ 01244 676431, **e-mail:** northshoe@mcmail.com, 9–6 MON–SAT, 10–4 SUN.

UNIT 1B, 2 GRAND JUNCTION RETAIL PARK, EARLE STREET, CREWE, CHESHIRE CW1 2RP, ☎ 01270 254156, **e-mail:** northshoe@mcmail.com, 10–8 MON–FRI, 9–6 SAT, 11–5 SUN.

UNIT 3, COCKHEDGE CENTRE, COCKHEADGE WAY, WARRINGTON, CHESHIRE WA1 2QQ, ☎ 01925 232306, **e-mail:** northshoe@mcmail.com, 9–6 MON–WED, SAT, 9–7 THUR, FRI, 10.30–4.30 SUN.

49 DEWHIRST ROAD, BIRCHWOOD, WARRINGTON, CHESHIRE WA3 7PG, ☎ 01925 822718, **e-mail:** northshoe@mcmail.com, 9–6 MON–WED, SAT, 9–8 THUR, FRI, 10.30–4.30 SUN. **PERMANENT DISCOUNT OUTLET**

Self-service discount store chain with 60 branches selling branded sportswear and sports footwear, such as Nike, Adidas and Reebok, as well as non-branded footwear at discounts of 50%. Also a reasonable selection of clothing and accessories. Phone the number above for details of your nearest branch.

TK MAXX

178–182 GRANGE ROAD, BIRKENHEAD, CHESHIRE CH41 2PF, ☎ 0151 647 2837, www.tkmaxx.com, 9–5.30 MON–FRI, 9–6 SAT, 10.30–4.30 SUN.

STANLEY GREEN RETAIL PARK, EARL ROAD, CHEADLE HULME, CHESHIRE, ☎ 0161 485 3734, www.tkmaxx.com, PHONE FOR DETAILS.

UNIT 3, CHESTER RETAIL PARK, CHESTER, CHESHIRE, www.tkmaxx.com, VISIT WEBSITE FOR DETAILS.

UNIT B, TRIDENT RETAIL PARK, RUNCORN, CHESHIRE WA7 2FQ, ☎ 01928 714050, www.tkmaxx.com, 9–6 MON, 9–7 TUE–WED, 9–8 THUR–FRI, 9–6 SAT, 11–5 SUN.

UNIT C, THE COCKHEDGE CENTRE, 2 PRINCE HENRY SQUARE, WARRINGTON, CHESHIRE, ☎ 01925 636262, www.tkmaxx.com, 9–6 MON–SAT, 9 ON THUR, 10–4. SUN. **PERMANENT DISCOUNT OUTLET**

See page 232 (BEDS)

TOG 24

MCARTHURGLEN DESIGNER OUTLET CHESHIRE OAKS, KINSEY ROAD, NEAR ELLESMERE PORT, JUNCTION 10 OF M53, CHESHIRE CH65 9JJ, ☎ 0151 356 7477, **e-mail:** mail-order@tog24.com, www.tog24.com, 10–8 MON–FRI, 9–6 SAT, 11–5 SUN. **FACTORY SHOP IN A FACTORY SHOPPING VILLAGE**

Tog 24 is the UK's fastest-growing brand name in outdoor clothing and leisurewear. The company utilises the world's finest performance fabrics, including GoreTex and Polartec, to produce merchandise which caters for all the family for all seasons. Their range includes fleeces and waterproofs for the winter, and trekking ranges, shorts and T-shirts for the summer. They also stock accessories, including sunglasses, toiletries and swimwear. All merchandise is available by mail order: phone 01924 236507 for a brochure. All prices here are at least 30% below RRP.

TOYWORLD STORE FACTORY OUTLET

MCARTHURGLEN DESIGNER OUTLET CHESHIRE OAKS, KINSEY ROAD, NEAR ELLESMERE PORT, JUNCTION 10 OF M53, CHESHIRE CH65 9JJ, ☎ 0151 355 9998, www.toyworldstore.com, 10–8 MON–FRI, 9–6 SAT, 11–5 SUN. **FACTORY SHOP IN A FACTORY SHOPPING VILLAGE**

Toyworld Store Factory Outlets are Europe's largest toy factory outlet retailer. They offer an enormous range of branded products which may be surplus stocks, end of ranges or cancelled orders, and are therefore able to sell their products at up to 70% off normal high street prices. Their range includes famous names such as: Action Man, Barbie, Bandai, Crayola, Corgi, Fisher-Price, Hasbro, Hornby, Lego, Little Tikes, Meccano, Tomy, V-Tech and many more, all at unbelievably low prices.

WILKINSONS HOME & GARDEN STORES

THE MARKET CENTRE, CREWE, CHESHIRE CW1 2NG, ☎ 01270 250754, www.wilko.co.uk, 8.30–5.30 MON–WED, 8.30–6.30 THUR–SAT, 10–4 SUN. **PERMANENT DISCOUNT OUTLET**

Family-owned business offering value on the high street through its 205 stores, selling 25,000 high quality, low-priced essential everyday products for all the family including clothes and toys. Phone 01909 505505 for details of your local outlet or visit their website.

WYNSORS WORLD OF SHOES

WARRINGTON ROAD, PENKETH, NR WARRINGTON, CHESHIRE WA2 7AP, ☎ 01925 727481 9–5.30 MON, TUE, WED, SAT, 9–8 THUR, FRI, 10–4 SUN AND BANK HOLIDAYS.

LONDON ROAD, HAZEL GROVE, STOCKPORT, CHESHIRE SK7 4AX, ☎ 0161 456 2632, 9–5.30 MON, TUE, SAT, 9–8 WED–FRI, 10–4 SUN. **PERMANENT DISCOUNT OUTLET**

Stocks top brand-name shoes at less than half price. Special monthly offers always available. There are shoes, trainers, slippers, sandals and boots for all the family, with a selection of bags, cleaners and polishes available, all at discount prices.

YOU & YOURS

UNIT 42, ORCHARD WALK, HALTON LEAS SHOPPING CENTRE, RUNCORN, CHESHIRE WA7 2GZ, ☎ 01928 795 792, 9–5.30 MON–SAT. **PERMANENT DISCOUNT OUTLET**

Sells surplus stock from both Grattan and Freemans catalogues. Womenswear, childrenswear, menswear and household items, at up to 50% off catalogue prices. Includes a wide range of brands from both designer and high street on a regularly changing basis. Electrical goods are sold at discounts of up to 30% off catalogue prices, and include many big-name brands. A 14-day refund policy is offered.

COUNTY DURHAM

CHARLES CLINKARD

JACKSONS LANDING, THE HIGHLIGHT, HARTLEPOOL, CO DURHAM TS24 0XN, ☎ 01429 866939, 10–6 MON–SAT, 11–5 SUN. **FACTORY SHOP IN A FACTORY SHOPPING VILLAGE**

Footwear for the family at discounts of between 30% and 50%. Labels on sale here include Rockport, Loake, Barker, Grenson, Base, Ecco, Gabor, Rohde, Van-Dal, Kickers, Clarks, Dr Martens, K Shoes and Lotus. At the time of going to print, the future of Jacksons Landing is uncertain. Please phone before making a special trip.

DEWHIRST IMPRESSIONS

MILL HILL NORTH WEST INDUSTRIAL ESTATE, PETERLEE, CO DURHAM SR8 2HR, ☎ 0191 586 4525, **e-mail:** kim.mcmaster@dewhirst.com, 9–6 MON–WED, FRI, SAT, 9–7 THUR, 10.30–4.30 SUN. **FACTORY SHOP**

Dewhirst Impressions sells garments from the manufacturing side of the business direct to the public as part of the Dewhirst Group plc which manufactures women's, men's and childrenswear for a leading high street retailer. You can choose from a huge selection of surplus production and slight seconds at bargain prices, making savings of more than 50% of the normal retail cost. For men there is a wide range of suits, formal shirts and casual wear. For example, suits from £60, formal and casual shirts from £7. For women there's a selection of blouses, smart tailoring and casual wear that includes a denim range. You can find women's jackets from £30, skirts, trousers and blouses from £8. There is also a selection of women's and men's underwear. Children's clothes start at £3. High street quality and style at wholesale prices.

DISCOUNT CLOTHING STORE

68 HOPE STREET, CROOK, CO DURHAM DL15 9HT, ☎ 01388 768272, 9.30–5.30 MON–SAT.

UNIT 5A, FOLLINGSBY PARK, WARDLEY, GATESHEAD, TYNE & WEAR NE10 8YA, ☎ 0191 415 4015, 9.30–5.30 MON–SAT. **PERMANENT DISCOUNT OUTLET**

With discounts of up to 50%, DCS offers a wide range of clothes for all the family and some bedlinen and towels, most of which are from high street stores.

FACTORY SHOP

LINGFIELD WAY, YARM ROAD BUSINESS PARK, DARLINGTON, CO DURHAM DL1 4XX, ☎ 01325 469181, FAX: 01325 381386, **e-mail:** tensorlimited@aol.com. www.tensormarketing.co.uk. 9–5 MON–FRI, 10–4.30 SAT. **FACTORY SHOP**

Part of Tensor Marketing Ltd, a marketing company specialising in innovative products with a huge range of goods covering home and garden, office, motoring, gifts, novelties, pets, pest control systems, security, health and fitness, sport and leisure. The garden section has a range of items including gutter flushes, hammer and edging fencing, mole chasers, foldaway wheelbarrows, garden lighting sets, weeders, garden thermometers, corner plant stands, garden hoses and obelisks. Order from the shop, the website or by mail order brochure.

LITTLEWOODS DISCOUNT STORE

UNIT 2A, METRO RETAIL PARK, GATESHEAD, TYNE & WEAR NE11 9XU, ☎ 0191 461 1491 10–8 MON–FRI, 9–6 SAT, 11–5 SUN. **PERMANENT DISCOUNT OUTLET**

Brand new, surplus women's, men's and children's clothing from last year's catalogue is on sale at greatly discounted prices. Returned and sometimes slightly damaged televisions and furniture can be found at as much as 70% below the original price. If you see an item you like, buy it there and then as stock is constantly changing and you are unlikely to see it on sale again. The store also has sales when stock is discounted even further.

LITTLEWOODS CATALOGUE DISCOUNT STORE

19 FAWCETT STREET, SUNDERLAND, TYNE & WEAR SR1 1RH, ☎ 0191 564 0684, 9–5 MON–THUR, 9–5.30 FRI, SAT. **FACTORY SHOP**

See page 237 (CHESH)

MATALAN

173 HIGH STREET WEST, GATESHEAD, TYNE & WEAR NE8 1EJ, ☎ 0191 478 8140, FAX: 0191 478 9480, www.matalan.co.uk, 10–8 MON–FRI, 9–6 SAT, 11–5 SUN.

48 CAMERON RETAIL PARK, METRO CENTRE, GATESHEAD, TYNE & WEAR NE11 9XU, ☎ 0191 461 0880, FAX: 0191 460 1340, www.matalan.co.uk, 9.30–8 MON–FRI, 9–6 SAT, 11–6 SUN.

ANCHOR RETAIL PARK, MARINA WAY, HARTLEPOOL, CO DURHAM TS24 0XR, ☎ 01429 855960, FAX: 01429 264028, www.matalan.co.uk, 10–8 MON–FRI, 9–6 SAT, 11–5 SUN.

BRIDGE ROAD RETAIL PARK, PARKFIELD ROAD, STOCKTON-ON-TEES, STOCKTON, CO DURHAM TS18 3AY, ☎ 01642 702410, FAX: 01642 702415, www.matalan.co.uk, 10–8 MON–FRI, 9–6 SAT, 11–5 SUN.

UNIT 1, HYLTON RIVERSIDE RETAIL PARK, SUNDERLAND, TYNE & WEAR SR5 3XG, ☎ 0191 516 0141, FAX: 0191 548 1572, www.matalan.co.uk, 10–8 MON–FRI, 9–6 SAT, 11–5 SUN. **PERMANENT DISCOUNT OUTLET**

See page 232 (BEDS)

SCOOPS CATALOGUE DISCOUNT STORE

UNIT 17, THE IN SHOP CENTRE, 1–2 WRIGHTON HOUSE, TRENCHARD AVENUE, THORNABY, TEESIDE TS17 9EP, ☎ 01642 751935, 9–5 MON–SAT. **PERMANENT DISCOUNT OUTLET**

Scoops the catalogue discount store sells surplus stock from both Grattan and Freeman's catalogues. Womenswear, menswear and childrenswear are on sale, as well as household items, all at up to 50% off catalogue prices. Stock changes on a regular basis, and includes a wide range of brands from both designer and high street. A 14-day refund policy is offered.

SEYMOUR'S OF DARLINGTON

1–3 EAST ROW, DARLINGTON DL1 5PZ, ☎ 01325 355272, FAX: 01325 355272, **e-mail:** jem@seymours.fsbusiness.co.uk, 9–5 MON–SAT. **PERMANENT DISCOUNT OUTLET**

Seymour's of Darlington is the longest-established household linen retailer in the area and takes great pride in maintaining its loyal customer base. This unique family-owned business combines old-fashioned quality and service with the newest designs and keenest prices. There is a constantly changing, stunning variety of stock from tea towels to the latest French and Italian designer bed linens. Customers of all ages will find trendy to traditional items at prices to suit all pockets. There are always special offers giving extra value and there is a full range of duvets, pillows, tablecloths, towels, throws, cushion covers, duvet covers and curtains (ready-made and made-to-measure), and bathroom fittings including shower curtains. Seymour's have their own high quality brand of polycotton sheets, valances and pillowcases, also available in percale. More unusual items include flannelette sheets, super king-size, 4ft and bunk-size bedding. Latest additions include a delightful Portugese range of bedding and towels by Piu Belle. Brands include current perfect ranges from Sanderson, Dorma, Nimbus, Snuggledown, Christy, Coloroll, Miller, Peter Reed and Ashley Wilde, plus economy lines and seconds. Chainstore seconds are often on offer and all prices are extremely competitive. For children, they stock Designers Guild quilt covers and fabric, as well as pattern books from which orders can be taken. Staff are friendly and obliging and will advise if required, and many items can be ordered if not in stock. Short-term parking is available right outside from Tuesday to Friday and there is wheelchair access. Debit and credit cards are accepted.

THE FACTORY SHOP

2–4 COMMERCIAL STREET, CROOK, CO DURHAM DL15 9HP, ☎ 01388 763211, 9–5.30 MON–SAT, 10.30–4.30 SUN. **FACTORY SHOP**

See page 243 (CHESH)

THE FAMOUS BRUNSWICK WAREHOUSE LTD

1-2 WEST ROW, DARLINGTON, CO DURHAM DL1 5PL, ☎ 01325 488446, **e-mail:** northshoe@mcmail.com, 9–5 MON–SAT.

25 JACKSON STREET, GATESHEAD, TYNE & WEAR, ☎ 0191 477 2364, **e-mail:** northshoe@mcmail.com, 9–5 MON–SAT.

UNIT 3 ANCHOR RETAIL PARK, MARINA WAY, HARTLEPOOL, CO DURHAM TS24 0XB, ☎ 01429 264519, **e-mail:** northshoe@mcmail.com, 10–7 MON–FRI, 9–6 SAT, 11–5 SUN.

UNIT 2, PETERLEE RETAIL DEVELOPMENT, HOWLETCH LANE, OFF EASTINGTON ROAD, PETERLEE, CO DURHAM SR8 2BL, ☎ 0191 587 0709, **e-mail:** northshoe@mcmail.com, 9–6 MON–SAT, 10–4 SUN.

UNIT 4, PALLION RETAIL PARK, WOODBINE TERRACE, SUNDERLAND, TYNE & WEAR SR4 6TY, ☎ 0191 565 7302, **e-mail:** northshoe@mcmail.com, 9.30–6 MON–WED, 9.30–7 THUR, FRI, 9–6 SAT, 10.30–4.30 SUN.

UNIT 4, OLD FULWELL ROAD, ROKER, SUNDERLAND, TYNE & WEAR SR6 0JD, ☎ 0191 565 0965, **e-mail:** northshoe@mcmail.com, 9–6 MON–SAT, 7 ON THUR, 10–4 SUN.

CHARLOTTE STREET, SOUTH SHIELDS, TYNE & WEAR NE33 1QQ, ☎ 0191 427 6545, **e-mail:** northshoe@mcmail.com, 9–5 MON–SAT, 9–6 THUR, 10–4 SUN.

42 WHITES MARKET, SUNDERLAND, TYNE & WEAR SR1 3DG, ☎ 0191 514 2653, **e-mail:** northshoe@mcmail.com, 9–5 MON–SAT.

UNIT 2A, SANDS INDUSTRIAL ESTATE, SWALWELL, GATESHEAD, TYNE & WEAR NE16 3DG, ☎ 0191 488 1333, **e-mail:** northshoe@mcmail.com, 9–7 MON–FRI, 9–6 SAT, 10–4 SUN.
PERMANENT DISCOUNT OUTLET

See page 240 (CHESH)

TK MAXX

TEAM VALLEY, RETAIL WORLD, GATESHEAD, TYNE & WEAR, ☎ 0191 487 4468, www.tkmaxx.com, PHONE FOR DETAILS.

UNIT 3, THE HIGHLIGHT RETAIL PARK, HARTLEPOOL MARINA, MARINA WAY, HARTLEPOOL, CO DURHAM TS24 0UX, ☎ 01429 222296, www.tkmaxx.com, 10–8 MON–FRI, 9–6 SAT, 11–5 SUN.

THE BRIDGES SHOPPING CENTRE, 34 CROWTREE ROAD, SUNDERLAND, TYNE & WEAR SR3 3JU, ☎ 0191 514 4484, www.tkmaxx.com, 9–5.30 MON–FRI, 9–6 SAT, 11–5 SUN.
PERMANENT DISCOUNT OUTLET

See page 232 (BEDS)

TOYMASTER FACTORY OUTLET

50–51 THE CORNMILL SHOPPING CENTRE, DARLINGTON, CO DURHAM DL1 1LT, ☎ 01325 363222, www.toyworldstore.com, 9–5.30 MON–SAT. **FACTORY SHOP**

Toymaster Factory Outlets are part of Europe's largest toy factory outlet retailer. They stock the very latest toys at amazing prices as well as TP outdoor products. They also offer an enormous range of branded products, which may be surplus stocks, end of ranges or cancelled orders, and are therefore able to sell those products at up to 70% off normal high street prices. Their range includes famous names such as: Action Man, Barbie, Bandai, Crayola, Corgi, Fisher-Price, Hasbro, Hornby, Lego, Little Tikes, Meccano, Tomy, V-Tech and many more, all at unbelievably low prices.

WYNSORS WORLD OF SHOES

PARKFIELD ROAD, OFF BRIDGE ROAD, STOCKTON-ON-TEES, CO DURHAM TS18 3DJ, ☎ 01642 672525, 9–5.30 MON, TUE, WED, SAT, 9–8 THUR, FRI, 10–4 SUN AND BANK HOLIDAYS. **PERMANENT DISCOUNT OUTLET**

See page 241 (CHESH)

CORNWALL

CORNISH MARKET WORLD

STADIUM RETAIL PARK, PAR, ST AUSTELL, CORNWALL PL25 3RP, ☎ 01726 812544, FAX: 01726 812346, **e-mail:** info@cornishmarketworld.co.uk, www.cornishmarketworld.co.uk, 9–5 SAT, SUN AND BANK HOLIDAYS, AND WED JUNE-SEPT.
PERMANENT DISCOUNT OUTLET

Huge indoor market that sells an enormous range of goods and food at very competitive prices: for example, a good quality breadmaker, £45. Sells clothes, fabrics, phones, bags, tools, electric equipment, motability equipment, jewellery and furniture. There is a good butchers, fish, and fruit and veg stands.

THE FACTORY SHOP

OLD STATION YARD, BERRYCOMBE ROAD, BODMIN, CORNWALL PL31 2NF, ☎ 01208 78492, 9–5.30 MON–SAT, 10.30–4.30 SUN.

MOUNT AMBROSE, SCORRIER, REDRUTH, CORNWALL TR15 1QT, ☎ 01209 219116, 9.30–5.30 MON–SAT, 10–4 SUN. **FACTORY SHOP**

See page 243 (CHESH)

TRAGO MILLS

ARWENACK STREET, FALMOUTH, CORNWALL, TR11 3LF, ☎ 01326 315738, www.trago.co.uk, 9–5.30 MON–SAT, 10.45–4.45 SUN.

TWOWATERSFOOT, LISKEARD, CORNWALL PL14 6HY, ☎ 01579 348877, www.trago.co.uk, 9–5.30 MON–SAT, 10.45- 4.45 SUN. **PERMANENT DISCOUNT OUTLET**

The historic Trago's original Cornish site is in the Glynn Valley on the A38 between Liskeard and Bodmin. You can bargain hunt here for brand name art materials, bathrooms and bedrooms and ceramics, carpets and rugs, clothing, DIY and home improvement, furniture, garden accessories, gifts, textiles, lighting, pet care, saddlery, stationery, tools, motoring products, toys and sport equipment and much more. There's a restaurant and picnic area by the beautiful Fowey river bank, free parking and disabled access. The Falmouth store is smaller, with only limited free car parking outside, but there is a public car park adjacent.

TRIPLE M FASHION

NEW PORTREATH ROAD, JUST OUTSIDE REDRUTH, CORNWALL TR16 4QL, ☎ 01209 842931 10–5.30 SEVEN DAYS A WEEK. **PERMANENT DISCOUNT OUTLET**

Large permanent discount shop selling men's and women's clothes, toys, bedding, footwear, bags, children's clothes.

CUMBRIA

BRIGGS SHOES

SOUTHEND ROAD, PENRITH, CUMBRIA CA11 8JH, ☎ 01768 899001, FAX: 01768 899001, www.briggsshoes.co.uk, 9.30–5.30 MON–SAT. **PERMANENT DISCOUNT OUTLET**

Vast selection of well-known brands of shoes with permanent clearance lines always on display. Some of the brands stocked include Hotter, Gabor, Equity, Hush Puppy, Van-Dal, Servas and the wider-fitting Elmdale range. Also stocks a large selection of children's clearance and sub-standards, from Start-Rite and Hush Puppy.

CATALOGUE BARGAIN SHOP

UNITS 4–5, SOUTH LAKELANDS RETAIL PARK, KENDAL, CUMBRIA LA9 6DU, ☎ 01539 740734, www.bargaincrazy.com, 9–8 MON–SAT, 11–5 SUN. **PERMANENT DISCOUNT OUTLET**

See page 234 (CAMBS)

FAMOUS FOOTWEAR

20–30 SANDES AVENUE, KENDAL, CUMBRIA LA9 4SG, ☎ 01539 738403, 9–5.30 MON–FRI, 9–6 SAT, 11–5 SUN. **FACTORY SHOP**

Wide range of brand names including Lilley & Skinner, Hush Puppies, Lotus, Wrangler, Frank Wright, Red Tape, Rohde, Brevitt, Padders, Rombah Wallace and Rieker, all at discount prices of up to 50%. Stand alone shop in Kendal which, as well as all the shoe brands, including clothing (Happit) and housewares.

FURNESS FOOTWEAR FACTORY SHOP

LONG LANE, DALTON-IN-FURNESS, CUMBRIA LA15 8PB, ☎ 01229 468837, 9–5.30 MON–SAT, 9–8 ON FRI, 10–4 SUN. **PERMANENT DISCOUNT OUTLET**

Stocks top brand-name shoes at less than half price. Special monthly offers always available. There are shoes, trainers, slippers, sandals and boots for all the family, with a selection of bags, cleaners and polishes available, all at discount prices.

K SHOES FACTORY SHOP

K VILLAGE, NETHERFIELD, KENDAL, CUMBRIA LA7 7BT, ☎ 01539 721892, 9.30–6 MON–FRI, 9–6 SAT, 11–5 SUN. **FACTORY SHOP**

Clarks International operate a chain of factory shops nationally which specialise in selling discontinued lines and slight sub-standards for men, women and children from Clarks, K Shoes and other famous brands. These shops trade under the name of K Shoes Factory Shop or Clarks Factory Shop and while not all are physically attached to a shoe factory, they are treated as factory shops by the company. Customers can expect to find an extensive range of quality shoes, sandals, walking boots, slippers, trainers, handbags, accessories and gifts, while their major outlets also offer luggage, sports clothing, sports equipment and outdoor clothing. Brands stocked include Clarks, K Shoes, Springer, CICA, Hi-Tec, Caterpillar, Timberland, Regatta, Craghoppers, Kangaroo Poo, Mercury, Antler, Eminent, Travelon, Hudson and Carlton, although not all are sold in every outlet. Phone first to find out what your particular store is offering. Discounts are from 30% to 60% off the normal high street price for perfect stock.

K VILLAGE OUTLET SHOPPING

LOUND ROAD, KENDAL, NEAR JUNCTION 36 OF M6, CUMBRIA LA9 7DA, ☎ 01539 732363, **e-mail:** mdixon@realm-ocm.com, www.kvillage.co.uk, 9.30–6 MON–FRI, 9–6 SAT, 11–5 SUN (9.30–5.30 MON–FRI NOVEMBER TO MARCH). **FACTORY SHOPPING VILLAGE**

Twelve outlets including Cotton Traders, Crabtree & Evelyn, Dartington Crystal selling Cloverleaf as well as glassware, Van Heusen, Denby Pottery, The Food Factory, Ponden Mill, Prices Candles, Tog 24, National Trust Gift Shop and a giant K Shoes factory shop selling a wide range of labels from K Shoes, Clarks, Cica, Delsey and Antler, as well as a full-price K Shop. There is also a heritage centre where you can discover the history of shoemaking, a 150-seater restaurant, a coffee shop, children's play area, baby changing facilities, a riverside picnic area, disabled facilities and free parking. Take the South Kendal exit and follow the signs for K Village.

LITTLEWOODS CATALOGUE DISCOUNT STORE

RAWLINSON STREET, BARROW-IN-FURNESS, CUMBRIA LA14 1BS, ☎ 01229 870668, 8.45–5.15 MON–SAT, 11–5 SUN. **PERMANENT DISCOUNT OUTLET**

See page 237 (CHESH)

MATALAN

WALNEY ROAD, BARROW-IN-FURNESS, CUMBRIA LA14 5UN, ☎ 01229 430899, FAX: 01229 430948, www.matalan.co.uk, 9.30–8 MON–FRI, 9–6 SAT, 11–5 SUN.

UNIT 2, 3, 4, STATION RETAIL PARK, WATER STREET, CARLISLE CUMBRIA CA2 5AF, ☎ 01228 403510, FAX: 01228 510068, www.matalan.co.uk, 10–8 MON–FRI, 9–6 SAT, 11–5 SUN.

DERWENT HOWE, SOLWAY ROAD, WORKINGTON, CUMBRIA CA14 3YA, ☎ 01900 870966, FAX: 01900 870967, www.matalan.co.uk, 9.30–8 MON–FRI, 9–6 SAT, 11–5 SUN. **PERMANENT DISCOUNT OUTLET**

See page 232 (BEDS)

NEW BALANCE ATHLETIC SHOES UK LTD

15 BANK STREET, KESWICK, CUMBRIA, ☎ 01768 774631, www.newbalance.co.uk, 9.30–5.30 MON–SAT, 10–5 SUN.

ST HELENS LANE, FLIMBY, MARYPORT, CUMBRIA CA15 8RY, ☎ 01900 602850, www.newbalance.co.uk, 9.30–5.30 MON–FRI, 9–5 SAT, 12–4 SUN.

MAIN STREET, SHAP, PENRITH, CUMBRIA CA10 3NL, ☎ 01931 716333, www.newbalance.co.uk, 9.30–5.30 MON–FRI, 9–5 SAT, 12–4 SUN. **FACTORY SHOP**

Factory shop selling running shoes, walking shoes and boots, fell running shoes, cross trainers, sports bags, sports clothing and children's trainers, all with discounts starting at 30% off normal retail prices.

THE FACTORY SHOP

EMPIRE BUILDINGS, MAIN STREET, EGREMONT, CUMBRIA CA22 2BD, ☎ 01946 820434, 9–5 MON–SAT. 10–4 SUN.

THE GILL, ULVERSTON, CUMBRIA LA12 7BN, ☎ 01229 583360, 9–5.30 MON–SAT, 10.30–4.30 SUN.

5 MARKET PLACE, WIGTON, CUMBRIA CA7 9NW, ☎ 01697 342171, 9–5.30 MON–SAT, 10.30–4.30 SUN. **FACTORY SHOP**

See page 243 (CHESH)

THE FAMOUS BRUNSWICK WAREHOUSE LTD

UNIT 5, THE BRIDGES RETAIL PARK, FLAT WALKS, WHITEHAVEN, CUMBRIA CA28 7RQ,

☎ 01946 694706, **e-mail:** northshoe@mcmail.com, 9–6 MON–SAT, 7 ON THUR, 10.30–4.30 SUN. **PERMANENT DISCOUNT OUTLET**

See page 240 (CHESH)

TK MAXX

THE EDEN CENTRE AND MARKET HALL, FISHER STREET, CARLISLE, CUMBRIA CA3 8JB, ☎ 01228 819292, www.tkmaxx.com, 9–5.30 MON–FRI, 8.30–6 SAT, 11–4 SUN. **PERMANENT DISCOUNT OUTLET**

See page 232 (BEDS)

TOG 24

UNIT 4, MARKET CROSS, AMBLESIDE, CUMBRIA LA22 9BT, ☎ 01539 433913, **e-mail:** mail-order@tog24.com, www.tog24.com, 9.30–6 MON–SAT, 10–5 SUN.

10 CRAG BROW, BOWNESS, CUMBRIA LA23 3BX, ☎ 01539 488656, **e-mail:** mail-order@tog24.com, www.tog24.com, 9.30–5.30 MON–THUR, 9.30–6 FRI, SAT, 10–5.30 SUN.

9 MARKET SQUARE, KESWICK, CUMBRIA CA12 5BJ, ☎ 01768 780876, **e-mail:** mail-order@tog24.com, www.tog24.com, 10–5 MON–FRI, 9.30–5.30 SAT, SUN. **FACTORY SHOP**

K VILLAGE, LOUND ROAD, KENDAL, CUMBRIA LA9 7DA, ☎ 01539 721555, **e-mail:** mail-order@tog24.com, www.tog24.com, 9.30–6 MON–FRI, 9–6 SAT, 11–5 SUN. **FACTORY SHOP IN A FACTORY SHOPPING VILLAGE**

See page 240 (CHESH)

WYNSORS WORLD OF SHOES

FURNESS FOOTWEAR, DALTON FIELDS LANE, DALTON-IN-FURNESS, CUMBRIA LA15 8PB, ☎ 01229 468837, 9–5.30 MON–SAT, 8 ON FRI, 10–4 SUN. **PERMANENT DISCOUNT OUTLET**

See page 241 (CHESH)

DERBYSHIRE

BROUGHTON SHOE WAREHOUSE

7 CROWN SQUARE, MATLOCK, DERBYSHIRE DE4 3AL, ☎ 01629 55616, 9–5.30 MON–SAT, 10–4 SUN. **PERMANENT DISCOUNT OUTLET**

Sells women's boots, shoes, sandals, handbags and slippers seasonally, as well as men's footwear, at savings of between 20% and 50%. Brands include Trickers and some Italian and Spanish designers.

DE BRADELEI JUNIOR

UNITY MILL HOUSE, DERWENT STREET, BELPER, DERBYSHIRE DE56 1WN, ☎ 01773 829830, FAX: 01773 829822, 9.30–5.30 MON–FRI, 9.30–6 SAT, 10.30–4.30 SUN. **PERMANENT DISCOUNT OUTLET**

It's difficult to find good children's discount shops – possibly because the unit prices are so low to start with. So it's good to see that that retailer with a lot of experience in the discount market, De Bradelei, has opened a De Bradelei Junior in Belper, Derbyshire. Opposite Thorntons Factory, the shop features for girls: Lily by Lily, OshKosh B'Gosh, Van Happen, Smarties, Vitamins and Zip-Zap; and for boys: Aribas, MCA, Osh Kosh, Zip-Zap and many more. Footwear includes Hush Puppies and Salamander. There are great gifts and accessories for all ages. The shoe section has qualified shoe fitters and car parking is easy.

GIFTTREE

38 MAIN CENTRE, DERBY, DERBYSHIRE DE1 2PE, ☎ 01332 204078, 9–5 MON–SAT.

36 HIGH STREET, SWADLINCOTE, DERBYSHIRE DE11 8HY, ☎ 01283 226700, 9–5 MON–SAT. **FACTORY SHOP**

Items from the Express Gifts mail order catalogues at reduced prices including cards, giftwrap, gifts, stationery, kitchenware, household products, clothes and toys, including Galt products. Discounts in most departments range from at least 50% off original catalogue selling prices.

HAWK FACTORY CYCLE STORES

960 LONDON ROAD, ALVASTON, DERBY, DERBYSHIRE DE24 8PY, ☎ 01332 756666, 9–6 MON–SAT, 9–4.30 SUN. **FACTORY SHOP**

Sells all types of adult's and children's bikes direct to the public at factory prices. Children's trikes start at £26.99, adults' mountain bikes £79.99 for women, £89.99 for men, normally £149.99. There are also clearance shops in South Yardley, Birmingham (0121 742 3332), Nottingham (0115 958 5900), Coventry (0247 622 2783), Shrewsbury (01743 344554), Cannock (01543 361656) and Cradley Heath (01384 636535).

LABEL TRADERS

30 MAIN CENTRE, DERBY, DERBYSHIRE DE1 2PE, ☎ 01332 381439, www.labeltraders.co.uk, 9–5 MON–SAT. **FACTORY SHOP**

Good quality ex-chainstore merchandise from well-known high street shops with all the labels cut out. Stock includes knitwear, dresses, suits, blouses, skirts, sportswear, nightwear, trousers for women, and childrenswear. Also stocks some household goods such as towels. Discounts range up to 50%. There are other branches in Sutton-in-Ashfield and Ruddington.

LEE COOPER

MCARTHURGLEN DESIGNER OUTLET MANSFIELD, MANSFIELD ROAD, SOUTH NORMANTON, ALFRETON, JUNCTION 28 OF M1, FOLLOW SIGNS FOR A38, DERBYSHIRE DE55 2ER, ☎ 01773 545153, 10–6 MON–FRI, 8 ON THUR, 9–6 SAT, 11–5 SUN. **FACTORY SHOP IN A FACTORY SHOPPING VILLAGE**

See page 238 (CHESH)

MARKS & SPENCER

MCARTHURGLEN DESIGNER OUTLET VILLAGE MANSFIELD, MANSFIELD ROAD, ALFRETON, DERBYSHIRE DE55 2ER, ☎ 01773 545342. 10–6 MON–FRI, 8 ON THUR, 9–6 SAT, 11–5 SUN. **FACTORY SHOP IN A FACTORY SHOPPING VILLAGE**

See page 238 (CHESH)

MASSON MILLS SHOPPING VILLAGE

DERBY ROAD, MATLOCK BATH, NEAR MATLOCK, DERBYSHIRE DE4 3PY, ☎ 01629 760208, FAX: 01629 761525, 10–5.30 MON–SAT, 11–5 SUN. **FACTORY SHOPPING VILLAGE**

Anchored by Edinburgh Woollen Mills and set on four floors, this shopping village is set in regenerated 18th century mill building with a working textile museum and conference facilities. There are shops selling fashion, golfwear and equipment, gifts, speciality foods and country goods and include Julian Graves food items, Woods of Windsor, and Ponden Mill selling bedlinen and towels. The top floor is a designer clothing store stocking labels such as DKNY, Kangol, Ben Sherman, Miss Sixty, Tommy Hilfiger and many others, all with up to 50% off normal retail prices. There is a riverside restaurant on site.

MATALAN

BRADSHAW RETAIL PARK, BRADSHAW WAY, DERBY, DERBYSHIRE DE24 5WA, ☎ 01332 223850, FAX: 01332 298020, www.matalan.co.uk, 9.30–8 MON–FRI, 9–6 SAT, 11–5 SUN. **PERMANENT DISCOUNT OUTLET**

See page 232 (BEDS)

MCARTHURGLEN DESIGNER OUTLET

MANSFIELD ROAD, SOUTH NORMANTON, ALFRETON, JUNCTION 28 OF M1, DERBYSHIRE DE55 2ER, ☎ 01773 545000, www.mcarthurglen.com/mansfiel, 10–6 MON–FRI, 8 ON THUR, 9–6 SAT, 11–5 SUN. **FACTORY SHOPPING VILLAGE**

The McArthurGlen Designer Outlet Mansfield has recently undergone a year-long development programme, transforming it from an open-plan department store layout to individual shops. The new look outlet is now bigger and better. Find all your favourite brands at discounts of up to 50% off typical retail prices. Facilities include a children's play area, a food court and plenty of free parking. Stores include: Antler, Banana Books, Bed & Bath Works, Big L, Camille Lingerie, Chapelle, Claire's Accessories, Coloroll, Cotton Traders, Donnay, Edinburgh Crystal, Harbi, Jaeger, Jane Shilton, Julian Graves, Kitch N Sync, Leading Labels, Lee Cooper, Mountain Warehouse, Pavers Shoes, Petroleum, Pilot, Price's Candles, Professional Cookware, Remington, Roman Originals, Sky, Soled Out, Speedo, Sportsmill, Suits You, Thorntons, Tog 24, Toyworld,

Revlon, Marks & Spencer Outlet, Windsmoor, Sportz, Reebok, Jumper, HKA, Proudfoot Leather, Garden Outlet, Lilley & Skinner, Adidas, Viyella, Whittards, XS Records and many more.

OAKHAM CLOTHING

BULLBRIDGE, AMBERGATE, DERBYSHIRE DE56 2HH, ☎ 01773 853473, 10–5.30 MON–FRI, 10–5 SAT, 10–4 SUN AND BANK HOLIDAYS. **FACTORY SHOP**

Previously Stevenson's of Ambergate, now under new ownership, this factory shop sells a wide range of women's knitwear, blouses, skirts, dresses, underwear, nightdresses, hosiery, men's trousers, outerwear, knitwear and childrenswear, as well as towels, face cloths and shoes for men and women. Women's clothes range from 8 to 22 in size, men's from 28in waist to 44in in season. There is a huge range of underwear, as well as wool coats, macs and anoraks in the outerwear. Childrenswear ranges from babies to teenwear.

PEAK VILLAGE

CHATSWORTH ROAD, ROWSLEY, (ON THE A6 BETWEEN BAKEWELL AND MATLOCK) DERBYSHIRE DE4 2JE, ☎ 01629 735326, www.peakvillage.co.uk, 9.30–5.30 MON–SAT, 10–5 SUN, EXCEPT CHRISTMAS DAY. **FACTORY SHOPPING VILLAGE**

More than 20 factory outlets including Leading Labels, Cotton Traders, Luggage & Bags, The Book Depot, Pavers Shoes, Sports & Mountain Warehouse, Yeoman Outdoors outdoor wear and equipment, Ponden Mill, Mansworld, New Beginnings and Woodlands Fitness Centre, all just 30 minutes from the M1 at the entrance to the Peak District National Park. On-site catering includes Massarella's Restaurant, which offers everything from an ice cream sundae to a traditional Sunday roast. The Wind in the Willows Attraction is a magical journey through the world of Ratty, Badger, Mole and of course the irrepressible Mr Toad. The latest sound and lighting effects bring Kenneth Grahame's classic tale to life in an enchanting recreation that's not just for kids! Free parking for up to 400 cars. Recently opened the Woodlands Fitness Centre.

R S DESIGNER LEISUREWEAR LTD

192–194 NORMAN STREET, COTMANHAY, ILKESTON, DERBYSHIRE DE7 8NR, ☎ 0115 932 3865, FAX: 0115 877 9915, **e-mail:** roger@sweatshirtsdirect.co.uk, www.sweatshirtsdirect.co.uk 9.30–3.30 MON–FRI. SAT: PHONE FIRST. **PERMANENT DISCOUNT OUTLET**

Sports, leisurewear, sweatshirts and cardigans for schoolwear in sizes from 1 year to XXXXL (60in waist) at discounts of up to 50%. Women's cardigans, sweatshirts and ski pants plus a variety of clothes, but no shoes, ranging from £1 to £12. All the merchandise is made up of overmakes, slight imperfects and end of season lines. There is a permanent sale rail. There is also a made-to-measure service which caters for all shapes and sizes, as well as an embroidery service.

TDP FACTORY SHOP

TDP HOUSE, RAWDON ROAD, MOIRA, SWADLINCOTE, DERBYSHIRE DE12 6DT, ☎ 01283 550400, www.tdptex-promotions.com, 9.30–5.30 MON–FRI, 10–4 SAT, SUN. **FACTORY SHOP**

In the heart of the National Forest, this factory shop sells clothes for children, mainly nightwear and underwear, at good discounts. Also women's and menswear at reasonable prices. TDP specialises in womenswear in sizes 16 to 30, and sells branded and ex-chainstore goods at a fraction of normal retail prices.

THE FAMOUS BRUNSWICK WAREHOUSE LTD

UNIT 4, SOUTHGATE RETAIL PARK, NORMANTON ROAD, DERBY, DERBYSHIRE DE23 6UX, ☎ 01332 204532, **e-mail:** northshoe@mcmail.com, 9–6 MON–WED, SAT, 9–8 THUR, FRI, 11–5 SUN. **PERMANENT DISCOUNT OUTLET**

See page 240 (CHESH)

THE SHOE FACTORY SHOP

UNIT 6, TRAFFIC STREET, EAGLE CENTRE, DERBY, DERBYSHIRE DE1 2NL, ☎ 01332 372823, 9–5 MON–SAT, 10.30–4.30 SUN. **FACTORY SHOP**

Men's and women's accessories which are bought in from other manufacturers including Spanish, Portuguese and Italian companies. All are unbranded. The range covers from mocassins to dressy shoes. Women's shoes from £10 to £30. Men's shoes from £20 upwards. They also sell slippers for men, women and children all year round.

TK MAXX

8 EAST STREET, DERBY, DERBYSHIRE, ☎ 01332 364225, www.tkmaxx.com, 9–5.30 MON–THUR, 9–6 FRI–SAT, 11–5 SUN. **PERMANENT DISCOUNT OUTLET**

See page 232 (BEDS)

TOG 24

DERBYSHIRE DESIGNER OUTLET VILLAGE, MANSFIELD ROAD, SOUTH NORMANTON, DERBYSHIRE DE55 2JW, ☎ 01773 545206, **e-mail:** mail-order@tog24.com, www.tog24.com, 10–6 MON–FRI, 8 ON THUR, 9–6 SAT, 11–5 SUN. **FACTORY SHOP IN A FACTORY SHOPPING VILLAGE**

See page 240 (CHESH)

TOYWORLD STORE FACTORY OUTLET

MCARTHURGLEN DESIGNER OUTLET MANSFIELD, MANSFIELD ROAD, SOUTH NORMANTON, ALFRETON, JUNCTION 28 OF M1, DERBYSHIRE DE55 2JH, ☎ 01773 545 333, www.toyworldstore.com, 10–6 MON–FRI, 8 ON THUR, 9–6 SAT, 11–5 SUN. **FACTORY SHOP IN A FACTORY SHOPPING VILLAGE**

See page 241 (CHESH)

WILKINSON STORES

13 INSTITUTE LANE, ALFRETON, DERBYSHIRE DE55 7BQ, ☎ 01773 836845, www.wilko.co.uk, 9–5.30 MON–THUR, SAT, 9–6 FRI, 10–2 SUN. MAIL ORDER. **PERMANENT DISCOUNT OUTLET**

See page 241 (CHESH)

WIRKSWORTH FACTORY SHOP

BENCO HOSIERY, NORTH END MILLS, WIRKSWORTH, DERBYSHIRE DE4 4FG, ☎ 01629 824731, 9–5 SEVEN DAYS A WEEK, 8 ON THUR. **FACTORY SHOP**

Wide selection of clothes for the family, household goods, giftware and linen. There are T-shirts, shorts, sun vests, skirts, blouses, shirts, sweatshirts, jeans, trousers, dresses, work shirts, swimwear, jog suits, underwear, babywear, socks, tea towels, pillows, duvets and towels. There is a children's play corner and snacks facility. Large, free car park. You can see machines making socks on most days.

WYNSORS WORLD OF SHOES

NETTO RETAIL DEVELOPMENT, SHEFFIELD ROAD, CHESTERFIELD, DERBYSHIRE S41 8JT, ☎ 01246 276690, 9–5.30 MON, TUE, WED, SAT, 9–8 THUR, FRI, 10–4 SUN AND BANK HOLIDAYS. **PERMANENT DISCOUNT OUTLET**

See page 241 (CHESH)

DEVON

ATLANTIC VILLAGE OUTLET CENTRE

CLOVELLY ROAD, OFF A39, WEST OF BIDEFORD, NORTH DEVON 01237 422544, **e-mail:** rmorris@realm-ocm.com, www.atlanticvillage.co.uk, JULY–MID SEPT, 9.30–7 MON–SAT, 11–5 SUN; MID SEPT–MID OCT AND EASTER TO JULY 9.30–6.30 MON–SAT, 11–5 SUN; MID OCT–EASTER 9.30–5 MON–SAT, 11–5 SUN. **FACTORY SHOPPING VILLAGE**

More than 30 shops with famous names and Devon's largest interactive maze make this village a good family day out. Shops include Banana Books; Claire's Accessories; Colony Candles; Cotton Traders, Designer Room, Ecco; Edinburgh Woollen Mill; Event Jewellery; Jane Shilton; Jean Scene; Julian Graves; Nickelby's; Pavers Shoes; Pilot; Ponden Mill; Puma; Roman Originals; Room, selling home accessories, fabrics and soft furnishings; Sportsmill; Suits You; Tog 24; Toyzone; Triumph; Warners; Windsmoor; XS Sound & Media. Free car parking, disabled and baby changing facilities. Atlantic Village also features an attractive piazza, cafés, a food court, visitor garden, arts and crafts market, open-air amphitheatre, and an adventure park set in an additional three-acre site linked to the shopping area by the piazza and amphitheatre. The Adventure Park features a mystery maze, adventure golf, wrecker's cove and adventure play boat.

BABE-EQUIP

9 LEAT STREET, TIVERTON, DEVON EX16 5LG, ☎ 01884 257938, FAX: 01884 257938, www.babe-equip.eclipse.co.uk, 9–5 MON–SAT. **HIRE SHOP**

Cots, highchairs, buggies, car seats, safety gates and other baby equipment.

BOB LOVELL SPORTS

36 FORE STREET, BRIXHAM, DEVON TQ5 8DZ, ☎ 01803 859115, FAX: 01803 859845, **e-mail:** Sales@Lovell-Rugby.co.uk, www.Lovell-Rugby.co.uk, MAIL ORDER. **PERMANENT DISCOUNT OUTLET**

Discounted rugby gear among other full-price stock.

CLARKS FACTORY SHOP

SHOE VALUE, 22 THE CROSSWAYS, HYDE ROAD, PAIGNTON, DEVON TQ4 5BL, ☎ 01803 553444, 9–5.30 MON–SAT. **FACTORY SHOP**

See page 236 (CHESH)

HUSH-A-BYE HIRE

16 WHITCHURCH AVENUE, EXETER, DEVON EX2 5NU, ☎ 01392 257636, OPEN SEVEN DAYS A WEEK: PHONE FOR AN APPOINTMENT. **HIRE SHOP**

Cots, highchairs, buggies, car seats, safety gates, travel cots, back packs: almost anything a parent of young children might want. Also supplies ball pools, bouncy castles etc, for children's parties. All items are bought new specially for hire.

MATALAN

UNIT 2, HAVEN BANKS, WATER LANE, EXETER, DEVON EX2 8DW, ☎ 01392 413375, FAX: 01392 413376, www.matalan.co.uk, 10–8 MON–FRI, 9–6 SAT, 11–5 SUN.

TRANSIT WAY, HONICKNOWLE, PLYMOUTH, DEVON PL5 3TW, ☎ 01752 237600, FAX: 01752 767216, www.matalan.co.uk, 9–8 MON–FRI, 9–6 SAT, 11–5 SUN. **PERMANENT DISCOUNT OUTLET**

See page 232 (BEDS)

NEXT TO NOTHING

30 EASTLAKE WALK, DRAKE CIRCUS, PLYMOUTH, DEVON PL1 1BL, ☎ 01752 229 487, www.next.co.uk, 9–5.30 MON–SAT, 11–5 SUN. **PERMANENT DISCOUNT OUTLET**

See page 239 (CHESH)

STEWART'S

58–60 FORE STREET, BRIXHAM, DEVON TQ5 8DZ, ☎ 01803 852000, FAX: 01803 852000, 9–5 MON–SAT, 10–4 SUN.

RICHMOND COURT, DAWLISH, DEVON EX7 9PL, ☎ 01626 895022, FAX: 01626 895022, 9–5 MON–SAT, 10.30–4.30 SUN.

24–26 QUEEN STREET, NEWTON ABBOT, DEVON TQ12 2EF, ☎ 01626 362721, FAX: 01626 36272, 9–5.30 MON–SAT.

9–15 STATION ROAD, TEIGNMOUTH, DEVON TQ14 8PE, ☎ 01626 775616, FAX: 01626 775616, 9–5.30 MON–SAT, 10.30–4.30 SUN.

37 FORE STREET, TOTNES, DEVON TG9 5HN, ☎ 01803 865093, FAX: 01803 865093, 9–5 MON–SAT, 10–4 SUN. **FACTORY SHOP**

Branded merchandise from most of the major UK chainstores, all well-known high street department store names, offered at a discount of 40% to 70% off normal high street prices. The garments are selected with great care by experienced buyers direct from factories worldwide to bring customers top quality merchandise at highly competitive prices.

TK MAXX

YEO BUILDING, 28 ROYAL PARADE, NEW GEORGE STREET, PLYMOUTH, DEVON PL1 1SA,

☎ 01752 255081, www.tkmaxx.com, 9–5.30 MON–WED, 9–8 THUR, 9–6 FRI–SAT, 11–5 SUN.

FIRST FLOOR, 56-62 FLEET WALK, FLEET WALK SHOPPING CENTRE, TORQUAY, DEVON TQ2 5EN, ☎ 01803 215682, www.tkmaxx.com, 9–5.30 MON–SAT, 7 ON THUR, 10–7 SAT, 11–5 SUN. **PERMANENT DISCOUNT OUTLET**

See page 232 (BEDS)

TOG 24

ATLANTIC VILLAGE, CLOVELLY ROAD, BIDEFORD, NORTH DEVON EX39 3QU, ☎ 01237 473799, **e-mail:** mail-order@tog24.com, www.tog24.com, 10–6 MON–SAT, 8 ON THUR, 10.30–4.30 SUN. **FACTORY SHOP IN A FACTORY SHOPPING VILLAGE**

See page 240 (CHESH)

TOYZONE

ATLANTIC VILLAGE, CLOVELLY ROAD, BIDEFORD, NORTH DEVON EX39 3QU, ☎ 01237 424324, FAX: 01237 473423, 9.30–7 MON–FRI, 9.30–6 SAT, 10.30–4.30 SUN. **FACTORY SHOP IN A FACTORY SHOPPING VILLAGE**

This shop sells a wide range of well-known children's brand names: Little Tikes, Corgi, Crayola, Tomy, Lego, Hasbro, Playskool, Mattel and Fisher-Price at discounts of up to 50%. They also stock a wide range of soft toys including TY Beanie Babies.

TRAGO MILLS SHOPPING AND LEISURE PARKS

LIVERTON, NEWTON ABBOT, DEVON TQ12 6JD, ☎ 01626 821111, www.trago.co.uk, 9–5.30 MON–SAT, 10.45–4.45 SUN. **PERMANENT DISCOUNT OUTLET**

The biggest range of discounted goods in the West Country, with a whole range of activities to keep the family amused on the 100 acre site. Sells virtually everything from men's, women's and childrenswear, gardening equipment and cookware to wallpaper, carpets and fitted kitchens. Most are branded goods and there is a café, pizza bar and petrol station. A reasonable amount of the women's fashion comes from high street multiples. The menswear offers a wide range of clothes, as well as all-leather classic brogues and Oxford shoes, and Doc Martens in the Shoes Yard. For the home, there are Black & Decker Dustbusters, Hotpoint dryers and washing machines with cosmetic blemishes; curtain fabrics from Monkwell, Sekers, Filigree, Laura Ashley as well as Janet Reger for Vantona double quilt covers, with matching sheets, pillow cases and valances. There is a vast range of tiles including Pilkington seconds. A huge gardening section with everything from hose pipes and garden machinery to imported trees and shrubs. An excellent leisure section offers bicycles and accessories, golf gear, keep-fit systems, fishing rods and flies. Comparison prices are not given here, although staff say most items are discounted by up to 50%, so if you're looking for a bargain, make sure you've done your homework on the high street first. The best deals are in fabrics, carpets, tiles and DIY. There is a leisure park with a giant free fall slide, supakart and family go-kart circuit, bumper boats, trawler rides, swan pedalos, pirate ship, aquablasters, orbiters, shooting gallery, remote control cars and cruisers, forklifts and mini-diggers, fun dungeon, animal park, model railway, narrow gauge steam railway, nature reserve, coarse fishing, Edwardian penny arcade and plenty of space to picnic and to park.

DORSET

MATALAN

TURBARY RETAIL PARK, RINGWOOD ROAD, BOURNEMOUTH, DORSET BH12 3JJ, ☎ 01202 590686, FAX: 01202 590697, www.matalan.co.uk, 10–8 MON–FRI, 9–6 SAT, 10–4 SUN.

JUBILEE RETAIL PARK, RADIPOLE PARK DRIVE, WEYMOUTH DORSET DT4 7BG, ☎ 01305 831300, FAX: 01305 830472, www.matalan.co.uk, 9–8 MON–FRI, 9–6 SAT, 10.30–4.30 SUN. **PERMANENT DISCOUNT OUTLET**

See page 232 (BEDS)

T J HUGHES

616–622 CHRISTCHURCH ROAD, BOSCOMBE, BOURNEMOUTH, DORSET BH1 4BR, ☎ 01202 300333, FAX: 01202 303515, **e-mail:** info@tjhughes.co.uk, www.tjhughes.co.uk, 9–5.30

MON–FRI, 9–6 SAT, 10–4 SUN. **PERMANENT DISCOUNT OUTLET**

See page 239 (CHESH)

THE CATALOGUE SHOP

401 LYMINGTON ROAD, HIGHCLIFFE, DORSET BH23 5HE, ☎ 01425 271202, FAX: 01425 278478, **e-mail:** thecatalogueshop@virgin.net, www.the catalogueshop.virgin.com, 9–5 MON–SAT, 10–5 SUN. **PERMANENT DISCOUNT OUTLET**

Returns, damaged and worn goods as well as clearance lines and ends of lines of branded merchandise from mail order catalogues. This includes men's, women's and children's wear, footwear, bedding, curtains, furniture, exercise equipment and leather coats. These items are always in stock but the shop also has an ever-changing range of items as well. Turnover is very fast with new deliveries every day. All items are sold at less than 50% of the catalogue price starting at 99p, with branded trainers from £14.99.

THE SHOE SHED

UNIT 9, QUADRANT ARCADE, HINTON ROAD, BOURNEMOUTH DORSET BH1 2AD, ☎ 01202 292992, 9–5.30 MON–SAT, 10–4 SUN. **FACTORY SHOP**

This shoe retailer, established for over 135 years, has a large factory shop selling a vast range of all types of women's, men's and children's shoes, all of which are perfects, at up to 30% below normal high street prices. Women's sandals cost from £2.99; shoes from £5. Men's shoes cost from £7.99; sports shoes from £5. Famous brands include Grenson, Loakes, Clarks, K Shoes, Elmdale, Caterpillar and Adidas. A large range of casual wear, including T-shirts and tracksuits for women, men and children, plus a selection of women's underwear. Kitchenware, ceramics, household goods and giftware are also stocked at discounted prices.

THE WARDROBE

422 LYMINGTON ROAD, HIGHCLIFFE, CHRISTCHURCH, DORSET BH23 5HE, ☎ 01425 276928, 10–5 MON–SAT, 10–1 WED. **DRESS AGENCY**

Stocks anything from Marks & Spencer to Ralph Lauren in sizes 8 to 20, with a wide range of shoes available. Bargain rail of older stock sold at half-price; sales in the summer and after Christmas. Large range of hats, handbags, scarves and jewellery.

TK MAXX

QUADRANT ARCADE, OLD CHRISTCHURCH ROAD, BOURNEMOUTH, DORSET BH1 2BX, ☎ 01202 316367, www.tkmaxx.com, 9–5.30 MON–FRI, 8 ON THUR, 9–6 SAT, 11–5 SUN. **PERMANENT DISCOUNT OUTLET**

See page 232 (BEDS)

ESSEX

BRANDLER GALLERIES

1 COPTFOLD ROAD, BRENTWOOD, ESSEX CM14 4BN, ☎ 01277 222269, **e-mail:** john@brandler-galleries.com, www.brandler-galleries.com/www.thomas-art.com/www.noddy-art.com, 10–5.30 TUE–SAT. PHONE FIRST IF LOOKING FOR A PARTICULAR ITEM. **PERMANENT DISCOUNT OUTLET**

Prints, sculptures and paintings of a high standard at prices which reflect the low overheads outside London. Works by Diana Armfield, Bill Bowyer, Fred Cuming, Bernard Dunstan, Mary Fedden, David Tindle, Carel Weight, Andy Warhol, David Hockney, Picasso and others of a similar calibre. Prices range from £45 to £20,000. for example, they sold a Turner watercolour for £18,500 which would have cost as much as £75,000 in Bond Street. There are original book illustrations for Noddy, Postman Pat, Captain Pugwash, Rupert etc. Also offer a framing service and free car park. Artwork for children's books including Noddy, Postman Pat, Thomas the Tank Engine, etc.

BURBERRY

FREEPORT RETAIL OUTLET VILLAGE, BRAINTREE, ESSEX CM7 8YH, ☎ 01376 554851 10–6 MON–SAT, 8 ON THUR, 11–5 SUN. **FACTORY SHOP IN A FACTORY SHOPPING VILLAGE**

See page 236 (CHESH)

CATALOGUE BARGAIN SHOP

ST JOHN'S WALK SHOPPING CENTRE, COLCHESTER, ESSEX CO2 7AL, ☎ 01206 563126, www.bargaincrazy.com, 9–5.30 MON–THUR, 9–7 FRI, 9–6 SAT, 10.30–4.30 SUN. **PERMANENT DISCOUNT OUTLET**

See page 234 (CAMBS)

CHARLES CLINKARD

CLACTON FACTORY OUTLET VILLAGE, STEPHENSON ROAD WEST, CLACTON-ON-SEA, ESSEX CO15 4TL, ☎ 01255 220384, FAX: 01255 230384, 10–6 MON–SAT, 8 ON THUR, 11–5 SUN. **FACTORY SHOP IN A FACTORY SHOPPING VILLAGE**

See page 241 (CO DURH)

CHOICE DISCOUNT STORES LIMITED

14–20 RECTORY ROAD, HADLEIGH, BENFLEET, ESSEX SS7 2ND, ☎ 01702 555245, 9–5.30 MON–THUR, 9–6 FRI, SAT.

26–28 HIGH STREET, BARKINGSIDE, ILFORD, ESSEX IG6 2DQ, ☎ 020 8551 2125, 9–5.30 MON–FRI, 9–6 SAT, 11–5 SUN.

10–11 LADYGATE CENTRE, HIGH STREET, WICKFORD, ESSEX SS12 9AJ, ☎ 01268 764893, 9–5.30 MON–FRI, 9–6 SAT.

UNIT 6A, MAYFLOWER RETAIL PARK, GARDINERS LINK, BASILDON, ESSEX SS14 3AP, ☎ 01268 288331, 10–6 MON–WED, 10–7 THUR, FRI, 9–6 SAT, 11–5 SUN.

14–16 HIGH STREET, GRAYS, ESSEX RM17 6LU, ☎ 01375 385780, 9–5.30 MON–FRI, 9–6 SAT.

CLACTON FACTORY SHOPPING VILLAGE, STEPHENSON ROAD WEST, CLACTON-ON-SEA, ESSEX CO15 4TL, ☎ 01255 474786, 10–6 MON–SAT, 11–5 SUN. **PERMANENT DISCOUNT OUTLET**

See page 235 (CAMBS)

CLACTON FACTORY SHOPPING VILLAGE

STEPHENSON ROAD WEST, CLACTON-ON-SEA, ESSEX CO15 4TL, ☎ 01255 479595, FAX: 01255 430777 INFORMATION LINE, 10–6 MON–SAT, 11–5 SUN. **FACTORY SHOPPING VILLAGE**

Forty eight units centred around a Victorian winter garden comprising the following: Banana Bookshop selling books, games and stationery; Because It's There (BIT) for sports and camping equipment; Bed & Bath Works, a homeware outlet with discounted branded linens and housewares from Janet Reger, Sheridan, Christy and Kingsley; Birthdays, stocking mainstream cards and gifts from manufacturers such as Andrew Brownsword, Disney, Parker, Galt and Warner Brothers; Camille for lingerie; Caterpillar selling foorwear from the Cat range; Choice, which sells family clothing from Next; Claire's Accessories; Clinkards family footwear from Church's, Gabor, Bally and Loake; Cook 'N Dine kitchenware, glass and ceramics; Cotton Traders casual wear; Dannimac outdoor wear; Designer Room selling designer fashion for men and women; Event fashion costume jewellery and watches from Accurist, Timberland, Seiko and Timex; Garden Store selling garden furniture, barbecues and equipment and, in season, Christmas decorations; Jacques Vert selling womenswear; JD Sports selling branded sports merchandise from Adidas, Nike, Reebok, Ellesse and Le Coq Sportif; Joanna Hall selling handbags from the Jane Shilton range; Julian Graves foods and nut mixes; Kids Play Factory with toys from ranges such as Fisher-Price and Lego; Leading Labels, with men's and women's fashions; Mobile Phone Shop; MX Active selling branded denim and casual wear for men, women and children; Nickelbys fashion wear for men and women; Olli Moda selling branded jeans and casual wear; Pilot, a young women's fashion outlet; Ponden Mill with a range of bedlinen and bathroom ware; Price's Candles; Roman Originals womenswear; Sasperilla for young women's fashions; Spotlight, a young women's fashion outlet; Suits You men's shirts, suits, and casual separates as well as wedding hire and Autonomy womenswear; Thorntons chocolates; Tog 24 outdoor activity wear; Windsmoor women's fashions; Travel Accessory Shop with travel goods from Delsey and Samsonite; Woods of Windsor toiletries and gift items; XS Music CDs and videos. There are also two restaurants, a tourist information centre, parking for 1,000 cars and a bus service link to Clacton-On-Sea town centre and railway station.

DESIGNER SHADES

FREEPORT ESSEX VILLAGE, CHARTER WAY, CHAPEL HILL, BRAINTREE, ESSEX CM77 8YH, ☎ 01376 334007, **e-mail:** info@sunglass-time.com, 10–6 MON–SAT, 8 ON THUR, 11–5 SUN. **FACTORY SHOP IN A FACTORY SHOPPING VILLAGE**

Designer Shades offer a wide selection of top-notch sunglasses and watches at more than 30% off typical high street prices. The frames are invitingly displayed on back-lit columns – no locked cabinets, messy stickers or hanging labels to contend with. Gucci, Polo Ralph Lauren, Valentino, Police, Christian Dior and Diesel are included in the ever-changing stock of top international brand names. Designer Shades ensure that all their sunglasses have quality lenses which protect against UVA and UVB rays, as well as filtering out damaging reflective blue light. Their range of high fashion unisex watches includes Dolce & Gabbana, Guess and Pulsar. They plan to have 20 shops throughout Europe by the end of 2003. For details of other locations, phone 01423 858007 or email info@sunglass-time.com.

FREEPORT BRAINTREE DESIGNER OUTLET VILLAGE

FREEPORT ESSEX VILLAGE, CHARTER WAY, CHAPEL HILL, BRAINTREE, JUNCTION 8 OF M11, THEN A120, ESSEX CM77 8YH, ☎ 01376 348168, www.freeportbraintree.com, 10–6 MON–SAT, 8 ON THUR, 11–5 SUN. **FACTORY SHOPPING VILLAGE**

Freeport Braintree is a designer outlet village with over 80 shops. Situated in the heart of Essex with easy access from the A120, Freeport Braintree has its own dedicated railway station and is only a one-hour journey from central London. Womenswear includes Aquascutum, Amazing Jeans, Antonio d'Errico, Box Fresh, Burberry, Christian Lacroix, Cotton Traders, Elle, Gossard, Karen Millen, Ted Baker, Tommy Hilfiger and Versace and The Designer Room with a host of designer labels. Menswear includes Aquascutum, Cecil Gee, Ciro Citterio, Cotton Traders, Kurt Muller, Nickleby's, Proibito, Ted Baker, Tommy Hilfiger, Van Heusen and Versace. For children there's Base 2 Base, Mexx and Toy Dome; there is also plenty to keep children entertained, such as the Cheeky Chimps indoor play area. Sportwear outlets include Brand Fusion, Donnay, Fila, Mountain Warehouse, Nike, Reebok, Regatta and Trespass. Footwear is covered by Ecco Shoes, Franchetti Bond, Hush Puppies, Jane Shilton, Lilley & Skinner, Soled Out and Vans Shoes. Shops selling household goods from kitchenware to pot pourri include Churchills, Denby, Edinburgh Crystal, Glen Eagles, Le Creuset, Professional Cookware, The Design House, Waterford Wedgwood and Villeroy & Boch. Other retail outlets, selling everything from luggage to music, include Body Shop, Carlton, Claire's Accessories, Designer Shades, Mobile Phone Store, Watch Store and XS Music, and there are no less than six cafés and restaurants on site.

HUSH PUPPIES

FREEPORT ESSEX VILLAGE, CHARTER WAY, CHAPEL HILL, BRAINTREE, ESSEX CM7 8YH, ☎ 01376 554682, 10–6 MON–SAT, 8 ON THUR, 11–5 SUN. **FACTORY SHOP**

Hush Puppies footwear sold at least 30% below normal retail prices. Also sells Loakes for men at £59.99.

KIDS COLLECTIONS

176C QUEENS ROAD, BUCKHURST HILL, ESSEX IG9 5BD, ☎ 020 8502 9600, 10–5.30 MON–SAT. **DRESS AGENCY**

Nearly-new designer wear children's clothes. Labels on sale at about one third of the retail price include Kenzo, Portofino, Oilily, Chipie and Levi's and all are in excellent condition. There are also new shoes, high chairs and a range of first Holy Communion accessories for sale.

KIDS PLAY FACTORY

UNIT 28, CLACTON FACTORY OUTLET SHOPPING CENTRE, STEVENSON ROAD, CLACTON-ON-SEA ESSEX CO15 4TL, ☎ 01255 222219, FAX: 01255 222654, 10–6 MON–SAT, 8 ON THUR, 11–5 SUN. **FACTORY SHOP IN A FACTORY SHOPPING VILLAGE**

This shop sells a wide range of well-known children's brand names: Little Tikes, Corgi, Crayola, Tomy, Lego, Hasbro, Playskool, Mattel and Fisher-Price at discounts of up to 50%. They also stock a wide range of soft toys including TY Beanie Babies.

LEE COOPER

FREEPORT ESSEX VILLAGE, CHARTER WAY, CHAPEL HILL, BRAINTREE, ESSEX CM7 8YH, ☎ 01376 554684, 10–6 MON–SAT, 8 ON THUR, 11–5 SUN. **FACTORY SHOP IN A FACTORY SHOPPING VILLAGE**

See page 238 (CHESH)

LILLEY & SKINNER

FREEPORT ESSEX VILLAGE, CHARTER WAY, CHAPEL HILL, BRAINTREE, ESSEX CM7 8YH, ☎ 01376 327490, 10–6 MON–SAT, 8 ON THUR, 11–5 SUN. **FACTORY SHOP IN A FACTORY SHOPPING VILLAGE**

Wide range of brand names including Lilley & Skinner, Hush Puppies, Lotus, Wrangler, Frank Wright, Red Tape, Rohde, Brevitt, Padders, Rombah Wallace and Rieker, all at discount prices of up to 50%.

MATALAN

CRICKETERS RETAIL PARK, CRICKETERS WAY, BASILDON, ESSEX SS13 1SA, ☎ 01268 290260, FAX: 01268 534860, www.matalan.co.uk, 10–8 MON–FRI, 9–6 SAT, 10–4 SUN.

UNIT 4, RIVERSIDE RETAIL PARK, VICTORIA ROAD, CHELMSFORD, ESSEX CM2 6LL, ☎ 01245 348787, FAX: 01245 348989, www.matalan.co.uk, 10–8 MON–FRI, 9–6 SAT, 11–5 SUN.

UNIT E, COLCHESTER RETAIL PARK, SHEEPPEN ROAD, COLCHESTER ESSEX CO3 3LE, ☎ 01206 812400, FAX: 01206 541716, www.matalan.co.uk, 10–8 MON–FRI, 9–6 SAT, 11–5 SUN.

TOWER RETAIL PARK, CRAYFORD ROAD, CRAYFORD, DARTFORD, ESSEX DA1 4LD, ☎ 01322 552140, FAX: 01322 522516, www.matalan.co.uk, 9 -8 MON–FRI, 9–6 SAT, 10–4 SUN.

117 NORTH STREET, ROMFORD ESSEX RM1 1EX, ☎ 01708 759780, FAX: 01708 760102, www.matalan.co.uk, 10–8 MON–FRI, 9–6 SAT, 10–4 SUN.

THE GREYHOUND RETAIL PARK, SUTTON ROAD, SOUTHEND, ESSEX SS2 5PY, ☎ 01702. 466248, FAX: 01702 617571, www.matalan.co.uk, 10 -8 MON–FRI, 9–6 SAT, 10–4 SUN.

UNIT 4B, THE TUNNEL ESTATE, LAKESIDE, WEST THURROCK, ESSEX RM20 3WZ, ☎ 01708 864350, FAX: 01708 864334, www.matalan.co.uk, 10–8 MON–FRI, 9–6 SAT, 11–5 SUN. **PERMANENT DISCOUNT OUTLET**

See page 232 (BEDS)

NIKE FACTORY STORE

FREEPORT ESSEX VILLAGE, CHARTER WAY, CHAPEL HILL, BRAINTREE, ESSEX CM7 8YH, ☎ 01376 320674, FAX: 01376 327469, www.nike.com, 10–6 MON–SAT, 8 ON THUR, 11–5 SUN. **FACTORY SHOP IN A FACTORY SHOPPING VILLAGE**

See page 239 (CHESH)

NIPPERS

WHITES FARM, BURES ROAD, WHITE COLNE, COLCHESTER, ESSEX CO6 2QF, ☎ 01787 228000, FAX: 01787 228560, **e-mail:** nipperscolchester@btinternet.com, www.nippers.co.uk, OPENING HOURS VARY SO PHONE FIRST. **PERMANENT DISCOUNT OUTLET**

See page 234 (BUCKS)

QD STORES

GREAT OAKS HOUSE, GREAT OAKS, BASILDON, ESSEX SS14 1JD, ☎ 01268 522999, 9–5.30 MON–SAT.

72–78 ROSEMARY ROAD, CLACTON-ON-SEA, ESSEX CO15 1TZ, ☎ 01255 479974, 9–5.30 MON–SAT, 10–4 SUN.

45–51 HIGH STREET, GRAYS, ESSEX RM16 5UF, ☎ 01375 385250, 9–5.30 MON–SAT.

UNITS 101–108, VICTORIA PLAZA, SOUTHEND-ON-SEA, ESSEX SS2 5FB, ☎ 01702 618777, 9–5.30 MON–SAT. **PERMANENT DISCOUNT OUTLET**

See page 232 (BEDS)

REGATTA

FREEPORT ESSEX VILLAGE, CHARTER WAY, CHAPEL HILL, BRAINTREE, ESSEX CM7 4YH, ☎ 01376 349755, FAX: 01376 349755, www.regatta.com, 10–6 MON–SAT, 8 ON THUR, 11–5 SUN. **FACTORY SHOP IN A FACTORY SHOPPING VILLAGE**

Regatta is the UK's biggest supplier of outdoor clothing and equipment for the whole family. The ranges comprise wovens, waterproofs, fleece, rucksacks and accessories for men, women and children, and are suitable for a whole range of outdoor activities. Regatta prides itself on offering excellent quality products at very reasonable prices. Craghoppers, the innovator in travel and outdoor wear, is a technical brand that leads with innovation. Its offering of waterproofs, fleece, wovens and rucksacks are intended for travel at home or abroad and suitable for a wide range of climates. All stock is sold here at discounted prices of at least 30%.

T J HUGHES

25–29 MARKET PLACE, ROMFORD, ESSEX RM1 3AB, ☎ 01708 747159, FAX: 01708 721126, **e-mail:** info@tjhughes.co.uk, www.tjhughes.co.uk, 9–5.30 MON–SAT, 10–4 SUN. **PERMANENT DISCOUNT OUTLET**

See page 239 (CHESH)

THE FACTORY SHOP LTD

THE GLOUCESTERS, LUCKYN LANE, PIPPS HILL INDUSTRIAL ESTATE, BASILDON, ESSEX SS14 3AX, ☎ 01268 520546, www.thefactoryshopsessexltd.co.uk, 9–6 MON–SAT, 10–5 SUN.

PURDEY'S INDUSTRIAL ESTATE, 1 MAGNOLIA WAY, ROCHFORD, ESSEX SS4 1ND, ☎ 01702 531153, www.thefactoryshopsessexltd.co.uk, 9–6 MON–SAT, 10–5 SUN. **FACTORY SHOP**

The Factory Shops carry a wide range of branded stock at discounted prices, from bed linen, towels, hardware, toys, party ware, electrical goods, tools and garden furniture to food, clothing, TY Beanies and much more. There is a large pet and aquatic department with a wide selection of pond and water features within its 14,000 square feet of selling space. At Christmas, a huge range of decorations, baubles, tinsel, trees, tree lights and gifts are available. Parking is easy with wheelchair/pushchair access. No membership is required; all major credit cards are accepted.

THE FACTORY SHOP LTD

THE CROSS ROADS, KELVEDON ROAD, TIPTREE, ESSEX CO5 0LJ, ☎ 01621 817662, 9–5.30 MON–SAT, 10–4 SUN. **FACTORY SHOP**

See page 243 (CHESH)

TK MAXX

93 EASTGATE SHOPPING CENTRE, SOUTHERNHAY, BASILDON, ESSEX SS14 1AF, ☎ 01268 273604, www.tkmaxx.com, 9–5.30 MON–SAT, 11–5 SUN.

26 SIR ISAAC WALK, CULVER SQUARE, COLCHESTER ESSEX CO1 1JJ, ☎ 01206 368745, www.tkmaxx.com, 9–6 MON, 9–7 TUE–WED, 9–8 THUR–FRI, 9–6 SAT, 11–5 SUN.

THE EXCHANGE, ILFORD, ESSEX IG1 1AS, ☎ 020 8514 1288, www.tkmaxx.com, 9.30–6 MON–FRI, 8 ON WED, 9–6 SAT, 11–5 SUN.

THE BREWERY, ROMFORD, ESSEX, ☎ 01708 761978, www.tkmaxx.com, PHONE FOR DETAILS.

THE ROYAL SHOPPING CENTRE, HIGH STREET, SOUTHEND ESSEX SS1, FAX: 01702 600020, www.tkmaxx.com, 9–5.30 MON–THUR, 9–6 FRI–SAT, 11–5 SUN.

UNIT 4, TUNNEL ESTATE RETAIL PARK WEST, LONDON ROAD, THURROCK, ESSEX RM22 3HH, ☎ 01708 860296, www.tkmaxx.com, 10–8 MON–FRI, 10–7 SAT, 11–5 SUN. **PERMANENT DISCOUNT OUTLET**

See page 232 (BEDS)

TOG 24

CLACTON FACTORY OUTLET VILLAGE, STEPHENSON ROAD WEST, CLACTON-ON-SEA ESSEX CO15 4TL, ☎ 01255 435035, **e-mail:** mail-order@tog24.com, www.tog24.com, 10–6 MON–SAT, 8 ON THUR DURING SUMMER AND AT CHRISTMAS, 11–5 SUN. **FACTORY SHOP IN A FACTORY SHOPPING VILLAGE**

See page 240 (CHESH)

VALROSE

610 CHIGWELL ROAD, WOODFORD BRIDGE, ESSEX 1G8 8AA, ☎ 020 8506 1667, 9.30–5 TUE–SAT. **DRESS AGENCY**

Valrose is a well-established dress agency dealing mostly in designer label womenswear for the past 16 years. A range of childrenswear is also stocked, from quality high street names to

Moschino. There is always plenty of stock available and friendly, helpful staff. Clothing is sectioned into skirts, trousers, blouses, jumpers, coats, swimwear, suits, bags, hats and shoes and then divided into sizes and seasons.

GLOUCESTERSHIRE

BRANDMART

WESTWARD ROAD, CAINSCROSS, STROUD, GLOUCESTERSHIRE GL5 4JE, ☎ 01453 756655, 9–5 MON–SAT, 10–4 SUN. **FACTORY SHOP**

The original factory shop in Cainscross, Stroud, has recently relocated next door into a 12,000 square foot premises and is now trading under the name of Brandmart, offering even more savings on branded household and family goods. The range includes men's, women's and children's clothing and footwear, household textiles, toiletries, hardware, luggage, lighting, electrical goods and bedding, most of which are chainstore and high street brands at discounts of between 30% and 50%. There are weekly deliveries and brands include famous names such as Calvin Klein, Adidas, Nike, Fcuk, Cat, Reebok, Ben Sherman, Kangol, Timberland and many more. There are kitchen and furniture displays and a new line in Cape Country furniture on sale. Ranges are continually changing and few factory shops offer such a variety under one roof. The shop has its own car park.

CATALOGUE BARGAIN SHOP

1–6 GROSVENOR HOUSE, STATION ROAD, GLOUCESTER, GLOUCESTERSHIRE GL1 1SZ, ☎ 01452 308779, www.bargaincrazy.com, 9–5.30 MON–SAT, 10.30–4.30 SUN. **PERMANENT DISCOUNT OUTLET**

See page 234 (CAMBS)

INFLATAMANIA

UNIT 8, MEAD PARK, MEAD ROAD, CHELTENHAM, GLOUCESTERSHIRE GL53 7EF, ☎ 01242 231231, FAX: 01242 231919, **e-mail:** info@inflatamania.co.uk, www.inflatamania.co.uk, 9–6 MON–FRI (WEEKENDS BY APPOINTMENT). **HIRE SHOP**

Exciting adventure play inflatables and bouncy castles including the popular balloon typhoon, bugsy caterpillar, games zone and play centre: ultra-light, ultra-bright, and ultra-safe. Available for hire and for sale. New for 2002 are fun wooden toys: traditional favourites for children and the young at heart. Puzzles, learning games and hand-puppets. Ideal for gifts and stocking fillers.

LEGS CLOTHING CO

7 THREADNEEDLE STREET, STROUD, GLOUCESTERSHIRE GL5 1AS, ☎ 01453 764621 9–5 MON–SAT. **FACTORY SHOP**

Exclusive outlet for Europe's leading trouser manufacturer. Sells trousers, jeans and shorts for all ages, at factory-direct prices, plus ancillary lines of casual wear at bargain prices.

MATALAN

27 SWINDON ROAD, CHELTENHAM, GLOUCESTERSHIRE GL50 4DF, ☎ 01242 579840, FAX: 01242 282142, www.matalan.co.uk, 10–8 MON–FRI, 9–6 SAT, 11–5 SUN.

QUEDGELEY DISTRICT CENTRE, GLOUCESTER, GLOUCESTERSHIRE GL2 4PF, ☎ 01452 726040, FAX: 01452 725216, www.matalan.co.uk, 9.30–8 MON–FRI, 9–6 SAT, 10–4 SUN. **PERMANENT DISCOUNT OUTLET**

See page 232 (BEDS)

STOCK EXCHANGE

14 CHURCH STREET, NEWENT, GLOUCESTER, GLOUCESTERSHIRE GL18 1PP, ☎ 01531 821681, 9–1 AND 2–5 MON, TUE, THUR, FRI, SAT, 9–1 WED. **DRESS AGENCY**

Dress agency stocking labels from Mondi to Marks & Spencer, Laura Ashley, Next, Wallis and

Principles. Also childrenswear from babygros to clothes for 14-year-olds, family videos and books, curtains, jewellery, children's and women's shoes and hats.

THE NATIONAL STAR STORE

10 MARKET PLACE, TETBURY, GLOUCESTERSHIRE GL8 8JG, ☎ 01666 502297, 9.30–4.30 TUE–SAT. **DRESS AGENCY**

A shop set up to support a charity, The National Star College (charity no 220239), a specialist residential college for students with a physical disability. It sells nearly new womenswear, shoes, handbags and accessories, as well as childrenswear, books, toys and bric-a-brac, as donated.

TK MAXX

REGENT ARCADE SHOPPING CENTRE, CHELTENHAM GLOUCESTERSHIRE GL50 1J2, FAX: 01242 513848, www.tkmaxx.com, 9–5.30 MON–WED, 9–8 THUR, 9–6 FRI–SAT. **PERMANENT DISCOUNT OUTLET**

See page 232 (BEDS)

TOP MARKS

SWISS COTTAGE, HIGH STREET, BOURTON-ON-THE-WATER, GLOUCESTERSHIRE, ☎ 01451 820369, 10–5 MON–SAT, 11–5 SUN.

23 HIGH STREET, MORETON-IN-MARSH, GLOUCESTERSHIRE GL56 0AF, ☎ 01608 651272, 9–5 MON–SAT. 10–4 SUN. **PERMANENT DISCOUNT OUTLET**

Sells seconds from leading chainstores for all the family. Most of the stock is made up of menswear and womenswear, with some childrenswear. The clothes are mainly Marks & Spencer seconds, sold at about one third cheaper than in the high street.

HAMPSHIRE

BENETTON

UNIT 8GF, GUNWHARF QUAYS, PORTSMOUTH, HAMPSHIRE PO1 3TA, ☎ 023 928 30099, FAX: 023 928 30066, www.benetton.co.uk, SUMMER: 10–6 MON–WED, 10–8 THUR–SAT, 11–5 SUN. WINTER: 10–6 MON–SAT, 10–5 SUN. **FACTORY SHOP IN A FACTORY SHOPPING VILLAGE**

Benetton stocks a wide range of clothes for women, men and children including colourful T-shirts, sweatshirts, men's button-neck T-shirts, swimwear, jeans, children's jackets, stretch shorts and all-in-one shorts. Some of the stock is marked seconds, but it is often difficult to tell why. Now also stocks luggage.

BURBERRY

GUNWHARF QUAYS, PORTSMOUTH, HAMPSHIRE PO1 3PZ, ☎ 02393 864620, 10–8 SUN–WED, 10–9 THUR–SAT IN SUMMER. 10–6 SEVEN DAYS A WEEK IN WINTER. **FACTORY SHOP IN A FACTORY SHOPPING VILLAGE**

See page 236 (CHESH)

CAMEO KIDZ

306 SHIRLEY ROAD, SOUTHAMPTON, HAMPSHIRE SO15 2HL, ☎ 02380 777 277, 10–5 MON–SAT. **SECONDHAND SHOPS**

Specialises in baby and childrenswear, all new items from uncollected parcels. Baby Gap, Next etc.

CLARKS FACTORY SHOP

UNIT 56 GUNWHARF QUAYS, PORTSMOUTH, HAMPSHIRE PO1 3TZ, ☎ 02392 838578, 10–6 MON–WED, 10–9 THUR–SAT, 10–6 SUN. **FACTORY SHOP**

See page 236 (CHESH)

DESIGNER SHADES

GUNWHARF QUAYS, PORTSMOUTH, HAMPSHIRE PO1 3TA, ☎ 0239 287 2007, **e-mail:** info@sunglass-time.com, 10–6 SEVEN DAYS A WEEK. **FACTORY SHOP IN A FACTORY SHOPPING VILLAGE**

See page 255 (ESSEX)

GAP

GUNWHARF QUAYS, PORTSMOUTH, HAMPSHIRE PO1 3TA, ☎ 023 92 755 493, 10–6 MON–WED, 10–8 THUR–SAT, 11–5 SUN. **FACTORY SHOP IN A FACTORY SHOPPING VILLAGE**

Gap sells casual clothes for men, women and children of all ages. Discounts at this factory outlet village range from 30% upwards. At the time of calling, they had women's trousers which usually retail for £38 on sale for 99p.

GUNWHARF QUAYS

PORTSMOUTH HARBOUR, HAMPSHIRE PO1 3TZ, ☎ 023 9283 6700, FAX: 023 9283 6701 **e-mail:** info@gunwharf-quays.com, www.gunwharf-quays.com, SUMMER: 10–6 MON–WED, 10–8 THUR–SAT, 11–5 SUN. WINTER: 10–6 MON–SAT, 11–5 SUN. **FACTORY SHOPPING VILLAGE**

Designer outlet shopping centre comprising 65 stores on a site next to Portsmouth Harbour station and Portsmouth Historic Dockyard, home to HMS Victory and the Mary Rose. As well as the designer outlets, which include Adidas, Benetton, Ben Sherman, Burberry, cK Calvin Klein, Crabtree & Evelyn, Ecco, Episode, Fenn Wright & Manson, Gap, Gieves & Hawkes, Marks & Spencer, Nicole Farhi, Nike, Tommy Hilfiger, Villeroy & Boch, Waterford Wedgwood and Whittard of Chelsea, there are 20 restaurants, bars and coffee shops, an 11-screen cinema, 26-lane bowling complex, comedy club and a year-round events programme.

HUSH PUPPIES

UNIT 26 NORTH PROMENADE BUILDING, GUNWHARF QUAYS, PORTSMOUTH, HAMPSHIRE PO1 3TR, ☎ 023 9286 4288, 10–6 MON, TUE, WED, SUN, 10–6 THUR, FRI, SAT. **FACTORY SHOP**

See page 255 (ESSEX)

JOKIDS

GUNWHARF QUAYS, PORTSMOUTH, HAMPSHIRE PO1 3TU, ☎ 0239 277 9545, FAX: 0239 277 9545, www.jokids.com, 9–6 MON–SAT, 11–5 SUN. **FACTORY SHOP IN A FACTORY SHOPPING VILLAGE**

See page 237 (CHESH)

LILLEY & SKINNER

WHITELEY VILLAGE OUTLET SHOPPING, WHITELEY WAY, WHITELEY, HAMPSHIRE PO15 7LJ, ☎ 01489 589026, 10–6 MON–SAT, 11–5 SUN. **FACTORY SHOP IN A FACTORY SHOPPING VILLAGE**

See page 256 (ESSEX)

MATALAN

CHANNON RETAIL PARK, WOODSIDE AVENUE, EASTLEIGH HAMPSHIRE SO50 9ER, ☎ 02380 626 150, FAX: 02380 650 749, www.matalan.co.uk, 10–8 MON–FRI, 9–6 SAT, 10–4 SUN. **PERMANENT DISCOUNT OUTLET**

STATION STREET, PORTSMOUTH, HAMPSHIRE PO1 1BE, ☎ 0239 285 1967, FAX: 0239 275 5316, www.matalan.co.uk, 9–8 MON–FRI, 9–6 SAT, 11–5 SUN. **PERMANENT DISCOUNT OUTLET**

See page 232 (BEDS)

NIKE FACTORY STORE

UNITS 4–6, GUNWHARF QUAYS, PORTSMOUTH, HAMPSHIRE PO1 1AA, ☎ 023 9275 2822, FAX: 023 9275 2903, www.nike.com, 10–6 MON–WED, 10–8 THUR–SAT, 11–5 SUN. **FACTORY SHOP IN A FACTORY SHOPPING VILLAGE**

See page 239 (CHESH)

PARTRIDGE

WHITELEY VILLAGE DESIGNER OUTLET CENTRE, WHITELEY WAY, FAREHAM, JUNCTION 9 OF M27, HAMPSHIRE PO15 7LJ, ☎ 01489 573804, 10–6 MON–SAT, 11–5 SUN. **FACTORY SHOP IN A FACTORY SHOPPING VILLAGE**

Partridge specialises in fashionable outdoor clothes and accessories. Ranges include waxed jackets, GoreTex jackets, waterproof jackets, tweeds, quilts, fleece jackets and waistcoats, knitwear, shirts, chinos, hats and caps. Discontinued lines are on sale at discounted prices with a minimum of 30% and up to 70% off during promotions.

PEPE JEANS

LEVI'S FACTORY OUTLET, 13 GUNWHARF QUAYS, PORTSMOUTH, HAMPSHIRE PO1 3TZ, ☎ 0239 275 5484, 10–6 MON–SAT, 8 ON THUR, 11–5 SUN. **FACTORY SHOP IN A FACTORY SHOPPING VILLAGE**

All stock at this store is discounted by at least 30% off normal retail prices. World-renowned Levi's clothing is sold here: stock is current and last seasons, including 501s, 507s (bootcut style), 525s and 544s (both flared styles) and the new engineered jeans with twisted seams. Other styles available include vintage look and acid wash jeans, and Dockers cotton twill trousers. Jeans range in size from 8 to 16 for women, and from 28 to 38 for men. Dockers are available in sizes 28 to 42. There are often special offers available if you buy two or more pairs. Students displaying an NUS card save an additional 10% off all purchases.

PRET A PORTER

SHOP ONE, 18–20 HIGH STREET, RINGWOOD, HAMPSHIRE BH24 1AF, ☎ 01425 476090, 10–5 MON–SAT. **DRESS AGENCY**

Dress agency selling top designer fashions including Versace, Dior and Jaeger, as well as wedding outfits from Condici, Jacques Vert, Frank Usher and many more, all at a fraction of their original price. Recently under new ownership and now on two floors. There is a newly-opened department specialising in sizes 20 to 30. Evening wear and clothing for cruises are available all year round. Hats are a passion at Pret à Porter: they have in excess of 100 hats at any time, ideal for weddings and Ascot. Hats can be 'dressed' with flowers, ribbons, feathers and hat pins if required. Day wear comes from quality brand names including Monsoon, Alexon, Principles, Wallis and Next. A range of skiwear, accessories and aprés skiwear is available from October to February. Stock is seasonal and around 200 new items are added to the range every week to ensure a continuous flow of new and exciting items. Accessories, including shoes, bags, scarves, jewellery and belts, are also stocked.

THE GALLERIES

HIGH STREET, ALDERSHOT, HAMPSHIRE GU11 1PE, ☎ 01252 341111, FAX: 01252 329800, **e-mail:** thegalleries@web-hq.com, www.thegalleriesaldershot.co.uk, 9–6 MON–SAT, 10–4 SUN. **FACTORY SHOPPING VILLAGE**

This town centre shopping mall has 20 discount shops on two levels such as Bed & Bath Works for bedlinen and bathroom ware; Cotton Traders casual wear; Designer Room selling women's and men's designer fashion; Hush Puppies shoes; Kitchen Kiosk with branded kitchen and homeware ranges including barbecues and some electrical goods such as bread making machines; Leading Labels selling men's, women's and childrenswear; MX Active for men's, women's and children's branded denim and casual wear; Optisave, an optician selling designer branded glasses; Pilot selling young women's fashions; Pocket Phone selling mobile phones and accessories; Roman Originals womenswear; Room for furniture and household accessories; Suits You men's shirts, suits and casual separates as well as Autonomy womenswear; and Young's dress hire; Surf Skate and Snow for branded casual and activity wear; Toyzone for children's toys; and XS Music selling CDs and videos. The centre also has a café, wheelchair access, a lottery kiosk and baby changing facilities.

TK MAXX

173–178 HIGH STREET (BELOW BAR), SOUTHAMPTON, HAMPSHIRE SO14 2BY, ☎ 023 80 631600, www.tkmaxx.com, 9–5.30 MON–FRI, 7 ON THUR, 9–6 SAT, 11–5 SUN.

2 WELLINGTON RETAIL PARK, HAMBLEDON ROAD, WATERLOOVILLE, HAMPSHIRE, ☎ 023 92 267626, www.tkmaxx.com, PHONE FOR DETAILS. **PERMANENT DISCOUNT OUTLET**

See page 232 (BEDS)

TOG 24

GUNWHARF QUAYS, PORTSMOUTH, HAMPSHIRE PO1 3TU, ☎ 0239 283 3717, **e-mail:** mail-order@tog24.com, www.tog24.com, 10–6 MON–WED, 10–8 THUR–SAT, 11–5 SUN. **FACTORY SHOP**

See page 240 (CHESH)

TOYZONE

ALDERSHOT GALLERIES, UNIT 5–6, THE WELLINGTON CENTRE, ALDERSHOT, HAMPSHIRE GU11 1DB, ☎ 01252 329652, FAX: 01252 329826, 10–6 MON–SAT, 10–4 SUN.

WHITELEY VILLAGE DESIGNER OUTLET CENTRE, WHITELEY WAY, FAREHAM, JUNCTION 9 OF M27, HAMPSHIRE PO15 7BS, ☎ 01489 565226, FAX: 01489 565227, 10–6 MON–SAT, 11–5 SUN.

UNIT 25, GUNWHARF QUAYS, PORTSMOUTH, HAMPSHIRE PO1 3TU, ☎ 02392 851110, FAX: 02392 865855, MON–WED 10–6, THUR–SAT 10–9, SUN 10–6. **FACTORY SHOP IN A FACTORY SHOPPING VILLAGE**

See page 252 (DEV)

UNITED FOOTWEAR

117–125 FRATTON ROAD, PORTSMOUTH, HAMPSHIRE, ☎ 0239 282 6799, 9–5.30 MON–SAT, 10–4 SUN. **PERMANENT DISCOUNT OUTLET**

This shoe retailer, established for over 135 years, sells shoes for all the family as well as clothes, handbags, sports shoes, boots, giftware and household goods, all at discounted prices. Famous brands include Clarks, K Shoes, Elmdale, Grenson, Loakes, Caterpillar and Adidas. Part of a national chain.

WHITELEY VILLAGE OUTLET SHOPPING

OFF THE M27 BETWEEN SOUTHAMPTON AND PORTSMOUTH, JUNCTION 9 OF M27, HAMPSHIRE PO15 7LJ, ☎ 01489 886886, FAX: 01489 886887, www.whiteleyvillage.com, 10–6 MON–SAT, 11- 5 SUN. **FACTORY SHOPPING VILLAGE**

Whiteley Village has more than 50 outlets, all offering shoppers up to 50% savings on high street prices. Top designer names fashion names are here – including Antonio D'Errico, Banana Bookshop, Camille Lingerie, Lilley & Skinner, Roman Originals, Surf, Skate & Snow, Top Table, High & Mighty, Chilli Pepper, Claire's Accessories, Helter Skelter, Cloverleaf, Marzotto, Cotton Traders, D2 Jeans, Elle, Emma Sommerset, Ethos, The Baggage Factory, Ghost, HKA, Jane Shilton, Jasper Conran Jeans, Jigsaw, John Jenkins, John Partridge, Joseph, Julian Graves, Mobile Phone Store, Outdoor Direct, Photo Optix, Pilot, Ponden Mill, Pringle, Proibito, Puma, Rio Jeweller and The Designer Room with a host of designer labels. Refreshments are available from Starbucks Coffee and Boswells Restaurant. There is free parking on site for 1,400 cars, as well as an area for coaches.

WILKINSON STORES

22–30 BRIDGE STREET, ANDOVER, HAMPSHIRE SP10 1BN, ☎ 01332 551241, www.wilko.co.uk, 9–5.30 MON–SAT, 10–4 SUN. MAIL ORDER. **PERMANENT DISCOUNT OUTLET**

See page 241 (CHESH)

HEREFORDSHIRE

E WALTERS FACTORY SHOP

STATION YARD, LEOMINSTER, HEREFORDSHIRE HR6 8TW, ☎ 01568 616127, 9–5 MON–SAT. **FACTORY SHOP**

Europe's leading trouser manufacturer sells ends of lines, cancelled orders and samples of jeans, trousers and shorts for all the family at factory direct prices. Also available ancillary lines of casual wear at bargain prices.

M & M SPORTS FACTORY SHOP

LEOMINSTER INDUSTRIAL ESTATE, SOUTHERN AVENUE, LEOMINSTER, HEREFORDSHIRE HR6 0SP, ☎ 01568 616161, FAX: 01568 619555, **e-mail:** sales@mandmsports.com, www.mandmsports.com, 10–8 THUR, 10–5 FRI, SAT, 10–4 SUN. MAIL ORDER. **FACTORY SHOP**

M & M Sports is the UK's largest sports and leisurewear mail order company, offering brand names for all the family at huge discounts including Nike, Adidas, Reebok, Fila, Ellesse, Berghaus and Rockport. Five catalogues a year are packed with all types of sports clothing, footwear and watches. M&M buys up huge quantities of end-of-line ranges direct from the manufacturers and passes on the massive savings to its customers. The M&M Factory Shop sells discontinued catalogue items. A football kit catalogue is available, while the Equipment Catalogue offers products for golf, tennis, cricket, cycling, fishing, snooker, fitness equipment plus a lot more. To order a catalogue, phone or fax the above telephone numbers or visit their website where orders can be placed and there are many internet-only sale offers. Click on the Exclusive Internet Offers logo.

ROSS LABELS LTD

ROSS PARK, OVERROSS, ROSS-ON-WYE, HEREFORDSHIRE HR9 7QJ, ☎ 01989 769000, www.rosslabels.co.uk, 9.30–6 MON–SAT, 10–4 SUN. **PERMANENT DISCOUNT OUTLET**

Factory outlet centre selling everything from women's and men's underwear and jeans to good, middle-of-the-road brand name outfits and suits bought direct from the manufacturer, as well as homewares. Over 100 leading brands are on sale. Discounts range from 20% to 50%.

STEWART'S SECONDS

33 HIGH STREET, ROSS-ON-WYE, HEREFORDSHIRE HR9 5HD, ☎ 01989 762403, 9.30–5 MON–WED, 9–5 THUR–SAT. **FACTORY SHOP**

See page 251 (DEV)

THE FACTORY SHOP

52 BROAD STREET, LEOMINSTER, HEREFORDSHIRE HR6 8BS, ☎ 01568 613944, 9–5.30 MON–SAT, 10–4 SUN. **FACTORY SHOP**

See page 243 (CHESH)

TK MAXX

5 TRINITY SQUARE, MAYLORD ORCHARD, HEREFORD, HEREFORDSHIRE HR1 2BX, ☎ 01432 355000, www.tkmaxx.com, 9–5.30 MON–FRI, 9–6 SAT, 11–5 SUN. **PERMANENT DISCOUNT OUTLET**

See page 232 (BEDS)

HERTFORDSHIRE

BhS FOR LESS

GALLERIA OUTLET CENTRE, COMET WAY, HATFIELD, HERTFORDSHIRE AL10 0XR, ☎ 01707 258351, 10–8 MON–FRI, 10–6 SAT, 11–5 SUN. **FACTORY SHOP IN A FACTORY SHOPPING VILLAGE**

BhS for Less sells the high street chain's men's, women's and childrenswear ranges, plus selections from its home and lighting ranges, at discounts of at least 30% and up to 75%.

CHARLES CLINKARD

GALLERIA OUTLET CENTRE, COMET WAY, HATFIELD, HERTFORDSHIRE AL10 0XS, ☎ 01707 258653, FAX: 01707 258653, 10–8 MON–FRI, 10–6 SAT, 11–5 SUN. **FACTORY SHOP IN A FACTORY SHOPPING VILLAGE**

See page 241 (CO DURH)

CHOICE DISCOUNT STORES LIMITED

GALLERIA OUTLET CENTRE, COMET WAY, HATFIELD, HERTFORDSHIRE AL10 0XR, ☎ 01707 258545, 10–8 MON–FRI, 10–6 SAT, 11–5 SUN.

46 HIGH STREET, WATFORD, HERTFORDSHIRE WD1 2BS, ☎ 01923 233255, 9–5.30 MON–FRI, 9–6 SAT. **FACTORY SHOP IN A FACTORY SHOPPING VILLAGE**

See page 235 (CAMBS)

CLARKS FACTORY SHOP

100 THE PARADE, HIGH STREET, WATFORD, HERTFORDSHIRE HD1 2AW, ☎ 01458 843155, 9.30–5.30 MON–FRI, 9–5.30 SAT. **FACTORY SHOP**

See page 236 (CHESH)

ECCO

GALLERIA OUTLET CENTRE, COMET WAY, HATFIELD, HERTFORDSHIRE AL10 0XR, ☎ 01707 258399, www.ecco.com, 10–8 MON–FRI, 10–6 SAT, 11–5 SUN. **FACTORY SHOP IN A FACTORY SHOPPING VILLAGE**

See page 236 (CHESH)

GALLERIA OUTLET CENTRE

COMET WAY, HATFIELD, HERTFORDSHIRE AL10 0XR, ☎ 01707 278301, www.factory-outlets.co.uk, 10–8 MON–FRI, 10–6 SAT, 11–5 SUN. **FACTORY SHOPPING VILLAGE**

The Galleria Outlet Centre, often referred to as the bargain hunter's best-kept secret, based in north London, houses more than 80 retail outlets. It offers a wide choice of shops for the discerning customer, providing up to 60% off designer labels and quality brands. The Designer Room is a must for branded men's and women's fashions at huge discounts, stocking DKNY, Jasper Conran, Ghost and Tommy Hilfiger clothing. Looking for a designer evening dress or smart-casual wear? Then visit Discount Dressing. For the latest in fashionable menswear, pay a visit to any of the leading menswear shops. City Menswear offers new season, discounted Yves Saint Laurent and Ben Sherman clothing; Choice sells ranges from Next; B52 Jeans stocks Levi's, Lee and Wrangler ranges; and Baron Jon sells a selection of international names from Versace to Valentino. Going on holiday or looking for a new set of luggage? Then visit the Baggage Factory which sells top quality brands including Carlton and Samsonite. For all your bathroom and bedroom needs pop in to Ponden Mill or the Bed and Bath Works, selling a selection of bedlinen, towels from Christy, soaps and duvets. BhS For Less sells a range of end-of-season men's women's and children's fashions, as well as homewares and lighting. For all your footwear fancies, take a stroll to Charles Clinkard, Ecco, Soled Out and Pavers, selling great brand names including Timberland, Loake, Grenson, Nike, Reebok and Kickers. For women, D Kaye Cosmetics stocks a host of leading beauty and skincare ranges including Revlon, Max Factor, Lancome and Yardley, all at up to 75% off normal retail prices. Walker & Hall represent the finest in jewellery, stocking Tag, Gucci and Raymond Weil watches all at affordable prices. It also sells gold by weight and guarantees savings of at least 30% per gram. While, for the home, Chinacraft specialises in glass, china and giftware, from Wedgwood to Royal Doulton. If interior soft furnishings are on the agenda, then the Furniture Zone is the largest of its type, selling Oriental, middle eastern and Continental rugs, plus great ranges of sofas and sofa-beds, teak, cherry and oak furniture from Wall Nuts and the Khokhar Collection. To complement any room, the Big Picture and Big Poster sell modern and classical pictures ranging from £5 to £20,000. Visit the Garden Outlet Store for all your outdoor gardening and furniture requirements. Music Surplus, the home entertainment store, is a recent addition to the centre, selling a wide range of imported jazz, pop, chart and classical CDs, as well as the latest DVDs. For the PC enthusiast, UK Software sells CD-Roms at up to 70% off the normal retail price. Tool Ware House sells DeWalt, considered by many to be the Armani of the tool worlds, as well as offering fantastic savings on Black & Decker. The centre also offers three cafés, six restaurants and an abundance of children's activities including Toddler World, a futuristic crazy golf course and bouncing slides as well as a mini go-karting track during weekends and holidays. With over 1,800 free car parking spaces and a nine-screen UCI cinema, the centre offers a complete family day out. The Galleria Outlet Centre is a 20-minute drive from north London, and is signposted from junction 3 and 4 of the A1M.

KIDS PLAY FACTORY

UNIT 16, GALLERIA OUTLET CENTRE, COMET WAY, HATFIELD, HERTFORDSHIRE AL10 0XR, ☎ 01707 258720, FAX: 01707 258721, 10–8 MON–FRI, 10–6 SAT, 11–5 SUN. **FACTORY SHOP IN A FACTORY SHOPPING VILLAGE**

See page 255 (ESSEX)

MARVELLOUS SECONDS

3 MOUNT PARADE, MOUNT PLEASANT, COCKFOSTERS, HERTFORDSHIRE EN4 9DD, ☎ 020 8441 5582, 10–5 MON–SAT. **FACTORY SHOP**

This tiny shop sells previous catalogue and end of season plus imperfects from the Blooming Marvellous catalogue label. Small baby and childrenswear section, from birth to three years, as well as a comprehensive maternity range including tights, trousers, dresses, skirts and tops. Prices are 50% less than shop or catalogue prices.

MATALAN

MADFORD RETAIL PARK, WARE ROAD, HERTFORD, HERTFORDSHIRE SG13 7EZ, ☎ 01992 512820, FAX: 01992 589515, www.matalan.co.uk, 10–8 MON–FRI, 9–6 SAT, 11–4 SUN.

DANESTRETE, STEVENAGE, HERTFORDSHIRE SG1 1XR, ☎ 01438 312433, FAX: 01438 312377, www.matalan.co.uk, 9–6 MON–SAT, 10–4 SUN. **PERMANENT DISCOUNT OUTLET**

See page 232 (BEDS)

MILLANO

GALLERIA OUTLET CENTRE, COMET WAY, HATFIELD, HERTFORDSHIRE AL10 0XR, ☎ 01707 259199, 10–8 MON–FRI, 10–6 SAT, 11–5 SUN. **FACTORY SHOP IN A FACTORY SHOPPING VILLAGE**

One of more than 70 shops in this glass and steel factory shopping centre straddling the A1. This outlet sells designer suede, leather and sheepskin jackets, coats and trousers for men, women and children at discount prices. Of particular interest are the highly fashionable Toscana lamb's coats. Larger than average sizes can sometimes be made on request. Prices can be up to 60% cheaper than in the high street, with samples, overruns or slight seconds as well as a selection of last and current season's perfects. Also stocked are leather and sheepskin soft furnishings such as beanbags, throws, cushions, etc and a selection of leather handbags and belts.

NIPPERS

LEYHILL FARM, 2 BRIDGE STREET, WHADDON, NR ROYSTON HERTFORDSHIRE SG8 5SQ, ☎ 01223 207071, FAX: 01223 208666, **e-mail:** Michaela.huffer@talk21.com, www.nippers.co.uk, OPENING HOURS VARY SO PHONE FIRST. **PERMANENT DISCOUNT OUTLET**

See page 234 (BUCKS)

OUTDOOR WEAR

10–14 POTTER STREET, BISHOPS STORTFORD, HERTFORDSHIRE CM23 3UL, ☎ 01279 653694, 9–5.30 TUE–SAT. **PERMANENT DISCOUNT OUTLET**

Ends of lines from Karrimor, Berghaus, Tenson, Barbour, Levi's, Rohan and Drizabone in shirts, jeans, hats, and skiwear, all sold at approximately 20% discount.

QD STORES

29 TOWN SQUARE, 38 QUEENSWAY, STEVENAGE, HERTFORDSHIRE SG1 1BP, ☎ 01438 747437, 9–5.30 MON–SAT. **PERMANENT DISCOUNT OUTLET**

See page 232 (BEDS)

TK MAXX

UNIT 30-31, A1 GALLERIA, COMET WAY, HATFIELD, HERTFORDSHIRE AL10 0XR, ☎ 01707 260066, www.tkmaxx.com, 10–8 MON–FRI, 8.30 ON THUR, 9–7 SAT, 11–5 SUN.

UNIT 50, 18 THE MALTINGS, ST ALBANS HERTFORDSHIRE AL1 3HL, ☎ 01727 855999, www.tkmaxx.com, 9.30–6 MON–TUE, 9.30–7 WED–FRI, 9–6 SAT, 11–5 SUN.

UNIT 10, FORUM SHOPPING CENTRE, STEVENAGE, HERTFORDSHIRE SG1 1ES, ☎ 01438 728408, www.tkmaxx.com, 9.30–8 MON–FRI, 9.30–6 SAT, 11–5 SUN. **PERMANENT DISCOUNT OUTLET**

See page 232 (BEDS)

TOG 24

GALLERIA OUTLET CENTRE, COMET WAY, HATFIELD, HERTFORDSHIRE AL10 OXS, ☎ 01707 258088, **e-mail:** mail-order@tog24.com, www.tog24.com, 10–8 MON–FRI, 10–6 SAT, 11–5 SUN. **FACTORY SHOP IN A FACTORY SHOPPING VILLAGE**

See page 240 (CHESH)

KENT

CATALOGUE BARGAIN SHOP

19A PRESTON STREET, FAVERSHAM, KENT ME13 8NZ, ☎ 01795 591203, www.bargaincrazy.com, 9–5.30 MON–SAT, 10–4 SUN. **PERMANENT DISCOUNT OUTLET**

See page 234 (CAMBS)

CLARKS FACTORY SHOP

UNITS 44–47 RETAIL OUTLET VILLAGE, ASHFORD, KENT TN24 0SD, ☎ 01233 637562, 10–6 MON–SAT, 8 ON THUR, 11–5 SUN. **FACTORY SHOP IN A FACTORY SHOPPING VILLAGE**

168 HIGH STREET, CHATHAM, KENT ME4 4AS, ☎ 01634 845215, 9–5.30 MON–SAT. **FACTORY SHOP**

See page 236 (CHESH)

DE BRADELEI WHARF

DE BRADELEI WHARF (DOVER) LTD, CAMBRIDGE ROAD, DOVER, KENT CT17 9BY, ☎ 01304 226616, FAX: 01304 226636, 9.30–5.30 MON–FRI, 9.30–6 SAT, 11–5 SUN. **PERMANENT DISCOUNT OUTLET**

Large outlet in superb maritime setting just off the Dover Seafront, selling top brand names for all the family, including shoes. The womenswear includes such names as Paul Costelloe, Dannimac, Windsmoor, Planet, Precis Petite, Alexon, Kaliko, Eastex, Minuet Petite, Country Casuals, Elle, French Connection, Tigi Wear, plus top American and German designer labels, handbags and much more including a new accessory department. The menswear range includes underwear, socks, coats, sweaters, jackets, suits and trousers from labels such as Wolsey, Countrywear, French Connection, Virgin and Tog 24. Robert Leonard's Menswear provide Greiff, Pierre Cardin, Gabicci, Gurteen, Oakman, Saville Row, John Slim and many more. For children, there are brands such as OshKosh B'Gosh, Lily by Lily, Smarties, Vitamins, Rebble Pebble, Zip-Zap, O'Neill, MCA and Hickory as well as fluffy toys and melamine tableware with Pokemon and Toy Story 2 designs as well as a new department selling clothing, shoes, books and scientific toys. There is a large shoe department featuring international shoes for all the family and a wonderful Home Furnishings Department. The Interior Design shops sell bedding, towels, top-name furnishing fabric, cushions, throws, furniture and curtains. The Glass and China Department has an amazing selection from Waterford/Wedgwood, Stuart Crystal, Royal Doulton, Arthur Price of England Silverware, Staffordshire Tableware, Churchill, Cloverleaf, Hornsea Pottery, Cristal d'Arques and much more. There is superb Liberty shop in the giftware department and a Cromwell and Morgan Cook Shop. Parking is easy with a large car park behind the store. The Waves Coffee Shop is open all day, serving delicious home-cooked food.

DEJA VU

OLD SEAL HOUSE, 19 CHURCH STREET, SEAL, NEAR SEVENOAKS, KENT TN15 0DA, ☎ 01732 762155, 10–4 TUE–FRI, 10–1 SAT. **DRESS AGENCY**

In this small, friendly shop, established in 1977, you will find British and European designers such as Paul Costelloe, Gerry Weber, Betty Barclay, Liz Claiborne, Patsy Seddon and Ouiset as well as old favourites such as Jaeger, Marks & Spencer and Laura Ashley. The price range is from £10 to £200. There is also a small range of children's dresses. After six to eight weeks, clothes which haven't sold or been collected are sent to charity. An alteration service is also offered for clothes purchased here.

GAP

MCARTHURGLEN DESIGNER OUTLET ASHFORD, KIMBERLEY WAY, ASHFORD, JUNCTION 10 OF M20, KENT TN23 1EZ, ☎ 01233 663951, 10–6 MON–FRI, 8 ON THUR, 9–6 SAT, 11–5 SUN.
FACTORY SHOP IN A FACTORY SHOPPING VILLAGE

Gap sells casual clothes for men, women, children and babies. Deliveries at this factory outlet are only six to eight weeks behind the high street, so this is not old stock. Discounts can be as much as 70%. There is a children's play area, restaurants and free car parking.

JOKIDS

MCARTHURGLEN DESIGNER OUTLET ASHFORD, KIMBERLEY WAY, ASHFORD, JUNCTION 10 OF M20, KENT TN24 0SD, ☎ 01233 612141, FAX: 01233 612141, www.jokids.com, 10–6 MON–FRI, 8 ON THUR, 9–6 SAT, 11–5 SUN. **FACTORY SHOP IN A FACTORY SHOPPING VILLAGE**

See page 237 (CHESH)

LEE COOPER

MCARTHURGLEN DESIGNER OUTLET ASHFORD, KIMBERLEY WAY, ASHFORD, JUNCTION 10 OF M20, KENT TN24 0SD, ☎ 01233 611186, 10–6 MON–SAT, 8 ON THUR, 11–5 SUN.
FACTORY SHOP IN A FACTORY SHOPPING VILLAGE

See page 238 (CHESH)

LITTLEWOODS CATALOGUE OUTLET STORE

MCARTHURGLEN DESIGNER OUTLET ASHFORD, KIMBERLEY WAY, ASHFORD, JUNCTION 10 OF M20, KENT TN24 0SD, ☎ 01233 625242, 10–6 MON–FRI, 8 ON THUR, 9–6 SAT, 11–5 SUN.
FACTORY SHOP IN A FACTORY SHOPPING VILLAGE

Littlewoods clearance shops offer up to 70% off the catalogue price for clothing and offer big discounts off electrical goods. Stock changes constantly and varies from day to day but can include well-known brand names such as Berlei and Gossard lingerie, Vivienne Westwood, Pamplemousse leisurewear, Nike and Adidas sports shoes, and Timberland and Caterpillar footwear. Stock depends on the size and location of the shop: larger shops get the longer discontinued runs, while smaller shops get overruns with only a small amount of colour and size variations left. Littlewoods also runs a mobile shop which operates in cities which don't have a sale shop. For details of venues for the sales, which usually take place once a month, write to Melanie Lamb, c/o Crosby DC Kershaw Avenue, Endbutt Lane, Crosby, Merseyside L70 1AH.

MARKS & SPENCER

MCARTHURGLEN DESIGNER OUTLET VILLAGE, KIMBERLEY WAY, ASHFORD, JUNCTION 10 OF M20, KENT TN24 0SD, ☎ 01233 662418, 9–6 MON–FRI, SAT, 8 ON THUR, 11–5 SUN.
FACTORY SHOP IN A FACTORY SHOPPING VILLAGE

See page 238 (CHESH)

MATALAN

BROOKFIELD ROAD, ASHFORD KENT TN24 8ME, ☎ 01233 898460, FAX: 01233 661438, www.matalan.co.uk, 10–8 MON–FRI, 9–6 SAT, 11–5 SUN.

STOUR RETAIL PARK, STURRY ROAD, CANTERBURY, KENT CT1 1AD, ☎ 01227 817910, FAX: 01227 764860, www.matalan.co.uk, 10–8 MON–FRI, 9–7 SAT, 10–4 SUN.

BROADWAY SHOPPING CENTRE, THE BROADWAY, MAIDSTONE, KENT ME16 8PS, ☎ 01622 675153, FAX: 01622 672841, www.matalan.co.uk, 10–8 MON–FRI, 9–6 SAT, 10–4 SUN.

STROOD RETAIL PARK, COMMERCIAL ROAD, STROOD, KENT ME2 2JG, ☎ 01634 731670, FAX: 01634 718048, www.matalan.co.uk, 10–8 MON–FRI, 9–6 SAT, 11–5 SUN.

WESTWOOD RETAIL PARK, WESTWOOD ROAD, BROADSTAIRS, THANET, KENT CT10 2RQ, ☎ 01843 608700, FAX: 01843 871248, www.matalan.co.uk, 10–8 MON–FRI, 9–6 SAT, 11–5 SUN. **PERMANENT DISCOUNT OUTLET**

See page 232 (BEDS)

MCARTHURGLEN DESIGNER OUTLET CENTRE

KIMBERLEY WAY, ASHFORD, JUNCTION 10 OF M20, KENT TN24 OSD, ☎ 01233 895900, www.mcarthurglen.com/ashford, 10–6 MON–FRI, 8 ON THUR, 9–6 SAT, 11–5 SUN. **FACTORY SHOPPING VILLAGE**

Voted 'Retail Destination of the Year' 2001 in the Retail Week awards, the McArthurGlen Designer Outlet Ashford in Kent is one of Europe's most spectacular shopping destinations. The outlet offers over 70 top brands and designer labels at up to 50% off typical retail prices. there is a food court, cafés, a children's play area, and parking for over 1,500 cars. A shuttle bus runs between the town centre, station and the outlet every eight minutes. Shops include: Ben Sherman, Cotton Traders, Designer Room/Classic Room, Daks, Fire Trap, Gap, Lee Cooper, Levi's Littlewoods Catalogue Outlet, Marks and Spencer, Mexx, Miss Sixty, Mountain Warehouse, Pilot, Polo Jeans Co. Factory Store, Proudfoot, Roman Originals, Thomas Pink, Tog 24, Tommy Hilfiger, Warehouse, Warner's, Windsmoor, Baron Jon, Ben Sherman, Cotton Traders, Daks, Fire Trap, Fred Perry, Gap, Lee Cooper, Levi's, Petroleum, Proudfoot, Suits You, The Suit Company, Thomas Pink, Van Heusen, Woodhouse, Donnay, Fila, Gap, JoKids, Mexx, Nike, Reebok, Toyzone, Clarks, Ecco, Jane Shilton Kiplings, Lilley & Skinner, Soled Out, Antler, Kipling, Samsonite Company Stores. Arran Aromatics, Body Shop, Chapelle Jewellery, Claire's Outlet, Gizmo, One 2 One, Picture Port, Revlon, Sekonda, Sunglass Hut International, Watch Station, Walker and Hall, Woods of Windsor, Bed and Bath Works, Bookends, Bose, China Place, Cloverleaf, Design House, Edinburgh Crystal, Le Creuset, Mountain Warehouse, Price's Candles, Professional Cookware Company, Spiegelau, Waterford Wedgwood, Whittard of Chelsea, XS Music and Video.

MERCIA SAFETY CENTRE

16 COVENTRY ROAD, TONBRIDGE, KENT TN10 4QE, ☎ 01732 357169, MAIL ORDER ONLY. **HIRE SHOP**

Safety equipment by post, including gates, guards and the Tiny Traveller for car seats. Phone for a brochure.

NIPPERS

CHALKPIT FARM, SCHOOL LANE, BEKESBOURNE, NR CANTERBURY KENT CT4 5EU, ☎ 01227 832008, FAX: 01227 831496, **e-mail:** nippers@farming.co.uk, www.nippers.co.uk, OPENING HOURS VARY SO PHONE FIRST. **PERMANENT DISCOUNT OUTLET**

See page 234 (BUCKS)

PANACHE

90–92 HIGH STREET, ROYAL TUNBRIDGE WELLS, KENT TN1 1YF, ☎ 01892 522 883, 10–5 MON–SAT. **DRESS AGENCY**

Panache sells women's nearly-new at savings of up to 50% on high street prices. The agency stocks a wide range of labels from Marella and Viyella to Paul Smith, LK Bennett, MaxMara and Escada. They also sell hats, evening wear, coats, shoes, jackets, handbags and belts.

PJN DISCOUNT WAREHOUSE

UNIT IB, EDDINGTON BUSINESS PARK, THANET WAY, HERNE BAY, KENT CT6 5TT, ☎ 01227 741112, FAX: 01227 365123, 9–5.30 MON–SAT, 10–4 SUN. **FACTORY SHOP**

Discontinued styles, slight seconds and end of line adult and children's shoes displayed in a 6,000 square foot warehouse with up to 10,000 pairs of shoes at any one time. Clarks, Lee, Pods, Lotus, Equity, Hush Puppies and Hi-Tec sportswear are typical names, available at up to 35% reductions. A GDD reader bought a pair of Clarks children's shoes for £20, usual price £29; and two pairs of sandals for £10 and £12, usual price, £29.95 and £34.95. Also sell bags. Small refreshment area, car parking and wheelchair accessibility. Also have a good range of clothing for men and women at very reasonable prices. For example, two pairs of men's trousers, £25; women's suit, £29.99. Labels include Klass and Elite, among others. Stock is constantly changing, so go with an open mind.

T J HUGHES

THE CHEQUERS SHOPPING CENTRE, PADS HILL, MAIDSTONE, KENT ME15 6AT, ☎ 01622 771600, FAX: 01622 753374, **e-mail:** info@tjhughes.co.uk, www.tjhughes.co.uk, 9–5.30 MON–SAT, 10–4 SUN. **PERMANENT DISCOUNT OUTLET**

See page 239 (CHESH)

THE FACTORY SHOP LTD

THE FOREMAN CENTRE, HIGH STREET, HEADCORN, KENT TN27 9NE, ☎ 01622 891651, 9–5.30 MON–SAT, 10–4 SUN. **FACTORY SHOP**

See page 243 (CHESH)

TK MAXX

BROADWAY SQUARE, BEXLEYHEATH BROADWAY, BEXLEYHEATH, KENT, ☎ 0208 301 0508, www.tkmaxx.com, 9–6 MON–SAT, 9 ON THUR, 10–4 SUN. **PERMANENT DISCOUNT OUTLET**

See page 232 (BEDS)

TOG 24

MCARTHURGLEN DESIGNER OUTLET ASHFORD, KIMBERLEY WAY, ASHFORD, JUNCTION 10 OF M20, KENT TN24 0SD, ☎ 01233 647357, **e-mail:** mail-order@tog24.com, www.tog24.com, 10–6 MON–FRI, 8 ON THUR, 9–6 SAT, 11–5 SUN.

DE BRADLEI WHARF, CAMBRIDGE ROAD, DOVER, KENT CT17 9BY, ☎ 01304 216126, **e-mail:** mail-order@tog24.com, www.tog24.com, 9.30–5.30 MON–FRI, 9.30–6 SAT, 11–5 SUN. **FACTORY SHOP IN A FACTORY SHOPPING VILLAGE**

See page 240 (CHESH)

TOYTIME

MEOPHAM BANK FARM, LEIGH ROAD, HILDENBOROUGH, NEAR TONBRIDGE, KENT TN11 9AQ, ☎ 01732 833695 OR 832416, FAX: 01732 835603, 9–12 AND 7.30–8.30 TUE, 9–12 THUR, 9–4 SAT. **PERMANENT DISCOUNT OUTLET**

Sells both new and secondhand toys – anything from a rattle to a climbing frame. The stock is always changing as you can get immediate cash for your used toys in good condition. There is a huge selection in three barns including bikes, trikes, doll's prams, doll's houses, trampolines, slides and sandpits. In addition, party bag fillers and baby toys abound. All the outdoor equipment (as well as Brio, Playmobil and Lego) is new and is sold at discounted prices. Climbing frames and swings are on display outside (as well as some animals) and advice is given, when required.

TOYZONE

MCARTHURGLEN DESIGNER OUTLET ASHFORD, KIMBERLEY WAY, ASHFORD, JUNCTION 10 OF M20, KENT TN24 0SD, ☎ 01233 662123, FAX: 01233 662646, 10–6 MON–FRI, 8 ON THUR, 9–6 SAT, 11–5 SUN. **FACTORY SHOP IN A FACTORY SHOPPING VILLAGE**

See page 252 (DEV)

LANCASHIRE

BARDEN MILL SHOP

BARDEN LANE, BURNLEY, LANCASHIRE BB12 0DX, ☎ 01282 420333, FAX: 01282 420336, **e-mail:** info@bardenmillshop.co.uk, 10–6 MON–SAT, 11–5 SUN (LATE NIGHTS TILL 8 THUR APRIL–SEPTEMBER). **FACTORY SHOP**

A true working mill full of bargains, most of which are high street brands at discounted prices. Full range of branded and non-branded merchandise includes Ladieswear from Tagg, Ambience, Affinity, Diva Design, Donna Bella, Prima Casamia, plus Solo from Italy and Camille lingerie; BMB Menswear from Jeff Banks, Regatta, Gola, Le Shark, Centaur, Jonathan Adams, Carabou, Umbro, Bentley, Alexandre and Gibson. Plus Musbury Fabrics selling towels, bedding, fabrics, curtains, from Dorma, Fogarty, Whiteheads, SMD Curtains, Zorbit and Swatch Box. Briggs Shoes with shoes for men, women and children from Hotter, Sterling and Hunt, Van Dal, Gabor and Hotter Subs. Plus Hothouse selling gifts, furniture, pictures, mirrors, candles, kitchenware, lighting, dried flowers, Staffordshire pottery, crystal and glassware. There is also a luggage, books and market stall section. A 140-seat tea room, ample free car and coach parking, disabled access and facilities and weekend boat trips and organised midweek tours.

BOUNDARY MILL STORES

BURNLEY ROAD, COLNE, LANCASHIRE BB8 8LS, ☎ 01282 865229, www.boundarymill.co.uk, 10–6 MON–FRI, 9 ON THUR, 9–6 SAT, 11–5 SUN, 10–6 BANK HOLIDAYS, OPENS AT 10 ON SUNDAYS FOR BREAKFAST AND BROWSING, PURCHASES CAN BE MADE FROM 11.
PERMANENT DISCOUNT OUTLET

One of the largest clearance stores in Britain, it covers more than 100,000 square feet with over 300 quality brands, all now under one roof. Many of the top end of the high street designer labels are on sale here for both women and men. Women's labels include: Alexon, Windsmoor, Austin Reed, Eastex, Planet, Jaeger, Jacques Vert, Liz Claiborne and Viyella. Men's labels include: Austin Reed, Centaur, Dannimac, Farah, Pierre Cardin, Lyle & Scott and Yves St Laurent. The women's and men's departments are very extensive – not to mention impressive – and cover the whole range from casual to evening wear with reductions of between 30% and 70%. There are also large leisurewear departments for women and men including Polo Ralph Lauren, Timberland, Wrangler and Tog 24, and a whole floor dedicated to women's lingerie. The new extension building, which links the fashion and home stores, contains a massive shoe department stocking Bally, Nine West and Hush Puppies, among others. On the ground floor, there is a huge new cookshop stocking up-to-the-minute ranges and a greatly extended luggage department including Globetrotter, Antler and Jane Shilton. The home store sells brand-name home furnishings, glass and china including Dorma, Sanderson, Denby, Edinburgh Crystal, Dartington Crystal, Portmeirion, Royal Worcester, Villeroy & Boch and Wedgwood. Four times a year, there are special sales at which prices are discounted further. Most of the stock is end of lines with the occasional marked seconds. There is a choice of food outlets: a large coffee shop, a restaurant and a pub, and there is extensive free parking.

BRAND CENTRE

1 STANLEY ROAD, WHITEFIELD, BURY, MANCHESTER, LANCASHIRE M45 6GT, ☎ 0161 796 2525, 10–8 MON–FRI, 9.30–6.30 SAT, 11–5 SUN. **PERMANENT DISCOUNT OUTLET**

Not a discount store as such, this department store stocking this season's fashions guarantees lower prices than any other UK competitor in non-sale periods. Stock includes menswear, womenswear, kidswear, lingerie, footwear, accessories and perfumes. Brands sold on a regular basis include Calvin Klein jeans, Calvin Klein underwear, Diesel, DKNY Jeans, DKNY Kids, Kenzo Kids, Kickers, French Connection, Morgan, Moschino Mare, Osh Kosh, Ted Baker, Versace Classic V2 and Yves St Laurent. A membership scheme operates with extra benefits such as big discounts on blue cross days and special sale previews. Membership costs just £3.

BRIGGS SHOES

BARDEN MILL, BARDEN LANE, BURNLEY, LANCASHIRE BB12 0DX, ☎ 01282 420333, FAX: 01282 420336, www.briggsshoes.co.uk, 10–6 MON–SAT, 10–5 SUN.

205 MARINE ROAD, MORECAMBE, LANCASHIRE LA4 4BU, ☎ 01524 419293, FAX: 01524 419293, www.briggsshoes.co.uk, 10–5.30 MON–SAT, 10.30–4.30 SUN. **PERMANENT DISCOUNT OUTLET**

See page 245 (CUMB)

CATALOGUE BARGAIN SHOP

UNIT 1, EASTGATE RETAIL PARK, ACCRINGTON, LANCASHIRE BB5 6PW, ☎ 01254 879195, www.bargaincrazy.com, 9–8 MON–FRI, 9–6 SAT, 10.30–4.30 SUN.

KINGSWAY, BURNLEY LANCASHIRE BB11 1AB, ☎ 01282 420202, www.bargaincrazy.com, 9–5 MON–SAT, 7 ON THUR, 10.30–4.30 SUN.

40–42 MARKET STREET, CHORLEY, LANCASHIRE PR7 2SE, ☎ 012572 68325, www.bargaincrazy.com, 9–5.30 MON–SAT, 10.30–4.30 SUN.

HALL BANK, WORSLEY RD, PATRICROFT, ECCLES, MANCHESTER, LANCASHIRE M30 8NR, ☎ 0161 787 7726, www.bargaincrazy.com, 10–5.30 MON–FRI, 8 ON THUR, 9–5 SAT, 10.30–4.30 SUN.

UNITS 1–2, HIGH STREET, HULME, MANCHESTER, LANCASHIRE M15 5AF, ☎ 0161 226 5379, www.bargaincrazy.com, 9–8 MON–SAT, 9 ON THUR, FRI, 11–5 SUN.

UNIT 3, THE PARSONAGE RETAIL PARK, LEIGH, LANCASHIRE WN7 5SJ, ☎ 01942 671911, www.bargaincrazy.com, 9–8 MON–FRI, 9–6 SAT, 11–5 SUN.

UNIT 4, QUEENS RETAIL PARK, QUEENS STREET, PRESTON, LANCASHIRE PR1 4HZ, ☎ 01772 884104, www.bargaincrazy.com, 9–8 MON–FRI, 9–6 SAT, 10.30–4.30 SUN.

82–83 EGARTON WALK, ELLESMERE CENTRE, WALKDEN, MANCHESTER, LANCASHIRE M28 3ZD, ☎ 0161 703 9311, www.bargaincrazy.com, 9–5.30 MON–SAT. **PERMANENT DISCOUNT OUTLET**

See page 234 (CAMBS)

CATALOGUE DISCOUNT STORE

1318–1324 ASHTON OLD ROAD, OPENSHAW, MANCHESTER M11 1JG, ☎ 0161 371 8243, 9–5.30 MON–SAT.

2 BURY OLD ROAD, CHEETHAM HILL, MANCHESTER M8 7JN, ☎ 0161 795 9312, FAX: 0161 7407 274, 9–5.30 MON–SAT. **PERMANENT DISCOUNT OUTLET**

Grattan catalogue store, selling a wide selection of items from those featured in the catalogue, including women's, men's, children's, home, electrics and toys. All items are discounted by up to 50% with regular special promotions. All stores offer a 14-day refund policy, and a 12-month guarantee on electrical items. A wide range of brands are in stock on a regularly changing basis. Each store carries a slightly different range, so please phone to check that they have what you want in stock.

CRAGHOPPERS

FREEPORT SHOPPING VILLAGE, ANCHORAGE ROAD, FLEETWOOD, LANCASHIRE FY7 6AE, ☎ 01253 778372, FAX: 01253 778372, www.regatta.com, 10–6 MON–WED, 10–8 THUR, FRI, 10–6 SAT, SUN. **FACTORY SHOP IN A FACTORY SHOPPING VILLAGE**

Craghoppers, the innovator in travel and outdoor wear, is a technical brand that leads with innovation. Its offering of waterproofs, fleece, wovens and rucksacks are intended for travel at home or abroad and suitable for a wide range of climates. All stock is sold here at discounted prices of at least 30%.

DALE MILL DISCOUNTS

DALE STREET, MILNROW, NEAR ROCHDALE, LANCASHIRE OL16 3NJ, ☎ 01706 359737, 9.30–6 MON–WED, FRI, 9.30–8 THUR, 9.30–5.30 SAT, 10–5.30 SUN. **PERMANENT DISCOUNT OUTLET**

A wide range of items from clothes and shoes for all the family to kitchenware, furniture, tablecloths, beds and bedding, televisions and general electrical goods, fridges, cookers, microwaves, kitchen and bedroom fittings and units, all on sale at discounted prices. On site there is also a designer clothes store and sportswear outlet, plus a new conservatory extension selling glassware, pottery, dried flowers, table lamps and other household goods.

DALESWEAR FACTORY OUTLET

LAUNDRY LANE, INGLETON, VIA CARNFORTH, LANCASHIRE LA6 3DF, ☎ 01524 241047, www.daleswear.co.uk, 9–5 MON–SAT, 9.30–5 SUN. **FACTORY SHOP**

Manufacturers and direct retailers of fleeces, waterproofs, caving suits and bags. Also children's fleeces, waterproofs and accessories. Non-standard sizes a speciality. They also stock boots, maps, walking poles etc.

FREEPORT FLEETWOOD OUTLET VILLAGE

ANCHORAGE ROAD, FLEETWOOD, 12 MILES FROM JUNCTION 3 OF M55, LANCASHIRE FY7 6AE, ☎ 01253 877377, www.freeportfleetwood.com, 10–6 SEVEN DAYS A WEEK, 8 ON THUR, FRI. **FACTORY SHOPPING VILLAGE**

Large, brightly-coloured New-England-style seaside shopping village. There are more than 40 shops selling at up to 50% off high street prices, as well as restaurants, family attractions and free parking. Women's fashions include Next to Nothing, Spotlight, Easy Jeans, VF Corp, Double Two, Warner's, Edinburgh Woollen Mill, The Designer Room, Giorgio, BhS for Less, Madhouse and Roman Originals. For men, there is Petroleum, Ciro Citterio, Double Two, Giorgio, VF Corp, Madhouse, Easy Jeans and BhS for Less. Sportswear and outdoor wear shops include Sports Mill, Craghoppers, Regatta and VF Corp. Footwear outlets comprise Lilley & Skinner, Jane Shilton, Shoe Sellers, BhS For Less, Next to Nothing and Petroleum. Sweet-toothed visitors can indulge at Thorntons or The Sweet Shop, and there is Julian Graves for nuts and dried fruits. Household outlets include Ponden Mill, Dartington Crystal, Home Zone, Picture Port and China Traders.

Childrenswear stockists include Next to Nothing, BhS for Less, Vecopri, VF Corp and Giorgio. Other stores include Woods of Windsor, Hallmark Cards and Gifts, XS Music & Video, Claire's Accessories, Watch Store and Book Depot.

GIFTTREE

CHURCHBRIDGE WORKS, HENRY STREET, ACCRINGTON, LANCASHIRE BB5 4EU, ☎ 01254 237324, 9–5 MON–SAT

REEDYFORD MILL, WESTFIELD ROAD, NELSON, LANCASHIRE BB9 7YM, ☎ 01282 619540, FAX: 01282 696639, 9–5 MON–SAT. **PERMANENT DISCOUNT OUTLET**

See page 247 (DERBY)

K SHOES FACTORY SHOP

UNIT 3, CLIFTON RETAIL PARK, BLACKPOOL, LANCASHIRE FY4 4RA, ☎ 01253 699380, 9.30–6 MON–FRI, 7 ON THUR, 9.30–5.30 SAT, 11–5 SUN.

18-19 WILLIAMSON SQUARE, LIVERPOOL, LANCASHIRE L1 LEJ, ☎ 0151 708 7564, 9.30–5.30 MON–SAT, 11–4 SUN. **FACTORY SHOP**

See page 245 (CUMB)

LAMBERT HOWARTH FOOTWEAR

GREENBRIDGE WORKS, FALBARN ROAD, OFF BOCHOLT WAY, RAWTENSTAL, ROSSENDALE, LANCASHIRE BB4 7NX, ☎ 01706 235160, FAX: 01706 235129, 9.30–5 MON–FRI, 9.30–4 SAT, 10–4 SUN. **FACTORY SHOP**

A real mixture of seconds and perfects. They sell clothes, handbags and towels. The seconds in footwear are from shoes made for major high street chainstores and all are at discounted prices. These include slippers, walking boots, flat shoes and sandals for men, women and children. The perfects in clothes, towels and bags are two-thirds of the high street prices. They also stock a large selection of pottery. There is an on-site creche and coffee shop serving drinks and light refreshments, wheelchair access and disabled facilities, plus free car parking.

LAMBERT HOWARTH MILL SHOP

FINSLEY GATE, BURNLEY, LANCASHIRE, ☎ 01282 471283, 9.30–5 MON–FRI, 9–4 SAT. **FACTORY SHOP**

A real mixture of seconds from their own factories and perfects from other sources – footwear, clothes, handbags and towels. The seconds in footwear are from shoes made for major high street chainstores and all are at discounted prices. These include slippers, walking boots, flat shoes and sandals for men, women and children. The perfects in clothes, towels and bags are two-thirds of the high street prices. Also sells home furnishings, pottery and curtains, from Marks & Spencer.

LILLEY & SKINNER

FREEPORT VILLAGE, ANCHORAGE ROAD, FLEETWOOD, LANCASHIRE FY7 9AE, ☎ 01253 877377, 10–6 SEVEN DAYS A WEEK, 8 ON THUR, FRI. **FACTORY SHOP IN A FACTORY SHOPPING VILLAGE**

See page 256 (ESSEX)

LITTLEWOODS CATALOGUE DISCOUNT STORE

185 STAMFORD STREET, ASHTON-UNDER-LYNE, LANCASHIRE OL6 7PY, ☎ 0161 339 0966, 9–5.30 MON–SAT.

UNIT 2, KINGS STREET, FARNWORTH, LANCASHIRE BL4 7AZ, ☎ 01204 861464, 9–5.30 MON–SAT, 10.30–4.30 SUN.

69–74 LORD STREET, FLEETWOOD, LANCASHIRE FY7 6DS, ☎ 01253 773418, 9–5.30 MON–SAT, 10.30–4.30 SUN.

UNIT 3, MONUMENT BUILDINGS, LONDON ROAD, LIVERPOOL L3 8JY, ☎ 0151 708 6118, 9–5 MON–SAT, 9.30–5.30 TUE, 11–5 SUN.

160 MARINE ROAD, CENTRAL MORECAMBE, LANCASHIRE LA4 4BU, ☎ 01524 412074, 9.30–5.30 MON, 9–5.30 TUE–SAT, 10.30–4.30 SUN. **PERMANENT DISCOUNT OUTLET**

See page 237 (CHESH)

MATALAN

FOUNTAIN RETAIL PARK, HYNDBURN ROAD, ACCRINGTON LANCASHIRE BB5 4AA, ☎ 01254 356100, FAX: 01254 879037, www.matalan.co.uk, 9.30–8 MON–FRI, 9–6 SAT, 11–5 SUN.
207 LOWER AUDLEY STREET, BLACKBURN, LANCASHIRE BB1 1DG, ☎ 01254 507200, www.matalan.co.uk, 10–8 MON–FRI, 9–6 SAT, 11–5 SUN.

UNIT 2, CLIFTON RETAIL PARK, CLIFTON ROAD, BLACKPOOL LANCASHIRE FY4 4UJ, ☎ 01253 697850, FAX: 01253 697852, www.matalan.co.uk, 10- 8 MON–FRI, 9–6 SAT, 11–5 SUN.

TURNER BRIDGE, TONGE MOOR ROAD, BOLTON, LANCASHIRE BL2 2DJ, ☎ 01204 383733, FAX: 01204 383542, www.matalan.co.uk, 10–8 MON–FRI, 9–6 SAT, 11–5 SUN.

SEFTON RETAIL PARK, DUNNINGS BRIDGE ROAD, BOOTLE, LIVERPOOL, LANCASHIRE L30 6UU, ☎ 0151 525 1190, FAX: 0151 525 3404, www.matalan.co.uk, 9.30–8 MON–FRI, 9–6 SAT, 11–5 SUN.

FOUNDRY STREET/GEORGE STREET, BURY, LANCASHIRE BL9 0BZ, ☎ 0161 705 4520, FAX: 0161 797 5680, www.matalan.co.uk, 9.30–8 MON–FRI, 9–6 SAT, 11–5 SUN.

NORTH VALLEY RETAIL PARK, NORTH VALLEY ROAD, COLNE, LANCASHIRE BB8 8LU, ☎ 01282 857700, FAX: 01282 859692, www.matalan.co.uk, 10–8 MON–FRI, 9–6 SAT, 11–5 SUN.

LANCASTER RETAIL PARK, MELLISHAW LANE, LANCASTER, LANCASHIRE LA1 5JR, ☎ 01524 541960, FAX: 01524 849911, www.matalan.co.uk, 10–8 MON–FRI, 9–6 SAT, 11–5 SUN.

UNITS G & H, THE TRIUMPH CENTRE, HUNTS CROSS, LIVERPOOL LANCASHIRE L24 9GB, ☎ 0151 486 0325, FAX: 0151 486 2952, www.matalan.co.uk, 9.30–8 MON–FRI, 9–6 SAT, 11–5 SUN.

BROOKWAY RETAIL PARK, 452 ALTRINCHAM ROAD, BAGULEY, MANCHESTER, LANCASHIRE M23 9BP, ☎ 0161 902 2500, FAX: 0161 945 1582, www.matalan.co.uk, 9.30–8 MON–FRI, 10–6 SAT, 11–5 SUN.

UNIT 3, ALEXANDRA CENTRE, PARK ROAD, OLDHAM, LANCASHIRE OL4 1SG, ☎ 0161 620 6686, FAX: 0161 620 6690, www.matalan.co.uk, 10–8 MON–FRI, 9–6 SAT, 11–5 SUN.

HOLME ROAD, BAMBER BRIDGE, PRESTON, LANCASHIRE PR5 6BP, ☎ 01772 627365, FAX: 01772 314856, www.matalan.co.uk, 10–8 MON–FRI, 9–6 SAT, 11–5 SUN.

CENTRAL RETAIL PARK, OLDHAM ROAD, ROCHDALE, LANCASHIRE OL11 1OZ, ☎ 01706 752320, FAX: 01706 527339, www.matalan.co.uk, 10–8 MON–FRI, 9–6 SAT, 11–5 SUN.

2 WATTS CLIFF WAY, TODD ROAD, ST HELENS, LANCASHIRE WA9 1JL, ☎ 01744 766200, FAX: 01744 750904, www.matalan.co.uk, 9.30–8 MON–FRI, 9–6 SAT, 11–5 SUN.

WESTOVER STREET, OFF STATION ROAD, SWINTON, LANCASHIRE M27 2AH, ☎ 0161 794 3441, FAX: 0161 794 3461, www.matalan.co.uk, 10–8 MON–FRI, 9–6 SAT, 11–5 SUN.

LOIRE DRIVE, ROBIN RETAIL PARK, WIGAN, LANCASHIRE WN5 0UH, ☎ 01942 629500, FAX: 01942 217625, www.matalan.co.uk, 10–6 MON–FRI, 10–6 SAT, 11–5 SUN. **PERMANENT DISCOUNT OUTLET**

See page 232 (BEDS)

NEWMANS FOOTWEAR FACTORY SHOP

GARDEN STREET WORKS, BLACKBURN, LANCASHIRE BB2 1TZ, ☎ 01254 676198, 10–6 MON–SAT, 10–4 SUN. **FACTORY SHOP**

Not just a shoes shop selling footwear for men, women and children but also a general product outlet with clothes, bedding, bags, belts, candles, glassware, dried flowers, ceramics and textiles.

NEXT TO NOTHING

FREEPORT SHOPPING VILLAGE, FLEETWOOD, LANCASHIRE L65 9JJ, ☎ 01253 779826, www.next.co.uk, 10–6 MON–SAT, 8 ON THUR, FRI, 12–6 SUN. **FACTORY SHOP IN A FACTORY SHOPPING VILLAGE**

See page 239 (CHESH)

QS FASHION

114–116 BOLTON ROAD, ATHERTON, LANCASHIRE M29 9JZ, ☎ 01942 873847, FAX: 01942 897954, 9–5.30 MON–WED, 9–7 THUR, FRI, 9–5 SAT, 11–5 SUN.

GREEN LANE/PRESTON OLD ROAD, CHERRY TREE, BLACKBURN, LANCASHIRE BB2 5LX, ☎ 01254 209800, FAX: 01254 209833, 10–8 MON–FRI, 10–5.30 SAT, 10–5 SUN.

11–14 PALL MALL, CHORLEY, LANCASHIRE PR7 2LA, ☎ 01257 267113, FAX: 01257 263485, 9–8 MON–FRI, 9–5.30 SAT, 10–4 SUN.

148 MARKET STREET, FARNWORTH, LANCASHIRE BL4 9AE, ☎ 01204 862625, FAX: 01204 701855, 9–5.30 MON–WED, SAT, 9–6 THUR, FRI, 10–4 SUN. **PERMANENT DISCOUNT OUTLET**

Fashion for all the family includes brands such as Timberland, Fila, Nike, Reebok, Adidas, Calvin Klein and Ralph Lauren and many more. Homeware products include towels, bedding, plastics, pictures, toys and mirrors. The stock is constantly changing so come with an open mind. QS Fashion has a price promise that if you can purchase the same item at a cheaper price at another store, QS will give you the product free.

REGATTA

FREEPORT SHOPPING VILLAGE, ANCHORAGE ROAD, FLEETWOOD, LANCASHIRE FY7 6AE, ☎ 01253 777705, FAX: 01253 777705, www.regatta.com, 10–6 MON, TUE, WED, SAT, SUN, 10–8 THUR, FRI. **FACTORY SHOP IN A FACTORY SHOPPING VILLAGE**

See page 256 (ESSEX)

SCOOPS

UNIT 56, ARNDALE CENTRE, MIDDLETON, MANCHESTER, LANCASHIRE M24 4EL, ☎ 0161 653 5435, FAX: 0161 653 9066, 9–5.30 MON–SAT.

1318–1324 ASHTON OLD ROAD, OPPENSHAW, MANCHESTER, LANCASHIRE M11 1JG, ☎ 0161 371 8243, 9–5.30 MON–SAT.

C/O DISCOUNT GIANT, SISSION STREET, OFF OLDHAM ROAD, FAILSWORTH LANCASHIRE M35 0EJ, ☎ 0161 682 5684, FAX: 0161 684 8991, 9–6 MON, TUE, SAT, 9–7 WED, 9–8 THUR, 9–7 FRI, 10–4 SUN.

LANCASHIRE L32 8VS, ☎ 0151 545 0226, FAX: 0151 546 2899, 9.30–5.30 MON–SAT.

984 STOCKPORT ROAD, LEVENSHULME, MANCHESTER, LANCASHIRE M19 3NN, ☎ 0161 257 3515, FAX: 0161 225 1390, 9–5.30 MON–SAT.

2 BURY OLD ROAD, CHEETHAM HILL, MANCHESTER, LANCASHIRE M8 7JN, ☎ 0161 795 9312, FAX: 0161 684 8991, 9–5.30 MON–SAT

UNIT 102, CONCOURSE SHOPPING CENTRE, SOUTH WAY, SKELMERSDALE, LANCASHIRE WN8 6LJ, ☎ 01695 50965, FAX: 01695 50759, 9–5.30 MON–SAT. **PERMANENT DISCOUNT OUTLET**

See page 243 (CO DURH)

SECOND INNINGS

6 WELLINGTON STREET, ASHTON-UNDER-LYNE, TAMESIDE, LANCASHIRE OL6 6AJ, ☎ 0161 343 1040, 10–4 TUE–FRI, 10–4.30 SAT. **DRESS AGENCY**

Good quality nearly-new designer clothes, mostly for children, at reasonable prices as well as some nursery equipment such as cots, prams etc. Also new clothes at less than half the normal recommended retail price. Labels on sale include Versace, Oilily, Miniman, Toff Togs, Mannalisa, DKNY, Armani, Elle, Pampolina, Little Darlings, Moschino, Kenzo, Timberland plus many more.

STAMPER ENTERPRISES & CO LTD

ALMA HOUSE, GRIMSHAW LANE, MIDDLETON, MANCHESTER, LANCASHIRE M24 1GQ, ☎ 0161 655 1000, www.sales@stamper.co.uk, 9–5.30 MON–FRI. **PERMANENT DISCOUNT OUTLET**

Permanent discount outlet selling vast stocks of high street names for men, women and children from shops such as Marks & Spencer, BhS, Debenhams, Gap, Next, Ladybird and Mothercare. All the items are end of season or slight seconds and are sold without labels.

SUNGLASS TIME

THE LOWRY CENTRE, QUAYS ROAD, SALFORD QUAYS, MANCHESTER, LANCASHIRE M5 2WZ, ☎ 0161 848 9007, **e-mail:** info@sunglass-time.com, 10–8 MON–FRI, 9–7 SAT, 11–5 SUN.
PERMANENT DISCOUNT OUTLET

Designer Shades offer a wide selection of top-notch sunglasses and watches at more than 30% off typical high street prices. The frames are invitingly displayed on back-lit columns – no locked cabinets, messy stickers or hanging labels to contend with. Gucci, Polo Ralph Lauren, Valentino, Police, Christian Dior and Diesel are included in the ever-changing stock of top international brand names. Designer Shades ensure that all their sunglasses have quality lenses which protect against UVA and UVB rays, as well as filtering out damaging reflective blue light. Their range of high fashion unisex watches includes Dolce & Gabbana, Guess and Pulsar. They plan to have 20 shops throughout Europe by the end of 2003. For details of other locations, phone 01423 858007 or email info@sunglass-time.com.

SUTTONS FACTORY SHOP

NEW CHURCH ROAD, BACUP, LANCASHIRE OL13 9DT, ☎ 01706 875578, 10–5.30 MON–FRI, 9–5.30 SAT, 10–4 SUN. **PERMANENT DISCOUNT OUTLET**

Stocks top brand-name shoes at less than half price. Special monthly offers always available. There are shoes, trainers, slippers, sandals and boots for all the family, with a selection of bags, cleaners and polishes available, all at discount prices.

T J HUGHES

59–63 CHURCH STREET, BLACKBURN, LANCASHIRE BB1 5AF, ☎ 01254 693333, FAX: 01254 693232, **e-mail:** info@tjhughes.co.uk, www.tjhughes.co.uk, 9–5.30 MON–SAT, 11–5 SUN.

MONS SQUARE, NEW STRAND, BOOTLE, LANCASHIRE L20 4SY, ☎ 0151 922 4397, FAX: 0151 933 1622, **e-mail:** info@tjhughes.co.uk, www.tjhughes.co.uk, 9–5.30 MON–SAT.

4 CURZON STREET, BURNLEY, LANCASHIRE BB11 1BB, ☎ 01282 838383, FAX: 01282 435400, **e-mail:** info@tjhughes.co.uk, www.tjhughes.co.uk, 9–5.30 MON–SAT, 11–4 SUN.

105 LONDON ROAD, LIVERPOOL, LANCASHIRE L3 8JA, ☎ 0151 207 2600, FAX: 0151 298 1339, **e-mail:** info@tjhughes.co.uk, www.tjhughes.co.uk, 9–5.30 MON–SAT, 11–5 SUN.

UNIT 32, TOWN SQUARE SHOPPING CENTRE, OLDHAM, MANCHESTER, LANCASHIRE OL1 1XF, ☎ 0161 628 3880, FAX: 0161 628 3886, **e-mail:** info@tjhughes.co.uk, www.tjhughes.co.uk, 9–5.30 MON–SAT.

FISHERGATE CENTRE, PRESTON, LANCASHIRE PR1 8HJ, ☎ 01772 887326, FAX: 01772 887328, **e-mail:** info@tjhughes.co.uk, www.tjhughes.co.uk, 9–5.30 MON–SAT, 8 ON WED, 11–5 SUN.

UNIT 6–7, THE WHEATSHEAF CENTRE, ROCHDALE LANCASHIRE OL16 1NZ, ☎ 01706 750555, FAX: 01706 750666, **e-mail:** info@tjhughes.co.uk, www.tjhughes.co.uk, 9–5.30 MON–SAT, 10.30–4.30 SUN.

86 RAVENS WAY, SALFORD SHOPPING CITY, SALFORD, MANCHESTER, LANCASHIRE M6 5JA, ☎ 0161 736 1472, FAX: 0161 736 0656, **e-mail:** info@tjhughes.co.uk, www.tjhughes.co.uk, 9–5.30 MON–SAT.

UNIT 1, THE HARDSHAW CENTRE, ST HELENS, LANCASHIRE WA10 1EB, ☎ 01744 453221, FAX: 01744 453065, **e-mail:** info@tjhughes.co.uk, www.tjhughes.co.uk, 9–5.30 MON–SAT, 10.30–4.30 SUN.

31–36 ARNDALE CENTRE, CHESTER ROAD, STRETFORD, MANCHESTER, LANCASHIRE M32 9BB, ☎ 0161 866 9733, FAX: 0161 864 4627, **e-mail:** info@tjhughes.co.uk, www.tjhughes.co.uk, 9–5.30 MON–SAT, 10–4 SUN.

27–31 SANKEY STREET, WARRINGTON, LANCASHIRE WA1 1XG, ☎ 01925 634 4321, FAX: 01925 445966, **e-mail:** info@tjhughes.co.uk, www.tjhughes.co.uk, 9–5.30 MON–SAT, 10.30–4.30 SUN. **PERMANENT DISCOUNT OUTLET**

See page 239 (CHESH)

TERRY'S STORES URMSTON LTD

47 STATION ROAD, URMSTON, MANCHESTER, LANCASHIRE M41 9JG, ☎ 0161 748 6011, 9.30–5 MON–SAT, CLOSED WED. **PERMANENT DISCOUNT OUTLET**

Described as 'the final resting-place for ex-catalogue stock', Terry's sells everything that is normally available by catalogue at half price. This includes leather jackets, jeans, shoes, trainers, dress and curtaining fabric, watnot stands, nests of tables, dining tables and chairs, bedlinen, curtains, electrical goods, wedding and bridesmaids dresses. The company has been in operation for 46 years and is privately owned.

THE ELITE DRESS AGENCY

35 KINGS STREET WEST, MANCHESTER, LANCASHIRE M3 2PW, ☎ 0161 832 3670, www.elitedressagency.co.uk, 9.30–5.30 MON–SAT, 11–4 SUN. **DRESS AGENCY**

Three floors of good quality men's, women's and children's clothing, many with a Continental flavour. Among the womenswear can be found labels such as Moschino, Escada, Prada, Armani and DKNY among others, with lots of chainstore makes, too. For men, there are Italian designer suits from £50 to £150, including Boss, Paul Smith and Armani. There are lots of hats from £8; also shoes, handbags, accessories and a selection of unwanted gifts for sale.

THE FACTORY SHOP

SHAWBRIDGE STREET, CLITHEROE, LANCASHIRE BB7 1NA, ☎ 01200 428784, 9–5.30 MON–SAT, 10.30–4.30 SUN.

LANCASTER LEISURE PARK, WYRESDALE ROAD, LANCASTER, LANCASHIRE LA1 3LA, ☎ 01524 846079, 10–5 MON–SAT, 11–5 SUN. **FACTORY SHOP**

See page 243 (CHESH)

THE FAMOUS BRUNSWICK WAREHOUSE LTD

UNIT 6, ASHTON RETAIL PARK, 102 WELLINGTON ROAD, ASHTON UNDER LYNE, LANCASHIRE OL6 6DJ, ☎ 0161 330 7400, **e-mail:** northshoe@mcmail.com, 9–5 MON–FRI, 6 ON THUR, SAT, 10.30–4.30 SUN.

UNIT C, 454 BROOKWAY RETAIL PARK, ALTRINGHAM ROAD, BAGULEY, MANCHESTER, LANCASHIRE M23 9BL, ☎ 0161 945 1441, **e-mail:** northshoe@mcmail.com, 10–6 MON–WED, 10–8 THUR, FRI, 9–6 SAT, 11–5 SUN.

UNIT B2, TOWNSMOOR RETAIL PARK, BLACKBURN, LANCASHIRE BB2 3DY, ☎ 01254 278772, **e-mail:** northshoe@mcmail.com, 9.30–6 MON–WED, 9.30–7 THUR, FRI, 9–6 SAT, 11–5 SUN.

CHURCHILL WAY, LEYLAND, LANCASHIRE PR25 2LZ, ☎ 01772 455053, **e-mail:** northshoe@mcmail.com, 9–6 MON–WED, SAT, 9–7 THUR, FRI, 10.30–4.30 SUN.

24 MIDDLETON GARDENS, MIDDLETON, LANCASHIRE M24 4DF, ☎ 0161 653 9905, **e-mail:** northshoe@mcmail.com, 9–6 MON–SAT.

UNIT 4B, CABLES RETAIL PARK, STELEY WAY, RAINHILL, PRESCOT, MERSEYSIDE, LANCASHIRE L34 5NO, ☎ 0151 426 8262, **e-mail:** northshoe@mcmail.com, 9–6 MON–WED, SAT, 9–7 THUR, FRI, 10–4 SUN.

UNIT 2C, QUEENS RETAIL PARK, PRESTON, LANCASHIRE PR1 4HZ, ☎ 01772 253003, **e-mail:** northshoe@mcmail.com, 9–6 MON, TUE, FRI, SAT, 9–7 WED, THUR, 10.30–4.30 SUN.

UNIT E1, REGENTS PARK, ORDSALL LANE, SALFORD, MANCHESTER, LANCASHIRE M5 3TP, ☎ 0161 833 2173, **e-mail:** northshoe@mcmail.com, 10–6 MON–WED, 10–7 THUR, FRI, 9–6 SAT, 11–5 SUN.

UNIT D, WARRINGTON NEW ROAD, ST HELENS RETAIL PARK, ST HELENS, LANCASHIRE WA9 1JJ, ☎ 01744 754410, **e-mail:** northshoe@mcmail.com, 9–6 MON–WED, SAT, 9–7 THUR, FRI, 10–4 SUN.

UNIT 19, ELLESMERE RETAIL PARK, WALKDEN, WORSLEY, LANCASHIRE M28 3ZD, ☎ 0161 790 330, **e-mail:** northshoe@mcmail.com, 9–6 MON–WED, SAT, 9–7 THUR, FRI, 10.30–4.30 SUN.

25 LOIRE DRIVE, ROBIN PARK, WIGAN, LANCASHIRE WN5 0UH, ☎ 01942 211901, **e-mail:** northshoe@mcmail.com, 10–6 MON, TUE, 10–7 WED, FRI, 10–8 THUR, 9–6 SAT, 11–5 SUN. **PERMANENT DISCOUNT OUTLET**

See page 240 (CHESH)

THE TOY FACTORY

UNIT F3, THE DESIGNER OUTLET AT THE LOWRY, SALFORD QUAYS, MANCHESTER, LANCASHIRE M5 2WZ, ☎ 0161 877 7745, www.thetoyfactory.co.uk, 10–8 MON–FRI, 9–7 SAT, 11–5 SUN. **FACTORY SHOP IN A FACTORY SHOPPING VILLAGE**

The Toy Factory Outlets are part of Europe's largest toy factory outlet retailer. They offer an enormous range of branded products which may be surplus stocks, end of ranges or cancelled orders, and are therefore able to sell their products at up to 70% off normal high street prices. Their range includes famous names such as: Action Man, Barbie, Bandai, Crayola, Corgi, Fisher-Price, Hasbro, Hornby, Lego, Little Tikes, Meccano, Tomy, V-Tech and many more, all at unbelievably low prices.

TK MAXX

76 BANK HEY STREET, BLACKPOOL, LANCASHIRE B19 0B7, FAX: 01253 752754, www.tkmaxx.com, PHONE FOR DETAILS.

1ST FLOOR, THE GATES SHOPPING CENTRE, MEALHOUSE LANE, BOLTON, LANCASHIRE, ☎ 01204 385527, www.tkmaxx.com, PHONE FOR DETAILS.

UNIT 1 AND 2, ANGOULEME RETAIL PARK, BURY, LANCASHIRE B19 0B7, FAX: 0161 7611700, www.tkmaxx.com, 9–5.30 MON–FRI, 7 ON THUR, 9–6 SAT, 11- 5 SUN.

1ST FLOOR, 15 PARKER ST, OFF CLAYTON SQUARE, LIVERPOOL, LANCASHIRE L1 1DP, ☎ 0151 708 9919, www.tkmaxx.com, 9–6 MON–SAT, 11–5 SUN.

BASEMENT LEVEL, LEWIS'S BUILDING, MARKET STREET, MANCHESTER, LANCASHIRE M60 1TX, ☎ 0161 236 1885, www.tkmaxx.com, 9–6.30 MON–FRI, 8 ON THUR, 9–6 SAT, 11–5 SUN.

FISHERGATE SHOPPING CENTRE, PRESTON, LANCASHIRE PR1 2BT, ☎ 01772 253220, www.tkmaxx.com, 9–5.30 MON–FRI, 8 ON WED, 9–6 SAT, 11–5 SUN.

THE POINT RETAIL PARK, MOLEWORTH STREET, ROCHDALE, LANCASHIRE, ☎ 01706 759187, www.tkmaxx.com, PHONE FOR DETAILS.

UNIT A1, REGENT ROAD RETAIL PARK, ORDSALL LANE, SALFORD, MANCHESTER LANCASHIRE M5 3TP, ☎ 0161 833 2200, www.tkmaxx.com, 9.30–8 MON, THUR, FRI, 9.30–6 TUE, WED, 9–6 SAT, 11–5 SUN.

7–9 MARBLE PLACE SHOPPING CENTRE, CHAPEL STREET, SOUTHPORT LANCASHIRE PR8 1DF, ☎ 01704 501900, www.tkmaxx.com, 9–5.30 MON–FRI, 9–6 SAT, 11–5 SUN.

ST HELEN'S RETAIL PARK, WARRINGTON NEW ROAD, LANCASHIRE, ☎ 01744 615847, www.tkmaxx.com, PHONE FOR DETAILS. **PERMANENT DISCOUNT OUTLET**

See page 232 (BEDS)

TOG 24

7 THE LINKWAY, HORWICH, BOLTON, LANCASHIRE BL6 6JA, ☎ 01204 469899, **e-mail:** mail-order@tog24.com, www.tog24.com, 10–6 MON–FRI, SAT, 8 ON WED, THUR, 11–5 SUN.

BOUNDARY MILLS STORE, BURNLEY ROAD, COLNE, LANCASHIRE BB8 8JN, ☎ 01282 870042, **e-mail:** mail-order@tog24.com, www.tog24.com, 10–6 MON–FRI, 9 ON THUR, 9–6 SAT, 10–5 SUN. **FACTORY SHOP**

See page 240 (CHESH)

TOMMY BALL'S

HART STREET, BLACKBURN, LANCASHIRE BB1 1HW, ☎ 01254 261910, 10–5 MON–SAT, 11–5 SUN. **PERMANENT DISCOUNT OUTLET**

Very large shop on several floors selling a variety of shoes, boots, Wellingtons, trainers, sandals etc which are fastened together in pairs rather than displayed on racks. Most of the brands are not well known though you will find a reasonable amount of Clarks and some Diesel trainers.

TOP MARKS

149–151 HOLLAND STREET, DENTON, MANCHESTER, LANCASHIRE M34 3GE, ☎ 0161 336 1279, 9.30–5.30 MON–SAT, 8 ON THUR, 11–5 SUN. **PERMANENT DISCOUNT OUTLET**

A two-floor, 7,000-foot warehouse selling famous chainstore clothing (cancelled orders, overstocks, ends-of-lines and some grade A seconds) at up to 50% off normal retail prices. Shoes and clothing for women are available in sizes 8 to 18; men's clothing ranges from small to XXL, 30 to 42in waist and 29 to 33in leg; children's clothing is available from birth up to nine years. Also stocks homeware, giftware and furniture at discounted prices. All major credit cards are accepted and free parking is available.

TOYWORLD STORE FACTORY OUTLET

FREEPORT SHOPPING VILLAGE, ANCHORAGE ROAD, FLEETWOOD, FYLDE LANCASHIRE FY7 6AE, ☎ 01253 773776, www.toyworldstore.com, 10–8 MON–FRI, 9–6 SAT, 11–5 SUN.
FACTORY SHOP IN A FACTORY SHOPPING VILLAGE

See page 241 (CHESH)

TRADEX

CARLISLE STREET, RINGWAY, PRESTON, LANCASHIRE PR1 1EH, ☎ 01772 888333, FAX: 01772 880015, 9.30–8.30 MON–FRI, 9–5.30 SAT, 10.30–4.30 SUN. **PERMANENT DISCOUNT OUTLET**
Clothing and shoes for all the family, jewellery, household goods, toiletries, bedding and home furnishings, food and confectionery. Leading and high street brand names can be found in all departments with discounts of up to 60% off recommended retail prices. To shop here, you have to be a member: bring two forms of identity showing your address and you can join instantly for £2. There is a coffee shop serving meals and snacks.

UNITED FOOTWEAR

12 LORD STREET, LEIGH, LANCASHIRE, ☎ 01942 604440, 9–5.30 MON–WED, 9–8 THUR, 9–6 FRI, 9–5.30 SAT.

68–70 OLDHAM STREET, MANCHESTER, LANCASHIRE, ☎ 0161 228 1706, 9–5.30 MON–SAT.

126 FRIARGATE BROW, PRESTON, LANCASHIRE, ☎ 01772 204410, 9–5.30 MON–SAT, 11–4.30 SUN.

CARRMILL ROAD, OFF EAST LANCS ROAD, ST HELENS LANCASHIRE, ☎ 01744 737777, 9–6 MON–WED, 9–8 THUR, FRI, 9–5.30 SAT, 10–4 SUN. **PERMANENT DISCOUNT OUTLET**

See page 262 (HAMPS)

WINFIELDS

HAZEL MILL, BLACKBURN ROAD, HASLINGDEN, ROSSENDALE, LANCASHIRE BB4 5DD, ☎ 01706 227916, FAX: 01706 831125, **e-mail:** info@winfields.co.uk, www.winfields.co.uk, 10–5.30 MON–FRI, 8 ON THUR, 9–5.30 SAT, 11–5 SUN. **PERMANENT DISCOUNT OUTLET**
Winfields is a big mill discount store with other outlets in Barrow-in-Furness, Middleton and Hull, offering tremendous savings on shoes (more than 100,000 pairs to choose from, including trainers, boots, dressy shoes and sandals), womenswear (casual wear, sportswear, swimwear, lingerie, suits and dresses and designer fashions), traditional and contemporary menswear (shirts, trousers, jeans, polo shirts, denim jackets, sleepsuits and underwear), and accessories such as leather belts and wallets. There is a young fashion department and a range for women in sizes 18 plus. Winfields is the word on the street for children and teens for footwear, sportswear and clothing in up-to-the-minute styles. In addition, Winfields has a massive selction of outdoor wear, fleeces, waterproofs, wellingtons, hiking boots, socks, hats, scarves and gloves for all the family. There is a wide variety of outdoor and indoor furniture, timber decking, garden tools, pet accessories, cookware, utensils, electrical goods, bath towels, mirrors, picture frames, and gifts such as watches, crystalware and beauty products, with new stock arriving weekly. Luggage can be found in the Winair holiday department. Dine or take a break at Cloggers, the restaurant. Free car parking. Wheelchair friendly.

WRANGLER LEE

FREEPORT SHOPPING VILLAGE, ANCHORAGE ROAD, FLEETWOOD, LANCASHIRE FY7 6AE, ☎ 01253 773988, 10–6 MON–WED, SAT, 10–8 THUR, FRI, 11–5 SUN. **FACTORY SHOP IN A FACTORY SHOPPING VILLAGE**
Men's, women's and children's denim jeans and jackets, cords, T-shirts, shirts, most of which are seconds. T-shirts and shirts are all perfects, as are some jeans. Discounts are at least one-third off the normal price. Brand names on sale include Lee, Wrangler and Sedgefield. Children's range starts at two years. Also sells Jan Sport bags, caps and hats.

WYNSORS WORLD OF SHOES

E SUTTON & SON LTD, NEWCHURCH ROAD, BACUP, LANCASHIRE OL13 9DT, ☎ 01706 875578, 10–5.30 MON–FRI, 9.30–5.30 SAT, 10–4 SUN.

DOCK STREET, FLEETWOOD, NEAR BLACKPOOL, LANCASHIRE FY7 6JW, ☎ 01253 779871, 9–5.30 MON–SAT, 8 ON THUR, FRI, 10–5 SUN.

EAST PRESCOTT ROAD, KNOTTY ASH, LIVERPOOL LANCASHIRE L14 5NA, ☎ 0151 228 6673, 9–5.30 MON, TUE, SAT, 9–8 WED, THUR, FRI, 10–4 SUN, BANK HOLIDAYS.

BOUNDARY ROAD, ST HELENS, LANCASHIRE WA10 2PX, ☎ 01744 454983, 8.30–8 MON, TUE, WED, 8–8 SAT, 8.30–9 THUR, FRI, 10–4 SUN, 9–6 BANK HOLIDAYS. **PERMANENT DISCOUNT OUTLET**

See page 241 (CHESH)

LEICESTERSHIRE

CATALOGUE BARGAIN SHOP

UNIT D, WHITWICK RETAIL PARK, COALVILLE, LEICESTERSHIRE LE67 3FA, ☎ 01530 830294, www.bargaincrazy.com, 9–8 MON–SAT, 9 ON THUR, FRI, 10–4 SUN. **PERMANENT DISCOUNT OUTLET**

See page 234 (CAMBS)

CHARTERHOUSE RETAIL OUTLET

173 CHARNWOOD ROAD, SHEPSHED, LOUGHBOROUGH, LEICESTERSHIRE LE12 9NN, ☎ 01509 505050, FAX: 01509 507373, **e-mail:** factoryshop@charterhouse-holdings.co.uk, www.charterhouseholdings.co.uk, 9.30–6 MON–SAT, 11–4 SUN. **FACTORY SHOP**

The Charterhouse Retail Outlet was established 30 years ago and now enjoys its reputation as probably the largest factory shop of its kind in the UK. With over £2 million worth of stock always available, Charterhouse offers family clothing, fashion, footwear, kitchenware, homeware and more – all ex-chain and branded products at a fraction of high street prices. Womenswear includes casual, evening, swimwear, nightwear and lingerie – all styles and sizes. Childrenswear ranges from babies upwards with a special department for early teen fashions. Men will also find an excellent selection of branded sportswear, smart and casual clothing as well as footwear. The expanded kitchenware and household department stocks a huge selection of home and gift ideas, including luggage and toiletries. There is free parking, a children's play area, parent and baby room, wheelchair access and café area. The outlet is only one mile from Junction 23 of the M1.

DE BRADELEI MILL SHOP LTD

LOWER LEICESTER ROAD, LUTTERWORTH, LEICESTERSHIRE LE17 4NF, ☎ 01455 557571, FAX: 01455 557332, 9.30–5.30 MON–FRI, 9.30–6 SAT, 10.30–4.30 SUN. **PERMANENT DISCOUNT OUTLET**

A light and airy outlet centre, easily accessible from M1 junction 20 and M6 junction 1, selling leading high street and designer labels with up to 70% discount. Brands include Windsmoor, Planet, Precis Petite, Jaegar Knitwear, Jacques Vert, Country Casuals, French Connection, Elle, Elvi, and Studio selling a small selection of designer labels. Lee Cooper has an extensive range of jeans and casuals. Menswear brands include French Connection, Wolsey, Lee Cooper, Farah, and Robert Leonards menswear selling Gabicci, Gurteen and Ben Sherman. The children's section stocks fashions from birth to 12 years plus. A large shoe department stocks well-known brands for all the family. Ponden Mill offers a wide range of soft furnishings and everything for the home. Liberty giftwear and Arran Aromatics toiletries also available. Car parking.

GEOFF'S TOYS

30 HIGH STREET, COALVILLE, LEICESTERSHIRE LE67 3ED, ☎ 01530 832795, FAX: 01530 810201, 9–5 MON–SAT, 9- 12.45 WED. **PERMANENT DISCOUNT OUTLET**

20 HIGH STREEET, LOUGHBOROUGH, LEICESTERSHIRE LE11 2PZ, ☎ 01509 216966, 9–5.30 MON–FRI, 9–5 SAT. **PERMANENT DISCOUNT OUTLET**

Vast array of toys at very low prices.

GIFTTREE

BRITANNIA CENTRE, HINCKLEY, LEICESTERSHIRE LE10 1RU, ☎ 01455 891920, 9–5 MON–SAT. **FACTORY SHOP**

See page 247 (DERBY)

MATALAN

100 CHURCHGATE, VAUGHAN WAY, LEICESTER, LEICESTERSHIRE LE1 4AL, ☎ 0116 242 6700, FAX: 0116 253 8398, www.matalan.co.uk, 9–8 MON–FRI, 9–6 SAT, 11–5 SUN. **PERMANENT DISCOUNT OUTLET**

See page 232 (BEDS)

ROHDE SHOES

FOSSE WAY, SYSTON, LEICESTER, LEICESTERSHIRE LE7 1PG, ☎ 0116 260 3443, www.rohdeshoes.co.uk, 10–4 WED–SUN. **FACTORY SHOP**

Factory shop where the majority of the stock is Rohde footwear, as well as some Daniel Hechter and occasionally other brands such as Ecco and Portland. Rohde have been making sandals, slippers, shoes and boots in Germany for the past 50 years, using the best craftsmen and materials. Their winter range includes a special selection of waterproof footwear incorporating the Sympatex membrane.

THE DOC SHOP

BRUCE WAY, CAMBRIDGE ROAD INDUSTRIAL ESTATE, WHETSTONE, LEICESTERSHIRE LE8 6HP, ☎ 0116 286 5958, 9–5.30 MON–SAT. **PERMANENT DISCOUNT OUTLET**

Sells Doc Martens shoes and boots, as well as clothing and a vast range of accessories at discounted prices.

THE UPPINGHAM DRESS AGENCY

2–6 ORANGE STREET, UPPINGHAM, RUTLAND, LEICESTERSHIRE LE15 9SQ, ☎ 01572 823276, FAX: 01572 823815, www.dressagency.co.uk, 9–5 MON–SAT, 12–4 SUN AND BANK HOLIDAYS **DRESS AGENCY**

One of Britain's largest, longest established and most reputable dress agencies packed with over 4,000 quality new, nearly-new and end of line garments from famous high street names to top designer labels. Featured on television and in numerous national newspapers and magazines, this agency, situated in a picturesque market town, has everything from casuals to occasion wear, evening wear, suits and separates, hats, shoes, handbags, scarves and costume jewellery. There are departments for men, women and children, and ten rooms to explore. Further discounts are available with the agency's own loyalty card – ask for details.

TK MAXX

HAYMARKET CENTRE, 10 KEMBLE SQUARE, LEICESTER, LEICESTERSHIRE LE1 3YD, ☎ 0116 251 0155, www.tkmaxx.com, 9–5.30 MON–THUR, 9–6 FRI–SAT, 11–5 SUN. **PERMANENT DISCOUNT OUTLET**

See page 232 (BEDS)

UNITED FOOTWEAR

114 MAIN STREET, NEWBOLD VERDON, LEICESTERSHIRE, ☎ 01455 822407, 9–8 MON–FRI, 9–5.30 SAT, 10–4 SUN. **PERMANENT DISCOUNT OUTLET**

See page 262 (HAMPS)

LINCOLNSHIRE

BOUNDARY MILL STORES

AT DOWNTOWN SUPERSTORE, GONERBY MOOR, A1, GRANTHAM, LINCOLNSHIRE NG32 2AB, ☎ 01476 591001, 9.30–5.30 MON–SAT, 11–5 SUN. **PERMANENT DISCOUNT OUTLET**

See page 270 (LANCS)

BROUGHTON SHOE WAREHOUSE

18 ST MARK'S SQUARE, LINCOLN, LINCOLNSHIRE LN5 7EX, ☎ 01522 532300, 9.30–6 MON–SAT, 8 ON THUR, 11–5 SUN. **PERMANENT DISCOUNT OUTLET**

See page 247 (DERBY)

CATALOGUE BARGAIN SHOP

12–14 SILVER STREET, GAINSBOROUGH, LINCOLNSHIRE DN21 2DP, ☎ 01427 810604, www.bargaincrazy.com, 9–5.30 MON, THUR, FRI, 8.30–5 TUE, 9–5 WED, 8.30–5.30 SAT, 10–4 SUN.

29–31 THE STRAIT, LINCOLN, LINCOLNSHIRE LN1 1JD, ☎ 01522 527276, www.bargaincrazy.com, 9–5.30 MON–SAT, 10.30–4.30 SUN. **PERMANENT DISCOUNT OUTLET**

See page 234 (CAMBS)

GYMPHLEX SPORTSWEAR

BOSTON ROAD, HORNCASTLE, LINCOLNSHIRE LN9 6HU, ☎ 01507 523243, **e-mail:** sales@gymphlex.co.uk, **DESIGNER SALES**

Holds a one day factory shop sale just once a year: phone 01507 523243 for details. Your chance to buy a huge range of sportswear for all the family: jogging pants, tracksuits, rugby and football shirts, rugby shorts, T-shirts, polo shirts, Lycra swimwear, leotards, tights, socks. Some of the stock is seconds, some overmakes. The rest is freshly-made stock which is specially reduced for the sale.

MATALAN

JOHN ADAMS WAY, BOSTON, LINCOLNSHIRE PE21 6TY, ☎ 01205 312040, FAX: 01205 352991, www.matalan.co.uk, 10–8 MON–FRI, 9–6 SAT, 11–5 SUN.

UNIT 1, HEWITTS CIRCUS, CLEETHORPES, GRIMSBY, LINCOLNSHIRE DN35 9QH, ☎ 01472 200255, FAX: 01472 200156, www.matalan.co.uk, 9–8 MON–FRI, 9–6 SAT, 11–5 SUN.

LINDIS RETAIL PARK, TRITTON ROAD, LINCOLN, LINCOLNSHIRE LN6 7QY, ☎ 01522 696541, FAX: 01522 684946, www.matalan.co.uk, 10–8 MON–FRI, 9–6 SAT, 11–5 SUN.

DUDLEY ROAD, SCUNTHORPE, LINCOLNSHIRE DN16 1BA, ☎ 01724 270958, FAX: 01724 270856, www.matalan.co.uk, 9.30–8 MON–FRI, 9–6 SAT, 11–5 SUN. **PERMANENT DISCOUNT OUTLET**

See page 232 (BEDS)

STAGE 2

TRITTON RETAIL PARK, TRITTON ROAD, LINCOLN, LINCOLNSHIRE LN6 7YA, ☎ 01522 560303, 10–8 MON–FRI, 9–6 SAT, 11–5 SUN AND BANK HOLIDAYS. **PERMANENT DISCOUNT OUTLET**

See page 235 (CAMBS)

SUNDAES SANDALS

THE CHASE, 18 HIGH STREET, MOULTON, SPALDING, LINCOLNSHIRE PE12 6QB, ☎ 01406 371370, FAX: 01406 371646, **e-mail:** sundaessandals@aol.com, 9–3.30 MON–FRI, SAT BY APPOINTMENT. MAIL ORDER. **FACTORY SHOP**

Handmade sandals in bright summer colours, top quality materials, including leather uppers, insoles and linings. Women's sandals are available up to size 10. Their small, informal factory shop sells the full range of sundaes made on the premises and usually has a selection of discontinued styles, colours and slight seconds at bargain prices. Visitors are always welcome, but do phone first.

THE FACTORY SHOP

MALT KILN ROAD, BARTON ON HUMBER, NORTH LINCOLNSHIRE DN18 5JT, ☎ 01652 636701, 9–7 MON, TUE, WED, 9–8 THUR, FRI, 8.30–7 SAT, 10–4 SUN.

43 HIGH STREET, MABLETHORPE, LINCOLNSHIRE LN12 1XA, ☎ 01507 473705, 9.30–6 MON–SAT, 10.30–4.30 SUN.

CARRE STREET, SLEAFORD, LINCOLNSHIRE NG34 7TW, ☎ 01529 410155, 9–5.30 MON–SAT, 10–4 SUN.

51 FLEET STREET, HOLBEACH, SPALDING, LINCOLNSHIRE PE12 7AU, ☎ 01406 422180, 9–5 MON–SAT, 10–4 SUN. **FACTORY SHOP**

See page 243 (CHESH)

THE FAMOUS BRUNSWICK WAREHOUSE LTD

UNIT A, VICTORIA RETAIL PARK, VICTORIA STREET NORTH, GRIMSBY, LINCOLNSHIRE DN31 1NX, ☎ 01472 250622, **e-mail:** northshoe@mcmail.com, 9–6 MON–WED, SAT, 9–7 THUR, FRI, 10.30–4.30 SUN.

THE CARLTON CENTRE, OUTER CIRCLE ROAD, LINCOLN, LINCOLNSHIRE LN2 4WA, ☎ 01522 520037, **e-mail:** northshoe@mcmail.com, 9–6 MON–WED, SAT, 9–7 THUR, FRI, 10–4 SUN.

UNIT 2, CARLTON STREET, OFF STATION ROAD, SCUNTHORPE, LINCOLNSHIRE DN15 6TZ, ☎ 01724 857307, **e-mail:** northshoe@mcmail.com, 9–6 MON–WED, SAT, 9–7 THUR, FRI, 10–4 SUN. **PERMANENT DISCOUNT OUTLET**

See page 240 (CHESH)

THE SHOE FACTORY SHOP

21 WELLOWGATE, GRIMSBY, LINCOLNSHIRE DN32 0RA, ☎ 01472 342415, 9–5 MON–SAT, 9–7 THUR. **FACTORY SHOP**

See page 249 (DERBY)

TK MAXX

FRESHNEY PLACE SHOPPING CENTRE, GRIMSBY, LINCOLNSHIRE, ☎ 01472 352842, www.tkmaxx.com, PHONE FOR DETAILS.

UNIT 16, ST MARK'S CENTRE, STATION STREET, LINCOLN, LINCOLNSHIRE LN5 7EY, ☎ 01522 530933, www.tkmaxx.com, 9–6 MON–SAT, 8 ON THUR, 11–5 SUN.

UNIT E, GALLAGHER RETAIL PARK, DONCASTER ROAD, SCUNTHORPE, LINCOLNSHIRE, ☎ 01724 868965, www.tkmaxx.com, PHONE FOR DETAILS. **PERMANENT DISCOUNT OUTLET**

See page 232 (BEDS)

TOG 24

BOUNDARY MILL STORES, GONERBY MOOR, ON THE A1, GRANTHAM, LINCOLNSHIRE NG32 2AB, ☎ 01476 591001, **e-mail:** mail-order@tog24.com, www.tog24.com, 9.30–5.30 MON–SAT, 11–5 SUN. **FACTORY SHOP IN A FACTORY SHOPPING VILLAGE**

See page 240 (BEDS)

TRADEX

MONKS ROAD, LINCOLN, LINCOLNSHIRE LN2 5HN, ☎ 01522 512251, FAX: 01522 513332, 9.30–8.30 MON–FRI, 9–5.30 SAT, 10.30–4.30 SUN. **PERMANENT DISCOUNT OUTLET**

See page 278 (LANCS)

WILKINSON STORES

2 THE BROADWAY, ASHBY, SCUNTHORPE, LINCOLNSHIRE NG5 7EL, ☎ 01724 867767, www.wilko.co.uk, 9–5.30 MON–FRI, 8.30–5.30 SAT, 10–4 SUN. MAIL ORDER. **PERMANENT DISCOUNT OUTLET**

See page 241 (CHESH)

WYNSORS WORLD OF SHOES

123 CROMWELL ROAD, GRIMSBY, LINCOLNSHIRE DN31 2BB, ☎ 01472 251627, 9–5.30 MON, TUE, WED, SAT, 9–8 THUR, FRI, 10–4 SUN AND BANK HOLIDAYS. **PERMANENT DISCOUNT OUTLET**

See page 241 (CHESH)

LONDON

AMAZON

1, 3, 7 AND 22 KENSINGTON CHURCH STREET, LONDON W8, FAX: 020 7937 4692,
PERMANENT DISCOUNT OUTLET

Amazon ranges over five shops at the Kensington High Street end of Kensington Church Street. Numbers 1, 3 and 22 feature much the same merchandise which changes from one week to the next according to what the buyers can get hold of. Number 7 features menswear in the left hand shop, women's shoes and childrenswear on the right. The most common labels seen here are In Wear, French Connection, Great Plains, Fenn, Wright & Manson, Nicole Farhi and Sticky Fingers. There's always plenty of stock in good condition and very reasonable prices.

BENNY DEE LTD

74–80 MIDDLESEX STREET, LONDON E1 7EZ, ☎ 020 7377 9067, FAX: 020 7247 7728, www.bennydee.com, 9–6 MON–FRI, 10–4 SAT, 9.30–4.30 SUN.

136–138 WALTHAMSTOW HIGH STREET, LONDON E17 7JS, ☎ 020 8520 4637, FAX: 020 8520 4637, www.bennydee.com, 9–6 MON–SAT. **PERMANENT DISCOUNT OUTLET**

110–114 KILBURN HIGH ROAD, LONDON NW6 4HY, ☎ 020 7624 2995, FAX: 020 7624 2995, 9–6 MON–SAT, 10–4 SUN. **PERMANENT DISCOUNT OUTLET**

4–6 HIGH ROAD, WOOD GREEN LONDON N22 6BX, ☎ 020 8881 8101, FAX: 020 8881 8101 **e-mail:** info@bennydee.com, www.bennydee.com, 9–6 MON–SAT, 10–4 SUN. **PERMANENT DISCOUNT OUTLET**

Discounted women's, men's and childrenswear, specialising in lingerie, with masses of bras, all brand names such as Marks & Spencer, Berlei, Gossard, Triumph and Warner. High street brands with at least 50% savings. Some of the brands there include Zorbit, Mothercare, Baby Gap, Baby Togs and Grasshopper. For men there are socks, ties, underwear, shirts, T-shirts, jogging bottoms and occasionally suits.

BURBERRY

29–53 CHATHAM PLACE, LONDON E9 6LP, ☎ 020 8985 3344, 11–6 MON–FRI, 10–5 SAT, 11–5 SUN. **FACTORY SHOP**

See page 236 (CHESH)

CATALOGUE BARGAIN SHOP

252 GREEN LANES, PALMERS GREEN, LONDON N13 5TU, ☎ 020 8886 9532, www.bargaincrazy.com, 9–5.30 MON–SAT, 10–4 SUN. **PERMANENT DISCOUNT OUTLET**

See page 234 (CAMBS)

CHANGE OF HABIT

65 ABBEVILLE ROAD, CLAPHAM, LONDON SW4 9JW, ☎ 020 8675 9475, 11–6 MON–FRI, 10–6 SAT. **DRESS AGENCY**

Day and evening wear as good as new from high street to designer label. Described by the owner as 'everyday clothes for everyday people at realistic prices'. Very high turnover. Also brand new clothes and accessories and recently added antiques and home furnishing for the garden and conservatory.

CHOICE DISCOUNT STORES LIMITED

67 GOLDERS GREEN ROAD, GOLDERS GREEN, LONDON NW11 8EL, ☎ 020 8458 8247, 9–6 MON–SAT, 11–5 SUN.

11 ARCADIA CENTRE, THE BROADWAY, EALING, LONDON W5 2ND, ☎ 020 8567 2747, 9.30–6 MON–SAT, 7 ON THUR, 11–5 SUN. **PERMANENT DISCOUNT OUTLET**

See page 235 (CAMBS)

CLARKS FACTORY SHOP

61-63 RYE LANE, PECKHAM, LONDON SE15 5EX, ☎ 020 7732 2530, 9.30–5 MON–SAT.

UNIT 2, 67-83 SEVEN SISTERS ROAD, LONDON N7 6BU, ☎ 020 7281 9364, 9.30–5.30 MON–SAT, 11–5 SUN.

113-117 POWIS STREET, WOOLWICH, LONDON SE18 6JB, ☎ 020 8854 3163, 9.30–5.15 MON–SAT. **FACTORY SHOP**

See page 236 (CHESH)

DAVID CHARLES

2–4 THANE WORKS, THANE VILLAS, LONDON N7 7NU, ☎ 020 7609 4797, **DESIGNER SALES**
Twice yearly showroom sale of this children's range at which prices are considerably reduced. Phone or write to put your name down on the mailing list for an automatic invitation.

DESIGNS

60 ROSSLYN HILL, LONDON NW3 1ND, ☎ 020 7435 0100, 10–5.45 MON–SAT, 6.30 ON THUR. **DRESS AGENCY**
Designs has been established for more than 18 years, and sells women's designer clothes and accessories. Their most sought-after labels include Hermes, Chanel, Donna Karan, Ralph Lauren, Giorgio Armani, Prada, Gucci, Joseph, Issey Miyake and Jil Sander and they have a constant supply of covetable Gucci and Prada handbags and shoes. They only accept perfect merchandise under two years old and have a rapid turnover with the most exciting pieces coming their way. Regular customers talk about the spacious, relaxed atmosphere and prices remain keenly competitive: ranging from £5 to £500. They have more than 6,000 clients and take in stock from the UK, America and Italy. They also keep a range of girls' clothes from birth to seven years.

DISPOSAL SERVICES AGENCY (DSA)

ROOM 727, MINISTRY OF DEFENCE, 6 HERCULES ROAD, LONDON SE1 7DJ, ☎ 020 7261 8968, www.disposalservices.agency.mod.uk. **PERMANENT DISCOUNT OUTLET**
The Disposal Services Agency is an agency of the Ministry of Defence set up to dispose of surplus equipment. It runs the largest disposal operation in the UK, organising the sale of both military equipment and commodities in use commercially, such as embassy furniture, government department office furniture, closed-down RAF-base vehicles and housing stock, ex-marine boats, ex-army tents, boots and ski equipment, medical and dental equipment, clothing, ship and aircraft spares, scrap metal and IT equipment. The DSA uses companies throughout the UK, each with their own specialist area, to dispose of stock. These companies also dispose of stock from a host of other, usually public sector, organisations varying from fire brigades and hospitals to health authorities and the police. Equipment from these companies varies from kitchen equipment and fax machines to mobile radios, cars, generators, jewellery and telecommunications equipment to food trolleys, X-ray equipment, telephones, uniforms, dinghies, fishing nets, photocopiers and chair lifts. Visit the website to find out which companies sell which products and how to contact them direct.

LA SCALA

39 ELYSTAN STREET, LONDON SW3 3NT, ☎ 020 7589 2784, 10–5.30 MON–SAT. **DRESS AGENCY**
La Scala sells women's nearly-new clothes, accessories, men's and children's clothes under the same roof. Top designer men's clothes including Armani, Prada and Gucci, and large quantities of women and men's cashmere as well as a range of shoes in immaculate condition. Owner Sandy Reid lived for 14 years in Northern Italy and uses her experience there in her shop behind the Conran Shop in Chelsea. There, she sells end of season Italian designer wear and current top designer nearly-new outfits from DKNY, Dolce & Gabbana, Voyage, MaxMara, Prada and Gucci. Italian is spoken in the shop which has a large Italian clientele. There's an emphasis on younger lines and the price reductions are fantastic.

LETTERBOX LIBRARY

71–73 ALLEN ROAD, LONDON N16 8RY, ☎ 020 7503 4801, FAX: 020 7503 4800, www.letterboxlibraray.com, 10–5 MON–FRI. **PERMANENT DISCOUNT OUTLET**
Run by a cooperative, Letterbox offers non-sexist, non-racist, multi-cultural books, as well as those about the environment, citizenship and disabilty for children of all ages. Books are sold at discounts of between 5% and 12%. Phone or fax the numbers above for a catalogue.

MATALAN

ALPINE RETAIL PARK, ALPINE WAY, EAST BECKTON, LONDON E6 6LA, ☎ 020 7473 9780, FAX: 020 7511 5554, www.matalan.co.uk, 10–8 MON–FRI, 9–6 SAT, 10–4 SUN.

HIGH ROAD, LEYTONSTONE, LONDON E11 1HH, ☎ 020 8988 8630, FAX: 020 8558 3048, www.matalan.co.uk, 10–8 MON–FRI, 9–6 SAT, 10–4 SUN.

317 EDGWARE ROAD, CRICKLEWOOD BROADWAY, CRICKLEWOOD, LONDON NW2 6PH, ☎ 020 8450 5667, FAX: 020 8450 8575, www.matalan.co.uk, 10–8 MON–FRI, 9–6 SAT, 11–5 SUN.

THURSTON ROAD, LOAMPIT VALE, LEWISHAM, LONDON SE13 7SN, ☎ 020 8463 9830, FAX: 020 8318 1936, www.matalan.co.uk, 10–8 MON–FRI, 9–6 SAT, 10–4 SUN.

59 BUGSBY WAY, CHARLTON, LONDON SE7 7SE, ☎ 020 8269 4290, FAX: 020 8858 6469, www.matalan.co.uk, 10–8 MON–FRI, 9–6 SAT, 11–5 SUN. **PERMANENT DISCOUNT OUTLET**

See page 232 (BEDS)

MORRY'S

39–40 THE BROADWAY, EDMONTON, LONDON N9 0TJ, ☎ 020 8807 6747, 8.30–5 MON–SAT, CLOSED 1 ON THUR. **PERMANENT DISCOUNT OUTLET**

Liquidation stock which includes some famous makes and can comprise anything from gardening equipment (shovels, forks and hoses) and household items to electrical equipment (CDs, radios, televisions, radio alarms) and clothing for men, women and children. For example, BhS padded jacket £3.99, normal retail price £30; Etam dress £2, normal retail price £40. Everything is at least half the retail price. Specialises in Philips electrical equipment from CD players and videos, car stereos and radio cassettes to shavers and baby alarms, all with full repair and spares back-up. If you live nearby, drop in frequently as stock is constantly changing.

OXFAM SUPER SAVING SHOP

570 KINGSLAND ROAD, LONDON E8 4AH, ☎ 020 7923 1532, 9.15–5.15 MON–SAT. **SECONDHAND SHOPS**

Vast secondhand shop selling loads of cheap bric a brac, records and clothes. Stock is made up of unsold items from Oxfam's other shops in London so it's very cheap indeed. For example, bric-a-brac items from 9p; items of clothing from £2.29; electrical items (which have all been tested), such as lamps, from £2.99. Other end-of-line Oxfam shops include Kilburn, Burnt Oak, Tooting and Walthamstow.

RAINBOW

249 AND 253 ARCHWAY ROAD, HIGHGATE, LONDON N6 5BS, ☎ 020 8340 8003, FAX: 0208 372 5484, 10.30–5.30 MON–SAT. **DRESS AGENCY**

Number 249 sells mainly secondhand items, while no. 253 is new merchandise and toys. At 249, the shop is divided into six selling areas which are rented out on a day-to-day basis. Examples of goods on sale are adults and children's clothing, baby equipment, toys, books, bric-a-brac, arts and crafts. The shop is in Highgate so there is a big variety of good quality designer clothes and other interesting goods. As there is no middle man, there are loads of bargains to be had. The shop at 253 has a large and fascinating selection of new toys at reasonable prices. They stock traditional wooden toys such as rocking horses, fots, trains, garages and dolls' houses from, among others, Brio, Galt, Escor and Plan Toys. They also sell Lego, Playmobil, TY Beanies, dressing up, books, creative kits, nostalgic pocket money toys and lots more. Ends of lines are discounted throughout the year. Highgate tube and buses are near by and there's free parking in the side streets and right outside to load and unload.

REAL NAPPY ASSOCIATION

PO BOX 3704, LONDON SE26 4RX, ☎ 020 8299 4519, www.realnappy.com. **PERMANENT DISCOUNT OUTLET**

Encourages the use of real nappies which, compared to disposable ones, are much cheaper. You can save £500-£1,250 on the cost of keeping your baby in nappies. Plus, they argue, your baby stays comfortable and healthy and you save resources and minimise pollution. Over two and a half years, or 5,020 nappy changes, disposables cost between £653 and £1,054 whereas real nappies can cost as little as £152 including all accessories, washing agents, energy and wear and tear on a washing machine. Nappy washing services are especially good value for families with two or more children in nappies. Send large SAE with two stamps for a free information pack. Some companies have payment plans to spread the cost of buying real nappies. The Real Nappy Exchange is a source of secondhand nappies.

ROCHELLE

LONDON NW7, FAX: 020 8906 2158, PHONE FOR APPOINTMENT. **DESIGNER SALES**

Home-based business selling designer childrenswear at discount prices including OshKosh B'Gosh, Double Dutch and Coco. There are dresses, jeans, tracksuits, pinafores and leggings for girls and boys aged from birth to eight years. Please phone for an appointment.

SWALLOWS & AMAZONS

91 NIGHTINGALE LANE, LONDON SW12 8NX, ☎ 020 8673 0275, 10–5.30 MON–SAT. **DRESS AGENCY**

Probably the largest good-as-new children's shop in London, S & A has a ground floor full of quality clothes from birth to 12 years: OshKosh, Oilily, Jean Le Bourget, Mexx etc, as well as a large basement with toys, books and baby equipment. The stock is constantly changing and they pride themselves on keeping standards high, but prices low: from 90p to £99. There is also children's hairdressing (with videos) on most afternoons and on Saturdays (appointments necessary). Friendly, helpful staff.

SWIMGEAR

11 STATION ROAD, FINCHLEY, LONDON N3 2SB, ☎ 020 8346 6106, FAX: 020 8346 7211, www.swimgear.co.uk, 9.30–5 MON–FRI. MAIL ORDER. **PERMANENT DISCOUNT OUTLET**

A mail order company which also operates via a retail outlet opposite Finchley Central station. As well as selling their swimwear at less than the normal retail price by not putting the full markup on their products, they also sell discontinued and ends of line ranges of swimwear for men, women and children at between 20% to 30% less than normal retail prices. They also stock swimming hats, bubble hats, kickboards, goggles and flippers in adult and children's sizes. Flippers normally cost about £18.50, but can be bought here for about £8 in black rubber; Lycra trunks, plain £7.35 up to £10 for patterned ones. Bikinis are on sale all year round, with women's swimwear ranging up to size 50 with Swimgear's own brand, full colour Mark One brochure or leaflet. Prices are lower than would be offered at swim meets and retail shops. As part of their service, they do not cash your cheque until your full order has been completed. Postage and packaging extra. Orders over £20 are post free, excluding heavy items such as flippers and shampoo on which p&p is charged.

THE NAPPY EXPRESS

128 HIGH ROAD, NEW SOUTHGATE, LONDON N11 1PG, ☎ 020 8361 4040, FAX: 020 8368 0132, **e-mail:** shopping@nappyexpress.co.uk, www.nappyexpress.co.uk, PHONE FIRST FOR BROCHURE. OFFICE OPEN 9.30–5.30 MON–FRI. **HIRE SHOP**

There is a free home delivery service aimed at new mothers in north, central and south London for Pampers and Huggies nappies, baby foods (including organic), baby toiletries, also large household items like washing powders, toilet rolls, bottled waters, fizzy drinks, beer etc, all at supermarket prices. A member of the Baby Equipment Hirers' Association (BEHA), which has members countrywide. A range of equipment can be hired from high chairs, cots and travel cots to baby car seats and buggies. BEHA runs an advice line which will try and answer any queries you have regarding hiring services for children. Phone the Babyline on 07831 310355.

TK MAXX

PENINSULA RETAIL PARK, BUGSBY WAY, CHARLTON, LONDON, ☎ 020 8293 1957, www.tkmaxx.com, PHONE FOR DETAILS.

THE ARCADIA CENTRE, THE BROADWAY, EALING, LONDON W5 2ND, ☎ 020 8566 0447, www.tkmaxx.com, 9.30–8 MON–FRI, 7.30 ON THUR, 9–7 SAT, 11–5 SUN.

UNIT B, FIRST FLOOR, WOOD GREEN SHOPPING CENTRE, LONDON N22 6YD, ☎ 020 888 88803, www.tkmaxx.com, 9–6 MON–SAT, 10–5 SUN. **PERMANENT DISCOUNT OUTLET**

See page 232 (BEDS)

TOG 24

PUTNEY EXCHANGE SHOPPING CENTRE, PUTNEY HIGH STREET, LONDON SW15 1TW, ☎ 020

8785 3565, **e-mail:** mail-order@tog24.com, www.tog24.com, 9–6 MON–SAT, 11–5 SUN. **FACTORY SHOP IN A FACTORY SHOPPING VILLAGE**

See page 240 (CHESH)

USA FASHION

111 FONTHILL ROAD, LONDON N4 3JH, ☎ 020 7272 3992, 9.30–5.30 MON–FRI, 9–4 SAT. **PERMANENT DISCOUNT OUTLET**

Specialists in special occasion wear: bridalwear, bridesmaid dresses and evening wear (more than 300 different styles) in sizes 8 to 26. They also stock women's casual wear from familiar high street and American designers, all at discounted prices. For example, a garment which would retail at £170 costs only £60 here. All the stock is brand new. There is also childrenswear from age 12.

MIDDLESEX

BRAND CENTRE

12 HAREFIELD ROAD, UXBRIDGE, MIDDLESEX UB8 1JS, ☎ 01895 814888, FAX: 01895 814222, 10–8 MON–FRI, 9.30–6.30 SAT, 11–5 SUN. **PERMANENT DISCOUNT OUTLET**

See page 270 (LANCS)

LITTLE STARS

33 ROYSTON PARK ROAD, HATCH END, MIDDLESEX HA5 4AA, ☎ 020 8537 0980, FAX: 020 8930 5340, **e-mail:** karoline@littlestars.co.uk, www.littlestars.co.uk, PHONE FIRST.

8 ANSELM ROAD, HATCH END, MIDDLESEX HA5 4LJ, ☎ 020 8621 4378, **e-mail:** karoline@littlestars.co.uk, www.littlestars.co.uk, PHONE FIRST. **HIRE SHOP**

Part of the Baby Equipment Hirers' Association (BEHA), which has members countrywide. A range of equipment can be hired from high chairs, cots and travel cots to baby car seats and buggies. Some members also hire out party equipment including child-sized tables and chairs. They also sell branded and unbranded equipment competitively, price list available on request by phoning the number below. BEHA runs an advice line which will try and answer any queries you have regarding hiring services for children. Phone the Babyline on 07831 310355.

MATALAN

PUMP LANE, HAYES, MIDDLESEX UB3 3NB, ☎ 020 8606 6700, FAX: 020 8573 5268, www.matalan.co.uk, 10–8 MON–FRI, 9–6 SAT, 11–5 SUN.

GREAT WESTERN INDUSTRIAL PARK, WINDMILL LANE, SOUTHALL, MIDDLESEX UB2 4SD, ☎ 020 8574 9660, FAX: 020 8574 4924, www.matalan.co.uk, 10–8 MON–FRI, 9–6 SAT, 11–5 SUN. **PERMANENT DISCOUNT OUTLET**

See page 232 (BEDS)

THE SALVAGE SHOP

34–40 WATLING AVENUE, BURNT OAK, MIDDLESEX HA8 0LR, ☎ 020 8952 4353, **e-mail:** lss@salvage1.co.uk, www.salvage1.co.uk, 9–5.30 MON–SAT, 10–4 SUN. **PERMANENT DISCOUNT OUTLET**

An Aladdin's cave of salvaged stock for the avid bargain hunter, most of which has been the subject of insurance claims for fire or flood, salvage, bankruptcy or is simply clearance stock. Stock changes every two or three days and regular visitors have found anything from half price Kenwood Chefs, televisions and toys to furniture, kitchen items, linens and especially fantastic bargains in designer clothing. Yves Saint Laurent, Armani, Ungaro, Hugo Boss and Valentino, as well as all major high street names, are just some of the names to be found (though the labels are often cut out). Discounts range from 50% to 80%. Phone first to check stock.

TK MAXX

UNIT 31, ST GEORGE'S CENTRE, ST ANNE'S ROAD, HARROW MIDDLESEX HA1 1HS, ☎ 020 8863 9292, www.tkmaxx.com, 9.30–8 MON–FRI, 9–7 SAT, 11–5 SUN. **PERMANENT DISCOUNT OUTLET**

See page 232 (BEDS)

NORFOLK

LATHAMS

BRIDGE STREET, POTTER HEIGHAM, GREAT YARMOUTH, NORFOLK NR29 5JE, ☎ 01692 670080, 9–5.30 MON–SAT, 10–4 SUN. **FACTORY SHOP**

Sell a wide range of fashions, hardware, china, fishing tackle, books, gardening equipment, linen, groceries and Christmas gifts at very reasonable prices. Most of the makes are high street labels and consist of discontinued lines and seconds. Also jewellery concessions, shoes, computer games kiosk, coffee shop and garden centre.

MATALAN

SOUTHTOWN ROAD, GREAT YARMOUTH NORFOLK NR31 0JB, ☎ 01493 444734, FAX: 01493 445636, www.matalan.co.uk, 9–8 MON–FRI, 9–6, 11–5 SUN.

BLACKFRIARS ROAD, KINGS LYNN, NORFOLK PE30 1RX, ☎ 01553 765696, FAX: 01553 764518, www.matalan.co.uk, 10–8 MON–FRI, 9–6 SAT, 11–5 SUN. **PERMANENT DISCOUNT OUTLET**

See page 232 (BEDS)

MR SHOE'S FACTORY SHOP

31 YAXHAM ROAD, DEREHAM, NORFOLK NR19 1HD, ☎ 01362 699599, 9–6 MON–SAT, 10.30–4.30 SUN. **PERMANENT DISCOUNT OUTLET**

Shoes for all the family, including well-known brands, at discounted prices.

MRS PICKERING'S DOLLS' CLOTHES

THE PINES, DECOY ROAD, POTTER HEIGHAM, GREAT YARMOUTH, NORFOLK NR29 5LX, ☎ 01692 670407, **e-mail:** dolls.clothes@virgin.net, www.dolls-clothes.com, MAIL ORDER. **PERMANENT DISCOUNT OUTLET**

A wide selection of well-made dolls' clothes which are easy to put on and take off and, especially for smaller children, will help them learn to use various methods of fastening. All the popular dolls are catered for including Baby Born, Tiny Tears, Timmy, Baby Annabell, Molly, Chou-Chou, Action Man, Sindy, Barbie, Ken, Skipper, Stacie, Shelly and Tommy as well as teddies. Special outfits, such as school uniforms to match the child's, can be made on request. Prices range from 50p for a Barbie-sized skirt to £3.50 for a wedding dress, and £1.40 for a nappy, £2.50 for a dress, and £7 for a Tiny Tears-sized snowsuit. Please send a stamped, self-addressed envelope for a catalogue, or visit the website, and mention The Good Deal Directory.

NORWICH CAMPING SPORTS AND LEISURE

52–56 MAGDALEN STREET, NORWICH, NORFOLK NR3 1JE, ☎ 01603 615525, FAX: 01603 623150, 9–5.45 MON–SAT. **PERMANENT DISCOUNT OUTLET**

Reductions of up to 50% on skiing jackets, one-pieces and salopettes all year round. This includes brand names such as Berghaus, O'Neill and Quiksilver, in children's sizes too. Also many ends of lines and last year's colours in fleeces, cagoules and waterproofs, as well as some reductions on ski boots and tents. Now stock an extensive range of climbing equipment at very competitive prices.

QD STORES

143 HIGH STREET, GORLESTON, GREAT YARMOUTH, NORFOLK NR31 6RB, ☎ 01493 652735, 9–5.30 MON–SAT.

128–132 NORFOLK STREET, KINGS LYNN, NORFOLK PE30 1AP, ☎ 01553 770068, 9–5.30 MON–SAT.

7–10 ANGLIA SQUARE, NORWICH, NORFOLK NR3 1DY, ☎ 01603 275201, 9–5.30 MON–SAT, 10–4 SUN.

48–54 ST STEPHENS STREET, NORWICH, NORFOLK NR1 3SL, ☎ 01603 622562, 9–5.30 MON–SAT. **PERMANENT DISCOUNT OUTLET, FOOD AND DRINK DISCOUNTERS**

See page 232 (BEDS)

ROYS

BOWTHORPE CENTRE, WENDENE, BOWTHORPE, NORWICH, NORFOLK NR5 9HA, ☎ 01603 746622, www.roys.co.uk, 8.30–8 MON–THUR, 8.30–9 FRI, 8–6 SAT, 10–4 SUN.

77–87 MAGDALEN STREET, NORWICH, NORFOLK NR3 1AA, ☎ 01603 612934, www.roys.co.uk, 9–5.30 MON–SAT, 10–4 SUN.

YAXHAM ROAD, DEREHAM NORFOLK NR19 1HD, ☎ 01362 690555, www.roys.co.uk, 9–8 MON–FRI, 9–6 SAT, 11–5 SUN.

10 YARMOUTH ROAD, NORTH WALSHAM, NORFOLK NR28 9BW, ☎ 01692 501058, www.roys.co.uk, 9–5.30 MON, TUE, 9–8 WED, THUR, FRI, 9–6 SAT, 10–4 SUN.

GUILDHALL STREET, THETFORD, NORFOLK IP24 2DP, ☎ 01842 766161, www.roys.co.uk, 9–5.30 MON–SAT, 10–4 SUN. **PERMANENT DISCOUNT OUTLET**

Roys sell branded household goods at what they call 'valued prices'. The Save 'n' Wear department deals with the cheaper end of the clothing market for men, women and children. They also include DIY, gardening, electrical, housewares, gifts, toiletries and some food lines.

ROYS OF WROXHAM LTD

WROXHAM, NORWICH, NORFOLK NR12 8DB, ☎ 01603 782131, www.roys.co.uk, 9–5.30 MON, TUE, 9–8 WED, THUR, FRI, 9–6 SAT, 10.30–4.30 SUN. **PERMANENT DISCOUNT OUTLET**
Reputed to be the largest village store in the world, Roys sell branded household goods at what they call 'valued prices'. The Save 'n' Wear department deals with the cheaper end of the clothing market for men, women and children. There is also a pharmacy department that deals with photography, records and toiletries, all at competitive prices. This branch has a coffee shop on site, as well as free parking.

START-RITE

8 HIGH STREET, KING'S LYNN, NORFOLK P30 1BX, ☎ 01553 760786, 9–5.30 MON–SAT. **FACTORY SHOP**
The children's shoe experts have a large factory shop selling clearance lines at discounted prices. They don't stock the full range – it's a matter of choosing from what's available. Rejects are sold at at least half price; end of sales stock with not quite such a high discount. There are also some senior sizes up to size 9. Feet are expertly measured by trained staff.

THE FACTORY SHOP LTD

NORWICH STREET, EAST DEREHAM, NORFOLK NR19 1AD, ☎ 01362 691868, 9–5.30 MON–SAT, 10–4 SUN.

52 LONDON ROAD, HARLESTON, NORFOLK IP20 9BZ, ☎ 01379 854860, 9–5.30 MON–SAT, 10.30–4 SUN.

LYNN ROAD, SNETTISHAM, NORFOLK PE31 7QG, ☎ 01485 544441, 9–5.30 MON–SAT, 10–4 SUN. **FACTORY SHOP**

See page 243 (CHESH)

NORTHAMPTONSHIRE

AIRWEAR

NENE PARK, STATION ROAD, NORTHAMPTONSHIRE NN9 5QG, ☎ 01933 653111, FAX: 01933 654506, www.drmartens.com, 9.30–5.30 MON–SAT, 10–4 SUN. **PERMANENT DISCOUNT OUTLET**
Sells Doc Martens shoes and boots, as well as clothing and a range of accessories at discounted prices. Nene Park is the only official outlet for Rushden and Diamonds' merchandise.

BARRATT'S SALE SHOP

BARRACK ROAD, KINGSTHORPE HOLLOW, NORTHAMPTON, NORTHAMPTONSHIRE NN2 6EL, ☎ 01604 718632, www.tall-small.com, 9–5.30 MON–SAT. **FACTORY SHOP**
This shop now stocks solely sales stock of trainers and shoes from last season for men, women

and children. Children's range from £5 to £10, men's from £20 to £40, and women's from £10 upwards. They also cater for small and large feet.

GLOVERALL FACTORY SHOP

LONDON ROAD, WELLINGBOROUGH, NORTHAMPTONSHIRE NN8 2QX, ☎ 01933 225666, OPEN 9–5 MON–FRI. **FACTORY SHOP**

Duffle coats, lightweight jackets, knitwear, silk ties and cufflinks. One reader bought a pure wool duffle coat for £90 whose original price was £395 and another made for Galeries Lafayette of Paris for £59, usual price £120.

MATALAN

UNIT 1, PHOENIX RETAIL PARK, PHOENIX PARKWAY, CORBY, NORTHAMPTONSHIRE NN17 5DT, ☎ 01536 408042, FAX: 01536 408750, www.matalan.co.uk, 9–8 MON–FRI, 9–6 SAT, 10–4 SUN.

UNIT 1, WEEDON ROAD INDUSTRIAL ESTATE, TYNE ROAD, NORTHAMPTON, NORTHAMPTONSHIRE NN5 5BE, ☎ 01604 597890, FAX: 01604 588068, www.matalan.co.uk, 9–8 MON–FRI, 9–6 SAT, 10.30–4.30 SUN.

VICTORIA ROAD, WELLINGBOROUGH, NORTHAMPTONSHIRE NN8 2EF, ☎ 01933 233890, FAX: 01933 272658, www.matalan.co.uk, 10–8 MON–FRI, 9–6 SAT, 11–5 SUN. **PERMANENT DISCOUNT OUTLET**

See page 232 (BEDS)

ORCHIDS BOUTIQUE

3 PARK STREET, TOWCESTER, NORTHAMPTON NN12 6DQ, ☎ 01327 358455, FAX: 01327 353961, 9.30–5 MON–SAT. **PERMANENT DISCOUNT OUTLET**

Sells womenswear and childrenswear casual clothing including end of ranges from the high street multiples at a fraction of the recommended retail price. Ladies sizes range from 8–24 and children's from birth to twelve years.

T J HUGHES

THE NEWLANDS CENTRE, GOLD STREET, KETTERING, NORTHAMPTONSHIRE NN16 8JA, ☎ 01536 419700, FAX: 01536 523041, **e-mail:** info@tjhughes.co.uk, www.tjhughes.co.uk, 9–5.30 MON–SAT, 10–4 SUN. **PERMANENT DISCOUNT OUTLET**

See page 239 (CHESH)

THE DOC SHOP

RUSHDEN AND DIAMONDS FOOTBALL CLUB, NENE PARK, DIAMOND WAY, IRTHLINGBOROUGH, NORTHAMPTONSHIRE NN9 5QF, ☎ 01933 652000, 9–5.30 MON–FRI, 9–5 SAT, 11–5 BANK HOLIDAYS, 10–6 ON MATCH DAYS.

71 HIGH STREET, WOLLASTON, NORTHAMPTONSHIRE NN9 5QF, ☎ 01933 666144, 9–5.30 MON–SAT, 11–5 BANK HOLIDAYS. **PERMANENT DISCOUNT OUTLET**

See page 280 (LEICS)

UNITED FOOTWEAR

75–79 STAMFORD ROAD, KETTERING, NORTHAMPTONSHIRE, ☎ 01536 481855, 9–5.30 MON–SAT, 10–4 SUN. **PERMANENT DISCOUNT OUTLET**

See page 262 (HAMPS)

NORTHUMBERLAND

BURBERRY

KITTY BREWSTER INDUSTRIAL ESTATE, BLYTH, NORTHUMBERLAND NE24 4RG, ☎ 01670 352524, 10–4 MON, 9.30–4 TUE–FRI, 8.45–3.30 SAT. **FACTORY SHOP**

See page 236 (CHESH)

CATALOGUE BARGAIN SHOP

51 SHIELDS ROAD, BYKER, NEWCASTLE UPON TYNE, TYNE & WEAR NE6 1DJ, ☎ 0191 265 6033, www.bargaincrazy.com, 9–6 MON–SAT, 8 ON THUR, FRI, 10.30–4.30 SUN. **PERMANENT DISCOUNT OUTLET**

See page 234 (CAMBS)

CATALOGUE DISCOUNT STORES

15 THE PRECINCT, THE IN CENTRE, JARROW, TYNE & WEAR, ☎ 0191 483 4318, 9–5 MON–SAT.

8 THE FORUM SHOPPING CENTRE, WALLSEND, NORTHUMBERLAND NE28 8JR, ☎ 0191 236 9501, 9–5 MON–SAT. **PERMANENT DISCOUNT OUTLET**

See page 271 (LANCS)

DEWHIRST IMPRESSIONS

NORTH SEATON INDUSTRIAL ESTATE, OFF NEWBIGGIN ROAD, ASHINGTON, NORTHUMBERLAND NE63 0YB, ☎ 01670 813493, **e-mail:** kim.mcmaster@dewhirst.com, 10–8 MON–FRI, 9–6 SAT, 10.30–4.30 SUN. **FACTORY SHOP**

See page 243 (CO DURH)

DISCOUNT CLOTHING STORE

UNIT 1, MORPETH ROAD, ASHINGTON, NORTHUMBERLAND NE53 8PX, ☎ 01670 858300, 9.30–5.30 MON–SAT.

UNIT 7, KINGSTON PARK CENTRE, KINGSTON PARK, NEWCASTLE, NORTHUMBERLAND NE3 2FP, ☎ 0191 271 4126, 9.30–5.30 MON–SAT.

UNIT 16-17, DONKIN ROAD, ARMSTRONG INDUSTRIAL ESTATE, WASHINGTON, TYNE & WEAR NE37 1PF, ☎ 0191 417 4910, 9.30–5.30 MON–SAT. **PERMANENT DISCOUNT OUTLET**

See page 243 (CO DURH)

J BARBOUR & SONS LTD

CUSTOMER SERVICE DEPARTMENT, MONKSWAY, JARROW, TYNE & WEAR NE32 3HL, ☎ 0191 428 4707, 9–5 MON–SAT, 10–4 SUN. **FACTORY SHOP**

The famous waterproof waxed jackets and outdoor wear, all of which are seconds or discontinued lines, at discounts of 20% to 25%. Jackets come in 15 different styles from short to full-length and in various colours, but you may not find the style, colour and size you want as quantities vary. There are also shooting jackets, tweed hats and caps, linings for coats, bags, waxed trousers, waders, waxed jackets, breathable jackets for men and women, fleeces, knitwear and quilted jackets. There is also a small selection of children's jackets. Free parking.

MATALAN

BELVEDERE RETAIL PARK, BRUNTON LANE, KINGSTON PARK, NEWCASTLE UPON TYNE TYNE & WEAR NE3 2PA, ☎ 0191 214 0352, FAX: 0191 271 0067, www.matalan.co.uk, 10–8 MON–FRI, 9–6 SAT, 11–5 SUN.

THE KILLINGWORTH CENTRE, CITADEL WEST, KILLINGWORTH, NORTHUMBERLAND NE12, FAX: 0191 216 5360, FAX: 0191 216 1336, www.matalan.co.uk, 10–8 MON–FRI, 9–6 SAT, 11–5 SUN. **PERMANENT DISCOUNT OUTLET**

See page 232 (BEDS)

MEXX INTERNATIONAL

ROYAL QUAYS FACTORY OUTLET CENTRE, NORTH SHIELDS, NEWCASTLE UPON TYNE, NEAR A19, TYNE & WEAR, ☎ 0191 257 5001, 10–6 MON–SAT, 8 ON THUR, 11–5 SUN. **FACTORY SHOP IN A FACTORY SHOPPING VILLAGE**

See page 238 (CHESH)

NIKE FACTORY STORE

UNIT 7, ROYAL QUAYS FACTORY OUTLET CENTRE, COBLE DENE, MAYHOLE ROAD, NORTH SHIELDS, NEWCASTLE UPON TYNE, NEAR A19, TYNE & WEAR NE29 6DW, ☎ 0191 270

8796, www.nike.com, 10–6 MON–SAT, 8 ON THUR, 11–5 SUN. **FACTORY SHOP IN A FACTORY SHOPPING VILLAGE**

See page 239 (CHESH)

ROYAL QUAYS OUTLET CENTRE

COBLE DENE, NORTH SHIELDS, NEWCASTLE UPON TYNE, NEAR A19, TYNE & WEAR NE29 6DW, ☎ 0191 296 3743, **e-mail:** outletcentres@realm-ocm.com, www.royalquaysoutletcentre.co.uk, 10–6 MON–SAT, 11–5 SUN. **FACTORY SHOPPING VILLAGE**

Forty-two shops with leisure facilities nearby including a full-scale steam railway, working harbour, Roman ruins and the usual seaside attractions. Adjacent to the Wet and Wild water park which attracts 350,000 visitors a year and next door to an international ferry terminal, the centre has a nautical feel to it. There is a great range of shops, many new, stocking famous name brands, all with up to 50% discounts off normal retail prices. Phone for more details.

SCOOPS CATALOGUE DISCOUNT STORE

15 THE PRECINCT, THE IN CENTRE, JARROW, TYNE & WEAR NE32 3LS, ☎ 0191 483 4318, 9–5 MON–SAT.

8 THE FORUM SHOPPING CENTRE, WALLSEND, TYNE & WEAR NE28 8JR, ☎ 0191 236 9501, 9–5 MON–SAT. **PERMANENT DISCOUNT OUTLET**

See page 243 (CO DURH)

SHARK GROUP

NORDSTROM HOUSE, NORTH BROOMHILL, NEAR AMBLE, MORPETH, NORTHUMBERLAND NE65 9UJ, ☎ 01670 760365, FAX: 01670 761343, **e-mail:** sales@sharkgroup.co.uk, www.sharkgroup.co.uk, 2–4 MON–FRI (ALL YEAR ROUND), 10–12 SAT (APRIL–MID-DEC). **FACTORY SHOP**

Manufactures and sells in the factory shop Shark wetsuits, cag tops, sailing suits, boots, gloves and accessories for men, women and children at factory prices. Children's one-piece wetsuits from £45, adults' two-piece wetsuits from £89, adults' one-piece wetsuits from £69. Also sell the Shark Country range of jackets, over trousers, fleeces and accessories in Real Tree camo and loden green. Special sales are held from time to time. The factory shop closes for the factory holidays in late May/early June and late July/early August and late October as well as bank holiday weekends.

SUNGLASS TIME

ROYAL QUAYS, COBLE DENE ROAD, NORTH SHIELDS, TYNE & WEAR NE29 6DW, ☎ 0161 848 9007, **e-mail:** info@sunglass-time.com, 10–6 MON–SAT, 8 ON THUR, 11–5 SUN. **PERMANENT DISCOUNT OUTLET**

See page 275 (LANCS)

THE FAMOUS BRUNSWICK WAREHOUSE LTD

UNIT 1A, ALBION RETAIL PARK, COWPEN ROAD, BLYTH, NORTHUMBERLAND NE24 5BS, ☎ 01670 367951, **e-mail:** northshoe@mcmail.com, 9–5.30 MON–SAT, 6 ON THUR, FRI, 9.530 SAT, 10–4.30 SUN.

2–3 GREEN MARKET, ELDON SQUARE, NEWCASTLE UPON TYNE, TYNE & WEAR NE1 6EP, ☎ 0191 261 2976, **e-mail:** northshoe@mcmail.com, 9–5 MON–SAT.

120–122 GRAINGER MARKET, NEWCASTLE UPON TYNE, TYNE & WEAR NE1 5QN, ☎ 0191 261 2903, **e-mail:** northshoe@mcmail.com, 9–5 MON–SAT.

UNIT 3, COAST ROAD RETAIL PARK, NORTHAM ROAD, NORTH SHIELDS, TYNE & WEAR, NE29 7PQ, ☎ 0191 257 2557, **e-mail:** northshoe@mcmail.com, 9–6 MON–WED, SAT, 9–7 THUR, FRI, 10–4.30 SUN.

UNIT 2B, GALLERIES RETAIL PARK, TOWN CENTRE, WASHINGTON, TYNE & WEAR NE38 7RW, ☎ 0191 417 7447, **e-mail:** northshoe@mcmail.com, 9–6 MON–WED, SAT, 9–7 THUR, FRI, 10–4 SUN. **PERMANENT DISCOUNT OUTLET**

See page 240 (CHESH)

TK MAXX

LOWER GROUND FLOOR, MONUMENT MALL SHOPPING CENTRE, NEWCASTLE UPON TYNE, TYNE & WEAR NE1 7AL, ☎ 0191 261 0404, www.tkmaxx.com, 9–5.30 MON–FRI, 8 ON THUR, 9–6 SAT, 11–5 SUN. **PERMANENT DISCOUNT OUTLET**

See page 232 (BEDS)

TOG 24

32 HIGH FRIARS, ELDON SQUARE, NEWCASTLE UPON TYNE, TYNE & WEAR NE1 7XG, ☎ 0191 260 2810, **e-mail:** mail-order@tog24.com, www.tog24.com, 9–5.30 MON–FRI, 8 ON THUR, 9–6 SAT, 11–5 SUN.

ROYAL QUAYS FACTORY OUTLET CENTRE, COBLE DENE, NORTH SHIELDS, NEWCASTLE UPON TYNE, NEAR A19, TYNE & WEAR NE29 6DW, ☎ 0191 258 3754, **e-mail:** mail-order@tog24.com, www.tog24.com, 9.30–6 MON–SAT, 9.30–8 THUR, 11–5 SUN. **FACTORY SHOP IN A FACTORY SHOPPING VILLAGE**

See page 240 (CHESH)

TOYWORLD STORE FACTORY OUTLET

ROYAL QUAYS **FACTORY SHOP**PING OUTLET, COBLE DENE, NORTH SHIELDS, NEWCASTLE UPON TYNE, NEAR A19, TYNE & WEAR NE29 6DW, ☎ 0191 257 3333, www.toyworldstore.com, 10–6 MON–SAT, 11–5 SUN. **FACTORY SHOP IN A FACTORY SHOPPING VILLAGE**

See page 241 (CHESH)

NOTTINGHAMSHIRE

ABSOLUTE BEGINNERS NURSERY HIRE

3 MUSTERS ROAD, RUDDINGTON, NOTTINGHAM, NOTTINGHAMSHIRE NG11 6JA, ☎ 0115 846 8967, **e-mail:** alisonhorspool@hot.com, PHONE FOR DETAILS. **HIRE SHOP**

Hires out a wide range of good quality baby and nursery equipment, such as travel cots, car seats and highchairs at competitive prices. Part of the Baby Equipment Hirers' Association (BEHA), which has more than 100 members countrywide. BEHA runs an advice line which will try and answer any queries you have regarding hiring services for children. Phone the Babyline on 07831 310355.

BROUGHTON SHOE WAREHOUSE

6 QUEENS COURT, LENTON LANE, NOTTINGHAM NOTTINGHAMSHIRE NG7 2NR, ☎ 0115 986 1945, 9–6 MON, TUE, FRI, 9–8 WED, THUR, 9–6 SAT 10–4 SUN.

32 KING STREET, SOUTHWELL, NOTTINGHAMSHIRE NG25 0EN, ☎ 01636 812078, 9.30–5 MON–SAT. **PERMANENT DISCOUNT OUTLET**

See page 247 (DERBY)

CATALOGUE BARGAIN SHOP

24–29 LEEMING STREET, MANSFIELD, NOTTINGHAMSHIRE NG18 1NE, ☎ 01623 623353, www.bargaincrazy.com, 9–5.30 MON–SAT, 10–4 SUN.

50 MAIN STREET, BULWELL, NOTTINGHAM, NOTTINGHAMSHIRE NG6 8EY, ☎ 0115 927 8373, www.bargaincrazy.com, 9–5.30 MON–SAT, 10–4 SUN. **PERMANENT DISCOUNT OUTLET**

See page 234 (CAMBS)

CLARKS FACTORY SHOP

111 FRONT STREET, ARNOLD, NOTTINGHAMSHIRE NG5 7ED, ☎ 0115 967 4212, 9–6 MON–SAT, 10–4 SUN. **FACTORY SHOP**

See page 236 (CHESH)

GIFTTREE

34 HIGH STREET, LONG EATON, NOTTINGHAMSHIRE NG10 1LL, ☎ 0115 973 6611 9–5.30 MON–SAT. **FACTORY SHOP**

See page 247 (DERBY)

HAWK FACTORY CYCLE STORES

CRAVEN ARMS SITE, WOODBURGH ROAD, NOTTINGHAM, NOTTINGHAMSHIRE NG3 1AA, ☎ 0115 958 5900, 9–6 MON–SAT, 9–4.30 SUN. **FACTORY SHOP**

See page 248 (DERBY)

LABEL TRADERS

PASTURE LANE, RUDDINGTON, NOTTINGHAMSHIRE NG1 6AJ, ☎ 0115 9405205, www.labeltraders.co.uk, 9–5 MON–FRI, 9–4 SAT, 10–4 SUN.

3 KIRKBY ROAD, SUTTON-IN-ASHFIELD, NOTTINGHAMSHIRE NG17 1GP, ☎ 01623 554026, www.labeltraders.co.uk, 9–5 MON–FRI, 10–5 SAT, 10–4 SUN. **FACTORY SHOP**

See page 248 (DERBY)

MATALAN

CHILWELL RETAIL PARK, BARTON LANE, BEESTON, NOTTINGHAM, NOTTINGHAMSHIRE NG9 6DS, ☎ 0115 946 9354, FAX: 0115 972 3184, www.matalan.co.uk, 10–8 MON–FRI, 9–6 SAT, 11–4 SUN.

SPRINGFIELD RETAIL PARK, HUCKNALL LANE, BULWELL, NOTTINGHAM NG6 8AJ, ☎ 0115 977 7800, FAX: 0115 976 3572, www.matalan.co.uk, 10–8 MON–FRI, 9–6 SAT, 10–4 SUN.

PORTLAND RETAIL PARK, STATION ROAD, SUTTON IN ASHFIELD, MANSFIELD, NOTTINGHAMSHIRE NG17 5GA, ☎ 01623 528710, FAX: 01623 554974, www.matalan.co.uk, 9.30–8 MON–FRI, 9–6 SAT, 11–5 SUN. **PERMANENT DISCOUNT OUTLET**

See page 232 (BEDS)

THE COURTAULDS FACTORY SHOP

HAYDN ROAD, NOTTINGHAM, NOTTINGHAMSHIRE NG5 1DH, ☎ 0115 924 6154, 9–5.30 MON–SAT, 7.30 ON WED, 10.30–4.30 SUN. **FACTORY SHOP**

Sells a wide range of women's, men's and childrens high street fashions at between 30% and 50% below high street prices. Also stocks a wide range of household textiles, luggage, shoes and accessories. There is now an on-site coffee shopping serving light meals, snacks and refreshments.

THE FACTORY SHOP

DONCASTER ROAD, LANGOLD, WORKSOP, NOTTINGHAMSHIRE DN22 7HY, ☎ 01909 731115, 9 -5.30 MON–SAT, 10–4.30 SUN. **FACTORY SHOP**

See page 243 (CHESH)

THE FAMOUS BRUNSWICK WAREHOUSE LTD

SPRINGFIELD RETAIL PARK, BULWELL, NOTTINGHAM, NOTTINGHAMSHIRE NG6 8AJ, ☎ 0115 951 9286, **e-mail:** northshoe@mcmail.com, 10–6 MON–WED, 10–7 THUR, FRI, 9–6 SAT, 10–4 SUN. **PERMANENT DISCOUNT OUTLET**

See page 240 (CHESH)

THE SHOE SHED

COURTAULDS TEXTILES FACTORY SHOP, ELLIS STREET, KIRKBY-IN-ASHFIELD, NOTTINGHAMSHIRE NG17 7AL, ☎ 01627 23083, 9–5.30 MON–SAT, 10.30–4.30 SUN. **FACTORY SHOP**

See page 253 (DORS)

TK MAXX

CHILWELL RETAIL PARK, BARTON LANE, BEESTON, NOTTINGHAM NOTTINGHAMSHIRE, ☎ 0115 946 3684, www.tkmaxx.com, PHONE FOR DETAILS. **PERMANENT DISCOUNT OUTLET**

See page 232 (BEDS)

TRADEX

QUEENS ROAD, BEESTON, NOTTINGHAM, NOTTINGHAMSHIRE NG9 2FE, ☎ 0115 922 0880, FAX: 0115 922 7333, 9.30–8.30 MON–FRI, 9–5.30 SAT, 10.30–4.30 SUN. **PERMANENT DISCOUNT OUTLET**

See page 278 (LANCS)

UNITED FOOTWEAR

BEECH AVENUE, OFF SHERWOOD RISE, OFF A60, NOTTINGHAM, NOTTINGHAMSHIRE, ☎ 0115 979 2799, 9–6.30 MON–FRI, 9–5.30 SAT, 10–4 SUN.

See page 262 (HAMPS)

WILKINSON STORES

2-6 FRONT STREET, ARNOLD, NOTTINGHAM, NOTTINGHAMSHIRE NG5 7EL, ☎ 0115 926 0805, www.wilko.co.uk, 9–5.30 MON–SAT, 10–4 SUN. MAIL ORDER.
PERMANENT DISCOUNT OUTLET

See page 241 (CHESH)

OXFORDSHIRE

BENETTON

BICESTER OUTLET SHOPPING VILLAGE, PINGLE DRIVE, BICESTER, JUNCTION 9 OF M40, OXFORDSHIRE OX26 7WD, ☎ 01869 320030, FAX: 01869 325518, **e-mail:** sstimpson@fibrenetname.co.uk, www.benetton.co.uk, 10–6 SEVEN DAYS A WEEK. **FACTORY SHOP IN A FACTORY SHOPPING VILLAGE**

See page 259 (HAMPS)

BICESTER OUTLET SHOPPING VILLAGE

PINGLE DRIVE, BICESTER, JUNCTION 9 OF M40, OXFORDSHIRE OX6 7WD, ☎ 01869 323200, 10–6 SEVEN DAYS A WEEK. **FACTORY SHOPPING VILLAGE**

Described as 'Bond Street comes to Bicester', Bicester Village has established itself as the UK's leading outlet shopping destination in terms of offering the largest selection of international brand names to choose from. Currently there are 90 outlet shops offering quality merchandise at discounts of up to 60%, sometimes even more. The choice of famous brands at Bicester Village is second to none. International names include a Polo Ralph Lauren store, which now stocks more goods from their women's sport and home collections, Donna Karan, Versace, Christian Lacroix, Escada, Cerruti 1881 and TSE Cashmere. New arrivals from the international fashion scene are La Perla, Nautica, Gieves & Hawkes, Tommy Hilfiger, Tod's, MaxMara, Salvatore Ferragamo, Zegna, Calvin Klein, Charles Tyrwhitt, Sand, Links, Nautica, Musto and Holland & Holland. Both of Britain's leading designers, Nicole Farhi and Paul Smith, have shops with goods from their men's and women's collections. Karen Millen and Whistles both cater for the younger set with much more women's fashion to be found in The Designer Room, Episode, Hobbs, Jigsaw and Inwear Matinique. Top high street names are also well represented by Benetton, Principles, French Connection, Monsoon and Racing Green. The more classic customer also has an unequalled choice with Burberry, Aquascutum, Jaeger, Mulberry and the Scandinavian company RedGreen, whose nautical style of casual wear is very popular. Rugged outdoor wear can be found at Helly Hansen, Tog 24, the climbing and walking specialist. Active sportswear, represented by Fred Perry and Reebok, has now been joined by one of America's most famous sports shoe brands, Vans. A comprehensive collection of shoes, including many ranges for children, can be found in Clarks, with elegant high fashion styles in Charles Jourdan from Paris. Also, for women's shoes, handbags and accessories, there is Jane Shilton; for luggage, there is the Samsonite shop, plus the exciting addition of the first TAG-Heuer outlet, which stocks end-of-line designer watches, all fully guaranteed, at very attractive prices. Lingerie and underwear is to be found at Warners and Triumph, with HOM, the French brand, for the men; and the finest French childrenswear at Petit Bateau; English fragrances at Penhaligon's; make-up, bath and body therapies at Molton Brown, and soaps and gifts at Woods of Windsor. For the home, there are Price's candles and towels and duvets from another leading French brand, Descamps; cutlery from Oneida; china and crystal from Villeroy & Boch and Waterford Wedgwood and fine linens and accessories for the home from The White Company. The Cosmetic Company stocks well-known skincare products, cosmetics and fragrances for men and women. Bicester Village is something akin to a 'one-floor department store' and menswear, which can often be found in the designer shops, is also well represented in its own right with Dunhill, Blazer, Sand, Savoy Taylors Guild, Oscar

Jacobson and Dockers, plus another international touch being provided by Cerruti Menswear, all offering good size ranges in a wide choice from very casual through to traditional business clothes. To complete the day out at Bicester Village, take home some popular titles from Books etc, get to know more about the location for a return visit from the Tourist Information Centre, and regain strength with top quality refreshment at Pret-A-Manger or Starbucks. There are cash machines, a children's play area, free parking and a shuttle bus (which is free from Thursday to Sunday) and taxi connection to Bicester North Station, which is on the Chiltern Railways line, and runs between Marylebone and Birmingham. Bicester Village is about one hour's drive from London, two miles from Junction 9 on the M40. Take the A41 and follow signs for Village Retail Park.

BURBERRY

BICESTER OUTLET SHOPPING VILLAGE, PINGLE DRIVE, BICESTER, JUNCTION 9 OF M40, OXFORDSHIRE OX6 7WD, ☎ 01869 354071, 10–6 SEVEN DAYS A WEEK. **FACTORY SHOP IN A FACTORY SHOPPING VILLAGE**

See page 236 (CHESH)

CLARKS FACTORY SHOP

BICESTER OUTLET SHOPPING VILLAGE, 27 PINGLE DRIVE, BICESTER, JUNCTION 9 OF M40, OXFORDSHIRE OX26 6WD, ☎ 01869 325646, 10–6 SEVEN DAYS A WEEK. **FACTORY SHOP IN A FACTORY SHOPPING VILLAGE**

See page 236 (CHESH)

IMPS

52 SHEEP STREET, BICESTER, OXFORDSHIRE OX26 7LG, ☎ 01869 243455, 9–5 MON–SAT
40 UPPER HIGH STREET, THAME, OXFORDSHIRE OX9 3AG, ☎ 01844 212985, 9–5 MON–SAT.

32 MARKET SQUARE, WITNEY, OXFORDSHIRE OX8 58A, ☎ 01993 779875, 9–5 MON–SAT.
PERMANENT DISCOUNT OUTLET

High street shops selling popular chainstore seconds fashion for all the family as well as towels, china, trays and flower cachepots. Men's women's and childrenswear from designer brands such as Ralph Lauren, Tommy Hilfiger, Timberland and Gap. Sportswear from Umbro, Adidas and Nike all at up to 50% off high street prices.

MATALAN

UNIT 5, THE JOHN ALLEN CENTRE, COWLEY, OXFORD OX4 3JP, ☎ 01865 336100, FAX: 01865 336107, www.matalan.co.uk, 10–8 MON–FRI, 9–6 SAT, 10–4 SUN. **PERMANENT DISCOUNT OUTLET**

See page 232 (BEDS)

PEPE JEANS

UNIT 3, BICESTER OUTLET SHOPPING VILLAGE, PINGLE DRIVE, BICESTER, JUNCTION 9 OF M40, OXFORDSHIRE OX26 6WD, ☎ 01869 325378, 10–6 SEVEN DAYS A WEEK.
FACTORY SHOP IN A FACTORY SHOPPING VILLAGE

See page 261 (HAMPS)

REVIVAL CLOTHES AGENCY

60 ST CLEMENT'S, OXFORD, OXFORDSHIRE OX4 1AH, ☎ 01865 251005, 10–4 TUE, WED, THUR, 10–5 FRI, SAT. **DRESS AGENCY**

A large shop containing two spacious rooms behind a showroom. All stock is less than two years old. The women's section includes labels from Wallis and Next to Whistles, Nicole Farhi, Jaeger and Karen Millen. There are also accessories such as hats, shoes, handbags and jewellery. All prices are well under half the original price and sizes range from 8 to 24. The evening dresses range from £30 to £100 and include many ballgowns. The menswear is not extensive but includes Armani, Next and Jaeger suits and dinner suits. Childrenswear includes Next, OshKosh and Laura Ashley. Soft furnishings and curtains are also stocked, and there is a small selection of new and nearly-new wedding dresses from £100 to £600.

THE FAMOUS BRUNSWICK WAREHOUSE LTD

THE CALTHORPE CENTRE, BANBURY, OXFORDSHIRE DX16 5HS, ☎ 01295 266519, **e-mail:** northshoe@mcmail.com, 9–6 MON–SAT, 11–5 SUN. **PERMANENT DISCOUNT OUTLET**

See page 240 (CHESH)

THE RED HOUSE

WINDRUSH PARK, WITNEY, OXFORDSHIRE OX29 0YD, ☎ 01993 893456, FAX: 01993 776813, www.redhouse.co.uk, MAIL ORDER.
PERMANENT DISCOUNT OUTLET

A no-commitment book club with an excellent catalogue of children's books, The Red House covers both educational matters, from reading skills to history, and practical activity books as well as fiction. The books are a mixture of hardback and paperback from a variety of different publishers, and good savings are to be made. Occasionally some CD-Roms are available. You can see the comprehensive range of books by visiting the website where you can also buy online. Here, they have introduced Bookends, books for children and adults at very low prices.

TK MAXX

CALTHORPE STREET, OFF HIGH STREET, BANBURY, OXFORDSHIRE OX16 8ES, ☎ 01295 277022, www.tkmaxx.com, 9–5.30 MON–FRI, 7 ON THUR, 9–6 SAT, 11–5 SUN. **PERMANENT DISCOUNT OUTLET**

See page 232 (BEDS)

TOG 24

BICESTER OUTLET SHOPPING VILLAGE, PINGLE DRIVE, BICESTER, JUNCTION 9 OF M40, OXFORDSHIRE OX6 7WD, ☎ 01869 323278, **e-mail:** mail-order@tog24.com, www.tog24.com, 10–6 SEVEN DAYS A WEEK. **FACTORY SHOP IN A FACTORY SHOPPING VILLAGE**

See page 240 (CHESH)

TOP MARKS

8 HIGH STREET, CHIPPING NORTON, OXFORDSHIRE OX7 5ND, ☎ 01608 642653, 9–5.30 MON–FRI, 9–5 SAT. **PERMANENT DISCOUNT OUTLET**

See page 259 (GLOS)

SHROPSHIRE

CATALOGUE SURPLUS CENTRE LTD

28–30 ST MARY'S STREET, NEWPORT, SHROPSHIRE TF10 7AB, ☎ 01952 825889, FAX: 01952 825545, 9–5 MON–SAT.

4 CLAREMONT STREET, SHREWSBURY, SHROPSHIRE SY1 1QG, ☎ 01743 243 629, 9–5 MON–SAT.

21 WILLOW STREET, OSWESTRY, SHROPSHIRE SY11 1AF, ☎ 01691 658155, 9–5 MON–SAT.

UNIT 3, OXFORD STREET, OAKENGATE, TELFORD, SHROPSHIRE TF2 6AA, ☎ 01952 617406, 9–5 MON–SAT. **PERMANENT DISCOUNT OUTLET**

Ex-catalogue clothes for men, women and children as well as shoes and bedlinen, all at a fraction of the cost of catalogue prices. There are other outlets at Telford, Oswestry, Shrewsbury and Stoke.

E WALTERS FACTORY SHOP

CHAPEL WORKS, OLD STREET, LUDLOW, SHROPSHIRE SY8 1NR, ☎ 01584 875595, 9–5 SAT, 11–5 SUN, SUMMER MONTHS.
FACTORY SHOP

See page 262 (HEREF)

HAWK FACTORY CYCLE STORES

15 CASTLE STREET, SHREWSBURY, SHROPSHIRE SY1 1QQ, ☎ 01743 344554, 9–6 MON–SAT, 9–4.30 SUN. **FACTORY SHOP**

See page 248 (DERBY)

LEGS CLOTHING CO

MARKET HOUSE, LISTLEY STREET, BRIDGNORTH, SHROPSHIRE WV16 4AW, ☎ 01746 769542, 9–5 MON–SAT, 11–5 SUN AND BANK HOLIDAYS, EASTER TO CHRISTMAS. **FACTORY SHOP**

See page 258 (GLOS)

MATALAN

HARLESCOTT RETAIL PARK, BRIXTON WAY, HARLESCOTT, SHREWSBURY, SHROPSHIRE SY1 3AZ, ☎ 01743 453040, FAX: 01743 462489, www.matalan.co.uk, 10–8 MON–FRI, 9–6 SAT, 11–5 SUN.

WREKIN RETAIL PARK, WELLINGTON, TELFORD, SHROPSHIRE TF1 2DE, ☎ 01952 641080, FAX: 01952 240155, www.matalan.co.uk, 10–8 MON–FRI, 9–6 SAT, 11–5 SUN. **PERMANENT DISCOUNT OUTLET**

See page 232 (BEDS)

STEWART'S

19–21 CROSS STREET, ELLESMERE, SHROPSHIRE SY12 0AW, ☎ 01691 624478, FAX: 01691 624478, 9.30–5.30 MON–FRI, 9–5.30 SAT, 10–4 SUN. **FACTORY SHOP**

See page 251 (DEV)

T J HUGHES

RIVERSIDE AND PRIDEHILL SHOPPING CENTRE, SHREWSBURY, SHROPSHIRE SY1 1BU, ☎ 01743 358359, FAX: 01743 271222, **e-mail:** info@tjhughes.co.uk, www.tjhughes.co.uk, 9–5.30 MON–SAT, 10.30–4.30 SUN. **PERMANENT DISCOUNT OUTLET**

See page 239 (CHESH)

THE FAMOUS BRUNSWICK WAREHOUSE LTD

UNIT K, WREKIN RETAIL PARK, TELFORD, SHROPSHIRE TF1 2DE, ☎ 01952 222802, **e-mail:** northshoe@mcmail.com, 10–6 MON–WED, 10–7 THUR, FRI, 9–6 SAT, 10–4 SUN. **PERMANENT DISCOUNT OUTLET**

See page 240 (CHESH)

TK MAXX

DARWIN SHOPPING CENTRE, RAVENS MEADOWS, SHREWSBURY, SHROPSHIRE SY1 1BW, ☎ 01743 341370, www.tkmaxx.com, 9–5.30 MON–FRI, 9–6 SAT, 11–5 SUN.

UNIT 16, TELFORD FORGE RETAIL PARK, ORDSALL LANE, TELFORD, SHROPSHIRE TF3 4AG, ☎ 01952 210200, www.tkmaxx.com, 10–8 MON–FRI, 9–6 SAT, 11–5 SUN. **PERMANENT DISCOUNT OUTLET**

See page 232 (BEDS)

SOMERSET

CHAPLINS SUPERSTORES HOME & GARDEN

BINDON ROAD, TAUNTON, SOMERSET TA2 6AA, ☎ 01823 288017, FAX: 01823 336189, 9–8 MON–FRI, 9–6 SAT, 10.30–4.30 SUN. **PERMANENT DISCOUNT OUTLET**

A wide range of merchandise for the bargain hunter, including garden tools, plants, fertilisers and accessories; toys; adults clothing and shoes; stationery; household textiles; electrical equipment; DIY items; glass and china; bathroom accessories; partyware; candles; food accessories. Spades are available at £4.99, trowels at 99p, shears at £5.99 (while stocks last).

CLARKS FACTORY SHOP

CLARKS VILLAGE FACTORY SHOPPING CENTRE, FARM ROAD, STREET, JUNCTION 23 OF M5, SOMERSET BA16 0BB, ☎ 01458 843163, 9–6 MON–SAT, 11–5 SUN. **FACTORY SHOP IN A FACTORY SHOPPING VILLAGE**

10A HIGH STREET, BURNHAM-ON-SEA, SOMERSET TA8 1NX, ☎ 01278 794668, 9–5.30 MON–SAT, 11–5 SUN.

112–114 HIGH STREET, STREET, SOMERSET BA16 0EW, ☎ 01458 442055, 9–5.30 MON–SAT, 10.30–4.30 SUN.

UNIT 2, WORLE DISTRICT SHOPPING CENTRE, WORLE, SOMERSET BS22 6BT, ☎ 01934 521693, 9–5.30 MON–FRI, 9–6 SAT, 10–4 SUN. **FACTORY SHOP**

See page 236 (CHESH)

CLARKS VILLAGE OUTLET SHOPPING

FARM ROAD, STREET, JUNCTION 23 OF M5, then A39, SOMERSET BA16 0BB, ☎ 01458 840064, **e-mail:** bgodwin@realm-ocm.com, www.clarksvillage.co.uk, APRIL–OCTOBER 9–5.30 MON–SAT, 11–5 SUN, NOVEMBER–MARCH 10–6, MON–SAT, 11–5 SUN. **FACTORY SHOPPING VILLAGE**

Purpose-built village of brick-built shops with extensive car parking facilities. Restaurant, fast food stands, carousel, indoor and outdoor play areas, and working village pottery and artists' studio. Here, there are 57 shops with more planned. Shops include: Body Shop, Reebok selling the Reebok brand, Rockport and the Greg Norman Collection; Monsoon/Accessorize, Benetton, Wrangler, The Designer Room, Jaeger, Viyella, Alexon, Triumph/Hom, Gossard, Clarks Factory Shop, Rohan, Windsmoor, Liz Claiborne, Calvin Klein, Van Heusen, Next, Warehouse, Tom Sayers men's sweaters and trousers, Warner's lingerie, Tog 24 outerwear, Jane Shilton handbags, luggage and shoes, The Suit Company and Blazer and Event jewellery. There is also a purpose-built china and glass pavilion and many other great stores, all with up to 50% off famous name brands.

DESIGNER SHADES

CLARKS VILLAGE FACTORY SHOPPING CENTRE, FARM ROAD, STREET, JUNCTION 23 OF M5 SOMERSET BA16 0BB, ☎ 01458 443007, **e-mail:** info@sunglass-time.com, 9–6 MON–SAT, 11–5 SUN. **PERMANENT DISCOUNT OUTLET**

See page 255 (ESSEX)

ECCO

82 HIGH STREET, STREET, SOMERSET BA16 0EN, ☎ 01458 443950, www.ecco.com, 9–5.30 MON–SAT, 11–4 SUN AND BANK HOLIDAYS. **FACTORY SHOP**

See page 236 (CHESH)

FINE SHOES

31–34 HIGH STREET, WELLS, SOMERSET BA5 2SG, ☎ 01749 679090, 9.30–5.30 mon–fri, 9–5.30 SAT, 10.30–4.30 SUN. **PERMANENT DISCOUNT OUTLET**

Men's and women's shoes, boots, plimsolls, sandals and trainers, with some children's up to size 5. Most of the shoes are from Bellina, but other brands on sale here include Roder, Hogl, Flexi, Dubarry, Hush Puppy, Barkers, Lec boots for men, Grensons and DB wider shoes for men.

JOKIDS

58 HIGH STREET, STREET, SOMERSET BA16 0EQ, ☎ 01458 8841909, www.jokids.com, 9–6 MON–SAT, 11–5 SUN. **FACTORY SHOP IN A FACTORY SHOPPING VILLAGE**

See page 237 (CHESH)

JPS FOOTWEAR LTD

2 HIGH STREET, BURNHAM-ON-SEA, SOMERSET TA8 1NX, ☎ 01278 780141, 9–5.30 MON–SAT, 11–5.30 SUN. **FACTORY SHOP**

Stock more than 10,000 pairs of shoes for men, women and children. The men's sizes range from 6 to 12; and women's from 4 to 9. Most of the stock consists of warehouse clearance lines and ends of lines.

MATALAN

LOCKING CASTLE DISTRICT CENTRE, WORLE, WESTON-SUPER-MARE, SOMERSET BS22 0BE, ☎ 01934 529830, FAX: 01934 521932, www.matalan.co.uk, 10–8 MON–FRI, 9–6 SAT, 10–4 SUN.

THE PEEL CENTRE, BABYLON HILL, YEOVIL, SOMERSET BA21 5BT, ☎ 01935 403110, FAX: 01935 426280, www.matalan.co.uk, 10–8 MON–FRI, 9–6 SAT, 11–5 SUN. **PERMANENT DISCOUNT OUTLET**

See page 232 (BEDS)

NEXT TO NOTHING

CLARKS VILLAGE FACTORY SHOPPING CENTRE, FARM ROAD, STREET, JUNCTION 23 OF M5, SOMERSET BA16 0BB, ☎ 01458 840828, www.next.co.uk, 9–6 MON–SAT, 11–5 SUN. **FACTORY SHOP IN A FACTORY SHOPPING VILLAGE**

See page 239 (CHESH)

NIPPERS

YARDE FARM, LANGFORD LANE, NORTON FITZWARREN, TAUNTON, SOMERSET TA2 6PA, ☎ 01823 350005, FAX 01823 350119, www.nippers.co.uk, OPENING HOURS VARY SO PHONE FIRST. **PERMANENT DISCOUNT OUTLET**

See page 234 (BUCKS)

PENNYWISE

10A WESTMINSTER STREET, YEOVIL, SOMERSET BA21 3PE, ☎ 01935 423938, 10–5 MON–SAT. **DRESS AGENCY**

Dress agency selling men's and women's day and evening business and casual clothes, shoes and accessories. Good quality and designer labels. Also, new to Pennywise, is a range of new ball-gowns, for sale at very reasonable prices. There is no parking available but the shop is near a large Tesco car park.

ROUNDABOUT

2 PRIOR PARK ROAD, WIDCOMBE, BATH, BANES, SOMERSET BA2 4NG, ☎ 01225 316696, 9–5 MON–SAT. **DRESS AGENCY**

Newly refurbished side by side shops, one selling nearly-new and sample childrenswear at discounts of about 50%, the other selling womenswear such as Gap. Roundabout has half-price brand new samples from Cakewalk and Oilily as well as nearly-new clothing from high street brands such as Gap and Next. They now also stock nearly-new curtains, furniture, nursery equipment, prams, cots, buggies, highchairs, toys, maternity wear, etc.

T J HUGHES

FAIRFAX HOUSE, HIGH STREET, WESTON-SUPER-MARE, SOMERSET BS23 1HA, ☎ 01934 414466, FAX: 01934 419911, **e-mail:** info@tjhughes.co.uk, www.tjhughes.co.uk, 9–5.30 MON–SAT, 11–5 SUN. **PERMANENT DISCOUNT OUTLET**

See page 239 (CHESH)

THE DOC SHOP

TOWNSEND ROAD, SHEPTON MALLET, SOMERSET BA4 5SB, ☎ 01794 347081, 9.30–4.30 MON–SAT. **PERMANENT DISCOUNT OUTLET**

See page 280 (LEICS)

THE FACTORY SHOP LTD
MART ROAD, MINEHEAD, SOMERSET TA24 5BJ, ☎ 01643 705911, 9.30–5.30 MON–SAT, 11–5 SUN. **FACTORY SHOP**

See page 243 (CHESH)

THE SPORTS FACTORY
CLARKS VILLAGE FACTORY SHOPPING CENTRE, FARM ROAD, STREET, JUNCTION 23 OF M5 SOMERSET BA16 0BB, ☎ 01458 843156, 9–6 MON–SAT, 11–5 SUN. **FACTORY SHOP IN A FACTORY SHOPPING VILLAGE**

Wide range of sports clothes and accessories, some of which are only stocked in season (for example, cricket bats and tennis rackets in summer only). There is also cricket gear and leisure clothing (Timberland and Regatta). All are discontinued lines and are between 10% and 40% cheaper than in the high street.

TOG 24
CLARKS VILLAGE FACTORY SHOPPING CENTRE, FARM ROAD, STREET, JUNCTION 23 OF M5 SOMERSET BA16 0ND, ☎ 01458 840468, **e-mail:** mail-order@tog24.com, www.tog24.com, 9–6 MON–SAT, 10–5 SUN. **FACTORY SHOP IN A FACTORY SHOPPING VILLAGE**

See page 240 (CHESH)

TOYZONE
CLARKS VILLAGE FACTORY SHOPPING CENTRE, FARM ROAD, STREET, JUNCTION 23 OF M5 SOMERSET BA16 0BB, ☎ 01458 440771, FAX: 01458 440748, 9–6 MON–SAT, 11–5 SUN. **FACTORY SHOP IN A FACTORY SHOPPING VILLAGE**

See page 252 (DEV)

STAFFORDSHIRE

BDF NEWLIFE
MARTINDALE, HAWK'S GREEN, CANNOCK, STAFFORDSHIRE WS11 2XN, ☎ 01543 468888, FAX: 01543 505989, **e-mail:** info@bdfnewlife.co.uk, 9.30–10 MON–SAT, 10–4 SUN, 10–5 BANK HOLIDAYS. **PERMANENT DISCOUNT OUTLET**

8,000 square foot charity superstore which sells both new merchandise donated by most of the top high street stores and nearly-new. This is the sort of shop where you can find anything from a girl's party dress to a two-seater rowing boat, men's shoes to a cooler bag, in between towels, jewellery, family clothes, furniture, mattresses (new with damaged packaging), beds, clocks, golf bags, umbrellas, wallpaper and designer dresses. Stock changes every 45 minutes. All the profits go to charity. Membership is by donation averaging £2. The shop is on one floor so is very accessible and has disabled toilet facilities. As the store also takes counterfeit goods from national Trading Standards departments' seizures, stress is put on not believing any labelling or assuring authenticity. There are also branches in Kirkby-in-Ashfield, Nottinghamshire and Stoke Aldermoor, Coventry.

CATALOGUE BARGAIN SHOP
95 CHURCH STREET, BILSTON, STAFFORDSHIRE WV14 0BJ, ☎ 01902 353624, www.bargaincrazy.com, 9–5.30 MON–SAT, 9.30–3.30 SUN.

UNIT 2, CHASE CENTRE, CHURCH STREET, CANNOCK, STAFFORDSHIRE WS11 1AP, ☎ 01543 468614, www.bargaincrazy.com, 9–8 MON–FRI, 9–6 SAT, 10.30–4.30 SUN.

FREEPORT TALKE OUTLET MALL, PIT LANE, TALKE PITS, STOKE-ON-TRENT, STAFFORDSHIRE ST7 1XD, ☎ 01782 775740, www.bargaincrazy.com, 9.30–8 MON–FRI, 9.30–6 SAT, 11–5 SUN. **PERMANENT DISCOUNT OUTLET**

See page 234 (CAMBS)

CATALOGUE DISCOUNT STORE

63 HIGH STREET, BROWNHILLS, STAFFORDSHIRE WS8 6HH, ☎ 01543 372933, 9–5.30 MON–SAT. **PERMANENT DISCOUNT OUTLET**

See page 271 (LANCS)

CATALOGUE SURPLUS CENTRE LTD

5 HIDE STREET, STOKE-ON-TRENT, STAFFORDSHIRE ST4 1NF, ☎ 01782 744445, 9–5 MON–SAT. **PERMANENT DISCOUNT OUTLET**

See page 297 (SHROP) .

CHARLES CLINKARD

FREEPORT TALKE OUTLET MALL, PIT LANE, TALKE PITS, STOKE-ON-TRENT, STAFFORDSHIRE ST7 1QE, ☎ 01782 787016, FAX: 01782 787016, 10–8 MON–SAT, 11–5 SUN. **FACTORY SHOP IN A FACTORY SHOPPING VILLAGE**

See page 241 (CO DURH)

COLOURS

3 PEPPER STREET, NEWCASTLE UNDER LYME, STAFFORDSHIRE ST5 1PR, ☎ 01782 714164, 9.30–5 MON–SAT. **DRESS AGENCY**

Dress agency catering for men and women. Men's labels include Armani, Boss, Joseph, Calvin Klein, Thomas Burberry and Ralph Lauren. Women's labels: Armani, Betty Barclay, Paul Costelloe, Nicole Farhi, Wallis and Next. There is always a marvellous selection of shoes.

FREEPORT TALKE OUTLET MALL

FREEPORT TALKE OUTLET MALL, PIT LANE, TALKE PITS, STOKE-ON-TRENT, OFF JUNCTION 16 OF M6 THEN TAKE THE A500 AND THE A34, FOLLOWING SIGNS TO TALKE, STAFFORDSHIRE ST7 1XD, ☎ 01782 774113, www.freeporttalke.com, 9.30–8 MON–FRI, 9.30–6 SAT, 11–5 SUN. **FACTORY SHOPPING VILLAGE**

Fully covered indoor outlet mall with a range of restaurants, including Burger King and Café Ritazza, and an indoor soft play area for children. Womenswear includes The Designer Room, Edinburgh Woollen Mill, Nickelby's, Pilot, Spotlight, Roman Originals and Leading Labels. Menswear includes The Suit Company, Double Two, Petroleum, Nickelby's, Madhouse and Tog 24. Childrenswear can be found at Used Co Kids. Other shops on site include: Claire's Accessories, Charles Clinkard, Jane Shilton, Bags Etc, Trespass, Streetwise Sports, The Golf Company, Catalogue Bargain Shop, Julian Graves, Kitchen and Table, Toy World, Thorntons, Birthdays, Room, Mobile Phone Store, Book Depot, Picture Port, Ponden Mill and XS Music.

GEOFF'S TOYS

43–44 CHURCH STREET, TAMWORTH, STAFFORDSHIRE B79 7DE, ☎ 01827 65333, 9–5 MON–SAT. **PERMANENT DISCOUNT OUTLET**

Vast array of toys at very low prices.

GIFTTREE

2 QUADRANT ROAD, POTTERIES SHOPPING CENTRE, HANLEY, STOKE-ON-TRENT, STAFFORDSHIRE ST1 1PP, ☎ 01782 202570, 9–5.30 MON–SAT, 8 ON THUR.

6 MARKET STREET, TAMWORTH, STAFFORDSHIRE B79 7LU, ☎ 01827 60266, 9–5 MON–SAT. **FACTORY SHOP**

See page 247 (DERBY) .

HAWK FACTORY CYCLE STORES

UNIT 1, WATLING STREET BUSINESS PARK, WATLING STREET, CANNOCK, STAFFORDSHIRE WS11 3NB, ☎ 01543 361656, 9–6 MON–SAT, 9–4.30 SUN.

FORGE LANE, CRADLEY HEATH, STAFFORDSHIRE B64 5AL, ☎ 01384 636535, 9–6 MON–SAT, 9–4.30 SUN. **FACTORY SHOP**

See page 248 (DERBY)

LILLEY & SKINNER TALKE

FREEPORT TALKE OUTLET MALL, PIT LANE, TALKE PITS, STOKE-ON-TRENT, STAFFORDSHIRE ST7 1XD, ☎ 01782 774113, 10–8 MON–SAT, 11–5 SUN. **FACTORY SHOP IN A FACTORY SHOPPING VILLAGE**

See page 256 (ESSEX)

MATALAN

UNIT A, LICHFIELD STREET, BURTON-ON-TRENT, STAFFORDSHIRE DE14 3QZ, ☎ 01283 540856, FAX: 01283 540873, www.matalan.co.uk, 10–8 MON–FRI, 9–6 SAT, 11–5 SUN.

QUEENSDALE RETAIL PARK, SILKMORE LANE, STAFFORD STAFFORDSHIRE ST17 4SU, ☎ 01785 226211, FAX: 01785 226279, www.matalan.co.uk, 10–8 MON–FRI, 9–6 SAT, 11–5 SUN.

WOLSTANTON RETAIL PARK, WOLSTANTON, NEWCASTLE, STOKE-ON-TRENT, STAFFORDSHIRE ST5 1DY, ☎ 01782 711731, FAX: 01782 714201, www.matalan.co.uk, 9.30–8 MON–FRI, 9–6 SAT, 11–5 SUN.

VENTURA RETAIL PARK, BONE HILL DRIVE, TAMWORTH, STAFFORDSHIRE B78 3HB, ☎ 01827 50900, FAX: 01827 509151, www.matalan.co.uk, 10–8 MON–FRI, 9–6 SAT, 11–5 SUN.

HOWARD STREET, BIRMINGHAM ROAD, WOLVERHAMPTON, STAFFORDSHIRE WV2 3LQ, ☎ 01902 352813, FAX: 01902 352908, www.matalan.co.uk, 10–8 MON–FRI, 9–6 SAT, 11–5 SUN. **PERMANENT DISCOUNT OUTLET**

See page 232 (BEDS)

NURSERY TO LEISURE

THE KELVIN WAY, WEST BROMWICH, STAFFORDSHIRE B70 7JW, ☎ 0121 525 5162, www.nurserytoleisure.co.uk, 9.30–4.30 MON–FRI. **PERMANENT DISCOUNT OUTLET**

Has a shop and a mail order service. The shop specialises in Maclaren pushchairs, but also sells reconditioned prams and pushchairs, as well as ends of lines which are particularly prevalent around the end of October after the nursery trade fair when fabric designs change. It also sells baby monitors, Zorbit baby cot linen, cots and mattresses and is a stockist for Jack Horner cots. For mail order please phone the number above.

PARTRIDGE ENGLAND LTD

POWER STATION ROAD, TRENT MEADOWS, RUGELEY, STAFFORDSHIRE WS15 2HS, ☎ 01889 584438, 9–5 MON–FRI, 9–4 SAT. **FACTORY SHOP**

See page 261 (HAMPS)

SCOOPS CATALOGUE DISCOUNT STORES

UNIT 3, 567–569 BEARWOOD SHOPPING CENTRE, SMETHWICK, STAFFORDSHIRE B66 4BH, ☎ 0121 434 3086, FAX: 0121 429 8488, 9–5.30 MON–SAT, 11–3 SUN. **PERMANENT DISCOUNT OUTLET**

See page 243 (CO DURH)

T J HUGHES

THREE SPIRES SHOPPING CENTRE, 46 BAKERS LANE, LICHFIELD, STAFFORDSHIRE WS13 6JF, ☎ 01543 418181, FAX: 01543 418185, **e-mail:** info@tjhughes.co.uk, www.tjhughes.co.uk, 9–5.30 MON–SAT, 10.30–4.30 SUN.

27 BELL STREET, MANDER CENTRE, WOLVERHAMPTON, WEST MIDLANDS WV1 3PT, ☎ 01902 428011, FAX: 01902 420248, **e-mail:** info@tjhughes.co.uk, www.tjhughes.co.uk, 9–5.30 MON–FRI, 8.30–5.30 SAT, 10.30–4.30 SUN. **PERMANENT DISCOUNT OUTLET**

See page 239 (CHESH)

THE FACTORY SHOP

QUEEN STREET CAR PARK, QUEEN STREET, MARKET DRAYTON, STAFFORDSHIRE TF9 1EQ, ☎ 01630 655673, 9–5 MON–SAT, 10–4 SUN. **FACTORY SHOP**

See page 243 (CHESH)

THE SHOE SHED

CASTLEFIELDS, NEWPORT ROAD, STAFFORD, STAFFORDSHIRE ST16 1BQ, ☎ 01785 211311
9–5.30 MON–SAT, 10–4 SUN. **FACTORY SHOP**

See page 253 (DORS)

TK MAXX

THE OCTAGON SHOPPING CENTRE, BURTON-ON-TRENT, STAFFORDSHIRE DE14 3TN, ☎ 01283 569891, www.tkmaxx.com, 9–5.30 MON–SAT, 10–4 SUN.

THE POTTERIES CENTRE, HANLEY, STOKE-ON-TRENT, STAFFORDSHIRE ST1 1PP, ☎ 01782 207509, www.tkmaxx.com, 9–5.30 MON–FRI, 9–6 SAT, 11–5 SUN, 8 ON THUR. **PERMANENT DISCOUNT OUTLET**

See page 232 (BEDS)

TOG 24

FREEPORT TALKE OUTLET MALL, PIT LANE, TALKE PITS, STOKE-ON-TRENT, STAFFORDSHIRE ST7 1QE, ☎ 01782 787558, **e-mail:** mail-order@tog24.com, www.tog24.com, 9.30–8 MON–FRI, 9.30–6 SAT, 11–5 SUN. **FACTORY SHOP IN A FACTORY SHOPPING VILLAGE**

See page 240 (CHESH)

TOYWORLD STORE FACTORY OUTLET

FREEPORT TALKE OUTLET MALL, PIT LANE, TALKE PITS, STOKE-ON-TRENT, STAFFORDSHIRE ST7 1QE, ☎ 01782 777744, www.toyworldstore.com, 10–8 MON–FRI, 10–6 SAT, 11–5 SUN. **FACTORY SHOP IN A FACTORY SHOPPING VILLAGE**

See page 241 (CHESH)

WEBB IVORY

QUEENSBRIDGE WORKS, QUEEN STREET, BURTON-ON-TRENT, STAFFORDSHIRE DE14 3LP, ☎ 01283 506371, 9–5 MON–FRI, 9–2 SAT. **FACTORY SHOP**

Items from the charity catalogues at reduced prices including cards, gifts, soft toys, books, pens, lamps, kitchenware and clothes. Stock is constantly changing, and discounts start from at least 50%.

WILKINSON STORES

OLD HALL STREET, HANLEY, STOKE-ON-TRENT, STAFFORDSHIRE, ☎ 01782 279225, www.wilko.co.uk, 8.30–6 MON–FRI, 8 ON THUR, 11–5 SUN. MAIL ORDER.

CASTLE HOUSE, 47–48 IRONMARKET, NEWCASTLE UNDER LYME, STAFFORDSHIRE ST5 1PD., ☎ 01782 714334, www.wilko.co.uk, 8.30–5.30 MON–SAT. **PERMANENT DISCOUNT OUTLET**

See page 241 (CHESH)

WYNSOR SHOES

151–153 MARSH STREET NORTH, HANLEY, STOKE-ON-TRENT, STAFFORDSHIRE ST1 5HR, ☎ 01782 266660, 9–5.30 MON, TUE, WED, SAT, 9–8 THUR, 9–6 FRI, 11–5 SUN.
PERMANENT DISCOUNT OUTLET

Stocks top brand-name shoes at less than half price. Special monthly offers always available. There are shoes, trainers, slippers, sandals and boots for all the family, with a selection of bags, cleaners and polishes available, all at discount prices.

SUFFOLK

BUYRIGHT OF HADLEIGH

CALAIS STREET, HADLEIGH, IPWICH, SUFFOLK IP7 5EW, ☎ 01473 822626, 9–5.30 MON–SAT, 10.30–4.30 SUN. **PERMANENT DISCOUNT OUTLET**

Discount shop selling a mixture of clothes, household textiles, ceramics, kitchenware, knitting yarn, garden tools, curtains, toys, stationery, dusters, Christmas decorations, masking tape, lingerie and a host of other items. Stock changes regularly because the low prices mean a quick turnover. Some items are seconds or end of season stock from the major chain stores.

GREENS CLOTHING COMPANY

GAOL LANE, SUDBURY, SUFFOLK CO10 1JL, ☎ 01787 881500, 9–5 MON–SAT, 9–1 WED.
PERMANENT DISCOUNT OUTLET

Women's clothes made by Frank Green, all brand new and at very cheap prices. For example, 100% cotton dresses, £12, jackets, £6, skirts, £6. Some in flowery prints, some plain. The shop also stocks good quality school clothing from nursery age to secondary school.

MATALAN

EASLEA ROAD, BURY ST EDMUNDS, SUFFOLK IP32 7BY, ☎ 01284 748300, FAX: 01284 749146, www.matalan.co.uk, 9–8 MON–FRI, 9–6 SAT, 10–4 SUN.

See page 232 (BEDS)

QD STORES

47–51 CARR STREET, THE EASTGATE CENTRE, IPSWICH, SUFFOLK IP4 1HB, ☎ 01473 284220, 9–5.30 MON–SAT.

UNIT 21–25, BRITTEN CENTRE, LOWESTOFT, SUFFOLK NR32 1LR, ☎ 01502 565222, 9–5.30 MON–SAT.

9 IPSWICH STREET, STOWMARKET, SUFFOLK IP14 1AH, ☎ 01449 770438, 9–5.30 MON–SAT. **PERMANENT DISCOUNT OUTLET**

See page 232 (BEDS)

ROYS OF BURY VARIETY STORE

88–89 RISBYGATE STREET, BURY ST EDMUNDS, SUFFOLK IP33 3AQ, ☎ 01284 753535, www.roys.co.uk, 9–5.30 MON–SAT, 8 ON THUR, 10.30–5.30 SUN.

GREAT EASTERN ROAD, SUDBURY, SUFFOLK CO10 6TJ, ☎ 01787 882800, www.roys.co.uk, 9–6 MON, TUE, WED, 8.30–8 THUR, FRI, 8.30–6 SAT, 10–4 SUN. **PERMANENT DISCOUNT OUTLET**

Roys sell branded household goods at what they call 'valued prices'. The Save 'n' Wear department deals with the cheaper end of the clothing market for men, women and children. They also include DIY, gardening, electrical, housewares, gifts, toiletries and some food lines.

THE FACTORY SHOP

BARTON BUSINESS CENTRE, BARTON ROAD, BURY ST EDMUNDS, SUFFOLK IP32 7BQ, ☎ 01284 701578, 9.30–5 MON–FRI, 10–6 SAT, 10–4 SUN.

LONDON ROAD, WRENTHAM, NR BECCLES, SUFFOLK NR34 7HJ, ☎ 01502 676100, 9–5.30 MON–SAT, 10.30–4.30 SUN. **FACTORY SHOP**

See page 243 (CHESH)

TK MAXX

1ST FLOOR, BUTTERMARKET SHOPPING CENTRE, IPSWICH, SUFFOLK IP1 1DT, ☎ 01473 226800, www.tkmaxx.com, 9–5.30 MON–FRI, 9–6 SAT, 11–5 SUN. **PERMANENT DISCOUNT OUTLET**

See page 232 (BEDS)

SURREY

ABACUS BABY HIRE

LONG LODGE, NIGHTINGALE AVENUE, WEST HORSLEY, SURREY KT24 6PA, ☎ 01483 285142, FAX: 01483 285142, **e-mail:** elizabeth/baxter@cs.com, www.babyhire.co.uk, PHONE FOR AN APPOINTMENT. **HIRE SHOP**

Part of the Baby Equipment Hirers' Association (BEHA) which has members countrywide. A range of equipment can be hired from one day to several months, including buggies, car seats, double buggies, baby swings, cots, travel cots and highchairs. Also party equipment, small tables and chairs, ball pond, roller coaster (suitable age one to five), outdoor and indoor play equipment, pop-up play equipment including castle, ride on cars, space hoppers, goal posts plus many other items.

Just ask if you want something special. For adults they hire out patio tables, chairs, umbrellas and gazebos. For information on members countrywide, phone the Babyline on 07831 310355.

BAMBINI

27 CHURCH STREET, WEYBRIDGE, SURREY KT13 8DG, ☎ 01932 857665, 9.30–5 MON–SAT.
DRESS AGENCY

Across the road from the women's dress agency, Ancora, Bambini sells mid-range and designer labels for children from birth to 10 years, including Gap, Gymboree, OshKosh, Monsoon, Next and Timberland, to name a few.

CHOICE DISCOUNT STORES LIMITED

1 WARWICK QUADRANT, LONDON ROAD, REDHILL, SURREY RH1 1NN, ☎ 01737 772777, 9–6 MON–WED, 9–7 THUR, 9–6 FRI–SAT. **PERMANENT DISCOUNT OUTLET**

See page 235 (CAMBS)

MATALAN

268–278 HIGH STREET, SUTTON, SURREY SM1 1PG, ☎ 020 8652 9600, FAX: 020 8770 3581, www.matalan.co.uk, 9–8 MON–FRI, 9–6 SAT, 11–5 SUN. **PERMANENT DISCOUNT OUTLET**

See page 232 (BEDS)

NIPPERS

THE WAFFRONS, WOODSTOCK LANE SOUTH, CHESSINGTON, SURREY KT9 1UF, ☎ 020 8398 3114, FAX: 020 8398 7553, **e-mail:** nippers@heppel.dircon.co.uk, www.nippers.co.uk, OPENING HOURS VARY SO PHONE FIRST. **PERMANENT DISCOUNT OUTLET**

See page 234 (BUCKS)

THE FACTORY SHOP LTD

THE ENGINE SHED, CONSORT WAY EAST, HORLEY, SURREY RH6 7AU, ☎ 01293 823883, 9–5.30 MON–SAT, 10–4 SUN. **FACTORY SHOP**

See page 243 (CHESH)

TINKERS

17 OLD OAK AVENUE, CHIPSTEAD, SURREY CR5 3PG, ☎ 01737 553761, PHONE FOR AN APPOINTMENT. **HIRE SHOP**

Tinkers hires out child-sized tables and chairs.

TK MAXX

THE DRUMMOND CENTRE, CROYDON, SURREY CR0 1TY, ☎ 020 8686 9753, www.tkmaxx.com, 9–6 MON–SAT, 9 ON THUR, 11–5 SUN.

102 HIGH STREET, EPSOM, SURREY, ☎ 01372 729060, www.tkmaxx.com, PHONE FOR DETAILS.

BISHOPS PALACE HOUSE, 2 CLARENCE STREET, KINGSTON, SURREY KT1 1PB, ☎ 020 8974 6296, www.tkmaxx.com, 9–6 MON–WED, 9–9 THUR–FRI, 8–7 SAT, 11–5. SUN.

TIMES SQUARE SHOPPING CENTRE, HIGH STREET, SUTTON, SURREY SM1 1LF, ☎ 020 8770 7786, www.tkmaxx.com, 9–5.30 MON–FRI, 8 ON THUR, 9–6 SAT, 11–5 SUN.

THE PEACOCKS CENTRE, WOKING, SURREY GU21 1GA, ☎ 01483 771660, www.tkmaxx.com, 9.30–6 MON–FRI, 8 ON THUR, 9–6 SAT, 11–5 SUN. **PERMANENT DISCOUNT OUTLET**

See page 232 (BEDS)

TOG 24

WHITGIFT CENTRE, CROYDON, SURREY CR0 1LP, ☎ 020 8680 7902, **e-mail:** mail-order@tog24.com, www.tog24.com, 10–6 MON–FRI, 8 ON THUR, 9–6 SAT, 10–5 SUN. **FACTORY SHOP IN A FACTORY SHOPPING VILLAGE**

See page 240 (CHESH)

SUSSEX

BRIGHTON MARINA OUTLET VILLAGE

CITY OF BRIGHTON AND HOVE, EAST SUSSEX BN2 5WB, ☎ 01273 818504, FAX: 01273 818701, 10–LATE SEVEN DAYS A WEEK. **FACTORY SHOPPING VILLAGE**

The UK and Europe's largest marina. Boasts an exciting range of outlet shops combined with excellent bars, restaurants and leisure facilities. Currently hosts 11 outlet stores, such as Pulse skating solutions, The Factory Shop, Leading Labels and many more. The marina is currently investing millions into additional facilities, planned to open at the end of 2002, which will include a further 16 outlet stores including some household names.

HEIRLOOMS LTD

2 ARUN BUSINESS PARK, BOGNOR REGIS, SUSSEX PO22 9SX, ☎ 01243 820252, FAX: 01243 821174, 10–5 EVERY FRIDAY AND ONE SAT MORNING EACH MONTH.
FACTORY SHOP

Sleep like a king, dine like a lord or lounge like a lady...the Heirlooms factory shop is brimming with luxurious linen at affordable prices, the majority of which are made on the premises. Elegant and exceptionally high quality bed linens in Egyptian cotton, cotton percale and the finest polycotton percale, in four sizes up to super-king, are sold in this 1,200 square foot outlet, together with the very best Egyptian cotton towels. There's also table linens using classic hem stitching or handmade laces, a cornucopia of gifts with exquisite laces and embroidery, and hand-made christening and baby wear. Sterling silver frames, waterproof picnic rugs, candles, night-wear, Isis ceramics and seasonal variations complete the diverse selection of really high quality products. Normally only found in the most exclusive shops, homes and palaces all over the world, here you can buy ends of lines and slight seconds at between 30% and 65% off the recommended retail price. This busy exporting company only opens the factory shop about once a week, so check before making what will be a worthwhile journey. As they manufacture, they can make bedlinen and tablecloths to order in any size. Free parking.

MATALAN

CARDEN AVENUE, HOLLINGBURY INDUSTRIAL ESTATE, BRIGHTON, EAST SUSSEX BN1 8AR, ☎ 01273 543800, FAX: 01273 502608, www.matalan.co.uk, 10–8 MON–FRI, 9–6 SAT, 10.30–4.30 SUN.

SOVEREIGN HARBOUR RETAIL PARK, PEVENSY BAY ROAD, EASTBOURNE, EAST SUSSEX BN23 6JH, ☎ 01323 470347, FAX: 01323 470601, www.matalan.co.uk, 10–8 MON–FRI, 9–6 SAT, 10.30–4.30 SUN. **PERMANENT DISCOUNT OUTLET**

See page 232 (BEDS)

PANACHE

5 STANFORD SQUARE, WARWICK ST, WORTHING, SUSSEX BN11 3EZ, ☎ 01903 212503, 10–5 MON–SAT. **DRESS AGENCY**
See page 268 (KENT)

RICARA

1 OLD MARKET AVENUE, CHICHESTER, SUSSEX PO19 1DR, ☎ 01243 778850, FAX: 01243 778850, www.ricara.co.uk, 9–5 MON–SAT.

12 SURREY STREET, LITTLEHAMPTON, SUSSEX BN17 5BG, ☎ 01903 723843, FAX: 01903 718401, www.ricara.co.uk, 9–5 MON–SAT, 10–4 SUN. **FACTORY SHOP**

Sells mainly schoolwear and men's casual wear, and branded sportswear such as unisex cycling shorts, track suits and leggings at very reasonable prices – discounts can be up to 50%. Brands include Nike and Adidas and specialised outfits for karate, kickboxing, boxing, tae kwon do, judo etc are also available.

STOCKLEY TRADING

UNIT N10–11, BRIDGE ROAD, RIVERSIDE INDUSTRIAL ESTATE, LITTLEHAMPTON, SUSSEX BN17 5DF, ☎ 01903 732392, FAX: 01903 732754, **e-mail:** sales@stockleytrading.co.uk, www.stockleytrading.co.uk, 9–6 MON–FRI, 9.30–5 SAT, 10–4 SUN. **PERMANENT DISCOUNT OUTLET**

Warehouse shop which sells a range of outdoor wear and sportswear at wholesale prices. There is a good selection of branded leisurewear from Adidas, Umbro, Nike, Reebok, Fila, CAT, Fred Perry, Ben Sherman and Timberland among others. Stock varies, so phone to check stock before visiting if you are after something in particular. The outdoor wear department sells everything from underwear to hats and coats from names such as Regatta, Champion and Opentrack, and the equestrian department offers value for money on leading brands such as Weatherbeeta, Dublin, Stylo and Harry Hall.

T J HUGHES

14–26 THE BROADWAY, CRAWLEY, SUSSEX RH10 1DT, ☎ 01293 537373, FAX: 01293 611676, **e-mail:** info@tjhughes.co.uk, www.tjhughes.co.uk, 9–5.30 MON–FRI, 8 ON THUR, 9–6 SAT, 11–5 SUN.

177–178 TERMINUS ROAD, EASTBOURNE, SUSSEX BN21 3NX, ☎ 01323 732222, FAX: 01323 730110, **e-mail:** info@tjhughes.co.uk, www.tjhughes.co.uk, 9–5.30 MON–FRI, 9–6 SAT, 10.30–4.30 SUN. **PERMANENT DISCOUNT OUTLET**

See page 239 (CHESH)

THE FACTORY SHOP LTD

BRIGHTON MARINA, THE VILLAGE SQUARE, BRIGHTON, SUSSEX BN2 5WA, ☎ 01273 818590, 10–6 MON–FRI, 10–6 SAT, 10.30–4.30 SUN. **FACTORY SHOP IN A FACTORY SHOPPING VILLAGE**

See page 243 (CHESH)

THE SHOE SHED

3 THE ARCADE, BOGNOR REGIS, SUSSEX PO21 1LH, ☎ 01243 829600, 9–5.30 MON–SAT, 10–4 SUN. **FACTORY SHOP**

See page 253 (DORS)

TK MAXX

36–37 NORTH STREET, BRIGHTON, SUSSEX BN1 1EB, ☎ 01273 727483, www.tkmaxx.com, 9–6 MON–SAT, 7 ON THUR, 11–5 SUN.

13 THE MONTAGUE CENTRE, WORTHING, SUSSEX BN11 1YJ, ☎ 01903 234141, www.tkmaxx.com, 9–6 MON–SAT, 11–5 SUN. **PERMANENT DISCOUNT OUTLET**

See page 232 (BEDS)

TOG 24

THE VILLAGE SQUARE SHOPS, BRIGHTON MARINA VILLAGE, BRIGHTON, SUSSEX BN2 5WA, ☎ 01273 818759, **e-mail:** mail-order@tog24.com, www.tog24.com, 10–6 MON–SAT, 10–5 SUN. **FACTORY SHOP IN A FACTORY SHOPPING VILLAGE**

See page 240 (CHESH)

WARWICKSHIRE

ALPINE ROSE FACTORY SHOP

BRIDGEMAN STREET, WALSALL, WEST MIDLANDS WS2 9XN, ☎ 01922 645105, FAX: 01922 616368, 8–5 MON–SAT. **FACTORY SHOP**

Alpine Rose have been supplying babywear to chainstores for more than sixteen years and this is their first ever factory shop selling high quality babywear at discount prices. Catering from new borns up to three year olds, there are sleep suits, body suits, dresses, bibs, hats and socks.

BABY EQUIPMENT COMPLETE

YEWS FARM, RUGBY ROAD, PAILTON, RUGBY, WARWICKSHIRE CV23 0QH, ☎ 01788 832219, FAX: 01788 833450, **e-mail:** enquiries@babyequipmentcomplete.co.uk, www.babyequipmentcomplete.co.uk, 9–5.30 MON–SAT, CLOSED WED AND SUN. **PERMANENT DISCOUNT OUTLET**

Sells a wide range of equipment for babies, including all leading makes of pushchairs, prams, cots, cot beds and toys, as well as new clothes, all at discounted prices. The shop is situated in a small village outside Rugby on a deer farm, where you can also buy country fresh produce such as eggs. There is car parking, a café, public toilets and baby changing facilities.

CATALOGUE BARGAIN SHOP

ROCK BOTTOM CLEARANCE, 24–28 KING STREET, DUDLEY, WEST MIDLANDS DY2 8NY, ☎ 01384 458112, www.bargaincrazy.com, 9.30–5.30 MON–SAT, 10–4 SUN.

78 HIGH STREET, STOURBRIDGE, WEST MIDLANDS DY8 1DX, ☎ 01384 374544, www.bargaincrazy.com, 9–5.30 MON–SAT, 10–4 SUN.

17 BRADFORD STREET, WALSALL, WEST MIDLANDS WS1 1PB, ☎ 01922 722286, www.bargaincrazy.com, 9–5.30 MON–SAT, 10.30–4.30 SUN. **PERMANENT DISCOUNT OUTLET**

See page 234 (CAMBS)

CATALOGUE DISCOUNT STORE

SWAN CENTRE, COVENTRY ROAD, YARDLEY, BIRMINGHAM, WEST MIDLANDS B26 1AJ, ☎ 0121 707 6585, 9–5.30 MON–SAT.

UNIT 67, THE MOOR CENTRE, BRIERLEY HILL, DUDLEY, WEST MIDLANDS DY5 3AH, ☎ 01384 262537, 9–5.30 MON–SAT. **PERMANENT DISCOUNT OUTLET**

See page 271 (LANCS)

GAMES CAROUSEL

129 REGENT STREET, LEAMINGTON SPA, WARWICKSHIRE CV32 4NX, ☎ 01926 335600, 10–5.30 MON–SAT. **PERMANENT DISCOUNT OUTLET**

Offer part-exchange deals and sells both new and used computer leisure and games software. All are in their original boxes with the original manuals and in good condition and savings of over half price are available. These include PCs, Play Station, Play Station II, Dreamcast and Nintendo entertainment.

HAWK FACTORY CYCLE STORES

82–92 FOLESHILL, FOLESHILL, COVENTRY, WARWICKSHIRE CV1 4JJ, ☎ 0247 622 2783, 9–6 MON–SAT, 9–4.30 SUN.

1781–1793 COVENTRY ROAD, SOUTH YARDLEY, BIRMINGHAM, WEST MIDLANDS B26 1DS, ☎ 0121 742 3332, 9–6 MON–SAT, 9–4.30 SUN. **FACTORY SHOP**

See page 248 (DERBY)

INTERNATIONAL STOCK LTD DIGBETH

95–100 REA STREET, DIGBETH, BIRMINGHAM, WEST MIDLANDS B5 6HA, ☎ 0121 622 3232, **e-mail:** mail@international-stock.co.uk, www.international-stock.co.uk, 9–5 MON–SAT, 10–4 SUN, CLOSED 1 ON WED.

1–17 SILVER STREET, KINGS HEATH, BIRMINGHAM, WEST MIDLANDS B14 7QX, ☎ 0121 443 3232, FAX: 0121 444 1792, **e-mail:** mail@international-stock.co.uk, www.international-stock.co.uk, 9–6 MON–SAT, CLOSED 1 ON WED. **PERMANENT DISCOUNT OUTLET**

Bankrupt, fire and flood damaged articles from CDs and videos, household goods and clothes to DIY tools and television sets, carpets and cookers. The King's Heath branch is a two-storey warehouse with ever-changing stock. The upper floor is devoted to electrical goods, some marked down to 30% of their normal retail cost. The Digbeth branch sells bigger items such as kitchens, flooring, tiles, dining room and lounge furniture, central heating radiators and a large clothing section for all the family, all of which is sold below wholesale price and in some cases below manufacturers' cost price. Top brand name kitchens, when in stock, are discounted by 75%.

LEGS CLOTHING CO

42 HIGH STREET, BLACKHEATH, ROWLEY REGIS, WEST MIDLANDS B65 0DR, ☎ 0121 559 0774, 9–5 MON–SAT. **FACTORY SHOP**

See page 258 (GLOS)

LILLIPUT

63 AVON CRESCENT, STRATFORD-UPON-AVON, WARWICKSHIRE CV37 7EZ, ☎ 01789 267991
10–4.30 TUE–SAT. **DRESS AGENCY**
Children's toys, secondhand clothes, and secondhand baby equipment from birth to 10 years as well as some maternity wear. Most of the children's merchandise is baby and toddler equipment and toys, though there is some end-of-line branded clothing and equipment, including quality secondhand and shop seconds. Short term hire is available on most equipment.

LITTLEWOODS CATALOGUE DISCOUNT STORE

14–16 NORTH STREET, RUGBY, WARWICKSHIRE CV21 2AF, ☎ 01788 565116, 9.30–5.45 MON–WED, 9–5.45 THUR–SAT.

236 HAWTHORN ROAD, KINGSTANDING, BIRMINGHAM, WEST MIDLANDS B44 8PP, ☎ 0121 373 1276, 9.30–5.30 MON–FRI, 9–5 SAT.

299–303 COVENTRY ROAD, SMALLHEATH, BIRMINGHAM, WEST MIDLANDS B10 0RA, ☎ 0121 772 1637, 9.30–5 MON–SAT, 10–5 WED, 11–4 SUN. **PERMANENT DISCOUNT OUTLET**

See page 237 (CHESH)

M LATIF & SONS

NEW CANAL STREET, DIGBETH, BIRMINGHAM, WEST MIDLANDS B5 5PL, ☎ 0121 643 2822, 9.30–5.30 MON–SAT, 8 ON THUR, 10–2.30 SUN. **PERMANENT DISCOUNT OUTLET**
Household and electrical goods, bedding, linens, ready-made curtains, clothes for all the family, pictures, garden equipment, toys, gifts and silk flowers, all of which are discounted as they arc ex-catalogue and department store surplus from high street stores.

MATALAN

SPRING VALE RETAIL PARK, BILSTON, WEST MIDLANDS WV14 0QL, ☎ 01902 406160, FAX: 01902 409534, www.matalan.co.uk, 10–8 MON–FRI, 9–6 SAT, 10–4 SUN.

DARTMOUTH CIRCUS, MIDDLEWAY, BIRMINGHAM, WEST MIDLANDS B6 4BA, ☎ 0121 503 4700, FAX: 0121 333 3870, www.matalan.co.uk, 9–8 MON–FRI, 9–6 SAT, 11–5 SUN.

GALLAGHER RETAIL PARK, STONEY STANTON ROAD, COVENTRY, WARWICKSHIRE CV6 5QQ, ☎ 0247 663 7320, FAX: 0247 663 8732, www.matalan.co.uk, 10–8 MON–FRI, 9–6 SAT, 11–5 SUN.

PORTWAY ROAD, PORTWAY GREEN, OLDBURY, BIRMINGHAM, WEST MIDLANDS B69 2BZ, ☎ 0121 544 4899, FAX: 0121 544 4394, www.matalan.co.uk, 10–8 MON–FRI, 9–6 SAT, 11–5 SUN.

2 FLAXLEY PARKWAY, STECHFORD RETAIL PARK, BIRMINGHAM, WEST MIDLANDS B33 9AN, ☎ 0121 789 5950, FAX: 0121 783 2170, www.matalan.co.uk, 10–8 MON–FRI, 9–6 SAT, 11–5 SUN.

MAYBIRD CENTRE, BIRMINGHAM ROAD, STRATFORD-UPON-AVON, WARWICKSHIRE CV37 0HZ, ☎ 01789 262223, FAX: 01789 262230, www.matalan.co.uk, 10–8 MON–FRI, 9–6 SAT, 11–5 SUN.

UNIT 9, BROADWAY RETAIL PARK, BESCOT CRESCENT, WALSALL, WEST MIDLANDS WS1 4DK, ☎ 01922 615188, FAX: 01922 611984, www.matalan.co.uk, 10–8 MON–FRI, 9–6 SAT, 11–5 SUN.

WALSALL RETAIL PARK, REEDSWOODS WAY, WALSALL, WEST MIDLANDS WS2 8XA, ☎ 01922 619830, FAX: 01922 746898, www.matalan.co.uk, 10–8 MON–FRI, 9–6 SAT, 10.30–4.30 SUN.

WHEELER ROAD, SEVEN STARS TRADING ESTATE, WHITELEY, COVENTRY SOUTH, WARWICKSHIRE CV3 2LB, ☎ 0247 621 7320, FAX: 0247 621 7321, www.matalan.co.uk, 9.30–8 MON–FRI, 9–6 SAT, 11–5 SUN. **PERMANENT DISCOUNT OUTLET**

See page 232 (BEDS)

MINOR MATTERS

54 ST MARY'S ROW, MOSELEY, BIRMINGHAM, WEST MIDLANDS B13 8JG, ☎ 0121 449 3553, 9.30–5 MON–SAT, 9.30–3.30 SUN. **DRESS AGENCY**

New and as-new children's and maternity clothing. Labels include Gap and Grobag as well as high street names. A selection of prams, cots and pushchairs, books, toys, games and maternity wear as well as new equipment is available. Also sells TY Beanie Babies. This shop has two floors and is next door to Encore women's and men's dress agency (see page 185).

NEXT TO NOTHING

104 CORPORATION STREET, BIRMINGHAM, WEST MIDLANDS B2 6SZ, ☎ 0121 233 0022, www.next.co.uk, 9–5.30 MON–SAT, 11–5 SUN. **PERMANENT DISCOUNT OUTLET**

See page 239 (CHESH)

NIPPERS

FIELDS FARM, MARTON, NEAR RUGBY, WARWICKSHIRE CV23 9RS, ☎ 01926 633100, FAX: 01926 633007, **e-mail:** lorraine@nippersw.globalnet.co.uk, www.nippers.co.uk, OPENING HOURS VARY SO PHONE FIRST. **PERMANENT DISCOUNT OUTLET**

See page 234 (BUCKS)

SCOOPS CATALOGUE DISCOUNT STORE

SWAN MARKET CENTRE, YARDLEY, BIRMINGHAM, WEST MIDLANDS, ☎ 0121 707 6585, 9–5.30 MON–SAT.

UNIT 6–7 MOOR CENTRE, BRIERLEY HILL, DUDLEY, WEST MIDLANDS DY5 3AH, ☎ 01384 262537, 9–5.30 MON–SAT.

63 HIGH STREET, BROWNHILLS, WEST MIDLANDS WS8 6HH, ☎ 01543 372933, 9–5.30 MON–SAT. **PERMANENT DISCOUNT OUTLET**

See page 243 (CO DURH)

STAGE 2

AUSTIN DRIVE, COURTHOUSE GREEN, COVENTRY, WARWICKSHIRE CV6 7NS, ☎ 024 76 681520, 10–8 MON–FRI, 10–5 SAT, 11–5 SUN. **PERMANENT DISCOUNT OUTLET**

See page 235 (CAMBS)

THE FAMOUS BRUNSWICK WAREHOUSE LTD

UNIT 12, ONE STOP SHOPPING CENTRE, 2 WALSALL ROAD, PERRY BARR, BIRMINGHAM, WEST MIDLANDS BA2 1AA, ☎ 0121 356 4107, **e-mail:** northshoe@mcmail.com, 9–6 MON–WED, SAT, 9–7.30 THUR, FRI, 11–5 SUN.

UNIT 2, TOWN WHARF, SHAW STREET, WALSALL, WEST MIDLANDS WA2 8PQ, ☎ 0192 616361, **e-mail:** northshoe@mcmail.com, 10–6 MON–WED, 10–8 THUR, FRI, 9–6 SAT, 11–5 SUN. **PERMANENT DISCOUNT OUTLET**

See page 240 (CHESH)

T J HUGHES

98–100 LOWER PRECINCT, COVENTRY, WARWICKSHIRE CV1 1DX, ☎ 0247 662 7450, FAX: 0247 663 3627, **e-mail:** info@tjhughes.co.uk, www.tjhughes.co.uk, 9–5.30 MON–SAT, 10.30–4.30 SUN. **PERMANENT DISCOUNT OUTLET**

See page 239 (CHESH)

TK MAXX

UNITS 3–4 CASTLE VALE RETAIL PARK, BIRMINGHAM, WEST MIDLANDS, ☎ 0121 7496122, www.tkmaxx.com, 9–8 MON–FRI, 9–6 SAT, 11–5 SUN.

ONE STOP SHOPPING CENTRE, WALSALL ROAD, PERRY BARR, BIRMINGHAM, WEST MIDLANDS, ☎ 0121 356 5807, www.tkmaxx.com, PHONE FOR DETAILS.

THE GALLAGHER RETAIL PARK, STONEY STANTON ROAD, COVENTRY, WARWICKSHIRE CV6 5QG, ☎ 02476 664158, www.tkmaxx.com, 10–8 MON–FRI, 9–6 SAT, 11–5 SUN.

7–8 CROWN WHARF RETAIL PARK, WOLVERHAMPTON STREET, WALSALL, WEST MIDLANDS, ☎ 01922 649742, www.tkmaxx.com, PHONE FOR DETAILS.

2 WULFRUN SQUARE, WOLVERHAMPTON, WEST MIDLANDS WV1 3HB, ☎ 01902 421004, www.tkmaxx.com, 9–5.30 MON–FRI, 9–6 SAT, 11–5 SUN. **PERMANENT DISCOUNT OUTLET**

See page 232 (BEDS)

UNITED FOOTWEAR BIRMINGHAM

926–928 STRATFORD ROAD, BIRMINGHAM, WEST MIDLANDS, ☎ 0121 778 1978, 9–5.30 MON–SAT, 10–4 SUN.

74 BRADFORD STREET, WALSALL, WEST MIDLANDS, ☎ 01922 641577, 9–5.30 MON–SAT, 10–4 SUN. **PERMANENT DISCOUNT OUTLET**

See page 262 (HAMPS)

WILTSHIRE

BURBERRY

MCARTHURGLEN DESIGNER OUTLET GREAT WESTERN, KEMBLE DRIVE, SWINDON, JUNCTION 16 OF M4, WILTSHIRE SN2 2DY, ☎ 01793 486861, 10–6 MON–FRI, 8 ON THUR, 9–6 SAT, 11–5 SUN. **FACTORY SHOP IN A FACTORY SHOPPING VILLAGE**

See page 236 (CHESH)

CASTAWAYS

GRANGE BARN, THE GRANGE, GRANGE LANE, MALMESBURY, WILTSHIRE SN16 0EP, ☎ 01666 829123, **e-mail:** castaways@bigfoot.com, www.bigfoot.com/~castaways, 9.30–4 MON–FRI, 9–4 SAT

WOODBOROUGH GARDEN CENTRE, NURSERY FARM, WOODBOROUGH, NEAR PEWSEY WILTSHIRE SN9 5PF, ☎ 01672 851999, **e-mail:** castaways@bigfoot.com, www.bigfoot.com/~castaways, 9–4 MON–FRI, 9–5 SAT, 11–5 SUN. **DRESS AGENCY**

Children's top quality nearly-new designer wear plus nursery equipment, toys and Polyotter float suits. Also do fittings for maternity bras, and act as an agency for Kingswood nursery equipment (all new).

CLARKS FACTORY SHOP

GREAT WESTERN VILLAGE, KEMBLE DRIVE, SWINDON, WILTSHIRE SN2 7AA, ☎ 01793 523723, 10–6 MON–FRI, 10–8 SAT, 9–6 SUN. **FACTORY SHOP**

See page 236 (CHESH)

ECCO

MCARTHURGLEN DESIGNER OUTLET GREAT WESTERN, KEMBLE DRIVE, SWINDON, JUNCTION 16 OF M4, WILTSHIRE SN2 2DY, ☎ 01793 422240, www.ecco.com, 10–6 MON–FRI, 8 ON THUR, 9–6 SAT, 11–5 SUN. **FACTORY SHOP IN A FACTORY SHOPPING VILLAGE**

See page 236 (CHESH)

GAP

MCARTHURGLEN DESIGNER OUTLET GREAT WESTERN, KEMBLE DRIVE, SWINDON, JUNCTION 16 OF M4, WILTSHIRE SN2 2DY, ☎ 01793 486696, 10–6 MON–FRI, 8 ON THUR, 9–6 SAT, 11–5 SUN. **FACTORY SHOP IN A FACTORY SHOPPING VILLAGE**

Gap sells casual clothes for men, women, babies and children, discounted at this factory outlet by a minimum of 30% up to as much as 80% off. There is a children's play area, restaurants and a large car park.

JOKIDS LTD

MCARTHURGLEN DESIGNER OUTLET GREAT WESTERN, KEMBLE DRIVE, SWINDON, JUNCTION 16 OF M4 WILTSHIRE SN2 2DY, ☎ 01793 436944, FAX: 01793 436944, www.jokids.com, 10–6 MON–FRI, 8 ON THUR, 9–6 SAT, 11–5 SUN. **FACTORY SHOP IN A FACTORY SHOPPING VILLAGE**

See page 237 (CHESH)

MATALAN

SOUTHAMPTON ROAD, SALISBURY, WILTSHIRE SP1 2LE, ☎ 01722 342360, FAX: 01722 413721, www.matalan.co.uk, 10–8 MON–FRI, 9–6 SAT, 10–4 SUN.

MANNINGTON RETAIL PARK, WOOTTON BASSETT ROAD, SWINDON, WILTSHIRE SN5 9NP, ☎ 01793 649500, FAX: 01793 431895, www.matalan.co.uk, 10–8 MON–FRI, 9–6 SAT, 10–4 SUN. **PERMANENT DISCOUNT OUTLET**

See page 232 (BEDS)

MCARTHURGLEN DESIGNER OUTLET GREAT WESTERN

KEMBLE DRIVE, SWINDON, JUNCTION 16 OF M4 WILTSHIRE SN2 2DY, ☎ 0800 316 4352 FREE INFORMATION LINE OR 01793 507600, www.mcarthurglen.com, 10–6 MON–FRI, 8 ON THUR, 9–6 SAT, 11–5 SUN. **FACTORY SHOPPING VILLAGE**

The McArthurGlen Designer Outlet Great Western offers over 100 stores selling top names and designer brands at up to 50% off typical retail prices. Housed in the restored Great Western Railway buildings, everything is conveniently located under one roof. A large open plan area dedicated to homewares has everything for the house and home. Facilities include a food court, children's play area, licensed creche and ample parking. Stores include: U Wear/I Wear, Warner UK Ltd, Antler, Ecco Shoes, Walker & Hall, Liz Claiborne, Viyella, Austin Reed, Suits You, Alexon, Jaeger, Windsmoor, Aquascutum, Olsen, Jacques Vert, Overland/Caterpillar, Episode, Long Tall Sally, Pilot, Triumph, Cotton Traders, Villeroy & Boch, Baron Jon, Clarks, HKA, Burberry, Remington, Regatta, Just Sweets, Easy Jeans, Ben Sherman, JoKids, Donnay, Le Creuset, Puma, Tog 24, XS, Gap, Big L, Soled Out, Ted Baker, Nike, Timberland, Quiksilver, Whittard, Marks and Spencer, Polo Jeans Company, Gant, Calp, The Design House, Darlington Crystal, Duvet and Pillow Shop, Henri Lloyd, Mexx, Ravel, The Luxury Beauty Store, Thomas Pink, Thorntons, Tie Rack, Julian Graves, Hanro, Jane Shilton, Birthday, Toy Zone, Bookends, Sofa Works, Designer Room, Petroleum, Next, Daks Simpson, Suit Company, Price's Candles, Claire's Accessories, Samsonite, Van Heusen, Cloverleaf, Poole Pottery, Spiegelau, Edinburgh Crystal, Woods of Windsor, Staffordshire Pottery, Waterford Wedgewood, Stuart Crystal, Gleneagles, The Garden Outlet, Ponden Mill, Jane Heath, Sheridan Australia, Tefal, Professional Cookware, and Oneida.

MEXX INTERNATIONAL

MCARTHURGLEN DESIGNER OUTLET GREAT WESTERN, KEMBLE DRIVE, SWINDON, JUNCTION 16 OF M4 WILTSHIRE SN2 2DY, ☎ 01793 692205, 10–6 MON–FRI, 8 ON THUR, 9–6 SAT, 11–5 SUN. **FACTORY SHOP IN A FACTORY SHOPPING VILLAGE**

See page 238 (CHESH)

NEXT TO NOTHING

MCARTHURGLEN DESIGNER OUTLET GREAT WESTERN, KEMBLE DRIVE, SWINDON, JUNCTION 16 OF M4, WILTSHIRE SN2 2DY, ☎ 01793 525555, www.next.co.uk, 10–6 MON–FRI, 8 ON THUR, 9–6 SAT, 11–5 SUN. **FACTORY SHOP IN A FACTORY SHOPPING VILLAGE**

See page 239 (CHESH)

NIKE FACTORY STORE

MCARTHURGLEN DESIGNER OUTLET GREAT WESTERN, KEMBLE DRIVE, SWINDON, JUNCTION 16 OF M4 WILTSHIRE SN2 2DY, ☎ 01793 484440, FAX: 01793 430092, 10–6 MON–FRI, 8 ON THUR, 9–6 SAT, 11–5 SUN. **FACTORY SHOP IN A FACTORY SHOPPING VILLAGE**

See page 239 (CHESH)

REGATTA

MCARTHURGLEN DESIGNER OUTLET GREAT WESTERN, KEMBLE DRIVE, SWINDON, JUNCTION 16 OF M4, WILTSHIRE SN2 2DY, ☎ 01793 520900, FAX: 01793 520900, www.regatta.com, 10–6 MON–FRI, 8 ON THUR, 9–6 SAT, 11–5 SUN. **FACTORY SHOP IN A FACTORY SHOPPING VILLAGE**

See page 256 (ESSEX)

THE FACTORY SHOP LTD

23–25 NEW PLACE, CORSHAM, WILTSHIRE SN13 0HL, ☎ 01249 712160, 9–5.30 MON–SAT, 10–4 SUN.

36–37 ROUNDSTONE STREET, TROWBRIDGE, WILTSHIRE BA14 8DE, ☎ 01225 751399, 9–5 MON–SAT.

24 MARKET PLACE, WARMINSTER, WILTSHIRE BA12 9AN, ☎ 01985 217532, 9–5 MON–SAT. **FACTORY SHOP**

See page 243 (CHESH)

TK MAXX

CROSS KEYS SHOPPING CENTRE, SALISBURY, WILTSHIRE, ☎ 01722 320644, www.tkmaxx.com, 9–5.30 MON–FRI, 8 ON THUR, 9–6 SAT, 10–4 SUN.

THE ARCADE, BRUNEL SHOPPING CENTRE, SWINDON, WILTSHIRE, ☎ 01793 532896, www.tkmaxx.com, PHONE FOR DETAILS. **PERMANENT DISCOUNT OUTLET**

See page 232 (BEDS)

TOG 24

MCARTHURGLEN DESIGNER OUTLET GREAT WESTERN, KEMBLE DRIVE, SWINDON, JUNCTION 16 OF M4 WILTSHIRE SN2 2DY, ☎ 01793 695966, **e-mail:** mail-order@tog24.com, www.tog24.com, 10–6 MON–FRI, 8 ON THUR, 9–6 SAT, 11–5 SUN. **FACTORY SHOP IN A FACTORY SHOPPING VILLAGE**

See page 240 (CHESH)

TOYZONE

UNIT 91, GREAT WESTERN OUTLET VILLAGE, KEMBLE DRIVE, SWINDON, JUNCTION 16 OF M4, WILTSHIRE SN2 2DY, ☎ 01793 695550, FAX: 01793 695016, 10–6 MON–FRI, 8 ON THUR, 9–6 SAT, 11–5 SUN. **FACTORY SHOP IN A FACTORY SHOPPING VILLAGE**

See page 252 (DEV)

UNITED FOOTWEAR

HORHAM CRESCENT, PARK SOUTH, SWINDON, WILTSHIRE SN3 2LX, ☎ 01793 435238, 9–5.30 MON–SAT, 10–4 SUN. **PERMANENT DISCOUNT OUTLET**

See page 262 (HAMPS)

WORCESTERSHIRE

BABY BARN

GANNOW GREEN FARM, GANNOW GREEN LANE, ROMSLEY, WORCESTERSHIRE B45 9AS, ☎ 01562 710220, FAX: 01562 711192, **e-mail:** rebecca@babybarn.freeserve.co.uk, 10–5 THUR–SAT, 11–4 SUN. MAIL ORDER. **PERMANENT DISCOUNT OUTLET**

Permanent discount outlet catering for nursery equipment and accessories. You can visit their outlet or phone for a leaflet outlining all the products they sell. These include buggies, prams, pram sheets, cotton blankets, foot muffs, baby nests, pushchair liners, shawls, pram bags, rain covers, net bags and clips, insect nets, cots, mattresses, Moses baskets, musical mobiles, nursery sheets, quilts, bumpers, valances with matching curtains, nappy stackers, waterproof sheets, travel cots, baby walkers, door bouncers, baby swings, arm bands, baby floats, rocking horses, car seats, car window sunshades, sterilisers, fireguards, highchairs, harnesses, baby food mixers, disposable bottles, non-spill cups, portable gates, baby monitors, rompers, mitts, Christening gowns, nappies, changing mats, layette boxes, toilet steps, nursery furniture potty and step stools, changing bags, changing mats, bath and carrycot stands, bath thermometers, shampoo shields, brush and comb sets and baby clothes hangers. Most of the merchandise is branded with names such as Bebe Car, Cosatto, Chicco, Britax, Pegasus, Maclaren, Mamas & Papas, Zorbit, Klippan, Avent, Kiddiproof and Tomy. They will also hire out some items such as travel cots. If you see what you want cheaper elsewhere, you can phone them and see if they can beat the price.

BLUNTS SHOE MARKET

51 UPPER TYTHING, WORCESTER, WORCESTERSHIRE WR1 1DT, ☎ 01905 27738, 9–5.30 MON–SAT. **PERMANENT DISCOUNT OUTLET**

This shoe retailer, established for over 135 years, sells shoes for all the family as well as clothes, handbags, sports shoes, boots, giftware and household goods, all at discounted prices. Famous brands include Clarks, K Shoes, Elmdale, Grenson, Loakes, Caterpillar and Adidas. Part of a national chain.

CATALOGUE BARGAIN SHOP

233 WORCESTER ROAD, MALVERN LINK, MALVERN WORCESTERSHIRE WR14 1SY, ☎ 01684 893062, www.bargaincrazy.com, 9–5.30 MON–SAT, 10.30–4.30 SUN. **PERMANENT DISCOUNT OUTLET**

See page 234 (CAMBS)

EVESHAM COUNTRY PARK

SHOPPING AND GARDENING CENTRE, COUNTRY PARK MANAGEMENT, EVESHAM, AT THE NORTHERN END OF THE EVESHAM BYPASS, AT ITS JUNCTION WITH THE STRATFORD ROAD WORCESTERSHIRE WR11 4TP, ENQUIRIES: 01386 41661; GARDEN CENTRE: 01386 761888; APPLE BARN RESTAURANT: 01386 761333; VALE WILDLIFE VISITOR CENTRE: 01386 443348; COARSE FISHING/GOTTFRIED: 07973 147323, 9–6 MON–SAT (WINTER 5.30), 10.30–4.30 SUN. **FACTORY SHOPPING VILLAGE**

Courtyard shops and garden centre providing a wide variety of goods at bargain prices. Designer and brand name men's and women's fashions from Leading Labels, leisurewear from Cotton Traders, coordinated soft furnishings, bedlinen and duvets from Ponden Mill, household goods from Lifestyles, dried fuits, nuts and packaged herbs from Julian Graves, an extensive range of books from The Book Depot, plus quality plants, colourful pots and garden equipment. Luggage & Bags sells a range of quality branded luggage and travel goods at great prices. There is also restaurant, wildlife centre, coarse fishing on the River Avon, and a miniature railway for a real country day out.

LEGS CLOTHING CO

29 HIGH STREET, PERSHORE, WORCESTERSHIRE WR10 1AA, ☎ 01386 550328, 9–5 MON–SAT. **FACTORY SHOP**

See page 258 (GLOS)

MATALAN

FORMER HOMEBASE, PARKER BUTTS, RINGWAY, KIDDERMINSTER, WORCESTERSHIRE DY11 6TQ, ☎ 01562 756880, FAX: 01562 753573, www.matalan.co.uk, 9–8 MON–FRI, 9–6 SAT, 10–4 SUN.

UNIT 10, MALVERN RETAIL PARK, ROMAN WAY, MALVERN, WORCESTERSHIRE WR14 1JQ, ☎ 01684 584800, FAX: 01684 584802, www.matalan.co.uk, 10–8 MON–FRI, 9–6 SAT, 11–4 SUN. **PERMANENT DISCOUNT OUTLET**

See page 232 (BEDS)

NIPPERS

ORCHARD COTTAGE FARM, CROOME ROAD, DEFFORD, WORCESTER, WORCESTERSHIRE WR8 9AS, ☎ 01386 750888, FAX: 01386 750333, **e-mail:** lorraine@nippersw.globalnet.co.uk, www.nippers.co.uk, OPENING HOURS VARY SO PHONE FIRST. **PERMANENT DISCOUNT OUTLET**

See page 234 (BUCKS)

T J HUGHES

1 HIGH STREET, KIDDERMINSTER, WORCESTERSHIRE DY10 2DS, ☎ 01562 745687, FAX: 01562 744025, **e-mail:** info@tjhughes.co.uk, www.tjhughes.co.uk, 9–5.30 MON–SAT, 10–4 SUN. **PERMANENT DISCOUNT OUTLET**

See page 239 (CHESH)

THE FACTORY SHOP LTD

NEW ROAD, PERSHORE, WORCESTERSHIRE WR10 1BY, ☎ 01386 556467, 9–5 MON–FRI, 9–5.30 SAT, 10.30–4.30 SUN. **FACTORY SHOP**

See page 243 (CHESH)

TK MAXX

UNIT 100, UPPER MALL, MERRYHILL CENTRE, DUDLEY, WORCESTERSHIRE DY5 1QX, ☎ 01384 77878, www.tkmaxx.com, 10–8 MON–FRI, 10–9 THUR, 9–7 SAT, 11–5 SUN.

EVESHAM WALK, KINGFISHER SHOPPING CENTRE, REDDITCH, WORCESTERSHIRE, ☎ 01527 598837, www.tkmaxx.com, PHONE FOR DETAILS. **PERMANENT DISCOUNT OUTLET**

See page 232 (BEDS)

TP ACTIVITY TOYS FACTORY SHOP

SEVERN ROAD, STOURPORT-ON-SEVERN, WORCESTERSHIRE DY13 9EX, ☎ 01299 872872, www.tptoys.com, 9–5 MON–FRI, 9–4.30 SAT. **FACTORY SHOP**

A full range of outdoor and indoor play equipment from swings and climbing frames to sand trays, some of which are discounted at certain times of the year as they are used as display items and aren't pristine. There is usually one big factory site sale every year, which is well worth going to: phone for details. Discounts for seconds are 20% on outdoor items only. Site shop also has Lego, Playmobil and Brio at competitive prices.

UNITED FOOTWEAR

80–81 HIGH STREET, DUDLEY, WORCESTERSHIRE, ☎ 01384 238492, 9–5.30 MON–SAT, 10–4 SUN.

NEW ROAD, KIDDERMINSTER, WORCESTERSHIRE, ☎ 01562 744022, 9–6 MON–SAT, 8 ON THUR, 9–1 SUN. **PERMANENT DISCOUNT OUTLET**

See page 262 (HAMPS)

YORKSHIRE

ALLDERS AT HOME

2 BRIDGE ROAD, KIRKSTALL, LEEDS, WEST YORKSHIRE LS5 3BL, ☎ 0113 230 5800, FAX: 0113 230 5888, 10–5.30 MON–WED, 10–8 THUR, FRI, 9.30–5.30 SAT, 10.30–4.30 SUN. **PERMANENT DISCOUNT OUTLET**

The fashion centre within the Allders department store is a clearance outlet for Allders stores selling men's, women's and children's reduced stock. Famous names include Morgan, Benetton, Planet, Precis, Windsmoor, Frank Usher, Jumper, Dannimac, Fenn Wright & Manson, French Connection, Gabicci, O'Neil, Matinique, Yves Saint Laurent, Shoe Studio. Samples are also available at competitive prices twice a year from Gerry Weber, Taifun, She, Ravens, Sigrid Olsen, Erfo and Samoon. The sports department sells a mix of reduced and full price stock.

BABY DIRECT

96 NEW ROAD SIDE, HORSFORTH, LEEDS, WEST YORKSHIRE LS18 4QB, ☎ 0113 225 0505, FAX: 0113 225 0505, **e-mail:** babydirect@aol.com, www.baby-direct.com/, www.allterrainpushchairs.co.uk, 10–5 MON–SAT. **HIRE SHOP**

Retail shop which also sells equipment from wooden cots and car seats to pushchairs and baby monitors. Baby Direct specialises in all terrain pushchairs.

BRANDMART

5 NORTH STREET, RIPON, NORTH YORKSHIRE HG4 1JY, ☎ 01765 601156, 9–5 MON–SAT. **FACTORY SHOP**

See page 258 (GLOS)

BROOKS FACTORY OUTLET STORES

SOUTH LANE, ELLAND, NEAR HALIFAX, WEST YORKSHIRE HX5 0HQ, ☎ 01422 377337, 9.30–5.30 MON–SAT, 8 ON THUR, 11–5 SUN. **PERMANENT DISCOUNT OUTLET**

Walk through the store and you can't fail to find a bargain. New stock arrives daily from well-known names such as Nike, French Connection, Gabicci, Klass, Camille and Ben Sherman. Apart from mens and women's clothes, they sell sportswear, linens, lingerie, shoes, accessories, luggage, towels, coordinated bed linen, household textiles, duvets, pillows and lots more from names such as Monogram and Ponden Mill. Everything under one roof at up to 50% off high street prices. The Elland store has a coffee shop.

BROUGHTON SHOE WAREHOUSE

44 NORTH BAR WITHIN, BEVERLEY, EAST YORKSHIRE HU7 8DG, ☎ 01482 863045, 9.30–5.30 MON–SAT. **PERMANENT DISCOUNT OUTLET**

12 GATEWAY COURT, PARKGATE, ROTHERHAM, SOUTH YORKSHIRE S62 5LH, ☎ 01709 719192, 10–6 MON–SAT, 10–4 SUN.

156–158 SHOREHAM STREET, SHEFFIELD, SOUTH YORKSHIRE S1 4SS, ☎ 0114 279 6037, 9–6 MON–SAT, 10–4 SUN. **PERMANENT DISCOUNT OUTLET**

See page 247 (DERBY)

BURBERRY

CORONATION MILLS, ALBION STREET, CASTLEFORD, WEST YORKSHIRE WS10 1QX, ☎ 01977 554411, 10–4.30 MON–FRI, 9.30–3 SAT.

WOODROW UNIVERSAL, JUNCTION MILLS, CROSS HILLS, NEAR KEIGHLEY, WEST YORKSHIRE BD20 7SE, ☎ 01535 631991, 10–4 MON–SAT.

141 MIDLAND ROAD, ROYSTON SOUTH YORKSHIRE S71 4BP, ☎ 01226 728030, 10–4.30 MON–FRI, 9.30–3.30 SAT, ONCE A MONTH ON SUNS.

OLD MARKET TAVERN, MARKET PLACE, WHITBY, NORTH YORKSHIRE YO22 4DD, ☎ 01947 606161, 9.30–4.30 MON–SAT, 11–4 SUN. **FACTORY SHOP**

MCARTHURGLEN DESIGNER OUTLET CENTRE, ST NICHOLAS AVENUE, FULFORD, YORK, NORTH YORKSHIRE YO19 4TA, ☎ 01904 679190, 10–6 MON–SAT, 8 ON THUR, 11–5 SUN. **FACTORY SHOP IN A FACTORY SHOPPING VILLAGE**

See page 236 (CHESH)

CATALOGUE BARGAIN SHOP

KAYS SHOP, HOLME LANE, OFF TONG STREET, BRADFORD, WEST YORKSHIRE BD4 6NA, ☎ 01274 681711, www.bargaincrazy.com, 9.30–5.30 MON–SAT, 7 ON THUR, 10.30–4.30 SUN.

FREEPORT DESIGNER OUTLET VILLAGE, CARRWOOD ROAD, GLASSHOUGHTON, CASTLEFORD, WEST YORKSHIRE WF10 4SB, ☎ 01977 519112, www.bargaincrazy.com, 10–8 MON–FRI, 10–6 SAT, 11–5 SUN.

UNITS 2–3, LEGER CENTRE, THORNE ROAD, DONCASTER, SOUTH YORKSHIRE DN2 4GB, ☎ 01302 341506, www.bargaincrazy.com, 9–8 MON–FRI, 10–6 SAT, 11–5 SUN.

57–59 MARKET PLACE, HECKMONDWIKE, WEST YORKSHIRE WF16 0EZ, ☎ 01924 402674, www.bargaincrazy.com, 9–5.30 MON–SAT, 10–4 SUN.

42 JOHN WILLIAM STREET, HUDDERSFIELD, WEST YORKSHIRE HD1 1ER, ☎ 01484 535112, www.bargaincrazy.com, 9–5.30 MON–SAT, 10.30–4.30 SUN.

28 NEW BRIGGATE, BRIGGATE, LEEDS, WEST YORKSHIRE LS1 6NU, ☎ 0113 243 6425, www.bargaincrazy.com, 9–5.30 MON–SAT, 11–5 SUN.

MARSHALL STREET, LEEDS, WEST YORKSHIRE LS1 1UL, ☎ 0113 254 2350, www.bargaincrazy.com, 10–5 MON–FRI, 7 ON THUR, 9–5.30 SAT, 10.30–4.30 SUN.

51 ACKLAM ROAD, MIDDLESBROUGH, NORTH YORKSHIRE TS5 5HA, ☎ 01642 825925, www.bargaincrazy.com, 9–5.30 MON–SAT, 10.30–4.30 SUN. **PERMANENT DISCOUNT OUTLET**

See page 234 (CAMBS)

CATALOGUE DISCOUNT STORES

UNIT 6, HILLSBOROUGH BARRACKS SHOPPING MALL, SHEFFIELD, SOUTH YORKSHIRE S6 2GY, ☎ 0114 234 5726, FAX: 0114 234 5006, 9–5.30 MON–SAT, 11–5 SUN.

UNIT 17, IN SHOP CENTRE, 1–2 WRIGHTON HOUSE, TRENCHARD AVENUE, THORNABY ON TEES, NORTH YORKSHIRE TS17 9EP, ☎ 01642 751935, 9–5 MON–SAT. **PERMANENT DISCOUNT OUTLET**

See page 271 (LANCS)

CHARLES CLINKARD

FREEPORT CASTLEFORD DESIGNER OUTLET VILLAGE, CARRWOOD ROAD, GLASSHOUGHTON, CASTLEFORD, JUNCTION 32 OF M52, WEST YORKSHIRE WF10 4SB, ☎ 01977 515391, FAX: 01255 515391, 10–8 MON–FRI, 10–6 SAT, 11–5 SUN. **FACTORY SHOP IN A FACTORY SHOPPING VILLAGE**

See page 241 (CO DURH)

CLARKS FACTORY SHOP

RAILWAY STREET RETAIL PARK, DEWSBURY, WEST YORKSHIRE WF12 8EQ, ☎ 01924 430444, 9.30–6 MON–FRI, 9–6 SAT, 10.30–4.30 SUN. **FACTORY SHOP**

FREEPORT DESIGNER OUTLET VILLAGE, CARRWOOD ROAD, GLASSHOUGHTON, CASTLEFORD, WEST YORKSHIRE WF10 4SB, ☎ 01977 522368, 10–8 MON–FRI, 10–6 SAT, 11–5 SUN.

THE YORKSHIRE OUTLET, WHITE ROSE WAY, DONCASTER, SOUTH YORKSHIRE DN4 5JH, ☎ 01302 322663, 10–6 MON–SAT, 11–5 SUN. **FACTORY SHOP IN A FACTORY SHOPPING VILLAGE**

See page 236 (CHESH)

CRAGHOPPERS

FREEPORT CASTLEFORD DESIGNER OUTLET VILLAGE, CARRWOOD ROAD, GLASSHOUGHTON, CASTLEFORD, JUNCTION 32 OF M52, WEST YORKSHIRE Wf10 4SB, ☎ 01977 667111, FAX: 01977 557771, www.craghoppers.com, 10–8 MON–FRI, 10–6 SAT, 11–5 SUN. **FACTORY SHOP IN A FACTORY SHOPPING VILLAGE**

See page 271 (LANCS)

DALESOX

6 SWADFORD STREET, SKIPTON, WEST YORKSHIRE BD23 1RD, ☎ 01756 796509, 9–5 MON–SAT, 11–5 SUN. **FACTORY SHOP**

Based in Skipton's main shopping area, Dalesox sells quality hosiery and accessories. Most are perfect women's, men's and children's socks made for the best high street chainstores selling at very competitive discounts. For example, three-pair packs of men's cotton/Lycra socks, £2.50, recommended retail price, £9.99.There is lots of design choice from Disney character socks to Christmas character socks. There are also ties, ski socks made for famous department stores, unusual design Swedish polyester ties, knickers, boxer shorts, pyjamas and nightshirts. Most of the stock is bought in from other manufacturers, cutting out the middleman.

DESIGNER SHADES

MCARTHURGLEN DESIGNER OUTLET YORK, FULFORD, JUNCTION OF A19 AND A64 SELBY JUNCTION, YORK, NORTH YORKSHIRE YO19 4TA, . ☎ 01904 679007, **e-mail:** info@sunglass-time.com, 10–6 MON–SAT, 8 ON THUR, 11–5 SUN. **FACTORY SHOP IN A FACTORY SHOPPING VILLAGE**

See page 255 (ESSEX)

DEWHIRST IMPRESSIONS REDCAR

WEST COATHAM LANE, DORMANSTOWN, REDCAR, NORTH YORKSHIRE TS10 5QD, ☎ 01642 474210, **e-mail:** kmcmaster@rtl.dewhirst.com, 10–8 MON–FRI, 9–6 SAT, 10.30–4.30 SUN. **FACTORY SHOP**

See page 243 (CO DURH)

EVERYTHING BUT THE BABY

19 KNARESBOROUGH RD, HARROGATE, NORTH YORKSHIRE HG2 7SR, ☎ 01423 888292, www.everythingbutthe baby.co.uk, 10–4 MON–SAT, 10–1 WED. **DRESS AGENCY**

Sells a wide range of nearly-new childrenswear from birth to 10 years, as well as baby bedding, toys and maternity wear. There is also an extensive range of pushchairs and other nursery equipment. All the equipment is fully checked and the clothes range from Mothercare and Ladybird to OshKosh, Oilily and some French designers.

FEELGOOD FACTORY FOOTWEAR

27 WEST END, HEBDEN BRIDGE, WEST YORKSHIRE HX7 8UQ, ☎ 01422 846800, 10–5.30 MON–SAT, 12–5 SUN. **FACTORY SHOP**

A factory shop for many factories selling a wide selection of quality footwear for all the family. They offer a range of branded leather shoes, wide fittings, cushioned footbeds, ex-high street store shoes and many one-off bargains. New stock arrives weekly. Find them near the main traffic lights in Hebden Bridge.

FREEPORT CASTLEFORD DESIGNER OUTLET VILLAGE

CARRWOOD ROAD, GLASSHOUGHTON, CASTLEFORD, JUNCTION 32 OF M52, WEST YORKSHIRE WF10 4SB, ☎ 01977 520153, www.freeportcastleford.com, 10–8 MON–FRI, 10–6 SAT, 11–5 SUN. **FACTORY SHOPPING VILLAGE**

Designer outlet village with over 75 shops, indoor and outdoor children's play areas and a wide range of restaurants with easy access from the M52 and 3,500 free car parking spaces. Shops include Amazing Jeans, Baron Jon, BhS For Less, Charles Clinkard, Clarks, Cromwells, Churchill, Ciro Citterio, Craghoppers, CBS, Claire's Accessories, Cotton Traders, Damart, Edinburgh Crystal, Donnay, Double Two, Event Jewellery, Easy Jeans, Edinburgh Woollen Mill, Elle, Fila, Giorgio, Gossard, XS Music, Jane Shilton, John Partridge, Kappa, Kitchen and Table, Kurt Muller, Leading Labels, Lee Cooper, Littlewoods, London Leathers, Mexx, Mobile Phone Store, Nike, Nickleby's, Next to Nothing, Outrage, Petroleum, Picture Port, Pilot, Ponden Mill, Proibito, Rio Jewellery, Roman Originals, Regatta, Room, Ice Jeans, Sergio Tacchini, Sportsmill, Spotlight, Startrite Shoes, Remainders Book Depot, Designer Room, Garden Outlet, Shoe Collection, Toy Factory, Time, X Catalogue Store, Thorntons, Trespass, Waterford Wedgwood, Windsmoor.

FREEPORT HORNSEA OUTLET VILLAGE

ROLSTON ROAD, HORNSEA, JUNCTION 38 OFF THE M62, EAST YORKSHIRE HU18 1UT, ☎ 01964 534211, www.freeporthornsea.com, 9.30–6 SEVEN DAYS A WEEK. **FACTORY SHOPPING VILLAGE**

The original British factory shopping village with over 40 shops offering discounts of up to 50% off high street prices. The village also boasts leisure attractions for all ages, ranging from an adventure playground to a themed soft play area and exciting rides for children. Womenswear labels include Alexon, Designer Room, Roman Originals, Arkwright's Mill, Select, Damart, Edinburgh Woollen Mill, Double Two, Mexx and London Leathers. Sportwear and outdoor clothing are available from Tog 24, Regatta and Sports Mill. Footwear is sold by Famous Footwear, Lilley & Skinner and Charles Clinkard. Menswear stores include The Suit Company, Double Two, Nickleby's, London Leathers and Giorgio. Other shops include Woods of Windsor, Thorntons, Masters Jewellery, Edinburgh Crystal, Waterford Wedgewood, Hallmark, Laura Ashley, The Book Depot, Claire's Accessories, Churchill China and Ponden Mill.

GAP

MCARTHURGLEN OUTLET VILLAGE, ST NICHOLAS AVENUE, YORK, NORTH YORKSHIRE YO19 4TA, ☎ 01904 634670, 10–6 MON–FRI, 8 ON THUR, 10–6 SAT, 11–4 SUN. **FACTORY SHOP IN A FACTORY SHOPPING VILLAGE**

Gap sells casual clothes for men, women, babies and children, discounted at this factory outlet village by a minimum of 30%.

HOLMSPUN CLOTHING

262 HUDDERSFIELD ROAD, HOLMFIRTH, HUDDERSFIELD, WEST YORKSHIRE HD9 2TT, ☎ 01484 687911, FAX: 01484 688754, 10–5 WED–SAT, 11–5 SUN. **FACTORY SHOP**

sources and supplies retail outlets throughout the country. This outlet sells end-of-lines and quality discounted branded items at factory shop prices. Stock includes quality branded clothing, ex-high street brands, plus imported, branded electrical items such as televisions, DVD players, CD players etc. Also sells designer ranges from Armani, Moschino, Versace, Iceberg, Burberry and Valentino at discounts of 50%. If you have a particular electrical item in mind, phone first to see if they can source and supply it for your at discounted prices.

HUSH PUPPIES

FREEPORT HORNSEA OUTLET VILLAGE, ROLSTON ROAD, HORNSEA, EAST YORKSHIRE HU18 1UT, ☎ 01964 534211, 9.30–6 SEVEN DAYS A WEEK. **FACTORY SHOP IN A FACTORY SHOPPING VILLAGE**

See page 255 (ESSEX)

JACK & JILL

1 WEST PARK DRIVE, WEST PARK, LEEDS, WEST YORKSHIRE LS16 5AS, ☎ 0113 278 5560, **HIRE SHOP**

Part of the Baby Equipment Hirers' Association (BEHA), which has members countrywide. A range of equipment can be hired from highchairs, cots and travel cots to baby car seats and buggies. Some members also hire out party equipment including child-sized tables and chairs. BEHA runs an advice line which will try and answer any queries you have regarding hiring services for children. Phone the Babyline on 07831 310355 for your nearest BEHA member.

JOKIDS LTD

THE YORKSHIRE OUTLET, WHITE ROSE WAY, DONCASTER, SOUTH YORKSHIRE DN4 5JH, ☎ 01302 760137, FAX: 01302 760137, www.jokids.com, 10–6 MON–SAT, 11–5 SUN.

MCARTHURGLEN DESIGNER OUTLET YORK, ST NICHOLAS AVENUE, YORK, NORTH YORKSHIRE, ☎ 0800 316 4352 FREE INFORMATION LINE, www.jokids.com, 10–6 MON–SAT, 8 ON THUR, 11–5 SUN. **FACTORY SHOP IN A FACTORY SHOPPING VILLAGE**

See page 237 (CHESH)

LEE COOPER

FREEPORT CASTLEFORD DESIGNER OUTLET VILLAGE, CARRWOOD ROAD, GLASSHOUGHTON, CASTLEFORD, JUNCTION 32 OF M52, WEST YORKSHIRE WF10 4SB, ☎ 01977 557011, 10–8 MON–FRI, 10–6 SAT, 11–5 SUN. **FACTORY SHOP IN A FACTORY SHOPPING VILLAGE**

See page 238 (CHESH)

LIGHTWATER VILLAGE AND FACTORY SHOPPING

NORTH STAINLEY, RIPON, NORTH YORKSHIRE HG4 3HT, ☎ 01765 634508, FAX: 01765 635359, www.lightwatervalley.co.uk, 10–5.30 MON–SUN. **FACTORY SHOPPING VILLAGE**

Large complex of retail and factory outlets with a wide range of branded womenswear including blouses, skirts, suits, dresses, lingerie, outerwear, shoes and accessories as well as menswear from jeans and outdoor wear to formal wear. Shoes, jewellery, home furnishings, crystal and glass, a large range of pottery, garden products, toys, cheese and confectionery. There is a restaurant and coffee shop serving snacks and refreshments, free parking and disabled facilities. A family theme park on site boasts the Ultimate Rollercoaster, the longest in Europe.

LILLEY & SKINNER CASTLEFORD

FREEPORT CASTLEFORD DESIGNER OUTLET VILLAGE, CARRWOOD ROAD, GLASSHOUGHTON, CASTLEFORD, JUNCTION 32 OF M52, WEST YORKSHIRE WF10 4SB, ☎ 01977 510910, 10–8 MON–FRI, 10–6 SAT, 11–5 SUN. **FACTORY SHOP IN A FACTORY SHOPPING VILLAGE**

See page 256 (ESSEX)

LITTLEWOODS CATALOGUE DISCOUNT STORE

FREEPORT CASTLEFORD DESIGNER OUTLET VILLAGE, CARRWOOD ROAD, GLASSHOUGHTON, CASTLEFORD, JUNCTION 32 OF M52, WEST YORKSHIRE WF10 4SB, ☎ 01977 517899, 10–8 MON–FRI, 10–6 SAT, 11–5 SUN.

602–608 ATTERCLIFFE ROAD, SHEFFIELD, SOUTH YORKSHIRE S9 3QS, ☎ 0114 244 1611, 9.30–5 MON–WED, 9–5.30 THUR–SAT. **PERMANENT DISCOUNT OUTLET**

See page 237 (CHESH)

MARKS & SPENCER

MCARTHURGLEN DESIGNER OUTLET VILLAGE, ST NICHOLAS WAY, FULFORD, YORK, NORTH YORKSHIRE YO19 4TA, ☎ 01904 677091, 10–6 MON–SAT, 8 ON THUR, 11–5 SUN.
FACTORY SHOP IN A FACTORY SHOPPING VILLAGE

See page 238 (CHESH)

MATALAN

1 WOMBWELL LANE, STAIRFOOT, BARNSLEY, SOUTH YORKSHIRE S70 3NS, ☎ 01226 733372, FAX: 01226 733368, www.matalan.co.uk, 9.30–8 MON–FRI, 9–6 SAT, 11–5 SUN.

FORSTER SQUARE RETAIL PARK, VALLEY ROAD, BRADFORD, WEST YORKSHIRE BD1 4RN, ☎ 01274 381000, FAX: 01274 306314, www.matalan.co.uk, 10–8 MON–FRI, 9–6 SAT, 11–5 SUN.

THE RISHWORTH CENTRE, RAILWAY STREET, DEWSBURY, WEST YORKSHIRE WF12 8EQ, ☎ 01924 868180, FAX: 01924 461623, www.matalan.co.uk, 9.30–8 MON–FRI, 9–6 SAT, 11–5 SUN.

THE WHEATLEY CENTRE, WHEATLEY HALL ROAD, DONCASTER, SOUTH YORKSHIRE DN2 4PE, ☎ 01302 760444, FAX: 01302 554520, www.matalan.co.uk, 10–8 MON–FRI, 9–6 SAT, 11–5 SUN.

GREENMOUNT RETAIL PARK, PELLON ROAD, HALIFAX, WEST YORKSHIRE HX1 5QN, ☎ 01422 383051, FAX: 01422 383053, www.matalan.co.uk, 10–8 MON–FRI, 9–6 SAT, 11–5 SUN.

RINGWAY INDUSTRIAL ESTATE, HUDDERSFIELD, WEST YORKSHIRE HD1 5DG, ☎ 01484 448800, FAX: 01484 452359, www.matalan.co.uk, 9.30–8 MON–FRI, 9–6 SAT, 11–5 SUN.

KINGSWOOD RETAIL PARK, BUDE ROAD, KINGSTON-UPON-HULL, EAST YORKSHIRE HU7 4AF, ☎ 01482 832880, FAX: 01482 587750, www.matalan.co.uk, 9–9 MON–FRI, 9–6 SAT, 11–5 SUN.

LOWER WORTLEY RING ROAD, LEEDS, WEST YORKSHIRE LS12 4SL, ☎ 0113 290 7400, FAX: 0113 279 5389, www.matalan.co.uk, 9.30–8 MON–FRI, 9–6 SAT, 11–5 SUN.

HALTON DISTRICT CENTRE, SELBY ROAD, LEEDS, WEST YORKSHIRE LS12 4SL, ☎ 0113 284 0110, FAX: 0113 264 1662, www.matalan.co.uk, 9.30–8 MON–FRI, 9–6 SAT, 11–5 SUN.

SKIPPERS LANE RETAIL PARK, SKIPPERS LANE, MIDDLESBROUGH, NORTH YORKSHIRE TS6 6UB, ☎ 01642 443930, FAX: 01642 430559, www.matalan.co.uk, 10–8 MON–FRI, 9–6 SAT, 11–5 SUN.

UNIT 4B, STADIUM WAY, PARKGATE RETAIL PARK, ROTHERHAM, SOUTH YORKSHIRE S60 1TG, ☎ 01709 780173, FAX: 01709 780772, www.matalan.co.uk, 10–8 MON–FRI, 9–6 SAT, 11–5 SUN.

HEELEY RETAIL PARK, CHESTERFIELD ROAD, SHEFFIELD, SOUTH YORKSHIRE S8 0RG, ☎ 0114 262 9400, FAX: 0114 255 4193, www.matalan.co.uk, 10–8 MON–FRI, 9–6 SAT, 11–5 SUN.

INGS ROAD RETAIL PARK, INGS ROAD, WAKEFIELD, WEST YORKSHIRE WF1 1RN, ☎ 01924 367395, FAX: 01924 298164, www.matalan.co.uk, 10–8 MON–FRI, 9–6 SAT, 11–5 SUN.

UNITS 10 & 11, CLIFTON MOORE RETAIL PARK, YORK, NORTH YORKSHIRE YO3 4XZ, ☎ 01904 693080, FAX: 01904 693797, www.matalan.co.uk, 9.30–8 MON–FRI, 9–6 SAT, 11–5 SUN. **PERMANENT DISCOUNT OUTLET**

See page 232 (BEDS)

MCARTHURGLEN DESIGNER OUTLET

ST NICHOLAS AVENUE, FULFORD, JUNCTION OF A19 AND A64, YORK, NORTH YORKSHIRE YO19 4TA, ☎ 01904 682720, www.mcarthurglen.com/york, 10–6 MON–SAT, 8 ON THUR, 11–5 SUN. **FACTORY SHOPPING VILLAGE**

The McArthurGlen Designer Outlet York is one of Europe's largest covered designer outlets with over 120 stores offering top brands and designer labels with discounts of up to 50% off typical retail prices. Find everything from men's, women's and children's clothing to accessories, shoes, sportswear, luggage, homewares, toys, books, and gifts. Facilities include a food court, a children's play area and free parking. Stores include: Armani, Autonomy, Ben Sherman, Burberry, Calvin Klein Jeans, Cerruti 1881, Chilli Pepper, Cotton Traders, Daks Simpson, Episode, Escada Sport, Gap Outlet, Guess, Hugo Boss, Jacques Vert, Jaeger/Viyella, Jesire/Esensual, Kabuki, Klass, Levi's, Margaret Howell, Marks & Spencer Outlet, Mergler, Mountain Warehouse, Nitya, Olsen, Pilot, Polo Ralph Lauren, Pringle, Proibito, Proudfoot Leather, Roman Originals, Ronit Zilkha, Ted Baker, The Designer Room, Thomas Pink, Tog 24, Tommy Hilfiger, Windsmoor, Alfred Dunhill, Baronjon, Ben Sherman, Haggar, HKA, Marlboro Classics, Paul Smith, Petroleum, Pour Homme, Rockport, Suit Company, Suits You, Timberland, Adidas, Diadora, Donnay, Reebok, Toyworld, Birthdays, Bodum, The Body Shop Depot, Bookends, Franchetti Bond, Le Creuset, Oneida, Paper Mill, Price's Candles, Remington, Scent To You, Whittard Kitchen, Woods of Windsor, XS Music & Video, Bed & Bath Works, China China, Coloroll, Descamps, Garden Outlet, Jane Heath, La Casa del Christallo, Lights 4 Less, Pictureport, Room, Slipperbox, Spiegelau, Professional Cookware, Daniel Footwear, Famous Footwear, Pavers, Rockport, Shoe Studio, Soled Out, Julian Graves, Thorntons, Antler, Kangol, Liberty, Travel Accessory, Chapelle Jewellery, Claire's Accessories, Designer Shades, Monet, Tie Rack, and The Watch Store.

MEXX INTERNATIONAL

FREEPORT CASTLEFORD DESIGNER OUTLET VILLAGE, CARRWOOD ROAD, GLASSHOUGHTON, JUNCTION 32 OF M62, WEST YORKSHIRE WF10 4SB, ☎ 01977 550886, 10–8 MON–FRI, 10–6 SAT, 11–5 SUN.

FREEPORT HORNSEA OUTLET VILLAGE, ROLSTON ROAD, HORNSEA, EAST YORKSHIRE HU18 1UT, ☎ 01964 537401, 9.30–6 SEVEN DAYS A WEEK. **FACTORY SHOP IN A FACTORY SHOPPING VILLAGE**

See page 238 (CHESH)

MR BABY

4 ST JOHN'S ROAD, HUDDERSFIELD, WEST YORKSHIRE HD1 5AT, ☎ 01484 515381 9.30–5.30 MON–FRI, 9–5.30 SAT. **PERMANENT DISCOUNT OUTLET**

Sells factory seconds, former showroom models and discounted items from the Mamas & Papas range and their nursery equipment, as well as everything for the nursery.

MR VALUE

KILLINGHALL ROAD, BRADFORD, WEST YORKSHIRE BD3 8DN, ☎ 01274 669674, 9–7 MON–FRI, 9–5.30 SAT, 10–4 SUN. **PERMANENT DISCOUNT OUTLET**

A discount store offering a wide selection of goods which are catalogue returns, factory rejects, seconds and ends of lines – everything from clothes for all the family with the labels cut out to tapes, kettles, televisions, microwaves, irons, toasters, bedlinen, towels, sweets, artificial flowers, batteries, toiletries, crockery, glass, stationery, pots and pans, toys and bins. Kitchen equipment brand names include Russell Hobbs and Morphy Richards. There is also a department for mobility, selling wheelchairs, scooters etc.

NEXT TO NOTHING

38 BROADWAY, BRADFORD, WEST YORKSHIRE BD1 1EY, ☎ 01274 301460, www.next.co.uk, 9–5.30 MON–SAT, 11–5 SUN.

FREEPORT CASTLEFORD DESIGNER OUTLET VILLAGE, CARRWOOD ROAD, GLASSHOUGHTON, CASTLEFORD, JUNCTION 32 OF M52, WEST YORKSHIRE WF10 4SB, ☎ 01997 522500, www.next.co.uk, 10–8 MON–FRI, 10–6 SAT, 11–5 SUN. **PERMANENT DISCOUNT OUTLET**

See page 239 (CHESH)

NIKE FACTORY STORE CASTLEFORD

FREEPORT CASTLEFORD DESIGNER OUTLET VILLAGE, CARRWOOD ROAD, GLASSHOUGHTON, CASTLEFORD, JUNCTION 32 OF M52, WEST YORKSHIRE WF10 4PS, ☎ 01977 517605, FAX: 01977 517704, www.nike.com, 10–8 MON–FRI, 10–6 SAT, 11–5 SUN. **FACTORY SHOP IN A FACTORY SHOPPING VILLAGE**

See page 239 (CHESH)

OPPORTUNITIES

13 PROVIDENCE STREET, WAKEFIELD, WEST YORKSHIRE WF1 3BG, ☎ 01924 290310, 10–5.30 MON–SAT, EVENINGS BY APPOINTMENT. **DRESS AGENCY**

Two floors of nearly-new outfits, from wedding outfits, evening wear and cruise wear to suits and separates for day wear. Larger sizes always in stock. Anything from Louis Feraud and Calvin Klein to Next and Principles. Childrenswear includes OshKosh, Oilily, Gap and Mothercare. New and gently-worn jewellery. A large selection of designer shoes, handbags and belts. Free parking, comfy sofas, and coffee and tea available.

PARTRIDGE

FREEPORT CASTLEFORD DESIGNER OUTLET VILLAGE, CARRWOOD ROAD, GLASSHOUGHTON, CASTLEFORD, JUNCTION 32 OF M52, WEST YORKSHIRE WF10 4SB, ☎ 01977 555341 10–8 MON–FRI, 9–6 SAT, 11–5 SUN. **FACTORY SHOP IN A FACTORY SHOPPING VILLAGE**

See page 261 (HAMPS)

PREMIER & CAROUSEL

78 STREET LANE, LEEDS, WEST YORKSHIRE LS8 2AL, ☎ 0113 266 6680, 11–5 TUE–FRI, 10–5 SAT. **DRESS AGENCY**

Premier & Carousel has an extensive range of nearly-new designer and high street fashion for all seasons and occasions at a fraction of the original cost. They stock evening wear, day wear, smart casual wear, special occasion outfits, costume jewellery, and accessories for men and women. Phone for more details if looking for that special something.

QLM LTD

IDLE ROAD, IDLE, BRADFORD, WEST YORKSHIRE BD2 2AL, ☎ 01274 642222, 9.30–6 MON–SAT, 5.30 ON WED, 11–5 SUN. **PERMANENT DISCOUNT OUTLET**

Toys, household goods, clothes, food, electrical equipment, garden implements, kitchenware and furniture, all sold at discounted prices. For example, reject garden forks £6.99, spades £4.99, pruning tools £2.99 to £19.99.

READMANS LTD

ALFRED HOUSE, SPENCE LANE, HOLBECK, LEEDS, WEST YORKSHIRE LS12 1EF, ☎ 0113 243 6355, FAX: 0113 242 3192, www.readmans.co.uk, CASH AND CARRY OPEN 9–9 MON–FRI, 8.30–6 SAT, 10–4 SUN.

HEALEY RETAIL PARK, CHESTERFIELD ROAD, SHEFFIELD, SOUTH YORKSHIRE, ☎ 0114 258 0077, FAX: 0113 242 3192, www.readmans.co.uk, 9–8 MON–FRI, 9–6 SAT, 11–5 SUN.

PARKGATE RETAIL WORLD, ROTHERHAM, SOUTH YORKSHIRE, ☎ 01709 781020, www.readmans.co.uk, 9–9 MON–FRI, 9–6 SAT, 10–5 SUN.

THE MILL DISCOUNT DEPARTMENT STORE, BATLEY, WEST YORKSHIRE, ☎ 01924 426634, www.readmans.co.uk, 9–5 MON–SAT, 9.30–8 THUR, 11–5 SUN. **PERMANENT DISCOUNT OUTLET**

Mainly women's, men's and children's clothing as well as bedding, textiles, toiletries, footwear, toys, children's books, shoes and towels at prices which are cheaper than the high street. Most of the stock is from well-known labels but they cannot be mentioned here as they are de-labelled before putting in the shop. A proportion of the stock is manufacturers' cancelled contracts and seconds; the rest is designed by the in-house team and is unbranded. The aim, however, is to sell products at 50% or less than the equivalent goods sold on the high street. Also has a café.

REGATTA

FREEPORT CASTLEFORD DESIGNER OUTLET VILLAGE, CARRWOOD ROAD, GLASSHOUGHTON, CASTLEFORD, JUNCTION 32 OF M52, WEST YORKSHIRE WS10 4SB, ☎ 01977 557771, FAX: 01977 557771, www.regatta.com, 10–8 MON–FRI, 10–6 SAT, 11–5 SUN.

FREEPORT SHOPPING VILLAGE, ROLSTON ROAD, HORNSEA, EAST YORKSHIRE HU18 1UT, ☎ 01964 536610, FAX: 01964 536610, www.regatta.com, 9.30–6 SEVEN DAYS A WEEK. **FACTORY SHOP IN A FACTORY SHOPPING VILLAGE**

See page 256 (ESSEX)

ROCK-A-BYE BABY

65 THE LARUN BEAT, YARM, STOCKTON-ON-TEES, NORTH YORKSHIRE TS15 9HR, ☎ 01642 898537, PHONE FIRST. **HIRE SHOP**

For hire: cots, travel cots, car seats, stair gates, fire guards, bed guards, portable high chairs, buggies, activity centres, door bouncers and toy packages. Terms are from one day to six months. They also specialise in a wide range of complete christening outfits and gowns from birth to 12 months from £8 to £25. Confirmation and communion dresses are also available for hire.

SCOOPS

ENTERPRISE 5, 5 LANE ENDS, IDLE, BRADFORD, WEST YORKSHIRE BD10 8EG, ☎ 01274 622300, 9–8 MON–FRI, 9–6 SAT, 10–4 SUN.

SHIRETHORNE CENTRE, 34–43 PROSPECT STREET, HULL, EAST YORKSHIRE HU2 8PX, ☎ 01482 224354, FAX: 01482 221729, 9–5.30 MON–SAT.

25 TOWN STREET, ARMLEY, LEEDS, WEST YORKSHIRE LS12 1UX, ☎ 0113 263 1825, FAX: 0113 231 9885, 9–5.30 MON–SAT.

41 BARNSLEY ROAD, SOUTH ELMSHALL, PONTEFRACT, WEST YORKSHIRE WF9 2RN, ☎ 01977 642256, FAX: 01977 650 629, 9–5.30 MON–SAT.

UNIT 6, SHOPPING MALL, HILLSBOROUGH BARRACKS, SHEFFIELD, SOUTH YORKSHIRE S6 2LR, ☎ 0114 234 5726, 9–7 MON, TUE, SAT, 9–8 WED, FRI, 9–9 THUR, 10–4 SUN. **PERMANENT DISCOUNT OUTLET**

See page 243 (CO DURH)

SOPHIE'S CHOICE

159 NEW ROADSIDE, HORSFORTH, LEEDS, WEST YORKSHIRE LS18 4DR, ☎ 0113 2743913, 10–5 MON–SAT. **DRESS AGENCY**

Nearly-new women's and children's clothes which caters for middle to upmarket labels. Also sells shoes, handbags, hats and children's accessories. Examples of prices include Dolce & Gabbana trouser suits, originally £800, now £95, and Joseph designer dresses, originally £200, now £35.

SPRINGFIELD CLOTHING

THE MILL SHOP, NORMAN ROAD, DENBY DALE, HUDDERSFIELD, WEST YORKSHIRE HD8 8TH, ☎ 01484 865082, 9–5 MON–SAT, 10–5 SUN. **PERMANENT DISCOUNT OUTLET**

Springfield Clothing sells clothes for all the family at up to 50% discount on high street prices such as Marks & Spencer, Principles, Next, Monsoon and Dorothy Perkins. Also stocks men's and women's underwear, a selection of basic bedding, duvets, sheets, pillows, pillowcases as well as tea towels, tablecloths, rugs, small carpets and Sheffield cutlery, all at discounted prices. They now also sell an exclusive range of handmade lingerie, swimwear and sportswear by EnVie. Also now incorporating instore boutique by Gasp at discounted prices.

START-RITE

FREEPORT CASTLEFORD DESIGNER OUTLET VILLAGE, CARRWOOD ROAD, GLASSHOUGHTON, CASTLEFORD, JUNCTION 32 OF M52, WEST YORKSHIRE WF10 4SB, ☎ 01977 555064, 10–6 MON–SAT, 11–5 SUN. **FACTORY SHOP IN A FACTORY SHOPPING VILLAGE**

See page 289 (NORF)

T J HUGHES

51–57 ST SEPULCHRE GATE, DONCASTER, SOUTH YORKSHIRE DN1 1UB, ☎ 01302 363119, FAX: 01302 363126, **e-mail:** info@tjhughes.co.uk, www.tjhughes.co.uk, 9–5.30 MON–SAT, 10–4 SUN.

121 FERENSWAY, HULL, EAST YORKSHIRE HU1 3UW, ☎ 01482 326174, FAX: 01482 329767, **e-mail:** info@tjhughes.co.uk, www.tjhughes.co.uk, 9–5.30 MON–SAT, 10.30–4.30 SUN.

18–19 CAPTAIN COOK SQUARE, MIDDLESBROUGH, NORTH YORKSHIRE TS1 5UB, ☎ 01642 220902, FAX: 01642 220903, **e-mail:** info@tjhughes.co.uk, www.tjhughes.co.uk, 9–5.30 MON–SAT, 11–5 SUN.

50 HIGH STREET, SHEFFIELD, SOUTH YORKSHIRE S1 1QH, ☎ 0114 272 8121, FAX: 0114

272 3146, **e-mail:** info@tjhughes.co.uk, www.tjhughes.co.uk, 9–5.30 MON–SAT, 11–5 SUN. **PERMANENT DISCOUNT OUTLET**

See page 239 (CHESH)

THE FACTORY SHOP

PARK ROSE POTTERY, CARNABY COVERT LANE, CARNABY, BRIDLINGTON, NORTH YORKSHIRE YO15 3QF, ☎ 01262 603518, 10–5 MON–SAT, 10.30–4.30 SUN.

WHEATLEY LANE, LEEDS ROAD, ILKLEY, WEST YORKSHIRE LS29 8BS, ☎ 01943 604514, 9–5.30 MON–SAT, 10.30–4.30 SUN.

LIGHTWATER VALLEY SHOPPING VILLAGE, NORTH STAINLEY, RIPON, NORTH YORKSHIRE HG4 3HT, ☎ 01765 635438, 10–6 MON–SAT, 11–5 SUN.

LAWKHOLME LANE, KEIGHLEY, WEST YORKSHIRE BD21 3JQ, ☎ 01535 611703, 9.30–5 MON–SAT, 10.30–4.30 SUN. **FACTORY SHOP**

See page 243 (CHESH)

THE FAMOUS BRUNSWICK WAREHOUSE LTD

UNIT 16, PHASE 2, FORSTER SQUARE RETAIL PARK, BRADFORD, WEST YORKSHIRE BD1 4BA, ☎ 01274 394699, **e-mail:** northshoe@mcmail.com, 9.30–6 MON, 9.30–8 TUE–FRI, 9–6 SAT, 11–5 SUN.

UNIT 2, THE WHEATLEY CENTRE, WHEATLEY HALL ROAD, DONCASTER, SOUTH YORKSHIRE DN2 4PE, ☎ 01302 343866, **e-mail:** northshoe@mcmail.com, 10–8 MON–FRI, 9–6 SAT, 10.30–4.30 SUN.

UNIT 1B, WESLEY SQUARE, GOOLE, SOUTH YORKSHIRE DN14 5EZ, ☎ 01405 768358, **e-mail:** northshoe@mcmail.com, 9–6 MON–SAT, 10–4 SUN.

UNIT 3, WESTSIDE RETAIL PARK, GUISELEY, LEEDS, WEST YORKSHIRE LS20 9NE, ☎ 01943 870565, **e-mail:** northshoe@mcmail.com, 10–6 MON–WED, SAT, 10–7 THUR, FRI, 10.30–4.30 SUN.

NORTHGATE RETAIL PARK, ALBION STREET, HECKMONDWIKE, WEST YORKSHIRE WF16 9LQ, ☎ 01924 408942, **e-mail:** northshoe@mcmail.com, 9–6 MON–WED, SAT, 9–7 THUR, FRI, 10 -4 SUN.

UNIT 7, KINGSTON SHOPPING CENTRE, HOLDERNESS ROAD, HULL, EAST YORKSHIRE HU9 2AA, ☎ 01482 211157, **e-mail:** northshoe@mcmail.com, 9–5.30 MON–WED, THUR, FRI, 9–6 SAT, 10–4 SUN.

UNIT 5A, HESSLE ROAD, HULL, EAST YORKSHIRE HU3 2AA, ☎ 01482 620519, **e-mail:** northshoe@mcmail.com, 9–5.30 MON–WED, 9–6 THUR–SAT, 10–4 SUN.

UNIT 16, KEIGHLEY RETAIL PARK, HARDINGS ROAD, KEIGHLEY, WEST YORKSHIRE BD21 3NJ, ☎ 01535 600793, **e-mail:** northshoe@mcmail.com, 10–6 MON–WED, SAT, 10–8 THUR, FRI, 11–5 SUN.

SEACROFT GREEN LEEDS, WEST YORKSHIRE LS14 6JD, ☎ 0113 265 1071, **e-mail:** northshoe@mcmail.com, 9–6 MON–SAT, 7 ON THUR, FRI, 11–5 SUN.

UNIT 2A, HEELEY RETAIL PARK, CHESTERFIELD ROAD, SHEFFIELD, SOUTH YORKSHIRE S8 0RG, ☎ 0114 258 3100, **e-mail:** northshoe@mcmail.com, 10–8 MON–FRI, 9–6 SAT, 11–5 SUN.

UNIT 20B, TEESIDE RETAIL PARK, TEESIDE, NORTH YORKSHIRE TS17 7BW, ☎ 01642 634163, **e-mail:** northshoe@mcmail.com, 10–8 MON–FRI, 9–6 SAT, 11–5 SUN.

UNIT 6, CLIFTON MOOR RETAIL PARK, CLIFTON MOOR, YORK, NORTH YORKSHIRE YO3 4WZ, ☎ 01904 690399, **e-mail:** northshoe@mcmail.com, 9–6 MON–WED, SAT, 9–7 THUR, FRI, 10.30–4.30 SUN. **PERMANENT DISCOUNT OUTLET**

See page 240 (CHESH)

THE GREAT CLOTHES FASHION STORE

84 YORK ROAD, LEEDS, WEST YORKSHIRE LS9 9AA, ☎ 0113 2350303, www.greatclothes.co.uk, 9.30–9 MON–FRI, 9.30–6 SAT, 11–5 SUN. **PERMANENT DISCOUNT OUTLET**

50,000 square feet of space with clothes for men, women and children from French Connection, Adidas, Berghaus, Pringle, Wolsey, Puma, Nike, Firetrap and Sonnetti, and including all brands of jeans. There are also accessories such as socks, shoes for adults, hats, scarves and underwear. Formal men's and boyswear includes hire of morning suits and kilts for weddings and a comprehensive 'big man's department' with sizes up to 54in chest. All stock is current season and is discounted by 20%. Free alterations carried out on site and there is a coffee shop and free parking.

THE MILL DISCOUNT DEPARTMENT STORE

BRADFORD ROAD, BATLEY, WEST YORKSHIRE WF17 5LZ, ☎ 01924 423172, FAX: 01924 446096, www.themillbatley.com, 9.30–5.30 MON–SAT, 10–4 SUN. **PERMANENT DISCOUNT OUTLET**

The Mill Discount Department Store is the largest Mill retail outlet in the UK, attracting more than one million visitors every year. Situated in a restored Victorian Mill in the heart of West Yorkshire, The Mill offers massive savings in a department-sotre format. This all-weather centre consists of four floors together with an external parade selling heavily discounted branded men's, women's and children's fashions, sportswear, homewares, accessories, music, vidoes, sunglasses, books, toys, perfumes, luggage, gifts, shoes, fabrics and lighting. Readmans, whose name is synonymous with unbeatable value, has opened there recently. This is the company's second major store, offering good quality women's, men's and children's wear, lingerie, shoes, homewares and linens at remarkably low prices. Among over 300 brand names sold at The Mill are Puma, Pilot, HKA, Leeds United, Liz Claiborne, Elle, Jumper, Kasper, Amazing Jeans, Spicy, Urban Turban, Chilli Pepper, Tigi Wear, Ponden Mill, Woods of Windsor, Gleneagles Crystal, Dartington, Arthur Price, Skopos home furnishings, Jane Shilton, Book Depot, Toy Factory, Eye Zone, Famous Footwear, Hush Puppies, Lee Cooper, MX Active, Berghaus, Craghopper, Julian Graves, Fox's Biscuits, John Bull and Lion Confectionery. The complex can be reached by car, coach and train. Junction 40 of the M1 and junctions 27 and 28 of the M62 are within five and six miles of the site respectively. Batley Station on the Trans-Pennine railway is just five minutes walk from The Mill, providing easy access to Leeds and Manchester. There are more than 500 car parking spaces and coach parking is available. Amenities include children's creche, self-service licensed restaurant serving hot and cold food and drinks, Yorkshire Board Information Centre and disabled access.

THE SHOE SHELTER

UNIT 16A SPRINGFIELD MILLS, DENBY-DALE, HUDDERSFIELD, WEST YORKSHIRE HD8 9TH, ☎ 01484 866221, 9.30–5 MON–FRI, 9–5 SAT, 10–5 SUN AND BANK HOLIDAYS. **PERMANENT DISCOUNT OUTLET**

Wide range of men's, women's and children's shoes with labels such as Ecco, Loake, Gabor, Start-Rite and Elefanten. Many of the shoes are discounted by up to 50%.

THE SPORTS FACTORY

THE YORKSHIRE OUTLET, WHITE ROSE WAY, DONCASTER, SOUTH YORKSHIRE DN4 5JH, ☎ 01302 322 663, 10–6 MON–SAT, 11–5 SUN. **FACTORY SHOP IN A FACTORY SHOPPING VILLAGE**

See page 301 (SOM)

THE TOY FACTORY

FREEPORT CASTLEFORD DESIGNER OUTLET VILLAGE, CARRWOOD ROAD, GLASSHOUGHTON WEST YORKSHIRE WF10 4SB, ☎ 01977 551900, www.thetoyfactory.co.uk, 10–8 MON–FRI, 10–6 SAT, 11–5 SUN. **FACTORY SHOP IN A FACTORY SHOPPING VILLAGE**

See page 277 (LANCS)

THE YORKSHIRE OUTLET

WHITE ROSE WAY, JUNCTION 3 OF M18, DONCASTER LAKESIDE, SOUTH YORKSHIRE DN4 5JH, ☎ 01302 366444, **e-mail:** cprimrose@realm-ocm.com, www.theyorkshireoutletcentre.co.uk, 10–6 MON–SAT, 11–5 SUN. **FACTORY SHOPPING VILLAGE**

The Yorkshire Outlet has a great range of stores offering up to 50% off recommended retail prices, with new products and bargains arriving daily. The centre has a range of restaurants, a children's play area, wheelchair hire, and free parking.

TK MAXX

THE ALHAMBRA CENTRE, CHEAPSIDE, UPPER NEW STREET, BARNSLEY, SOUTH YORKSHIRE S70 1SB, ☎ 01226 770078, www.tkmaxx.com, 9–5.30 MON–SAT, 10.30–4.30 SUN.

UNITS 11 AND 12, FORSTER SQUARE RETAIL PARK, 53 VALLEY ROAD, BRADFORD WEST YORKSHIRE BD1 4RN, ☎ 01274 738600, www.tkmaxx.com, 9.30–8 MON–FRI, 9–6 SAT, 11-5 SUN.

8 THE WHEATLEY CENTRE, WHEATLEY HALL ROAD, DONCASTER, SOUTH YORKSHIRE, ☎ 01302 327 707, www.tkmaxx.com, PHONE FOR DETAILS.

2ND FLOOR, THE VICTORIA SHOPPING CENTRE, HARROGATE, NORTH YORKSHIRE HG1 1AG, ☎ 01423 536636, www.tkmaxx.com, 9–5.30 MON–SAT, 11–4 SUN.

2 KINGSGATE, KING STREET, HUDDERSFIELD, WEST YORKSHIRE, ☎ 01484 519095, www.tkmaxx.com, PHONE FOR DETAILS.

PRINCES QUAY SHOPPING CENTRE, HULL, EAST YORKSHIRE HU1 2PQ, ☎ 01482 223202, www.tkmaxx.com, 9–5.30 MON–FRI, 9–6 SAT, 11–5 SUN.

LEEDS SHOPPING PLAZA, 27 ALBION ARCADE, LEEDS, WEST YORKSHIRE LS1 5ER, ☎ 0113 246 7990, www.tkmaxx.com, 9–5.30 MON–FRI, 9–6 SAT, 11–5 SUN.

12 CAPTAIN COOK SQUARE, MIDDLESBROUGH, NORTH YORKSHIRE TS1 5UB, ☎ 01642 222220, www.tkmaxx.com, 9–5.30 MON–FRI, 9–6 SAT, 11–5 SUN.

ORCHARD SQUARE SHOPPING CENTRE, FARGATE, SHEFFIELD, SOUTH YORKSHIRE S1 2FB, ☎ 0114 275 0755, www.tkmaxx.com, 9–6 MON–SAT, 11–5 SUN.

90-93 CATHEDRAL WALK, WAKEFIELD, WEST YORKSHIRE WF1 1YD, ☎ 01924 382828, www.tkmaxx.com, 9–5.30 MON–WED, 9–7.30 THUR, 9–5.30 FRI–SAT.

UNIT 2 MONKS CROSS RETAIL PARK, MONKS CROSS DRIVE, YORK SOUTH YORKSHIRE Y032 9GX, ☎ 01904 659996, www.tkmaxx.com, 9–8 MON–FRI, 9–6 SAT, 10.30–5 SUN.
PERMANENT DISCOUNT OUTLET

See page 232 (BEDS)

TOG 24

THE YORKSHIRE OUTLET, WHITE ROSE WAY, DONCASTER, SOUTH YORKSHIRE DN4 5PH, ☎ 01302 364123, **e-mail:** mail-order@tog24.com, www.tog24.com, 10–6 MON–SAT, 11–5 SUN.

SPEN VALE MILLS, STATION LANE, HECKMONDWIKE, WEST YORKSHIRE WF16 0NQ, ☎ 01924 409314, **e-mail:** mail-order@tog24.com, www.tog24.com, 10–5 MON–SAT, 11–5 SUN.

FREEPORT HORNSEA OUTLET VILLAGE, ROLSTON ROAD, HORNSEA, EAST YORKSHIRE HU18 1UT, ☎ 01964 535308, **e-mail:** mail-order@tog24.com, www.tog24.com, 9.30–6 SEVEN DAYS A WEEK.

UNIT 23, BRUNSWICK PAVILION, SCARBOROUGH, NORTH YORKSHIRE YO11 2PA, ☎ 01723 377760, **e-mail:** mail-order@tog24.com, www.tog24.com, 9.30–5 MON–SAT, 11–5 SUN.

93–94 CHURCH STREET, WHITBY, NORTH YORKSHIRE YO22 4BH, ☎ 01947 820456, **e-mail:** mail-order@tog24.com, www.tog24.com, 10–5 EVERY DAY.

MCARTHURGLEN DESIGNER OUTLET YORK, ST NICHOLAS AVENUE, FULFORD, JUNCTION OF A19 AND A64, YORK, NORTH YORKSHIRE YO19 4TA, ☎ 01904 677814, **e-mail:** mail-order@tog24.com, www.tog24.com, 10–6 MON–SAT, 8 ON THUR, 11–5 SUN. **FACTORY SHOP IN A FACTORY SHOPPING VILLAGE**

See page 240 (CHESH)

TOYWORLD STORE FACTORY OUTLET

UNIT 28, NORTH POINT SHOPPING CENTRE, BRANSHOLME, HULL, EAST YORKSHIRE HU7 4EE, ☎ 01482 833540, www.toyworldstore.com, 9–5.30 MON–SAT.

BUTTERLEY STREET, HUNSLET, LEEDS, WEST YORKSHIRE LS10 1ES, ☎ 0113 234 2221, www.toyworldstore.com, 10–5 FRI–SAT, 11–5 SUN. **FACTORY SHOP**

MCARTHURGLEN DESIGNER OUTLET, NABURN, YORK, ST NICHOLAS AVENUE, FULFORD, JUNCTION OF A19 AND A64, YORK, NORTH YORKSHIRE YO19 4TA, ☎ 01904 639 333, www.toyworldstore.com, 10–6 MON–SAT, 8 ON THUR, 11–5 SUN.

THE YORKSHIRE OUTLET, WHITE ROSE WAY, DONCASTER, SOUTH YORKSHIRE DN4 5JH, ☎ 01302 365511, www.toyworldstore.com, 10–6 MON–SAT, 11–5 SUN. **FACTORY SHOP IN A FACTORY SHOPPING VILLAGE**

See page 241 (CHESH)

TRADEX

RINGWAY INDUSTRIAL ESTATE, BECK WAY, HUDDERSFIELD, WEST YORKSHIRE HD1 5ND, ☎ 01484 448000, FAX: 01484 448001, 9.30–8.30 MON–FRI, 9–5.30 SAT, 10.30–4.30 SUN.

CHATSWORTH ROAD, LEEDS, WEST YORKSHIRE LS8 3QE, ☎ 0113 240 7407, FAX: 0113 200 9819, 9.30–8.30 MON–FRI, 9–5.30 SAT, 10.30–4.30 SUN.

BRADFORD ROAD, PUDSEY, WEST YORKSHIRE LS28 5AS, ☎ 0113 239 3377, 9.30–8.30 MON–FRI, 9–5.30 SAT, 10.30–4.30 SUN. **PERMANENT DISCOUNT OUTLET**

See page 278 (DERBY)

UNITED FOOTWEAR

ROOLEY LANE, DUDLEY HILL, (A6036 RING ROAD), BRADFORD, WEST YORKSHIRE, ☎ 01274 680322, 9–8 MON–FRI, 9–5.30 SAT, 10–4 SUN.

178 EASTERLY ROAD, LEEDS, WEST YORKSHIRE, ☎ 0113 249 3244, 9–5.30 MON–SAT, 10–4 SUN. **PERMANENT DISCOUNT OUTLET**

See page 262 (HAMPS)

WYNSORS WORLD OF SHOES

90 DONCASTER ROAD, BARNSLEY, SOUTH YORKSHIRE S70 1TW, 9–5.30 MON, TUE, WED, SAT, 9–8 THUR, 9–6 FRI, 10–4 SUN.

339 THORNTON ROAD, BRADFORD, WEST YORKSHIRE BD8 9ER, ☎ 01274 495016, 9–5.30 MON, TUE, WED, SAT, 9–8 THUR, FRI, 10–4 SUN AND BANK HOLIDAYS.

ENTERPRISE WAY, CASTLEFORD, WEST YORKSHIRE WF10 1EQ, ☎ 01977 514774, 9–5.30 MON, TUE, WED, SAT, 9–8 THUR, FRI, 10–4 SUN AND BANK HOLIDAYS.

CASTLE MILLS, HORNCASTLE STREET, CLECKHEATON, WEST YORKSHIRE BD19 3HJ, ☎ 01274 851366, 9–5.30 MON, TUE, WED, SAT, 9–8 THUR, FRI.

438 HESSEL ROAD, KINGSTON UPON HULL, EAST YORKSHIRE HU3 3SE, ☎ 01482 223585, 9–5.30 MON, TUE, WED, SAT, 9–8 THUR, FRI, 10–4 SUN AND BANK HOLIDAYS.

MIDDLETON SHOPPING CENTRE, LEEDS, WEST YORKSHIRE LS10 4AX, ☎ 0113 2710849, 9–5.30 MON, TUE, WED, SAT, 9–8 THUR, FRI, 10–4 SUN AND BANK HOLIDAYS.

WOODHOUSE GREEN, THURCROFT, NEAR ROTHERHAM, SOUTH YORKSHIRE S66 9AN, ☎ 01709 540876, 9–5.30 MON, TUE, WED, SAT, 9–8 THUR, FRI, 10–4 SUN AND BANK HOLIDAYS.

INFIRMARY ROAD, SHEFFIELD, SOUTH YORKSHIRE S6 3DG, ☎ 0114 273 7903, 9–5.30 MON, TUE, WED, SAT, 9–8 THUR, FRI, 10–4 SUN AND BANK HOLIDAYS.

12 THE STONEBOW, YORK, NORTH YORKSHIRE YO1 7NY, ☎ 01904 637611, 9–5.30 MON, TUE, WED, SAT, 9–8 THUR, FRI, 11–5 SUN AND BANK HOLIDAYS. **PERMANENT DISCOUNT OUTLET**

See page 241 (CHESH)

YOU & YOURS

UNIT 9, CROWN POINT RETAIL PARK, HUNSLET ROAD, LEEDS, WEST YORKSHIRE LS10 1ET, ☎ 0113 234 1924, 10–5 MON, 10–7 TUE–FRI, 9.30–6 SAT, 11–5 SUN.

98–100 NEW STREET, HUDDERSFIELD, WEST YORKSHIRE HD1 2UD, ☎ 01484 543301, 9–5.30 MON–SAT.

WESTFIELD, INGLEBY ROAD (OPPOSITE GRATTAN), BRADFORD, WEST YORKSHIRE BD99 2XE, ☎ 01274 624611, 10–5.30 MON, 10–8 TUE–FRI, 9–5.30 SAT, 11–5 SUN. **PERMANENT DISCOUNT OUTLET**

See page 241 (CHESH)

YOYO

61 EASTGATE, BEVERLEY, EAST YORKSHIRE HU17 0DR, ☎ 01482 861713, 10.30–3 TUE, 10–3 WED–SAT. **DRESS AGENCY**

YoYo sells good quality, nearly-new childrenswear at prices from one quarter to one third of the original cost. The labels range from Marks & Spencer, Next, Gap, Debenhams and BhS to Little Darlings, Jean Bourget, Babi-Mini, Miniman, Clayeaux and Absorba. Most items are under £10 and generally you can clothe a child for the price of one week's family allowance. Age range from birth to about 10 years. They also sell maternity wear and children's dance wear.

SOUTH WALES

BURBERRY

YNYSWEN ROAD, TREORCHY, RHONDDA, MID GLAMORGAN, SOUTH WALES, ☎ 01443 772020, 9–4 TUE–THUR, 9–2 FRI, 9–1.30 SAT. **FACTORY SHOP**

See page 236 (CHESH)

CATALOGUE BARGAIN SHOP

FFALDS ROAD SHOPPING CENTRE, PYLE CROSS, PYLE, BRIDGEND, SOUTH WALES CF33 6BH, ☎ 01656 746426, www.bargaincrazy.com, 9–8 MON–FRI, 9–6 SAT, 10.30–4.30 SUN.

PIONEER SUPERSTORE, BRYN-SERTH ROAD, RHD-Y-BLEW, EBBW VALE, GWENT, SOUTH WALES NP3 5YD, ☎ 01495 309297, www.bargaincrazy.com, 9–8 MON–THUR, 9–9 FRI, 9–6 SAT, 10–4 SUN.

61 HIGH STREET, MERTHYR TYDFIL, MID GLAMORGAN, SOUTH WALES CF47 8DE, ☎ 01685 385653, www.bargaincrazy.com, 9–5.30 MON–SAT.

MIDWAY RETAIL PARK, PONTYPRIDD, SOUTH WALES CF37 5NX, ☎ 01443 843718, www.bargaincrazy.com, 9–8 MON–FRI, 9–6 SAT, 11–5 SUN.

UNIT 1A, HAVENS HEAD RETAIL CENTRE, MILFORD HAVEN, PEMBROKESHIRE, SOUTH WALES SA73 3AU, ☎ 01646 697407, www.bargaincrazy.com, 9–8 MON–FRI, 9–6 SAT, 10.30–4.30 SUN.

31 STATION ROAD, PORT TALBOT, WEST GLAMORGAN, SOUTH WALES SA13 1NN, ☎ 01639 899419, www.bargaincrazy.com, 9–5.30 MON–SAT.

229–230 HIGH STREET, SWANSEA, WEST GLAMORGAN, SOUTH WALES SA1 1NY, ☎ 01792 456748, www.bargaincrazy.com, 9–5.30 MON–SAT, 10–4 SUN. **PERMANENT DISCOUNT OUTLET**

See page 234 (CAMBS)

CLARKS FACTORY SHOP

42–43 MACARTHUR GLEN OUTLET CENTRE, THE DERWEN, BRIDGEND, SOUTH WALES CF32 9SU, ☎ 01656 651151, 10–8 MON– FRI, 10–6 SAT, 11–5 SUN. **FACTORY SHOP IN A FACTORY SHOPPING VILLAGE**

See page 236 (CHESH)

CRAZY MAC'S

PONTARDULAIS ROAD, FFORESTFACH, SWANSEA, SOUTH WALES SA5 4BA, ☎ 01792 585828, FAX: 01792 585566, **e-mail:** lss@salvage1.co.uk, www.salvage1.co.uk, 9.30–6 MON–THUR, 9.30–8 FRI, 9–6 SAT, 11–5 SUN. **PERMANENT DISCOUNT OUTLET**

An Aladdin's cave of salvaged stock for the avid bargain hunter, most of which has been the subject of insurance claims for fire or flood, salvage, bankruptcy or is simply clearance stock. Stock changes every two or three days and regular visitors have found anything from half price Kenwood Chefs, televisions and toys to furniture, kitchen items, linens and especially fantastic bargains in designer clothing. Yves Saint Laurent, Armani, Ungaro, Hugo Boss and Valentino, as well as all major high street names, are just some of the names to be found (though the labels are often cut out). Discounts range from 50% to 80%. Phone first to check stock.

DEWHIRST IMPRESSIONS FFORESTFACH

UNIT 22, KINGSWAY, FFORESTFACH INDUSTRIAL ESTATE, FFORESTFACH, SWANSEA, SOUTH WALES SA5 4DL, ☎ 01792 584621, **e-mail:** kim.mcmaster@dewhirst.com, 9–5.30 MON–SAT, 11–5 SUN. **FACTORY SHOP**

See page 243 (CO DURH)

ECCO

MCARTHURGLEN DESIGNER OUTLET WALES, THE DERWEN, BRIDGEND, JUNCTION 36 OF M4, SOUTH WALES CF32 9SU, ☎ 01656 767202, www.ecco.com, 10–8 MON–FRI, 10–6 SAT, 11–5 SUN. **FACTORY SHOP IN A FACTORY SHOPPING VILLAGE**

See page 236 (CHESH)

FESTIVAL PARK FACTORY SHOPPING VILLAGE

FESTIVAL PARK, VICTORIA, EBBW VALE, GWENT, SOUTH WALES NP23 8FP, ☎ 01495 350010, FAX: 01495 307363, 9.30–5.30 MON–SAT, 7 ON THUR, 11–5 SUN. **FACTORY SHOPPING VILLAGE**

Factory shopping village with over 40 shops offering a wide range of top brand goods and designer labels, many at half the recommended retail price. Factory shops include: fashion from Windsmoor, Designer Room, Leading Labels, Double Two, Pilot and Roman Originals; shoes from Pavers; china and crystal from Wedgwood and Stuart Crystal; golfing and sports equipment from Edinburgh Woollen Mill and Sportz; chocolates from Thorntons; leisurewear from Cotton Traders; luggage and bags from Antler; accessories from Claire's and lots more. Built on the former site of the National Garden Festival of Wales, there are over 70 acres of woodland and parkland to explore either on foot or on the land train which operates from Easter to September on weekends and during school holidays, weather permitting. Within the park you can visit the woodland craft centre, owl sanctuary and lakes. There is a 200-seat restaurant, with panoramic views over the valley, serving both snacks and cooked meals. The free car park has dedicated spaces for both the disabled and parent and toddler. There is free wheelchair hire and baby changing facilities.

JOJO MAMAN BEBE

WAREHOUSE SALES SHOP, OXWICH ROAD, REEVESLAND PARK, NEWPORT, SOUTH WALES NP19 4PU, ☎ 01633 294465, www.jojomamonbebe.co.uk, 10–3 WED AND FRI. **FACTORY SHOP**

Maternity wear, children's and baby clothes as well as some gifts, toys and nursery equipment. There is no current season stock, only ends of ranges, seconds and samples from the company's catalogue. Many items discounted by more than 50%. The type and amount of stock varies from week to week so more than one visit may be necessary.

JOKIDS

MCARTHURGLEN DESIGNER OUTLET WALES, THE DERWEN, BRIDGEND, JUNCTION 36 OF M4, SOUTH WALES CF32 9SU, ☎ 01656 651225, FAX: 01656 651225, www.jokids.com, 10–8 MON–FRI, 10–6 SAT, 11–5 SUN. **FACTORY SHOP IN A FACTORY SHOPPING VILLAGE**

See page 237 (CHESH)

KIDS PLAY FACTORY

UNIT 34B, FESTIVAL PARK SHOPPING CENTRE, VICTORIA, EBBW VALE, GWENT, SOUTH WALES NP2 8FP, ☎ 01495 309333, FAX: 01495 309323, 9.30–5.30 MON–SAT, 7 ON THUR, 11–5 SUN. **FACTORY SHOP IN A FACTORY SHOPPING VILLAGE**

See page 255 (ESSEX)

LEE COOPER

MCARTHURGLEN DESIGNER OUTLET WALES, THE DERWEN, BRIDGEND, JUNCTION 36 OFF THE M4, SOUTH WALES CF32 9SU, ☎ 01656 645992, 10–8 MON–FRI, 10–6 SAT, 11–5 SUN. **FACTORY SHOP IN A FACTORY SHOPPING VILLAGE**

See page 238 (CHESH)

LITTLEWOODS CATALOGUE DISCOUNT STORE

MCARTHURGLEN DESIGNER OUTLET WALES, THE DERWEN, BRIDGEND, JUNCTION 36 OF M4, SOUTH WALES CF32 9SU, ☎ 01656 665700, 10–8 MON–FRI, 10–6 SAT, 11–5 SUN. **FACTORY SHOP**

See page 237 (CHESH)

MARKS & SPENCER

MCARTHURGLEN DESIGNER OUTLET VILLAGE, THE DERWEN, BRIDGEND, SOUTH WALES CF32 9SU, ☎ 01656 662063, 10–8 MON–FRI, 10–6 SAT, 11–5 SUN. **FACTORY SHOP IN A FACTORY SHOPPING VILLAGE**

See page 238 (CHESH)

MATALAN

UNIT 2, 383–384 NEWPORT ROAD, CARDIFF, SOUTH WALES CF3 7AE, ☎ 02920 491781, FAX: 02920 49782, www.matalan.co.uk, 10–8 MON–FRI, 9–6 SAT, 11–5 SUN.

UNIT 4B, CWMBRAN RETAIL PARK, CWMBRAN DRIVE, CWMBRAN, GWENT, SOUTH WALES NP44 3JQ, ☎ 01633 866944, FAX: 01633 868400, www.matalan.co.uk, 9.30–8 MON–FRI, 9–6 SAT, 11–5 SUN.

UNIT 8, GLAMORGAN VALE RETAIL PARK, LLANTRISANT, MID-GLAMORGAN, SOUTH WALES CF72 8RP, ☎ 01443 224854, FAX: 01443 227138, www.matalan.co.uk, 10–8 MON–FRI, 9–8 SAT, 11–5 SUN.

NEWPORT RETAIL PARK, 7 STILES AVENUE, NEWPORT, SOUTH WALES NP19 4TX, ☎ 01633 636030, FAX: 01633 281271, www.matalan.co.uk, 10–8 MON–FRI, 9–6 SAT, 11–5 SUN.

FOUNDRY ROAD, MORRISTON, SWANSEA, SOUTH WALES SA6 8DU, ☎ 01792 792229, FAX: 01792 702455, www.matalan.co.uk, 10–8 MON–FRI, 9–6 SAT, 11–5 SUN.

CARMARTHEN ROAD, SWANSEA, CARMARTHEN, SOUTH WALES SA5 8LL, ☎ 01792 560010, FAX: 01792 582979, www.matalan.co.uk, 10–8 MON–FRI, 9–6 SAT, 11–5 SUN. **PERMANENT DISCOUNT OUTLET**

See page 232 (BEDS)

MCARTHURGLEN DESIGNER OUTLET WALES

THE DERWEN, BRIDGEND, JUNCTION 36 OF M4, SOUTH WALES CF32 9SU, ☎ 01656 665700, www.mcarthurglen.com/bridgend, 10–8 MON–FRI, 10–6 SAT, 11–5 SUN. **FACTORY SHOPPING VILLAGE**

The McArthurGlen Designer Outlet in Bridgend is Wales' premier designer outlet. Set out in a friendly village street style the outlet has over 80 stores with everything from men's, women's and children's clothing to accessories, shoes, sportswear, luggage, homewares, toys, books, and gifts. All stock is excess stock sold by the retailers themselves at 30% to 50% off typical retail prices. The outlet also has over 1,800 free parking spaces, a food court, two children's play areas and a nine-screen Odeon cinema. Stores include: Reebok, Calvin Klein, Tie Rack, Ciro Pearls, Monet, Picture Port, Ciro Citterio, Bookends, Bed & Bath, Clover House, Overland, Pepe, Famous Footwear, Nickelbys, The Suit Company, Birthdays, Toyzone, Vans, Red/Green, Whittards, Travel Accessories, Ecco, Jacques Vert, Warners, Next, Windsmoor, Pilot, Petroleum, Roman Originals, Antler, Julian Graves,

The Watch Shop, Knickerbox, Wedgewood, The Garden Outlet, Claire's Accessories, Clarks, Donnay, JoKids, Ben Sherman, Smiths Signature, Spiegelau, Royal Worcester/Edinburgh Crystal, Littlewoods, Helly Hansen, Woodies, Lee Cooper, Van Heusen/Viyella/Jaeger, Ted Baker, Cotton Traders, Royal Doulton, Walker and Hall, Professional Cookware Co, Thorntons, Price's Candles, Mountain Warehouse, John Partridge, Remington, U Wear/I Wear, Nike, The Body Shop, Mexx, Suits You, Designer Rooms, Winning Line, Tog 24, Elle, Chilli Pepper/Watsons, HKA, XS, Soled Out, Timberland, Carphone Warehouse, Levi's and The Craft Outlet.

MEXX INTERNATIONAL

MCARTHURGLEN DESIGNER OUTLET WALES, THE DERWEN, BRIDGEND, JUNCTION 36 OF M4, SOUTH WALES CF32 9SU, ☎ 01656 766870, 10–8 MON–FRI, 10–6 SAT, 11–5 SUN. **FACTORY SHOP IN A FACTORY SHOPPING VILLAGE**

See page 238 (CHESH)

NEXT TO NOTHING

MCARTHURGLEN DESIGNER OUTLET WALES, THE DERWEN, BRIDGEND, JUNCTION 36 OF M4, SOUTH WALES CF32 9SU, ☎ 01656 641950, www.next.co.uk, 10–8 MON–FRI, 10–6 SAT, 11–5 SUN. **FACTORY SHOP IN A FACTORY SHOPPING VILLAGE**

See page 239 (CHESH)

NIKE FACTORY STORE

MCARTHURGLEN DESIGNER OUTLET WALES, THE DERWEN, BRIDGEND, JUNCTION 36 OF M4, SOUTH WALES CF32 9SU, ☎ 01656 655588, FAX: 01656 655056, www.nike.com, 10–8 MON–FRI, 9–6 SAT, 11–5 SUN. **FACTORY SHOP IN A FACTORY SHOPPING VILLAGE**

See page 239 (CHESH)

START-RITE

FESTIVAL PARK SHOPPING VILLAGE, VICTORIA ROAD, EBBW VALE, SOUTH WALES NP23 6UF, ☎ 01495 305700, 9.30–5.30 MON–FRI, SAT, 7 ON THUR, 11–5 SUN. **FACTORY SHOP**

See page 289 (NORF)

STEWART'S

12 PIER STREET, ABERYSTWYTH, CEREDIGION, SOUTH WALES SY23 2LJ, ☎ 01970 611437, FAX: 01970 611437, 9–5. MON–SAT.

UNIT 4, BETHEL SQUARE SHOPPING CENTRE, BRECON, POWYS, SOUTH WALES LD3 7HU, ☎ 01874 610260, FAX: 01874 610260, 9–5.30 MON–SAT, 11–4 SUN.

MARLAS ROAD, PYLE CROSS, NR BRIDGEND, MID GLAMORGAN, SOUTH WALES CF33 6AY, ☎ 01656 744988, FAX: 01656 744988, 9.30–5.30 MON–SAT, 12–4 SUN.

2–4 CARDIFF ROAD, Y TWYN, CAERPHILLY, MID GLAMORGAN, SOUTH WALES CF83 1JN, ☎ 02920 888054, FAX: 02920 888054, 9–5.30 MON–SAT.

21–22 GREYFRIARS, CARMARTHEN, CARMARTHENSHIRE, SOUTH WALES SA31 3NB, ☎ 01267 232208, FAX: 01267 232021, 9–5.30 MON–SAT, 11–4 SUN.

LONDON HOUSE, HARFORD SQUARE, LAMPETER, CEREDIGION, SOUTH WALES SA48 7HD, ☎ 01570 422205, 9.30–5.30 MON–SAT, 5 ON WED.

52 STEPNEY STREET, LLANELLI, CARMARTHENSHIRE, SOUTH WALES SA15 3TR, ☎ 01554 776957, FAX: 01554 776957, 9–5 MON–SAT.

7–11 MONNOW STREET, MONMOUTH, MONMOUTHSHIRE, SOUTH WALES NP5 3EF, ☎ 01600 716926, FAX: 01600 716926, 9.30–5.30 MON–SAT.

GLAMORE TERRACE, NEW QUAY, CEREDIGION, SOUTH WALES SA45 9PL, ☎ 01545 560740, FAX: 01545 560740, 9.30–5.30 MON–SAT, 11–5 SUN.

144 HIGH STREET, PORTHMADOG, GWYNEDD, SOUTH WALES LL49 9NU, ☎ 01766 514166, FAX: 01766 514166, 9–5.30 MON–SAT, 12–4 SUN.

THE STRAND, SAUNDERSFOOT, PEMBROKESHIRE, SOUTH WALES SA69 9GE, ☎ 01834 812579, FAX: 01834 812579, 9–5.30 MON–SAT, 10–5.30 SUN.

BREWERY TERRACE, SAUNDERSFOOT, PEMBROKESHIRE, SOUTH WALES SA69 9HG, ☎ 01834 813169, FAX: 01834 813169, 9.30–5.30 MON–SAT, 10–5.30 SUN.

HIGH STREET, TENBY, PEMBROKESHIRE, SOUTH WALES SA70 7EW, ☎ 01834 844621, FAX: 01834 844621, 9.30–5.30 MON–SAT, 10–5.30 SUN. **FACTORY SHOP**

See page 251 (DEV)

THE FACTORY SHOP

SNOWDROP LANE, HAVERFORDWEST, PEMBROKESHIRE, SOUTH WALES SA61 1ET, ☎ 01437 766000, 9–5.30 MON–SAT, 10.30–4.30 SUN. **FACTORY SHOP**

See page 243 (CHESH)

TK MAXX

UNIT 11, QUEENS WEST CENTRE, QUEEN STREET, CARDIFF, SOUTH WALES CF10 2AQ, ☎ 02920 341290, www.tkmaxx.com, 9–5.30 MON–WED, 9–7 THUR, 9–6 FRI–SAT, 11–5 SUN.

UNIT 25, GREYFRIARS SHOPPING CENTRE, CARMARTHEN, SOUTH WALES SA31 3BN, ☎ 01267 220934, www.tkmaxx.com, 9–5.30 MON–TUE, 9–6 WED– SAT, 9–8 THUR, 10–4 SUN.

2–3 OXFORD STREET, SWANSEA, SOUTH WALES SA1 3AE, ☎ 01792 642055, www.tkmaxx.com, 9–5.30 MON–THUR, 9– 6 FRI–SAT, 11–5 SUN. **PERMANENT DISCOUNT OUTLET**

See page 232 (BEDS)

TOG 24

MCARTHURGLEN DESIGNER OUTLET WALES, THE DERWEN, BRIDGEND, JUNCTION 36 OF M4, SOUTH WALES CF32 9SU, ☎ 01656 767033, **e-mail:** mail-order@tog24.com, www.tog24.com, 10–8 MON–FRI, 10–6 SAT, 11–5 SUN.

FESTIVAL PARK OUTLET CENTRE, VICTORIA, EBBW VALE, GWENT, SOUTH WALES NP23 8FP, ☎ 01495 301902, **e-mail:** mail-order@tog24.com, www.tog24.com, 9.30–5.30 MON–SAT, 7 ON THUR, 11–5 SUN. **FACTORY SHOP IN A FACTORY SHOPPING VILLAGE**

See page 240 (CHESH)

TOYZONE

UNIT 19, MCARTHURGLEN DESIGNER OUTLET WALES, THE DERWEN, BRIDGEND, JUNCTION 36 OF M4, SOUTH WALES CF32 9SU, ☎ 01656 652265, FAX: 01656 652300, 10–8 MON–FRI, 10–6 SAT, 11–5 SUN. **FACTORY SHOP IN A FACTORY SHOPPING VILLAGE**

See page 252 (DEV)

WILKINSON STORES

10–13 CARDIFF STREET, ABERDARE, MID-GLAMORGAN, SOUTH WALES CF44 7DP, ☎ 01685 870393, www.wilko.co.uk, 9–5.30 MON–THUR, 9–6 FRI, SAT, 10–4 SUN. MAIL ORDER.

CIBI WALK SHOPPING CENTRE, FOGMORE STREET, ABERGAVENNY, SOUTH WALES NP7 5AJ, ☎ 01685 870393, www.wilko.co.uk, 8.30–5.30 MON–THUR, 8.30–6 FRI, SAT, 10–4 SUN. MAIL ORDER. **PERMANENT DISCOUNT OUTLET**

See page 241 (CHESH)

NORTH WALES

CATALOGUE BARGAIN SHOP

UNITS F1–F2, FLINTSHIRE RETAIL CENTRE, FLINT, NORTH WALES CH6 5RR, ☎ 01352 732460, www.bargaincrazy.com, 9–8 MON–FRI, 9–6 SAT, 10.30–4.30 SUN.

6–8 MADOC STREET, LLANDUDNO, GWYNEDD, NORTH WALES LL30 2TP, ☎ 01492 877561, www.bargaincrazy.com, 9–5 MON–SAT, 10.30–4.30 SUN.

OLD KERRY ROAD, NEWTOWN, POWYS NORTH WALES SY16 1BJ, ☎ 01686 628283, www.bargaincrazy.com, 9–5.30 MON–SAT, 10–4 SUN. **PERMANENT DISCOUNT OUTLET**

See page 234 (CAMBS)

KIDS STOCK AND EXCHANGE

24 WELLINGTON ROAD, RHYL, CLWYD, NORTH WALES LL18 1BD, ☎ 01745 330115, FAX: 01745 330115, **e-mail:** sgray@fsnet.com, 10–5 MON–SAT. **SECONDHAND SHOP, AND HIRE SHOP**

Sells and hires out new and nearly-new baby equipment. There are buggies, stair gates, parasols, raincovers, cots, prams, Moses baskets – and everything parents of young children could want, including items with famous brand names such as Jané. Old prams are exchanged for nearly-new or new. Hire charges start at £1.50 per day for a baby walker, £2.50 for a pushchair, £3.50 for a travel cot and £1.50 for a stairgate. No children's clothes are stocked.

LEGS CLOTHING CO

39 HIGH STREET, BUILTH WELLS, POWYS, NORTH WALES LD2 3AB, ☎ 01982 551043, 9–5 MON–SAT, 11–5 BANK HOLIDAYS. **FACTORY SHOP**

See page 258 (GLOS)

MATALAN

UNIT 1A AND 1B, CAERNARFON ROAD, BANGOR, GWYNEDD, NORTH WALES LL57 4SU, ☎ 01248 362778, FAX: 01248 362779, www.matalan.co.uk, 9.30–8 MON–FRI, 9–6 SAT, 11–5 SUN.

UNIT 1, MOUNT STREET RETAIL, MOUNT STREET, WREXHAM, NORTH WALES LL1 2BN, ☎ 01978 346850, FAX: 01978 262933, www.matalan.co.uk, 10–8 MON–FRI, 9–6 SAT, 11–5 SUN. **PERMANENT DISCOUNT OUTLET**

See page 232 (BEDS)

SCOOPS

FORYD ROAD, KIMMEL BAY, RHYL, NORTH WALES LL18 5EQ, ☎ 01745 353947, 9–5.30 MON–SAT, 10–4 SUN. **PERMANENT DISCOUNT OUTLET**

See page 243 (CO DURH)

STEWART'S

23 MOSTYN STREET, LLANDUDNO, GWYNEDD, NORTH WALES LL30 2NL, ☎ 01492 870733, FAX: 01492 870733, 9–5.30 MON–SAT, 10–4 SUN.

Y MAES, PWLLHELI, GWYNEDD, NORTH WALES LL53 5HG, ☎ 01758 701130, FAX: 01758 701130, 9.30–5 MON–SAT. **FACTORY SHOP**

See page 251 (DEV)

T J HUGHES

UNIT B, HENBLAS SQUARE, CHESTER STREET, WREXHAM, CLWYD, NORTH WALES LL13 8BA, ☎ 01978 359555, FAX: 01978 359500, **e-mail:** info@tjhughes.co.uk, www.tjhughes.co.uk, 9–5.30 MON– SAT, 11–5 SUN. **PERMANENT DISCOUNT OUTLET**

See page 239 (CHESH)

THE FACTORY SHOP

BRUNSWICK ROAD, BUCKLEY, CLYWD, NORTH WALES CH7 2EF, ☎ 01555 759017, FAX: 01555 759018, 9.30–5.30 MON–SAT, 10.30–4.30 SUN. **FACTORY SHOP**

See page 243 (CHESH)

THE FAMOUS BRUNSWICK WAREHOUSE LTD

UNIT H, FLINTSHIRE RETAIL PARK, HOLYWELL ROAD, FLINTSHIRE, NORTH WALES CH6 5GB, ☎ 01352 731942, **e-mail:** northshoe@mcmail.com, 9–6 MON–WED, SAT, 9–7 THUR, FRI, 10–4 SUN.

UNIT 4, ISLAND GREEN RETAIL PARK, WREXHAM, CLWYD, NORTH WALES LL13 7NB, ☎ 01978 310999, **e-mail:** northshoe@mcmail.com, 9–6 MON–SAT, 11–5 SUN. **PERMANENT DISCOUNT OUTLET**

See page 240 (CHESH)

TK MAXX

UNIT 12, ISLAND GREEN, WREXHAM, CLWYD LL13 7LW, ☎ 01978 261133, www.tkmaxx.com, 9–5.30 MON–FRI, 9–6 SAT, 11–5 SUN. **PERMANENT DISCOUNT OUTLET**

See page 232 (BEDS)

SOUTHERN SCOTLAND

BALMORAL MILL SHOP

16 CHURCH LANE, GALSTON, AYRSHIRE, SCOTLAND KA4 8HF, ☎ 01563 820213, FAX: 01563 821740, **e-mail:** millshop@balmoralknitwear.co.uk, www.balmoralmill.com, 9–5 MON–SAT, 12–5 SUN, ALSO BANK HOLIDAYS. **FACTORY SHOP**

Sells cashmere and lambswool knitwear, embroidered knitwear, sweatshirts, polo shirts, bowling and golf attire and schoolwear, some of which is brand name and some own label, but all sold at factory direct prices. Women's, men's, children's and babywear are all stocked. Popular ranges are Alice Collins, Emreco, Lyle and Scott, Gabicci, Farah, Hodgsons and Poppy. Examples of prices include embroidered sweatshirts £14.95, polo shirts from £4.95, lambswool jumpers £22.95, seconds from £1.95. Telephone, mail and email orders welcome.

GRETNA GATEWAY OUTLET VILLAGE

GLASGOW ROAD, GRETNA, SCOTLAND DG16 6GG, ☎ 01461 339028, FAX: 01461 339100 INFORMATION LINE, **e-mail:** info@gretnagateway.com, www.gretnagateway.com, 10–6 SEVEN DAYS A WEEK. **FACTORY SHOPPING VILLAGE**

Thirty trading outlets with a planned second phase of 20 shops. Includes Episode, Bags Etc, Designer Room, Directions Design Studio, Design House, DKNY, Edinburgh Woollen Mill, Jane Shilton, John Partridge, Price's Candles, Polo Ralph Lauren (stocking clothes for men, women and children as well as homewares), Reebok, Rockport, Tag Heuer, The Golf Company, Tog 24, Tommy Hilfiger, La Casa del Cristallo, Book Depot, Mexx, Claire's Accessories, Pavers Shoes, Chapelle Jewellery, Thorntons, Van Heusen and Whittards. There is a children's play area, disabled access, free parking and restaurants.

PARTRIDGE

GRETNA GATEWAY OUTLET VILLAGE, GLASGOW ROAD, GRETNA, SCOTLAND DG16 5GG, ☎ 01461 338959, 10–6 SEVEN DAYS A WEEK. **FACTORY SHOP IN A FACTORY SHOPPING VILLAGE**

See page 261 (HAMPS)

THE FACTORY SHOP LTD

DRAKEMYRE, DALRY, AYRSHIRE, SCOTLAND KA24 5JD, ☎ 01294 832791, 10–5 MON–SAT, 11–5 SUN.

54–60 HIGH STREET, ANNAN, DUMFRIES SCOTLAND DG12 6AJ, ☎ 01461 207687, 9–5 MON–SAT, 10.30–4.30 SUN. **FACTORY SHOP**

See page 243 (CHESH)

THE FAMOUS BRUNSWICK WAREHOUSE LTD

UNIT 14, THE LOREBURN CENTRE, HIGH STREET, DUMFRIES, SCOTLAND DG1 2BD, ☎ 01387 268758, **e-mail:** northshoe@mcmail.com, 9–5.30 MON–SAT, 12–4 SUN. **PERMANENT DISCOUNT OUTLET**

See page 240 (CHESH)

TOG 24

GRETNA GATEWAY OUTLET VILLAGE, GLASGOW ROAD, GRETNA, AYRSHIRE, SCOTLAND DG16 5GG, ☎ 01461 339080, **e-mail:** mail-order@tog24.com, www.tog24.com, 10–6 SEVEN DAYS A WEEK. **FACTORY SHOP IN A FACTORY SHOPPING VILLAGE**

See page 240 (CHESH)

CENTRAL SCOTLAND

ANTARTEX VILLAGE VISITOR CENTRE

LOMOND INDUSTRIAL ESTATE, ALEXANDRIA, DUMBARTONSHIRE G83 0TP, ☎ 01389 752393, FAX: 01389 750656, 10–6 SEVEN DAYS A WEEK. **FACTORY SHOP**

Large, rambling building with a coffee shop, well signposted off the A82, which has a vast retail area and additional manufacturing workshops where you can watch sheepskin jackets being made, or enjoy whisky tasting. It's difficult to tell how good the prices are as most are not double ticketed to show the original and sale price, but there are bargain sections. Edinburgh Woollen Mill has a large area, and other labels on sale include Pitlochry, Country Rose and Regatta. As well as clothes and shoes for men (new One Valley range of waterproof jackets, Hippo and PG Fields) and women and children, there are tea towels, toys, books, food, gifts, blankets, mugs, candles, CDs and tapes, table mats, sports equipment and countrywear. There is a big golf department selling Wilson, Spalding and Arnold Palmer equipment at discounts of 20% to 30% and lots of different workshops. Close to the Loch Lomond outlet village.

BABYGRO LTD

HAYFIELD INDUSTRIAL ESTATE, KIRKCALDY, FIFE, SCOTLAND KY2 5DN, ☎ 01592 647859, FAX: 01592 205284, 10.30–4.30 MON, 9.30–4.30 TUE–SAT (CLOSED FOR LUNCH BETWEEN 1.30 AND 2, MON–SAT), 12.30–4.30 SUN. **FACTORY SHOP**

Sells baby and childrenswear from birth to 16 years, all Marks & Spencer, at discounts of up to 50%. Also womenswear and menswear from Marks & Spencer, Dorothy Perkins, Principles, Next and many other high street stores, all at 50% discount.

BROUGHTON SHOE WAREHOUSE

62 CRAIGENTINNEY AVENUE, EDINBURGH, SCOTLAND EH6 7LW
9.30–6 MON–SAT, 8 ON THUR, 11–5 SUN. **PERMANENT DISCOUNT OUTLET**

See page 247 (DERBY)

CATALOGUE BARGAIN SHOP

315–317 HIGH STREET, COWDENBEATH, FIFE, SCOTLAND KY4 9QJ, ☎ 01383 611054, www.bargaincrazy.com, 9–5.30 MON–SAT, 11–4 SUN.

12–16 CADZOW STREET, HAMILTON, LANARKSHIRE, SCOTLAND ML3 6DG, ☎ 01698 421112, www.bargaincrazy.com, 9–5.30 MON–SAT, 12–4 SUN.

THE FORGE SHOPPING CENTRE, PARKHEAD, GLASGOW, SCOTLAND G31 4EB, ☎ 0141 556 5352, www.bargaincrazy.com, 9–6 MON–SAT, 11–5 SUN. **PERMANENT DISCOUNT OUTLET**

See page 234 (CAMBS)

CHARLES CLINKARD

STERLING MILLS DESIGNER OUTLET VILLAGE, DEVONVALE, TILLICOULTRY, CLACKMANNANSHIRE FK13 6HQ, ☎ 01259 753001, FAX: 01259 753001, 10–6 MON–SAT, 10–5 SUN.

FREEPORT LEISURE SCOTLAND, FIVE SISTERS, WEST WOOD, WEST CALDER, WEST LOTHIAN SCOTLAND EH55 8BQ, ☎ 01501 763650, FAX: 01501 763650, 10–6 MON–SAT, 8 ON THUR, 11–5 SUN. **FACTORY SHOP IN A FACTORY SHOPPING VILLAGE**

See page 241 (CO DURH)

CLARKS FACTORY SHOP

UNIT 26, PARKHEAD FORGE SHOPPING CENTRE, PARKHEAD, GLASGOW, LANARKSHIRE SCOTLAND G31 4EB, ☎ 0141 556 5290, 9.30–5.30 MON–SAT, 12–4.30 SUN.

UNITS 31–35, ALMONDVALE AVENUE, LIVINGSTON, WEST LOTHIAN, SCOTLAND EH54 6HR, ☎ 01506 461376, 10–6 MON–SAT, 8 ON THUR, 10–6 SUN. **FACTORY SHOP**

See page 236 (CHESH)

DESIGNER SHADES

MCARTHURGLEN DESIGNER OUTLET LIVINGSTON, ALMONDVALE AVENUE, LIVINGSTON, WEST LOTHIAN, JUNCTION 3 OFF THE M8, BETWEEN EDINBURGH AND GLASGOW, SCOTLAND EH54 6QX, ☎ 01506 461177, **e-mail:** info@sunglass-time.com, 10–6 MON–WED, SAT, SUN. 10–8 THUR, FRI. **PERMANENT DISCOUNT OUTLET**

See page 255 (ESSEX)

FREEPORT SCOTLAND OUTLET VILLAGE

FIVE SISTERS, WESTWOOD, WEST CALDER, NEAR JUNCTION 4 OF THE M8, WEST LOTHIAN, SCOTLAND EH55 8QB, ☎ 01501 763488, www.freeportscotland.com, 10–6 SEVEN DAYS A WEEK. **FACTORY SHOPPING VILLAGE**

Designer outlet village with more than 25 shops offering up to 50% off high street prices, as well as a café and free parking. Outlets for women include The Designer Room, Mexx, London Leathers, Versace, Klass, Select, Iceberg and Jean Scene. Menswear is available from Ciro Citterio, Versace, Double Two, Madhouse, Leading Labels, Iceberg, Mexx, Nickleby's and Proibito. Sweet-toothed visitors can savour the chocolates at Thorntons. Other shops include Tog 24, Bags Etc, Charles Clinkard, Outdoor Adventure, Book Depot, Churchill China and Ponden Mill.

GAP

MCARTHURGLEN OUTLET VILLAGE, ALMONDVALE AVENUE, LIVINGSTON, WEST LOTHIAN, JUNCTION 3 OFF THE M8, BETWEEN EDINBURGH AND GLASGOW, SCOTLAND EH54 6QX, ☎ 01506 419899, 10–6 MON, TUE, 10–8 WED, THUR, FRI, 10–6 SAT, SUN. **FACTORY SHOP IN A FACTORY SHOPPING VILLAGE**

Gap sells casual clothes for men, women, babies and children, discounted at this factory outlet village by a minimum of 30% and as much as 80% to 90%.

HAVEN

473 HILLINGTON ROAD, HILLINGTON INDUSTRIAL ESTATE, GLASGOW, DUMBARTONSHIRE G52 4QX, ☎ 0141 883 4801, 7.50–4 MON–THUR, 7.50–2.50 FRI. **PERMANENT DISCOUNT OUTLET**

A sheltered workshop owned by the Haven Products Trust to whom all the profits go. It sells women's, men's and children's knitwear. Many of the products are high street and brand names at reduced prices.

JOKIDS

MCARTHURGLEN DESIGNER OUTLET LIVINGSTON, ALMONDVALE AVENUE, LIVINGSTON, WEST LOTHIAN, JUNCTION 3 OFF THE M8, SCOTLAND EH54 6QX, ☎ 01506 416663, www.jokids.com, 9–6 MON–SAT, 11–5 SUN. **FACTORY SHOP IN A FACTORY SHOPPING VILLAGE**

See page 237 (CHESH)

LILLEY & SKINNER

ALMONDVALE AVENUE, LIVINGSTON, MCARTHURGLEN DESIGNER OUTLET LIVINGSTON, WEST LOTHIAN, JUNCTION 3 OFF THE M8, BETWEEN EDINBURGH AND GLASGOW, SCOTLAND EH54 6QX, ☎ 0800 3164352 FREE INFORMATION LINE, www.mcarthurglen.com, 10–8 MON–FRI, 10–7 SAT, 10–6 SUN. **FACTORY SHOP IN A FACTORY SHOPPING VILLAGE**

See page 256 (ESSEX)

LOCH LOMOND FACTORY OUTLETS

MAIN STREET, ALEXANDRIA, JUNCTION 17 OF M8 THEN A82, LOCH LOMOND, SCOTLAND G83 0UG, ☎ 01389 710077, 01389 605500 INFORMATION LINE, FAX: 01389 607259, **e-mail:**

info@lochlomondoutlets.co.uk, www.lochlomondoutletcentre.co.uk, 9.30–5.30 SEVEN DAYS A WEEK. **FACTORY SHOPPING VILLAGE**

Just off the A82, the main route between Glasgow and the West Highlands and Islands, and only one mile from Loch Lomond, this factory outlet centre combines history, heritage, adventure and shopping under one roof. Shops include Bags Etc selling luggage items; Book Depot, Designer Room (Klass, DKNY, Elle), Global Emporium for gifts, Jean Scene for branded denim wear; Julian Graves foods and nut mixes; Leading Labels, Nickleby's, Pavers Shoes, Ponden Mill for bed-linen and bathroom ware; Ramseys womenswear; Room offering homes accessories and furniture; Stuart Crystal; Sportz selling sportswear from Adidas, Nike, etc; Tog 24 for outdoor wear; Trespass; Card & Party Place (greetings cards and posters). There is also Ceramic Experience (a unique opportunity to decorate your own ceramics and pottery merchandise plus a children's soft play area), a Motoring Heritage Centre telling the history of the Scottish motor car industry with a collection of vintage cars, and The Gallery Cafe selling meals, snacks and sandwiches.

MARKS & SPENCER

MCARTHURGLEN DESIGNER OUTLET VILLAGE LIVINGSTON, ALMONDVALE AVENUE, WEST LOTHIAN, SCOTLAND EH54 6QX, ☎ 01506 418206, 10–6 MON, TUE, SAT, SUN, 10–8 WED–FRI. **FACTORY SHOP IN A FACTORY SHOPPING VILLAGE**

See page 238 (CHESH)

MATALAN

UNIT 13A, WEST LODGE ROAD, RENFREW, BLYTHSWOOD SCOTLAND PA4 9EN, ☎ 0141 886 8050, FAX: 0141 886 2447, www.matalan.co.uk, 9.30–8 MON–FRI, 9.30–5.30 SAT, 10–6 SUN.

CLYDE RETAIL PARK, LIVINGSTONE STREET, CLYDEBANK, GLASGOW SCOTLAND G81 2XA, ☎ 0141 435 7450, FAX: 0141 952 0415, www.matalan.co.uk, 10–8 MON–FRI, 8–5.30 SAT, 10–6 SUN.

UNIT 2, FARADAY RETAIL PARK, WHIFFLET STREET/COATBANK STREET, COATBRIDGE, LANARKSHIRE ML5 3SP, ☎ 01244 665260, FAX: 01236 423950, www.matalan.co.uk, 10–8 MON–FRI, 10–6 SAT, 10–6 SUN.

NITSHILL ROAD, DARNLEY, GLASGOW SCOTLAND G53 7BW, ☎ 0141 880 3900, FAX: 0141 880 4958, www.matalan.co.uk, 10–8 MON–FRI, 9.30–6 SAT, 10–6 SUN.

155 SLATEFORD ROAD, EDINBURGH SCOTLAND EH14 1NZ, ☎ 0131 455 7224, FAX: 0131 443 2570, www.matalan.co.uk, 10–8 MON–FRI, 8.30–5.30 SAT, 10–6 SUN.

CARRON ROAD, BAINESFORD, FALKIRK, SCOTLAND FK1, FAX: 01324 614130, FAX: 01324 627149, www.matalan.co.uk, 10–8 MON–FRI, 10–6 SAT, SUN.

SALTAIRE RETAIL PARK, PENTLAND PARK, GLENROTHES, SCOTLAND KY6 2AL, ☎ 01592 776860, FAX: 01592 773354, www.matalan.co.uk, 10–8 MON–FRI, 9.30–5.30 SAT, 10–6 SUN.

LORENY INDUSTRIAL ESTATE, UMBERLEY ROAD, KILMARNOCK SCOTLAND KA1 5LB, ☎ 01563 555040, FAX: 01563 549832, www.matalan.co.uk, 10–8 MON–FRI, 9.30–5.30 SAT, 10–6 SUN.

3–4 SEAFIELD WAY, SEAFIELD ROAD, LEITH, EDINBURGH, SCOTLAND EH15 1TB, ☎ 0131 657 5045, FAX: 0131 657 5046, www.matalan.co.uk, 10–8 MON–FRI, 9.30–5.30 SAT, 10–6 SUN.

PHOENIX RETAIL PARK, LINWOOD ROAD, PAISLEY, SCOTLAND PA1 2AB, ☎ 0141 840 5120, FAX: 0141 849 7109, www.matalan.co.uk, 10–8 MON–FRI, 9–6 SAT, 10–6 SUN.

UNIT 5, CALEDONIAN CENTRE, NEW ASHTREE INDUSTRIAL ESTATE, WISHAW, LANARKSHIRE ML2 7UR, ☎ 01698 357075, FAX: 01698 357072, www.matalan.co.uk, 10–9 MON–FRI, 9.30–6.30 SAT, 10–6 SUN. **PERMANENT DISCOUNT OUTLET**

See page 232 (BEDS)

MCARTHURGLEN DESIGNER OUTLET

ALMONDVALE AVENUE, LIVINGSTON, WEST LOTHIAN, JUNCTION 3 OFF THE M8, BETWEEN EDINBURGH AND GLASGOW, SCOTLAND EH54 6QX, ☎ 01506 423600, FAX: 01506 423602, www.mcarthurglen.com/livingston, 10–6 SEVEN DAYS A WEEK, 8 ON THUR. **FACTORY SHOPPING VILLAGE**

The McArthurGlen Designer Outlet Livingston offers over 80 stores full of top brands and designer labels at up to 50% off typical retail prices. There is a food court, cafés and restaurants as well as an eight-screen licensed cinema, health and fitness club and free parking for 1,800 cars. Stores include: Gap Outlet, XS, Designer Shades, Marks & Spencer Outlet, The Body Shop Outlet, Van Heusen/Jaeger/Viyella, One to One, Antler, Clarks, Suits You, Chappelle, Banana Books, Toyworld, Donnay, Whittard, Price's Candles, Aquascutum, Revlon, The Paper Mill Shop, Regatta, Jane Shilton, Brand Fushion, Early Learning Centre, CK Jeans, Jockey, Autonomy, Cotton Traders, Black and Decker, Room, Surf, Skate and Snow, Ronit Zilkha, Ted Baker, Proudfoot, Thornton's, Arran Aromatics, Bon Bleu, Jokids, Soled Out, Windsmoor, Suit Co, Easy Jeans, Roman Originals, Julian Graves, Directions, Sportz, Lilley & Skinner, Armani, Ben Sherman, Petroleum, Samsonite, Tog 24, Outdoor Scene, Trespass, Logo, Levi's, Professional Cookware, Coloroll, Jane Heath, Bed & Bath, Denby, Pictureport, Waterford/Wedgewood, Poole Pottery, Lights 4 Less, Cloverhouse, Gleneagles, Edinburgh Crystal, and Speigelau.

MEXX INTERNATIONAL

FREEPORT VILLAGE FIVE SISTERS, WESTWOOD, WEST CALDER, NEAR JUNCTION 4 OF THE M8, WEST LOTHIAN, SCOTLAND EH55 8QB, ☎ 01501 763320, 10–6 SEVEN DAYS A WEEK, 8 ON THUR. **FACTORY SHOP**

See page 238. (CHESH)

NEXT TO NOTHING

49–53 UNION STREET, GLASGOW, SCOTLAND G1 3RB, ☎ 0141 221 7100, www.next.co.uk, 10–6 MON–FRI, 7 ON THUR, 9–6 SAT, 11–5 SUN. **PERMANENT DISCOUNT OUTLET**

See page 239. (CHESH)

NIKE FACTORY STORE

UNIT 28, STERLING MILLS DESIGNER OUTLET VILLAGE, TILLICOULTRY, CLACKMANNANSHIRE, SCOTLAND FK13 6HN, ☎ 01259 750148, FAX: 01259 753867, www.nike.com, 10–6 SEVEN DAYS A WEEK. **FACTORY SHOP IN A FACTORY SHOPPING VILLAGE**

See page 239. (CHESH)

REGATTA

MCARTHURGLEN DESIGNER OUTLET VILLAGE, ALMONDALE AVENUE, LIVINGSTON, SCOTLAND EH54 6QX, ☎ 01506 429813, FAX: 01506 429813, www.regatta.com, 10–6 SEVEN DAYS A WEEK, 8 ON THUR. **FACTORY SHOP IN A FACTORY SHOPPING VILLAGE**

See page 256 (ESSEX)

STERLING MILLS DESIGNER OUTLET VILLAGE

TILLICOULTRY, NEAR STIRLING, CLACKMANNANSHIRE, MIDWAY BETWEEN M9 AND M90, SCOTLAND FK13 6HQ, ☎ 01259 752100, www.sterlingmills.com, 10–6 SEVEN DAYS A WEEK. **FACTORY SHOPPING VILLAGE**

This factory shopping centre guarantees prices of at least 30% off typical high street prices and sometimes as much as 70%. Outlets so far include Mountain Warehouse, Adidas, Penny Plain, Enigma Candles, Jacques Vert, The Officers' Club, Bed & Bath Works, Book Depot, Claire's Accessories, Cotton Traders, Denby Pottery, Designer Room, Double Two, Julian Graves, Nike, Nickelby's, Pavers Shoes, Proibito, Roman Originals, Thorntons, Tog 24, Bags Etc, USA Golf Wear House, VF Corporation Factory Store, Winning Line, XS Music, Charles Clinkard, Naf Naf Chevignon, The Toy Factory, Pilot, Real Jewellery, The Sweet Factory, The Design House, Watson Chilli Pepper, Regatta, Blue Ridge, Playtex and more. There's a restaurant on site, and the very large Sterling Furniture Centre is situated opposite.

T J HUGHES

127–135 TRONGATE, GLASGOW, SCOTLAND G1 5HG, ☎ 0141 548 8400, FAX: 0141 552 6297, **e-mail:** info@tjhughes.co.uk, www.tjhughes.co.uk, 9–5.30 MON– FRI, 8 ON THUR, 9–6 SAT, 11–5 SUN. **PERMANENT DISCOUNT OUTLET**

See page 239 (CHESH)

THE FACTORY SHOP LTD

56 CHAPEL STREET, CARLUKE, SOUTH LANARKSHIRE, SCOTLAND ML8 4BA, ☎ 01555 759017, FAX: 01555 759018, 9–5 MON–FRI, 9–5.30 SAT, 10–5 SUN.

BURNSIDE MILL, CUPAR, FIFE SCOTLAND KY15 4DQ, ☎ 01334 650661, FAX: 01334 656772, 9.30–5.30 MON–SAT, 10–5 SUN. **FACTORY SHOP**

See page 243 (CHESH)

THE FAMOUS BRUNSWICK WAREHOUSE LTD

UNIT 1, KILBOWIE RETAIL PARK, CLYDEBANK, SCOTLAND G81 4QH, ☎ 0141 952 4914, **e-mail:** northshoe@mcmail.com, 10–6 MON–SAT, 7 ON THUR, 10–5 SUN.

UNIT 3, FARADAY RETAIL PARK, COATBRIDGE, SCOTLAND ML5 3SQ, ☎ 01236 449095, **e-mail:** northshoe@mcmail.com, 10–6 MON–WED, 10–8 THUR, FRI, 9–6 SAT, 10–6 SUN.

ST JAMES RETAIL PARK, DUMBARTON, SCOTLAND G82 1RB, ☎ 01389 762897, **e-mail:** northshoe@mcmail.com, 10–6 MON–WED, SAT, SUN, 10–7 THUR, 9–6 FRI.

UNIT 8, MEADOWBANK RETAIL PARK, MARIONVILLE ROAD, EDINBURGH, SCOTLAND EH7, FAX: 0131 652 2885, **e-mail:** northshoe@mcmail.com, 10–6 MON–WED, 10–8 THUR, 10–7 FRI, 9–6 SAT, 11–5 SUN.

11 GRAHAMS ROAD, CENTRAL RETAIL PARK, FALKIRK, SCOTLAND FK1 1LD, ☎ 01324 671177, **e-mail:** northshoe@mcmail.com, 10–6 MON–WED, 10–7 THUR, FRI, 9–6 SAT, 10–5 SUN.

UNIT 9, HAMILTON RETAIL PARK, DOUGLAS STREET, HAMILTON, SCOTLAND ML3 0DF, ☎ 01698 286120, **e-mail:** northshoe@mcmail.com, 10–7 MON–FRI, 8 ON THUR, 9–6 SAT, 10–6 SUN.

UNIT 4, PHASE 2, RIVERWAY RETAIL PARK, IRVINE, SCOTLAND KA12 8AG, ☎ 01294 204042, **e-mail:** northshoe@mcmail.com, 9–6 MON–WED, SAT, 9–7 THUR, FRI, 10–6 SUN.

PORTLAND GATE, KILMARNOCK, SCOTLAND KA1 1HZ, ☎ 01563 537145, **e-mail:** northshoe@mcmail.com, 9–5.30 MON–WED, 9–6 THUR–SAT, 11–5 SUN.

8–20 HIGH STREET, KIRKCALDY, SCOTLAND KY1 1LU, ☎ 01592 205257, **e-mail:** northshoe@mcmail.com, 9–6 MON–SAT, 11–5 SUN.

UNITS 55A AND 25, THE PLAZA SHOPPING CENTRE, PAISLEY, SCOTLAND PA1 1EL, ☎ 0141 848 9127, **e-mail:** northshoe@mcmail.com, 9–6 MON–SAT, 11–5 SUN.

UNIT 3A, WEST END RETAIL PARK, CROW ROAD, PARTICK, GLASGOW, SCOTLAND G11 7SA, ☎ 0141 337 3822, **e-mail:** northshoe@mcmail.com, 10–6 MON–WED, 10–8 THUR, 10–7 FRI, 9–6 SAT, 10–6 SUN.

181 NETHERAULD HOUSE ROAD, POLLOCKSHAWS, GLASGOW, SCOTLAND G43 2YP, ☎ 0141 632 5841, **e-mail:** northshoe@mcmail.com, 10–6 MON–WED, 10–7 THUR, FRI, 9–6 SAT, 10–5.30 SUN.

UNIT 10, THE CALEDONIAN CENTRE, NEW ASHTREE STREET, WISHAW, SCOTLAND ML2 7UR, ☎ 01698 350055, **e-mail:** northshoe@mcmail.com, 10–6 MON–WED, 10–8 THUR, FRI, 9–6 SAT, 10–6 SUN. **PERMANENT DISCOUNT OUTLET**

See page 240 (CHESH)

THE TOY FACTORY

UNIT 12, STERLING MILLS DESIGNER OUTLET VILLAGE, DEVONDALE, TILLICOULTRY, CLACKMANNANSHIRE, SCOTLAND FK13 6HQ, ☎ 01259 751951, www.thetoyfactory.co.uk, 10–6 SEVEN DAYS A WEEK.
FACTORY SHOP IN A FACTORY SHOPPING VILLAGE

See page 277 (LANCS)

TK MAXX

UNIT 10 MEADOW BANK RETAIL PARK, EDINBURGH, SCOTLAND EH7 5TS, ☎ 0131 661 6611, www.tkmaxx.com, 10–8 MON–FRI, 9–6 SAT, 11–5 SUN.

UNIT C1261, CALLENDER SQUARE SHOPPING CENTRE, HIGH STREET, FALKIRK, SCOTLAND FK1 1UU, ☎ 01324 619881, www.tkmaxx.com, 9–5.30 MON–WED, 7.30 ON THUR, 9–6 FRI–SAT, 12–5 SUN.

THE SAUCHIEHALL CENTRE, GLASGOW, SCOTLAND G2 3ER, ☎ 0141 331 0411, www.tkmaxx.com, 9–5.30 MON–FRI, 7 ON THUR, 9–6 SAT, 12–5 SUN.

UNIT 5, ST ENOCH'S CENTRE, 55 ST ENOCH'S SQUARE, GLASGOW, SCOTLAND G1 4BW, ☎ 0141 221 9393, www.tkmaxx.com, 9–6 MON–FRI, 8 ON THUR, 9.30–6 SAT, 11–5 SUN.

GLENCAIRN RETAIL PARK, KILMARNOCK, SCOTLAND, ☎ 01563 532486, www.tkmaxx.com, PHONE FOR DETAILS.

UNIT 25–26 MERCAT CENTRE, KIRKCALDY, FIFE, SCOTLAND KY1 1N1, FAX: 01592 644488, www.tkmaxx.com, 9–5.30 MON– SAT, 11–5 SUN.

UNIT 5, ALMONDVALE WEST RETAIL PARK, ALMONDVALE ROAD, LIVINGSTON, SCOTLAND EH54 6QX, ☎ 01506 462060, www.tkmaxx.com, 10–8 MON–FRI, 9–6 SAT, 11–5 SUN.

THE PHOENIX RETAIL PARK, LINWOOD ROAD, PAISLEY, SCOTLAND, ☎ 0141 849 6796, www.tkmaxx.com, PHONE FOR DETAILS.

ST CATHERINE'S RETAIL PARK, SCOTLAND, ☎ 01738 636751, www.tkmaxx.com, PHONE FOR DETAILS. **PERMANENT DISCOUNT OUTLET**

See page 232 (BEDS)

TOG 24

LOCH LOMOND FACTORY OUTLETS, MAIN STREET, ALEXANDRIA, STRATHCLYDE, SCOTLAND G83 0UG, ☎ 01389 607175, **e-mail:** mail-order@tog24.com, www.tog24.com, 9.30–5.30 SEVEN DAYS A WEEK.

MCARTHURGLEN DESIGNER OUTLET LIVINGSTON, ALMONDVALE AVENUE, LIVINGSTON, SCOTLAND EH54 6QX, ☎ 01506 413630, **e-mail:** mail-order@tog24.com, www.tog24.com, 10–6 SEVEN DAYS A WEEK, 8 ON THUR.

STERLING MILLS DESIGNER OUTLET VILLAGE, TILLICOULTRY, CLACKMANNANSHIRE, SCOTLAND FK13 6HN, ☎ 01259 753911, **e-mail:** mail-order@tog24.com, www.tog24.com, 10–6 SEVEN DAYS A WEEK.

FREEPORT VILLAGE FIVE SISTERS, WEST CALDER, JUNCTION 4 OF M8, WEST LOTHIAN, SCOTLAND EH55 8QB, ☎ 01501 762823, **e-mail:** mail-order@tog24.com, www.tog24.com, 10–6 SEVEN DAYS A WEEK. **FACTORY SHOP IN A FACTORY SHOPPING VILLAGE**

See page 240. (CHESH)

TOYWORLD STORE FACTORY OUTLET

MCARTHURGLEN DESIGNER OUTLET, ALMONDVALE AVENUE, LIVINGSTON, WEST LOTHIAN, SCOTLAND EH54 6QX, ☎ 01506 462 221, www.thetoyfactory.co.uk, 10–6 SEVEN DAYS, 8 ON THUR. **FACTORY SHOP IN A FACTORY SHOPPING VILLAGE**

See page 241 (CHESH)

SCOTTISH HIGHLANDS AND ISLANDS

FOOTWEAR DISCOUNT CENTRE

JOHN STREET, OBAN, SCOTLAND PA34 5NS, ☎ 01631 563633, **e-mail:** billyt@eggconnect.net 9–5.30 MON–SAT, 11–4 SUN. **PERMANENT DISCOUNT OUTLET**

Two floors of more than 10,000 pairs of quality branded footwear such as Ecco, Lotus, Nil Simile and Equity, some of which are seconds, discontinued lines, factory directs and Italian imports. Women's shoes, fashion courts to leather walking shoes, from size 2 to 9. Men's leather shoes in sizes 5 to 13, including walking boots, trainers, work boots and safety boots. Children's shoes and Wellingtons.

K SHOES FACTORY SHOP

UNIT 26A, WELLGATE, DUNDEE, ANGUS, SCOTLAND DD1 1DB, ☎ 01382 322048, 9.30–5.30 MON– SAT, 12–4 SUN. **FACTORY SHOP**

See page 245 (CUMB)

MATALAN

CONSTITUTION STREET, ABERDEEN SCOTLAND AB24 5ET, ☎ 01224 650690, FAX: 01224 624235, www.matalan.co.uk, 10–8 MON–FRI, 9.30–5.30 SAT, 10–6 SUN.

UNIT1, INCHES RETAIL PARK, INVERNESS, SCOTLAND IV2 3TW, ☎ 01463 227250, FAX: 01463 224772, www.matalan.co.uk, 10–8 MON–FRI, 9.30–5.30 SAT, 10–6 SUN.

VICTORIA ROAD, PERTH, SCOTLAND PH8 9LW, ☎ 01738 587020, FAX: 01738 443883, www.matalan.co.uk, 10–8 MON–FRI, 9.30–5.30 SAT, 10–6 SUN. **PERMANENT DISCOUNT OUTLET**

See page 232 (BEDS)

TK MAXX

KITTY BREWSTER RETAIL PARK, BEDFORD ROAD, ABERDEEN, SCOTLAND, ☎ 01224 497810, www.tkmaxx.com, PHONE FOR DETAILS.

WELLGATE SHOPPING CENTRE, DUNDEE SCOTLAND DD1 2DB, ☎ 01382 322288, www.tkmaxx.com, 9–5.30 MON–WED, FRI, SAT, 9–8 THUR, 12–5 SUN.

UNIT 2, ACADEMY RETAIL PARK, STROTHERS LANE, INVERNESS, SCOTLAND, ☎ 01463 729729, www.tkmaxx.com, 9–5.30 MON–FRI, 7 ON THUR, 9–6 SAT. **PERMANENT DISCOUNT OUTLET**

See page 232 (BEDS)

TOG 24

CITY QUAY, CAMPERDOWN STREET, DUNDEE, SCOTLAND DD1 3ND, ☎ 01382 223883, **e-mail:** mail-order@tog24.com, www.tog24.com, 9.30–5.30 MON–SAT, 11–5 SUN. **FACTORY SHOP**

See page 240 (CHESH)

TOYWORLD STORE FACTORY OUTLET

CITY QUAY FACTORY OUTLET VILLAGE, VICTORIA DOCK, CAMPERDOWN STREET, DUNDEE, SCOTLAND DD1 3ND, ☎ 01382 206333, www.thetoyfactory.co.uk, 9.30–5.30 MON–SAT, 11–5 SUN. **FACTORY SHOP IN A FACTORY SHOPPING VILLAGE**

See page 241 (CHESH)

DIY/Renovation

BEDFORDSHIRE

ARCHITECTURAL ANTIQUES

70 PEMBROKE STREET, BEDFORD, BEDFORDSHIRE MK40 3RQ, ☎ 01234 213131, FAX: 01234 309858, 12–5 MON–FRI, 9–5 SAT. **ARCHITECTURAL SALVAGE**

Buy and sell antiques, good quality furniture, original fireplaces and all architectural salvage. They have a large selection of original Georgian, Victorian and Edwardian fireplaces in marble, slate, cast iron, mahogany, oak and pine, and provide a restoration and installation service. All types and sizes of internal and external doors and cupboards, glazed doors and bookshelves; rolltop baths, basins, glazed and stone sinks, brass taps, radiators and towel rails, stone flooring, tiles, bricks, floorboards, moulded skirting and architrave. Balustrades, chimney pots, garden edging, grates and timber; good quality antique chests of drawers, wardrobes, dressing tables, dining chairs, dressers, bookcases, mirrors, clocks, lamps, radios and other unusual items.

D S & A G PRIGMORE & SON,

MILL COTTAGE, MILL ROAD, COLMWORTH, BEDFORDSHIRE MK44 2NU, ☎ 01234 376264, 8–4 MON–FRI, 8–12 SAT. **ARCHITECTURAL SALVAGE**

Reclaimed building materials, oak and pine beams, slates, tiles, bricks, woodblock flooring, doors and other quality items including a good selection of 2-inch Tudor-style bricks. Also RSJs.

NO FRILLS DIY STORE

WINGATE ROAD, LUTON, BEDFORDSHIRE LU4 8PX, ☎ 01582 585 509, FAX: 01582 562780, 9–8 MON–SAT, 10–4 SUN. **PERMANENT DISCOUNT OUTLET**

Not a discount operator as such but a great place for bargains. Now part of the Focus DIY Group, they stock everything you would find in B&Q or Homebase but at cheaper prices. Paints, tiles, bathroom equipment, patio furniture, toiletries, sheds, lighting, crockery, bedding, pans, kitchen units, barbecues in season.

BERKSHIRE

BATHROOM WORLD

51 HIGH STREET, ASCOT, BERKSHIRE SL5 7GH, ☎ 01344 873366, FAX: 01344 626688, www.bathrooms-showers.co.uk, 9–5.30 MON–SAT, 10.30–4 SUN. **PERMANENT DISCOUNT OUTLET**

Fantastic, extensive bathroom showrooms pandering to any taste or budget. Many products are exclusive to the group who are continually expanding their already large product portfolio. The buying power of the group ensures that prices are always extremely competitive. Experienced staff and designers guide customers through styles and specifications as part of a free service.

BMJ POWER

27 BOULTON ROAD, READING, BERKSHIRE RG2 0NH, ☎ 0118 975 8822, FAX: 0118 975 2212, www.bmjdirect.com, 8.30–5 MON–FRI, 9.30–5 ON WED, 8.30–4 SAT, 10–4 SUN.

295 HIGH STREET, SLOUGH, BERKSHIRE SL1 1BD, ☎ 01753 820445, www.bmjdirect.com, 8.30–5 MON–SAT, 9–5 ON WED. **FACTORY SHOP**

Once owned by Black & Decker to provide after-sale service to their customers and to sell discounted end of line and returned products, BMJ Power Ltd is now an independent company specialising in the sale and repair of electrical products. As well as selling a full range of power tools and electrical garden products from Black & Decker, many of them discontinued lines or with damaged packaging or returns, they also offer returned products from a number of other manufacturers through their 38 retail stores, which also deal with repairs. Factory reconditioned products carry the Gold Seal of Approval which means they come complete with a manufacturers full guarantee, but at a substantial savings. Other manufacturers stocked include De Walt, power tools primarily for the professional user and tradesman; Flymo, electric garden products; Alto-Kew, electric powered pressure washers; Delta, electric powered woodworking products; Kress electric power tools. BMJ also produce a quarterly catalogue for those unable to visit their stores. Phone 0870 7323 023 for details of your nearest outlet. You can also phone this number to find out if BMJ s nationwide network of repair collection agents operate near you.

BRISTOL

AU TEMPS PERDU

28 30 MIDLAND ROAD, ST PHILIP, BRISTOL BS2 0JY, ☎ 0117 929 9143, **e-mail:** mail@autempsperdu.com, www.autempsperdu.com, 10–5 TUE–SAT. **ARCHITECTURAL SALVAGE**

General architectural salvage with French and English stock: bathroom fittings, fire surrounds, door and furniture stripping, landscaping materials, paving and Victorian fireplaces.

CROYDEX FACTORY SHOP

169 WHITELADIES ROAD, CLIFTON, BRISTOL BS8 2SQ, ☎ 0117 946 7361, 11–5.30 MON–SAT. **FACTORY SHOP**

Factory shop selling the Croydex range of branded bathroom equipment and accessories: shower curtains, towels rails, toilet roll holders, brushes, shelves, bathroom cabinets, mats, mirrors, bath panels, ceramic and wooden accessories, at discounts averaging 40% but up to 70%.

SOUTH WEST ARCHITECTURAL SALVAGE

2830 MIDLAND ROAD, ST PHILIPS, BRISTOL BS2 0JY, ☎ 0117 929 9143, www.autempsperdu.com, 10–5 TUE–SAT. **ARCHITECTURAL SALVAGE**

Established for more than 21 years, this architectural salvage specialist stocks more than 300 stripped doors and general salvage. Au Temps Perdu is also located on this site selling fireplaces, bathroom ware and general fixtures and fittings for period houses. Also sells stained glass and has a cabinet maker on site. Restoration ironwork also carried out on site.

CAMBRIDGESHIRE

CHARLTON RECYCLED AUTOPARTS LTD

GRAVEL PIT HILL, THRIPLOW, NEAR DUXFORD, CAMBRIDGESHIRE SG8 7HZ, ☎ 01223 863386, FAX: 01223 837010, **e-mail:** admin@charltonautoparts.co.uk, www.charltonautoparts.co.uk, 8.30–5.30 MON–FRI, 8.30–5 SAT. **PERMANENT DISCOUNT OUTLET**

Sells car spares and accessories, but its not like any usual spares or salvage yard. All parts have been checked, tagged and stored in a warehouse on a computer-controlled inventory. The shop is clean, efficient and all parts have a 101-day guarantee. Although the main business is used car parts, they also often stock brand new parts, either from bankrupt or flood damaged stock. Specialises in spare parts for vehicles including Mercedes, Chrysler, Jeep and Mitsubishi.

RAMSEY PAINT COMPANY

16 LITTLE WHYTE, RAMSEY, CAMBRIDGESHIRE PE26 1DS, ☎ 01487 710876, 8–5 MON–FRI, 9–12 SAT.

19A EAST STREET, ST IVES, CAMBRIDGESHIRE PE27 5PD, ☎ 01480 465002, 8–5 MON–FRI, 9–12 SAT, CLOSED WEEKDAYS BETWEEN 1–2. **PERMANENT DISCOUNT OUTLET**

Paints, paint accessories, wood stains and wallpapers at discounted prices. Stocks most major paint brands including Crown and holds 100 wallpaper books which you can order from at discounts of 20%. Mainly caters for the trade, but will serve the public, too. More than 6,000 colours to choose from. An electronic spectrometer colour matching service is also available to enable an exact paint match with fabrics, wallpapers etc.

SOLOPARK PLC

STATION ROAD, NR PAMPISFORD, CAMBRIDGESHIRE CB2 4HB, ☎ 01223 834663, FAX: 01223 834 780, **e-mail:** info@solopark.co.uk, www.solopark.co.uk, 8–5 MON–THUR, 8–4 FRI, SAT, 9–1 SUN. **ARCHITECTURAL SALVAGE**

Reclaimed bricks including soft reds, Suffolk whites, Cambridge stocks, Tudors, roofing tiles, slates, timbers, oak beams, doors, wood block, flooring, railway sleepers, chimney pots, York stone, paviors, granite setts, gates, fireplaces, statuary, garden furniture, etc.

ST IVES TILES

HIGH STREET, BLUNTISHAM, HUNTINGDON, CAMBRIDGESHIRE PE28 3LD, ☎ 01487 840471, FAX: 01487 843124, **e-mail:** info@trademarktiles.co.uk, 8.30–6 MON–FRI, 9–4 SAT, 10–3 SUN. **PERMANENT DISCOUNT OUTLET**

Importers of top quality floor and wall tiles, mainly Italian and Spanish terracotta and quarry style and sold at discounts of one third on selected lines. Warehouse-type shop with a wide selection of tiles displayed and laid to give you some idea of what they look like. One reader saved 50% on their floor tiles here, having been quoted £600 elsewhere. They also offer a fixing service at very competitive rates.

TILE CLEARING HOUSE

UNIT 12, CORAL PARK TRADING ESTATE, COLDHAMS LANE, CAMBRIDGE, CAMBRIDGESHIRE CB1 3EA, ☎ 01223 305953, FAX: 01223 305950, 8–6 MON–FRI, 9–6 SAT, 10–4 SUN.

UNIT 1, BRASSEY CLOSE, LINCOLN ROAD, PETERBOROUGH, CAMBRIDGESHIRE PE1 2A2, FAX: 01733 553222, 8–6 MON–FRI, 9–6 SAT, 10–4 SUN. **PERMANENT DISCOUNT OUTLET**

Over 500 ranges of top quality ceramic wall and floor tiles permanently in stock, plus a comprehensive range of grouts, adhesives, tools and accessories to complete the job. By buying direct from the manufacturer and passing the savings on to the customer, their prices are very competitive. Moreover, everything you see is in stock, so there's no waiting for orders to be processed. Save up to 75% on manufacturer's recommended selling prices.

CHESHIRE

ABAKHAN FABRICS

65–67 CHURCH ROAD, BIRKENHEAD, CHESHIRE L42 5LE, ☎ 0151 647 6983, FAX: 0151 650 0726, 9–5 MON–SAT.

812 GREENWAY ROAD, BIRKENHEAD, CHESHIRE L42 0NG, ☎ 0151 652 5195, FAX: 0151 653 8942, 9–5 MON–SAT, 8 ON THUR, 10–4 SUN. **FACTORY SHOP**

With five outlets in the North West and one in Staffordshire, Abakhan Fabrics are as well known for the emphasis they put on value for money as they are for the huge variety of fabrics, needlecrafts, haberdashery, gifts, knitting yarns and soft furnishings, all gathered from around the world. The large mill shop complex in Wales has a new home and garden department, baskets of remnant fabrics, wools, yarns and unrivalled selections of fabrics sold by the metre from evening wear, bridal wear and crepe de Chine to curtaining, nets and velvets. There are more than ten tonnes of remnant fabrics and 10,000 rolls, all at mill shop prices. Abakhan is able to offer such bargains through bulk buying, or selling clearance lines, job lots and seconds.

CHESHIRE BRICK & SLATE COMPANY

BROOK HOUSE FARM, SALTERS BRIDGE, TARVIN SANDS, NR CHESTER, CHESHIRE CH3 8NR, ☎ 01829 740883, FAX: 01829 740481, 8–5.30 MON–FRI, 8–4.30 SAT, 10–4 SUN. **ARCHITECTURAL SALVAGE**

Reclaimed bricks, slates, setts, tiles, lamposts, doors, Victorian bathroom suites, fireplaces, ranges, garden ornaments, beams, Yorkshire paving and brass door furniture.

CUT-PRICE WALLPAPERS

13–17 MILL STREET, CREWE, CHESHIRE CW2 7AE, ☎ 01270 250117, FAX: 01270 257083, 9–5.30 MON–SAT, 10–4 SUN. **PERMANENT DISCOUNT OUTLET**

Offers much more than the name suggests: paint, bedding, curtains, fabrics, curtain poles, pictures, mirrors and a host of other decorative and furnishing items. Brands stocked include Crown,

Vymura, Shand-Kydd, Coloroll, Graham & Brown and Zen. There are two floors of wallpaper in stock but if you can't find what you want, pattern books are available.

CWV BRANDS AT HOME FACTORY SHOP

TALBOT ROAD, HYDE, CHESHIRE SK14 4EJ, ☎ 0161 351 3070, **e-mail:** pamhindle@englewood.co.uk, 9.30–5.30 MON–FRI, 9–5 SAT, 10–4 SUN, 10–5 BANK HOLIDAYS. **FACTORY SHOP**

One of two CWV factory shops offering discontinued lines or seconds of bedlinen, wallpaper and fabrics by Coloroll, Vymura and Wilman Interiors at discounted prices. Savings of more than 50% can be made. For example, Coloroll, Vymura and Wilman wallpaper at £1.99 a roll or less, vinyls £1.99 a roll or less. Coloroll single quilt cover and pillow case, £6.50. Wilman curtain fabric, £3.50 a metre or less; Wilman upholstery fabric, £5 a metre or less. Towels, lamps, candles, kitchen accessories, bathroom accessories and baby products are available, too. Free car parking. Disabled access. They also maintain a data base to inform customers of offers and sale dates.

GLYN WEBB

UNIT 1C, THE BOUGHTON CENTRE, BOUGHTON, CHESTER, CHESHIRE CH3 5AF, ☎ 01244 344 144, 9–8 MON–FRI, 9–6 SAT, 10–4 SUN AND BANK HOLIDAYS. **PERMANENT DISCOUNT OUTLET**

Established in 1974, Glyn Webb are now one of the largest stockists of discount branded wallpaper and paint in the UK, with 25 stores across the country. They specialise in discontinued and end-of-line branded stock, as well as perfect quality products, clearance stock and own-brand paint and wallpaper. Top brand names include Johnston, Coloroll, Graham & Brown, Pilkingtons and Ronseal. The company's strong point is the sheer variety of goods available under one roof, all at bargain prices. For details of your nearest branch phone 0161 621 4500.

GREAT NORTHERN ARCHITECTURAL ANTIQUES

NEW RUSSIA HALL, CHESTER ROAD, TATTENHALL, CHESHIRE CH3 9AH, ☎ 01829 770796, FAX: 01829 770971, **e-mail:** archantique@greatnorthern.co.uk, www.greatnothern.co.uk, 9.30–5 SEVEN DAYS A WEEK. **ARCHITECTURAL SALVAGE**

Doors, panelled rooms, sanitary fittings, stained glass, garden furniture, York stone flags, fireplaces, gates, railings, curios, bric-a-brac and decorative stonework.

NOSTALGIA ANTIQUE FIREPLACE

61 SHAW HEATH, STOCKPORT, CHESHIRE SK3 8BH, ☎ 0161 477 7706, FAX: 0161 477 2267, **e-mail:** info@nostalgiafireplaces.co.uk, www.nostalgia-uk.com, 10–6 TUE–FRI, 10–5 SAT. **ARCHITECTURAL SALVAGE**

A constant stock of more than 1,200 genuine antique fireplaces of all descriptions and materials dating from 1750 to 1920. Also lots of Victorian and Edwardian washbasins and toilets. Expert restoration is carried out on this extensive stock and a wealth of advice is available.

THE BATH RE-ENAMELLING COMPANY

55 MAIN ROAD, WORLESTON, NANTWICH, CHESHIRE CW5 CDN, ☎ 01270 626554, FAX: 01270 627632, www.bathreenamelling.co.uk, 9–5 MON, TUE, THUR, FRI, 9–1 SAT. **ARCHITECTURAL SALVAGE**

Bath re-enamelling carried out by fully trained operatives in your home for £178 or baths can be collected for stove enamelling or vitreous enamelling at 1100 degrees Centigrade. Reclaimed baths for sale. The service is available throughout mainland Britain.

TILE CLEARING HOUSE

WHITEHALL INDUSTRIAL ESTATE, HERROD AVENUE, REDDISH, STOCKPORT, CHESHIRE, ☎ 0161 476 4355, 8–6 MON–FRI, 9–6 SAT, 10–4 SUN. **PERMANENT DISCOUNT OUTLET**

See page 345 (CAMBS)

WILKINSONS HOME & GARDEN STORES

THE MARKET CENTRE, CREWE, CHESHIRE CW1 2NG, ☎ 01270 250754, www.wilko.co.uk, 8.30–5.30 MON–WED, 8.30–6.30 THUR–SAT, 10–4 SUN. **PERMANENT DISCOUNT OUTLET**

Family-owned business offering value on the high street through its 205 stores, selling 25,000 high quality, low-priced essential everyday products for all the family including kitchenware, household disposables, clothing, DIY decoration, stationery, homewares, bedlinen, picture frames, china, cutlery, toys, pet foot, curtains, mirrors, gardening equipment including outdoor furniture, Christmas decorations, confectionery and seasonal goods. It also caters for the ardent gardener with fertiliser, grass seed loose or boxed plants, insecticides, composts both multi-purpose or tub and basket garden tools, strimmers, hoses and attachments, watering cans, water butts, wheelbarrows, and reels on wheels. In season, they sell bedding plants, garden lights, coolboxes, paint, paint brushes and rollers, and climbing plants such as honeysuckle, but as the summer progresses these are replaced by barbecues and picnic ranges. Phone 01909 505505 for details of your local outlet or visit their website.

WOOD LAMINATES DIRECT

166 NANTWICH ROAD, CREWE, CHESHIRE CW2 6BG, ☎ 01270 255992, **e-mail:** allwoodfloors@yahoo.co.uk, www.allwoodfloors.co.uk, 10–5 MON–SAT, 11–4 SUN. **PERMANENT DISCOUNT OUTLET**

Wood Laminates Direct supply and fit laminate and real wood flooring at very competitive prices: laminate from £7.50 to £18.99 a metre; real wood from £29.99 a metre.

COUNTY DURHAM

BMJ POWER LTD

C/O BLACK & DECKER, GREEN LANE, SPENNYMOOR, CO DURHAM DL16 6JG, ☎ 01388 813888, www.bmjdirect.com, 8.30–5 MON–FRI, 9–5 WED, 8.30–2 SAT. **FACTORY SHOP**

See page 343 (BERKS)

GLYN WEBB

BRIDGE ROAD, CHANDLERS WHARF, STOCKTON ON TEES, CO DURHAM TS18 3BA, ☎ 01642 606699, 9–8 MON–FRI, 9–6 SAT, 10–4 SUN AND BANK HOLIDAYS. **PERMANENT DISCOUNT OUTLET**

See page 346 (CHESH)

NO FRILLS DIY STORE

MEYNELL ROAD, OFF WHESSOE ROAD, DARLINGTON, CO DURHAM DL3 0XZ, ☎ 01325 481414, FAX: 01325 464020, 9–8 MON–SAT, 10–4 SUN. **PERMANENT DISCOUNT OUTLET**

See page 343 (BEDS)

TECAZ

TECAZ HOUSE, PORTRACK LANE, STOCKTON, CO DURHAM TS18 2HQ, ☎ 01642 670100, FAX: 0191 523 8148, **e-mail:** northshields@swift957ltd.com, www.swift957ltd.com, 9–6 MON–FRI, 9–5 SAT, 10–4 SUN.

TECAZ HOUSE, RYHOPE STREET, RYHOPE, SUNDERLAND, TYNE & WEAR SR2 9QR, ☎ 0191 523 8164, FAX: 0191 523 8148, **e-mail:** northshields@swift957ltd.com, www.swift957ltd.com, 9–6 MON–FRI, 9–5 SAT, 10–4 SUN. **PERMANENT DISCOUNT OUTLET**

Vast area displaying over 150 bathroom suites, 50 shower cubicles from manufacturers like Heritage, Armitage Shanks, Shires, Vitra, Twyfords and Rocca, as well as 50 kitchen and bedroom ranges from Symphony and PWS, including the electrical equipment to go in them by well-known brands. There are tiles, baths, sinks, taps, shower trays, showers, soap dishes, toilets, loo roll holders and mirrors, and they carry huge stocks of many of the ranges. Because Tecaz buy in large numbers, they can get better discounts from the manufacturer, many of which they pass on to the customer. They offer a free, no-obligation planning and design service, interest free credit on many ranges, and delivery can be arranged.

TILE CLEARING HOUSE

UNIT A & B, NORTH ROAD INDUSTRIAL ESTATE, MEYNELL ROAD, DARLINGTON, CO DURHAM DL3 0XA, ☎ 01325 466868, FAX: 01325 353275, 8–6 MON–FRI, 9–6 SAT, 10–4 SUN. **PERMANENT DISCOUNT OUTLET**

See page 345 (CAMBS)

CORNWALL

CORNISH MARKET WORLD

STADIUM RETAIL PARK, PAR, ST AUSTELL, CORNWALL PL25 3RP, ☎ 01726 812544, FAX: 01726 812346, **e-mail:** info@cornishmarketworld.co.uk, www.cornishmarketworld.co.uk, 9–5 SAT, SUN AND BANK HOLIDAYS, AND WED JUNE-SEPT. **PERMANENT DISCOUNT OUTLET**

Huge indoor market that sells an enormous range of goods and food at very competitive prices: for example, a good quality breadmaker, £45. Sells clothes, fabrics, phones, bags, tools, electric equipment, motability equipment, jewellery and furniture. There is a good butchers, fish, and fruit and veg stands.

NO FRILLS DIY STORE

STADIUM PARK, ST AUSTELL, CORNWALL PL25 3RP, ☎ 01726 814791, FAX: 01726 817953, 9–8 MON–SAT, 10–4 SUN. **PERMANENT DISCOUNT OUTLET**

See page 343 (BEDS)

TRAGO MILLS

ARWENACK STREET, FALMOUTH, CORNWALL TR11 3LF, ☎ 01326 315738, www.trago.co.uk, 9–5.30 MON–SAT, 10.45–4.45 SUN.

TWOWATERSFOOT, LISKEARD, CORNWALL PL14 6HY, ☎ 01579 348877, www.trago.co.uk, 9–5.30 MON–SAT, 10.45- 4.45 SUN. **PERMANENT DISCOUNT OUTLET**

The historic Tragos original Cornish site is in the Glynn Valley on the A38 between Liskeard and Bodmin. You can bargain hunt here for brand name art materials, bathrooms and bedrooms and ceramics, carpets and rugs, clothing, DIY and home improvement, furniture, garden accessories, gifts, textiles, lighting, pet care, saddlery, stationery, tools, motoring products, toys and sport equipment and much more. There is a restaurant and picnic area by the beautiful Fowey river bank, free parking and disabled access. The Falmouth store is smaller, with only limited free car parking outside, but there is a public car park adjacent.

CUMBRIA

CUMBRIA ARCHITECTURAL SALVAGE

BIRKS HILL, RAUGHTON HEAD, CARLISLE, CUMBRIA CA5 7DH, ☎ 01697 476420, FAX: 01697 476754, 9–5 MON–FRI, 9–12 SAT. **ARCHITECTURAL SALVAGE**

Period fireplaces, ranges, old free-standing baths, reclaimed doors, oak beams, cast iron radiators, church pews, building materials and general fittings from old houses. Also stocks additional bathroom fittings.

WILSON RECLAMATION SERVICES

YEW TREE BARN, LOW NEWTON, NEAR GRANGE-OVER-SANDS, CUMBRIA LA11 6JP, ☎ 01539 531498, www.yewtreebarn.co.uk, 10–5 MON–SAT, 11–5 SUN. **ARCHITECTURAL SALVAGE**

Fireplaces, oak beams, doors, bathroom fittings, flagstones, chimney pots, quoins and antiques. They also offer antique restoration, and there is a café on site.

DERBYSHIRE

GLYN WEBB

ASCOT DRIVE, DERBY, DERBYSHIRE DE24 8QZ, ☎ 01332 204282, 9–8 MON–SAT, 10–4 SUN AND BANK HOLIDAYS. **PERMANENT DISCOUNT OUTLET**

See page 346 (CHESH)

WILKINSON STORES

13 INSTITUTE LANE, ALFRETON, DERBYSHIRE DE55 7BQ, ☎ 01773 836845, www.wilko.co.uk, 9–5.30 MON–THUR, SAT, 9–6 FRI, 10–2 SUN. MAIL ORDER. **PERMANENT DISCOUNT OUTLET**

See page 346 (CHESH)

DEVON

ADRIAN AGER

GREAT HALL, NORTH STREET, ASHBURTON, DEVON TQ13 7QD, ☎ 01364 653189, FAX: 01364 653189, **e-mail:** enquiries@adrianager.co.uk, www.adrianfager.co.uk, 8–5 MON–FRI, 10–4 SAT. **ARCHITECTURAL SALVAGE**

An extensive array of items are on offer at Ashburton Marbles' 18th century showrooms. These include period marble and wood chimney pieces, cast iron inserts, fire baskets, fenders, guards, etc and anything related to your fireplace spanning 250 years. There is also a varied selection of furnishings, including Art Deco suites, Victorian chaise longues, comfortable Victorian sofas, gilt overmantels and mirrors, chandeliers and wall lights from country-made cast iron to French ormolu. For the garden, there are cast iron fountains, stone bird baths, sun dials, staddle stones, Moroccan pots, reconstituted stone bird baths, stone sundial stands, lead planters, massive olive jars, planters, garden statuary and furniture. Delivery can be arranged throughout the UK.

CLASSIC COUNTRY RANGES

4 WEBBERS YARD, DARTINGTON, NR TOTNES, SOUTH DEVON TQ9 6JY, ☎ 01803 865555, FAX: 01803 867267, **e-mail:** info@classiccountryranges.com, www.classiccountryranges.com, 9–5 MON–FRI, 10–1 SAT. **PERMANENT DISCOUNT OUTLET**

Specialist suppliers of factory renovated Aga and Rayburn cookers, plus a range of new appliances for cooking or central heating, all at very competitive prices. Old Agas are completely dismantled, sandblasted inside, all the enamel parts re-enamelled in the customer's choice of colour, and re-assembled with new burners and fully tested. Savings of at least £1,000 can be made compared with buying a new Aga or Rayburn. Also sells an Aga equivalent, the Trianco Redfyre, which costs about £1,000 less than an Aga but has the equivalent insides, although the outside looks different. Main agent for Nobel and Sandyford products, spares and discount heating materials especially flue products. Installations undertaken at competitive prices. Also sell a range of Bridgewater pottery.

COLIN BAKER

CROWN HILL, HALBERTON, TIVERTON, DEVON EX16 7AY, ☎ 01884 820152, 91884 820152, www.colinbaker.co.uk, 8.30–5 MON–FRI, 8.30–12 SAT. PHONE FIRST. **ARCHITECTURAL SALVAGE**

Reclaimed oak beams and joists, oak floorboards and period joinery. Quality timber for furniture making and flooring, doors, mullioned windows. Also new kiln-dried seasoned oak floorboards.

M C SLATES

BOW STATION YARD, BOW, NEAR CREDITON, DEVON EX17 6JD, ☎ 01363 82598, 8–4.30 MON–FRI, 9–1 SAT. **ARCHITECTURAL SALVAGE**

Reclaimed roofing slates and new terracotta flooring natural not ceramic.

TILE CLEARING HOUSE

12 TRUSHAM ROAD, BARTON TRADING ESTATE, EXETER, DEVON EX2 8HQ, ☎ 01392 411110, FAX: 01392 411270, 8–6 MON–FRI, 9–6 SAT, 10–4 SUN. **PERMANENT DISCOUNT OUTLET**

See page 345 (CAMBS)

TOBYS (THE OLD BUILDERS YARD AND STORE)

EXMINSTER STATION, EXMINSTER, EXETER, DEVON EX6 8DZ, ☎ 01392 833499, 9–5 MON–FRI, 9.30–4.30 SAT, 10.30–4.30 SUN.

BRUNEL ROAD INDUSTRIAL ESTATE, NEWTON ABBOT, DEVON TQ12 4PB, ☎ 01626 351767, 8.30–4.30 MON–FRI, 9.30–4.30 SAT.

TORRE STATION, TORQUAY ROAD, TORQUAY, DEVON, ☎ 01803 212222, 10–5 MON–SAT, 10.30–4.30 SUN, BANK HOLIDAYS. **ARCHITECTURAL SALVAGE**

Ten thousand square feet of reclaimed doors, windows, slates, sanitaryware, bricks, chimney pots, roof tiles, timber and pine stripping. Also sell antique and imported furniture, bric-a-brac and much more.

TRAGO MILLS SHOPPING AND LEISURE PARKS

LIVERTON, NEWTON ABBOT, DEVON TQ12 6JD, ☎ 01626 821111, www.trago.co.uk, 9–5.30 MON–SAT, 10.45–4.45 SUN. **PERMANENT DISCOUNT OUTLET**

The biggest range of discounted goods in the West Country, with a whole range of activities to keep the family amused on the 100 acre site. Sells virtually everything from men's, women's and childrenswear, gardening equipment and cookware to wallpaper, carpets and fitted kitchens. Most are branded goods and there is a café, pizza bar and petrol station. A reasonable amount of the women's fashion comes from high street multiples. The menswear offers a wide range of clothes, as well as all-leather classic brogues and Oxford shoes, and Doc Martens in the Shoes Yard. For the home, there are Black & Decker Dustbusters, Hotpoint dryers and washing machines with cosmetic blemishes; curtain fabrics from Monkwell, Sekers, Filigree, Laura Ashley as well as Janet Reger for Vantona double quilt covers, with matching sheets, pillow cases and valances. There is a vast range of tiles including Pilkington seconds. A huge gardening section with everything from hose pipes and garden machinery to imported trees and shrubs. An excellent leisure section offers bicycles and accessories, golf gear, keep-fit systems, fishing rods and flies. Comparison prices are not given here, although staff say most items are discounted by up to 50%, so if you're looking for a bargain, make sure you've done your homework on the high street first. The best deals are in fabrics, carpets, tiles and DIY. There is a leisure park with a giant free fall slide, supakart and family go-kart circuit, bumper boats, trawler rides, swan pedalos, pirate ship, aquablasters, orbiters, shooting gallery, remote control cars and cruisers, forklifts and mini-diggers, fun dungeon, animal park, model railway, narrow gauge steam railway, nature reserve, coarse fishing, Edwardian penny arcade and plenty of space to picnic and to park.

WINKLEIGH TIMBER SHOWROOM

SECKINGTON CROSS, INDUSTRIAL ESTATE, WINKLEIGH, DEVON EX19 8DQ, ☎ 01837 83832, FAX: 01837 83026, **e-mail:** winkleigh@garden-online.co.uk, 9–5 MON–SAT, 10–4 SUN. **ARCHITECTURAL SALVAGE**

Traditional country-style furniture handmade in reclaimed pine. Over 150 lines are available, many of which are displayed in the showroom. Winkleigh timber yard also offers the largest stock of reclaimed timber in the south of England, including pine, oak and pitch pine planks. Parquet flooring in oak, mahogany, maple, meranti; strip flooring in maple, mahogany, oak and pitch pine. Joinery grade timber, beams and new random width oak and elm. Large stocks of handmade furniture in reclaimed timber always on display in showroom. Also now includes a small range of slate, stone and granite cobbles, as well as new, pre-finished, hardwood flooring.

DORSET

DORSET RECLAMATION

COW DROVE, BERE REGIS, DORSET BH20 7JZ, ☎ 01929 472200, **e-mail:** info@dorsetrec.u-net.com, www.dorset-reclamation.co.uk, 8–5 MON–FRI, 9–4 SAT **ARCHITECTURAL SALVAGE**

Bathroom fittings, fireplaces, garden statuary and fountains, stained glass, Dorset bricks, flagstones, quarry tiles, clay peg and ridge tiles, doors, oak beams, reclaimed wood flooring, garden statuary, chimney pots, and lead garden figures. Take the business park exit off the A31/A35 roundabout at Bere Regis.

IN EXCESS

354–358 ASHLEY ROAD, PARKSTONE, POOLE, DORSET BH14 9DF, ☎ 01202 740188, 9–5.30 MON–SAT, 10–4 SUN.

80–83 DOLPHIN CENTRE, POOLE, DORSET, ☎ 01202 673534, 9–5.30 MON–SAT, 10–4 SUN.

SOMERFORD ROAD, CHRISTCHURCH, DORSET BH23 3PH, ☎ 01202 481438, 9–5.30 MON–SAT, 10–4 SUN. **PERMANENT DISCOUNT OUTLET**

In Excess is stacked full of bankrupt stock from stationery and paint to DIY tools and cleaning materials, plumbing materials, screws, bolts, nuts, and telephone accessories. It also houses, in season, garden furniture and pots aimed at the starter garden lover and decking. Plastic tables and chairs start at 2.95 for a chair and from £5.95 to £12.95 for a table; terracotta pots start from 50p and there are also 'antiqued' stone pots.

PILKINGTON'S TILES FACTORY SHOP

BLANDFORD ROAD, HAMWORTHY, POOLE, DORSET BH15 4AR, ☎ 01202 675200, 8.30–5.30 MON–FRI, 9–5 SAT, 10–4 SUN. **FACTORY SHOP**

Sells seconds of the well-known Pilkington's bathroom and kitchen wall and floor tiles and DIY tiling equipment at discount prices of up to 75% off manufacturers prices. Two hundred and fifty ranges of wall and floor tiles to choose from. Now also stock laminate wood floor and glazed floor tiles.

ESSEX

GLYN WEBB

ST ANDREW AVENUE, COLCHESTER, ESSEX
CO4 3BQ, ☎ 01206 798407, 9–8 MON–SAT, 10–4 SUN AND BANK HOLIDAYS. **PERMANENT DISCOUNT OUTLET**

See page 346 (CHESH)

VICTORIAN WOOD WORKS

54 RIVER ROAD, CREEKMOUTH, BARKING, ESSEX IG11 0DW, ☎ 020 8534 1000, FAX: 020 8534 2000, **e-mail:** sales@victorianwoodworks.co.uk, www.victorianwoodworks.co.uk, 8.30–5.30 MON–FRI, 10–2 SAT. **ARCHITECTURAL SALVAGE**

Reclaimed antique and new hardwood flooring manufacturers, suppliers and installers.

GLOUCESTERSHIRE

COXS YARD

10 FOSSE WAY BUSINESS CENTRE, MORETON-IN-MARSH, GLOUCESTERSHIRE GL56 9NQ, ☎ 01608 652505, FAX: 01608 652887, **e-mail:** coxs@fsbdial.co.uk, www.salvoweb.com/dealers/coxs, 9–5 MON–SAT. **ARCHITECTURAL SALVAGE**

Architectural antiques, reclamation oak, pine, elm and pitch beams and boards. Can make traditional oak doors from reclaimed oak to your dimensions.

MARLBOROUGH TILES

14 MONTPELLIER STREET, CHELTENHAM, GLOUCESTERSHIRE GL50 1SX, ☎ 01242 224870, **e-mail:** admin@marlborough-tiles.co.uk, www.marlborough-tiles.co.uk, 9.30–5 MON–SAT.

10 BLACKJACK STREET, CIRENCESTER, GLOUCESTERSHIRE GL7 2AA, ☎ 01242 224870, **e-mail:** admin@marlborough-tiles.co.uk, www.marlborough-tiles.co.uk, 9.30–5 MON–SAT. **PERMANENT DISCOUNT OUTLET**

Wall and floor tiles from Marlborough and other top quality, specialist manufacturers. Seconds come mostly from Marlborough's own factory with discounts of up to 50% on first quality prices, when available. For general enquiries, phone the factory on 01672 512422.

MINCHINHAMPTON ARCHITECTURAL SALVAGE CO

CIRENCESTER ROAD, CHALFORD, NEAR STROUD, GLOUCESTERSHIRE GL6 8PE, ☎ 01285 760886, FAX: 01285 760838, **e-mail:** masco@catbrain.com, www.catbrain.com, 9–5 MON–FRI, 9–3 SAT. **ARCHITECTURAL SALVAGE**

Antique statuary, bespoke chimney pieces, period fireplaces, columns, arches, cornice, pediments, porches, mullions, capitals, gargoyles, sundials, troughs, staddlestones, coping, ridge, stone tiles, quarry tiles, stone walling, flagstones, setts, bricks, floorboards, building stone, woodstrip, pine beams, boarding, baths, basins and taps. Specialists in hardwood floors. Reclaimed materials bought and sold. Garden design, project management and consultancy. Export shipping facilities.

THE ORIGINAL ARCHITECTURAL ANTIQUES CO LTD

ERMINE FARM, A419, CIRENCESTER, GLOUCESTERSHIRE GL7 5PN, ☎ 01285 869222, FAX: 01285 862221, **e-mail:** john@orignaluk.com, www.originaluk.com, 9–5 MON–SAT, 10–4 SUN. **ARCHITECTURAL SALVAGE**

Architectural antiques including period and reproduction fireplaces, doors, floor tiles, chairs, baths, beams, busts, columns, fire surrounds, sirebacks, kitchen ranges, marble fireplaces, mirrors, oak floorboards, objets d'art, paintings, pews, prints, radiators, shutters, sinks, stained glass, taps, towel rails. Also gardenware, including stone troughs, pond surrounds, fountains, flagstones, stone artefacts, sundials, terracotta pots, weather vanes, windows, wrought ironwork, gates, lead cisterns and many other one-off architectural features.

HAMPSHIRE

BATHROOM WORLD

9 SOLARTON ROAD, FARNBOROUGH, HAMPSHIRE GU14 7QL, ☎ 01252 373366, FAX: 01252 370333, www.bathrooms-showers.co.uk, 9–5.30 MON–SAT, 10.30–4 SUN. **PERMANENT DISCOUNT OUTLET**

See page 343 (BERKS)

C J ROGERS DEMOLITION AND SALVAGE

33–43 EMPRESS ROAD, BEVOIS VALLEY, PORTSWOOD, SOUTHAMPTON, HAMPSHIRE SO14 0JU, ☎ 0238 023 5777, FAX: 0238 366133, **e-mail:** cjrogersdemolition@yahoo.co.uk, www.cjrogers.co.uk, 8–5.45 MON–FRI, 8–4 SAT. **ARCHITECTURAL SALVAGE**

Literally anything that can be salvaged from architectural demolition, including sheds, barns, gates and railings. Huge selection of timber as well as fireplaces, bricks and tiles. Pine furniture made to order.

HOME PLUS DIY SURPLUS STORE

8 WATER LANE, TOTTON, HAMPSHIRE SO40 3DP, ☎ 023 8066 1041, OPEN 9–5.30 MON–SAT. **PERMANENT DISCOUNT OUTLET**

Brand new items bought as a result of shop closures or bankruptcy. Specialises in DIY products – paints, tiles, wallpaper, tools, nails, batteries, screws – but also sells kitchen items such as kettles, stationery, lampshades and gardening products. There is another branch at Sainsburys Parade, Lordswood, Southampton.

IN EXCESS

43–45 HIGH STREET, WEST END, SOUTHAMPTON, HAMPSHIRE SO30 3LU, ☎ 0238 046 4545, 9–5.30 MON–SAT, 10–4 SUN.

64–66 SHIRLEY HIGH STRREET, SHIRLEY, SOUTHAMPTON, HAMPSHIRE SO15 3TE, ☎ 02380 771657, 9–5.30 MON–SAT. **PERMANENT DISCOUNT OUTLET**

See page 350 (DORS)

ROMSEY RECLAMATION

STATION APPROACH, RAILWAY STATION, ROMSEY, HAMPSHIRE SO51 8DU, ☎ 01794 524174 OR 515486, FAX: 01794 514344, **e-mail:** trevor.halfacre@virgin.net, www.romseyreclamation.com, 8–5 MON–FRI, 8.30–12 SAT. **ARCHITECTURAL SALVAGE**

Chimney pots, reclaimed slates, railway sleepers, bricks, tiles, motorway crash barriers, Yorkshire flags, quarry tiles, fixtures and fitting, telegraph poles and other reclaimed materials. Also stocks architectural antiques such as fancy masonry blocks, ornate gates, fireplaces, and now real stone.

THE BATHROOM WAREHOUSE WINCHESTER LTD

UNIT 3, WYKEHAM ESTATE, MOORSIDE ROAD, WINNALL, NEAR WINCHESTER, HAMPSHIRE SO23 7RX, ☎ 01962 862554, FAX: 01962 840927, www.bathroomwarehousewinchester.co.uk, 9–5.30 MON–SAT, 10.30–4 SUN. **PERMANENT DISCOUNT OUTLET**

Fantastic, extensive bathroom showrooms pandering to any taste or budget. Many products are exclusive to the Group who are continually expanding their already large product portfolio. The buying power of the Group ensures that prices are always extremely competitive. Experienced staff and designers guide customers through styles and specifications as part of a free service.

THE MALTHOUSE

CHURCH LANE, BOTLEY, HAMPSHIRE SO30 2EJ, ☎ 01489 786272, FAX: 01489 787774, **e-mail:** admin@bathsetc.co.uk, www.bathsetc.co.uk, 9–5 MON–SAT. **PERMANENT DISCOUNT OUTLET**

The ground floor of this 200-year-old Malting House, which incorporates The Botley Bathroom Centre, is full of DIY, bric a brac, discontinued items of yesteryear. The local saying is, "If it's not in The Malthouse, you won't get it!" On the first floor, there are more than 20 displays of bathroom furniture, including showers, taps, whirlpool baths. They are one of the largest suppliers of discontinued sanitary ware in the UK, holding more than 3,000 items of china, taps, toilet seats and accessories. With over 25 years' experience and full manufacturers' backing, they always do their best to help with any enquiry.

WILKINSON STORES

22–30 BRIDGE STREET, ANDOVER, HAMPSHIRE SP10 1BN, ☎ 01332 551241, www.wilko.co.uk, 9–5.30 MON–SAT, 10–4 SUN. MAIL ORDER. **PERMANENT DISCOUNT OUTLET**

See page 346 (CHESH)

HEREFORDSHIRE

BAILEYS HOME & GARDEN

THE ENGINE SHED, STATION APPROACH, ROSS-ON-WYE, HEREFORDSHIRE HR9 7BW, ☎ 01989 563015, FAX: 01989 768172, **e-mail:** sales@baileys-home-garden.co.uk, www.baileyshomeandgarden.com, 9–5 MON–SAT. **ARCHITECTURAL SALVAGE**

Bathroom fittings, fireplaces, garden furniture, gates, ironwork, lighting, Belfast sinks and dressers. They also sell a range of garden statuary and items made from reconstituted stone as well as original troughs, staddle stones, repro Regency-style distressed metal benches with Gothic arched backs, French folding chairs, and lots of terracotta plant pots. This company specialises in antique garden tools and horticultural antiques.

HERTFORDSHIRE

WATFORD BATHROOMS

60–62 QUEEN'S ROAD, WATFORD, HERTFORDSHIRE WD17 2LA, ☎ 01923 250663, FAX: 01923 442046, **e-mail:** sales@watfordbathrooms.fsnet.co.uk, 9–5.30 MON–SAT, 10.30–4 SUN. **PERMANENT DISCOUNT OUTLET**

Good quality bathrooms at competitive prices including Sottini, Heritage, Daryl, Showerlux and Aqualisa. Bathroom accessories are also competitively priced. Free parking.

KENT

B & A WHELAN

52 HIGH STREET, BLUE TOWN, NEXT TO SHEERNESS DOCKS, KENT ME12 1RW, ☎ 01795 663879, FAX: 01795 661934, 9–5 SEVEN DAYS A WEEK. **PERMANENT DISCOUNT OUTLET**

Manufacturers of concrete garden ornaments, they sell more than 2,500 different items including benches, gnomes, bird baths and sundials, all sold at prices which are about 50% less than those charged in most garden centres. Parking.

BROMLEY DEMOLITION

75 SIWARD ROAD, BROMLEY, KENT BR2 9JY, ☎ 020 8464 3610, FAX: 020 8313 3623, **e-mail:** info@bromleydem.co.uk, www.bromleydem.co.uk, 9–5 MON–FRI. **ARCHITECTURAL SALVAGE**

Bromley Demolition reclaim whatever is usable from demolished properties including doors, old bricks and assorted sizes of timbers.

IN DOORS

BEECHINWOOD LANE, PLATT, SEVENOAKS, KENT TN15 8QN, ☎ 01732 887445, FAX: 01732 887446, www.indoorsltd.co.uk, 9–5 MON–FRI, 9–12.30 SAT. **ARCHITECTURAL SALVAGE**

Over 500 original period doors in stock. New doors made to measure from English oak and reclaimed pine. Free on-site parking.

TILE CLEARING HOUSE

UNIT 5A, NUGENT INDUSTRIAL ESTATE, CRAY WAY, ST MARY CRAY, ORPINGTON, KENT BR5 3RP, ☎ 01689 890 511, 8–6 MON–FRI, 9–6 SAT, 10–4 SUN. **PERMANENT DISCOUNT OUTLET**

See page 345 (CAMBS)

LANCASHIRE

AL MURAD DIY

839 ASTON OLD ROAD, MANCHESTER, LANCASHIRE M11 2NL, ☎ 0161 220 8798, www.almurad.co.uk, 9.30–4.45 MON–WED, THUR, SAT.

94 CHORLTON ROAD, OLD TRAFFORD, MANCHESTER M15 4AL, ☎ 0161 226 3929, www.almurad.co.uk, 9.30–5.30 MON–THUR, SAT. **PERMANENT DISCOUNT OUTLET**

Sells a wide range of branded paints Dulux, Crown and Johnsons at discount prices. With 35 shops in Yorkshire, Lancashire and Lincolnshire, they bulk buy and pass on savings to customers. They also offer a range of discounted wallpapers from Vymura, Crown, Super Fresco, Pride and Knightsbridge which, if not in stock, can be ordered from their range of books, as well as ceramic tiles, grouting and grouting tools.

ARCHITECTURAL WALL AND FLOOR CO.

UNIT 3, PREMIER MILL, BEGONIA STREET, DARWEN, LANCASHIRE BB3 2DR, ☎ 01254 873994, FAX: 01254 702243, **e-mail:** john@fireclaysinks.com, www.architecturalwallandfloor.com, 9–5 MON–FRI, 9–12 SAT. **ARCHITECTURAL SALVAGE**

Ceramics, terracotta, floor coverings, traditional sanitaryware, glazed brick, Belfast sinks, architectural antiques, reclaimed building materials, timber, stone, slate and pine doors.

BRUCE KILNER ARCHITECTURAL SALVAGE

ASHTON'S FIELD FARM, WINDMILL ROAD, WALKDEN, WORSLEY, MANCHESTER, LANCASHIRE M28 3RP, ☎ 0161 702 8604, OPEN DAILY. PHONE FOR DETAILS OF OPENING HOURS. **ARCHITECTURAL SALVAGE**

Original doors, baths, radiators, sinks, sash windows, Victorian stable fittings, cart wheels, troughs.

CWV BRANDS AT HOME FACTORY SHOP

HEASANDFORD INDUSTRIAL ESTATE, WIDOW HILL ROAD, BURNLEY, LANCASHIRE BB10 2TJ, ☎ 01282 727272, **e-mail:** pamhindle@englewood.co.uk, 9.30–5.30 MON–FRI, 9–5 SAT, 10–4 SUN, 10–5 BANK HOLIDAYS. **FACTORY SHOP**

See page 346 (CHESH)

DALE STREET WAREHOUSE

77 DALE STREET, MANCHESTER, LANCASHIRE M1 2HG, ☎ 0161 236 4645, 9–5 MON–FRI, 10–4 SAT, 11–3 SUN. **FACTORY SHOP**

Makes baths which it sells direct to the public at competitive prices. Unlike most acrylic baths which are made from 5mm deep sheets of acrylic, Dale's baths are handmade from 10mm sheets, making them strong, durable and heat retentive. The factory shop also sells a full range of bathroom and shower accessories, sinks, stone resin shower trays, shower cubicles, showers which work off a standard hot water system, and tiles which are imported directly from Spain.

GLYN WEBB

144–146 BLACKBURN ROAD, ACCRINGTON, LANCASHIRE BB5 0AB, ☎ 01254 236831, 9–8 MON–FRI, 9–6 SAT, 10–4 SUN AND BANK HOLIDAYS.

231 VICARAGE LANE, BLACKPOOL, LANCASHIRE FY4 4NG, ☎ 01253 692549, 9–8 MON–SAT, 10–4 SUN AND BANK HOLIDAYS.

UNIT A, ORLANDO STREET, OFF MANCHESTER ROAD, BOLTON, LANCASHIRE BL2 1DU, ☎ 01204 365806, 9–8 MON–SAT, 10–4 SUN AND BANK HOLIDAYS.

641 HYDE ROAD, BELLEVUE, MANCHESTER, LANCASHIRE M12 5PS, ☎ 0161 230 8240, 9–8 MON–SAT, 10–4 SUN AND BANK HOLIDAYS.

HILL STREET, OFF HUDDERSFIELD ROAD, OLDHAM, LANCASHIRE OL4 2AG, ☎ 0161 620 4415, 9–8 MON–SAT, 10–4 SUN AND BANK HOLIDAYS.

126 RIBBLETON LANE, PRESTON, LANCASHIRE PR1 5LB, ☎ 01772 794373, 9–8 MON–SAT, 10–4 SUN AND BANK HOLIDAYS.

DENTONS GREEN LANE, DENTONS GREEN, ST HELENS, LANCASHIRE WA10 2QB, ☎ 01744 454798, 9–8 MON–SAT, 10–4 SUN AND BANK HOLIDAYS. **PERMANENT DISCOUNT OUTLET**

See page 346 (CHESH)

GRAHAM & BROWN

UNIT 7, SHUTTLEWORTH MEAD, PADIHAM, LANCASHIRE BB12 7NG, ☎ 01282 680442, 9.30–5.30 MON–FRI, 9.30–5 SAT, 10–4 SUN. **FACTORY SHOP**

Wallpaper manufacturers under the brand name Graham & Brown, which is stocked by B&Q and Great Mills, among others. Here, they sell overstocks and ends of lines of lining paper, vinyls, blown vinyls and top quality wallpaper. A wide range at good prices.

HEYWOOD DISCOUNT WALLPAPERS

ADELAIDE STREET, HEYWOOD, LANCASHIRE DL10 4HQ, ☎ 01706 365 5555, 9–6 MON–FRI, 8 ON THUR, 9–5.30 SAT, 10–4 SUN. **PERMANENT DISCOUNT OUTLET**

Discounted wallpapers from names such as Vymura, Coloroll and Shankeys either from stock or from the book bar which has a greater selection. Also Johnstons paints at trade prices.

IN SITU

TALBOT MILL, 44 ELLESMERE STREET, HULME, MANCHESTER M15 4JY, ☎ 0161 839 5525, FAX: 0161 839 5525, 10–5.30 MON–SAT.

LONGFORD ROAD, STRETFORD, MANCHESTER M32 0HQ, ☎ 0161 865 2110, 9–5.30 MON–SAT. **ARCHITECTURAL SALVAGE**

Church interiors, period fireplaces, doors, leaded glass, antique bathrooms, garden ware, staircases, chimney pots, furniture, flooring. Deliver anywhere. Period fireplaces cost from £80 for a small cast-iron bedroom fireplace; baths from £300; reclaimed maple flooring from £18 per square yard.

OVALWORLD

BASTFIELD MILL, BEECH STREET, LITTLE HARWOOD, BLACKBURN, LANCASHIRE BB1 6LT, ☎ 01254 582735, 9–5.30 MON–FRI, 9.30–5 SAT, 10.30–4 SUN. **FACTORY SHOP**

Large mill shop with three warehouses behind stocking thousands of different designs of wallpapers from many different manufacturers at very competitive prices. Some matching paint and fabrics can be ordered from samples. Brands sold include Vymura, Coloroll, Tim Wilman, Country Decor, Holder and Crown. Most expensive wallpaper costs £9.99 a roll.

PILKINGTON'S TILES FACTORY SHOP

BURY FACTORY SHOP, 1 DERBY STREET, ROCHDALE ROAD, LANCASHIRE BL9 0NW, ☎ 0161 761 7771, 8.30–5.30 MON–FRI, 9–5 SAT, 10–4 SUN.

RAKE LANE, CLIFTON JUNCTION, MANCHESTER M27 8LP, ☎ 0161 727 7088, 8.30–5.30 MON–FRI, 9–5 SAT, 10–4 SUN. **FACTORY SHOP**

See page 351 (DORS)

TILE CLEARING HOUSE

13A CROSBY ROAD NORTH, WATERLOO, LIVERPOOL L22 0LD, ☎ 0151 920 3400, 8–6 MON–FRI, 9–6 SAT, 10–4 SUN.

1326 ASHTON OLD ROAD, HIGHER OPENSHAW, MANCHESTER, LANCASHIRE M11 1LG, ☎ 0161 370 6449, 8–6 MON–FRI, 9–6 SAT, 10–4 SUN.

UNIT 3 AND 4, LAUREL TRADING ESTATE, HIGGINSHAW LANE, ROYTON, OLDHAM LANCASHIRE OL2 6LH, ☎ 0161 628 9462, 8–6 MON–FRI, 9–6 SAT, 10–4 SUN.

UNIT 2, RIBBLETON LANE, PRESTON, LANCASHIRE PR1 5LR, ☎ 01772 705 990, 8–6 MON–FRI, 9–6 SAT, 10–4 SUN. **PERMANENT DISCOUNT OUTLET**

See page 345 (CAMBS)

LEICESTERSHIRE

GLYN WEBB

10A BURTON STREET, HUMBERSTONE GATE, LEICESTER LE1 1TE, ☎ 0116 251 6622, 9–6 MON–SAT, 10.30–4.30 SUN AND BANK HOLIDAYS. **PERMANENT DISCOUNT OUTLET**

See page 346 (CHESH)

TILE CLEARING HOUSE

253–255 BELGRAVE GATE, LEICESTER, LEICESTERSHIRE LE1 3HV, ☎ 0116 262 7299, FAX: 0116 253 9695, 8–6 MON–FRI, 9–6 SAT, 10–4 SUN. **PERMANENT DISCOUNT OUTLET**

See page 345 (CAMBS)

LINCOLNSHIRE

GLYN WEBB

TRITTON ROAD, LINCOLN, LINCOLNSHIRE LN6 7QY, ☎ 01522 575252, 9–8 MON–SAT, 10–4 SUN AND BANK HOLIDAYS. **PERMANENT DISCOUNT OUTLET**

See page 346 (CHESH)

WILKINSON STORES

2 THE BROADWAY, ASHBY, SCUNTHORPE, LINCOLNSHIRE NG5 7EL, ☎ 01724 867767, www.wilko.co.uk, 9–5.30 MON–FRI, 8.30–5.30 SAT, 10–4 SUN. MAIL ORDER. **PERMANENT DISCOUNT OUTLET**

See page 346 (CHESH)

LONDON

BATHROOMS @ SOURCE

312–314 BATTERSEA PARK ROAD, LONDON SW11 3BX, ☎ 020 7738 0808, FAX: 020 8871 1155, **e-mail:** bathroomsatsource@hotmail.com, 8.30–5.30 MON–FRI, 10–6 SAT. PHONE TO CHECK FIRST.

128 GARRETT LANE, LONDON SW18 3DJ, ☎ 020 8870 0066, FAX: 020 8871 1155, **e-mail:** bathroomsatsource@hotmail.com, 8.30–5.30 MON–FRI, 10–6 SAT. PHONE TO CHECK FIRST. **PERMANENT DISCOUNT OUTLET**

Retailers of discounted bathrooms, selling a very extensive range to suit all tastes and budgets. Quality service and installation.

BLUE MANTLE

THE OLD FIRE STATION, 306-312 OLD KENT ROAD, LONDON SE1 5UE, ☎ 020 7703 7437, FAX: 020 7703 7437, www.bluemantle.co.uk, 10.30–5.30 MON–SAT. **ARCHITECTURAL SALVAGE**

Salvage yard with well priced range of old fireplaces, stoves, grates, mirrors, bric a brac, chimney pots, radiators, Butler sinks.

BRONDESBURY ARCHITECTURAL RECLAMATION

THE YARD, 136 WILLESDEN LANE, LONDON NW6 7TE, ☎ 020 7328 0820, FAX: 020 7328 0280, www.brondesburyarchitectural.com, 10–6 MON–SAT. **ARCHITECTURAL SALVAGE**

Architectural salvage up to the Thirties including Art Deco,Victorian, Edwardian and Georgian with the occasional French piece. Lots of fireplaces, baths, sinks, taps, towel rails, kitchen ranges, marble surrounds and cast-iron. Garden department stocks garden tables, sundials, bird baths and chimney pots. Everything you could want to convert a modernised house back to its former glory all originals, no copies.

CARPET TILE CENTRE

227 WOODHOUSE ROAD, NORTH FINCHLEY, LONDON N12 9BD, ☎ 020 8361 1261, FAX: 020 8361 3147, **e-mail:** carpetcentre@btconnect.com, www.carpetcentre@barclays.net
9–5 MON–FRI, 9–1 SAT. **PERMANENT DISCOUNT OUTLET**

Offers a wide range of seconds as well as end of line carpet tiles, specials and non-standard colours of Heuga and Interface brands. Prices start at £1.95 to £2.95 for tiles which normally cost £5. Even the perfect tiles are competitively priced.

CHESNEYS ANTIQUE FIREPLACE WAREHOUSE LTD

194–202 BATTERSEA PARK ROAD, LONDON SW11 4ND, ☎ 020 7627 1410, FAX: 020 7622 1078, **e-mail:** sales@chesney's.co.uk, www.chesney's.co.uk, 9–5.30 MON–FRI, 10–5 SAT.
ARCHITECTURAL SALVAGE

Antique and reproduction fireplaces with at least 120 in stock at any one time. Full fitting service. Marble fireplaces range from £450 to £6,000; stone from £495 to £3,000; pine from £230 to £900. Bespoke fireplaces available to order: please phone for more information.

DISCOUNT DECORATING

157–159 RYE LANE, PECKHAM, LONDON SE15 4TL, ☎ 020 7732 3986, 8–5.30 MON–FRI, 9–5.30 SAT. **PERMANENT DISCOUNT OUTLET**

Three thousand square foot warehouse selling top of the range wallpapers, including Contour, Crown, Sanderson,Vymura and Hill & Knowles at between 10% and 50% discount. Dulux paints and decorating equipment are available at low prices. There is a large stock of DIY equipment. All current, last season's or discontinued stock no seconds sold.

DISPOSAL SERVICES AGENCY (DSA)

ROOM 727, MINISTRY OF DEFENCE, 6 HERCULES ROAD, LONDON SE1 7DJ, ☎ 020 7261 8968, www.disposalservices.agency.mod.uk
PERMANENT DISCOUNT OUTLET

The Disposal Services Agency is an agency of the Ministry of Defence set up to dispose of surplus equipment. It runs the largest disposal operation in the UK, organising the sale of both military equipment and commodities in use commercially, such as embassy furniture, government department office furniture, closed-down RAF-base vehicles and housing stock, ex-marine boats, ex-army tents, boots and ski equipment, medical and dental equipment, clothing, ship and aircraft spares, scrap metal and IT equipment. The DSA uses companies throughout the UK, each with their own specialist area, to dispose of stock. These companies also dispose of stock from a host of other, usually public sector, organisations varying from fire brigades and hospitals to health authorities and the police. Equipment from these companies varies from kitchen equipment and fax machines to mobile radios, cars, generators, jewellery and telecommunications equipment to food trolleys, X-ray equipment, telephones, uniforms, dinghies, fishing nets, photocopiers and chair lifts. Visit the website to find out which companies sell which products and how to contact them direct.

FENS RESTORATION

46 LOTS ROAD, CHELSEA, LONDON SW10 0QF, ☎ 020 7352 9883, **e-mail:** fensrestoration@hotmail.com, 8–5 MON–FRI, BY APPOINTMENT SAT. **ARCHITECTURAL SALVAGE**

Sells furniture and carries out restoration work and repairs, and metal polishing and caustic stripping. Bathroom fittings are also available to order.

FIREPLACE DESIGN SERVICE

39 COURT ROAD, ELTHAM, LONDON SE9 5AF, ☎ 020 8355 1419, FAX: 020 8355 7044, www.seersfireplaces.co.uk, VIEWING BY APPOINTMENT ONLY. **SECONDHAND SHOP**

Fireplaces designed and built to your own specifications. They claim that anything is possible and that no flue will present a problem. They specialise in funky, modern, hole-in-wall designs with pebbles and stoves to fit. Home visits and estimates are free.

GARDEN MASTERS

39 COURT ROAD, ELTHAM, LONDON SE9 5AF, ☎ 020 8355 1419, FAX: 020 8355 7044, www.seersfireplaces.co.uk, VIEWING BY APPOINTMENT ONLY. **PERMANENT DISCOUNT OUTLET**

Specialist design and build garden makeover company. Your design can be transformed into reality, with full advice given if required. Their buying power means the plants are often 50% cheaper than in DIY stores or garden centres. Free estimates given within the M25.

G THORNFIELD LTD

321 GRAY'S INN ROAD, LONDON WC1X 8PX, ☎ 020 7837 2996, FAX: 020 7278 2515, **e-mail:** dave.daybyday@virgin.net, 8–6 MON–FRI, 9–2 SAT. **PERMANENT DISCOUNT OUTLET**

Offers from 20% to 50% off wallcovering brands such as Sanderson and Kingfisher. The more you buy, the greater your discount. Also up to one-third off coordinating fabrics. Doesn't hold stocks of wallpapers and fabrics but you can order from their books with next day delivery. Also sells frames, prints and posters at very low prices. Access to nearly 10,000 picture and prints from stock or to order, including limited editions. Dulux paint colours are mixed on the premises, with 1,800 shades to choose from.

HOUSE OF STEEL

400 CALEDONIAN ROAD, LONDON N1 1DN, ☎ 020 7607 5889, FAX: 020 7607 5889, 11.30–5 MON–FRI, BY APPOINTMENT ON SAT. **ARCHITECTURAL SALVAGE**

Five thousand square foot warehouse devoted to reclaimed metalwork of every kind including wrought-iron gates, railings, old grilles, wrought-iron panels, arched gates, beds, spiral staircases, balconies and lighting. Also designs and makes steel furniture. Anything in metal designed, made and fitted, where appropriate, from a pin to an anchor. Repairs and restoration undertaken.

KEW ARCHITECTURAL ANTIQUES

4 KEWBRIDGE ARCHES, STRAND ON THE GREEN, LONDON W4 3NG, ☎ 020 8987 2610, 10–6.30 MON–FRI, 11–5 SAT, 1–5 SUN. **ARCHITECTURAL SALVAGE**

Lots of door fittings, door knobs, door knockers, coat hooks, finger plates, period bathroom fittings, cast iron radiators, wood flooring and antique furniture (Edwardian and Victorian) etc. Also shades and refurbished French light fittings. If you are looking for something special, it's worth ringing first to see what they have in stock.

KINGS CROSS TILES

29 MIDLAND ROAD, KING'S CROSS, LONDON NW1 2AD, ☎ 020 7387 3886, FAX: 020 7387 1012, www.kingscrosstiles.com, 8–6 MON–FRI, 9–5 SAT. **PERMANENT DISCOUNT OUTLET**

Wall tiles, floor tiles, mosaics, slates, marbles, borders, limestone and bathroom suites, all at very competitive prices. The tiles are imported directly from Spain and Italy so there is no middleman taking a cut, which is why prices are so good. The company don't produce glossy brochures so can offer the bathroom suites at prices lower than most of their competitors. Full range of exterior patio tiles also good value. At the time of going to press, King's Cross Tiles was relocating. Please phone the number above for details of the new address.

LASSCO FLOORING

41 MALTBY STREET, LONDON SE1 3PA, ☎ 020 7237 4488, **e-mail:** flooring@lassco.co.uk, www.lassco.co.uk, 10–5 MON–SAT. OPEN LATE ON THURSDAYS BY APPOINTMENT. **ARCHITECTURAL SALVAGE**

Supplies more than 150 lines of reclaimed, antique and new timber flooring in parquet strip and board. Two galleries in Bermondsey display finished samples. Recent stocks are burgeoning with the arrival of a quarter of a million feet of Oregon pine salvaged from Whitfield Barracks, Dover, dating from the 1930s. The Tate & Lyle building in Silvertown has also yielded enormous quantities of Muhuhu parquet, an unusual East African hardwood of extreme durability in a marbled, honeyed colour. Lassco's sawmill has produced a new range of traditional French chevron flooring as an alternative to the English herringbone style parquet. Mainland delivery and worldwide export can be arranged.

LASSCO HOUSE & GARDEN

MARK STREET (OFF PAUL STREET), LONDON EC2A 4ER, ☎ 020 7231 7278, **e-mail:** replicas@lassco.co.uk, www.lassco.co.uk, 10–5 MON–SAT. **ARCHITECTURAL SALVAGE**

LASSCO House & Garden is a range of replica architectural elements and authentic ornament for the period English house and garden. From door furniture to garden statuary, their stock ranges from the small and delicate to the large and majestic. A comprehensive catalogue is available, as well as a fully illustrated and searchable website.

LASSCO RBK

41 MALTBY STREET, LONDON SE1 3PA, ☎ 020 7394 7788, **e-mail:** rbk@lassco.co.uk, www.lassco.co.uk, 10–5 MON–SAT. OPEN LATE ON THURSDAYS BY APPOINTMENT.
ARCHITECTURAL SALVAGE

LASSCO RBK (radiators, bathrooms and kitchens) has an eclectic stock of reclaimed cast iron radiators, many with decorative casting and unusual examples. Radiators are restored, guaranteed and finished to order. Many finishes are available including burnishing, priming and powder coating. Continually changing and expanding stocks of bathtubs in enamel, porcelain, tin and copper; Art Deco suites, Edwardian shower units, original and antique taps, sinks, nauticalia plus much more. A colour brochure is available.

LASSCO ST MICHAELS

ST MICHAEL S CHURCH, MARK STREET, OFF PAUL STREET, LONDON EC2A 4ER, ☎ 020 7749 9944, **e-mail:** st.michaels@lassco.co.uk, www.lassco.co.uk. 10–5 MON–SAT. **ARCHITECTURAL SALVAGE**

Fine architectural antiques, chimney pieces, panelled rooms, garden ornaments, lighting, door furniture and much more. See also LASSCO Flooring at Maltby Street, Bermondsey and Lassco RBK (radiators, bathrooms, kitchens) in Islington.

LASSCO WAREHOUSE

BRITANNIA WALK, ISLINGTON, LONDON N1 7LU, ☎ 020 7490 1000, **e-mail:** warehouse@lassco.co.uk, www.lassco.co.uk, 10–5 MON–SAT. **ARCHITECTURAL SALVAGE**

LASSCO Warehouse offers discounted architectural elements, doors and panelled rooms, marine salvage, counters, shop fittings, etc, many sourced from famous hotels, museums, theatres, department stores and public buildings.

LAZDAN

218 BOW COMMON LANE, LONDON E3 4HH, ☎ 020 8981 4632, FAX: 020 8980 5395, 8–5 MON–FRI, 8–12.30 SAT. **ARCHITECTURAL SALVAGE**

Secondhand bricks, reclaimed slates, sash weights and chimney pots.

LEYLAND SDM

9 THE MALL, LONDON W5, FAX: 020 8566 0481, **e-mail:** info@leylandsdm.co.uk, www.leylandsdm.co.uk, 7–6 MON–SAT.

88–90 FARRINGDON ROAD, LONDON EC1, FAX: 020 7278 8933, **e-mail:** info@leylandsdm.co.uk, www.leylandsdm.co.uk, 7–6 MON–SAT.

7–15 CAMDEN ROAD, LONDON NW1 9QL, ☎ 020 7284 4366, **e-mail:** info@leylandsdm.co.uk, www.leylandsdm.co.uk, 7–6 MON–SAT, 9.30–3 SUN.

683–685 FINCHLEY ROAD, LONDON NW2 2PJ, ☎ 020 7794 5927, **e-mail:** info@leylandsdm.co.uk, www.leylandsdm.co.uk, 7–6 MON–SAT.

6–8 WARWICK WAY, LONDON SW1, FAX: 020 7828 8695, **e-mail:** info@leylandsdm.co.uk, www.leylandsdm.co.uk, 7–6 MON–SAT.

335–337 KING'S ROAD, LONDON SW3 5EU, ☎ 020 7352 4742, **e-mail:** info@leylandsdm.co.uk, www.leylandsdm.co.uk, 7–6 MON–SAT, 9.30–3 SUN.

314–316 OLD BROMPTON ROAD, LONDON SW5, FAX: 020 7370 6600, **e-mail:** info@leylandsdm.co.uk, www.leylandsdm.co.uk, 7–6 MON–SAT.

25 GOODGE STREET, LONDON W1P 1FD, ☎ 020 7636 2995, **e-mail:** info@leylandsdm.co.uk, www.leylandsdm.co.uk, 7–6 MON–SAT.

361–365 KENSINGTON HIGH STREET, LONDON W14 8QY, ☎ 020 7602 9099, **e-mail:** info@leylandsdm.co.uk, www.leylandsdm.co.uk, 7–6 MON–SAT.

371–373 EDGWARE ROAD LONDON W2 1BS, ☎ 020 7723 8048, **e-mail:** info@leylandsdm.co.uk, www.leylandsdm.co.uk, 7–6 MON–SAT, 9.30–3 SUN.

167–169 SHAFTESBURY AVENUE LONDON WC2 8AN, ☎ 020 7836 7337, **e-mail:** info@leylandsdm.co.uk, www.leylandsdm.co.uk, 7–6 MON–SAT. **PERMANENT DISCOUNT OUTLET**

Everything the enthusiastic DIYer could possibly need; power tools, hand tools, decorating tools, wallpapers, decorative mouldings, plumbing, electrics and paint. Over 10,000 paint colours to choose from with colour matching facility, all sold at competive prices. Many branches throughout Central London. Phone 020 7405 8985 during office hours for more information.

PAINTERS CASH AND CARRY

294–296 FIRS LANE, PALMERS GREEN, LONDON N13, FAX: 020 8807 3539, FAX: 020 8803 3818, 7.30–5 MON–FRI, 9–12 SAT. **PERMANENT DISCOUNT OUTLET**

A painter's and decorator's cash and carry with computerised mixing machines for Dulux, Cuprinol, Crown, Sandtex, Woodsheen, Johnstones, Leyland, Manders, Sadolin, Glidden, Macpherson and Berger. Wallpaper brands include Kingfisher, Mayfair, Crown and Vymura, among others, from a range of 300 wallpaper books at discounts of up to 40%. Anaglyptas at half price. Next day ordering for wallpapers. Discount fabrics also available. Aimed at the trade, The Decor Store also caters for members of the public who benefit from the discounts available.

RENAISSANCE

193–195 CITY ROAD, LONDON EC1 1JN, ☎ 020 7251 8844, FAX: 020 7251 8844, **e-mail:** renaissance1@easynet.co.uk, www.renaissancelondon.com, 9–5 Mon–Sat, 12–4 Sun. **ARCHITECTURAL SALVAGE**

Specialist in antique, reproduction and contemporary fireplaces. On show is a large selection of antique stone fireplaces, with at least 50 on display at any one time. The showroom boasts seven rooms and a warehouse packed with fireplaces from 16th century Art Nouveau and Art Deco originals to reproduction pieces and stunning modern versions. There are also displays of crucifixed original doors, shutters, radiators, chairs, gates, grates, chandeliers, window boxes and decorative objects, as well as on-site restoration services and bespoke designing. There is also a range of garden ornaments: urns, sundials, statues etc.

RENUBATH SERVICES

248 LILLIE ROAD, LONDON SW6 7QA, ☎ 020 7381 8337, FAX: 020 7381 8907, **e-mail:** london@renubath.co.uk, www.renubath.co.uk, 9–5.30 MON–THUR, 9–5 FRI. **PERMANENT DISCOUNT OUTLET**

If you've got a good quality bath that looks a bit tatty and chipped, why not have it resurfaced, polished or cleaned by the experts? Phone for details of their surface repair service which covers UPVC windows, sanitary ware, shower trays and other acrylic-based products.

SDM INTERIORS

424 EDGWARE ROAD, LONDON W2 1EG, ☎ 020 7706 1099, 8.30–5.30 MON–SAT, CLOSED 1.30–2. **PERMANENT DISCOUNT OUTLET**

Numerous types of wooden flooring from laminate to hardwood at competitive prices. Also floor and wall tiles, wallpapers and decorative mouldings.

SEERS FIREPLACES

THE BANK, 213 TRAFALGAR ROAD, GREENWICH, LONDON SE10 9EQ, ☎ 020 8293 0293, FAX: 020 8305 2305, 10–6 TUE–SAT, 10–5 SUN. **SECONDHAND SHOP**

Huge shop with over 50 fireplaces on display ranging from modern to antique. Largest display of stoves in London. Great selection of over-mantles and mirrors at bargain prices. Mail order available, nationwide delivery, free within M25.

THE ANTIQUE FIREPLACE WAREHOUSE

LONDON SE9, FAX: 0800 068 1515, www.seersfireplaces.co.uk, VIEWING BY APPOINTMENT ONLY. **SECONDHAND SHOP**

Hundreds of antique fireplaces, inserts, surrounds, combinations and spare parts. A full restoration service is available, as are a specialist matching service and a fitting service. For free estimate, please phone the number above.

THE HARDWOOD FLOORING CO LTD

146–152 WEST END LANE, WEST HAMPSTEAD, LONDON NW6 1SD, ☎ 020 7328 8481, FAX: 020 7625 5951, www.hardwoodflooringcompany.com, 8.30–5.30 MON–FRI, 8 ON THUR.

151 ESSEX ROAD, ISLINGTON, LONDON N1, FAX: 020 7354 3500, FAX: 020 7354 8822, www.hardwoodflooringcompany.com, 9–5.30 MON–SAT **ARCHITECTURAL SALVAGE**

Established for more than 16 years, there are over 200 different types of new hardwood floorings ranging from pre-finished strip and block to American white oak wide board planking and American black walnut. A full installation service is available, if required. They have recently introduced bamboo flooring (ideal for bathrooms) and exterior hardwood decking to their extensive range. Also stocks the new locking system from Kahrs. This sandable, real hardwood flooring uses no adhesive and is reusable up to seven times, so you can take them with you when you move house, or change the room they are in.

THE HOUSE HOSPITAL

UNIT 9, FERRIER STREET INDUSTRIAL ESTATE, WANDSWORTH, LONDON SW18 1SW, ☎ 020 8870 8202, 10–5 MON–SAT. **ARCHITECTURAL SALVAGE**

Cast iron radiators, bathroom fittings, brass mixer taps, doors, door handles, chimney pots and fireplaces.

THE NATURAL WOOD FLOOR COMPANY

20 SMUGGLERS WAY, WANDSWORTH, LONDON SW18 1EQ, ☎ 020 8871 9771, FAX: 020 8877 0273, see website, www.naturalwoodfloor.co.uk, 9–6 MON–FRI, 9–4 SAT. **ARCHITECTURAL SALVAGE**

Up to 170 different wood-flooring materials including reclaimed wooden floorboards: beechwood woodblock from £18, pine, douglas fir and pitch pine. Pine floorboards cost from £17 per square metre; while oak starts at £18 per square metre. Also sells new solid wood floors at prices which they claim are cheaper than anything offered in the same style. For example, 20mm thick redwood, £18.13 per square metre. The largest range of quality, solid wood floors in the London area are on sale here at very competitive prices.

THE OLD STATION

72 LOAMPIT HILL, LEWISHAM, LONDON SE13 7SX, ☎ 020 8694 6540/MOBILE 07710 489 895 OR 07956 251 180, www.the-old-station.co.uk, 10–5.30 MON–SAT, 11–4 SUN OR BY APPOINTMENT. **ARCHITECTURAL SALVAGE**

The Old Station in Lewisham is a salvage yard based in a converted station with a garden at the rear. While the salvage yard section houses Victorian reclaimed items from roll-top baths and original and reproduction fireplaces to Butler sinks, doors, heated towel rails, and French patterned as well as English Victorian radiators, the garden features repro garden statues which start at £30; urns on plinths, £300; garden railings, old slate sculptures and Victorian chimney pots from £20. Since 2000 they have been importing European pine furniture including dressers, chests of drawers, kitchen units, tables and chairs. All are sold at very competitive prices. Out of hours appointments are available for committed buyers: please phone for details. Worldwide shipping can be arranged.

THE REJECT TILE SHOP

2A ENGLANDS LANE LONDON NW3 4TG, ☎ 020 7483 2608, FAX: 020 7483 2609, www.criterion-tiles.co.uk, 10–6 MON–FRI, 10–5 SAT.

178 WANDSWORTH BRIDGE ROAD, LONDON SW6 2UQ, ☎ 020 7731 6098, FAX: 020 7736 3693, www.criterion-tiles.co.uk, 9.30–5.30 MON–FRI, 9.30–5 SAT. **PERMANENT DISCOUNT OUTLET**

Specialises in second quality and low cost ceramic wall and floor tiles as well as terracotta tiles. Most tiles are sold at approximately half the cost of first quality equivalent products. Quality control is so tight nowadays that seconds are usually given this status due to minor glazing defects, barely perceptible pinholing in the glaze or slightly off-standard colour shades. Many tiles are imported exclusively from Italy and there is also a wide selection of fine quality English and Victorian style decorated tiles, borders and dados, as well as a wide choice of discontinued and special purchase first quality tiles.

TILE CLEARING HOUSE

NEW SOUTHGATE INDUSTRIAL ESTATE, LOWER PARK ROAD, LONDON N11 1QD, ☎ 020 8361 6180, 8–6 MON–FRI, 9–6 SAT, 10–4 SUN.

ACE CORNER, STONEBRIDGE PARK, NORTH CIRCULAR ROAD, WEMBLEY, LONDON NW10 7UI, ☎ 020 8965 8062, 8–6 MON–FRI, 9–6 SAT, 10–4 SUN.

MARITIME INDUSTRIAL ESTATE, HORIZON WAY, CHARLTON, LONDON SE7 7SW, ☎ 020 8858 9955, FAX: 020 8453 0392, 8–6 MON–FRI, 9–6 SAT, 10–4 SUN. **PERMANENT DISCOUNT OUTLET**

See page 345 (CAMBS)

TILES GALORE

1 CROSS WAYS PARADE, SELSDON PARK ROAD, ADDINGTON, LONDON CR2 8JJ, ☎ 020 8651 3782, 7.30–5 MON–SAT.

GRACEFIELD GARDENS, STREATHAM, LONDON SW16 2ST, ☎ 020 8677 6068, 8–5.30 MON–SAT. **PERMANENT DISCOUNT OUTLET**

Sells perfect tiles from around the world at discount prices by buying direct from the factories, unlike the large department stores which buy from distributors. There are hundreds of designs to choose from. The Addington Shop is small, while the Streatham shop has 10,000 square feet of tiles. All necessary equipment is also stocked and staff give helpful advice and tips if needed.

TOWNSENDS

96A CLIFTON HILL, LONDON NW8 0JN, ☎ 020 7372 4327, 10–6 MON–FRI, 10–5 SAT.

106 BOUNDARY ROAD, LONDON NW8 0RH, ☎ 020 7372 4327, 10–6 MON–FRI, 10–5 SAT.

81 ABBEY ROAD, ST JOHNS WOOD, LONDON NW8 0AE, ☎ 020 7625 6762, FAX: 020 7624 4756, 10–6 MON–FRI, 10–5 SAT. **ARCHITECTURAL SALVAGE**

Antique fireplaces, related items, and antique stained glass. More than 800 fireplaces in stock at prices from £250 to £30,000 in wood, marble, cast-iron and natural stone. This business has been established for more than 20 years and offers a full survey and fitting service and free delivery in the London area. They also restore antique stained glass, acid-etched and sandblasted glass from £30 per square foot to £100.

WARD & STEVENS

248 HIGH STREET NORTH, MANOR PARK, LONDON E12 6SB, ☎ 020 8472 4067, FAX: 020 8470 9091, www.wardandstevens.co.uk, 9–5.30 MON–SAT, 11–4 SUN. **PERMANENT DISCOUNT OUTLET**

Budget ranges of floor and wall tiles including standard quality and excellent seconds. Specialise in low cost quarry floor tiles at prices starting from £6.80 per square metre plus VAT. Also 300 x 300 floors in a wide range available from stock. Wall tiles from £2 per metre to 25 per metre. A wide range of ceramic borders are available from stock. Budget range of wallcoverings from stock. Full range of British Standard and NCS paints (10,000 plus colours) at less than trade prices. Sells mirrors cut to size. Budget priced top quality laminate flooring from £4.99 a metre.

MIDDLESEX

EUROTILES

UNIT 2C, TWICKENHAM TRADING ESTATE, RUGBY ROAD, MIDDLESEX TW1 1DG, ☎ 020 8744 0088, www.eurotiles.co.uk, 8–5 MON–FRI, 9–4 SAT, 11–3 SUN. **PERMANENT DISCOUNT OUTLET**

Opposite the main entrance to Twickenham Rugby Ground, this showroom displays tiles and some bathroom suites. There are regular changes of merchandise which offer good deals.

PECO

72 STATION ROAD, HAMPTON, MIDDLESEX TW12 2BT, ☎ 020 8979 8310, FAX: 020 8941 3319, www.peco-of-hampton.co.uk, 8.15–5 MON–SAT. **ARCHITECTURAL SALVAGE**

One of the largest door and fireplace warehouses in the country with two floors of display area and three additional shops featuring at least 600 fireplaces, 100 in marble and slate. Stocks about 2,000 period doors up to the Thirties, as well as oak beams, pot stoves from France and cast-iron fireplaces. Also offers marble restoration, fireplace restoration, and made-to-order stained-glass panels and doors. Please phone for more details.

THE DECOR STORE

4 ENFIELD ROAD, ENFIELD, MIDDLESEX, ☎ 020 8363 1680, FAX: 020 8366 6618, 8.30–5 MON–FRI, 9–12 SAT. **PERMANENT DISCOUNT OUTLET**

A painter's and decorator's cash and carry with computerised mixing machines for Dulux, Cuprinol, Crown, Sandtex, Woodsheen, Johnstones, Leyland, Manders, Sadolin, Glidden, Macpherson and Berger. Wallpaper brands include Kingfisher, Mayfair, Crown and Vymura, among others, from a range of 300 wallpaper books at discounts of up to 40%. Anaglyptas at half price. Next day ordering for wallpapers. Discount fabrics also available. Aimed at the trade, The Decor Store also caters for members of the public who benefit from the discounts available.

THE SALVAGE SHOP

34–40 WATLING AVENUE, BURNT OAK, MIDDLESEX HA8 0LR, ☎ 020 8952 4353, **e-mail:** lss@salvage1.co.uk, www.salvage1.co.uk, 9–5.30 MON–SAT, 10–4 SUN. **PERMANENT DISCOUNT OUTLET**

An Aladdin's cave of salvaged stock for the avid bargain hunter, most of which has been the subject of insurance claims for fire or flood, salvage, bankruptcy or is simply clearance stock. Stock changes every two or three days and regular visitors have found anything from half price Kenwood Chefs, televisions and toys to furniture, kitchen items, linens and especially fantastic bargains in designer clothing. Yves Saint Laurent, Armani, Ungaro, Hugo Boss and Valentino, as well as all major high street names, are just some of the names to be found (though the labels are often cut out). Discounts range from 50% to 80%. Phone first to check stock.

NORFOLK

AYLSHAM BATHROOM & KITCHEN

BURGH ROAD, AYLSHAM, NORFOLK NR11 6AR, ☎ 01263 735396, FAX: 01263 734800, **e-mail:** aylsham.bathrooms@virgin.net, www.abkc.co.uk, 8.30–5 MON–FRI, 9–5 SAT, 10–4 SUN. **PERMANENT DISCOUNT OUTLET**

Bathroom equipment, kitchen displays, all at reduced prices of between 15% to 25% less than normal retail prices. Top brands such as Sanitan, Heritage, Ideal Standard and Armitage Shanks are some of the 70 bathrooms displayed here; and there are 30 display kitchens with appliances by Neff, Philips, Whirlpool and Zanussi, including kitchen and bathroom taps from the main manufacturers such as Franke, Blanco as well as Lefroy Brooks, Tre Mercati, Briston, Sottini and Villeroy & Boch.

BMJ POWER

SCANDIC HOUSE, 85 MOUNTERGATE, NORWICH, NORFOLK NR1 1PY, ☎ 01603 627600, FAX: 01603 615650, www.bmjdirect.com, 8.30–5.30 MON–FRI, 9.30–5.30 ON WED, 9–5.30 SAT. **FACTORY SHOP**

See page 343 (BERKS)

HODGSON'S FORGE

THE FORGE, 2 WESLEY ROAD, TERRINGTON ST CLEMENT, NEAR KINGS LYNN, NORFOLK PE34 4NG, ☎ 01553 828637, 8–5 MON–FRI, WEEKENDS BY APPOINTMENT. **ARCHITECTURAL SALVAGE**

Hand-forged wrought iron work, including restoration. Anything from fenders to gates.

NORTHAMPTONSHIRE

BATHCRAFT

4A HAVELOCK STREET, KETTERING, NORTHAMPTONSHIRE NN16 9PZ, ☎ 01536 417009, FAX: 01536 417009, www.antiquebaths.co.uk, 9.30–5.30 WED–SAT. **ARCHITECTURAL SALVAGE**

Old fashioned rolltop baths, taps, bath fittings, showers and re-enamelling.

SHOWHOME WAREHOUSE

11–17 FRANCIS COURT, WELLINGBOROUGH ROAD, RUSHDEN, NORTHAMPTONSHIRE NN10 6AY, ☎ 01933 411695, 10–5 TUE–SUN, 11–3 MON. **PERMANENT DISCOUNT OUTLET**

The contents of quality show homes are sold seven days a week at this 20,000 square foot warehouse. Savings normally range from 50% to 70% off store prices. About 50% of their stock is sold each week and different stock arrives daily. Choose from a range of kitchen appliances, lounge furniture, three-piece suites, dining tables and chairs, rugs, study and bedroom furniture, oil paintings, mirrors, ornaments, televisions and videos, patio and garden furniture and gym equipment. The range is eclectic: from suits of armour to lions heads, Tiffany lampshades to leather zebras, hand-painted furniture to mahogany classics, alien-shaped CD racks to antique carts made into bookcases or sets of oars turned into coat racks. Because a high percentage of their business comes from trade, prices exclude VAT but still represent very good value for money. For example, elaborate metal bed, £175, normally £750; dining room table and chairs, £350, normally £1,500; washer-dryer, £300, usually £500 to £600. Occasional auctions take place during the year: phone for details.

NORTHUMBERLAND

NO FRILLS DIY STORE

WHITLEY ROAD, LONGBENTON, NEWCASTLE UPON TYNE, TYNE & WEAR NE12 9SZ, ☎ 0191 270 0393, FAX: 0191 215 0823, 9–8 MON–SAT, 10–4 SUN. **PERMANENT DISCOUNT OUTLET**

See page 343 (BEDS)

TECAZ

SWIFT 957, TECAZ HOUSE, NORHAM ROAD, CHIRTON INDUSTRIAL ESTATE, NORTH SHIELDS, NEWCASTLE UPON TYNE, TYNE & WEAR NE29 7TN, ☎ 0191 257 6511, FAX: 0191 296 1943, **e-mail:** northshields@swift957ltd.com, www.swift957ltd.com, 9–6 MON–FRI, 9–5 SAT, 10–4 SUN. **PERMANENT DISCOUNT OUTLET**

See page 347 (CO DURH)

NOTTINGHAMSHIRE

BMJ POWER

361 CARLTON HILL, NOTTINGHAM, NOTTINGHAMSHIRE NG4 1HX, ☎ 0115 987 3012, FAX: 0115 940 1014, www.bmjdirect.com, 8.30–5.30 MON, TUE, FRI, 9.30–5.30 WED, 8.30–7.30 THUR, 8.30–4 SAT. **FACTORY SHOP**

See page 343 (BERKS)

OLD FLAMES ARCHITECTURAL ANTIQUES

531 WOODBOROUGH ROAD, NOTTINGHAM, NOTTINGHAMSHIRE NG3 5FR, ☎ 0115 960 5665, 10–5 MON–SAT. **ARCHITECTURAL SALVAGE**

Garden ornaments, bathroom fittings, Victorian fireplaces, doors, radiators, and stained and etched glass, all sold at very competitive prices.

TILE CLEARING HOUSE

POULTON DRIVE, OFF DALESIDE ROAD, NOTTINGHAM, NOTTINGHAMSHIRE NG4 4DH, ☎ 0115 985 1921, 8–6 MON–FRI, 9–6 SAT, 10–4 SUN. **PERMANENT DISCOUNT OUTLET**

See page 345 (CAMBS)

WILKINSON STORES

2-6 FRONT STREET, ARNOLD, NOTTINGHAM, NOTTINGHAMSHIRE NG5 7EL, ☎ 0115 926 0805, www.wilko.co.uk, 9–5.30 MON–SAT, 10–4 SUN. MAIL ORDER. **PERMANENT DISCOUNT OUTLET**

See page 346 (CHESH)

OXFORDSHIRE

FIRED EARTH

TWYFORD MILL, OXFORD ROAD, ADDERBURY, OXFORDSHIRE OX17 3HP, ☎ 01295 814399, 9.30–5.30 MON–SAT, 12–4 SUN. **FACTORY SHOP**

Fired Earth sells seconds and discontinued ranges of tiles, fabric and natural fibre floor coverings from its countryside venue, as well as rugs, kelims, gabbehs and other tribal weaving at full price. Terracotta and slate floor tiles are sold from around £15 a square metre upwards; some glazed tiles from around £5 a square metre. There is a lifestyle range comprising furniture, lamps and glassware. Bathroom suites are available, too. Fired Earth also produces the V&A range of historic and traditional paints and dented paint tins are sold at a discount alongside other bruised accessories. Fired Earth is now part of the Aga Group so a full range of Agas are also displayed in this outlet.

SHROPSHIRE

GLYN WEBB

UNIT 3, SUNDORNE RETAIL PARK, SHREWSBURY, SHROPSHIRE SY1 4YA, ☎ 01743 460993, 9–8 MON–SAT, 10–4 SUN AND BANK HOLIDAYS. **PERMANENT DISCOUNT OUTLET**

See page 346 (CHESH)

ORANGERY HOME AND GARDEN

140 CORVE STREET, LUDLOW, SHROPSHIRE SY8 2PG, ☎ 01584 876207, **e-mail:** info@orangeryhome.com, www.orangeryhome.com, 9.30–5 MON–SAT. **ARCHITECTURAL SALVAGE**

A growing family business, Orangery Home & Garden was originally founded in 1985 as an architectural antiques business. By striving to source the very best period items for homes and garden, the business has built its reputation on always having unique and beautiful original pieces. In particular, they specialise in period bathrooms and fittings, fireplaces and grates, dramatic lighting, doors and door furniture, Belfast sinks and mixer taps, leaded light and garden features. Based in spacious showrooms in Ludlow, Orangery provides an ideal environment for finding those period features that are increasingly hard to find. The business also offers a bespoke service to help those planning a major renovation. By carefully understanding the property and the customers requirements, Orangery will help source the prefect pieces at the required times during the project. To complement the core range of period items, Orangery have also sourced the best in craftsman made accessories where original items have become almost impossible to find. Examples include spun-brass door knobs and blacksmith-made ironmongery. Recalimed, recycled and re-thought items are also stocked to provide that finishing touch to the home.

SOMERSET

BLACK & DECKER

CLARKS VILLAGE FACTORY SHOPPING CENTRE, FARM ROAD, STREET, JUNCTION 23 OF M5, SOMERSET BA16 0BB, ☎ 01458 840205, 9–6 MON–SAT, 11–5 SUN. **FACTORY SHOP IN A FACTORY SHOPPING VILLAGE**

Reconditioned tools and acccessories from the famous Black & Decker range, all with full manufacturer's warranty. Often, stock consists of goods returned from the shops because of damaged packaging or which are part of a line which is being discontinued. Lots of seasonal special offers.

BRIDGWATER RECLAMATION

THE OLD CO-OP DAIRY, MONMOUTH STREET, BRIDGWATER, SOMERSET TA6 5EJ, ☎ 01278 424636, FAX: 01934 512308, **e-mail:** chrisw-b.rec@talk21.com, www.reclaiming.it, 8–5 MON–FRI, 8–12 SAT. **ARCHITECTURAL SALVAGE**

Building materials including reclaimed bricks, Bridgwater-made clay roof and ridge tiles, Welsh slates, flagstones, chimney pots, doors, baths, fireplaces, reproduction furniture and purpose-made joinery from the on-site workshop.

CHAPLINS SUPERSTORES HOME & GARDEN

BINDON ROAD, TAUNTON, SOMERSET TA2 6AA, ☎ 01823 288017, FAX: 01823 336189, 9–8 MON–FRI, 9–6 SAT, 10.30–4.30 SUN. **PERMANENT DISCOUNT OUTLET**

A wide range of merchandise for the bargain hunter, including garden tools, plants, fertilisers and accessories; toys; adults clothing and shoes; stationery; household textiles; electrical equipment; DIY items; glass and china; bathroom accessories; partyware; candles; food accessories. Spades are available at £4.99, trowels at 99p, shears at £5.99 (while stocks last).

OLD HARRYS RECLAMATION LTD

FAIRWATER YARD, HIGHER PALMERSTON ROAD, OFF STAPLEGROVE ROAD, TAUNTON, SOMERSET TA1 1DP, ☎ 01823 337035, FAX: 01823 337035, www.reclaimationsuk.com, 9–5.30 MON–FRI, 10–12 SAT, OR AFTER HOURS BY APPOINTMENT. **ARCHITECTURAL SALVAGE**

Clay roof tiles, slates, secondhand bricks, chimney pots, recycled timber, floorboards, fireplaces, windows, doors, sanitaryware, staircases, RSJ's, channel-crushed concrete and interesting curios discovered during demolition. Old Harrys recycles all available materials from buildings, from chimney pots to flagstones. Visitors are welcome to come and browse, and if they do not have a particular item that you are seeking in stock, they will try to locate it for you.

SCREWFIX DIRECT (MAIL ORDER)

SCREWFIX DIRECT, FREEPOST, YEOVIL, SOMERSET BA22 8BF, ☎ 0500 414141, www.screwfix.com, MAIL ORDER. PHONE LINES AVAILABLE 7–10 MON–FRI, 8–8 SAT, SUN AND BANK HOLIDAYS.

PERMANENT DISCOUNT OUTLET

DIY materials by mail order: everything including the kitchen sink, from nails, screws, torches and bulbs to electric screwdrivers, plumbing materials and sealants at prices which, one reader claims, are lower than the DIY superstores. Send for a comprehensive catalogue, which is updated and expanded quarterly. All products are available for next working day delivery. Warehouse shop on site also sells ends of lines and one-off samples at discounted prices.

SCREWFIX DIRECT (SHOP)

MEAD AVENUE, HOUNDSTONE BUSINESS PARK, YEOVIL, SOMERSET BA22 8RT, ☎ 0500 414141, FAX: 0800 056 2256, **e-mail:** online@screwfix.com, www.screwfix.com, 7–6 MON–WED, 7–8 THUR, FRI, 8–6 SAT AND SUN. **PERMANENT DISCOUNT OUTLET**

DIY materials by mail order: everything including the kitchen sink, from nails, screws, torches and bulbs to electric screwdrivers, plumbing materials and sealants at prices which, one reader claims, are lower than the DIY superstores. Send for a comprehensive catalogue, which is updated and expanded quarterly. All products are available for next working day delivery. Warehouse shop on site also sells ends of lines and one-off samples at discounted prices.

TOTAL BATHROOMS

BRASSMILL TRADING ESTATE, BRASSMILL LANE, NEWBRIDGE, BATH, SOMERSET BA1 3JF, ☎ 01225 481815, 9–5 TUE–FRI, 9–4 SAT. **FACTORY SHOP**

Largest suppliers of bathroom accessories to the retail trade. Supplying accessories for well-known DIY and homewares stores, here they sell ends of lines and overstocks of bathroom accessories such as towel rails, mirrors, toilet brushes, toothbrush holders as well as vanity units, bath panels, bathroom cabinets. They now stock larger bathroom items such as shower cubicles and baths with some display room sets. Phone or call in for more information. Total Bathrooms is the exclusive supplier of Rhoper Rhodes Seconds and end-of-line products.

WALCOT RECLAMATION

108 WALCOT STREET, BATH, SOMERSET BA1 5BG, ☎ 01225 444404, FAX: 01225 448163, **e-mail:** vick@walcot.com, www.walcot.com, 8.30–5.30 MON–FRI, 9–5 SAT. **ARCHITECTURAL SALVAGE**

Ideas and advice for the period home owner. Everything from panelling to paving, doors, flagstones, flooring, bathroom fittings, fireplaces, radiators, garden ornaments, railings and gates. High quality replicas also available from 'The Repro Shop'. Stone carving, wood and metal-working restoration workshops on site.

WELLS RECLAMATION COMPANY

COXLEY, NR WELLS, SOMERSET BA5 1RQ, ☎ 01749 677087, FAX: 01749 671089, www.wellsreclamation.com, 8.30–5.30 MON–FRI, 9–4 SAT. **ARCHITECTURAL SALVAGE**

Reclaimed timber: pine and oak beams, pine doors, flooring; bathroom accessories, quarry tiles and flagstones (pennent and blue lias), fireplaces and bricks sold from this four-acre site.

STAFFORDSHIRE

CAWARDEN BRICK COMPANY

CAWARDEN SPRINGS FARM, BLITHBURY ROAD, RUGELEY, STAFFORDSHIRE WS15 3HL, ☎ 01889 574066, FAX: 01889 575695, **e-mail:** sales@cawardenreclaim.co.uk, www.cawardenreclaim.co.uk, 8–5 MON–FRI, 8–4 SAT, 9–3 SUN. **ARCHITECTURAL SALVAGE**

New showroom with fireplaces, large quantities of reclaimed handmade bricks, also tiles, flagstone and block stone. Oak flooring, doors, cupboards, garden ornaments and oak beams.

GLYN WEBB

122–126 BROAD STREET, HANLEY, STOKE-ON-TRENT, STAFFORDSHIRE ST1 4EQ, ☎ 01782 214471, 9–8 MON–SAT, 10–4 SUN AND BANK HOLIDAYS. **PERMANENT DISCOUNT OUTLET**

See page 346 (CHESH)

H & R JOHNSON FACTORY SHOP

HAREWOOD STREET, TUNSTALL, STOKE-ON-TRENT, STAFFORDSHIRE ST6 4JX, ☎ 01782 524040, 8.30–4 MON–SAT, 10–4 SUN. **PERMANENT DISCOUNT OUTLET**

Seconds of wall tiles from many of the biggest manufacturers in the UK, as well as best quality imported ceramic floor tiles. The flaws in the wall tiles are visual only – there are no cracks or chips. There is a vast selection including plain and patterned tiles, borders, white tiles and 400mm x 300mm marble effect bathroom tiles. Free parking.

HOUSEHOLD BARGAIN CENTRE

23 COMMERCE STREET, LONGTON, STOKE-ON-TRENT, STAFFORDSHIRE ST3 5RH, ☎ 01782 314016, OPEN 9–10 AND 11–6 MON–WED, FRI, SAT. **PERMANENT DISCOUNT OUTLET**

Stocks a selection of blinds from 32 different UK manufacturers and seven continental companies including vertical, venetian, pleated and roller blinds. Offers a 10% discount if you measure and fit yourself.

HYDE PARK TILES

UNIT 6, HYDE PARK INDUSTRIAL ESTATE, CITY ROAD, STOKE-ON-TRENT, STAFFORDSHIRE ST4 1DS, ☎ 01782 747547, 8.30–5.30 MON, WED, FRI, 8.30–8 TUE, THUR, 8.30–5 SAT, 10–2 SUN. **PERMANENT DISCOUNT OUTLET**

Part of a tile distribution company, which means that when they sell the tiles themselves, they are their own middleman and can cut out most of that cost to pass savings on to their customers. For example, they sell tiles at £16.95 a square yard which are on sale at other tile shops for £29.50. They specialise in top Italian and Spanish companies such as Apperici, Richetti and Gomez Gomez and deal in sizes from 10cm x 10cm to 45cm x 45cm. Free parking.

PAINT 'N' PAPER

CLOUGH STREET, HANLEY, STOKE-ON-TRENT, STAFFORDSHIRE ST1 4BA, ☎ 01782 205201, **e-mail:** lyndon@slanns.net or michelle@slanns.net, www.rugshop.co.uk, 9–6 MON–FRI, 9–5.30 SAT, 10–4 SUN. **PERMANENT DISCOUNT OUTLET**

Leyland paint, Coloroll wallpaper, Crown paint and wallpaper, Graham & Brown super fresco, borders and vinyls at discount prices. Over 10,000 colours are always in stock, and if you are looking for a particular colour that they don't stock, they can mix it for you. Also sells a full range of decorating accessories, and a range of Stanley tools at competitive prices. Lincrusta wallcoverings are also available.

PARK LANE TILES

UNIT 7, EMERALD WAY, STONE BUSINESS PARK, STONE, STAFFORDSHIRE ST15 0SR, ☎ 01785 816161, 9–5.30 MON–FRI, 9–5 SAT. **PERMANENT DISCOUNT OUTLET**

Retail shop for Creta Ceramica, a company which imports good quality Italian and Spanish wall and floor tiles. You can find their tiles in shops countrywide, but at varying prices depending on the local competition and almost always more expensive than they are in this shop, which is on the same industrial estate as the wholesale warehouse. For the floor, they offer terracotta lookalike tiles averaging £14 a square yard, quarry tiles, porcelain tiles, both glazed and unglazed, octagon, dot, hexagon, square and lozenge shaped. For walls, the tiles are glazed in a variety of finishes from satin and glossy to eggshell and come in sizes from four inches square to 14 inches square by nine inches. They also offer a range of glass mosaic tiles on sheets in 10 different colours with 144 tiles to a one foot square sheet, as well as all necessary adhesives and grouts for DIY or professional use, all at very competitive prices.

TILE CLEARING HOUSE

104–106 CITY ROAD, FENTON, STOKE-ON-TRENT STAFFORDSHIRE ST4 2PH, ☎ 01782 849966, 8–6 MON–FRI, 9–6 SAT, 10–4 SUN.

BROWNHILLS ROAD, TUNSTALL, STOKE-ON-TRENT, STAFFORDSHIRE ST6 4OU, ☎ 01782 833248, 8–6 MON–FRI, 9–6 SAT, 10–4 SUN. **PERMANENT DISCOUNT OUTLET**

See page 345 (CAMBS)

TOPPS TILES

UNIT 4, LIME COURT, LIME VALLEY ROAD, NEWCASTLE UNDER LYME, STAFFORDSHIRE ST5 3TF, ☎ 01782 711083, 8–6 MON–FRI, 8 ON THUR, 9–5.30 SAT, 10–4 SUN.

UNIT B, SCOTIA ROAD, BURSLEM, STOKE-ON-TRENT, STAFFORDSHIRE ST6 4HE, ☎ 01782 819111, 8–6 MON–FRI, 8 ON THUR, 9–5.30 SAT, 10–4 SUN. **PERMANENT DISCOUNT OUTLET**

Owners of the Tile Clearing House whose shops are detailed in this book, their main business also offers tiles at competitive prices. They sell wall and floor tiles from names such as Johnsons, Pilkingtons and Platta as well as Spanish and Bulgarian tiles. Here, if you buy more than four square metres, you get a discount of 30%. They also sell real wood and laminate flooring, and are now official stockists of Bal adhesives and grouts. For a catalogue phone free on 0800 783 6262. Also has branches in Inverness, Greenock, Perth, Aberdeen and Edinburgh.

UNIT DISCOUNT

53 UPPER HUNTBACH STREET, HANLEY, STOKE-ON-TRENT, STAFFORDSHIRE ST1 2BX, ☎ 01782 268977, 9–5.30 MON–SAT. **PERMANENT DISCOUNT OUTLET**

Unit Discount sell competitively priced baths, sinks, toilets, bidets, shower trays, kitchen sink units, as well as the plumbing materials to complete your own DIY installation: copper tubes and plastic waste pipes.

WILKINSON STORES

OLD HALL STREET, HANLEY, STOKE-ON-TRENT, STAFFORDSHIRE, ☎ 01782 279225, www.wilko.co.uk, 8.30–6 MON–FRI, 8 ON THUR, 11–5 SUN. MAIL ORDER.

CASTLE HOUSE, 4748 IRONMARKET, NEWCASTLE UNDER LYME, STAFFORDSHIRE ST5 1PD., ☎ 01782 714334, www.wilko.co.uk, 8.30–5.30 MON–SAT. **PERMANENT DISCOUNT OUTLET**

See page 346 (CHESH)

SUFFOLK

GLYN WEBB

204 RANELAGH ROAD, IPSWICH, SUFFOLK IP2 0AG, ☎ 01473 236333, 9–8 MON–SAT, 10–4 SUN AND BANK HOLIDAYS. **PERMANENT DISCOUNT OUTLET**

See page 346 (CHESH)

ORWELL PINE CO LTD

HALIFAX MILL, 427 WHERSTEAD ROAD, IPSWICH, SUFFOLK IP2 8LH, ☎ 01473 680091, FAX: 01473 691542, **e-mail:** sales@orwells.co.uk, www.orwells.co.uk, 8.30–5.30 MON–FRI, 8–4 SAT. **ARCHITECTURAL SALVAGE**

Buys old pine floorboards and joists to make new 'old' pine furniture, including kitchens. Stockists of old pine doors and manufacturers of good quality cottage doors at £75 plus VAT. The manufacture of bespoke furniture for any room in the house made in oak, cherry, maple, painted, etc. Suppliers of granite and marble cut to size.

TERRACOTTA DIRECT

PINFORD END FARM, PINFORD END, HAWSTEAD, BURY ST EDMUNDS, SUFFOLK IP29 5NU, ☎ 01284 388002, FAX: 01284 388003, **e-mail:** info@terracottadirect.com, www.terracottadirect.com, BY APPOINTMENT ONLY. **PERMANENT DISCOUNT OUTLET**

Handmade Spanish terracotta floor tiles in different sizes and shades at prices which are discounted by one third. Delivery within three days. Colour brochure available.

THE TOOL SHOP

78 HIGH STREET, NEEDHAM MARKET, SUFFOLK IP6 8AW, ☎ 01449 722992, FAX: 01449 722683, **e-mail:** tony@antiquetools.co.uk/mike@uktoolshop.com, www.antiquetools.co.uk/www.uktoolshop.com, 10–5 MON–SAT. MAIL ORDER. **SECONDHAND SHOP**

Specialises in antique and usable tools with a vast selection always in stock and 25 new types added each week. They always have more than 1,500 carving tools (planes, chisels, gauges) at the shop as well as many tools associated with other trades. They also send tools by mail all over the world and will always try and find a specific tool. Four times a year, they hold tool auctions at the Limes Hotel, opposite the shop. Three of these auctions contain mixed quality tools, ranging from 'as found condition' to items of collectable quality. There is also a fishing tackle section and a 'bygones' section containing items of interest, kitchenalia, old golf clubs etc. Once a year, there is also an international tool sale. This comprises more than 1,500 lots of superior quality tools for the user and collector. In order to qualify for this sale, the tools have to be in superb condition and they are presented in a large-format, colour catalogue. Also sells a fine range of new Japanese tools and French Auriou handmade chisels. They now have a website which specialises in new tools: www.uktoolshop.com.

SURREY

ALFRED G CAWLEY

HAVERING FARM, GUILDFORD ROAD, SUTTON GREEN, SURREY GU4 7QA, ☎ 01483 232398, 8–5 MON–FRI, 8–1 SAT. **ARCHITECTURAL SALVAGE**

Demolition experts, they stock bathroom fittings, floorboards, railway sleepers, roof tiles, bricks, windows, doors and beams.

ANTIQUE BUILDINGS LIMITED

ALFOLD ROAD, DUNSFOLD, GODALMING, SURREY GU8 4NP, ☎ 01483 200477, **e-mail:** info@antiquebuildings.com, www.antiquebuildings.com, 8.15–4.30 MON–FRI, OR BY APPOINTMENT. **ARCHITECTURAL SALVAGE**

Stocks an immense number of ancient oak beams, ceiling joists, bressumes, oak and pine floorboard, handmade clay tiles, bricks and walling stone, reclaimed handmade bricks and peg tiles. Specialises in ancient timber framed buildings, with more than 35 barns, cartsheds, hovels, granary and house frames available for re-erection, each of which has been measured, drawn and photographed before being dismantled.

BMJ POWER

20 THE BROADWAY, TOLWORTH, SURREY KT6 7HL, ☎ 020 8399 6411, FAX: 020 8390 4848, www.bmjdirect.com, 8.30–5 MON–FRI, 9.30–5 ON WED, 8.30–4 SAT. **FACTORY SHOP**

See page 343 (BERKS)

PEW CORNER LTD

ARTINGTON MANOR FARM, OLD PORTSMOUTH ROAD, GUILDFORD, SURREY GU3 1LP, ☎ 01483 533337, FAX: 01483 535554, **e-mail:** sales@pewcorner.co.uk, www.pewcorner.co.uk, 10–5 MON–SAT, 11–5 SUN. **ARCHITECTURAL SALVAGE**

Reclaimed church furniture, fixtures and fittings and makers of traditional handmade furniture. Hundreds of original church pews in oak, pine and elm; church chairs; altars; pulpits; lecterns; fonts; balcony fonts; Gothic screens; candlesticks; wood flooring, in fact anything that exists inside a church. Also creates handmade furniture from solid oak, several styles of dining table, refectory, double and single pedestal, scissor brace, vaulted and round. Dining chairs, sideboards, dressers, bookshelves, beds etc. Most items are made to order and are available in a variety of colours and finishes. Large showroom with plenty of free parking. Phone for brochure and map or visit website for further details.

SIESTA CORK TILES CO

UNIT 21, TAIT ROAD, GLOUCESTER ROAD, CROYDON, SURREY CRO 2DP, ☎ 020 8683 4055, FAX: 020 8683 4480, www.siestacorktiles.co.uk, 9–5 MON–FRI. CLOSED BETWEEN 1 AND 2. MAIL ORDER. **PERMANENT DISCOUNT OUTLET**

Cork importers, who supply on a mail order basis, a complete range of cork floor tiles in all thicknesses unsealed, acrylic varnished, hard wax or PVC surfaced, plus a coloured range. Special offers usually available. Details and samples sent on request. They also sell cork for walls and ceilings, decoration, insulation and for noticeboards. A large range of tiles are stocked in thicknesses of 3mm, 6mm and 8mm, and in sizes 300 x 300mm and 600 x 300mm. Composition cork (fine grain) comes in rolls up to 1.22m x 5m in a variety of thicknesses: 2mm, 3mm and 6mm, ideal for large noticeboards. Unsealed floor cork can be coloured using diluted water-based paints then clear varnished when laid with quick-dry, water-based floor sealant. Please phone for more details.

SILVERLAND STONE

HOLLOWAY HILL, CHERTSEY, SURREY KT16 0AE, ☎ 01932 569277, FAX: 01932 563588, www.silverlandstone.co.uk, 8–5 MON–FRI, 10–4 SAT, SUN (WINTER) 7.30–5.30 MON–FRI, 8.30–4 SAT, 10–4 SUN (SUMMER). **ARCHITECTURAL SALVAGE**

Natural stone floors for both interior and exterior and fireplaces. Extensive range of hard landscaping materials sold including rockery and pebbles.

SUSSEX

BATH SHIELD

BLENHEIM STUDIO, LEWES ROAD, FOREST ROW, SUSSEX RH18 5EZ, ☎ 01342 823243, FAX: 01342 823097, **e-mail:** sales@chadder.com, www.chadder.com, 8.30–5.30 MON–FRI, 8.30–2 SAT. PHONE FIRST FOR AN APPOINTMENT. **ARCHITECTURAL SALVAGE**

If you've got a good quality bath which is looking a bit tatty, have it re-enamelled in situ or in the workshop. While it will cost from £325 plus VAT, just think of the savings made by not having to rip out an old bath, hire a plumber, redo tiling etc. And because the re-enamelled bath is baked with infra-red lamps and polished, it will repel calcium and dirt and be easier to clean in the future. Also provides traditional and Victorian bathroom equipment, taps, shower roses and fittings and old-fashioned bathrooms. Up to 150 different baths and accessories on display at any one time at the retail shop, Chadder & Co. Delivers in the London area and abroad.

BRIGHTON ARCHITECTURAL SALVAGE

33–34 GLOUCESTER ROAD, BRIGHTON, EAST SUSSEX BN1 4AQ, ☎ 01273 681656, FAX: 01273 681656, 10–5 TUE–SAT. **ARCHITECTURAL SALVAGE**

Lots of fireplaces including marble, cast iron and wood surrounds; reclaimed flooring; cast-iron inserts from Regency to Art Nouveau; doors, pine furniture, columns, stained and etched glass, panelling, railings and garden ornaments.

THE WEST SUSSEX ANTIQUE TIMBER COMPANY LTD

RELIANCE WORKS, NEWPOUND, WISBOROUGH GREEN, SUSSEX RH14 0AZ, ☎ 01403 700139, FAX: 01403 700936, www.wsatimber@aol.com, 8.30–5 MON–FRI, 9–12.30 SAT. **ARCHITECTURAL SALVAGE**

Specialists in oak beams, oak flooring and mouldings (the oak flooring is supplied and laid). Also sells pine and oak doors and old timber furniture. Also carries out barn restoration and conversion: please phone for more details.

WARWICKSHIRE & WEST MIDLANDS

BMJ POWER

LONG ACRE, BIRMINGHAM, WEST MIDLANDS B7 5SL, ☎ 0121 327 3411, www.bmjdirect.com, 8–5.30 MON–FRI, 9–5.30 WED, 8–2 SAT. **FACTORY SHOP**

See page 343 (BERKS)

CONSERVATION BUILDING PRODUCTS LTD

FORGE WORKS, FORGE LANE, CRADLEY HEATH, WARLEY, WEST MIDLANDS B64 5AL, ☎ 01384 564219, FAX: 01384 410625, **e-mail:** conservationbuildingproducts@ukonline.co.uk, www.conservationbuildingproducts.co.uk, 8–4.30 MON–FRI, 8–12 SAT. **ARCHITECTURAL SALVAGE**

Bricks, roof tiles, slates, quarry tiles, flooring beams, decorative ironwork, staircase parts, complete oak-framed buildings, garden statuary and interesting artefacts for period property renovations.

DISCOUNT CERAMICS

7 MILLFIELDS ROAD, BILSTON, WOLVERHAMPTON, WEST MIDLANDS WV1 0QS, ☎ 01902 405526, 8–6 MON–FRI, 8–5.30 SAT, 10–4 SUN. **PERMANENT DISCOUNT OUTLET**

Stocks a vast range of imported wall and floor tiles. As they buy direct from the importer, they can cut costs to below that of most of their competitors, though in areas with a wide selection of tile shops, prices will be on a par.

GLYN WEBB

UNIT 1, KEYWAY RETAIL PARK, ARMSTRONG WAY, WILLENHALL, WEST MIDLANDS WV13 2QU, ☎ 01902 630704, 9–8 MON–SAT, 10–4 SUN AND BANK HOLIDAYS. **PERMANENT DISCOUNT OUTLET**

See page 346 (CHESH)

INTERNATIONAL STOCK LTD

95–100 REA STREET, DIGBETH, BIRMINGHAM, WEST MIDLANDS B5 6HA, ☎ 0121 622 3232, **e-mail:** mail@international-stock.co.uk, www.international-stock.co.uk, 9–5 MON–SAT, 10–4 SUN, CLOSED 1 ON WED.

1–17 SILVER STREET, KING'S HEATH, BIRMINGHAM, WEST MIDLANDS B14 7QX, ☎ 0121 443 3232, FAX: 0121 444 1792, **e-mail:** mail@international-stock.co.uk, www.international-stock.co.uk, 9–6 MON–SAT, CLOSED 1 ON WED. **PERMANENT DISCOUNT OUTLET**

Bankrupt, fire and flood damaged articles from CDs and videos, household goods and clothes to DIY tools and television sets, carpets and cookers. The King's Heath branch is a two-storey warehouse with ever-changing stock. The upper floor is devoted to electrical goods, some marked down to 30% of their normal retail cost. The Digbeth branch sells bigger items such as kitchens, flooring, tiles, dining room and lounge furniture, central heating radiators and a large clothing section for all the family, all of which is sold below wholesale price and in some cases below manufacturers cost price. Top brand name kitchens, when in stock, are discounted by 75%.

ROBERTSON & PARTNERS LTD

JODRELL STREET, NUNEATON, CV11 5EH, ☎ 02476 384110, FAX: 01203 642403, 9–5 MON–FRI, 9–1 SAT. **ARCHITECTURAL SALVAGE**

Reclaimed materials from demolition sites, including doors, chimney pots, staircase parts, baths, steel shelving, slabs, reclaimed timber, reinforced steel joists, roof tiles and slates. In fact anything from a demolished building will be available here.

TILE CLEARING HOUSE

UNIT 1, OLD WALSALL ROAD, GREAT BARR, BIRMINGHAM, WEST MIDLANDS B42 1EA, ☎ 0121 357 1247, 8–6 MON–FRI, 9–6 SAT, 10–4 SUN.

BRANDON ROAD, BINLEY, COVENTRY, WARWICKSHIRE CV3 2AG, ☎ 02476 441313, FAX: 02476 457865, 8–6 MON–FRI, 9–6 SAT, 10–4 SUN. **PERMANENT DISCOUNT OUTLET**

See page 345 (CAMBS)

WILTSHIRE

IN EXCESS

131 NETHERHAMPTON ROAD, SALISBURY, WILTSHIRE SP2 8NA, ☎ 01722 414444, 9–5.30 MON–SAT, 10–4 SUN. **PERMANENT DISCOUNT OUTLET**

See page 350 (DORS)

MARLBOROUGH TILES FACTORY SHOP

16 HIGH STREET, MARLBOROUGH, WILTSHIRE SN8 1AA, ☎ 01672 515287, **e-mail:** admin@marlborough-tiles.co.uk, www.marlborough-tiles.co.uk, 9.30–5 MON–SAT.

13 MILFORD STREET, SALISBURY, WILTSHIRE SP1 2AJ, ☎ 01722 328010, **e-mail:** admin@marlborough-tiles.co.uk, www.marlborough-tiles.co.uk, 9.30–5 MON–SAT. **PERMANENT DISCOUNT OUTLET**

See page 351 (GLOS)

TILE CLEARING HOUSE

UNIT 12, HAWKESWORTH INDUSTRIAL ESTATE, BRIDGEWATER ROAD, SWINDON, WILTSHIRE SN2 5TZ, ☎ 01793 490123, FAX: 01793 719097, 8–6 MON–FRI, 9–6 SAT, 10–4 SUN. **PERMANENT DISCOUNT OUTLET**

See page 345 (CAMBS)

WORCESTERSHIRE

HOLLOWAYS

LOWER COURT, SUCKLEY, WORCESTERSHIRE WR6 5DE, ☎ 01886 884665, www.holloways.co.uk, 9–5 MON–SAT, 10–4 SUN FROM APRIL–AUGUST **ARCHITECTURAL SALVAGE**

Conservatory furniture specialists, with perhaps the best range of furniture and garden furniture in the country. They also sell antique and reproduction garden statuary, urns, troughs, gates, Coalbrookdale benches, cider mills, staddle stones. The conservatory furniture includes a wide selection of rattan, English willow, metal and Lloyd Loom. Among the huge choice they have an exclusive range of rattan with elegant sofas, chairs and dining furniture with driftwood-coloured frames, leather bindings and woven banana fibre panels. The cushions can be covered in any fabric. There is also more rustic, casual furniture made from unpeeled woven rattan which is waxed to a deep patina and traditional English willow with deep feather cushions. They also sell plantation-grown teak garden furniture steamer chairs, folding chairs, loungers, benches, rectangular and round tables plus a good selection of other hardwood and cast-aluminium furniture. Among the antique and reproduction garden items are antique stone benches, sundials and figures, 19th-century Coalbrookdale cast iron seats and farm artefacts. Ornaments such as stone vases, urns, birdbaths and statues are made from reconstituted limestone with a surface texture like Portland stone and coloured to resemble Portland, Bath or Cotswold stone or terracotta. This stone soon develops a covering of moss and lichen to look genuinely old. Original Coalbrookdale benches cost from £1,250, repro ones from £300; antique cider mills from £1,200.

POSTERITY ARCHITECTURAL ANTIQUES

UNDERHILL FARM, LITTLE MALVERN, WORCESTERSHIRE WR14 4JN, ☎ 01684 541254, **e-mail:** posterity80@hotmail.com, www.posterityantiques.co.uk, 9–5 MON–SAT. **ARCHITECTURAL SALVAGE**

Sells all types of old building materials and artefacts, internal fittings, bathrooms, fireplaces, kitchen church pews, stained glass, doors, lighting, garden urns, benches, mouldings and radiators. Whether it's a lamp post for the garden, a butler's sink, a 17th century doorway or a pile of handmade bricks, you may well find what you're looking for here.

TILE CLEARING HOUSE

UNIT 13, SHERIFF STREET, WORCESTER, WORCESTERSHIRE WR4 9AB, ☎ 01905 731931, FAX: 01905 611465, 8–6 MON–FRI, 9–6 SAT, 10–4 SUN. **PERMANENT DISCOUNT OUTLET**

See page 345 (CAMBS)

YORKSHIRE

ANDY THORNTON LTD

VICTORIA MILLS, STAINLAND ROAD, GREETLAND, HALIFAX, WEST YORKSHIRE HX4 8AD, ☎ 01422 377314, FAX: 01422 310372, **e-mail:** antiques@ataa.co.uk, www.andythorntonltd.co.uk, 8.30–5.30 MON–FRI, 9–5 SAT. **ARCHITECTURAL SALVAGE**

Doors, fireplaces, panelled rooms, church interiors, radiators, balustrades, chandeliers, stained glass, marble, pews and light-fittings all situated in an enormous converted mill. If you can't find the original piece you want, they will make you a reproduction. One of the five floors is devoted to reproduction furniture, lamps and decor. Outside are plenty of garden urns, statuary and cast-iron gates.

AQUAROOF LTD

13 BOWLING COURT INDUSTRIAL ESTATE, MARY STREET, BRADFORD, WEST YORKSHIRE BD4 8TT, ☎ 01274 737828, **e-mail:** info@aquaroof.co.uk, www.aquaroof.co.uk, 10–4 MON–THUR BY APPOINTMENT ONLY. MAIL ORDER. **FACTORY SHOP**

Aquaroof import and sell epdm rubber, a synthetic rubber which is used on flat roofs worldwide, which they sell both to the trade and direct to the DIY market by mail order or to personal shoppers. The epdm is cut to size so there is no waste. It is guaranteed for 20 years. Visit the website for more information; a free instructional video is available with any order.

BLACK & DECKER

THE YORKSHIRE OUTLET, WHITE ROSE WAY, DONCASTER, SOUTH YORKSHIRE DN4 5JH, ☎ 01302 344488, 10–6 MON–SAT, 11–5 SUN. **FACTORY SHOP IN A FACTORY SHOPPING VILLAGE**

See page 365 (SOM)

CHAPEL HOUSE FIREPLACES

ST GEORGE'S ROAD, SCHOLES, HOLMFIRTH, HUDDERSFIELD, WEST YORKSHIRE HD9 1UH, ☎ 01484 682275, FAX: 01484 682275, **e-mail:** info@chapelhousefireplaces.co.uk, www.chapelhousefireplaces.co.uk, TUE–SAT BY APPOINTMENT ONLY. **ARCHITECTURAL SALVAGE**

Antique fireplaces with correct grates, baskets and inserts, including French fireplaces, dating from 1750 to 1910. Usually 200 to 300 in stock at any one time with surrounds in pine, marble, oak, mahogany, stone and occasionally beach and teak. Grates range from Georgian hobs, free-standing, suspended baskets, early Victorian hobs, arched fire grates and early Victorian and Edwardian grates. Prices range from £245 to £10,500. This is a family business which has been in operation for 23 years.

DOLMENS

79 LATHAM LANE, GOMERSAL, CLECKHEATON, WEST YORKSHIRE BD19 4AP, ☎ 01274 872368, FAX: 01274 869953, www.dolmens.freeserve.co.uk, BY APPOINTMENT ONLY. **ARCHITECTURAL SALVAGE**

Old and new York stone paving flags. Various prices and quality. Worldwide delivery.

GLYN WEBB

KINGS ROAD, BRADFORD, WEST YORKSHIRE BD2 1EY, ☎ 01274 722122, 9–8 MON–SAT, 10–4 SUN AND BANK HOLIDAYS.

UNIT 2, THORNE RETAIL PARK, OGDEN ROAD, DONCASTER, SOUTH YORKSHIRE DN2 4SG, ☎ 01302 556556, 9–8 MON–SAT, 10–4 SUN AND BANK HOLIDAYS.

SHAY SYKE, HALIFAX, WEST YORKSHIRE HX1 2ND, ☎ 01422 349249, 9–8 MON–SAT, 10–4 SUN AND BANK HOLIDAYS.

100 WAKEFIELD ROAD, HUDDERSFIELD, WEST YORKSHIRE HD1 3PD, ☎ 01484 539330,

OSLO ROAD, SUTTON FIELDS, HULL, EAST YORKSHIRE, HU8 0JU, ☎ 01482 836344, 9–8 MON–SAT, 10–4 SUN AND BANK HOLIDAYS. 9–8 MON–SAT, 10–4 SUN AND BANK HOLIDAYS.

UNIT C KILNER WAY, OFF HALIFAX ROAD, SHEFFIELD, SOUTH YORKSHIRE S6 1NN, ☎ 0114 2312665, 9–8 MON–SAT, 10–4 SUN AND BANK HOLIDAYS.

INGS ROAD, WAKEFIELD, WEST YORKSHIRE WF1 1RN, ☎ 01924 298600, 9–8 MON–SAT, 10–4 SUN AND BANK HOLIDAYS. **PERMANENT DISCOUNT OUTLET**

See page 346 (CHESH)

NO FRILLS DIY STORE

115–125 LEADMILL ROAD, SHEFFIELD, SOUTH YORSHIRE S2 4AZ, ☎ 0114 276 1454, FAX: 0114 272 5083, 9–8 MON–SAT, 10–4 SUN.

NAVIGATION YARD, WAKEFIELD, WEST YORKSHIRE, ☎ 01924 369660, FAX: 01924 364421, 9–8 MON–SAT, 10–4 SUN. **PERMANENT DISCOUNT OUTLET**

See page 343 (BEDS)

TILE CLEARING HOUSE

UNIT 1, SPROTBROUGH ROAD, OFF YORK ROAD, DONCASTER, SOUTH YORKSHIRE DN5 8BN, ☎ 01302 787 000, 8–6 MON–FRI, 9–6 SAT, 10–4 SUN.

149–150 CLOUGH ROAD, HULL, HUMBERSIDE HU5 1SW, ☎ 01482 470 711, 8–6 MON–FRI, 9–6 SAT, 10–4 SUN.

RING ROAD, LOWER WORTLEY, LEEDS, WEST YORKSHIRE LS12 5DS, ☎ 0113 279 3443, FAX: 0113 2793101, 8–6 MON–FRI, 9–6 SAT, 10–4 SUN.

107 MEADOWHALL ROAD, MEADOWHALL, SHEFFIELD SOUTH YORKSHIRE S9 1HE, ☎ 0114 243 2444, 8–6 MON–FRI, 9–6 SAT, 10–4 SUN. **PERMANENT DISCOUNT OUTLET**

See page 345 (CAMBS)

W MACHELL & SONS LTD

LOW MILLS, GUISELEY, LEEDS, WEST YORKSHIRE LS20 9LT, ☎ 0113 250 5043, FAX: 0113 250 0315, **e-mail:** lisamachell@btconnect.com, www.machells.co.uk, 8–5 MON–FRI, 8–12 SAT.
ARCHITECTURAL SALVAGE

Manufacturers of Machells unique period oak flooring. Solid English and European oak supplied tongue and groove, sanded, stained and sealed. Available in a selection of delightfully characterful stains, finished with a hard-wearing, low-maintenance lacquer that requires no polishing or buffing. Period joinery work, including panelling, doors, staircases, etc, also undertaken by their team of skilled craftsmen. One of the country's largest stock of reclaimed building materials including recycled oak and pine beams and reclaimed flooring. Six full-time masons handcrafting genuine period stone fireplaces, mullioned window sets and stone doorways, all tailor-made to individual specifications.

YORK HANDMADE BRICK CO LTD

FOREST LANE, ALNE, YORK, NORTH YORKSHIRE YO61 1TU, ☎ 01347 838881, **e-mail:** sales@yorkhandmade.co.uk, www.yorkhandmade.co.uk. 9–5 MON–FRI, 9–12 SAT, SUN.
ARCHITECTURAL SALVAGE

One of the few businesses still producing handmade bricks, as well as pavers and terracotta floor tiles. They can provide bricks for archways, slopes, edges, ledges and corners and do all the British Standards specials as well as taking special orders.

SOUTH WALES

CARDIFF RECLAMATION

SITE 7, TREMORFA INDUSTRIAL ESTATE, CARDIFF, SOUTH WALES CF2 2SD, ☎ 02920 458995, 9–5 MON–FRI, 9–1 SAT, 10–1 SUN. **ARCHITECTURAL SALVAGE**

Flagstones, Victorian fireplaces, pine doors, church pews, handrails, chimney pots, quarry tiles, oak beams and lots more.

CRAZY MAC'S

PONTARDULAIS ROAD, FFORESTFACH, SWANSEA, SOUTH WALES SA5 4BA, ☎ 01792 585828, FAX: 01792 585566, **e-mail:** lss@salvage1.co.uk, www.salvage1.co.uk, 9.30–6 MON–THUR, 9.30–8 FRI, 9–6 SAT, 11–5 SUN. **PERMANENT DISCOUNT OUTLET**

An Aladdin's cave of salvaged stock for the avid bargain hunter, most of which has been the subject of insurance claims for fire or flood, salvage, bankruptcy or is simply clearance stock. Stock changes every two or three days and regular visitors have found anything from half price Kenwood Chefs, televisions and toys to furniture, kitchen items, linens and especially fantastic bargains in designer clothing. Yves Saint Laurent, Armani, Ungaro, Hugo Boss and Valentino, as well as all major high street names, are just some of the names to be found (though the labels are often cut out). Discounts range from 50% to 80%. Phone first to check stock.

DYFED ANTIQUES & ARCHITECTURAL SALVAGE

WESLEYAN CHAPEL, PERROTS ROAD, HAVERFORDWEST, PEMBROKESHIRE, SOUTH WALES SA61 2JD, ☎ 01437 760496, 10–5 MON–SAT. **ARCHITECTURAL SALVAGE**

Slate slabs, quarry tiles, oak beams and flooring, doors, Victorian fireplaces, tiled insets, surrounds in wood, marble and cast iron, antique furniture, many huge dressers and curios, gardenware including urns. Furniture and fire surrounds made to measure in new or old wood. Specialising in slate slabs, they sell half slabs which measure 4ft by 18 inches, slates for flooring which usually measure 2ft or old billiard table slates which are 2 inches thick and really smooth and measure 7ft by 3ft. Wood stripping service also available.

GLYN WEBB

PONTARDULAIS ROAD, CADLE, SWANSEA, SOUTH WALES SA5 4BA, ☎ 01792 579955, 9–8 MON–SAT, 10–4 SUN AND BANK HOLIDAYS. **PERMANENT DISCOUNT OUTLET**

See page 346 (CHESH)

HARRY TUFFINS SUPERMARKET AND PETROL STATION

KNIGHTON SHELL GARAGE, POWYS, SOUTH WALES LD17 1DA, ☎ 01547 528645, 8–6 MON–WED, SAT, 8–8 THUR, FRI, 10–4 SUN. **PERMANENT DISCOUNT OUTLET**

Supermarket selling foodstuffs, garden furniture and household goods at incredibly competitive prices. Newly refurbished, the store offers a vast range of groceries, wine, household cleaning products, kitchen equipment, stationery, DIY, hardware, clothing and gardening items. Instore fruit and vegetables. The 'Quids In Shop' stocks more than 1,000 items at just £1. Harry Tuffins bottled mineral water is available at Churchstoke.

TILE CLEARING HOUSE

DAVID CLOSE, DAVID STREET, BRIDGEND INDUSTRIAL ESTATE, BRIDGEND, GLAMORGAN, SOUTH WALES CF1 3SA, ☎ 01656 651666, FAX: 01656 647392, 8–6 MON–FRI, 9–6 SAT, 10–4 SUN. **PERMANENT DISCOUNT OUTLET**

See page 345 (CAMBS)

WILKINSON STORES

10–13 CARDIFF STREET, ABERDARE, MID-GLAMORGAN, SOUTH WALES CF44 7DP, ☎ 01685 870393, www.wilko.co.uk, 9–5.30 MON–THUR, 9–6 FRI, SAT, 10–4 SUN. MAIL ORDER.

CIBI WALK SHOPPING CENTRE, FOGMORE STREET, ABERGAVENNY, SOUTH WALES NP7 5AJ, ☎ 01685 870393, www.wilko.co.uk, 8.30–5.30 MON–THUR, 8.30–6 FRI, SAT, 10–4 SUN. MAIL ORDER. **PERMANENT DISCOUNT OUTLET**

See page 346 (CHESH)

NORTH WALES

ABAKHAN FABRICS

LLANERCH-Y-MOR, COAST ROAD, MOSTYN, FLINTSHIRE, NORTH WALES CH8 9DX, ☎ 01745 562100, FAX: 01745 562101, **e-mail:** enquiries@abakhan-fabrics.co.uk, 9–5.15 MON–SAT, 8 ON THUR, 10.30–4.30 SUN. **FACTORY SHOP**

See page 345 (CHESH)

SCOTLAND

BMJ POWER

280 GREAT WESTERN ROAD, ST GEORGE'S CROSS, GLASGOW, SCOTLAND G4 9EJ, ☎ 0141 332 8000, www.bmjdirect.com, 8.30–5 MON–SAT, 9–5 WED. **FACTORY SHOP**

See page 343 (BERKS)

CAPONES

UNITS 5–6, LOCK STREET, COATBRIDGE, SCOTLAND ML5 3RT, ☎ 01236 710990, FAX: 01236 710993, **e-mail:** sales@capones.co.uk, www.capones.co.uk, 8–8 MON–FRI, 9–5.30 SAT, 10–5.30 SUN.

1–7 MOLENDINAR STREET, GLASGOW, SCOTLAND G1 5AT, ☎ 0141 552 4399, FAX: 0141 552 4263, 9–5.30 MON–SAT, 10–5.30 SUN. **PERMANENT DISCOUNT OUTLET**

Wallpaper and paint clearance warehouse which also sells paste, borders, brushes, rollers. Stocks Crown, Norvar, Berger paints; Crown, Belgravia and wallpaper with thousands of rolls in stock at any one time.

EDINBURGH ARCHITECTURAL SALVAGE YARD (EASY)

UNIT 6, COUPER STREET, OFF COBURG STREET, LEITH, EDINBURGH, SCOTLAND EH6 6HH, ☎ 0131 554 7077, www.easy-arch-salv.co.uk, 9–5 MON–SAT. **ARCHITECTURAL SALVAGE**

Antique fireplaces, fire surrounds, fire inserts, cast iron spiral staircases, original fixtures and fittings, panelled wooden doors, shutters, baths, sinks, radiators and general architectural salvage.

HENDERSON ROOFING SUPPLIES LTD

31 WESTERBURN STREET, CARNTYNE, GLASGOW, SCOTLAND G32 6AT, ☎ 0141 778 3602, www.hrs-slates.com, 8–4.30 MON–THUR, 8–3.30 FRI. **ARCHITECTURAL SALVAGE**

Slate merchants and specialists in new and secondhand slates. Free car park.

REJECTS

123 ST CLAIR STREET, KIRKCALDY, FIFE, SCOTLAND KY1 2BS, ☎ 01592 655955, FAX: 01592 655722, **e-mail:** info@rejectsonline.com, 9–5.30 MON–SAT, 12.30–4.30 SUN. **PERMANENT DISCOUNT OUTLET**

Rejects Department Store sells curtain and dress fabric, china, pottery, carpets, silk flower, glassware, home decoration equipment and materials, lighting, basketware, carpet and flooring and has a cookshop. The shop is 100,000 square feet and claims to be the best value department store in the UK, although it isn't a discount store as such. For example, the curtain shop is larger than Harrods curtain department with thousands of rolls of material. There is a particularly large selection of pottery and china, bedding, cushions, pictures, mirrors, wallpaper, paint, hardware and garden tools. The shop also has a self-service café. Free parking for 300 cars at the rear of the building.

NORTHERN IRELAND

ALEXANDER THE GRATE

126–128 DONEGAL PASS, BELFAST, NORTHERN IRELAND BT7 1BZ, ☎ 028 9023 2041, FAX: 028 9047 1559, www.alexanderthegrate.co.uk, 10–5 MON–SAT. **ARCHITECTURAL SALVAGE**

A specialist in antique fireplaces, as well as leaded windows, doors and general architectural salvage. There is also garden furniture in the spring and summer. The owner also runs an antiques market on the first floor of the same premises every Saturday from 9.30am to 5pm with four different stallholders. Phone before visiting as the owner has plans to move premises in late 2002.

Furniture & Soft Furnishings

BEDFORDSHIRE

THE CURTAIN CONNECTION LTD

AMPTHILL ANTIQUES EMPORIUM 6 BEDFORD STREET, AMPTHILL, BEDFORDSHIRE, ☎ 01525 402131, 10–5 MON, WED–SUN. **SECONDHAND SHOP**

Sister shop to the secondhand curtain shop in St Albans, it sells good quality curtains, as well as a wide range of soft furnishings and accessories. Designer fabrics from all the main labels are represented here, including Liberty, Designers Guild, Anna French, Colefax and Fowler and Laura Ashley. Prices generally vary from £20 to £400 for a full-length pair of top-name interlined curtains complete with pelmet and tie-backs. The Emporium houses three floors of town, country and decorative antiques, garden antiques, fireplaces, reclaimed chimney pots and a variety of services such as chair caning and stool weaving, upholstery, metal polishing and restoration.

THE FABRIC FACTORY SHOP

2 ASTON ROAD, CAMBRIDGE ROAD, BEDFORD, BEDFORDSHIRE MK42 0JN, ☎ 01234 217788, FAX: 01234 217469, **e-mail:** sales@boynett.com, www.boynett.com, 8–5 MON–FRI, 10–1.30 SAT. **FACTORY SHOP**

This Boynett fabric factory shop offers customers the chance to buy ends of ranges and overruns direct at highly competitive prices. The company supplies the leading department stores and interior designers with high quality curtain and upholstery fabrics which you can purchase here at discounted prices from only £2.95 per metre.

TK MAXX

UNIT 14, THE HOWARD CENTRE, BEDFORD, BEDFORDSHIRE MK40 1UH, ☎ 01234 270787, www.tkmaxx.com, 9–5.30 MON–FRI, 8.30–6 SAT, 10–4 SUN.

BEACON RETAIL PARK, WATLING STREET, BLETCHLEY, BEDFORDSHIRE MK1 1BN, ☎ 01908 644406, www.tkmaxx.com, 10–8 MON–FRI, 9–6 SAT, 11–5 SUN. **PERMANENT DISCOUNT OUTLET**

TK Maxx is a unique shopping experience, based on an American concept, offering an ever-changing range of famous names, high street brands and designer labels at up to 60% off normal retail prices. The majority of the stock is current season which makes the savings even more amazing. With 50,000 items in store and 10,000 new pieces arriving each week there is always something fresh and exciting to be found in every department: womenswear, menswear, childrenswear, sports and leisurewear, shoes, accessories and homewares. The stores are spacious and functional, with wide aisles enabling easy disabled and pushchair access. There are individual changing rooms, the stores accept all major credit and debit cards, and there is a return and refund policy. There are now over 120 easily accessible stores, often situated in main shopping centres or retail parks. All stores are open seven days a week and late in the evenings, though times vary from store to store. For details of your nearest store and opening hours, visit the website at www.tkmaxx.com.

BERKSHIRE

FABRIC WAREHOUSE

WHITEHOUSE DEVELOPMENT, LONDON ROAD, NEWBURY, BERKSHIRE RG14 2BP, ☎ 01635 31463, 9–8 MON, 9–5.30 TUE–SAT, 10–4 SUN. **PERMANENT DISCOUNT OUTLET**

Large warehouse chain, now with 40 outlets countrywide, selling upholstery fabric, cushions, ready-made curtains and net curtains. Most of the merchandise is made up of clearance material from mills and manufacturers. Some of the outlets also stock a full range of bed linen, towels and bathroom accessories while others sells tracks, poles, blinds of all kinds, brassware, crafts and occasional furniture.

FREELANCE FABRICS

130 CROCKHAM WELL, WOODLEY, READING, BERKSHIRE RG5 8JH, ☎ 0118 969 9611 9–5.30 MON–SAT, 10–4 SUN. **PERMANENT DISCOUNT OUTLET**

Large warehouse chain, now with 40 outlets countrywide, selling upholstery fabric, cushions, ready-made curtains and net curtains. Most of the merchandise is made up of clearance material from mills and manufacturers. Some of the outlets also stock a full range of bed linen, towels and bathroom accessories while others sells tracks, poles, blinds of all kinds, brassware, crafts and occasional furniture.

KNICKERBEAN

8 BARTHOLOMEW STREET, NEWBURY, BERKSHIRE RG14 5LL, ☎ 01635 529016, FAX: 01635 528636, **e-mail:** info@knickerbean.com, www.knickerbean.com, 9–5.30 MON–SAT.
PERMANENT DISCOUNT OUTLET

Recommended by countless interior and decorating magazines and much loved by bargain hunters, Knickerbean offers a continuous stream of stylish and sumptuous fabrics (the kind found at the Chelsea Harbour Design Centre and Decorex), all at affordable prices. You can find many famous name bargains here, but increasingly their fabrics are sourced directly from the same mills and manufacturers as the top names, both here and abroad. This allows them to offer the same top quality in the most current colours and designs but at much lower prices than normal because they buy direct from the source and sell directly, cutting out the middlemen. Their selection of curtain and upholstery fabrics is mostly in the mid to upper end of the market and caters for both contemporary and traditional homemakers with formal glazed chintzes, regal damasks, toiles de jouy and luxurious chenilles displayed next to basic neutrals, bright, modern prints, airy voiles and earthy, ethnic patterns. They also have large ranges of checks and stripes, self-patterned weaves, simple prints for a child's room as well as a huge range of upholstery brocades and tapestries. Prices range fromt £5.95 for prints to £24.95 and occasionally more for some of their tapestries, chenilles and damasks. Knickerbean's outlets are bright and pleasant, more like an interior designer's showroom – there's no warehouse feeling here. Their trained staff are helpful with all sorts of advice on fabrics, colours and interiors and they offer a complete home visit service with interior measuring and design advice. They have a hand-finished making-up service for curtains, blinds and loose covers, as well as a range of custom made furniture with footstools, sofas, etc. Those living close to their five shops can keep a look-out in their local newspapers or keep in touch with their branch to snap up even bigger bargains.

SOUL HOME LIMITED

21 LABURNHAM ROAD, MAIDENHEAD, BERKSHIRE SL6 4DB, ☎ 01628 418 988, FAX: 01628 418 977, **e-mail:** enquiries@soulhomeuk.com, www.soulhomeuk.com, 9–5.30 MON–FRI. MAIL ORDER. **PERMANENT DISCOUNT OUTLET**

The vision behind Soul Home, a contemporary gift and soft-furnishing mail order company, was to translate the fabrics, textures and detail of high fashion into stylish yet affordable home furnishings. Designed in the UK, these beautiful products are made exclusively by some of the world's best manufacturers – this is Contran chic at a fraction of the price. Gifts range from exquisite silver-grey tissue faille notebooks to quilted satin bags and embroidered notebooks. In the bedroom, choose from the clean simplicity of the Kashmir percale bedlinen, or the beautiful sheer organdy Fern collection. Bring the Fern collection into your dining room with delicate table mats, napkins and tiny coasters. Or spice up the table with the burnt orange, rich burgundy and cool chartreuse of their Sari hand-woven tableware. And dress your windows stylishly but inexpensively with distinctively embroidered tab-top organdy curtains. Secure online shopping, or order by post.

TK MAXX

6 THE MALL, THE KENNETT CENTRE, NEWBURY, BERKSHIRE RG14 5EN, ☎ 01635 522323, www.tkmaxx.com, 9–5.30 MON–FRI, 7 ON THUR, 9–6 SAT, 11–5 SUN.

UNIT A39, BROAD STREET MALL, BROAD STREET, READING, BERKSHIRE RG1 7QE, ☎ 0118 951 1117, www.tkmaxx.com, 9–5.30 MON–FRI, 9–6 SAT, 11–5 SUN.

UNIT 30–40, OBSERVATORY CENTRE, HIGH STREET, SLOUGH, BERKSHIRE SL1 1LL, ☎ 01753 572550, www.tkmaxx.com, 9–5.30 MON–FRI, 8 ON THUR, 9–6 SAT, 11–5 SUN. **PERMANENT DISCOUNT OUTLET**

See page 377 (BEDS)

BRISTOL

FABRIC WAREHOUSE

BATH ROAD, BRISLINGTON, BRISTOL BS4 3LP, ☎ 0117 972 3505, 9–6 MON–FRI, 9–5 SAT, 10.30–4.30 SUN. **PERMANENT DISCOUNT OUTLET**

See page 378 (BERKS)

THE CAPE

10 MERCHANT STREET, BROADMEAD, BRISTOL BS1 3ET, ☎ 0117 929 7919, FAX: 0117 929 7460, **e-mail:** sc@thefactory-shop.co.uk, www.thecape.co.uk, 9–5.30 MON–FRI, 9–6 SAT, 11–5 SUN. **FACTORY SHOP**

High quality, high density pine furniture made in South Africa from trees grown in managed forests, is sold at factory direct prices with home delivery throughout the UK. The range includes beds, wardrobes, blanket boxes, chests of drawers, tallboys, dressing tables, cheval mirrors, headboards, mattresses, a kitchen range, dining room tables, Welsh dressers, hi-fi units, bookcases. Also on sale in this shop is a range of African accessories and artefacts from Zimbabwe encompassing mirrors, prints, serpentine (stone) ornaments, recycled stationery, handmade wirework, candles and other ethnic and traditional gifts. Colour brochure and price list available on 01535 650940.

TK MAXX

THE GALLERIES CENTRE, 31–32 CASTLE GALLERY, BROADMEAD, BRISTOL BS1 3XE, ☎ 0117 930 4404, www.tkmaxx.com, 9–5.30 MON–SAT, 7 ON THUR, 11–5 SUN. **PERMANENT DISCOUNT OUTLET**

See page 377 (BEDS)

BUCKINGHAMSHIRE

ASB BLINDS LTD

31 HIGH STREET, IVER, BUCKINGHAMSHIRE SLO 9ND, ☎ 01753 655155, 9–5 MON–FRI, 9.30–1 SAT. **FACTORY SHOP**

Blinds of all type: venetian, roller, vertical, pleated (suitable for conservatory roofs) and Roman. Also blind fabric and vertical headrow tracks.

FABRIC WAREHOUSE

UNIT 5, CAMBRIDGE RETAIL PARK, AYLESBURY, BUCKINGHAMSHIRE HP20 1DF, ☎ 01296 337717, 9.30–5.30 MON–SAT, 10–4 SUN. **PERMANENT DISCOUNT OUTLET**

See page 378 (BERKS)

WORLD OF WOOD

7 CORNWALL PLACE, BUCKINGHAM, BUCKINGHAMSHIRE MK18 1SB, ☎ 01280 822003, FAX: 01280 822003, **e-mail:** worldofwood@hotmail.com, 9–5.30 MON–SAT. **PERMANENT DISCOUNT OUTLET**

Furniture for the home which offers everything except the bath! All the furniture is designed by craftsmen in Italy and much of it is made from original wood reclaimed from houses in Italy, mainly Verona, and made by small Italian manufacturers. If you're looking for modern glass-topped tables to massive semi-distressed sideboards, World of Wood has something to offer at prices which are very competitive, and in a variety of woods including chestnut, oak, cherry and walnut, among others. For example, there are 200 different solid dining chairs to choose from at prices starting from £90. You can choose your own finish for the wood or have a piece custom made.

CAMBRIDGESHIRE

CHELFORD FABRICS

CHELFORD HOUSE, STATION ROAD, GAMLINGAY, CAMBRIDGESHIRE SG19 3HQ, ☎ 01767 651888, FAX: 01767 651886, **e-mail:** sales@chelfordfabrics.freeserve.co.uk, www.chelfordfabrics.com, 9.30–5.30 MON–SAT. **PERMANENT DISCOUNT OUTLET**

A large, out-of-town showroom selling only perfect regular curtain and upholstery fabrics at greatly reduced prices, including everything from glazed cotton chintzes to prints, tapestries and damasks from all leading manufacturers. Choose from more than 4,000 rolls, order from the extensive range of manufacturers pattern books or buy own-brand fabrics which are one-third less expensive than branded material. A full high quality making-up service is available. Curtain accessories, rails, tapes and hooks are also on sale at reduced prices. There is also a huge selection of towels, cushions, pillows and duvets. There is another branch in Harpenden, Hertfordshire. Phone 01582 763636.

CHOICE DISCOUNT STORES LIMITED

UNITS 5–6 VIKING WAY, BARHILL, CAMBRIDGESHIRE CB3 8EL, 10–6 MON–WED, 10–7 THUR, FRI, 9–6 SAT, 11–5 SUN. **PERMANENT DISCOUNT OUTLET**

Surplus stock including women's, men's and children's fashions from Next plc, Next Directory, other high street fashion houses, Next Interiors and footwear. You can save up to 50% off normal retail prices for first quality; up to two thirds for seconds. There are special sales each January and September. Easy access for wheelchairs and pushchairs.

COUNTRYWIDE INTERIORS

8 TOWER SQUARE, HUNTINGDON, CAMBRIDGESHIRE PE29 7DT, ☎ 01480 52440, FAX: 01480 433476, 9.30–5 MON–SAT, CLOSED WED. **PERMANENT DISCOUNT OUTLET**

Furniture including beds, carpets and curtains at substantial discounts. Up to 50% off bedroom, lounge, dining room and cane furniture. Underlay costs from £2.40 a square yard.

FABRIC WAREHOUSE

UNIT 15, LONDON ROAD INDUSTRIAL ESTATE, SAWSTON, CAMBRIDGESHIRE CB2 4EE, ☎ 01223 832810, www.fabric-warehouse.com, 9–5.30 MON–FRI, 9–5 SAT, 10–4 SUN. **PERMANENT DISCOUNT OUTLET**

Wide range of soft-furnishing fabrics: chenille; tapestries from £14.99 with a bargain section from £5.99; flat weaves from £12.99; curtain fabrics from £3.50 for ends-of-lines and £5.99 for standard ranges; muslins and voiles. Foam cutting service for cushion pads etc also available, as well as satin and polycotton linings, upholstery sundries, a good range of wooden and metal curtain poles, curtain rails, net rods and wires, trimmings, tie-backs and accessories. In-house curtain-making service available at competitive prices. New for 2002 is a curtain gallery offering thousands of permutations of designs and colours to choose and order from .

THE CURTAIN CONNECTION LTD

HUNTINGDON TRADING POST, 1ST MARY STREET, HUNTINGDON, CAMBRIDGESHIRE PE29 3PE, ☎ 01480 450998, FAX: 01727 874515, www.huntingdontradingpost.co.uk, 9–5 MON–SAT, 10–2 SUN. **SECONDHAND SHOP**

See page 377 (BEDS)

THE CURTAIN EXCHANGE

16 NORFOLK STREET, CAMBRIDGE, CAMBRIDGESHIRE CB1 2LF, ☎ 01223 212500, www.thecurtainexchange.net, 10–5 MON–SAT 9–8 MON–SAT, 11–5 SUN AND OPEN ALL BANK HOLIDAYS. **SECONDHAND SHOP**

The Curtain Exchange is a franchised group of shops selling beautiful top quality new and secondhand curtains, blinds, pelmets, etc at between one-third and one half of the brand new price. Their stock comes from a variety of sources: people who are moving house; people who have curtains made and then feel they are wrong for the room; show houses, where the builder wants to recoup some of his outgoings; and interior designers' mistakes. Stock changes constantly and ranges from rich brocades, damasks and velvets to chintzes, linens and cottons. Designer names include Colefax and Fowler, Designers Guild, Laura Ashley, Warner, Sanderson, Osborne & Little, Fortuny and Bennison. A team of fitters and alteration experts are available if required. They also offer a 24-hour fitting and alteration service. The Curtain Exchange also supply bespoke ranges with samples of curtains hanging. These fabrics are chosen from suppliers all over the world and are an excellent buy. They also offer lined, ready-made curtains designed exclusively for them which come in lengths up to 305cm (120in). These are outstanding value: for example, 80in wide, 120in drop start at £175 including VAT.

THE WINDOW SCENE

105 NORFOLK STREET, WISBECH, CAMBRIDGESHIRE PE13 2LD, ☎ 01945 474335, www.thewindowscene.co.uk, 10–5 MON–FRI, CLOSED WED, 10–4 SAT. **PERMANENT DISCOUNT OUTLET**

Tiny, back-street shop crammed with everything to do with soft furnishings including curtain fabrics, velvets, chintzes, nets, blind tapes, linings, heading tapes, foam, track, upholstery fabrics, at very competitive prices. Brands sold include Moygashel, Texcraft, Bill Beaumont, Imago, Philtex, Corniche, Prestigious, SMD Textiles, Ashley Wilde, Glen Fabrics and Anna & Robert Swaffer.

CHANNEL ISLANDS

THE FABRIC FACTORY

INTERNATIONAL HOUSE, 41 THE PARADE, ST HELIER, JERSEY, CHANNEL ISLANDS JE2 3QQ, ☎ 01534 739551, 9–5.30 MON–SAT. **PERMANENT DISCOUNT OUTLET**

The Fabric Factory sells dress and furnishing fabrics at discounted prices. Stock is regular and clearance, and they also sell tracks, poles, and offer a made-to-measure service.

CHESHIRE

ABAKHAN FABRICS

4 DELAMERE STREET, CHESTER, CHESHIRE CH1 4DS, ☎ 01244 320300, 9.30–5.15 MON–SAT, 8 ON THUR, 11–4 SUN.

65–67 CHURCH ROAD, BIRKENHEAD, CHESHIRE L42 5LE, ☎ 0151 647 6983, FAX: 0151 650 0726, 9–5 MON–SAT.

8–12 GREENWAY ROAD, BIRKENHEAD, CHESHIRE L42 0NG, ☎ 0151 652 5195, FAX: 0151 653 8942, 9–5 MON–SAT, 8 ON THUR, 10–4 SUN. **FACTORY SHOP**

With five outlets in the North West and one in Staffordshire, Abakhan Fabrics are as well known for the emphasis they put on value for money as they are for the huge variety of fabrics, needlecrafts, haberdashery, gifts and knitting yarns, soft furnishings, all gathered from around the world. The large mill shop complex in Wales has a new home and garden department, baskets of remnant fabrics, wools, yarns and unrivalled selections of fabrics sold by the metre from evening wear, bridal wear and crêpe de Chine to curtaining, nets and velvets. Abakhan is able to offer such bargains through bulk buying, or selling clearance lines, job lots and seconds.

BRAMHALL INTERIOR DESIGN

8–10 BUXTON ROAD, STOCKPORT, CHESHIRE SK2 6NU, ☎ 0161 477 7173, FAX: 0161 477 7173, **e-mail:** sales@bramhallinteriors.co.uk, www.bramhallinteriors.co.uk, 9–5 MON–FRI, 9–4.30 SAT. **PERMANENT DISCOUNT OUTLET**

Sells fabrics and wallpapers at discounts of 20%. As agents for most leading makes, you can find almost anything you want here. If you pay full price for the fabric you choose, curtains will be made free of charge.

CLASSIC INTERIORS

FOUNDRY BANK, CONGLETON, CHESHIRE CW12 1EE, ☎ 01260 281071, FAX: 01260 281071, 10–5 MON–SAT. **FACTORY SHOP**

Recently taken over, this former lamp factory shop now sells furniture, too. Specialising in recovering shades as well as making new ones to order. They also stock assorted lamps made from many different materials. Most of the stock is seconds and reduced by about one-third. Set in a delightful market town adjacent to the town centre, this Victorian mill has recently been extensively refurbished to offer a variety of independent shops displaying a huge array of merchandise. Chainstore merchandise, including bed, carpets, glassware, fabric, mirrors and lighting. Coffee shop. Ample parking.

CWV BRANDS AT HOME FACTORY SHOP

TALBOT ROAD, HYDE, CHESHIRE SK14 4EJ, ☎ 0161 351 3070, **e-mail:** pamhindle@englewood.co.uk, 9.30–5.30 MON–FRI, 9–5 SAT, 10–4 SUN, 10–5 BANK HOLIDAYS. **FACTORY SHOP**

One of two CWV factory shops offering discontinued lines or seconds of bedlinen, wallpaper and fabrics by Coloroll, Vymura and Wilman Interiors at discounted prices. Savings of more than 50% can be made. For example, Coloroll, Vymura and Wilman wallpaper at £1.99 a roll or less, vinyls £1.99 a roll or less. Coloroll single quilt cover and pillow case, £6.50. Wilman curtain fabric, £3.50 a metre or less; Wilman upholstery fabric, £5 a metre or less. Towels, lamps, candles, kitchen accessories, bathroom accessories and baby products are available, too. Free car parking. Disabled access. They also maintain a data base to inform customers of offers and sale dates.

JOHN TURNER INTERIORS

9 SPRINGMOUNT MILL, NORTHGATE ROAD, STOCKPORT, CHESHIRE SK3 0JX, ☎ 0161 477 4919, 10–4.30 MON–SAT. **PERMANENT DISCOUNT OUTLET**

Sells a wide selection of leading middle market brand name fabrics including Wilman, Prestigious and Imago ranging from lining fabric to upholstery fabrics at trade prices. They usually have a very large stock of clearance lines from £2 a metre while Wilman curtain fabric costs £16-£36 a metre, discounted by 20%, and traditional tapestry fabric costs £50 a metre, also discounted by 20%. Also sells carpets by many of the main manufacturers at trade prices and wallpapers. The company run a free interior design service and also provide free estimates, supply and fitting services.

SIMON BOYD

SANSBURY RETAIL PARK, CALDY VALLEY ROAD, CHESTER, CHESHIRE CH3 5QZ, ☎ 01244 311160, **e-mail:** simonboyd@freewire.net, 9.30–5.30 MON–SAT, 10–4 SUN.

FABRIC HOUSE, PRINCESS STREET, KNUTSFORD, CHESHIRE WA16 6DD, ☎ 01565 633855, **e-mail:** simonboyd@freewire.net, 9.30–5.30 MON–SAT. **PERMANENT DISCOUNT OUTLET**

Stocks thousands of rolls of curtain fabric including chenilles, tapestries, cotton satin and chintzes from brands such as Monkwell, Sanderson and Crowson. For example a chenille costing £25 a yard costs £15.99 here. Also tie-backs, cushions, throws, ready-made curtains. Free measuring, plus making-up service available.

SUNRIDGE UPHOLSTERY

19 FARNWORTH ROAD, PENKETH, WARRINGTON, CHESHIRE WA5 2RZ, ☎ 01925 727610, FAX: 01925 727610, 8–4 MON–FRI. **FACTORY SHOP**

A small factory with a showroom, principally making sofas and suites for showhouses. It sells three-piece suites, sofas and upholstery fabrics. Sunridge are willing to customise the sofa design based on the half dozen or so sofas they have on display. Two-seater sofas cost from £600; armchairs from £350 and foot stools from £130. There are hundreds of upholstery fabrics to choose from including Monkwell, Crowsons, Romo and John Wilman. Delivery, which is free in the northwest only, takes six weeks.

THE BANKRUPT SHOP LTD

371–375 BOROUGH ROAD, BIRKENHEAD, CHESHIRE CH42 0HA, ☎ 0151 653 6685, 9.30–5.30 MON–SAT, 10.30–4.30 SUN. **PERMANENT DISCOUNT OUTLET**

Fabric retailers with 11 shops in the Northwest. First class fabrics, including many leading brands. Top quality curtaining and upholstery fabrics all at one price: £2.90 a metre. Also linings at £1.40 a metre and heading tape from 20p a metre. Select from more than 500,000 metres. This chain claims to be the biggest and best of the fabric superstores in the Northwest.

THE CAPE

114 FOREGATE STREET, CHESTER, CHESHIRE CH1 1HB, ☎ 01244 329880, FAX: 01244 829880, **e-mail:** sc@thefactory-shop.co.uk, www.thecape.co.uk, 9–5.30 MON–SAT, 10.30–4.30 SUN. **FACTORY SHOP**

See page 379 (BRIS)

THE CURTAIN EXCHANGE

3 HAWTHORN LANE, WILMSLOW, CHESHIRE SK9 1AQ, ☎ 01625 536060, www.thecurtainexchange.net, 10–5 MON–SAT, CLOSED WED. **SECONDHAND SHOP**

See page 381 (CAMBS)

THE FACTORY SHOP LTD

UNIT 1 EDDISBURY SQUARE, FRODSHAM, CHESHIRE WA6 6QS, ☎ 01928 734624, FAX: 01928 734906, 9–5.30 MON–SAT, 10.30–4 SUN. **FACTORY SHOP**

Wide range on sale includes men's, women's and children's clothing and footwear; household textiles; toiletries; hardware; luggage; lighting; electrical goods; and bedding, most of which are chainstore and high street brands at discounts of approximately 30% to 50%. There are kitchen and furniture displays and on sale is the Cape Country Furniture range with free-standing kitchens, as well as living, bedroom and dining furniture. There are weekly deliveries and brands include famous names such as Adidas, Nike, Joe Bloggs and Brabantia, among others. Lines are continually changing and few factory shops offer such a variety under one roof. Parking is free.

TK MAXX

UNIT B, TRIDENT RETAIL PARK, RUNCORN, CHESHIRE WA7 2FQ, ☎ 01928 714050, www.tkmaxx.com, 9–6 MON, 9–7 TUE–WED, 9–8 THUR–FRI, 9–6 SAT, 11–5 SUN.

UNIT C, THE COCKHEDGE CENTRE, 2 PRINCE HENRY SQUARE, WARRINGTON, CHESHIRE, ☎ 01925 636262, www.tkmaxx.com, 9–6 MON–SAT, 9 ON THUR, 10–4. SUN.

UNIT 12, ISLAND GREEN, WREXHAM, CHESHIRE LL13 7LW, ☎ 01978 261133, www.tkmaxx.com, 9–5.30 MON–FRI, 9–6 SAT, 11–5 SUN. **PERMANENT DISCOUNT OUTLET**

See page 377 (BEDS)

VICTORIA MILL RETAIL AND FACTORY OUTLETS

FOUNDRY BANK, CONGLETON, CHESHIRE CW12 1EE, ☎ 01260 297642, FAX: 01260 290068, **e-mail:** vicmill@talk21.com, 9.30–5 MON–SAT. **FACTORY SHOP**

An emporium of homewares and fashion at ex-factory prices. Set in a delightful market town adjacent to the town centre, this Victorian mill has recently been extensively refurbished to offer a variety of independent shops displaying a huge array of merchandise. Everything from cane furniture to beds, mirrors and lighting. Coffee shop. Ample parking.

WILKINSONS HOME & GARDEN STORES

THE MARKET CENTRE, CREWE, CHESHIRE CW1 2NG, ☎ 01270 250754, www.wilko.co.uk, 8.30–5.30 MON–WED, 8.30–6.30 THUR–SAT, 10–4 SUN. **PERMANENT DISCOUNT OUTLET**

Family-owned business offering value on the high street through its 205 stores, selling 25,000 high quality, low-priced essential everyday products for all the family including kitchenware, household disposables, clothing, DIY decoration, stationery, homewares, bedlinen, picture frames, china, cutlery, toys, pet foot, curtains, mirrors, gardening equipment including outdoor furniture, Christmas decorations, confectionery and seasonal goods. It also caters for the ardent gardener with fertiliser, grass seed – loose or boxed – plants, insecticides, composts – both multi-purpose or tub and basket – garden tools, strimmers, hoses and attachments, watering cans, water butts, wheelbarrows, and reels on wheels. In season, they sell bedding plants, garden lights, coolboxes, paint, paint brushes and rollers, and climbing plants such as honeysuckle, but as the summer progresses these are replaced by barbecues and picnic ranges. Phone 01909 505505 for details of your local outlet or visit their website.

WOORE HOUSE INTERIORS

7–8 NANTWICH ROAD, WOORE, NEAR CREWE, CHESHIRE CW3 9SA, ☎ 01630 647888, FAX: 01630 647888, BY APPOINTMENT ONLY, PLEASE PHONE FIRST. **SECONDHAND SHOP**

The Old Sofa Warehouse buys Victorian, Edwardian and later furniture, drop-end sofas, chaise longues, winged-back armchairs or the odd dining chair in their original condition. They stock a selection of designer fabrics and swatches – from Thomas Dare, Andrew Martin, Titley and Marr, Hill & Knowles, Ian Sanderson, Linwood and Abbot & Boyd for example. They offer an upholstery service with customers choosing their own fabric or one from Woore House Interiors.

YOU & YOURS

UNIT 42, ORCHARD WALK, HALTON LEAS SHOPPING CENTRE, RUNCORN, CHESHIRE WA7 2GZ, ☎ 01928 795 792, 9–5.30 MON–SAT. **PERMANENT DISCOUNT OUTLET**

Sells surplus stock from both Grattan and Freemans catalogues. Womenswear, childrenswear, menswear and household items, at up to 50% off catalogue prices. Includes a wide range of brands from both designer and high street on a regularly changing basis. Electrical goods are sold at discounts of up to 30% off catalogue prices, and include many big-name brands. There is a 14-day refund policy.

COUNTY DURHAM

CATALOGUE DISCOUNT STORES

UNIT 17, IN SHOP CENTRE, 1–2 WRIGHTON HOUSE, TRENCHARD AVENUE, THORNABY ON TEES, CO DURHAM TS17 9EP, ☎ 01642 751935, 9–5 MON–SAT. **PERMANENT DISCOUNT OUTLET**

Grattan catalogue store, selling a wide selection of items from those featured in the catalogue, including women's, men's, children's, home, electrics and toys. All items are discounted by up to 50% with regular special promotions. All stores offer a 14-day refund policy, and a 12-month guarantee on electrical items. A wide range of brands are in stock on a regularly changing basis. Each store carries a slightly different range, so please phone to check that they have what you want in stock.

LITTLEWOODS DISCOUNT STORE

UNIT 2A, METRO RETAIL PARK, GATESHEAD, TYNE & WEAR NE11 9XU, ☎ 0191 461 1491 10–8 MON–FRI, 9–6 SAT, 11–5 SUN. **PERMANENT DISCOUNT OUTLET**

Brand new, surplus women's, men's and children's clothing from last year's catalogue is on sale at greatly discounted prices. Returned and sometimes slightly damaged televisions and furniture can be found at as much as 70% below the original price. If you see an item you like, buy it there and then as stock is constantly changing and you are unlikely to see it on sale again. The store also has sales when stock is discounted even further.

MAGNET LTD CLEARANCE CENTRE

JOHN STREET, DARLINGTON, CO DURHAM DL1 1LG, ☎ 01642 344564, 8–5 MON–FRI, 9–1 SAT. **FACTORY SHOP**

With more than 200 branches countrywide, when Magnet Kitchens discontinue one of their ranges, there are always some shops with spare stock they can no longer sell. This applies to equipment such as ovens, hob, hoods, fridge/freezers and fridges, too as, when manufacturers upgrade their ranges, Magnet customers don't want to buy the old model currently in situ in the showroom. Old stock is sent to three sites in Birmingham, Darlington and Keighley, West Yorkshire. Prices on average are about 70% less than the high street price. If you are looking for a particular kitchen from the current catalogue, you may need to make three or four trips to buy sufficient quantities but you take the risk that you may never find enough doors to finish the kitchen. On the other hand, you could find half your kitchen at the factory shop and, as long as it is a current model, pay full price for the other half – it's still a substantial saving. The Keighley outlet has the most stock, followed by the Birmingham outlet and then Darlington, which doesn't stock any joinery items. Electrical equipment is all top brands – Neff and Smeg ovens, Stoves range cookers, as well as Magnet's own brand range which is made by Whirlpool. Some is ex-display, some discontinued models, some just overstock which is still boxed or returns from customers, which is unboxed. The best value are ex-display models which can be reduced by two-thirds; otherwise, returns from customers who have been sent a wrong order are reduced but not significantly. Single ovens cost from £80, double from £150; gas/electric hobs from £40 to £250; ceramics hobs from £80 and halogen hobs from £110. There are also wood and PVC glazed window frames, conservatory panels (from £25 for panels which normally cost £100), patio doors and French doors.

PONDEN MILL

UNIT 192, SOUTH MALL, MIDDLETON GRANGE SHOPPING CENTRE, HARTLEPOOL, CO DURHAM TS24 7RR, ☎ 01429 894239, 10–6 MON–SAT, 11–5 SUN. **FACTORY SHOP IN A FACTORY SHOPPING VILLAGE**

Famous branded products at direct-from-the-mill prices. A fabulous assortment of towels, duvets, pillows, throws, bedspreads, and up-to-the-minute coordinated bed linen, from names including Crown, Coloroll and Jeff Banks Ports-of-Call. Something for every room in the house. At the time of going to print, the future of Jacksons Landing is uncertain. Please phone before making a special trip.

SEYMOUR'S OF DARLINGTON

1–3 EAST ROW, DARLINGTON, CO DURHAM DL1 5PZ, ☎ 01325 355272, FAX: 01325 355272, **e-mail:** jem@seymours.fsbusiness.co.uk, 9–5 MON–SAT. **PERMANENT DISCOUNT OUTLET**

Seymour's of Darlington is the longest-established household linen retailer in the area and takes great pride in maintaining its loyal customer base. This unique family-owned business combines old-fashioned quality and service with the newest designs and keenest prices. There is a constantly changing, stunning variety of stock from tea towels to the latest French and Italian designer bed linens. Customers of all ages will find trendy to traditional items at prices to suit all pockets. There are always special offers giving extra value and there is a full range of duvets, pillows, tablecloths, towels, throws, cushion covers, duvet covers and curtains (ready-made and made-to-measure), and bathroom fittings including shower curtains. Seymour's have their own high quality brand of polycotton sheets, valances and pillowcases, also available in percale. More unusual items include flannelette sheets, super king-size, 4ft and bunk-size bedding. Latest additions include a delightful Portugese range of bedding and towels by Piu Belle. Brands include current perfect ranges from Sanderson, Dorma, Nimbus, Snuggledown, Christy, Coloroll, Miller, Peter Reed and Ashley Wilde, plus economy lines and seconds. Chainstore seconds are often on offer and all prices are extremely competitive. For children, they stock Designers Guild quilt covers and fabric, as well as pattern books from which orders can be taken. Staff are friendly and obliging and will advise if required, and many items can be ordered if not in stock. Short-term parking is available right outside from Tuesday to Friday and there is wheelchair access. Debit and credit cards are accepted.

TECAZ

TECAZ HOUSE, PORTRACK LANE, STOCKTON, CO DURHAM TS18 2HQ, ☎ 01642 670100, FAX: 0191 523 8148, **e-mail:** northshields@swift957ltd.com, www.swift957ltd.com, 9–6 MON–FRI, 9–5 SAT, 10–4 SUN.

TECAZ HOUSE, RYHOPE STREET, RYHOPE, SUNDERLAND, TYNE & WEAR SR2 9QR, ☎ 0191 523 8164, FAX: 0191 523 8148, **e-mail:** northshields@swift957ltd.com, www.swift957ltd.com, 9–6 MON–FRI, 9–5 SAT, 10–4 SUN. **PERMANENT DISCOUNT OUTLET**

Vast area displaying over 150 bathroom suites, 50 shower cubicles from manufacturers like Heritage, Armitage Shanks, Shires, Vitra, Twyfords and Rocca, as well as 50 kitchen and bedroom ranges from Symphony and PWS, including the electrical equipment to go in them by well-known brands. There are tiles, baths, sinks, taps, shower trays, showers, soap dishes, toilets, loo roll holders and mirrors, and they carry huge stocks of many of the ranges. Because Tecaz buy in large numbers, they can get better discounts from the manufacturer, many of which they pass on to the customer. They offer a free, no-obligation planning and design service, interest free credit on many ranges, and delivery can be arranged.

THE CAPE

UNIT F43, THE FORUM, METRO CENTRE, GATESHEAD, TYNE & WEAR NE11 9XR, ☎ 0191 493 2379, FAX: 0191 493 2382, **e-mail:** sc@thefactory-shop.co.uk, www.thecape.co.uk, 10–8 MON–WED, 10–9 THUR, 10–8 FRI, 9–7 SAT, 11–5 SUN. **FACTORY SHOP**

See page 379 (BRIS)

THE FACTORY SHOP

2–4 COMMERCIAL STREET, CROOK, CO DURHAM DL15 9HP, ☎ 01388 763211, 9–5.30 MON–SAT, 10.30–4.30 SUN. **FACTORY SHOP**

See page 383 (CHESH)

TK MAXX

TEAM VALLEY, RETAIL WORLD, GATESHEAD, TYNE & WEAR, ☎ 0191 487 4468, www.tkmaxx.com, PHONE FOR DETAILS.

UNIT 3, THE HIGHLIGHT RETAIL PARK, HARTLEPOOL MARINA, MARINA WAY, HARTLEPOOL, CO DURHAM TS24 0UX, ☎ 01429 222296, www.tkmaxx.com, 10–8 MON–FRI, 9–6 SAT, 11–5 SUN.

THE BRIDGES SHOPPING CENTRE, 34 CROWTREE ROAD, SUNDERLAND, TYNE & WEAR SR3 3JU, ☎ 0191 514 4484, www.tkmaxx.com, 9–5.30 MON–FRI, 9–6 SAT, 11–5 SUN. **PERMANENT DISCOUNT OUTLET**

See page 377 (BEDS)

CORNWALL

CHILD'S PLAY

TREWORTHAL BARN, TREWORTHAL, CRANTOCK, CORNWALL TR8 5PJ, ☎ 01637 830896, www.itschildsplay.co.uk, OPEN 8.30–5 MON–FRI, 10.30–2 SAT. **FACTORY SHOP**

Child's Play design, make and sell traditional toys and children's furniture from hardwood and pine. The factory shop adjoining the workshop sells overstocks including children's size chairs, stools, rocking chairs, toy boxes, old-fashioned desks and educational toys.

CORNISH MARKET WORLD

STADIUM RETAIL PARK, PAR, ST AUSTELL, CORNWALL PL25 3RP, ☎ 01726 812544, FAX: 01726 812346, **e-mail:** info@cornishmarketworld.co.uk, www.cornishmarketworld.co.uk, 9–5 SAT, SUN AND BANK HOLIDAYS, AND WED JUNE-SEPT. **PERMANENT DISCOUNT OUTLET**

Huge indoor market that sells an enormous range of goods and food at very competitive prices: for example, a good quality breadmaker, £45. Sells clothes, fabrics, phones, bags, tools, electric equipment, motability equipment, jewellery and furniture. There is a good butchers, fish, and fruit and veg stands.

JUST FABRICS AT INSCAPE

THE BRIDEWELL, DOCKACRE ROAD, LAUNCESTON, CORNWALL PL15 8YY, ☎ 01566 776279, FAX: 01566 773239, **e-mail:** justfabric@btinternet.com, www.justfab.co.uk, 9–5 MON–SAT. MAIL ORDER ALSO. **PERMANENT DISCOUNT OUTLET**

Based in a very attractive, converted, stone-built warehouse at the edge of the picturesque town of Launceston on the Devon/Cornwall border and within easy reach of Exeter, Plymouth and Truro, Just Fabrics holds the largest sample library in the country of all types of designer furnishing fabrics for curtains and upholstery. More than 150 famous brand names are represented, among them British designers such as Jane Churchill, Zoffany, Harlequin, GP & J Baker, Monkwell & Design Archives, John Wilman and Crowson. European suppliers such as JAB, Zimmer & Rohde, Christian Fischbacher, Sandberg and Garlin provide a flavour of international interior fashion with wallpapers, fabrics and voiles, trimmings, rugs and throws. India and the Far East provide a kaleidoscope of colours from bright cottons through to shimmering silks and organzas. The trimmings room holds every type of braid, rope and tassel imaginable, to complement your chosen interior design and colour scheme. Wallpapers, borders, Heritage paints by Sanderson, Farrow & Ball, Zoffany, Cole's and Paint Library, as well as every type, finish and size of curtain track, fitting or pole are supplied. The company offers a research service to find or match any soft furnishing item you may require. The website at www.justfab.co.uk gives further details. A worldwide delivery service is available. The showroom carries extensive stocks of designer fabrics plus all making-up accessories like linings, interlinings, heading tapes and accessories at unbeatable prices. The helpful and expert staff are able to guide you through this Aladdin's cave of choice and can demonstrate the look of a chosen decorations scheme with the help of a sophisticated computer-aided design system. For customers relocating to the West Country, an architectural and interior design service by Inscape Design is available on the same premises. The recent addition of a stylish coffee shop and restaurant will make your visit even more relaxing and rewarding.

THE CURTAIN EXCHANGE

UNIT 3, NEWPORT INDUSTRIAL ESTATE, LAUNCESTON, CORNWALL PL15 8EX, ☎ 01566 776001, www.thecurtainexchange.net, 9–5 MON–FRI, 10–4 SAT. **SECONDHAND SHOP**

See page 381 (CAMBS)

THE FACTORY SHOP

OLD STATION YARD, BERRYCOMBE ROAD, BODMIN, CORNWALL PL31 2NF, ☎ 01208 78492, 9–5.30 MON–SAT, 10.30–4.30 SUN.

MOUNT AMBROSE, SCORRIER, REDRUTH, CORNWALL TR15 1QT, ☎ 01209 219116, 9.30–5.30 MON–SAT, 10–4 SUN. **FACTORY SHOP**

See page 383 (CHESH)

TRAGO MILLS

ARWENACK STREET, FALMOUTH, CORNWALL TR11 3LF, ☎ 01326 315738, www.trago.co.uk, 9–5.30 MON–SAT, 10.45–4.45 SUN.

TWOWATERSFOOT, LISKEARD, CORNWALL PL14 6HY, ☎ 01579 348877, www.trago.co.uk, 9–5.30 MON–SAT, 10.45- 4.45 SUN. **PERMANENT DISCOUNT OUTLET**

The historic Trago's original Cornish site is in the Glynn Valley on the A38 between Liskeard and Bodmin. You can bargain hunt here for brand name art materials, bathrooms and bedrooms and ceramics, carpets and rugs, clothing, DIY and home improvement, furniture, garden accessories, gifts, textiles, lighting, pet care, saddlery, stationery, tools, motoring products, toys and sport equipment and much more. There's a restaurant and picnic area by the beautiful Fowey river bank, free parking and disabled access. The Falmouth store is smaller, with only limited free car parking outside, but there is a public car park adjacent.

CUMBRIA

FABRIC WAREHOUSE

SOUTH LAKELAND RETAIL PARK, QUEEN KATHERINE AVENUE, KENDAL, CUMBRIA LA9 6HZ, ☎ 01539 721552, 9–5.30 MON–SAT, 6 ON WED, 11–5 SUN. **PERMANENT DISCOUNT OUTLET**

See page 378 (BERKS)

FACTORY BEDDING SHOP

ATLAS HOUSE, NELSON STREET, DENTON HOLME, CARLISLE, CUMBRIA CA2 5NB, ☎ 01228 514703, 10–5 MON–FRI, 9–5 SAT. **FACTORY SHOP**

Bedding, curtains, duvets, duvet covers, pillows, towels, cushions, and curtain fabrics bought in direct from the manufacturer at factory shop prices. No brand names, but all sold in high street department stores. Pillows from £1.99; quilts from £5.99; curtains from £6.99; double fitted sheets from £4.99; double duvet covers from £12.99; double valances from £10.99. Wide range of curtain fabrics from £1.99 a metre and a curtain-making service.

SEKERS FABRICS

HENSINGHAM, WHITEHAVEN, CUMBRIA CA28 8QT, ☎ 01946 692691, 9–7 THUR, 9–3 FRI, 9–1 SAT. **FACTORY SHOP**

Discontinued curtain and upholstery fabrics and braiding sold off at weekly sales. There are 5,000 to 6,000 metres to choose from at discounts of up to 75% off normal retail prices.

STEAD McALPIN & CO LTD

CUMMERSDALE PRINT WORKS, CARLISLE, CUMBRIA CA2 6BT, ☎ 01228 599589, 9–4.15 MON–SAT, 11–2.45 SUN AND BANK HOLIDAY MONDAY. **FACTORY SHOP**

This genuine factory shop has been refurbished and expanded over the last three years. There is a wide variety of prints in traditional and modern designs from £6.50 per metre produced in the factory, together with plain dyed fabrics and upholstery weaves from a sister company in Lancashire, priced from £7.50. The mill prints fabric for the top end of the furnishing trade. The fabrics are seconds but are checked for suitability before sale. The staff are always pleased to help you with calculations for making up. Also available are curtain poles, haberdashery, pillows and cushions, duvets, bed linen and occasional specials such as wallpaper or ready-made curtains. The stock varies according to factory production, so phone before travelling if there is something special you are looking for.

THE FACTORY SHOP

EMPIRE BUILDINGS, MAIN STREET, EGREMONT, CUMBRIA CA22 2BD, ☎ 01946 820434, 9–5 MON–SAT. 10–4 SUN.

THE GILL, ULVERSTON, CUMBRIA LA12 7BN, ☎ 01229 583360, 9–5.30 MON–SAT, 10.30–4.30 SUN.

5 MARKET PLACE, WIGTON, CUMBRIA CA7 9NW, ☎ 01697 342171, 9–5.30 MON–SAT, 10.30–4.30 SUN. **FACTORY SHOP**

See page 383 (CHESH)

TK MAXX

THE EDEN CENTRE AND MARKET HALL, FISHER STREET, CARLISLE, CUMBRIA CA3 8JB, ☎ 01228 819292, www.tkmaxx.com, 9–5.30 MON–FRI, 8.30–6 SAT, 11–4 SUN. **PERMANENT DISCOUNT OUTLET**

See page 377 (BEDS)

DERBYSHIRE

AJ FABRICS AND CRAFTS

6 EAGLE STREET, HEAGE, DERBYSHIRE DE56 2AJ, ☎ 01773 853552, FAX: 01773 853552, **e-mail:** info@fabrics&crafts.co.uk, 9–4.30 MON–FRI, 9.30–4.30 SAT. **PERMANENT DISCOUNT OUTLET**

Fabrics and haberdashery including curtaining, upholstery and dress and fur fabrics at discounted prices. Remnants are a speciality, and they also manufacture scatter cushions from a huge choice of designer fabrics. They also now stock a range of crafts, sold at full price.

DE BRADELEI MILL SHOPS LTD

DE BRADELEI HOUSE, CHAPEL STREET, BELPER, DERBYSHIRE DE56 1AR, ☎ 01773 882442, FAX: 01773 829830, 9.30–5.30 MON–FRI, 9.30–6 SAT, 10.30–4.30 SUN. **PERMANENT DISCOUNT OUTLET**

A delightful Mill centre with individual shops based round a central courtyard, each one selling top brand names in fashions and footwear for men and women, along with Liberty giftware. The womenswear includes such names as Paul Costelloe, Windsmoor, Planet, Precis Petite, Alexon, Kaliko, Eastex, Minuet Petite, Liz Claiborne, Jaeger Knitwear Shop, French Connection, Elle, Country Casuals, Elvi, top American and German designer labels, plus many more. The menswear range includes underwear, socks, sweaters, trousers, jackets, coats and suits from labels such as Wolsey, French Connection, Jaeger Knitwear Shop and Glenmuir. Robert Leonard's Menswear provides Pierre Cardin, Gabicci, Gurteen, Oakman and many more. There is a large shoe department with an excellent range of shoes and accessories for men and women. A Tenson department sells outerwear for men and women. The giftware department offers a superb collection of Liberty giftware with scented candles, Arran Aromatic toiletires, photo frames, baskets, toilet bags and chocolates from Italo Suisse. Chevin Coffee Shop serves delicious home-cooked food throughout the day. De Bradelei Mill Shop has its own car park with alternative parking nearby; coach parties are always welcome though booking is preferred.

END OF THE LINE FURNITURE

32 DERBY ROAD, AMBERGATE, DERBYSHIRE DE56 2GE, ☎ 01773 856082, www.endofthelinefurniture.com, 10–5 TUE, THUR, FRI, SAT, 1–5 SUN. **FACTORY SHOP**

Quality upholstery at factory direct prices.

FABRIC DESIGN

10–12 NORTH PARADE, MATLOCK BATH, DERBYSHIRE DE4 3NS, ☎ 01629 584747, **e-mail:** fabricdesign@aol.com, 1.30–5 MON, THUR, SUN, 11–5 TUE, WED, FRI, SAT, CLOSED BANK HOLIDAYS. **PERMANENT DISCOUNT OUTLET**

Situated in a beautiful spa town, the Matlock Bath outlet is a busy, exciting Victorian shop on the parade by the river, which carries a huge range of designer clearance fabrics from £4.25 per metre, heavy linens from £5.99 per metre and an ever-changing range of bargain one-off buys such as £42 per metre fabric reduced to £9.99 per metre. Fabrics sold in the shop include such names as Sanderson, Monkwell, Jane Churchill, Warner, Anna French and Liberty, but a range of natural fabrics – calico, twills and cream weaves – is also available. Those looking for good quality fabric for upholstery and curtaining should be prepared to buy on the day as the good deals don't stay in the shop for long. Huge range of discounted, one-off, end of lines and a discount is also offered on perfect fabrics and wallpapers ordered from pattern books in store.

FILIGREE LTD

CARTER LANE EAST, SOUTH NORMANTON, JUNCTION 28 OF M1, (OPPOSITE MCARTHURGLEN DESIGNER OUTLET), DERBYSHIRE DE55 2EG, ☎ 01773 811630 EXT 296, 9–4.30 MON–THUR, 9–5 FRI, 9–1.30 SAT, 10–2 SUN. **FACTORY SHOP**

Real factory shop behind factory. Manufactures Filigree and Stiebel of Nottingham lace curtains and printed curtains. Makes curtains on the premises for well-known high street department stores and mail order companies and sells them here at reduced prices. Nets range from 50p a metre to £6 with fabric from £1.99 a metre to £5.99 a metre and remnants from 50p. Also stocks ready-made curtains, curtain accessories and bedding.

MCARTHURGLEN DESIGNER OUTLET

MANSFIELD ROAD, SOUTH NORMANTON, ALFRETON, JUNCTION 28 OF M1, DERBYSHIRE DE55 2ER, ☎ 01773 545000, www.mcarthurglen.com/mansfield, 10–6 MON–FRI, 8 ON THUR, 9–6 SAT, 11–5 SUN. **FACTORY SHOPPING VILLAGE**

The McArthurGlen Designer Outlet Mansfield has recently undergone a year-long development programme, transforming it from an open-plan department store layout to individual shops. The new look outlet is now bigger and better. Find all your favourite brands at discounts of up to 50% off typical retail prices. Facilities include a children's play area, a food court and plenty of free parking. Stores include: Antler, Banana Books, Bed & Bath Works, Big L, Camille Lingerie, Chapelle, Claire's Accessories, Coloroll, Cotton Traders, Donnay, Edinburgh Crystal, Harbi, Jaeger, Jane Shilton, Julian Graves, Kitch N Sync, Leading Labels, Lee Cooper, Mountain Warehouse, Pavers Shoes, Petroleum, Pilot, Price's Candles, Professional Cookware, Remington, Roman Originals, Sky, Soled Out, Speedo, Sportsmill, Suits You, Thorntons, Tog 24, Toyworld, Revlon, Marks & Spencer Outlet, Windsmoor, Sportz, Reebok, Jumper, HKA, Proudfoot Leather, Garden Outlet, Lilley & Skinner, Adidas, Viyella, Whittards, XS Records and many more.

PEAK VILLAGE

CHATSWORTH ROAD, ROWSLEY, (ON THE A6 BETWEEN BAKEWELL AND MATLOCK) DERBYSHIRE DE4 2JE, ☎ 01629 735326, www.peakvillage.co.uk, 9.30–5.30 MON–SAT, 10–5 SUN, EXCEPT CHRISTMAS DAY. **FACTORY SHOPPING VILLAGE**

More than 20 factory outlets including Leading Labels, Cotton Traders, Luggage & Bags, The Book Depot, Pavers Shoes, Sports & Mountain Warehouse, Yeoman Outdoors outdoor wear and equipment, Ponden Mill, Mansworld, New Beginnings and Woodlands Fitness Centre, all just 30 minutes from the M1 at the entrance to the Peak District National Park. On-site catering includes Massarella's Restaurant, which offers everything from an ice cream sundae to a traditional Sunday roast. The Wind in the Willows Attraction is a magical journey through the world of Ratty, Badger, Mole and of course the irrepressible Mr Toad. The latest sound and lighting effects bring Kenneth Grahame's classic tale to life in an enchanting recreation that's not just for kids! Free parking for up to 400 cars. Recently opened the Woodlands Fitness Centre.

TK MAXX

8 EAST STREET, DERBY, DERBYSHIRE, ☎ 01332 364225, www.tkmaxx.com, 9–5.30 MON–THUR, 9–6 FRI–SAT, 11–5 SUN. **PERMANENT DISCOUNT OUTLET**

See page 377 (BEDS)

WILKINSON STORES

13 INSTITUTE LANE, ALFRETON, DERBYSHIRE DE55 7BQ, ☎ 01773 836845, www.wilko.co.uk, 9–5.30 MON–THUR, SAT, 9–6 FRI, 10–2 SUN. MAIL ORDER. **PERMANENT DISCOUNT OUTLET**

See page 383 (CHESH)

DEVON

ATLANTIC VILLAGE OUTLET CENTRE

CLOVELLY ROAD, OFF A39, WEST OF BIDEFORD, NORTH DEVON, ☎ 01237 422544, **e-mail:** rmorris@realm-ocm.com, www.atlanticvillage.co.uk, JULY–MID SEPT, 9.30–7 MON–SAT, 11–5 SUN; MID SEPT–MID OCT AND EASTER TO JULY 9.30–6.30 MON–SAT, 11–5 SUN; MID OCT–EASTER 9.30–5 MON–SAT, 11–5 SUN. **FACTORY SHOPPING VILLAGE**

More than 30 shops with famous names and Devon's largest interactive maze make this village a good family day out. Shops include Banana Books; Claire's Accessories; Colony Candles; Cotton Traders, Designer Room, Ecco; Edinburgh Woollen Mill; Event Jewellery; Jane Shilton; Jean Scene; Julian Graves; Nickelby's; Pavers Shoes; Pilot; Ponden Mill; Puma; Roman Originals; Room, selling home accessories, fabrics and soft furnishings; Sportsmill; Suits You; Tog 24; Toyzone; Triumph; Warners; Windsmoor; XS Sound & Media. Free car parking, disabled and baby changing facilities. Atlantic Village also features an attractive piazza, cafés, a food court, visitor garden, arts and crafts market, open-air amphitheatre, and an adventure park set in an additional three-acre site linked to the shopping area by the piazza and amphitheatre. The Adventure Park features a mystery maze, adventure golf, wrecker's cove and adventure play boat.

CURTAIN TRADER

52 HIGH STREET, HONITON, DEVON EX14 1LQ, ☎ 01404 45451, **e-mail:** flatcatco@yahoo.co.uk, 9–5 MON–SAT. **SECONDHAND SHOP**

Secondhand curtain agency, they are also specialists in discontinued and seconds designer fabrics and sale stock from £2 to £20 a metre, selling curtain fabrics, linings and accessories from many different labels. Also incorporating Flat Cat Cushion Co, individual cushions, trade and retail, and Old Devon Pine, made-to-measure furniture.

EXETER SURPLUS

BAKERS YARD, ALPHINBROOK ROAD, MARSH BARTON INDUSTRIAL ESTATE, EXETER, DEVON EX2 8SS, ☎ 01392 427508, 8.30–5 MON–SAT. **PERMANENT DISCOUNT OUTLET**

Operates from a 4,000 square foot retail unit and a 10,000 square foot trade site half a mile away on Christow Road, the latter specialising in quality, nearly-new office furniture and shelving. Retail goods include engineering equipment, hand tools, clothing, a large range of outdoor goods, chandlery, a range of tents, bedding and domestic furniture, kayaks, rope and chain, canvas sheets, rucksacks, boots and shoes, overalls, ceremonial clothing and an enormous amount of miscellaneous one-off items, all very competitively priced. The outdoor leisure market is their new specialisation.

FABRIC WAREHOUSE

BISHOPS COURT ESTATE, SIDMOUTH ROAD, EXETER, DEVON EX2 7JH, ☎ 01392 447267, 9–5.30 MON–SAT, 10–4 SUN. **PERMANENT DISCOUNT OUTLET**

See page 378 (BERKS)

HARVEY BAKER DESIGNS

RODGERS INDUSTRIAL ESTATE, YALBERTON ROAD, PAIGNTON, DEVON TQ4 7PJ, ☎ 01803 521515, www.harvey-baker-design.co.uk, 8–5 MON–FRI. **FACTORY SHOP**

Supplies unpainted MDF and galvanised accessories, such as wastepaper baskets, tables, deskware, lanterns and gardenware, all available mail order. Send £1 and a stamped, self-addressed envelope for a brochure.

HEATHCOAT FABRICS

RETAIL SHOP, WESTEXE, TIVERTON, DEVON EX16 5LL, ☎ 01884 254949, 9–4.30 MON–FRI, 9–1 SAT. **PERMANENT DISCOUNT OUTLET**

Furnishing fabrics from £3 a metre, dress fabrics, cottons, sequins, header tapes and linings.

THE EXETER FABRIC WAREHOUSE

7–9 FARADAY MILL, PRINCE ROCK, PLYMOUTH DEVON PL4 0ST, ☎ 01752 253351 **e-mail:** sales@boynett.com, www.boynett.com, 9–5 MON–SAT, 10–4 SUN. **PERMANENT DISCOUNT OUTLET**

This Boynett fabric factory shop offers customers the chance to buy ends of ranges and overruns direct at highly competitive prices. The company supplies the leading department stores and interior designers with high quality curtain and upholstery fabrics which you can purchase here at discounted prices from only £2.95 per metre.

TK MAXX

YEO BUILDING, 28 ROYAL PARADE, NEW GEORGE STREET, PLYMOUTH, DEVON PL1 1SA, ☎ 01752 255081, www.tkmaxx.com, 9–5.30 MON–WED, 9–8 THUR, 9–6 FRI–SAT, 11–5 SUN.

FIRST FLOOR, 56–62 FLEET WALK, FLEET WALK SHOPPING CENTRE, TORQUAY, DEVON TQ2 5EN, ☎ 01803 215682, www.tkmaxx.com, 9–5.30 MON–SAT, 7 ON THUR, 10–7 SAT, 11–5 SUN. **PERMANENT DISCOUNT OUTLET**

See page 377 (BEDS)

TRAGO MILLS SHOPPING AND LEISURE PARKS

LIVERTON, NEWTON ABBOT, DEVON TQ12 6JD, ☎ 01626 821111, www.trago.co.uk, 9–5.30 MON–SAT, 10.45–4.45 SUN. **PERMANENT DISCOUNT OUTLET**

The biggest range of discounted goods in the West Country, with a whole range of activities to keep the family amused on the 100 acre site. Sells virtually everything from men's, women's and childrenswear, gardening equipment and cookware to wallpaper, carpets and fitted kitchens. Most are branded goods and there is a café, pizza bar and petrol station. A reasonable amount of the women's fashion comes from high street multiples. The menswear offers a wide range of clothes, as well as all-leather classic brogues and Oxford shoes, and Doc Martens in the Shoes Yard. For the home, there are Black & Decker Dustbusters, Hotpoint dryers and washing machines with cosmetic blemishes; curtain fabrics from Monkwell, Sekers, Filigree, Laura Ashley as well as Janet Reger for Vantona double quilt covers, with matching sheets, pillow cases and valances. There is a vast range of tiles including Pilkington seconds. A huge gardening section with everything from hose pipes and garden machinery to imported trees and shrubs. An excellent leisure section offers bicycles and accessories, golf gear, keep-fit systems, fishing rods and flies. Comparison prices are not given here, although staff say most items are discounted by up to 50%, so if you're looking for a bargain, make sure you've done your homework on the high street first. The best deals are in fabrics, carpets, tiles and DIY. There is a leisure park with a giant free fall slide, supakart and family go-kart circuit, bumper boats, trawler rides, swan pedalos, pirate ship, aquablasters, orbiters, shooting gallery, remote control cars and cruisers, forklifts and mini-diggers, fun dungeon, animal park, model railway, narrow gauge steam railway, nature reserve, coarse fishing, Edwardian penny arcade and plenty of space to picnic and to park.

WINKLEIGH TIMBER SHOWROOM

SECKINGTON CROSS, INDUSTRIAL ESTATE, WINKLEIGH, DEVON EX19 8DQ, ☎ 01837 83832, FAX: 01837 83026, **e-mail:** winkleigh@garden-online.co.uk, 9–5 MON–SAT, 10–4 SUN. **ARCHITECTURAL SALVAGE**

Traditional country-style furniture handmade in reclaimed pine. Over 150 lines are available, many of which are displayed in the showroom. Winkleigh timber yard also offers the largest stock of reclaimed timber in the south of England, including pine, oak and pitch pine planks. Parquet flooring in oak, mahogany, maple, meranti; strip flooring in maple, mahogany, oak and pitch pine.

Joinery grade timber, beams and new random width oak and elm. Large stocks of handmade furniture in reclaimed timber always on display in showroom. Also now includes a small range of slate, stone and granite cobbles, as well as new, pre-finished, hardwood flooring.

DORSET

BAILIE HOUSE WAREHOUSE

STURMINSTER MARSHALL, DORSET BH21 4AE, ☎ 01258 857112, www.middleditchsalvage.com, OPEN 10–6 FRI, 10–5 SAT, 10–2 SUN. **PERMANENT DISCOUNT OUTLET**

Wide range of goods which are the result of insurance claims due to fire, flood, burglary or other insurance problems. A salvage warehouse which has been in operation for 38 years, stock includes sports clothing from names such as Nike, Adidas and Reebox; cricket, tennis and keep fit outfits; men's casual clothing including Fred Perry, underwear and socks; women's fashion including jeans, jackets, tops, many from top London boutiqes; records, CDs, books, pine furniture, curtain and upholstery fabrics.

BALMAIN & BALMAIN

DORSET, DT9 4SB, ☎ 01963 220247, FAX: 01963 220580, **e-mail:** sales@balmain.co.uk, PHONE FOR APPOINTMENT. **FACTORY SHOP**

Buying a sofa is one of the biggest home purchases you make, particularly for good quality. Balmain & Balmain offers traditional, handmade furniture which is custom-made and can be delivered throughout the country at workshop-direct prices. The sofas and chairs are built on best beechwood frames, with coil-sprung seats and feather cushions, using absolutely no foam, and carry a ten-year guarantee. The furniture can be tight or loose-covered in your choice from thousands of fabrics from all the major fabric houses including Colefax and Fowler, Osborne & Little, Romo, Monkwell, and Sanderson. Prices are 20% to 40% less than the equivalent quality in the high street.

CURTAINS ENCORE

57 SALISBURY STREET, BLANDFORD FORUM, DORSET DT11 7PX, ☎ 01258 458871, FAX: 01258 455221, 9–4 MON–TUE, THUR AND FRI, 9–12 WED AND SAT. **SECONDHAND SHOP**

Quality new and secondhand curtains, lined and interlined, as well as headboards, tablecloths, bedspreads, stencils and blanks. Alteration service also available.

FABRIC SUPERSTORE

MANNINGS HEATH RETAIL PARK, POOLE, DORSET BH12 4QV, ☎ 01202 717181 9–5.30 MON–SAT, 10–4 SUN. **PERMANENT DISCOUNT OUTLET**

Large warehouse chain, now with 40 outlets countrywide, selling upholstery fabric, cushions, ready-made curtains and net curtains. Most of the merchandise is made up of clearance material from mills and manufacturers. Some of the outlets also stock a full range of bed linen, towels and bathroom accessories while others sells tracks, poles, blinds of all kinds, brassware, crafts and occasional furniture.

HANSONS FABRICS

STATION ROAD, STURMINSTER NEWTON, DORSET DT10 1BD, ☎ 01258 472698, FAX: 01258 473813, 9–5 MON–SAT. **PERMANENT DISCOUNT OUTLET**

Fabric specialist which also sells sewing machines, haberdashery, craft fabrics and other items, patterns and knitting wools. It stocks all the well-known names and the full range of fabric weights. Lots of choice for wedding dress fabric: polyester, satin, silk dupion, taffeta, tulles, veiling and lining and plenty of bridal pattern books available. If you spend more than £25, you get a 5% discount; more than £125 and you receive a 7.5% discount; more than £250 and your discount is 10%. All leading makes of sewing machines, including Bernina, Brother and Janomi, are very competitively priced, and they also offer a machine repair service. Stocks specialist craft books and sells seasonal fabrics out of season. Sewing and craft workshops are organised during the autumn: send for a brochure. Free parking.

THE CATALOGUE SHOP

401 LYMINGTON ROAD, HIGHCLIFFE, DORSET BH23 5HE, ☎ 01425 271202, FAX: 01425

278478, **e-mail:** thecatalogueshop@virgin.net, www.the catalogueshop.virgin.com, 9–5 MON–SAT, 10–5 SUN. **PERMANENT DISCOUNT OUTLET**

Returns, damaged and worn goods as well as clearance lines and ends of lines of branded merchandise from mail order catalogues. This includes men's, women's and children's wear, footwear, bedding, curtains, furniture, exercise equipment and leather coats. These items are always in stock but the shop also has an ever-changing range of items as well. Turnover is very fast with new deliveries every day. All items are sold at less than 50% of the catalogue price starting at 99p, with branded trainers from £14.99.

THE OLD MILL FACTORY SHOP

PYMORE MILLS, BRIDPORT, DORSET DT6 5PJ, ☎ 01308 420969, FAX: 01308 455001 **e-mail:** info@oldmillshop.co.uk, www.oldmillshop.co.uk, 9.30–5 MON–SAT. CLOSED BANK HOLIDAYS. **FACTORY SHOP**

Beds, mattresses, sofabeds, bedroom and occasional furniture. Traditional style brass, cast and forged bedsteads, top quality handmade sofabeds and mattresses, slight seconds and discontinued lines of which are on sale at huge discounts. The beds are from a well-known brand name, Relyon, made for top quality stores. Also sells brass curtain poles and end of roll upholstery fabric.

ESSEX

BRANDLER GALLERIES

1 COPTFOLD ROAD, BRENTWOOD, ESSEX CM14 4BN, ☎ 01277 222269, **e-mail:** john@brandler-galleries.com, www.brandler-galleries.com/www.thomas-art.com/www.noddy-art.com, 10–5.30 TUE–SAT. PHONE FIRST IF LOOKING FOR A PARTICULAR ITEM. **PERMANENT DISCOUNT OUTLET**

Prints, sculptures and paintings of a high standard at prices which reflect the low overheads outside London. Works by Diana Armfield, Bill Bowyer, Fred Cuming, Bernard Dunstan, Mary Fedden, David Tindle, Carel Weight, Andy Warhol, David Hockney, Picasso and others of a similar calibre. Prices range from £45 to £20,000. for example, they sold a Turner watercolour for £18,500 which would have cost as much as £75,000 in Bond Street. There are original book illustrations for Noddy, Postman Pat, Captain Pugwash, Rupert etc. Also offer a framing service and free car park. Artwork for children's books including Noddy, Postman Pat, Thomas the Tank Engine, etc.

CHOICE DISCOUNT STORES LIMITED

14–20 RECTORY ROAD, HADLEIGH, BENFLEET, ESSEX SS7 2ND, ☎ 01702 555245, 9–5.30 MON–THUR, 9–6 FRI, SAT.

26–28 HIGH STREET, BARKINGSIDE, ILFORD, ESSEX IG6 2DQ, ☎ 020 8551 2125, 9–5.30 MON–FRI, 9–6 SAT, 11–5 SUN.

UNIT 6A, MAYFLOWER RETAIL PARK, GARDINERS LINK, BASILDON, ESSEX SS14 3AP, ☎ 01268 288331, 10–6 MON–WED, 10–7 THUR, FRI, 9–6 SAT, 11–5 SUN.

14–16 HIGH STREET, GRAYS, ESSEX RM17 6LU, ☎ 01375 385780, 9–5.30 MON–FRI, 9–6 SAT.

CLACTON **FACTORY SHOP**PING VILLAGE, STEPHENSON ROAD WEST, CLACTON-ON-SEA, ESSEX CO15 4TL, ☎ 01255 474786, 10–6 MON–SAT, 11–5 SUN. **PERMANENT DISCOUNT OUTLET**

See page 380 (CAMBS)

CITY BEDS

20–22 FOWLER ROAD, HAINAULT INDUSTRIAL ESTATE, ILFORD, ESSEX IG6 3UT, ☎ 020 8501 2426, FAX: 020 8500 3398, **e-mail:** sales@citybeds.co.uk, www.citybeds.co.uk, 8.30–5 MON–FRI, 9.30–4 SAT, 10–3.30 SUN.

10 CLAYDON LANE, RAYLEIGH, WEIR, ESSEX SS6 7UP, ☎ 01268 772422, FAX: 01268 772422, **e-mail:** sales@citybeds.co.uk, www.citybeds.co.uk, 8.30–5 MON–FRI, 9.30–4 SAT, 10–3.30 SUN. **PERMANENT DISCOUNT OUTLET**

Family-owned bed specialist selling mostly UK-made, quality, brand-name beds such as Sealy, Sprung Slumber, Silent Night, Nestledown, Staples and Myers, and many others. The metal beds are imported from Holland and Malaysia. Single beds cost from £75 to top of the range beds, £1,600, normal price £2,300. Also branches at Hainault and Rayleigh.

FABRIC WAREHOUSE

SAINSBURY'S HOMEBASE, BASILDON, ESSEX SS16 4PR, ☎ 01268 552224, 9.30–5.30 MON–FRI, 9–5.30 SAT, 10–4 SUN. **PERMANENT DISCOUNT OUTLET**

See page 378 (BERKS)

FAIRHEADS

60–64 CRANBROOK ROAD, ILFORD, ESSEX IG1 4NQ, ☎ 020 8478 0328, 9–5.30 MON–SAT. **PERMANENT DISCOUNT OUTLET**

There are 13 different departments at Fairheads, including household, linen, soft furnishings, lingerie, fashion, hosiery, craft and haberdashery. There are often 'blue ticket' specials: for example, buy three pairs of Sloggi briefs and get a fourth free. Best quality stock at the lowest price possible and always special offers and reduced lines throughout the store. At sale time stock is half price or less. There are two genuine sales a year: after Christmas and at the end of June. Phone for details.

FREEPORT BRAINTREE DESIGNER OUTLET VILLAGE

FREEPORT ESSEX VILLAGE, CHARTER WAY, CHAPEL HILL, BRAINTREE, JUNCTION 8 OF M11, THEN A120, ESSEX CM77 8YH, ☎ 01376 348168, www.freeportbraintree.com, 10–6 MON–SAT, 8 ON THUR, 11–5 SUN. **FACTORY SHOPPING VILLAGE**

Freeport Braintree is a designer outlet village with over 80 shops. Situated in the heart of Essex with easy access from the A120, Freeport Braintree has its own dedicated railyway station and is only a one-hour journey from central London. Shops selling household goods from kitchenware to pot pourri include Churchills, Denby, Edinburgh Crystal, Glen Eagles, Le Creuset, Professional Cookware, The Design House, Waterford Wedgwood and Villeroy & Boch. Womenswear includes Aquascutum, Amazing Jeans, Antonio d'Errico, Box Fresh, Burberry, Christian Lacroix, Cotton Traders, Elle, Gossard, Karen Millen, Ted Baker, Tommy Hilfiger and Versace and The Designer Room with a host of designer labels. Menswear includes Aquascutum, Cecil Gee, Ciro Citterio, Cotton Traders, Kurt Muller, Nickleby's, Proibito, Ted Baker, Tommy Hilfiger, Van Heusen and Versace. For children there's Base 2 Base, Mexx and Toy Dome; there is also plenty to keep children entertained, such as the Cheeky Chimps indoor play area. Sportwear outlets include Brand Fusion, Donnay, Fila, Mountain Warehouse, Nike, Reebok, Regatta and Trespass. Footwear is covered by Ecco Shoes, Franchetti Bond, Hush Puppies, Jane Shilton, Lilley & Skinner, Soled Out and Vans Shoes. Other retail outlets, selling everything from luggage to music, include Body Shop, Carlton, Claire's Accessories, Designer Shades, Mobile Phone Store, Watch Store and XS Music, and there are no less than six cafés and restaurants on site.

JUST FABRICS

102D HIGH STREET, MALDON, ESSEX CM9 5ET, ☎ 01621 852552, 9–5.30 MON–SAT. **PERMANENT DISCOUNT OUTLET**

This fabric shop sells discounted fabric from dress material to net curtains, fleece, tapestry, curtaining, voile, cushion covers, toy making fabric, buttons, zips, tapes and a full range of haberdashery. If it's not end of line, it's always reasonably priced. For example, at the time of writing, they had designer fabric at £2.99 per metre and fabric which would normally cost between £8 and £17.99 at £2.99. Upholstery-weight fabric which would retail at £9.99 to £25.99 a metre is available at £6.99.

THE CAPE

58 HIGH STREET, COLCHESTER, ESSEX CO1 1DH, ☎ 01206 368183, FAX: 01206 368184, **e-mail:** sc@thefactory-shop.co.uk, www.thecape.co.uk, 9–5.30 MON–FRI, 9–6 SAT, 10–4.30 SUN. **FACTORY SHOP**

See page 379 (BRIS)

THE CURTAIN EXCHANGE

11 MARKET HILL, COGGESHALL, ESSEX CO6 1TS, ☎ 01376 561199, FAX: 01376 562806, www.thecurtainexchange.net, 10–5 MON–SAT. **SECONDHAND SHOP**

See page 381 (CAMBS)

THE FABRIC FACTORY DISCOUNT WAREHOUSE

33–35 EAST WALK, BASILDON, ESSEX CM9 5ET, ☎ 01268 521887, 9–5.30 MON–SAT.
PERMANENT DISCOUNT OUTLET

The Fabric Factory sells dress, bridal and furnishing fabrics at discounted prices. Stock is regular and clearance. They also sell tracks and poles, and offer a made-to-measure service. Haberdashery and a good selection of trimmings are also availalbe.

THE FACTORY SHOP LTD

THE CROSS ROADS, KELVEDON ROAD, TIPTREE, ESSEX CO5 0LJ, ☎ 01621 817662, 9–5.30 MON–SAT, 10–4 SUN. **FACTORY SHOP**

See page 383 (CHESH)

THE LAMPSHADE & LIGHTING FACTORY SHOP

UNIT 1, HASTINGWOOD ROAD, HASTINGWOOD, NEAR HARLOW, ESSEX CM17 9JH, ☎ 01279 413466, 10–4 MON–SAT. **FACTORY SHOP**

Makes lamp bases and fabric shades with coordinating trims, and also sells outdoor lights, lamps, chandeliers, bulbs, lamp bases, shades, all at factory shop prices.

THE REMNANT SHOP

12–14 HEAD STREET, COLCHESTER, ESSEX CO1 1NY, ☎ 01206 763432, 9–5.30 MON–SAT.
PERMANENT DISCOUNT OUTLET

Although not strictly a discount fabric shop, they sell cut-price ends of rolls and remnants in curtain materials, dressmaking fabrics (satins, silks, dupions, polyesters) and patterns. They always have a good range of curtain fabrics and hold thousands of rolls of fabric in stock. Lines change constantly so you should always find something to suit. Also hold a substantial stock of haberdashery at very competitive prices. Friendly staff are always on hand should you need help with any purchase.

TK MAXX

93 EASTGATE SHOPPING CENTRE, SOUTHERNHAY, BASILDON, ESSEX SS14 1AF, ☎ 01268 273604, www.tkmaxx.com, 9–5.30 MON–SAT, 11–5 SUN.

26 SIR ISAAC WALK, CULVER SQUARE, COLCHESTER ESSEX CO1 1JJ, ☎ 01206 368745, www.tkmaxx.com, 9–6 MON, 9–7 TUE–WED, 9–8 THUR–FRI, 9–6 SAT, 11–5 SUN.

THE EXCHANGE, ILFORD, ESSEX IG1 1AS, ☎ 020 8514 1288, www.tkmaxx.com, 9.30–6 MON–FRI, 8 ON WED, 9–6 SAT, 11–5 SUN.

THE BREWERY, ROMFORD, ESSEX, ☎ 01708 761978, www.tkmaxx.com, PHONE FOR DETAILS.

THE ROYAL SHOPPING CENTRE, HIGH STREET, SOUTHEND ESSEX SS1, FAX: 01702 600020, www.tkmaxx.com, 9–5.30 MON–THUR, 9–6 FRI–SAT, 11–5 SUN.

UNIT 4, TUNNEL ESTATE RETAIL PARK WEST, LONDON ROAD, THURROCK, ESSEX RM22 3HH, ☎ 01708 860296, www.tkmaxx.com, 10–8 MON–FRI, 10–7 SAT, 11–5 SUN. **PERMANENT DISCOUNT OUTLET**

See page 377 (BEDS)

YOU'RE FURNISHED

UNIT 6, REAR OF 14 CAMBRIDGE ROAD, STANSTED, ESSEX CM24 8BZ, ☎ 01279 815028 SHOWROOM, FAX: 07947 890467 WAREHOUSE, ☎ 01279 815541, 10–5 TUE–SAT, 11–4 SUN. **PERMANENT DISCOUNT OUTLET**

Home merchandise and furniture from the Marks & Spencer catalogue at discounts of up to half price. Most of the stock is customer's cancelled orders and turnover is brisk with two or three large deliveries a week. There is a small showroom at the above address and a warehouse which is ten times the size just before Stansted airport at Unit 1, Waltham Hall Industrial Estate, Essex CM22 6PF (take the right hand turning at the last roundabout before Stansted car park, first left and about one mile down the road near a sign saying Open Network is the industrial estate). There are up to 900 sofas and sofabeds at any one time, dining room tables and chairs, beds, wardrobes – anything in the M&S catalogue, though they can't guarantee that, having seen it in the catalogue, they will have it on sale.

GLOUCESTERSHIRE

BRANDMART

WESTWARD ROAD, CAINSCROSS, STROUD, GLOUCESTERSHIRE GL5 4JE, ☎ 01453 756655, 9–5 MON–SAT, 10–4 SUN. **FACTORY SHOP**

The original factory shop in Cainscross, Stroud, has recently relocated next door into a 12,000 square foot premises and is now trading under the name of Brandmart, offering even more savings on branded household and family goods. The range includes men's, women's and children's clothing and footwear, household textiles, toiletries, hardware, luggage, lighting, electrical goods and bedding, most of which are chainstore and high street brands at discounts of between 30% and 50%. There are weekly deliveries and brands include famous names such as Calvin Klein, Adidas, Nike, Fcuk, Cat, Reebok, Ben Sherman, Kangol, Timberland and many more. There are kitchen and furniture displays and a new line in Cape Country furniture on sale. Ranges are continually changing and few factory shops offer such a variety under one roof. The shop has its own car park.

COTSWOLD FABRIC WAREHOUSE

5 TEWKESBURY ROAD, CHELTENHAM, GLOUCESTERSHIRE GL51 9AH, ☎ 01242 255959, FAX: 01242 257373, 9–5.30 MON–FRI, 9–5.30 SAT, 10–4 SUN. **PERMANENT DISCOUNT OUTLET**

Thousands of rolls of curtain and upholstery fabric from £2.99 per metre. Huge range of ready made curtains, tracks, poles and accessories, as well as dress fabrics. Now also stocks rugs at 50% of RRP. New lines arrive every week. Senior citizens can save 10% every Wednesday.

PAINSWICK FABRICS

NEW STREET, PAINSWICK, GLOUCESTERSHIRE GL6 6XH, ☎ 01452 812616, 9.30–5 WED–FRI, 9.30–5.30 SAT. **PERMANENT DISCOUNT OUTLET**

A veritable Aladdin's cave brimming with fine quality furnishing fabrics often seen in the glossy magazines. You will find some of the best linens, chintzes, damasks and chenilles among their stock which is collected from around the globe. Their aim is to stock something with a difference, at savings of up to 75% off normal retail prices. Their prices range from next to nothing up to £25 per metre. They also stock a range of trimmings. Set in the picturesque village of Painswick, known as the queen of the Cotswolds, the shop is well worth a visit.

SPRING GRAND SALE

SUDELEY CASTLE, WINCHCOMBE, NEAR CHELTENHAM, GLOUCESTERSHIRE, ☎ 01367 860017, FAX: 01367 860177, **e-mail:** nheslam@aol.com, 10–6 THUR, FRI, SAT. **DESIGNER SALES**

There are now three annual Grand Sales taking place countrywide. The Christmas Grand Sale in London, with over 120 different small companies selling their merchandise to the public, is the largest. This takes place in mid-late November each year. Quality is high and covers everything from dried flowers to bath accessories, Amish quilts to silverware, wooden toys to hand-painted kitchenware, antiques to handmade furniture, luxurious bedlinen to faux fur throws, pewter cutlery to glass vases, garden furniture to deck chairs, often at discount because they are ends of lines. There is a Spring Grand Sale at Sudeley Castle, Winchcombe, near Cheltenham, Gloucestershire, usually at the end of April/beginning of May, and a Summer Grand Sale at Ripley Castle, near Harrogate, North Yorkshire, in June. Both feature gardening furniture and equipment as well as decorative home accessories. Phone the above number for more details. A proportion of the ticket revenue goes to charity.

THE CAPE

25 REGENT ARCADE, CHELTENHAM, GLOUCESTERSHIRE GL50 1JZ, ☎ 01242 519021, FAX: 01242 519021, **e-mail:** sc@thefactory-shop.co.uk, www.thecape.co.uk, 9–5.30 MON–SAT, 10.30–4.30 SUN. **FACTORY SHOP**

See page 379 (BRIS)

THE CURTAIN EXCHANGE

9 THE WOOLMARKET, CIRENCESTER, GLOUCESTERSHIRE GL7 2PR, ☎ 01285 643303, www.thecurtainexchange.net, 10–5 MON–FRI, 10–4 SAT. **SECONDHAND SHOP**

See page 381 (CAMBS)

THE ORIGINAL ARCHITECTURAL ANTIQUES CO LTD

ERMIN FARM, A419, CIRENCESTER, GLOUCESTERSHIRE GL7 5PN, ☎ 01285 869222, FAX: 01285 862221, **e-mail:** john@orignaluk.com, www.originaluk.com, 9–5 MON–SAT, 10–4 SUN.
ARCHITECTURAL SALVAGE

Architectural antiques including period and reproduction fireplaces, doors, floor tiles, chairs, baths, beams, busts, columns, fire surrounds, sirebacks, kitchen ranges, marble fireplaces, mirrors, oak floorboards, objets d'art, paintings, pews, prints, radiators, shutters, sinks, stained glass, taps, towel rails. Also gardenware, including stone troughs, pond surrounds, fountains, flagstones, stone artefacts, sundials, terracotta pots, weather vanes, windows, wrought ironwork, gates, lead cisterns and many other one-off architectural features.

TK MAXX

REGENT ARCADE SHOPPING CENTRE, CHELTENHAM GLOUCESTERSHIRE GL50 1J2, FAX: 01242 513848, www.tkmaxx.com, 9–5.30 MON–WED, 9–8 THUR, 9–6 FRI–SAT. **PERMANENT DISCOUNT OUTLET**

See page 377 (BEDS)

HAMPSHIRE

FABRIC WAREHOUSE

RAEBURN HOUSE, 326 LONDON ROAD, WATERLOOVILLE, HAMPSHIRE PO7 7DU, ☎ 0239 225 5682, 9.30–5.30 MON–FRI, 9–5.30 SAT, 10–4 SUN.

WINNAL TRADING ESTATE, WINCHESTER, HAMPSHIRE SO23 7SI, ☎ 01962 859544, 9–5.30 MON–SAT, 8 ON THUR, 10–4 SUN. **PERMANENT DISCOUNT OUTLET**

See page 378 (BERKS)

FREELANCE FABRICS LTD

WEST QUAY ROAD, SOUTHAMPTON, HAMPSHIRE SO15 1GZ, ☎ 0238 033 6410, 9–5.30 MON–SAT, 10–4 SUN. **PERMANENT DISCOUNT OUTLET**

See page 378 (BERKS)

GRANDFORD CARPET MILLS

UNIT 11, BRIDGE INDUSTRIES, BROAD CUT, FAREHAM, HAMPSHIRE PO16 8ST, ☎ 01329 289612 OR 0500 717124, 9–4.30 MON–FRI, 9–3.30 SAT. **FACTORY SHOP**

Family-run factory which sells the majority of their carpets direct to the consumer. Good quality 80/20 carpets at half the price you would pay in high street shops. The top price is £15.50 a square yard for carpet which you would pay at least £30 for in the high street due to its top quality weight of 50 oz. Seconds, which may be due to uneven dyeing, are £6.50 per square yard. Carpets can be dyed and made to customer's own colour requirements in 80/20 twist. Measuring and fitting can be undertaken and underlay and accessories are available.

RICHARD EADE & SONS FURNITURE WAREHOUSE

THE WAREHOUSE, FOREST ROAD, WHITEHILL, BORDON, HAMPSHIRE GU35 9BA, ☎ 01420 472783, **e-mail:** sales@richard-eade.co.uk, www.richard-eade.co.uk, 9–5 MON–FRI, 10–5 SAT, 10.30–1 SUN. **PERMANENT DISCOUNT OUTLET**

Quality furniture at warehouse prices. Richard Eade & Sons is a family-owned business, established in 1892. Three-piece suites and sofas are bulk purchased from most leading manufacturers including Christie Tyler, Lebus, Buoyant, Alstons, Ultra, Celebrity, Kevin France and many more. All stock is available for immediate delivery. Beds and mattresses from Silentnight, Myers, Jay-Be, Slumberland, Kingkoil Kaymed, Airsprung, Healthbeds, Layezee, Rest Assured. All at discount prices without compromising quality and service. Pine beds and bedroom furniture are imported direct from Scandinavia providing unbeatable value for money. Local delivery, enquiries welcome.

SUE FOSTER FABRICS

14 QUEENS STREET, EMSWORTH, HAMPSHIRE PO10 7YA, ☎ 01243 378831, FAX: 01243 373734, **e-mail:** mail@suefoster.co.uk, www.suefoster.co.uk, 9.30–5 MON–FRI, 9.30–1 SAT.
PERMANENT DISCOUNT OUTLET

Supplies top name furnishing fabrics at discounts. Her showroom has one of the widest ranges of pattern books outside London, where customers can choose perfect fabrics and wallpapers, usually 15% to 20% below retail price and where they can also find trimmings, cushions, sofas and chairs. Also takes orders over the phone and sends out samples and undertakes sample searches – send for the questionnaire. Interior design and curtain making service also available.

THE WILTON CARPET SHOP

105 WINCHESTER ROAD, CHANDLERS FORD, EASTLEIGH, SOUTHAMPTON, HAMPSHIRE SO53 2GH, ☎ 02380 273732, 9.30–5.30 MON–SAT, 11–5 SUN. **FACTORY SHOP**

Wilton weave plain carpets, plain tufted carpets and Axminsters in both big patterns and tonals (smaller designs). As the carpets aren't manufactured here, but on the site at Wilton in Wiltshire, customers order from samples and pattern books but at factory shop prices.

TK MAXX

173–178 HIGH STREET (BELOW BAR), SOUTHAMPTON, HAMPSHIRE SO14 2BY, ☎ 023 80 631600, www.tkmaxx.com, 9–5.30 MON–FRI, 7 ON THUR, 9–6 SAT, 11–5 SUN.

2 WELLINGTON RETAIL PARK, HAMBLEDON ROAD, WATERLOOVILLE, HAMPSHIRE, ☎ 023 92 267626, www.tkmaxx.com, PHONE FOR DETAILS.
PERMANENT DISCOUNT OUTLET

See page 377 (BEDS)

WESTHOUSE TEXTILES

103–105 LYNCHFORD ROAD, NORTH CAMP, FARNBOROUGH, HAMPSHIRE GU14 6ET, ☎ 01252 372701, 9–5 MON–SAT. **PERMANENT DISCOUNT OUTLET**

CORNWALL ROAD, FRATTON, PORTSMOUTH, HAMPSHIRE PO1 5AA, ☎ 023 9285 1275, FAX: 023 9287 6249, 9–5 MON–SAT. **PERMANENT DISCOUNT OUTLET**

Sells quality fabrics, curtaining, sheeting, dress fabrics and haberdashery as well as housing one of the biggest ranges of craft fabrics in the south. Most of the major fabric names are sold here. Some of the stock is clearance, ends of lines and seconds sold at discounts of 50%; most is perfect stock sold at discounts of about 20%. Also offers a bespoke curtain making service.

WILKINSON STORES

22–30 BRIDGE STREET, ANDOVER, HAMPSHIRE SP10 1BN, ☎ 01332 551241, www.wilko.co.uk, 9–5.30 MON–SAT, 10–4 SUN. MAIL ORDER. **PERMANENT DISCOUNT OUTLET**

See page 383 (CHESH)

HEREFORDSHIRE

AFFORDABLE FABRICS

THE GRANARY, LOWER COURT, CLIFFORD, HAY-ON-WYE, HEREFORDSHIRE HR3 5ER, ☎ 01497 831309, **e-mail:** enquiries@affordablefabrics.co.uk, www.affordablefabrics.co.uk, 10–5 MON–SAT. **PERMANENT DISCOUNT OUTLET**

Ends of lines and overstocks of designer fabrics (traditional designs and hand embroidered) from names such as Zoffany, Monkwell, Malabar and G P & J Baker at discounted prices. They specialise in crewel work imported direct from India at affordable prices and provide a full curtain making and design service.

THE FACTORY SHOP

52 BROAD STREET, LEOMINSTER, HEREFORDSHIRE HR6 8BS, ☎ 01568 613944, 9–5.30 MON–SAT, 10–4 SUN. **FACTORY SHOP**

See page 383 (CHESH)

TK MAXX

5 TRINITY SQUARE, MAYLORD ORCHARD, HEREFORD, HEREFORDSHIRE HR1 2BX, ☎ 01432 355000, www.tkmaxx.com, 9–5.30 MON–FRI, 9–6 SAT, 11–5 SUN. **PERMANENT DISCOUNT OUTLET**

See page 377 (BEDS)

TWYFORD COOKERS

UNIT 31–32, THREE ELMS TRADING ESTATE, BAKERS LANE, HEREFORD, HEREFORDSHIRE HR4 9PU, ☎ 01432 355924, FAX: 01432 272664, www.twyford-cookers.com, 9–5 MON–FRI, SAT 10–3. **SECONDHAND SHOP**

Renovated Agas at prices which are very competitive with other similar outlets. They also supply Aga parts and re-fit lids with new chrome parts while you wait. They specialise in old Agas, even those as far back as the Forties style before the casing changed. As well as offering a complete renovation, which will still save you about £1,000 compared with a new Aga, they also offer a 'part-renovation' which will save you even more money. For those who like their Agas looking lived in, this involves restoring the insides, vitreous enamelling the top and replacing the lids but not re-enamelling the front. Also supply gas, CE-approved Agas and offer an installation service. They also stock a range of new Rayburns and Aga Masterchef, Mercury and Falcon ranges. They claim to offer best prices for your old Aga: please phone for details.

HERTFORDSHIRE

CHELFORD FABRICS LTD

CHELFORD HOUSE, COLDHARBOUR LANE, HARPENDEN, HERTFORDSHIRE AL5 4SR, ☎ 01582 763636, FAX: 01582 461114, **e-mail:** sales@chelfordfabrics.freeserve.co.uk, www.chelfordfabrics.com, 9.30–5.30 MON–SAT. **PERMANENT DISCOUNT OUTLET**

See page 380 (BRIS)

CHOICE DISCOUNT STORES LIMITED

GALLERIA OUTLET CENTRE, COMET WAY, HATFIELD, HERTFORDSHIRE AL10 0XR, ☎ 01707 258545, 10–8 MON–FRI, 10–6 SAT, 11–5 SUN. **PERMANENT DISCOUNT OUTLET**

See page 380 (CAMBS)

FABRIC WAREHOUSE

184 EAST BARNET ROAD, NEW BARNET, HERTFORDSHIRE EN4 8RD, ☎ 020 8441 3114, FAX: 01223 830582, www.fabric-warehouse.com, 10–6 MON–SAT. **PERMANENT DISCOUNT OUTLET**

Wide range of soft-furnishing fabrics: chenille; tapestries from £14.99 with a bargain section from £5.99; flat weaves from £12.99; curtain fabrics from £3.50 for ends-of-lines and £5.99 for standard ranges; muslins and voiles. Foam cutting service for cushion pads etc also available, as well as satin and polycotton linings, upholstery sundries, a good range of wooden and metal curtain poles, curtain rails, net rods and wires, trimmings, tie-backs and accessories. In-house curtain-making service available at competitive prices. New for 2002 is a curtain gallery offering thousands of permutations of designs and colours to choose and order from .

GALLERIA OUTLET CENTRE

COMET WAY, HATFIELD, HERTFORDSHIRE AL10 0XR, ☎ 01707 278301, www.factory-outlets.co.uk, 10–8 MON–FRI, 10–6 SAT, 11–5 SUN. **FACTORY SHOPPING VILLAGE**

The Galleria Outlet Centre, often referred to as the bargain hunter's best-kept secret, based in north London, houses more than 80 retail outlets. It offers a wide choice of shops for the discerning customer, providing up to 60% off designer labels and quality brands. The Designer Room is a must for branded men's and women's fashions at huge discounts, stocking DKNY, Jasper Conran, Ghost and Tommy Hilfiger clothing. Looking for a designer evening dress or smart-casual wear? Then visit Discount Dressing. For the latest in fashionable menswear, pay a visit to any of the leading menswear shops. City Menswear offers new season, discounted Yves Saint Laurent and Ben Sherman clothing; Choice sells ranges from Next; B52 Jeans stocks Levi's, Lee and Wrangler ranges; and Baron Jon sells a selection of international names from Versace to

Valentino. Going on holiday or looking for a new set of luggage? Then visit the Baggage Factory which sells top quality brands including Carlton and Samsonite. For all your bathroom and bedroom needs pop in to Ponden Mill or the Bed and Bath Works, selling a selection of bedlinen, towels from Christy, soaps and duvets. BhS For Less sells a range of end-of-season men's women's and children's fashions, as well as homewares and lighting. For all your footwear fancies, take a stroll to Charles Clinkard, Ecco, Soled Out and Pavers, selling great brand names including Timberland, Loake, Grenson, Nike, Reebok and Kickers. For women, D Kaye Cosmetics stocks a host of leading beauty and skincare ranges including Revlon, Max Factor, Lancome and Yardley, all at up to 75% off normal retail prices. Walker & Hall represent the finest in jewellery, stocking Tag, Gucci and Raymond Weil watches all at affordable prices. It also sells gold by weight and guarantees savings of at least 30% per gram. While, for the home, Chinacraft specialises in glass, china and giftware, from Wedgwood to Royal Doulton. If interior soft furnishings are on the agenda, then the Furniture Zone is the largest of its type, selling Oriental, middle eastern and Continental rugs, plus great ranges of sofas and sofa-beds, teak, cherry and oak furniture from Wall Nuts and the Khokhar Collection. To complement any room, the Big Picture and Big Poster sell modern and classical pictures ranging from £5 to £20,000. Visit the Garden Outlet Store for all your outdoor gardening and furniture requirements. Music Surplus, the home entertainment store, is a recent addition to the centre, selling a wide range of imported jazz, pop, chart and classical CDs, as well as the latest DVDs. For the PC enthusiast, UK Software sells CD-Roms at up to 70% off the normal retail price. Tool Ware House sells DeWalt, considered by many to be the Armani of the tool worlds, as well as offering fantastic savings on Black & Decker. The centre also offers three cafés, six restaurants and an abundance of children's activities including Toddler World, a futuristic crazy golf course and bouncing slides as well as a mini go-karting track during weekends and holidays. With over 1,800 free car parking spaces and a nine-screen UCI cinema, the centre offers a complete family day out. The Galleria Outlet Centre is a 20-minute drive from north London, and is signposted from junction 3 and 4 of the A1M.

KNICKERBEAN

11 HOLYWELL HILL, ST ALBANS, HERTFORDSHIRE AL1 1EZ, ☎ 01727 866662, FAX: 01727 866453, **e-mail:** info@knickerbean.com, www.knickerbean.com, 9–5.30 MON–SAT.
PERMANENT DISCOUNT OUTLET

See page 378 (BERKS)

MILLANO

GALLERIA OUTLET CENTRE, COMET WAY, HATFIELD, HERTFORDSHIRE AL10 0XR, ☎ 01707 259199, 10–8 MON–FRI, 10–6 SAT, 11–5 SUN. **FACTORY SHOP IN A FACTORY SHOPPING VILLAGE**

One of more than 70 shops in this glass and steel factory shopping centre straddling the A1. This outlet sells designer suede, leather and sheepskin jackets, coats and trousers for men, women and children at discount prices. Of particular interest are the highly fashionable Toscana lamb's coats. Larger than average sizes can sometimes be made on request. Prices can be up to 60% cheaper than in the high street, with samples, overruns or slight seconds as well as a selection of last and current season's perfects. Also stocked are leather and sheepskin soft furnishings such as beanbags, throws, cushions, etc and a selection of leather handbags and belts.

THE CURTAIN CONNECTION LTD

108 LONDON ROAD, ST ALBANS, HERTFORDSHIRE AL1 1NX, ☎ 01727 868368, FAX: 01727 874515, 10–2.30 MON–FRI, 10–4 SAT. **SECONDHAND SHOP**

A secondhand curtain shop with a well-deserved reputation for service and value for money. The shop is now in its ninth year and has recently been extended with currently over 450 pairs of good quality curtains, as well as a wide range of soft furnishings and accessories. Designer fabrics from all the main labels are represented here, including Liberty, Designers Guild, Anna French, Colefax and Fowler and Laura Ashley. Prices generally vary from £20 to £400 for a full-length pair of top-name interlined curtains complete with pelmet and tie-backs. At the back of the shop there is a special section which caters for the growing number of clients who are renting out properties. The curtains represented here, at the lower end of the price scale, are excellent value for money. To get the best out of your visit, bring your measurements with you together with a sample of fabric, if possible.

THE CURTAIN MILL

19 GREYCAINE ROAD, WATFORD, HERTFORDSHIRE WD24 7GP, ☎ 01923 220339, 9–5.30 MON–SAT, 10–4 SUN. **PERMANENT DISCOUNT OUTLET**

Huge choice of fabrics at really low prices: from £1.99 a metre and including excellent discounts on many designer labels. A large warehouse that stocks Ashley Wilde and Swatchbox, among other leading names at discount prices. Also supplies ready made curtains, bespoke curtains, blinds, venetian verticals, all types of window treatments and has its own making up service.

TK MAXX

UNIT 30-31, A1 GALLERIA, COMET WAY, HATFIELD, HERTFORDSHIRE AL10 0XR, ☎ 01707 260066, www.tkmaxx.com, 10–8 MON–FRI, 8.30 ON THUR, 9–7 SAT, 11–5 SUN.

UNIT 50, 18 THE MALTINGS, ST ALBANS HERTFORDSHIRE AL1 3HL, ☎ 01727 855999, www.tkmaxx.com, 9.30–6 MON–TUE, 9.30–7 WED–FRI, 9–6 SAT, 11–5 SUN.

UNIT 10, FORUM SHOPPING CENTRE, STEVENAGE, HERTFORDSHIRE SG1 1ES, ☎ 01438 728408, www.tkmaxx.com, 9.30–8 MON–FRI, 9.30–6 SAT, 11–5 SUN.

PRINCES QUAY SHOPPING CENTRE, HULL, HUMBERSIDE HU1 2PQ, ☎ 01482 223202, www.tkmaxx.com, 9–5.30 MON–FRI, 9–6 SAT, 11–5 SUN. **PERMANENT DISCOUNT OUTLET**

See page 377 (BEDS)

KENT

BELL HOUSE FABRICS

HIGH STREET, CRANBROOK, KENT TN17 3DN, ☎ 01580 712555, **e-mail:** bellhouse-fabrics@talk21.com, 9–5.30 MON–SAT. **PERMANENT DISCOUNT OUTLET**

This two-storey shop is a Sanderson specialist, but also offers an extensive range of beautiful fabrics from manufacturers such as Anne Swaffer, Jane Churchill, Monkwell and John Wilman, with 400 books to order from other well-known suppliers. Everything is sold at competitive prices, with current, seconds and discontinued lines at less than half price. Printed cottons from £6.99; upholstery fabrics – brocades, tapestries and damasks – from £13.99; Sanderson's linens from £10.99; and silks. They also offer a quality design, make-up and fitting service. Haberdashery, wallpapers and all soft furnishing accessories either in stock or to order.

DE BRADELEI WHARF

DE BRADELEI WHARF (DOVER) LTD, CAMBRIDGE ROAD, DOVER, KENT CT17 9BY, ☎ 01304 226616, FAX: 01304 226636, 9.30–5.30 MON–FRI, 9.30–6 SAT, 11–5 SUN. **PERMANENT DISCOUNT OUTLET**

Large outlet in superb maritime setting just off the Dover Seafront, selling top brand names for all the family, including shoes. The womenswear includes such names as Paul Costelloe, Dannimac, Windsmoor, Planet, Precis Petite, Alexon, Kaliko, Eastex, Minuet Petite, Country Casuals, Elle, French Connection, Tigi Wear, plus top American and German designer labels, handbags and much more including a new accessory department. The menswear range includes underwear, socks, coats, sweaters, jackets, suits and trousers from labels such as Wolsey, Countrywear, French Connection, Virgin and Tog 24. Robert Leonard's Menswear provide Greiff, Pierre Cardin, Gabicci, Gurteen, Oakman, Saville Row, John Slim and many more. For children, there are brands such as OshKosh B'Gosh, Lily by Lily, Smarties, Vitamins, Rebble Pebble, Zip-Zap, O'Neill, MCA and Hickory as well as fluffy toys and melamine tableware with Pokemon and Toy Story 2 designs as well as a new department selling clothing, shoes, books and scientific toys. There is a large shoe department featuring international shoes for all the family and a wonderful Home Furnishings Department. The Interior Design shops sell bedding, towels, top-name furnishing fabric, cushions, throws, furniture and curtains. The Glass and China Department has an amazing selection from Waterford/Wedgwood, Stuart Crystal, Royal Doulton, Arthur Price of England Silverware, Staffordshire Tableware, Churchill, Cloverleaf, Hornsea Pottery, Cristal d'Arques and much more. There is superb Liberty shop in the giftware department and a Cromwell and Morgan Cook Shop. Parking is easy with a large car park behind the store. The Waves Coffee Shop is open all day, serving delicious home-cooked food.

ELITE LIGHTING

7 GOODWOOD PARADE, UPPER ELMERS END ROAD, BECKENHAM, KENT BR3 3QZ, ☎ 020 8639 0050, FAX: 020 8639 0051, **e-mail:** sales@elitelighting.co.uk, www.elitelighting.co.uk, 9.30–5.30 MON–SAT. ALSO MAIL ORDER. **PERMANENT DISCOUNT OUTLET**

Elite sells all types of lighting for the home and garden, including a spectacular range of crystal chandeliers and wall brackets dressed with Swarovski strass crystal. Crystal components are also available. As a leading importer, their prices are very competitive. Visit their website or phone for a brochure.

FABRIC WAREHOUSE

INDUSTRIAL BUSINESS CENTRE, ST PETERS STREET, MAIDSTONE, KENT WE16 0ST, ☎ 01622 763030, 9–5.30 MON -SAT, 10–4 SUN. **PERMANENT DISCOUNT OUTLET**

See page 378 (BERKS)

THE CURTAIN SHOP – PETER HOARE LTD

12 GOODS STATION ROAD, TUNBRIDGE WELLS, KENT TN1 2BL, ☎ 01892 527202, FAX: 01892 522682, 9.45–5.30 MON–SAT. **SECONDHAND SHOP**

Interior designers with showroom stocking new and secondhand quality curtains. Prices range from £30 for a pair of cottage or nursery curtains to more than £1,000 for antique silk curtains. New curtains for a large bay window would average £460 to £520 for a 10ft. drop. They also offer a design and advice service for all new curtain and pelments, and a complete track and pelmet board fitting service. Fabric is also available on the roll and to order.

THE FACTORY SHOP LTD

THE FOREMAN CENTRE, HIGH STREET, HEADCORN, KENT TN27 9NE, ☎ 01622 891651, 9–5.30 MON–SAT, 10–4 SUN. **FACTORY SHOP**

See page 383 (CHESH)

TK MAXX

BROADWAY SQUARE, BEXLEYHEATH BROADWAY, BEXLEYHEATH, KENT, ☎ 0208 301 0508, www.tkmaxx.com, 9–6 MON–SAT, 9 ON THUR, 10–4 SUN. **PERMANENT DISCOUNT OUTLET**

See page 377 (BEDS)

TRACKS AND TRIMMINGS

50 THE PANTILES, TUNBRIDGE WELLS, KENT TN2 5TN, ☎ 01892 515288, 9.30–5.30 MON–SAT, 9.30–1 WED. MAIL ORDER. **PERMANENT DISCOUNT OUTLET**

Small shop with a lot of stock; what they don't have you can order. Everything for the curtain maker and upholsterer, as well as roller and Venetian blinds and exterior awnings. Tracks and trimmings, upholstery and curtains, cushions, tie-backs, from £3.99 each; plaited and rope tie-backs, from £9.99; pelmet boards and handmade lampshades. Extensive fabric and pole ranges. Cafe clips (decorative or plain), café clip hooks, swag creators, rings and brackets in all sizes, pelmet brackets, weights, tie-back hooks, silicon lubricant, soil guard, new tab inserts, roller and Austrian blind kits, Velcro, nail studs, net wire, webbing, curved/mattress/spring needles, key tassels. Clearance lines of trimmings and tie-backs can be discounted by up to 50%. Friendly and helpful staff are always on hand to give advice if needed.

LANCASHIRE

ABAKHAN FABRICS

34–44 STAFFORD STREET, LIVERPOOL, LANCASHIRE L3 8LX, ☎ 0151 207 4029, FAX: 0151 298 1809, 9.30–5 MON–SAT, 10–4 SUN.

111–115 OLDHAM STREET, MANCHESTER, LANCASHIRE M4 1LN, ☎ 0161 839 3229, FAX: 0161 839 3339, 9.30–5.15 MON–SAT, 7 ON THUR.

20–22 MANCHESTER ROAD, PRESTON, LANCASHIRE PR1 3YH, ☎ 01772 202677, 9.30–5.15 MON–SAT, 7 ON THUR. **FACTORY SHOP**

See page 381 (CHESH)

ANGLO FELT INDUSTRIES LTD

TONG LANE, WHITWORTH, ROCHDALE, LANCASHIRE OL12 8BG, ☎ 01706 853153, FAX: 01706 853625, **e-mail:** info@anglofelt.com, www.anglofelt.com, 9–5 MON–FRI. **FACTORY SHOP**

Quieter, safer, more durable, greener – quality underlay in traditional hair felt and felt/rubber combination at factory prices. Seconds and short rolls are available. Minimum order of one roll but the prices are so reasonable that this is still a great bargain. Go to reception where samples of the different thicknesses and types are available to view before buying.

BARDEN MILL SHOP

BARDEN LANE, BURNLEY, LANCASHIRE BB12 0DX, ☎ 01282 420333, FAX: 01282 420336, **e-mail:** info@bardenmillshop.co.uk, 10–6 MON–SAT, 11–5 SUN (LATE NIGHTS TILL 8 THUR APRIL–SEPTEMBER). **FACTORY SHOP**

A true working mill full of bargains, most of which are high street brands at discounted prices. Full range of branded and non-branded merchandise includes Ladieswear from Tagg, Ambience, Affinity, Diva Design, Donna Bella, Prima Casamia, plus Solo from Italy and Camille lingerie; BMB Menswear from Jeff Banks, Regatta, Gola, Le Shark, Centaur, Jonathan Adams, Carabou, Umbro, Bentley, Alexandre and Gibson. Plus Musbury Fabrics selling towels, bedding, fabrics, curtains, from Dorma, Fogarty, Whiteheads, SMD Curtains, Zorbit and Swatch Box. Briggs Shoes with shoes for men, women and children from Hotter, Sterling and Hunt, Van Dal, Gabor and Hotter Subs. Plus Hothouse selling gifts, furniture, pictures, mirrors, candles, kitchenware, lighting, dried flowers, Staffordshire pottery, crystal and glassware. There is also a luggage, books and market stall section. A 140-seat tea room, ample free car and coach parking, disabled access and facilities and weekend boat trips and organised midweek tours.

BOND STREET FABRICS

48–56 BOND STREET, BLACKPOOL, LANCASHIRE FY4 1BW, ☎ 01253 343333, 9–5.30 MON–SAT. **PERMANENT DISCOUNT OUTLET**

Large warehouse chain, now with 40 outlets countrywide, selling upholstery fabric, cushions, ready-made curtains and net curtains. Most of the merchandise is made up of clearance material from mills and manufacturers. Some of the outlets also stock a full range of bed linen, towels and bathroom accessories while others sells tracks, poles, blinds of all kinds, brassware, crafts and occasional furniture.

BOUNDARY MILL STORES

BURNLEY ROAD, COLNE, LANCASHIRE BB8 8LS, ☎ 01282 865229, www.boundarymill.co.uk, 10–6 MON–FRI, 9 ON THUR, 9–6 SAT, 11–5 SUN, 10–6 BANK HOLIDAYS, OPENS AT 10 ON SUNDAYS FOR BREAKFAST AND BROWSING, PURCHASES CAN BE MADE FROM 11. **PERMANENT DISCOUNT OUTLET**

One of the largest clearance stores in Britain, it covers more than 100,000 square feet with over 300 quality brands, all now under one roof. Many of the top end of the high street designer labels are on sale here for both women and men. Women's labels include: Alexon, Windsmoor, Austin Reed, Eastex, Planet, Jaeger, Jacques Vert, Liz Claiborne and Viyella. Men's labels include: Austin Reed, Centaur, Dannimac, Farah, Pierre Cardin, Lyle & Scott and Yves St Laurent. The women's and men's departments are very extensive – not to mention impressive – and cover the whole range from casual to evening wear with reductions of between 30% and 70%. There are also large leisurewear departments for women and men including Polo Ralph Lauren, Timberland, Wrangler and Tog 24, and a whole floor dedicated to women's lingerie. The new extension building, which links the fashion and home stores, contains a massive shoe department stocking Bally, Nine West and Hush Puppies, among others. On the ground floor, there is a huge new cookshop stocking up-to-the-minute ranges and a greatly extended luggage department including Globetrotter, Antler and Jane Shilton. The home store sells brand-name home furnishings, glass and china including Dorma, Sanderson, Denby, Edinburgh Crystal, Dartington Crystal, Portmeirion, Royal Worcester, Villeroy & Boch and Wedgwood. Four times a year, there are special sales at which prices are discounted further. Most of the stock is end of lines with the occasional marked seconds. There is a choice of food outlets: a large coffee shop, a restaurant and a pub, and there is extensive free parking.

BRONTE CARPETS

BANKFIELD MILL, GREENFIELD ROAD, COLNE, LANCASHIRE BB8 9PD, ☎ 01282 871141
OPEN 8–5 MON–FRI, 10–4 SAT. **FACTORY SHOP**

Factory shop manufacturing high quality 100% wool and 80/20 wool mix carpets, all of which are plain, although some of the classic naturals have a pattern in the loop. They buy in yarn from other manufacturers where the yarn colour match between different rolls of the same carpet may not match so they can also make to measure for customers.

CANE AND WICKER FACTORY SHOP

CARSFIELD ROAD OFF LEESTONE ROAD, SHARSTON INDUSTRIAL AREA, SHARSTON, MANCHESTER LANCASHIRE M22 4TJ, ☎ 0161 428 7300, www.caneandwicker.com, 10–5 MON–SAT, 11–4 SUN, CLOSED WED. **FACTORY SHOP**

One of the largest cane and wicker furniture showroom in the country, with over 80 suites on display at any one time. This importer and wholesaler runs three factory shops (here, Walsall, and a smaller outlet in Shrewsbury) to clear stock which has been returned by retailers. The furniture is assembled and all the cushions are made and finished in our own production unit. It comes in a wide range of finishes including light and dark antique, honey, mahogany and walnut. There is also a Mexican pine furniture range and fabric for curtains (though because the fabric is back coated for fire retardancy, it is very heavy). The cheapest cane suites cost from £399, the most expensive, £2,500. A saving of about 15% to 20% can be made on normal retail prices. Matching dining sets and occasional furniture also available. There is immediate delivery for furniture in stock; orders are fulfilled within about one week.

CATALOGUE DISCOUNT STORES

2 BURY OLD ROAD, CHEETHAM HILL, MANCHESTER, LANCASHIRE M8 7JN, ☎ 0161 795 9312, FAX: 0161 7407 274, 9–5.30 MON–SAT, **PERMANENT DISCOUNT OUTLET**

See page 384 (CO DURH)

COLOUR BLIND

FARRINGTON ROAD INDUSTRIAL ESTATE, OFF ROSSENDALE ROAD, BURNLEY, LANCASHIRE BB11 5SS, ☎ 01282 425504. OPEN 10–5.30 MON–FRI, 10–4 SAT. **FACTORY SHOP**

Manufactures roller and vertical blinds and buys in to sell at competitive prices venetian blinds and conservatory roof blinds. There is a large selection of colours and fabrics. Verticals blinds start at £7 per width (regardless of drop) plus VAT; venetian blinds, size 6ft width by 4ft drop, £75; pleated roof blinds to fit a Victorian conservatory roof, approx. £1,500.

CRESTA FURNITURE

RIBBLETON LANE, PRESTON, LANCASHIRE PR1 5LB, ☎ 01772 797474, FAX: 01772 792704, **e-mail:** office@cresta.co.uk, www.cresta.co.uk, 9–6 MON–SAT, 11–5 SUN.
PERMANENT DISCOUNT OUTLET

Permanent discount outlet which endeavours to offer top of the range leather furniture at competive prices by buying large quantities from the largest manufacturers. They offer both 'family' leather sofas made of a coarser grade of leather, designed to withstand heavy usage and the softer, supple, aniline leathers, which are more expensive. Their range starts at £389 for a three-seater Chesterfield up to £4,000.

CROFT MILL

LOWTHER LANE, FOULRIDGE, COLNE, LANCASHIRE BB8 7NG, ☎ 01282 869625, FAX: 01282 870038, **e-mail:** info@croftmill.co.uk, www.croftmill.co.uk, 10–4 SEVEN DAYS A WEEK. ALSO MAIL ORDER. **FACTORY SHOP**

Sells fabrics, dress and furnishing, haberdashery and sheeting material, both in the shop and by mail order. Also stock high quality upholstery fabrics and chenilles and offer a home make up service. Most of the fabrics are overruns, samples, ends of lines, bankrupt stock and some seconds. Nearly all, including the dress fabrics, are 60in (150cm) wide and range in price from £1 to £30 or so a metre. They include cottons, jerseys, sweatshirting, drills, linings, anorak fabric, coatings, and suitings. They send out a catalogue describing their current stock every two months or so and will supply samples up to ten items for £1; up to 30 items for £2; up to 50 items for £5, all of which is refundable if you make a purchase. Most have been manufactured for high street store clothes for shops such as Marks & Spencer, BhS, Laura Ashley and for Dorma. There are also pillows, cushion pads, tea towels and quilts, all at factory shop prices.

CWV BRANDS AT HOME FACTORY SHOP

HEASANDFORD INDUSTRIAL ESTATE, WIDOW HILL ROAD, BURNLEY, LANCASHIRE BB10 2TJ, ☎ 01282 727272, **e-mail:** pamhindle@englewood.co.uk, 9.30–5.30 MON–FRI, 9–5 SAT, 10–4 SUN, 10–5 BANK HOLIDAYS. **FACTORY SHOP**

See page 382 (CHESH)

DALE MILL DISCOUNTS

DALE STREET, MILNROW, NEAR ROCHDALE, LANCASHIRE OL16 3NJ, ☎ 01706 359737, 9.30–6 MON–WED, FRI, 9.30–8 THUR, 9.30–5.30 SAT, 10–5.30 SUN. **PERMANENT DISCOUNT OUTLET**

A wide range of items from clothes and shoes for all the family to kitchenware, furniture, tablecloths, beds and bedding, televisions and general electrical goods, fridges, cookers, microwaves, kitchen and bedroom fittings and units, all on sale at discounted prices. On site there is also a designer clothes store and sportswear outlet, plus a new conservatory extension selling glassware, pottery, dried flowers, table lamps and other household goods.

FABRIC WAREHOUSE

MANCHESTER ROAD, BROADHEATH, ALTRINCHAM, LANCASHIRE WA14 5UN, ☎ 0161 929 8878, 9.30–5.30 MON, WED, FRI, 9.30–8 TUE, THUR, 9–5.30 SAT, 10.30–4.30 SUN.

MANCHESTER ROAD, BOLTON, LANCASHIRE BL2 6TW, ☎ 01204 532518, 9.30–5.30 MON–SAT, 7.30 ON THUR, 10–4 SUN.

5–9 KING STREET, SOUTHPORT, MERSEYSIDE, LANCASHIRE PR3 1LB, ☎ 01704 537433, 9–5.30 MON–SAT, 6 ON THUR, 11–5 SUN. **PERMANENT DISCOUNT OUTLET**

See page 378 (BERKS)

FREEPORT FLEETWOOD OUTLET VILLAGE

ANCHORAGE ROAD, FLEETWOOD, 12 MILES FROM JUNCTION 3 OF M55, LANCASHIRE FY7 6AE, ☎ 01253 877377, www.freeportfleetwood.com, 10–6 SEVEN DAYS A WEEK, 8 ON THUR, FRI. **FACTORY SHOPPING VILLAGE**

Large, brightly-coloured New-England-style seaside shopping village. There are more than 40 shops selling at up to 50% off high street prices, as well as restaurants, family attractions and free parking. Women's fashions include Next to Nothing, Spotlight, Easy Jeans, VF Corp, Double Two, Warner's, Edinburgh Woollen Mill, The Designer Room, Giorgio, BhS for Less, Madhouse and Roman Originals. For men, there is Petroleum, Ciro Citterio, Double Two, Giorgio, VF Corp, Madhouse, Easy Jeans and BhS for Less. Sportswear and outdoor wear shops include Sports Mill, Craghoppers, Regatta and VF Corp. Footwear outlets comprise Lilley & Skinner, Jane Shilton, Shoe Sellers, BhS For Less, Next to Nothing and Petroleum. Sweet-toothed visitors can indulge at Thorntons or The Sweet Shop, and there is Julian Graves for nuts and dried fruits. Household outlets include Ponden Mill, Dartington Crystal, Home Zone, Picture Port and China Traders. Childrenswear stockists include Next to Nothing, BhS for Less, Vecopri, VF Corp and Giorgio. Other stores include Woods of Windsor, Hallmark Cards and Gifts, XS Music & Video, Claire's Accessories, Watch Store and Book Depot.

GDS DISCOUNT FURNITURE STORE

66–77 CAROLINE STREET, WIGAN, LANCASHIRE WN3 4EL, ☎ 01942 826400, 9–5.30 MON–THUR, 9.30–5 FRI, SAT, 10.30–4.30 SUN. **PERMANENT DISCOUNT OUTLET**

Up to 70 suites on show at this store, which features both top of the market and mass market suites. By buying overruns and cancelled orders from the main manufacturers, it is able to stock some of the best names including Lebus, Christie Tyler, Lifestyle, and Pendragon, the leather specialists. Suites range from £490 to £3,000. Bedroom furniture also available. Immediate delivery.

GIFTTREE

CHURCHBRIDGE WORKS, HENRY STREET, ACCRINGTON, LANCASHIRE BB5 4EU, ☎ 01254 237324, 9–5 MON–SAT

REEDYFORD MILL, WESTFIELD ROAD, NELSON, LANCASHIRE BB9 7YM, ☎ 01282 619540, FAX: 01282 696639, 9–5 MON–SAT. **PERMANENT DISCOUNT OUTLET**

Items from the Express Gifts mail order catalogues at reduced prices including cards, giftwrap, gifts, stationery, kitchenware, household products, clothes and toys, including Galt products. Discounts in most departments range from at least 50% off original catalogue selling prices.

HABITAT CLEARANCE DEPARTMENT

SOUTHMOOR ROAD, WYTHENSHAWE, LANCASHIRE M23 9LR, ☎ 0161 902 0441
OPEN 9.30–6 MON – WED, 9.30 – 7 THUR, FRI, 9–6 SAT, 11–5 SUN. **PERMANENT DISCOUNT OUTLET**

Ends of ranges and slightly damaged stock from the famous Habitat stores displayed in one section of this full-price shop. Specialises in furniture, rather than china, glass and rugs, though there is usually a selection of the latter, too. Plenty of sofas, tables and fitted kitchen units.

HARTLEYS MAIL ORDER LTD

REGENT HOUSE, WHITEWALLS INDUSTRIAL ESTATE, COLNE, LANCASHIRE BB8 8LJ,
☎ 01282 861350, **e-mail:** info@hartleys.co.uk, www.hartleysmo.co.uk, 9.30–4.30 MON–FRI.
MAIL ORDER. **PERMANENT DISCOUNT OUTLET**

Clearance lines and regular ranges from manufacturers who supply well-known high street names, Hartleys, which has been established for 38 years, sells calico, voile, muslin, sheeting, pillows, dress fabric, towels, quilts, ready made bedding, curtaining, many of which are well-known brand names, as well as selected garden accessories and furniture. Examples of prices include 70in to 110in sheeting from £2 to £4.95 a metre; huge savings on casement stitched 13.5 tog goose down quilts from £78 for singles, £110 for doubles and £135 for king sizes; polyester quilts from £7.95 for singles, £9.95 for doubles and £11.95 for king size. Curtaining is available from £2 to £20 plus a metre, enhanced by a craftsman-quality curtain and drape making service, which is available economically, using fabric supplied by Hartleys. Dress fabrics cost from 99p a metre; plus large stocks of polycottons, cottons and wool and silks. Curtaining can also be ordered from the curtain range books in the shop which include Crowson and Moygashel. Prices are the same whether you buy through the on-site shop or by mail order or via the website, although many offers are available through the shop only. UK order, C & H charge only £3.50, overseas charge on request. Parking available. Send five second class stamps for samples and a free copy of Hartleys' most recent offers.

HOLLIN HALL CRAFT & SEWING CENTRE

EMPRESS MILLS (1927) LTD, HOLLIN HALL MILL, TRAWDEN, COLNE, LANCASHIRE BB8 8SS,
☎ 01282 863181, FAX: 01282 870935, **e-mail:** chris@empressmills.co.uk,
www.empressmills.co.uk, 9–5 MON–FRI, 10–4 SAT, SUN. MAIL ORDER. **FACTORY SHOP**

At Hollin Craft & Sewing Centre, you will find a modern, working thread mill. The centre houses all the threads and yarns previously only available to industry. Here, you can buy extraordinary threads at factory prices. Hand and machine quilting, endless overlocking types, tailoring, household textiles, tacking, speciality bookbinding, machine and hand embroidery are all on show. The haberdashery section stocks a similarly huge variety including many types of zip fastener. There is an extensive fabric gallery stocking furnishing fabrics, muslins and silks. The large, two-floor shop also accommodates the Thread Collection, plus books, kits, and innumerable crafts including stencilling, stamping and embossing, American innovations, decoupage, beading, hardanger, dolls houses and furniture. There are also ceramics, glassware, wood, candles and wicker in the exclusive gift and homewares section. All this is available by mail order, worldwide. Set in the heart of the countryside, there are workshops, demonstrations and good walking routes nearby.

J B CARPETS LTD

UNIT F2, TOLLBAR BUSINESS PARK, NEW CHURCH ROAD, STACKSTEADS, BACUP,
LANCASHIRE OL13 ONA, ☎ 01706 875709, 9–5 MON–FRI, 9–4.30 SAT, 10–4 SUN.
PERMANENT DISCOUNT OUTLET

Most of the stock here is clearance stock from mid-market brand names such as Berbers, Wilton and Saxony, at discounts of at least 50%. 80/20 twists and 50/50 wool twists from £4.99 to £8.99, free delivery. Bigger, better and cheaper than before: the more you spend, the bigger the discount. Plenty of end of roll bargains.

JORGUS CARPETS

GRIMEFORD MILL, GRIMEFORD LANE, ANDERTON, NEAR CHORLEY, LANCASHIRE PR6 9HL,
☎ 01257 482636, 8–5 MON–FRI, 9–3 SAT, 11–3 SUN. **PERMANENT DISCOUNT OUTLET**

Genuine factory shop selling direct to the public twist, plain, tweed and wool carpets at discounted prices, although most of the stock is plain. Bedroom quality carpets 80% wool/20% nylon cost £8.99 a square yard. Lounge quality carpet, 40 ounce twist pile, costs £10.99 a square yard, which represents a 50% discount. Also stocks 50oz quality at £13.99 a square yard.

MILLENNIUM FURNITURE IMPORTERS LTD

UNITED BUILDINGS, 80 OLDHAM STREET, MANCHESTER, LANCASHIRE M4 1LF, ☎ 0161 228 2377, FAX: 0161 833 4466, 9.30–5.30 MON–FRI, 11–5 SAT. **PERMANENT DISCOUNT OUTLET**

Imports furniture, predominantly dining room and bedroom furniture from Italy, and sofas and chairs from Belgium. By buying directly from the Continental manufacturers, they can sell at very competitive prices. For example, they claim you can buy a complete set of bedroom furniture for £1,000. They also sell 23 different types of leather suites. They are situated opposite Abakhan Fabrics.

MUSBURY FABRICS MILL SHOP

PARK MILL, HOLCOMBE ROAD, HELMSHORE, ROSSENDALE, LANCASHIRE BB4 4NP, ☎ 01706 244280, FAX: 01706 212121, **e-mail:** orders@musburyfabrics.co.uk, www.musburyfabrics.co.uk, 9.30–4.30 MON–SAT, 10–4 SUN. **PERMANENT DISCOUNT OUTLET**

Hundreds of rolls of fabric from SMD, Tyrone, Bill Beaumont and Fryetts, all at greatly reduced prices. Bedlinen by Dorma, Horrockses, Rectella and Coelima. Ready-made curtains by SMD, Tyrone and Whiteheads. All high street brands are stocked at low prices and all are greatly reduced. Throughout the year, they also buy in hundreds of discontinued lines, clearance and slight seconds from various suppliers, many sold off at less than 50% of the recommended retail price. Huge stocks of towels, sheets, pillows, duvets, tablelinen, curtain poles and cushion covers, all at low mill shop prices. January and summer sales see even greater bargains.

NEW ENGLAND FACTORY SHOP

SLADEN WOOD MILL, TODMORDEN ROAD, LITTLEBOROUGH, LANCASHIRE OL15 9EW, ☎ 01706 813563, www.newenglanddesign.co.uk, 10–5 SEVEN DAYS A WEEK.

PORTSMOUTH MILL, BURNLEY RD, TODMORDEN, LANCASHIRE OL14 7EZ, ☎ 01706 813563, www.newenglanddesign.co.uk, 10–5 SEVEN DAYS A WEEK. **FACTORY SHOP**

Manufacturers of furniture, they sell beds, sofas and three-piece suites. They tailor-make three-piece suites which can be delivered in two weeks, primarily in the North West of England. They also sell furniture, bedroom furniture, mirrors, pictures, candelabras and cushions, all at very competitive prices.

NEWBOLD TEXTILES

SHAW ROAD, ROCHDALE, LANCASHIRE OL16 4SQ, ☎ 01706 640211, 9–3.30 MON–WED, 9–6.30 THUR, 9–12 FRI, 10–4 SAT. PHONE FIRST. **PERMANENT DISCOUNT OUTLET**

Two-storey mill shop in residential area which sells an enormous variety of different types of fabric: curtaining, novelty prints, dress material, voiles, sheeting, bedding and upholstery fabrics. Also sells bedding boxes and toy boxes, children's chairs, curtain poles and track, tie-backs, tassels, fringing and accessories. Names on sale include Bill Beaumont and Prestigious. Also stocks haberdashery items and children's prints, and offers a making-up service. Swatches are available and if they don't stock what you want you can order it. Open to trade and public. Free car parking.

OAK MOUNT MILL SHOP

WISEMAN STREET, BURNLEY, LANCASHIRE BB11 1RU, ☎ 01282 414950, 9.15–5 MON–SAT. **FACTORY SHOP**

Reasonably-sized factory shop selling a small range of dress and a wide range of curtain fabrics.

PENDLE VILLAGE SHOPPING OUTLET

HOLLIN BANK, BRIERFIELD, NELSON, JUNCTION 12 OF M65, LANCASHIRE, ☎ 01282 605004 HOMEWARES, FAX: 01282 605023 FASHION. OPEN 10–5.30 MON–SAT, 10.30–4.30 SUN. **PERMANENT DISCOUNT OUTLET**

A huge mill shop with different areas selling fashion for men and women, home furnishings, bedding, towels, pine and cane furniture, dining sets, three-piece suites, carpets and rugs. The fashion department boasts many famous high street names and features lingerie and footwear while the homewares department offers a wide range of bedding with matching accessories, ready-made curtains, cushions, towels in a wide range of colours and sizes and a collection of cookware and gifts. The furniture showroom offers a wide range of upholstery in modern fabrics, chenilles and leathers; traditional dining room furniture; kitchen sets; pine bedroom, dining and occasional furniture; and an extensive selection of different types of beds. The carpet department offers an extensive selection of rolls and roll ends in carpets and vinyls as well as wood flooring and more than 600 traditional Chinese, Indian and Oriental rugs in a variety of sizes and colours.

SANDERSON CLEARANCE OUTLET SHOP

2 POLLARD STREET, ANCOATS, MANCHESTER, LANCASHIRE M4 7DS, ☎ 0161 272 8501, FAX: 0161 272 8628, 10–6 MON–SAT, 10–4 SUN. **FACTORY SHOP**

Seconds in furnishing fabrics from discontinued patterns, lines and end of ranges; wallpapers and ready made curtains, duvet covers, most of which cost about half price. Lots of remnants and ends of ranges and slight seconds of bedding. Also sells furniture, including sofas and chairs, at discounted prices. Free parking. Payment by Visa, MasterCard, Switch and Delta accepted.

SPRINGVALE LEATHER

UNIT 2, HOLMEBANK WORKS, FOUNDRY STREET, RAWTENSTALL, ROSSENDALE, LANCASHIRE BB4 6HQ, ☎ 01706 225005/211830, FAX: 01706 229170, **e-mail:** springv@springvaleleather.co.uk, www.springvaleleather.co.uk, 9–4.45 MON–FRI, 9–1 SAT. MAIL ORDER. **PERMANENT DISCOUNT OUTLET**

Manufacturers of leather furniture, suites, occasional and office furniture available by mail order or direct from the factory showroom. Suites start at £2,000. Recliners and bedsettees also available. Phone for a free colour brochure.

STANDFAST FACTORY FABRIC SHOP

CATON ROAD, LANCASTER, LANCASHIRE LA1 3PA, ☎ 01524 64334, 9.30–1 MON–FRI, 10–12.30 SAT. **FACTORY SHOP**

Genuine factory shop selling a wide range of well-known designer named fabrics, which are suitable for all soft furnishings, at discounted prices. Stocks vary according to factory production and all fabrics are seconds. Prices range from £2 to £7 per metre. They always stock plenty of pieces for cushion covers and patchwork from 30p each to £3 for small sackful. Usually they have some fabrics on special offer, ranging from £1.50 per metre to £7 a metre. None of the fabric is flame retardant but once treated, can be used for upholstery.

STAPLES

UNIT 4, TRINITY RETAIL PARK, SPRINGFIELD BRADFORD STREET, BOLTON, LANCASHIRE BL2 1HY, ☎ 01204 365307, www.staples.co.uk, 8–8 MON–FRI, 9–6 SAT, 11–5 SUN. **PERMANENT DISCOUNT OUTLET**

Office equipment and furniture supplier which is aimed at businesses, but is also open to the public. The owner buys in bulk and so is able to sell a range of goods from paper clips to personal computers at very competitive prices. Customers do not have to buy in bulk to make savings. A mail order catalogue with details of over 4,000 products is available. Delivery on mail order items is free on purchases of over £30 (area permitting). There are more than 70 branches countrywide – for your nearest store, phone Talking Pages on 0800 600 900.

TERRY'S STORES URMSTON LTD

47 STATION ROAD, URMSTON, MANCHESTER, LANCASHIRE M41 9JG, ☎ 0161 748 6011, 9.30–5 MON–SAT, CLOSED WED. **PERMANENT DISCOUNT OUTLET**

Described as 'the final resting-place for ex-catalogue stock', Terry's sells everything that is normally available by catalogue at half price. This includes leather jackets, jeans, shoes, trainers, dress and curtaining fabric, whatnot stands, nests of tables, dining tables and chairs, bedlinen, curtains, electrical goods, wedding and bridesmaids dresses. The company has been in operation for 46 years and is privately owned.

THE BANKRUPT SHOP LTD

29 STAFFORD STREET, LIVERPOOL, LANCASHIRE L3 8LX, ☎ 0151 207 0531, FAX: 0151 207 1880, www.bankrupt-shop.com, 9.30–5.30 MON–SAT, 10.30–4.30 SUN.

88 GREAT ANCOATS, STREET, MANCHESTER, LANCASHIRE M4 5BG, ☎ 0161 228 3547, 9.30–5.30 MON–SAT, 10.30–4.30 SUN.

450 NEW HALL LANE, PRESTON LANCASHIRE PR1 4TA, ☎ 01772 654442, 9.30–5.30 MON–SAT, 10.30–4.30 SUN.

85 WALLGATE, WIGAN, LANCASHIRE WN3 4EA, ☎ 01942 242668, 9.30–5.30 MON–SAT, 10.30–4.30 SUN. **PERMANENT DISCOUNT OUTLET**

See page 383 (CHESH)

THE FABRIC WAREHOUSE

UNIT 2B, QUEENS RETAIL PARK, QUEENS STREET, PRESTON, LANCASHIRE PR1 4HZ, ☎ 01772 202066, www.homestylegroupplc.com, 9–5.30 Mon–sat, 8 on wed, 11–5 sun. **PERMANENT DISCOUNT OUTLET**

Massive outlet, heaving with shelves of fabric, net and voiles, as well as haberdashery from needles and cotton to braid and Velcro. Brand names on sale here include Prestigious, Ashley Wilde, Fairfield Mills, Rectella and Style. Ready-made curtains also for sale with an express service available in which curtains can be made in five days.

THE FACTORY SHOP

LANCASTER LEISURE PARK, WYRESDALE ROAD, LANCASTER, LANCASHIRE LA1 3LA, ☎ 01524 846079, 10–5 MON–SAT, 11–5 SUN. **FACTORY SHOP**

See page 383 (CHESH)

THE PINE FACTORY SHOP

ADEPT PINT LTD, TAMEWATER MILL, DELPH NEW ROAD, DOBCROSS, NEAR OLDHAM, LANCASHIRE OL3 5BE, ☎ 01457 877155, www.pine-factory.shop.co.uk, 9–5 MON–FRI, 8 ON THUR, 10–5 SAT, SUN. **FACTORY SHOP**

Good selection of their own pine furniture made on the premises. Offers finishes in situ which can be matched to existing furniture. Custom-made furniture can be made to your own design. Delivery service also available.

TK MAXX

BASEMENT LEVEL, LEWIS'S BUILDING, MARKET STREET, MANCHESTER, LANCASHIRE M60 1TX, ☎ 0161 236 1885, www.tkmaxx.com, 9–6.30 MON–FRI, 8 ON THUR, 9–6 SAT, 11–5 SUN.

THE POINT RETAIL PARK, MOLEWORTH STREET, ROCHDALE, LANCASHIRE, ☎ 01706 759187, www.tkmaxx.com, PHONE FOR DETAILS.

UNIT A1, REGENT ROAD RETAIL PARK, ORDSALL LANE, SALFORD, MANCHESTER LANCASHIRE M5 3TP, ☎ 0161 833 2200, www.tkmaxx.com, 9.30–8 MON, THUR, FRI, 9.30–6 TUE, WED, 9–6 SAT, 11–5 SUN.

ST HELEN'S RETAIL PARK, WARRINGTON NEW ROAD, LANCASHIRE, ☎ 01744 615847, www.tkmaxx.com, PHONE FOR DETAILS. **PERMANENT DISCOUNT OUTLET**

See page 377 (BEDS)

WINFIELDS

HAZEL MILL, BLACKBURN ROAD, HASLINGDEN, ROSSENDALE, LANCASHIRE BB4 5DD, ☎ 01706 227916, FAX: 01706 831125, **e-mail:** info@winfields.co.uk, www.winfields.co.uk, 10–5.30 MON–FRI, 8 ON THUR, 9–5.30 SAT, 11–5 SUN. **PERMANENT DISCOUNT OUTLET**

Winfields is a big mill discount store with other outlets in Barrow-in-Furness, Middleton and Hull, offering tremendous savings on shoes (more than 100,000 pairs to choose from, including trainers, boots, dressy shoes and sandals), womenswear (casual wear, sportswear, swimwear, lingerie, suits and dresses and designer fashions), traditional and contemporary menswear (shirts, trousers, jeans, polo shirts, denim jackets, sleepsuits and underwear), and accessories such as leather belts and wallets. There is a young fashion department and a range for women in sizes 18 plus. Winfields is the word on the street for children and teens for footwear, sportswear and clothing in up-to-the-minute styles. In addition, Winfields has a massive selction of outdoor wear, fleeces, waterproofs, wellingtons, hiking boots, socks, hats, scarves and gloves for all the family. There is a wide variety of outdoor and indoor furniture, timber decking, garden tools, pet accessories, cookware, utensils, electrical goods, bath towels, mirrors, picture frames, and gifts such as watches, crystalware and beauty products, with new stock arriving weekly. Luggage can be found in the Winair holiday department. Dine or take a break at Cloggers, the restaurant. Free car parking. Wheelchair friendly.

LEICESTERSHIRE

CREATIVE CARPETS LTD

UNIT 8, MILL HILL INDUSTRIAL ESTATE, QUARRY LANE, ENDERBY, LEICESTERSHIRE LE9 5AU, ☎ 0116 284 1455, FAX: 0116 275 2550, **e-mail:** info@creativecarpetsltd.co.uk, 9–3 SAT, WEEKDAYS BY APPOINTMENT ONLY. CLOSED CHRISTMAS.

FACTORY SHOP

Genuine factory shop where carpets are manufactured on the premises. All carpets are quality heavy domestic, 80/20 wool, hessian backed. There is a large choice of colour including plain dyed, berbers and heather tweeds. Savings of 50% can be made by buying direct from the factory. Prices for the perfects start at about £10.70 a square metre. Seconds, underlay and a full fitting service are also available.

CURTAINS COMPLETE

THE STABLES, EAST FARNDON HALL, MARKET HARBOROUGH, LEICESTERSHIRE LE16 9SE, ☎ 01858 466671, FAX: 01858 432112, 9.30–3 TUE, OTHER TIMES BY APPOINTMENT.

SECONDHAND SHOP

Owner Caroline Everard spent a five-year apprenticeship in London making for most of the top interior decorators, and 20 years making top quality hand-made curtains and soft furnishings for private clients. Now, the stables at her home, East Farndon Hall, house more than 200 pairs of nearly-new curtains ranging in price from £35 to £800, many in top quality fabrics such as Colefax & Fowler, Jane Churchill and Designers Guild. A large number are in almost perfect condition, but for those needing repairs or alterations, these can be easily organised. Linings, interlinings, hooks and tapes are also available for those wishing to do their own alterations. She also sells new made-to-measure curtains from a wide range of fabrics. Curtains can also be taken home on approval.

DE BRADELEI MILL SHOP LTD LUTTERWORTH

LOWER LEICESTER ROAD, LUTTERWORTH, LEICESTERSHIRE LE17 4NF, ☎ 01455 557571, FAX: 01455 557332, 9.30–5.30 MON–FRI, 9.30–6 SAT, 10.30–4.30 SUN. **PERMANENT DISCOUNT OUTLET**

A light and airy outlet centre, easily accessible from M1 junction 20 and M6 junction 1, selling leading high street and designer labels with up to 70% discount. Brands include Windsmoor, Planet, Precis Petite, Jaegar Knitwear, Jacques Vert, Country Casuals, French Connection, Elle, Elvi, and Studio selling a small selection of designer labels. Lee Cooper has an extensive range of jeans and casuals. Menswear brands include French Connection, Wolsey, Lee Cooper, Farah, and Robert Leonards menswear selling Gabicci, Gurteen and Ben Sherman. The children's section stocks fashions from birth to 12 years plus. A large shoe department stocks well-known brands for all the family. Ponden Mill offers a wide range of soft furnishings and everything for the home. Liberty giftwear and Arran Aromatics toiletries akso available. Car parking. Coaches welcome.

LOW WOODS FURNISHINGS

LOW WOODS LANE, BELTON, NR LOUGHBOROUGH, LEICESTERSHIRE LE12 9TR, ☎ 01530 222246, FAX: 01530 223932, www.lowwoodsfurnishings.co.uk, 9–5.30 TUE–SAT, 9–1 SUN, CLOSED MON. **PERMANENT DISCOUNT OUTLET**

Low Woods sells discounted designer curtain and upholstery fabrics including tapestries, voiles, silks, chenille, cotton satin, weaves, damasks, etc. They have thousands of metres in stock at one third normal retail price. Brands include Crowson, Sanderson, Harlequin, John Wilman and many more. Prices can be as low as £2.50 a metre in sale times which are January, April and August. A professional make-up service is also available in on-site workrooms. They also stock a range of painted French furniture: wardrobes, beds, chests of drawers, tables, chairs as well as accessories such as candle holders and mirrors. Sofas and chairs are also stocked at hugely discounted prices. Unlimited free parking; coaches welcome.

TK MAXX

HAYMARKET CENTRE, 10 KEMBLE SQUARE, LEICESTER, LEICESTERSHIRE LE1 3YD, ☎ 0116 251 0155, www.tkmaxx.com, 9–5.30 MON–THUR, 9–6 FRI–SAT, 11–5 SUN. **PERMANENT DISCOUNT OUTLET**

See page 377 (BEDS)

LINCOLNSHIRE

ASHCROFT FABRICS

HORNCASTLE ROAD, COWBRIDGE, BOSTON, LINCOLNSHIRE PE22 7DJ, ☎ 01205 360888, FAX: 01205 311803, 9–5.30 MON–SAT, 12–4 SUN. **PERMANENT DISCOUNT OUTLET**

Large mixed store with car parking selling furnishing fabrics, foam, cane furniture, beanbags, throwovers, braiding, towels, bedding, mats, cushion pads, ready-made curtains and lampshades.

CLOTH MARKET

UNIT 5, STAMFORD WALK, ST MARY'S STREET, STAMFORD, LINCOLNSHIRE PE9 2JE, ☎ 01780 753409, 9.30–5.30 MON–SAT, CLOSED THUR. **PERMANENT DISCOUNT OUTLET**

Small shop selling upholstery and furnishing fabric by Liberty, Sanderson, G P & J Baker, Monkwell and other good quality makes. Apart from offering a cut-length service on new collections, they specialise in discontinued designs and seconds in current designs, including undyed natural weaves and damasks, at prices starting at £3.90 a metre. Here, customers can see it all in stock, check out the good prices and walk away with it. Some even borrow a roll to look at against their home colours. There is also a marvellous stock of dress fabrics, with couture wools at 25% of the regular price, starting at £10 a metre. Friendly, personal service.

DESIGNER FABRIC WAREHOUSE

UNIT 5, GREYFRIARS, GRANTHAM, LINCOLNSHIRE NG31 6PG, ☎ 01476 570022, FAX: 01476 579333, 9.30–5.30 MON–SAT, 10–4 SUN. **PERMANENT DISCOUNT OUTLET**

Stocks up to 8,000 rolls of curtain, upholstery and dress fabrics from 99p a metre. This warehouse is packed to the rafters with voiles, muslins, chintz, nets, velvets, calicos, readymade curtains, superb tapestries, cushions, braids and fringes, tracks, poles and blinds, as well as brassware, crafts and occasional furniture. 35,000 square feet on two floors, incorporating craft workshops, Benson's beds and Husquarna Sewing Centre.

FABRIC WAREHOUSE

ROUNDTREE WAY, MOUSEHOLD, NORWICH, LINCOLNSHIRE DN15 8NW, ☎ 01724 858949, 10–6 MON–SAT, 8 ON THUR, FRI, 10–4 SUN. **PERMANENT DISCOUNT OUTLET**

See page 378 (BERKS)

HEMSWELL CLIFF ANTIQUE CENTRE

NEAR CAENBY CORNER, HEMSWELL, LINCOLNSHIRE DN21 5JJ, ☎ 01427 668389, **e-mail:** info@hemswell-antiques.com, www.hemswell-antiques.com, 10–5 SEVEN DAYS A WEEK. **SECONDHAND SHOP**

Created from the former RAF Hemswell, it claims to be the largest centre for antiques, collectables and retro items in Europe, with about 300 stalls spread over three separate buildings selling everything from furniture and china to glass, beds, bedlinen, clocks and with a whole room of taps and knobs. There is also a major craft centre. Many of the antiques are of high quality though the prices seem to be below most recognised major centres. Avoid Sundays when there is a very popular car boot sale/market making car parking difficult.

MAGPIE FABRICS

22 BRIDGE STREET, SAXILBY, LINCOLN, LINCOLNSHIRE LN1 2PZ, ☎ 01522 702137, 10–1 MON, WED, 10–5 TUE, THUR, FRI, 10–4 SAT. **PERMANENT DISCOUNT OUTLET**

Sells quality low-priced fabrics for curtaining and upholstery as well as fabrics and wallpapers to order from Blendworth, Malthouse, John Wilman, Nouveau, Wemyss, Sanderson, Dovedale and others at competitive prices. Curtaining from £7.50 per yard, upholstery from £8.50 per yard. Also stocks lining fabric (100% cotton sateen), heading tapes (from standard to diamond and pinch pleat), cording, haberdashery, tassels, tie-backs, wooden holdbacks and cotton thread. Phone for the price of any of the fabrics you want. Making-up service available. The shop is five minutes out of Lincoln on the A57, with easy parking.

THE CAPE

UNIT 1A, 233–235 HIGH STREET, LINCOLN, LINCOLNSHIRE LN2 1AT, ☎ 01522 522462, FAX: 01522 522464, **e-mail:** sc@thefactory-shop.co.uk, www.thecape.co.uk, 9–5.30 MON–FRI, 9–6 SAT, 11–5 SUN. **FACTORY SHOP**

See page 379 (BRIS)

THE FACTORY SHOP

MALT KILN ROAD, BARTON ON HUMBER, NORTH LINCOLNSHIRE DN18 5JT, ☎ 01652 636701, 9–7 MON, TUE, WED, 9–8 THUR, FRI, 8.30–7 SAT, 10–4 SUN.

43 HIGH STREET, MABLETHORPE, LINCOLNSHIRE LN12 1XA, ☎ 01507 473705, 9.30–6 MON–SAT, 10.30–4.30 SUN.

CARRE STREET, SLEAFORD, LINCOLNSHIRE NG34 7TW, ☎ 01529 410155, 9–5.30 MON–SAT, 10–4 SUN.

51 FLEET STREET, HOLBEACH, SPALDING, LINCOLNSHIRE PE12 7AU, ☎ 01406 422180, 9–5 MON–SAT, 10–4 SUN. **FACTORY SHOP**

See page 383 (CHESH)

WILKINSON STORES

2 THE BROADWAY, ASHBY, SCUNTHORPE, LINCOLNSHIRE NG5 7EL, ☎ 01724 867767, www.wilko.co.uk, 9–5.30 MON–FRI, 8.30–5.30 SAT, 10–4 SUN. MAIL ORDER. **PERMANENT DISCOUNT OUTLET**

See page 383 (CHESH)

LONDON

ALEXANDER FURNISHINGS

51–61 WIGMORE STREET, LONDON W1U 1PU, ☎ 020 7935 2624, FAX: 020 7224 3275, 9–6 MON–SAT, 7 ON THUR. **PERMANENT DISCOUNT OUTLET**

The largest independent curtain retailer in the UK, Alexander Furnishings has been operating from the same base for nearly 50 years. Famous for curtaining, they also sell upholstery fabric and wallpapers and trimmings. There's always a discount on fabrics and the biggest bargains are the discontinued lines which can be discounted by up to 50%. There is also a trimming shop on the premises and sofas and sofabeds are on sale. Fabric prices can start as low as £1.95 and there is a vast selection below £10 but this varies over the year.

ANDREW'S OFFICE FURNITURE

97–101 HACKNEY ROAD, LONDON E2 8ET, ☎ 020 7256 1269, FAX: 020 7613 1399, **e-mail:** eddyandrews@lineone.net, www.andrewoffco.co.uk, 7.30–5.30 MON–FRI, 8–2 SAT. **SECONDHAND SHOP**

Two floors and a labyrinthian courtyard packed with really cheap office furniture. Stock is mostly from bankrupt companies or comprises new but discontinued styles, with prices 50% lower than at usual retail outlets. Outdoors, there is a huge selection of stacking chairs and old rickety desks. For details of other branches, phone 020 7405 6816.

ART IN IRON 2001 LTD

557–561 BATTERSEA PARK ROAD, LONDON SW11 3BL, ☎ 020 7924 2332, FAX: 020 7924 2744, **e-mail:** sales@artiniron.demon.co.uk, www.zzz4u.com, 10–6 MON–FRI, 11–5 SAT, SUN. **FACTORY SHOP**

They handmake all their bed in their forge in Battersea, London, and sell direct to the public through their showroom on Battersea Park Road. Art in Iron specialise in simple, unfussy contemporary designs, some minimalist, some Gothic and some classic. Prices here are a lot lower than the same beds would be in department stores. Single beds from £260 to £360; three-quarters and doubles from £320 to £600; kings from £340 to £660; and superkings from £390 to £750. Most beds can be made into four-posters for an extra £220.

BUCKS FURNITURE WAREHOUSE

125 EVELYN STREET, DEPTFORD, LONDON SE8 5RJ, ☎ 020 8692 4447, FAX: 020 8469 3136, 10–7 MON–FRI, 10–5 SAT, 10–4 SUN. **PERMANENT DISCOUNT OUTLET**

20,000 square foot warehouse selling cancelled orders, ex-display and ex-photo shoot furniture from famous department stores and other well-known brand names. Some of the department store furniture is from the current catalogue. Some has been marked or damaged during display or photography, but they are all clearly signposted. A lot of stock is brand new. Furniture includes three-piece suites, wardrobes, a very large stock of beds, bedsteads (modern and traditional), tables, chairs and dressing tables. Most of the three-piece suites are reduced by 40% to 50% and the other items are all substantially discounted. Free car parking.

CARPET TILE CENTRE

227 WOODHOUSE ROAD, NORTH FINCHLEY, LONDON N12 9BD, ☎ 020 8361 1261, FAX: 020 8361 3147, **e-mail:** carpetcentre@btconnect.com, www.carpetcentre@barclays.net, 9–5 MON–FRI, 9–1 SAT. **PERMANENT DISCOUNT OUTLET**

Offers a wide range of seconds as well as end of line carpet tiles, specials and non-standard colours of Heuga and Interface brands. Prices start at £1.95 to £2.95 for tiles which normally cost £5. Even the perfect tiles are competitively priced.

CHANGE OF HABIT

65 ABBEVILLE ROAD, CLAPHAM, LONDON SW4 9JW, ☎ 020 8675 9475, 11–6 MON–FRI, 10–6 SAT. **DRESS AGENCIES**

This dress agency has recently added antiques and home furnishing both for the garden and for the conservatory.

CHRISTMAS GRAND SALE

ROYAL HORTICULTURAL HALLS, ELVERTON STREET, VICTORIA, LONDON SW1, FAX: 01367 860017 (ENQUIRIES: OPEN 9.30–5.30 MON–FRI), ☎ 01367 860177, **e-mail:** nheslam@aol.com, 6–9 WED, 10–6 THUR–SAT. **DESIGNER SALES**

There are now three annual Grand Sales taking place countrywide. The Christmas Grand Sale in London, with over 120 different small companies selling their merchandise to the public, is the largest, taking place over three days plus a charity preview evening. This takes place in mid-late November each year. Quality is high and covers everything from from swags and garlands, smoked trout pate, French lavender sachets, hand-painted furniture, made-to-measure blinds, 19th century wall clocks, Continental Advent cards, boozy Christmas cakes, unusual watercolours, cinammon-scented apple wreaths, traditional American tinware, children's pyjama cases, candle sconces, handmade Indian pickles, bamboo placemats, embossed copper sketchbooks, Art Deco mirrors, silk embroidered cushions, herbal tinctures, stunning tree decorations, English garden trugs, African shopping baskets, handmade wrapping paper, elegant kitchen woodware, beaded handbags, bespoke Ottomans, fine champagne, baby sleeping bags, nautical mirrors, painted dog and cat beds, ties and matching cufflinks, foie gras, antique Bergeres suites, Egyptian cotton bedlinen, often at discount because they are ends of lines. There is a three-day Spring Grand Sale at Sudeley Castle, Winchcombe, near Cheltenham, Gloucestershire, usually at the end of April/beginning of May, and a four-day Summer Grand Sale at Ripley Castle, near Harrogate, North Yorkshire, in early-mid June. Both feature gardening furniture and equipment as well as decorative home accessories. Phone the above number for more details. A proportion of the ticket revenue goes to charity.

CITY BEDS

17–39 GIBBINS ROAD, OFF CARPENTER'S ROAD, LONDON E15 2HU, ☎ 020 8534 9000, FAX: 020 8519 8450, **e-mail:** sales@citybeds.co.uk, www.citybeds.net, 8.30–5 MON–FRI, 9.30–4 SAT. **PERMANENT DISCOUNT OUTLET**

See page 393 (ESSEX)

COLEFAX AND FOWLER

19–23 GROSVENOR HILL, LONDON W1X 9HG, ☎ 020 7493 2231, **DESIGNER SALES**

Annual sales of Colefax and Fowler and Jane Churchill ranges, held at the Royal Horticultural Halls in London's SW1 usually in January. Ask for trade and put your name on the mailing list.

DAVID J WILKINS

27 PRINCESS ROAD, LONDON NW1 8JR, ☎ 020 7722 7608, www.orientalrugexperts.com, OPEN BY APPOINTMENT. **PERMANENT DISCOUNT OUTLET**

Handmade rugs from Iran, Turkey, Afghanistan and Russia at what are claimed to be wholesale prices, giving members of the public average discounts of 25% compared with normal retail prices. Customers can spend the whole morning or afternoon looking at stock at London's wholesale warehouses which specialises in large and unusual sizes. Free car parking on site.

DESIGNERS' GUILD

RELAY ROAD, OFF ARIEL WAY, WOOD LANE, LONDON W12 7SJ, ☎ 020 7351 5775, www.designersguild.com, PHONE TO BE PUT ON MAILING LIST. **DESIGNER SALES**

Twice-yearly warehouse clearance sale which is usually advertised in London newspapers. Stock usually comprises some large furniture – such as sofas and chairs – masses of rolls of fabric at greatly reduced prices, wallpaper borders, cushion covers and upholstery fabrics, bed-linen, towels, throws and blankets. Come with measurements and exact lengths required as it can be very busy.

DISPOSAL SERVICES AGENCY (DSA)

ROOM 727, MINISTRY OF DEFENCE, 6 HERCULES ROAD, LONDON SE1 7DJ, ☎ 020 7261 8968, www.disposalservices.agency.mod.u. **PERMANENT DISCOUNT OUTLET**

The Disposal Services Agency is an agency of the Ministry of Defence set up to dispose of surplus equipment. It runs the largest disposal operation in the UK, organising the sale of both military equipment and commodities in use commercially, such as embassy furniture, government department office furniture, closed-down RAF-base vehicles and housing stock, ex-marine boats, ex-army tents, boots and ski equipment, medical and dental equipment, clothing, ship and aircraft spares, scrap metal and IT equipment. The DSA uses companies throughout the UK, each with their own specialist area, to dispose of stock. These companies also dispose of stock from a host of other, usually public sector, organisations varying from fire brigades and hospitals to health authorities and the police. Equipment from these companies varies from kitchen equipment and fax machines to mobile radios, cars, generators, jewellery and telecommunications equipment to food trolleys, X-ray equipment, telephones, uniforms, dinghies, fishing nets, photocopiers and chair lifts. Visit the website to find out which companies sell which products and how to contact them direct.

G THORNFIELD LTD

321 GRAY'S INN ROAD, LONDON WC1X 8PX, ☎ 020 7837 2996, FAX: 020 7278 2515, **e-mail:** dave.daybyday@virgin.net, 8–6 MON–FRI, 9–2 SAT. **PERMANENT DISCOUNT OUTLET**

Offers from 20% to 50% off wallcovering brands such as Sanderson and Kingfisher. The more you buy, the greater your discount. Also up to one-third off coordinating fabrics. Doesn't hold stocks of wallpapers and fabrics but you can order from their books with next day delivery. Also sells frames, prints and posters at very low prices. Access to nearly 10,000 picture and prints from stock or to order, including limited editions. Dulux paint colours are mixed on the premises, with 1,800 shades to choose from.

HENRY BUTCHER INTERNATIONAL LTD

BROWNLOW HOUSE, 50–51 HIGH HOLBORN, LONDON WC1V 6EG, ☎ 020 7405 8411 **e-mail:** london@henrybutcher.com, www.henrybutcher.com, 9.15–6 MON–FRI. **PERMANENT DISCOUNT OUTLET**

Established more than 100 years ago, Henry Butcher International are global auctioneers and valuers, dealing with all types of industrial plant, machinery and equipment. They have a mailing list of some 30,000 names under the categories of equipment which they are looking for, from heavy engineering to office furniture and computers. They sell anything from boardroom tables to typists' chairs, computers to manufacturing plants. Put your name on their mailing list for a colour flysheet of sales which you might be interested in.

KEW ARCHITECTURAL ANTIQUES

4 KEWBRIDGE ARCHES, STRAND ON THE GREEN, LONDON W4 3NG, ☎ 020 8987 2610, 10–6.30 MON–FRI, 11–5 SAT, 1–5 SUN. **ARCHITECTURAL SALVAGE**

Lots of door fittings, door knobs, door knockers, coat hooks, finger plates, period bathroom fittings, cast iron radiators, wood flooring and antique furniture (Edwardian and Victorian) etc. Also shades and refurbished French light fittings. If you are looking for something special, it's worth ringing first to see what they have in stock.

LONDON WAREHOUSES LTD

UNIT 2A, ENDEAVOUR WAY, WIMBLEDON, LONDON SW19 8UH, ☎ 020 8947 9878, www.showhousefurniture.co.uk, 10–5 SAT, SUN. **PERMANENT DISCOUNT OUTLET**

Sales every weekend of ex-showhouse furniture direct from designers and national house builders, plus manufacturers end of line and surplus stocks. Three-piece suites, tables, chairs, bedroom furniture plus much, much more, all at affordable prices.

LUNN ANTIQUES LTD

86 NEW KING'S ROAD, PARSONS GREEN, LONDON SW6 4LU, ☎ 020 7736 4638, FAX: 020 7371 7113, **e-mail:** lunnantiques@aol.com, 10–6 MON–SAT. **SECONDHAND AND VINTAGE CLOTHES**

UNIT 8, ADMIRAL VERNON ARCADE, PORTOBELLO ROAD, LONDON W11, FAX: 020 7736 4638, 7.30–3.30 SAT ONLY. **SECONDHAND AND VINTAGE CLOTHES**

Stockists of antique and modern linen and lace. Its headquarters are at the New King's Road shop where it specialises in antique and modern bedlinen, sheets, duvet covers and bedcovers. Here, they also sell top quality antique christening robes and modern reproductions and there is an expert laundry and restoration service for antique linen and lace. Period clothing includes Victorian nightwear, Edwardian camisoles and blouses, Twenties' beaded dresses, Thirties' silk chiffon and Forties', Fifties' and Sixties' outfits. Also risque silk lingerie, luxurious lace and elaborate embroidery and a rich profusion of antique textiles. All wholesale and trade enquiries should be made here. The Portobello Road shop is Lunn Antique's lace outlet with a good selection from four centuries: 17th century needlepoints: 18th century Brussels, Mechlin, Valenciennes and White work; 19th century Alencon, Point de Gaze, Chantilly, Honiton and Youghal, plus 20th century bed and table linen decorated with filet, cutwork, drawnwork, embroidery and needlepoint.

MAISON DU MONDE

UNIT 24-26 ARIEL WAY, SHEPHERDS BUSH, LONDON W12 7SH, ☎ 020 8740 1314, FAX: 020 8740 8914, **e-mail:** query@maisondumonde.com, www.maisondumonde.com, 10–6 TUE–SAT, 11–5 SUN. **PERMANENT DISCOUNT OUTLET**

Outdoor and indoor furniture at up to 60% less than the top high-street stores which they supply. From Thailand are benches and swing seats made from reclaimed cartwheels which follow the curve of the wheel with the spokes forming the seat. They also stock wrought-iron Moroccan benches with Arabesque detail and cushions that can be covered in protective fabric – from £395 for a 3-seater that would cost £750. And Indian bullock cart seats and Moroccan mosaic tables, the latter being just over one-third of the price of top department stores.

MODERN AGE FURNITURE

AT MARTIN BARNETT, 68–72 MARYLEBONE LANE, OFF WIGMORE STREET, LONDON W1M 5FF, ☎ 020 7487 2997, FAX: 020 7487 2717, 10–6 MON–SAT, 12–5 SUN. **PERMANENT DISCOUNT OUTLET**

Offers a trio of different money-saving packages: Rooms To Go, which is perfect for those owning properties which they rent out or those aiming to furnish a whole flat/house in one week. You can furnish a two-bedroom flat in one week for £2,700 plus VAT choosing from either traditional or contemporary furniture and including a dining table and four chairs, two side tables, two pictures and a lamp, two beds, one coffee table and one leather sofa. The company claims that this package would normally cost anything up to £8.500. The other side of the business is manufacturing furniture and custom making leather sofas and designer fabric sofas. Finally, the company also offers hand-coloured Chesterfields and chairs and classically modern imported Italian furniture at quick turnover prices.

ORIENT EXPRESSIONS

STUDIO 3B2, COOPER HOUSE, 2 MICHAEL ROAD, LONDON SW6 2AD, ☎ 020 7610 9311, FAX: 020 7610 6872, **e-mail:** amandaleader@cs.com, www.orientexpressions.com, 10–5 MON–SAT AND BY APPOINTMENT. **PERMANENT DISCOUNT OUTLET**

Specialises in buying 19th century Chinese furniture and decorative accessories. All items are handpicked for their appearance and practical potential. Restorations is kept to a minimum so that the pieces retain as much of their original character as possible. Sourced from the rural provinces of China, the stock includes simple, chunky domestic pieces in natural woods, sophisticated lacquered items and highly decorative, lacquered and gilded accessories. Orient Expressions keeps its overheads to a minimum and offers really good value, undercutting its main competitors. Orient Expressions has outlets in London and Bath. (See page 428)

OSBORNE & LITTLE

LONDON, ☎ 020 7352 1456, FAX: 020 7351 7813, **e-mail:** showroom@osborneandlittle.com, www.osborneandlittle.com. **DESIGNER SALES**

Annual sales of fabrics, wallpapers and accessories from Osborne & Little, Nina Campbell and Liberty Furnishings ranges, usually held at London's Battersea Town Hall. Please contact the showroom on the telephone number above in early January for sale dates, usually in January/February.

POETSTYLE LTD

UNIT 1, BAYFORD STREET INDUSTRIAL CENTRE, MARE STREET, LONDON E8 3SE, ☎ 020 8533 0915, **e-mail:** sofachairs@aol.com, www.sofachairs.com, 7–6 MON–FRI, 10–5 SAT, 10–3 SUN. **FACTORY SHOP**

This factory shop, established for more than 16 years, sells quality, made-to-order sofas, sofa beds and chairs, displayed in their on-site showroom. They also sell ex-display model sofas and sofa beds from their own showroom at greatly reduced prices. All furniture is upholstered using Sanderson, Liberty, Monkwell, Colefax and Fowler, Andrew Martin, Osborne & Little, Jane Churchill, Nina Campbell, Designers Guild, Parkertex and many other leading fabrics. Also Ottomans, stools, armchairs. All goods sold here are manufactured on the premises using traditional methods. Interior designers are welcome. Phone for a brochure, or visit the website.

POSNERS: THE FLOOR STORE

35A–37 FAIRFAX ROAD, SWISS COTTAGE, LONDON NW6 4EW, ☎ 020 7625 8899, FAX: 020 7625 8866, **e-mail:** posners@compuserve.com, 9–6 MON–SAT. **PERMANENT DISCOUNT OUTLET**

Posners: The Floor Store is London's largest hardwood flooring showroom where you will get unbiased advice based on three generations of experience in timber and carpets. Posners, an independent family business since 1946, specialises in fitted carpets and pre-finished hardwood floors. Recommended installers for all major brands, you will find most brands supplied at trade prices. Posners are the London stockist for Pergo, the high pressure laminate floor that's difficult to distinguish from real wood and which is scratch, dent and burn resistant. Posners have more than 2,000 ranges of flooring and carpeting, with various promotional ranges available at any time from £11.99 (including VAT) for carpet and £22 net for 14/15mm pre-finished flooring from stock. Posners are unique for the almost overwhelming choice on offer and for the in-house fitting service available.

POT LUCK

84 COLUMBIA ROAD, LONDON E2 0HQ, ☎ 020 7722 6892, FAX: 020 7722 7162, **e-mail:** potluck@braidman.freeserve.co.uk, 10–2 FRI, 8–2.30 SUN. **PERMANENT DISCOUNT OUTLET**

Pot Luck specialises in selling famous-name 'blanks' (pure white china) in bone china, porcelain and hotel-ware. They sell plates in all sizes from 6in to 13in; huge pasta plates as used in all the trendiest restaurants; plus numerous shapes in cups and saucers, mugs, jugs, creamers and teapots. In addition they offer plain white oven-to-tableware in every shape and size at less than 50% of normal retail prices. They also now sell pure wool, completely washable, natural white Flokati rugs with a lovely long, shaggy pile: also great to use as throws bed or covers. Trade supplied: phone for appointment.

R F GREASBY LONDON LTD

211 LONGLEY ROAD, TOOTING, LONDON SW17 9LG, ☎ 020 8672 2972 OR 020 8682 4564, FAX: 020 8767 8616, **e-mail:** staff@greasbys.co.uk, www.greasbys.com, 9–5 MON–THUR, 9–4 FRI, VIEWING 4–8.30 EVERY OTHER MONDAY. **PERMANENT DISCOUNT OUTLET**

Want to buy a computer for £30, a leather briefcase for £20, a dozen umbrellas for the price of one good one? R F Greasby Ltd (Public Auctioneers) deal in goods from the lost property offices of London Transport, major airlines, and customs and excise, among others, plus those obtained because of outstanding debt. Merchandise has included Nepal rugs, cases of good quality wine, built-in ovens, fridges and freezers, office equipment, clothing, computers, furniture, coffins, garden and agricultural equipment, television sets and hi-fis. This is the place where dealers get great bargains, but there's still some left for members of the public. Regular buyers are admitted first, then entry is on a first-come, first-served basis every second Tuesday. The catalogue can be obtained by annual subscription (phone the number above). There are also catalogues available (including a map) on the website as above.

ROCOCO FRAMES

19 JERDAN PLACE, FULHAM BROADWAY, LONDON SW6 1BE, ☎ 020 7385 9929, FAX: 020 7385 4729, **e-mail:** enquiries@rococoframes.com, www.rococoframes.com, 10–6 MON–SAT, 11–4 SUN. **PERMANENT DISCOUNT OUTLET**

Rococo has recently moved back into its original building after a multi-million pound site redevelopment at Jerdan Place. The fabulously refurbished shop is a showroom for Rococo Mirrors: interior design-led mirrors at good prices with UK nationwide home delivery. Phone for catalogue. Rococo has an unpretentious gallery room with good value original art. The stable of artists includes undiscovered student talent. Rococo offers an excellent bespoke framing service, with hundreds of samples to suit all types of artwork, specialising in contemporary and traditional gallery-type framing. The shop has not forgotten its roots: with a budget-priced range of ready-made frames and a good range of inexpensive mirrors to take away. Trade shop here for their cheap and chic wall fillers. The shop also has a gorgeous gift and card room with inexpensive presents and home accessories. An eclectic mix of old and new furniture decorating the shop and all available to buy completes the shopping experience at Rococo. Phone for more information. They are closed on some bank holidays so do phone first before travelling. The nearest tube is Fulham Broadway. Parking at local pay and display.

RUG CONNECTIONS

13 PRIOR STREET, GREENWICH, LONDON SE10 8SF, ☎ 020 8853 3358, FAX: 020 8305 2867, **e-mail:** rugs@greenwich.demon.co.uk, www.rugconnections.com, PHONE FOR AN APPOINTMENT. **PERMANENT DISCOUNT OUTLET**

Carpet broking service set up to provide independent advice on purchasing an Oriental rug. By providing clients with access to the rarified atmosphere of London's bonded warehouses which are never usually open to the public, they can offer the largest selection of rugs from Persia, Afghanistan, India, Turkey, China and many more countries in styles from traditional to contemporary. The prices are significantly below retail, saving hundreds of pounds. Based in Greenwich, Rug Connections operates on a one-to-one, by-appointment basis, offering home counties customers their professional skills.

RUSSELL & CHAPPLE LTD

68 DRURY LANE, LONDON WC2B 5SP, ☎ 020 7836 7521, FAX: 020 7497 0554, **e-mail:** info@randc.net, 9–5.30 MON–FRI, CLOSED WEEKENDS. **PERMANENT DISCOUNT OUTLET**

Specialists in artists' and theatrical supplies, they also sell natural upholstery fabrics at rock bottom prices for hessians, calicos and muslins. Prices from £1.30 per metre for muslin to £22.70 per metre for linen which is 120 inches wide. The more you buy, the bigger the discount. There are also flame retardant materials on sale.

S & M MYERS LTD

81–85 EAST END ROAD, EAST FINCHLEY, LONDON N2 0Sp, ☎ 020 8444 3457, FAX: 020 8444 3467, 8.30–5.30 MON–FRI, 8.30–5 SAT.

100–106 MACKENZIE ROAD, HOLLOWAY, LONDON N7 8RG, ☎ 020 7609 0091, FAX: 020 7609 2457, 8–5.30 MON–FRI, 9.30–2 SAT. **PERMANENT DISCOUNT OUTLET**

Permanent discount outlet specialising in plain wool carpets, rugs and natural flooring. The company, which was established in 1819, offers end-of-range carpets at discount prices, as well as value-for-money, quality carpets by buying direct from the manufacturer. Mainly 80% wool twists, such as New Hampshire from Cormars at £12.50 per square metre, or Royal Palace from Wilton Royal at £12.99 per square metre. Examples of natural flooring include Seagrass at £8.99 per square metre and Sisal at £13.95 per square metre. All prices include VAT.

SDM INTERIORS

424 EDGWARE ROAD, LONDON W2 1EG, ☎ 020 7706 1099, 8.30–5.30 MON–SAT, CLOSED 1.30–2. **PERMANENT DISCOUNT OUTLET**

Numerous types of wooden flooring from laminate to hardwood at competitive prices. Also floor and wall tiles, wallpapers and decorative mouldings.

SEERS

49 NEW KINGS ROAD, FULHAM LONDON SW6, FAX: 020 7371 8999, FAX: 0207 371 8666, www.seersfireplaces.co.uk, 10–6 MON–SAT, 10–5 SUN (OR LATER BY APPOINTMENT). **SECONDHAND SHOP**

Specialises in antique and reproduction fireplaces with an enormous selection of surrounds in marble and stone at competitive prices. The furniture is a mixture of antique and modern. There is a vast array of mirrors at bargain prices. Everything is clearly priced. Friendly atmosphere. A mail order service is available, with nationwide delivery, free within the M25.

SOFAS TO GO

SOFA WORKSHOP, 8 HIGH STREET, EALING BROADWAY CENTRE, LONDON W5 5DB, ☎ 020 8579 0693, www.sofaworkshop.com, 9.30–6 MON–SAT, 7 ON THUR, 11–5 SUN. **PERMANENT DISCOUNT OUTLET**

Sofas To Go is the clearance department for Sofa Workshop. The majority of sofas on offer are ex-display models, discounted by up to 50% or more. You can take away furniture immediately.

SOVIET CARPET AND ART GALLERIES

303–305 CRICKLEWOOD BROADWAY, LONDON NW2 6PG, ☎ 020 8452 2445, FAX: 020 8450 2642, **e-mail:** rr@soviet-world.fsnet.co.uk, 10.30–5 SUN ONLY, BY APPOINTMENT MON–FRI. **PERMANENT DISCOUNT OUTLET**

Sells Oriental rugs and Russian art at trade prices, giving savings of about 50% on high street prices. The company has only been open to the public since 1992 and then only on Sundays (established in 1983, it was exclusively a wholesale operation for the first nine years of its existence). It imports handmade rugs directly from all the main rug-producing centres of the East (Persia, Turkey, Afghanistan, Pakistan, China) and is one of the principal world distributors of rugs from the former Soviet Union. This explains why the superb Caucasian and Turkmenian (Bukhara) rugs are a speciality. They also stock one of the largest collections of quality Russian art in Europe. Only a small fraction of this is displayed, the remaining thousands of paintings can be chosen from photographs, and will then be brought out from storage. All styles in Russian art are covered from museum-quality greatest names of the 19th century through propaganda art of the Stalin years to leading contemporary artists. All works are offered at prices well below retail/auction price levels, and in extreme cases paintings sold in West End galleries for thousands can be picked up here for a few hundred pounds.

TEMPTATION ALLEY

359–361 PORTOBELLO ROAD, LONDON W10 5SA, ☎ 020 8964 2004, **e-mail:** sales@temptat.demon.co.uk, www.temptationalley.com, 10–5.30 MON–SAT. **PERMANENT DISCOUNT OUTLET**

A trade warehouse which is also open to the public selling a wide range of tie-backs, trimmings (2,000 different types of upholstery trimmings), fabric, cords, braids and general haberdashery. Tie-backs cost from £2.50 to £28, the latter normally costing £60 in top department stores. Fabrics are mostly plain ranging from calico and muslin at £1.65 a metre to velvets, basic cotton drills, silks, organza and slub cotton imported from India to their own design.

THE CLOTH SHOP

290 PORTOBELLO ROAD, LONDON W10 5TE, ☎ 020 8968 6001
020 8960 2719, www.clothshop.co.uk, 10–6 MON–SAT. **PERMANENT DISCOUNT OUTLET**

The Cloth Shop is one of the few small one-off fabric shops left in London that sells fabrics for all purposes. It stocks a wide range of Indian cotton furnishings in a myriad of colours, plus a selection of canvas, calicoes and muslins in a variety of creams and colours, as well as linens, wools, fleeces and cottons for both furnishings and dress-making. It also stocks a large range of beautiful antique French linen sheets, including sheets from World War II. There is an extensive range of household linen goods from France, including antique linen by the metre, and a colourful selection of antique Welsh blankets. Prices are reasonable: fabrics range from £1.50 to £12.50 a metre; antique sheets from £45 to £100.

THE CURTAIN EXCHANGE

54 ABBEY GARDENS, LONDON NW8 9HT, ☎ 020 7372 1044, www.thecurtainexchange.net
10–5 MON–SAT.

80 PARK HALL ROAD, DULWICH, LONDON SE21 8BW, ☎ 020 8670 5570,
www.thecurtainexchange.net, 10–5 MON–SAT.

129–131 STEPHENDALE ROAD, LONDON SW6 2PG, ☎ 020 7610 6844,
www.thecurtainexchange.net, 10–5 MON–SAT, 7 ON WED. **SECONDHAND SHOP**

See page 381 (CAMBS)

THE CURTAIN FABRIC FACTORY SHOP

230–236 NORTH END ROAD, LONDON W14 9NU, ☎ 020 7381 1777, FAX: 020 7381 8879,
e-mail: cfpolytrad@aol.com, www.curtainfabricfactory.co.uk, 9.30–5.30 MON–SAT. **FACTORY SHOP**

Genuine factory shop which prints curtain fabric on site and sells overstocks, seconds and cancelled orders at trade prices here – there are 1,000 rolls in stock. Makes for hundreds of shops countrywide and exports to 12 different countries. There are hundreds of different designs and qualities from which to choose at prices starting at £1.99 a metre. There are also quilted bedspreads available to match the fabrics, a curtain making and track fitting service, and a large stock of upholstery fabrics.

THE CURTAIN MILL

46–52 FAIRFIELD ROAD, BOW, LONDON E3 2QB, ☎ 020 8980 9000, 9–5.30 MON–SAT,
10–4 SUN.

15–17 COLINDALE AVENUE, LONDON NW9 9DB, ☎ 020 8205 2220, 9–5.30 MON–SAT,
10–4 SUN.

2 THE VALE, ACTON, LONDON W3 7SB, ☎ 020 8743 2299, 9–5.30 MON–SAT, 10–4 SUN.
PERMANENT DISCOUNT OUTLET

See page 401 (HERTS)

THE GALLERIES LTD

157 TOWER BRIDGE ROAD, LONDON SE1 3LW, ☎ 020 7407 5371, 9.30–5.30 MON–THUR,
8–4.30 FRI, 12–6 SAT, SUN. **SECONDHAND SHOP**

This branch is a 30,000 square foot warehouse with antique furniture, some from pub fittings, garden and pine furniture. Periods include Art Deco, Art Nouveau, Victoriana and Americana. There's everything from kitchen sinks to Millennium Dome memorabilia. Chairs start at £20, art deco dining room suites from £400 to £2,000, Victorian dining tables from £900.

THE LONDON PICTURE CENTRE

287–289 HACKNEY ROAD LONDON E2 8NA, ☎ 020 7739 6624,
www.thelondonpicturecentre.co.uk, 8–5 MON–FRI, 10–4 SAT, 10–2 SUN.

152 HACKNEY ROAD, LONDON E2 1QL, ☎ 020 7729 0881,
www.thelondonpicturecentre.co.uk, 9–5 MON–FRI, 10–2 SAT.

75 LEATHER LANE, LONDON EC1 7UJ, ☎ 020 7404 4110, www.thelondonpicturecentre.co.uk,
9–4 MON–FRI.

709 FULHAM ROAD, LONDON SW6 5UL, ☎ 020 7371 5737, www.thelondonpicturecentre.co.uk, 9–5.30 MON–FRI, 10–6 SAT 11–3 SUN.

723 FULHAM ROAD, LONDON SW6 5HA, ☎ 020 7731 4883, www.thelondonpicturecentre.co.uk, 9–5.30 MON–FRI, 10–6 SAT, 11–3 SUN.

18 CRAWFORD STREET, LONDON W1 1PF, ☎ 020 7487 2895, www.thelondonpicturecentre.co.uk, 9.30–5.30 MON–FRI, 10–4 SAT. **PERMANENT DISCOUNT OUTLET**

Manufacturers and global importers of mirrors and frames with large wholesale premises with own retail showroom offering an enormous selection of mirrors in all sizes and types from gilt frames to baroque style, as well as oil paintings and framed prints. Prices range from £2 to £1,000. Framing is very reasonable, too, and the service is used regularly by local artists. The branch at 709 Fulham Road is a mirror gallery offering competitively priced mirrors to any specification. This branch has now been established for over 25 years. Picture framing is available at all branches. All the showrooms now stock an extensive range of contemporary art.

THE OLD CINEMA

160 CHISWICK HIGH ROAD, LONDON W4 1PR, ☎ 020 8995 4166, 10–6 MON–SAT, 12–5 SUN. **SECONDHAND SHOP**

This branch holds ten thousand square feet of antique furniture, some in complete room settings. Wide range of Victorian, Georgian, Edwardian and art nouveau. Items range from light fittings and mirrors to dining tables, decorative metalware and jewellery.

THE SHUTTLE FABRIC SHOP

52–54 LAVENDER HILL, BATTERSEA, LONDON SW11 5RJ, ☎ 020 7738 9589, 9.30–5.30 MON–SAT. **PERMANENT DISCOUNT OUTLET**

Sells discounted dress fabrics and some furnishing fabrics from well-known designers as well as furnishing sheeting, curtain lining, plastic fabrics for tablecloths, wadding, patterns and general haberdashery. Many are ends of lines and there are always special offers.

TK MAXX

THE ARCADIA CENTRE, THE BROADWAY, EALING, LONDON W5 2ND, ☎ 020 8566 0447, www.tkmaxx.com, 9.30–8 MON–FRI, 7.30 ON THUR, 9–7 SAT, 11–5 SUN.

UNIT B, FIRST FLOOR, WOOD GREEN SHOPPING CENTRE, LONDON N22 6YD, ☎ 020888 88803, www.tkmaxx.com, 9–6 MON–SAT, 10–5 SUN. **PERMANENT DISCOUNT OUTLET**

See page 377 (BEDS)

WALL TO WALL

549 BATTERSEA PARK ROAD, BATTERSEA, LONDON SW11 3BL, ☎ 020 7585 3335, FAX: 020 7228 5080, 10–6 MON–SAT. **PERMANENT DISCOUNT OUTLET**

Top name designer brand wallpaper, all at £9.95 a roll, with very many different designs from which to choose. All their bargain lines are discontinued patterns, or ends of ranges so you have to buy the right quantity when you see it as there won't be any more. Names on sale include Anna French, Monkwell, Hill & Knowles and GP&J Baker. Also designer-name fabrics at clearance prices from £9.95 a metre: 10,000 metres always in stock. Full making-up and fitting service, which is particularly good for people who want to do places up quickly as there is a very fast free measuring and estimating service. There's also a free design service on the premises.

MIDDLESEX

FABRIC WAREHOUSE

36 HIGH STREET, WEALDSTONE, HARROW, MIDDLESEX HA3 7AA, ☎ 020 8863 6333, 9–5 MON–SAT, 10–4 SUN.

WHITEHOUSE DEVELOPMENT, LONDON ROAD, WEMBLEY, MIDDLESEX HA9 0NP, ☎ 020 890 5510, 9–5.30 MON–SAT, 10–5 SUN. **PERMANENT DISCOUNT OUTLET**

See page 378 (BERKS)

KENTON WAREHOUSE SUPERSTORE

DAWNCROFT LTD, 2A CHARLTON ROAD, KENTON, MIDDLESEX HA3 9HF, ☎ 020 8732 2525, FAX: 020 8732 2626, **e-mail:** dawncroft@btinternet.com, 9.30–5.30 MON–SAT. **PERMANENT DISCOUNT OUTLET**

Carpet and bed warehouse which sells Sealy beds at up to 30% off the recommended retail price; Relyon beds at up to 50% off RRP, brand-name carpets at highly competitive prices, as well as carpet rolls, room size ends of rolls, laminate flooring and vinyls. Free delivery inside M25 area if you spend £250.

LONDON WAREHOUSES LTD SOUTH

802 FIELDEND ROAD, SOUTH RUISLIP, MIDDLESEX HA4 0QP, ☎ 020 8422 7326, 10–5 SAT, SUN. **PERMANENT DISCOUNT OUTLET**

See page 415 (LOND)

THE CURTAIN MILL

13–19 LONDON ROAD, ENFIELD, MIDDLESEX EN2 6BS, ☎ 020 8364 6515, 9–5.30 MON–SAT, 10–4 SUN. **PERMANENT DISCOUNT OUTLET**

See page 401 (HERTS)

THE SALVAGE SHOP

34–40 WATLING AVENUE, BURNT OAK, MIDDLESEX HA8 0LR, ☎ 020 8952 4353, **e-mail:** lss@salvage1.co.uk, www.salvage1.co.uk, 9–5.30 MON–SAT, 10–4 SUN. **PERMANENT DISCOUNT OUTLET**

An Aladdin's cave of salvaged stock for the avid bargain hunter, most of which has been the subject of insurance claims for fire or flood, salvage, bankruptcy or is simply clearance stock. Stock changes every two or three days and regular visitors have found anything from half price Kenwood Chefs, televisions and toys to furniture, kitchen items, linens and especially fantastic bargains in designer clothing. Yves Saint Laurent, Armani, Ungaro, Hugo Boss and Valentino, as well as all major high street names, are just some of the names to be found (though the labels are often cut out). Discounts range from 50% to 80%. Phone first to check stock.

TK MAXX

UNIT 31, ST GEORGE'S CENTRE, ST ANNE'S ROAD, HARROW, MIDDLESEX HA1 1HS, ☎ 020 8863 9292, www.tkmaxx.com, 9.30–8 MON–FRI, 9–7 SAT, 11–5 SUN. **PERMANENT DISCOUNT OUTLET**

See page 377 (BEDS)

NORFOLK

FABRIC WAREHOUSE

NORTH STREET, KINGS LYNN, NORFOLK PE30 1QW, ☎ 01553 660491, 9.30–5.30 MON–FRI, 9–5.30 SAT, 10–4 SUN.

ROUNDTREE WAY, MOUSEHOLD, NORWICH, NORFOLK NR3 8SQ, ☎ 01603 408454, 9–5.30 MON–SAT, 10–4 SUN. **PERMANENT DISCOUNT OUTLET**

See page 378 (BERKS)

MARSTON & LANGINGER FACTORY SHOP

GEORGE EDWARDS ROAD, FAKENHAM, NORFOLK NR21 8NL, ☎ 01328 852540, FAX: 01328 852552, **e-mail:** factoryshop@marston-and-langinger.com, www.marston-and-langinger.com, 10–5 MON–FRI, 10–4 SAT FROM EASTER TO END SEPT. **FACTORY SHOP**

Marston & Langinger, top quality conservatory manufacturers and designers, with a showroom in London's Ebury Street, operate a factory shop in Norfolk selling former display stock from exhibitions such as the Chelsea Flower Show, as well as ends of ranges and prototypes. Because they offer a complete design service from making conservatories to supplying blinds, floors, lighting, furniture and furnishings, the factory shop can feature a variety of items, which comprise end of line, ex-display and some slightly imperfect products at discounts ranging from 30% to 60%. Items available at the factory shop include various styles and sizes of ceramic, terracotta and lead flowerpots and vases; a selection of garden items including bamboo ladders, cast iron border edging, and baskets; a good selection of interior and exterior lighting, candlesticks, lanterns and lampshades; a range of beautifully made exterior hardwood doors and window casements; lots of discontinued furnishing fabrics, ready-made cushions, scatter cushions in woven cottons; a good selection of furniture including English willow, wirework, solid oak and many glass and stone table tops and metal bases; various hardware items such as doorknobs, hinges, escutcheons, casement stays, letter plates, rim locks, cabin hooks and round doorknobs. For an extra cost, any item of sale furniture can be painted in colours from the Marston & Langinger paint range.

THE CURTAIN EXCHANGE

6 BRIDEWELL ALLEY, NORWICH, NORFOLK NR2 1AQ, ☎ 01603 631 407, FAX: 01603 631 407, www.thecurtainexchange.net, 10–5 MON–SAT. **SECONDHAND SHOP**

See page 381 (CAMBS)

THE FACTORY SHOP LTD

NORWICH STREET, EAST DEREHAM, NORFOLK NR19 1AD, ☎ 01362 691868, 9–5.30 MON–SAT, 10–4 SUN.

52 LONDON ROAD, HARLESTON, NORFOLK IP20 9BZ, ☎ 01379 854860, 9–5.30 MON–SAT, 10.30–4 SUN.

LYNN ROAD, SNETTISHAM, NORFOLK PE31 7QG, ☎ 01485 544441, 9–5.30 MON–SAT, 10–4 SUN. **FACTORY SHOP**

See page 383 (CHESH)

NORTHAMPTONSHIRE

SHOWHOME WAREHOUSE

11–17 FRANCIS COURT, WELLINGBOROUGH ROAD, RUSHDEN, NORTHAMPTONSHIRE NN10 6AY, ☎ 01933 411695, 10–5 TUE–SUN, 11–3 MON. **PERMANENT DISCOUNT OUTLET**

The contents of quality show homes are sold seven days a week at this 20,000 square foot warehouse. Savings normally range from 50% to 70% off store prices. About 50% of their stock is sold each week and different stock arrives daily. Choose from a range of kitchen appliances, lounge furniture, three-piece suites, dining tables and chairs, rugs, study and bedroom furniture, oil paintings, mirrors, ornaments, televisions and videos, patio and garden furniture and gym equipment. The range is eclectic: from suits of armour to lion's heads, Tiffany lampshades to leather zebras, handpainted furniture to mahogany classics, alien-shaped CD racks to antique carts made into bookcases or sets of oars turned into coat racks. Because a high percentage of their business comes from trade, prices exclude VAT but still represent very good value for money. For example, elaborate metal bed, £175, normally £750; dining room table and chairs, £350, normally £1,500; washer-dryer, £300, usually £500 to £600. Occasional auctions take place during the year: phone for details.

STUART BUGLASS INTERIOR DESIGN IRONWORK

THE BUGLASS METALWORK GALLERY, CLIFFORD MILL HOUSE, LITTLE HOUGHTON, NORTHAMPTONSHIRE NN7 1AL, ☎ 01604 890366, FAX: 01604 890 372, **e-mail:** sbuglass@aol.com, www.stuartbuglass.co.uk, 10–5 MON–FRI. **FACTORY SHOP**

Hand-crafted interior design wrought-iron work including candleholders, wine racks, electric lighting (including wall sconces and chandeliers) curtain poles, as well as furniture, including beds, tables, chairs and shelving, are all on sale in this converted barn at direct-to-the-public prices. The showroom was extended in 1998 and is now twice its original size. There is now a high street outlet at 26 Regent Street, Leamington Spa and another at 311 Wellingborough Road, Northampton, both of which are open 10-5 Tuesday to Saturday. They also sell soft furnishings, bedding, light shades and gift items.

THE FABRIC WAREHOUSE

HARVEY REEVES ROAD, ST JAMES MILL INDUSTRIAL ESTATE, NORTHAMPTON, NORTHAMPTONSHIRE NN5 5JR, ☎ 01604 759312, FAX: 01604 755577, 9.30–5.30 MON–SAT, 10–4 SUN. **PERMANENT DISCOUNT OUTLET**

Stocks up to 8,000 rolls of upholstery and dress fabric from £2.99 a metre with remnants at £1 a metre. Chenilles are from £9.99 to £25 a metre, damask £10.99 a metre and heavy-duty prints £7.99 a metre. In addition, there are made-up curtains, cushions, pillows, net curtains, tassle tie-backs, curtain poles, tracks, lining, braid, bean bags. They will also take orders for fabric.

NORTHUMBERLAND

A M S FABRICS

UNIT 7, MAURICE ROAD INDUSTRIAL ESTATE, WALLSEND, NORTHUMBERLAND NE28 6BY, ☎ 0191 263 4095, 10–4 TUE, WED, SAT. **FACTORY SHOP**

Factory shop selling mainly dress and suiting fabric and linings and also plain curtain fabrics such as organzas, voiles and jacquards. Large range of accessories such as header tape, thread, needles, curtain tape, hooks, zips, buttons, elastic.

ASHINGTON BEDDING CENTRE

UNIT 10A, NORTH SEATON INDUSTRIAL ESTATE, ASHINGTON, NORTHUMBERLAND NE63 0YB, ☎ 01670 852522, FAX: 01670 852522, 9.30–5.30 MON–FRI, 9.30–5.15 SAT, 11–3 SUN. **PERMANENT DISCOUNT OUTLET**

Sells a wide variety of beds from the bottom end of the market to the pocket sprung top end, and including electric bed, ranging in price from £75 to £799. Prices have the edge over the same beds sold elsewhere, with one bed costing £499 here on sale for £799 in a local department store. Brands sold here include Silent Night, Rest Assured and Airsprung.

ATTICA

2 OLD GEORGE YARD, OFF HIGHBRIDGE, NEWCASTLE UPON TYNE, TYNE & WEAR NE1 1EZ, ☎ 0191 261 4062, 10.30–5.30 MON–SAT. **SECONDHAND AND VINTAGE CLOTHES**

Two floors of vintage clothing for men and women from the Victorian era to the 1960s. Stock includes a vast range of glamorous evening wear, as well as 1960s furniture and decor.

CATALOGUE DISCOUNT STORES

15 THE PRECINCT, THE IN CENTRE, JARROW, TYNE & WEAR, ☎ 0191 483 4318, 9–5 MON–SAT.

8 THE FORUM SHOPPING CENTRE, WALLSEND, NORTHUMBERLAND NE28 8JR, ☎ 0191 236 9501, 9–5 MON–SAT. **PERMANENT DISCOUNT OUTLET**

See page 384 (CO DURH)

CURTAIN FABRICS FACTORY SHOP

36 GRASSMER WAY, KITTY BREWSTER INDUSTRIAL ESTATE, BLYTH, NORTHUMBERLAND NE24 4RR, ☎ 01670 540240, FAX: 01670 540240, 10–3 MON–SAT. **PERMANENT DISCOUNT OUTLET**

Low prices on curtains, fabrics, made-to-measure curtains or ready-made curtains. Lots of fabrics on the roll or you can order through books.

FACTORY SHOP CENTRE

TUNDRY WAY, CHAINBRIDGE INDUSTRIAL ESTATE, BLAYDON, NORTHUMBERLAND NE21 5SJ, ☎ 0191 414 4515, 10–5 MON–FRI, 9–5 SAT, 10–4 SUN. **PERMANENT DISCOUNT OUTLET**

Large industrial estate on which a variety of discount shops operate selling everything from brand-name wallpaper and paint, fire surrounds, bedding and fabrics, cane suites, curtains, bedding, towels, upholstery fabrics and textiles to Axminster and Wilton carpets, and Rest Assured and Silent Night beds as well as pet foods and pet products.

TECAZ

SWIFT 957, TECAZ HOUSE, NORHAM ROAD, CHIRTON INDUSTRIAL ESTATE, NORTH SHIELDS, NEWCASTLE UPON TYNE, TYNE & WEAR NE29 7TN, ☎ 0191 257 6511, FAX: 0191 296 1943, **e-mail:** northshields@swift957ltd.com, www.swift957ltd.com, 9–6 MON–FRI, 9–5 SAT, 10–4 SUN. **PERMANENT DISCOUNT OUTLET**

See page 385 (CO DURH)

THE FABRIC AND TAPESTRY SHOP

1 HILL STREET, CORBRIDGE, NORTHUMBERLAND NE45 5AA, ☎ 01434 632902, 10–5 MON–SAT. **PERMANENT DISCOUNT OUTLET, SECONDHAND SHOP**

Designer discount fabric in 2 to 3 metre lengths from £8, including names such as Colefax and Fowler and Ramm Son & Crocker. They also take in and sell good quality secondhand curtains at very good prices. There are leading brand tapestry kits, such as Elizabeth Bradley, Beth Russell, Stitchery, Beverly etc, all at full price.

TK MAXX

LOWER GROUND FLOOR, MONUMENT MALL SHOPPING CENTRE, NEWCASTLE UPON TYNE, TYNE & WEAR NE1 7AL, ☎ 0191 261 0404, www.tkmaxx.com, 9–5.30 MON–FRI, 8 ON THUR, 9–6 SAT, 11–5 SUN. **PERMANENT DISCOUNT OUTLET**

See page 377 (BEDS)

TYNEDALE RETAIL PARK

HEXHAM, NORTHUMBERLAND NE46 3PJ, ☎ 01434 607788, 10–6 MON–FRI, 9.30–6 SAT, 11–5 SUN. **PERMANENT DISCOUNT OUTLET**

With 15,000 square feet of retail selling across a 10 acre site, all at ground level except the restaurant which has access via a lift, the Tynedale Retail Park is accessible to all. Here you will find overstocks and clearance lines at up to 50% off normal retail prices. Quality names such as Windsmoor, Jaegar, French Connection, Timberland, Elle and Edinburgh Woollen Mill are just a few of the brands available. The clothing is just for adults, but there are shoes for adults and children. There is also furniture, linen, electrical items, bath accessories, toys, gifts and DIY equipment. The main section is a garden centre which also has pets, golf, sporting and outdoor wear departments. The child-friendly restaurant has a kids zone, parking is free and there are disabled facilities on site.

NOTTINGHAMSHIRE

DESIGNER FABRIC WAREHOUSE

HUCKNALL LANE, BULWELL, NOTTINGHAM, NOTTINGHAMSHIRE NG6 8AJ, ☎ 0115 975 3311, 9.30–5.30 MON–SAT, 10–4 SUN. **PERMANENT DISCOUNT OUTLET**

See page 411 (LINCS)

ESSENTIAL ITEMS

CHURCH HOUSE, PLUNGAR, NOTTINGHAMSHIRE NG13 0JA, ☎ 01949 861172, FAX: 01949 861320, **e-mail:** pcmc@philida.freeserve.co.uk, 8–8 SEVEN DAYS A WEEK. MAIL ORDER. **PERMANENT DISCOUNT OUTLET**

Essential Items is one of the country's most established companies manufacturing and designing stools and Ottomans. Other items new to their range are elegant window seats and bed-end stools, all made to order and covered in the customers' own fabric. Because of their low overheads, their mail order service offers much more competitive prices than similar items bought in department stores. Although items can be covered in calico, most lines are covered in customers' own material at no extra charge. Now specialising in hand made curtains as well as re-upholstery. The upholstered filing cabinet Ottoman is one of their best sellers – either as a single at £195 or as a double at £250.

LABELS OF EDWINSTOWE

25 HIGH STREET, EDWINSTOWE, NOTTINGHAMSHIRE NG21 9QP, ☎ 01623 825479, 10–5.30 MON–SAT. **DRESS AGENCIES**

Friendly and accommodating shop, concentrating on barely worn upmarket and designer labels, stocking garments, accessories and jewellery in immaculate condition. The emporium at Edwinstone is set on two floors and also incorporates gifts, beauty salon and sought after pieces for the home such as Persian rugs, old olive jars and other decorative items. In addition, a range of imported Indonesian and Asian furniture is also displayed, although the main business is still women's clothes from beachwear to designer evening and day wear. (Business terms are 50:50%.)

P W SHEPHERD UPHOLSTERY

195 STATION ROAD, LANGLEY MILL, NOTTINGHAMSHIRE NG16 4AF, ☎ 01773 769395, 9–5.30 MON–FRI, 9–5 SAT, 10–2 SUN. **FACTORY SHOP**

Manufacturer of quality three-piece suites, storage boxes, cushions and curtains.

THE FACTORY SHOP

DONCASTER ROAD, LANGOLD, WORKSOP, NOTTINGHAMSHIRE DN22 7HY, ☎ 01909 731115, 9–5.30 MON–SAT, 10–4.30 SUN. **FACTORY SHOP**

See page 383 (CHESH)

WILKINSON STORES

2–6 FRONT STREET, ARNOLD, NOTTINGHAM, NOTTINGHAMSHIRE NG5 7EL, ☎ 0115 926 0805, www.wilko.co.uk, 9–5.30 MON–SAT, 10–4 SUN. MAIL ORDER. **PERMANENT DISCOUNT OUTLET**

See page 383 (CHESH)

OXFORDSHIRE

HAYNES OF CHALLOW LTD

ROADSIDE, EAST CHALLOW, NEAR FARINGDON, OXFORDSHIRE OX12 9TB, ☎ 01235 762747, 9–5 SEVEN DAYS A WEEK. **SECONDHAND SHOP**

House, school and office clearance specialists, part of this business stocks secondhand furniture and the larger part brand new. Beds, mattresses, garden ornaments, sofas, tables, pictures, pine furniture, fencing panels, slabs, plants, garden ornaments, tools, toys, ladders, kitchen utensils etc.

JUST FABRICS

BURFORD ANTIQUES CENTRE, CHELTENHAM ROAD, BURFORD, OXFORDSHIRE OX18 4JA, ☎ 01993 823391, **e-mail:** fabrics@justfabrics.co.uk, www.justfabrics.co.uk, 9.30–5.30 MON–SAT, 12–4 SUN AND BANK HOLIDAYS. MAIL ORDER. **PERMANENT DISCOUNT OUTLET**

Just Fabrics offers huge savings on a comprehensive selection of quality furnishing fabrics from stock. Whether choosing a leading designer name, clearance or from their own range of exclusive weaves or prints, all are very competitively priced. Their telephone enquiry service is also very popular. After discussing your fabric requirements, samples are then despatched. A mail order service is available. They do not order from pattern books. The enquiry line on 01993 823391 is open during shop hours, with an answerphone out of hours.

MILL OUTLETS LTD

51 HIGH STREET, BANBURY, OXFORDSHIRE OX16 8LA, ☎ 01295 264455, 9–5 MON–SAT. **PERMANENT DISCOUNT OUTLET**

Specialises in curtains, net curtains, bedding, bed linens, towels, kitchen textiles and other household textiles. They also offer ranges of hand knitting yarns, men's and women's socks, hosiery and underwear. Merchandise comes direct from the manufacturers, often made up of clearance stock or chainstore overmakes and seconds. Prices are very competitive with savings of up to 50% and more off manufacturer's recommended prices.

REVIVAL CLOTHES AGENCY

60 ST CLEMENT'S, OXFORD, OXFORDSHIRE OX4 1AH, ☎ 01865 251005, 10–4 TUE, WED, THUR, 10–5 FRI, SAT. **DRESS AGENCY**

Dress agency which also stocks soft furnishings and curtains.

SHIRLEY LALLY INTERIORS

78 HIGH STREET, WITNEY, OXFORDSHIRE OX8 6HL, ☎ 01993 773508, 9.30–5 MON–SAT. **PERMANENT DISCOUNT OUTLET**

All perfects fabrics stock at reasonable prices. Shirley Lally supplies a free design, measurement and quote service. Excellent make-up service plus free delivery and hanging within a 10 mile radius. Choose fabrics in the comfort of your own home and avoid the hassle of parking and looking through endless fabric sample books. They also supply carpets, soft furnishings, upholstery and loose covers. Situated in the busy high street, with a car park nearby.

THE CURTAIN EXCHANGE

85 HIGH STREET, THAME, OXFORDSHIRE OX9 3EH, ☎ 01844 261566, www.thecurtainexchange.net, 9.30–4.30 MON–SAT. **SECONDHAND SHOP**

See page 381 (CAMBS)

TK MAXX

CALTHORPE STREET, OFF HIGH STREET, BANBURY, OXFORDSHIRE OX16 8ES, ☎ 01295 277022, www.tkmaxx.com, 9–5.30 MON–FRI, 7 ON THUR, 9–6 SAT, 11–5 SUN. **PERMANENT DISCOUNT OUTLET**

See page 377 (BEDS)

WESLEY BARRELL

3 BRIDGE STREET, OFF HIGH STREET, WITNEY, OXFORDSHIRE, ☎ 01993 776682, www.wesley-barrell.co.uk, 9–5.30 MON–SAT. **PERMANENT DISCOUNT OUTLET**

Wesley Barrell design, hand make and selll their own exclusive range of sofas and armchairs through a network of shops countrywdie. The second floor of the full-price showroom in Witney always has a selection of 'sell-offs' at discounts of up to 50%. Every Easter, there is a special clearance sale with scores more sofas brought in from Wesley Barrell showrooms countrywide.

WESTCOTE DESIGN

THRESHERS YARD, WEST STREET, KINGHAM, OXFORDSHIRE, ☎ 01608 659091 OPEN 10–4 SAT OR BY APPOINTMENT. **FACTORY SHOP**

Buy more than 20 styles of sofas and chairs direct from the manufacturers at lower prices including the traditional Knote Sofa. Most of the sofas contain beech frames, coil springs and duck feather cushions and are traditionally made. You can choose from their range of fabrics or match your own.

SHROPSHIRE

CANE AND WICKER FACTORY SHOP

MONKMOOR INDUSTRIAL ESTATE, SHREWSBURY, SHROPSHIRE SY2 5ST, ☎ 01743 240261, www.caneandwicker.com, 9.30–5 MON–SAT, CLOSED SUN. **FACTORY SHOP**

See page 404 (LANCS)

FABRIC BARN

UPPER ASTON FARM, NEAR CLAVERLY (OFF A454 WOLVERHAMPTON TO BRIDGNORTH ROAD), SHROPSHIRE WV5 7EE, ☎ 01746 710237, 9–5 MON–FRI, 10.30–4.30 SAT. **PERMANENT DISCOUNT OUTLET**

Top quality designer curtain and upholstery fabrics imported from Italy and Belgium from £3.50 a metre, as well as linings from £2 a metre, craft poles and tracks. Lots of trimmings, tie-backs and accessories.

SIMON BOYD

SMITHFIELD ROAD, SHREWSBURY, SHROPSHIRE SY1 1PB, ☎ 01743 363006, **e-mail:** simonboyd@freewire.net, 9–5.30 MON–SAT. **PERMANENT DISCOUNT OUTLET**

See page 382 (CHESH)

STANWAY FABRICS AND INTERIORS

SHIPTON HALL BARN, SHIPTON, NEAR MUCH WENLOCK, SHROPSHIRE TF13 6JZ, ☎ 01746 785151, FAX: 01746 785152, www.stanwayfabrics.co.uk, 10–4 MON–SAT. **PERMANENT DISCOUNT OUTLET**

Leading suppliers of top designer fabric seconds and clearances at prices from as little as £3.95 per metre for fabrics which would normally retail between £25 and £85. Thousands of metres of curtain and upholstery fabrics always in stock, together with linings, interlinings, tape etc, at extremely competitive prices. They stock a wide range of tassels, tie-backs, trimmings and accessories, with many more available to order. Curtains, cushions, loose covers and headboards can be made to customers' specifications by their experienced in house team at affordable prices. They also have a swap shop where customers can buy or sell beautiful curtains. Situated in a converted barn next to the 16th-century Shipton Hall in the beautiful Corvedale area of south Shropshire, close to the historic towns of Ludlow, Much Wenlock and Shrewsbury, there is also a coffee shop within the barn and parking is right outside the door.

TEXTILE EXPRESS

42 CHURCH STREET, OSWESTRY, SHROPSHIRE SY11 2SY, ☎ 01691 670277, **e-mail:** pauline@textileexpress.co.uk, www.textile-express.co.uk, 9–5 MON–FRI, 9–5.30 SAT. **PERMANENT DISCOUNT OUTLET**

Regular line first quality fabrics sold alongside clearance fabrics suitable for bedding, curtaining, upholstery, bridal, craft and dressmaking – from hessian to silk. Large remnant department where prices start at £1 a metre. Curtain accessories such as poles and blinds are also sold, and a making up service is available. The large stock at this business which wholesales and exports is constantly changing. Limited free parking is available.

TK MAXX

DARWIN SHOPPING CENTRE, RAVENS MEADOWS, SHREWSBURY, SHROPSHIRE SY1 1BW, ☎ 01743 341370, www.tkmaxx.com, 9–5.30 MON–FRI, 9–6 SAT, 11–5 SUN.

UNIT 16, TELFORD FORGE RETAIL PARK, ORDSALL LANE, TELFORD, SHROPSHIRE TF3 4AG, ☎ 01952 210200, www.tkmaxx.com, 10–8 MON–FRI, 9–6 SAT, 11–5 SUN. **PERMANENT DISCOUNT OUTLET**

See page 377 (BEDS)

SOMERSET

BRAINGE LTD TRADING AS SOMERSET CREATIVE PRODUCTS

LAUREL FARM, WESTHAM, WEDMORE, SOMERSET BS28 4UZ, ☎ 01934 712416, FAX: 01934 712210, **e-mail:** info@cowparsley.com, www.cowparsley.com, MAIL ORDER. BY APPOINTMENT ONLY. **FACTORY SHOP**

A range of interior and garden furniture and accessories made from new and reclaimed timber. They also stock a selection of traditional mild steel benches, tables and chairs with curled arms and legs, from £100. Seconds are on sale here at discount prices. Please phone to request a brochure. Westham is about eight miles from Clarks Village Factory Shopping Centre in Street: phone for directions.

FABRIC WAREHOUSE

BABYLON HILL, BRADFORD ABBAS, YEOVIL, SOMERSET BA21 5BT, ☎ 01935 415573, 9–6 MON–SAT, 8 ON THUR, 10–4 SUN. **PERMANENT DISCOUNT OUTLET**

See page 378 (BERKS)

FURNITURE FACTORY SHOP

WELLS ROAD, GLASTONBURY, SOMERSET BS28 4AW, ☎ 01458 830188, 11–4 MON–WED, 11–5 THUR–FRI, 10–5 SAT, 12–4 SUN, CLOSED TUE. **FACTORY SHOP**

Good discounts on flat-pack furniture to take away, including lounge and bedroom furniture (but not beds), bookcases, cube units, computer workstations, desks and home office furniture.

JAMES GAUNT

1 CHURCH STREET, FROME, SOMERSET BA11 1PW, ☎ 01373 452344, 9–5.30 MON–SAT. **PERMANENT DISCOUNT OUTLET**

Specialist interior designers James Gaunt sells regular lines and some clearance fabrics. The range includes well known names such as Andrew Martin, Malabar and GP & J Baker, as well as an exclusive range of Italian jacquards and tapestries. The emphasis throughout this shop is on designer stock at bargain prices.

KNICKERBEAN

5 WALCOT STREET, BATH, SOMERSET BA1 5BN, ☎ 01225 445741, FAX: 01225 448862, **e-mail:** info@knickerbean.com, www.knickerbean.com, 9–5.30 MON–SAT. **PERMANENT DISCOUNT OUTLET**

See page 378 (BERKS)

MULBERRY

THE OLD SCHOOL HOUSE, KILVER STREET ON THE A37, SHEPTON MALLET, SOMERSET BA4 5NF, ☎ 01749 340583, www.mulberry.com, 10–6 MON–SAT, 11–5 SUN AND BANK HOLIDAYS. **FACTORY SHOP**

A very popular large, attractive, factory outlet situated in an old school house with parking outside, which sells a wide variety of end of line stock and seconds including men's and women's leather bags, accessories, tech product cases, planners, agendas and stationery. It also sells last season's clothes and home goods which include a selection of furniture, cushions, lamps, china and fabric. Small coffee shop and toilet and disabled facilities. There are other Mulberry factory shops in York and at Bicester Village, Oxfordshire.

ORIENT EXPRESSIONS

LANSDOWN PLACE EAST, BATH, SOMERSET BA1 5ET, ☎ 01225 313399, FAX: 01225 425446, **e-mail:** Trishwilks@aol.com, www.orientexpressions.com, OPEN BY APPOINTMENT. **PERMANENT DISCOUNT OUTLET**

See page 416 (LOND)

SANDPITS HEATING CENTRE

HIGH STREET, CURRY RIVEL, LANGPORT, SOMERSET TA10 0ES, ☎ 01458 251476, 8–5.30 MON–SAT, 10–4 SUN. **SECONDHAND SHOP**

Stockists of multi-fuel stoves and cookers at discount prices. Specialises in new and reconditioned Rayburns and Agas. The reconditioned models are considerably cheaper than the new and some can incorporate a domestic heating system for hot water and radiators. They also stock Stanley, Alpha and Redfyre cookers at full price, a selection of wood burning stoves, and a large selection of flue accessories. A DIY and hardware store, and now a garden centre, sells plants, trees, shrubs etc, all at competitive prices.

THE CURTAIN EXCHANGE

11 WIDCOMBE PARADE, BATH SOMERSET BA2 4JT, ☎ 01225 422078, www.thecurtainexchange.net, 10–4 MON–SAT, 1 ON FRI.

LONGALLER MILL, BISHOPS HULL, TAUNTON, SOMERSET TA4 1AD, ☎ 01823 326071, www.thecurtainexchange.net, 10–4 WED–SAT OR BY APPOINTMENT. **SECONDHAND SHOP**

See page 381 (CAMBS)

THE FABRIC BARN

CLOCK HOUSE, QUEEN CAMEL, YEOVIL, SOMERSET BA22 7NB, ☎ 01935 851025, 10–4 TUE–FRI OR BY APPOINTMENT ON SATURDAY. **PERMANENT DISCOUNT OUTLET**

Designer furnishing fabrics off the roll from Monkwell, Malabar, Warwick, G P & J Baker and Swaffer, among others. All at clearance prices at discounts of up to 50% and many available in 40 to 50-metre rolls. Sited in a converted barn in a farmyard setting and run by two former curtain makers who can offer advice and recommend a local making-up service. They also import sumptuous designer fabrics direct from Spain also at discounted prices which offer excellent value.

THE FACTORY SHOP LTD

MART ROAD, MINEHEAD, SOMERSET TA24 5BJ, ☎ 01643 705911, 9.30–5.30 MON–SAT, 11–5 SUN. **FACTORY SHOP**

See page 383 (CHESH)

THE FURNITURE FACTORY SHOP

THE WELLS TRADING ESTATE, WELLS ROAD, GLASTONBURY, SOMERSET BA6 9AG, ☎ 01458 830188, 11–4 MON, WED, 11–5 THUR, FRI, 10–5 SAT, 10–4 SUN. **FACTORY SHOP**

Manufacturers of flat-packed furniture for home and office for shops such as Argos, Littlewoods, MFI, Staples, Comet and Tiny, overstocks and end of catalogue lines are sold here at bargain prices. Large space allows excellent display of flat pack furniture including lounge pieces, desks and computer work stations.

THE IRON MAID COMPANY

PO BOX 3229, WELLS, SOMERSET BA5 2WL, ☎ 01749 670017, FAX: 020 7378 1533, www.ironmaid.co.uk, MAIL ORDER ONLY. **PERMANENT DISCOUNT OUTLET**

Stunning collection of garden and conservatory folding and flat packed iron furniture, combining contemporary designs with quality workmanship – and all at affordable prices. Range includes iron love seats, decorative outdoor benches and seats, folding outdoor iron furniture, side tables, wine storage and magazine racks. Phone for a brochure and price list.

THE OLD CREAMERY

WATERCOMBE PARK, LYNX TRADING ESTATE, YEOVIL, SOMERSET BA20 2EB, ☎ 01935 410500, OPEN 9–5 MON–SAT, 10–4 SUN. **PERMANENT DISCOUNT OUTLET**

27,000 square foot showroom which claims to be the biggest pine warehouse in the south west, selling at very competitive prices. Stocks includes beds (without mattresses), wardrobes, dressers, tables, chairs, bookcases.

STAFFORDSHIRE

ABAKHAN FABRICS

12 OLD HALL STREET, HANLEY, STOKE-ON-TRENT, STAFFORDSHIRE ST1 1QT, ☎ 01782 274200, FAX: 01745 562101, **e-mail:** enquiries@abakhan-fabrics.co.uk, 9.30–5.15 MON–SAT, 10.30–4.30 SUN. **FACTORY SHOP**

See page 381 (CHESH)

ALLSORTS FURNITURE

23 HAMILL ROAD, BURSLEM, STOKE-ON-TRENT, STAFFORDSHIRE ST6 1AJ, ☎ 01782 833006, FAX: 01782 833006, 10–5 MON–SAT. **PERMANENT DISCOUNT OUTLET**

Household goods, furniture and exercise equipment at discounts of up to 60%. Furniture includes new three-piece suites, pine tables and chairs, television cabinets, nests of tables and kitchen furniture, as well as pine furniture imported from Denmark. Household goods include pots and pans, ovenware, casserole dishes, kettles etc. There are also suitcases, exercise bikes, step striders, walking and running machines, but no clothes, fabrics or curtains.

BDF NEWLIFE

MARTINDALE, HAWK'S GREEN, CANNOCK, STAFFORDSHIRE WS11 2XN, ☎ 01543 468888, FAX: 01543 505989, **e-mail:** info@bdfnewlife.co.uk, 9.30–10 MON–SAT, 10–4 SUN, 10–5 BANK HOLIDAYS. **PERMANENT DISCOUNT OUTLET**

8,000 square foot charity superstore which sells both new merchandise donated by most of the top high street stores and nearly-new. This is the sort of shop where you can find anything from a girl's party dress to a two-seater rowing boat, men's shoes to a cooler bag, in between towels, jewellery, family clothes, furniture, mattresses (new with damaged packaging), beds, clocks, golf bags, umbrellas, wallpaper and designer dresses. Stock changes every 45 minutes. All the profits go to charity. Membership is by donation averaging £2. The shop is on one floor so is very accessible and has disabled toilet facilities. As the store also takes counterfeit goods from national Trading Standards departments' seizures, stress is put on not believing any labelling or assuring authenticity. There are also branches in Kirkby-in-Ashfield, Nottinghamshire and Stoke Aldermoor, Coventry.

CARPET MILL FACTORY SHOP

WATERLOO ROAD, BURSLEM, STOKE-ON-TRENT, STAFFORDSHIRE ST6 2QB, ☎ 01782 833823, FAX: 01782 833823, www.unitedcarpets.co.uk, 9–7 MON, FRI, 9–6 TUE–THUR, SAT, 10–4 SUN. **FACTORY SHOP**

Factory clearance specialist, and the biggest carpet warehouse in Stoke-on-Trent, it usually has at least 3,000 remnants in all sizes as well as 500 rolls and samples from which customers can order. They also stock Axminsters and a good selection of Wiltons (from £10 a yard), Berbers and Saxony, both plain and patterned. Prices are obviously cheaper for the remnants and roll stock, although carpets to order are still very competitive. Also stock laminate wood flooring.

DOMESTIC APPLIANCES

92 HIGH STREET, TUNSTALL, STOKE-ON-TRENT, STAFFORDSHIRE ST6 5TJ, ☎ 01782 833303, 9–5 MON–SAT. **PERMANENT DISCOUNT OUTLET**

Reconditioned Hotpoint washing machines as well as fridge freezers, tumble dryers and cookers from different manufacturers. Also new repro tables, beds and chairs imported from abroad and sold at low profit margins.

FABRIC WAREHOUSE

ANGLESEY BUSINESS PARK, ANGLESEY ROAD, BURTON-ON-TRENT, STAFFORDSHIRE DE44 3PF, ☎ 01283 544266, 9–5.30 MON–SAT, 10–4 SUN. **PERMANENT DISCOUNT OUTLET**

See page 378 (BERKS)

FRAYLING FURNITURE

SALEM STREET, ETRURIA, NEAR HANLEY, STOKE-ON-TRENT, STAFFORDSHIRE ST1 5PR, ☎ 01782 811041, FAX: 01782 818329, 2–8 FRI, 10–4 SAT, SUN. **DESIGNER SALES**

Quarterly sales are held at this manufacturer of leather furniture to clear overstocks. Prices are discounted by up to 50%. Telephone for the sale dates.

FREEPORT TALKE OUTLET MALL

FREEPORT TALKE OUTLET MALL, PIT LANE, TALKE PITS, STOKE-ON-TRENT, OFF JUNCTION 16 OF M6 THEN TAKE THE A500 AND THE A34, FOLLOWING SIGNS TO TALKE, STAFFORDSHIRE ST7 1XD, ☎ 01782 774113, www.freeporttalke.com, 9.30–8 MON–FRI, 9.30–6 SAT, 11–5 SUN. **FACTORY SHOPPING VILLAGE**

Fully covered indoor outlet mall with a range of restaurants, including Burger King and Café Ritazza, and an indoor soft play area for children. Womenswear includes The Designer Room, Edinburgh Woollen Mill, Nickelby's, Pilot, Spotlight, Roman Originals and Leading Labels. Menswear includes The Suit Company, Double Two, Petroleum, Nickelby's, Madhouse and Tog 24. Childrenswear can be found at Used Co Kids. Other shops on site include: Claire's Accessories, Charles Clinkard, Jane Shilton, Bags Etc, Trespass, Streetwise Sports, The Golf Company, Catalogue Bargain Shop, Julian Graves, Kitchen and Table, Toy World, Thorntons, Birthdays, Room, Mobile Phone Store, Book Depot, Picture Port, Ponden Mill and XS Music.

GOODMANS CARPETS

MILL CLEARANCE WAREHOUSE, UNIT 1, HEATHCOTE STREET, CHESTERTON, NEWCASTLE UNDER LYME, STAFFORDSHIRE, ☎ 01782 563060, 11–6 MON–SAT, CLOSED THUR. **FACTORY SHOP**

Offcuts and remnants of carpets sold direct to the public at sale prices.

HADIDA BATHROOM INTERIORS

OLD FOLEY POTTERY, KING STREET, FENTON, STOKE-ON-TRENT, STAFFORDSHIRE ST4 3DH, ☎ 01782 597739, FAX: 01782 597702, **e-mail:** enquiries@hadida.co.uk, www.hadida.co.uk, 9–4.30 MON–SAT, 11–4 SUN. **FACTORY SHOP**

Hadida Bathroom Interiors offers a wide range of seconds and discontinued ceramic bathroom accessories complemented by matching fabric shower curtains, Austrian blinds, window drapes, bath pillows, tissue box covers etc. All the shower curtains are specially treated to make them mildew resistant, and come in standard 180cm and longer lengths. Examples of prices include: toilet roll holder, £6.40, normal price £16.00; soap dish, £2.80, normally £7.00; frilled shower curtain, £14.00, normally £50.00; plain shower curtain, £9.95, normally £35.00. Also in stock are Chortex/Horrockses towels, candles, soaps, bathroom toiletries, shower rails and shower curtain hooks. Hadida also manufactures James Kent Floral Chintzware which is sold as seconds in the shop at heavily discounted prices. Free parking.

HEART OF THE COUNTRY

SWINFEN, NEAR LICHFIELD, STAFFORDSHIRE WS14 9QR, ☎ 01543 481612, PHONE FOR SALE DATES. **PERMANENT DISCOUNT OUTLET**

This wholesaler of American textiles and gift items who usually supplies garden centres and gift shops, holds sales of discontinued stock in a barn. These sales are normally held on bank holiday weekends – phone for details.

HOME FURNITURE (UK) LTD

LEEK ROAD, HANLEY, STOKE-ON-TRENT, STAFFORDSHIRE ST1 6AT, ☎ 01782 273500, 9–5.30 MON–SAT, 11–5 SUN. **PERMANENT DISCOUNT OUTLET**

Furniture at discounted prices. They specialise in three-piece suites, beds and dining sets, some of which are recognisable brand names. For example, a five-foot double divan bed costing £199 at Home Furniture would normally sell elsewhere for £399.

HOUSEHOLD BARGAIN CENTRE

23 COMMERCE STREET, LONGTON, STOKE-ON-TRENT, STAFFORDSHIRE ST3 5RH, ☎ 01782 314016, OPEN 9–10 AND 11–6 MON–SAT, CLOSED THUR. **PERMANENT DISCOUNT OUTLET**

Sells vertical, venetian, roller and pleated blinds from 32 different UK manufacturers and 7 continental ones in a wide variety of sizes, colours and fabrics. Vertical blinds measuring 6ft wide by 4ft drop, £50 include VAT, fitting and 10-year guarantee; same size pleated blinds, £71; 10% reduction for self-fitting.

PATTENS

HIGH STREET, WOLSTANTON, NEWCASTLE UNDER LYME, STAFFORDSHIRE ST5 0HE, ☎ 01782 719101, www.pattensfurniture.co.uk, 9–5.30 MON–SAT. **PERMANENT DISCOUNT OUTLET**

Every houshold item you could possibly want can be found here, from a fridge–freezer to a bed, all at discounted prices. Stock also includes some ex-catalogue (Kays, Freemans, Argos) furniture including chairs, beds, wardrobes, wall units, three-piece suites, coffee tables and console tables.

PHOENIX WORKS

500 KING STREET, LONGTON, STOKE-ON-TRENT, STAFFORDSHIRE ST3 1EZ, ☎ 01782 595922, 9–5.30 MON–SAT, 11–4 SUN. **PERMANENT DISCOUNT OUTLET**

Victorian pottery factory restored to create a retail and visitor centre with a number of different businesses ranging from furniture from India, Thailand and the Philippines to leather goods, picture frames, white tableware, gifts and arts and crafts. All are competitively priced.

SCOOPS CATALOGUE DISCOUNT STORES

UNIT 3, 567–569 BEARWOOD SHOPPING CENTRE, SMETHWICK, STAFFORDSHIRE B66 4BH, ☎ 0121 434 3086, FAX: 0121 429 8488, 9–5.30 MON–SAT, 11–3 SUN. **PERMANENT DISCOUNT OUTLET**

Scoops the catalogue discount store sells surplus stock from both Grattan and Freeman's catalogues. Womenswear, menswear and childrenswear are on sale, as well as household items, all at up to 50% off catalogue prices. Stock changes on a regular basis, and includes a wide range of brands from both designer and high street. A 14-day refund policy is offered.

SUITES DIRECT

MINSTER MILLS, WALLEY STREET, BIDDULPH, STOKE-ON-TRENT, STAFFORDSHIRE ST8 6EA, ☎ 01782 510007, FAX: 01782 510007, 9–5 MON–FRI, 10–5 SAT, 11–4 SUN. **FACTORY SHOP**

Manufacturers of three-piece suites mainly, as well as some beds and carpets, they sell to the public at excellent prices as there is no middleman. There are three showrooms here so you can see lots of examples of their products or choose to have something unique made up – perhaps a three-and-a-half seater sofa. Sofas can be manufactured and delivered within 10 days. Plenty of fabric from which to choose covers.

TERRY'S FABRIC WAREHOUSE

CARTLIDGE STREET, OFF SHELTON NEW ROAD, NEWCASTLE UNDER LYME, STAFFORDSHIRE ST4 6DJ, ☎ 01782 710777, **e-mail:** sales@terrysfabrics.co.uk, www.terrysfabrics.co.uk, 9–5.30 MON–SAT, 11–5 SUN. **PERMANENT DISCOUNT OUTLET**

A large fabric warehouse with thousands of rolls of upholstery and curtain fabrics on sale from £1 to £17 a metre. One of the most popular names stocked here is Prestigious, but there is also Crowson and some of the finest Italian damasks. They also sell accessories including curtain poles and tie-backs. Everything is sold at very competitive prices. There is a complete manufacturing service on site, as well as an interior design and fitting service. The staff are fully trained with years of experience and are on hand with help and advice if needed. Ample free parking.

THE BANKRUPT SHOP LTD

1 BOROUGH ROAD, NEWCASTLE UNDER LYME, STAFFORDSHIRE ST5 1TT, ☎ 01782 711494, 9.30–5.30 MON–SAT, 10.30–4.30 SUN. **PERMANENT DISCOUNT OUTLET**

See page 383 (CHESH)

THE FACTORY SHOP

QUEEN STREET CAR PARK, QUEEN STREET, MARKET DRAYTON, STAFFORDSHIRE TF9 1EQ, ☎ 01630 655673, 9–5 MON–SAT, 10–4 SUN. **FACTORY SHOP**

See page 383 (CHESH)

THE PINE WAREHOUSE

UNIT 2, ETRUSCAN TRADING ESTATE, ETRURIA ROAD, HANLEY, STOKE-ON-TRENT, STAFFORDSHIRE ST1 5NH, ☎ 01782 204500, 10–5.30 MON–SAT, 11–4 SUN. **PERMANENT DISCOUNT OUTLET**

The Pine Warehouse sells stained and finished furniture made from redwood pine. There are five or six bedroom ranges, as well as tables, chairs, dressers and hi-fi units in 10 different finishes. Unlike more expensive competitors, they aren't able to incorporate intricate design details, but their prices are very reasonable.

TK MAXX

THE OCTAGON SHOPPING CENTRE, BURTON-ON-TRENT, STAFFORDSHIRE DE14 3TN, ☎ 01283 569891, www.tkmaxx.com, 9–5.30 MON–SAT, 10–4 SUN.

THE POTTERIES CENTRE, HANLEY, STOKE-ON-TRENT, STAFFORDSHIRE ST1 1PP, ☎ 01782 207509, www.tkmaxx.com, 9–5.30 MON–FRI, 9–6 SAT, 11–5 SUN, 8 ON THUR. **PERMANENT DISCOUNT OUTLET**

See page 377 (BEDS)

VOGUE CARPETS

11 BRUNSWICK STREET, NEWCASTLE UNDER LYME, STAFFORDSHIRE ST5 1HF, ☎ 01782 630569, 9–5 MON–SAT. **FACTORY SHOP**

All types and styles of carpets including Axminsters and Wilton at very competitive prices. Vogue work on small margins and buy direct as part of a large group from the manufacturers, thereby buying in at good prices. Also now sell laminate and wood flooring at competitive prices.

WILKINSON STORES

OLD HALL STREET, HANLEY, STOKE-ON-TRENT, STAFFORDSHIRE, ☎ 01782 279225, www.wilko.co.uk, 8.30–6 MON–FRI, 8 ON THUR, 11–5 SUN. MAIL ORDER.

CASTLE HOUSE, 47–48 IRONMARKET, NEWCASTLE UNDER LYME, STAFFORDSHIRE ST5 1PD., ☎ 01782 714334, www.wilko.co.uk, 8.30–5.30 MON–SAT. **PERMANENT DISCOUNT OUTLET**

See page 383 (CHESH)

SUFFOLK

FABRIC WAREHOUSE

1–3 COMMERCIAL ROAD, IPSWICH, SUFFOLK IP1 1DZ, ☎ 01473 213090, 9–5 MON–THUR, 9–6 FRI, SAT, 11–5 SUN. **PERMANENT DISCOUNT OUTLET**

See page 378 (BERKS)

KNICKERBEAN

4 OUT NORTHGATE, BURY ST EDMUNDS, SUFFOLK IP33 1JQ, ☎ 01284 704055, FAX: 01284 701647, **e-mail:** info@knickerbean.com, www.knickerbean.com, 9–5.30 MON–SAT. **PERMANENT DISCOUNT OUTLET**

See page 378 (BERKS)

THE CURTAIN AGENCY AND PERIOD HOUSE INTERIORS

73 HIGH STREET, NEEDHAM MARKET, IPSWICH, SUFFOLK IP6 8AN, ☎ 01449 722885, 10–5 MON–FRI, 10–1 SAT. **SECONDHAND SHOP**

An emporium of quality secondhand and new made-to-measure or ready-to-hang curtains. There is also a great range of permanently cut-price, quality fabrics available by the metre. These include designer names such as Gainsborough Silk Weaving Co for classic brocades; Linwood chenille, Archive printed linens, and Toile de Jouy from GP & J Baker; Parker Knoll fabrics for upholstery; and many others. Old and new Continental accessories, including tie-backs and trimmings, are also available. The shop also has a large stock of old French linen sheets, many hand woven and monogrammed, which are made into sumptuous curtains and Roman blinds as well as being used for luxurious bed linen and upholstery. Decorative, French garden and occasional furniture, period chandeliers, wall lights, old armchairs (for re-upholstering), traditional curtain poles and fittings, together with unusual gifts makes this an Aladdin's cave of inspiration for anyone wanting something special for their home.

THE CURTAIN EXCHANGE

75 ST JOHN'S STREET, BURY ST EDMUNDS, SUFFOLK IP33 1SN, ☎ 01284 760059, www.thecurtainexchange.net, 10–5 MON–SAT. **SECONDHAND SHOP**

See page 381 (CAMBS)

THE FACTORY SHOP

BARTON BUSINESS CENTRE, BARTON ROAD, BURY ST EDMUNDS, SUFFOLK IP32 7BQ, ☎ 01284 701578, 9.30–5 MON–FRI, 10–6 SAT, 10–4 SUN.

LONDON ROAD, WRENTHAM, NR BECCLES, SUFFOLK NR34 7HJ, ☎ 01502 676100, 9–5.30 MON–SAT, 10.30–4.30 SUN. **FACTORY SHOP**

See page 383 (CHESH)

THE REMNANT SHOP

3–5 HAMILTON ROAD, FELIXSTOWE, SUFFOLK IP11 7AX, ☎ 01394 283186, 9 -5.30 MON–SAT. **PERMANENT DISCOUNT OUTLET**

See page 395 (ESSEX)

TK MAXX

1ST FLOOR, BUTTERMARKET SHOPPING CENTRE, IPSWICH, SUFFOLK IP1 1DT, ☎ 01473 226800, www.tkmaxx.com, 9–5.30 MON–FRI, 9–6 SAT, 11–5 SUN. **PERMANENT DISCOUNT OUTLET**

See page 377 (BEDS)

SURREY

ANGELA MARBER'S PRIVATE BUY

TRANQUILLITY HOUSE, COOMBE PARK, KINGSTON, SURREY KT2 7JA, ☎ 020 8549 8453, FAX: 020 8541 5049, **e-mail:** angelamarber@hotmail.com, www.privatebuy.co.uk, **DESIGNER SALES**

Private Buy arranges for its club members to purchase current and next season's top label European and American samples and stock in the agents' intimate and friendly London showrooms nine months ahead of the season at half the cost. Also available at trade prices are household linens, fabrics and wallpapers. Usually a recommendation-only club; due to this exclusivity, some personal references may be required. Membership costs £70 a year and £40 for size 14 and over and includes a regular newsletter informing you of future showroom visits, restaurant reviews and member-to-member recommendations.

C H FURNITURE LTD

21 NORTH STREET, GUILDFORD, SURREY GU1 4TB, ☎ 01483 573405, FAX: 01483 539094, 9–5.30 MON–SAT. **PERMANENT DISCOUNT OUTLET**

Privately owned by the same owner since 1932, this shop sells better end furniture of the same sort of quality as seen in John Lewis and Harrods. They stock cabinets, beds, upholstery, dining tables (both modern and traditional in glass, iron and painted), sofas, wardrobes, etc at very competitive prices. The cabinets are all imported, the upholstery English. Most of the furniture comes from Italy, Denmark and France with some from Germany, India, Belgium and Holland. metal tables and chairs and a Mexican mosaic range which can be used outdoors as long as they're not left out in winter, can be ordered via brochures.

CHOICE DISCOUNT STORES LIMITED

1 WARWICK QUADRANT, LONDON ROAD, REDHILL, SURREY RH1 1NN, ☎ 01737 772777, 9–6 MON–WED, 9–7 THUR, 9–6 FRI–SAT. **PERMANENT DISCOUNT OUTLET**

See page 380 (CAMBS)

COBHAM FURNITURE CENTRE

43-47 HIGH STREET, COBHAM, SURREY KT11 3DP, ☎ 01932 865814, www.cobhamfurniture.com, 9.30–5.30 MON–SAT, 10–4 WED. **PERMANENT DISCOUNT OUTLET**

Medium-sized shop with lots of catalogues from which you can order quality furniture, lamps, carpets etc at discounts of up to 20%. They work by cutting their own margins.

CORCORAN & MAY'S FABRIC SUPERSTORE

31–35 BLAGDON ROAD, NEW MALDEN, SURREY KT3 4AH, ☎ 020 8949 0234, FAX: 020 8949 1774, 9.30–5.30 MON–SAT, 11–5 SUN, BANK HOLIDAYS. **PERMANENT DISCOUNT OUTLET**

Huge fabric superstore with what they claim to be the best selection of fabrics within the M25. The store draws on Corcoran & May's long years of expertise in the industry where they are known for getting the best of clearance and overstocks from a whole host of designers such as Andrew Martin, Anna French, Crowson, Monkwell and the Malabar Cotton Company. They also have a vast range of repeatable designs from the brightest newcomers, as well as traditional damasks, plains and weaves. Prices range from £1.99 to £19.99 per metre, and there's everything in store for the home curtain maker, plus an expert curtain making service, ready-made curtains and blinds, feather cushions at wholesale prices, and plenty of friendly advice.

CURTAIN CALL

52 FRIARS STILE ROAD, RICHMOND, SURREY TW10 6NQ, ☎ 020 8332 6250, FAX: 020 8940 6137, **e-mail:** curtaincall@blueyonder.co.uk, www.curtain-call.co.uk, 9.30–5.30 MON–FRI, 10–6 SAT, CLOSED WED. **SECONDHAND SHOP**

Curtain Call in Richmond sells nearly-new curtains for at least half of their original price. The current stock of over 400 pairs includes Colefax and Fowler, Osborne & Little and Designers Guild fabrics. The curtains range in price from £50 to £1,500 for sets which may include valances, swags and tails, as well as headboards and matching bedspreads. All the nearly-new curtains can be taken home overnight on approval, so that you can see the curtains in your own home before you buy. If you have curtains to sell, they will agree a price with you and, once the curtains have sold, you receive 60% of the selling price. An alteration service is also available on the premises, as well as a making-up service using your own fabric. New curtains can usually be made within a three week time span. They have a large range of tassels and tie-backs, as well as a comprehensive range of trimmings to order, which can really update and finish off new or nearly-new curtains. They also have a large selection of made-to-measure fabrics which can be made up in three weeks. This range encompasses everything from natural textured cottons through to more elaborate toiles, damask, tapestry fabrics and silk in 50 different colours. The samples of these fabrics are made up as full-sized curtains for you to borrow overnight to try at home, before ordering. They now offer a wide range of luxurious and unusual cushions in tapestry and velvet designs, as well as some individual one-off special hand-printed designs by local designers, and a range of small gifts such as hand-beaded photo frames, handbags and embroidered voile panels.

FABRIC WAREHOUSE

UNIT F2, FELNEX TRADING ESTATE, 190 LONDON ROAD, OFF HACKBRIDGE ROAD, WALLINGTON, NEAR SUTTON, SURREY SM6 7EL, ☎ 020 8647 3313, 9–5 MON–SAT, 10–4 SUN.

10A CHURCH STREET, WEYBRIDGE, SURREY XT13 8DX, ☎ 01932 828684, 9.30–5.30 MON–SAT, 10–4 SUN. **PERMANENT DISCOUNT OUTLET**

See page 378 (BERKS)

FABRIC WORLD

6–10 BRIGHTON ROAD, SOUTH CROYDON, SURREY CR2 6AA, ☎ 020 8688 6282, **e-mail:** info@fabricworldlondon.co.uk, www.fabricworldlondon.co.uk, 9–5.30 MON–SAT.

287–289 HIGH STREET, SUTTON, SURREY SM1 1LL, ☎ 020 8643 5127, **e-mail:** info@fabricworldlondon.co.uk, www.fabricworldlondon.co.uk, 9–5.30 MON–SAT. **PERMANENT DISCOUNT OUTLET**

A family business which claims to be the largest factory warehouse of designer curtain and upholstery fabrics in England. It stocks at least 2,000 rolls of material, most selling at between £5 and £20 a metre for fabric which would normally cost between £25 and £55 a metre. Designer names on sale include Warners and Sandersons, and stock is all perfect and includes current lines. The company imports from all over the world: tapestries, damasks, natural fabrics, checks, stripes, linens, cottons and satins, and also stocks their own range of silk fabrics, exclusive to Fabric World. There is a making-up service available and a free interior design service.

LONDON CURTAIN AGENCY

298 SANDYCOMBE ROAD, KEW, SURREY TW9 3NG, ☎ 020 8940 5959, FAX: 020 8977 2654, **e-mail:** info@curtain agency.com, www.curtainagency.com, 10–4 TUE–FRI 10–5 SAT. **SECONDHAND SHOP**

A mixture of new and secondhand curtains. Some of the curtains are refurbishment stock from London's five-star hotels, others designer samples and former display stock from fabric houses and interior designers. Stock ranges from curtains for small windows for £50 up to £800 for drapes for huge bay windows with swags and tails. Designer fabrics include Designer's Guild, Osborne & Little and Colefax and Fowler. There are also curtain rails, cushions, blinds, tie-backs and pelmets. All the curtains are lined or interlined. Fantastic bargains at approximately one third of the original cost. Their made-to-measure collection of calico and cream cotton damask curtains handmade to individual requirements, as recommended in Homes & Gardens magazine, are for sale at competitive prices. The made-to-measure collection also includes silks and linen.

LONDON WAREHOUSES LTD

ST CLEMENTS HOUSE, CHURCH STREET, WALTON-ON-THAMES, SURREY KT12 2QN, ☎ 01932 252522, www.showhousefurniture.co.uk, 10–5 SAT, SUN. **PERMANENT DISCOUNT OUTLET**

See page 415 (LOND)

THE CURTAIN AGENCY

231 LONDON ROAD, CAMBERLEY, SURREY GU15 3EY, ☎ 01276 671672, FAX: 01276 671672, **e-mail:** jackie-curtains@lineone.net, www.thecurtainagency.co.uk, 10–5 MON–SAT.

103 WEST STREET, FARNHAM, SURREY GU9 7EN, ☎ 01252 714711, FAX: 01252 714711, **e-mail:** jackie-curtains@lineone.net, www.thecurtainagency.co.uk, 10–5 MON–SAT **SECONDHAND SHOP**

Two shops offering a wide range of quality secondhand curtains from designer elegance to practical and functional. Many are from ex-display stock and executive home relocations. All the curtains are ready to hang, but if alterations are required an excellent service is available and a 24-hour sale or return option can be requested at both shops. A good range of new fabrics and wallpapers are stocked for making up to customers' own requirements, and these include names such as Malabar, Anna French and John Wilman. A selection of antique poles supplement a large choice of new wood and metal poles. Bay poles are our speciality.

THE FACTORY SHOP LTD

THE ENGINE SHED, CONSORT WAY EAST, HORLEY, SURREY RH6 7AU, ☎ 01293 823883, 9–5.30 MON–SAT, 10–4 SUN. **FACTORY SHOP**

See page 383 (CHESH)

THE LIGHTING AGENCY & TRADING COMPANY

LION & LAMB YARD, FARNHAM, SURREY GU9 7LL, ☎ 01252 719192, FAX: 01252 719192, www.lightingagency.co.uk, 10–5.30 MON–SAT. **PERMANENT DISCOUNT OUTLET**

Lighting Agency and Trading Company in Farnham offers a wide variety of quality secondhand and antique chandeliers and wall lights, many of which have been rewired to a tested and certified UK standard. Others which have not been wired have the electrical or gas parts removed for easy rewiring. A wiring service can be provided. The Lighting Agency also offers a unique range of small chandeliers available in many colours and sizes. This Aladdin's Cave of shades, lamps and chandeliers is often the haunt of dealers and design decorators.

TK MAXX

THE DRUMMOND CENTRE, CROYDON, SURREY CR0 1TY, ☎ 020 8686 9753, www.tkmaxx.com, 9–6 MON–SAT, 9 ON THUR, 11–5 SUN.

102 HIGH STREET, EPSOM, SURREY, ☎ 01372 729060, www.tkmaxx.com, PHONE FOR DETAILS.

BISHOPS PALACE HOUSE, 2 CLARENCE STREET, KINGSTON, SURREY KT1 1PB, ☎ 020 8974 6296, www.tkmaxx.com, 9–6 MON–WED, 9–9 THUR–FRI, 8–7 SAT, 11–5. SUN.

TIMES SQUARE SHOPPING CENTRE, HIGH STREET, SUTTON, SURREY SM1 1LF, ☎ 020 8770 7786, www.tkmaxx.com, 9–5.30 MON–FRI, 8 ON THUR, 9–6 SAT, 11–5 SUN.

THE PEACOCKS CENTRE, WOKING, SURREY GU21 1GA, ☎ 01483 771660, www.tkmaxx.com, 9.30–6 MON–FRI, 8 ON THUR, 9–6 SAT, 11–5 SUN. **PERMANENT DISCOUNT OUTLET**

See page 377 (BEDS)

SUSSEX

ANSELL'S FURNITURE WAREHOUSE

KIRDFORD ROAD, WISBOROUGH GREEN, NR BILLINGSHURST, SUSSEX RH14 0DD, ☎ 01403 700359, FAX: 01403 700604, 10–4 SAT, SUN OR BY APPOINTMENT. **PERMANENT DISCOUNT OUTLET**

Established for 40 years, Ansell's specialises in three-piece suites and beds from most of the leading names such as Collins & Hayes, Heirloom Wade, G-Plan, Durestur, Christy Tyler, Peter Guild, Derwent, Parker Knoll and Cintique and beds from Nestledown, Rest Assured and Relyon. There are 10 big buildings full of sofas and beds so come prepared to spend some time walking round. Offers excellent value for money all year round. This is the only warehouse in the UK allowed to sell these brands direct.

COLLINS AND HAYES

PONSWOOD INDUSTRIAL ESTATE, MENZIES ROAD, ST LEONARDS, HASTINGS, SUSSEX TN34 1XF, ☎ 01424 443834, **e-mail:** sales@collinsandhayes.com, www.collinsandhayes.com, 9–5 MON–SAT. **FACTORY SHOP**

Manufacturers of upholstered furniture and with their own collection of fabrics, this is Collins and Hayes only factory shop. Here, they sell ends of lines, discontinued models and cancelled orders of sofas and chairs, as well as fabrics, at half price or less. Upholstered furniture is a fashion industry and accordingly new collections are brought out once or twice a year, so there is a steady supply of ends of lines.

FABRIC WAREHOUSE

HAMPDEN RETAIL PARK, LOFTBRIDGE DRIVE, MARSHALL ROAD, EASTBOURNE, SUSSEX, ☎ 01323 503040, 9–5.30 MON -SAT, 10–4 SUN. **PERMANENT DISCOUNT OUTLET**

See page 378 (BERKS)

FURNITURE WAREHOUSE

UNIT 1, QUAY SIDE, BASIN ROAD SOUTH, PORTSLADE, HOVE, BRIGHTON, SUSSEX BN41 1NS, ☎ 01273 430355, www.furniturecentre.co.uk, 9–6 MON–SAT, 10–5 SUN. **PERMANENT DISCOUNT OUTLET**

High street quality furniture at warehouse prices. Also antique pine furniture, wardrobes, chests of drawers and a range of repro furniture. Local delivery.

HEIRLOOMS LTD

2 ARUN BUSINESS PARK, BOGNOR REGIS, SUSSEX PO22 9SX, ☎ 01243 820252, FAX: 01243 821174, 10–5 EVERY FRIDAY AND ONE SAT MORNING EACH MONTH. **FACTORY SHOP**

Sleep like a king, dine like a lord or lounge like a lady . . . the Heirlooms factory shop is brimming with luxurious linen at affordable prices, the majority of which are made on the premises. Elegant and exceptionally high quality bed linens in Egyptian cotton, cotton percale and the finest polycotton percale, in four sizes up to super-king, are sold in this 1,200 square foot outlet, together with the very best Egyptian cotton towels. There's also table linens using classic hem stitching or handmade laces, a cornucopia of gifts with exquisite laces and embroidery, and handmade christening and baby wear. Sterling silver frames, waterproof picnic rugs, candles, nightwear, Isis ceramics and seasonal variations complete the diverse selection of really high quality products. Normally only found in the most exclusive shops, homes and palaces all over the world, here you can buy ends of lines and slight seconds at between 30% and 65% off the recommended retail price. This busy exporting company only opens the factory shop about once a week, so check before making what will be a worthwhile journey. As they manufacture, they can make bedlinen and tablecloths to order in any size. Free parking.

THE CURTAIN EXCHANGE

45 HIGH STREET, CUCKFIELD, SUSSEX RH17 5JU, ☎ 01444 417000, www.thecurtainexchange.net, 10–4 MON–SAT. **SECONDHAND SHOP**

See page 381 (CAMBS)

THE FABRIC WAREHOUSE

42 GEORGE STREET, BRIGHTON, SUSSEX BN2 1RJ, ☎ 01273 620744, 9.30–5 MON–SAT, 2 ON WED. **PERMANENT DISCOUNT OUTLET**

Curtain and upholstery fabric including names such as Monkwell, Voyager, Whiteheads and Prestigious. Stock depends on what is available on the end-of-line market, so changes constangly. If you are particularly interested in one label, phone first to check that they have it in stock.

THE FACTORY SHOP LTD

BRIGHTON MARINA, THE VILLAGE SQUARE, BRIGHTON, SUSSEX BN2 5WA, ☎ 01273 818590, 10–6 MON–FRI, 10–6 SAT, 10.30–4.30 SUN. **FACTORY SHOP IN A FACTORY SHOPPING VILLAGE**

See page 383 (CHESH)

THE FURNISHING CENTRE

HIGH STREET, BUXTED, EAST SUSSEX TN22 4LA, ☎ 01825 733353, 9–5 MON–SAT. **PERMANENT DISCOUNT OUTLET**

Specialises in Crowson fabrics, selling current stock both on the roll and to order from this season's pattern books at discounted prices, as well as some end of rolls at £3.99 a metre. Lightweight voiles start at £7.99 a metre while curtain and upholstery fabrics range from £14.99 to £18.99 a metre for fabric which would cost £19.99 to £24.99 a metre in department stores. Also sells furniture, some of which has been used in photo shoots or as display stock and is heavily discounted; for example, sofas reduced from £895 to £495. Wallpaper can be ordered from pattern books.

THE OLD LOOM MILL

MULBROOKS FARM, ERSHAM ROAD, HAILSHAM, SUSSEX BN27 2RH, ☎ 01323 848007, 9–5 MON–SAT, 10–5 SUN & BANK HOLIDAYS. **FACTORY SHOP**

One of the largest stockists in the area selling fabric and wool, curtaining, sheeting, lining and dress fabric. Curtaining ranges from £2.99 to £5 per metre; sheeting is £6 per kilo, £4.20 per metre (96in wide); 54in wide lining £1.99 per metre; dress fabrics from £1 to £4.50. All material is perfect unless otherwise stated. There are lots of well-known brands here, adding up to savings of about 60% on the high street. Stock is constantly changing so phone first if you have a special something in mind. The outlet also offers a curtain-making service, a tea room and a craft hall. Easy off road free parking and wheelchair access makes this a lovely place in the countryside for a visit to browse or buy.

TK MAXX

36–37 NORTH STREET, BRIGHTON, SUSSEX BN1 1EB, ☎ 01273 727483, www.tkmaxx.com, 9–6 MON–SAT, 7 ON THUR, 11–5 SUN.

13 THE MONTAGUE CENTRE, WORTHING, SUSSEX BN11 1YJ, ☎ 01903 234141, www.tkmaxx.com, 9–6 MON–SAT, 11–5 SUN. **PERMANENT DISCOUNT OUTLET**

See page 377 (BEDS)

WARWICKSHIRE AND WEST MIDLANDS

CANE AND WICKER FACTORY SHOP

TAME BRIDGE, WEST BROMWICH ROAD, WALSALL, WEST MIDLANDS WS5 4AN, ☎ 01922 63 63 64, www.caneandwicker.com, 10–5 MON–SAT, 11–4 SUN, CLOSED TUE. **FACTORY SHOP**

See page 404 (LANCS)

FABRIC WAREHOUSE

UNIT 2–3, OAK PARK, STOURBRIDGE ROAD, BRIERLEY HILL, WEST MIDLANDS DV5 1HR, ☎ 01384 482424, 9.30–5.30 MON–SAT, 8 ON FRI, 10–4 SUN.

STAFFORD STREET, CANNOCK ROAD, WOLVERHAMPTON, WEST MIDLANDS WV1 1NT, ☎ 01902 428472, 9–5.30 MON–SAT, 8 ON THUR, 10.30–4.30 SUN. **PERMANENT DISCOUNT OUTLET**

See page 378 (BERKS)

INTERNATIONAL STOCK LTD

95–100 REA STREET, DIGBETH, BIRMINGHAM, WEST MIDLANDS B5 6HA, ☎ 0121 622 3232, **e-mail:** mail@international-stock.co.uk, www.international-stock.co.uk, 9–5 MON–SAT, 10–4 SUN, CLOSED 1 ON WED.

1–17 SILVER STREET, KINGS HEATH, BIRMINGHAM, WEST MIDLANDS B14 7QX, ☎ 0121 443 3232, FAX: 0121 444 1792, **e-mail:** mail@international-stock.co.uk, www.international-stock.co.uk, 9–6 MON–SAT, CLOSED 1 ON WED. **PERMANENT DISCOUNT OUTLET**

Bankrupt, fire and flood damaged articles from CDs and videos, household goods and clothes to DIY tools and television sets, carpets and cookers. The King's Heath branch is a two-storey warehouse with ever-changing stock. The upper floor is devoted to electrical goods, some marked down to 30% of their normal retail cost. The Digbeth branch sells bigger items such as kitchens, flooring, tiles, dining room and lounge furniture, central heating radiators and a large clothing section for all the family, all of which is sold below wholesale price and in some cases below manufacturers' cost price. Top brand name kitchens, when in stock, are discounted by 75%.

MAGNET LTD CLEARANCE CENTRE

CHESTON ROAD, ASTON, BIRMINGHAM, WEST MIDLANDS B7 5EL, ☎ 0121 327 3201, 8–5 MON–FRI, 9–1 SAT. **FACTORY SHOP**

See page 384 (CO DURH)

MILL OUTLETS LTD

2 CANNON PARK CENTRE, CANLEY, COVENTRY, WARWICKSHIRE CV4 7AY, ☎ 024 7641 8441, 9–5.30 MON–WED, 9–6 THUR, FRI, 8.30–5 SAT, 10–4 SUN.

33 SOUTHAM ROAD, DUNCHURCH, RUGBY, WARWICKSHIRE CV22 6NL, ☎ 01788 816008, 9–5 MON–SAT, 10–4 SUN.

134 THE PARADE, LEAMINGTON SPA, WARWICKSHIRE CV32 4AG, ☎ 01926 744332, 9–5.30 MON–SAT, 11–5 SUN.

ABBEYGATE SHOPPING CENTRE, NUNEATON, WARWICKSHIRE CV11 5HL, ☎ 0247 638 6669, 9–5 MON–SAT.

3 ALBERT STREET, RUGBY, WARWICKSHIRE WARWICKSHIRE CV21 2RZ, ☎ 01788 542947, 9–5 MON–SAT. **PERMANENT DISCOUNT OUTLET**

See page 425 (OXON)

RMJ (ALLOYS) LTD

46–48 BAYTON ROAD, COVENTRY, WARWICKSHIRE CV7 9EJ, ☎ 02476 367508, 9–4.30 MON–THUR, 9–3.30 FRI. **FACTORY SHOP**

Made to measure staircases in metal or wood for indoors or outdoors – spiral, straight or fire escapes – all at factory prices.

THE CURTAIN EXCHANGE

10 WEST STREET, WARWICK WARWICKSHIRE CV34 6AN, ☎ 01926 492947, www.thecurtainexchange.net, 10–5 TUE–SAT, OR BY APPOINTMENT. **SECONDHAND SHOP**

See page 381 (CAMBS)

TK MAXX

UNITS 3–4 CASTLE VALE RETAIL PARK, BIRMINGHAM, WEST MIDLANDS, ☎ 0121 7496122, www.tkmaxx.com, 9–8 MON–FRI, 9–6 SAT, 11–5 SUN.

ONE STOP SHOPPING CENTRE, WALSALL ROAD, PERRY BARR, BIRMINGHAM, WEST MIDLANDS, ☎ 0121 356 5807, www.tkmaxx.com, PHONE FOR DETAILS.

THE GALLAGHER RETAIL PARK, STONEY STANTON ROAD, COVENTRY, WARWICKSHIRE CV6 5QG, ☎ 02476 664158, www.tkmaxx.com, 10–8 MON–FRI, 9–6 SAT, 11–5 SUN.

7–8 CROWN WHARF RETAIL PARK, WOLVERHAMPTON STREET, WALSALL, WEST MIDLANDS, ☎ 01922 649742, www.tkmaxx.com, PHONE FOR DETAILS.

2 WULFRUN SQUARE, WOLVERHAMPTON, WEST MIDLANDS WV1 3HB, ☎ 01902 421004, www.tkmaxx.com, 9–5.30 MON–FRI, 9–6 SAT, 11–5 SUN. **PERMANENT DISCOUNT OUTLET**

See page 377 (BEDS)

WILTSHIRE

FROCK FOLLIES

34 HIGH STREET, CORSHAM, WILTSHIRE SN13 0HB, ☎ 01249 713981
OPEN 10–4 MON, TUE, THUR–SAT, CLOSED 1–1.30 DAILY, 10–1 WED.
SECONDHAND SHOP

Dress agency on two floors with womenswear on one floor and secondhand curtains on another.

LOOSE ENDS

PRIORY PLACE, HANKERTON, MALMESBURY, WILTSHIRE SN16 9JZ, ☎ 01666 575300, FAX: 01666 575300, **e-mail:** looseendsfabrics@aol.com, 9–4 MON–SAT. **PERMANENT DISCOUNT OUTLET**

Loose Ends offers end of line furnishing fabric, both classic and contemporary, from their rural showroom. They buy from the top houses such as Ramm Son & Crocker, Malibar, Warners, Monkwell, Voyage, Zoffany, and many others. Large stocks, including 40m rolls, are available at amazing prices, some as low as one third of the normal retail price. Also stocks lining, interlining and wallpaper. They have a skilled 'maker upper' on hand to advise or quote for curtains and upholstery.

MCARTHURGLEN DESIGNER OUTLET GREAT WESTERN

KEMBLE DRIVE, SWINDON, JUNCTION 16 OF M4, WILTSHIRE SN2 2DY, ☎ 0800 316 4352 FREE INFORMATION LINE OR 01793 507600, www.mcarthurglen.com, 10–6 MON–FRI, 8 ON THUR, 9–6 SAT, 11–5 SUN. **FACTORY SHOPPING VILLAGE**

The McArthurGlen Designer Outlet Great Western offers over 100 stores selling top names and designer brands at up to 50% off typical retail prices. Housed in the restored Great Western Railway buildings, everything is conveniently located under one roof. A large open plan area dedicated to homewares has everything for the house and home. Facilities include a food court, children's play area, licensed creche and ample parking. Stores include: U Wear/I Wear, Warner UK Ltd, Antler, Ecco Shoes, Walker & Hall, Liz Claiborne, Viyella, Austin Reed, Suits You, Alexon, Jaeger, Windsmoor, Aquascutum, Olsen, Jacques Vert, Overland/Caterpillar, Episode, Long Tall Sally, Pilot, Triumph, Cotton Traders, Villeroy & Boch, Baron Jon, Clarks, HKA, Burberry, Remington, Regatta, Just Sweets, Easy Jeans, Ben Sherman, JoKids, Donnay, Le Creuset, Puma, Tog 24, XS, Gap, Big L, Soled Out, Ted Baker, Nike, Timberland, Quiksilver, Whittard, Marks and Spencer, Polo Jeans Company, Gant, Calp, The Design House, Darlington Crystal, Duvet and Pillow Shop, Henri Lloyd, Mexx, Ravel, The Luxury Beauty Store, Thomas Pink, Thorntons, Tie Rack, Julian Graves, Hanro, Jane Shilton, Birthday, Toy Zone, Bookends, Sofa Works, Designer Room, Petroleum, Next, Daks Simpson, Suit Company, Price's Candles, Claire's Accessories, Samsonite, Van Heusen, Cloverleaf, Poole Pottery, Spiegelau, Edinburgh Crystal, Woods of Windsor, Staffordshire Pottery, Waterford Wedgewood, Stuart Crystal, Gleneagles, The Garden Outlet, Ponden Mill, Jane Heath, Sheridan Australia, Tefal, Professional Cookware, and Oneida.

S & M HUGHES ORIENTAL RUGS

SOUTHVIEW, MARLOWE WAY, WOOTTON BASSETT, WILTSHIRE SN4 8LG, ☎ 01793 840147, FAX: 07721 860147, www.hughesorientalrugs.co.uk, BY APPOINTMENT. **PERMANENT DISCOUNT OUTLET**

Oriental Rugs Direct supply a range of handmade and machine-made Persian, Turkish, Afghan, Pakistani, Indian and Chinese rugs in all sizes. This family-run business will do the looking for you and bring a selection of rugs or carpets to your home so you can see them in situ and colour match them with your existing furnishings.

THE CURTAIN TRADERS

1ST FLOOR, 123 HIGH STREET, MARLBOROUGH, WILTSHIRE SN8 1LZ, ☎ 01672 516994, FAX: 01672 512400, **e-mail:** ali@curtaintraders.uk.com, www.curtaintraders.uk.com, 10–4.30 MON–FRI, SAT BY APPOINTMENT ONLY. **SECONDHAND SHOP**

Specialises in value for money, selling high quality, pre-loved curtains and accessories at rock-bottom prices. With two floors of constantly-changing stock, they offer an extensive variety to suit most tastes and needs and most fabrics can be obtained on request. They stock many designer names such as Osborne & Little, Colefax and Fowler, Sanderson, Warner and Designers Guild in natural linens, cottons, damasks, brocades, designer chintzes and velvets. They have extended their range of services to provide a fast make-up, alterations and fitting team and can source most materials. They also offer a professional interior design service at their in-house workshop, which includes loose covers, upholstery, carpets and flooring without the expensive design prices.

THE FACTORY SHOP LTD

23–25 NEW PLACE, CORSHAM, WILTSHIRE SN13 0HL, ☎ 01249 712160, 9–5.30 MON–SAT, 10–4 SUN.

36–37 ROUNDSTONE STREET, TROWBRIDGE, WILTSHIRE BA14 8DE, ☎ 01225 751399, 9–5 MON–SAT.

24 MARKET PLACE, WARMINSTER, WILTSHIRE BA12 9AN, ☎ 01985 217532, 9–5 MON–SAT. **FACTORY SHOP**

See page 383 (CHESH)

THE MAGNIFICENT MATERIAL COMPANY

CHAPEL BARN YARD, DEPTFORD, WYLYE, WILTSHIRE BA12 0QQ, ☎ 01985 248404, 9.30–12.30 MON, THUR AND BY APPOINTMENT. **PERMANENT DISCOUNT OUTLET**

Sells a wide variety of discontinued lines, overstocks, first and seconds, including traditional chintzes, linens, damasks, checks and upholstery. These fabrics come from many of the top designer warehouses, both here and on the continent, and are sold at less than half the retail price.

THE WILTON CARPET FACTORY SHOP

KING STREET, WILTON, SALISBURY, WILTSHIRE SP2 0AY, ☎ 01722 742733, 9.30–5.340 MON–SAT, 11–5 SUN. **FACTORY SHOP**

Factory shop where plain Wilton weave carpets are manufactured on site. Also sells plain tufted carpets and Axminsters in both big patterns and tonals (smaller designs). Room-sized remnants, end of rolls, as well as discontinued patterns on the roll. They offer a measuring service and fitters can be recommended.

TK MAXX

CROSS KEYS SHOPPING CENTRE, SALISBURY, WILTSHIRE, ☎ 01722 320644, www.tkmaxx.com, 9–5.30 MON–FRI, 8 ON THUR, 9–6 SAT, 10–4 SUN.

THE ARCADE, BRUNEL SHOPPING CENTRE, SWINDON, WILTSHIRE, ☎ 01793 532896, www.tkmaxx.com, PHONE FOR DETAILS. **PERMANENT DISCOUNT OUTLET**

See page 377 (BEDS)

WILTON SHOPPING VILLAGE

MINSTER STREET, WILTON, SALISBURY, WILTSHIRE SP2 0RS, ☎ 01722 741 211, www.thewsv@eagleone.co.uk, 9.30–5.30 MON–SAT, 11–5 SUN. **FACTORY SHOPPING VILLAGE**

On the former site of the Royal Wilton Carpet Factory, this village uses the refurbished original factory dye houses and 300-year-old, listed, historic courtyard buildings to house factory shops selling fashion and homewares at discounted prices. It includes shops such as Cotton Traders, Double Two, Edinburgh Woollen Mill, Julian Graves, Old Traditions, Ponden Mill, Remainders Books, Roman Originals, Scotts of Stow and the Wilton Carpet Factory Shop. Free parking, coffee shop, children's play area and disabled facilities. A riverside café is also open during the summer, serving homemade food and refreshments.

WORCESTERSHIRE

CARPETS OF WORTH LTD

TOWNSHEND WORKS, PUXTON LANE, KIDDERMINSTER, DY11 5DF, ☎ 01562 745000, **e-mail:** sales@carpetsofworth.co.uk, www.carpetsofworth.co.uk, 8.30–5 MON–FRI, 8–1 SAT. **FACTORY SHOP**

Sells Axminster tufted carpets and rugs made out of carpet overmakes. All the carpets are patterned and 80/20. These are usually seconds or overmakes, discontinued lines or end of contract rolls and are sold at half the usual retail price. Credit cards accepted.

EDINBURGH CRYSTAL

ROYAL WORCESTER VISITOR CENTRE, SEVERN STREET, WORCESTER, WORCESTERSHIRE WR1 2NE, ☎ 01905 746000 (CENTRE TEL NO), ☎ 01905 619503, **e-mail:** general@royal-worcester.co.uk, www.royal-worcester.co.uk, 9–5.30 MON–SAT, 11–5 SUN. MAIL ORDER. **FACTORY SHOP**

The Victorian buildings of Royal Worcester's visitor centre lead into the heart of a world famous porcelain industry that was founded in 1751. Wide range of Edinburgh Crystal crystalware, among others, from glasses and vases to tumblers and bowls at discounts of between 33% and 50%. The shop sells firsts and seconds of crystal from one third off the normal price. There are also special promotional lines at discount prices up to 70% off seconds. Visitors can also shop in Wigornia Court where a myriad of home accessories and factory outlets selling cutlery, crystal, candles, linen, kitchen utensils, rugs and giftware can be found. Parking and disabled facilities.

ROYAL WORCESTER VISITOR CENTRE

SEVERN STREET, WORCESTER, WORCESTERSHIRE WR1 2NE, ☎ 01905 746000, FAX: 01905 619503, **e-mail:** general@royal-worcester.co.uk, www.royal-worcester.co.uk, 9–5.30 MON–SAT, 11–5 SUN. MAIL ORDER. **FACTORY SHOP**

The Victorian buildings of Royal Worcester's visitor centre lead into the heart of a world famous porcelain industry that was founded in 1751. Royal Worcester's factory shops carry an extensive range of quality bone china tableware, porcelain oven-to-tableware, giftware and figurines. The factory seconds shop offers quality seconds at greatly reduced prices. Visitors can also shop in Wigornia Court where a myriad of home accessories and factory outlets selling cutlery, crystal, candles, linen, kitchen utensils, rugs and giftware can be found. Parking and disabled facilities.

THE CAPE

40 THE SHAMBLES, WORCESTER, WORCESTERSHIRE WR1 2RE, ☎ 01905 729291, FAX: 01905 24111, **e-mail:** sc@thefactory-shop.co.uk, www.thecape.co.uk, 9–5.30 MON–FRI, 9–6 SAT, 10.30–4.30 SUN. **FACTORY SHOP**

See page 379 (BRIS)

THE CURTAIN RACK

25 HIGH STREET, PERSHORE, WORCESTERSHIRE WR10 1AA, ☎ 01386 556105, 10–5 MON–SAT, CLOSED WED. **SECONDHAND SHOP**

Three large showrooms specialising in good quality secondhand curtains, readymades and fabrics. The curtains vary from some cheap and cheerful through to lined curtains, some with matching valances, cushion covers etc. One section of the shop has a large variety of brocades and damask fabrics sold by the metre or they tailor at very competitive prices. They also offer a choice of six companies for a selection of top quality ready-made lined curtains at discounted prices, all of which have optional accessories. There is also a large showroom, packed with sumptuous designer curtains, some interlined, some with swags, tails, tie-backs and others beautifully fringed. They can cater for extremely large windows, all at unbeatable prices.

THE FACTORY SHOP LTD

NEW ROAD, PERSHORE, WORCESTERSHIRE WR10 1BY, ☎ 01386 556467, 9–5 MON–FRI, 9–5.30 SAT, 10.30–4.30 SUN. **FACTORY SHOP**

See page 383 (CHESH)

THE WEAVERS SHOP

DUKE PLACE, KIDDERMINSTER, WORCESTERSHIRE DY10 2JR, ☎ 01562 820680, FAX: 01562 820030, **e-mail:** weavers.shop@tomkinsons.co.uk, 9–5 MON–FRI, 9–12 SAT. **FACTORY SHOP**

Offers a large selection of tufted and Axminster plain and patterned carpets from the factory. Also has a wide collection of natural floor coverings and rugs at a considerable discount off high street prices. All goods sold here are returns, discontinued, contract overmakes, ends or slight seconds and therefore represent excellent value for money. Fitters can be suggested and delivery arranged.

TK MAXX

UNIT 100, UPPER MALL, MERRYHILL CENTRE, DUDLEY, WORCESTERSHIRE DY5 1QX, ☎ 01384 77878, www.tkmaxx.com, 10–8 MON–FRI, 10–9 THUR, 9–7 SAT, 11–5 SUN.

EVESHAM WALK, KINGFISHER SHOPPING CENTRE, REDDITCH, WORCESTERSHIRE, ☎ 01527 598837, www.tkmaxx.com, PHONE FOR DETAILS. **PERMANENT DISCOUNT OUTLET**

See page 377 (BEDS)

YORKSHIRE

BEST BARGAINS

REAR OF 140-152 WESTBOURNE ROAD, MARSH, HUDDERSFIELD, WEST YORKSHIRE HD1 2LF, ☎ 01484 434999, 9–5 MON–SAT, 10–4 SUN. **PERMANENT DISCOUNT OUTLET**

Large building selling beds, television cabinets, drinks cabinets, chests of drawers, wardrobes, bunk beds, suites, dining rooms sets, as well as some housewares, DIY, lighting and mirrors at very competitive prices. For example, single mattress, from £32; double bed frame, from £100.

BRANDMART

5 NORTH STREET, RIPON, NORTH YORKSHIRE HG4 1JY, ☎ 01765 601156, 9–5 MON–SAT. **FACTORY SHOP**

See page 396 (GLOS)

BROOKS FACTORY OUTLET STORES HALIFAX

SOUTH LANE, ELLAND, NEAR HALIFAX, WEST YORKSHIRE HX5 0HQ, ☎ 01422 377337, 9.30–5.30 MON–SAT, 8 ON THUR, 11–5 SUN.

BUYWELL RETAIL PARK, THORP ARCH, WETHERBY, NORTH YORKSHIRE LS23 7BJ, ☎ 01937 541895, 9.30–5.30 MON–SAT, 11–5 SUN. **PERMANENT DISCOUNT OUTLET**

Walk through the store and you can't fail to find a bargain. New stock arrives daily from well-known names such as Nike, Reebok, Gabicci, Gossard, Camille and Klass. Apart from mens and women's clothes, they sell sportswear, linens, lingerie, shoes, accessories, luggage, towels, coordinated bed linen, household textiles, duvets, pillows and lots more from names such as Jeff Banks, Ports of Call, Hamilton McBride, Broomhill, Monogram and Ponden Mill. Everything under one roof at up to 50% off high street prices. The Elland store has a coffee shop.

BURMATEX LTD

VICTORIA MILLS, THE GREEN, OSSETT, WEST YORKSHIRE WF5 0AN, ☎ 01924 276 333, FAX: 01924 280033, www.burmatex.co.uk, 9.30–4 MON–FRI, 8–11 SAT. **FACTORY SHOP**

A factory shop selling end-of-range carpet tiles at prices that are significantly less than those found in the high street, and which range from £1.65 to £2.

CATALOGUE DISCOUNT STORES

UNIT 6, HILLSBOROUGH BARRACKS SHOPPING MALL, SHEFFIELD, SOUTH YORKSHIRE S6 2GY, ☎ 0114 234 5726, FAX: 0114 234 5006, 9–5.30 MON–SAT, 11–5 SUN. **PERMANENT DISCOUNT OUTLET**

See page 384 (CO DURH)

CJ FURNITURE DIRECT

THE FURNITURE FACTORY, LEEDS ROAD, OTLEY, WEST YORKSHIRE LS21 1QX, ☎ 01943 461888, FAX: 01943 850763, **e-mail:** cjfurniture@bigfoot.com, www.cjfurniture.com, MAIL ORDER. **FACTORY SHOP**

Contemporary, handcrafted wooden furniture sold direct to the public without the overheads of the high street so that they promise always to be significantly better value than competitors. By selling direct, they can be at least 20% cheaper than the shops for similar furniture and they are so confident of this, that they promise to refund the difference if proved wrong. Phone or fax or e-mail for a brochure.

CLASSIC CARPET COMPANY

MIALL STREET, OFF PELLON LANE, HALIFAX, WEST YORKSHIRE HX1 4AE, ☎ 01422 343324, FAX: 01422 343321, **e-mail:** classiccarpet@supanet.com, 9–5.30 MON–FRI, 9–5 SAT, 11–3 SUN. **FACTORY SHOP**

Huge selection of carpets, some vinyls, also rugs. Fitting and delivery service.

CURTAIN TRANSFER

BACK TEWIT WELL ROAD, OFF SOUTH DRIVE, HARROGATE, NORTH YORKSHIRE HG2 8JF, ☎ 01423 505520, FAX: 01423 520051, www.curtain-transfer.com, 10–5 TUE–SAT, WED BY APPOINTMENT. **SECONDHAND SHOP**

Curtain Transfer is a treasure trove of secondhand curtains and upmarket furnishing accessories – pictures, lamps and lampshades, cushions and throws. A new addition is unused linen sheets and tablecloths, which can be hung as minimalist curtains and Swedish and French-style painted occasional furniture. Goods are accepted on sale-or-return agency terms – plain weaves, damasks and velvets are especially welcome. Over 200 pairs of lined of interlined curtains are imaginatively hung in an old stable opposite the owner's home – including prints by Monkwell, GP & J Baker, Sanderson, Osborne & Little, Colefax and Fowler, and Zoffany. Phone for directions: Curtain Transfer is off South Drive, behind Tewit Well Road, which is off the Leeds Road on the south side of Harrogate town centre. Children are welcome and parking is in the yard.

FABRIC WAREHOUSE

75A BRADFORD ROAD, RIDDLESDEN, KEIGHLEY, WEST YORKSHIRE BD21 4HD, ☎ 01535 692999, 9–5 MON–SAT. **PERMANENT DISCOUNT OUTLET**

Sells unbranded fabric direct from the same mills which manufacture for well-known brand names at a discount of about 30%. They stock prints, plains, brocades, silks, chenilles, voiles, muslin, damask, weaves, chenilles, lining fabric and a wide range of accessories from heading tape and cushion pads to tracks and poles. Prices average £2.99-£9.99 a linear metre with flat weaves costing £19 a metre for fabric which would cost £35 a metre in the high street and muslin for 99p a metre.

FABRIC WAREHOUSE

GIBRALTAR STREET, BROOKSHAW PARK, SHALESMOOR, SHEFFIELD, SOUTH YORKSHIRE S3 8UB, ☎ 0114 275 5657, 9.30–5.30 MON–SAT, 7 ON WED, 11–5 SUN.

WESTGATE RETAIL PARK, WAKEFIELD, WEST YORKSHIRE WF2 9SD, ☎ 01924 299373, 9.30–8 MON, THUR, 9.30–6 TUE, WED, FRI, 9–6 SAT, 11–5 SUN. **PERMANENT DISCOUNT OUTLET**

See page 378 (BERKS)

FABRICS FROM THE MILLS

ARCH 9, VIADUCT STREET, HUDDERSFIELD, WEST YORKSHIRE HD1 5DL, ☎ 01484 450509, 9.30–5.30 MON–SAT. **PERMANENT DISCOUNT OUTLET**

A place where you can change that room without breaking the bank. There's a huge choice of quality curtain and upholstery fabric in as many designs and colours. The stock is mainly first quality, but there are clearances and seconds of famous labels such as Next, Marks & Spencer, Prestigious, etc: all at a fraction of their original price. There's also a speedy, professional made-to-measure service.

FREEPORT CASTLEFORD DESIGNER OUTLET VILLAGE

CARRWOOD ROAD, GLASSHOUGHTON, CASTLEFORD, JUNCTION 32 OF M52, WEST YORKSHIRE WF10 4SB, ☎ 01977 520153, www.freeportcastleford.com, 10–8 MON–FRI, 10–6 SAT, 11–5 SUN. **FACTORY SHOPPING VILLAGE**

Designer outlet village with over 75 shops, indoor and outdoor children's play areas and a wide range of restaurants with easy access from the M52 and 3,500 free car parking spaces. Shops include Amazing Jeans, Baron Jon, BhS For Less, Charles Clinkard, Clarks, Cromwells, Churchill, Ciro Citterio, Craghoppers, CBS, Claire's Accessories, Cotton Traders, Damart, Edinburgh Crystal, Donnay, Double Two, Event Jewellery, Easy Jeans, Edinburgh Woollen Mill, Elle, Fila, Giorgio, Gossard, XS Music, Jane Shilton, John Partridge, Kappa, Kitchen and Table, Kurt Muller, Leading Labels, Lee Cooper, Littlewoods, London Leathers, Mexx, Mobile Phone Store, Nike, Nickleby's, Next to Nothing, Outrage, Petroleum, Picture Port, Pilot, Ponden Mill, Proibito, Rio Jewellery, Roman Originals, Regatta, Room, Ice Jeans, Sergio Tacchini, Sportsmill, Spotlight, Startrite Shoes, Remainders Book Depot, Designer Room, Garden Outlet, Shoe Collection, Toy Factory, Time, X Catalogue Store, Thorntons, Trespass, Waterford Wedgwood, Windsmoor,

GARDNER CARPETS

LEE BRIDGE INDUSTRIAL ESTATE, DEAN CLOUGH, HALIFAX, WEST YORKSHIRE, ☎ 01422 355010, 9–4.30 MON–FRI, 9.30–4 SAT, 12.30–4 SUN. **FACTORY SHOP**

Hundreds of rolls of carpet in stock and even more remnants, many room-sized, or you can order from samples. Offer measuring and fitting service.

GREENHOLME MILLS CARPET CENTRE

GREENHOLME MILL, BURLEY IN WHARFEDALE, NORTH YORKSHIRE LS29 7DB, ☎ 01943 864656, OPEN 9–5 MON–SAT, 12–4 SUN. **FACTORY SHOP**

Fcatory shop selling carpets, rugs and carpet tiles at exceptionally good prices. They will measure up and fit.

HABITAT CLEARANCE DEPARTMENT

REDBRICK MILL LTD, 218 BRADFORD ROAD, BATLEY, WEST YORKSHIRE WF17 6JF, ☎ 01924 468960, OPEN 9.30–5.30 MON–FRI, 9–6 SAT, 11–5 SUN. **PERMANENT DISCOUNT OUTLET**

See page 406 (LANCS)

HOUSE OF FABRICS

HIRST LANE, SALTAIRE, SHIPLEY, WEST YORKSHIRE BD18 4ND, ☎ 01274 595952, FAX: 01274 593019, 9–5 MON–SAT, 10–4 SUN. **PERMANENT DISCOUNT OUTLET**

Curtaining and upholstery fabrics from a range which includes plain cotton, chintz, damasks and heavy upholstery fabric. Prices from £2.99 a metre. The upholstery fabric is sold at greatly reduced prices. There are many brands to choose from, including Rectella, Prestigious and Wilson Wilcox. They can supply all accessories too, such as braid, tie-backs, brassware, corded and uncorded tracks; metal, wood and brass poles; brass tie-backs, holdbacks, embracers, braids, cords and trims, and offer a complete measure, make-up and fitting service, including upholstery.

HOWKEL CARPETS

60 LOWER VIADUCT STREET, HUDDERSFIELD, WEST YORKSHIRE HD1 6BN, ☎ 01484 425422, 9–5 MON–FRI, 9–4.30 SAT. **FACTORY SHOP**

Warehouse-type building on three floors stacked with quality carpets and ends of lines, all perfect, specialising in 80% wool twist pile carpets. For example 40oz wool twist off the roll costs £10.50 a square yard, while room-sized remnants are even less. Nothing costs more than £10.50 a square yard, about half the shop price. There is a small off-shoot shop selling their seconds, offcuts, contract division carpeting and vinyls at Blackmoorfoot Road.

LAURA ASHLEY HORNSEA

FREEPORT HORNSEA OUTLET VILLAGE, ROLSTON ROAD, HORNSEA, EAST YORKSHIRE HU18 1UT, ☎ 01964 536503, 9.30–6 SEVEN DAYS A WEEK. **FACTORY SHOP IN A FACTORY SHOPPING VILLAGE**

Home furnishings on two floors. Most of the merchandise is made up of perfect carry-overs from the high street shops around the country, though there are also some discontinued lines. Stock reflects the normal high street variety, though at least one season later and with less choice in colours. The shopping village has restaurants, play centres, a vintage car collection, water games, and plenty for the family to do and see.

LINDSAY'S ALLSORTS

STANLEY MILL, BRITANNIA ROAD, MILNSBRIDGE, HUDDERSFIELD, WEST YORKSHIRE HD3 4QS, ☎ 01484 648670, 9–5.30 MON–SAT, 10–4 SUN. **PERMANENT DISCOUNT OUTLET**

Claims to be Yorkshire's largest furniture warehouse. Three huge floors with at least 400 suites, some from names such as Christie-Tyler and Buoyant, and 100 dining room sets plus beds, coffee tables, chairs etc. Most have been manufactured for the well-known high street and out-of-town furniture chains and are sold here at prices which are lower than the chains at sale time. Instant delivery.

MAGNET LTD CLEARANCE CENTRE

ROYDINGS AVENUE, KEIGHLEY, WEST YORKSHIRE BD21 4BY, ☎ 01535 680461, 8–5 MON–FRI, 9–1 SAT. **FACTORY SHOP**

See page 384 (CO DURH)

MCARTHURGLEN DESIGNER OUTLET YORK

ST NICHOLAS AVENUE, FULFORD, JUNCTION OF A19 AND A64, YORK, NORTH YORKSHIRE YO19 4TA, ☎ 01904 682720, www.mcarthurglen.com/york, 10–6 MON–SAT, 8 ON THUR, 11–5 SUN. **FACTORY SHOP IN A FACTORY SHOPPING VILLAGE**

The McArthurGlen Designer Outlet York is one of Europe's largest covered designer outlets with over 120 stores offering top brands and designer labels with discounts of up to 50% off typical retail prices. Find everything from men's, women's and children's clothing to accessories, shoes, sportswear, luggage, homewares, toys, books, and gifts. Facilities include a food court, a children's play area and free parking. Stores include: Armani, Autonomy, Ben Sherman, Burberry, Calvin Klein Jeans, Cerruti 1881, Chilli Pepper, Cotton Traders, Daks Simpson, Episode, Escada Sport, Gap Outlet, Guess, Hugo Boss, Jacques Vert, Jaeger/Viyella, Jesire/Esensual, Kabuki, Klass, Levi's, Margaret Howell, Marks & Spencer Outlet, Mergler, Mountain Warehouse, Nitya, Olsen, Pilot, Polo Ralph Lauren, Pringle, Proibito, Proudfoot Leather, Roman Originals, Ronit Zilkha, Ted Baker, The Designer Room, Thomas Pink, Tog 24, Tommy Hilfiger, Windsmoor, Alfred Dunhill, Baronjon, Ben Sherman, Haggar, HKA, Marlboro Classics, Paul Smith, Petroleum, Pour Homme, Rockport, Suit Company, Suits You, Timberland, Adidas, Diadora, Donnay, Reebok, Toyworld, Birthdays, Bodum, The Body Shop Depot, Bookends, Franchetti Bond, Le Creuset, Oneida, Paper Mill, Price's Candles, Remington, Scent To You, Whittard Kitchen, Woods of Windsor, XS Music & Video, Bed & Bath Works, China China, Coloroll, Descamps, Garden Outlet, Jane Heath, La Casa del Christallo, Lights 4 Less, Pictureport, Room, Slipperbox, Spiegelau, Professional Cookware, Daniel Footwear, Famous Footwear, Pavers, Rockport, Shoe Studio, Soled Out, Julian Graves, Thorntons, Antler, Kangol, Liberty, Travel Accessory, Chapelle Jewellery, Claire's Accessories, Designer Shades, Monet, Tie Rack, and The Watch Store.

MULBERRY CLEARANCE SHOP

23–25 SWINEGATE, YORK, NORTH YORKSHIRE YO1 2AB, ☎ 01904 611055, FAX: 01904 640717, www.mulberry.com, 10–6 MON–SAT. **PERMANENT DISCOUNT OUTLET**

Clearance shop for the famous Mulberry brands with some full-price goods also on sale. Sale items include last season's clothing for men and women, leather goods, handbags, personal organisers, wallets, cushions, lamps, china, throws and fabric. The shop is all on one level.

NEXT TO NOTHING

38 BROADWAY, BRADFORD, WEST YORKSHIRE BD1 1EY, ☎ 01274 301460, www.next.co.uk, 9–5.30 MON–SAT, 11–5 SUN. **PERMANENT DISCOUNT OUTLET**

Sells perfect surplus stock from Next stores and the Next Directory catalogue – from belts, jewellery and underwear to day and evening wear – at discounts of 50% or more. The ranges are usually last season's and overruns. Stock consists of women's, men's and children's clothing, with some homeware and shoes. One reader bought sufficient wallpaper here for £10 to paper a room (£1 a roll reduced from £7.99)and matching curtains for £20, reduced from £70.

NUMBER 36

36 PIERCY END, KIRKBYMOORSIDE, YORK, NORTH YORKSHIRE YO62 6DF, ☎ 01751 433253, FAX: 01751 433253, 10–5 TUE, WED, FRI, SAT. **PERMANENT DISCOUNT OUTLET**

This shop sells international designer fabrics with the emphasis on high class designs with a difference. More unusually, they also stock a vast range of quality trimmings, cords, bullions, tassels, tiebacks, etc. Regular customers describe the shop as an Aladdin's cave, with its tapestries, handmade quilts, Egyptian cotton bedding, throws, cushions and traditional household textiles. Those who have tried the famous Knaresborough linen dishcloth vow never to use anything else again. Most of the stock is overmakes, bankrupt merchandise, bought from the US or imported from all over the world. Although the shop is small, it is bursting with incredible soft furnishing bargains, including fabric from as little as £1 per metre and a good selection of trimmings and accessories at budget prices. A making-up service is available. Kirkbymoorside is a picturesque market town, well served with restaurants and cafés, and perfect for a day out in the North York Moors countryside.

PEASE & JAY FURNITURE DIRECT

LEEDS ROAD, OTLEY, WEST YORKSHIRE LS21 1QX, ☎ 01943 850764, FAX: 01943 850763, **e-mail:** peaseandjay@bigfoot.com, wwwpeaseandjay.co.uk, 10–5 MON–SAT, 11–4 SUN. MAIL ORDER. **FACTORY SHOP**

High quality traditional English furniture at factory direct prices from this manufacturer with more than 50 years experience in design and production. By cutting out the middleman and selling to customers direct from their factory, they can offer the same high quality products you see in high street shops at significantly lower prices. All their furniture is made in the UK by specialist craftsmen and is available in mahogany or yew. Items on sale include coffee tables, curio cabinets, bow front hall tables, chests of drawers, bedside chests, circular tables, lamp tables, octagonal drum tables, swag and drape chairs, lamp trolleys, desks, bureaux, television cabinets, hi-fi storage units, sideboards, dining tables, book cases and corner cabinets. Discounted items of furniture are due to Pease & Jay getting better deals on their raw materials and passing the benefits onto customers. They offer a five-year guarantee and 7-day trial period to decide whether or not you like the furniture.

PONDEN MILL

FREEPORT CASTLEFORD DESIGNER OUTLET VILLAGE, CARWOOD ROAD, GLASSHOUGHTON, CASTLEFORD, JUNCTION 32 OF M52, WEST YORKSHIRE WF10 4SB, ☎ 01977 518327, 10–8 MON–FRI, 10–6 SAT, 11–5 SUN.

THE YORKSHIRE OUTLET, WHITE ROSE WAY, DONCASTER, SOUTH YORKSHIRE DN4 5JH, ☎ 01302 360117, 10–6 MON–SAT, 11–5 SUN.

FREEPORT HORNSEA OUTLET VILLAGE, ROLSTON ROAD, HORNSEA, EAST YORKSHIRE HU18 1UT, ☎ 01964 537452, 9.30–6 MON–SAT, 11–5 SUN.

THE MILL, BRADFORD ROAD, BATLEY, WEST YORKSHIRE WF17 5LZ, ☎ 01924 444948, 9.30–5.30 MON–FRI, 9–5.30 SAT, 11–5 SUN. **FACTORY SHOP IN A FACTORY SHOPPING VILLAGE**

See page 385 (CO DURH)

QLM LTD

IDLE ROAD, IDLE, BRADFORD, WEST YORKSHIRE BD2 2AL, ☎ 01274 642222, 9.30–6 MON–SAT, 5.30 ON WED, 11–5 SUN. **PERMANENT DISCOUNT OUTLET**

Toys, household goods, clothes, food, electrical equipment, garden implements, kitchenware and furniture, all sold at discounted prices. For example, reject garden forks £6.99, spades £4.99, pruning tools £2.99 to £19.99.

RL & CM BOND LTD

93–99 TOWN STREET, FARSLEY, PUDSEY, NEAR LEEDS, WEST YORKSHIRE LS28 5HX, ☎ 0113 257 4905, 9–4.30 WED–SAT. **PERMANENT DISCOUNT OUTLET**

Customers travel from all over the country to this Aladdin's cave with a range that is second to none. Two-storey shop selling everything for the needlecraft and cross stitch enthusiast at very competitive prices. There are tapestry kits, silks, zips, threads, buttons, ribbons, cross stitch books galore, as well as a host of items for curtain makers including rufflette tape, braid, trimmings, fringing, bullion fringe, curtain hooks, header tape for Austrian and festoon blinds and tie-backs. All sewing supplies and haberdashery at unbelievable prices. Coach parties welcome by appointment.

SHAWS CARPET FACTORY SHOP

DARTON, BARNSLEY, SOUTH YORKSHIRE S75 5QX, ☎ 01226 390133, 10–5 MON–SAT, 8 ON THUR, 10–4 SUN. **FACTORY SHOP**

Huge selection of carpets, many made from top quality wool direct from the factory at discounted prices. Fitting and delivery service available.

SIMPLY DUTCH

DARTON HOUSE, BEDALE ROAD, LEEMING BAR, NORTH YORKSHIRE DL7 9AS, ☎ 01677 427800, 9.30–5 MON–SAT, 10–4 SUN. **PERMANENT DISCOUNT OUTLET**

Large, warehouse-style shop on two floors selling nearly-new, old and antique Dutch furniture including solid oak and other tables, chairs, dressers, cabinets, coffee tables, television cabinets and free standing panelled kitchen furniture. Oak tables and chairs, cheese racks, chests and boxes. From China, there are cast iron patio sets, planters, lampposts, water features, water pumps and cast iron and wood garden benches, as well as reclaimed antique-style furniture from panelled four posters to small carved side tables, dressers, sideboards, book cases, wall brackets, wine cabinets and table and chairs. From elsewhere in the world, bronze fountains, herons, parrots, dogs, pewter stem glasses, painted ware, wood burning clay stoves, Mexican chimneas and ceramics. New stock arrives weekly. Free local delivery service.

SMITH'S MILL SHOP

THOMAS STREET, HALIFAX, WEST YORKSHIRE HX1 1QX, ☎ 01422 343432, FAX: 01422 347569, 9–5 MON–SAT. **PERMANENT DISCOUNT OUTLET**

Perfect stock and some seconds in a wide range of curtain fabrics at discounts of 50%, as well as tracks, poles and haberdashery. Fabrics cost from £1 per metre and range from voiles, chenilles and fur to dress materials. Brands include Prestigious, Ashley Wilde, SMD, Voyage and many more. Full measuring, fitting and sewing service is available on site. Special offers are always available.

SOFAS TO GO

SOFA WORKSHOP, 10 COPPERGATE, YORK, NORTH YORKSHIRE YO1 1NR, ☎ 01904 612189, www.sofaworkshop.com, 9–5.30 MON–SAT, 11–5 SUN. **PERMANENT DISCOUNT OUTLET**

See page 418 (LOND)

SPRINGFIELD CLOTHING

THE MILL SHOP, NORMAN ROAD, DENBY DALE, HUDDERSFIELD, WEST YORKSHIRE HD8 8TH, ☎ 01484 865082, 9–5 MON–SAT, 10–5 SUN. **PERMANENT DISCOUNT OUTLET**

Springfield Clothing sells clothes for all the family at up to 50% discount on high street prices such as Marks & Spencer, Principles, Next, Monsoon and Dorothy Perkins. Also stocks men's and women's underwear, a selection of basic bedding, duvets, sheets, pillows, pillowcases as well as tea towels, tablecloths, rugs, small carpets and Sheffield cutlery, all at discounted prices.

STAPLES, THE OFFICE SUPERSTORE

UNIT 11B, JUNCTION STREET, CROWN POINT RETAIL PARK, HUNSLET LANE, LEEDS, WEST YORKSHIRE LS10 1EL, ☎ 0113 2421061, www.staples.co.uk, 8–8 MON–FRI, 9–6 SAT, 11–5 SUN. MAIL ORDER ALSO. **PERMANENT DISCOUNT OUTLET**

See page 408 (LANCS)

SUMMER GRAND SALE

RIPLEY CASTLE, RIPLEY, NEAR HARROGATE, NORTH YORKSHIRE, ENQUIRIES: 01367 860017, FAX: 01367 860177, **e-mail:** nheslam@aol.com, 9.30–5.30 MON–FRI. **DESIGNER SALES**

There are now three annual Grand Sales taking place countrywide. The Christmas Grand Sale in London, with over 120 different small companies selling their merchandise to the public, is the largest. This takes place in mid-late November each year. Quality is high and covers everything from French lavender sachets, hand-painted furniture, made-to-measure blinds, 19th century wall clocks, unusual watercolours, cinammon-scented apple wreaths, traditional American tinware, children's pyjama cases, candle sconces, handmade Indian pickles, bamboo placemats, embossed copper sketchbooks, Art Deco mirrors, silk embroidered cushions, herbal tinctures, English garden trugs, African shopping baskets, handmade wrapping paper, elegant kitchen woodware, beaded handbags, bespoke Ottomans, fine champagne, baby sleeping bags, nautical mirrors, painted dog and cat beds, ties and matching cufflinks, antique Bergeres suites, Egyptian cotton bedlinen, often at discount because they are ends of lines. There is a three-day Spring Grand Sale at Sudeley Castle, Winchcombe, near Cheltenham in Gloucestershire, usually at the end of April/beginning of May, and a four-day Summer Grand Sale at Ripley Castle, near Harrogate, North Yorkshire, in June. Both feature gardening furniture and equipment as well as decorative home accessories. Phone the above number to put your name on the mailing list. A proportion of the ticket revenue goes to charity.

TEXERE YARNS

COLLEGE MILL, BARKEREND ROAD, BRADFORD, WEST YORKSHIRE BD1 4AU, ☎ 01274 722191, 9–5 MON–FRI. **FACTORY SHOP**

Factory shop selling every type of yarn you can imagine: wool, cotton, silk, linen, viscose, acrylic, alpaca, fine metallics, Lurex yarns, braid making yarns for rugs, textured colours for creative embroidery, but no mohair or cashmere. A must visit for the hand or machine knitter, the embroiderer, weaver or rug maker.

THE CAPE

REDBRICK MILL, 218 BRADFORD ROAD, BATLEY CARR, WEST YORKSHIRE WF17 6JF, ☎ 01924 466228, FAX: 01924 466228, **e-mail:** sc@thefactory-shop.co.uk, www.thecape.co.uk, 9–5.30 MON–FRI, 9.30–5.30 SAT, 11–5 SUN. **FACTORY SHOP**

See page 379 (BRIS)

THE CURTAIN EXCHANGE

162 HIGH STREET, BOSTON SPA, WEST YORKSHIRE LS23 6BW, ☎ 01937 849755, www.thecurtainexchange.net, 10–5 MON–SAT. **SECONDHAND SHOP**

See page 381 (CAMBS)

THE DARLEY MILL CENTRE

DARLEY, NEAR HARROGATE, NORTH YORKSHIRE HG3 2QQ, ☎ 01423 780857, 9.30–5.30 MON–SAT, 11–5 SUN. **PERMANENT DISCOUNT OUTLET**

The centre offers a great day out for the whole family, combining great bargains in clothing, crockery, linens, crafts and exclusive gifts, with lots for children to see and do. This 17th-century corn mill has one of the largest water wheels in Yorkshire and there's a licensed restaurant with an outdoor dining terrace.

THE FABRIC EMPORIUM

KIDD HOUSE, WHITEHALL ROAD, LEEDS, WEST YORKSHIRE LS12 1AP, ☎ 0113 2458601, 9–6 MON–SAT, 10–4 SUN. **PERMANENT DISCOUNT OUTLET**

Curtain and upholstery own brand fabrics and those from many well-known high street brands such as Laura Ashley, Next and Marks & Spencer. Because they buy job lots from the USA, Europe and the UK, prices range from 99p a metre to £25.99 a metre although the normal recommended retail price of many items ranges from £16 to £30 a metre. Most goods are first quality and the majority are priced in the range of £3.99 to £7.99 a metre. Stock is continually changing and brands include Prestigious, Voyage, Chess, Select etc. All curtain accessories are available and there is an in-house making up service.

THE FABRIC SHOP

82 MAIN STREET, ADDINGHAM, NEAR ILKLEY, NORTH YORKSHIRE LS29 0PL, ☎ 01943 830982, 9–5 MON–SAT. **PERMANENT DISCOUNT OUTLET**

Great fabric bargains in this rabbit warren of interconnecting rooms, stacked high to the ceiling with bolts of perfects and seconds of furnishing fabrics. Brands include Moygashel, Monkwell and Designers Guild. Most of the fabric, tapestries and damasks are from Italian and English–Italian manufacturers. Prints on the roll cost no more than £8.80 per metre, upholstery fabric costs no more than £20 per metre. Fabrics range from £2 to £20 a metre, curtain lining from £2.40 to £3 a metre, tapes from 45p a metre and interlining from £3 a metre. No making up service; telephone orders taken. The staff are very helpful and knowledgeable and there is parking directly outside or in the next side street at the village car park.

THE FACTORY SHOP

PARK ROSE POTTERY, CARNABY COVERT LANE, CARNABY, BRIDLINGTON, NORTH YORKSHIRE YO15 3QF, ☎ 01262 603518, 10–5 MON–SAT, 10.30–4.30 SUN.

WHEATLEY LANE, LEEDS ROAD, ILKLEY, WEST YORKSHIRE LS29 8BS, ☎ 01943 604514, 9–5.30 MON–SAT, 10.30–4.30 SUN.

LIGHTWATER VALLEY SHOPPING VILLAGE, NORTH STAINLEY, RIPON, NORTH YORKSHIRE HG4 3HT, ☎ 01765 635438, 10–6 MON–SAT, 11–5 SUN. **FACTORY SHOP**

See page 383 (CHESH)

THE FACTORY VALUE SHOP

LAWKHOLME LANE, KEIGHLEY, WEST YORKSHIRE BD21 3JQ, ☎ 01535 611703, 9.30–5 MON–SAT, 10.30–4.30 SUN. **FACTORY SHOP**

Wide range on sale includes men's, women's and children's clothing and footwear; household textiles; toiletries; hardware; luggage; lighting, electrical goods and bedding, most of which are chainstore and high street brands at discounts of approximately 30% to 50%. There are kitchen and furniture displays. The Cape Country Furniture range is on sale with free-standing kitchens, as well as living, bedroom and dining furniture. There are weekly deliveries and brands include famous names such as Adidas, Nike, Joe Bloggs and Brabantia, among others. Lines are continually changing. Few factory shops offer such a variety under one roof. To round off your visit, there are excellent tea rooms offering homemade foods and home baking.

THE MILL DISCOUNT DEPARTMENT STORE

BRADFORD ROAD, BATLEY, WEST YORKSHIRE WF17 5LZ, ☎ 01924 423172, FAX: 01924 446096, www.themillbatley.com, 9.30–5.30 MON–SAT, 10–4 SUN. **PERMANENT DISCOUNT OUTLET**

The Mill Discount Department Store is the largest Mill retail outlet in the UK, attracting more than one million visitors every year. Situated in a restored Victorian Mill in the heart of West Yorkshire, The Mill offers massive savings in a department-store format. This all-weather centre consists of four floors together with an external parade selling heavily discounted branded men's, women's and children's fashions, sportswear, homewares, accessories, music, vidoes, sunglasses, books, toys, perfumes, luggage, gifts, shoes, fabrics and lighting. Readmans, whose name is synonymous with unbeatable value, has opened there recently. This is the company's second major stores, offering good quality women's, men's and children's wear, lingerie, shoes, homewares and linens at remarkably low prices. Among over 300 brand names sold at The Mill are Puma, Pilot, HKA, Leeds United, Liz Claiborne, Elle, Jumper, Kasper, Amazing Jeans, Spicy, Urban Turban, Chilli Pepper, Tigi Wear, Ponden Mill, Woods of Windsor, Gleneagles Crystal, Dartington, Arthur Price, Skopos home furnishings, Jane Shilton, Book Depot, Toy Factory, Eye Zone, Famous Footwear, Hush Puppies, Lee Cooper, MX Active, Berghaus, Craghopper, Julian Graves, Fox's Biscuits, John Bull and Lion Confectionery. The complex can be reached by car, coach and train. Junction 40 of the M1 and junctions 27 and 28 of the M62 are within five and six miles of the site respectively. Batley Station on the Trans-Pennine railway is just five minutes walk from The Mill, providing easy access to Leeds and Manchester. There are more than 500 car parking spaces and coach parking is available. Amenities include children's creche, self-service licensed restaurant serving hot and cold food and drinks, Yorkshire Board Information Centre and disabled access.

THE SHUTTLE FABRIC SHOP

BAILDON BRIDGE, OTLEY ROAD, SHIPLEY, WEST YORKSHIRE BD17 7AA, ☎ 01274 587171
9–5.30 MON–SAT. **PERMANENT DISCOUNT OUTLET**

See page 420 (LOND)

TK MAXX

THE ALHAMBRA CENTRE, CHEAPSIDE, UPPER NEW STREET, BARNSLEY, SOUTH YORKSHIRE S70 1SB, ☎ 01226 770078, www.tkmaxx.com, 9–5.30 MON–SAT, 10.30–4.30 SUN.

UNITS 11 AND 12, FORSTER SQUARE RETAIL PARK, 53 VALLEY ROAD, BRADFORD, WEST YORKSHIRE BD1 4RN, ☎ 01274 738600, www.tkmaxx.com, 9.30–8 MON–FRI, 9–6 SAT, 11-5 SUN.

2ND FLOOR, THE VICTORIA SHOPPING CENTRE, HARROGATE, NORTH YORKSHIRE HG1 1AG, ☎ 01423 536636, www.tkmaxx.com, 9–5.30 MON–SAT, 11–4 SUN.

LEEDS SHOPPING PLAZA, 27 ALBION ARCADE, LEEDS, WEST YORKSHIRE LS1 5ER, ☎ 0113 246 7990, www.tkmaxx.com, 9–5.30 MON–FRI, 9–6 SAT, 11–5 SUN.

12 CAPTAIN COOK SQUARE, MIDDLESBROUGH, NORTH YORKSHIRE TS1 5UB, ☎ 01642 222220, www.tkmaxx.com, 9–5.30 MON–FRI, 9–6 SAT, 11–5 SUN.

ORCHARD SQUARE SHOPPING CENTRE, FARGATE, SHEFFIELD, SOUTH YORKSHIRE S1 2FB, ☎ 0114 275 0755, www.tkmaxx.com, 9–6 MON–SAT, 11–5 SUN.

90-93 CATHEDRAL WALK, WAKEFIELD, WEST YORKSHIRE WF1 1YD, ☎ 01924 382828, www.tkmaxx.com, 9–5.30 MON–WED, 9–7.30 THUR, 9–5.30 FRI–SAT.

UNIT 2 MONKS CROSS RETAIL PARK, MONKS CROSS DRIVE, YORK SOUTH YORKSHIRE YO32 9GX, ☎ 01904 659996, www.tkmaxx.com, 9–8 MON–FRI, 9–6 SAT, 10.30–5 SUN.
PERMANENT DISCOUNT OUTLET

See page 377 (BEDS)

TOMLINSON'S FINE FURNITURE CLUB

TOMLINSON FURNITURE GROUP, MOORSIDE, BETWEEN TOCKWITH AND COWTHORPE, NEAR YORK, NORTH YORKSHIRE YO26 7QG, ☎ 01423 358777, www.antique-furniture.co.uk, 9–4.30 SAT AND BANK HOLIDAYS, 10–4 SUN. **SECONDHAND SHOP**

One of the UK's leading wholesalers and exporters of antique and reproduction furniture and artefacts, with over 5,000 items of antique furniture under one roof. They are open to the public on Saturdays, Sundays and bank holidays only. Membership is £3 to this huge emporium selling everything from antique china services to original and reproduction nests of tables, rocking horses, dining tables, beds, sideboards and wardrobes. If you see something you like which needs restoration work, this can be quoted for on site. Tomlinson's can also make bespoke furniture to your requirements. They also now stock a range of garden furniture and accessories, from small statues to large urns, cast iron benches to picnic tables. A range of leather-upholstered goods suitable for the living room and study is also available. There is a café on site specialising in freshly-cooked organic food.

WALTONS MILL SHOP

41 TOWER STREET, HARROGATE, NORTH YORKSHIRE HG1 1HS, ☎ 01423 520980, FAX: 01423 520920, 10–5 MON–SAT. **PERMANENT DISCOUNT OUTLET**

The Harrogate shop is a high street retail outlet which sells international designer fabrics with the emphasis on high class designs with a difference. More unusually, they also stock a vast range of quality trimmings, cords, bullions, tassels, tie-backs, etc. Regular customers really do describe the shop as an Aladdin's cave, with its tapestries, handmade quilts, Egyptian cotton bedding, throws, cushions and traditional household textiles. Those who have tried the famous Knaresborough linen dishcloth vow never to use anything else again. Most of the stock is over-makes, bankrupt merchandise, bought from the US or imported from all over the world. Tucked away, you have to take the A61 Leeds road into Harrogate, and take the first right hand turn after the Prince of Wales roundabout at the long-term car park sign. The shop is 200 yards up on the left hand side.

YOU & YOURS

UNIT 9, CROWN POINT RETAIL PARK, HUNSLET ROAD, LEEDS, WEST YORKSHIRE LS10 1ET, ☎ 0113 234 1924, 10–5 MON, 10–7 TUE–FRI, 9.30–6 SAT, 11–5 SUN. **PERMANENT DISCOUNT OUTLET**

See page 384 (CHESH)

SOUTH WALES

CLASSIC CHOICE FURNISHINGS LIMITED

BRYNMENYN INDUSTRIAL ESTATE, BRYNMENYN, BRIDGEND, GLAMORGAN, SOUTH WALES CF32 9TD, ☎ 01656 725111, FAX: 01656 725404, **e-mail:** sales@classicchoice.co.uk, www.classicchoice.co.uk, SHOWROOM OPEN 10–4 SEVEN DAYS A WEEK. MAIL ORDER. **PERMANENT DISCOUNT OUTLET**

Save money on high quality furniture by purchasing direct. Choose from modern and traditional designs in suites or separates – all fully guaranteed for quality and supplied with a 21-day, full refund, no-quibble guarantee. There is an excellent choice of fabric and leather furniture in a wide choice of covers. Phone or write for free catalogue. Once a month, a selection of furniture is set out in hotels countrywide for customers to try out.

CRAZY MAC'S

PONTARDULAIS ROAD, FFORESTFACH, SWANSEA, SOUTH WALES SA5 4BA, ☎ 01792 585828, FAX: 01792 585566, **e-mail:** lss@salvage1.co.uk, www.salvage1.co.uk, 9.30–6 MON–THUR, 9.30–8 FRI, 9–6 SAT, 11–5 SUN. **PERMANENT DISCOUNT OUTLET**

An Aladdin's cave of salvaged stock for the avid bargain hunter, most of which has been the subject of insurance claims for fire or flood, salvage, bankruptcy or is simply clearance stock. Stock changes every two or three days and regular visitors have found anything from half price Kenwood Chefs, televisions and toys to furniture, kitchen items, linens and especially fantastic bargains in designer clothing. Yves Saint Laurent, Armani, Ungaro, Hugo Boss and Valentino, as well as all major high street names, are just some of the names to be found (though the labels are often cut out). Discounts range from 50% to 80%. Phone first to check stock.

DIVANI

MAERDY INDUSTRIAL ESTATE, RYHMNEY, SOUTH WALES NP22 5YD, ☎ 01685 844444, FAX: 01685 844911, MAIL ORDER ONLY. **FACTORY SHOP**

Divani manufacture and supply direct from their factory in South Wales with no retail overheads or margins to cover. Thus you pay factory prices direct from the manufacturer. Owned and managed by the same family for the past 19 years, they offer products made with hardwood frames which have all passed the relevant British standards and come with a two-year guarantee. There are six styles in a variety of fabrics and colours, including three-seaters, two-seaters, sofabeds, chairs, footstool as well as extra scatter cushions and arm caps. Orders take four weeks to manufacture and deliver and you have 21 days following delivery to return the product if you change your mind. Phone for a brochure and fabric swatches.

FABRIC WAREHOUSE

MICHAELSTON ROAD, CULVERHOUSE CROSS, CARDIFF, SOUTH WALES CF5 4SY, ☎ 02920 670236, 9.30–6 MON–FRI, 7 ON THUR, 9–6 SAT, 10.30–4.30 SUN. **PERMANENT DISCOUNT OUTLET**

See page 378 (BERKS)

GLAMOURLINE BLINDS

UNIT 2, CAMBRIAN PARK, CLYDACH VALE, TONYPANDY, SOUTH WALES CF40 2XX, ☎ 01443 433232, 9–5 MON–THUR, 9–2 FRI, CLOSED 1–1.30 DAILY, CLOSED SAT. **FACTORY SHOP**

Specialises in blinds of all types – venetian, roller, vertical, Austrian and Roman – overstocks of which they sell in the factory shop from £6. Also offer bespoke service in conservatory blinds and awnings which are sold at normal, though competitive, prices. Operates a home visit and fitting service.

MCARTHURGLEN DESIGNER OUTLET

THE DERWEN, BRIDGEND, JUNCTION 36 OF M4, SOUTH WALES CF32 9SU, ☎ 01656 665700, www.mcarthurglen.com/bridgend, 10–8 MON–FRI, 10–6 SAT, 11–5 SUN. **FACTORY SHOPPING VILLAGE**

The McArthurGlen Designer Outlet in Bridgend is Wales' premier designer outlet. Set out in a friendly village street style the outlet has over 80 stores with everything from men's, women's and children's clothing to accessories, shoes, sportswear, luggage, homewares, toys, books, and gifts. All stock is excess stock sold by the retailers themselves at 30% to 50% off typical retail prices. The outlet also has over 1,800 free parking spaces, a food court, two children's play areas and a nine-screen Odeon cinema. Stores include: Reebok, Calvin Klein, Tie Rack, Ciro Pearls, Monet, Picture Port, Ciro Citterio, Bookends, Bed & Bath, Clover House, Overland, Pepe, Famous Footwear, Nickelbys, The Suit Company, Birthdays, Toyzone, Vans, Red/Green, Whittards, Travel Accessories, Ecco, Jacques Vert, Warners, Next, Windsmoor, Pilot, Petroleum, Roman Originals, Antler, Julian Graves, The Watch Shop, Knickerbox, Wedgewood, The Garden Outlet, Claire's Accessories, Clarks, Donnay, JoKids, Ben Sherman, Smiths Signature, Spiegelau, Royal Worcester/Edinburgh Crystal, Littlewoods, Helly Hansen, Woodies, Lee Cooper, Van Heusen/Viyella/Jaeger, Ted Baker, Cotton Traders, Royal Doulton, Walker and Hall, Professional Cookware Co, Thorntons, Price's Candles, Mountain Warehouse, John Partridge, Remington, U Wear/I Wear, Nike, The Body Shop, Mexx, Suits You, Designer Rooms, Winning Line, Tog 24, Elle, Chilli Pepper/Watsons, HKA, XS, Soled Out, Timberland, Carphone Warehouse, Levi's, and The Craft Outlet.

OAKRIDGE DIRECT

MAERDY INDUSTRIAL ESTATE, RHYMNEY, SOUTH WALES NP22 5YD, ☎ 01685 844000, FAX: 01685 844911, 9–4.30 MON–FRI. MAIL ORDER. **PERMANENT DISCOUNT OUTLET**

Two and three seater sofas, suites and sofabeds delivered direct at comfortable prices. A fabric sample service is available. Phone for a copy of their brochure, which contains the full range or visit the showroom in Cardiff.

ODEON FURNITURE COMPANY

THE ASHVALE INDUSTRIAL ESTATE, TREDEGAR, GWENT, SOUTH WALES NP22 3HA, ☎ 01495 717170, www.odeonfurniture.co.uk, 10–4 mon–fri by appointment only. **FACTORY SHOP**

A manufacturer which also offers a mail order and a showroom service. They offer four, three and two-seaters, sofabeds, recliners, high back and club chairs and footstools. Four-seaters cost £499, three seaters, £399 and two seaters £349 from any one of the six models. Phone for a brochure or visit them at the factory showroom, now at Newport Road, St Mellons, Cardiff.

SOFA CONCEPTS

1 MILLERS AVENUE, BRYNMENYN, BRIDGEND, SOUTH WALES CF32 9TD, ☎ 01656 726148, **e-mail:** sales@sofaconcepts, www.sofaconcepts.co.uk, 10–4 SEVEN DAYS A WEEK (SHOWROOM). **PERMANENT DISCOUNT OUTLET**

Save money by purchasing high quality furniture direct. A range of contemporary smaller furniture, sofas, chairs and sofa beds, for the modern home in fabric and leather. Phone for a free catalogue or visit the website.

SOFA WORKSHOP DIRECT

COED CAE LANE, PONTYCLUN, SOUTH WALES CF72 9DX, ☎ 01443 238699, FAX: 01443 237752, www.sofaworkshopdirect.co.uk, 9–8 mon–fri, 9–5 SAT, SUN. MAIL ORDER. **FACTORY SHOP**

Based in Wales, Sofa Workshop Direct have been making furniture for 21 years and supplying direct to the customer at factory prices. There are 12 ranges to choose from in a variety of fabrics, both loose cover and fixed, with a choice of large or small sofa, sofabed, chair or footstool. Fabric options range from brushed cotton twill and soft chenille to a striking patterned chenille and a chunky plain cotton with a textured floral pattern. Chairs cost from £249 to £299 and large sofas (up to 220cms long) from £379 to £499. Phone for a brochure or visit the website. They also stock the modern, contemporary Viva range of sofas, chairs and corner sofas. The range has its own website at www.vivasofa.co.uk, or you can phone the number above to request a mail order catalogue. There are 21 showrooms around the country. Phone the number above for details of your nearest showroom.

THE FACTORY SHOP

SNOWDROP LANE, HAVERFORDWEST, SOUTH WALES SA61 1ET, ☎ 01437 766000, 9–5.30 MON–SAT, 10.30–4.30 SUN. **FACTORY SHOP**

See page 383 (CHESH)

TK MAXX

UNIT 11, QUEENS WEST CENTRE, QUEEN STREET, CARDIFF, SOUTH WALES CF10 2AQ, ☎ 029 2034 1290, www.tkmaxx.com, 9–5.30 MON–WED, 9–7 THUR, 9–6 FRI–SAT, 11–5 SUN.

UNIT 25, GREYFRIARS SHOPPING CENTRE, CARMARTHEN, SOUTH WALES SA31 3BN, ☎ 01267 220934, www.tkmaxx.com, 9–5.30 MON–TUE, 9–6 WED– SAT, 9–8 THUR, 10–4 SUN.

2-3 OXFORD STREET, SWANSEA, SOUTH WALES SA1 3AE, ☎ 01792 642055, www.tkmaxx.com, 9–5.30 MON–THUR, 9– 6 FRI–SAT, 11–5 SUN. **PERMANENT DISCOUNT OUTLET**

See page 377 (BEDS)

WILKINSON STORES

10–13 CARDIFF STREET, ABERDARE, MID-GLAMORGAN, SOUTH WALES CF44 7DP, ☎ 01685 870393, www.wilko.co.uk, 9–5.30 MON–THUR, 9–6 FRI, SAT, 10–4 SUN. MAIL ORDER.

CIBI WALK SHOPPING CENTRE, FOGMORE STREET, ABERGAVENNY SOUTH WALES NP7 5AJ, ☎ 01685 870393, www.wilko.co.uk, 8.30–5.30 MON–THUR, 8.30–6 FRI, SAT, 10–4 SUN. MAIL ORDER. **PERMANENT DISCOUNT OUTLET**

See page 383 (CHESH)

NORTH WALES

ABAKHAN FABRICS

LLANERCH-Y-MOR, COAST ROAD, MOSTYN, FLINTSHIRE, NORTH WALES CH8 9DX, ☎ 01745 562100, FAX: 01745 562101, **e-mail:** enquiries@abakhan-fabrics.co.uk, 9–5.15 MON–SAT, 8 ON THUR, 10.30–4.30 SUN. **FACTORY SHOP**

See page 381 (CHESH)

DEESIDE FURNITURE LTD

UNIT 47 GREENFIELD BUSINESS PARK, BAGILLT ROAD, HOLYWELL, FLINTSHIRE, NORTH WALES CH8 7FF, ☎ 01352 711196, 7.30–4.30 TUE–THUR, 7.30–12.30 FRI, 9–2 SAT, 10–2 SUN. **PERMANENT DISCOUNT OUTLET**

Large furniture warehouse selling sofas, curtains and soft furnishings at factory direct prices. Many of the sofas are made for top high street stores.

SIMON BOYD

ISLAND GREEN SHOPPING CENTRE, WREXHAM, CLWYD, NORTH WALES LL13 7NW, ☎ 01978 313628, **e-mail:** simonboyd@freewire.net, 9.30–5.30 MON–SAT, 10–4 SUN. **PERMANENT DISCOUNT OUTLET**

See page 382 (CHESH)

THE BANKRUPT SHOP LTD

COAST ROAD, GREENFIELD, NORTH WALES CH8 9DN, ☎ 01352 714484, 9.30–5.30 MON–SAT, 10.30–4.30 SUN. **PERMANENT DISCOUNT OUTLET**

See page 383 (CHESH)

THE FACTORY SHOP LTD

BRUNSWICK ROAD, BUCKLEY, CLYWD, NORTH WALES CH7 2EF, ☎ 01555 759017, FAX: 01555 759018, 9.30–5.30 MON–SAT, 10.30–4.30 SUN. **FACTORY SHOP**

See page 383 (CHESH)

THE TWEEDMILL FACTORY OUTLETS

LLANNERCH PARK, ST ASAPH, DENBIGHSHIRE, (OFF A55), NORTH WALES LL17 0UY, ☎ 01745 730072, FAX: 01745 731008, **e-mail:** enquiries@tweedmill.co.uk, www.tweedmill.co.uk, 9.30–6 MON–SAT, 8 ON THUR, 11–5 SUN. **FACTORY SHOP**

Stocks a wide range of clothes for both men and women, luggage, giftware, handbags and home accessories with savings of up to 50% off normal high street prices. Selling directly to the public from the manufacturers, there are always at least 50,000 garments in stock and 5,000 pairs of shoes as well as 100,000 homeware items, all of which are perfects. Labels on sale include Regatta, Klass, Roman, Wolsey, French Connection, Easy Jeans, Glenmuir, James Barry, Double Two, Lotus, Salisbury's and Farah for clothes and shoes; Coloroll, Ponden Mill, Price's Candles, Cloverleaf and Dartington Crystal for homewares. Everything is labelled with the original retail price, so you can see the discounts of up to 50%.

TREFRIW WOOLLEN MILLS LTD

TREFRIW, CONWAY COUNTY, NORTH WALES LL27 0NQ, ☎ 01492 640462, FAX: 01492 641821, www.trefriw-woollen-mills.co.uk, 9.30–5.30 MON–FRI, 10–5 SAT. **FACTORY SHOP**

Sells products manufactured on the premises: there are traditional Welsh 'tapestry' bedspreads from £82, travel rugs from £26, tweed fabrics from £15.20 a metre, tweed sports jackets, ruanas, and knitting wool at £2.95 per 100g. There is also a tearoom selling light refreshments.

SOUTHERN SCOTLAND

J & W CARPETS

24 BACK MAIN STREET, AYR, SCOTLAND KA8 8BZ, ☎ 01292 265539, FAX: 01292 265539, 9–8 MON–FRI, 9–5.30 SAT, 12–5 SUN. **PERMANENT DISCOUNT OUTLET**

Sells carpets from polyproplene and wool twists to Axminsters at discounts of up to 50%. They also sell Chinese rugs from £20 to £175, representing discounts of 20% to 30% on the high street. Carpets range from £1.50 to £20 a square yard. Carpet fitting accessories are also supplied at discounted prices.

THE FACTORY SHOP LTD

DRAKEMYRE, DALRY, AYRSHIRE, SCOTLAND KA24 5JD, ☎ 01294 832791, 10–5 MON–SAT, 11–5 SUN.

54–60 HIGH STREET, ANNAN, DUMFRIES SCOTLAND DG12 6AJ, ☎ 01461 207687, 9–5 MON–SAT, 10.30–4.30 SUN. **FACTORY SHOP**

See page 383 (CHESH)

CENTRAL SCOTLAND

BETHANY

60 HAMILTON PLACE, STOCKBRIDGE, EDINBURGH, SCOTLAND EH3 9ZA, ☎ 0131 220 5656, OPEN 10–5 MON–SAT. **SECONDHAND SHOP**

Charity shop for the Bethany Christian Trust which one reader has recommended as selling excellent condition and restored antique furniture, paintings, books, games and clothes.

FABRIC WAREHOUSE

SPRINGBANK INDUSTRIAL ESTATE, LAMONT DRIVE, IRVINE, SCOTLAND KA12 8HD, ☎ 01294 278040, 9.30–5.30 MON -SAT, 11–5 SUN. **PERMANENT DISCOUNT OUTLET**

UNIT 9, SPRINGKERSE RETAIL PARK, STIRLING, SCOTLAND FX7 7TL, ☎ 01786 449104, 9–5.30 MON -SAT, 11–5 SUN. **PERMANENT DISCOUNT OUTLET**

See page 378 (BERKS)

J & W CARPETS

WAREHOUSE 1, LOCH STREET, COATBRIDGE SCOTLAND ML5 3RT, ☎ 01236 440090, FAX: 01236 440090, 9–8 MON–FRI, 9–5.30 SAT, 12–5 SUN.

12 LITHGOW PLACE, EAST KILBRIDE, SCOTLAND G74 1PW, ☎ 01355 570562, FAX: 01355 570562, 9–8 MON–FRI, 9–5.30 SAT, 12–5 SUN.

WAREHOUSE 1, CARRON ROAD, FALKIRK, SCOTLAND FK2 7RR, ☎ 01324 610210, 9–8 MON–FRI, 9–5.30 SAT, 12–5 SUN.

32 POSSIL ROAD, GLASGOW SCOTLAND G4 9SR, ☎ 0141 333 1212, FAX: 0141 333 1212, 9–8 MON–FRI, 9–5.30 SAT, 12–5 SUN.

9 PORTLAND ROAD, IRVINE, SCOTLAND KA12 8HY, ☎ 01294 274724, FAX: 01294 274724, 9–8 MON–FRI, 9–5.30 SAT, 12–5 SUN.

UNIT 1, FORGE INDUSTRIAL ESTATE, BONNYTON ROAD, KILMARNOCK SCOTLAND KA1 2QP, ☎ 01563 535397, FAX: 01563 535397, 9–8 MON–FRI, 9–5.30 SAT, 12–5 SUN.

3 RUTHERGLEN ROAD, RUTHERGLEN SCOTLAND G73 1SX, ☎ 0141 647 9442, FAX: 0141 647 9442, 9–8 MON–FRI, 9–5.30 SAT, 12–5 SUN. **PERMANENT DISCOUNT OUTLET**

See page 454 (S. SCOT)

JOHN BAILLIE CARPETS

22 GREENHILL ROAD, PAISLEY, SCOTLAND PA3 1RN, ☎ 0141 848 5502, www.bcarpets.com, 9–8 MON–FRI, 9–5.30 SAT, 11–5 SUN. **PERMANENT DISCOUNT OUTLET**

Sells carpets from polyproplene and wool twists to Axminsters at discounts of up to 50%. Carpets range from £1.50 a square yard to £20. Hardwood flooring also available at discounts of up to 20%.Vinyls start from £4 a square yard, underlay £1.75 to £3.63 per square yard.

LOCH LOMOND FACTORY OUTLETS

MAIN STREET, ALEXANDRIA, JUNCTION 17 OF M8 THEN A82, LOCH LOMOND, SCOTLAND G83 0UG, ☎ 01389 710077 , FAX: 01389 605500 INFORMATION LINE., ☎ 01389 607259, **e-mail:** info@lochlomondoutlets.co.uk, www.lochlomondoutletcentre.co.uk, 9.30–5.30 SEVEN DAYS A WEEK. **FACTORY SHOPPING VILLAGE**

Just off the A82, the main route between Glasgow and the West Highlands and Islands, and only one mile from Loch Lomond, this factory outlet centre combines history, heritage, adventure and shopping under one roof. Shops include Bags Etc selling luggage items; Book Depot, Designer Room (Klass, DKNY, Elle), Global Emporium for gifts, Jean Scene for branded denim wear; Julian Graves foods and nut mixes; Leading Labels, Nicklebys, Pavers Shoes, Ponden Mill for bed-linen and bathroom ware; Ramseys womenswear; Room offering homes accessories and furniture; Stuart Crystal; Sportz selling sportswear from Adidas, Nike, etc; Tog 24 for outdoor wear; Trespass; Card & Party Place (greetings cards and posters). There is also Ceramic Experience (a unique opportunity to decorate your own ceramics and pottery merchandise plus a children's soft play area), a Motoring Heritage Centre telling the history of the Scottish motor car industry with a collection of vintage cars, and The Gallery Cafe selling meals, snacks and sandwiches.

REJECTS

123 ST CLAIR STREET, KIRKCALDY, FIFE, SCOTLAND KY1 2BS, ☎ 01592 655955, FAX: 01592 655722, **e-mail:** info@rejectsonline.com, 9–5.30 MON–SAT, 12.30–4.30 SUN. **PERMANENT DISCOUNT OUTLET**

Rejects Department Store sells curtain and dress fabric, china, pottery, carpets, silk flower, glassware, home decoration equipment and materials, lighting, basketware, carpet and flooring and has a cookshop. The shop is 100,000 square feet and claims to be the best value department store in the UK, although it isn't a discount store as such. For example, the curtain shop is larger than Harrods curtain department with thousands of rolls of material. There is a particularly large selection of pottery and china, bedding, cushions, pictures, mirrors, wallpaper, paint, hardware and garden tools. The shop also has a self-service café. Free parking for 300 cars at the rear of the building.

SUNRITE BLINDS FACTORY SHOP

BLACKCHAPEL ROAD, NEWCRAIGHALL, EDINBURGH, SCOTLAND EH15 3HL, ☎ 0131 669 2345, 9–5 MON–FRI, 9.30–1 SAT BUT PHONE FIRST. **FACTORY SHOP**

Blinds of all type: venetian, roller, vertical, pleated (suitable for conservatory roofs) and Roman. Also blind fabric and vertical headrow tracks.

THE CLOTH SHOP

169 BONNINGTON ROAD, EDINBURGH, SCOTLAND EH6 5BQ, ☎ 0131 554 7733, 9.30–5 MON–SAT, 8 ON THUR, 11–4 SUN. **PERMANENT DISCOUNT OUTLET**

Large warehouse chain, now with 40 outlets countrywide, selling upholstery fabric, cushions, ready-made curtains and net curtains. Most of the merchandise is made up of clearance material from mills and manufacturers. Some of the outlets also stock a full range of bed linen, towels and bathroom accessories while others sells tracks, poles, blinds of all kinds, brassware, crafts and occasional furniture.

THE COTTON PRINT FACTORY SHOP

58 ADMIRAL STREET, GLASGOW, SCOTLAND G41 1HU, ☎ 0141 420 1855, 9–5.30 MON–SAT, 10–5 SUN. **FACTORY SHOP**

Three floors housing the largest selection of top quality curtain fabric at discount prices in Scotland as well as wallpaper and borders. There are up to 6,000 rolls of curtaining fabric, heading tapes, tie-backs, curtain pulls, cushion pads, track fabrics. They claim no one in Scotland can beat their prices. The top floor has clearance lines of discontinued stocks, end of rolls and remnants, but all are first quality with no seconds. Fabrics cost from 99p to £20 a metre.

THE FACTORY SHOP LTD

56 CHAPEL STREET, CARLUKE, SOUTH LANARKSHIRE SCOTLAND ML8 4BA, ☎ 01555 759017, FAX: 01555 759018, 9–5 MON–FRI, 9–5.30 SAT, 10–5 SUN.

BURNSIDE MILL, CUPAR, FIFE SCOTLAND KY15 4DQ, ☎ 01334 650661, FAX: 01334 656772, 9.30–5.30 MON–SAT, 10–5 SUN. **FACTORY SHOP**

See page 383 (CHESH)

TK MAXX EDINBURGH

UNIT 10 MEADOW BANK RETAIL PARK, EDINBURGH SCOTLAND EH7 5TS, ☎ 0131 661 6611, www.tkmaxx.com, 10–8 MON–FRI, 9–6 SAT, 11–5 SUN.

UNIT C1261, CALLENDER SQUARE SHOPPING CENTRE, HIGH STREET, FALKIRK SCOTLAND FK1 1UU, ☎ 01324 619881, www.tkmaxx.com, 9–5.30 MON–WED, 7.30 ON THUR, 9–6 FRI–SAT, 12–5 SUN.

THE SAUCHIEHALL CENTRE, GLASGOW, SCOTLAND G2 3ER, ☎ 0141 331 0411, www.tkmaxx.com, 9–5.30 MON–FRI, 7 ON THUR, 9–6 SAT, 12–5 SUN.

UNIT 5, ST ENOCHS CENTRE, 55 ST ENOCH S SQUARE, GLASGOW, SCOTLAND G1 4BW, ☎ 0141 221 9393, www.tkmaxx.com, 9–6 MON–FRI, 8 ON THUR, 9.30–6 SAT, 11–5 SUN.

GLENCAIRN RETAIL PARK, KILMARNOCK, SCOTLAND, ☎ 01563 532486, www.tkmaxx.com, PHONE FOR DETAILS.

UNIT 25-26 MERCAT CENTRE, KIRKCALDY, FIFE SCOTLAND KY1 1N1, FAX: 01592 644488, www.tkmaxx.com, 9–5.30 MON– SAT, 11–5 SUN.

UNIT 5, ALMONDVALE WEST RETAIL PARK, ALMONDVALE ROAD, LIVINGSTON SCOTLAND EH54 6QX, ☎ 01506 462060, www.tkmaxx.com, 10–8 MON–FRI, 9–6 SAT, 11–5 SUN.

THE PHOENIX RETAIL PARK, LINWOOD ROAD, PAISLEY, SCOTLAND, ☎ 0141 849 6796, www.tkmaxx.com, PHONE FOR DETAILS. **PERMANENT DISCOUNT OUTLET**

See page 377 (BEDS)

SCOTTISH HIGHLANDS & ISLANDS

OUT LINES

TRINITY GASK, AUCHTERARDER, PERTHSHIRE, SCOTLAND PH3 1LG, ☎ 01764 683733, FAX: 01764 683462, **e-mail:** info@outlines.co.uk, www.northwooddesign.com, 9.30–5 MON–FRI, 9–1 SAT. **PERMANENT DISCOUNT OUTLET**

Out Lines is an Aladdins cave of designer furnishing fabrics at bargain prices. Suppliers include Designers Guild, Osborne & Little, Nina Campbell, Zofany, Bakers, Monkwell and many others.

Wallpapers, paint and furnishing accessories are also available, as well as a soft furnishing make-up service. Many products are suitable for commercial interiors and private houses. All products can be delivered in the UK by carrier. Phone for further details. For information of their professional interior design service, which is available throughout the UK, send full details of your requirements to Northwood Design and Interiors Ltd at the same address.

TK MAXX

KITTY BREWSTER RETAIL PARK, BEDFORD ROAD, ABERDEEN, SCOTLAND, ☎ 01224 497810, www.tkmaxx.com, PHONE FOR DETAILS.

WELLGATE SHOPPING CENTRE, DUNDEE SCOTLAND DD1 2DB, ☎ 01382 322288, www.tkmaxx.com,

ST CATHERINE'S RETAIL PARK, PERTH, SCOTLAND, ☎ 01738 636751, www.tkmaxx.com, PHONE FOR DETAILS. 9–5.30 MON–WED, FRI, SAT, 9–8 THUR, 12–5 SUN.

UNIT 2, ACADEMY RETAIL PARK, STROTHERS LANE, INVERNESS, SCOTLAND, ☎ 01463 729729, www.tkmaxx.com, 9–5.30 MON–FRI, 7 ON THUR, 9–6 SAT. **PERMANENT DISCOUNT OUTLET**

See page 377 (BEDS)

NORTHERN IRELAND

THE LIGHTHOUSE COLLECTION

10 MAIN STREET, HILLSBOROUGH, COUNTY DOWN BT26 6AE, ☎ 02892 688188, www.lighthousecollection.com, 10–5 MON–SAT. MAIL ORDER. **PERMANENT DISCOUNT OUTLET**
The Lighthouse Collection of teak furniture is made from teak exclusively grown on the plantations of East Java and not in the tropical forest. These plantations are under the control of the Indonesian Government and are strictly managed by the Forest Commission. The Lighthouse Collection currently manufactures teak garden furniture. They encourage price comparisons with other suppliers of teak furniture as they claim to be by far the best value for money. The garden furniture is available by mail order: phone for a catalogue and price list.

TK MAXX

UNIT 70, FIRST FLOOR, CASTLE COURT SHOPPING CENTRE, ROYAL AVENUE, BELFAST, NORTHERN IRELAND BT1 1DD, ☎ 028 9033 1151, www.tkmaxx.com, 9–6 MON–SAT, 9 ON THUR, 1–6 SUN.

1 MILL ROAD, SHORE ROAD, NEWTON ABBEY, BELFAST, NORTHERN IRELAND, www.tkmaxx.com, VISIT WEBSITE FOR DETAILS.

UNIT 31, RUSHMERE SHOPPING CENTRE, CRAIGAVON, NORTHERN IRELAND BT64 1AA, ☎ 028 3834 4544, www.tkmaxx.com, 9–5.30 MON–TUE, 9–9 WED–FRI, 9–6 SAT, 1–6 SUN.

MERCHANTS QUAY, NEWRY, NORTHERN IRELAND, ☎ 028 3025 2465, www.tkmaxx.com, PHONE FOR DETAILS. **PERMANENT DISCOUNT OUTLET**

See page 377 (BEDS)

Household

BEDFORDSHIRE

DUNELM MILL SHOP

LUTON ROAD, DUNSTABLE, BEDFORDSHIRE LU5 4JN, ☎ 01582 606090, FAX: 01582 606690, www.dunelm-mill.co.uk, 9–6 MON–SAT, 8 ON THUR, FRI, 10–4 SUN. **PERMANENT DISCOUNT OUTLET**

Part of a chain of shops selling brand-name and chainstore curtains, masses of bedlinen, towels, wickerware, pictures and frames, all at great value for money. Fabric shop in store. Free parking.

MATALAN

RACE MEADOWS WAY, AMPTHILL ROAD, BEDFORD, BEDFORDSHIRE MK42 7AZ, ☎ 01234 365077, FAX: 01234 360671, www.matalan.co.uk, 10–8 MON–FRI, 9–6 SAT, 11–5 SUN.

UNIT 2, LONDON ROAD INDUSTRIAL ESTATE, BIGGLESWADE BEDFORDSHIRE SG18 8PW, ☎ 01767 310810, FAX: 01767 601876, www.matalan.co.uk, 10–8 MON–FRI, 9–6 SAT, 11–5 SUN. **PERMANENT DISCOUNT OUTLET**

Matalan is a fashion and homewares value retailer giving customers what they claim to be unbeatable value for money with huge savings on a wide range of products including high quality fashionable clothing for men, women and children at up to 50% off high street prices. Matalan is situated out of town and stores are open seven days a week all year round. This is one of 145 stores nationwide. The Matalan website contains maps of how to get to any of the stores.

NO FRILLS DIY STORE

WINGATE ROAD, LUTON, BEDFORDSHIRE LU4 8PX, ☎ 01582 585 509, FAX: 01582 562780, 9–8 MON–SAT, 10–4 SUN. **PERMANENT DISCOUNT OUTLET**

Not a discount operator as such but a great place for bargains. Now part of the Focus DIY Group, they stock everything you would find in B&Q or Homebase but at cheaper prices. Paints, tiles, bathroom equipment, patio furniture, toiletries, sheds, lighting, crockery, bedding, pans, kitchen units, barbecues in season.

QD STORES

22–30 GREYFRIARS, BEDFORD, BEDFORDSHIRE MK40 1HP, ☎ 01234 345204, 9–5.30 MON–SAT. **PERMANENT DISCOUNT OUTLET**

Discount shop selling a mixture of clothes, household textiles, ceramics, kitchenware, knitting wool, garden tools, curtains, toys, stationery, dusters, Christmas decorations, masking tape, lingerie and a host of other items. Stock changes regularly because the low prices mean a quick turnover. Some items are seconds or end of season stock from the major chain stores.

TK MAXX

UNIT 14, THE HOWARD CENTRE, BEDFORD, BEDFORDSHIRE MK40 1UH, ☎ 01234 270787, www.tkmaxx.com, 9–5.30 MON–FRI, 8.30–6 SAT, 10–4 SUN. **PERMANENT DISCOUNT OUTLET**

TK Maxx is a unique shopping experience, based on an American concept, offering an ever-changing range of famous names, high street brands and designer labels at up to 60% off normal retail prices. The majority of the stock is current season which makes the savings even more amazing. With 50,000 items in store and 10,000 new pieces arriving each week there is always something fresh and exciting to be found in every department: womenswear, menswear, childrenswear, sports and leisurewear, shoes, accessories and homewares. The stores are spacious and functional, with wide aisles enabling easy disabled and pushchair access. There are individual changing rooms, the stores accept all major credit and debit cards, and there is a return and refund policy. There are now over 120 easily accessible stores, often situated in main shopping centres or retail parks. All stores are open seven days a week and late in the evenings, though times vary from store to store. For details of your nearest store and opening hours, visit the website at www.tkmaxx.com.

BERKSHIRE

MATALAN

ROSE KILN LANE, READING, BERKSHIRE RG2 0SN, ☎ 0118 939 1958, FAX: 0118 939 4605, www.matalan.co.uk, 10–8 MON–FRI, 9–6 SAT, 11–5 SUN.

217A BATH ROAD, SLOUGH, BERKSHIRE SL1 4AA, ☎ 01753 487900, FAX: 01753 523353, www.matalan.co.uk, 10–8 MON–FRI, 9–6 SAT, 11–5 SUN. **PERMANENT DISCOUNT OUTLET**

See page 458 (BEDS)

REJECT CHINA SHOPS

1 CASTLE HILL, WINDSOR, BERKSHIRE SL4 1PD, ☎ 01753 850870, FAX: 01753 855272, www.tableware.uk.com, 9–5.30 MON–SAT, 11–5 SUN. **PERMANENT DISCOUNT OUTLET**

Sells china, crystal and gifts of overstocks and imperfect lines from mainly well-known makes. Most of the stock is first quality, but often sold at discounted prices and includes Portmeirion, Wedgwood, Crown Derby and Royal Doulton. Also seconds dinner sets from Spode, Royal Doulton, Aynsley, and Royal Worcester at up to 50% off. Other manufacturers available.

SOUL HOME LIMITED

21 LABURNHAM ROAD, MAIDENHEAD, BERKSHIRE SL6 4DB, ☎ 01628 418 988, FAX: 01628 418 977, **e-mail:** enquiries@soulhomeuk.com, www.soulhomeuk.com, 9–5.30 MON–FRI. MAIL ORDER. **PERMANENT DISCOUNT OUTLET**

The vision behind Soul Home, a contemporary gift and soft-furnishing mail order company, was to translate the fabrics, textures and detail of high fashion into stylish yet affordable home furnishings. Designed in the UK, these beautiful products are made exclusively by some of the world's best manufacturers – this is Contran chic at a fraction of the price. Gifts range from exquisite silver-grey tissue faille notebooks to quilted satin bags and embroidered notebooks. In the bedroom, choose from the clean simplicity of the Kashmir percale bedlinen, or the beautiful sheer organdy Fern collection. Bring the Fern collection into your dining room with delicate table mats, napkins and tiny coasters. Or spice up the table with the burnt orange, rich burgundy and cool chartreuse of their Sari hand-woven tableware. And dress your windows stylishly but inexpensively with distinctively embroidered tab-top organdy curtains. Secure online shopping, or order by post.

TK MAXX

6 THE MALL, THE KENNETT CENTRE, NEWBURY, BERKSHIRE RG14 5EN, ☎ 01635 522323, www.tkmaxx.com, 9–5.30 MON–FRI, 7 ON THUR, 9–6 SAT, 11–5 SUN.

UNIT A39, BROAD STREET MALL, BROAD STREET, READING, BERKSHIRE RG1 7QE, ☎ 0118 951 1117, www.tkmaxx.com, 9–5.30 MON–FRI, 9–6 SAT, 11–5 SUN.

UNIT 30-40, OBSERVATORY CENTRE, HIGH STREET, SLOUGH, BERKSHIRE SL1 1LL, ☎ 01753 572550, www.tkmaxx.com, 9–5.30 MON–FRI, 8 ON THUR, 9–6 SAT, 11–5 SUN. **PERMANENT DISCOUNT OUTLET**

See page 458 (BEDS)

BRISTOL

MATALAN

ALDERMOOR WAY, LONGWELL GREEN, BRISTOL BS15 7AD, ☎ 0117 935 2828, FAX: 0117 935 3035, www.matalan.co.uk, 10–8 MON–FRI, 9–6 SAT, 11–5 SUN.

ABBEY RETAIL PARK, STATION ROAD, FILTON, BRISTOL BS2 7JW, ☎ 0117 974 8000, FAX: 0117 969 5904, www.matalan.co.uk, 10–8 MON–FRI, 9–6 SAT, 11–5 SUN. **PERMANENT DISCOUNT OUTLET**

See page 458 (BEDS)

THE CAPE

10 MERCHANT STREET, BROADMEAD, BRISTOL BS1 3ET, ☎ 0117 929 7919, FAX: 0117 929 7460, **e-mail:** sc@thefactory-shop.co.uk, www.thecape.co.uk, 9–5.30 MON–FRI, 9–6 SAT, 11–5 SUN. **FACTORY SHOP**

High quality, high density pine furniture made in South Africa from trees grown in managed forests, is sold at factory direct prices with home delivery throughout the UK. The range includes beds, wardrobes, blanket boxes, chests of drawers, tallboys, dressing tables, cheval mirrors, headboards, mattresses, a kitchen range, dining room tables, Welsh dressers, hi-fi units, bookcases. Also on sale in this shop is a range of African accessories and artefacts from Zimbabwe encompassing mirrors, prints, serpentine (stone) ornaments, recycled stationery, handmade wirework, candles and other ethnic and traditional gifts. Colour brochure and price list available on 01535 650940.

TK MAXX

THE GALLERIES CENTRE, 31-32 CASTLE GALLERY, BROADMEAD, BRISTOL BS1 3XE, ☎ 0117 930 4404, www.tkmaxx.com, 9–5.30 MON–SAT, 7 ON THUR, 11–5 SUN. **PERMANENT DISCOUNT OUTLET**

See page 458 (BEDS)

BUCKINGHAMSHIRE

MATALAN

103 WATLING STREET, BLETCHLEY, MILTON KEYNES, BUCKINGHAMSHIRE MK1 1HS, ☎ 01908 625400, FAX: 01908 641935, www.matalan.co.uk, 10–8 MON–FRI, 9–6 SAT, 11–4 SUN. **PERMANENT DISCOUNT OUTLET**

See page 458 (BEDS)

QD STORES

HAMPDEN HOUSE, HIGH STREET AYLESBURY, BUCKINGHAMSHIRE HP20 1RE, ☎ 01296 428231, 9–5.30 MON–SAT. **PERMANENT DISCOUNT OUTLET**

See page 458 (BEDS)

SILVER EDITIONS

UNITEK HOUSE, CHURCHFIELD ROAD, CHALFONT ST PETER, BUCKINGHAMSHIRE SL9 9EW, ☎ 01753 888810, FAX: 01753 888830, **e-mail:** sales@silver-editions.co.uk, www.collection925.co.uk, SHOWROOM OPEN 9–5 MON–FRI. MAIL ORDER. **FACTORY SHOP**

Specialises in selling fine English sterling silver and silver-plated gifts and cutlery at wholesale prices, often half the sum for the same items in high street shops. Their catalogue features an exceptionally wide range of gifts and cutlery at prices from £2.50 to several thousand pounds. Canteens of cutlery, photo frames, desk sets, serving pieces, children's christening gifts and a new range of sterling silver jewellery are just a few of the categories on offer. The catalogue also carries the complete range of Hagerty silver cleaning products. Write to the address above for a copy of the catalogue. Or visit their new showroom/factory shop for other special offers available throughout the year.

TK MAXX

BEACON RETAIL PARK, WATLING STREET, BLETCHLEY BUCKINGHAMSHIRE MK1 1BN, ☎ 01908 644406, www.tkmaxx.com, 10–8 MON–FRI, 9–6 SAT, 11–5 SUN. **PERMANENT DISCOUNT OUTLET**

See page 458 (BEDS)

CAMBRIDGESHIRE

CATALOGUE BARGAIN SHOP

51 WEST STREET, WISBECH, CAMBRIDGESHIRE PE13 2LY, ☎ 01945 584327, www.bargaincrazy.com, 9–4.30 MON–SAT, 10–4 SUN. **PERMANENT DISCOUNT OUTLET**

Catalogue Bargain Shop is a growing national chain of stores which obtains the majority of its goods from mail order giants Great Universal and Kays, and offers a range of clothing for all the family, a wide selection of shoes, bed linen, household goods, electrical equipment and hundreds of other catalogue items at very competitive prices. The merchandise consists of ends of ranges and previous season's stock for which there is no longer space when the catalogues change.

CHOICE DISCOUNT STORES LIMITED

UNITS 5–6 VIKING WAY, BARHILL, CAMBRIDGESHIRE CB3 8EL, 10–6 MON–WED, 10–7 THUR, FRI, 9–6 SAT, 11–5 SUN. **PERMANENT DISCOUNT OUTLET**

Surplus stock including women's, men's and children's fashions from Next plc, Next Directory, other high street fashion houses, Next Interiors and footwear. You can save up to 50% off normal retail prices for first quality; up to two thirds for seconds. There are special sales each January and September. Easy access for wheelchairs and pushchairs.

DUNELM MILL SHOP

UNIT 7, STUKELEY MEADOWS TRADING ESTATE, STUKELEY ROAD, HUNTINGDON, CAMBRIDGESHIRE PE18 6EB, ☎ 01480 417807, FAX: 01480 459222, www.dunelm-mill.co.uk, 9–6 MON–SAT, 8 ON THUR, FRI, 10–4 SUN.

35 WESTGATE, PETERBOROUGH, CAMBRIDGESHIRE PE1 1PZ, ☎ 01733 349848, FAX: 01733 557646, www.dunelm-mill.co.uk, 9–5.30 MON–SAT, 8 ON THUR. **PERMANENT DISCOUNT OUTLET**

See page 458 (BEDS)

MATALAN

EAST STATION ROAD, PETERBOROUGH, CAMBRIDGESHIRE PE2 8AA, ☎ 01733 341229, FAX: 01733 341246, www.matalan.co.uk, 10–8 MON–FRI, 9–6 SAT, 11–5 SUN. **PERMANENT DISCOUNT OUTLET**

See page 458 (BEDS)

QD STORES

ORTON CENTRE, PETERBOROUGH, CAMBRIDGESHIRE PE2 0UD, ☎ 01733 237311, 9–5.30 MON–SAT, 10–4 SUN.

62 BURLEIGH STREET, CAMBRIDGE, CAMBRIDGESHIRE CB1 1DG, ☎ 01223 323174, 9–5.30 MON–SAT, 10–4 SUN.

16–17 MARKET PLACE, WISBECH, CAMBRIDGESHIRE PE13 1DY, ☎ 01945 466756, 9–5.30 MON–SAT. **PERMANENT DISCOUNT OUTLET**

See page 458 (BEDS)

STAGE 2

SAVILLE ROAD, PETERBOROUGH, CAMBRIDGESHIRE PE3 7RP, ☎ 01733 263308, 10–8 MON–FRI, 9–6 SAT, 10–4 SUN, BANK HOLIDAYS. **PERMANENT DISCOUNT OUTLET**

Sells surplus stock from both Grattan and Freemans catalogues. Womenswear, childrenswear, menswear and household items, at up to 50% off catalogue prices. Includes a wide range of brands from both designer and high street on a regularly changing basis. Electrical goods are sold at discounts of up to 30% off catalogue prices, and include many big-name brands. There is a 14-day refund policy.

CHANNEL ISLANDS

STONELAKE LTD

5 SMITH STREET, ST PETER PORT, GUERNSEY, CHANNEL ISLANDS GY1 2JN, ☎ 01481 720053, FAX: 01481 713808, **e-mail:** hersch@guernsey.net, 9–5.15 MON–SAT. MAIL ORDER AVAILABLE. **PERMANENT DISCOUNT OUTLET**

Family-run business which has operated in Guernsey for more than 80 years serving both locals and tourists alike. In recent years, they have added a mail order service. They have two shops – one a pharmacy and perfumery, the other selling perfume and cosmetics – and specialise in fragrance bargains from UK and French companies, in aftershaves, cosmetics, perfumes, toilet waters, soaps, and talcs. Being duty-free, and with no VAT, they have competitive prices on standard ranges and by buying excess stocks and ends of lines, they have a large list of extra special offers including ranges no longer sold in the UK. Brand names stocked include Yves Saint Laurent, Paloma Picasso, Cacharel, Boss, Georgio, Paco Rabanne, Gucci, Safari, Elizabeth Arden, Givenchy, Oscar de la Renta, Nina Ricci, Rochas, Davidoff, Ghost, Armani, Royal Secret, Apple Blossom and lots of other old favourites. Free postage and packaging on orders of over £40.

CHESHIRE

BED & BATH WORKS

MCARTHURGLEN DESIGNER OUTLET CHESHIRE OAKS, KINSEY ROAD, NEAR ELLESMERE PORT, JUNCTION 10 OF M53, CHESHIRE CH65 9JJ, ☎ 0151 356 7377, **e-mail:** hello@bedandbathworks.co.uk, www.bedandbathworks.co.uk, 10–8 MON–FRI, 9–6 SAT, 11–5 SUN. **FACTORY SHOP IN A FACTORY SHOPPING VILLAGE**

Bed & Bath Works sells bedlinen and towels from famous-name companies, as well as brushes, sponges, bath mitts, bath mats, flannels, cushions and throws. Discounts range from 30% upwards.

BIRTHDAYS

MCARTHURGLEN DESIGNER OUTLET CHESHIRE OAKS, KINSEY ROAD, NEAR ELLESMERE PORT, JUNCTION 10 OF M53, CHESHIRE CH65 9JJ, ☎ 0151 356 7393, 10–8 MON–FRI, 9–6 SAT, 11–5 SUN. **FACTORY SHOP IN A FACTORY SHOPPING VILLAGE**

Cards, notelets, stationery sets, colouring books, soft toys, photo albums, picture frames, gifts, giftwrap, tissue paper, party packs, Christmas crackers and string puppets all at discounts of up to 30%. Some are special purchases, some seconds.

CATALOGUE BARGAIN SHOP

ROYAL AVENUE, WIDNES, CHESHIRE WA8 7BR, ☎ 0151 424 6161, www.bargaincrazy.com, 10–6 MON–FRI, 9–5 SAT. **PERMANENT DISCOUNT OUTLET**

See page 461 (CAMBS)

CHESHIRE WORKSHOPS

BURWARDSLEY, NEAR CHESTER, CHESHIRE CH3 9PF, ☎ 01829 770401, FAX: 01829 770440, www.guides.co.uk/www.themap.co.uk, 10–5 SEVEN DAYS A WEEK. **FACTORY SHOP**

Cheshire Workshops offer a day out for all the family as well as the opportunity to choose from a large range of candles at factory shop prices. You can watch skilled craftspeople carving candles by hand, and see the unique candle dipping ferris wheel, standing over 30 feet high. Most of the candles made here are exported throughout the world. There are also hundreds of other gift ideas in the shop. Candles start from 15p, much cheaper than the equivalent quality in the high street and are available in a wide range of colours, shapes and sizes. There is free parking, a restaurant, and a play area with hands-on activities for children.

CHRISTY, THE MILL SHOP

NEWTON STREET, HYDE, CHESHIRE SK14 4NR, ☎ 0161 368 1961 EXT 4603, 9–5 MON–WED, 9–6.30 THUR, 9–5 FRI, 9–4 SAT. **FACTORY SHOP**

Top quality seconds and discontinued lines from the UK's brand leader in towels. The finest quality Christy towels are available, plus well-known high street names as well as Prettywise bedding, Zorbit baby goods and a range of other goods including flannelette sheets and tea towels.

CLASSIC INTERIORS

FOUNDRY BANK, CONGLETON, CHESHIRE CW12 1EE, ☎ 01260 281071, FAX: 01260 281071, 10–5 MON–SAT. **FACTORY SHOP**

Recently taken over, this former lamp factory shop now sells furniture, too. Specialising in recovering shades as well as making new ones to order. They also stock assorted lamps made from different materials. Most of the stock is seconds and reduced by about one-third. Set in a delightful market town adjacent to the town centre, this Victorian mill has recently been extensively refurbished to offer a variety of independent shops displaying a huge array of merchandise. Chainstore merchandise, including bed, carpets, glassware, fabric, mirrors and lighting. Coffee shop. Ample parking.

CWV BRANDS AT HOME FACTORY SHOP

TALBOT ROAD, HYDE, CHESHIRE SK14 4EJ, ☎ 0161 351 3070, **e-mail:** pamhindle@englewood.co.uk, 9.30–5.30 MON–FRI, 9–5 SAT, 10–4 SUN, 10–5 BANK HOLIDAYS. **FACTORY SHOP**

One of two CWV factory shops offering discontinued lines or seconds of bedlinen, wallpaper and fabrics by Coloroll, Vymura and Wilman Interiors at discounted prices. Savings of more than 50% can be made. For example, Coloroll, Vymura and Wilman wallpaper at £1.99 a roll or less, vinyls £1.99 a roll or less. Coloroll single quilt cover and pillow case, £6.50. Wilman curtain fabric, £3.50 a metre or less; Wilman upholstery fabric, £5 a metre or less. Towels, lamps, candles, kitchen accessories, bathroom accessories and baby products are available, too. Free car parking. Disabled access. They also maintain a data base to inform customers of offers and sale dates.

DENBY FACTORY SHOP

CHESHIRE OAKS DESIGNER OUTLET VILLAGE, KINSEY ROAD, NEAR ELLESMERE PORT, CHESHIRE CH65 9JJ, ☎ 0151 356 4943, www.denby.co.uk, 10–8 MON–FRI, 9–6 SAT, 11–5 SUN. **FACTORY SHOP IN A FACTORY SHOPPING VILLAGE**

This outlet stocks quality seconds in new and popular patterns. A bridal gift service is available. Discounts on seconds start at 20% off the first quality RRP. There are special offers throughout the year (see web site for dates and details).

EDINBURGH CRYSTAL

MCARTHURGLEN DESIGNER OUTLET CHESHIRE OAKS, KINSEY ROAD, NEAR ELLESMERE PORT, JUNCTION 10 OF M53, CHESHIRE CH65 9HN, ☎ 0151 357 3661, 10–8 MON–FRI, 9–6 SAT, 11–5 SUN. **FACTORY SHOP IN A FACTORY SHOPPING VILLAGE**

Wide range of crystalware from glasses and vases to tumblers and bowls at discounts of between 30% to 40%. The shop sells firsts and seconds of crystal from one third off the normal price. There are also special promotional lines at discount prices of up to 70% off seconds.

HOME AND BEAUTY DISCOUNTS

29 MILL STREET, CONGLETON, CHESHIRE CW12 1AG, ☎ 01260 273009, 9–5 MON–SAT, 9–1.15 WED. **PERMANENT DISCOUNT OUTLET**

Three-storey shop with a picture gallery also selling mirrors downstairs, café upstairs and in the middle a floor full of competitively-priced items for the kitchen and household. These include cleaning materials, make-up, toys, ornaments, pottery, aromatherapy oils, shampoo, toothpaste, soaps, lipsticks. They claim prices here are cheaper than in supermarkets and high street shops. Some of the brands are well-known: Flex shampoo, for instance, and Colgate toothpaste.

MATALAN

UNITS 3, 4 & 5A, THE ROCK RETAIL PARK, GREEN LANE, BIRKENHEAD CHESHIRE CH41 9AG, ☎ 0151 650 6820, FAX: 0151 650 0487, www.matalan.co.uk, 10–8 MON–FRI, 9.30–6 SAT, 11–5 SUN.

NEW CHESTER ROAD, BROMBOROUGH, SOUTH WIRRAL, CHESHIRE CH62 7EK, ☎ 0151 343 9494, FAX: 0151 343 9321, www.matalan.co.uk, 9.30–8 MON–FRI, 9–6 SAT, 11–5 SUN.

STADIUM WAY, CHESTER, CHESHIRE CH1 4PZ, ☎ 01244 665260, FAX: 01244 665908, www.matalan.co.uk, 9.30–8 MON–FRI, 9–6 SAT, 11–5 SUN.

KERFOOT STREET, OFF WINWICK ROAD, WARRINGTON, CHESHIRE WA2 8NU, ☎ 01925 235365, FAX: 01925 230371, www.matalan.co.uk, 9.30–8 MON–FRI, 9–6 SAT, 11–5 SUN. **PERMANENT DISCOUNT OUTLET**

See page 458 (BEDS)

MCARTHURGLEN DESIGNER OUTLET

KINSEY ROAD, NEAR ELLESMERE PORT, JUNCTION 10 OF M53, CHESHIRE CH65 9JJ, ☎ 0800 316 4352 FREE INFORMATION LINE OR 0151 348 5600, FAX: 0151 357 3744, www.mcarthurglen.com/cheshireoaks, 10–8 MON–FRI, 9–6 SAT, 11–5 SUN. **FACTORY SHOPPING VILLAGE**

The McArthurGlen Designer Outlet Cheshire Oaks is Europe's largest designer outlet with over 140 stores selling top brands and designer names at up to 50% off typical retail prices. Facilities include a food court, a children's play area and free parking. Stores include: Gap Outlet, Big L, Fruit of the Loom, Monsoon, Timberland, Tie Rack, Principles, Petroleum, James Barry, Donnay, Aquascutum, Burberrys, Viyella, Warehouse, Racing Green, Famous Footwear, Jeffrey Rogers, Liz Claiborne, Winning Line, Overland, Ciro Pearls, Diesel, Jokids, Fred Perry, Travel Accessory Outlet, Baron Jon, La Senza, Nike, Next to Nothing, Helly Hansen, Jane Shilton, Joe Bloggs, Birthdays, Thorntons, Toyworld, D2, Pilot, Jumper, Clarks, Villeroy & Boch, Episode, Windsmoor, Jaeger, Daks Simpson, Mexx, Bed & Bath Works, Woods of Windsor, The Suit Company, XS Music & Video, Suits You, Claire's Accessories, Lee Cooper, Tog 24, Fila, Warners, Cecil Gee, Remington, Whittard of Chelsea, Kitchen Store, Denby, Edinburgh Crystal, Price's Candles, Reebok, Hobbs, Kurt Muller, Bookends, Pictureport, Kappa, Easy Jeans, Woodhouse, Designer Room, DKNY, Ponden Mill, U Wear/I Wear, Penn, Le Coq Sportif, Roman Originals, Revlon, Monet, Walker and Hall, Ben Sherman, Van Heusen, Austin Reed, Antler, Ecco, Blazer, Watson/Chillii Pepper, Red/Green, Soled Out, Carphone Warehouse, Cotton Traders, Royal Doulton, Royal Worcester, Oneida, Proibito, Vans, Reiss, Garden Outlet, Proudfoot Leather, Playtime Toys, Wedgwood, Prima Tessuti, Natural World, WHSmith, Littlewoods, Bose, The Body Shop, Samsonite, Adidas, Kangol, Dune, Marks & Spencer Outlet, Daniel Footwear, Polo Jeans Company, The North Face, Elle, Sergio Tacchini, Autonomy, Chapelle, Fiorelli, Julian Graves, Spiegelau, Bose, Kitch N Sync, Early Learning Centre, Tommy Hilfiger, Triumph and Professional Cookware.

ONEIDA

MCARTHURGLEN DESIGNER OUTLET CHESHIRE OAKS, KINSEY ROAD, NEAR ELLESMERE PORT, JUNCTION 10 OF M53, CHESHIRE CH65 9JJ, ☎ 0151 356 1024, 10–8 MON–FRI, 9–6 SAT, 11–5 SUN. **FACTORY SHOP IN A FACTORY SHOPPING VILLAGE**

Oneida is the world's largest cutlery company and originates from the USA. In addition to cutlery, it sells silver and silver plate at discounts of between 30% and 50%, plus frames, candlesticks and trays. Now sells Viners cookware with an average discount of 50%.

PONDEN MILL

MCARTHURGLEN DESIGNER OUTLET CHESHIRE OAKS, KINSEY ROAD, NEAR ELLESMERE PORT, JUNCTION 10 OF M53, CHESHIRE CH65 9JJ, ☎ 0151 356 4411, 10–8 MON–THUR, 9–6 FRI–SAT, 11–5 SUN. **FACTORY SHOP IN A FACTORY SHOPPING VILLAGE**

Famous branded products at direct-from-the-mill prices. A fabulous assortment of towels, duvets, pillows, throws, bedspreads, and up-to-the-minute coordinated bed linen, from names including Crown, Coloroll and Jeff Banks Ports-of-Call. Something for every room in the house.

PRICE'S CANDLES

MCARTHURGLEN DESIGNER OUTLET CHESHIRE OAKS, KINSEY ROAD, NEAR ELLESMERE PORT, JUNCTION 10 OF M53, CHESHIRE CH65 9JJ, ☎ 0151 356 0248, 10–8 MON–FRI, 9–6 SAT, 11–5 SUN. **FACTORY SHOP IN A FACTORY SHOPPING VILLAGE**

Factory outlets stocking most current ranges from spring, summer and Christmas, including seconds and discontinued lines. Products include: church candles, dinner candles, tealights, scented candles, fashion ranges and accessories, all at discounted prices. Perfect for gifts.

QS FASHION SALE

1–5 BROAD ROAD, SALE, CHESHIRE M33 2AE, ☎ 0161 976 2747, FAX: 0161 962 9244, 9–8 MON–FRI, 9–5.30 SAT, 11–5 SUN. **PERMANENT DISCOUNT OUTLET**

Fashion for all the family includes brands such as Timberland, Fila, Nike, Reebok, Adidas, Calvin Klein and Ralph Lauren and many more. Homeware products include towels, bedding, plastics, pictures, toys and mirrors. The stock is constantly changing so come with an open mind. QS Fashion has a price promise that if you can purchase the same item at a cheaper price at another store, QS will give you the product free.

ROYAL WORCESTER & SPODE FACTORY SHOP

MCARTHURGLEN DESIGNER OUTLET CHESHIRE OAKS, KINSEY ROAD, NEAR ELLESMERE PORT, JUNCTION 10 OF M53, CHESHIRE CH65 9JJ, ☎ 0151 356 9199, www.royal-worcester.co.uk, 10–8 MON–FRI, 9–6 SAT, 11–5 SUN. **FACTORY SHOP IN A FACTORY SHOPPING VILLAGE**

Porcelain and china seconds at 25% less than 'perfect' prices. This outlet stocks Gleneagles, Country Artists, Worcester Ornamental Studios, Caithness Glass, Fo-Frame, Six Trees and Pimpernel table mats. There is a vast range with special offers throughout the year on anything from crystal decanters and bowls to figurines, cookware and dinner sets. Shipping can be organised worldwide.

T J HUGHES

BOROUGH PAVEMENT, GRANGE PRECINCT, BIRKENHEAD, CHESHIRE L41 2XX, ☎ 0151 647 5151, FAX: 0151 666 1610, **e-mail:** info@tjhughes.co.uk, www.tjhughes.co.uk, 9–5.30 MON–SAT, 10–4 SUN.

THE FORUM, HAMILTON PLACE, CHESTER, CHESHIRE CH1 2BH, ☎ 01244 316600, FAX: 01244 316646, **e-mail:** info@tjhughes.co.uk, www.tjhughes.co.uk, 9–5.30 MON–SAT, 11–5 SUN.

2 MERCIER WALK, SOUTH WIRRAL CHESHIRE CH65 0AP, ☎ 0151 357 3151, FAX: 0151 357 3174, **e-mail:** info@tjhughes.co.uk, www.tjhughes.co.uk, 9–5.30 MON–SAT, 10–4 SUN.

EXCHANGE STREET, MACCLESFIELD, CHESHIRE SK11 6UZ, ☎ 01625 611807, FAX: 01625 611859, **e-mail:** info@tjhughes.co.uk, www.tjhughes.co.uk, 9–5.30 MON–SAT, 10–4 SUN.

GREENOAKS SHOPPING CENTRE, WIDNES, CHESHIRE WA8 6UD, ☎ 0151 420 1010, FAX: 0151 423 4570, **e-mail:** info@tjhughes.co.uk, www.tjhughes.co.uk, 9–5.30 MON–SAT, 10–4 SUN. **PERMANENT DISCOUNT OUTLET**

Expanding chain of shops offering, not discounts as such, but very competitively priced goods including clothes for all the family, china, towels, bedlinen, duvets, pots and pans, kettles, vacuum cleaners, television sets, CDs, toasters, many from top brand names.

THE CAPE

114 FOREGATE STREET, CHESTER, CHESHIRE CH1 1HB, ☎ 01244 329880, FAX: 01244 829880, **e-mail:** sc@thefactory-shop.co.uk, www.thecape.co.uk, 9–5.30 MON–SAT, 10.30–4.30 SUN. **FACTORY SHOP**

See page 460 (BRIS)

THE FACTORY SHOP LTD

UNIT 1 EDDISBURY SQUARE, FRODSHAM, CHESHIRE WA6 6QS, ☎ 01928 734624, FAX: 01928 734906, 9–5.30 MON–SAT, 10.30–4 SUN. **FACTORY SHOP**

Wide range on sale includes men's, women's and children's clothing and footwear; household textiles; toiletries; hardware; luggage; lighting; electrical goods; and bedding, most of which are chainstore and high street brands at discounts of approximately 30% to 50%. There are kitchen and furniture displays and on sale is the Cape Country Furniture range with free-standing kitchens, as well as living, bedroom and dining furniture. There are weekly deliveries and brands include famous names such as Adidas, Nike, Joe Bloggs and Brabantia, among others. Lines are continually changing and few factory shops offer such a variety under one roof. Parking is free.

TIVIOT PRINTS LTD FABRIC MILL SHOP

LYMEFIELD MILL, BROADBOTTOM, NR HYDE, CHESHIRE SK14 6AG, ☎ 01457 763297/764399, **e-mail:** tiviot@hotmail.com, 10–4 THUR–FRI, 10–3 SAT. **FACTORY SHOP**

Extensive range of printed cotton fabrics in various colours and designs, both modern and traditional, as well as some tea towels, oven gloves and pottery.

TK MAXX

178–182 GRANGE ROAD, BIRKENHEAD, CHESHIRE CH41 2PF, ☎ 0151 647 2837, www.tkmaxx.com, 9–5.30 MON–FRI, 9–6 SAT, 10.30–4.30 SUN.

STANLEY GREEN RETAIL PARK, EARL ROAD, CHEADLE HULME, CHESHIRE, ☎ 0161 485 3734, www.tkmaxx.com, PHONE FOR DETAILS OF OPENING TIMES.

UNIT 3, CHESTER RETAIL PARK, CHESTER, CHESHIRE, www.tkmaxx.com, PHONE FOR DETAILS OF OPENING TIMES.

UNIT B, TRIDENT RETAIL PARK, RUNCORN, CHESHIRE WA7 2FQ, ☎ 01928 714050, www.tkmaxx.com, 9–6 MON, 9–7 TUE–WED, 9–8 THUR–FRI, 9–6 SAT, 11–5 SUN.

UNIT C, THE COCKHEDGE CENTRE, 2 PRINCE HENRY SQUARE, WARRINGTON, CHESHIRE, ☎ 01925 636262, www.tkmaxx.com, 9–6 MON–SAT, 9 ON THUR, 10–4. SUN. **PERMANENT DISCOUNT OUTLET**

See page 458 (BEDS)

VICTORIA MILL RETAIL AND FACTORY OUTLETS

FOUNDRY BANK, CONGLETON, CHESHIRE CW12 1EE, ☎ 01260 297642, FAX: 01260 290068, **e-mail:** vicmill@talk21.com, 9.30–5 MON–SAT. **FACTORY SHOP**

An emporium of homewares and fashion at ex-factory prices. Set in a delightful market town adjacent to the town centre, this Victorian mill has recently been extensively refurbished to offer a variety of independent shops displaying a huge array of merchandise. Everything from cane furniture to chainstore merchandise, including beds, mirrors and lighting. Coffee shop. Parking.

VILLEROY & BOCH (UK) LIMITED

MCARTHURGLEN DESIGNER OUTLET CHESHIRE OAKS, KINSEY ROAD, NEAR ELLESMERE PORT, JUNCTION 10 OF M53, CHESHIRE CH65 9JJ, ☎ 0151 355 7771, 10–8 MON–FRI, 9–6 SAT, 11–5 SUN. **FACTORY SHOP IN A FACTORY SHOPPING VILLAGE**

One of six factory outlets for Villeroy & Boch, this shop carries an exclusive range of tableware, crystal and cutlery from Europe's largest tableware manufacturer. A varied and constantly changing stock, including seconds, hotelware and discontinued lines, on sale at excellent reductions, always makes for a worthwhile visit.

WHITTARD

MCARTHURGLEN DESIGNER OUTLET, ELLESMERE PORT, SOUTH WIRRAL CHESHIRE CH65 9JJ, ☎ 0151 356 3300, 10–8 MON–FRI, 9–6 SAT, 11–5 SUN. **FACTORY SHOP IN A FACTORY SHOPPING VILLAGE**

Sells tea, coffee, coffee-making equipment (cafetieres and stove-top espressos), a wide range of china, colourful tableware, corkscrews, trays, bins, and kitchen containers at discount prices.

WILKINSONS HOME & GARDEN STORES

THE MARKET CENTRE, CREWE, CHESHIRE CW1 2NG, ☎ 01270 250754, www.wilko.co.uk, 8.30–5.30 MON–WED, 8.30–6.30 THUR–SAT, 10–4 SUN. **PERMANENT DISCOUNT OUTLET**

Family-owned business offering value on the high street through its 205 stores, selling 25,000 high quality, low-priced essential everyday products for all the family including kitchenware, household disposables, clothing, DIY decoration, stationery, homewares, bedlinen, picture frames, china, cutlery, toys, pet foot, curtains, mirrors, gardening equipment including outdoor furniture, Christmas decorations, confectionery and seasonal goods. It also caters for the ardent gardener with fertiliser, grass seed – loose or boxed – plants, insecticides, composts – both multi-purpose or tub and basket – garden tools, strimmers, hoses and attachments, watering cans, water butts, wheelbarrows, and reels on wheels. In season, they sell bedding plants, garden lights, coolboxes, paint, paint brushes and rollers, and climbing plants such as honeysuckle, but as the summer progresses these are replaced by barbecues and picnic ranges. Phone 01909 505505 for details of your local outlet or visit their website.

WOODS OF WINDSOR

UNIT 54, CHESHIRE OAKS DESIGNER OUTLET VILLAGE, KINSEY ROAD, ELLESMERE PORT, JUNCTION 10 OF M53, CHESHIRE CH65 9JJ, ☎ 0151 355 8170, www.woodsofwindsor.co.uk, 10–6 MON–SAT, 8 ON THUR, 11–5 SUN. **FACTORY SHOP IN A FACTORY SHOPPING VILLAGE**

Sells gift sets, soaps, perfume, bath gel, room fragrance sprays, hand and body lotions and talc at discounts of 30% for standard ranges and 50% for discounted ranges.

YOU & YOURS

UNIT 42, ORCHARD WALK, HALTON LEAS SHOPPING CENTRE, RUNCORN, CHESHIRE WA7 2GZ, ☎ 01928 795 792, 9–5.30 MON–SAT. **PERMANENT DISCOUNT OUTLET**

Sells surplus stock from both Grattan and Freemans catalogues. Womenswear, childrenswear, menswear and household items, at up to 50% off catalogue prices. Includes a wide range of brands from both designer and high street on a regularly changing basis. Electrical goods are sold at discounts of up to 30% off catalogue prices, and include many big-name brands. They offer a 14-day refund policy.

COUNTY DURHAM

DISCOUNT CLOTHING STORE

68 HOPE STREET, CROOK, CO DURHAM DL15 9HT, ☎ 01388 768272, 9.30–5.30 MON–SAT.

UNIT 5A, FOLLINGSBY PARK, WARDLEY, GATESHEAD, TYNE & WEAR NE10 8YA, ☎ 0191 415 4015, 9.30–5.30 MON–SAT.

UNIT 16-17, DONKIN ROAD, ARMSTRONG INDUSTRIAL ESTATE, WASHINGTON, CO DURHAM NE37 1PF, ☎ 0191 417 4910, 9.30–5.30 MON–SAT. **PERMANENT DISCOUNT OUTLET**

With discounts of up to 50%, DCS offers a wide range of clothes for all the family and some bedlinen and towels, most of which are from high street stores.

FACTORY SHOP

LINGFIELD WAY, YARM ROAD BUSINESS PARK, DARLINGTON, CO DURHAM DL1 4XX, ☎ 01325 469 181, FAX: 01325 381386, **e-mail:** tensorlimited@aol.com, www.tensormarketing.co.uk. 9–5 MON–FRI, 10–4.30 SAT. **FACTORY SHOP**

Part of Tensor Marketing Ltd, a marketing company specialising in innovative products with a huge range of goods covering home and garden, office, motoring, gifts, novelties, pets, pest control systems, security, health and fitness, sport and leisure. The garden section has a range of items including gutter flushes, hammer and edging fencing, mole chasers, foldaway wheelbarrows, garden lighting sets, weeders, garden thermometers, corner plant stands, garden hoses and obelisks. Order from the shop, the website or by mail order brochure.

LITTLEWOODS DISCOUNT STORE

UNIT 2A, METRO RETAIL PARK, GATESHEAD, TYNE & WEAR NE11 9XU, ☎ 0191 461 1491 10–8 MON–FRI, 9–6 SAT, 11–5 SUN. **PERMANENT DISCOUNT OUTLET**

Brand new, surplus women's, men's and children's clothing from last year's catalogue is on sale at greatly discounted prices. Returned and sometimes slightly damaged televisions and furniture can be found at as much as 70% below the original price. If you see an item you like, buy it there and then as stock is constantly changing and you are unlikely to see it on sale again. The store also has sales when stock is discounted even further.

MATALAN

173 HIGH STREET WEST, GATESHEAD, TYNE & WEAR NE8 1EJ, ☎ 0191 478 8140, FAX: 0191 478 9480, www.matalan.co.uk, 10–8 MON–FRI, 9–6 SAT, 11–5 SUN.

48 CAMERON RETAIL PARK, METRO CENTRE, GATESHEAD, TYNE & WEAR NE11 9XU, ☎ 0191 461 0880, FAX: 0191 460 1340, www.matalan.co.uk, 9.30–8 MON–FRI, 9–6 SAT, 11–6 SUN.

ANCHOR RETAIL PARK, MARINA WAY, HARTLEPOOL, CO DURHAM TS24 0XR, ☎ 01429 855960, FAX: 01429 264028, www.matalan.co.uk, 10–8 MON–FRI, 9–6 SAT, 11–5 SUN.

BRIDGE ROAD RETAIL PARK, PARKFIELD ROAD, STOCKTON-ON-TEES, STOCKTON, CO DURHAM TS18 3AY, ☎ 01642 702410, FAX: 01642 702415, www.matalan.co.uk, 10–8 MON–FRI, 9–6 SAT, 11–5 SUN.

UNIT 1, HYLTON RIVERSIDE RETAIL PARK, SUNDERLAND, TYNE & WEAR SR5 3XG, ☎ 0191 516 0141, FAX: 0191 548 1572, www.matalan.co.uk, 10–8 MON–FRI, 9–6 SAT, 11–5 SUN. **PERMANENT DISCOUNT OUTLET**

See page 458 (BEDS)

NO FRILLS DIY STORE

MEYNELL ROAD, OFF WHESSOE ROAD, DARLINGTON, CO DURHAM DL3 0XZ, ☎ 01325 481414, FAX: 01325 464020, 9–8 MON–SAT, 10–4 SUN. **PERMANENT DISCOUNT OUTLET**

See page 458 (BEDS)

PONDEN MILL

UNIT 192, SOUTH MALL, MIDDLETON GRANGE SHOPPING CENTRE, HARTLEPOOL, CO DURHAM TS24 7RR, ☎ 01429 894239, 10–6 MON–SAT, 11–5 SUN. **FACTORY SHOP IN A FACTORY SHOPPING VILLAGE**

See page 464 (CHESH)

SCOOPS CATALOGUE DISCOUNT STORE

UNIT 17, THE IN SHOP CENTRE, 1–2 WRIGHTON HOUSE, TRENCHARD AVENUE, THORNABY, TS17 9EP, ☎ 01642 751935, 9–5 MON–SAT. **PERMANENT DISCOUNT OUTLET**

Scoops the catalogue discount store sells surplus stock from both Grattan and Freeman's catalogues. Womenswear, menswear and childrenswear are on sale, as well as household items, all at up to 50% off catalogue prices. Stock changes on a regular basis, and includes a wide range of brands from both designer and high street. A 14-day refund policy is offered.

SEYMOUR'S OF DARLINGTON

1–3 EAST ROW, DARLINGTON, CO DURHAM DL1 5PZ, ☎ 01325 355272, FAX: 01325 355272, **e-mail:** jem@seymours.fsbusiness.co.uk, 9–5 MON–SAT. **PERMANENT DISCOUNT OUTLET**

Seymour's of Darlington is the longest-established household linen retailer in the area and takes great pride in maintaining its loyal customer base. This unique family-owned business combines old-fashioned quality and service with the newest designs and keenest prices. There is a constantly changing, stunning variety of stock from tea towels to the latest French and Italian designer bed linens. Customers of all ages will find trendy to traditional items at prices to suit all pockets. There are always special offers giving extra value and there is a full range of duvets, pillows, tablecloths, towels, throws, cushion covers, duvet covers and curtains (ready-made and made-to-measure), and bathroom fittings including shower curtains. Seymour's have their own high quality brand of poly-cotton sheets, valances and pillowcases, also available in percale. More unusual items include flannelette sheets, super king-size, 4ft and bunk-size bedding. Latest additions include a delightful Portugese range of bedding and towels by Piu Belle. Brands include current perfect ranges from Sanderson, Dorma, Nimbus, Snuggledown, Christy, Coloroll, Miller, Peter Reed and Ashley Wilde, plus economy lines and seconds. Chainstore seconds are often on offer and all prices are extremely competitive. For children, they stock Designers Guild quilt covers and fabric, as well as pattern books from which orders can be taken. Staff are friendly and obliging and will advise if required, and many items can be ordered if not in stock. Short-term parking is available right outside from Tuesday to Friday and there is wheelchair access. Debit and credit cards are accepted.

THE CAPE

UNIT F43, THE FORUM, METRO CENTRE, GATESHEAD, TYNE & WEAR NE11 9XR, ☎ 0191 493 2379, FAX: 0191 493 2382, **e-mail:** sc@thefactory-shop.co.uk, www.thecape.co.uk, 10–8 MON–WED, 10–9 THUR, 10–8 FRI, 9–7 SAT, 11–5 SUN. **FACTORY SHOP**

See page 460 (BRIS)

THE FACTORY SHOP

2–4 COMMERCIAL STREET, CROOK, CO DURHAM DL15 9HP, ☎ 01388 763211, 9–5.30 MON–SAT, 10.30–4.30 SUN. **FACTORY SHOP**

See page 465 (CHESH)

TK MAXX

TEAM VALLEY, RETAIL WORLD, GATESHEAD, TYNE & WEAR, ☎ 0191 487 4468, www.tkmaxx.com, PHONE FOR DETAILS OF OPENING TIMES..

UNIT 3, THE HIGHLIGHT RETAIL PARK, HARTLEPOOL MARINA, MARINA WAY, HARTLEPOOL CO DURHAM TS24 0UX, ☎ 01429 222296, www.tkmaxx.com, 10–8 MON–FRI, 9–6 SAT, 11–5 SUN.

THE BRIDGES SHOPPING CENTRE, 34 CROWTREE ROAD, SUNDERLAND, TYNE & WEAR SR3 3JU, ☎ 0191 514 4484, www.tkmaxx.com, 9–5.30 MON–FRI, 9–6 SAT, 11–5 SUN. **PERMANENT DISCOUNT OUTLET**

See page 458 (BEDS)

CORNWALL

ART CANDLES

DUNMERE ROAD, BODMIN, CORNWALL PL31 2QN, ☎ 01208 73258, FAX: 01208 73258, www.artcandles.co.uk, 10–6 MON–FRI, 10–5 SAT, 11–6 SUN, EASTER TO SEPTEMBER. WEEKDAYS ONLY OCTOBER–EASTER, 10–12 SATS OCT–CHRISTMAS. **FACTORY SHOP**

A family business with a factory outlet selling candles and candleholders of every shape and design from decorative to scented, figurative holders to pottery. They specialise in marbled candles, and there are also 3-foot-high stalagmite candles, owl, tortoise and Buddha-shaped candles. There are tubs of seconds at even cheaper prices. They also sell candle-making materials, joss sticks and oil burners, boxes or kilos of wax, moulds, colours and wicks, and pottery, including handmade pottery dragons which smoke with incense. Stock changes constantly.

CORNISH MARKET WORLD

STADIUM RETAIL PARK, PAR, ST AUSTELL, CORNWALL PL25 3RP, ☎ 01726 812544, FAX: 01726 812346, **e-mail:** info@cornishmarketworld.co.uk, www.cornishmarketworld.co.uk, 9–5 SAT, SUN AND BANK HOLIDAYS, AND WED JUNE-SEPT. **PERMANENT DISCOUNT OUTLET**

Huge indoor market that sells an enormous range of goods and food at very competitive prices: for example, a good quality breadmaker, £45. Sells clothes, fabrics, phones, bags, tools, electric equipment, motability equipment, jewellery and furniture. There is a good butchers, fish, and fruit and veg stands.

DARTINGTON CRYSTAL

KERNOW MILL, TRERULEFOOT, SALTASH, CORNWALL PL12 5BL, ☎ 01752 851161, FAX: 01752 851856, 9.30–5.30 MON–SAT, 11–5 SUN. **FACTORY SHOP**

An extensive range of Dartington Crystal seconds at greatly reduced prices as well as some perfect crystal at full price. Range includes wine suites, sherry glasses, tankards, decanters, rippled glass, and fruit and salad bowls.

NO FRILLS DIY STORE

STADIUM PARK, ST AUSTELL, CORNWALL PL25 3RP, ☎ 01726 814791, FAX: 01726 817953, 9–8 MON–SAT, 10–4 SUN. **PERMANENT DISCOUNT OUTLET**

See page 458 (BEDS)

THE FACTORY SHOP

OLD STATION YARD, BERRYCOMBE ROAD, BODMIN, CORNWALL PL31 2NF, ☎ 01208 78492, 9–5.30 MON–SAT, 10.30–4.30 SUN.

MOUNT AMBROSE, SCORRIER, REDRUTH, CORNWALL TR15 1QT, ☎ 01209 219116, 9.30–5.30 MON–SAT, 10–4 SUN. **FACTORY SHOP**

See page 465 (CHESH)

TRAGO MILLS

ARWENACK STREET, FALMOUTH, CORNWALL TR11 3LF, ☎ 01326 315738, www.trago.co.uk, 9–5.30 MON–SAT, 10.45–4.45 SUN.

TWOWATERSFOOT, LISKEARD, CORNWALL PL14 6HY, ☎ 01579 348877, www.trago.co.uk, 9–5.30 MON–SAT, 10.45- 4.45 SUN. **PERMANENT DISCOUNT OUTLET**

Sister stores to the historic Trago's original Cornish site, which is in the Glynn Valley on the A38 between Liskeard and Bodmin. You can bargain hunt at both places for brand name art materials, bathrooms and bedrooms and ceramics, carpets and rugs, clothing, DIY and home improvement, furniture, garden accessories, gifts, textiles, lighting, pet care, saddlery, stationery, tools, motoring products, toys and sport equipment and much more. There's a restaurant and picnic area by the beautiful Fowey river bank, free parking and disabled access. The Falmouth store is smaller, with only limited free car parking outside, but there is a public car park adjacent.

TRIPLE M FASHION

NEW PORTREATH ROAD, JUST OUTSIDE REDRUTH, CORNWALL TR16 4QL, ☎ 01209 842931 10–5.30 SEVEN DAYS A WEEK. **PERMANENT DISCOUNT OUTLET**

Large permanent discount shop selling men's and women's clothes, toys, bedding, footwear, bags, children's clothes.

WILLIAMSON'S FACTORY SHOP

NEW PORTREATH ROAD, REDRUTH, CORNWALL TR16 4QL, ☎ 01209 843366, 10–5 SEVEN DAYS A WEEK. **FACTORY SHOP**

Two factory shops in one, the smaller one sells shoes and household goods, mainly textiles, in equal quantities. The shoes are very reasonably priced and include some designer trainers, shoes by Moshulu, Wrangler, R and Ricker, and deck shoes. The household textiles include bedlinen, tea towels, towels, duvets and pillows. The larger shop opposite sells men's and women's middle market clothes including coats, underwear and socks from names such as Regatta, Double TwoWrangler, Outdoor Scene and HJ socks at discounted prices.

CUMBRIA

CATALOGUE BARGAIN SHOP

UNITS 4–5, SOUTH LAKELANDS RETAIL PARK, KENDAL, CUMBRIA LA9 6DU, ☎ 01539 740734, www.bargaincrazy.com, 9–8 MON–SAT, 11–5 SUN. **PERMANENT DISCOUNT OUTLET**

See page 461 (CAMBS)

DARTINGTON CRYSTAL

K VILLAGE, KENDAL, CUMBRIA LA9 7BT, ☎ 01539 737834, 9–6 MON–SAT, 9–6 SAT, 11–5 SUN. **FACTORY SHOP IN A FACTORY SHOPPING VILLAGE**

See page 469 (CORN)

DENBY FACTORY SHOP

K VILLAGE, LOUND ROAD, KENDAL, CUMBRIA LA9 7DA, ☎ 01539 735418, www.denby.co.uk, 9.30–5.30 MON–FRI (WINTER), 9.30–6 MON–FRI (SUMMER), 9 -6 SAT, 11–5 SUN, 10–6 BANK HOLIDAYS. **FACTORY SHOP IN A FACTORY SHOPPING VILLAGE**

See page 463 (CHESH)

FACTORY BEDDING SHOP

ATLAS HOUSE, NELSON STREET, DENTON HOLME, CARLISLE, CUMBRIA CA2 5NB, ☎ 01228 514703, 10–5 MON–FRI, 9–5 SAT. **FACTORY SHOP**

Bedding, curtains, duvets, duvet covers, pillows, towels, cushions, and curtain fabrics bought in direct from the manufacturer at factory shop prices. No brand names, but all sold in high street department stores. Pillows from £1.99; quilts from £5.99; curtains from £6.99; double fitted sheets from £4.99; double duvet covers from £12.99; double valances from £10.99. Wide range of curtain fabrics from £1.99 a metre and a curtain-making service.

FAMOUS FOOTWEAR

20–30 SANDES AVENUE, KENDAL, CUMBRIA LA9 4SG, ☎ 01539 738403, 9–5.30 MON–FRI, 9–6 SAT, 11–5 SUN. **FACTORY SHOP**

Wide range of brand names including Lilley & Skinner, Hush Puppies, Lotus, Wrangler, Frank Wright, Red Tape, Rohde, Brevitt, Padders, Rombah Wallace and Rieker, all at discount prices of up to 50%. Stand alone shop in Kendal which, as well as all the shoe brands, including clothing (Happit) and housewares.

K VILLAGE OUTLET SHOPPING

LOUND ROAD, KENDAL, NEAR JUNCTION 36 OF M6, CUMBRIA LA9 7DA, ☎ 01539 732363, **e-mail:** mdixon@realm-ocm.com, www.kvillage.co.uk, 9.30–6 MON–FRI, 9–6 SAT, 11–5 SUN (9.30–5.30 MON–FRI NOVEMBER TO MARCH). **FACTORY SHOPPING VILLAGE**

Twelve outlets including Cotton Traders, Crabtree & Evelyn, Dartington Crystal selling Cloverleaf as well as glassware, Van Heusen, Denby Pottery, The Food Factory, Ponden Mill, Prices Candles, Tog 24, National Trust Gift Shop and a giant K Shoes factory shop selling a wide range of labels from K Shoes, Clarks, Cica, Delsey and Antler, as well as a full-price K Shop. There is also a heritage centre where you can discover the history of shoemaking, a 150-seater restaurant, a coffee shop, children's play area, baby changing facilities, a riverside picnic area, disabled facilities and free parking. Take the South Kendal exit and follow the signs for K Village.

MATALAN

WALNEY ROAD, BARROW-IN-FURNESS, CUMBRIA LA14 5UN, ☎ 01229 430899, FAX: 01229 430948, www.matalan.co.uk, 9.30–8 MON–FRI, 9–6 SAT, 11–5 SUN.

UNIT 2, 3, 4, STATION RETAIL PARK, WATER STREET, CARLISLE CUMBRIA CA2 5AF, ☎ 01228 403510, FAX: 01228 510068, www.matalan.co.uk, 10–8 MON–FRI, 9–6 SAT, 11–5 SUN.

DERWENT HOWE, SOLWAY ROAD, WORKINGTON, CUMBRIA CA14 3YA, ☎ 01900 870966, FAX: 01900 870967, www.matalan.co.uk, 9.30–8 MON–FRI, 9–6 SAT, 11–5 SUN.
PERMANENT DISCOUNT OUTLET

See page 458 (BEDS)

PONDEN MILL

UNIT 14, MARKET CROSS SHOPPING CENTRE, AMBLESIDE, CUMBRIA LA22 9BT, ☎ 01539 434656, PHONE FOR DETAILS OF OPENING TIMES.

CRAG BROW, LAKE ROAD, BOWNESS-ON-WINDERMERE, CUMBRIA LA23 3BT, ☎ 01539 448640, PHONE FOR DETAILS OF OPENING TIMES.

K VILLAGE, LOUND ROAD, KENDAL, CUMBRIA LA9 1DA, ☎ 01539 737116, 9.30–6 MON–FRI, 9–6 SAT, 11–5 SUN.

15–17 STRICKLANDGATE, KENDAL, CUMBRIA LA9 7DA, ☎ 01539 736691, 9.30–6 MON–FRI, 9–6 SAT, 11–5 SUN. **FACTORY SHOP IN A FACTORY SHOPPING VILLAGE**

See page 464 (CHESH)

PRICE'S CANDLES

K VILLAGE, KENDAL, NEAR JUNCTION 36 OF M6, CUMBRIA LA9 7DA, ☎ 01539 733736, 9.30–6 MON–FRI, 9–6 SAT, 11–5 SUN, 9–6 BANK HOLIDAYS. **FACTORY SHOP**

See page 464 (CHESH)

ROYAL WORCESTER & SPODE FACTORY SHOP

DUNMAIL SHOPPING PARK, MARYPORT ROAD, WORKINGTON, CUMBRIA CA14 1NQ, ☎ 01900 62950, www.royal-worcester.co.uk, 9–9 MON–FRI, 9–6 SAT, 11–5 SUN. **FACTORY SHOP**

See page 465 (CHESH)

THE COLONY COUNTRY STORE

LINDAL-IN-FURNESS, ULVERSTON, CUMBRIA LA12 0LD, ☎ 01229 461102, 9–5 MON–SAT, 10.30–4 SUN. **FACTORY SHOP**

This is one of the biggest outlets for factory price candles, scented candles, candle holders and lamps in Britain, with some stock selling at between 10% and 50% of the normal retail price. There are normally 3,000 candles on display, both perfect and seconds. A special section called Waxworks sells goods at a fraction of their usual retail price, and there is a one-off sample area where you can buy original designs. The store also sells pot pourri and gift soaps, and a Christmas shop with Santa's grotto is open all year round. You can watch the candles being made from a viewing gallery, there is a large children's area and also a dipping area where you can create candles of your own design to buy and take home.

THE FACTORY SHOP

EMPIRE BUILDINGS, MAIN STREET, EGREMONT, CUMBRIA CA22 2BD, ☎ 01946 820434, 9–5 MON–SAT. 10–4 SUN. **FACTORY SHOP**

THE GILL, ULVERSTON, CUMBRIA LA12 7BN, ☎ 01229 583360, 9–5.30 MON–SAT, 10.30–4.30 SUN.

5 MARKET PLACE, WIGTON, CUMBRIA CA7 9NW, ☎ 01697 342171, 9–5.30 MON–SAT, 10.30–4.30 SUN. **FACTORY SHOP**

See page 465 (CHESH)

THE PAPER MILL SHOP COMPANY LTD

BURNESIDE MILLS, NEAR KENDAL, CUMBRIA LA9 6PZ, ☎ 01539 818484, www.thepapermillshop.co.uk, 10–4.30 MON–THUR, 10–4 FRI, 9–3 SAT.

RHEGED DISCOVERY CENTRE, PENRITH, CUMBRIA CA11 0DQ, ☎ 01768 868000, www.thepapermillshop.c.uk, 10–6 APR–OCT, 10–5.30 NOV–MAR, SEVEN DAYS A WEEK. **FACTORY SHOP**

Pick'n'mix coloured paper and card, artists' pads, designer pads, coloured envelopes, stationery sets, Creative Kiddies children's range, all sold at unbeatable prices. Threre are card making accessories, stamps, punches and peel offs.

THE TEA POTTERY

CENTRAL CAR PARK ROAD, KESWICK, CUMBRIA CA12 5DF, ☎ 01768 773983, **e-mail:** info@teapottery.co.uk, www.teapottery.co.uk, 9–5 SEVEN DAYS A WEEK. **FACTORY SHOP**

Paradise for collectors of novelty teapots, all of which are manufactured on site in up to 50 different designs and in sizes from one cup to five cups. Designs include Welsh dressers, caravans, Agas, cookers, scarecrows, washbasins and a host of others, many of which are collectors' items. Prices range from £12 to £65 for perfects, which represents a 10% to 20% saving on retail prices, and good discounts on seconds. This factory shop is smaller than its sister shop in Leyburn and light refreshments are served. Also you can watch a short video showing the teapots being made.

TK MAXX

THE EDEN CENTRE AND MARKET HALL, FISHER STREET, CARLISLE, CUMBRIA CA3 8JB, ☎ 01228 819292, www.tkmaxx.com, 9–5.30 MON–FRI, 8.30–6 SAT, 11–4 SUN. **PERMANENT DISCOUNT OUTLET**

See page 458 (BEDS)

DERBYSHIRE

BED & BATH WORKS

MCARTHURGLEN DESIGNER OUTLET, MANSFIELD ROAD, SOUTH NORMANTON, ALFRETON, JUNCTION 28 OF M1, DERBYSHIRE DB55 2JW, ☎ 01773 545190, FAX: 01773 545194, **e-mail:** hello@bedandbathworks.co.uk, www.bedandbathworks.co.uk, 10–6 MON–FRI, 8 ON THUR, 9–6 SAT, 11–5 SUN. **FACTORY SHOP IN A FACTORY SHOPPING VILLAGE**

See page 462 (CHESH)

DARTINGTON CRYSTAL

DENBY POTTERY CO, DENBY, DERBYSHIRE DE5 8NX, ☎ 01773 513116, 9–5 MON–SAT, 10–5 SUN. **FACTORY SHOP**

See page 469 (CORN)

DE BRADELEI MILL SHOPS LTD

DE BRADELEI HOUSE, CHAPEL STREET, BELPER, DERBYSHIRE DE56 1AR, ☎ 01773 882442, FAX: 01773 829830, 9.30–5.30 MON–FRI, 9.30–6 SAT, 10.30–4.30 SUN. **PERMANENT DISCOUNT OUTLET**

A delightful Mill centre with individual shops based round a central courtyard, each one selling top brand names in fashions and footwear for men and women, along with Liberty giftware. The womenswear includes such names as Paul Costelloe, Windsmoor, Planet, Precis Petite, Alexon, Kaliko, Eastex, Minuet Petite, Liz Claiborne, Jaeger Knitwear Shop, French Connection, Elle, Country Casuals, Elvi, top American and German designer labels, plus many more. The menswear range includes underwear, socks, sweaters, trousers, jackets, coats and suits from labels such as Wolsey, French Connection, Jaeger Knitwear Shop and Glenmuir. Robert Leonard's Menswear provides Pierre Cardin, Gabicci, Gurteen, Oakman and many more. There is a large shoe department with an excellent range of shoes and accessories for men and women. A Tenson department sells outerwear for men and women. The giftware department offers a superb collection of Liberty giftware with scented candles, Arran Aromatic toiletries, photo frames, baskets, toilet bags and chocolates from Italo Suisse. Chevin Coffee Shop serves delicious home-cooked food throughout the day. De Bradelei Mill Shop has its own car park with alternative parking nearby; coach parties always welcome though booking is preferred.

DENBY POTTERY VISITOR CENTRE

DERBY ROAD, DENBY, NR RIPLEY, DERBYSHIRE DE5 8NX, ☎ 01773 740799, www.denbyvisitorcentre.co.uk, 9.30–5 MON–SAT, 10–5 SUN (CENTRE), 11–5 SUN (FACTORY SHOP). **FACTORY SHOP**

Denby has been welcoming visitors to its pottery for many years. The largest of the Denby Factory Shops is located in the Visitor Centre. It sells both seconds and first quality pieces. Discounts on the large range of seconds start at 20% off the first quality RRP, with regular bargains offering much greater savings all the year round (see Factory Shops on their web site for dates and details). At the Visitor Centre you can go on a fascinating tour of the factory to see how Denby is made, then browse around the shops, which include an award-winning Cookshop (with free cookery demonstrations daily), Garden Centre, Dartington Crystal Factory Shop, Gift Shop, Artists Gallery area and Restaurant. Entry to the centre and parking are free and there are picnic and children's play areas. You can also watch traditional skills on a visit to the new Glass Studio at Denby.

DERWENT CRYSTAL LTD

SHAWCROFT, ASHBOURNE, DERBYSHIRE DE6 1GH, ☎ 01335 345219, FAX: 01335 300225, **e-mail:** enquiries@derwentcrystal.co.uk, www.derwentcrystal.co.uk, 9–5 MON–SAT. **FACTORY SHOP**

A wide selection of glassware and fancy items at factory shop prices. Lead crystal from liqueur glasses to vases and bowls, ring stands and dressing-table novelties. More than 200 different items on sale. Gift wrapping and mail order available. Also engraving for special occasions.

DUNELM MILL SHOP

OSMASTON PARK INDUSTRIAL ESTATE, ASCOT DRIVE, DERBY, DERBYSHIRE DE24 8GW, ☎ 01332 362526, FAX: 01332 362059, www.dunelm-mill.co.uk, 9–5.30 MON–WED, 9–8 THUR, FRI, 9–6 SAT, 10–4 SUN. **PERMANENT DISCOUNT OUTLET**

See page 458 (BEDS)

EDINBURGH CRYSTAL

MCARTHUR GLEN DESIGNER OUTLET VILLAGE, HOMEWARES BUILDING, SOUTH NORMANTON, DERBYSHIRE DE55 2ER, ☎ 01773 545186, 10–6 MON–SAT, 8 ON THUR, 11–5 SUN. **FACTORY SHOP IN A FACTORY SHOPPING VILLAGE**

See page 463 (CHESH)

GIFTTREE

38 MAIN CENTRE, DERBY, DERBYSHIRE DE1 2PE, ☎ 01332 204078, 9–5 MON–SAT.
36 HIGH STREET, SWADLINCOTE, DERBYSHIRE DE11 8HY, ☎ 01283 226700, 9–5 MON–SAT.
FACTORY SHOP

Items from the Express Gifts mail order catalogues at reduced prices including cards, giftwrap, gifts, stationery, kitchenware, household products, clothes and toys, including Galt products. Discounts in most departments range from at least 50% off original catalogue selling prices.

LABEL TRADERS

30 MAIN CENTRE, DERBY, DERBYSHIRE DE1 2PE, ☎ 01332 381439, www.labeltraders.co.uk, 9–5 MON–SAT. **FACTORY SHOP**

Good quality ex-chainstore merchandise from well-known high street shops with all the labels cut out. Stock includes knitwear, dresses, suits, blouses, skirts, sportswear, nightwear, trousers for women, and childrenswear. Also stocks some household goods such as towels. Discounts range up to 50%. There are other branches in Sutton-in-Ashfield and Ruddington.

MASSON MILLS SHOPPING VILLAGE

DERBY ROAD, MATLOCK BATH, NEAR MATLOCK, DERBYSHIRE DE4 3PY, ☎ 01629 760208, FAX: 01629 761525, 10–5.30 MON–SAT, 11–5 SUN. **FACTORY SHOPPING VILLAGE**

Anchored by Edinburgh Woollen Mills and set on four floors, this shopping village is set in regenerated 18th century mill building with a working textile museum and conference facilities. There are shops selling fashion, golfwear and equipment, gifts, speciality foods and country goods and include Julian Graves food items, Woods of Windsor, and Ponden Mill selling bedlinen and towels. The top floor is a designer clothing store stocking labels such as DKNY, Kangol, Ben Sherman, Miss Sixty, Tommy Hilfiger and many others, all with up to 50% off normal retail prices. There is a riverside restaurant on site.

MATALAN

BRADSHAW RETAIL PARK, BRADSHAW WAY, DERBY, DERBYSHIRE DE24 5WA, ☎ 01332 223850, FAX: 01332 298020, www.matalan.co.uk, 9.30–8 MON–FRI, 9–6 SAT, 11–5 SUN. **PERMANENT DISCOUNT OUTLET**

See page 458 (BEDS)

MCARTHURGLEN DESIGNER OUTLET

MANSFIELD ROAD, SOUTH NORMANTON, ALFRETON, JUNCTION 28 OF M1, DERBYSHIRE DE55 2ER, ☎ 01773 545000, www.mcarthurglen.com/mansfield, 10–6 MON–FRI, 8 ON THUR, 9–6 SAT, 11–5 SUN. **FACTORY SHOPPING VILLAGE**

The McArthurGlen Designer Outlet Mansfield has recently undergone a year-long development programme, transforming it from an open-plan department store layout to individual shops. The new look outlet is now bigger and better. Find all your favourite brands at discounts of up to 50% off typical retail prices. Facilities include a children's play area, a food court and plenty of free parking. Stores include: Antler, Banana Books, Bed & Bath Works, Big L, Camille Lingerie, Chapelle, Claire's Accessories, Coloroll, Cotton Traders, Donnay, Edinburgh Crystal, Harbi, Jaeger, Jane Shilton, Julian Graves, Kitch N Sync, Leading Labels, Lee Cooper, Mountain Warehouse, Pavers Shoes, Petroleum, Pilot, Price's Candles, Professional Cookware, Remington, Roman Originals, Sky, Soled Out, Speedo, Sportsmill, Suits You, Thorntons, Tog 24, Toyworld, Revlon, Marks & Spencer Outlet, Windsmoor, Sportz, Reebok, Jumper, HKA, Proudfoot Leather, Garden Outlet, Lilley & Skinner, Adidas, Viyella, Whittards, XS Records and many more.

OAKHAM CLOTHING

BULLBRIDGE, AMBERGATE, DERBYSHIRE DE56 2HH, ☎ 01773 853473, 10–5.30 MON–FRI, 10–5 SAT, 10–4 SUN AND BANK HOLIDAYS. **FACTORY SHOP**

Previously Stevenson's of Ambergate, now under new ownership, this factory shop sells a wide range of women's knitwear, blouses, skirts, dresses, underwear, nightdresses, hosiery, men's trousers, outerwear, knitwear and childrenswear, as well as towels, face cloths and shoes for men and women. Women's clothes range from 8 to 22 in size, men's from 28in waist to 44in in season. There is a huge range of underwear, as well as wool coats, macs and anoraks in the outerwear. Childrenswear ranges from babies to teenwear.

PEAK VILLAGE

CHATSWORTH ROAD, ROWSLEY, (ON THE A6 BETWEEN BAKEWELL AND MATLOCK) DERBYSHIRE DE4 2JE, ☎ 01629 735326, www.peakvillage.co.uk, 9.30–5.30 MON–SAT, 10–5 SUN, EXCEPT CHRISTMAS DAY. **FACTORY SHOPPING VILLAGE**

More than 20 factory outlets including Leading Labels, Cotton Traders, Luggage & Bags, The Book Depot, Pavers Shoes, Sports & Mountain Warehouse, Yeoman Outdoors outdoor wear and equipment, Ponden Mill, Mansworld, New Beginnings and Woodlands Fitness Centre, all just 30 minutes from the M1 at the entrance to the Peak District National Park. On-site catering includes Massarella's Restaurant, which offers everything from ice cream to a traditional Sunday roast. The Wind in the Willows Attraction is a magical journey through the world of Ratty, Badger, Mole and of course the irrepressible Mr Toad. The latest sound and lighting effects bring Kenneth Grahame's classic tale to life in an enchanting recreation that's not just for kids! Free parking for up to 400 cars. Recently opened the Woodlands Fitness Centre.

PONDEN MILL LINENS

PONDEN MILL FACTORY SHOP, DE BRADELEI MILL SHOPS, DE BRADELEI HOUSE, CHAPEL STREET, BELPER, DERBYSHIRE DE56 1AR, ☎ 01773 882815, 9.30–5.30 MON–FRI, 9.30–6 SAT, 11–5 SUN.

PEAK VILLAGE, CHATSWORTH ROAD, ROWSLEY, DERBYSHIRE DE4 2JE, ☎ 01629 733857, 9.30–5.30 MON–SAT, 10–5 SUN. **FACTORY SHOP**

See page 464 (CHESH)

PORTMEIRION

MCARTHURGLEN DESIGNER OUTLET, MANSFIELD ROAD, SOUTH NORMANTON, ALFRETON, JUNCTION 28 OF M1, DERBYSHIRE DE55 2ER, ☎ 01773 545186, www.portmeirion.co.uk, 10–6 MON–SAT, 8 ON THUR, 11–5 SUN (OPEN UNTIL 9 IN WINTER: PHONE FIRST). **FACTORY SHOP IN A FACTORY SHOPPING VILLAGE**

This factory shop sells Portmeirion seconds in all patterns alongside Edinburgh Crystal. The selection includes tableware (tea, coffee and dinner set); giftware (vases, planters, mugs, candlesticks, salad and fruit bowls) and coordinating accessories (placemats, cookware, textiles, tumblers). Discounts are approximately one third but vary from item to item. There are monthly promotions where stock is further reduced. Phone if you would like to be added to the mailing list to be advised of forthcoming promotions. Good coach parking facilities (please book) and wheelchair access.

PRICE'S CANDLES

MCARTHURGLEN DESIGNER OUTLET, MANSFIELD ROAD, SOUTH NORMANTON, ALFRETON, JUNCTION 28 OF M1, DERBYSHIRE DE55 2ER, ☎ 01773 545202, 10–6 MON–FRI, 8 ON THUR, 9–6 SAT, 11–5 SUN. **FACTORY SHOP IN A FACTORY SHOPPING VILLAGE**

See page 464 (CHESH)

ROYAL CROWN

194 OSMASTON ROAD, DERBY, DERBYSHIRE DE23 8JZ, ☎ 01332 712833, www.royal-crown-derby.co.uk, 9–5 MON–SAT, 10.30–4.30 SUN. **FACTORY SHOP**

One third of the stock in this shop is made up of seconds of bone china at discount prices reduced by about one third of recommended retail prices. This includes giftware, tableware and paperweights. Factory tours can be arranged on weekdays, while a seven-day visitor centre allows you to see Royal Crown Derby being made and have a go at it yourself.

T G GREEN POTTERY FACTORY OUTLET

JOHN STREET, CHURCH GRESLEY, DERBYSHIRE DE11 8EF, ☎ 01283 226696, 9.30–4.30 MON–FRI, 9.30–4 SAT, 10–3.30 SUN. PHONE FOR CHRISTMAS OPENING HOURS. MAIL ORDER. **FACTORY SHOP**

This factory shop sells table mats, dinner sets, clocks, coasters, trays, pottery and end-of-line stock from chainstores most of which are either discontinued lines or seconds of ongoing ranges. Many items are half the normal retail price. They will send you a price list and catalogue for £2.50 and you can order by phone. They hold ad hoc sales throughout the year: phone for details.

TK MAXX

8 EAST STREET, DERBY, DERBYSHIRE, ☎ 01332 364225, www.tkmaxx.com, 9–5.30 MON–THUR, 9–6 FRI–SAT, 11–5 SUN. **PERMANENT DISCOUNT OUTLET**

See page 458 (BEDS)

WILKINSON STORES

13 INSTITUTE LANE, ALFRETON, DERBYSHIRE DE55 7BQ, ☎ 01773 836845, www.wilko.co.uk, 9–5.30 MON–THUR, SAT, 9–6 FRI, 10–2 SUN. MAIL ORDER. **PERMANENT DISCOUNT OUTLET**

See page 466 (CHESH)

WIRKSWORTH FACTORY SHOP

BENCO HOSIERY, NORTH END MILLS, WIRKSWORTH, DERBYSHIRE DE4 4FG, ☎ 01629 824731, 9–5 SEVEN DAYS A WEEK, 8 ON THUR. **FACTORY SHOP**

Wide selection of clothes for the family, household goods, giftware and linen. There are T-shirts, shorts, sun vests, skirts, blouses, shirts, sweatshirts, jeans, trousers, dresses, work shirts, swimwear, jog suits, underwear, babywear, socks, tea towels, pillows, duvets and towels. There is a children's play corner and snacks facility. Men's shirts are up to 19-inch collar. For women, the stockings are less than half shop prices and there is cotton, thermal and woollen underwear. Large, free car park. You can see machines making socks on most days.

WOODS OF WINDSOR MASSON MILLS

UNIT 10, MASSON SHOPPING VILLAGE AND HISTORIC MILLS, MASSON MILLS, MATLOCK BATH, DERBYSHIRE DE4 3PY, ☎ 01629 760952, www.woodsofwindsor.co.uk, 10–6 MON–SAT, 8 ON THUR, 11–5 SUN. **FACTORY SHOP IN A FACTORY SHOPPING VILLAGE**

See page 466 (CHESH)

DEVON

ATLANTIC VILLAGE OUTLET CENTRE

CLOVELLY ROAD, OFF A39, WEST OF BIDEFORD, NORTH DEVON, ☎ 01237 422544, **e-mail:** rmorris@realm-ocm.com, www.atlanticvillage.co.uk, JULY–MID SEPT, 9.30–7 MON–SAT, 11–5 SUN; MID SEPT–MID OCT AND EASTER TO JULY 9.30–6.30 MON–SAT, 11–5 SUN; MID OCT–EASTER 9.30–5 MON–SAT, 11–5 SUN. **FACTORY SHOPPING VILLAGE**

More than 30 shops with famous names and Devon's largest interactive maze make this village a good family day out. Shops include Banana Books; Claire's Accessories; Colony Candles; Cotton Traders, Designer Room, Ecco; Edinburgh Woollen Mill; Event Jewellery; Jane Shilton; Jean Scene; Julian Graves; Nickelby's; Pavers Shoes; Pilot; Ponden Mill; Puma; Roman Originals; Room, selling home accessories, fabrics and soft furnishings; Sportsmill; Suits You; Tog 24; Toyzone; Triumph; Warners; Windsmoor; XS Sound & Media. Free car parking, disabled and baby changing facilities. Atlantic Village also features an attractive piazza, cafés, a food court, visitor garden, arts and crafts market, open-air amphitheatre, and an adventure park set in an additional three-acre site linked to the shopping area by the piazza and amphitheatre. The Adventure Park features a mystery maze, adventure golf, wrecker's cove and adventure play boat.

BED & BATH WORKS

UNIT 24C, HOMESTYLE, ATLANTIC VILLAGE, CLOVELLY ROAD, BIDEFORD, NORTH DEVON EX39 3QU, ☎ 01237 470774, FAX: 01237 470774, **e-mail:** hello@bedandbathworks.co.uk, www.bedandbathworks.co.uk, 10–6 MON–SAT, 8 ON THUR, 10.30–4.30 SUN. **FACTORY SHOP IN A FACTORY SHOPPING VILLAGE**

See page 462 (CHESH)

C H BRANNAM LTD

ROUNDSWELL INDUSTRIAL ESTATE, BARNSTAPLE, DEVON EX31 3NJ, ☎ 01271 376853, FAX: 01271 379400, **e-mail:** brannam@brannam.com, 9–5 MON–SAT, 10–4 SUN FROM MAY–SEPT ONLY. **FACTORY SHOP**

On-site factory shop selling terracotta gardening and cookware, including many different forms of pots, especially glazed pots. Seconds are usually available. Phone for details of factory tours.

CLASSIC COUNTRY RANGES

4 WEBBERS YARD, DARTINGTON, NR TOTNES, SOUTH DEVON TQ9 6JY, ☎ 01803 865555, FAX: 01803 867267, **e-mail:** info@classiccountryranges.com, www.classiccountryranges.com, 9–5 MON–FRI, 10–1 SAT. **PERMANENT DISCOUNT OUTLET**

Specialist suppliers of factory renovated Aga and Rayburn cookers, plus a range of new appliances for cooking or central heating, all at very competitive prices. Old Agas are completely dismantled, sandblasted inside, all the enamel parts re-enamelled in the customer's choice of colour, and re-assembled with new burners and fully tested. Savings of at least £1,000 can be made compared with buying a new Aga or Rayburn. Also sells an Aga equivalent, the Trianco Redfyre, which costs about £1,000 less than an Aga but has the equivalent insides, although the outside looks different. Main agent for Nobel and Sandyford products, spares and discount heating materials especially flue products. Installations undertaken at competitive prices. Also sell a range of Bridgewater pottery.

CLAYTON MUNROE LTD

KINGSTON WEST DRIVE, KINGSTON, STAVERTON, TOTNES, DEVON TQ9 6AR, ☎ 01803 762626, FAX: 01803 762584, **e-mail:** mail@claytonmunroe.com, www.claytonmunroe.com, 9–5 MON–FRI. **FACTORY SHOP**

Clayton Munroe Ltd manufacture innovative high quality door furniture with a French feel, specialising in a patine finish, a rust-proof pewter colour. The factory in Devon has a factory shop area where ends of line of these and their cabinet knobs, electrical fittings, coat hooks, pull handles and towel rings are on sale at discount prices. The website also includes details of discounted discontinued lines and slight imperfects which can be ordered by post. Items on sale include patine skirting door stop, £8.82 each; patine fleur de lys door bolt, £23.86; patine Celtic hat and coat hook £18.71 each; black hanging bracket, £8.77; ornate patine hinge, £3.95; patine twisted towel ring, £10.61.

CLOVERLEAF

HOMESTYLE, ATLANTIC VILLAGE, BIDEFORD, NORTH DEVON EX39 3QU, ☎ 01237 473998, 10–6 MON–SAT, 11–5 SUN. **FACTORY SHOP**

Part of the large household department at this large factory shopping complex, one section sells a range of melamine products, such as place mats, coasters and trays, oven-to-tableware and storage jars. Seconds and discontinued lines are sold here at reduced prices.

CURTAIN TRADER

52 HIGH STREET, HONITON, DEVON EX14 1LQ, ☎ 01404 45451, **e-mail:** flatcatco@yahoo.co.uk, 9–5 MON–SAT. **SECONDHAND SHOP**

Secondhand curtain agency, they are also specialists in discontinued and seconds designer fabrics and sale stock from £2 to £20 a metre, selling curtain fabrics, linings and accessories from many different labels. Also incorporating Flat Cat Cushion Co, individual cushions, trade and retail, and Old Devon Pine, made-to-measure furniture.

DARTINGTON CRYSTAL

ATLANTIC VILLAGE, CLOVELLY ROAD, BIDEFORD, NORTH DEVON EX39 3QU, ☎ 01237 473998, 9.30–6 MON–SAT, 11–5 SUN.

BARBICAN GLASSWORKS, THE BARBICAN, PLYMOUTH, DEVON PL1 2LT, ☎ 01752 224777, FAX: 01752 253354, 9–6 MON–SAT, 11–5 SUN. **FACTORY SHOP**

See page 469 (CORN)

DARTINGTON CRYSTAL

GREAT TORRINGTON, NORTH DEVON EX38 7AN, ☎ 01805 626262, FAX: 01805 626263, www.dartington.co.uk, 9.30–5 MON–SAT, 10.30–4 SUN. FACTORY TOURS 9.30–10.15, 12–3.15. **FACTORY SHOP**

The factory shop at Torrington has an extensive range of Dartington Crystal seconds at greatly reduced prices. Shopping opportunities include a giftware shop selling Portmeirion, Cloverleaf and Denby, locally produced quality goods, gifts and candles as well as The Edinburgh Woollen Mill with a large selection of classic knitwear and coordinated clothing. For a small charge, there are factory tours where you can watch skilled craftsmen blowing and shaping beautiful crystal. The visitor centre now includes a family activity centre where you can try your hand at glass art, paint or engrave your own designs on a piece of glass. There is a restaurant serving hot and cold meals. The other outlets sell crystal of first and second quality, all at discounted prices.

DARTMOUTH POTTERY

WARFLEET, DARTMOUTH, DEVON TQ6 9BY, ☎ 01803 832258, 10–5 SEVEN DAYS A WEEK. **FACTORY SHOP**

Discontinued lines and some perfects of Dartmouth pottery at varied discounts. There is always something on special offer: prices range from 50p to £15. Cafe, gallery retail area and working factory (free admission).

EXETER SURPLUS

BAKERS YARD, ALPHINBROOK ROAD, MARSH BARTON INDUSTRIAL ESTATE, EXETER, DEVON EX2 8SS, ☎ 01392 427508, 8.30–5 MON–SAT. **PERMANENT DISCOUNT OUTLET**

Operates from a 4,000 square foot retail unit and a 10,000 square foot trade site half a mile away on Christow Road, the latter specialising in quality, nearly-new office furniture and shelving. Retail goods include engineering equipment, hand tools, clothing, a large range of outdoor goods, chandlery, a range of tents, bedding and domestic furniture, kayaks, rope and chain, canvas sheets, rucksacks, boots and shoes, overalls, ceremonial clothing and an enormous amount of miscellaneous one-off items, all very competitively priced. The outdoor leisure market is their new specialisation.

HOUSE OF MARBLES & TEIGN VALLEY GLASS

THE OLD POTTERY, POTTERY ROAD, BOVEY TRACEY, DEVON TQ13 9DS, ☎ 01626 835358, 9–5 SEVEN DAYS A WEEK. **FACTORY SHOP**

Traditional games, glassware and gifts for all occasions, with lots of discounted seconds at up to 50% off. There are museums of pottery, glass marbles and games and a coffee shop and licensed restaurant. Glass blowing can be viewed from 9am to 4.30pm Monday to Friday and from 10am to 3pm on Sundays all year round. No entrance charge and free parking.

MATALAN

UNIT 2, HAVEN BANKS, WATER LANE, EXETER, DEVON EX2 8DW, ☎ 01392 413375, FAX: 01392 413376, www.matalan.co.uk, 10–8 MON–FRI, 9–6 SAT, 11–5 SUN.

TRANSIT WAY, HONICKNOWLE, PLYMOUTH, DEVON PL5 3TW, ☎ 01752 237600, FAX: 01752 767216, www.matalan.co.uk, 9–8 MON–FRI, 9–6 SAT, 11–5 SUN. **PERMANENT DISCOUNT OUTLET**

See page 458 (BEDS)

PONDEN MILL LINENS

ATLANTIC VILLAGE, CLOVELLEY ROAD, BIDEFORD, NORTH DEVON EX39 5TB, ☎ 01237 472127, 9–6 MON–SAT, 10.30–4.30 SUN. **FACTORY SHOP IN A FACTORY SHOPPING VILLAGE**

See page 464 (CHESH)

STEWART'S

58–60 FORE STREET, BRIXHAM, DEVON TQ5 8DZ, ☎ 01803 852000, FAX: 01803 852000, 9–5 MON–SAT, 10–4 SUN.

RICHMOND COURT, DAWLISH, DEVON EX7 9PL, ☎ 01626 895022, FAX: 01626 895022, 9–5 MON–SAT, 10.30–4.30 SUN.

24–26 QUEEN STREET, NEWTON ABBOT, DEVON TQ12 2EF, ☎ 01626 362721, FAX: 01626 362721, 9–5.30 MON–SAT.

9–15 STATION ROAD, TEIGNMOUTH, DEVON TQ14 8PE, ☎ 01626 775616, FAX: 01626 775616, 9–5.30 MON–SAT, 10.30–4.30 SUN.

37 FORE STREET, TOTNES, DEVON TG9 5HN, ☎ 01803 865093, FAX: 01803 865093, 9–5 MON–SAT, 10–4 SUN. **FACTORY SHOP**

Branded merchandise from most of the major UK chainstores, all well-known department store names, offered at a discount of 40% to 70% off normal high street prices. The garments are selected with great care by experienced buyers direct from factories worldwide to bring customers top quality merchandise at highly competitive prices.

THE CARDEW TEAPOT POTTERY

NEWTON ROAD, BOVEY TRACEY, DEVON TQ13 9DX, ☎ 01626 832172, FAX: 01626 834773, www.cardewdesign.com, 10–5.30 SEVEN DAYS A WEEK. **FACTORY SHOP**

It's said that Josiah Wedgwood used to personally smash any pottery which didn't come up to his exacting standards; Paul Cardew has much the same philosophy. As Cardew don't sell anything other than first quality perfect goods to retailers, here in Bovey Tracey they sell a selected range of slightly imperfect teapots, miniature teapots and other ceramics at up to 50% less than the normal price. Their shop is also a Mecca for all other things to do with tea, from tea itself to teatowels, and from books about tea to tea cosies. There are free tours when you can see these collectable teapots being made. Large free car park and tea room. Opening hours change seasonally so do phone first.

THE FAMOUS LEE MILL FACTORY OUTLET

PLYMOUTH ROAD, NEAR IVYBRIDGE, DEVON PL21 9EE, ☎ 01752 691100, 9.30–5 MON–SAT, 10–4 SUN. **PERMANENT DISCOUNT OUTLET**

A factory outlet selling fashion for men and women including golf clothes from Glenmuir and Lyle & Scott. There is also a selection of childrenswear from three to 16 years, and kitchenware, including wooden kitchen goods and a wide range of gifts from key rings to mugs. There is a coffee shop on site which serves cream teas, light meals and refreshments. Free parking.

THE SHERIDAN AUSTRALIA FACTORY SHOP

27 KENNEDY WAY INDUSTRIAL ESTATE, MOUNTBATTEN ROAD, TIVERTON, DEVON EX16 6SW, ☎ 01884 255997, FAX: 01884 258644, www.sheridan.com.au, 9–5 MON–SAT. **PERMANENT DISCOUNT OUTLET**

Sells bed linen from Australia to 60 concessions countrywide. Full range of bedlinen including sheets, bedspreads and curtains with prices from 30% to 70% off. Designed in Australia, unusual designs with a high thread count made to last. Other outlet in the UK include the Designer Outlet Village in Swindon and Boundary Mill Stores.

TK MAXX

YEO BUILDING, 28 ROYAL PARADE, NEW GEORGE STREET, PLYMOUTH, DEVON PL1 1SA, ☎ 01752 255081, www.tkmaxx.com, 9–5.30 MON–WED, 9–8 THUR, 9–6 FRI–SAT, 11–5 SUN.

FIRST FLOOR, 56-62 FLEET WALK, FLEET WALK SHOPPING CENTRE, TORQUAY, DEVON TQ2 5EN, ☎ 01803 215682, www.tkmaxx.com, 9–5.30 MON–SAT, 7 ON THUR, 10–7 SAT, 11–5 SUN. **PERMANENT DISCOUNT OUTLET**

See page 458 (BEDS)

TRAGO MILLS SHOPPING AND LEISURE PARKS

LIVERTON, NEWTON ABBOT, DEVON TQ12 6JD, ☎ 01626 821111, www.trago.co.uk, 9–5.30 MON–SAT, 10.45–4.45 SUN. **PERMANENT DISCOUNT OUTLET**

The biggest range of discounted goods in the West Country, with a whole range of activities to keep the family amused on the 100 acre site. Sells virtually everything from men's, women's and childrenswear, gardening equipment and cookware to wallpaper, carpets and fitted kitchens. Most are branded goods and there is a café, pizza bar and petrol station. A reasonable amount of the women's fashion comes from high street multiples. The menswear offers a wide range of clothes, as well as all-leather classic brogues and Oxford shoes, and Doc Martens in the Shoes Yard. For the home, there are Black & Decker Dustbusters, Hotpoint dryers and washing machines with cosmetic blemishes; curtain fabrics from Monkwell, Sekers, Filigree, Laura Ashley as well as Janet Reger for Vantona double quilt covers, with matching sheets, pillow cases and valances. There is a vast range of tiles including Pilkington seconds. A huge gardening section with everything from hose pipes and garden machinery to imported trees and shrubs. An excellent leisure section offers bicycles and accessories, golf gear, keep-fit systems, fishing rods and flies. Comparison prices are not given here, although staff say most items are discounted by up to 50%, so if you're looking for a bargain, make sure you've done your homework on the high street first. The best deals are in fabrics, carpets, tiles and DIY. There is a leisure park with a giant free fall slide, supakart and family go-kart circuit, bumper boats, trawler rides, swan pedalos, pirate ship, aquablasters, orbiters, shooting gallery, remote control cars and cruisers, forklifts and mini-diggers, fun dungeon, animal park, model railway, narrow gauge steam railway, nature reserve, coarse fishing, Edwardian penny arcade and plenty of space to picnic and to park.

TURNSTYLE DESIGNS

BARON WAY, ROUNDSWELL BUSINESS PARK, BARNSTAPLE, DEVON EX31 3TB, ☎ 01271 325325, FAX: 01271 328248, **e-mail:** sales@turnstyle-designs.com, www.turnstyle-designs.com, 9–6 MON–THUR, 9–5 FRI. **FACTORY SHOP**

Factory shop area within the new showroom at its Devon warehouse selling seconds and overstock of its stylish, co-ordinating functional fittings: door handles, cabinet knobs, window bolts, light pulls, door locks, latches, hinges, slot keyhole covers and electric switch plates. A one-stop shop for architectural ironmongery, both traditional and contemporary, products come in a variety of different materials including alupewt, black bronze, ochre, bone and ebony, and designs including frog-shaped, ammomite, fish, rope, deco etc.

DORSET

DARTINGTON CRYSTAL

POOLE POTTERY, THE QUAY, POOLE, DORSET BH15 1RF, ☎ 01202 668615, FAX: 01202 682894, 9–6 MON–SAT, 10–5 SUN. **FACTORY SHOP**

See page 469 (CORN)

IN EXCESS

354–358 ASHLEY ROAD, PARKSTONE, POOLE, DORSET BH14 9DF, ☎ 01202 740188, 9–5.30 MON–SAT, 10–4 SUN.

80–83 DOLPHIN CENTRE, POOLE, DORSET, ☎ 01202 673534, 9–5.30 MON–SAT, 10–4 SUN.

SOMERFORD ROAD, CHRISTCHURCH, DORSET BH23 3PH, ☎ 01202 481438, 9–5.30 MON–SAT, 10–4 SUN. **PERMANENT DISCOUNT OUTLET**

In Excess is stacked full of bankrupt stock from stationery and paint to DIY tools and cleaning materials, plumbing materials, screws, bolts, nuts, and telephone accessories. It also houses, in season, garden furniture and pots aimed at the starter garden lover and decking. Plastic tables and chairs start at £2.95 for a chair and from £5.95 to £12.95 for a table; terracotta pots start from 50p and there are also 'antiqued' stone pots.

MATALAN

TURBARY RETAIL PARK, RINGWOOD ROAD, BOURNEMOUTH, DORSET BH12 3JJ, ☎ 01202 590686, FAX: 01202 590697, www.matalan.co.uk, 10–8 MON–FRI, 9–6 SAT, 10–4 SUN.

JUBILEE RETAIL PARK, RADIPOLE PARK DRIVE, WEYMOUTH DORSET DT4 7BG, ☎ 01305 831300, FAX: 01305 830472, www.matalan.co.uk, 9–8 MON–FRI, 9–6 SAT, 10.30–4.30 SUN. **PERMANENT DISCOUNT OUTLET**

See page 458 (BEDS)

PONDEN MILL LINENS

POOLE POTTERY, THE QUAY, POOLE, DORSET BH15 1RF, ☎ 01202 684024, 9–5.30 MON–SAT, 10–5 SUN. **FACTORY SHOP**

See page 464 (CHESH)

T J HUGHES

616–622 CHRISTCHURCH ROAD, BOSCOMBE, BOURNEMOUTH, DORSET BH1 4BR, ☎ 01202 300333, FAX: 01202 303515, **e-mail:** info@tjhughes.co.uk, www.tjhughes.co.uk, 9–5.30 MON–FRI, 9–6 SAT, 10–4 SUN. **PERMANENT DISCOUNT OUTLET**

See page 465 (CHESH)

THE CATALOGUE SHOP

401 LYMINGTON ROAD, HIGHCLIFFE, DORSET BH23 5HE, ☎ 01425 271202, FAX: 01425 278478, **e-mail:** thecatalogueshop@virgin.net, www.the catalogueshop.virgin.com, 9–5 MON–SAT, 10–5 SUN. **PERMANENT DISCOUNT OUTLET**

Returns, damaged and worn goods as well as clearance lines and ends of lines of branded merchandise from mail order catalogues. This includes men's, women's and children's wear, footwear, bedding, curtains, furniture, exercise equipment and leather coats. These items are always in stock but the shop also has an ever-changing range of items as well. Turnover is very fast with new deliveries every day. All items are sold at less than 50% of the catalogue price starting at 99p, with branded trainers from £14.99.

THE POOLE POTTERY FACTORY SHOP

THE QUAY, POOLE, DORSET BH15 1RF, ☎ 01202 668681, FAX: 01202 649082, 9–5.30 MON–SAT, 10.30–4.30 SUN. PHONE FOR SEASONAL OPENING TIMES. **FACTORY SHOP**

The Poole Factory Shop is still the cheapest place to buy the widest selection of Poole Pottery. All the old favourite ranges such as Dorset Fruit, Vincent and Vineyard are joined by new exciting ranges like Fresco. The critically acclaimed new 'Living Glaze' gift range which uses a glazing method pioneered at Poole nearly 40 years ago is now also available. The shop has long ceased to be just an outlet for Poole Pottery. It now boasts some of the top brands in giftware such as Dartington, Colony Candles and, more recently, Julian Graves. All these plus the new cook shop makes it the perfect place for the first-time housebuyer to buy practically all their home essentials – it is fast becoming the biggest gift shop in the south. Poole Pottery has recently undertaken an extensive site redevelopment responding to their own research which suggested that both parents and children prefer a separate area to paint plates, throw pots and learn the ancient skills of the potter. The activity area can now be found on a floor of its own offering more freedom and security. This can now be found on the ground floor at the rear of the building. Glass blowing demonstrations are regularly held. In addition you can enjoy an a la carte, table d'hote meal with fine wines and unique harbour views at Carters restaurant, or opt for a light snack in the tea room or self-service area. A new, exciting fashion floor is now also here, with labels available including Excel, Reflection, Morgan and many others. Top quality suits, lingerie, shoes etc are all on sale at factory shop prices.

THE SHOE SHED

UNIT 9, QUADRANT ARCADE, HINTON ROAD, BOURNEMOUTH DORSET BH1 2AD, ☎ 01202 292992, 9–5.30 MON–SAT, 10–4 SUN. **FACTORY SHOP**

This shoe retailer, established for over 135 years, has a large factory shop selling a vast range of all types of women's, men's and children's shoes, all of which are perfects, at up to 30% below normal high street prices. Women's sandals cost from £2.99; shoes from £5. Men's shoes cost from £7.99; sports shoes from £5. Famous brands include Grenson, Loakes, Clarks, K Shoes, Elmdale, Caterpillar and Adidas. A large range of casual wear, including T-shirts and tracksuits for women, men and children, plus a selection of women's underwear. Kitchenware, ceramics, household goods and giftware are also stocked at discounted prices.

TK MAXX

QUADRANT ARCADE, OLD CHRISTCHURCH ROAD, BOURNEMOUTH, DORSET BH1 2BX, ☎ 01202 316367, www.tkmaxx.com, 9–5.30 MON–FRI, 8 ON THUR, 9–6 SAT, 11–5 SUN. **PERMANENT DISCOUNT OUTLET**

See page 458 (BEDS)

ESSEX

BED & BATH WORKS

CLACTON FACTORY OUTLET VILLAGE, STEPHENSON ROAD WEST, CLACTON-ON-SEA, ESSEX CO15 4XA, ☎ 01255 222585, FAX: 01255 223950, **e-mail:** hello@bedandbathworks.co.uk, www.bedandbathworks.co.uk, 10–6 MON–SAT, 11–5 SUN. **FACTORY SHOP IN A FACTORY SHOPPING VILLAGE**

See page 462 (CHESH)

BIRTHDAYS

UNIT 24, CLACTON COMMON FACTORY OUTLET, STEPHENSON ROAD WEST, CLACTON-ON-SEA, ESSEX CO16 9HB, ☎ 01255 223460, 10–6 SEVEN DAYS A WEEK. **FACTORY SHOPPING VILLAGE**

See page 462 (CHESH)

CATALOGUE BARGAIN SHOP

ST JOHN'S WALK SHOPPING CENTRE, COLCHESTER, ESSEX CO2 7AL, ☎ 01206 563126, www.bargaincrazy.com, 9–5.30 MON–THUR, 9–7 FRI, 9–6 SAT, 10.30–4.30 SUN. **PERMANENT DISCOUNT OUTLET**

See page 461 (CAMBS)

CHOICE DISCOUNT STORES LIMITED

14–20 RECTORY ROAD, HADLEIGH, BENFLEET, ESSEX SS7 2ND, ☎ 01702 555245, 9–5.30 MON–THUR, 9–6 FRI, SAT.

26–28 HIGH STREET, BARKINGSIDE, ILFORD, ESSEX IG6 2DQ, ☎ 020 8551 2125, 9–5.30 MON–FRI, 9–6 SAT, 11–5 SUN.

UNIT 6A, MAYFLOWER RETAIL PARK, GARDINERS LINK, BASILDON, ESSEX SS14 3AP, ☎ 01268 288331, 10–6 MON–WED, 10–7 THUR, FRI, 9–6 SAT, 11–5 SUN.

14–16 HIGH STREET, GRAYS, ESSEX RM17 6LU, ☎ 01375 385780, 9–5.30 MON–FRI, 9–6 SAT.

CLACTON FACTORY SHOPPING VILLAGE, STEPHENSON ROAD WEST, CLACTON-ON-SEA, ESSEX CO15 4TL, ☎ 01255 474786, 10–6 MON–SAT, 11–5 SUN. **PERMANENT DISCOUNT OUTLET**

See page 461 (CAMBS)

CHRISTMAS IN THE EASTERS

EASTER HALL, AYTHORPE RODING, GREAT DUNMOW, ESSEX CM6 1PE, ☎ 01245 231628, FAX: 01245 231827, **e-mail:** info@christmasintheeasters.com, www.christmasintheeasters.com, 8–6 SEVEN DAYS A WEEK. 20 OCT–CHRISTMAS EVE. **PERMANENT DISCOUNT OUTLET**

A Christmas tree farm with a seasonal discount outlet in the form of a themed Christmas barn selling everything you need for the festive season. The season starts with the sale of fireworks from Standard and Blackcat, all of which are priced so that you can enjoy more than one 'flash bang' as an excellent start to the season. A wide selection of top quality, home grown Christmas trees are available, including cut, potted, non-drop and pot-grown. This is the largest selection of big trees at competitive prices. Artificial trees of all sizes and a fantastic selection of tree and wall decorations are also available, including homemade, decorated Noble fir wreaths and artificial wreaths and tree stands. Fresh garlands can be made to order, to trail down staircases and above mantelpieces. Also stocks everything you need to make your own wreaths, including orange slices, dried roses, chillies, pine cones, apple slices, and many, many more. Well-known designer names in Christmas decorations in every colour feature in this barn which is full of trees decorated in different themes and colours to give you ideas not seen in the high street. A Santa's grotto is open at weekends while a special cartoon corner is set aside in the barn where children can watch television while you browse the two floors of this extensive barn.

CLACTON FACTORY SHOPPING VILLAGE

STEPHENSON ROAD WEST, CLACTON-ON-SEA, ESSEX CO15 4TL, ☎ 01255 479595, FAX: 01255 430777 INFORMATION LINE, 10–6 MON–SAT, 11–5 SUN. **FACTORY SHOPPING VILLAGE**

Forty eight units centred around a Victorian winter garden comprising the following: Banana Bookshop selling books, games and stationery; Because It's There (BIT) for sports and camping equipment; Bed & Bath Works, a homeware outlet with discounted branded linens and housewares from Janet Reger, Sheridan, Christy and Kingsley; Birthdays, stocking mainstream cards and gifts from manufacturers such as Andrew Brownsword, Disney, Parker, Galt and Warner Brothers; Camille for lingerie; Caterpillar selling foorwear from the Cat range; Choice, which sells family clothing from Next; Claire's Accessories; Clinkards family footwear from Church's, Gabor, Bally and Loake; Cook 'N Dine kitchenware, glass and ceramics; Cotton Traders casual wear; Dannimac outdoor wear; Designer Room selling designer fashion for men and women; Event fashion costume jewellery and watches from Accurist, Timberland, Seiko and Timex; Garden Store selling garden furniture, barbecues and equipment and, in season, Christmas decorations; Jacques Vert selling womenswear; JD Sports selling branded sports merchandise from Adidas, Nike, Reebok, Ellesse and Le Coq Sportif; Joanna Hall selling handbags from the Jane Shilton range; Julian Graves foods and nut mixes; Kids Play Factory with toys from ranges such as Fisher-Price and Lego; Leading Labels, with men's and women's fashions; Mobile Phone Shop; MX Active selling branded denim and casual wear for men, women and children; Nickelbys fashion wear for men and women; Olli Moda selling branded jeans and casual wear; Pilot, a young women's fashion outlet; Ponden Mill with a range of bedlinen and bathroom ware; Price's Candles; Roman Originals womenswear; Sasperilla for young women's fashions; Spotlight, a young women's fashion outlet; Suits You men's shirts, suits, and casual separates as well as wedding hire and Autonomy womenswear; Thorntons chocolates; Tog 24 outdoor activity wear; Windsmoor women's fashions; Travel Accessory Shop with travel goods from Delsey and Samsonite; Woods of Windsor toiletries and gift items; XS Music CDs and videos. There are also two restaurants, a tourist information centre, parking for 1,000 cars and a bus service link to Clacton-On-Sea town centre and railway station.

DENBY FACTORY SHOP

BRAINTREE FREEPORT, DESIGNER OUTLET VILLAGE, CHARTER WAY, CHAPEL HILL, BRAINTREE, ESSEX CM7 8YH, ☎ 01376 343032, www.denby.co.uk, 10–6 MON–WED AND FRI–SAT, 10–8 THUR, 11–5 SUN. **FACTORY SHOP IN A FACTORY SHOPPING VILLAGE**

See page 463 (CHESH)

DESIGN HOUSE

FREEPORT ESSEX VILLAGE, CHARTER WAY, CHAPEL HILL, BRAINTREE, ESSEX CM7 8YH, ☎ 01376 343004, 10–6 MON–SAT, 8 ON THUR, 11–5 SUN. **FACTORY SHOP IN A FACTORY SHOPPING VILLAGE**

A fantastic opportunity to acquire designer led home funishings at up to 50% off high street prices. With leading names such as Designers Guild, Caroline Charles, Benetton, Cawo and Bedeck, you'll be amazed at the fabulous assortment of bedding, duvets, throws, kitchen and dining co-ordinates, and much more.

EDINBURGH CRYSTAL

FREEPORT ESSEX, CHARTER WAY, CHAPEL HILL, BRAINTREE, ESSEX CM7 8YH, ☎ 01376 344797, 10–6 MON–SAT, 8 ON THUR, 11–5 SUN. **FACTORY SHOP IN A FACTORY SHOPPING VILLAGE**

See page 463 (CHESH)

FAIRHEADS

60–64 CRANBROOK ROAD, ILFORD, ESSEX IG1 4NQ, ☎ 020 8478 0328, 9–5.30 MON–SAT. **PERMANENT DISCOUNT OUTLET**

There are 13 different departments at Fairheads, including household, linen, soft furnishings, lingerie, fashion, hosiery, craft and haberdashery. There are often 'blue ticket' specials: for example, buy three pairs of Sloggi briefs and get a fourth free. Best quality stock at the lowest price possible and always special offers and reduced lines throughout the store. At sale time stock is half price or less. There are two genuine sales a year: after Christmas and at the end of June. Phone for details.

FREEPORT BRAINTREE DESIGNER OUTLET VILLAGE

FREEPORT ESSEX VILLAGE, CHARTER WAY, CHAPEL HILL, BRAINTREE, JUNCTION 8 OF M11, THEN A120, ESSEX CM77 8YH, ☎ 01376 348168, www.freeportbraintree.com, 10–6 MON–SAT, 8 ON THUR, 11–5 SUN. **FACTORY SHOPPING VILLAGE**

Freeport Braintree is a designer outlet village with over 80 shops. Situated in the heart of Essex with easy access from the A120, Freeport Braintree has its own dedicated railway station and is only a one-hour journey from central London. Womenswear includes Aquascutum, Amazing Jeans, Antonio d'Errico, Box Fresh, Burberry, Christian Lacroix, Cotton Traders, Elle, Gossard, Karen Millen, Ted Baker, Tommy Hilfiger and Versace and The Designer Room with a host of designer labels. Menswear includes Aquascutum, Cecil Gee, Ciro Citterio, Cotton Traders, Kurt Muller, Nickleby's, Proibito, Ted Baker, Tommy Hilfiger, Van Heusen and Versace. For children there's Base 2 Base, Mexx and Toy Dome; there is also plenty to keep children entertained, such as the Cheeky Chimps indoor play area. Sportwear outlets include Brand Fusion, Donnay, Fila, Mountain Warehouse, Nike, Reebok, Regatta and Trespass. Footwear is covered by Ecco Shoes, Franchetti Bond, Hush Puppies, Jane Shilton, Lilley & Skinner, Soled Out and Vans Shoes. Shops selling household goods from kitchenware to pot pourri include Churchills, Denby, Edinburgh Crystal, Glen Eagles, Le Creuset, Professional Cookware, The Design House, Waterford Wedgwood and Villeroy & Boch. Other retail outlets, selling everything from luggage to music, include Body Shop, Carlton, Claire's Accessories, Designer Shades, Mobile Phone Store, Watch Store and XS Music, and there are no less than six cafés and restaurants on site.

LE CREUSET

FREEPORT ESSEX VILLAGE, CHARTER WAY, CHAPEL HILL, BRAINTREE, ESSEX CM7 8YH, ☎ 01376 329584, 10–6 MON–SAT, 8 ON THUR, 11–5 SUN. **FACTORY SHOP IN A FACTORY SHOPPING VILLAGE**

Items from the famous Le Creuset range – casseroles, saucepans, frying pans etc – plus their pottery collection at discounts of at least 30%.

MATALAN

CRICKETERS RETAIL PARK, CRICKETERS WAY, BASILDON, ESSEX SS13 1SA, ☎ 01268 290260, FAX: 01268 534860, www.matalan.co.uk, 10–8 MON–FRI, 9–6 SAT, 10–4 SUN.

UNIT 4, RIVERSIDE RETAIL PARK, VICTORIA ROAD, CHELMSFORD, ESSEX CM2 6LL, ☎ 01245 348787, FAX: 01245 348989, www.matalan.co.uk, 10–8 MON–FRI, 9–6 SAT, 11–5 SUN.

UNIT E, COLCHESTER RETAIL PARK, SHEEPHEN ROAD, COLCHESTER, ESSEX CO3 3LE, ☎ 01206 812400, FAX: 01206 541716, www.matalan.co.uk, 10–8 MON–FRI, 9–6 SAT, 11–5 SUN.

TOWER RETAIL PARK, CRAYFORD ROAD, CRAYFORD, DARTFORD, ESSEX DA1 4LD, ☎ 01322 552140, FAX: 01322 522516, www.matalan.co.uk, 9 -8 MON–FRI, 9 -6 SAT, 10–4 SUN.

117 NORTH STREET, ROMFORD ESSEX RM1 1EX, ☎ 01708 759780, FAX: 01708 760102, www.matalan.co.uk, 10–8 MON–FRI, 9–6 SAT, 10–4 SUN.

THE GREYHOUND RETAIL PARK, SUTTON ROAD, SOUTHEND ESSEX SS2 5PY, ☎ 01702 466248, FAX: 01702 617571, www.matalan.co.uk, 10 -8 MON–FRI, 9 -6 SAT, 10–4 SUN.

UNIT 4B, THE TUNNEL ESTATE, LAKESIDE, WEST THURROCK, ESSEX RM20 3WZ, ☎ 01708 864350, FAX: 01708 864334, www.matalan.co.uk, 10–8 MON–FRI, 9–6 SAT, 11–5 SUN.
PERMANENT DISCOUNT OUTLET

See page 458 (BEDS)

NORPAR FLOWERS

NAVESTOCK HALL, NAVESTOCK, ROMFORD, ESSEX RM4 1HA, ☎ 01277 374968, **e-mail:** norparflowers@ukgateway.net, www.norpar.co.uk, 9–5 MON–SAT. **FACTORY SHOP**

Dried flowers direct from the grower, silk flowers, basket arrangements, natural ingredients for Christmas decorations and Easter gifts. A family-run business in the inspiring surroundings of a medieval granary, 30 years experience of growing and drying flowers has led to a large range of English dried flowers as well as an impressive range of imported preserved and articial flowers and foliage. They also sell all the items you need to create your own arrangements from mosses and sprays to oases, pots, glue, ribbons, wires, dishes and dried fruit. To complement, they also sell a full range of stylish products for the home and, in the summer, a selected range of garden living decor and patio ware.

PONDEN MILL

CLACTON SHOPPING VILLAGE, STEPHENSON ROAD WEST, CLACTON-ON-SEA, ESSEX CO15 4TL, ☎ 01255 423412, 10–6 MON–SAT, 11–5 SUN. **FACTORY SHOP IN A FACTORY SHOPPING VILLAGE**

See page 464 (CHESH)

PRICE'S CANDLES

CLACTON FACTORY OUTLET VILLAGE, STEPHENSON ROAD WEST, CLACTON-ON-SEA, ESSEX CO15 4TL, ☎ 01255 426331, 10–6 MON–SAT, 8 ON THUR, 11–5 SUN. **FACTORY SHOP IN A FACTORY SHOPPING VILLAGE**

See page 464 (CHESH)

QD STORES

GREAT OAKS HOUSE, GREAT OAKS, BASILDON, ESSEX SS14 1JD, ☎ 01268 522999, 9–5.30 MON–SAT.

72–78 ROSEMARY ROAD, CLACTON-ON-SEA, ESSEX CO15 1TZ, ☎ 01255 479974, 9–5.30 MON–SAT, 10–4 SUN.

45–51 HIGH STREET, GRAYS, ESSEX RM16 5UF, ☎ 01375 385250, 9–5.30 MON–SAT.

UNITS 101–108, VICTORIA PLAZA, SOUTHEND-ON-SEA, ESSEX SS2 5FB, ☎ 01702 618777, 9–5.30 MON–SAT. **PERMANENT DISCOUNT OUTLET**

See page 458 (BEDS)

T J HUGHES

25–29 MARKET PLACE, ROMFORD, ESSEX RM1 3AB, ☎ 01708 747159, FAX: 01708 721126, **e-mail: e-mail:** info@tjhughes.co.uk, www.tjhughes.co.uk, 9–5.30 MON–SAT, 10–4 SUN. **PERMANENT DISCOUNT OUTLET**

See page 465 (CHESH)

THE CAPE

58 HIGH STREET, COLCHESTER, ESSEX CO1 1DH, ☎ 01206 368183, FAX: 01206 368184, **e-mail:** sc@thefactory-shop.co.uk, www.thecape.co.uk, 9–5.30 MON–FRI, 9–6 SAT, 10–4.30 SUN. **FACTORY SHOP**

See page 460 (BRIS)

THE FACTORY SHOP LTD

THE GLOUCESTERS, LUCKYN LANE, PIPPS HILL INDUSTRIAL ESTATE, BASILDON, ESSEX SS14 3AX, ☎ 01268 520546, www.thefactoryshopsessexltd.co.uk, 9–6 MON–SAT, 10–5 SUN.

PURDEY'S INDUSTRIAL ESTATE, 1 MAGNOLIA WAY, ROCHFORD, ESSEX SS4 1ND, ☎ 01702 531153, www.thefactoryshopsessexltd.co.uk, 9–6 MON–SAT, 10–5 SUN. **FACTORY SHOP**

The Factory Shops carry a wide range of branded stock at discounted prices, from bed linen, towels, hardware, toys, party ware, electrical goods, tools and garden furniture to food, clothing, TY Beanies and much more. There is a large pet and aquatic department with a wide selection of pond and water features within its 14,000 square feet of selling space. At Christmas, a huge range of decorations, baubles, tinsel, trees, tree lights and gifts are available. Parking is easy with wheelchair/pushchair access. No membership is required, and major credit cards are accepted.

THE FACTORY SHOP LTD

THE CROSS ROADS, KELVEDON ROAD, TIPTREE, ESSEX CO5 0LJ, ☎ 01621 817662, 9–5.30 MON–SAT, 10–4 SUN. **FACTORY SHOP**

See page 465 (CHESH)

TK MAXX

93 EASTGATE SHOPPING CENTRE, SOUTHERNHAY, BASILDON, ESSEX SS14 1AF, ☎ 01268 273604, 9–5.30 MON–SAT, 11–5 SUN.

26 SIR ISAAC WALK, CULVER SQUARE, COLCHESTER, ESSEX CO1 1JJ, ☎ 01206 368745, 9–6 MON, 9–7 TUE-WED, 9–8 THU-FRI, 9–6 SAT, 11–5 SUN.

THE EXCHANGE, ILFORD, ESSEX IG1 1AS, ☎ 020 8514 1288, www.tkmaxx.com, 9.30–6 MON–FRI, 8 ON WED, 9–6 SAT, 11–5 SUN.

THE BREWERY, ROMFORD, ESSEX, ☎ 01708 761978, PHONE FOR DETAILS OF OPENING TIMES.

THE ROYAL SHOPPING CENTRE, HIGH STREET, SOUTHEND SS1, FAX: 01702 600020, www.tkmaxx.com, 9–5.30 MON–SAT, 11–5 SUN.

UNIT 4, TUNNEL ESTATE RETAIL PARK WEST, LONDON ROAD, THURROCK, ESSEX RM22 3HH, ☎ 01708 860296, www.tkmaxx.com, 10–8 MON–FRI, 10–7 SAT, 11–5 SUN. **PERMANENT DISCOUNT OUTLET**

See page 458 (BEDS)

VILLEROY & BOCH (UK) LIMITED

FREEPORT ESSEX VILLAGE, CHARTER WAY, CHAPEL HILL, BRAINTREE, ESSEX CM7 8YH, ☎ 01376 348168, 10–6 MON–SAT, 8 ON THUR, 11–5 SUN. **FACTORY SHOP IN A FACTORY SHOPPING VILLAGE**

See page 466 (CHESH)

WOODS OF WINDSOR

UNIT P6, FREEPORT BRAINTREE DESIGNER OUTLET VILLAGE, CHARTER WAY, BRAINTREE, ESSEX CM7 8YH, ☎ 01376 839960, FAX: 01376 839960, www.woodsofwindsor.co.uk, 9–6 MON–SAT, 9 ON THUR, 11–5 SUN.

UNIT 31, CLACTON FACTORY OUTLET CENTRE, STEPHENSON ROAD, CLACTON-ON-SEA, ESSEX CO15 4TL, ☎ 01255 479475, www.woodsofwindsor.co.uk, 10–6 MON–SAT, 8 ON THUR, 11–5 SUN. **FACTORY SHOP IN A FACTORY SHOPPING VILLAGE**

See page 466 (CHESH)

YOU'RE FURNISHED

UNIT 6, REAR OF 14 CAMBRIDGE ROAD, STANSTED, ESSEX CM24 8BZ, ☎ 01279 815028 SHOWROOM, FAX: 07947 890467 WAREHOUSE, 01279 815541, 10–5 TUE–SAT, 11–4 SUN. **PERMANENT DISCOUNT OUTLET**

Home merchandise and furniture from the Marks & Spencer catalogue at discounts of up to half price. Most of the stock is customer's cancelled orders and turnover is brisk with two or three large deliveries a week. There is a small showroom at the above address and a warehouse which is ten times the size just before Stansted airport at Unit 1, Waltham Hall Industrial Estate, Essex CM22 6PF (take the right hand turning at the last roundabout before Stansted car park, first left and about one mile down the road near a sign saying Open Network is the industrial estate). There are up to 900 sofas and sofabeds at any one time, dining room tables and chairs, beds, wardrobes – anything in the M&S catalogue, though they can't guarantee that, having seen it in the catalogue, they will have it on sale.

GLOUCESTERSHIRE

BRANDMART

WESTWARD ROAD, CAINSCROSS, STROUD, GLOUCESTERSHIRE GL5 4JE, ☎ 01453 756655, 9–5 MON SAT, 10–4 SUN. **FACTORY SHOP**

The original factory shop in Cainscross, Stroud, has recently relocated next door into a 12,000 square foot premises and is now trading under the name of Brandmart, offering even more savings on branded household and family goods. The range includes men's, women's and children's clothing and footwear, household textiles, toiletries, hardware, luggage, lighting, electrical goods and bedding, most of which are chainstore and high street brands at discounts of between 30% and 50%. There are weekly deliveries and brands include famous names such as Calvin Klein, Adidas, Nike, Fcuk, Cat, Reebok, Ben Sherman, Kangol, Timberland and many more. There are kitchen and furniture displays and a new line in Cape Country furniture on sale. Ranges are continually changing and few factory shops offer such a variety under one roof. Car park.

CATALOGUE BARGAIN SHOP

1–6 GROSVENOR HOUSE, STATION ROAD, GLOUCESTER, GLOUCESTERSHIRE GL1 1SZ, ☎ 01452 308779, www.bargaincrazy.com, 9–5.30 MON–SAT, 10.30–4.30 SUN. **PERMANENT DISCOUNT OUTLET**

See page 461 (CAMBS)

COTSWOLD WOOLLEN WEAVERS

FILKINS, OFF A361 BETWEEN BURFORD AND LECHLADE, GLOUCESTERSHIRE GL7 3JJ, ☎ 01367 860491, FAX: 01367 860661, **e-mail:** wool.weavers@dial.pipex.com, www.naturalbest.co.uk, 10–6 MON–SAT, 2–6 SUN. **FACTORY SHOP**

Cotswold Woollen Weavers make their rugs and throws on site using traditional Dobcross looms. Regarded as the elite of looms, their slow action is gentler on yarns than modern machines, resulting in cloth with more depth, resilience and texture. CWW also produce "organic" rugs and cloth made from merino yarn which is naturally coloured and washed using soap rather than synthetic detergent. The on-site shop sells rugs for £36, which are on sale in the high street for up to £80, as well as a wide range of clothing, throws and accessories.

CROCK SHOP

DIGBETH STREET, STOW-ON-THE-WOLD, GLOUCESTERSHIRE GL54 1BN, ☎ 01451 870340, 9.30–6 SEVEN DAYS A WEEK. **PERMANENT DISCOUNT OUTLET**

China, glass and cookware and giftware direct from the factories of the manufacturers of Churchill, BhS, Wood and Sons and Portmeirion at discounts of up to 50%. Now in bigger premises so an even wider range is available.

DISCOUNT CHINA

HIGH STREET, BOURTON-ON-THE-WATER, NEAR CHELTENHAM, GLOUCESTERSHIRE GL54 2AP, ☎ 01451 820662, 10–5 SEVEN DAYS A WEEK. **PERMANENT DISCOUNT OUTLET**

Retailers of china and cookware direct from the factories of Staffordshire. Supplies are sourced from different manufacturers so stock varies according to what is available at the time, but includes china fancies, beakers, cookware, planters and dinner sets.

DUNELM MILL SHOP

CARRIAGE BUILDINGS, BRUTON WAY, GLOUCESTER, GLOUCESTERSHIRE GL1 1BZ, ☎ 01452 385063, FAX: 01452 303669, www.dunelm-mill.co.uk, 9–5 MON–THUR, 9–5.30 FRI, SAT, 10.30–4.30 SUN. **PERMANENT DISCOUNT OUTLET**

See page 458 (BEDS)

ENGLISH COUNTRY POTTERY

STATION ROAD, WICKWAR, WOTTON-UNDER-EDGE, GLOUCESTERSHIRE GL12 8NB, ☎ 01454 299100, FAX: 01454 294053, 9–4 MON–FRI. MAIL ORDER. **FACTORY SHOP**

English Country Pottery has a factory shop on site just down the stairs from where the large range of pottery is made. Each pot is taken through eight traditional processes, before being handpainted and signed by the painters. Finally, the pattern is sealed under the glaze and fired, making it very durable: oven, dishwasher and microwave proof. Here, seconds and discontinued pottery from their own ranges are sold at discounted prices. Some of the pottery has been made by special commission for department stores, galleries and mail order companies, some is wholesaled to the independent gift trade. Because of this, and the fact that they design and manufacture their own pottery, the variety of styles is very wide, resulting in a vibrant, individualistic and very English style of pottery. The designs include farm animals, traditional countryside scenes and a selection of very modern designs. The range also includes tableware, children's items, giftware and bathroom accessories, as well as a large range of wall tiles, hand decorated with sea, animal and floral motifs with coordinating plain coloured tiles.

KEYSTONES (DISCONTINUED DENBY TABLEWARE)

UNIT 3, FIRST FLOOR, GLOUCESTER ANTIQUES CENTRE, SEVERN ROAD, GLOUCESTER DOCKS, GLOUCESTER, GLOUCESTERSHIRE GL1 2LE, ☎ 01785 256648, FAX: 01785 256648, **e-mail:** gkey@keystones.demon.co.uk, www.keystones.co.uk, 10–5 MON–SAT, 1–5 SUN AND MAIL ORDER. **PERMANENT DISCOUNT OUTLET**

A long-established business operated by husband and wife team Graham and Alva Key, leading specialists in old Denby pottery for the last decade. There are two retail outlets selling discontinued Denby pottery both here and at Dagfields Antiques and Craft Centre, at Waigherton, near Nantwich, Cheshire (off the A51 near the Bridgemere Garden Centre) and they also operate a mail order business, saving you from wasting your old dinner/tea service by supplying replacement items for discontinued designs. A free, no-obligation search sevice is provided if they cannot supply from existing stocks. A worldwide ordering service is available and deliveries are by post or private carrier.

MASH

INNSWORTH TECHNOLOGY PARK, INNSWORTH LANE, GLOUCESTER, GLOUCESTERSHIRE GL3 1DL, ☎ 01452 730577, FAX: 01452 731999, **e-mail:** tim@dowco.co.uk, www.mashcamping.com, 8.30–5.30 MON–FRI, 8.30–5 SAT, 10–4 SUN, BANK HOLIDAYS. **SECONDHAND SHOP**

Warehouse/shop carrying an extensive range of backpacking and camping equipment, outdoor clothing, tools, Gelert tents, Sunngas cookers, Victorinox knives, Maglite torches and government surplus stock at discount prices.

MATALAN

27 SWINDON ROAD, CHELTENHAM, GLOUCESTERSHIRE GL50 4DF, ☎ 01242 579840, FAX: 01242 282142, www.matalan.co.uk, 10–8 MON–FRI, 9–6 SAT, 11–5 SUN.

QUEDGELEY DISTRICT CENTRE, GLOUCESTER, GLOUCESTERSHIRE GL2 4PF, ☎ 01452 726040, FAX: 01452 725216, www.matalan.co.uk, 9.30–8 MON–FRI, 9–6 SAT, 10–4 SUN. **PERMANENT DISCOUNT OUTLET**

See page 458 (BEDS)

PONDEN MILL

HIGH STREET, BOURTON-ON-THE-WATER, NEAR CHELTENHAM, GLOUCESTERSHIRE GL54 2AP, ☎ 01451 822699, PHONE FOR DETAILS OF OPENING TIMES. **FACTORY SHOP IN A FACTORY SHOPPING VILLAGE**

See page 464 (CHESH)

SPRING GRAND SALE

SUDELEY CASTLE, WINCHCOMBE, NEAR CHELTENHAM, GLOUCESTERSHIRE, ☎ 01367 860017, FAX: 01367 860177, **e-mail:** nheslam@aol.com, 10–6 THUR, FRI, SAT. **DESIGNER SALES**

There are now three annual Grand Sales taking place countrywide. The Christmas Grand Sale in London, with over 120 different small companies selling their merchandise to the public, is the largest. This takes place in mid-late November each year. Quality is high and covers everything from dried flowers to bath accessories, Amish quilts to silverware, wooden toys to hand-painted kitchenware, antiques to handmade furniture, luxurious bedlinen to faux fur throws, pewter cutlery to glass vases, garden furniture to deck chairs, often at discount because they are ends of lines. There is a Spring Grand Sale at Sudeley Castle, Winchcombe, near Cheltenham, Gloucestershire, usually at the end of April/beginning of May, and a Summer Grand Sale at Ripley Castle, near Harrogate, North Yorkshire, in June. Both feature gardening furniture and equipment as well as decorative home accessories. Phone the above number for more details. A proportion of the ticket revenue goes to charity.

STANCOMB STONE

WAYSIDE FARM, THE CAMP, STROUD, NEAR PAINSWICK, GLOUCESTERSHIRE GL6 7EW, ☎ 01285 821839, 8–4 MON–FRI. **FACTORY SHOP**

Imperfect garden pots and troughs – in fact, anything for the garden made from stone.

THE CAPE

25 REGENT ARCADE, CHELTENHAM, GLOUCESTERSHIRE GL50 1JZ, ☎ 01242 519021, FAX: 01242 519021, **e-mail:** sc@thefactory-shop.co.uk, www.thecape.co.uk, 9–5.30 MON–SAT, 10.30–4.30 SUN. **FACTORY SHOP**

See page 460 (BRIS)

THE ORIGINAL ARCHITECTURAL ANTIQUES CO LTD

ERMIN FARM, A419, CIRENCESTER, GLOUCESTERSHIRE GL7 5PN, ☎ 01285 869222, FAX: 01285 862221, **e-mail:** john@orignaluk.com, www.originaluk.com, 9–5 MON–SAT, 10–4 SUN. **ARCHITECTURAL SALVAGE**

Architectural antiques including period and reproduction fireplaces, doors, floor tiles, chairs, baths, beams, busts, columns, fire surrounds, sirebacks, kitchen ranges, marble fireplaces, mirrors, oak floorboards, objets d'art, paintings, pews, prints, radiators, shutters, sinks, stained glass, taps, towel rails. Also gardenware, including stone troughs, pond surrounds, fountains, flagstones, stone artefacts, sundials, terracotta pots, weather vanes, windows, wrought ironwork, gates, lead cisterns and many other one-off architectural features.

TK MAXX

REGENT ARCADE SHOPPING CENTRE, CHELTENHAM GLOUCESTERSHIRE GL50 1J2, FAX: 01242 513848, www.tkmaxx.com, 9–5.30 MON–WED, 9–8 THUR, 9–6 FRI–SAT. **PERMANENT DISCOUNT OUTLET**

See page 458 (BEDS)

WINCHCOMBE POTTERY

BROADWAY ROAD, WINCHCOMBE CHELTENHAM, GLOUCESTERSHIRE GL54 5NU, ☎ 01242 602462, **e-mail:** mike@winchcombepottery.co.uk, www.winchcombepottery.co.uk, 8–5 MON–FRI, 10–4 SAT, 12–4 SUN, FROM MAY–SEP. MAIL ORDER. **FACTORY SHOP**

The pottery produces a wide range of hand-thrown stoneware pots for domestic use. Prices start at £3.20 for an eggcup; platters from £6.20; coffee mugs from £6.40; salad bowls from £11.75; casseroles from £13.10. Visitors are welcome to look round the showroom and, at most times, the workshop. Payment in Euros accepted.

HAMPSHIRE

BAGGAGE FACTORY

52 WHITELEY VILLAGE, WHITELEY WAY, FAREHAM, HAMPSHIRE PO14 7LJ, ☎ 01489 573333, www.baggagefactory.co.uk, 10–6 MON–SAT, 11–5 SUN. **FACTORY SHOP IN A FACTORY SHOPPING VILLAGE**

This outlet sells bags, cases and wallets, some well-known brand names such as Antler, Carlton, Skyway and Samsonite, at prices from 10% to 40% lower than the high street.

BED & BATH WORKS

UNIT 13, ALDERSHOT GALLERIES, WELLINGTON CENTRE, WELLINGTON STREET, ALDERSHOT, HAMPSHIRE GU11 1DX, ☎ 01252 328581, FAX: 01252 328598, **e-mail:** hello@bedandbathworks.co.uk, www.bedandbathworks.co.uk, 9–6 MON–SAT, 10–4 SUN. **FACTORY SHOP IN A FACTORY SHOPPING VILLAGE**

See page 462 (CHESH)

CHINAMATCHING

23 KILN ROAD, FAREHAM, HAMPSHIRE PO16 7UA, ☎ 01329 282785, FAX: 01329 282785, **e-mail:** Sue.holder@talk21.com, www.thechinamatcher.co.uk, 8–8 SEVEN DAYS A WEEK. **PERMANENT DISCOUNT OUTLET**

Stocks and searches for English and some European patterns from the 1940s to the present. Brands stocked include Wedgwood, Colclough, Denby, Royal Doulton, Royal Worcester, Spode, Royal Albert, Paragon and Hornsea. There is no registration fee.

CLOVERLEAF

WHITELEY VILLAGE DESIGNER OUTLET CENTRE, WHITELEY WAY, FAREHAM, JUNCTION 9 OF M27, HAMPSHIRE PO15 7BS, ☎ 01489 571 021, 10–6 MON–SAT, 11–5 SUN. **FACTORY SHOP**

See page 477 (DEV)

DARTINGTON CRYSTAL

CLOVERLEAF LTD, WHITELEY VILLAGE DESIGNER OUTLET CENTRE, WHITELEY WAY, FAREHAM, JUNCTION 9 OF M27, HAMPSHIRE PO15 7BS, ☎ 01489 571021, FAX: 01489 571014, 10–6 MON–SAT, 11-5 SUN. **FACTORY SHOP IN A FACTORY SHOPPING VILLAGE**

See page 469 (CORN)

DESIGN HOUSE

GUNWHARF QUAYS, PORTSMOUTH, HAMPSHIRE PO1 3TA, ☎ 02392 865696, 10–6 SUN–THUR, 10–9 FRI–SAT. **FACTORY SHOP IN A FACTORY SHOPPING VILLAGE**

See page 483 (ESSEX)

GUNWHARF QUAYS

PORTSMOUTH HARBOUR, HAMPSHIRE PO1 3TZ, ☎ 023 9283 6700, FAX: 023 9283 6701 **e-mail:** info@gunwharf-quays.com, www.gunwharf-quays.com, SUMMER: 10–6 MON–WED, 10–8 THUR–SAT, 11–5 SUN. WINTER: 10–6 MON–SAT, 11–5 SUN. **FACTORY SHOPPING VILLAGE**

Designer outlet shopping centre comprising 65 stores on a site next to Portsmouth Harbour station and Portsmouth Historic Dockyard, home to HMS Victory and the Mary Rose. As well as the designer outlets, which include Adidas, Benetton, Ben Sherman, Burberry, cK Calvin Klein, Crabtree & Evelyn, Ecco, Episode, Fenn Wright & Manson, Gap, Gieves & Hawkes, Marks & Spencer, Nicole Farhi, Nike, Tommy Hilfiger, Villeroy & Boch, Waterford Wedgwood and Whittard of Chelsea, there are 20 restaurants, bars and coffee shops, an 11-screen cinema, 26-lane bowling complex, comedy club and a year-round events programme.

HOME PLUS DIY SURPLUS STORE

8 WATER LANE, TOTTON, HAMPSHIRE SO40 3DP, ☎ 023 8066 1041, OPEN 9–5.30 MON–SAT. **PERMANENT DISCOUNT OUTLET**

Brand new items bought as a result of shop closures or bankruptcy. Specialises in DIY products – paints, tiles, wallpaper, tools, nails, batteries, screws – but also sells kitchen items such as kettles, stationery, lampshades and gardening products. There is another branch at Sainsburys Parade, Lordswood, Southampton.

IN EXCESS

43–45 HIGH STREET, WEST END, SOUTHAMPTON, HAMPSHIRE SO30 3LU, ☎ 0238 046 4545, 9–5.30 MON–SAT, 10–4 SUN.

64–66 SHIRLEY HIGH STRREET, SHIRLEY, SOUTHAMPTON, HAMPSHIRE SO15 3TE, ☎ 02380 771657, 9–5.30 MON–SAT. **PERMANENT DISCOUNT OUTLET**

See page 480 (DORS)

JOHN JENKINS & SON LTD

NYEWOOD, ROGATE, PETERSFIELD, HAMPSHIRE GU31 5HZ, ☎ 01730 821495, FAX: 01730 821698, 9.30–5 MON–SAT. **FACTORY SHOP**

Factory shop selling cut crystal, plain glass and porcelain. Quality ranges from plain glass to 24% cut lead crystal including champagne flutes, sherry/white wine/red wine glasses and decanters, vases and bowls. The factory shop also sells candles, porcelain, ceramics, pictures, mirrors, Crabtree & Evelyn toiletries, costume jewellery and many other gifts for the home.

KENWOOD SERVICE SHOP

NEW LANE, HAVANT, HAMPSHIRE PO9 2NH, ☎ 02392 392 111, FAX: 02392 392393, **e-mail:** kshop@kenwood.co.uk, www.kenwood.co.uk, 9–4 MON–THUR, 9–1 FRI, SAT. **FACTORY SHOP**

Wide range of Kenwood items from food processors, coffee makers and deep fryers to irons, can openers, water filters, juice extractors and toasters at factory prices. This usually means 20% off the normal retail price. All items are in perfect condition and come with a one year's guarantee. On-site parking available.

MATALAN

CHANNON RETAIL PARK, WOODSIDE AVENUE, EASTLEIGH, HAMPSHIRE SO50 9ER, ☎ 02380 626 150, FAX: 02380 650 749, www.matalan.co.uk, 10–8 MON–FRI, 9–6 SAT, 10–4 SUN.

STATION STREET, PORTSMOUTH, HAMPSHIRE PO1 1BE, ☎ 0239 285 1967, FAX: 0239 275 5316, www.matalan.co.uk, 9–8 MON–FRI, 9–6 SAT, 11–5 SUN. **PERMANENT DISCOUNT OUTLET**

See page 458 (BEDS)

MOUNTJOY PICTURE FRAMES

61 WINCHESTER ROAD, FOUR MARKS, ALTON, HAMPSHIRE GU34 5HR, ☎ 01420 561220, FAX: 01420 561223, 9–5 TUE–FRI, 9–4 SAT. **FACTORY SHOP**

Sells ready-made picture frames, framed chalkboards and letter boards, manufactured on the premises, at about 20% less than high street retail.

ONEIDA

GUNWHARF QUAYS, PORTSMOUTH, HAMPSHIRE PO1 3TN, ☎ 023 9283 7616, 10–6 MON–WED, 10–8 THUR–SAT, 11–5 SUN. **FACTORY SHOP IN A FACTORY SHOPPING VILLAGE**

See page 464 (CHESH)

PONDEN MILL LINENS

WHITELEY VILLAGE DESIGNER OUTLET CENTRE, WHITELEY WAY, FAREHAM, JUNCTION 9 OF M27, HAMPSHIRE PO15 7BS, ☎ 01489 571075, 10–6 MON–SAT, 11–5 SUN. **FACTORY SHOP IN A FACTORY SHOPPING VILLAGE**

See page 464 (CHESH)

PRICE'S PATENT CANDLE CO

WHITELEY VILLAGE DESIGNER OUTLET CENTRE, WHITELEY WAY, FAREHAM, JUNCTION 9 OF M27, HAMPSHIRE PO15 7BS, ☎ 01489 565150, 10–6 MON–SAT, 11–5 SUN.

UNIT 24, GUNWHARF QUAYS, PORTSMOUTH, HAMPSHIRE, ☎ 023 92 851579, 10–6 MON–WED, 10–8 THUR–SAT, 11–5 SUN. **FACTORY SHOP IN A FACTORY SHOPPING VILLAGE**

Factory outlets stocking most current ranges from spring, summer and Christmas, including seconds and discontinued lines. Products include: church candles, dinner candles, tealights, scented candles, fashion ranges and accessories, all at discounted prices. Perfect for gifts.

THE GALLERIES

HIGH STREET, ALDERSHOT, HAMPSHIRE GU11 1PE, ☎ 01252 341111, FAX: 01252 329800, **e-mail:** thegalleries@web-hq.com, www.thegalleriesaldershot.co.uk, 9–6 MON–SAT, 10–4 SUN. **FACTORY SHOPPING VILLAGE**

This town centre shopping mall has 20 discount shops on two levels such as Bed & Bath Works for bedlinen and bathroom ware; Cotton Traders casual wear; Designer Room selling women's and men's designer fashion; Hush Puppies shoes; Kitchen Kiosk with branded kitchen and homeware ranges including barbecues and some electrical goods such as bread making machines; Leading Labels selling men's, women's and childrenswear; MX Active for men's, women's and children's branded denim and casual wear; Optisave, an optician selling designer branded glasses; Pilot selling young women's fashions; Pocket Phone selling mobile phones and accessories; Roman Originals womenswear; Room for furniture and household accessories; Suits You men's shirts, suits and casual separates as well as Autonomy womenswear; and Young's dress hire; Surf Skate and Snow for branded casual and activity wear; Toyzone for children's toys; and XS Music selling CDs and videos. The centre also has a café, wheelchair access, a lottery kiosk and baby changing facilities.

TK MAXX

173–178 HIGH STREET (BELOW BAR), SOUTHAMPTON, HAMPSHIRE SO14 2BY, ☎ 023 80 631600, www.tkmaxx.com, 9–5.30 MON–FRI, 7 ON THUR, 9–6 SAT, 11–5 SUN.

2 WELLINGTON RETAIL PARK, HAMBLEDON ROAD, WATERLOOVILLE, HAMPSHIRE, ☎ 023 92 267626, www.tkmaxx.com, PHONE FOR DETAILS OF OPENING TIMES. **PERMANENT DISCOUNT OUTLET**

See page 458 (BEDS)

VILLEROY & BOCH (UK) LIMITED

GUNWHARF QUAYS, PORTSMOUTH, HAMPSHIRE PO1 3TA, ☎ 0239 275 5940 (CENTRE INFORMATION LINE), 9–5 SEVEN DAYS A WEEK. **FACTORY SHOP IN A FACTORY SHOPPING VILLAGE**

See page 466 (CHESH)

WHITELEY VILLAGE OUTLET SHOPPING

OFF THE M27 BETWEEN SOUTHAMPTON AND PORTSMOUTH, JUNCTION 9 OF M27, HAMPSHIRE PO15 7LJ, ☎ 01489 886886, FAX: 01489 886887, www.whiteleyvillage.com, 10–6 MON–SAT, 11- 5 SUN. **FACTORY SHOPPING VILLAGE**

Whiteley Village has more than 50 outlets, all offering shoppers up to 50% savings on high street prices. Top designer names fashion names are here – including Antonio D'Errico, Banana Bookshop, Camille Lingerie, Lilley & Skinner, Roman Originals, Surf, Skate & Snow, Top Table, High & Mighty, Chilli Pepper, Claire's Accessories, Helter Skelter, Cloverleaf, Marzotto, Cotton Traders, D2 Jeans, Elle, Emma Sommerset, Ethos, The Baggage Factory, Ghost, HKA, Jane Shilton, Jasper Conran Jeans, Jigsaw, John Jenkins, John Partridge, Joseph, Julian Graves, Mobile Phone Store, Outdoor Direct, Photo Optix, Pilot, Ponden Mill, Pringle, Proibito, Puma, Rio Jeweller and The Designer Room with a host of designer labels. Refreshments are available from Starbucks Coffee and Boswells Restaurant. There is free parking on site for 1, 400 cars, as well as an area for coaches.

WHITTARD

GUNWHARF QUAYS, PORTSMOUTH, HAMPSHIRE PO1 3TX, ☎ 02392 811135, 10–6 MON–WED, 10–9 THUR–SAT, 10–6 SUN. **FACTORY SHOP IN A FACTORY SHOPPING VILLAGE**

See page 466 (CHESH)

WILKINSON STORES

22–30 BRIDGE STREET, ANDOVER, HAMPSHIRE SP10 1BN, ☎ 01332 551241, www.wilko.co.uk, 9–5.30 MON–SAT, 10–4 SUN. MAIL ORDER. **PERMANENT DISCOUNT OUTLET**

See page 466 (CHESH)

HEREFORDSHIRE

DARTINGTON CRYSTAL

ROSS LABELS LTD, OVERROSS, ROSS-ON-WYE, HEREFORDSHIRE HR9 7QJ, ☎ 01989 769000, FAX: 01989 768855, 9.30–6 MON–SAT, 10–4 SUN. **FACTORY SHOP**

See page 469 (CORN)

DUNELM MILL SHOP

2–3A UNION WALK, HEREFORD HEREFORDSHIRE HR1 2EP, ☎ 01432 266466, FAX: 01432 352396, www.dunelm-mill.co.uk, 9–5.30 MON–SAT, 10.30–4.30 SUN.

SALMON RETAIL PARK, HOLMER ROAD, HEREFORD, HEREFORDSHIRE HR4 9SA, ☎ 01432 264265, FAX: 01432 264364, www.dunelm-mill.co.uk, 9–6 MON–SAT, 8 ON THUR, FRI, 10.30–4.30 SUN. **PERMANENT DISCOUNT OUTLET**

See page 458 (BEDS)

PONDEN MILL

ROSS LABELS LTD, OVEROSS, ROSS-ON-WYE, HEREFORDSHIRE HR9 7AS, ☎ 01989 564348, 10–6 MON–SAT, 11–5 SUN. **FACTORY SHOP**

See page 464 (CHESH)

ROSS LABELS LTD

ROSS PARK, OVERROSS, ROSS-ON-WYE, HEREFORDSHIRE HR9 7QJ, ☎ 01989 769000, www.rosslabels.co.uk, 9.30–6 MON–SAT, 10–4 SUN. **PERMANENT DISCOUNT OUTLET**
Factory outlet centre selling everything from women's and men's underwear and jeans to good, middle-of-the-road brand name outfits and suits bought direct from the manufacturer, as well as homewares. Over 100 leading brands arc on sale. Discounts range from 20% to 50%.

STEWART'S

33 HIGH STREET, ROSS-ON-WYE, HEREFORDSHIRE HR9 5HD, ☎ 01989 762403, FAX: 01989 762403, 9.30–5.30 MON–SAT, 10–5.30 SUN. **FACTORY SHOP**

See page 478 (DEV)

STEWART'S SECONDS

33 HIGH STREET, ROSS-ON-WYE, HEREFORDSHIRE HR9 5HD, ☎ 01989 762403, 9.30–5 MON–WED, 9–5 THUR–SAT. **FACTORY SHOP**
Branded merchandise from most of the major UK chainstores, all well-known high street department store names, offered at a discount of 40% to 70% off normal high street prices. The garments are selected with great care by experienced buyers direct from factories worldwide to bring customers top quality merchandise at highly competitive prices.

THE FACTORY SHOP

52 BROAD STREET, LEOMINSTER, HEREFORDSHIRE HR6 8BS, ☎ 01568 613944, 9–5.30 MON–SAT, 10–4 SUN. **FACTORY SHOP**

See page 465 (CHESH)

TK MAXX

5 TRINITY SQUARE, MAYLORD ORCHARD, HEREFORD, HEREFORDSHIRE HR1 2BX, ☎ 01432 355000, www.tkmaxx.com, 9–5.30 MON–FRI, 9–6 SAT, 11–5 SUN. **PERMANENT DISCOUNT OUTLET**

See page 458 (BEDS)

HERTFORDSHIRE

BAGGAGE FACTORY

GALLERIA OUTLET CENTRE, COMET WAY, HATFIELD, HERTFORDSHIRE AL10 0XR, ☎ 01707 257779, www.baggagefactory.co.uk, 10–8 MON–FRI, 10–6 SAT, 11–5 SUN. **FACTORY SHOP IN A FACTORY SHOPPING VILLAGE**

See page 489 (HAMPS)

BED & BATH WORKS

GALLERIA OUTLET CENTRE, COMET WAY, HATFIELD, HERTFORDSHIRE AL10 0XR, ☎ 01707 259202, FAX: 01707 259204, **e-mail:** hello@bedandbathworks.co.uk, www.bedandbathworks.co.uk, 10–8 MON–FRI, 10–6 SAT, 11–5 SUN. **FACTORY SHOP IN A FACTORY SHOPPING VILLAGE**

See page 462 (CHESH)

BhS FOR LESS

GALLERIA OUTLET CENTRE, COMET WAY, HATFIELD, HERTFORDSHIRE AL10 0XR, ☎ 01707 258351, 10–8 MON–FRI, 10–6 SAT, 11–5 SUN. **FACTORY SHOP IN A FACTORY SHOPPING VILLAGE**

BhS for Less sells the high street chain's men's, women's and childrenswear ranges, plus selections from its home and lighting ranges, at discounts of at least 30% and up to 75%.

CHOICE DISCOUNT STORES LIMITED

GALLERIA OUTLET CENTRE, COMET WAY, HATFIELD, HERTFORDSHIRE AL10 0XR, ☎ 01707 258545, 10–8 MON–FRI, 10–6 SAT, 11–5 SUN.

46 HIGH STREET, WATFORD, HERTFORDSHIRE WD1 2BS, ☎ 01923 233255, 9–5.30 MON–FRI, 9–6 SAT. **PERMANENT DISCOUNT OUTLET**

See page 461 (CAMBS)

GALLERIA OUTLET CENTRE

COMET WAY, HATFIELD, HERTFORDSHIRE AL10 0XR, ☎ 01707 278301, www.factory-outlets.co.uk, 10–8 MON–FRI, 10–6 SAT, 11–5 SUN. **FACTORY SHOPPING VILLAGE**

The Galleria Outlet Centre, often referred to as the bargain hunter's best-kept secret, based in north London, houses more than 80 retail outlets. It offers a wide choice of shops for the discerning customer, providing up to 60% off designer labels and quality brands. The Designer Room is a must for branded men's and women's fashions at huge discounts, stocking DKNY, Jasper Conran, Ghost and Tommy Hilfiger clothing. Looking for a designer evening dress or smart-casual wear? Then visit Discount Dressing. For the latest in fashionable menswear, pay a visit to any of the leading menswear shops. City Menswear offers new season, discounted Yves Saint Laurent and Ben Sherman clothing; Choice sells ranges from Next; B52 Jeans stocks Levi's, Lee and Wrangler ranges; and Baron Jon sells a selection of international names from Versace to Valentino. Going on holiday or looking for a new set of luggage? Then visit the Baggage Factory which sells top quality brands including Carlton and Samsonite. For all your bathroom and bedroom needs pop in to Ponden Mill or the Bed and Bath Works, selling a selection of bedlinen, towels from Christy, soaps and duvets. BhS For Less sells a range of end-of-season men's women's and children's fashions, as well as homewares and lighting. For all your footwear fancies, take a stroll to Charles Clinkard, Ecco, Soled Out and Pavers, selling great brand names including Timberland, Loake, Grenson, Nike, Reebok and Kickers. For women, D Kaye Cosmetics stocks a host of leading beauty and skincare ranges including Revlon, Max Factor, Lancome and Yardley, all at up to 75% off normal retail prices. Walker & Hall represent the finest in jewellery, stocking Tag, Gucci and Raymond Weil watches all at affordable prices. It also sells gold by weight and guarantees savings of at least 30% per gram. While, for the home, Chinacraft specialises in glass, china and giftware, from Wedgwood to Royal Doulton. If interior soft furnishings are on the agenda, then the Furniture Zone is the largest of its type, selling Oriental, middle eastern and Continental rugs, plus great ranges of sofas and sofa-beds, teak, cherry and oak furniture from Wall Nuts and the Khokhar Collection. To complement any room, the Big Picture and Big Poster sell modern and classical pictures ranging from £5 to £20,000. Visit the Garden Outlet Store for all your outdoor gardening and furniture requirements. Music Surplus, the home entertainment store, is a recent addition to the centre, selling a wide range of imported jazz, pop, chart and classical CDs, as well as the latest DVDs. For the PC enthusiast, UK Software sells CD-Roms at up to 70% off the normal retail price. Tool Ware House sells DeWalt, considered by many to be the Armani of the tool worlds, as well as offering fantastic savings on Black & Decker. The centre also offers three cafés, six restaurants and an abundance of children's activities including Toddler World, a futuristic crazy golf course and bouncing slides as well as a mini go-karting track during weekends and holidays. With over 1, 800 free car parking spaces and a nine-screen UCI cinema, the centre offers a complete family day out. The Galleria Outlet Centre is a 20-minute drive from north London, and is signposted from junction 3 and 4 of the A1M.

MATALAN

MADFORD RETAIL PARK, WARE ROAD, HERTFORD, HERTFORDSHIRE SG13 7EZ, ☎ 01992 512820, FAX: 01992 589515, www.matalan.co.uk, 10–8 MON–FRI, 9–6 SAT, 11–4 SUN.

DANESTRETE, STEVENAGE, HERTFORDSHIRE SG1 1XR, ☎ 01438 312433, FAX: 01438 312377, www.matalan.co.uk, 9–6 MON–SAT, 10–4 SUN. **PERMANENT DISCOUNT OUTLET**

See page 458 (BEDS)

NAZEING GLASS

NAZEING NEW ROAD, BROXBOURNE, HERTFORDSHIRE EN10 6SU, ☎ 01992 464485, FAX: 01992 450966, **e-mail:** sales@nazeing-glass.co.uk, www.nazeing-glass.co.uk, 9.30–4.30 MON–FRI, 9.30–3 SAT. **FACTORY SHOP**

Bespoke handmade glass makers since 1610, Nazeing don't design their own ranges but make to other companies' designs, many of them limited edition or exclusive ranges. The factory shop sells ends of lines and seconds at discontinued prices. You can also find first quality, 24% lead crystal, thin-stemmed and very thin-stemmed elegant plain or cut glassware, including decanters, coloured glassware in modern and contemporary designs, reproduction glass in eighteenth century styles and Bristol Blue glassware in champagne flutes, red and white wine glasses, water goblets and decanters.

PONDEN MILL

GALLERIA OUTLET CENTRE, COMET WAY, HATFIELD, HERTFORDSHIRE AL10 0XR, ☎ 01707 270053, 10–8 MON–FRI, 10–6 SAT, 11–5 SUN. **FACTORY SHOP IN A FACTORY SHOPPING VILLAGE**

See page 464 (CHESH)

QD STORES

29 TOWN SQUARE, 38 QUEENSWAY, STEVENAGE, HERTFORDSHIRE SG1 1BP, ☎ 01438 747437, 9–5.30 MON–SAT. **PERMANENT DISCOUNT OUTLET**

See page 458 (BEDS)

TK MAXX

UNIT 30-31, A1 GALLERIA, COMET WAY, HATFIELD, HERTFORDSHIRE AL10 0XR, ☎ 01707 260066, www.tkmaxx.com, 10–8 MON–FRI, 8.30 ON THUR, 9–7 SAT, 11–5 SUN.

UNIT 50, 18 THE MALTINGS, ST ALBANS HERTFORDSHIRE AL1 3HL, ☎ 01727 855999, www.tkmaxx.com, 9.30–6 MON–TUE, 9.30–7 WED–FRI, 9–6 SAT, 11–5 SUN.

UNIT 10, FORUM SHOPPING CENTRE, STEVENAGE, HERTFORDSHIRE SG1 1ES, ☎ 01438 728408, www.tkmaxx.com, 9.30–8 MON–FRI, 9.30–6 SAT, 11–5 SUN. **PERMANENT DISCOUNT OUTLET**

See page 458 (BEDS)

KENT

BED & BATH WORKS

MCARTHURGLEN DESIGNER OUTLET ASHFORD, KIMBERLEY WAY, ASHFORD, JUNCTION 10 OF M20, KENT TN24 0FD, ☎ 01233 630133, FAX: 01233 635820, **e-mail:** hello@bedandbathworks.co.uk, www.bedandbathworks.co.uk, 10–6 MON–FRI, 9–6 SAT, 11–5 SUN. **FACTORY SHOP IN A FACTORY SHOPPING VILLAGE**

See page 462 (CHESH)

CATALOGUE BARGAIN SHOP

19A PRESTON STREET, FAVERSHAM, KENT ME13 8NZ, ☎ 01795 591203, www.bargaincrazy.com, 9–5.30 MON–SAT, 10–4 SUN. **PERMANENT DISCOUNT OUTLET**

See page 461 (CAMBS)

CLOVERLEAF

MCARTHURGLEN DESIGNER OUTLET ASHFORD, KIMBERLEY WAY, ASHFORD, JUNCTION 10 OF M20, KENT TN23 1EZ, ☎ 01233 626561, 10–6 MON–SAT, 11–5 SUN.

DE BRADELEI WHARF, CAMBRIDGE ROAD, DOVER, KENT CT17 9BY, ☎ 01304 226616, 9.30–5.30 MON–FRI, 9.30–6 SAT, 11–5 SUN. **FACTORY SHOP**

See page 477 (DEV)

DE BRADELEI WHARF

DE BRADELEI WHARF (DOVER) LTD, CAMBRIDGE ROAD, DOVER, KENT CT17 9BY, ☎ 01304 226616, FAX: 01304 226636, 9.30–5.30 MON–FRI, 9.30–6 SAT, 11–5 SUN. **PERMANENT DISCOUNT OUTLET**

Large outlet in superb maritime setting just off the Dover Seafront, selling top brand names for all the family, including shoes. The womenswear includes such names as Paul Costelloe, Dannimac, Windsmoor, Planet, Precis Petite, Alexon, Kaliko, Eastex, Minuet Petite, Country Casuals, Elle, French Connection, Tigi Wear, plus top American and German designer labels, handbags and much more including a new accessory department. The menswear range includes underwear, socks, coats, sweaters, jackets, suits and trousers from labels such as Wolsey, Countrywear, French Connection, Virgin and Tog 24. Robert Leonard's Menswear provide Greiff, Pierre Cardin, Gabicci, Gurteen, Oakman, Saville Row, John Slim and many more. For children, there are brands such as OshKosh B'Gosh, Lily by Lily, Smarties, Vitamins, Rebble Pebble, Zip-Zap, O'Neill, MCA and Hickory as well as fluffy toys and melamine tableware with Pokemon and Toy Story 2 designs as well as a new department selling clothing, shoes, books and scientific toys. There is a large shoe department featuring international shoes for all the family and a wonderful Home Furnishings Department. The Interior Design shops sell bedding, towels, top-name furnishing fabric, cushions, throws, furniture and curtains. The Glass and China Department has an amazing selection from Waterford/Wedgwood, Stuart Crystal, Royal Doulton, Arthur Price of England Silverware, Staffordshire Tableware, Churchill, Cloverleaf, Hornsea Pottery, Cristal d'Arques and much more. There is superb Liberty shop in the giftware department and a Cromwell and Morgan Cook Shop. Parking is easy with a large car park behind the store. The Waves Coffee Shop is open all day, serving delicious home-cooked food.

DESIGN HOUSE

MCARTHURGLEN DESIGNER OUTLET ASHFORD, KIMBERLEY WAY, ASHFORD, JUNCTION 10 OF M20, KENT TN24 0SD, ☎ 01233 620106, 10–6 MON–FRI, 8 ON THUR, 9–6 SAT, 11–5 SUN. **FACTORY SHOP IN A FACTORY SHOPPING VILLAGE**

See page 483 (ESSEX)

EDINBURGH CRYSTAL

MCARTHURGLEN DESIGNER OUTLET ASHFORD, KIMBERLEY WAY, ASHFORD, JUNCTION 10 OF M20, KENT TN24 0SD, ☎ 0800 316 4352 FREE CENTRE INFORMATION LINE, 10–6 MON–FRI, 8 ON THUR, 9–6 SAT, 11–5 SUN. **FACTORY SHOP IN A FACTORY SHOPPING VILLAGE**

See page 463 (CHESH)

ELITE LIGHTING

7 GOODWOOD PARADE, UPPER ELMERS END ROAD, BECKENHAM, KENT BR3 3QZ, ☎ 020 8639 0050, FAX: 020 8639 0051, **e-mail:** sales@elitelighting.co.uk, www.elitelighting.co.uk, 9.30–5.30 MON–SAT. ALSO MAIL ORDER. **PERMANENT DISCOUNT OUTLET**

Elite sells all types of lighting for the home and garden, including a spectacular range of crystal chandeliers and wall brackets dressed with Swarovski strass crystal. Crystal components are also available. As a leading importer, their prices are very competitive. Visit their website or phone for a brochure.

LE CREUSET

MCCARTHURGLEN DESIGNER OUTLET, KIMBERLEY WAY, ASHFORD, JUNCTION 10 OF M20, KENT TN24 0SD, ☎ 01233 611635, 10–6 MON–FRI, 8 ON THUR, 9–6 SAT, 11–5 SUN. **FACTORY SHOP IN A FACTORY SHOPPING VILLAGE**

See page 483 (ESSEX)

MATALAN

BROOKFIELD ROAD, ASHFORD, KENT TN24 8ME, ☎ 01233 898460, FAX: 01233 661438, www.matalan.co.uk, 10–8 MON–FRI, 9–6 SAT, 11–5 SUN.

STOUR RETAIL PARK, STURRY ROAD, CANTERBURY, KENT CT1 1AD, ☎ 01227 817910, FAX: 01227 764860, www.matalan.co.uk, 10–8 MON–FRI, 9–7 SAT, 10–4 SUN.

BROADWAY SHOPPING CENTRE, THE BROADWAY, MAIDSTONE, KENT ME16 8PS, ☎ 01622 675153, FAX: 01622 672841, www.matalan.co.uk, 10–8 MON–FRI, 9–6 SAT, 10–4 SUN.

STROOD RETAIL PARK, COMMERCIAL ROAD, STROOD, KENT ME2 2JG, ☎ 01634 731670, FAX: 01634 718048, www.matalan.co.uk, 10–8 MON–FRI, 9–6 SAT, 11–5 SUN.

WESTWOOD RETAIL PARK, WESTWOOD ROAD, BROADSTAIRS, THANET, KENT CT10 2RQ, ☎ 01843 608700, FAX: 01843 871248, www.matalan.co.uk, 10–8 MON–FRI, 9–6 SAT, 11–5 SUN. **PERMANENT DISCOUNT OUTLET**

See page 458 (BEDS)

MCARTHURGLEN DESIGNER OUTLET CENTRE

KIMBERLEY WAY, ASHFORD, JUNCTION 10 OF M20, KENT TN24 0SD, ☎ 01233 895900, www.mcarthurglen.com/ashford, 10–6 MON–FRI, 8 ON THUR, 9–6 SAT, 11–5 SUN. **FACTORY SHOPPING VILLAGE**

Voted 'Retail Destination of the Year' 2001 in the Retail Week awards, the McArthurGlen Designer Outlet Ashford in Kent is one of Europe's most spectacular shopping destinations. The outlet offers over 70 top brands and designer labels at up to 50% off typical retail prices. there is a food court, cafés, a children's play area, and parking for over 1,500 cars. A shuttle bus runs between the town centre, station and the outlet every eight minutes. Shops include: Ben Sherman, Cotton Traders, Designer Room/Classic Room, Daks, Fire Trap, Gap, Lee Cooper, Levi's Littlewoods Catalogue Outlet, Marks and Spencer, Mexx, Miss Sixty, Mountain Warehouse, Pilot, Polo Jeans Co. Factory Store, Proudfoot, Roman Originals, Thomas Pink, Tog 24, Tommy Hilfiger, Warehouse, Warner's, Windsmoor, Baron Jon, Ben Sherman, Cotton Traders, Daks, Fire Trap, Fred Perry, Gap, Lee Cooper, Levi's, Petroleum, Proudfoot, Suits You, The Suit Company, Thomas Pink, Van Heusen, Woodhouse, Donnay, Fila, Gap, JoKids, Mexx, Nike, Reebok, Toyzone, Clarks, Ecco, Jane Shilton Kiplings, Lilley & Skinner, Soled Out, Antler, Kipling, Samsonite Company Stores. Arran Aromatics, Body Shop, Chapelle Jewellery, Claire's Outlet, Gizmo, One 2 One, Picture Port, Revlon, Sekonda, Sunglass Hut International, Watch Station, Walker and Hall, Woods of Windsor, Bed and Bath Works, Bookends, Bose, China Place, Cloverleaf, Design House, Edinburgh Crystal, Le Creuset, Mountain Warehouse, Price's Candles, Professional Cookware Company, Spiegelau, Waterford Wedgwood, Whittard of Chelsea, XS Music and Video.

PONDEN MILL

DE BRADLEI WHARF, CAMBRIDGE ROAD, DOVER, KENT CT17 9BY, ☎ 01304 225821, 9.30–5.30 MON–FRI, 9.30–6 SAT, 11–5 SUN. **FACTORY SHOP**

See page 464 (CHESH)

PRICE'S PATENT CANDLE CO

MCARTHURGLEN DESIGNER OUTLET ASHFORD, KIMBERLEY WAY, ASHFORD, JUNCTION 10 OF M20, KENT TN24 0SD, ☎ 01233 611828, 10–6 MON–FRI, 8 ON THUR, 9–6 SAT, 11–5 SUN. **FACTORY SHOP**

See page 464 (HAMPS)

ROYAL WORCESTER & SPODE FACTORY SHOP

MCARTHURGLEN DESIGNER OUTLET, OFF ROMNEY MARSH ROAD, ASHFORD, JUNCTION 10 OF M20, KENT TN23 1EL, ☎ 01233 621640, www.royal-worcester.co.uk, 10–6 MON–FRI, 8 ON THUR, 9–6 SAT, 11–5 SUN. **FACTORY SHOP**

See page 465 (CHESH)

T J HUGHES

THE CHEQUERS SHOPPING CENTRE, PADS HILL, MAIDSTONE, KENT ME15 6AT, ☎ 01622 771600, FAX: 01622 753374, **e-mail:** info@tjhughes.co.uk, www.tjhughes.co.uk, 9–5.30 MON–SAT, 10–4 SUN. **PERMANENT DISCOUNT OUTLET**

See page 465 (CHESH)

THE FACTORY SHOP LTD

THE FOREMAN CENTRE, HIGH STREET, HEADCORN, KENT TN27 9NE, ☎ 01622 891651, 9–5.30 MON–SAT, 10–4 SUN. **FACTORY SHOP**

See page 465 (CHESH)

TK MAXX

BROADWAY SQUARE, BEXLEYHEATH BROADWAY, BEXLEYHEATH, KENT, ☎ 0208 301 0508, www.tkmaxx.com, 9–6 MON–SAT, 9 ON THUR, 10–4 SUN. **PERMANENT DISCOUNT OUTLET**

See page 458 (BEDS)

WHITTARD

MCARTHURGLEN DESIGNER OUTLET, ASHFORD, KENT TN24 0SD, ☎ 01233 663061 10–6 MON–SAT, 8 ON THUR, 11–5 SUN. **FACTORY SHOP IN A FACTORY SHOPPING VILLAGE**

See page 466 (CHESH)

WOODS OF WINDSOR

UNIT 84, MCARTHUR GLEN DESIGNER OUTLET VILLAGE, KIMBERLEY WAY, ASHFORD, KENT TN24 0SD, ☎ 01233 647424, www.woodsofwindsor.co.uk, 10–6 MON–SAT, 8 ON THUR, 11–5 SUN. **FACTORY SHOP IN A FACTORY SHOPPING VILLAGE**

219 THE GLADES SHOPPING CENTRE, BROMLEY, KENT BR1 1DN, ☎ 020 8460 5580, www.woodsofwindsor.co.uk, 9–6 MON–SAT, 9 ON THUR, 11–5 SUN. **FACTORY SHOP IN A FACTORY SHOPPING VILLAGE**

See page 466 (CHESH)

LANCASHIRE

ALLWEIS CHINA

GEORGE STREET NORTH, BURY OLD ROAD, MANCHESTER, LANCASHIRE M7 4PX, ☎ 0161 740 2409, FAX: 0161 795 9814, **e-mail:** info@allweis.co.uk, www.allweis.co.uk, 9.15–5.30 MON–FRI, CLOSED SAT, 10.30–3.30 SUN. **PERMANENT DISCOUNT OUTLET**

Branded china, crystal and cutlery at good discounts including Waterford Wedgwood, Royal Doulton, Royal Worcester and many others. None of the stock is seconds. Wedding lists a speciality. Stockists for Alessi, Arthur Price, Boda Nova, Bugatti, George Butler, Oneida, Rosenthal, Villeroy & Boch, and Wilkens. Many of the designers in cutlery are modern Italian and there is a variety ranging from stainless steel to silver plate.

BARDEN MILL SHOP

BARDEN LANE, BURNLEY, LANCASHIRE BB12 0DX, ☎ 01282 420333, FAX: 01282 420336, **e-mail:** info@bardenmillshop.co.uk, 10–6 MON–SAT, 11–5 SUN (LATE NIGHTS TILL 8 THUR APRIL–SEPTEMBER). **FACTORY SHOP**

A true working mill full of bargains, most of which are high street brands at discounted prices. Full range of branded and non-branded merchandise includes Ladieswear from Tagg, Ambience, Affinity, Diva Design, Donna Bella, Prima Casamia, plus Solo from Italy and Camille lingerie; BMB Menswear from Jeff Banks, Regatta, Gola, Le Shark, Centaur, Jonathan Adams, Carabou, Umbro, Bentley, Alexandre and Gibson. Plus Musbury Fabrics selling towels, bedding, fabrics, curtains, from Dorma, Fogarty, Whiteheads, SMD Curtains, Zorbit and Swatch Box. Briggs Shoes with shoes for men, women and children from Hotter, Sterling and Hunt, Van Dal, Gabor and Hotter Subs. Plus Hothouse selling gifts, furniture, pictures, mirrors, candles, kitchenware, lighting, dried flowers, Staffordshire pottery, crystal and glassware. There is also a luggage, books and market stall section. A 140-seat tea room, ample free car and coach parking, disabled access and facilities and weekend boat trips and organised midweek tours.

BEDDING BOX HOMESTYLE

53 QUEEN STREET, GREAT HARWOOD, LANCASHIRE BB6 6PQ, ☎ 01254 885859, FAX: 01254 888338, 9–5 MON–THUR, 9–4 FRI, 10–4 SAT. MAIL ORDER. **PERMANENT DISCOUNT OUTLET**

Bedding and textiles: fitted sheets, flat sheet, base valances, duvet cover, pillowcases, cot quilt covers in 50/50 cotton/polyester, cotton percale, 100% pure cotton and flannelette. Also Early's of Witney blankets, mattress and pillow protectors, duvets for adults and children including white goose feather and down, pillows, cushions, towels and flame retardant curtains, bedspreads, duvet covers and pillows, bath and shower mats, tablecloths and napkins.

BOTTOMS MILL CO LTD

ROCHDALE ROAD, WALSDEN, LANCASHIRE OL14 7UB, ☎ 01706 812691, FAX: 01706 815389, **e-mail:** enquiries@bottomsmill.co.uk, 9.30–5 MON–SAT, 10.30–4.30 SUN. **FACTORY SHOP**

Cotton textile manufacturers, the factory shop sells a wide range of household textiles, pottery, tea towels, sheets, cleaning cloths, lighting and fabrics. Opposite Gordon Rigg's Garden Centre.

BOUNDARY MILL STORES

BURNLEY ROAD, COLNE, LANCASHIRE BB8 8LS, ☎ 01282 865229, www.boundarymill.co.uk, 10–6 MON–FRI, 9 ON THUR, 9–6 SAT, 11–5 SUN, 10–6 BANK HOLIDAYS, OPENS AT 10 ON SUNDAYS FOR BREAKFAST AND BROWSING, PURCHASES CAN BE MADE FROM 11. **PERMANENT DISCOUNT OUTLET**

One of the largest clearance stores in Britain, it covers more than 100,000 square feet with over 300 quality brands, all now under one roof. Many of the top end of the high street designer labels are on sale here for both women and men. Women's labels include: Alexon, Windsmoor, Austin Reed, Eastex, Planet, Jaeger, Jacques Vert, Liz Claiborne and Viyella. Men's labels include: Austin Reed, Centaur, Dannimac, Farah, Pierre Cardin, Lyle & Scott and Yves St Laurent. The women's and men's departments are very extensive – not to mention impressive – and cover the whole range from casual to evening wear with reductions of between 30% and 70%. There are also large leisurewear departments for women and men including Polo Ralph Lauren, Timberland, Wrangler and Tog 24, and a whole floor dedicated to women's lingerie. The new extension building, which links the fashion and home stores, contains a massive shoe department stocking Bally, Nine West and Hush Puppies, among others. On the ground floor, there is a huge new cookshop stocking up-to-the-minute ranges and a greatly extended luggage department including Globetrotter, Antler and Jane Shilton. The home store sells brand-name home furnishings, glass and china including Dorma, Sanderson, Denby, Edinburgh Crystal, Dartington Crystal, Portmeirion, Royal Worcester, Villeroy & Boch and Wedgwood. Four times a year, there are special sales at which prices are discounted further. Most of the stock is end of lines with the occasional marked seconds. There is a choice of food outlets: a large coffee shop, a restaurant and a pub, and there is extensive free parking.

CATALOGUE BARGAIN SHOP

UNIT 1, EASTGATE RETAIL PARK, ACCRINGTON, LANCASHIRE BB5 6PW, ☎ 01254 879195, www.bargaincrazy.com, 9–8 MON–FRI, 9–6 SAT, 10.30–4.30 SUN.

KINGSWAY, BURNLEY LANCASHIRE BB11 1AB, ☎ 01282 420202, www.bargaincrazy.com, 9–5 MON–SAT, 7 ON THUR, 10.30–4.30 SUN.

40–42 MARKET STREET, CHORLEY, LANCASHIRE PR7 2SE, ☎ 012572 68325, www.bargaincrazy.com, 9–5.30 MON–SAT, 10.30–4.30 SUN.

HALL BANK, WORSLEY RD, PATRICROFT, ECCLES, MANCHESTER, LANCASHIRE M30 8NR, ☎ 0161 787 7726, www.bargaincrazy.com, 10–5.30 MON–FRI, 8 ON THUR, 9–5 SAT, 10.30–4.30 SUN.

UNITS 1–2, HIGH STREET, HULME, MANCHESTER, LANCASHIRE M15 5AF, ☎ 0161 226 5379, www.bargaincrazy.com, 9–8 MON–SAT, 9 ON THUR, FRI, 11–5 SUN.

UNIT 3, THE PARSONAGE RETAIL PARK, LEIGH, LANCASHIRE WN7 5SJ, ☎ 01942 671911, www.bargaincrazy.com, 9–8 MON–FRI, 9–6 SAT, 11–5 SUN.

UNIT 4, QUEENS RETAIL PARK, QUEENS STREET, PRESTON, LANCASHIRE PR1 4HZ, ☎ 01772 884104, www.bargaincrazy.com, 9–8 MON–FRI, 9–6 SAT, 10.30–4.30 SUN.

82–83 EGARTON WALK, ELLESMERE CENTRE, WALKDEN, MANCHESTER, LANCASHIRE M28 3ZD, ☎ 0161 703 9311, www.bargaincrazy.com, 9–5.30 MON–SAT. **PERMANENT DISCOUNT OUTLET**

See page 461 (CAMBS)

CATALOGUE DISCOUNT STORES

2 BURY OLD ROAD, CHEETHAM HILL, MANCHESTER, LANCASHIRE M8 7JN, ☎ 0161 795 9312, FAX: 0161 7407 274, 9–5.30 MON–SAT

PERMANENT DISCOUNT OUTLET

Grattan catalogue store, selling a wide selection of items from those featured in the catalogue, including women's, men's, children's, home, electrics and toys. All items are discounted by up to 50% with regular special promotions. All stores offer a 14-day refund policy, and a 12-month guarantee on electrical items. A wide range of brands are in stock on a regularly changing basis. Each store carries a slightly different range, so please phone to check that they have what you want in stock.

CHORTEX TOWEL MILL SHOP

VICTORIA MILL, CHORLEY NEW ROAD, HORWICH, NEAR BOLTON, LANCASHIRE BL6 6ER, ☎ 01204 673073, FAX: 01204 696680, **e-mail:** millshop@chortex.com, www.chortex.com, 9–4.45 MON–FRI, 7 ON THUR, 10–3 SAT. **FACTORY SHOP**

Sells top quality plain dyed towels in every colour imaginable, produced in their own factory in Horwich. Embellished towels, towelling robes, beach towels, bath mats and shower curtains are also stocked, together with other bathroom accessories. Brand names include Chortex and Horrockses. Personal shoppers only.

CWV BRANDS AT HOME FACTORY SHOP

HEASANDFORD INDUSTRIAL ESTATE, WIDOW HILL ROAD, BURNLEY, LANCASHIRE BB10 2TJ, ☎ 01282 727272, **e-mail:** pamhindle@englewood.co.uk, 9.30–5.30 MON–FRI, 9–5 SAT, 10–4 SUN, 10–5 BANK HOLIDAYS. **FACTORY SHOP**

See page 463 (CHESH)

DALE MILL DISCOUNTS

DALE STREET, MILNROW, NEAR ROCHDALE, LANCASHIRE OL16 3NJ, ☎ 01706 359737, 9.30–6 MON–WED, FRI, 9.30–8 THUR, 9.30–5.30 SAT, 10–5.30 SUN. **PERMANENT DISCOUNT OUTLET**

A wide range of items from clothes and shoes for all the family to kitchenware, furniture, table-cloths, beds and bedding, televisions and general electrical goods, fridges, cookers, microwaves, kitchen and bedroom fittings and units, all on sale at discounted prices. On site there is also a designer clothes store and sportswear outlet, plus a new conservatory extension selling glassware, pottery, dried flowers, table lamps and other household goods.

DARTINGTON CRYSTAL

BOUNDARY MILL, BURNLEY ROAD, COLNE, LANCASHIRE BB8 8LS, ☎ 01282 865229, 10–6 MON–FRI, 9 ON THUR, 10–8 SAT, 10.30–5 SUN.

FREEPORT VILLAGE, ANCHORAGE ROAD, FLEETWOOD LANCASHIRE FY7 6AE, ☎ 01253 872272, 10–8 MON–FRI, 10–6 SAT, 10–6 SUN. **FACTORY SHOP IN A FACTORY SHOPPING VILLAGE**

See page 469 (CORN)

DENBY FACTORY SHOP

BOUNDARY MILL, BURNLEY ROAD, COLNE, LANCASHIRE BB8 8LS, ☎ 01282 865229, www.denby.co.uk, 10–6 MON–FRI, 8 ON THUR, 9–6 SAT, 10–5 SUN. **FACTORY SHOP**

See page 463 (CHESH)

DESIGN HOUSE

UNIT G8, THE DESIGNER OUTLET AT THE LOWRY, THE QUAYS, SALFORD QUAYS, MANCHESTER, LANCASHIRE M5 2WZ, ☎ 0161 877 5015, 10–8 MON–FRI, 9–7 SAT, 11–5 SUN. **FACTORY SHOP IN A FACTORY SHOPPING VILLAGE**

See page 483 (ESSEX)

DUNELM MILL SHOP

GREEN STREET, RADCLIFFE, MANCHESTER, LANCASHIRE M26 3AD, ☎ 0161 724 1004, FAX: 0161 724 6631, www.dunelm-mill.co.uk, 9–5.30 MON–FRI, 9–6 SAT, 11–5 SUN.

THE CAPITOL CENTRE, LONDON WAY, WALTON LE DALE, PRESTON, LANCASHIRE PR5 4AW, ☎ 01772 888801, FAX: 01772 888892, www.dunelm-mill.co.uk, 9–6 MON–SAT, 8 ON THUR, FRI, 10–4 SUN.

WHITWORTH ROAD, ROCHDALE, LANCASHIRE OL12 0TR, ☎ 01706 342222, FAX: 01706 868 023, www.dunelm-mill.co.uk, 9–6 MON–SAT, 8 ON THUR, FRI, 10–4 SUN. **PERMANENT DISCOUNT OUTLET**

See page 458 (BEDS)

EDINBURGH CRYSTAL

BOUNDARY MILL, LIBRA TEXTILE LTD, BURNLEY ROAD, COLNE, LANCASHIRE BB8 8LS, ☎ 01282 865229 BOUNDARY MILL, 10–6 MON–FRI, 9 ON THUR, 9–6 SAT, 10–5 SUN. **FACTORY SHOP**

See page 463 (CHESH)

FREEPORT FLEETWOOD OUTLET VILLAGE

ANCHORAGE ROAD, FLEETWOOD, 12 MILES FROM JUNCTION 3 OF M55, LANCASHIRE FY7 6AE, ☎ 01253 877377, www.freeportfleetwood.com, 10–6 SEVEN DAYS A WEEK, 8 ON THUR, FRI. **FACTORY SHOPPING VILLAGE**

Large, brightly-coloured New-England-style seaside shopping village. There are more than 40 shops selling at up to 50% off high street prices, as well as restaurants, family attractions and free parking. Women's fashions include Next to Nothing, Spotlight, Easy Jeans, VF Corp, Double Two, Warner's, Edinburgh Woollen Mill, The Designer Room, Giorgio, BhS for Less, Madhouse and Roman Originals. For men, there is Petroleum, Ciro Citterio, Double Two, Giorgio, VF Corp, Madhouse, Easy Jeans and BhS for Less. Sportswear and outdoor wear shops include Sports Mill, Craghoppers, Regatta and VF Corp. Footwear outlets comprise Lilley & Skinner, Jane Shilton, Shoe Sellers, BhS For Less, Next to Nothing and Petroleum. Sweet-toothed visitors can indulge at Thorntons or The Sweet Shop, and there is Julian Graves for nuts and dried fruits. Household outlets include Ponden Mill, Dartington Crystal, Home Zone, Picture Port and China Traders. Childrenswear stockists include Next to Nothing, BhS for Less, Vecopri, VF Corp and Giorgio. Other stores include Woods of Windsor, Hallmark Cards and Gifts, XS Music & Video, Claire's Accessories, Watch Store and Book Depot.

GIFTTREE

CHURCHBRIDGE WORKS, HENRY STREET, ACCRINGTON, LANCASHIRE BB5 4EU, ☎ 01254 237324, 9–5 MON–SAT

REEDYFORD MILL, WESTFIELD ROAD, NELSON, LANCASHIRE BB9 7YM, ☎ 01282 619540, FAX: 01282 696639, 9–5 MON–SAT. **PERMANENT DISCOUNT OUTLET**

See page 473 (DERBY)

GORSE MILL LIGHTING

GORDON STREET, OFF JARDINE WAY, BROADWAY, CHADDERTON, OLDHAM, LANCASHIRE OL9 9QW, ☎ 0161 628 4202, FAX: 0161 652 0947, 9.30–5 MON–FRI, 7 ON THUR, 10–5 SAT, 11–5 SUN. **PERMANENT DISCOUNT OUTLET**

240,000 square feet dedicated to lighting up your home. One of Britain's largest decorative light manufacturers, this shop claims to house the biggest display of lighting in the country. The range includes halogen, garden and security lights as well as crystal fittings at savings of between 30% and 75% off high street prices. Lampshades start at as little as 50p and also come in a variety of sizes, patterns and colours. Gorse Mill supplies major chainstores and has vast ranges of decorative lighting, outdoor lighting, crystal chandeliers and ceiling fans, as well as Chinese and Portuguese pottery. Coffee shop, parking for 300 cars, disabled facilities.

HABITAT CLEARANCE DEPARTMENT

SOUTHMOOR ROAD, WYTHENSHAWE, LANCASHIRE M23 9LR, ☎ 0161 902 0441
OPEN 9.30–6 MON–WED, 9.30–7 THUR, FRI, 9 -6 SAT, 11 -5 SUN. **PERMANENT DISCOUNT OUTLET**

Ends of ranges and slightly damaged stock from the famous Habitat stores displayed in one section of this full-price shop. Specialises in furniture rather than china, glass and rugs though there is usually a selection of the latter, too. Plenty of sofas, tables and fitted kitchen units.

HARTLEYS MAIL ORDER LTD

REGENT HOUSE, WHITEWALLS INDUSTRIAL ESTATE, COLNE, LANCASHIRE BB8 8LJ, ☎ 01282 861350, **e-mail:** info@hartleys.co.uk, www.hartleysmo.co.uk, 9.30–4.30 MON–FRI. MAIL ORDER. **PERMANENT DISCOUNT OUTLET**

Clearance lines and regular ranges from manufacturers who supply well-known high street names, Hartleys, which has been established for 38 years, sells calico, voile, muslin, sheeting, pillows, dress fabric, towels, quilts, ready made bedding, curtaining, many of which are well-known brand names, as well as selected garden accessories and furniture. Examples of prices include 70in to 110in sheeting from £2 to £4.95 a metre; huge savings on casement stitched 13.5 tog goose down quilts from £78 for singles, £110 for doubles and £135 for king sizes; polyester quilts from £7.95 for singles, £9.95 for doubles and £11.95 for king size. Curtaining is available from £2 to £20 plus a metre, enhanced by a craftsman-quality curtain and drape making service, which is available economically, using fabric supplied by Hartleys. Dress fabrics cost from 99p a metre; plus large stocks of polycottons, cottons and wool and silks. Curtaining can also be ordered from the curtain range books in the shop which include Crowson and Moygashel. Prices are the same whether you buy through the on-site shop or by mail order or via the website, although many offers are available through the shop only. UK order, C & H charge only £3.50, overseas charge on request. Parking available. Send five second class stamps for samples and a free copy of Hartleys' most recent offers.

HOLLIN HALL CRAFT & SEWING CENTRE

EMPRESS MILLS (1927) LTD, HOLLIN HALL MILL, TRAWDEN, COLNE, LANCASHIRE BB8 8SS, ☎ 01282 863181, FAX: 01282 870935, **e-mail:** chris@empressmills.co.uk, www.empressmills.co.uk, 9–5 MON–FRI, 10–4 SAT, SUN. MAIL ORDER. **PERMANENT DISCOUNT OUTLET**

At Hollin Craft & Sewing Centre, you will find a modern, working thread mill. The centre houses all the threads and yarns previously only available to industry. Here, you can buy extraordinary threads at factory prices. Hand and machine quilting, endless overlocking types, tailoring, household textiles, tacking, speciality bookbinding, machine and hand embroidery are all on show. The haberdashery section stocks a similarly huge variety including many types of zip fastener. There is an extensive fabric gallery stocking furnishing fabrics, muslins and silks. The large, two-floor shop also accommodates the Thread Collection, plus books, kits, and crafts including stencilling, stamping and embossing, American innovations, decoupage, beading, hardanger, dolls houses and furniture. There are also ceramics, glassware, wood, candles and wicker in the exclusive gift and homewares section. All this is available by mail order, worldwide. Set in the heart of the countryside, there are workshops, demonstrations and good walking routes nearby.

LAMBERT HOWARTH FOOTWEAR

GREENBRIDGE WORKS, FALBARN ROAD, OFF BOCHOLT WAY, RAWTENSTAL, ROSSENDALE, LANCASHIRE BB4 7NX, ☎ 01706 235160, FAX: 01706 235129, 9.30–5 MON–FRI, 9.30–4 SAT, 10–4 SUN.

FINSLEY GATE, BURNLEY, LANCASHIRE, ☎ 01282 471283, 9.30–5 MON–FRI, 9–4 SAT.
FACTORY SHOP
A real mixture of seconds and perfects. They sell clothes, handbags and towels. The seconds in footwear are from shoes made for major high street chainstores and all are at discounted prices. These include slippers, walking boots, flat shoes and sandals for men, women and children. The perfects in clothes, towels and bags are two-thirds of the high street prices. They also stock a large selection of pottery. There is an on-site creche and coffee shop serving drinks and light refreshments, wheelchair access and disabled facilities, plus free car parking.

LOWRY DESIGNER OUTLET

THE QUAYS, SALFORD QUAYS, MANCHESTER, LANCASHIRE M5 2WZ, ☎ 0161 848 1800, FAX: 0161 848 1801, **e-mail:** peter.cronin@emerson.co.uk, www.lowrydesigneroutlet.co.uk, 10–8 MON–FRI, 9–7 SAT, 11–5 SUN. **FACTORY SHOPPING VILLAGE**
A new outlet shopping centre with 80 shops in a site next to the Manchester Ship Canal. The site includes a hotel, Warner Village multiplex cinema, 15 cafés/restaurants and a health and fitness club. It is built alongside the £127 million Lowry Millennium Project for the Arts. The newly-opened Imperial War Museum North, is just a bridge away. Names with outlets here include Whistles, Karen Millen, Cotton Traders, Proibito (selling Moschino, Armani, Diesel, Calvin Klein, Gianfranco Ferre, Replay, Guess, Boss, Fendi and Valentino), Marks & Spencer, Donnay International, Carphone WArehouse, Antler, Scotts and Diadora Italian sportswear, among others.

MATALAN

FOUNTAIN RETAIL PARK, HYNDBURN ROAD, ACCRINGTON LANCASHIRE BB5 4AA, ☎ 01254 356100, FAX: 01254 879037, www.matalan.co.uk, 9.30–8 MON–FRI, 9–6 SAT, 11–5 SUN.

207 LOWER AUDLEY STREET, BLACKBURN, LANCASHIRE BB1 1DG, ☎ 01254 507200, www.matalan.co.uk, 10–8 MON–FRI, 9–6 SAT, 11–5 SUN.

UNIT 2, CLIFTON RETAIL PARK, CLIFTON ROAD, BLACKPOOL LANCASHIRE FY4 4UJ, ☎ 01253 697850, FAX: 01253 697852, www.matalan.co.uk, 10- 8 MON–FRI, 9–6 SAT, 11–5 SUN.

TURNER BRIDGE, TONGE MOOR ROAD, BOLTON, LANCASHIRE BL2 2DJ, ☎ 01204 383733, FAX: 01204 383542, www.matalan.co.uk, 10–8 MON–FRI, 9–6 SAT, 11–5 SUN.

SEFTON RETAIL PARK, DUNNINGS BRIDGE ROAD, BOOTLE, LIVERPOOL, LANCASHIRE L30 6UU, ☎ 0151 525 1190, FAX: 0151 525 3404, www.matalan.co.uk, 9.30–8 MON–FRI, 9–6 SAT, 11–5 SUN.

FOUNDRY STREET/GEORGE STREET, BURY, LANCASHIRE BL9 0BZ, ☎ 0161 705 4520, FAX: 0161 797 5680, www.matalan.co.uk, 9.30–8 MON–FRI, 9–6 SAT, 11–5 SUN.

NORTH VALLEY RETAIL PARK, NORTH VALLEY ROAD, COLNE, LANCASHIRE BB8 8LU, ☎ 01282 857700, FAX: 01282 859692, www.matalan.co.uk, 10–8 MON–FRI, 9–6 SAT, 11–5 SUN.

LANCASTER RETAIL PARK, MELLISHAW LANE, LANCASTER, LANCASHIRE LA1 5JR, ☎ 01524 541960, FAX: 01524 849911, www.matalan.co.uk, 10–8 MON–FRI, 9–6 SAT, 11–5 SUN.

UNITS G & H, THE TRIUMPH CENTRE, HUNTS CROSS, LIVERPOOL LANCASHIRE L24 9GB, ☎ 0151 486 0325, FAX: 0151 486 2952, www.matalan.co.uk, 9.30–8 MON–FRI, 9–6 SAT, 11–5 SUN.

BROOKWAY RETAIL PARK, 452 ALTRINCHAM ROAD, BAGULEY, MANCHESTER, LANCASHIRE M23 9BP, ☎ 0161 902 2500, FAX: 0161 945 1582, www.matalan.co.uk, 9.30–8 MON–FRI, 10–6 SAT, 11–5 SUN.

UNIT 3, ALEXANDRA CENTRE, PARK ROAD, OLDHAM LANCASHIRE OL4 1SG, ☎ 0161 620 6686, FAX: 0161 620 6690, www.matalan.co.uk, 10–8 MON–FRI, 9–6 SAT, 11–5 SUN.

HOLME ROAD, BAMBER BRIDGE, PRESTON, LANCASHIRE PR5 6BP, ☎ 01772 627365, FAX: 01772 314856, www.matalan.co.uk, 10–8 MON–FRI, 9–6 SAT, 11–5 SUN.

CENTRAL RETAIL PARK, OLDHAM ROAD, ROCHDALE, LANCASHIRE OL11 1OZ, ☎ 01706 752320, FAX: 01706 527339, www.matalan.co.uk, 10–8 MON–FRI, 9–6 SAT, 11–5 SUN.

2 WATTS CLIFF WAY, TODD ROAD, ST HELENS, LANCASHIRE WA9 1JL, ☎ 01744 766200, FAX: 01744 750904, www.matalan.co.uk, 9.30–8 MON–FRI, 9–6 SAT, 11–5 SUN.

WESTOVER STREET, OFF STATION ROAD, SWINTON LANCASHIRE M27 2AH, ☎ 0161 794 3441, FAX: 0161 794 3461, www.matalan.co.uk, 10–8 MON–FRI, 9–6 SAT, 11–5 SUN.

LOIRE DRIVE, ROBIN RETAIL PARK, WIGAN, LANCASHIRE WN5 0UH, ☎ 01942 629500, FAX: 01942 217625, www.matalan.co.uk, 10–6 MON–FRI, 10–6 SAT, 11–5 SUN. **PERMANENT DISCOUNT OUTLET**

See page 458 (BEDS)

MUSBURY FABRICS MILL SHOP

PARK MILL, HOLCOMBE ROAD, HELMSHORE, ROSSENDALE, LANCASHIRE BB4 4NP, ☎ 01706 244280, FAX: 01706 212121, **e-mail:** orders@musburyfabrics.co.uk, www.musburyfabrics.co.uk, 9.30–4.30 MON–SAT, 10–4 SUN. **PERMANENT DISCOUNT OUTLET**

Hundreds of rolls of fabric from SMD, Tyrone, Bill Beaumont and Fryetts, all at greatly reduced prices. Bedlinen by Dorma, Horrockses, Rectella and Coelima. Ready-made curtains by SMD, Tyrone and Whiteheads. All high street brands are stocked at low prices and all are greatly reduced. Throughout the year, they also buy in hundreds of discontinued lines, clearance and slight seconds from various suppliers, many sold off at less than 50% of the recommended retail price. Huge stocks of towels, sheets, pillows, duvets, tablelinen, curtain poles and cushion covers, all at low mill shop prices. January and summer sales see even greater bargains.

NEWMANS FOOTWEAR FACTORY SHOP

GARDEN STREET WORKS, BLACKBURN, LANCASHIRE BB2 1TZ, ☎ 01254 676198, 10–6 MON–SAT, 10–4 SUN. **FACTORY SHOP**

Not just a shoes shop selling footwear for men, women and children but also a general product outlet with some clothes, bedding, bags, belts, candles, glassware, dried flowers, ceramics and textiles.

OAK BANK MILL FACTORY SHOP

CASTERTON AVENUE, BURNLEY, LANCASHIRE BB10 2PG, ☎ 01282 425280, 9–5 MON–FRI, 10–12 SAT. **FACTORY SHOP**

Large range of bedding and curtains with Horrocks towels, flannelette sheets, duvet covers, quilts, pillows and cushions, most of which are made in the next door factory.

ONEIDA

BOUNDARY MILL, BURNLEY ROAD, COLNE, LANCASHIRE BB8 8LS, ☎ 01282 865 229, 10–6 MON–FRI, 9 ON THUR, 9–6 SAT, 10–5 SUN, 10–6 BANK HOLIDAYS. **FACTORY SHOP**

See page 464 (CHESH)

OSWALDTWISTLE MILLS

MOSCOW MILL, COLLIER ST, OSWALDTWISTLE, ACCRINGTON, LANCASHIRE BB5 3DF, ☎ 01254 871025, FAX: 01254 770790, **e-mail:** info@o-mills.co.uk, www.o-mills.co.uk, 9–5 MON–SAT, 11–5 SUN, 8 ON THUR. MAIL ORDER ALSO. **FACTORY SHOP**

A working mill which manufactures for top hotels and restaurants within the UK, with lots of attractions for families, apart from the bargains on offer. There are landscaped grounds with mini golf, Wendy House village, Gnomeland, wildfowl reserve and picnic area. Musbury Fabrics sell bedding, quilts, sheets and towels; Hot House sell dried flowers, mirrors, ceramics, kitchenware and pictures. Also sells a selection of women's clothes plus cards and books. Craft House sells everything from salt dough to decoupage; Body Shop sells shampoo and bathroom products; and there are other shops selling furniture, handicrafts, jewellery and sweets (made on the premises), all at competitive prices. There is also a weaver, silk painting, garden centre and a children's play area. Part of the complex sells everything from Egyptian cotton to household textiles, plus everything you need to keep the house clean, including brand-names such as Cif, Comfort and Flash – and you don't have to bulk buy.

OSWALDTWISTLE MILLS LINEN COLLECTION

OSWALDTWISTLE MILLS, MOSCOW MILL, COLLIER STREET, OSWALDTWISTLE, NEAR ACCRINGTON, LANCASHIRE BB5 3DE, ☎ 01254 871025, FAX: 01254 770790, **e-mail:** rclarke@o-mills.co.uk, www.o-mills.co.uk/linencol, 9–5 SEVEN DAYS A WEEK. MAIL ORDER.

46 MARKET STREET, LANCASTER LANCASHIRE LA1 1HF, ☎ 01524 843591, **e-mail:** rclarke@o-mills.co.uk, www.o-mills.co.uk/linencol, 9–5 MON–SAT, 11–4 SUN. **PERMANENT DISCOUNT OUTLET**

Collection of quality UK woven Damask tablelinen and bedlinen, luxury robes and towels, duvets and pillows. Products are sold exclusively in their retail outlets and can be delivered to your door if ordered from the Internet or from their mail order catalogue. White 100% cotton double sheets are priced from £6.84, luxury bath robes from £14.89, and dyed 100% cotton tablecloths from £4.86.

PENDLE VILLAGE SHOPPING OUTLET

HOLLIN BANK, BRIERFIELD, NELSON, JUNCTION 12 OF M65, LANCASHIRE, ☎ 01282 605004 HOMEWARES, FAX: 01282 605023 FASHION, OPEN 10–5.30 MON–SAT, 10.30–4.30 SUN. **PERMANENT DISCOUNT OUTLET**

A huge mill shop with different areas selling fashion, home furnishings, bedding, towels, pine and cane furniture, dining sets, three-piece suites, carpets and rugs. The fashion department boasts many famous high street names and features lingerie and footwear while the homewares department offers a wide range of bedding with matching accessories, ready-made curtains, cushions, towels in a wide range of colours and sizes and a collection of cookware and gifts. The furniture showroom offers a wide range of upholstery in modern fabrics, chenilles and leathers; traditional dining room furniture; kitchen sets; pine bedroom, dining and occasional furniture; and an extensive selection of different types of beds. The carpet department offers an extensive selection of rolls and roll ends in carpets and vinyls as well as wood flooring and more than 600 traditional Chinese, Indian and Oriental rugs in a variety of sizes and colours.

PONDEN MILL

FREEPORT SHOPPING VILLAGE, ANCHORAGE ROAD, FLEETWOOD, LANCASHIRE FY7 6AE, ☎ 01253 777252, 10–6 SEVEN DAYS A WEEK, 8 ON THUR, FRI. **FACTORY SHOP IN A FACTORY SHOPPING VILLAGE**

See page 464 (CHESH)

QS FASHION

114–116 BOLTON ROAD, ATHERTON, LANCASHIRE M29 9JZ, ☎ 01942 873847, FAX: 01942 897954, 9–5.30 MON–WED, 9–7 THUR, FRI, 9–5 SAT, 11–5 SUN.

GREEN LANE/PRESTON OLD ROAD, CHERRY TREE, BLACKBURN, LANCASHIRE BB2 5LX, ☎ 01254 209800, FAX: 01254 209833, 10–8 MON–FRI, 10–5.30 SAT, 10–5 SUN.

11–14 PALL MALL, CHORLEY, LANCASHIRE PR7 2LA, ☎ 01257 267113, FAX: 01257 263485, 9–8 MON–FRI, 9–5.30 SAT, 10–4 SUN.

148 MARKET STREET, FARNWORTH, LANCASHIRE BL4 9AE, ☎ 01204 862625, FAX: 01204 701855, 9–5.30 MON–WED, SAT, 9–6 THUR, FRI, 10–4 SUN. **PERMANENT DISCOUNT OUTLET**

Fashion for all the family includes brands such as Timberland, Fila, Nike, Reebok, Adidas, Calvin Klein and Ralph Lauren and many more. Homeware products include towels, bedding, plastics, pictures, toys and mirrors. The stock is constantly changing so come with an open mind. QS Fashion has a price promise that if you can purchase the same item at a cheaper price at another store, QS will give you the product free.

ROYAL WORCESTER & SPODE FACTORY SHOP

BOUNDARY MILL, BURNLEY ROAD, COLNE, LANCASHIRE BB8 8LS, ☎ 01282 865 229 EXTENSION 510, www.royal-worcester.co.uk, 10–6 MON–SAT, 8 ON THUR, 11–5 SUN. **FACTORY SHOP**

See page 465 (CHESH)

SECOND CHANCE

8 PORTLAND STREET, SOUTHPORT, LANCASHIRE PR8 1JU, ☎ 01704 538329, 9.30–5 MON–SAT. **PERMANENT DISCOUNT OUTLET**

Sells mostly good quality seconds in white English bone china. Examples of prices include: cup and saucer £4.25, 10 inch dinner plate £3.99, side plate £2.99, teapots from £4.99, decorated bone china mugs from £1.99. Also stocks Burgess & Leigh seconds at 30% discounts, cut glass tableware, oven-to-tableware, drinking glasses from 75p and giftware.

SHERRY'S LANCASHIRE MILL SHOP

STOCKBRIDGE MILL, STOCKBRIDGE ROAD, PADIHAM, BURNLEY, LANCASHIRE BB12 7HA, ☎ 01282 778416, 9.30–5.30 MON -F RI, 9.30–5 SAT, 11–5 SUN. **FACTORY SHOP**

Factory shop next to the weaving mill selling mainly towels and bedding, and also including net curtains, voiles, fabrics, candles, candleholders, pot pourri, picture frames, table cloths, swags and giftware.

STANDFAST FACTORY FABRIC SHOP

CATON ROAD, LANCASTER, LANCASHIRE LA1 3PA, ☎ 01524 64334, 9.30–1 MON–FRI, 10–12.30 SAT. **FACTORY SHOP**

Genuine factory shop selling a wide range of well-known designer named fabrics, which are suitable for all soft furnishings, at discounted prices. Stocks vary according to factory production and all fabrics are seconds. Prices range from £2 to £7 per metre. They always stock plenty of pieces for cushion covers and patchwork from 30p each to £3 for small sackful. Usually they have some fabrics on special offer, ranging from £1.50 per metre to £7 a metre. None of the fabric is flame retardant but once treated, can be used for upholstery.

T J HUGHES

59–63 CHURCH STREET, BLACKBURN, LANCASHIRE BB1 5AF, ☎ 01254 693333, FAX: 01254 693232, **e-mail:** info@tjhughes.co.uk, www.tjhughes.co.uk, 9–5.30 MON–SAT, 11–5 SUN.

MONS SQUARE, NEW STRAND, BOOTLE, LANCASHIRE L20 4SY, ☎ 0151 922 4397, FAX: 0151 933 1622, **e-mail:** info@tjhughes.co.uk, www.tjhughes.co.uk, 9–5.30 MON–SAT.

4 CURZON STREET, BURNLEY, LANCASHIRE BB11 1BB, ☎ 01282 838383, FAX: 01282 435400, **e-mail:** info@tjhughes.co.uk, www.tjhughes.co.uk, 9–5.30 MON–SAT, 11–4 SUN.

105 LONDON ROAD, LIVERPOOL, LANCASHIRE L3 8JA, ☎ 0151 207 2600, FAX: 0151 298 1339, **e-mail:** info@tjhughes.co.uk, www.tjhughes.co.uk, 9–5.30 MON–SAT, 11–5 SUN.

31–36 ARNDALE CENTRE, CHESTER ROAD, STRETFORD, MANCHESTER, LANCASHIRE M32 9BB, ☎ 0161 866 9733, FAX: 0161 864 4627, **e-mail:** info@tjhughes.co.uk, www.tjhughes.co.uk, 9–5.30 MON–SAT, 10–4 SUN.

UNIT 32, TOWN SQUARE SHOPPING CENTRE, OLDHAM, MANCHESTER, LANCASHIRE OL1 1XF, ☎ 0161 628 3880, FAX: 0161 628 3886, **e-mail:** info@tjhughes.co.uk, www.tjhughes.co.uk, 9–5.30 MON–SAT.

FISHERGATE CENTRE, PRESTON, LANCASHIRE PR1 8HJ, ☎ 01772 887326, FAX: 01772 887328, **e-mail:** info@tjhughes.co.uk, www.tjhughes.co.uk, 9–5.30 MON–SAT, 8 ON WED, 11–5 SUN.

UNIT 6–7, THE WHEATSHEAF CENTRE, ROCHDALE LANCASHIRE OL16 1NZ, ☎ 01706 750555, FAX: 01706 750666, **e-mail:** info@tjhughes.co.uk, www.tjhughes.co.uk, 9–5.30 MON–SAT, 10.30–4.30 SUN.

86 RAVENS WAY, SALFORD SHOPPING CITY, SALFORD, MANCHESTER, LANCASHIRE M6 5JA, ☎ 0161 736 1472, FAX: 0161 736 0656, **e-mail:** info@tjhughes.co.uk, www.tjhughes.co.uk, 9–5.30 MON–SAT.

UNIT 1, THE HARDSHAW CENTRE, ST HELENS, LANCASHIRE WA10 1EB, ☎ 01744 453221, FAX: 01744 453065, **e-mail:** info@tjhughes.co.uk, www.tjhughes.co.uk, 9–5.30 MON–SAT, 10.30–4.30 SUN.

27–31 SANKEY STREET, WARRINGTON, LANCASHIRE WA1 1XG, ☎ 01925 634 4321, FAX: 01925 445966, **e-mail:** info@tjhughes.co.uk, www.tjhughes.co.uk, 9–5.30 MON–SAT, 10.30–4.30 SUN. **PERMANENT DISCOUNT OUTLET**

See page 465 (CHESH)

THE EAST LANCASHIRE TOWEL COMPANY

PARK MILL, HOLSTEAD LANE, BARROWFORD, NELSON, LANCASHIRE BB9 6HJ, ☎ 01282 612193, FAX: 01282 697736, www.towelcompany.co.uk, 8.30–5 MON–FRI. MAIL ORDER.

FACTORY SHOP

The East Lancashire Towel Company still produces towels by the traditional method – making them both highly absorbent and hard wearing – and are able to keep costs down by selling direct to the general public. They produce a wide variety of towels: bath sheets, jacquard woven with intricate floral patterns in a variety of designs, kitchen and terry roller towels, souvenir and promotional towels, football club towels, dishcloths, tea towels, sheets, duvets, pillows, face cloths, dusters and hankies, all at about half price. Toilets and car parking. Please phone if you would like a copy of their brochure.

THE FACTORY SHOP

SHAWBRIDGE STREET, CLITHEROE, LANCASHIRE BB7 1NA, ☎ 01200 428784, 9–5.30 MON–SAT, 10.30–4.30 SUN.

LANCASTER LEISURE PARK, WYRESDALE ROAD, LANCASTER, LANCASHIRE LA1 3LA, ☎ 01524 846079, 10–5 MON–SAT, 11–5 SUN. **FACTORY SHOP**

See page 465 (CHESH)

TK MAXX

76 BANK HEY STREET, BLACKPOOL, LANCASHIRE B19 0B7, FAX: 01253 752754, www.tkmaxx.com, PHONE FOR DETAILS OF OPENING TIMES.

1ST FLOOR, THE GATES SHOPPING CENTRE, MEALHOUSE LANE, BOLTON, LANCASHIRE, ☎ 01204 385527, www.tkmaxx.com, PHONE FOR DETAILS OF OPENING TIMES.

UNIT 1 AND 2, ANGOULEME RETAIL PARK, BURY, LANCASHIRE B19 0B7, FAX: 0161 7611700, www.tkmaxx.com, 9–5.30 MON–FRI, 7 ON THUR, 9–6 SAT, 11–5 SUN.

1ST FLOOR, 15 PARKER ST, OFF CLAYTON SQUARE, LIVERPOOL, LANCASHIRE L1 1DP, ☎ 0151 708 9919, www.tkmaxx.com, 9–6 MON–SAT, 11–5 SUN.

BASEMENT LEVEL, LEWIS'S BUILDING, MARKET STREET, MANCHESTER, LANCASHIRE M60 1TX, ☎ 0161 236 1885, www.tkmaxx.com, 9–6.30 MON–FRI, 8 ON THUR, 9–6 SAT, 11–5 SUN.

FISHERGATE SHOPPING CENTRE, PRESTON, LANCASHIRE PR1 2BT, ☎ 01772 253220, www.tkmaxx.com, 9–5.30 MON–FRI, 8 ON WED, 9–6 SAT, 11–5 SUN.

THE POINT RETAIL PARK, MOLEWORTH STREET, ROCHDALE, LANCASHIRE, ☎ 01706 759187, www.tkmaxx.com, PHONE FOR DETAILS OF OPENING TIMES.

UNIT A1, REGENT ROAD RETAIL PARK, ORDSALL LANE, SALFORD, MANCHESTER LANCASHIRE M5 3TP, ☎ 0161 833 2200, www.tkmaxx.com, 9.30–8 MON, THUR, FRI, 9.30–6 TUE, WED, 9–6 SAT, 11–5 SUN.

7–9 MARBLE PLACE SHOPPING CENTRE, CHAPEL STREET, SOUTHPORT LANCASHIRE PR8 1DF, ☎ 01704 501900, www.tkmaxx.com, 9–5.30 MON–FRI, 9–6 SAT, 11–5 SUN.

ST HELEN'S RETAIL PARK, WARRINGTON NEW ROAD, LANCASHIRE, ☎ 01744 615847, www.tkmaxx.com, PHONE FOR DETAILS OF OPENING TIMES. **PERMANENT DISCOUNT OUTLET**

See page 458 (BEDS)

TOP MARKS

149–151 HOLLAND STREET, DENTON, MANCHESTER, LANCASHIRE M34 3GE, ☎ 0161 336 1279, 9.30–5.30 MON–SAT, 8 ON THUR, 11–5 SUN. **PERMANENT DISCOUNT OUTLET**

A two-floor, 7,000-foot warehouse selling famous chainstore clothing (cancelled orders, overstocks, ends-of-lines and some grade A seconds) at up to 50% off normal retail prices. Shoes and clothing for women are available in sizes 8 to 18; men's clothing ranges from small to XXL, 30in to 42in waist and 29in to 33in leg; children's clothing is available from birth up to nine years. Also stocks homeware, giftware and furniture at discounted prices. All major credit cards are accepted and free parking is available.

TRADEX

CARLISLE STREET, RINGWAY, PRESTON, LANCASHIRE PR1 1EH, ☎ 01772 888333, FAX: 01772 880015, 9.30–8.30 MON–FRI, 9–5.30 SAT, 10.30–4.30 SUN. **PERMANENT DISCOUNT OUTLET**

Clothing and shoes for all the family, jewellery, household goods, toiletries, bedding and home furnishings, food and confectionery. Leading and high street brand names can be found in all departments with discounts of up to 60% off recommended retail prices. To shop here, you have to be a member: bring two forms of identity showing your address and you can join instantly for £2. There is a coffee shop serving meals and snacks.

VANILLA

OSWALDTWISTLE MILLS, COLLIER STREET, OSWALDTWISTLE, LANCASHIRE BB5 3DF, ☎ 01254 871025, **e-mail:** christina@vanilla-ossy.fsnet.co.uk, 10–5 MON–SAT, 8 ON THUR, 11–5 SUN. **FACTORY SHOP**

Sells fantasy flowers and provides every aspect of imitation decor. They stock hundreds of different single stems from 49p – bunches, foliage and trees, many at wholesale prices. Arrangements average £40. Their bridal department offers a personal service. Phone or email for brochure.

WINFIELDS

HAZEL MILL, BLACKBURN ROAD, HASLINGDEN, ROSSENDALE, LANCASHIRE BB4 5DD, ☎ 01706 227916, FAX: 01706 831125, **e-mail:** info@winfields.co.uk, www.winfields.co.uk, 10–5.30 MON–FRI, 8 ON THUR, 9–5.30 SAT, 11–5 SUN. **PERMANENT DISCOUNT OUTLET**

Winfields is a big mill discount store with other outlets in Barrow-in-Furness, Middleton and Hull, offering tremendous savings on shoes (more than 100,000 pairs to choose from, including trainers, boots, dressy shoes and sandals), womenswear (casual wear, sportswear, swimwear, lingerie, suits and dresses and designer fashions), traditional and contemporary menswear (shirts, trousers, jeans, polo shirts, denim jackets, sleepsuits and underwear), and accessories such as leather belts and wallets. There is a young fashion department and a range for women in sizes 18 plus. Winfields is the word on the street for children and teens for footwear, sportswear and clothing in up-to-the-minute styles. In addition, Winfields has a massive selction of outdoor wear, fleeces, waterproofs, wellingtons, hiking boots, socks, hats, scarves and gloves for all the family. There is a wide variety of outdoor and indoor furniture, timber decking, garden tools, pet accessories, cookware, utensils, electrical goods, bath towels, mirrors, picture frames, and gifts such as watches, crystalware and beauty products, with new stock arriving weekly. Luggage can be found in the Winair holiday department. Dine or take a break at Cloggers, the restaurant. Free car parking. Wheelchair friendly.

WOODS OF WINDSOR

UNIT 1A2, FREEPORT VILLAGE, ANCHORAGE ROAD, FLEETWOOD, LANCASHIRE FY7 6AE, ☎ 01253 877270, www.woodsofwindsor.co.uk, 10–6 MON–SAT, 8 ON THUR, 11–5 SUN.

THE DESIGNER OUTLET AT THE LOWRY, SALFORD QUAYS, MANCHESTER, LANCASHIRE M5 2WZ, ☎ 0161 873 8740, www.woodsofwindsor.co.uk, 10–8 MON–FRI, 9–7 SAT, 11–5 SUN. **FACTORY SHOP IN A FACTORY SHOPPING VILLAGE**

See page 466 (CHESH)

LEICESTERSHIRE

BECK MILL FACTORY SHOP

33 KINGS ROAD, MELTON MOWBRAY, LEICESTERSHIRE LE13 1QF, ☎ 01664 501105, 10–5 MON–SAT, 11–4 SUN. **FACTORY SHOP**

Top high street women's and menswear at discounts of up to 70%. Excellent selection of giftware. There is easy parking at the side of the shop.

CATALOGUE BARGAIN SHOP

UNIT D, WHITWICK RETAIL PARK, COALVILLE, LEICESTERSHIRE LE67 3FA, ☎ 01530 830294, www.bargaincrazy.com, 9–8 MON–SAT, 9 ON THUR, FRI, 10–4 SUN. **PERMANENT DISCOUNT OUTLET**

See page 461 (CAMBS)

CHARTERHOUSE RETAIL OUTLET

173 CHARNWOOD ROAD, SHEPSHED, LOUGHBOROUGH, LEICESTERSHIRE LE12 9NN, ☎ 01509 505050, FAX: 01509 507373, **e-mail:** factoryshop@charterhouse-holdings.co.uk, www.charterhouseholdings.co.uk, 9.30–6 MON–SAT, 11–4 SUN. **FACTORY SHOP**

The Charterhouse Retail Outlet was established 30 years ago and now enjoys its reputation as probably the largest factory shop of its kind in the UK. With over £2 million worth of stock always available, Charterhouse offers family clothing, fashion, footwear, kitchenware, homeware and more – all ex-chain and branded products at a fraction of high street prices. Womenswear includes casual, evening, swimwear, nightwear and lingerie – all styles and sizes. Childrenswear ranges from babies upwards with a special department for early teen fashions. Men will also find an excellent selection of branded sportswear, smart and casual clothing as well as footwear. The expanded kitchenware and household department stocks a huge selection of home and gift ideas, including luggage and toiletries. There is free parking, a children's play area, parent and baby room, wheelchair access and café area. The outlet is only one mile from Junction 23 of the M1.

DE BRADELEI MILL SHOP LTD

LOWER LEICESTER ROAD, LUTTERWORTH, LEICESTERSHIRE LE17 4NF, ☎ 01455 557571, FAX: 01455 557332, 9.30–5.30 MON–FRI, 9.30–6 SAT, 10.30–4.30 SUN. **PERMANENT DISCOUNT OUTLET**

A light and airy outlet centre, easily accessible from M1 junction 20 and M6 junction 1, selling leading high street and designer labels with up to 70% discount. Ponden Mill offers a wide range of soft furnishings and everything for the home. Liberty giftwear and Arran Aromatics toiletries akso available. Car parking. Coaches welcome.

DUNELM MILL SHOP

THE REX, MARLBOROUGH SQUARE, COALVILLE LEICESTERSHIRE LE67 3LT, ☎ 01530 510004, FAX: 01530 510631, www.dunelm-mill.co.uk, 9–5 MON–FRI, 9–5.30 SAT, 10.30–4.30 SUN.

BRITANNIA CENTRE, HINCKLEY, LEICESTERSHIRE LE10 1RU, ☎ 01455 619044, FAX: 01455 891598, www.dunelm-mill.co.uk, 9–5 MON–FRI, 9–5.30 SAT.

40–44 CASTLE STREET, HINCKLEY LEICESTERSHIRE LE10 1DD, ☎ 01455 234908, FAX: 01455 615264, www.dunelm-mill.co.uk, 9–5 MON–FRI, 9–5.30 SAT.

17–25 EAST STREET, LEICESTER LEICESTERSHIRE LE1 6NB, ☎ 01162 470592, FAX: 01162 550990, www.dunelm-mill.co.uk, 9–5.30 MON–SAT, 11–5 SUN.

BARKBY THORPE LANE, THURMASTON, LEICESTER, LEICESTERSHIRE LE4 8GP, ☎ 0116 260 7606, FAX: 0116 260 5114, www.dunelm-mill.co.uk, 9–6 MON–SAT, 8 ON THUR, FRI, 10–4 SUN.

3–6 THE RUSHES, LOUGHBOROUGH, LEICESTERSHIRE LE11 0BJ, ☎ 01509 234717, FAX: 01509 269698, www.dunelm-mill.co.uk, 9–5 MON–THUR, 9–5.30 FRI, SAT. **PERMANENT DISCOUNT OUTLET**

See page 458 (BEDS)

GIFTTREE

BRITANNIA CENTRE, HINCKLEY, LEICESTERSHIRE LE10 1RU, ☎ 01455 891920, 9–5 MON–SAT. **FACTORY SHOP**

See page 473 (DERBY)

LOW WOODS FURNISHINGS

LOW WOODS LANE, BELTON, NR LOUGHBOROUGH, LEICESTERSHIRE LE12 9TR, ☎ 01530 222246, FAX: 01530 223932, www.lowwoodsfurnishings.co.uk, 9–5.30 TUE–SAT, 9–1 SUN, CLOSED MON. **PERMANENT DISCOUNT OUTLET**

Low Woods sells discounted designer curtain and upholstery fabrics including tapestries, voiles, silks, chenille, cotton satin, weaves, damasks, etc. They have thousands of metres in stock at one third normal retail price. Brands include Crowson, Sanderson, Harlequin, John Wilman and many more. Prices can be as low as £2.50 a metre in sale times which are January, April and August. A professional make-up service is also available in on-site workrooms. They also stock a range of painted French furniture: wardrobes, beds, chests of drawers, tables, chairs as well as accessories such as candle holders and mirrors. Sofas and chairs are also stocked at hugely discounted prices. Unlimited free parking; coaches welcome.

MATALAN

100 CHURCHGATE, VAUGHAN WAY, LEICESTER, LEICESTERSHIRE LE1 4AL, ☎ 0116 242 6700, FAX: 0116 253 8398, www.matalan.co.uk, 9–8 MON–FRI, 9–6 SAT, 11–5 SUN. **PERMANENT DISCOUNT OUTLET**

See page 458 (BEDS)

STANDARD SOAP CO

DERBY ROAD, ASHBY-DE-LA-ZOUCH LEICESTERSHIRE LE65 2HG, ☎ 01530 410 000, 10–3 MON–THUR, 10–1 FRI. **FACTORY SHOP**

This factory shop sells soaps of all shapes and sizes, including glycerine soaps and novelty soaps, as well as bubble bath and other toiletries.

TK MAXX

HAYMARKET CENTRE, 10 KEMBLE SQUARE, LEICESTER, LEICESTERSHIRE LE1 3YD, ☎ 0116 251 0155, www.tkmaxx.com, 9–5.30 MON–THUR, 9–6 FRI–SAT, 11–5 SUN. **PERMANENT DISCOUNT OUTLET**

See page 458 (BEDS)

UNITED FOOTWEAR

114 MAIN STREET, NEWBOLD VERDON, LEICESTERSHIRE, ☎ 01455 822407, 9–8 MON–FRI, 9–5.30 SAT, 10–4 SUN. **PERMANENT DISCOUNT OUTLET**

This shoe retailer, established for over 135 years, sells shoes for all the family as well as clothes, handbags, sports shoes, boots, giftware and household goods, all at discounted prices. Famous brands include Clarks, K Shoes, Elmdale, Grenson, Loakes, Caterpillar and Adidas. Part of a national chain.

UPPINGHAM YARNS

22 NORTH STREET EAST, UPPINGHAM, RUTLAND, LEICESTER LE15 9QL, ☎ 01572 823747, **e-mail:** uppyarn@wools.co.uk, www.wools.co.uk, 10–5 MON–SAT. MAIL ORDER. **PERMANENT DISCOUNT OUTLET**

Large warehouse selling wide range of materials for seamstresses, embroiderers, tailors and knitters. Exciting threads and metallics on cones sold by weight, yarns, patterns and accessories for knitting machines. They also stock silk, linen, viscose, Lycra, cashmere, angora, mohair, alpaca, tape, Lurex, buttons, chenille and boucle and, for knitters, yarn wax, needles, ribber combs, table clamps, electronic and standard blank cards, ribber wires, brushes, stitch cams, strippers, deco card clips, latch tools and knitting tables.

LINCOLNSHIRE

CATALOGUE BARGAIN SHOP

12–14 SILVER STREET, GAINSBOROUGH, LINCOLNSHIRE DN21 2DP, ☎ 01427 810604, www.bargaincrazy.com, 9–5.30 MON, THUR, FRI, 8.30–5 TUE, 9–5 WED, 8.30–5.30 SAT, 10–4 SUN.

29–31 THE STRAIT, LINCOLN LINCOLNSHIRE LN1 1JD, ☎ 01522 527276, www.bargaincrazy.com, 9–5.30 MON–SAT, 10.30–4.30 SUN. **PERMANENT DISCOUNT OUTLET**

See page 461 (CAMBS)

DUNELM MILL SHOP

LAWRENCE LANE, BOSTON LINCOLNSHIRE PE21 8QD, ☎ 01205 353787, FAX: 01205 364329, www.dunelm-mill.co.uk, 9–5 MON, TUE, THUR, FRI, 9–5.30 WED, SAT, 10.30–4.30 SUN.

13 WEST STREET, BOSTON, LINCOLNSHIRE PE21 8QE, ☎ 01205 310772, FAX: 01205 353182, www.dunelm-mill.co.uk, 9–5 MON, TUE, THUR, FRI, 9–5.30 SAT, 10.30–4.30 SUN.

SOUTH PARADE, LONDON ROAD, GRANTHAM, LINCOLNSHIRE NG31 6HT, ☎ 01476 566996, FAX: 01476 566565, www.dunelm-mill.co.uk, 9–6 MON–SAT, 8 ON THUR, FRI, 10.30–4.30 SUN.

OUTER CIRCLE ROAD, PROCTORS ROAD, LINCOLN, LINCOLNSHIRE LN2 4LA, ☎ 01522 589737, FAX: 01522 538886, www.dunelm-mill.co.uk, 9–5.30 MON–WED, 9–8 THUR, FRI, 9–6 SAT, 10.30–4.30 SUN.

HOLYROOD DRIVE, SKIPPINGDALE INDUSTRIAL ESTATE, SCUNTHORPE, LINCOLNSHIRE DN15 8NN, ☎ 01724 277866, FAX: 01724 277855, www.dunelm-mill.co.uk, 9–6 MON–SAT, 8 ON THUR, FRI, 10–4 SUN. **PERMANENT DISCOUNT OUTLET**

See page 458 (BEDS)

MATALAN

JOHN ADAMS WAY, BOSTON LINCOLNSHIRE PE21 6TY, ☎ 01205 312040, FAX: 01205 352991, www.matalan.co.uk, 10–8 MON–FRI, 9–6 SAT, 11–5 SUN.

UNIT 1, HEWITTS CIRCUS, CLEETHORPES, GRIMSBY LINCOLNSHIRE DN35 9QH, ☎ 01472 200255, FAX: 01472 200156, www.matalan.co.uk, 9–8 MON–FRI, 9–6 SAT, 11–5 SUN.

LINDIS RETAIL PARK, TRITTON ROAD, LINCOLN, LINCOLNSHIRE LN6 7QY, ☎ 01522 696541, FAX: 01522 684946, www.matalan.co.uk, 10–8 MON–FRI, 9–6 SAT, 11–5 SUN.

DUDLEY ROAD, SCUNTHORPE LINCOLNSHIRE DN16 1BA, ☎ 01724 270958, FAX: 01724 270856, www.matalan.co.uk, 9.30–8 MON–FRI, 9–6 SAT, 11–5 SUN. **PERMANENT DISCOUNT OUTLET**

See page 458 (BEDS)

RUTLAND LIGHTING

10–12 WATERGATE, GRANTHAM, LINCOLNSHIRE NG31 6PR, ☎ 01476 591049, 9–5.30 MON–SAT. **PERMANENT DISCOUNT OUTLET**

Sells a full range of lampshades, table and floor lamps, chandeliers, bulbs, outdoor and indoor lights, plus other manufacturers' ends of lines and chainstore seconds. Most lines have genuine reductions on normal retail prices. This shop, unlike its sister shop in Market Overton, Rutland, is large and on the high street. Stock is mainly manufactured on site at the Market Overton branch, although some is bought in or imported.

STAGE 2

TRITTON RETAIL PARK, TRITTON ROAD, LINCOLN, LINCOLNSHIRE LN6 7YA, ☎ 01522 560303, 10–8 MON–FRI, 9–6 SAT, 11–5 SUN AND BANK HOLIDAYS. **PERMANENT DISCOUNT OUTLET**

See page 461 (CAMBS)

THE CAPE

UNIT 1A, 233–235 HIGH STREET, LINCOLN, LINCOLNSHIRE LN2 1AT, ☎ 01522 522462, FAX: 01522 522464, **e-mail:** sc@thefactory-shop.co.uk, www.thecape.co.uk, 9–5.30 MON–FRI, 9–6 SAT, 11–5 SUN. **FACTORY SHOP**

See page 460 (BRIS)

THE FACTORY SHOP

MALT KILN ROAD, BARTON ON HUMBER, NORTH LINCOLNSHIRE DN18 5JT, ☎ 01652 636701, 9–7 MON, TUE, WED, 9–8 THUR, FRI, 8.30–7 SAT, 10–4 SUN.

43 HIGH STREET, MABLETHORPE, LINCOLNSHIRE LN12 1XA, ☎ 01507 473705, 9.30–6 MON–SAT, 10.30–4.30 SUN.

CARRE STREET, SLEAFORD, LINCOLNSHIRE NG34 7TW, ☎ 01529 410155, 9–5.30 MON–SAT, 10–4 SUN.

51 FLEET STREET, HOLBEACH, SPALDING, LINCOLNSHIRE PE12 7AU, ☎ 01406 422180, 9–5 MON–SAT, 10–4 SUN. **FACTORY SHOP**

See page 465 (CHESH)

TK MAXX

FRESHNEY PLACE SHOPPING CENTRE, GRIMSBY, LINCOLNSHIRE, ☎ 01472 352842, www.tkmaxx.com, PHONE FOR DETAILS OF OPENING TIMES.

UNIT 16, ST MARK'S CENTRE, STATION STREET, LINCOLN, LINCOLNSHIRE LN5 7EY, ☎ 01522 530933, www.tkmaxx.com, 9–6 MON–SAT, 8 ON THUR, 11–5 SUN.

UNIT E, GALLAGHER RETAIL PARK, DONCASTER ROAD, SCUNTHORPE LINCOLNSHIRE, ☎ 01724 868965, www.tkmaxx.com, PHONE FOR DETAILS OF OPENING TIMES.

PERMANENT DISCOUNT OUTLET

See page 458 (BEDS)

TRADEX

MONKS ROAD, LINCOLN, LINCOLNSHIRE LN2 5HN, ☎ 01522 512251, FAX: 01522 513332, 9.30–8.30 MON–FRI, 9–5.30 SAT, 10.30–4.30 SUN. **PERMANENT DISCOUNT OUTLET**

See page 507 (LANCS)

WILKINSON STORES

2 THE BROADWAY, ASHBY, SCUNTHORPE, LINCOLNSHIRE NG5 7EL, ☎ 01724 867767, www.wilko.co.uk, 9–5.30 MON–FRI, 8.30–5.30 SAT, 10–4 SUN. MAIL ORDER. **PERMANENT DISCOUNT OUTLET**

See page 466 (CHESH)

LONDON

BUCKS FURNITURE WAREHOUSE

125 EVELYN STREET, DEPTFORD, LONDON SE8 5RJ, ☎ 020 8692 4447, FAX: 020 8469 3136, 10–7 MON–FRI, 10–5 SAT, 10–4 SUN. **PERMANENT DISCOUNT OUTLET**
20,000 square foot warehouse selling cancelled orders, ex-display and ex-photo shoot furniture from famous department stores and other well-known brand names. Some of the department store furniture is from the current catalogue. Some has been marked or damaged during display or photography, but they are all clearly signposted. A lot of stock is brand new. Furniture includes three-piece suites, wardrobes, a very large stock of beds, bedsteads (modern and traditional), tables, chairs and dressing tables. Most of the three-piece suites are reduced by 40% to 50% and the other items are all substantially discounted. Free car parking.

CATALOGUE BARGAIN SHOP

252 GREEN LANES, PALMERS GREEN, LONDON N13 5TU, ☎ 020 8886 9532, www.bargaincrazy.com, 9–5.30 MON–SAT, 10–4 SUN. **PERMANENT DISCOUNT OUTLET**

See page 461 (CAMBS)

CHOICE DISCOUNT STORES LIMITED

67 GOLDERS GREEN ROAD, GOLDERS GREEN, LONDON NW11 8EL, ☎ 020 8458 8247, 9–6 MON–SAT, 11–5 SUN.

11 ARCADIA CENTRE, THE BROADWAY, EALING, LONDON W5 2ND, ☎ 020 8567 2747, 9.30–6 MON–SAT, 7 ON THUR, 11–5 SUN. **PERMANENT DISCOUNT OUTLET**

See page 461 (CAMBS)

CHOMETTE

307 MERTON ROAD, LONDON SW18 5JS, ☎ 020 8877 7000, FAX: 020 8874 8627, www.chomette.co.uk, 10–5 MON–FRI. **FACTORY SHOP**

A wide selection of French porcelain oven-to-tableware, including plates, bowls, cups and saucers, serving dishes, roasting dishes, ramekins, soufflé and flan dishes. They also stock SKK cookware, noted for its durability and non-stick properties, and Italian stainless steel cutlery. Top professional brands include Pillivuyt, Pinti and de Buyer. There is a combination of seconds and ends of lines at excellent reductions. Just 50 metres from the Villeroy & Boch factory shop.

CHRISTMAS GRAND SALE

ROYAL HORTICULTURAL HALLS, ELVERTON STREET, VICTORIA, LONDON SW1, FAX: 01367 860017 (ENQUIRIES: OPEN 9.30–5.30 MON–FRI), ☎ 01367 860177, **e-mail:** nheslam@aol.com, 6–9 WED, 10–6 THUR–SAT. **DESIGNER SALES**

There are now three annual Grand Sales taking place countrywide. The Christmas Grand Sale in London, with over 120 different small companies selling their merchandise to the public, is the largest, taking place over three days plus a charity preview evening. This takes place in mid-late November each year. Quality is high and covers everything from from swags and garlands, smoked trout pate, French lavender sachets, hand-painted furniture, made-to-measure blinds, 19th century wall clocks, Continental Advent cards, boozy Christmas cakes, unusual water-colours, cinammon-scented apple wreaths, traditional American tinware, children's pyjama cases, candle sconces, handmade Indian pickles, bamboo placemats, embossed copper sketchbooks, Art Deco mirrors, silk embroidered cushions, herbal tinctures, stunning tree decorations, English garden trugs, African shopping baskets, handmade wrapping paper, elegant kitchen woodware, beaded handbags, bespoke Ottomans, fine champagne, baby sleeping bags, nautical mirrors, painted dog and cat beds, ties and matching cufflinks, foie gras, antique Bergeres suites, Egyptian cotton bedlinen, often at discount because they are ends of lines. There is a three-day Spring Grand Sale at Sudeley Castle, Winchcombe, near Cheltenham, Gloucestershire, usually at the end of April/beginning of May, and a four-day Summer Grand Sale at Ripley Castle, near Harrogate, North Yorkshire, in early-mid June. Both feature gardening furniture and equipment as well as decorative home accessories. Phone the above number for more details. A proportion of the ticket revenue goes to charity.

CONRAN 2

THE SALE SHOP, 350 KING'S ROAD, LONDON SW35UU, ☎ 020 7559 1140, 10–6 MON–SAT, 11–5 SUN. **PERMANENT DISCOUNT OUTLET**

Small shop next to the Bluebird selling discontinued ranges from Conran at discounts up to 50%. There will be very little furniture, due to the size of the store, apart from a few garden and office chairs. Instead, products will be sold on a themed basis. Thus, for instance, in spring they will concentrate on vases, outdoor living, candles etc. Occasional sales of larger items such as sofas and dining suites are held at their Merton warehouse. Phone to put your name on the mailing list.

DAVID RICHARDS & SONS

10 NEW CAVENDISH STREET, LONDON W1G 8UL, ☎ 020 7935 3206, FAX: 020 7224 4423, 9.30–6 MON–FRI. **PERMANENT DISCOUNT OUTLET**

David Richards & Sons are really wholesalers, but they are pleased to help retail customers from their showroom. Their shop is stacked high with solid silver, silver plate and silver picture frames, christening presents, models of animals, candlesticks, salvers and silver jewellery. Also, they can provide wedding lists, personalised corporate gifts, customer repairs and valuations. Service is well informed and courteous, and prices are much more reasonable than comparable prices in the high street. This is due to the fact that because the shop wholesales in Britain and Europe, it buys enormous quantities and is thus able to pass on bulk-buying savings to customers.

DISPOSAL SERVICES AGENCY (DSA)

ROOM 727, MINISTRY OF DEFENCE, 6 HERCULES ROAD, LONDON SE1 7DJ, ☎ 020 7261 8968, www.disposalservices.agency.mod.uk. **PERMANENT DISCOUNT OUTLET**

The Disposal Services Agency is an agency of the Ministry of Defence set up to dispose of surplus equipment. It runs the largest disposal operation in the UK, organising the sale of both military equipment and commodities in use commercially, such as embassy furniture, government department office furniture, closed-down RAF-base vehicles and housing stock, ex-marine boats, ex-army tents, boots and ski equipment, medical and dental equipment, clothing, ship and aircraft spares, scrap metal and IT equipment. The DSA uses companies throughout the UK, each with their own specialist area, to dispose of stock. These companies also dispose of stock from a host of other, usually public sector, organisations varying from fire brigades and hospitals to health authorities and the police. Equipment from these companies varies from kitchen equipment and fax machines to mobile radios, cars, generators, jewellery and telecommunications equipment to food trolleys, X-ray equipment, telephones, uniforms, dinghies, fishing nets, photocopiers and chair lifts. Visit the website to find out which companies sell which products and how to contact them direct.

G THORNFIELD LTD

321 GRAY'S INN ROAD, LONDON WC1X 8PX, ☎ 020 7837 2996, FAX: 020 7278 2515, **e-mail:** dave.daybyday@virgin.net, 8–6 MON–FRI, 9–2 SAT. **PERMANENT DISCOUNT OUTLET**

Offers from 20% to 50% off wallcovering brands such as Sanderson and Kingfisher. The more you buy, the greater your discount. Also up to one-third off coordinating fabrics. Doesn't hold stocks of wallpapers and fabrics but you can order from their books with next day delivery. Also sells frames, prints and posters at very low prices. Access to nearly 10,000 picture and prints from stock or to order, including limited editions. Dulux paint colours are mixed on the premises, with 1, 800 shades to choose from.

HOT & COLD INC

13–15 GOLBORNE ROAD, LONDON W10 5NY, ☎ 020 8960 1200 OR 1300, 10–5.30 MON–FRI, 10–5 SAT. **PERMANENT DISCOUNT OUTLET**

Supplies domestic appliances from nearly one hundred brands. Range now includes American fridge freezers and range cookers. A total of about 10,000 different items, at prices which they claim will beat any genuine competitor's. In fact, they are so sure of this that they promise to refund the difference if you find you could have bought the same product elsewhere at the same time for a lower price, provided you give them proof of that within two weeks of purchase. All goods are brand new, perfect and guaranteed. They specialise in built-in equipment, but they can also supply freestanding appliances. Also ends of lines, some at less than half the original price. Prices include VAT. Delivery can be arranged countrywide.

LLOYDS INTERNATIONAL AUCTION GALLERIES

9 LYDDEN ROAD, LONDON SW18, FAX: 020 8788 7777, FAX: 020 8874 5390, **e-mail:** lloyds_international@compuserve.com, www.lloyds-auction.co.uk, PHONE FOR OPENING TIMES. **PERMANENT DISCOUNT OUTLET**

Auctioneers who specialise in Victorian and Edwardian furniture and carpets as well as china, glass, art and collectables, also offer unclaimed goods from the customs department and Metropoliton Police lost property which is sold here by auction. Furniture sales are held fortnightly on a Saturday, viewing is on the Friday. Miscellaneous sales are held fortnightly on a Wednesday with viewing on the same day. Phone for the date of the next auction.

MATALAN

ALPINE RETAIL PARK, ALPINE WAY, EAST BECKTON, LONDON E6 6LA, ☎ 020 7473 9780, FAX: 020 7511 5554, www.matalan.co.uk, 10–8 MON–FRI, 9–6 SAT, 10–4 SUN.

HIGH ROAD, LEYTONSTONE, LONDON E11 1HH, ☎ 020 8988 8630, FAX: 020 8558 3048, www.matalan.co.uk, 10–8 MON–FRI, 9–6 SAT, 10–4 SUN.

317 EDGWARE ROAD, CRICKLEWOOD BROADWAY, CRICKLEWOOD, LONDON NW2 6PH, ☎ 020 8450 5667, FAX: 020 8450 8575, www.matalan.co.uk, 10–8 MON–FRI, 9–6 SAT, 11–5 SUN.

THURSTON ROAD, LOAMPIT VALE, LEWISHAM LONDON SE13 7SN, ☎ 020 8463 9830, FAX: 020 8318 1936, www.matalan.co.uk, 10–8 MON–FRI, 9–6 SAT, 10–4 SUN.

59 BUGSBY WAY, CHARLTON, LONDON SE7 7SE, ☎ 020 8269 4290, FAX: 020 8858 6469, www.matalan.co.uk, 10–8 MON–FRI, 9–6 SAT, 11–5 SUN. **PERMANENT DISCOUNT OUTLET**

See page 458 (BEDS)

NOTTING HILL HOUSING TRUST

33 SOUTH END ROAD, HAMPSTEAD, LONDON NW3 2PY, **e-mail:** charityshop@nhhg.org.uk, www.nottinghillonline.com/supporters, 10–6 MON–SAT, 12–5 SUN.

53 ST JOHN'S WOOD HIGH STREET, LONDON NW8 7NJ, ☎ 020 7586 9493, **e-mail:** charityshop@nhhg.org.uk, www.nottinghillonline.com/supporters, 10–6 MON–SAT, 12–5 SUN.

309 FULHAM ROAD, LONDON SW10 9QH, ☎ 020 7352 7986, FAX: 020 8357 5344, **e-mail:** charityshop@nhhg.org.uk, www.nottinghillonline.com/supporters, 10–6 MON–SAT, 12–4 SUN.

3 BARNES HIGH STREET, LONDON SW13 9LB, ☎ 020 8878 6170, **e-mail:** charityshop@nhhg.org.uk, www.nottinghillonline.com/supporters, 10–6 MON–SAT, 12–5 SUN.

288 UPPER RICHMOND ROAD, LONDON SW15 6TH, ☎ 020 8788 5763, **e-mail:** charityshop@nhhg.org.uk, www.nottinghillonline.com/supporters, 10–6 MON–SAT.

36 HIGH STREET, TOOTING, LONDON SW17 0RG, ☎ 020 8767 3431, **e-mail:** charityshop@nhhg.org.uk, www.nottinghillonline.com/supporters, 10–6 MON–SAT, 12–5 SUN.

211 BROMPTON ROAD, LONDON SW3 2EJ, ☎ 020 7581 7987, **e-mail:** charityshop@nhhg.org.uk, www.nottinghillonline.com/supporters, 10.30–6.30 MON–SAT, 12–5 SUN.

303 KINGS ROAD, LONDON SW3, FAX: 020 7352 8606, **e-mail:** charityshop@nhhg.org.uk, www.nottinghillonline.com/supporters, 10–6 MON–SAT, 12–5 SUN.

654A FULHAM ROAD, LONDON SW6 5RU, **e-mail:** charityshop@nhhg.org.uk, www.nottinghillonline.com/supporters, 10–6 MON–SAT, 12–5 SUN.

3 BUTE STREET, SOUTH KENSINGTON, LONDON SW7 3EY, ☎ 020 7581 9458, **e-mail:** charityshop@nhhg.org.uk, www.nottinghillonline.com/supporters, 10–6 MON–SAT, 12–5 SUN.

24 GOODGE STREET, LONDON W1T 2QF, ☎ 020 7636 4201, **e-mail:** charityshop@nhhg.org.uk, www.nottinghillonline.com/supporters, 10–6 MON–SAT.

59 NOTTING HILL GATE, LONDON W11 3JS, ☎ 020 7229 1476, **e-mail:** charityshop@nhhg.org.uk, www.nottinghillonline.com/supporters, 10–7 MON–SAT, 1–6 SUN.

76 ASKEW ROAD, LONDON W12 9BJ, ☎ 020 8740 4878, **e-mail:** charityshop@nhhg.org.uk, www.nottinghillonline.com/supporters, 10–6 MON–SAT.

178 QUEENSWAY, LONDON W2 6LY, ☎ 020 7221 8582, **e-mail:** charityshop@nhhg.org.uk, www.nottinghillonline.com/supporters, 10–6 MON–SAT, 1–6 SUN.

46 TURNHAM GREEN TERRACE, LONDON W4 1QP, ☎ 020 8995 8864, **e-mail:** charityshop@nhhg.org.uk, www.nottinghillonline.com/supporters, 10–6 MON–SAT, 1–6 SUN.

40 HIGH STREET, EALING, LONDON W5 5DB, ☎ 020 8567 8003, **e-mail:** charityshop@nhhg.org.uk, www.nottinghillonline.com/supporters, 10–6 MON–SAT, 12–5 SUN.
57 KENSINGTON CHURCH STREET, LONDON W8 4BA, ☎ 020 7937 5274, **e-mail:** charityshop@nhhg.org.uk, www.nottinghillonline.com/supporters, 10–6 MON–SAT. **DRESS AGENCIES**

Notting Hill Housing Trust has over 20 shops around London, well-known for their unique findings: designer wares including Duffer of St George, Gucci, Valentino, Armani, even Versace can be found, as well as other little gems. The shops also feature a brand new range of home furnishings, glassware, wooden items etc. A delight for bargain-hunters.

OXFAM SUPER SAVING SHOP

570 KINGSLAND ROAD, LONDON E8 4AH, ☎ 020 7923 1532, 9.15–5.15 MON–SAT. **SECONDHAND SHOP**

Vast secondhand shop selling loads of cheap bric a brac, records and clothes. Stock is made up of unsold items from Oxfam's other shops in London so it's very cheap indeed. For example, bric-a-brac items from 9p; items of clothing from £2.29; electrical items (which have all been tested), such as lamps, from £2.99. Other end-of-line Oxfam shops include Kilburn, Burnt Oak, Tooting and Walthamstow.

POT LUCK

84 COLUMBIA ROAD, LONDON E2 0HQ, ☎ 020 7722 6892, FAX: 020 7722 7162, **e-mail:** potluck@braidman.freeserve.co.uk, 10–2 FRI, 8–2.30 SUN. **PERMANENT DISCOUNT OUTLET**

Pot Luck specialises in selling famous-name 'blanks' (pure white china) in bone china, porcelain and hotel-ware. They sell plates in all sizes from 6in to 13in; huge pasta plates as used in all the trendiest restaurants; plus numerous shapes in cups and saucers, mugs, jugs, creamers and teapots. In addition they offer plain white oven-to-tableware in every shape and size at less than 50% of normal retail prices. They also now sell pure wool, completely washable, natural white Flokati rugs with a lovely long, shaggy pile: also great to use as throws bed or covers. Trade supplied: phone for appointment.

PRICE'S PATENT CANDLE CO

100 YORK ROAD, LONDON SW11 3RU, ☎ 020 7924 6336, 9.30–5.30 MON–SAT, 11–5 SUN. **FACTORY SHOP**

See page 464 (HAMPS)

RAINBOW

249 AND 253 ARCHWAY ROAD, HIGHGATE, LONDON N6 5BS, ☎ 020 8340 8003, FAX: 0208 372 5484, 10.30–5.30 MON–SAT. **DRESS AGENCY**

Number 249 sells mainly secondhand items, while no. 253 is new merchandise and toys. At 249, the shop is divided into six selling areas which are rented out on a day-to-day basis. Examples of goods on sale are adults and children's clothing, baby equipment, toys, books, bric-a-brac, arts and crafts. The shop is in Highgate so there is a big variety of good quality designer clothes and other interesting goods. As there is no middle man, there are loads of bargains to be had. The shop at 253 has a large and fascinating selection of new toys at reasonable prices. They stock traditional wooden toys such as rocking horses, fots, trains, garages and dolls' houses from, among others, Brio, Galt, Escor and Plan Toys. They also sell Lego, Playmobil, TY Beanies, dressing up, books, creative kits, nostalgic pocket money toys and lots more. Ends of lines are discounted throughout the year. Highgate tube and buses are near by and there's free parking in the side streets and right outside to load and unload.

REJECT CHINA SHOPS

UNIT 26, COVENT GARDEN, LONDON WC2E 8AH, ☎ 020 7379 8374, FAX: 020 7836 7735, www.tableware.uk.com, 10–7 MON–SAT, 11–5 SUN.

183 BROMPTON ROAD, KNIGHTSBRIDGE, LONDON SW3 1NU, ☎ 020 7581 0739, FAX: 020 7225 2283, **e-mail:** reject183@china.uk.com, www.tableware.uk.com, 9–6 MON–SAT, 7 ON WED, 12–6 SUN.

71 REGENT STREET, LONDON W1R 7HG, ☎ 020 7734 4915, FAX: 020 7734 2652, www.tableware.uk.com, 9–6 MON–SAT, 7.30 ON THUR, 11–5 SUN. **PERMANENT DISCOUNT OUTLET**

See page 459 (BERKS)

REJECT POT SHOP

56 CHALK FARM ROAD, LONDON NW1, FAX: 020 7485 2326, FAX: 020 7485 2326, **e-mail:** sales@rejectpotshop.co.uk, www.rejectpotshop.co.uk, 11–5.30 TUE–SUN. **PERMANENT DISCOUNT OUTLET**

Reject shop selling white china seconds and some decorated china seconds at great prices. The china comes from a variety of manufacturers including Royal Stafford, Royal Doulton and Portmeirion, although there are no manufacturers' names on the underside of the china. Most are rejected before stamping.

ROCOCO FRAMES

19 JERDAN PLACE, FULHAM BROADWAY, LONDON SW6 1BE, ☎ 020 7385 9929, FAX: 020 7385 4729, **e-mail:** enquiries@rococoframes.com, www.rococoframes.com, 10–6 MON–SAT, 11–4 SUN. **PERMANENT DISCOUNT OUTLET**

Rococo has recently moved back into its original building after a multi-million pound site redevelopment at Jerdan Place. The fabulously refurbished shop is a showroom for Rococo Mirrors: interior design-led mirrors at good prices with UK nationwide home delivery. Phone for catalogue. Rococo has an unpretentious gallery room with good value original art. The stable of artists includes undiscovered student talent. Rococo offers an excellent bespoke framing service, with hundreds of samples to suit all types of artwork, specialising in contemporary and traditional gallery-type framing. The shop has not forgotten its roots: with a budget-priced range of ready-made frames and a good range of inexpensive mirrors to take away. Trade shop here for their cheap and chic wall fillers. The shop also has a gorgeous gift and card room with inexpensive presents and home accessories. An eclectic mix of old and new furniture decorating the shop and all available to buy compeltes the shopping experience at Rococo. Phone for more information. They are closed on some bank holidays so do phone first before travelling. The nearest tube is Fulham Broadway. Parking at local pay and display.

S & B EVANS & SONS

7A EZRA STREET, LONDON E2 7RH, ☎ 020 7729 6635, FAX: 0207 613558, **e-mail:** evans@thecitygardenpottery.co.uk, www.thecitygardenpottery.co.uk, 9–5 FRI, 9–1.30 SUN, OTHER TIMES BY APPOINTMENT. **PERMANENT DISCOUNT OUTLET**

Seconds from the kiln are half price on the first Sunday of each month. The rest of the time, the shop is full-priced. Their stock is mostly for the garden and ranges from flower pots to terracotta ware, mugs, jugs and bowls. Situated near to Columbia Road Flower Market which is open from 8am to 2pm every Sunday.

SOVIET CARPET AND ART GALLERIES

303–305 CRICKLEWOOD BROADWAY, LONDON NW2 6PG, ☎ 020 8452 2445, FAX: 020 8450 2642, **e-mail:** rr@soviet-world.fsnet.co.uk, 10.30–5 SUN ONLY, BY APPOINTMENT MON–FRI. **PERMANENT DISCOUNT OUTLET**

Sells Oriental rugs and Russian art at trade prices, giving savings of about 50% on high street prices. The company has only been open to the public since 1992 and then only on Sundays (established in 1983, it was exclusively a wholesale operation for the first nine years of its existence). It imports handmade rugs directly from all the main rug-producing centres of the East (Persia, Turkey, Afghanistan, Pakistan, China) and is one of the principal world distributors of rugs from the former Soviet Union. This explains why the superb Caucasian and Turkmenian (Bukhara) rugs are a speciality. They also stock one of the largest collections of quality Russian art in Europe. Only a small fraction of this is displayed, the remaining thousands of paintings can be chosen from photographs, and will then be brought out from storage. All styles in Russian art are covered from museum-quality greatest names of the 19th century through propaganda art of the Stalin years to leading contemporary artists. All works are offered at prices well below retail/auction price levels, and in extreme cases paintings sold in West End galleries for thousands can be picked up here for a few hundred pounds.

TABLEWHERE?

4 QUEEN'S PARADE CLOSE, FRIERN BARNET, LONDON N11 3FY, ☎ 020 8361 6111, FAX: 0845 130 6111, FAX: 020 8361 4143, **e-mail:** mail@tablewhere.co.uk, www.tablewhere.co.uk 9–5.30 MON–SAT. **PERMANENT DISCOUNT OUTLET**

A china matching service, Tablewhere stocks thousands of patterns from the world's leading manufacturers including Wedgwood, Royal Doulton, Spode, Denby, Minton, Royal Albert, Johnson Bros, Royal Worcester and Aynsley, some of which go back 40 or 50 years. By buying up discontinued lines from all over the country, Tablewhere? has built up a stock of over one million pieces which are available through the London-based mail order service. Specialist staff maintain detailed computer and photographic records of all the patterns and shapes in stock so that they can locate any replacement pieces from egg cups to soup tureens, although tea cups and dinner plates are in most demand. Replacement pieces usually cost around the equivalent of today's retail prices. There is no charge to register requirements – phone or write with details of the manufacturer, pattern name and the replacement pieces needed. If there is no pattern name on the service, then a photograph or colour photocopy showing both sides of a dinner plate with a colour description will help identification. You can also visit their website or e-mail them.

THE AFFORDABLE ART FAIR

BATTERSEA PARK, LONDON SW11, FAX: 0870 739 9555. TICKET HOTLINE: 020 7371 8787, www.affordableartfair.co.uk, 11–6 THUR–SUN. **DESIGNER SALES**

The Affordable Art Fair is where artworks by famous names such as David Hockney vie for space with works by recent art school graduates. It takes place twice a year here, usually in March and mid October and also in Bristol in June. There are thousands of original paintings, prints, photographs and sculptures, exhibited by some of Britain's leading galleries and professional artists groups. All work for sale is priced at under £2,500 and the range is enormous. Whether you are a first time art buyer or a serious collector, there is something for everyone. Traditional landscapes jostle for space with large abstract canvases, limited edition screenprints from world famous names are displayed next to funky artworks by talented young graduates and fine art studio groups. Tickets cost £7 in advance or £8 on the door Free shuttle bus from Sloane Square tube.

THE CANDLE SHOP

50 NEW KING'S ROAD, LONDON SW6 4LS, ☎ 020 7736 0740, **e-mail:** info@candlesontheweb.co.uk, www.candlesontheweb.co.uk, 10–6 MON–SAT, 11–5 SUN. MAIL ORDER. **PERMANENT DISCOUNT OUTLET**

Warehouse outlet servicing the shop in Covent Garden's Piazza which sells candles at what they claim are the lowest prices in the country. You can buy anything from bulk boxes of 200 8in cream candles from £29.95 to church candles at wholesale prices, as well as floating, scented and novelty candles. Candle-making supplies are also available. Mail order catalogue on request. Or visit the website to compare prices.

THE CASH EXCHANGE

352 HOLLOWAY ROAD, LONDON N7, FAX: 020 7609 2100, FAX: 020 7609 9070, www.cashexchangelondon.co.uk, 10–6 MON–SAT. **PERMANENT DISCOUNT OUTLET**

Permanent discount outlet which operates rather like a pawn brokers. It takes unwanted household and electrical items and gives you cash. Unredeemed items are sold off at very low prices. For example, laptop computers from £200, top of the range televisions, worth £1,500, for £700. International money transfer services are available, and a 24-hour electrical repair service, offering very competitive rates, is also on site.

THE CLOTH SHOP

290 PORTOBELLO ROAD, LONDON W10 5TE, ☎ 020 8968 6001, FAX: 020 8960 2719, www.clothshop.co.uk, 10–6 MON–SAT. **PERMANENT DISCOUNT OUTLET**

The Cloth Shop is one of the few small one-off fabric shops left in London that sells fabrics for all purposes. It stocks a wide range of Indian cotton furnishings in a myriad of colours, plus a selection of canvas, calicoes and muslins in a variety of creams and colours, as well as linens, wools, fleeces and cottons for both furnishings and dress-making. It also stocks a large range of beautiful antique French linen sheets, including sheets from World War II. There is an extensive range of household linen goods from France, including antique linen by the metre, and a colourful selection of antique Welsh blankets. Prices are reasonable: fabrics range from £1.50 to £12.50 a metre; antique sheets from £45 to £100.

TK MAXX

PENINSULA RETAIL PARK, BUGSBY WAY, CHARLTON, LONDON, ☎ 020 8293 1957, www.tkmaxx.com, PHONE FOR DETAILS OF OPENING TIMES..

THE ARCADIA CENTRE, THE BROADWAY, EALING, LONDON W5 2ND, ☎ 020 8566 0447, www.tkmaxx.com, 9.30–8 MON–FRI, 7.30 ON THUR, 9–7 SAT, 11–5 SUN.

UNIT B, FIRST FLOOR, WOOD GREEN SHOPPING CENTRE, LONDON N22 6YD, ☎ 020888 88803, www.tkmaxx.com, 9–6 MON–SAT, 10–5 SUN. **PERMANENT DISCOUNT OUTLET**

See page 458 (BEDS)

TOP VALUE DRUGSTORE

23 TEMPLE FORTUNE PARADE, OPPOSITE MARKS & SPENCER, FINCHLEY ROAD, LONDON NW11 0QS, ☎ 020 8905 5448, **e-mail:** topvalue-drugstore@pgen.net, 8.30–6 MON–SAT, 9.30–1.30 SUN. **PERMANENT DISCOUNT OUTLET**

One of those rare, family-run businesses which manages to undercut the competition, including, with many items, Boots and Superdrug. They claim to set prices which others can't match. Well-stocked shop which is divided into sections such as haircare, skincare, toiletries, baby equipment, household cleaning (Cif, Comfort, Pledge, Flash, Dettol, Ajax, Mr Muscle, Astonish etc), bathroom cleaning products, oven cleaners, window cleaning products, polishes, scourers, brushes, cloths, sponges, air fresheners etc, bakeware and non-pharmaceutical drugs. The shop also stocks a selection of cards, toys and fancy goods and offers same-day developing for £2.99 for up to 40 prints with an extra set costing £1.49 if ordered at time of processing. Prices are generally 30% cheaper than other chemist chains, and special price promotions are held every week. You can phone your order through and there is a delivery service if you spend a minimum of £35.

VILLEROY & BOCH (UK) LIMITED

267 MERTON ROAD, LONDON SW18 5JS, ☎ 020 8875 6006, 10–5 SEVEN DAYS A WEEK. **FACTORY SHOP**

See page 466 (CHESH)

ZEON

39 WATERLOO ROAD, LONDON NW2 7TT, ☎ 020 8208 1833, FAX: 020 8208 0350, **e-mail:** sales@zeonltd.co.uk, www.zeonltd.co.uk, 9–5.30 MON–FRI. PHONE FOR APPOINTMENT. **FACTORY SHOP**

Zeon is the UK's largest timepiece importer. Brands include Zeon, Ingersoll, Red or Dead, Kookai, Fiorelli, Fila, Mikey and Head. Zeon is also a specialist in children's and young people's watches and clocks such as Barbie, Action Man, Harry Potter, Thunderbirds, Clangers, Bagpuss, SClub 7, and Westlife. The products on sale here include watches of all types, clocks and executive gifts.

MIDDLESEX

MATALAN

PUMP LANE, HAYES, MIDDLESEX UB3 3NB, ☎ 020 8606 6700, FAX: 020 8573 5268, www.matalan.co.uk, 10–8 MON–FRI, 9–6 SAT, 11–5 SUN.

GREAT WESTERN INDUSTRIAL PARK, WINDMILL LANE, SOUTHALL, MIDDLESEX UB2 4SD, ☎ 020 8574 9660, FAX: 020 8574 4924, www.matalan.co.uk, 10–8 MON–FRI, 9–6 SAT, 11–5 SUN. **PERMANENT DISCOUNT OUTLET**

See page 458 (BEDS)

THE SALVAGE SHOP

34–40 WATLING AVENUE, BURNT OAK, MIDDLESEX HA8 0LR, ☎ 020 8952 4353, **e-mail:** lss@salvage1.co.uk, www.salvage1.co.uk, 9–5.30 MON–SAT, 10–4 SUN. **PERMANENT DISCOUNT OUTLET**

An Aladdin's cave of salvaged stock for the avid bargain hunter, most of which has been the subject of insurance claims for fire or flood, salvage, bankruptcy or is simply clearance stock. Stock changes every two or three days and regular visitors have found anything from half price Kenwood Chefs, televisions and toys to furniture, kitchen items, linens and especially fantastic bargains in designer clothing. Yves Saint Laurent, Armani, Ungaro, Hugo Boss and Valentino, as well as all major high street names, are just some of the names to be found (though the labels are often cut out). Discounts range from 50% to 80%. Phone first to check stock.

TK MAXX

UNIT 31, ST GEORGE'S CENTRE, ST ANNE'S ROAD, HARROW, MIDDLESEX HA1 1HS, ☎ 020 8863 9292, www.tkmaxx.com, 9.30–8 MON–FRI, 9–7 SAT, 11–5 SUN. **PERMANENT DISCOUNT OUTLET**

See page 458 (BEDS)

WHEELHOUSE LTD

9–21 BELL ROAD, HOUNSLOW, MIDDLESEX TW3 3NS, ☎ 020 8570 3501, 8.30–5.30 MON–SAT, 10–4.30 SUN. **PERMANENT DISCOUNT OUTLET**

Sells all sorts of household goods (plates, cups, cutlery, Addis bins, tea towels etc), DIY, garden equipment (flowers, plants, lawn seed), everything to do with cars, etc. There is an extensive tool section on the upper floor – everything for the DIY enthusiast. There is an electrical and lighting department selling sockets, plugs, telephone extension kits, cable etc. You need to visit regularly as stock is constantly changing, but prices are very competitive and there is easy access and helpful staff. They buy branded products in bulk, adding new lines every week. There is a car park in front of the store and another across the road.

NORFOLK

CAITHNESS CRYSTAL VISITOR CENTRE

8–12 PAXMAN ROAD, HARDWICK INDUSTRIAL ESTATE, KINGS LYNN, NORFOLK PE30 4NE, ☎ 01553 765111, FAX: 01553 767628, **e-mail:** visitor@caithnessglass.co.uk, www.caithnessglass.co.uk, 9–5 MON–SAT, 10.15–4.15 SUN. **FACTORY SHOP**

Well-stocked factory shop with many bargains all year round in glass and crystal, giftware and tableware. Also stocks a selection of Royal Worcester products and other great gift ideas.

EDINBURGH CRYSTAL

CAITHNESS CRYSTAL, 8–12 PAXMAN ROAD, HARDWICK INDUSTRIAL ESTATE, KINGS LYNN, NORFOLK PE30 4NE, ☎ 01553 765111 (CENTRE TEL NO), ☎ 01553 767628, **e-mail:** visitor@caithnessglass.co.uk, www.caithnessglass.co.uk, 9–5 MON–SAT, 10.15–4.15 SUN. **FACTORY SHOP**

See page 463 (CHESH)

LATHAMS

BRIDGE STREET, POTTER HEIGHAM, GREAT YARMOUTH, NORFOLK NR29 5JE, ☎ 01692 670080, 9–5.30 MON–SAT, 10–4 SUN. **FACTORY SHOP**

Sell a wide range of fashions, hardware, china, fishing tackle, books, gardening equipment, linen, groceries and Christmas gifts at very reasonable prices. Most of the makes are high street labels and consist of discontinued lines and seconds. Also jewellery concessions, shoes, computer games kiosk, coffee shop and garden centre.

MATALAN

SOUTHTOWN ROAD, GREAT YARMOUTH, NORFOLK NR31 0JB, ☎ 01493 444734, FAX: 01493 445636, www.matalan.co.uk, 9–8 MON–FRI, 9–6, 11–5 SUN.

BLACKFRIARS ROAD, NORFOLK PE30 1RX, ☎ 01553 765696, FAX: 01553 764518, www.matalan.co.uk, 10–8 MON–FRI, 9–6 SAT, 11–5 SUN. **PERMANENT DISCOUNT OUTLET**

See page 458 (BEDS)

QD STORES

143 HIGH STREET, GORLESTON, GREAT YARMOUTH, NORFOLK NR31 6RB, ☎ 01493 652735, 9–5.30 MON–SAT.

128–132 NORFOLK STREET, KINGS LYNN, NORFOLK PE30 1AP, ☎ 01553 770068, 9–5.30 MON–SAT.

7–10 ANGLIA SQUARE, NORWICH, NORFOLK NR3 1DY, ☎ 01603 275201, 9–5.30 MON–SAT, 10–4 SUN.

48–54 ST STEPHENS STREET, NORWICH, NORFOLK NR1 3SL, ☎ 01603 622562, 9–5.30 MON–SAT. **PERMANENT DISCOUNT OUTLET, FOOD AND DRINK DISCOUNTERS**

See page 458 (BEDS)

THE FACTORY SHOP LTD

NORWICH STREET, EAST DEREHAM, NORFOLK NR19 1AD, ☎ 01362 691868, 9–5.30 MON–SAT, 10–4 SUN.

52 LONDON ROAD, HARLESTON, NORFOLK IP20 9BZ, ☎ 01379 854860, 9–5.30 MON–SAT, 10.30–4 SUN.

LYNN ROAD, SNETTISHAM, NORFOLK PE31 7QG, ☎ 01485 544441, 9–5.30 MON–SAT, 10–4 SUN. **FACTORY SHOP**

See page 465 (CHESH)

NORTHAMPTONSHIRE

CURVER CONSUMER PRODUCTS

CURVER WAY, WILLOWBROOK INDUSTRIAL ESTATE, CORBY, NORTHAMPTONSHIRE NN17 5XN, ☎ 01536 200550, 1–6 THUR–FRI, 9–1.30 SAT. **PERMANENT DISCOUNT OUTLET**

Branded housewares, including buckets, bins and bowls, as well as storage boxes and drawers for home organisation, plus toolboxes and related DIY equipment. All made from durable plastic in a wide range of sizes and colours. Seconds priced from 50p to £5. New stock every week.

MATALAN

UNIT 1, PHOENIX RETAIL PARK, PHOENIX PARKWAY, CORBY, NORTHAMPTONSHIRE NN17 5DT, ☎ 01536 408042, FAX: 01536 408750, www.matalan.co.uk, 9–8 MON–FRI, 9–6 SAT, 10–4 SUN.

UNIT 1, WEEDON ROAD INDUSTRIAL ESTATE, TYNE ROAD, NORTHAMPTON, NORTHAMPTONSHIRE NN5 5BE, ☎ 01604 597890, FAX: 01604 588068, www.matalan.co.uk, 9–8 MON–FRI, 9–6 SAT, 10.30–4.30 SUN.

VICTORIA ROAD, WELLINGBOROUGH, NORTHAMPTONSHIRE NN8 2EF, ☎ 01933 233890, FAX: 01933 272658, www.matalan.co.uk, 10–8 MON–FRI, 9–6 SAT, 11–5 SUN. **PERMANENT DISCOUNT OUTLET**

See page 458 (BEDS)

SHOWHOME WAREHOUSE

11–17 FRANCIS COURT, WELLINGBOROUGH ROAD, RUSHDEN, NORTHAMPTONSHIRE NN10 6AY, ☎ 01933 411695, 10–5 TUE–SUN, 11–3 MON. **PERMANENT DISCOUNT OUTLET**

The contents of quality show homes are sold seven days a week at this 20,000 square foot warehouse. Savings normally range from 50% to 70% off store prices. About 50% of their stock is sold each week and different stock arrives daily. Choose from a range of kitchen appliances, lounge furniture, three-piece suites, dining tables and chairs, rugs, study and bedroom furniture, oil paintings, mirrors, ornaments, televisions and videos, patio and garden furniture and gym equipment. The range is eclectic: from suits of armour to lion's heads, Tiffany lampshades to leather zebras, handpainted furniture to mahogany classics, alien-shaped CD racks to antique carts made into bookcases or sets of oars turned into coat racks. Because a high percentage of their business comes from trade, prices exclude VAT but still represent very good value for money. For example, elaborate metal bed, £175, normally £750; dining room table and chairs, £350, normally £1,500; washer-dryer, £300, usually £500 to £600. Occasional auctions take place during the year: phone for details.

STUART BUGLASS INTERIOR DESIGN IRONWORK

THE BUGLASS METALWORK GALLERY, CLIFFORD MILL HOUSE, LITTLE HOUGHTON, NORTHAMPTONSHIRE NN7 1AL, ☎ 01604 890366, FAX: 01604 890 372, **e-mail:** sbuglass@aol.com, www.stuartbuglass.co.uk, 10–5 MON–FRI. **FACTORY SHOP**

Hand-crafted interior design wrought-iron work including candleholders, wine racks, electric lighting (including wall sconces and chandeliers) curtain poles, as well as furniture, including beds, tables, chairs and shelving, are all on sale in this converted barn at direct-to-the-public prices. The showroom was extended in 1998 and is now twice its original size. There is now a high street outlet at 26 Regent Street, Leamington Spa and another at 311 Wellingborough Road, Northampton, both of which are open 10-5 Tuesday to Saturday. They also sell soft furnishings, bedding, light shades and gift items.

T J HUGHES

THE NEWLANDS CENTRE, GOLD STREET, KETTERING, NORTHAMPTONSHIRE NN16 8JA, ☎ 01536 419700, FAX: 01536 523041, **e-mail:** info@tjhughes.co.uk, www.tjhughes.co.uk, 9–5.30 MON–SAT, 10–4 SUN. **PERMANENT DISCOUNT OUTLET**

See page 465 (CHESH)

THE FABRIC WAREHOUSE

HARVEY REEVES ROAD, ST JAMES MILL INDUSTRIAL ESTATE, NORTHAMPTON, NORTHAMPTONSHIRE NN5 5JR, ☎ 01604 759312, FAX: 01604 755577, 9.30–5.30 MON–SAT, 10–4 SUN. **PERMANENT DISCOUNT OUTLET**

Stocks up to 8,000 rolls of upholstery and dress fabric from £2.99 a metre with remnants at £1 a metre. Chenilles are from £9.99 to £25 a metre, damask £10.99 a metre and heavy-duty prints £7.99 a metre. In addition, there are made-up curtains, cushions, pillows, net curtains, tassle tie-backs, curtain poles, tracks, lining, braid, bean bags. They will also take orders for fabric.

NORTHUMBERLAND

ATTICA

2 OLD GEORGE YARD, OFF HIGHBRIDGE, NEWCASTLE UPON TYNE, TYNE & WEAR NE1 1EZ, ☎ 0191 261 4062, 10.30–5.30 MON–SAT. **SECONDHAND SHOP**

1960s furniture and decor in this shop which specialises in vintage clothing for men and women from the Victorian era to the 1960s.

BIRTHDAYS

UNIT 51, ROYAL QUAYS FACTORY OUTLET CENTRE, COBLE DENE ROAD, NORTH SHIELDS, NEWCASTLE UPON TYNE, NEAR A19, TYNE & WEAR NE29 6DW, ☎ 0191 257 1729, 10–6 MON–SAT, 8 ON THUR, 11–5 SUN. **FACTORY SHOPPING VILLAGE**

See page 462 (CHESH)

CATALOGUE BARGAIN SHOP

51 SHIELDS ROAD, BYKER, NEWCASTLE UPON TYNE, TYNE & WEAR NE6 1DJ, ☎ 0191 265 6033, www.bargaincrazy.com, 9–6 MON–SAT, 8 ON THUR, FRI, 10.30–4.30 SUN. **PERMANENT DISCOUNT OUTLET**

See page 461 (CAMBS)

CATALOGUE DISCOUNT STORE

15 THE PRECINCT, THE IN CENTRE, JARROW, TYNE & WEAR, ☎ 0191 483 4318, 9–5 MON–SAT.

8 THE FORUM SHOPPING CENTRE, WALLSEND, NORTHUMBERLAND NE28 8JR, ☎ 0191 236 9501, 9–5 MON–SAT. **PERMANENT DISCOUNT OUTLET**

See page 499 (LANCS)

CHINA TIME

FENWICK STEAD, BELFORD, NORTHUMBERLAND NE70 7PL, ☎ 01289 381363, MAIL ORDER. **PERMANENT DISCOUNT OUTLET**

Specialises in fine bone china as individual pieces or complete antique tea and coffee sets. Please phone for details.

DISCOUNT CLOTHING STORE

UNIT 1, MORPETH ROAD, ASHINGTON, NORTHUMBERLAND NE53 8PX, ☎ 01670 858300, 9.30–5.30 MON–SAT. **PERMANENT DISCOUNT OUTLET**

See page 467 (CO DURH)

ERRINGTON REAY POTTERY,

TYNESIDE POTTERY WORKS, BARDON MILL, HEXHAM, NORTHUMBERLAND NE47 7HU, ☎ 01434 344245, www.erringtonreay.co.uk, 9–5 SEVEN DAYS A WEEK. **FACTORY SHOP**

Large, salt-glazed garden and domestic clay pots in all sizes. Lots of storage pot seconds available from this supplier to garden centres, as well as ornamental garden animals and water features.

LE CREUSET

UNIT 50, ROYAL QUAYS OUTLET SHOPPING CENTRE, COBLE DENE, NORTH SHIELDS, TYNE & WEAR NE29 6DW, ☎ 0191 257 1533, 10–6 MON–SAT, 8 ON THUR. **FACTORY SHOP IN A FACTORY SHOPPING VILLAGE**

See page 483 (ESSEX)

MATALAN

THE KILLINGWORTH CENTRE, CITADEL WEST, KILLINGWORTH, NORTHUMBERLAND NE12, ☎ 0191 216 5360, FAX: 0191 216 1336, www.matalan.co.uk, 10–8 MON–FRI, 9–6 SAT, 11–5 SUN.

BELVEDERE RETAIL PARK, BRUNTON LANE, KINGSTON PARK, NEWCASTLE UPON TYNE, TYNE & WEAR NE3 2PA, ☎ 0191 214 0352, FAX: 0191 271 0067, www.matalan.co.uk, 10–8 MON–FRI, 9–6 SAT, 11–5 SUN. **PERMANENT DISCOUNT OUTLET**

See page 458 (BEDS)

MCINTOSH'S FACTORY SHOP

UNIT 1, THE FACTORY SHOP CENTRE, TUNDRY WAY, CHAINBRIDGE INDUSTRIAL ESTATE, BLAYDON ON TYNE, TYNE & WEAR NE21 5SJ, ☎ 0191 414 8598, 10–5 MON–FRI, 9–5 SAT, 10–4 SUN. **FACTORY SHOP**

Quilts, duvet covers, towels, beach towels, bedlinen, dusters, bath mat sets and ceramic kitchenware at bargain prices. Most of the household textiles are perfect with some seconds. Parking is easy and there is a coffee shop.

NO FRILLS DIY STORE

WHITLEY ROAD, LONGBENTON, NEWCASTLE UPON TYNE, TYNE & WEAR NE12 9SZ, ☎ 0191 270 0393, FAX: 0191 215 0823, 9–8 MON–SAT, 10–4 SUN. **PERMANENT DISCOUNT OUTLET**

See page 458 (BEDS)

PONDEN MILL

ROYAL QUAYS FACTORY OUTLET CENTRE, COBLE DENE ROAD, NORTH SHIELDS, NEWCASTLE UPON TYNE, NEAR A19, TYNE & WEAR NE29 6DY, ☎ 0191 257 4607, 10–6 MON–SAT, 11–5 SUN. **FACTORY SHOP IN A FACTORY SHOPPING VILLAGE**

See page 464 (CHESH)

ROYAL QUAYS OUTLET CENTRE

COBLE DENE, NORTH SHIELDS, NEWCASTLE UPON TYNE, NEAR A19, TYNE & WEAR NE29 6DW, ☎ 0191 296 3743, **e-mail:** outletcentres@realm-ocm.com, www.royalquaysoutletcentre.co.uk, 10–6 MON–SAT, 11–5 SUN. **FACTORY SHOPPING VILLAGE**

Forty-two shops with leisure facilities nearby including a full-scale steam railway, working harbour, roman ruins and the usual seaside attractions. Adjacent to the Wet and Wild water park which attracts 350,000 visitors a year and next door to an international ferry terminal, the centre has a nautical feel to it. There is a great range of shops, stocking famous name brands, all with up to 50% discounts off normal retail prices. Phone the above number for more details.

SCOOPS CATALOGUE DISCOUNT STORE

15 THE PRECINCT, THE IN CENTRE, JARROW, TYNE & WEAR NE32 3LS, ☎ 0191 483 4318, 9–5 MON–SAT.

8 THE FORUM SHOPPING CENTRE, WALLSEND, TYNE & WEAR NE28 8JR, ☎ 0191 236 9501, 9–5 MON–SAT. **PERMANENT DISCOUNT OUTLET**

See page 468 (CO DURH)

TK MAXX

LOWER GROUND FLOOR, MONUMENT MALL SHOPPING CENTRE, NEWCASTLE UPON TYNE, TYNE & WEAR NE1 7AL, ☎ 0191 261 0404, www.tkmaxx.com, 9–5.30 MON–FRI, 8 ON THUR, 9–6 SAT, 11–5 SUN. **PERMANENT DISCOUNT OUTLET**

See page 458 (BEDS)

TYNEDALE RETAIL PARK

HEXHAM, NORTHUMBERLAND NE46 3PJ, ☎ 01434 607788, 10–6 MON–FRI, 9.30–6 SAT, 11–5 SUN. **PERMANENT DISCOUNT OUTLET**

With 15,000 square feet of retail selling across a 10 acre site, all at ground level except the restaurant which has access via a lift, the Tynedale Retail Park is accessible to all. Here you will find overstocks and clearance lines at up to 50% off normal retail prices. Quality names such as Windsmoor, Jaegar, French Connection, Timberland, Elle and Edinburgh Woollen Mill are just a few of the brands available. The clothing is just for adults, but there are shoes for adults and children. There is also furniture, linen, electrical items, bath accessories, toys, gifts and DIY equipment. The main section is a garden centre which also has pets, golf, sporting and outdoor wear departments. The child-friendly restaurant has a kids zone, parking is free and there are disabled facilities on site.

NOTTINGHAMSHIRE

CATALOGUE BARGAIN SHOP

24–29 LEEMING STREET, MANSFIELD, NOTTINGHAMSHIRE NG18 1NE, ☎ 01623 623353, www.bargaincrazy.com, 9–5.30 MON–SAT, 10–4 SUN.

50 MAIN STREET, BULWELL, NOTTINGHAM, NOTTINGHAMSHIRE NG6 8EY, ☎ 0115 927 8373, www.bargaincrazy.com, 9–5.30 MON–SAT, 10–4 SUN. **PERMANENT DISCOUNT OUTLET**

See page 461 (CAMBS)

DENBY FACTORY SHOP

DURY WALK, BROADMARSH SHOPPING CENTRE, NOTTINGHAM, NOTTINGHAMSHIRE NG1 7LP, ☎ 0115 948 3932, www.denby.co.uk, 9–5.30 MON–SAT, 9.30–5.30 TUE, 10.30–4.30 SUN. **FACTORY SHOP**

See page 463 (CHESH)

DUNELM MILL SHOP

CASTLE RETAIL PARK, RADFORD BOULEVARD, NOTTINGHAM, NOTTINGHAMSHIRE NG7 5QJ, ☎ 0115 924 4200, FAX: 0115 924 4221, www.dunelm-mill.co.uk, 9–6 MON–SAT, 8 ON THUR, FRI, 11–5 SUN. **PERMANENT DISCOUNT OUTLET**

See page 458 (BEDS)

GIFTTREE

34 HIGH STREET, LONG EATON, NOTTINGHAMSHIRE NG10 1LL, ☎ 0115 973 6611, 9–5.30 MON–SAT. **FACTORY SHOP**

See page 473 (DERBY)

LABEL TRADERS

PASTURE LANE, RUDDINGTON, NOTTINGHAMSHIRE NG1 6AJ, ☎ 0115 9405205, www.labeltraders.co.uk, 9–5 MON–FRI, 9–4 SAT, 10–4 SUN.

3 KIRKBY ROAD, SUTTON-IN-ASHFIELD, NOTTINGHAMSHIRE NG17 1GP, ☎ 01623 554026, www.labeltraders.co.uk, 9–5 MON–FRI, 10–5 SAT, 10–4 SUN. **FACTORY SHOP**

See page 473 (DERBY)

LABELS OF EDWINSTOWE

25 HIGH STREET, EDWINSTOWE, NOTTINGHAMSHIRE NG21 9QP, ☎ 01623 825479, 10–5.30 MON–SAT. **DRESS AGENCY**

Friendly and accommodating shop, concentrating on barely worn upmarket and designer labels, stocking garments, accessories and jewellery in immaculate condition. The emporium at Edwinstone is set on two floors and also incorporates gifts, beauty salon and sought after pieces for the home such as Persian rugs, old olive jars and other decorative items. In addition, a range of imported Indonesian and Asian furniture is also displayed, although the main part of the business is still women's clothes from beachwear to designer evening and day wear. (Business terms are 50:50%.)

MATALAN

CHILWELL RETAIL PARK, BARTON LANE, BEESTON, NOTTINGHAM, NOTTINGHAMSHIRE NG9 6DS, ☎ 0115 946 9354, FAX: 0115 972 3184, www.matalan.co.uk, 10–8 MON–FRI, 9–6 SAT, 11–4 SUN.

SPRINGFIELD RETAIL PARK, HUCKNALL LANE, BULWELL, NOTTINGHAM NOTTINGHAMSHIRE NG6 8AJ, ☎ 0115 977 7800, FAX: 0115 976 3572, www.matalan.co.uk, 10–8 MON–FRI, 9–6 SAT, 10–4 SUN.

PORTLAND RETAIL PARK, STATION ROAD, SUTTON IN ASHFIELD, MANSFIELD, NOTTINGHAMSHIRE NG17 5GA, ☎ 01623 528710, FAX: 01623 554974, www.matalan.co.uk, 9.30–8 MON–FRI, 9–6 SAT, 11–5 SUN. **PERMANENT DISCOUNT OUTLET**

See page 458 (BEDS)

THE COURTAULDS FACTORY SHOP

HAYDN ROAD, NOTTINGHAM, NOTTINGHAMSHIRE NG5 1DH, ☎ 0115 924 6154, 9–5.30 MON–SAT, 7.30 ON WED, 10.30–4.30 SUN. **FACTORY SHOP**

Sells a wide range of women's, men's and childrens high street fashions at between 30% and 50% below high street prices. Also stocks a wide range of household textiles, luggage, shoes and accessories. There is now an on-site coffee shopping serving light meals, snacks and refreshments.

THE FACTORY SHOP

DONCASTER ROAD, LANGOLD, WORKSOP, NOTTINGHAMSHIRE DN22 7HY, ☎ 01909 731115, 9 -5.30 MON–SAT, 10–4.30 SUN. **FACTORY SHOP**

See page 465 (CHESH)

THE SHOE SHED

COURTAULDS TEXTILES **FACTORY SHOP**, ELLIS STREET, KIRKBY-IN-ASHFIELD, NOTTINGHAMSHIRE NG17 7AL, ☎ 01627 23083, 9–5.30 MON–SAT, 10.30–4.30 SUN. **FACTORY SHOP**

See page 481 (DORS)

TK MAXX

CHILWELL RETAIL PARK, BARTON LANE, BEESTON, NOTTINGHAM NOTTINGHAMSHIRE, ☎ 0115 946 3684, www.tkmaxx.com, PHONE FOR DETAILS OF OPENING TIMES. **PERMANENT DISCOUNT OUTLET**

See page 458 (BEDS)

TRADEX

QUEENS ROAD, BEESTON, NOTTINGHAM, NOTTINGHAMSHIRE NG9 2FE, ☎ 0115 922 0880, FAX: 0115 922 7333, 9.30–8.30 MON–FRI, 9–5.30 SAT, 10.30–4.30 SUN. **PERMANENT DISCOUNT OUTLET**

See page 507 (LANCS)

UNITED FOOTWEAR

BEECH AVENUE, OFF SHERWOOD RISE, OFF A60, NOTTINGHAM, NOTTINGHAMSHIRE, ☎ 0115 979 2799, 9–6.30 MON–FRI, 9–5.30 SAT, 10–4 SUN. **FACTORY SHOP**

See page 509 (LEICS)

WESTON MILL POTTERY

EGG PACKERS WORKSHOP, NAVIGATION YARD, MILLGATE, NEWARK, NOTTINGHAMSHIRE NG24 4TY, ☎ 01636 676835, www.wmpot.co.uk, 9.30–4.30 MON–SAT, 11–4.30 SUN, BANK HOLIDAYS. SOMETIMES CLOSED SUN IN JAN AND FEB SO PHONE FIRST. **FACTORY SHOP**

Manufacturer of terracotta wares, which they supply to many high street retailers. Garden pots in a variety of shapes and sizes are handthrown on the premises. Quality clay and high-firing make these frost resistant. A range of imported troughs, urns and large pots are also available at discounted prices. Weston Mill also produces items for the kitchen and home, including chicken roasters, tandori pots, garlic cellars and egg racks. Seconds and discounted items are always on sale at bargain prices. A large range of bird care products is also available.

WILKINSON STORES

2–6 FRONT STREET, ARNOLD, NOTTINGHAM, NOTTINGHAMSHIRE NG5 7EL, ☎ 0115 926 0805, www.wilko.co.uk, 9–5.30 MON–SAT, 10–4 SUN. MAIL ORDER. **PERMANENT DISCOUNT OUTLET**

See page 466 (CHESH)

WILLIS OWEN LTD

98 MANSFIELD ROAD, NOTTINGHAM, NOTTINGHAMSHIRE NG1 3HD, ☎ 0115 947 2595, www.willisowen.co.uk, 24 HOURS A DAY SEVEN DAYS A WEEK.

They will send you free guides to investing in ISAs, With Profit Bonds, Investment Bonds, etc. Top discounts available on all investments. Fully independent recommendations.

OXFORDSHIRE

BICESTER OUTLET SHOPPING VILLAGE

PINGLE DRIVE, BICESTER, JUNCTION 9 OF M40, OXFORDSHIRE OX6 7WD, ☎ 01869 323200, 10–6 SEVEN DAYS A WEEK. **FACTORY SHOPPING VILLAGE**

Described as 'Bond Street comes to Bicester', Bicester Village has established itself as the UK's leading outlet shopping destination in terms of offering the largest selection of international brand names to choose from. Currently there are 90 outlet shops offering quality merchandise at discounts of up to 60%, sometimes even more. The choice of famous brands at Bicester Village is second to none. International names include a Polo Ralph Lauren store, which now stocks more goods from their women's sport and home collections, Donna Karan, Versace, Christian Lacroix, Escada, Cerruti 1881 and TSE Cashmere. New arrivals from the international fashion scene are La Perla, Nautica, Gieves & Hawkes, Tommy Hilfiger, Tod's, MaxMara, Salvatore Ferragamo, Zegna, Calvin Klein, Charles Tyrwhitt, Sand, Links, Nautica, Musto and Holland & Holland. Both of Britain's leading designers, Nicole Farhi and Paul Smith, have shops with goods from their men's and women's collections. Karen Millen and Whistles both cater for the younger set with much more women's fashion to be found in The Designer Room, Episode, Hobbs, Jigsaw and Inwear Matinique. Top high street names are also well represented by Benetton, Principles, French Connection, Monsoon and Racing Green. The more classic customer also has an unequalled choice with Burberry, Aquascutum, Jaeger, Mulberry and the Scandinavian company RedGreen, whose nautical style of casual wear is very popular. Rugged outdoor wear can be found at Helly Hansen, Tog 24, the climbing and walking specialist. Active sportswear, represented by Fred Perry and Reebok, has now been joined by one of America's most famous sports shoe brands, Vans. A comprehensive collection of shoes, including many ranges for children, can be found in Clarks, with elegant high fashion styles in Charles Jourdan from Paris. Also, for women's shoes, handbags and accessories, there is Jane Shilton; for luggage, there is the Samsonite shop, plus the exciting addition of the first TAG-Heuer outlet, which stocks end-of-line designer watches, all fully guaranteed, at very attractive prices. Lingerie and underwear is to be found at Warners and Triumph, with HOM, the French brand, for the men; and the finest French childrenswear at Petit Bateau; English fragrances at Penhaligon's; make-up, bath and body therapies at Molton Brown, and soaps and gifts at Woods of Windsor. For the home, there are Price's candles and towels and duvets from another leading French brand, Descamps; cutlery from Oneida; china and crystal from Villeroy & Boch and Waterford Wedgwood and fine linens and accessories for the home from The White Company. The Cosmetic Company stocks well-known skincare products, cosmetics and fragrances for men and women. Bicester Village is something akin to a 'one-floor department store' and menswear, which can often be found in the designer shops, is also well represented in its own right with Dunhill, Blazer, Sand, Savoy Taylors Guild, Oscar Jacobson and Dockers, plus another international touch being provided by Cerruti Menswear, all offering good size ranges in a wide choice from very casual through to traditional business clothes. To complete the day out at Bicester Village, take home some popular titles from Books etc, get to know more about the location for a return visit from the Tourist Information Centre, and regain strength with top quality refreshment at Pret-A-Manger or Starbucks. There are cash machines, a children's play area, free parking and a shuttle bus (which is free from Thursday to Sunday) and taxi connection to Bicester North Station, which is on the Chiltern Railways line, and runs between Marylebone and Birmingham. The Village is about one hour's drive from London, two miles from Junction 9 on the M40. Take the A41 and follow signs for Village Retail Park.

DESCAMPS

BICESTER OUTLET SHOPPING VILLAGE, PINGLE DRIVE, BICESTER, JUNCTION 9 OF M40, OXFORDSHIRE OX26 7WD, ☎ 01869 323636, 10–6 SEVEN DAYS A WEEK. **FACTORY SHOP IN A FACTORY SHOPPING VILLAGE**

French designer range of bedlinen, towels and dressing gowns at prices discounted by between 30% and 70% off normal retail prices. By using a very high cotton count (the amount of thread used per square metre), their bedlinen is very soft. The higher the density of cotton, the better the quality.

DISCOUNT CHINA

HIGH STREET, BURFORD, OXFORDSHIRE OX18 4QA, ☎ 01993 823452, 10–5 SEVEN DAYS A WEEK. **PERMANENT DISCOUNT OUTLET**

See page 487 (GLOS)

ELLIS BAUGHAN DESIGN

THE STABLE, KINGSWAY FARM, ASTON, OXFORDSHIRE OX18 2BT, ☎ 01993 852031, FAX: 01993 851877, 9–5 MON–SAT, 10.30–4.30 SUN, BANK HOLIDAYS. **FACTORY SHOP**

Set in a converted barn next to their workshop, Jane and Stephen Baughan's factory shop sells seconds and overmakes of their hand-decorated pottery. The pottery is made using traditional methods of slip-casting and jollying before being decorated by hand using a combination of fresh colours and a wide variety of surface designs. They have also developed their own specialised technique of hand stencilling on pottery. Designs range from Sunflower and Blue Wild Clematis to birds and animals, and all products are microwave and dishwasher safe. Stephen and Jane supply more than 200 shops, as well as English Heritage. There is now a visitors' centre open on weekdays from 9am to 5pm. From 1 June to 30 September, tours and demonstrations take place four time a day on Wednesdays, Thursdays and Fridays. The first tour is at 11am and the last tour begins at 4pm. Tours cost £2 for adults and £1.50 for children. Coffee shop and free parking.

IMPS

52 SHEEP STREET, BICESTER, OXFORDSHIRE OX26 7LG, ☎ 01869 243455, 9–5 MON–SAT

40 UPPER HIGH STREET, THAME OXFORDSHIRE OX9 3AG, ☎ 01844 212985, 9–5 MON–SAT.

32 MARKET SQUARE, WITNEY, OXFORDSHIRE OX8 58A, ☎ 01993 779875, 9–5 MON–SAT. **PERMANENT DISCOUNT OUTLET**

High street shops selling popular chainstore seconds fashion for all the family as well as towels, china, trays and flower cachepots. Men's women's and childrenswear from designer brands such as Ralph Lauren, Tommy Hilfiger, Timberland and Gap. Sportswear from Umbro, Adidas and Nike all at up to 50% off high street prices.

ISIS CERAMICS

WEST HILL FARM, CHURCH LANE, HORTON CUM STUDLEY, OXFORDSHIRE OX33 1AP, ☎ 01865 358000, FAX: 01865 358333, 10–4 MON–FRI BY APPOINTMENT ONLY. **DESIGNER SALES**

Makers of ceramics which are handpainted in the style of 17th and 18th century Delftware, Isis has a range of cut-price seconds on sale at their central Oxford showroom twice a year, while their manufacturing base in a restored barn is open by appointment only. The company's most popular seller is the flower brick followed by lamps and colander bowls, all painted in traditional colours: blue, ox-blood, sage green, manganese, plum, sepia, black, saffron and watermelon pink. They also do complete dinner services, platters with tulips, birds and farmyard animals, dessert plates with scalloped edges, teapots and cream jugs, vases, baluster vases and cachepots. Seconds range from £15, high quality seconds enjoy discounts of at least 25%. Phone for address and sale dates.

MATALAN

UNIT 5, THE JOHN ALLEN CENTRE, COWLEY, OXFORDSHIRE OX4 3JP, ☎ 01865 336100, FAX: 01865 336107, www.matalan.co.uk, 10–8 MON–FRI, 9–6 SAT, 10–4 SUN. **PERMANENT DISCOUNT OUTLET**

See page 458 (BEDS)

MILL OUTLETS LTD BANBURY

51 HIGH STREET, BANBURY, OXFORDSHIRE OX16 8LA, ☎ 01295 264455, 9–5 MON–SAT.
PERMANENT DISCOUNT OUTLET

Specialises in curtains, net curtains, bedding, bed linens, towels, kitchen textiles and other household textiles. They also offer ranges of hand knitting yarns, men's and women's socks, hosiery and underwear. Merchandise comes direct from the manufacturers, often made up of clearance stock or chainstore overmakes and seconds. Prices are very competitive with savings of up to 50% and more off manufacturer's recommended prices.

ONEIDA

BICESTER OUTLET SHOPPING VILLAGE, PINGLE DRIVE, BICESTER, JUNCTION 9 OF M40, OXFORDSHIRE OX6 7WD, ☎ 01869 324789, 10–6 SEVEN DAYS A WEEK. **FACTORY SHOP IN A FACTORY SHOPPING VILLAGE**

See page 464 (CHESH)

PONDEN MILL

8 HIGH STREET, BANBURY, OXFORDSHIRE OX16 8DZ, ☎ 01295 253635, PHONE FOR DETAILS OF OPENING TIMES. **FACTORY SHOP**

See page 464 (CHESH)

PRICE'S CANDLES

BICESTER OUTLET SHOPPING VILLAGE, PINGLE DRIVE, BICESTER, JUNCTION 9 OF M40, OXFORDSHIRE OX6 7WD, ☎ 01869 325520, 10–6 SEVEN DAYS A WEEK. **FACTORY SHOP IN A FACTORY SHOPPING VILLAGE**

See page 464 (CHESH)

TK MAXX

CALTHORPE STREET, OFF HIGH STREET, BANBURY, OXFORDSHIRE OX16 8ES, ☎ 01295 277022, www.tkmaxx.com, 9–5.30 MON–FRI, 7 ON THUR, 9–6 SAT, 11–5 SUN. **PERMANENT DISCOUNT OUTLET**

See page 458 (BEDS)

VILLEROY & BOCH (UK) LIMITED

BICESTER OUTLET SHOPPING VILLAGE, PINGLE DRIVE, BICESTER, JUNCTION 9 OF M40, OXFORDSHIRE OX6 7WD, ☎ 01869 324646, 10–6 SEVEN DAYS A WEEK. **FACTORY SHOP IN A FACTORY SHOPPING VILLAGE**

See page 466 (CHESH)

WOODS OF WINDSOR

UNIT 29, BICESTER RETAIL VILLAGE, PINGLE DRIVE, BICESTER, JUNCTION 9 OF M40, OXFORDSHIRE OX26 7WD, ☎ 01869 325307, www.woods of windsor.co.uk, 10–6 SEVEN DAYS A WEEK. **FACTORY SHOP IN A FACTORY SHOPPING VILLAGE**

See page 466 (CHESH)

SHROPSHIRE

AMANDA BRISBANE GLASS

THE GLASSBARN, CHURCH FARM BARNS, STANTON LACY, LUDLOW, SHROPSHIRE SY8 2AE, ☎ 01584 856292, **e-mail:** amanda@amandabrisbaneglass.com, www.amandabrisbaneglass.com, **FACTORY SHOP**

The UK's foremost sand-glass artist usually has some experimental pieces and discontinued lines at her Ludlow showroom. Her range includes shell design soap dishes, ashtrays, stand-alone glass fish, bowls, unusual vases and a variety of decorative ware.

CATALOGUE SURPLUS CENTRE LTD

28–30 ST MARY'S STREET, NEWPORT, SHROPSHIRE TF10 7AB, ☎ 01952 825889, FAX: 01952 825545, 9–5 MON–SAT.

4 CLAREMONT STREET, SHREWSBURY, SHROPSHIRE SY1 1QG, ☎ 01743 243 629, 9–5 MON–SAT.

21 WILLOW STREET, OSWESTRY SHROPSHIRE SY11 1AF, ☎ 01691 658155, 9–5 MON–SAT.

UNIT 3, OXFORD STREET, OAKENGATE, TELFORD SHROPSHIRE TF2 6AA, ☎ 01952 617406, 9–5 MON–SAT. **PERMANENT DISCOUNT OUTLET**

Ex-catalogue clothes for men, women and children as well as shoes and bedlinen, all at a fraction of the cost of catalogue prices.

DUNELM MILL SHOP

18 MARKET STREET, SHREWSBURY, SHROPSHIRE SY1 1LE, ☎ 01743 271478, FAX: 01743 243384, www.dunelm-mill.co.uk, 9–5 MON–THUR, 9–5.30 FRI, SAT, 10–4 SUN.

BRIDGE ROAD, WELLINGTON SHROPSHIRE TF1 1ED, ☎ 01952 245593, FAX: 01952 245118, www.dunelm-mill.co.uk, 9–5.30 MON–THUR, 9–8 FRI, 9–6 SAT, 10.30–4.30 SUN. **PERMANENT DISCOUNT OUTLET**

See page 458 (BEDS)

MATALAN

HARLESCOTT RETAIL PARK, BRIXTON WAY, HARLESCOTT, SHREWSBURY SHROPSHIRE SY1 3AZ, ☎ 01743 453040, FAX: 01743 462489, www.matalan.co.uk, 10–8 MON–FRI, 9–6 SAT, 11–5 SUN.

WREKIN RETAIL PARK, WELLINGTON, TELFORD, SHROPSHIRE TF1 2DE, ☎ 01952 641080, FAX: 01952 240155, www.matalan.co.uk, 10–8 MON–FRI, 9–6 SAT, 11–5 SUN. **PERMANENT DISCOUNT OUTLET**

See page 458 (BEDS)

STANWAY FABRICS AND INTERIORS

SHIPTON HALL BARN, SHIPTON, NEAR MUCH WENLOCK, SHROPSHIRE TF13 6JZ, ☎ 01746 785151, FAX: 01746 785152, www.stanwayfabrics.co.uk, 10–4 MON–SAT. **PERMANENT DISCOUNT OUTLET**

Leading suppliers of top designer fabric seconds and clearances at prices from as little as £3.95 per metre for fabrics which would normally retail between £25 and £85. Thousands of metres of curtain and upholstery fabrics always in stock, together with linings, interlinings, tape etc, at extremely competitive prices. They stock a wide range of tassels, tie-backs, trimmings and accessories, with many more available to order. Curtains, cushions, loose covers and headboards can be made to customers' specifications by their experienced in house team at affordable prices. They also have a swap shop where customers can buy or sell beautiful curtains. Situated in a converted barn next to the 16th-century Shipton Hall in the beautiful Corvedale area of south Shropshire, close to the historic towns of Ludlow, Much Wenlock and Shrewsbury, there is also a coffee shop within the barn and parking is right outside the door.

STEWART'S

19–21 CROSS STREET, ELLESMERE, SHROPSHIRE SY12 0AW, ☎ 01691 624478, FAX: 01691 624478, 9.30–5.30 MON–FRI, 9–5.30 SAT, 10–4 SUN. **FACTORY SHOP**

See page 478 (DEV)

T J HUGHES

RIVERSIDE AND PRIDEHILL SHOPPING CENTRE, SHREWSBURY, SHROPSHIRE SY1 1BU, ☎ 01743 358359, FAX: 01743 271222, **e-mail:** info@tjhughes.co.uk, www.tjhughes.co.uk, 9–5.30 MON–SAT, 10.30–4.30 SUN. **PERMANENT DISCOUNT OUTLET**

See page 465 (CHESH)

TK MAXX

DARWIN SHOPPING CENTRE, RAVENS MEADOWS, SHREWSBURY, SHROPSHIRE SY1 1BW, ☎ 01743 341370, www.tkmaxx.com, 9–5.30 MON–FRI, 9–6 SAT, 11–5 SUN.

UNIT 16, TELFORD FORGE RETAIL PARK, ORDSALL LANE, TELFORD, SHROPSHIRE TF3 4AG, ☎ 01952 210200, www.tkmaxx.com, 10–8 MON–FRI, 9–6 SAT, 11–5 SUN. **PERMANENT DISCOUNT OUTLET**

See page 458 (BEDS)

SOMERSET

CHAPLINS SUPERSTORES HOME & GARDEN

BINDON ROAD, TAUNTON, SOMERSET TA2 6AA, ☎ 01823 288017, FAX: 01823 336189, 9–8 MON–FRI, 9–6 SAT, 10.30–4.30 SUN. **PERMANENT DISCOUNT OUTLET**

A wide range of merchandise for the bargain hunter, including garden tools, plants, fertilisers and accessories; toys; adults clothing and shoes; stationery; household textiles; electrical equipment; DIY items; glass and china; bathroom accessories; partyware; candles; food accessories. Spades are available at £4.99, trowels at 99p, shears at £5.99 (while stocks last).

CLARKS VILLAGE OUTLET SHOPPING

FARM ROAD, STREET, JUNCTION 23 OF M5, THEN A39, SOMERSET BA16 0BB, ☎ 01458 840064, **e-mail:** bgodwin@realm-ocm.com, www.clarksvillage.co.uk, APRIL–OCTOBER 9–5.30 MON–SAT, 11–5 SUN, NOVEMBER–MARCH 10–6, MON–SAT, 11–5 SUN. **FACTORY SHOPPING VILLAGE**

Purpose-built village of brick-built shops with extensive car parking facilities. Restaurant, fast food stands, carousel, indoor and outdoor play areas, and working village pottery and artists' studio. Here, there are 57 shops with more planned. Shops include: Body Shop, Reebok selling the Reebok brand, Rockport and the Greg Norman Collection; Monsoon/Accessorize, Benetton, Wrangler, The Designer Room, Jaeger, Viyella, Alexon, Triumph/Hom, Gossard, Clarks Factory Shop, Rohan, Windsmoor, Liz Claiborne, Calvin Klein, Van Heusen, Next, Warehouse, Tom Sayers men's sweaters and trousers, Warner's lingerie, Tog 24 outerwear, Jane Shilton handbags, luggage and shoes, The Suit Company and Blazer and Event jewellery. There is also a purpose-built china and glass pavilion and many other stores, all with up to 50% off famous name brands.

CLOVERLEAF

CHINA AND GLASS PAVILION, CLARKS VILLAGE FACTORY SHOPPING CENTRE, FARM ROAD, STREET, JUNCTION 23 OF M5 SOMERSET BA16 0BB, ☎ 01458 447788, 10–6 MON–SAT, 11–5 SUN. **FACTORY SHOP**

See page 477 (DEV)

CRAFTS

16 CHEAP STREET, BATH, SOMERSET BA1 1NA, ☎ 01225 464397, 9.30–5.30 MON–SAT, 10.30–4.30 SUN. **FACTORY SHOP**

Crafts is a cooperative selling direct to the public at makers' direct prices. Items range from ceramics to wood, clocks, musical instruments and glassware. Everything is hand-made and commissions are welcome. They also sell a small amount of English Country Pottery.

DARTINGTON CRYSTAL

CLARKS VILLAGE FACTORY SHOPPING CENTRE, FARM ROAD, STREET, JUNCTION 23 OF M5 SOMERSET BA16 0BB, ☎ 01458 841618, 9–6 MON–SAT, 11–5 SUN. **FACTORY SHOP IN A FACTORY SHOPPING VILLAGE**

See page 469 (CORN)

DENBY FACTORY SHOP

CLARKS VILLAGE, FARM ROAD, STREET, JUNCTION 23 OF M5 SOMERSET BA16 0BB, ☎ 01458 840940, www.denby.co.uk, 9–6 MON–SAT, 11–5 SUN. **FACTORY SHOP IN A FACTORY SHOPPING VILLAGE**

See page 463 (CHESH)

DESIGN HOUSE

CLARKS VILLAGE FACTORY SHOPPING CENTRE, FARM ROAD, STREET, JUNCTION 23 OF M5 SOMERSET BA16 0BB, ☎ 01458 448470, 9–6 MON–SAT, 11–5 SUN. **FACTORY SHOP IN A FACTORY SHOPPING VILLAGE**

See page 483 (ESSEX)

DUNELM MILL SHOP

UNIT D, WESTON RETAIL PARK, MARCHFIELDS WAY, WESTON-SUPER-MARE, SOMERSET BS23 3YZ, ☎ 01934 641004, FAX: 01934 641139, www.dunelm-mill.co.uk, 9–6 MON–SAT, 8 ON THUR, FRI, 10.30–4.30 SUN. **PERMANENT DISCOUNT OUTLET**

See page 458 (BEDS)

EDINBURGH CRYSTAL

50 THE HIGH STREET, CLARKS VILLAGE, STREET, SOMERSET BA16 0EQ, ☎ 01458 441977, 9–6 MON–SAT, 10–4 SUN. **FACTORY SHOP IN A FACTORY SHOPPING VILLAGE**

See page 463 (CHESH)

HYBURY CHINA

27 NORTH STREET, CREWKERNE, SOMERSET TA18 7AL, ☎ 08707 380380, FAX: 08707 353637, **e-mail:** sales@hyburychina.co.uk, www.hyburychina.co.uk, MAIL ORDER ONLY **PERMANENT DISCOUNT OUTLET**

Sells high quality pure white English bone china seconds, all from famous manufacturers, delivered to your door by mail order. Brilliant value at very competitive prices and all items are dishwasher safe and hard-wearing. The classic good looks and contemporary styles of the china make it ideal for use at home or in restaurants, rented properties, B&Bs, boardrooms, offices or the perfect wedding gift. The china comes from major English companies selected prior to being stamped with the manufacturer's brand name. A perfect bone china dinner plate would normally cost from £17 to £35; Hybury offer their dinner plates from £4.75 and have also included a new and exciting giftware collection to solve that difficult present problem. Phone for a free brochure or visit their website for monthly special offers throughout the year.

LE CREUSET

UNIT 40, CLARKS VILLAGE FACTORY SHOPPING CENTRE, FARM ROAD, STREET, JUNCTION 23 OF M5 SOMERSET BA16 0BB, ☎ 01458 440123, 9–5.30 MON SAT, 11–5 SUN. **FACTORY SHOP IN A FACTORY SHOPPING VILLAGE**

See page 483 (ESSEX)

MATALAN

LOCKING CASTLE DISTRICT CENTRE, WORLE, WESTON-SUPER-MARE, SOMERSET BS22 0BE, ☎ 01934 529830, FAX: 01934 521932, www.matalan.co.uk, 10–8 MON–FRI, 9–6 SAT, 10–4 SUN.

THE PEEL CENTRE, BABYLON HILL, YEOVIL, SOMERSET BA21 5BT, ☎ 01935 403110, FAX: 01935 426280, www.matalan.co.uk, 10–8 MON–FRI, 9–6 SAT, 11–5 SUN. **PERMANENT DISCOUNT OUTLET**

See page 458 (BEDS)

MULBERRY

THE OLD SCHOOL HOUSE, KILVER STREET ON THE A37, SHEPTON MALLET, SOMERSET BA4 5NF, ☎ 01749 340583, www.mulberry.com, 10–6 MON–SAT, 11–5 SUN AND BANK HOLIDAYS. **FACTORY SHOP**

A very popular large, attractive, factory outlet situated in an old school house with parking outside, which sells a wide variety of end of line stock and seconds including men's and women's leather bags, accessories, tech product cases, planners, agendas and stationery. It also sells last season's clothes and home goods which include a selection of furniture, cushions, lamps, china and fabric. Small coffee shop and toilet and disabled facilities. There are other Mulberry factory shops in York and at Bicester Village, Oxfordshire.

PRICE'S CANDLES

CLARKS VILLAGE FACTORY SHOPPING CENTRE, FARM ROAD, STREET, JUNCTION 23 OF M5, SOMERSET BA16 0BB, ☎ 01458 440006, 9–6 MON–SAT, 10–5 SUN. **FACTORY SHOP IN A FACTORY SHOPPING VILLAGE**

See page 464 (CHESH)

ROYAL WORCESTER & SPODE FACTORY SHOP

CLARKS VILLAGE FACTORY SHOPPING CENTRE, FARM ROAD, STREET, JUNCTION 23 OF M5 SOMERSET BA16 0BB, ☎ 01458 840554, www.royal-worcester.co.uk, 9–6 MON–SAT, 11–5 SUN. **FACTORY SHOP IN A FACTORY SHOPPING VILLAGE**

See page 465 (CHESH)

T J HUGHES

FAIRFAX HOUSE, HIGH STREET, WESTON-SUPER-MARE, SOMERSET BS23 1HA, ☎ 01934 414466, FAX: 01934 419911, **e-mail:** info@tjhughes.co.uk, www.tjhughes.co.uk, 9–5.30 MON–SAT, 11–5 SUN. **PERMANENT DISCOUNT OUTLET**

See page 465 (CHESH)

TAYLORS OF TAUNTON

RICHMOND ROAD, OFF STAPLEGROVE ROAD, TAUNTON, SOMERSET TA1 1EN, ☎ 01823 272961, www.users.globalnet.co.uk/taylorcg, 9–5.30 MON–SAT. **PERMANENT DISCOUNT OUTLET**

Large shop, with a free car park and a coffee shop, which sells both perfect and seconds in a wide range of china and glassware, as well as cutlery, cooking utensils, baskets, wrapping paper, cards, napkins, table mats, garden pots, logs and pet baskets and sundials. There are always special offers in the china and glassware sections such as Denby Pottery reduced by 20%, Johnson Bros dinner services reduced by 25%, seconds of Churchill tableware; George Butler stainless steel 44-piece canteens reduced from £390 to £195, special offers on Edinburgh crystal and half-price offers on Dartington Crystal as well as run of kiln Spode Blue Italian at reductions of 25% (run of kiln means the factory hasn't checked the products – while there are certain to be a few seconds, the majority of the products are fine). Also now stock leather good, briefcases, executive cases and conference folders at savings of up to 50%.

THE FACTORY SHOP LTD

MART ROAD, MINEHEAD, SOMERSET TA24 5BJ, ☎ 01643 705911, 9.30–5.30 MON–SAT, 11–5 SUN. **FACTORY SHOP**

See page 465 (CHESH)

THE IRON MAID COMPANY

PO BOX 3229, WELLS, SOMERSET BA5 2WL, ☎ 01749 670017, FAX: 020 7378 1533, www.ironmaid.co.uk, MAIL ORDER ONLY. **PERMANENT DISCOUNT OUTLET**

Stunning collection of garden and conservatory folding and flat packed iron furniture, combining contemporary designs with quality workmanship – and all at affordable prices. Range includes iron love seats, decorative outdoor benches and seats, folding outdoor iron furniture, side tables, wine storage and magazine racks. Phone for a brochure and price list.

TOTAL BATHROOMS

BRASSMILL TRADING ESTATE, BRASSMILL LANE, NEWBRIDGE, BATH, SOMERSET BA1 3JF, ☎ 01225 481815, 9–5 TUE–FRI, 9–4 SAT. **FACTORY SHOP**

Largest suppliers of bathroom accessories to the retail trade. Supplying accessories for well-known DIY and homewares stores, here they sell ends of lines and overstocks of bathroom accessories such as towel rails, mirrors, toilet brushes, toothbrush holders as well as vanity units, bath panels, bathroom cabinets. They now stock larger bathroom items such as shower cubicles and baths with some display room sets. Phone or call in for more information. Total Bathrooms is the exclusive supplier of Rhoper Rhodes Seconds and end-of-line products.

STAFFORDSHIRE

ALLSORTS FURNITURE

23 HAMILL ROAD, BURSLEM, STOKE-ON-TRENT, STAFFORDSHIRE ST6 1AJ, ☎ 01782 833006, FAX: 01782 833006, 10–5 MON–SAT. **PERMANENT DISCOUNT OUTLET**

Household goods, furniture and exercise equipment at discounts of up to 60%. Furniture includes new three-piece suites, pine tables and chairs, television cabinets, nests of tables and kitchen furniture, as well as pine furniture imported from Denmark. Household goods include pots and pans, ovenware, casserole dishes, kettles etc. There are also suitcases, exercise bikes, step striders, walking and running machines, but no clothes, fabrics or curtains.

ARGYLE CHINA

WATERLOO ROAD, BURSLEM, STOKE-ON-TRENT, STAFFORDSHIRE ST6 2EL, ☎ 01782 834561 9.30–4.30 MON–THUR, 9.30–3.30 FRI. **FACTORY SHOP**

Small factory shop selling china tableware, china ornaments, wedding gifts and souvenirs.

ARTHUR PRICE OF ENGLAND

BRITANNIA WAY, BRITANNIA ENTERPRISE PARK, LICHFIELD, STAFFORDSHIRE WS14 9UY, ☎ 01543 257775, FAX: 01543 414488, **e-mail:** marketing@arthur-price.co.uk, www.arthur-price.co.uk, 9–5 MON–FRI, 10–1 SAT. **FACTORY SHOP**

This factory shop in Lichfield sells seconds, discontinued lines and shop-soiled samples of silver-plated and stainless steel cutlery. There are sets as well as loose items on sale at half price or less. Also on sale is giftware consisting of candelabras, cruet sets, tea services, tankards and trays, most at half price. There are usually four sales a year – in March, June, September and December – when there is up to 50% off.

AYNSLEY CHINA

UNIT 14, LOWER MALL, POTTERIES SHOPPING CENTRE, HANLEY, STOKE-ON-TRENT, STAFFORDSHIRE ST1 1PS, ☎ 01782 204108, **e-mail:** customer.services@aynsley.co.uk, www.aynsley.co.uk, 9–5.30 MON–SAT, TILL 8 THUR PRE CHRISTMAS.

SUTHERLAND ROAD, LONGTON, STOKE-ON-TRENT, STAFFORDSHIRE ST3 1HS, ☎ 01782 339420, FAX: 01782 339420, **e-mail:** customer.services@aynsley.co.uk, www.aynsley.co.uk, 9–5.30 MON–SAT, 11–4 SUN. MAIL ORDER. **FACTORY SHOP**

The chance to buy beautiful fine bone china at affordable prices from a selection of seconds and discontinued lines at factory shop prices. The giftware range includes handmade china flowers, clocks, table lamps, vases, photograph frames and trinket boxes. For formal or informal dining, Aynsley China has a tableware pattern for every occasion.

BDF NEWLIFE

MARTINDALE, HAWK'S GREEN, CANNOCK, STAFFORDSHIRE WS11 2XN, ☎ 01543 468888, FAX: 01543 505989, **e-mail:** info@bdfnewlife.co.uk, 9.30–10 MON–SAT, 10–4 SUN, 10–5 BANK HOLIDAYS. **PERMANENT DISCOUNT OUTLET**

8,000 square foot charity superstore which sells both new merchandise donated by most of the top high street stores and nearly-new. This is the sort of shop where you can find anything from a girl's party dress to a two-seater rowing boat, men's shoes to a cooler bag, in between towels, jewellery, family clothes, furniture, mattresses (new with damaged packaging), beds, clocks, golf bags, umbrellas, wallpaper and designer dresses. Stock changes every 45 minutes. All the profits go to charity. Membership is by donation averaging £2. The shop is on one floor so is very accessible and has disabled toilet facilities. As the store also takes counterfeit goods from national Trading Standards departments' seizures, stress is put on not believing any labelling or assuring authenticity. There are also branches in Kirkby-in-Ashfield, Nottinghamshire and Stoke Aldermoor, Coventry.

BIRTHDAYS

UNIT 41, FREEPORT TALKE OUTLET MALL, PIT LANE, TALKE PITS, STOKE-ON-TRENT, STAFFORDSHIRE ST7 1QE, ☎ 01782 775013, 9.30–8 MON–FRI, 9.30–6 SAT, 11–5 SUN. **FACTORY SHOP IN A FACTORY SHOPPING VILLAGE**

See page 462 (CHESH)

BRIDGEWATER

EASTWOOD WORKS, LICHFIELD STREET, HANLEY, STOKE-ON-TRENT, STAFFORDSHIRE ST1 3EJ, ☎ 01782 201328, FAX: 01782 271508, **e-mail:** bridge.water@btinternet.com, www.bridgewater-pottery.co.uk, 9.30–5.30 MON–SAT, 11–4 SUN. MAIL ORDER. **FACTORY SHOP**

Emma Bridgewater's distinctive hand decorated and sponge painted pottery, textiles and cookware ranges at discounts of 30% and 40% for seconds and discontinued lines. All pottery on sale here has been made on site. Also on sale across the courtyard at the Bridgewater Decorating Studio and café are a collection of first quality Bridgewater pottery plus a selection of quality brand giftwares. You can paint your own design on a piece of Bridgewater pottery here, too. Hot and cold drinks and snacks available. Mail order service for both shops.

BURLEIGH

MIDDLEPORT POTTERY, PORT STREET, BURSLEM, STOKE-ON-TRENT, STAFFORDSHIRE ST6 3PE, ☎ 01782 577866, 9–5 MON–SAT, 10–4 SUN. **FACTORY SHOP**

Factory shop selling blue and white earthenware pottery as well as black and green pottery. Full dinnerware range as well as mugs, bowls, jugs, teapots, vases, plates, bowls and storage jars.

CATALOGUE BARGAIN SHOP

95 CHURCH STREET, BILSTON, STAFFORDSHIRE WV14 0BJ, ☎ 01902 353624, www.bargaincrazy.com, 9–5.30 MON–SAT, 9.30–3.30 SUN.

UNIT 2, CHASE CENTRE, CHURCH STREET, CANNOCK, STAFFORDSHIRE WS11 1AP, ☎ 01543 468614, www.bargaincrazy.com, 9–8 MON–FRI, 9–6 SAT, 10.30–4.30 SUN.

FREEPORT TALKE OUTLET MALL, PIT LANE, TALKE PITS, STOKE-ON-TRENT, STAFFORDSHIRE ST7 1XD, ☎ 01782 775740, www.bargaincrazy.com, 9.30–8 MON–FRI, 9.30–6 SAT, 11–5 SUN. **PERMANENT DISCOUNT OUTLET**

See page 461 (CAMBS)

CATALOGUE DISCOUNT STORE

63 HIGH STREET, BROWNHILLS, STAFFORDSHIRE WS8 6HH, ☎ 01543 372933, 9–5.30 MON–SAT. **PERMANENT DISCOUNT OUTLET**

See page 499 (LANCS)

CATALOGUE SURPLUS CENTRE LTD

5 HIDE STREET, STOKE-ON-TRENT, STAFFORDSHIRE ST4 1NF, ☎ 01782 744445, 9–5, MON–SAT. **PERMANENT DISCOUNT OUTLET**

See page 527 (SHROP)

CHINACAVE

LEWIS'S ARCADE, THE POTTERIES SHOPPING CENTRE, HANLEY, STOKE-ON-TRENT, STAFFORDSHIRE ST1 1PS, ☎ 01782 204156, 9–5.30 MON–SAT, 8 ON THUR, 11–4 SUN. **FACTORY SHOP**

This outlet sells seconds in Royal Doulton, Royal Albert crystal, Beatrix Potter figurines and Royal Minton at discounts of up to 50%. In the same complex is Royal Aynsley and the general discount shop, TK Maxx.

CHURCHILL CHINA

THE QUEENS POTTERY, WHIELDON ROAD, STOKE-ON-TRENT, STAFFORDSHIRE ST4 4HQ, ☎ 01253 773927, 9–5 MON–SAT, 10–4 SUN. **FACTORY SHOP**

Top quality fine bone china, tableware and mugs from Queens and earthenware from Churchill at discount prices of up to 30%. All are seconds.

CHURCHILL CHINA

ANCHOR POTTERY, BRIDGEWOOD STREET, LONGTON, STOKE-ON-TRENT, STAFFORDSHIRE ST3 1JJ, ☎ 01782 329785, 9–5 MON–SAT. **FACTORY SHOP**

Factory shop selling a large range of china and earthenware. There are dinner services, as well as individual mugs, cups, plates etc.

COBRIDGE STONEWARE

PHOENIX WORKS, NILE STREET, COBRIDGE, STOKE-ON-TRENT, STAFFORDSHIRE ST6 2BH, ☎ 01782 820505, 10–5 MON–FRI, 9.30–4.30 SAT. **FACTORY SHOP**

Factory shop making and selling handmade painted vases and lamps, ginger jars and sculptures.

DOULTON & CO OUTLET SUPERSTORE

FORGE LANE, ETRURIA VALLEY, STOKE-ON-TRENT, NEAR HANLEY, STAFFORDSHIRE ST1 5NN, ☎ 01782 284056, www.royal-doulton.com, 10–8 MON–FRI, 9–6 SAT, 11–5 SUN. **FACTORY SHOP**

Royal Doulton, Minton and Royal Albert ranges, focussing on tableware complemented by kitchenware and kitchen linen as well as Country Artist range, Bunnykins, Winnie the Pooh and Harry Potter.

DOULTON VISITOR CENTRE

NILE STREET, BURSLEM, STOKE-ON-TRENT STAFFORDSHIRE ST6 2AJ, ☎ 01782 292451 9.- 5.30 MON–SAT, 10–4 SUN. **FACTORY SHOP**

Factory shop attached to the factory selling Royal Doulton, Minton and Royal Albert ranges, focusing on tableware as well as Country Artist, Bunnykins, Winnie the Pooh and Harry Potter.

DUDSON LTD

NILE STREET, BURSLEM, STOKE-ON-TRENT, STAFFORDSHIRE ST6 2BA, ☎ 01782 821075, 9–5 MON–FRI, 9–12 SAT. **FACTORY SHOP**

Factory shop selling hotelware so there will be dinner services and individual plates, cups, bowls, saucers etc.

DUNELM FABRIC SHOP

FABRIC SHOP, 81 HIGH GREEN, CANNOCK, STAFFORDSHIRE WS1 3BH, ☎ 01543 462505, FAX: 01543 469168, www.dunelm-mill.co.uk, 9–5 MON–FRI, 9–5.30 SAT, 10–4 SUN.
PERMANENT DISCOUNT OUTLET

Part of a chain of shops selling brand-name and chainstore curtains, masses of bedlinen, towels, wickerware, pictures and frames, all at great value for money.

DUNELM MILL SHOP

4 WORTHINGTON WALK, BURTON-ON-TRENT, STAFFORDSHIRE DE14 1BU, ☎ 01283 512803, FAX: 01283 545180, www.dunelm-mill.co.uk, 9–5 MON–FRI, 9–5.30 SAT, 10–4 SUN.

89 HIGH STREET, CANNOCK, STAFFORDSHIRE WS1 1BH, ☎ 01543 503437, FAX: 01543 469168, www.dunelm-mill.co.uk, 9–5 MON–FRI, 9–5.30 SAT, 10–4 SUN.

98–104 HIGH STREET, NEWCASTLE UNDER LYME, STAFFORDSHIRE ST5 1QQ, ☎ 01782 713400, FAX: 01782 636395, www.dunelm-mill.co.uk, 9–5.30 MON–SAT.

UNIT 3, QUEENSVILLE RETAIL PARK, SILKMORE LANE, STAFFORD STAFFORDSHIRE ST17 4SU, ☎ 01785 248433, FAX: 01785 226322, www.dunelm-mill.co.uk, 10–6 MON–WED, 10–8 THUR, FRI, 9–6 SAT, 11–5 SUN.

GUNGATE PRECINCT, LOWER GUNGATE, TAMWORTH STAFFORDSHIRE B79 7AG, ☎ 01827 69504, FAX: 01827 314034, www.dunelm-mill.co.uk, 9–5 MON–FRI, 9–5.30 SAT.
PERMANENT DISCOUNT OUTLET

See page 458 (BEDS)

FREEPORT TALKE OUTLET MALL

FREEPORT TALKE OUTLET MALL, PIT LANE, TALKE PITS, STOKE-ON-TRENT, OFF JUNCTION 16 OF M6 THEN TAKE THE A500 AND THE A34, FOLLOWING SIGNS TO TALKE, STAFFORDSHIRE ST7 1XD, ☎ 01782 774113, www.freeporttalke.com, 9.30–8 MON–FRI, 9.30–6 SAT, 11–5 SUN. **FACTORY SHOPPING VILLAGE**

Fully covered indoor outlet mall with a range of restaurants, including Burger King and Café Ritazza, and an indoor soft play area for children. Womenswear includes The Designer Room, Edinburgh Woollen Mill, Nickelby's, Pilot, Spotlight, Roman Originals and Leading Labels. Menswear includes The Suit Company, Double Two, Petroleum, Nickelby's, Madhouse and Tog 24. Childrenswear can be found at Used Co Kids. Other shops on site include: Claire's Accessories, Charles Clinkard, Jane Shilton, Bags Etc, Trespass, Streetwise Sports, The Golf Company, Catalogue Bargain Shop, Julian Graves, Kitchen and Table, Toy World, Thorntons, Birthdays, Room, Mobile Phone Store, Book Depot, Picture Port, Ponden Mill and XS Music.

GEORGIAN CRYSTAL FACTORY SHOP

SILK MILL LANE, TUTBURY, BURTON-ON-TRENT, STAFFORDSHIRE DE13 9LE, ☎ 01283 814534, FAX: 01283 520186, **e-mail:** enquiries@georgiancrystal.co.uk, www.georgiancrystal.co.uk, 9–5 MON–SAT, 10–4 SUN. **FACTORY SHOP**

The only retail outlet for the lead crystal glassware manufactured on site. One of the few UK manufacturers of handmade, full lead crystal, you can buy first quality lead crystal only here at 75% less than the high street price for the same quality, with seconds at even bigger discounts. Full lead crystal handmade sherry glasses cost £5.50 each compared with between £15 and £20 in department stores. The range extends from liqueur glasses to 16-inch chalices, and includes decanters and salad bowls. Call and see a free demonstration of glass being made on the premises, from Monday to Thursday.

GIFTTREE

2 QUADRANT ROAD, POTTERIES SHOPPING CENTRE, HANLEY, STOKE-ON-TRENT, STAFFORDSHIRE ST1 1PP, ☎ 01782 202570, 9–5.30 MON–SAT, 8 ON THUR.

6 MARKET STREET, TAMWORTH, STAFFORDSHIRE B79 7LU, ☎ 01827 60266, 9–5 MON–SAT. **FACTORY SHOP**

See page 473 (DERBY)

HADIDA BATHROOM INTERIORS

OLD FOLEY POTTERY, KING STREET, FENTON, STOKE-ON-TRENT, STAFFORDSHIRE ST4 3DH, ☎ 01782 597739, FAX: 01782 597702, **e-mail:** enquiries@hadida.co.uk, www.hadida.co.uk, 9–4.30 MON–SAT, 11–4 SUN. **FACTORY SHOP**

Hadida Bathroom Interiors offers a wide range of seconds and discontinued ceramic bathroom accessories complemented by matching fabric shower curtains, Austrian blinds, window drapes, bath pillows, tissue box covers etc. All the shower curtains are specially treated to make them mildew resistant, and come in standard 180cm and longer lengths. Examples of prices include: toilet roll holder, £6.40, normal price £16.00; soap dish, £2.80, normally £7.00; frilled shower curtain, £14.00, normally £50.00; plain shower curtain, £9.95, normally £35.00. Also in stock are Chortex/Horrocks towels, candles, soaps, bathroom toiletries, shower rails and shower curtain hooks. Hadida also manufactures James Kent Floral Chintzware which is sold as seconds in the shop at heavily discounted prices. Free parking.

HARRY HANCOCK LTD

NEWFIELD CHINA WAREHOUSE, SUMMERBANK ROAD, TUNSTALL, STOKE-ON-TRENT, STAFFORDSHIRE ST6 5EZ, ☎ 01782 837303, FAX: 01782 838612, 8.30–4.45 MON–FRI, CLOSED 1–2 DAILY, 9.30–11.30 SAT. **PERMANENT DISCOUNT OUTLET**

Trade warehouse also dealing with members of the public. The majority of the stock here is lead crystal from Czechoslovakia and Poland, although there is also imported china, some English bone china, giftware such as figurines and ornaments, and earthenware dinner sets. All sold at trade prices. Open to the public. Free parking.

HARTLEY GREEN'S LEEDS POTTERY

ANCHOR ROAD, LONGTON, STOKE-ON-TRENT, STAFFORDSHIRE ST4 3DH, ☎ 01782 599959, 9–3.30 MON–THUR, 9–12.30 FRI, 10–2 LAST SAT EACH MONTH. **FACTORY SHOP**

Tableware and giftware which is very fancy, much of it being creamware. Dinner services, jugs, vases as well as gifts.

HUDSON AND MIDDLETON

SUTHERLAND WORKS, NORMACOT ROAD, LONGTON, STOKE-ON-TRENT, STAFFORDSHIRE ST3 1PP, ☎ 01782 319256, 8.30–5 MON–THUR, 8.30–1 FRI. **FACTORY SHOP**

Factory shop selling bone china mugs, wall plates and giftware; no dinner services sold.

L & M EUROTRADING

WOODLANDS, LEYCETT LANE, NEWCASTLE, STOKE-ON-TRENT, STAFFORDSHIRE ST5 6AD, ☎ 01782 839555, FAX: 01782 839555, 9–6 MON–SAT. **SECONDHAND SHOP**

Clearance company for businesses which relocate or shut down, specialising in the catering market, especially pubs, clubs, restaurants and supermarkets. When they go in, they take everything from bulbs to desks, chairs, computers, racking and shelving. You can find almost anything here, but if you're looking for anything to do with preparing food, there are fridges, freezers, cookers, microwaves, plates, saucepans, stainless steel sinks and tables. Cookers range from domestic size to commercial six-burner versions; freezers from domestic to 20ft by 18ft walk-in types, stainless steel sinks from 6ft to 14ft.

MATALAN

UNIT A, LICHFIELD STREET, BURTON-ON-TRENT, STAFFORDSHIRE DE14 3QZ, ☎ 01283 540856, FAX: 01283 540873, www.matalan.co.uk, 10–8 MON–FRI, 9–6 SAT, 11–5 SUN.

QUEENSDALE RETAIL PARK, SILKMORE LANE, STAFFORD STAFFORDSHIRE ST17 4SU, ☎ 01785 226211, FAX: 01785 226279, www.matalan.co.uk, 10–8 MON–FRI, 9–6 SAT, 11–5 SUN.

WOLSTANTON RETAIL PARK, WOLSTANTON, NEWCASTLE, STOKE-ON-TRENT, STAFFORDSHIRE ST5 1DY, ☎ 01782 711731, FAX: 01782 714201, www.matalan.co.uk, 9.30–8 MON–FRI, 9–6 SAT, 11–5 SUN.

VENTURA RETAIL PARK, BONE HILL DRIVE, TAMWORTH, STAFFORDSHIRE B78 3HB, ☎ 01827 50900, FAX: 01827 509151, www.matalan.co.uk, 10–8 MON–FRI, 9–6 SAT, 11–5 SUN. **PERMANENT DISCOUNT OUTLET**

See page 458 (BEDS)

MOORLAND POTTERY

CHELSEA WORKS, 72A MOORLAND ROAD, BURSLEM, STOKE-ON-TRENT, STAFFORDSHIRE ST6 1DY, ☎ 01782 834631, www.moorlandpottery.co.uk, 9–5 MON–FRI, 10–5 SAT. **FACTORY SHOP**

The place where Susie Cooper started her business, Moorland Pottery is one of the few art-ware potteries still producing hand-thrown, hand-turned and hand-painted pottery for the modern collector. The small factory shop sells tableware, giftware, reproduction Art Deco, reproduction Staffordshire dogs, and flatbacks and hand decorated spongeware – all manufactured at the works – at reasonable prices. There is a collectors' club which produces exclusive products for members and there are plans for a complete restoration of this 19th century building complete with original bottle kiln and enclosed cobbled yard.

ONEIDA

CHURCH STREET, STOKE-ON-TRENT, STAFFORDSHIRE ST4 1BX, ☎ 01782 749367, 9–5 MON–SAT, 10–4 SUN. **FACTORY SHOP**

See page 464 (CHESH)

PHOENIX WORKS

500 KING STREET, LONGTON, STOKE-ON-TRENT, STAFFORDSHIRE ST3 1EZ, ☎ 01782 595922, 9–5.30 MON–SAT, 11–4 SUN. **PERMANENT DISCOUNT OUTLET**

Victorian pottery factory restored to create a retail and visitor centre with a number of different businesses ranging from furniture from India, Thailand and the Philippines to leather goods, picture frames, white tableware, gifts and arts and crafts. All are competitively priced.

PONDEN MILL

UNIT 14–15, FREEPORT OUTLET MALL, PIT LANE, TALKE PITS, STOKE-ON-TRENT, STAFFORDSHIRE ST4 1BX, ☎ 01782 787150, 9–5 MON–SAT, 10–4 SUN. **FACTORY SHOP IN A FACTORY SHOPPING VILLAGE**

See page 464 (CHESH)

PORTMEIRION

LONDON ROAD, STOKE-ON-TRENT, STAFFORDSHIRE ST4 7QQ, ☎ 01782 411756, FAX: 01782 411756, www.portmeirion.co.uk, 9–5.30 MON–SAT, 10–4 SUN.

VICTORIA ROAD, FENTON, STOKE-ON-TRENT, STAFFORDSHIRE ST4 2HS, ☎ 01782 749131, FAX: 01782 749131, www.portmeirion.co.uk, 9–5.30 MON–SAT, 10–4 SUN.

SILVAN WORKS, NORMACOTT ROAD, LONGTON, STOKE-ON-TRENT, STAFFORDSHIRE ST3 1PL, ☎ 01782 326412, FAX: 01782 326412, **e-mail:** dmoss@portmeirion.co.uk, www.portmeirion.co.uk, 9–5.30 MON–SAT, 10–4 SUN. **FACTORY SHOP**

See page 475 (DERBY)

PRICE AND KENSINGTON POTTERIES

TRUBSHAW CROSS, LONGPORT, STOKE-ON-TRENT, STAFFORDSHIRE ST6 4LR, ☎ 01782 838631, FAX: 01782 811734, **e-mail:** pricekensington@ukonline.co.uk, 9.15–5 MON–FRI, 9.30–4.30 SAT, 10.30–4.30 SUN. **FACTORY SHOP**

Price & Kensington Pottery are a member of the Arthur Wood group and are renowned for their traditionally hand-decorated spongeware, novelty teapots and cottageware, although it now also produces an extensive selection of quality earthenware kitchen items. The on-site factory shop boasts a wide selection of selected seconds from both Price and Kensington and its parent company, Arthur Wood and Son.

ROYAL BRIERLEY CRYSTAL AT SPODE

CHURCH STREET, STOKE-ON-TRENT, STAFFORDSHIRE ST4 1BX, ☎ 01782 417510, www.royalbrierley.com, 9–5 MON–SAT, 10–4 SUN. **FACTORY SHOP**

Sells seconds of Royal Brierley crystal at 30% to 50% off retail price, with two special sales (phone for details). Poole Pottery and Royal Winton are also available, as is first quality crystal at discounted prices.

ROYAL DOULTON

LEEK NEW ROAD, BADDELEY GREEN, STOKE-ON-TRENT STAFFORDSHIRE ST2 7HS, ☎ 01782 291700, 9–5.30 MON–SAT, 11–5 SUN.

BESWICK FACTORY SHOP, BARFORD STREET, STOKE-ON-TRENT STAFFORDSHIRE ST3 2NN, ☎ 01782 291237, 9–5.30 MON–FRI. FORGE LANE, ETRURIA, STOKE-ON-TRENT, STAFFORDSHIRE ST3, FAX: 01782 284056, 10–8 MON–FRI, 9–6 SAT, 11–5 SUN.

REGENT WORKS, LAWLEY STREET, LONGTON, STOKE-ON-TRENT STAFFORDSHIRE ST3 2PH, ☎ 01782 291172, 9–5.30 MON–SAT, 10.30–4.30 SUN. **FACTORY SHOP**

Royal Doulton's factory shops which, as well as selling at normal retail prices, also offer a variety of discontinued and slightly imperfect pieces at reduced prices. The shops sell the company's three main brands: Minton, Royal Albert and Royal Doulton itself. For a tour of china factory shops in this area, go to the railway station and take the potteries tour. You can phone the information service on 01782 292292.

ROYAL DOULTON

VICTORIA ROAD, FENTON, STAFFORDSHIRE ST4 2PJ, ☎ 01782 291869, 9.- 5.30 MON–SAT, 10–4 SUN. **FACTORY SHOP**

Royal Doulton, Minton and Royal Albert ranges, focussing on tableware complemented by kitchenware and kitchen linen as well as Country Artist range, Bunnykins, Winnie the Pooh and Harry Potter.

SCOOPS CATALOGUE DISCOUNT STORES

UNIT 3, 567–569 BEARWOOD SHOPPING CENTRE, SMETHWICK, STAFFORDSHIRE B66 4BH, ☎ 0121 434 3086, FAX: 0121 429 8488, 9–5.30 MON–SAT, 11–3 SUN. **PERMANENT DISCOUNT OUTLET**

See page 468 (CO DURH)

SPODE

ELENORE STREET, STOKE-ON-TRENT, STAFFORDSHIRE ST4 1BX, ☎ 01782 744011, FAX: 01782 572526, **e-mail:** visitorcentre@spode, co.uk, www.spode.co.uk, 9–5 MON–SAT, 10–4 SUN. **FACTORY SHOP**

Spode, the oldest pottery in England, still on its original site, has two factory shops selling Spode china and earthenware at least 25% below the normal retail price, as well as holding regular sales at which further discounts are available on some discontinued lines. All the stock, including seconds, is current patterns and includes tableware, wall plaques, fine bone china dinner sets, tea and coffee sets and giftware. Also exceptional bargains in the whiteware shop. There is a museum and visitor centre which is open seven days a week with fully guided factory tours running every week day. There are conference facilities and an Italian restaurant on site and a selection of national and international concession shops selling at factory shop prices.

T J HUGHES

THREE SPIRES SHOPPING CENTRE, 46 BAKERS LANE, LICHFIELD, STAFFORDSHIRE WS13 6JF, ☎ 01543 418181, FAX: 01543 418185, **e-mail:** info@tjhughes.co.uk, www.tjhughes.co.uk, 9–5.30 MON–SAT, 10.30–4.30 SUN. **PERMANENT DISCOUNT OUTLET**

See page 465 (CHESH)

TAMS GROUP

SUTHERLAND ROAD, LONGTON, STOKE-ON-TRENT, STAFFORDSHIRE ST3 1JB, ☎ 01782 599667, FAX: 01782 598952, 9–4.30 MON–FRI, 9–4 SAT. 11–4 SUN. **FACTORY SHOP**

Discounted prices of between 50% and 75% for seconds and discontinued lines of Royal Grafton, Duchess, Tams and other chinaware, as well as Poole Pottery and a wide range of glassware and giftware.

THE FACTORY SHOP

QUEEN STREET CAR PARK, QUEEN STREET, MARKET DRAYTON, STAFFORDSHIRE TF9 1EQ, ☎ 01630 655673, 9–5 MON–SAT, 10–4 SUN. **FACTORY SHOP**

See page 465 (CHESH)

THE SHOE SHED

CASTLEFIELDS, NEWPORT ROAD, STAFFORD, STAFFORDSHIRE ST16 1BQ, ☎ 01785 211311 9–5.30 MON–SAT, 10–4 SUN. **FACTORY SHOP**

See page 481 (DORS)

TK MAXX

THE OCTAGON SHOPPING CENTRE, BURTON-ON-TRENT, STAFFORDSHIRE DE14 3TN, ☎ 01283 569891, www.tkmaxx.com, 9–5.30 MON–SAT, 10–4 SUN.

THE POTTERIES CENTRE, HANLEY, STOKE-ON-TRENT, STAFFORDSHIRE ST1 1PP, ☎ 01782 207509, www.tkmaxx.com, 9–5.30 MON–FRI, 9–6 SAT, 11–5 SUN, 8 ON THUR. **PERMANENT DISCOUNT OUTLET**

See page 458 (BEDS)

TUTBURY CRYSTAL FACTORY SHOP

BURTON STREET, TUTBURY, BURTON-ON-TRENT, STAFFORDSHIRE DE13 9NG, ☎ 01283 813281, **e-mail:** info@tutburycrystal.co.uk, www.tutburycrystal.co.uk, 9–5 MON–SAT, 10–4 SUN. **FACTORY SHOP**

Cut-glass from liqueur glasses and goblets to tumblers, jugs, decanters, rose bowls and vases, seconds of which are sold at discounts of up to 50%. There is also a tea room and large free car park with wheelchair access. Now has a visitor centre with free admission open six days a week, and factory tours can be booked: phone for details.

WATERFORD WEDGWOOD FACTORY SHOP

KING STREET, FENTON, STOKE-ON-TRENT, STAFFORDSHIRE ST4 3DQ, ☎ 01782 316161 **e-mail:** factory.shop@wedgwood.com, www.wedgwood.com, 9–5.30 MON–SAT, 11–5 SUN, 9–5.30 BANK HOLIDAYS. **FACTORY SHOP**

The Waterford Wedgwood factory shop features brands including Waterford Crystal, Wedgwood, Stuart Crystal, Coalport, Masons and Johnsons Brs. Whether looking for tableware, crystal or gifts, there's something here for everyone. Waterford and Stuart crystal ranges include many discontinued stemware and gift items, and for Wedgwood, you'll find a whole host of patterns available as seconds as well as discontinued lines, all at knock-down prices. And if you can't find the exact item you want as a second, there is also a best quality ordering service on a limited number of current patterns. There's always a bargain to be found and as well as the usual range of products, particular ranges are often promoted in the store. There is a large car park and facilities for the disabled.

WEBB IVORY

QUEENSBRIDGE WORKS, QUEEN STREET, BURTON-ON-TRENT, STAFFORDSHIRE DE14 3LP, ☎ 01283 506371, 9–5 MON–FRI, 9–2 SAT. **FACTORY SHOP**

Items from the charity catalogues at reduced prices including cards, gifts, soft toys, books, pens, lamps, kitchenware and clothes. Stock is constantly changing, and discounts start from 50%.

WILKINSON STORES

OLD HALL STREET, HANLEY, STOKE-ON-TRENT, STAFFORDSHIRE, ☎ 01782 279225, www.wilko.co.uk, 8.30–6 MON–FRI, 8 ON THUR, 11–5 SUN. MAIL ORDER.

CASTLE HOUSE, 47–48 IRONMARKET, NEWCASTLE UNDER LYME, STAFFORDSHIRE ST5 1PD., ☎ 01782 714334, www.wilko.co.uk, 8.30–5.30 MON–SAT. **PERMANENT DISCOUNT OUTLET**

See page 466 (CHESH)

SUFFOLK

BUYRIGHT OF HADLEIGH

CALAIS STREET, HADLEIGH, IPWICH, SUFFOLK IP7 5EW, ☎ 01473 822626, 9–5.30 MON–SAT, 10.30–4.30 SUN. **PERMANENT DISCOUNT OUTLET**

Discount shop selling a mixture of clothes, household textiles, ceramics, kitchenware, knitting yarn, garden tools, curtains, toys, stationery, dusters, Christmas decorations, masking tape, lingerie and a host of other items. Stock changes regularly because the low prices mean a quick turnover. Some items are seconds or end of season stock from the major chain stores.

MATALAN

EASLEA ROAD, BURY ST EDMUNDS, SUFFOLK IP32 7BY, ☎ 01284 748300, FAX: 01284 749146, www.matalan.co.uk, 9–8 MON–FRI, 9–6 SAT, 10–4 SUN. **PERMANENT DISCOUNT OUTLET**

See page 458 (BEDS)

QD STORES

47–51 CARR STREET, THE EASTGATE CENTRE, IPSWICH, SUFFOLK IP4 1HB, ☎ 01473 284220, 9–5.30 MON–SAT.

UNIT 21–25, BRITTEN CENTRE, LOWESTOFT, SUFFOLK NR32 1LR, ☎ 01502 565222, 9–5.30 MON–SAT.

9 IPSWICH STREET, STOWMARKET, SUFFOLK IP14 1AH, ☎ 01449 770438, 9–5.30 MON–SAT. **PERMANENT DISCOUNT OUTLET**

See page 458 (BEDS)

THE CROCKERY BARN

ASHLEIGH FARM, ASHBOCKING, IPSWICH, SUFFOLK IP6 9JS, ☎ 01473 890123, FAX: 01473 890123, www.thecrockerybarn.co.uk, 10–5 MON–SAT, 11–4 SUN. **PERMANENT DISCOUNT OUTLET**

Mountains of white tableware, huge stocks of Portmeirion, Spode, Emma Bridgewater, Nicholas Mosse and imported ceramics. Stock bought directly from Italy and Portugal can be found nowhere else in the UK and is good value. Fresh deliveries arrive weekly so there is always something new to see. Also now stocks an extensive range of basketwear, in a barn of its own called the Long Barn. Refreshments and light lunches are available in the Barnyard Café.

THE CURTAIN AGENCY AND PERIOD HOUSE INTERIORS

73 HIGH STREET, NEEDHAM MARKET, IPSWICH, SUFFOLK IP6 8AN, ☎ 01449 722885, 10–5 MON–FRI, 10–1 SAT. **SECONDHAND SHOP**

An emporium of quality secondhand and new made-to-measure or ready-to-hang curtains. There is also a great range of permanently cut-price, quality fabrics available by the metre. These include designer names such as Gainsborough Silk Weaving Co for classic brocades; Linwood chenille, Archive printed linens, and Toile de Jouy from GP & J Baker; Parker Knoll fabrics for upholstery; and many others. Old and new Continental accessories, including tie-backs and trimmings, are also available. The shop also has a large stock of old French linen sheets, many hand woven and monogrammed, which are made into sumptuous curtains and Roman blinds as well as being used for luxurious bed linen and upholstery. Decorative, French garden and occasional furniture, period chandeliers, wall lights, old armchairs (for re-upholstering), traditional curtain poles and fittings, together with unusual gifts makes this an Aladdin's cave of inspiration for anyone wanting something special for their home.

THE FACTORY SHOP

BARTON BUSINESS CENTRE, BARTON ROAD, BURY ST EDMUNDS, SUFFOLK IP32 7BQ, ☎ 01284 701578, 9.30–5 MON–FRI, 10–6 SAT, 10–4 SUN.

LONDON ROAD, WRENTHAM, NR BECCLES, SUFFOLK NR34 7HJ, ☎ 01502 676100, 9–5.30 MON–SAT, 10.30–4.30 SUN. **FACTORY SHOP**

See page 465 (CHESH)

TK MAXX

1ST FLOOR, BUTTERMARKET SHOPPING CENTRE, IPSWICH, SUFFOLK IP1 1DT, ☎ 01473 226800, www.tkmaxx.com, 9–5.30 MON–FRI, 9–6 SAT, 11–5 SUN. **PERMANENT DISCOUNT OUTLET**

See page 458 (BEDS)

SURREY

CHINA 2 REPLACE

57 DEEPCUT BRIDGE ROAD, CAMBERLEY, SURREY GU16 6QT, ☎ 08707 509889, FAX: 01252 837231, **e-mail:** jill@chinareplacements.co.uk, www.china2replace.co.uk, 10–5 THUR–SAT, THEN ON ANSWERPHONE AND FAX. MAIL ORDER. **PERMANENT DISCOUNT OUTLET**

Specialist stockists and finders of discontinued English 20th-century tableware such as Royal Doulton, Wedgwood, Royal Worcester, Spode and Denby. Single or multiple pieces bought and sold. Mail order or collections close to M3 Junction 3/M4. Don't buy an entire new service when you can replenish your treasured collection. Now, you can visit their shop full of antique and collectable china and the warehouse with over 1,000 different patterns available. Open 10am to 5pm Thursday to Saturday; phone first to check availability.

CHOICE DISCOUNT STORES LIMITED

1 WARWICK QUADRANT, LONDON ROAD, REDHILL, SURREY RH1 1NN, ☎ 01737 772777, 9–6 MON–WED, 9–7 THUR, 9–6 FRI–SAT. **PERMANENT DISCOUNT OUTLET**

See page 461 (CAMBS)

CURTAIN CALL

52 FRIARS STILE ROAD, RICHMOND, SURREY TW10 6NQ, ☎ 020 8332 6250, FAX: 020 8940 6137, **e-mail:** curtaincall@blueyonder.co.uk, www.curtain-call.co.uk, 9.30–5.30 MON–FRI, 10–6 SAT, CLOSED WED. **SECONDHAND SHOP**

Curtain Call in Richmond sells nearly-new curtains for at least half of their original price. The current stock of over 400 pairs includes Colefax and Fowler, Osborne & Little and Designers Guild fabrics. The curtains range in price from £50 to £1,500 for sets which may include valances, swags and tails, as well as headboards and matching bedspreads. All the nearly-new curtains can be taken home overnight on approval, so that you can see the curtains in your own home before you buy. If you have curtains to sell, they will agree a price with you and, once the curtains have sold, you receive 60% of the selling price. An alteration service is also available on the premises, as well as a making-up service using your own fabric. New curtains can usually be made within a three week time span. They have a large range of tassels and tie-backs, as well as a comprehensive range of trimmings to order, which can really update and finish off new or nearly-new curtains. They also have a large selection of made-to-measure fabrics which can be made up in three weeks. This range encompasses everything from natural textured cottons through to more elaborate toiles, damask, tapestry fabrics and silk in 50 different colours. The samples of these fabrics are made up as full-sized curtains for you to borrow overnight to try at home, before ordering. They now offer a wide range of luxurious and unusual cushions in tapestry and velvet designs, as well as some individual one-off special hand-printed designs by local designers, and a range of small gifts such as hand-beaded photo frames, handbags and embroidered voile panels.

GENEVIEVE THE GALLERY

13 VICTORIA STREET, ENGLEFIELD GREEN, SURREY TW20 0QY, ☎ 01784 430516, **e-mail:** genevieveneilson@hotmail.com, www.genevieves.co.uk, 10–5 TUE–SAT 10–8 THUR. **FACTORY SHOP**

A ceramicist of handmade and handpainted items with bright floral, fruit and foliage designs, Genevieve Neilson is now manufacturing and retailing from the same outlet. At the back is the workshop; at the front, the shop where she sells her own products at factory direct prices. Among other items on sale are mirrors, candles, candlesticks, clocks, soft toys, cards and gift wrap. Commissions taken for specific orders. You can also try your hand at painting your own plate or pot.

MATALAN

268–278 HIGH STREET, SUTTON, SURREY SM1 1PG, ☎ 020 8652 9600, FAX: 020 8770 3581, www.matalan.co.uk, 9–8 MON–FRI, 9–6 SAT, 11–5 SUN. **PERMANENT DISCOUNT OUTLET**

See page 458 (BEDS)

NOTTING HILL HOUSING TRUST RICHMOND

394 RICHMOND ROAD, SURREY TW1 2DY, ☎ 020 8891 6819, **e-mail:** charityshop@nhhg.org.uk, www.nottinghillonline.com/supporters, 10–6 MON–SAT, 12.30–5.30 SUN. **SECONDHAND SHOP**

See page 514 (LOND)

THE FACTORY SHOP LTD

THE ENGINE SHED, CONSORT WAY EAST, HORLEY, SURREY RH6 7AU, ☎ 01293 823883, 9–5.30 MON–SAT, 10–4 SUN. **FACTORY SHOP**

See page 465 (CHESH)

THE LIGHTING AGENCY & TRADING COMPANY

LION & LAMB YARD, FARNHAM, SURREY GU9 7LL, ☎ 01252 719192, FAX: 01252 719192, www.lightingagency.co.uk, 10–5.30 MON–SAT. **PERMANENT DISCOUNT OUTLET**

Lighting Agency and Trading Company in Farnham offers a variety of quality secondhand and antique chandeliers and wall lights, many of which have been rewired to a tested and certified UK standard. Others which have not been wired have the electrical or gas parts removed for easy rewiring. A wiring service can be provided. The Lighting Agency also offers a unique range of small chandeliers available in many colours and sizes. This Aladdin's Cave of shades, lamps and chandeliers is often the haunt of dealers and design decorators.

TK MAXX

THE DRUMMOND CENTRE, CROYDON, SURREY CR0 1TY, ☎ 020 8686 9753, www.tkmaxx.com, 9–6 MON–SAT, 9 ON THUR, 11–5 SUN.

102 HIGH STREET, EPSOM, SURREY, ☎ 01372 729060, www.tkmaxx.com, PHONE FOR DETAILS OF OPENING TIMES..

BISHOPS PALACE HOUSE, 2 CLARENCE STREET, KINGSTON SURREY KT1 1PB, ☎ 020 8974 6296, www.tkmaxx.com, 9–6 MON–WED, 9–9 THUR–FRI, 8–7 SAT, 11–5. SUN.

TIMES SQUARE SHOPPING CENTRE, HIGH STREET, SUTTON, SURREY SM1 1LF, ☎ 020 8770 7786, www.tkmaxx.com, 9–5.30 MON–FRI, 8 ON THUR, 9–6 SAT, 11–5 SUN.

THE PEACOCKS CENTRE, WOKING, SURREY GU21 1GA, ☎ 01483 771660, www.tkmaxx.com, 9.30–6 MON–FRI, 8 ON THUR, 9–6 SAT, 11–5 SUN. **PERMANENT DISCOUNT OUTLET**

See page 458 (BEDS)

SUSSEX

BAGGAGE FACTORY

8 THE VILLAGE SQUARE, BRIGHTON MARINA, BRIGHTON, WEST SUSSEX BN2 5WA, ☎ 01273 699996, www.baggagefactory.co.uk, 10–6 MON–SUN. **FACTORY SHOP IN A FACTORY SHOPPING VILLAGE**

See page 489 (HAMPS)

BRIGHTON MARINA

CITY OF BRIGHTON AND HOVE, EAST SUSSEX BN2 5WB, ☎ 01273 818504, FAX: 01273 818701, 10–LATE SEVEN DAYS A WEEK. **FACTORY SHOPPING VILLAGE**

The UK and Europe's largest marina. Boasts an exciting range of outlet shops combined with excellent bars, restaurants and leisure facilities. Currently hosts 11 outlet stores, such as PULSE skating solutions, The Factory Shop, Leading Labels and many more. The marina is currently investing millions into additional facilities, planned to open at the end of 2002, which will include a further 16 outlet stores including some household names.

HEIRLOOMS LTD

2 ARUN BUSINESS PARK, BOGNOR REGIS, SUSSEX PO22 9SX, ☎ 01243 820252, FAX: 01243 821174, 10–5 EVERY FRIDAY AND ONE SAT MORNING EACH MONTH. **FACTORY SHOP**

Sleep like a king, dine like a lord or lounge like a lady . . . the Heirlooms factory shop is brimming with luxurious linen at affordable prices, the majority of which are made on the premises. Elegant and exceptionally high quality bed linens in Egyptian cotton, cotton percale and the finest polycotton percale, in four sizes up to super-king, are sold in this 1, 200 square foot outlet, together with the very best Egyptian cotton towels. There's also table linens using classic hem stitching or handmade laces, a cornucopia of gifts with exquisite laces and embroidery, and handmade christening and baby wear. Sterling silver frames, waterproof picnic rugs, candles, nightwear, Isis ceramics and seasonal variations complete the diverse selection of really high quality products. Normally only found in the most exclusive shops, homes and palaces all over the world, here you can buy ends of lines and slight seconds at between 30% and 65% off the recommended retail price. This busy exporting company only opens the factory shop about once a week, so check before making what will be a worthwhile journey. As they manufacture, they can make bedlinen and tablecloths to order in any size. Free parking.

MATALAN

CARDEN AVENUE, HOLLINGBURY INDUSTRIAL ESTATE, BRIGHTON, EAST SUSSEX BN1 8AR, ☎ 01273 543800, FAX: 01273 502608, www.matalan.co.uk, 10–8 MON–FRI, 9–6 SAT, 10.30–4.30 SUN.

SOVEREIGN HARBOUR RETAIL PARK, PEVENSY BAY ROAD, EASTBOURNE, EAST SUSSEX BN23 6JH, ☎ 01323 470347, FAX: 01323 470601, www.matalan.co.uk, 10–8 MON–FRI, 9–6 SAT, 10.30–4.30 SUN. **PERMANENT DISCOUNT OUTLET**

See page 458 (BEDS)

RYE POTTERY LTD

77 FERRY ROAD, RYE, SUSSEX TN31 7DJ, ☎ 01797 223038, FAX: 01797 225802, **e-mail:** sales@ryepottery.sagehost.co.uk, 9.30–12.30, 1.30–4 SAT. **FACTORY SHOP**

There is always a selection of seconds available in distinctive, hand-decorated designs. No two items of this Majolica or Delft decorated pottery are the same. Choose from Chaucer figures, American folk heroes or Pastoral Primitives. Seconds are usually two-thirds of retail price.

SECOND EDITION

46–48 HIGH STREET, BOGNOR REGIS, SUSSEX PO21 1SP, ☎ 01243 868319, 9.30–5 MON–SAT. **PERMANENT DISCOUNT OUTLET**

Second Edition sells a wide range of household goods including lamps, china ornaments, tablecloths, giftware, garden ornaments, cushion covers, duvets, pillows and kitchenware. Some are seconds, some perfects and discounts range from 25% to 50%. There's a wide range of high street and chainstore brand names. Kitchenware includes storage jars, assorted mugs, assorted melamine and various designs in kitchen linens.

T J HUGHES

14–26 THE BROADWAY, CRAWLEY, SUSSEX RH10 1DT, ☎ 01293 537373, FAX: 01293 611676, **e-mail:** info@tjhughes.co.uk, www.tjhughes.co.uk, 9–5.30 MON–FRI, 8 ON THUR, 9–6 SAT, 11–5 SUN.

177–178 TERMINUS ROAD, EASTBOURNE, SUSSEX BN21 3NX, ☎ 01323 732222, FAX: 01323 730110, **e-mail:** info@tjhughes.co.uk, www.tjhughes.co.uk, 9–5.30 MON–FRI, 9–6 SAT, 10.30–4.30 SUN. **PERMANENT DISCOUNT OUTLET**

See page 465 (CHESH)

THE DENBY SHOWROOM

BROWNINGS FARM, BLACKBOYS, UCKFIELD, SUSSEX TN22 5HG, ☎ 01825 890 664, www.chinahunt.co.uk, 10-1 SAT. **PERMANENT DISCOUNT OUTLET**

Buys and sells discontinued tableware from Denby, Poole and Marks & Spencer, among others. A china matching service is available. Phone for more details.

THE FACTORY SHOP LTD

BRIGHTON MARINA, THE VILLAGE SQUARE, BRIGHTON SUSSEX BN2 5WA, ☎ 01273 818590, 10–6 MON–FRI, 10–6 SAT, 10.30–4.30 SUN. **FACTORY SHOP IN A FACTORY SHOPPING VILLAGE**

See page 465 (CHESH)

THE SHOE SHED

3 THE ARCADE, BOGNOR REGIS, SUSSEX PO21 1LH, ☎ 01243 829600, 9–5.30 MON–SAT, 10–4 SUN. **FACTORY SHOP**

See page 481 (DORS)

THE TRUGGERY

COOPERS CROFT, HERSTMONCEUX, SUSSEX BN27 1QL, ☎ 01323 832314, www.truggery.co.uk, 10–5 TUE–FRI, SAT 10–1. **FACTORY SHOP**

Manufacturers of traditional Sussex trugs, shallow wooden gardening baskets made from sweet chestnut and willow and particular to the region. Prices range from £15 to £50. Also supply English willow baskets, all shapes and sizes from £15 to £40, kitchen storage shelf baskets, prawning baskets, duck nesters, and local wooden crafts such as hay rakes, dibbers and miniature sheep hurdles to use as borders. Parking provided.

TK MAXX

36–37 NORTH STREET, BRIGHTON, SUSSEX BN1 1EB, ☎ 01273 727483, www.tkmaxx.com, 9–6 MON–SAT, 7 ON THUR, 11–5 SUN.

13 THE MONTAGUE CENTRE, WORTHING, SUSSEX BN11 1YJ, ☎ 01903 234141, www.tkmaxx.com, 9–6 MON–SAT, 11–5 SUN. **PERMANENT DISCOUNT OUTLET**

See page 458 (BEDS)

WARWICKSHIRE AND WEST MIDLANDS

CATALOGUE BARGAIN SHOP

ROCK BOTTOM CLEARANCE, 24–28 KING STREET, DUDLEY, WEST MIDLANDS DY2 8NY, ☎ 01384 458112, www.bargaincrazy.com, 9.30–5.30 MON–SAT, 10–4 SUN.

78 HIGH STREET, STOURBRIDGE, WEST MIDLANDS DY8 1DX, ☎ 01384 374544, www.bargaincrazy.com, 9–5.30 MON–SAT, 10–4 SUN.

17 BRADFORD STREET, WALSALL WEST MIDLANDS WS1 1PB, ☎ 01922 722286, www.bargaincrazy.com, 9–5.30 MON–SAT, 10.30–4.30 SUN. **PERMANENT DISCOUNT OUTLET**

See page 461 (CAMBS)

CATALOGUE DISCOUNT STORE

SWAN CENTRE, COVENTRY ROAD, YARDLEY, BIRMINGHAM, WEST MIDLANDS B26 1AJ, ☎ 0121 707 6585, 9–5.30 MON–SAT.

UNIT 67, THE MOOR CENTRE, BRIERLEY HILL, DUDLEY, WEST MIDLANDS DY5 3AH, ☎ 01384 262537, 9–5.30 MON–SAT. **PERMANENT DISCOUNT OUTLET**

See page 499 (LANCS)

CHINASEARCH

PO BOX 1202, KENILWORTH, WARWICKSHIRE CV8 2WW, ☎ 01926 512402, FAX: 01926 859311, **e-mail:** jackie@chinasearch.uk.com, **e-mail:** helen@chinasearch.uk.com, www.chinasearch.uk.com, 9–5 MON–SAT. MAIL ORDER. VISITORS WELCOME BY APPOINTMENT ONLY. **PERMANENT DISCOUNT OUTLET**

Your chance to find the discontinued items of tableware that you thought you would never see again. Chinasearch, who are frequently featured in the national press and on television and radio, are leading specialists in finding and supplying china and pottery tableware and collectables. In their impressive Kenilworth warehouse, which is frequently described as 'an Aladdin's cave', they are continually adding to their stock of over 3,000 patterns. Most of these patterns have been discontinued over the last 50 years and are unobtainable from the original suppliers. Manufacturers include Royal Doulton, Minto, Crown Derby, Royal Albert, Paragon, Colclough, Crown Staffordshire, Booths, Wedgwood, Coalport, Susie Cooper, Adams, Johnsons, Masons, Meakin, Midwinter, Churchill, Royual Worcester, Palissy, Copeland Spode, Aynsley, Denby, Hornsea, Poole, Marks & Spencer, Portmeirion, Noritake, Burleigh, T G Green, Thomas and Villeroy & Boch. Friendly staff are always willing to help. If Chinasearch cannot supply the required items immediately, details are kept on file until the pieces are obtained. There is no registration fee and no obligation to buy. They are also pleased to hear from people who wish to sell unwanted tableware or collectables and can arrange collection countrywide. Please enclose an SAE with correspondence.

DJ GOLD DEPOT LTD

37 VYSE STREET, BIRMINGHAM, WEST MIDLANDS B18 6JY, ☎ 0121 554 6165, FAX: 0121 554 2438, 9–4 MON–SAT, SUN BEFORE CHRISTMAS ONLY. **PERMANENT DISCOUNT OUTLET**

Manufacturers of wedding rings, engagement rings, bracelets, necklaces, earrings and pendants, with the emphasis on diamond jewellery. As you are dealing directly with the manufacturer, you benefit from savings of at least 30% off the high street equivalent. Gold jewellery can be made to customer's own design with any gem stones. Also sells glassware and pewter items.

DUNELM MILL SHOP

20 QUEENS ROAD, NUNEATON, WARWICKSHIRE CV11 5JW, ☎ 024 7634 4711, FAX: 024 7637 5097, www.dunelm-mill.co.uk, 9–5 MON–SAT, 5.30 ON FRI.

REGENT STREET, NUNEATON, WARWICKSHIRE CV11 4BL, ☎ 024 7637 0090, FAX: 024 7637 0092, www.dunelm-mill.co.uk, 9–6 MON–SAT, 8 ON THUR, FRI, 10–4 SUN.

UNIT D, BIRCHLEY INDUSTRIAL ESTATE, BIRCHFIELD LANE, OLDBURY, WEST MIDLANDS B69 1DT, ☎ 0121 544 7755, FAX: 0121 544 3204, www.dunelm-mill.co.uk, 9–6 TUES–THUR, SAT, 9–8 MON, FRI, 10.30–4.30 SUN.

CLOCK TOWERS CENTRE, MANNINGS WALK, RUGBY, WARWICKSHIRE CV21 2JT, ☎ 01788 541171, FAX: 01788 551947, www.dunelm-mill.co.uk, 9–5.30 MON–SAT, 10–4 SUN.
PERMANENT DISCOUNT OUTLET

See page 458 (BEDS)

INTERNATIONAL STOCK LTD

95–100 REA STREET, DIGBETH, BIRMINGHAM, WEST MIDLANDS B5 6HA, ☎ 0121 622 3232, **e-mail:** mail@international-stock.co.uk, www.international-stock.co.uk, 9–5 MON–SAT, 10–4 SUN, CLOSED 1 ON WED.

1–17 SILVER STREET, KINGS HEATH, BIRMINGHAM, WEST MIDLANDS B14 7QX, ☎ 0121 443 3232, FAX: 0121 444 1792, **e-mail:** mail@international-stock.co.uk, www.international-stock.co.uk, 9–6 MON–SAT, CLOSED 1 ON WED. **PERMANENT DISCOUNT OUTLET**

Bankrupt, fire and flood damaged articles from CDs and videos, household goods and clothes to DIY tools and television sets, carpets and cookers. The King's Heath branch is a two-storey warehouse with ever-changing stock. The upper floor is devoted to electrical goods, some marked down to 30% of their normal retail cost. The Digbeth branch sells bigger items such as kitchens, flooring, tiles, dining room and lounge furniture, central heating radiators and a large clothing section for all the family, all of which is sold below wholesale price and in some cases below manufacturers' cost price. Top brand name kitchens, when in stock, are discounted by 75%.

M LATIF & SONS

NEW CANAL STREET, DIGBETH, BIRMINGHAM, WEST MIDLANDS B5 5PL, ☎ 0121 643 2822, 9.30–5.30 MON–SAT, 8 ON THUR, 10–2.30 SUN. **PERMANENT DISCOUNT OUTLET**

Household and electrical goods, bedding, linens, ready-made curtains, clothes for all the family, pictures, garden equipment, toys, gifts and silk flowers, all of which are discounted as they are ex-catalogue and department store surplus from high street stores.

MATALAN

GALLAGHER RETAIL PARK, STONEY STANTON ROAD, COVENTRY, WARWICKSHIRE CV6 5QQ, ☎ 0247 663 7320, FAX: 0247 663 8732, www.matalan.co.uk, 10–8 MON–FRI, 9–6 SAT, 11–5 SUN.

WHEELER ROAD, SEVEN STARS TRADING ESTATE, WHITELEY, COVENTRY SOUTH, WARWICKSHIRE CV3 2LB, ☎ 0247 621 7320, FAX: 0247 621 7321, www.matalan.co.uk, 9.30–8 MON–FRI, 9–6 SAT, 11–5 SUN.

SPRING VALE RETAIL PARK, BILSTON, WEST MIDLANDS WV14 0QL, ☎ 01902 406160, FAX: 01902 409534, www.matalan.co.uk, 10–8 MON–FRI, 9–6 SAT, 10–4 SUN.

DARTMOUTH CIRCUS, MIDDLEWAY, BIRMINGHAM, WEST MIDLANDS B6 4BA, ☎ 0121 503 4700, FAX: 0121 333 3870, www.matalan.co.uk, 9–8 MON–FRI, 9–6 SAT, 11–5 SUN.

PORTWAY ROAD, PORTWAY GREEN, OLDBURY, BIRMINGHAM, WEST MIDLANDS B69 2BZ, ☎ 0121 544 4899, FAX: 0121 544 4394, www.matalan.co.uk, 10–8 MON–FRI, 9–6 SAT, 11–5 SUN.

2 FLAXLEY PARKWAY, STECHFORD RETAIL PARK, BIRMINGHAM, WEST MIDLANDS B33 9AN, ☎ 0121 789 5950, FAX: 0121 783 2170, www.matalan.co.uk, 10–8 MON–FRI, 9–6 SAT, 11–5 SUN.

MAYBIRD CENTRE, BIRMINGHAM ROAD, STRATFORD-UPON-AVON, WARWICKSHIRE CV37 OHZ, ☎ 01789 262223, FAX: 01789 262230, www.matalan.co.uk, 10–8 MON–FRI, 9–6 SAT, 11–5 SUN.

UNIT 9, BROADWAY RETAIL PARK, BESCOT CRESCENT, WALSALL, WEST MIDLANDS WS1 4DK, ☎ 01922 615188, FAX: 01922 611984, www.matalan.co.uk, 10–8 MON–FRI, 9–6 SAT, 11–5 SUN.

WALSALL RETAIL PARK, REEDSWOODS WAY, WALSALL, WEST MIDLANDS WS2 8XA, ☎ 01922 619830, FAX: 01922 746898, www.matalan.co.uk, 10–8 MON–FRI, 9–6 SAT, 10.30–4.30 SUN.

HOWARD STREET, BIRMINGHAM ROAD, WOLVERHAMPTON, WEST MIDLANDS WV2 3LQ, ☎ 01902 352813, FAX: 01902 352908, www.matalan.co.uk, 10–8 MON–FRI, 9–6 SAT, 11–5 SUN. **PERMANENT DISCOUNT OUTLET**

See page 458 (BEDS)

MILL OUTLETS LTD

2 CANNON PARK CENTRE, CANLEY, COVENTRY WARWICKSHIRE CV4 7AY, ☎ 024 7641 8441, 9–5.30 MON–WED, 9–6 THUR, FRI, 8.30–5 SAT, 10–4 SUN.

33 SOUTHAM ROAD, DUNCHURCH, RUGBY, WARWICKSHIRE CV22 6NL, ☎ 01788 816008, 9–5 MON–SAT, 10–4 SUN.

134 THE PARADE, LEAMINGTON SPA, WARWICKSHIRE CV32 4AG, ☎ 01926 744332, 9–5.30 MON–SAT, 11–5 SUN.

ABBEYGATE SHOPPING CENTRE, NUNEATON, WARWICKSHIRE CV11 5HL, ☎ 0247 638 6669, 9–5 MON–SAT.

3 ALBERT STREET, RUGBY, WARWICKSHIRE WARWICKSHIRE CV21 2RZ, ☎ 01788 542947, 9–5 MON–SAT. **PERMANENT DISCOUNT OUTLET**

Specialises in curtains, net curtains, bedding, bed linens, towels, kitchen textiles and other household textiles. They also offer ranges of hand knitting yarns, men's and women's socks, hosiery and underwear. Merchandise comes direct from the manufacturers, often made up of clearance stock or chainstore overmakes and seconds. Prices are very competitive with savings of up to 50% and more off manufacturer's recommended prices.

PROBUS MAYFAIR PLC

UNIT 20, EMPIRE CLOSE, EMPIRE INDUSTRIAL PLC, ALDRIDGE, WEST MIDLANDS WS9 8UQ, ☎ 01922 453040, 10–4 THUR–SUN. **FACTORY SHOP**

Probus Mayfair plc manufacture a wide range of small items for the kitchen for top Knightsbridge and mail order names. Kitchenware overstocks and seconds are sold off at factory shop at substantial discounts. The shop also stocks some cookware imported from the Far East. As well as utensils, oven gloves, cookware and chopping boards, there are aprons, tea towels, icing cookware and tablecloths. Most of the stock they make is textile-based and there are no ceramics or saucepans.

ROYAL BRIERLEY CRYSTAL

TIPTON ROAD, DUDLEY, WEST MIDLANDS DY1 4SH, ☎ 0121 530 5600, www.royalbrierley.com, 9–5.30 MON–SAT, 10–4 SUN. **FACTORY SHOP**

Sells seconds of Royal Brierley crystal at 30% to 50% off retail price, with two special sales (phone for details). Poole Pottery, David Bradbury, Halcyon Days, Woods of Windsor, Ponden Mill, Lifestyle Products, La Casa Del Cristallo, Arthur Price, Royal Doulton and Royal Winton are also available, as is first quality crystal at discounted prices. There is also a museum and factory tours where you can watch a traditional craftsman blowing and cutting English lead crystal. An on-site restaurant serves hot and cold food and drinks, there is free parking, wheelchair access and disabled facilities.

ROYAL DOULTON

CRYSTAL GLASS CENTRE, CHURTON HOUSE, STOURBRIDGE, WEST MIDLANDS DY8 4AJ, ☎ 01384 354400, 9–5.30 MON–SAT. **FACTORY SHOP**

See page 537 (STAFFS)

ROYAL WORCESTER & SPODE FACTORY SHOP

THE CRYSTAL GLASS CENTRE, CHURTON HOUSE, AUDNAM, STOURBRIDGE, WEST MIDLANDS DY8 4AJ, ☎ 01384 354718, www.royal-worcester.co.uk, 9.30–5.30 MON–SAT, 10–4 SUN. **FACTORY SHOP**

See page 465 (CHESH)

SCOOPS CATALOGUE DISCOUNT STORE

63 HIGH STREET, BROWNHILLS, WEST MIDLANDS WS8 6HH, ☎ 01543 372933, 9–5.30 MON–SAT.

UNIT 6–7 MOOR CENTRE, BRIERLEY HILL, DUDLEY, WEST MIDLANDS DY5 3AH, ☎ 01384 262537, 9–5.30 MON–SAT.

SWAN MARKET CENTRE, YARDLEY, BIRMINGHAM, WEST MIDLANDS, ☎ 0121 707 6585, 9–5.30 MON–SAT. **PERMANENT DISCOUNT OUTLET**

See page 468 (CO DURH)

STAGE 2

AUSTIN DRIVE, COURTHOUSE GREEN, COVENTRY, WARWICKSHIRE CV6 7NS, ☎ 024 76 681520, 10–8 MON–FRI, 10–5 SAT, 11–5 SUN. **PERMANENT DISCOUNT OUTLET**

See page 461 (CAMBS)

STUART CRYSTAL

RED HOUSE GLASSWORKS, WORDSLEY, STOURBRIDGE, DUDLEY, WEST MIDLANDS DY8 4AA, ☎ 01384 261777, 9–5 MON–SAT, 10–4 SUN. **FACTORY SHOP**

Seconds of Stuart Crystal sold at about 30% discount. The selection includes wine glasses, flower holders, perfume holders, everyday tableware, salt and pepper sets, wine coolers, cutlery and photo frames Also seasonal special offers. First quality is also for sale at the appropriate price as is a Jasper Conran range.

T J HUGHES

98–100 LOWER PRECINCT, COVENTRY, WARWICKSHIRE CV1 1DX, ☎ 0247 662 7450, FAX: 0247 663 3627, **e-mail:** info@tjhughes.co.uk, www.tjhughes.co.uk, 9–5.30 MON–SAT, 10.30–4.30 SUN.

27 BELL STREET, MANDER CENTRE, WOLVERHAMPTON, WEST MIDLANDS WV1 3PT, ☎ 01902 428011, FAX: 01902 420248, **e-mail:** info@tjhughes.co.uk, www.tjhughes.co.uk, 9–5.30 MON–FRI, 8.30–5.30 SAT, 10.30–4.30 SUN. **PERMANENT DISCOUNT OUTLET**

See page 465 (CHESH)

THE CRAFT COMPANY

23 COTEN END, WARWICK, WARWICKSHIRE CV34 4NT, ☎ 01926 492505, FAX: 01926 492535, **e-mail:** heather@craftcompany.co.uk, 9–5.30 MON–SAT. MAIL ORDER ALSO.
PERMANENT DISCOUNT OUTLET

Needlecraft warehouse which also operates a mail order leaflet. Due to bulk buying, savings are between 5% and 10%. There is every type of thread, tapestry wool, stranded cotton, shade cards, metallic threads, crochet cotton, flexi-hoops, needles, tapestry frames, scissors, beads, anchor accessories such as organiser boxes, as well as fabrics (Aida, Evenweave and Zweigart linens). They also sell sugar craft equipment, marzipan, fondant, cutters, drums, boards, boxes, pillars, sugar craft colours, wires, stamens, ribbons, nozzles, sugarcraft tools, crimpers, candles, mottoes, special occasion cakes and veiners by retail and mail order.

THE OUTLET

HATTON COUNTRY WORLD, DARK LANE, HATTON, NEAR WARWICK, WARWICKSHIRE CV35 8XA, ☎ 01926 842761, **e-mail:** hatton@hattonworld.com, www.hattonworld.com, 10–5 SEVEN DAYS A WEEK. **PERMANENT DISCOUNT OUTLET**

Hatton Country World consists of a Shopping Village with 25 craft and specialist shops and an antiques centre and, for bargain hunters, The Outlet, a department-style store selling discounted brand names in women's and men's clothes, kitchenware and gifts. All are housed in a charming cluster of converted Victorial farm buildings. There is a farm park and outdoor activity centre.

TK MAXX

THE GALLAGHER RETAIL PARK, STONEY STANTON ROAD, COVENTRY, WARWICKSHIRE CV6 5QG, ☎ 02476 664158, www.tkmaxx.com, 10–8 MON–FRI, 9–6 SAT, 11–5 SUN.

UNITS 3-4 CASTLE VALE RETAIL PARK, BIRMINGHAM, WEST MIDLANDS, ☎ 0121 7496122, www.tkmaxx.com, 9–8 MON–FRI, 9–6 SAT, 11–5 SUN.

ONE STOP SHOPPING CENTRE, WALSALL ROAD, PERRY BARR, BIRMINGHAM, WEST MIDLANDS, ☎ 0121 356 5807, www.tkmaxx.com, PHONE FOR DETAILS OF OPENING TIMES.

7–8 CROWN WHARF RETAIL PARK, WOLVERHAMPTON STREET, WALSALL, WEST MIDLANDS, ☎ 01922 649742, www.tkmaxx.com, PHONE FOR DETAILS OF OPENING TIMES.

2 WULFRUN SQUARE, WOLVERHAMPTON, WEST MIDLANDS WV1 3HB, ☎ 01902 421004, www.tkmaxx.com, 9–5.30 MON–FRI, 9–6 SAT, 11–5 SUN. **PERMANENT DISCOUNT OUTLET**

See page 458 (BEDS)

WILTSHIRE

BIRTHDAYS

MCARTHURGLEN DESIGNER OUTLET GREAT WESTERN, KEMBLE DRIVE, SWINDON, JUNCTION 16 OF M4, WILTSHIRE SN2 2DY, ☎ 01793 719751, 10–6 MON–FRI, 8 ON THUR, 9–6 SAT, 11–5 SUN. **FACTORY SHOP IN A FACTORY SHOPPING VILLAGE**

See page 462 (CHESH)

CLOVERLEAF

ARKWRIGHT ROAD, GROUNDWELL INDUSTRIAL ESTATE, SWINDON, WILTSHIRE SN2 5BB, ☎ 01793 720709, 9.30–4.30 MON–SAT, 10–4 SUN, BANK HOLIDAYS. **FACTORY SHOP**

MCARTHURGLEN DESIGNER OUTLET GREAT WESTERN, KEMBLE DRIVE, SWINDON, JUNCTION 16 OF M4 WILTSHIRE SN2 2DY, ☎ 01793 617486, 10–6 MON–SAT, 11–5 SUN. **FACTORY SHOP**

See page 477 (DEV)

DARTINGTON CRYSTAL

CLOVERLEAF RETAIL SHOP, ARKWRIGHT ROAD, GROUNDWELL, SWINDON, WILTSHIRE SN2 5BB, ☎ 01793 720709, 9.30–4.30 MON–SAT, 10–4 SUN. **FACTORY SHOP**

MCARTHURGLEN DESIGNER OUTLET GREAT WESTERN, KEMBLE DRIVE, SWINDON, JUNCTION 16 OF M4 WILTSHIRE SN2 2DY, ☎ 01793 530222, 10–6 MON–FRI, 8 ON THUR, 9–6 SAT, 11–5 SUN. **FACTORY SHOP**

See page 469 (CORN)

EDINBURGH CRYSTAL

AT HOME, KEMBLE DRIVE, GREAT WESTERN VILLAGE, CHURCH WARD PARK, SWINDON, WILTSHIRE SN2 2DZ, ☎ 01793 692311, 10–6 MON–SAT, 8 ON THUR, 11–5 SUN. **FACTORY SHOP IN A FACTORY SHOPPING VILLAGE**

See page 463 (CHESH)

IN EXCESS

131 NETHERHAMPTON ROAD, SALISBURY, WILTSHIRE SP2 8NA, ☎ 01722 414444, 9–5.30 MON–SAT, 10–4 SUN. **PERMANENT DISCOUNT OUTLET**

See page 480 (DORS)

LE CREUSET

MCARTHURGLEN DESIGNER OUTLET GREAT WESTERN, KEMBLE DRIVE, SWINDON, JUNCTION 16 OF M4 WILTSHIRE SN2 2DZ, ☎ 01793 641587, 10–6 MON–FRI, 8 ON THUR, 9–6 SAT, 11–5 SUN, 10–5 BANK HOLIDAYS. **FACTORY SHOP IN A FACTORY SHOPPING VILLAGE**

See page 483 (ESSEX)

MATALAN

SOUTHAMPTON ROAD, SALISBURY, WILTSHIRE SP1 2LE, ☎ 01722 342360, FAX: 01722 413721, www.matalan.co.uk, 10–8 MON–FRI, 9–6 SAT, 10–4 SUN.

MANNINGTON RETAIL PARK, WOOTTON BASSETT ROAD, SWINDON, WILTSHIRE SN5 9NP, ☎ 01793 649500, FAX: 01793 431895, www.matalan.co.uk, 10–8 MON–FRI, 9–6 SAT, 10–4 SUN. **PERMANENT DISCOUNT OUTLET**

See page 458 (BEDS)

MCARTHURGLEN DESIGNER OUTLET GREAT WESTERN

KEMBLE DRIVE, SWINDON, JUNCTION 16 OF M4 WILTSHIRE SN2 2DY, ☎ 0800 316 4352 FREE INFORMATION LINE OR 01793 507600, www.mcarthurglen.com, 10–6 MON–FRI, 8 ON THUR, 9–6 SAT, 11–5 SUN. **FACTORY SHOPPING VILLAGE**

The McArthurGlen Designer Outlet Great Western offers over 100 stores selling top names and designer brands at up to 50% off typical retail prices. Housed in the restored Great Western Railway buildings, everything is conveniently located under one roof. A large open plan area dedicated to homewares has everything for the house and home. Facilities include a food court, children's play area, licensed creche and ample parking. Stores include: U Wear/I Wear, Warner UK Ltd, Antler, Ecco Shoes, Walker & Hall, Liz Claiborne, Viyella, Austin Reed, Suits You, Alexon, Jaeger, Windsmoor, Aquascutum, Olsen, Jacques Vert, Overland/Caterpillar, Episode, Long Tall Sally, Pilot, Triumph, Cotton Traders, Villeroy & Boch, Baron Jon, Clarks, HKA, Burberry, Remington, Regatta, Just Sweets, Easy Jeans, Ben Sherman, JoKids, Donnay, Le Creuset, Puma, Tog 24, XS, Gap, Big L, Soled Out, Ted Baker, Nike, Timberland, Quiksilver, Whittard, Marks and Spencer, Polo Jeans Company, Gant, Calp, The Design House, Darlington Crystal, Duvet and Pillow Shop, Henri Lloyd, Mexx, Ravel, The Luxury Beauty Store, Thomas Pink, Thorntons, Tie Rack, Julian Graves, Hanro, Jane Shilton, Birthday, Toy Zone, Bookends, Sofa Works, Designer Room, Petroleum, Next, Daks Simpson, Suit Company, Price's Candles, Claire's Accessories, Samsonite, Van Heusen, Cloverleaf, Poole Pottery, Spiegelau, Edinburgh Crystal, Woods of Windsor, Staffordshire Pottery, Waterford Wedgewood, Stuart Crystal, Gleneagles, The Garden Outlet, Ponden Mill, Jane Heath, Sheridan Australia, Tefal, Professional Cookware, and Oneida.

ONEIDA

MCARTHURGLEN DESIGNER OUTLET GREAT WESTERN, KEMBLE DRIVE, SWINDON, JUNCTION 16 OF M4 WILTSHIRE SN2 2DY, ☎ 01793 514103, 10–6 MON–FRI, 8 ON THUR, 9–6 SAT, 11–5 SUN. **FACTORY SHOP IN A FACTORY SHOPPING VILLAGE**

See page 464 (CHESH)

PONDEN MILL LINENS

WILTON SHOPPING VILLAGE, KING STREET, WILTON, NEAR SALISBURY, WILTSHIRE SP2 0RS, ☎ 01722 741271, 9.30–5.30 MON–SAT, 11–5 SUN.

MCARTHURGLEN DESIGNER OUTLET GREAT WESTERN, KEMBLE DRIVE, SWINDON, JUNCTION

16 OF M4 WILTSHIRE SN2 2DY, ☎ 01793 531880, 10–6 MON–FRI, 8 ON THUR, 9–6 SAT, 11–5 SUN. **FACTORY SHOP IN A FACTORY SHOPPING VILLAGE**

See page 464 (CHESH)

PRICE'S CANDLES

MCARTHURGLEN DESIGNER OUTLET GREAT WESTERN, KEMBLE DRIVE, SWINDON, JUNCTION 16 OF M4 WILTSHIRE SN2 2DY, ☎ 01793 693745, 10–6 MON–FRI, 8 ON THUR, 9–6 SAT, 11–5 SUN. **FACTORY SHOP IN A FACTORY SHOPPING VILLAGE**

See page 464 (CHESH)

THE FACTORY SHOP LTD

23–25 NEW PLACE, CORSHAM, WILTSHIRE SN13 0HL, ☎ 01249 712160, 9–5.30 MON–SAT, 10–4 SUN.

36–37 ROUNDSTONE STREET, TROWBRIDGE, WILTSHIRE BA14 8DE, ☎ 01225 751399, 9–5 MON–SAT.

24 MARKET PLACE, WARMINSTER, WILTSHIRE BA12 9AN, ☎ 01985 217532, 9–5 MON–SAT. **FACTORY SHOP**

See page 465 (CHESH)

TK MAXX

CROSS KEYS SHOPPING CENTRE, SALISBURY, WILTSHIRE, ☎ 01722 320644, www.tkmaxx.com, 9–5.30 MON–FRI, 8 ON THUR, 9–6 SAT, 10–4 SUN.

THE ARCADE, BRUNEL SHOPPING CENTRE, SWINDON, WILTSHIRE, ☎ 01793 532896, www.tkmaxx.com, PHONE FOR DETAILS OF OPENING TIMES. **PERMANENT DISCOUNT OUTLET**

See page 458 (BEDS)

UNITED FOOTWEAR

HORHAM CRESCENT, PARK SOUTH, SWINDON, WILTSHIRE SN3 2LX, ☎ 01793 435238, 9–5.30 MON–SAT, 10–4 SUN. **PERMANENT DISCOUNT OUTLET**

See page 509 (LEICS)

VILLEROY & BOCH (UK) LIMITED

MCARTHURGLEN DESIGNER OUTLET GREAT WESTERN, KEMBLE DRIVE, SWINDON, JUNCTION 16 OF M4 WILTSHIRE SN2 2DY, ☎ 01793 480944, 10–6 MON–FRI, 8 ON THUR, 9–6 SAT, 11–5 SUN. **FACTORY SHOP IN A FACTORY SHOPPING VILLAGE**

See page 466 (CHESH)

WHITTARD

MCARTHURGLEN DESIGNER OUTLET CENTRE, KEMBLE DRIVE, SWINDON, WILTSHIRE SN2 2DY, ☎ 01793 618392, 10–6 MON–FRI, 8 ON THUR, 9–6 SAT, 11–5 SUN. **FACTORY SHOP IN A FACTORY SHOPPING VILLAGE**

See page 466 (CHESH)

WILTON SHOPPING VILLAGE

MINSTER STREET, WILTON, SALISBURY, WILTSHIRE SP2 0RS, ☎ 01722 741 211, www.thewsv@eagleone.co.uk, 9.30–5.30 MON–SAT, 11–5 SUN. **FACTORY SHOPPING VILLAGE**

On the former site of the Royal Wilton Carpet Factory, this village uses the refurbished original factory dye houses and 300-year-old, listed, historic courtyard buildings to house factory shops selling fashion and homewares at discounted prices. It includes shops such as Cotton Traders, Double Two, Edinburgh Woollen Mill, Julian Graves, Old Traditions, Ponden Mill, Remainders Books, Roman Originals, Scotts of Stow and the Wilton Carpet Factory Shop. Free parking, coffee shop, children's play area and disabled facilities. A riverside café is also open during the summer, serving homemade food and refreshments.

WOODS OF WINDSOR

AT HOME AREA, GREAT WESTERN DESIGNER OUTLET VILLAGE, KEMBLE DRIVE, CHURCHWARD VILLAGE, SWINDON, WILTSHIRE SN2 7AA, ☎ 01793 423443, FAX: 01793 423449, www.woodsofwindsor.co.uk, 10–6 MON–SAT, 8 ON THUR, 11–5 SUN. **FACTORY SHOP IN A FACTORY SHOPPING VILL3AGE**

See page 466 (CHESH)

WORCESTERSHIRE

G R PRATLEY & SONS

THE SHAMBLES, WORCESTER WR1 2RG, ☎ 01905 22678 OR 28642, FAX: 01905 745031, www.jks.org/grpratleyandsons, 9–5.30 MON–SAT, CLOSES AT 1 ON THUR. **PERMANENT DISCOUNT OUTLET**

A family business which specialises in bone china and earthenware, selling famous designer names at 18% lower than normal retail prices. Manufacturers include Royal Worcester, Spode, Royal Doulton, Wedgwood, Johnsons and many others, and individual pieces as well as sets can be bought. Good country furniture, tribal rugs and carpet specialists.

BLUNTS SHOE MARKET

51 UPPER TYTHING, WORCESTER, WORCESTERSHIRE WR1 1DT, ☎ 01905 27738, 9–5.30 MON–SAT. **PERMANENT DISCOUNT OUTLET**

This shoe retailer, established for over 135 years, sells shoes for all the family as well as clothes, handbags, sports shoes, boots, giftware and household goods, all at discounted prices. Famous brands include Clarks, K Shoes, Elmdale, Grenson, Loakes, Caterpillar and Adidas. Part of a national chain.

CATALOGUE BARGAIN SHOP

233 WORCESTER ROAD, MALVERN LINK, MALVERN WORCESTERSHIRE WR14 1SY, ☎ 01684 893062, www.bargaincrazy.com, 9–5.30 MON–SAT, 10.30–4.30 SUN. **PERMANENT DISCOUNT OUTLET**

See page 461 (CAMBS)

CHINAMATCH

PO BOX 30, DROITWICH LDO, WORCESTERSHIRE WR9 7ZJ, ☎ 01905 391520, FAX: 01905 391520, **e-mail:** chinamatch_uk@compuserve.com, www.chinamatch.uk.com, MAIL ORDER. **PERMANENT DISCOUNT OUTLET**

Would you like to add to your dinner or tea service or replace breakages, but find the pattern is no longer available? Or perhaps you want to buy a new service but need to sell on your old service first. China Match registers your requirements and checks them constantly against existing and incoming stock: they stock most English manufacturers and Noritake. There are no registration fees. The company buys stock daily and only supplies pieces in new or little used condition. Most customers are supplied with their requirements from stock, but in those instances where stock is not available, every effort is made to find the piece you need as quickly as possible, although success cannot be guaranteed. Established since 1980, this company prides itself on its proactive, personal service.

DARTINGTON CRYSTAL

SECONDS SHOP, ROYAL WORCESTER PORCELAIN, SEVERN STREET, WORCESTER, WORCESTERSHIRE WR1 2NE, ☎ 01905 23221, FAX: 01905 23601, 10–5.30 MON–SAT, 11–5 SUN. **FACTORY SHOP**

See page 469 (CORN)

DUNELM MILL SHOP

F17 CROWNGATE SHOPPING CENTRE, FRIARY WALK, WORCESTER, WORCESTERSHIRE WR1 3LE, ☎ 01905 611159, FAX: 01905 613004, www.dunelm-mill.co.uk, 9–5.30 MON–SAT. **PERMANENT DISCOUNT OUTLET**

See page 458 (BEDS)

EDINBURGH CRYSTAL

ROYAL WORCESTER VISITOR CENTRE, SEVERN STREET, WORCESTER, WORCESTERSHIRE WR1 2NE, ☎ 01905 746000 (CENTRE TEL NO), FAX: 01905 619503, **e-mail:** general@royal-worcester.co.uk, www.royal-worcester.co.uk, 9–5.30 MON–SAT, 11–5 SUN. MAIL ORDER. **FACTORY SHOP**

See page 463 (CHESH)

EVESHAM COUNTRY PARK

SHOPPING AND GARDENING CENTRE, COUNTRY PARK MANAGEMENT, EVESHAM, AT THE NORTHERN END OF THE EVESHAM BYPASS, AT ITS JUNCTION WITH THE STRATFORD ROAD WORCESTERSHIRE WR11 4TP, ENQUIRIES: 01386 41661; GARDEN CENTRE: 01386 761888; APPLE BARN RESTAURANT: 01386 761333; VALE WILDLIFE VISITOR CENTRE: 01386 443348; COARSE FISHING/GOTTFRIED: 07973 147323, 9–6 MON–SAT (WINTER 5.30), 10.30–4.30 SUN. **FACTORY SHOPPING VILLAGE**

Courtyard shops and garden centre providing a wide variety of goods at bargain prices. Designer and brand name men's and women's fashions from Leading Labels, leisurewear from Cotton Traders, coordinated soft furnishings, bedlinen and duvets from Ponden Mill, household goods from Lifestyles, dried fuits, nuts and packaged herbs from Julian Graves, an extensive range of books from The Book Depot, plus quality plants, colourful pots and garden equipment. Luggage & Bags sells a range of quality branded luggage and travel goods at great prices. There is also restaurant, wildlife centre, coarse fishing on the River Avon, and a miniature railway for a real country day out.

FARMHOUSE FLORA

CHURCH FARM, SHRAWLEY, WORCESTERSHIRE WR6 6TS, ☎ 01905 620283, FAX: 01905 621608, **e-mail:** information@farmhouseflora.com, www.farmhouseflora.com, OPENING HOURS VARY – PHONE FIRST. **FACTORY SHOP**

Set in the heart of the Worcestershire countryside, this 16th century farmhouse is the site for a rural business centred arond the 60-plus varieties of flowers and Christmas trees grown on the farm and sold direct to the public. Here, during the spring and summer months, you can buy a selection of home-grown, freshly dried flowers, arrangements, and all the ribbons, containers and other accessories you need to make your own arrangements. As well as flower designs, there are sweetly scented herbs, rolls of vivid ribbons and bunches of colourful delphiniums, roses and majestic sunflowers. At Christmas time, you can find one-off fresh or dried flower arrangements, garlands, wreaths, naturally-dried flowers, nuts, berries, fragrant fruits and spices, candles, ribbons, Christmas decorations, gilded grasses and silver seedheads, plus a huge variety of traditional and modern Christmas arrangements and unusual gifts. The Yuletide Barn next door sells home-grown Christmas trees (potted or cut), Norway and Blue Spruce, Scots Pine and Nodrnamm, fresh berried hollies, mistletoe and ivy.

MATALAN

FORMER HOMEBASE, PARKER BUTTS, RINGWAY, KIDDERMINSTER WORCESTERSHIRE DY11 6TQ, ☎ 01562 756880, FAX: 01562 753573, www.matalan.co.uk, 9–8 MON–FRI, 9–6 SAT, 10–4 SUN.

UNIT 10, MALVERN RETAIL PARK, ROMAN WAY, MALVERN, WORCESTERSHIRE WR14 1JQ, ☎ 01684 584800, FAX: 01684 584802, www.matalan.co.uk, 10–8 MON–FRI, 9–6 SAT, 11–4 SUN. **PERMANENT DISCOUNT OUTLET**

See page 458 (BEDS)

PONDEN MILL

EVESHAM COUNTRY PARK, EVESHAM, WORCESTERSHIRE WR11 4TP, ☎ 01386 47407, 9–6 MON–SAT, 10.30–4.30 SUN. **FACTORY SHOP IN A FACTORY SHOPPING VILLAGE**

ROYAL WORCESTER FACTORY SHOP, SEVERN STREET, WORCESTER, WORCESTERSHIRE WR1 2NE, ☎ 01905 726708, 9–5.30 MON–SAT, 11–5 SUN. **FACTORY SHOP**

See page 464 (CHESH)

ROYAL WORCESTER VISITOR CENTRE

SEVERN STREET, WORCESTER, WORCESTERSHIRE WR1 2NE, ☎ 01905 746000, FAX: 01905 619503, **e-mail:** general@royal-worcester.co.uk, www.royal-worcester.co.uk, 9–5.30 MON–SAT, 11–5 SUN. MAIL ORDER. **FACTORY SHOP**

The Victorian buildings of Royal Worcester's visitor centre lead into the heart of a world famous porcelain industry that was founded in 1751. Royal Worcester's factory shops carry an extensive range of quality bone china tableware, porcelain oven-to-tableware, giftware and figurines. The factory seconds shop offers quality seconds at greatly reduced prices. Visitors can also shop in Wigornia Court where a myriad of home accessories and factory outlets selling cutlery, crystal, candles, linen, kitchen utensils, rugs and giftware can be found. Parking and disabled facilities.

T J HUGHES

1 HIGH STREET, KIDDERMINSTER, WORCESTERSHIRE DY10 2DS, ☎ 01562 745687, FAX: 01562 744025, **e-mail:** info@tjhughes.co.uk, www.tjhughes.co.uk, 9–5.30 MON–SAT, 10–4 SUN. **PERMANENT DISCOUNT OUTLET**

See page 465 (CHESH)

THE CAPE

40 THE SHAMBLES, WORCESTER, WORCESTERSHIRE WR1 2RE, ☎ 01905 729291, FAX: 01905 24111, **e-mail:** sc@thefactory-shop.co.uk, www.thecape.co.uk, 9–5.30 MON–FRI, 9–6 SAT, 10.30–4.30 SUN. **FACTORY SHOP**

See page 460 (BRIS)

THE FACTORY SHOP LTD

NEW ROAD, PERSHORE, WORCESTERSHIRE WR10 1BY, ☎ 01386 556467, 9–5 MON–FRI, 9–5.30 SAT, 10.30–4.30 SUN. **FACTORY SHOP**

See page 465 (CHESH)

THE WEAVERS SHOP

DUKE PLACE, KIDDERMINSTER, WORCESTERSHIRE DY10 2JR, ☎ 01562 820680, FAX: 01562 820030, **e-mail:** weavers.shop@tomkinsons.co.uk, 9–5 MON–FRI, 9–12 SAT. **FACTORY SHOP**

Offers a large selection of tufted and Axminster plain and patterned carpets from the factory. Also has a wide collection of natural floor coverings and rugs at a considerable discount off high street prices. All goods sold here are returns, discontinued, contract overmakes, ends or slight seconds and therefore represent excellent value for money. Fitters can be suggested and delivery arranged.

TK MAXX

UNIT 100, UPPER MALL, MERRYHILL CENTRE, DUDLEY, WORCESTERSHIRE DY5 1QX, ☎ 01384 77878, www.tkmaxx.com, 10–8 MON–FRI, 10–9 THUR, 9–7 SAT, 11–5 SUN.

EVESHAM WALK, KINGFISHER SHOPPING CENTRE, REDDITCH, WORCESTERSHIRE, ☎ 01527 598837, www.tkmaxx.com, PHONE FOR DETAILS OF OPENING TIMES. **PERMANENT DISCOUNT OUTLET**

See page 458 (BEDS)

UNITED FOOTWEAR

NEW ROAD, KIDDERMINSTER, WORCESTERSHIRE, ☎ 01562 744022, 9–6 MON–SAT, 8 ON THUR, 9–1 SUN. **PERMANENT DISCOUNT OUTLET**

See page 509 (LANCS)

YORKSHIRE

BED & BATH WORKS

MCARTHURGLEN DESIGNER OUTLET YORK, ST NICHOLAS AVENUE, FULFORD, JUNCTION OF A19 AND A64, YORK, NORTH YORKSHIRE YO19 4TA, ☎ 01904 636598, FAX: 01904 646598, **e-mail:** hello@bedandbathworks.co.uk, www.bedandbathworks.co.uk, 10–6 MON–SAT, 8 ON THUR, 11–5 SUN. **FACTORY SHOP IN A FACTORY SHOPPING VILLAGE**

See page 462 (CHESH)

BIRTHDAYS

THE YORKSHIRE OUTLET, WHITE ROSE WAY, DONCASTER, SOUTH YORKSHIRE DN4 5JH, ☎ 01302 325803, 10–6 MON–SAT, 11–5 SUN.

UNIT 202, MCARTHURGLEN DESIGNER OUTLET, NABURN, YORK, ST NICHOLAS AVENUE, FULFORD, JUNCTION OF A19 AND A64, YORK, NORTH YORKSHIRE YO19, FAX: 01904 679367, 10–6 MON–SAT, 8 ON THUR, 11–5 SUN. **FACTORY SHOPPING VILLAGE**

See page 462 (CHESH)

BRANDMART

5 NORTH STREET, RIPON, NORTH YORKSHIRE HG4 1JY, ☎ 01765 601156, 9–5 MON–SAT. **FACTORY SHOP**

See page 486 (GLOS)

BRK CRYSTAL LTD

TREEFIELD ESTATE, OFF GELDERD ROAD, GILDERSOME, LEEDS, WEST YORKSHIRE LS27 7LB, ☎ 0113 252 2922, FAX: 0113 238 1445, **e-mail:** b_metcalfe@brk-group.co.uk, www.brk-group.co.uk, 9–5 MON–FRI, 10–4 SAT. **FACTORY SHOP**

Factory shop selling 24% lead crystal stemware and giftware. Available boxed as gift sets or unboxed at slightly lower prices, large wine glasses cost £6.50 each, champagne flutes £5.75 each, vases £17, and compote dishes £17. Located just down the road from the Lighting Factory Shop.

BROOKS FACTORY OUTLET STORES

SOUTH LANE, ELLAND, NEAR HALIFAX, WEST YORKSHIRE HX5 0HQ, ☎ 01422 377337, 9.30–5.30 MON–SAT, 8 ON THUR, 11–5 SUN.

BUYWELL RETAIL PARK, THORP ARCH, WETHERBY, NORTH YORKSHIRE LS23 7BJ, ☎ 01937 541895, 9.30–5.30 MON–SAT, 11–5 SUN. **PERMANENT DISCOUNT OUTLET**

Walk through the store and you can't fail to find a bargain. New stock arrives daily from well-known names such as Nike, French Connection, Gabicci, Klass, Camille and Ben Sherman. Apart from men's and women's clothes, they sell sportswear, linens, lingerie, shoes, accessories, luggage, towels, coordinated bed linen, household textiles, duvets, pillows and lots more from names such as Monogram and Ponden Mill. Everything under one roof at up to 50% off high street prices. The Elland store has a coffee shop.

CARD & GIFT

DAWSON LANE, DUDLEY HILL, BRADFORD, WEST YORKSHIRE BD4 6HW, ☎ 01274 689399, 10–5.30 MON–FRI, 10–2 SAT. **FACTORY SHOP**

Wedding novelties, cards, gift wrap, toys, soft toys, banners, balloons, badges, candlesticks and stationery, all of which is perfect stock at reduced prices.

CATALOGUE BARGAIN SHOP

KAYS SHOP, HOLME LANE, OFF TONG STREET, BRADFORD, WEST YORKSHIRE BD4 6NA, ☎ 01274 681711, www.bargaincrazy.com, 9.30–5.30 MON–SAT, 7 ON THUR, 10.30–4.30 SUN.

FREEPORT DESIGNER OUTLET VILLAGE, CARRWOOD ROAD, GLASSHOUGHTON, CASTLEFORD, WEST YORKSHIRE WF10 4SB, ☎ 01977 519112, www.bargaincrazy.com, 10–8 MON–FRI, 10–6 SAT, 11–5 SUN.

UNITS 2–3, LEGER CENTRE, THORNE ROAD, DONCASTER, SOUTH YORKSHIRE DN2 4GB, ☎ 01302 341506, www.bargaincrazy.com, 9–8 MON–FRI, 10–6 SAT, 11–5 SUN.

57–59 MARKET PLACE, HECKMONDWIKE, WEST YORKSHIRE WF16 0EZ, ☎ 01924 402674, www.bargaincrazy.com, 9–5.30 MON–SAT, 10–4 SUN.

42 JOHN WILLIAM STREET, HUDDERSFIELD, WEST YORKSHIRE HD1 1ER, ☎ 01484 535112, www.bargaincrazy.com, 9–5.30 MON–SAT, 10.30–4.30 SUN.

28 NEW BRIGGATE, BRIGGATE, LEEDS, WEST YORKSHIRE LS1 6NU, ☎ 0113 243 6425, www.bargaincrazy.com, 9–5.30 MON–SAT, 11–5 SUN.

MARSHALL STREET, LEEDS, WEST YORKSHIRE LS1 1UL, ☎ 0113 254 2350, www.bargaincrazy.com, 10–5 MON–FRI, 7 ON THUR, 9–5.30 SAT, 10.30–4.30 SUN.

51 ACKLAM ROAD, MIDDLESBROUGH, NORTH YORKSHIRE TS5 5HA, ☎ 01642 825925, www.bargaincrazy.com, 9–5.30 MON–SAT, 10.30–4.30 SUN. **PERMANENT DISCOUNT OUTLET**

See page 461 (CAMBS)

CATALOGUE DISCOUNT STORES

UNIT 6, HILLSBOROUGH BARRACKS SHOPPING MALL, SHEFFIELD, SOUTH YORKSHIRE S6 2GY, ☎ 0114 234 5726, FAX: 0114 234 5006, 9–5.30 MON–SAT, 11–5 SUN. **PERMANENT DISCOUNT OUTLET**

See page 499 (LANCS)

CLOVERLEAF

THE YORKSHIRE OUTLET, WHITE ROSE WAY, DONCASTER, SOUTH YORKSHIRE DN4 5JH, ☎ 01302 367021, 10–6 MON–SAT, 11–5 SUN. **FACTORY SHOP IN A FACTORY SHOPPING VILLAGE**

See page 477 (DEV)

DARTINGTON CRYSTAL

BACCHANALIA, THE MILL VILLAGE, BRADFORD ROAD, WEST YORKSHIRE WF17 5LZ, ☎ 01924 424000, 9.30–5.30 MON–SAT, 8 ON THUR, 11–5 SUN. **FACTORY SHOP IN A FACTORY SHOPPING VILLAGE**

See page 469 (CORN)

DAVID MELLOR FACTORY SHOP

THE ROUND BUILDING, HATHERSAGE, SHEFFIELD S32 1BA, ☎ 01433 650220, www.davidmellordesign.com, 10–5 MON–SAT, 11- 5 SUN. **FACTORY SHOP**

Up to 10% discount on most David Mellor cutlery designs to personal shoppers. The shop, situated in a former industrial workshop at an old gasworks in the Peak District, also sells, at normal prices, handthrown pottery with which David Mellor has been involved in design or development, as well as kitchen racks, basketware and cutlery boxes. Also sells lots of wooden utensils and good quality kitchenware.

DUNELM FABRIC AND MILL SHOP

UNITS 1 & 3, CANKLOW MEADOWS, WEST BAWTRY ROAD, ROTHERHAM SOUTH YORKSHIRE S60 2XL, ☎ 01709 820374 (MILL SHOP), ☎ 01709 360320 (FABRIC SHOP), FAX: 01709 820403 (MILL SHOP), FAX: 01709 364964 (FABRIC SHOP), www.dunelm-mill.co.uk, 10–8 MON–FRI, 9–6 SAT, 11–5 SUN.

UNIT 3, THORNE ROAD RETAIL PARK, OGDEN ROAD, DONCASTER, SOUTH YORKSHIRE DN2 4SE, ☎ 01302 366007, FAX: 01302 322006, www.dunelm-mill.co.uk, 9–6 MON–SAT, 8 ON THUR, FRI, 10–4 SUN.

CLOUGH ROAD RETAIL PARK, HULL, HUMBERSIDE HU5 1SP, ☎ 01482 447666, FAX: 01482 491020, www.dunelm-mill.co.uk, 9–6 MON–SAT, 8 ON THUR, FRI, 10.30–4.30 SUN.

151 BRADFIELD ROAD, HILLSBOROUGH, SHEFFIELD, SOUTH YORKSHIRE S6 2BY, ☎ 01142 315600, FAX: 01142 344049, www.dunelm-mill.co.uk, 9–5 MON–SAT, 10–4 SUN.

CLIFTON MOOR CENTRE, STIRLING ROAD, YORK, NORTH YORKSHIRE YO3 4WZ, ☎ 01904 692229, FAX: 01904 692259, www.dunelm-mill.co.uk, 9–6 MON–SAT, 8 ON THUR, FRI, 10.30–4.30 SUN. **PERMANENT DISCOUNT OUTLET**

See page 458 (STAFFS)

EDINBURGH CRYSTAL

FREEPORT CASTLEFORD, CARRWOOD ROAD, GLASS HOUGHTON WEST YORKSHIRE WS10 4SB, ☎ 01977 667500, 10–8 MON–FRI, 10–6 SAT, 11–5 SUN.

FREEPORT HORNSEA OUTLET VILLAGE, ROLSTON ROAD, HORNSEA, EAST YORKSHIRE HU18 1UT, ☎ 01964 534260, 9.30–6 SEVEN DAYS A WEEK. **FACTORY SHOP IN A FACTORY SHOPPING VILLAGE**

See page 463 (CHESH)

FABRIC WAREHOUSE

75A BRADFORD ROAD, RIDDLESDEN, KEIGHLEY, WEST YORKSHIRE BD21 4HD, ☎ 01535 692999, 9–5 MON–SAT. **PERMANENT DISCOUNT OUTLET**

Sells unbranded fabric direct from the same mills which manufacture for well-known brand names at a discount of about 30%. They stock prints, plains, brocades, silks, chenilles, voiles, muslin, damask, weaves, chenilles, lining fabric and a wide range of accessories from heading tape and cushion pads to tracks and poles. Prices average £2.99-£9.99 a linear metre with flat weaves costing £19 a metre for fabric which would cost £35 a metre in the high street and muslin for 99p a metre.

FREEPORT CASTLEFORD DESIGNER OUTLET VILLAGE

CARRWOOD ROAD, GLASSHOUGHTON, CASTLEFORD, JUNCTION 32 OF M52, WEST YORKSHIRE WF10 4SB, ☎ 01977 520153, www.freeportcastleford.com, 10–8 MON–FRI, 10–6 SAT, 11–5 SUN. **FACTORY SHOPPING VILLAGE**

Designer outlet village with over 75 shops, indoor and outdoor children's play areas and a wide range of restaurants with easy access from the M52 and 3,500 free car parking spaces. Shops include Amazing Jeans, Baron Jon, BhS For Less, Charles Clinkard, Clarks, Cromwells, Churchill, Ciro Citterio, Craghoppers, CBS, Claire's Accessories, Cotton Traders, Damart, Edinburgh Crystal, Donnay, Double Two, Event Jewellery, Easy Jeans, Edinburgh Woollen Mill, Elle, Fila, Giorgio, Gossard, XS Music, Jane Shilton, John Partridge, Kappa, Kitchen and Table, Kurt Muller, Leading Labels, Lee Cooper, Littlewoods, London Leathers, Mexx, Mobile Phone Store, Nike, Nickleby's, Next to Nothing, Outrage, Petroleum, Picture Port, Pilot, Ponden Mill, Proibito, Rio Jewellery, Roman Originals, Regatta, Room, Ice Jeans, Sergio Tacchini, Sportsmill, Spotlight, Startrite Shoes, Remainders Book Depot, Designer Room, Garden Outlet, Shoe Collection, Toy Factory, Time, X Catalogue Store, Thorntons, Trespass, Waterford Wedgwood, Windsmoor.

FREEPORT HORNSEA OUTLET VILLAGE

ROLSTON ROAD, HORNSEA, JUNCTION 38 OFF THE M62, EAST YORKSHIRE HU18 1UT, ☎ 01964 534211, www.freeporthornsea.com, 9.30–6 SEVEN DAYS A WEEK. **FACTORY SHOPPING VILLAGE**

The original British factory shopping village with over 40 shops offering discounts of up to 50% off high street prices. The village also boasts leisure attractions for all ages, ranging from an adventure playground to a themed soft play area and exciting rides for children. Womenswear labels include Alexon, Designer Room, Roman Originals, Arkwright's Mill, Select, Damart, Edinburgh Woollen Mill, Double Two, Mexx and London Leathers. Sportwear and outdoor clothing are available from Tog 24, Regatta and Sports Mill. Footwear is sold by Famous Footwear, Lilley & Skinner and Charles Clinkard. Menswear stores include The Suit Company, Double Two, Nickleby's, London Leathers and Giorgio. Other shops include Woods of Windsor, Thorntons, Masters Jewellery, Edinburgh Crystal, Waterford Wedgewood, Hallmark, Laura Ashley, The Book Depot, Claire's Accessories, Churchill China and Ponden Mill.

HABITAT CLEARANCE DEPARTMENT

REDBRICK MILL LTD, 218 BRADFORD RD., BATLEY, WEST YORKSHIRE WF17 6JF, ☎ 01924 468960, OPEN 9.30–5.30 MON–FRI, 9–6 SAT, 11 -5 SUN. **PERMANENT DISCOUNT OUTLET**

See page 501 (LANCS)

LE CREUSET

MCARTHURGLEN DESIGNER OUTLET YORK, ST NICHOLAS AVENUE, FULFORD, JUNCTION OF A19 AND A64, YORK, NORTH YORKSHIRE YO19 4TA, ☎ 01904 630485, 10–6 MON–SAT, 8 ON THUR, 11–5 SUN. **FACTORY SHOP IN A FACTORY SHOPPING VILLAGE**

See page 483 (ESSEX)

LIGHTWATER VILLAGE AND FACTORY SHOPPING

NORTH STAINLEY, RIPON, NORTH YORKSHIRE HG4 3HT, ☎ 01765 634508, FAX: 01765 635359, www.lightwatervalley.co.uk, 10–5.30 MON–SUN. **FACTORY SHOPPING VILLAGE**

Large complex of retail and factory outlets with a wide range of branded womenswear including blouses, skirts, suits, dresses, lingerie, outerwear, shoes and accessories as well as menswear from jeans and outdoor wear to formal wear. Shoes, jewellery, home furnishings, crystal and glass, a large range of pottery, garden products, toys, cheese and confectionery. There is a restaurant and coffee shop serving snacks and refreshments, free parking and disabled facilities. A family theme park on site boasts the Ultimate Rollercoaster, the longest in Europe.

MATALAN

1 WOMBWELL LANE, STAIRFOOT, BARNSLEY SOUTH YORKSHIRE S70 3NS, ☎ 01226 733372, FAX: 01226 733368, www.matalan.co.uk, 9.30–8 MON–FRI, 9–6 SAT, 11–5 SUN.

FORSTER SQUARE RETAIL PARK, VALLEY ROAD, BRADFORD WEST YORKSHIRE BD1 4RN, ☎ 01274 381000, FAX: 01274 306314, www.matalan.co.uk, 10–8 MON–FRI, 9–6 SAT, 11–5 SUN.

THE RISHWORTH CENTRE, RAILWAY STREET, DEWSBURY, WEST YORKSHIRE WF12 8EQ, ☎ 01924 868180, FAX: 01924 461623, www.matalan.co.uk, 9.30–8 MON–FRI, 9–6 SAT, 11–5 SUN.

THE WHEATLEY CENTRE, WHEATLEY HALL ROAD, DONCASTER, SOUTH YORKSHIRE DN2 4PE, ☎ 01302 760444, FAX: 01302 554520, www.matalan.co.uk, 10–8 MON–FRI, 9–6 SAT, 11–5 SUN.

GREENMOUNT RETAIL PARK, PELLON ROAD, HALIFAX, WEST YORKSHIRE HX1 5QN, ☎ 01422 383051, FAX: 01422 383053, www.matalan.co.uk, 10–8 MON–FRI, 9–6 SAT, 11–5 SUN.

RINGWAY INDUSTRIAL ESTATE, HUDDERSFIELD WEST YORKSHIRE HD1 5DG, ☎ 01484 448800, FAX: 01484 452359, www.matalan.co.uk, 9.30–8 MON–FRI, 9–6 SAT, 11–5 SUN.

KINGSWOOD RETAIL PARK, BUDE ROAD, KINGSTON-UPON-HULL, EAST YORKSHIRE HU7 4AF, ☎ 01482 832880, FAX: 01482 587750, www.matalan.co.uk, 9–9 MON–FRI, 9–6 SAT, 11–5 SUN.

LOWER WORTLEY RING ROAD, LEEDS WEST YORKSHIRE LS12 4SL, ☎ 0113 290 7400, FAX: 0113 279 5389, www.matalan.co.uk, 9.30–8 MON–FRI, 9–6 SAT, 11–5 SUN.

HALTON DISTRICT CENTRE, SELBY ROAD, LEEDS, WEST YORKSHIRE LS12 4SL, ☎ 0113 284 0110, FAX: 0113 264 1662, www.matalan.co.uk, 9.30–8 MON–FRI, 9–6 SAT, 11–5 SUN.

SKIPPERS LANE RETAIL PARK, SKIPPERS LANE, MIDDLESBROUGH, NORTH YORKSHIRE TS6 6UB, ☎ 01642 443930, FAX: 01642 430559, www.matalan.co.uk, 10–8 MON–FRI, 9–6 SAT, 11–5 SUN.

UNIT 4B, STADIUM WAY, PARKGATE RETAIL PARK, ROTHERHAM SOUTH YORKSHIRE S60 1TG, ☎ 01709 780173, FAX: 01709 780772, www.matalan.co.uk, 10–8 MON–FRI, 9–6 SAT, 11–5 SUN.

HEELEY RETAIL PARK, CHESTERFIELD ROAD, SHEFFIELD SOUTH YORKSHIRE S8 0RG, ☎ 0114 262 9400, FAX: 0114 255 4193, www.matalan.co.uk, 10–8 MON–FRI, 9–6 SAT, 11–5 SUN.

INGS ROAD RETAIL PARK, INGS ROAD, WAKEFIELD, WEST YORKSHIRE WF1 1RN, ☎ 01924 367395, FAX: 01924 298164, www.matalan.co.uk, 10–8 MON–FRI, 9–6 SAT, 11–5 SUN.

UNITS 10 & 11, CLIFTON MOORE RETAIL PARK, YORK, NORTH YORKSHIRE YO3 4XZ, ☎ 01904 693080, FAX: 01904 693797, www.matalan.co.uk, 9.30–8 MON–FRI, 9–6 SAT, 11–5 SUN. **PERMANENT DISCOUNT OUTLET**

See page 458 (BEDS)

MCARTHURGLEN DESIGNER OUTLET YORK

ST NICHOLAS AVENUE, FULFORD, JUNCTION OF A19 AND A64, YORK, NORTH YORKSHIRE YO19 4TA, ☎ 01904 682720, www.mcarthurglen.com/york, 10–6 MON–SAT, 8 ON THUR, 11–5 SUN. **FACTORY SHOPPING VILLAGE**

The McArthurGlen Designer Outlet York is one of Europe's largest covered designer outlets with over 120 stores offering top brands and designer labels with discounts of up to 50% off typical retail prices. Find everything from men's, women's and children's clothing to accessories, shoes, sportswear, luggage, homewares, toys, books, and gifts. Facilities include a food court, a children's play area and free parking. Stores include: Armani, Autonomy, Ben Sherman, Burberry, Calvin Klein Jeans, Cerruti 1881, Chilli Pepper, Cotton Traders, Daks Simpson, Episode, Escada Sport, Gap Outlet, Guess, Hugo Boss, Jacques Vert, Jaeger/Viyella, Jesire/Esensual, Kabuki, Klass, Levi's, Margaret Howell, Marks & Spencer Outlet, Mergler, Mountain Warehouse, Nitya, Olsen, Pilot,

Polo Ralph Lauren, Pringle, Proibito, Proudfoot Leather, Roman Originals, Ronit Zilkha, Ted Baker, The Designer Room, Thomas Pink, Tog 24, Tommy Hilfiger, Windsmoor, Alfred Dunhill, Baronjon, Ben Sherman, Haggar, HKA, Marlboro Classics, Paul Smith, Petroleum, Pour Homme, Rockport, Suit Company, Suits You, Timberland, Adidas, Diadora, Donnay, Reebok, Toyworld, Birthdays, Bodum, The Body Shop Depot, Bookends, Franchetti Bond, Le Creuset, Oneida, Paper Mill, Price's Candles, Remington, Scent To You, Whittard Kitchen, Woods of Windsor, XS Music & Video, Bed & Bath Works, China China, Coloroll, Descamps, Garden Outlet, Jane Heath, La Casa del Christallo, Lights 4 Less, Pictureport, Room, Slipperbox, Spiegelau, Professional Cookware, Daniel Footwear, Famous Footwear, Pavers, Rockport, Shoe Studio, Soled Out, Julian Graves, Thorntons, Antler, Kangol, Liberty, Travel Accessory, Chapelle Jewellery, Claire's Accessories, Designer Shades, Monet, Tie Rack, and The Watch Store.

MR VALUE

KILLINGHALL ROAD, BRADFORD, WEST YORKSHIRE BD3 8DN, ☎ 01274 669674, 9–7 MON–FRI, 9–5.30 SAT, 10–4 SUN. **PERMANENT DISCOUNT OUTLET**

A discount store offering a wide selection of goods which are catalogue returns, factory rejects, seconds and ends of lines – everything from clothes with the labels cut out to tapes, kettles, televisions, microwaves, irons, toasters, bedlinen, towels, sweets, artificial flowers, batteries, toiletries, crockery, glass, stationery, pots and pans, toys and bins. Kitchen equipment brand names include Russell Hobbs and Morphy Richards. There is also a department for mobility, selling wheelchairs, scooters etc.

MULBERRY CLEARANCE SHOP

23–25 SWINEGATE, YORK, NORTH YORKSHIRE YO1 2AB, ☎ 01904 611055, FAX: 01904 640717, www.mulberry.com, 10–6 MON–SAT. **PERMANENT DISCOUNT OUTLET**

See page 530 (SOM)

MULBERRY HALL

STONEGATE, YORK, NORTH YORKSHIRE YO1 8ZW, ☎ 01904 620736, FAX: 01904 620251 **e-mail:** mailorder@mulberryhall.co.uk, www.mulberryhall.co.uk, 9–5.30 MON–SAT. **DESIGNER SALES**

Mulberry Hall's once-a-year-only January sale is the greatest sale of top quality china, crystal and cutlery in the north of England. Held in Mulberry Hall's majestic medieval premises in Stonegate, there are reductions of between 30% and 70% on many thousands of items of tableware including hundreds of dinner and tea services, giftware from leading European manufacturers including Royal Crown Derby, Royal Doulton, Royal Worcester, Spode, Wedgwood, Ginori, Dartington, Cristoffe and Stuart Crystal. Phone to add your name to the mailing list.

NAYLOR GARDENWARE

CLOUGH GREEN, CAWTHORNE, BARNSLEY, SOUTH YORKSHIRE S75 4AD, ☎ 01226 790591 **e-mail:** info@naylor.co.uk, www.bigpots.co.uk, 9–4.30 SEVEN DAYS A WEEK. **FACTORY SHOP**

Naylor, manufacturer of natural clay products since 1890, offers a range of planters at its factory shop, including plain flowerpots, bedding bowls, long toms, bell pots, wall pots, urns, strawberry pots and baskets. The Naylor Toad in the Hole 'Potty Abode for Frog or Toad' is available in a presentation box – an ideal gift for a gardener. Naylor uses local clays and all products are fired in excess of 1000 deg C.

NO FRILLS DIY STORE

NAVIGATION YARD, WAKEFIELD, WEST YORKSHIRE ☎ 01924 369660, FAX: 01924 364421 9–8 MON–SAT, 10–4 SUN.

115–125 LEADMILL ROAD, SHEFFIELD, SOUTH YORKSHIRE S2 4AZ, ☎ 0114 276 1454, FAX: 0114 272 5083, 9–8 MON–SAT, 10–4 SUN. **PERMANENT DISCOUNT OUTLET**

See page 458 (BEDS)

ONEIDA

MCARTHURGLEN DESIGNER OUTLET YORK, ST NICHOLAS AVENUE, FULFORD, JUNCTION OF A19 AND A64, YORK, NORTH YORKSHIRE YO19 4TA, ☎ 01904 610675, 10–6 MON–SAT, 8 ON THUR, 11–5 SUN. **FACTORY SHOP IN A FACTORY SHOPPING VILLAGE**

See page 464 (CHESH)

OSBORNE SILVERSMITHS (SHEFFIELD) LTD

WESTWICK WORKS, SOLLY STREET, WEST BAR, SHEFFIELD, SOUTH YORKSHIRE S1 4BA, ☎ 0114 272 4929, **e-mail:** john@osbornesilversmiths.co.uk, www.osbornesilversmiths.co.uk, 9.30–4 MON–THUR, 9.30–3 FRI; CLOSED END JULY/BEGINNING AUGUST AND SPRING WEEK.

FACTORY SHOP

For almost 300 years, the Osborne family have been Sheffield craftsmen; they are now one of Britain's leading cutlery manufacturers, supplying many of the top stores in London's West End. The factory shop sells slightly blemished or surplus perfect items of cutlery at special prices direct to the public. Their extensive ranges cover both English and Continental patterns in sterling silver, silver plate and stainless steel. In addition to canteens, place sets or individual pieces, they also manufacture an extensive selection of servicing and accessory items difficult to find elsewhere.

OSWALDTWISTLE MILLS LINEN COLLECTION

LIGHTWATER VALLEY PARK, NORTH STAINLEY, RIPON NORTH YORKSHIRE HG4 3NT, ☎ 01765 634519, **e-mail:** rclarke@o-mills.co.uk, www.o-mills.co.uk/linencol 10–5.30 SEVEN DAYS A WEEK.

15–17 COACH STREET, SKIPTON, NORTH YORKSHIRE BD23 1LH, ☎ 01756 796701 **e-mail:** rclarke@o-mills.co.uk, www.o-mills.co.uk/linencol, 10–5 MON–SAT, 11–4 SUN.

PERMANENT DISCOUNT OUTLET

Collection of quality UK woven Damask tablelinen and bedlinen, luxury robes and towels, duvets and pillows. Products are sold exclusively in their retail outlets and can be delivered to your door if ordered from the Internet or from their mail order catalogue. White 100% cotton double sheets are priced from £6.84, luxury bath robes from £14.89, and dyed 100% cotton tablecloths from £4.86.

PONDEN MILL

FREEPORT CASTLEFORD DESIGNER OUTLET VILLAGE, CARWOOD ROAD, GLASSHOUGHTON, CASTLEFORD, JUNCTION 32 OF M52, WEST YORKSHIRE WF10 4SB, ☎ 01977 518327, 10–8 MON–FRI, 10–6 SAT, 11–5 SUN.

THE YORKSHIRE OUTLET, WHITE ROSE WAY, DONCASTER, SOUTH YORKSHIRE DN4 5JH, ☎ 01302 360117, 10–6 MON–SAT, 11–5 SUN.

FREEPORT HORNSEA OUTLET VILLAGE, ROLSTON ROAD, HORNSEA, EAST YORKSHIRE HU18 1UT, ☎ 01964 537452, 9.30–6 MON–SAT, 11–5 SUN.

THE MILL, BRADFORD ROAD, BATLEY, WEST YORKSHIRE WF17 5LZ, ☎ 01924 444948, 9.30–5.30 MON–FRI, 9–5.30 SAT, 11–5 SUN. **FACTORY SHOP IN A FACTORY SHOPPING VILLAGE**

See page 464 (CHESH)

PREMIER DISCOUNT STORES

CLOUGH LANE, PADDOCK, HUDDERSFIELD, WEST YORKSHIRE HD1 4UW, ☎ 01484 519007, 9–5.30 MON, TUE, WED, 9–7 THUR, FRI, 9–5 SAT, 10–4 SUN. **PERMANENT DISCOUNT OUTLET**

Converted cinema, now a warehouse selling toiletries, soap powders, bleach, tinned goods, biscuits, chocolates, pet food, beers, wines and gift items.

PRICE'S CANDLES

THE YORKSHIRE OUTLET, WHITE ROSE WAY, DONCASTER, SOUTH YORKSHIRE DN4 5JH, ☎ 01302 325362, 10–6 MON–SAT, 11–5 SUN.

MCARTHURGLEN DESIGNER OUTLET YORK, ST NICHOLAS AVENUE, FULFORD, JUNCTION OF A19 AND A64, YORK, NORTH YORKSHIRE YO19 4TA, ☎ 01904 677997, 10–6 MON–SAT, 8 ON THUR, 11–5 SUN. **FACTORY SHOP IN A FACTORY SHOPPING VILLAGE**

See page 464 (CHESH)

QLM LTD

IDLE ROAD, IDLE, BRADFORD, WEST YORKSHIRE BD2 2AL, ☎ 01274 642222, 9.30–6 MON–SAT, 5.30 ON WED, 11–5 SUN. **PERMANENT DISCOUNT OUTLET**

Toys, household goods, clothes, food, electrical equipment, garden implements, kitchenware and furniture, all sold at discounted prices. For example, reject garden forks £6.99, spades £4.99, pruning tools £2.99 to £19.99.

READMANS LTD

ALFRED HOUSE, SPENCE LANE, HOLBECK, LEEDS, WEST YORKSHIRE LS12 1EF, ☎ 0113 243 6355, FAX: 0113 242 3192, www.readmans.co.uk, CASH AND CARRY OPEN 9–9 MON–FRI, 8.30–6 SAT, 10–4 SUN.

HEALEY RETAIL PARK, CHESTERFIELD ROAD, SHEFFIELD, SOUTH YORKSHIRE, ☎ 0114 258 0077, FAX: 0113 242 3192, www.readmans.co.uk, 9–8 MON–FRI, 9–6 SAT, 11–5 SUN.

PARKGATE RETAIL WORLD, ROTHERHAM, SOUTH YORKSHIRE, ☎ 01709 781020, www.readmans.co.uk, 9–9 MON–FRI, 9–6 SAT, 10–5 SUN.

THE MILL DISCOUNT DEPARTMENT STORE, BATLEY, WEST YORKSHIRE, ☎ 01924 426634, www.readmans.co.uk, 9–5 MON–SAT, 9.30–8 THUR, 11–5 SUN. **PERMANENT DISCOUNT OUTLET**

Mainly women's, men's and children's clothing as well as bedding, textiles, toiletries, footwear, toys, children's books, shoes and towels at prices which are cheaper than the high street. Most of the stock is from well-known labels but they cannot be mentioned here as they are de-labelled before putting in the shop. A proportion of the stock is manufacturers' cancelled contracts and seconds; the rest is designed by the in-house team and is unbranded. The aim, however, is to sell products at 50% or less than the equivalent goods sold on the high street. Also has a café.

SCOOPS

ENTERPRISE 5, 5 LANE ENDS, IDLE, BRADFORD, WEST YORKSHIRE BD10 8EG, ☎ 01274 622300, 9–8 MON–FRI, 9–6 SAT, 10–4 SUN.

25 TOWN STREET, ARMLEY, LEEDS, WEST YORKSHIRE LS12 1UX, ☎ 0113 263 1825, FAX: 0113 231 9885, 9–5.30 MON–SAT.

SCOOPS, SHIRETHORNE CENTRE, 34–43 PROSPECT STREET, HULL, HUMBERSIDE HU2 8PX, ☎ 01482 224354, FAX: 01482 221729, 9–5.30 MON–SAT.

41 BARNSLEY ROAD, SOUTH ELMSHALL, PONTEFRACT WEST YORKSHIRE WF9 2RN, ☎ 01977 642256, FAX: 01977 650 629, 9–5.30 MON–SAT. **PERMANENT DISCOUNT OUTLET**

See page 468 (CO DURH)

SPRINGFIELD CLOTHING

THE MILL SHOP, NORMAN ROAD, DENBY DALE, HUDDERSFIELD, WEST YORKSHIRE HD8 8TH, ☎ 01484 865082, 9–5 MON–SAT, 10–5 SUN. **PERMANENT DISCOUNT OUTLET**

Springfield Clothing sells clothes for all the family at up to 50% discount on high street prices such as Marks & Spencer, Principles, Next, Monsoon and Dorothy Perkins. Also stocks men's and women's underwear, a selection of basic bedding, duvets, sheets, pillows, pillowcases as well as tea towels, tablecloths, rugs, small carpets and Sheffield cutlery, all at discounted prices. They now also sell an exclusive range of handmade lingerie, swimwear and sportswear by EnVie. Also now incorporating instore boutique by Gasp at discounted prices.

SUMMER GRAND SALE

RIPLEY CASTLE, RIPLEY, NEAR HARROGATE, NORTH YORKSHIRE, ENQUIRIES: 01367 860017, FAX: 01367 860177, **e-mail:** nheslam@aol.com, 9.30–5.30 MON–FRI. **DESIGNER SALES**

There are now three annual Grand Sales taking place countrywide. The Christmas Grand Sale in London, with over 120 different small companies selling their merchandise to the public, is the largest. This takes place in mid-late November each year. Quality is high and covers everything from French lavender sachets, hand-painted furniture, made-to-measure blinds, 19th century wall clocks, unusual watercolours, cinammon-scented apple wreaths, traditional American tinware, children's pyjama cases, candle sconces, handmade Indian pickles, bamboo placemats, embossed copper sketchbooks, Art Deco mirrors, silk embroidered cushions, herbal tinctures, English garden trugs, African shopping baskets, handmade wrapping paper, elegant kitchen woodware, beaded handbags, bespoke Ottomans, fine champagne, baby sleeping bags, nautical mirrors, painted dog and cat beds, ties and matching cufflinks, antique Bergeres suites, Egyptian cotton bedlinen, often at discount because they are ends of lines. There is a three-day Spring Grand Sale at Sudeley Castle, Winchcombe, near Cheltenham in Gloucestershire, usually at the end of April/beginning of May, and a four-day Summer Grand Sale at Ripley Castle, near Harrogate, North Yorkshire, in June. Both feature gardening furniture and equipment as well as decorative home accessories. Phone the above number to put your name on the mailing list. A proportion of the ticket revenue goes to charity.

T J HUGHES

51–57 ST SEPULCHRE GATE, DONCASTER, SOUTH YORKSHIRE DN1 1UB, ☎ 01302 363119, FAX: 01302 363126, **e-mail:** info@tjhughes.co.uk, www.tjhughes.co.uk, 9–5.30 MON–SAT, 10–4 SUN.

121 FERENSWAY, HULL, HUMBERSIDE HU1 3UW, ☎ 01482 326174, FAX: 01482 329767, **e-mail:** info@tjhughes.co.uk, www.tjhughes.co.uk, 9–5.30 MON–SAT, 10.30–4.30 SUN.

18–19 CAPTAIN COOK SQUARE, MIDDLESBROUGH, NORTH YORKSHIRE TS1 5UB, ☎ 01642 220902, FAX: 01642 220903, **e-mail:** info@tjhughes.co.uk, www.tjhughes.co.uk, 9–5.30 MON–SAT, 11–5 SUN.

50 HIGH STREET, SHEFFIELD, SOUTH YORKSHIRE S1 1QH, ☎ 0114 272 8121, FAX: 0114 272 3146, **e-mail:** info@tjhughes.co.uk, www.tjhughes.co.uk, 9–5.30 MON–SAT, 11–5 SUN.
PERMANENT DISCOUNT OUTLET

See page 465 (CHESH)

THE CAPE

REDBRICK MILL, 218 BRADFORD ROAD, BATLEY CARR WEST YORKSHIRE WF17 6JF, ☎ 01924 466228, FAX: 01924 466228, **e-mail:** sc@thefactory-shop.co.uk, www.thecape.co.uk, 9–5.30 MON–FRI, 9.30–5.30 SAT, 11–5 SUN. **FACTORY SHOP**

See page 460 (BRIS)

THE DARLEY MILL CENTRE

DARLEY, NEAR HARROGATE, NORTH YORKSHIRE HG3 2QQ, ☎ 01423 780857, 9.30–5.30 MON–SAT, 11–5 SUN. **PERMANENT DISCOUNT OUTLET**

The centre offers a great day out for the whole family, combining great bargains in clothing, crockery, linens, crafts and exclusive gifts, with lots for children to see and do. This fine 17th-century corn mill has one of the largest water wheels in Yorkshire and there's a licensed restaurant with an outdoor dining terrace.

THE DINING WAREHOUSE

STONEGATE, YORK, NORTH YORKSHIRE YO1 8ZW, ☎ 01904 620736, FAX: 01904 620251 **e-mail:** mailorder@diningwarehouse.co.uk, www.diningwarehouse.co.uk, 9–5.30 MON–SAT.
DESIGNER SALES

The Dining Warehouse at Mulberry Hall contains all you need to entertain in contemporary style. Their once-a-year January sale is the best of its kind in the north of England. There are reductions of between 25% and 70% on hundreds of items from manufacturers including Alessi, Bridgewater Pottery, Villeroy & Boch and cookware from Berndes, Cuisinox and Le Pentole. Also runs an efficient mail order service.

THE FACTORY SHOP

PARK ROSE POTTERY, CARNABY COVERT LANE, CARNABY, BRIDLINGTON, NORTH YORKSHIRE YO15 3QF, ☎ 01262 603518, 10–5 MON–SAT, 10.30–4.30 SUN.

WHEATLEY LANE, LEEDS ROAD, ILKLEY, WEST YORKSHIRE LS29 8BS, ☎ 01943 604514, 9–5.30 MON–SAT, 10.30–4.30 SUN.

LIGHTWATER VALLEY SHOPPING VILLAGE, NORTH STAINLEY, RIPON, NORTH YORKSHIRE HG4 3HT, ☎ 01765 635438, 10–6 MON–SAT, 11–5 SUN.

LAWKHOLME LANE, KEIGHLEY, WEST YORKSHIRE BD21 3JQ, ☎ 01535 611703, 9.30–5 MON–SAT, 10.30–4.30 SUN. **FACTORY SHOP**

See page 465 (CHESH)

THE MILL DISCOUNT DEPARTMENT STORE

BRADFORD ROAD, BATLEY, WEST YORKSHIRE WF17 5LZ, ☎ 01924 423172, FAX: 01924 446096, www.themillbatley.com, 9.30–5.30 MON–SAT, 10–4 SUN. **PERMANENT DISCOUNT OUTLET**

The Mill Discount Department Store is the largest Mill retail outlet in the UK, attracting more than one million visitors every year. Situated in a restored Victorian Mill in the heart of West Yorkshire, The Mill offers massive savings in a department-store format. This all-weather centre consists of four floors together with an external parade selling heavily discounted branded men's, women's and children's fashions, sportswear, homewares, accessories, music, vidoes, sunglasses, books, toys, perfumes, luggage, gifts, shoes, fabrics and lighting. Readmans, whose name is synonymous with unbeatable value, has opened there recently. This is the company's second major stores, offering good quality women's, men's and children's wear, lingerie, shoes, homewares and linens at remarkably low prices. Among over 300 brand names sold at The Mill are Puma, Pilot, HKA, Leeds United, Liz Claiborne, Elle, Jumper, Kasper, Amazing Jeans, Spicy, Urban Turban, Chilli Pepper, Tigi Wear, Ponden Mill, Woods of Windsor, Gleneagles Crystal, Dartington, Arthur Price, Skopos home furnishings, Jane Shilton, Book Depot, Toy Factory, Eye Zone, Famous Footwear, Hush Puppies, Lee Cooper, MX Active, Berghaus, Craghopper, Julian Graves, Fox's Biscuits, John Bull and Lion Confectionery. The complex can be reached by car, coach and train. Junction 40 of the M1 and junctions 27 and 28 of the M62 are within five and six miles of the site respectively. Batley Station on the Trans-Pennine railway is just five minutes walk from The Mill, providing easy access to Leeds and Manchester. There are more than 500 car parking spaces and coach parking is available. Amenities include children's creche, self-service licensed restaurant serving hot and cold food and drinks, Yorkshire Board Information Centre and disabled access.

THE PAPER MILL SHOP COMPANY LTD

MCARTHUR GLEN DESIGNER OUTLET VILLAGE, ST NICHOLAS AVENUE, FULFORD, NORTH YORKSHIRE YO19 4TA, ☎ 01904 674822, www.thepapermillshop. co.uk, 10–6 MON–SAT, 8 ON THUR, 11–5 SUN. **FACTORY SHOP IN A FACTORY SHOPPING VILLAGE**

See page 472 (CUMB)

THE TEA POTTERY

BUSINESS PARK, HARMBY ROAD, LEYBURN, WENSLEYDALE, NORTH YORKSHIRE DL8 5QA, ☎ 01969 623839, FAX: 01969 624079, **e-mail:** info@teapottery.co.uk, www.teapottery.co.uk, 9–5 SEVEN DAYS A WEEK. **FACTORY SHOP**

See page 472 (CUMB)

THE YORKSHIRE OUTLET

WHITE ROSE WAY, JUNCTION 3 OF M18, DONCASTER LAKESIDE, SOUTH YORKSHIRE DN4 5JH, ☎ 01302 366444, **e-mail:** cprimrose@realm-ocm.com, www.theyorkshireoutletcentre.co.uk, 10–6 MON–SAT, 11–5 SUN. **FACTORY SHOPPING VILLAGE**

The Yorkshire Outlet has a great range of stores offering up to 50% off recommended retail prices, with new products and bargains arriving daily. The centre has a range of restaurants, a children's play area, wheelchair hire, and free parking.

TK MAXX

THE ALHAMBRA CENTRE, CHEAPSIDE, UPPER NEW STREET, BARNSLEY, SOUTH YORKSHIRE S70 1SB, ☎ 01226 770078, www.tkmaxx.com, 9–5.30 MON–SAT, 10.30–4.30 SUN.

UNITS 11 AND 12, FORSTER SQUARE RETAIL PARK, 53 VALLEY ROAD, BRADFORD WEST YORKSHIRE BD1 4RN, ☎ 01274 738600, www.tkmaxx.com, 9.30–8 MON–FRI, 9–6 SAT, 11-5 SUN.

8 THE WHEATLEY CENTRE, WHEATLEY HALL ROAD, DONCASTER, SOUTH YORKSHIRE, ☎ 01302 327 707, www.tkmaxx.com, PHONE FOR DETAILS OF OPENING TIMES.

2ND FLOOR, THE VICTORIA SHOPPING CENTRE, HARROGATE, NORTH YORKSHIRE HG1 1AG, ☎ 01423 536636, www.tkmaxx.com, 9–5.30 MON–SAT, 11–4 SUN.

2 KINGSGATE, KING STREET, HUDDERSFIELD, WEST YORKSHIRE, ☎ 01484 519095, www.tkmaxx.com, PHONE FOR DETAILS OF OPENING TIMES.

PRINCES QUAY SHOPPING CENTRE, HULL, HUMBERSIDE HU1 2PQ, ☎ 01482 223202, www.tkmaxx.com, 9–5.30 MON–FRI, 9–6 SAT, 11–5 SUN.

LEEDS SHOPPING PLAZA, 27 ALBION ARCADE, LEEDS, WEST YORKSHIRE LS1 5ER, ☎ 0113 246 7990, www.tkmaxx.com, 9–5.30 MON–FRI, 9–6 SAT, 11–5 SUN.

12 CAPTAIN COOK SQUARE, MIDDLESBROUGH, NORTH YORKSHIRE TS1 5UB, ☎ 01642 222220, www.tkmaxx.com, 9–5.30 MON–FRI, 9–6 SAT, 11–5 SUN.

ORCHARD SQUARE SHOPPING CENTRE, FARGATE, SHEFFIELD, SOUTH YORKSHIRE S1 2FB, ☎ 0114 275 0755, www.tkmaxx.com, 9–6 MON–SAT, 11–5 SUN.

90–93 CATHEDRAL WALK, WAKEFIELD, WEST YORKSHIRE WF1 1YD, ☎ 01924 382828, www.tkmaxx.com, 9–5.30 MON–WED, 9–7.30 THUR, 9–5.30 FRI–SAT.

UNIT 2 MONKS CROSS RETAIL PARK, MONKS CROSS DRIVE, YORK SOUTH YORKSHIRE Y032 9GX, ☎ 01904 659996, www.tkmaxx.com, 9–8 MON–FRI, 9–6 SAT, 10.30–5 SUN.
PERMANENT DISCOUNT OUTLET

See page 458 (BEDS)

TOMLINSON'S FINE FURNITURE CLUB

TOMLINSON FURNITURE GROUP, MOORSIDE, BETWEEN TOCKWITH AND COWTHORPE, NEAR YORK, NORTH YORKSHIRE YO26 7QG, ☎ 01423 358777, www.antique-furniture.co.uk, 9–4.30 SAT AND BANK HOLIDAYS, 10–4 SUN. **SECONDHAND SHOP**

One of the UK's leading wholesalers and exporters of antique and reproduction furniture and artefacts, with over 5,000 items under one roof. They are open to the public on Saturdays, Sundays and bank holidays only. Membership is £3 to this huge emporium selling everything from antique china services to original and reproduction nests of tables, rocking horses, dining tables, beds, sideboards and wardrobes. If you see something you like which needs restoration work, this can be quoted for on site. Tomlinson's can also make bespoke furniture to your requirements. They also now stock a range of garden furniture and accessories, from small statues to large urns, cast iron benches to picnic tables. A range of leather-upholstered goods suitable for the living room and study is also available. There is a café on site specialising in freshly-cooked organic food.

TRADEX

RINGWAY INDUSTRIAL ESTATE, BECK WAY, HUDDERSFIELD, WEST YORKSHIRE HD1 5ND, ☎ 01484 448000, FAX: 01484 448001, 9.30–8.30 MON–FRI, 9–5.30 SAT, 10.30–4.30 SUN.

CHATSWORTH ROAD, LEEDS WEST YORKSHIRE LS8 3QE, ☎ 0113 240 7407, FAX: 0113 200 9819, 9.30–8.30 MON–FRI, 9–5.30 SAT, 10.30–4.30 SUN.

BRADFORD ROAD, PUDSEY, WEST YORKSHIRE LS28 5AS, ☎ 0113 239 3377, 9.30–8.30 MON–FRI, 9–5.30 SAT, 10.30–4.30 SUN. **PERMANENT DISCOUNT OUTLET**

See page 507 (LANCS)

UREDALE GLASS

MARKET PLACE, MASHAM, RIPON, NORTH YORKSHIRE HG4 4EF, ☎ 01765 689780, FAX: 01765 689780, **e-mail:** info@uredale.co.uk, www.uredale.co.uk, 10–4.30 SEVEN DAYS A WEEK IN WINTER, 10–5 IN SUMMER. **FACTORY SHOP**

Individual style of glass making, with an extravagant use of colour, making each piece unique. Also a range of lighting, both hand blown and stained glass. Some slight seconds usually available. There is a small gift section selling items such as animals, paperweights and hearts, plus much more. You can watch the glass-making from Monday to Friday, and admission is free.

WALKLEYS CANALSIDE MILL SHOPPING

BURNLEY ROAD, HEBDEN BRIDGE, WEST YORKSHIRE HX7 7NH, ☎ 01422 842061, 10–5 MON–FRI, 10–5.30 SAT, SUN. **PERMANENT DISCOUNT OUTLET**

Three-storey shop selling a wide selection of goods at discount prices: linen, textiles, footwear, clothes, gifts, crafts, china, fine art and collectables. The ground floor houses the clearance stock or merchandise which is bought in bulk and sold at very competitive prices. Also situated on the ground floor is a comprehensive nursery section sellings prams, buggies, cots etc. The first floor clothes for men and women at 30% to 50% discounts, the third floor houses the china and art shop as well as craft stalls.

WHITE ROSE CANDLES WORKSHOP

WENSLEY MILL, WENSLEY, LEYBURN, NORTH YORKSHIRE DL8 4HR, ☎ 01969 623544, FAX: 01969 623544, www.whiterosecandles.co.uk, 10–5 MON, TUE, THUR, FRI, SUN JUNE–NOVEMBER. MAIL ORDER. **FACTORY SHOP**

Based in an old watermill, and situated beside a waterfall, this candle workshop has been selling direct to the public for the past 30 years. All types of candles are made in simple shapes from hand-dipped and cast dinner table candles to church candles. Sizes range up to 5 feet high x 3 inches in diameter. There are also aromatherapy candles and a wide range of candle holders.

WHITTARD

THE YORKSHIRE OUTLET, WHITE ROSE WAY, DONCASTER, SOUTH YORKSHIRE DN4 5PM, ☎ 01302 739020, 10–6 MON–FRI, 11–5 SAT, SUN.

MCARTHURGLEN DESIGNER OUTLET CENTRE, ST NICHOLAS AVENUE, FULFORD, YORK, NORTH YORKSHIRE YO19 4TA, ☎ 01904 679317, 10–6 MON–FRI, 8 ON THUR, 10–6 SAT, 11–5 SUN. **FACTORY SHOP IN A FACTORY SHOPPING VILLAGE**

See page 466 (CHESH)

WOODS OF WINDSOR

UNIT 4, THE YORKSHIRE OUTLET, WHITE ROSE WAY, DONCASTER, SOUTH YORKSHIRE DN4 5JH, ☎ 01302 368617, www.woodsofwindsor.co.uk, 10–6 MON–SAT, 8 ON THUR, 11–5 SUN.

UNIT 14, FREEPORT VILLAGE, ROLSTON ROAD, HORNSEA, EAST YORKSHIRE HU18 1UT, ☎ 01964 533617, www.woodsofwindsor.co.uk, 10–6 MON–SAT, 8 ON THUR, 11–5 SUN.

UNIT 56, MCARTHURGLEN DESIGNER OUTLET VILLAGE, SELBY ROAD, NABURN, YORK, NORTH YORKSHIRE YO19 4TA, ☎ 01904 624688, www.woodsofwindsor.co.uk, 10–6 MON–SAT, 8 ON THUR, 11–5 SUN. **FACTORY SHOP IN A FACTORY SHOPPING VILLAGE**

See page 466 (CHESH)

YOU & YOURS

UNIT 9, CROWN POINT RETAIL PARK, HUNSLET ROAD, LEEDS, WEST YORKSHIRE LS10 1ET, ☎ 0113 234 1924, 10–5 MON, 10–7 TUE–FRI, 9.30–6 SAT, 11–5 SUN.

98–100 NEW STREET, HUDDERSFIELD, WEST YORKSHIRE HD1 2UD, ☎ 01484 543301, 9–5.30 MON–SAT.

WESTFIELD, INGLEBY ROAD (OPPOSITE GRATTAN), BRADFORD WEST YORKSHIRE BD99 2XE, ☎ 01274 624611, 10–5.30 MON, 10–8 TUE–FRI, 9–5.30 SAT, 11–5 SUN. **PERMANENT DISCOUNT OUTLET**

See page 466 (CHESH)

SOUTH WALES

BED & BATH WORKS

MCARTHURGLEN DESIGNER OUTLET WALES, THE DERWEN, BRIDGEND, JUNCTION 36 OF M4, SOUTH WALES CF32 9SU, ☎ 01656 661335, FAX: 01656 645991, **e-mail:** hello@bedandbathworks.co.uk, www.bedandbathworks.co.uk, 10–8 MON–FRI, 10–6 SAT, 11–5 SUN. **FACTORY SHOP IN A FACTORY SHOPPING VILLAGE**

See page 462 (CHESH)

BIRTHDAYS

UNIT 18, MCARTHURGLEN DESIGNER OUTLET WALES, THE DERWEN, BRIDGEND, JUNCTION 36 OF M4, SOUTH WALES CF32 9FU, ☎ 01656 663822, 10–8 MON–FRI, 10–6 SAT, 11–5 SUN.

UNIT 24, FESTIVAL PARK, VICTORIA, EBBW VALE, SOUTH WALES NP23 5EX, ☎ 01495 306434, 9.30–5.30 MON–SAT, 7 ON THUR, 11–5 SUN. **FACTORY SHOP IN A FACTORY SHOPPING VILLAGE**

See page 462 (CHESH)

CATALOGUE BARGAIN SHOP

FFALDS ROAD SHOPPING CENTRE, PYLE CROSS, PYLE, BRIDGEND, SOUTH WALES CF33 6BH, ☎ 01656 746426, www.bargaincrazy.com, 9–8 MON–FRI, 9–6 SAT, 10.30–4.30 SUN.

PIONEER SUPERSTORE, BRYN-SERTH ROAD, RHD-Y-BLEW, EBBW VALE, GWENT, SOUTH WALES NP3 5YD, ☎ 01495 309297, www.bargaincrazy.com, 9–8 MON–THUR, 9–9 FRI, 9–6 SAT, 10–4 SUN.

61 HIGH STREET, MERTHYR TYDFIL, MID GLAMORGAN, SOUTH WALES CF47 8DE, ☎ 01685 385653, www.bargaincrazy.com, 9–5.30 MON–SAT.

MIDWAY RETAIL PARK, PONTYPRIDD, SOUTH WALES CF37 5NX, ☎ 01443 843718, www.bargaincrazy.com, 9–8 MON–FRI, 9–6 SAT, 11–5 SUN.

UNIT 1A, HAVENS HEAD RETAIL CENTRE, MILFORD HAVEN, PEMBROKESHIRE, SOUTH WALES SA73 3AU, ☎ 01646 697407, www.bargaincrazy.com, 9–8 MON–FRI, 9–6 SAT, 10.30–4.30 SUN.

31 STATION ROAD, PORT TALBOT, WEST GLAMORGAN, SOUTH WALES SA13 1NN, ☎ 01639 899419, www.bargaincrazy.com, 9–5.30 MON–SAT.

229–230 HIGH STREET, SWANSEA, WEST GLAMORGAN, SOUTH WALES SA1 1NY, ☎ 01792 456748, www.bargaincrazy.com, 9–5.30 MON–SAT, 10–4 SUN. **PERMANENT DISCOUNT OUTLET**

See page 461 (CAMBS)

CRAZY MAC'S

PONTARDULAIS ROAD, FFORESTFACH, SWANSEA, SOUTH WALES SA5 4BA, ☎ 01792 585828, FAX: 01792 585566, **e-mail:** lss@salvage1.co.uk, www.salvage1.co.uk, 9.30–6 MON–THUR, 9.30–8 FRI, 9–6 SAT, 11–5 SUN. **PERMANENT DISCOUNT OUTLET**

An Aladdin's cave of salvaged stock for the avid bargain hunter, most of which has been the subject of insurance claims for fire or flood, salvage, bankruptcy or is simply clearance stock. Stock changes every two or three days and regular visitors have found anything from half price Kenwood Chefs, televisions and toys to furniture, kitchen items, linens and especially fantastic bargains in designer clothing. Yves Saint Laurent, Armani, Ungaro, Hugo Boss and Valentino, as well as all major high street names, are just some of the names to be found (though the labels are often cut out). Discounts range from 50% to 80%. Phone first to check stock.

DUNELM MILL SHOP

CITY LINK RETAIL PARK, NEWPORT ROAD, CARDIFF, SOUTH WALES CF2 1PQ, ☎ 02920 482555, FAX: 0290 496160, www.dunelm-mill.co.uk, 9–5 MON–SAT, 8 ON THUR, FRI, 10.30–4.30 SUN.

SPYTTY ROAD, NEWPORT, GWENT, SOUTH WALES NP9 0TG, ☎ 01633 282200, FAX: 01633 281970, www.dunelm-mill.co.uk, 9–6 MON–SAT, 8 ON THUR, FRI, 11–5 SUN. **PERMANENT DISCOUNT OUTLET**

See page 458 (BEDS)

EDINBURGH CRYSTAL

MCARTHURGLEN DESIGNER OUTLET WALES, THE DERWEN, BRIDGEND, JUNCTION 36 OF M4, SOUTH WALES CF32 9SU, ☎ 0800 316 4352 FREE CENTRE INFORMATION LINE 10–8 MON–FRI, 10–6 SAT, 11–5 SUN. **FACTORY SHOP IN A FACTORY SHOPPING VILLAGE**

See page 463 (CHESH)

FESTIVAL PARK FACTORY SHOPPING VILLAGE

FESTIVAL PARK, VICTORIA, EBBW VALE, GWENT, SOUTH WALES NP23 8FP, ☎ 01495 350010, FAX: 01495 307363, 9.30–5.30 MON–SAT, 7 ON THUR, 11–5 SUN. **FACTORY SHOPPING VILLAGE**

Factory shopping village with over 40 shops offering a wide range of top brand goods and designer labels, many at half the recommended retail price. Factory shops include: fashion from Windsmoor, Designer Room, Leading Labels, Double Two, Pilot and Roman Originals; shoes from Pavers; china and crystal from Wedgwood and Stuart Crystal; golfing and sports equipment from Edinburgh Woollen Mill and Sportz; chocolates from Thorntons; leisurewear from Cotton Traders; luggage and bags from Antler; accessories from Claire's and lots more. Built on the former site of the National Garden Festival of Wales, there are over 70 acres of woodland and parkland to explore either on foot or on the land train which operates from Easter to September on weekends and during school holidays, weather permitting. Within the park you can visit the woodland craft centre, owl sanctuary and lakes. There is a 200-seat restaurant, with panoramic views over the valley, serving both snacks and cooked meals. The free car park has dedicated spaces for both the disabled and parent and toddler. There is free wheelchair hire and baby changing facilities.

HARRY TUFFINS SUPERMARKET AND PETROL STATION

KNIGHTON SHELL GARAGE, POWYS, SOUTH WALES LD17 1DA, ☎ 01547 528645, 8–6 MON–WED, SAT, 8–8 THUR, FRI, 10–4 SUN. **PERMANENT DISCOUNT OUTLET**

Supermarket selling foodstuffs, garden furniture and household goods at incredibly competitive prices. Newly refurbished, the store offers a vast range of groceries, wine, household cleaning products, kitchen equipment, stationery, DIY, hardware, clothing and gardening items. Instore fruit and vegetables. The 'Quids In Shop' stocks more than 1,000 items at just £1. Harry Tuffins bottled mineral water is available at Churchstoke.

HYPER VALUE HOLDINGS LTD

BROWN LENNOX RETAIL PARK, YUYSANGHARAD ROAD, PONTYPRIDD, SOUTH WALES CF37 4DA, ☎ 01443 480115, 9–8 MON–FRI, 9–6 SAT, 11–5 SUN. **PERMANENT DISCOUNT OUTLET**

Housed in old supermarket premises, this Aladdin's cave holds a huge array of just about everything, some of which are great value. Dig around among the frames, mirrors, socks, tights, toiletries, tools, carpets, stationery, shirts, ornaments, paint, wallpaper borders and garden furniture, and you may find the odd gem such as the natural canvas parasol, Habitat-style, £20, or Christian Dior tights, 40p. There are 22 branches in South Wales, 27 in total, some in retail parks, others in stand-alone shops.

MATALAN

UNIT 2, 383–384 NEWPORT ROAD, CARDIFF, SOUTH WALES CF3 7AE, ☎ 02920 491781, FAX: 02920 49782, www.matalan.co.uk, 10–8 MON–FRI, 9–6 SAT, 11–5 SUN.

UNIT 4B, CWMBRAN RETAIL PARK, CWMBRAN DRIVE, CWMBRAN, GWENT, SOUTH WALES NP44 3JQ, ☎ 01633 866944, FAX: 01633 868400, www.matalan.co.uk, 9.30–8 MON–FRI, 9–6 SAT, 11–5 SUN.

UNIT 8, GLAMORGAN VALE RETAIL PARK, LLANTRISANT, MID-GLAMORGAN, SOUTH WALES CF72 8RP, ☎ 01443 224854, FAX: 01443 227138, www.matalan.co.uk, 10–8 MON–FRI, 9–8 SAT, 11–5 SUN.

NEWPORT RETAIL PARK, 7 STILES AVENUE, NEWPORT, SOUTH WALES NP19 4TX, ☎ 01633 636030, FAX: 01633 281271, www.matalan.co.uk, 10–8 MON–FRI, 9–6 SAT, 11–5 SUN.

FOUNDRY ROAD, MORRISTON, SWANSEA, SOUTH WALES SA6 8DU, ☎ 01792 792229, FAX: 01792 702455, www.matalan.co.uk, 10–8 MON–FRI, 9–6 SAT, 11–5 SUN.

CARMARTHEN ROAD, SWANSEA CARMARTHEN, SOUTH WALES SA5 8LL, ☎ 01792 560010, FAX: 01792 582979, www.matalan.co.uk, 10–8 MON–FRI, 9–6 SAT, 11–5 SUN. **PERMANENT DISCOUNT OUTLET**

See page 458 (BEDS)

MCARTHURGLEN DESIGNER OUTLET WALES

THE DERWEN, BRIDGEND, JUNCTION 36 OF M4, SOUTH WALES CF32 9SU, ☎ 01656 665700, www.mcarthurglen.com/bridgend, 10–8 MON–FRI, 10–6 SAT, 11–5 SUN. **FACTORY SHOPPING VILLAGE**

The McArthurGlen Designer Outlet in Bridgend is Wales' premier designer outlet. Set out in a friendly village street style the outlet has over 80 stores with everything from men's, women's and children's clothing to accessories, shoes, sportswear, luggage, homewares, toys, books, and gifts. All stock is excess stock sold by the retailers themselves at 30% to 50% off typical retail prices. The outlet also has over 1, 800 free parking spaces, a food court, two children's play areas and a nine-screen Odeon cinema. Stores include: Reebok, Calvin Klein, Tie Rack, Ciro Pearls, Monet, Picture Port, Ciro Citterio, Bookends, Bed & Bath, Clover House, Overland, Pepe, Famous Footwear, Nickelbys, The Suit Company, Birthdays, Toyzone, Vans, Red/Green, Whittards, Travel Accessories, Ecco, Jacques Vert, Warners, Next, Windsmoor, Pilot, Petroleum, Roman Originals, Antler, Julian Graves, The Watch Shop, Knickerbox, Wedgewood, The Garden Outlet, Claire's Accessories, Clarks, Donnay, JoKids, Ben Sherman, Smiths Signature, Spiegelau, Royal Worcester/Edinburgh Crystal, Littlewoods, Helly Hansen, Woodies, Lee Cooper, Van Heusen/Viyella/Jaeger, Ted Baker, Cotton Traders, Royal Doulton, Walker and Hall, Professional Cookware Co, Thorntons, Price's Candles, Mountain Warehouse, John Partridge, Remington, U Wear/I Wear, Nike, The Body Shop, Mexx, Suits You, Designer Rooms, Winning Line, Tog 24, Elle, Chilli Pepper/Watsons, HKA, XS, Soled Out, Timberland, Carphone Warehouse, Levi's, and The Craft Outlet.

PONDEN MILL

FESTIVAL PARK SHOPPING VILLAGE, VICTORIA, EBBW VALE, SOUTH WALES NP3 6FP, ☎ 01495 302765, 9.30–5.30 MON–SAT, 7 ON THUR, 11–5 SUN. **FACTORY SHOP IN A FACTORY SHOPPING VILLAGE**

See page 464 (CHESH)

PRICE'S CANDLES

MCARTHURGLEN DESIGNER OUTLET WALES, THE DERWEN, BRIDGEND, JUNCTION 36 OF M4, SOUTH WALES CF32 9SU, ☎ 01656 767001, 10–8 MON–FRI, 10–6 SAT, 11–5 SUN. **FACTORY SHOP IN A FACTORY SHOPPING VILLAGE**

See page 464 (CHESH)

ROYAL WORCESTER & SPODE FACTORY SHOP

MCARTHURGLEN DESIGNER OUTLET WALES, THE DERWEN, BRIDGEND, JUNCTION 36 OF M4, SOUTH WALES CF32 9SU, ☎ 01656 651444, www.royal-worcester.co.uk, 10–8 MON–FRI, 10–6 SAT, 11–5 SUN. **FACTORY SHOP IN A FACTORY SHOPPING VILLAGE**

See page 465 (CHESH)

STEWART'S

12 PIER STREET, ABERYSTWYTH, CEREDIGION, SOUTH WALES SY23 2LJ, ☎ 01970 611437, FAX: 01970 611437, 9–5. MON–SAT.

UNIT 4, BETHEL SQUARE SHOPPING CENTRE, BRECON, POWYS, SOUTH WALES LD3 7HU, ☎ 01874 610260, FAX: 01874 610260, 9–5.30 MON–SAT, 11–4 SUN.

MARLAS ROAD, PYLE CROSS, NR BRIDGEND, MID GLAMORGAN, SOUTH WALES CF33 6AY, ☎ 01656 744988, FAX: 01656 744988, 9.30–5.30 MON–SAT, 12–4 SUN.

2–4 CARDIFF ROAD, Y TWYN, CAERPHILLY, MID GLAMORGAN SOUTH WALES CF83 1JN, ☎ 02920 888054, FAX: 02920 888054, 9–5.30 MON–SAT.

21–22 GREYFRIARS, CARMARTHEN, CARMARTHENSHIRE, SOUTH WALES SA31 3NB, ☎ 01267 232208, FAX: 01267 232021, 9–5.30 MON–SAT, 11–4 SUN.

LONDON HOUSE, HARFORD SQUARE, LAMPETER, CEREDIGION, SOUTH WALES SA48 7HD, ☎ 01570 422205, 9.30–5.30 MON–SAT, 5 ON WED.

52 STEPNEY STREET, LLANELLI, CARMARTHENSHIRE, SOUTH WALES SA15 3TR, ☎ 01554 776957, FAX: 01554 776957, 9–5 MON–SAT.

7–11 MONNOW STREET, MONMOUTH, MONMOUTHSHIRE, SOUTH WALES NP5 3EF, ☎ 01600 716926, FAX: 01600 716926, 9.30–5.30 MON–SAT.

GLAMORE TERRACE, NEW QUAY, CEREDIGION, SOUTH WALES SA45 9PL, ☎ 01545 560740, FAX: 01545 560740, 9.30–5.30 MON–SAT, 11–5 SUN.

144 HIGH STREET, PORTHMADOG, GWYNEDD, SOUTH WALES LL49 9NU, ☎ 01766 514166, FAX: 01766 514166, 9–5.30 MON–SAT, 12–4 SUN.

THE STRAND, SAUNDERSFOOT, PEMBROKESHIRE SOUTH WALES SA69 9GE, ☎ 01834 812579, FAX: 01834 812579, 9–5.30 MON–SAT, 10–5.30 SUN.

BREWERY TERRACE, SAUNDERSFOOT, PEMBROKESHIRE, SOUTH WALES SA69 9HG, ☎ 01834 813169, FAX: 01834 813169, 9.30–5.30 MON–SAT, 10–5.30 SUN.

HIGH STREET, TENBY, PEMBROKESHIRE, SOUTH WALES SA70 7EW, ☎ 01834 844621, FAX: 01834 844621, 9.30–5.30 MON–SAT, 10–5.30 SUN. **FACTORY SHOP**

See page 478 (DEV)

STUART CRYSTAL

BRIDGE STREET, CHEPSTOW, MONMOUTHSHIRE, SOUTH WALES NP16 5EZ, ☎ 01291 620136, 9–5 MON–SAT APRIL–SEPTEMBER, 10–5 OCTOBER–MARCH, 11–5 SUN. **FACTORY SHOP**

See page 546 (WARW)

THE ABBEY WOOLLEN MILLS

MUSEUM SQUARE, MARITIME QUARTER, SWANSEA, SOUTH WALES SA1 1SN, ☎ 01792 650351, FAX: 01792 654200, www.swansea.maritime.museum@business.ntl.com, 10–5 TUE–SUN, CLOSED MON EXCEPT FOR BANK HOLIDAYS. **PERMANENT DISCOUNT OUTLET**

Housed in the Swansea Maritime and Industrial Museum. Because its products are woven on the restored 19th-century looms housed there, Abbey Woollen Mills makes blankets woven from the raw fleece of the Welsh Radno breed of sheep. The mills dye, lubricate, card and spin the fleece into yarn which is woven using traditional colours and patterns. Unlike blankets which are acrylic or wool blends and can therefore use a cheap fleece, these products are hard-wearing, long-lasting and wash well. Only available through the on-site shop, you can save at least 50% on shop prices for the same quality blankets. The mills specialise in pure wool shawls, rugs and blankets, which are sold at discounts of one third off the normal retail price, with occasional seconds selling at half price. Scarves start at £4.99, picnic rugs from £13 to £20, large throw 100in x 70in, £40 in various colours and patterns. There is a small tea room open from Easter to September.

THE FACTORY SHOP

SNOWDROP LANE, HAVERFORDWEST, SOUTH WALES SA61 1ET, ☎ 01437 766000, 9–5.30 MON–SAT, 10.30–4.30 SUN. **FACTORY SHOP**

See page 465 (CHESH)

TK MAXX

UNIT 11, QUEENS WEST CENTRE, QUEEN STREET, CARDIFF, SOUTH WALES CF10 2AQ, ☎ 02920 341290, www.tkmaxx.com, 9–5.30 MON–WED, 9–7 THUR, 9–6 FRI–SAT, 11–5 SUN. **PERMANENT DISCOUNT OUTLET**

UNIT 25, GREYFRIARS SHOPPING CENTRE, CARMARTHEN, SOUTH WALES SA31 3BN, ☎ 01267 220934, www.tkmaxx.com, 9–5.30 MON–TUE, 9–6 WED–SAT, 9–8 THUR, 10–4 SUN.

2–3 OXFORD STREET, SWANSEA, SOUTH WALES SA1 3AE, ☎ 01792 642055, www.tkmaxx.com, 9–5.30 MON–THUR, 9–6 FRI–SAT, 11–5 SUN. **PERMANENT DISCOUNT OUTLET**

See page 458 (BEDS)

WHITTARD

MCARTHURGLEN DESIGNER OUTLET WALES, THE DERWEN, BRIDGEND, JUNCTION 36 OF M4, SOUTH WALES CF32 9SU, ☎ 01656 658434, 10–8 MON–FRI, 10–6 SAT, 11–5 SUN. **FACTORY SHOP IN A FACTORY SHOPPING VILLAGE**

See page 466 (CHESH)

WILKINSON STORES

10–13 CARDIFF STREET, ABERDARE, MID-GLAMORGAN, SOUTH WALES CF44 7DP, ☎ 01685 870393, www.wilko.co.uk, 9–5.30 MON–THUR, 9–6 FRI, SAT, 10–4 SUN. MAIL ORDER.

CIBI WALK SHOPPING CENTRE, FOGMORE STREET, ABERGAVENNY SOUTH WALES NP7 5AJ, ☎ 01685 870393, www.wilko.co.uk, 8.30–5.30 MON–THUR, 8.30–6 FRI, SAT, 10–4 SUN. MAIL ORDER. **PERMANENT DISCOUNT OUTLET**

See page 466 (CHESH)

NORTH WALES

CATALOGUE BARGAIN SHOP

UNITS F1–F2, FLINTSHIRE RETAIL CENTRE, FLINT, NORTH WALES CH6 5RR, ☎ 01352 732460, www.bargaincrazy.com, 9–8 MON–FRI, 9–6 SAT, 10.30–4.30 SUN.

6–8 MADOC STREET, LLANDUDNO, GWYNEDD, NORTH WALES LL30 2TP, ☎ 01492 877561, www.bargaincrazy.com, 9–5 MON–SAT, 10.30–4.30 SUN.

OLD KERRY ROAD, NEWTOWN, POWYS, NORTH WALES SY16 1BJ, ☎ 01686 628283, www.bargaincrazy.com, 9–5.30 MON–SAT, 10–4 SUN. **PERMANENT DISCOUNT OUTLET**

See page 461 (CAMBS)

CHINA CHASE

LONG BYRE, BORRAS HEAD, WREXHAM, NORTH WALES LL13 9TL, ☎ 01978 856400, FAX: 01978 856400, **e-mail:** chinachase@aol.com, www.chinachase.co.uk, PHONE OR WRITE ENCLOSING AN SAE FOR DETAILS. **PERMANENT DISCOUNT OUTLET**

If you wish to buy or sell discontinued or obsolete china patterns, China Chase can help you, sourcing from stock and the company's vast database of clients. Whether it be Royal Doulton, Royal Albert, Royal Worcester, Royal Grafton or Wedgwood, Minton, Coalport, Spode or Denby, China Chase is worth a call.

DARTINGTON CRYSTAL

C/O JAMES PRINGLE WEAVERS, HOLYHEAD ROAD, LLANFAIRPWLLGWYNGYLL, ANGLESEY, NORTH WALES LL61 5UJ, ☎ 01248 715255, FAX: 01248 713110, 9–5.30 MON–SAT, 11–5 SUN.

TWEEDMILL, LLANERCH PARK, ST ASAPH, NORTH WALES LL17 0UY, ☎ 01745 730072, FAX: 01745 731008, 9.30–6 MON–SAT, 8 ON THUR, 11–5 SUN. **FACTORY SHOP**

See page 469 (CORN)

MATALAN

UNIT 1A AND 1B, CAERNARFON ROAD, BANGOR, GWYNEDD, NORTH WALES LL57 4SU, ☎ 01248 362778, FAX: 01248 362779, www.matalan.co.uk, 9.30–8 MON–FRI, 9–6 SAT, 11–5 SUN.

UNIT 1, MOUNT STREET RETAIL, MOUNT STREET, WREXHAM, NORTH WALES LL1 2BN, ☎ 01978 346850, FAX: 01978 262933, www.matalan.co.uk, 10–8 MON–FRI, 9–6 SAT, 11–5 SUN. **PERMANENT DISCOUNT OUTLET**

See page 458 (BEDS)

STEWART'S

23 MOSTYN STREET, LLANDUDNO, GWYNEDD, NORTH WALES LL30 2NL, ☎ 01492 870733, FAX: 01492 870733, 9–5.30 MON–SAT, 10 – 4 SUN.

Y MAES, PWLLHELI, GWYNEDD, NORTH WALES LL53 5HG, ☎ 01758 701130, FAX: 01758 701130, 9.30–5 MON–SAT. **FACTORY SHOP**

See page 478 (DEV)

T J HUGHES

UNIT B, HENBLAS SQUARE, CHESTER STREET, WREXHAM, CLWYD, NORTH WALES LL13 8BA, ☎ 01978 359555, FAX: 01978 359500, **e-mail:** info@tjhughes.co.uk, www.tjhughes.co.uk, 9–5.30 MON– SAT, 11–5 SUN. **PERMANENT DISCOUNT OUTLET**

See page 465 (CHESH)

THE FACTORY SHOP LTD

BRUNSWICK ROAD, BUCKLEY, CLYWD, NORTH WALES CH7 2EF, ☎ 01555 759017, FAX: 01555 759018, 9.30–5.30 MON–SAT, 10.30–4.30 SUN. **FACTORY SHOP**

See page 465 (CHESH)

THE TWEEDMILL FACTORY OUTLETS

LLANNERCH PARK, ST ASAPH, DENBIGHSHIRE, (OFF A55), NORTH WALES LL17 0UY, ☎ 01745 730072, FAX: 01745 731008, **e-mail:** enquiries@tweedmill.co.uk, www.tweedmill.co.uk, 9.30–6 MON–SAT, 8 ON THUR, 11–5 SUN. **FACTORY SHOP**

Stocks a wide range of clothes for both men and women, luggage, giftware, handbags and home accessories with savings of up to 50% off normal high street prices. Selling directly to the public from the manufacturers, there are always at least 50,000 garments in stock and 5,000 pairs of shoes as well as 100,000 homeware items, all of which are perfects. Coloroll, Ponden Mill, Price's Candles, Cloverleaf and Dartington Crystal for homewares. Everything is labelled with the original retail price, so you can see the discounts of up to 50%.

SOUTHERN SCOTLAND

DESIGN HOUSE

GRETNA GATEWAY OUTLET CENTRE, GRETNA GREEN, SCOTLAND DG16 5GG, ☎ 01461 337332, 10–6 SEVEN DAYS A WEEK. **FACTORY SHOP IN A FACTORY SHOPPING VILLAGE**

See page 483 (ESSEX)

GRETNA GATEWAY OUTLET VILLAGE

GLASGOW ROAD, GRETNA, SCOTLAND DG16 6GG, ☎ 01461 339028, FAX: 01461 339100 INFORMATION LINE, **e-mail:** info@gretnagateway.com, www.gretnagateway.com, 10–6 SEVEN DAYS A WEEK. **FACTORY SHOPPING VILLAGE**

Thirty trading outlets with a planned second phase of 20 shops. Includes Episode, Bags Etc, Designer Room, Directions Design Studio, Design House, DKNY, Edinburgh Woollen Mill, Jane Shilton, John Partridge, Price's Candles, Polo Ralph Lauren (stocking clothes for men, women and children as well as homewares), Reebok, Rockport, Tag Heuer, The Golf Company, Tog 24, Tommy Hilfiger, La Casa del Cristallo, Book Depot, Mexx, Claire's Accessories, Pavers Shoes, Chapelle Jewellery, Thorntons, Van Heusen and Whittards. There is a children's play area, disabled access, free parking and restaurants.

PRICE'S CANDLES

GRETNA GATEWAY OUTLET VILLAGE, JUNCTION 22 OF A74, DUMFRIESSHIRE, SCOTLAND DG16 5GG, ☎ 01461 339050, 10–6 SEVEN DAYS A WEEK. **FACTORY SHOP IN A FACTORY SHOPPING VILLAGE**

See page 464 (CHESH)

THE FACTORY SHOP LTD

54–60 HIGH STREET, ANNAN, DUMFRIES, SCOTLAND DG12 6AJ, ☎ 01461 207687, 9–5 MON–SAT, 10.30–4.30 SUN. **FACTORY SHOP**

See page 465 (CHESH)

WHITTARD

GRETNA GATEWAY OUTLET VILLAGE, GRETNA GREEN, DUMFRIES, SCOTLAND DG16 5GG 10461 339151, 10–6 SEVEN DAYS A WEEK. **FACTORY SHOP IN A FACTORY SHOPPING VILLAGE**

See page 466 (CHESH)

CENTRAL SCOTLAND

ANTARTEX VILLAGE VISITOR CENTRE

LOMOND INDUSTRIAL ESTATE, ALEXANDRIA, DUMBARTONSHIRE G83 0TP, ☎ 01389 752393, FAX: 01389 750656, 10–6 SEVEN DAYS A WEEK. **FACTORY SHOP**

Large, rambling building with a coffee shop, well signposted off the A82, which has a vast retail area and additional manufacturing workshops where you can watch sheepskin jackets being made, or enjoy whisky tasting. It's difficult to tell how good the prices are as most are not double ticketed to show the original and sale price, but there are bargain sections. Edinburgh Woollen Mill has a large area, and other labels on sale include Pitlochry, Country Rose and Regatta. As well as clothes and shoes for men (new One Valley range of waterproof jackets, Hippo and PG Fields) and women and children, there are tea towels, toys, books, food, gifts, blankets, mugs, candles, CDs and tapes, table mats, sports equipment and countrywear. There is a big golf department selling Wilson, Spalding and Arnold Palmer equipment at discounts of 20% to 30% and lots of different workshops. Close to the Loch Lomond outlet village.

BED & BATH WORKS

MCARTHURGLEN DESIGNER OUTLET LIVINGSTON, ALMONDVALE AVENUE, LIVINGSTON, WEST LOTHIAN, JUNCTION 3 OFF THE M8, BETWEEN EDINBURGH AND GLASGOW, SCOTLAND EH54 6OX, ☎ 01506 418454, FAX: 01506 418316, **e-mail:** hello@bedandbathworks.co.uk, www.bedandbathworks.co.uk, 10–6 SEVEN DAYS A WEEK, 8 ON THUR.

STERLING MILLS DESIGNER OUTLET VILLAGE, MOSS ROAD, TILLICOULTRY, CLACKMANNANSHIRE, SCOTLAND FK13 6HN, ☎ 01259 753750, FAX: 01259 753751, **e-mail:** hello@bedandbathworks.co.uk, www.bedandbathworks.co.uk, 10–8 MON–FRI, 9–6 SAT, 11–5 SUN. **FACTORY SHOP IN A FACTORY SHOPPING VILLAGE**

See page 462 (CHESH)

CATALOGUE BARGAIN SHOP

315–317 HIGH STREET, COWDENBEATH, FIFE, SCOTLAND KY4 9QJ, ☎ 01383 611054, www.bargaincrazy.com, 9–5.30 MON–SAT, 11–4 SUN.

12–16 CADZOW STREET, HAMILTON, LANARKSHIRE SCOTLAND ML3 6DG, ☎ 01698 421112, www.bargaincrazy.com, 9–5.30 MON–SAT, 12–4 SUN.

THE FORGE SHOPPING CENTRE, PARKHEAD, GLASGOW, SCOTLAND G31 4EB, ☎ 0141 556 5352, www.bargaincrazy.com, 9–6 MON–SAT, 11–5 SUN. **PERMANENT DISCOUNT OUTLET**

See page 461 (CAMBS)

DARTINGTON CRYSTAL

STERLING MILL, MOSS ROAD, TILLICOULTRY, CLACKMANNANSHIRE, SCOTLAND FK13 6NS, ☎ 01259 755181, 10–6 MON–SAT, 11–5 SUN. **FACTORY SHOP IN A FACTORY SHOPPING VILLAGE**

See page 469 (CORN)

DENBY FACTORY SHOP

MCARTHURGLEN DESIGNER OUTLET VILLAGE, ALMONDVALE AVENUE, LIVINGSTON, WEST LOTHIAN, SCOTLAND EH54 6QX, ☎ 01506 461442, www.denby.co.uk, 10–6 MON–SUN, 8 ON THUR.

STERLING MILLS DESIGNER OUTLET VILLAGE, MOSS ROAD, TILLICOULTRY, CLACKMANNANSHIRE, SCOTLAND FK13 6HN, ☎ 01259 753939, www.denby.co.uk, 10–6 DAILY. **FACTORY SHOP IN A FACTORY SHOPPING VILLAGE**

See page 463 (CHESH)

DESIGN HOUSE

STERLING MILLS DESIGNER OUTLET VILLAGE, DEVONDALE, TILLICOULTRY, CLACKMANNANSHIRE, SCOTLAND FK13 6HQ, ☎ 01259 753773, 10–6 SEVEN DAYS A WEEK. **FACTORY SHOP IN A FACTORY SHOPPING VILLAGE**

See page 483 (ESSEX)

EDINBURGH CRYSTAL

MCARTHUR GLEN DESIGNER OUTLET VILLAGE, ALMONDALE AVENUE, LIVINGSTON, SCOTLAND EH54 6QX, ☎ 01506 417411, 10–6 MON–SAT, 8 ON THUR, 11–5 SUN. **FACTORY SHOP IN A FACTORY SHOPPING VILLAGE**

EASTFIELD, PENICUIK, LOTHIAN, SCOTLAND EH26 8HB, ☎ 01968 675128, 9–5 MON–SAT, 11–5 SUN. **FACTORY SHOP**

See page 463 (CHESH)

FREEPORT SCOTLAND OUTLET VILLAGE

FIVE SISTERS, WESTWOOD, WEST CALDER, NEAR JUNCTION 4 OF THE M8, WEST LOTHIAN, SCOTLAND EH55 8QB, ☎ 01501 763488, www.freeportscotland.com, 10–6 SEVEN DAYS A WEEK. **FACTORY SHOPPING VILLAGE**

Designer outlet village with more than 25 shops offering up to 50% off high street prices, as well as a café and free parking. Outlets for women include The Designer Room, Mexx, London Leathers, Versace, Klass, Select, Iceberg and Jean Scene. Menswear is available from Ciro Citterio, Versace, Double Two, Madhouse, Leading Labels, Iceberg, Mexx, Nickleby's and Proibito. Sweet-toothed visitors can savour the chocolates at Thorntons. Other shops include Tog 24, Bags Etc, Charles Clinkard, Outdoor Adventure, Book Depot, Churchill China and Ponden Mill.

GLENEAGLES CRYSTAL

9 SIMPSON ROAD, EAST MAIN INDUSTRIAL ESTATE, BROXBURN, LOTHIAN, SCOTLAND EH52 5NP, ☎ 01506 852566, 10–5 MON–SAT, 11–4 SUN. **FACTORY SHOP**

Hand-cut crystal, wine glasses, tumblers, ornaments, giftware, china and ceramics at discounts of about 15% for seconds. There are usually promotions on various ranges. Tableware, dinner sets, complete china range from names such as Villeroy & Boch, Wedgwood, Royal Doulton, Royal Worcester, Spode, Denby, Portmeirion and Arthur Price cutlery.

LOCH LOMOND FACTORY OUTLETS

MAIN STREET, ALEXANDRIA, JUNCTION 17 OF M8 THEN A82, LOCH LOMOND, SCOTLAND G83 0UG, ☎ 01389 710077 , FAX: 01389 605500 INFORMATION LINE., ☎ 01389 607259, **e-mail:** info@lochlomondoutlets.co.uk, www.lochlomondoutletcentre.co.uk, 9.30–5.30 SEVEN DAYS A WEEK. **FACTORY SHOPPING VILLAGE**

Just off the A82, the main route between Glasgow and the West Highlands and Islands, and only one mile from Loch Lomond, this factory outlet centre combines history, heritage, adventure and shopping under one roof. Shops include Bags Etc selling luggage items; Book Depot, Designer Room (Klass, DKNY, Elle), Global Emporium for gifts, Jean Scene for branded denim wear; Julian Graves foods and nut mixes; Leading Labels, Nickleby's, Pavers Shoes, Ponden Mill for bedlinen and bathroom ware; Ramseys womenswear; Room offering homes accessories and furniture; Stuart Crystal; Sportz selling sportswear from Adidas, Nike, etc; Tog 24 for outdoor wear; Trespass; Card & Party Place (greetings cards and posters). There is also Ceramic Experience (a unique opportunity to decorate your own ceramics and pottery merchandise plus a children's soft play area), a Motoring Heritage Centre telling the history of the Scottish motor car industry with a collection of vintage cars, and The Gallery Cafe selling meals, snacks and sandwiches.

MACKINNON MILLS

KIRKSHAW ROAD, COATBRIDGE, SCOTLAND ML5 4SL, ☎ 01236 440702, 10–5.30 MON–FRI, 10–6 SAT–SUN. **FACTORY SHOP**

Working woollen mill that sells some seconds and perfect woollens with labels such as Lyle & Scott, Antartex and Edinburgh Woollen Mill. They also sell golf equipment, Scottish music tapes, dress jewellery, books, shoes, bags and bedding. Meals are served in the coffee shop.

MATALAN

UNIT 13A, WEST LODGE ROAD, RENFREW, BLYTHSWOOD, SCOTLAND PA4 9EN, ☎ 0141 886 8050, FAX: 0141 886 2447, www.matalan.co.uk, 9.30–8 MON–FRI, 9.30–5.30 SAT, 10–6 SUN.

CLYDE RETAIL PARK, LIVINGSTONE STREET, CLYDEBANK, GLASGOW SCOTLAND G81 2XA, ☎ 0141 435 7450, FAX: 0141 952 0415, www.matalan.co.uk, 10–8 MON–FRI, 8–5.30 SAT, 10–6 SUN.

UNIT 2, FARADAY RETAIL PARK, WHIFFLET STREET/COATBANK STREET, COATBRIDGE, LANARKSHIRE ML5 3SP, ☎ 01244 665260, FAX: 01236 423950, www.matalan.co.uk, 10–8 MON–FRI, 10–6 SAT, 10–6 SUN.

NITSHILL ROAD, DARNLEY, GLASGOW, SCOTLAND G53 7BW, ☎ 0141 880 3900, FAX: 0141 880 4958, www.matalan.co.uk, 10–8 MON–FRI, 9.30–6 SAT, 10–6 SUN.

CARRON ROAD, BAINESFORD, FALKIRK SCOTLAND FK1, FAX: 01324 614130, FAX: 01324 627149, www.matalan.co.uk, 10–8 MON–FRI, 10–6 SAT, SUN.

SALTAIRE RETAIL PARK, PENTLAND PARK, GLENROTHES, SCOTLAND KY6 2AL, ☎ 01592 776860, FAX: 01592 773354, www.matalan.co.uk, 10–8 MON–FRI, 9.30–5.30 SAT, 10–6 SUN.

LORENY INDUSTRIAL ESTATE, UMBERLEY ROAD, KILMARNOCK, SCOTLAND KA1 5LB, ☎ 01563 555040, FAX: 01563 549832, www.matalan.co.uk, 10–8 MON–FRI, 9.30–5.30 SAT, 10–6 SUN.

3–4 SEAFIELD WAY, SEAFIELD ROAD, LEITH, EDINBURGH, SCOTLAND EH15 1TB, ☎ 0131 657 5045, FAX: 0131 657 5046, www.matalan.co.uk, 10–8 MON–FRI, 9.30–5.30 SAT, 10–6 SUN.

PHOENIX RETAIL PARK, LINWOOD ROAD, PAISLEY, SCOTLAND PA1 2AB, ☎ 0141 840 5120, FAX: 0141 849 7109, www.matalan.co.uk, 10–8 MON–FRI, 9–6 SAT, 10–6 SUN.

155 SLATEFORD ROAD, EDINBURGH, SCOTLAND EH14 1NZ, ☎ 0131 455 7224, FAX: 0131 443 2570, www.matalan.co.uk, 10–8 MON–FRI, 8.30–5.30 SAT, 10–6 SUN.

UNIT 5, CALEDONIAN CENTRE, NEW ASHTREE INDUSTRIAL ESTATE, WISHAW, LANARKSHIRE ML2 7UR, ☎ 01698 357075, FAX: 01698 357072, www.matalan.co.uk, **PERMANENT DISCOUNT OUTLET**

See page 458 (BEDS)

MCARTHURGLEN DESIGNER OUTLET

ALMONDVALE AVENUE, LIVINGSTON, WEST LOTHIAN, JUNCTION 3 OFF THE M8, BETWEEN EDINBURGH AND GLASGOW, SCOTLAND EH54 6QX, ☎ 01506 423600, FAX: 01506 423602, www.mcarthurglen.com/livingston, 10–6 SEVEN DAYS A WEEK, 8 ON THUR. **FACTORY SHOPPING VILLAGE**

The McArthurGlen Designer Outlet Livingston offers over 80 stores full of top brands and designer labels at up to 50% off typical retail prices. There is a food court, cafés and restaurants as well as an eight-screen licensed cinema, health and fitness club and free parking for 1, 800 cars. Stores include: Gap Outlet, XS, Designer Shades, Marks & Spencer Outlet, The Body Shop Outlet, Van Heusen/Jaeger/Viyella, One to One, Antler, Clarks, Suits You, Chappelle, Banana Books, Toyworld, Donnay, Whittard, Price's Candles, Aquascutum, Revlon, The Paper Mill Shop, Regatta, Jane Shilton, Brand Fushion, Early Learning Centre, CK Jeans, Jockey, Autonomy, Cotton Traders, Black and Decker, Room, Surf, Skate and Snow, Ronit Zilkha, Ted Baker, Proudfoot, Thornton's, Arran Aromatics, Bon Bleu, Jokids, Soled Out, Windsmoor, Suit Co, Easy Jeans, Roman Originals, Julian Graves, Directions, Sportz, Lilley & Skinner, Armani, Ben Sherman, Petroleum, Samsonite, Tog 24, Outdoor Scene, Trespass, Logo, Levi's, Professional

Cookware, Coloroll, Jane Heath, Bed & Bath, Denby, Pictureport, Waterford/Wedgewood, Poole Pottery, Lights 4 Less, Cloverhouse, Gleneagles, Edinburgh Crystal, and Speigelau.

ONEIDA

STERLING WAREHOUSE FURNITURE GROUP LTD, TILLICOULTRY, SCOTLAND FK13 6NS, ☎ 01259 750655, 10–8 MON–FRI, 10–6 SAT, 12–5.30 SUN. **FACTORY SHOP**

See page 464 (CHESH)

PONDEN MILL LINENS

FREEPORT SHOPPING VILLAGE, FIVE SISTERS, WESTWOOD, WEST CALDER, WEST LOTHIAN, SCOTLAND EH55 8QB, ☎ 01501 763053, 10–6 SEVEN DAYS A WEEK, 8 ON THUR.

LOCH LOMOND FACTORY OUTLET, ARGYLE WORKS, MAIN STREET, ALEXANDRIA, LOCH LOMOND SCOTLAND G83 0UG, ☎ 01389 607200, 10–6 SEVEN DAYS A WEEK. **FACTORY SHOP IN A FACTORY SHOPPING VILLAGE**

See page 464 (CHESH)

PRICE'S CANDLES

MCARTHURGLEN DESIGNER OUTLET LIVINGSTON, ALMONDVALE AVENUE, LIVINGSTON, WEST LOTHIAN, JUNCTION 3 OFF THE M8, BETWEEN EDINBURGH AND GLASGOW, SCOTLAND, ☎ 01506 461481, 10–6 SEVEN DAYS A WEEK 8 ON THUR. **FACTORY SHOP IN A FACTORY SHOPPING VILLAGE**

See page 464 (CHESH)

REJECTS

123 ST CLAIR STREET, KIRKCALDY, FIFE, SCOTLAND KY1 2BS, ☎ 01592 655955, FAX: 01592 655722, **e-mail:** info@rejectsonline.com, 9–5.30 MON–SAT, 12.30–4.30 SUN. **PERMANENT DISCOUNT OUTLET**

Rejects Department Store sells curtain and dress fabric, china, pottery, carpets, silk flower, glassware, home decoration equipment and materials, lighting, basketware, carpet and flooring and has a cookshop. The shop is 100,000 square feet and claims to be the best value department store in the UK, although it isn't a discount store as such. For example, the curtain shop is larger than Harrods curtain department with thousands of rolls of material. There is a particularly large selection of pottery and china, bedding, cushions, pictures, mirrors, wallpaper, paint, hardware and garden tools. The shop also has a self-service café. Free parking for 300 cars.

SCOTTISH FINE SOAPS FACTORY SHOP

UNIT 2, OCHILTERRACE, CARRON GROVE INDUSTRIAL ESTATE, CARRON, FALKIRK, SCOTLAND FK2 8DZ, ☎ 01324 551377, 9.30–3.30 MON–THUR, 9–3 FRI. **FACTORY SHOP**

Makes soap, pot pourri, bubble bath and a novelty range of soaps in the shape of cats, pigs, elephants and dogs. Prices are half those you would expect to pay on the high street for discontinued lines in soaps which are made for many of the major department stores. Soaps are priced from 10p upwards.

STERLING MILLS DESIGNER OUTLET VILLAGE

TILLICOULTRY, NEAR STIRLING, CLACKMANANSHIRE, MIDWAY BETWEEN M9 AND M90, SCOTLAND FK13 6HQ, ☎ 01259 752100, www.sterlingmills.com, 10–6 SEVEN DAYS A WEEK. **FACTORY SHOPPING VILLAGE**

This factory shopping centre guarantees prices of at least 30% off typical high street prices and sometimes as much as 70%. Outlets so far include Mountain Warehouse, Adidas, Penny Plain, Enigma Candles, Jacques Vert, The Officers' Club, Bed & Bath Works, Book Depot, Claire's Accessories, Cotton Traders, Denby Pottery, Designer Room, Double Two, Julian Graves, Nike, Nickelby's, Pavers Shoes, Proibito, Roman Originals, Thorntons, Tog 24, Bags Etc, USA Golf Wear House, VF Corporation Factory Store, Winning Line, XS Music, Charles Clinkard, Naf Naf Chevignon, The Toy Factory, Pilot, Real Jewellery, The Sweet Factory, The Design House, Watson Chilli Pepper, Regatta, Blue Ridge, Playtex and more. There's a restaurant on site, and the very large Sterling Furniture Centre is situated opposite.

T J HUGHES

127–135 TRONGATE, GLASGOW, SCOTLAND G1 5HG, ☎ 0141 548 8400, FAX: 0141 552 6297, **e-mail:** info@tjhughes.co.uk, www.tjhughes.co.uk, 9–5.30 MON– FRI, 8 ON THUR, 9–6 SAT, 11–5 SUN. **PERMANENT DISCOUNT OUTLET**

See page 465 (CHESH)

THE FACTORY SHOP LTD

56 CHAPEL STREET, CARLUKE, SOUTH LANARKSHIRE SCOTLAND ML8 4BA, ☎ 01555 759017, FAX: 01555 759018, 9–5 MON–FRI, 9–5.30 SAT, 10–5 SUN.

BURNSIDE MILL, CUPAR, FIFE SCOTLAND KY15 4DQ, ☎ 01334 650661, FAX: 01334 656772, 9.30–5.30 MON–SAT, 10–5 SUN.

DRAKEMYRE, DALRY, AYRSHIRE, SCOTLAND KA24 5JD, ☎ 01294 832791, 10–5 MON–SAT, 11–5 SUN. **FACTORY SHOP**

See page 465 (CHESH)

THE PAPER MILL SHOP COMPANY LTD

MCARTHURGLEN DESIGNER OUTLET, LIVINGSTON, WEST LOTHIAN EH54 6QX, ☎ 01506 426995, www.thepapermillshop.c.uk, 10–6 SEVEN DAYS A WEEK, 8 ON THUR. **FACTORY SHOP IN A FACTORY SHOPPING VILLAGE**

See page 472 (CUMB)

TK MAXX

UNIT 10 MEADOW BANK RETAIL PARK, EDINBURGH SCOTLAND EH7 5TS, ☎ 0131 661 6611, www.tkmaxx.com, 10–8 MON–FRI, 9–6 SAT, 11–5 SUN.

UNIT C1261, CALLENDER SQUARE SHOPPING CENTRE, HIGH STREET, FALKIRK, SCOTLAND FK1 1UU, ☎ 01324 619881, www.tkmaxx.com, 9–5.30 MON–WED, 7.30 ON THUR, 9–6 FRI–SAT, 12–5 SUN.

THE SAUCHIEHALL CENTRE, GLASGOW, SCOTLAND G2 3ER, ☎ 0141 331 0411, www.tkmaxx.com, 9–5.30 MON–FRI, 7 ON THUR, 9–6 SAT, 12–5 SUN.

UNIT 5, ST ENOCH'S CENTRE, 55 ST ENOCH'S SQUARE, GLASGOW, SCOTLAND G1 4BW, ☎ 0141 221 9393, www.tkmaxx.com, 9–6 MON–FRI, 8 ON THUR, 9.30–6 SAT, 11–5 SUN.

GLENCAIRN RETAIL PARK, KILMARNOCK, SCOTLAND, ☎ 01563 532486, www.tkmaxx.com, PHONE FOR DETAILS OF OPENING TIMES.

UNIT 25-26 MERCAT CENTRE, KIRKCALDY, FIFE, SCOTLAND KY1 1N1, FAX: 01592 644488, www.tkmaxx.com, 9–5.30 MON– SAT, 11–5 SUN.

UNIT 5, ALMONDVALE WEST RETAIL PARK, ALMONDVALE ROAD, LIVINGSTON, SCOTLAND EH54 6QX, ☎ 01506 462060, www.tkmaxx.com, 10–8 MON–FRI, 9–6 SAT, 11–5 SUN.

THE PHOENIX RETAIL PARK, LINWOOD ROAD, PAISLEY, SCOTLAND, ☎ 0141 849 6796, www.tkmaxx.com, PHONE FOR DETAILS OF OPENING TIMES. **PERMANENT DISCOUNT OUTLET**

See page 458 (BEDS)

WHITTARD

MCARTHURGLEN DESIGNER OUTLET VILLAGE, ALMONDVALE AVENUE, LIVINGSTON, SCOTLAND EH54 6XA, ☎ 01506 410116, 10–6 SEVEN DAYS A WEEK, 8 ON THUR. **FACTORY SHOP IN A FACTORY SHOPPING VILLAGE**

See page 466 (CHESH)

WILD ROSE ANTIQUES

15 HENDERSON ROW, EDINBURGH SCOTLAND EH3 5DH, ☎ 0131 557 1916
10.30–6 TUE–SAT.
SECONDHAND SHOP
A distinctive specialist shop selling decorative/functional silver, women's and men's jewellery, porcelain, pottery, glass and metalware.

SCOTTISH HIGHLANDS AND ISLANDS

CAITHNESS GLASS

THE WATERFRONT CENTRE, RAILWAY PIER, OBAN, ARGYLL, SCOTLAND PA34 4LW, ☎ 01631 563386, FAX: 01631 563386, www.caithnessglass.co.uk, 9–5 MON–SAT, MARCH–OCTOBER, CHANGING IN WINTER, PHONE FIRST. **FACTORY SHOP**

AIRPORT INDUSTRIAL ESTATE, WICK, CAITHNESS, SCOTLAND KW1 5BP, ☎ 01955 602286, FAX: 01955 605200, www.caithnessglass.co.uk, 9–5 MON–SAT, 11–5 SUN EASTER–DECEMBER. **FACTORY SHOP**

See page 519 (NORF)

DARTINGTON CRYSTAL

STUART CRYSTAL, MUTHILL ROAD, CRIEFF, PERTHSHIRE, SCOTLAND PH7 4HQ, ☎ 01764 655632, 10–6 MON–SAT, 11–5 SUN. **FACTORY SHOP**

See page 469 (CORN)

MATALAN

CONSTITUTION STREET, ABERDEEN SCOTLAND AB24 5ET, ☎ 01224 650690, FAX: 01224 624235, www.matalan.co.uk, 10–8 MON–FRI, 9.30–5.30 SAT, 10–6 SUN.

UNIT1, INSHES RETAIL PARK, INVERNESS SCOTLAND IV2 3TW, ☎ 01463 227250, FAX: 01463 224772, www.matalan.co.uk, 10–8 MON–FRI, 9.30–5.30 SAT, 10–6 SUN.

VICTORIA ROAD, PERTH, SCOTLAND PH8 9LW, ☎ 01738 587020, FAX: 01738 443883, www.matalan.co.uk, 10–8 MON–FRI, 9.30–5.30 SAT, 10–6 SUN. **PERMANENT DISCOUNT OUTLET**

See page 458 (BEDS)

PONDEN MILL

CAMPERDOWN STREET, UNIT 16B-17, CITY QUAY, DUNDEE, SCOTLAND DD1 3HW, ☎ 01382 224373, 9.30–5.30 MON–SAT, 11–5 SUN. **FACTORY SHOP**

See page 464 (CHESH)

STUART CRYSTAL

MUTHILL ROAD, CRIEFF, PERTHSHIRE, SCOTLAND PH7 4HQ, ☎ 01764 654004, 10–6 SEVEN DAYS A WEEK JUNE–SEPT, 10–5 OTHERWISE.
FACTORY SHOP

See page 546 (WARW)

TK MAXX

KITTY BREWSTER RETAIL PARK, BEDFORD ROAD, ABERDEEN, SCOTLAND, ☎ 01224 497810, www.tkmaxx.com, PHONE FOR DETAILS OF OPENING TIMES.

WELLGATE SHOPPING CENTRE, DUNDEE SCOTLAND DD1 2DB, ☎ 01382 322288, www.tkmaxx.com, 9–5.30 MON–WED, FRI, SAT, 9–8 THUR, 12–5 SUN.

UNIT 2, ACADEMY RETAIL PARK, STROTHERS LANE, INVERNESS, SCOTLAND, ☎ 01463 729729, www.tkmaxx.com, 9–5.30 MON–FRI, 7 ON THUR, 9–6 SAT.

ST CATHERINE'S RETAIL PARK, SCOTLAND, ☎ 01738 636751, www.tkmaxx.com, PHONE FOR DETAILS OF OPENING TIMES. **PERMANENT DISCOUNT OUTLET**

See page 458 (BEDS)

NORTHERN IRELAND

ULSTER WEAVERS

10 LINEN GREEN, MOYGASHEL, DUNGANNON, CO TYRONE, NORTHERN IRELAND BT71 7HB, ☎ 028 8772 4004, 9.30–5 MON–SAT.

MALDON STREET, DONEGAL ROAD, WEST BELFAST, NORTHERN IRELAND, ☎ 028 9033 4650, **FACTORY SHOP**

Ulster Weavers is the largest linen manufacturer in Europe, established more than 170 years ago and now famous worldwide for their kitchen textiles and accessories. The shop here sells not just their kitchen textiles – tea towels and tablecloths – but a range of ceramics and pottery.

Electrical Equipment

BEDFORDSHIRE

NO FRILLS DIY STORE

WINGATE ROAD, LUTON, BEDFORDSHIRE LU4 8PX, ☎ 01582 585 509, FAX: 01582 562780, 9–8 MON–SAT, 10–4 SUN. **PERMANENT DISCOUNT OUTLET**

Not a discount operator as such but a great place for bargains. Now part of the Focus DIY Group, they stock everything you would find in B&Q or Homebase but at cheaper prices. Paints, tiles, bathroom equipment, patio furniture, toiletries, sheds, lighting, crockery, bedding, pans, kitchen units, barbecues in season.

BERKSHIRE

GD EVANS

331–333 HIGH STREET, SLOUGH, BERKSHIRE SL1 1TX, ☎ 01753 524188 OR 535138, **e-mail:** gdevans@talk21.com, www.gdevans.co.uk, 9–5.30 MON–SAT. **PERMANENT DISCOUNT OUTLET**

Established for nearly 50 years, this is the place to come for built-in appliances. Great discounts on new boxed, ex-display and discontinued models of up to 50%. Former exhibition Bosch, Neff and Siemens appliances. Phone for free brochure.

CAMBRIDGESHIRE

CATALOGUE BARGAIN SHOP

51 WEST STREET, WISBECH, CAMBRIDGESHIRE PE13 2LY, ☎ 01945 584327, www.bargaincrazy.com, 9–4.30 MON–SAT, 10–4 SUN. **PERMANENT DISCOUNT OUTLET**

Catalogue Bargain Shop is a growing national chain of stores which obtains the majority of its goods from mail order giants Great Universal and Kays, and offers a range of clothing for all the family, a wide selection of shoes, bed linen, household goods, electrical equipment and hundreds of other catalogue items at very competitive prices. The merchandise consists of ends of ranges and previous season's stock for which there is no longer space when the catalogues change.

REMARK

16 TRESHAM ROAD, ORTON, SOUTHGATE, PETERBOROUGH, CAMBRIDGESHIRE PE2 6SG, ☎ 01733 231639, www.remarktelecom.co.uk, 8–5 MON–FRI. **PERMANENT DISCOUNT OUTLET**

Sells new and reconditioned telecommunication systems at competitive prices. Can install equipment, voice and data networks, arrange service and maintenance.

STAGE 2

SAVILLE ROAD, PETERBOROUGH, CAMBRIDGESHIRE, PE3 7RP, ☎ 01733 263308, 10–8 MON–FRI, 9–6 SAT, 10–4 SUN, BANK HOLIDAYS. **PERMANENT DISCOUNT OUTLET**

Sells surplus stock from both Grattan and Freemans catalogues. Womenswear, childrenswear, menswear and household items, at up to 50% off catalogue prices. Includes a wide range of brands from both designer and high street on a regularly changing basis. Electrical goods are sold at discounts of up to 30% off catalogue prices, and include many big-name brands. A 14-day refund policy is offered.

CHESHIRE

A C COMPUTER WAREHOUSE

MOTTRAM STREET, MIDDLE HILLGATE, STOCKPORT, CHESHIRE SK1 3PA, ☎ 0161 476 2220, **e-mail:** sales@accomp.co.uk, www.accomp.co.uk, 9.30–6 MON–FRI, 10–5 SAT. MAIL ORDER. **PERMANENT DISCOUNT OUTLET**

Computers, monitors, scanners and printers, all at competitive prices. Phone for a product and price list.

CATALOGUE BARGAIN SHOP

ROYAL AVENUE, WIDNES, CHESHIRE WA8 7BR, ☎ 0151 424 6161, www.bargaincrazy.com, 10–6 MON–FRI, 9–5 SAT. **PERMANENT DISCOUNT OUTLET**

See page 577 (CAMBS)

LITTLEWOODS CATALOGUE DISCOUNT STORE

MCARTHURGLEN DESIGNER OUTLET CHESHIRE OAKS, KINSEY ROAD, NEAR ELLESMERE PORT, JUNCTION 10 OF M53, CHESHIRE CH65 9JJ, ☎ 0151 356 0501, 10–8 MON–FRI, 9–6 SAT, 11–5 SUN. **FACTORY SHOP IN A FACTORY SHOPPING VILLAGE**

Littlewoods clearance shops offer up to 70% off the catalogue price for clothing and offer big discounts off electrical goods. Stock changes constantly and varies from day to day but can include well-known brand names such as Berlei and Gossard lingerie, Vivienne Westwood, Pamplemousse leisurewear, Nike and Adidas sports shoes, and Timberland and Caterpillar footwear. Stock depends on the size and location of the shop: larger shops get the longer discontinued runs, while smaller shops get overruns with only a small amount of colour and size variations left. Littlewoods also runs a mobile shop which operates in cities which don't have a sale shop. For details for the sales, which usually take place once a month, write to Melanie Lamb, c/o Crosby DC Kershaw Avenue, Endbutt Lane, Crosby, Merseyside L70 1AH.

MCARTHURGLEN DESIGNER OUTLET

KINSEY ROAD, NEAR ELLESMERE PORT, JUNCTION 10 OF M53, CHESHIRE CH65 9JJ, ☎ 0800 316 4352 FREE INFORMATION LINE OR 0151 348 5600, FAX: 0151 357 3744, www.mcarthurglen.com/cheshireoaks, 10–8 MON–FRI, 9–6 SAT, 11–5 SUN. **FACTORY SHOPPING VILLAGE**

The McArthurGlen Designer Outlet Cheshire Oaks is Europe's largest designer outlet with over 140 stores selling top brands and designer names at up to 50% off typical retail prices. Facilities include a food court, a children's play area and free parking. Stores include: Gap Outlet, Big L, Fruit of the Loom, Monsoon, Timberland, Tie Rack, Principles, Petroleum, James Barry, Donnay, Aquascutum, Burberrys, Viyella, Warehouse, Racing Green, Famous Footwear, Jeffrey Rogers, Liz Claiborne, Winning Line, Overland, Ciro Pearls, Diesel, Jokids, Fred Perry, Travel Accessory Outlet, Baron Jon, La Senza, Nike, Next to Nothing, Helly Hansen, Jane Shilton, Joe Bloggs, Birthdays, Thorntons, Toyworld, D2, Pilot, Jumper, Clarks, Villeroy & Boch, Episode, Windsmoor, Jaeger, Daks Simpson, Mexx, Bed & Bath Works, Woods of Windsor, The Suit Company, XS Music & Video, Suits You, Claire's Accessories, Lee Cooper, Tog 24, Fila, Warners, Cecil Gee, Remington, Whittard of Chelsea, Kitchen Store, Denby, Edinburgh Crystal, Price's Candles, Reebok, Hobbs, Kurt Muller, Bookends, Pictureport, Kappa, Easy Jeans, Woodhouse, Designer Room, DKNY, Ponden Mill, U Wear/I Wear, Penn, Le Coq Sportif, Roman Originals, Revlon, Monet, Walker and Hall, Ben Sherman, Van Heusen, Austin Reed, Antler, Ecco, Blazer, Watson/Chillii Pepper, Red/Green, Soled Out, Carphone Warehouse, Cotton Traders, Royal Doulton, Royal Worcester, Oneida, Proibito, Vans, Reiss, Garden Outlet, Proudfoot Leather, Playtime Toys, Wedgwood, Prima Tessuti, Natural World, WHSmith, Littlewoods, Bose, The Body Shop, Samsonite, Adidas, Kangol, Dune, Marks & Spencer Outlet, Daniel Footwear, Polo Jeans Company, The North Face, Elle, Sergio Tacchini, Autonomy, Chapelle, Fiorelli, Julian Graves, Spiegelau, Bose, Kitch N Sync, Early Learning Centre, Tommy Hilfiger, Triumph and Professional Cookware.

REMINGTON

MCARTHURGLEN DESIGNER OUTLET CHESHIRE OAKS, KINSEY ROAD, NEAR ELLESMERE PORT, JUNCTION 10 OF M53, CHESHIRE CH65 9JJ, ☎ 0151 357 2477, 10–8 MON–FRI, 9–6 SAT, 11–5 SUN. **FACTORY SHOP IN A FACTORY SHOPPING VILLAGE**

Lots of famous names here from Oneida cutlery to Braun, Philips, Remington, Clairol, Wahl and Swan electrical goods. There is small kitchen equipment as well as a wide range of hair, beauty and male grooming accessories, all at reduced prices. It's a great place to buy gifts or replenish your kitchen equipment with combi stylers, turbo travel hairdryers, air purifiers, liquidisers, food processors, batteries, clocks and cutlery. Occasionally some of the packaging may be damaged, but the products are in perfect working order.

T J HUGHES

BOROUGH PAVEMENT, GRANGE PRECINCT, BIRKENHEAD, CHESHIRE L41 2XX, ☎ 0151 647 5151, FAX: 0151 666 1610, **e-mail:** info@tjhughes.co.uk, www.tjhughes.co.uk, 9–5.30 MON–SAT, 10–4 SUN.

THE FORUM, HAMILTON PLACE, CHESTER, CHESHIRE CH1 2BH, ☎ 01244 316600, FAX: 01244 316646, **e-mail:** info@tjhughes.co.uk, www.tjhughes.co.uk, 9–5.30 MON– SAT, 11–5 SUN.

2 MERCIER WALK, SOUTH WIRRAL, CHESHIRE CH65 0AP, ☎ 0151 357 3151, FAX: 0151 357 3174, **e-mail:** info@tjhughes.co.uk, www.tjhughes.co.uk, 9–5.30 MON– SAT, 10–4 SUN.

EXCHANGE STREET, MACCLESFIELD, CHESHIRE SK11 6UZ, ☎ 01625 611807, FAX: 01625 611859, **e-mail:** info@tjhughes.co.uk, www.tjhughes.co.uk, 9–5.30 MON– SAT, 10–4 SUN.

GREENOAKS SHOPPING CENTRE, WIDNES, CHESHIRE WA8 6UD, ☎ 0151 420 1010, FAX: 0151 423 4570, **e-mail:** info@tjhughes.co.uk, www.tjhughes.co.uk, 9–5.30 MON– SAT, 10–4 SUN. **PERMANENT DISCOUNT OUTLET**

Expanding chain of shops offering, not discounts as such, but very competitively priced goods including clothes for all the family, china, towels, bedlinen, duvets, pots and pans, kettles, vacuum cleaners, television sets, CDs, toasters, many from top brand names.

TELEVIEW DIRECT LTD

PHOENIX HOUSE, GOLBOURNE, WARRINGTON, CHESHIRE WA3 3DP, ☎ 0800 900 009, FAX: 0942 270500, **e-mail:** televiewdirect@yahoo.com, www.teleview-direct.co.uk, 8 TILL LATE **PERMANENT DISCOUNT OUTLET**

Discounted televisions, videos, DVDs and hi-fi units to rent or buy, from manufacturers such as Toshiba, Samsung and Philips.

THE FACTORY SHOP LTD

UNIT 1 EDDISBURY SQUARE, FRODSHAM, CHESHIRE WA6 6QS, ☎ 01928 734624, FAX: 01928 734906, 9–5.30 MON–SAT, 10.30–4 SUN. **FACTORY SHOP**

Wide range on sale includes men's, women's and children's clothing and footwear; household textiles; toiletries; hardware; luggage; lighting; electrical goods; and bedding, most of which are chainstore and high street brands at discounts of approximately 30% to 50%. There are kitchen and furniture displays and on sale is the Cape Country Furniture range with free-standing kitchens, as well as living, bedroom and dining furniture. There are weekly deliveries and brands include famous names such as Adidas, Nike, Joe Bloggs and Brabantia, among others. Lines are continually changing and few factory shops offer such a variety under one roof. Parking is free.

YOU & YOURS

UNIT 42, ORCHARD WALK, HALTON LEAS SHOPPING CENTRE, RUNCORN, CHESHIRE WA7 2GZ, ☎ 01928 795 792, 9–5.30 MON–SAT. **PERMANENT DISCOUNT OUTLET**

Sells surplus stock from both Grattan and Freemans catalogues. Womenswear, childrenswear, menswear and household items, at up to 50% off catalogue prices. Includes a wide range of brands from both designer and high street on a regularly changing basis. Electrical goods are sold at discounts of up to 30% off catalogue prices, and include many big-name brands. A 14-day refund policy is offered.

COUNTY DURHAM

CATALOGUE DISCOUNT STORES

UNIT 17, IN SHOP CENTRE, 1–2 WRIGHTON HOUSE, TRENCHARD AVENUE, THORNABY ON TEES, CO DURHAM TS17 9EP, ☎ 01642 751935, 9–5 MON–SAT. **PERMANENT DISCOUNT OUTLET**

Grattan catalogue store, selling a wide selection of items from those featured in the catalogue, including women's, men's, children's, home, electrics and toys. All items are discounted by up to 50% with regular special promotions. All stores offer a 14-day refund policy, and a 12-month guarantee on electrical items. A wide range of brands are in stock on a regularly changing basis. Each store carries a slightly different range, so please phone to check that they have what you want in stock.

COOKERS PLUS

23 NORTHFIELD WAY, NEWTON AYCLIFFE INDUSTRIAL ESTATE, NEWTON AYCLIFFE, CO DURHAM DL5 6EJ, ☎ 01325 301916, FAX: 01325 300552, 7.30–4.30 MON–FRI, 8–4 SAT. **PERMANENT DISCOUNT OUTLET**

Independent retailers of domestic appliances and white goods from top manufacturers, including free-standing and built-in models. Most appliances have slight cosmetic damage, but still carry the manufacturer's full warranty. They can supply models from the majority of manufacturers, including AEG, Zanussi, Tricity Bendix and Electrolux. They are also agents for the Britannia Leisure range of cookers, offering prices at £50 to £200 below the retail price guide.

EBAC

ST HELENS TRADING ESTATE, BISHOP AUCKLAND, CO DURHAM DL14 9AL, ☎ 01388 602602, 9–3 MON–FRI. **FACTORY SHOP**

Quality end of range dehumidifiers at discount prices, plus graded ex-display models in perfect working order.

LITTLEWOODS DISCOUNT STORE

UNIT 2A, METRO RETAIL PARK, GATESHEAD, TYNE & WEAR NE11 9XU, ☎ 0191 461 1491 10–8 MON–FRI, 9–6 SAT, 11–5 SUN. **PERMANENT DISCOUNT OUTLET**

Brand new, surplus women's, men's and children's clothing from last year's catalogue is on sale at greatly discounted prices. Returned and sometimes slightly damaged televisions and furniture can be found at as much as 70% below the original price. If you see an item you like, buy it there and then as stock is constantly changing and you are unlikely to see it on sale again. The store also has sales when stock is discounted even further.

LITTLEWOODS CATALOGUE DISCOUNT STORE

19 FAWCETT STREET, SUNDERLAND, TYNE & WEAR SR1 1RH, ☎ 0191 564 0684, 9–5 MON–THUR, 9–5.30 FRI, SAT. **PERMANENT DISCOUNT OUTLET**

See page 578 (CHESH)

NO FRILLS DIY STORE

MEYNELL ROAD, OFF WHESSOE ROAD, DARLINGTON, CO DURHAM DL3 0XZ, ☎ 01325 481414, FAX: 01325 464020, 9–8 MON–SAT, 10–4 SUN. **PERMANENT DISCOUNT OUTLET**

See page 577 (BEDS)

THE FACTORY SHOP

2–4 COMMERCIAL STREET, CROOK, CO DURHAM DL15 9HP, ☎ 01388 763211, 9–5.30 MON–SAT, 10.30–4.30 SUN. **FACTORY SHOP**

See page 579 (CHESH)

SCOOPS CATALOGUE DISCOUNT STORE

15 THE PRECINCT, THE IN CENTRE, JARROW, TYNE & WEAR NE32 3LS, ☎ 0191 483 4318, 9–5 MON–SAT.

UNIT 17, THE IN SHOP CENTRE, 1–2 WRIGHTON HOUSE, TRENCHARD AVENUE, THORNABY, TYNE & WEAR TS17 9EP, ☎ 01642 751935, 9–5 MON–SAT. **PERMANENT DISCOUNT OUTLET**

Scoops the catalogue discount store sells surplus stock from both Grattan and Freeman's catalogues. Womenswear, menswear and childrenswear are on sale, as well as household items, all at up to 50% off catalogue prices. Stock changes on a regular basis, and includes a wide range of brands from both designer and high street. A 14-day refund policy is offered.

CORNWALL

CORNISH MARKET WORLD

STADIUM RETAIL PARK, PAR, ST AUSTELL, CORNWALL PL25 3RP, ☎ 01726 812544, FAX: 01726 812346, **e-mail:** info@cornishmarketworld.co.uk, www.cornishmarketworld.co.uk, 9–5 SAT, SUN AND BANK HOLIDAYS, AND WED JUNE-SEPT. **PERMANENT DISCOUNT OUTLET**

Huge indoor market that sells an enormous range of goods and food at very competitive prices: for example, a good quality breadmaker, £45. Sells clothes, fabrics, phones, bags, tools, electric equipment, motability equipment, jewellery and furniture. There is a good butchers, fish, and fruit and veg stands.

DARTINGTON CRYSTAL

KERNOW MILL, TRERULEFOOT, SALTASH, CORNWALL PL12 5BL, ☎ 01752 851161, FAX: 01752 851856, 9.30–5.30 MON–SAT, 11–5 SUN. **FACTORY SHOP**

An extensive range of Dartington Crystal seconds at greatly reduced prices as well as some perfect crystal at full price. Range includes wine suites, sherry glasses, tankards, decanters, rippled glass, and fruit and salad bowls.

NO FRILLS DIY STORE

STADIUM PARK, ST AUSTELL, CORNWALL PL25 3RP, ☎ 01726 814791, FAX: 01726 817953, 9–8 MON–SAT, 10–4 SUN. **PERMANENT DISCOUNT OUTLET**

See page 577 (BEDS)

THE FACTORY SHOP

OLD STATION YARD, BERRYCOMBE ROAD, BODMIN, CORNWALL PL31 2NF, ☎ 01208 78492, 9–5.30 MON–SAT, 10.30–4.30 SUN. **FACTORY SHOP**

MOUNT AMBROSE, SCORRIER, REDRUTH, CORNWALL TR15 1QT, ☎ 01209 219116, 9.30–5.30 MON–SAT, 10–4 SUN. **FACTORY SHOP**

See page 579 (CHESH)

CUMBRIA

CATALOGUE BARGAIN SHOP

UNITS 4–5, SOUTH LAKELANDS RETAIL PARK, KENDAL, CUMBRIA LA9 6DU, ☎ 01539 740734, www.bargaincrazy.com, 9–8 MON–SAT, 11–5 SUN. **PERMANENT DISCOUNT OUTLET**

See page 577 (CAMBS)

LITTLEWOODS CATALOGUE DISCOUNT STORE

RAWLINSON STREET, BARROW-IN-FURNESS, CUMBRIA LA14 1BS, ☎ 01229 870668, 8.45–5.15 MON–SAT, 11–5 SUN. **PERMANENT DISCOUNT OUTLET**

See page 578 (CHESH)

THE FACTORY SHOP

EMPIRE BUILDINGS, MAIN STREET, EGREMONT, CUMBRIA CA22 2BD, ☎ 01946 820434, 9–5 MON–SAT. 10–4 SUN.

THE GILL, ULVERSTON, CUMBRIA LA12 7BN, ☎ 01229 583360, 9–5.30 MON–SAT, 10.30–4.30 SUN.

5 MARKET PLACE, WIGTON, CUMBRIA CA7 9NW, ☎ 01697 342171, 9–5.30 MON–SAT, 10.30–4.30 SUN. **FACTORY SHOP**

See page 579 (CHESH)

DERBYSHIRE

MCARTHURGLEN DESIGNER OUTLET

MANSFIELD ROAD, SOUTH NORMANTON, ALFRETON, JUNCTION 28 OF M1, DERBYSHIRE DE55 2ER, ☎ 01773 545000, www.mcarthurglen.com/mansfield, 10–6 MON–FRI, 8 ON THUR, 9–6 SAT, 11–5 SUN. **FACTORY SHOPPING VILLAGE**

The McArthurGlen Designer Outlet Mansfield has recently undergone a year-long development programme, transforming it from an open-plan department store layout to individual shops. The new look outlet is now bigger and better. Find all your favourite brands at discounts of up to 50% off typical retail prices. Facilities include a children's play area, a food court and plenty of free parking. Stores include: Antler, Banana Books, Bed & Bath Works, Big L, Camille Lingerie, Chapelle, Claire's Accessories, Coloroll, Cotton Traders, Donnay, Edinburgh Crystal, Harbi, Jaeger, Jane Shilton, Julian Graves, Kitch N Sync, Leading Labels, Lee Cooper, Mountain Warehouse, Pavers Shoes, Petroleum, Pilot, Price's Candles, Professional Cookware, Remington, Roman Originals, Sky, Soled Out, Speedo, Sportsmill, Suits You, Thorntons, Tog 24, Toyworld, Revlon, Marks & Spencer Outlet, Windsmoor, Sportz, Reebok, Jumper, HKA, Proudfoot Leather, Garden Outlet, Lilley & Skinner, Adidas, Viyella, Whittards, XS Records and many more.

REMINGTON

MCARTHURGLEN DESIGNER OUTLET MANSFIELD, MANSFIELD ROAD, SOUTH NORMANTON, ALFRETON, JUNCTION 28 OF M1, DERBYSHIRE DE55 2JW, ☎ 01773 545062, 10–6 MON–FRI, 8 ON THUR, 9–6 SAT, 11–5 SUN. **FACTORY SHOP IN A FACTORY SHOPPING VILLAGE**

See page 579 (CHESH)

DEVON

ATLANTIC VILLAGE OUTLET CENTRE

CLOVELLY ROAD, OFF A39, WEST OF BIDEFORD, NORTH DEVON, ☎ 01237 422544, **e-mail:** rmorris@realm-ocm.com, www.atlanticvillage.co.uk, JULY–MID SEPT, 9.30–7 MON–SAT, 11–5 SUN; MID SEPT–MID OCT AND EASTER TO JULY 9.30–6.30 MON–SAT, 11–5 SUN; MID OCT–EASTER 9.30–5 MON–SAT, 11–5 SUN. **FACTORY SHOPPING VILLAGE**

More than 30 shops with famous names and Devon's largest interactive maze make this village a good family day out. Shops include Banana Books; Claire's Accessories; Colony Candles; Cotton Traders, Designer Room, Ecco; Edinburgh Woollen Mill; Event Jewellery; Jane Shilton; Jean Scene; Julian Graves; Nickelby's; Pavers Shoes; Pilot; Ponden Mill; Puma; Roman Originals; Room, selling home accessories, fabrics and soft furnishings; Sportsmill; Suits You; Tog 24; Toyzone; Triumph; Warners; Windsmoor; XS Sound & Media. Free car parking, disabled and baby changing facilities. Atlantic Village also features an attractive piazza, cafés, a food court, visitor garden, arts and crafts market, open-air amphitheatre, and an adventure park set in an additional three-acre site linked to the shopping area by the piazza and amphitheatre. The Adventure Park features a mystery maze, adventure golf, wrecker's cove and adventure play boat.

DORSET

IN EXCESS

354–358 ASHLEY ROAD, PARKSTONE, POOLE, DORSET BH14 9DF, ☎ 01202 740188, 9–5.30 MON–SAT, 10–4 SUN.

80–83 DOLPHIN CENTRE, POOLE, DORSET, ☎ 01202 673534, 9–5.30 MON–SAT, 10–4 SUN.

SOMERFORD ROAD, CHRISTCHURCH, DORSET BH23 3PH, ☎ 01202 481438, 9–5.30 MON–SAT, 10–4 SUN. **PERMANENT DISCOUNT OUTLET**

In Excess is stacked full of bankrupt stock from stationery and paint to DIY tools and cleaning materials, plumbing materials, screws, bolts, nuts, and telephone accessories. It also houses, in season, garden furniture and pots aimed at the starter garden lover and decking. Plastic tables and chairs start at £2.95 for a chair and from £5.95 to £12.95 for a table; terracotta pots start from 50p and there are also 'antiqued' stone pots.

T J HUGHES

616–622 CHRISTCHURCH ROAD, BOSCOMBE, BOURNEMOUTH, DORSET BH1 4BR, ☎ 01202 300333, FAX: 01202 303515, **e-mail:** info@tjhughes.co.uk, www.tjhughes.co.uk, 9–5.30 MON–FRI, 9–6 SAT, 10–4 SUN. **PERMANENT DISCOUNT OUTLET**

See page 579 (CHESH)

ESSEX

CATALOGUE BARGAIN SHOP

ST JOHN'S WALK SHOPPING CENTRE, COLCHESTER, ESSEX CO2 7AL, ☎ 01206 563126, www.bargaincrazy.com, 9–5.30 MON–THUR, 9–7 FRI, 9–6 SAT, 10.30–4.30 SUN. **PERMANENT DISCOUNT OUTLET**

See page 577 (CAMBS)

CLACTON FACTORY SHOPPING VILLAGE

STEPHENSON ROAD WEST, CLACTON-ON-SEA, ESSEX CO15 4TL, ☎ 01255 479595, FAX: 01255 430777 INFORMATION LINE, 10–6 MON–SAT, 11–5 SUN. **FACTORY SHOPPING VILLAGE**

Forty eight units centred around a Victorian winter garden comprising the following: Banana Bookshop selling books, games and stationery; Because It's There (BIT) for sports and camping equipment; Bed & Bath Works, a homeware outlet with discounted branded linens and housewares from Janet Reger, Sheridan, Christy and Kingsley; Birthdays, stocking mainstream cards and gifts from manufacturers such as Andrew Brownsword, Disney, Parker, Galt and Warner Brothers; Camille for lingerie; Caterpillar selling foorwear from the Cat range; Choice, which sells family clothing from Next; Claire's Accessories; Clinkards family footwear from Church's, Gabor, Bally and Loake; Cook 'N Dine kitchenware, glass and ceramics; Cotton Traders casual wear; Dannimac outdoor wear; Designer Room selling designer fashion for men and women; Event fashion costume jewellery and watches from Accurist, Timberland, Seiko and Timex; Garden Store selling garden furniture, barbecues and equipment and, in season, Christmas decorations; Jacques Vert selling womenswear; JD Sports selling branded sports merchandise from Adidas, Nike, Reebok, Ellesse and Le Coq Sportif; Joanna Hall selling handbags from the Jane Shilton range; Julian Graves foods and nut mixes; Kids Play Factory with toys from ranges such as Fisher-Price and Lego; Leading Labels, with men's and women's fashions; Mobile Phone Shop; MX Active selling branded denim and casual wear for men, women and children; Nickelbys fashion wear for men and women; Olli Moda selling branded jeans and casual wear; Pilot, a young women's fashion outlet; Ponden Mill with a range of bedlinen and bathroom ware; Price's Candles; Roman Originals womenswear; Sasperilla for young women's fashions; Spotlight, a young women's fashion outlet; Suits You men's shirts, suits, and casual separates as well as wedding hire and Autonomy womenswear; Thorntons chocolates; Tog 24 outdoor activity wear; Windsmoor women's fashions; Travel Accessory Shop with travel goods from Delsey and Samsonite; Woods of Windsor toiletries and gift items; XS Music CDs and videos. There are also two restaurants, a tourist information centre, parking for 1,000 cars and a bus service link to Clacton-On-Sea town centre and railway station.

FREEPORT BRAINTREE DESIGNER OUTLET VILLAGE

FREEPORT ESSEX VILLAGE, CHARTER WAY, CHAPEL HILL, BRAINTREE, JUNCTION 8 OF M11, THEN A120, ESSEX CM77 8YH, ☎ 01376 348168, www.freeportbraintree.com, 10–6 MON–SAT, 8 ON THUR, 11–5 SUN. **FACTORY SHOPPING VILLAGE**

Freeport Braintree is a designer outlet village with over 80 shops. Situated in the heart of Essex with easy access from the A120, Freeport Braintree has its own dedicated railyway station and is only a one-hour journey from central London. Womenswear includes Aquascutum, Amazing Jeans, Antonio d'Errico, Box Fresh, Burberry, Christian Lacroix, Cotton Traders, Elle, Gossard, Karen Millen, Ted Baker, Tommy Hilfiger and Versace and The Designer Room with a host of designer labels. Menswear includes Aquascutum, Cecil Gee, Ciro Citterio, Cotton Traders, Kurt Muller, Nickleby's, Proibito, Ted Baker, Tommy Hilfiger, Van Heusen and Versace. For children there's Base 2 Base, Mexx and Toy Dome; there is also plenty to keep children entertained, such as the Cheeky Chimps indoor play area. Sportwear outlets include Brand Fusion, Donnay, Fila, Mountain Warehouse, Nike, Reebok, Regatta and Trespass. Footwear is covered by Ecco Shoes, Franchetti Bond, Hush Puppies, Jane Shilton, Lilley & Skinner, Soled Out and Vans Shoes. Shops selling household goods from kitchenware to pot pourri include Churchills, Denby, Edinburgh Crystal, Glen Eagles, Le Creuset, Professional Cookware, The Design House, Waterford Wedgwood and Villeroy & Boch. Other retail outlets, selling everything from luggage to music, include Body Shop, Carlton, Claire's Accessories, Designer Shades, Mobile Phone Store, Watch Store and XS Music, and there are no less than six cafés and restaurants on site.

LEIGH LIGHTING COMPANY

1591–1593 LONDON ROAD, LEIGH-ON-SEA, ESSEX SS9 2SG, ☎ 01702 477633, FAX: 01702 470112, 9–5 MON–FRI, 9.30–5 SAT. MAIL ORDER. **FACTORY SHOP**

Thousands of lighting fixtures at between 10% and 50% below normal retail prices. Selling to both the commercial and domestic market, they offer recessed lights, table lamps, chandeliers, wall lights and outdoor security lighting, some of which are bought direct from the manufacturer. They can supply virtually any lighting seen elsewhere at very competitive prices. Catalogues available for mail order.

STELLISONS LTD

350 HARWICH ROAD, COLCHESTER, ESSEX CO4 3HP, ☎ 01206 871151, FAX: 01206 871809, 9–6 MON–SAT, 10–4 SUN. **PERMANENT DISCOUNT OUTLET**

Excellent display of electrical goods from television sets and videos to cookers, fridges, freezers, washing machines, tumble dryers and fitted kitchens by Comera and Arthur Bonnet. They claim to sell at prices which are lower than any other shop in Essex. Sell only mainstream brands and local delivery is free.

T J HUGHES

25-29 MARKET PLACE, ROMFORD, ESSEX RM1 3AB, ☎ 01708 747159, FAX: 01708 721126, **e-mail: e-mail:** info@tjhughes.co.uk, www.tjhughes.co.uk, 9–5.30 MON– SAT, 10–4 SUN. **PERMANENT DISCOUNT OUTLET**

See page 579 (CHESH)

THE FACTORY SHOP LTD

THE GLOUCESTERS, LUCKYN LANE, PIPPS HILL INDUSTRIAL ESTATE, BASILDON, ESSEX SS14 3AX, ☎ 01268 520546, www.thefactoryshopsessexltd.co.uk, 9–6 MON–SAT, 10–5 SUN.

PURDEY'S INDUSTRIAL ESTATE, 1 MAGNOLIA WAY, ROCHFORD, ESSEX SS4 1ND, ☎ 01702 531153, www.thefactoryshopsessexltd.co.uk, 9–6 MON–SAT, 10–5 SUN.

THE CROSS ROADS, KELVEDON ROAD, TIPTREE, ESSEX CO5 0LJ, ☎ 01621 817662, 9–5.30 MON–SAT, 10–4 SUN. **FACTORY SHOP**

The Factory Shops carry a wide range of branded stock at discounted prices, from bed linen, towels, hardware, toys, party ware, electrical goods, tools and garden furniture to food, clothing, TY Beanies and much more. There is a large pet and aquatic department with a wide selection of pond and water features within its 14,000 square feet of selling space. At Christmas, a huge range of decorations, baubles, tinsel, trees, tree lights and gifts are available. Parking is easy with wheelchair/pushchair access. No membership is required, and major credit cards are accepted.

GLOUCESTERSHIRE

BRANDMART

WESTWARD ROAD, CAINSCROSS, STROUD, GLOUCESTERSHIRE GL5 4JE, ☎ 01453 756655, 9–5 MON–SAT, 10–4 SUN. **FACTORY SHOP**

The original factory shop in Cainscross, Stroud, has recently relocated next door into a 12,000 square foot premises and is now trading under the name of Brandmart, offering even more savings on branded household and family goods. The range includes men's, women's and children's clothing and footwear, household textiles, toiletries, hardware, luggage, lighting, electrical goods and bedding, most of which are chainstore and high street brands at discounts of between 30% and 50%. There are weekly deliveries and brands include famous names such as Calvin Klein, Adidas, Nike, Fcuk, Cat, Reebok, Ben Sherman, Kangol, Timberland and many more. There are kitchen and furniture displays and a new line in Cape Country furniture on sale. Ranges are continually changing and few factory shops offer such a variety under one roof. Car park.

CATALOGUE BARGAIN SHOP

1–6 GROSVENOR HOUSE, STATION ROAD, GLOUCESTER, GLOUCESTERSHIRE GL1 1SZ, ☎ 01452 308779, www.bargaincrazy.com, 9–5.30 MON–SAT, 10.30–4.30 SUN. **PERMANENT DISCOUNT OUTLET**

See page 577 (CAMBS)

HAMPSHIRE

DIRECT ELECTRICAL

UNIT 2, FAREHAM ENTERPRISE CENTRE, NEWGATE LANE, FAREHAM, HAMPSHIRE PO14 1TH, ☎ 01329 319999, FAX: 01329 510111, **e-mail:** directelectrical@bun.com, www.directelectricalsales.co.uk, PHONE FOR OPENING TIMES, MAIL ORDER. **PERMANENT DISCOUNT OUTLET**

A trade warehouse offering trade prices direct to the public, they specialise in widescreen televisions from 24 inch to 46 inch. For example, 28-inch Philips silver widescreen, £299; 32-inch with DVD players, £499; 14-inch Philips televideo, £139. Also has an excellent range of camcorders on offer at almost half price. For example, Hitachi 500x zoom, £189; JVC Digital, £399. Mail order available.

IN EXCESS

43–45 HIGH STREET, WEST END, SOUTHAMPTON, HAMPSHIRE SO30 3LU, ☎ 0238 046 4545, 9–5.30 MON–SAT, 10–4 SUN.

64–66 SHIRLEY HIGH STREET, SHIRLEY, SOUTHAMPTON, HAMPSHIRE SO15 3TE, ☎ 02380 771657, 9–5.30 MON–SAT. **PERMANENT DISCOUNT OUTLET**

See page 582 (DORS)

SOUTHERN DOMESTIC ELECTRICAL SERVICES

4–6 BRIDGE ROAD, WOOLSTON, SOUTHAMPTON, HAMPSHIRE SO19 7GQ, ☎ 0238 032 8428 OR 0238 040 3222 WAREHOUSE, www.southern-domestic.com, 8.30–6 MON–FRI, 9–5 SAT. **PERMANENT DISCOUNT OUTLET**

Domestic electrical kitchen goods – washing machines, fridges, cookers, tumble dryers, freezers – usually 10% to 25% cheaper than their competitors. Also sell goods that are slight seconds – perhaps with a damaged box or a small scratch – which are priced even lower, from Bosch, Neff, Siemens, Creda, Zanussi, Lacanche, White Knight, Baumatic, Cannon, Belling, Hotpoint, Flavel Leisure, Miele, Electrolux, Panasonic, Technic, Britannia, Amana, Liebherr, De Dietrich, AEG, Stoves, Elica, Fisher-Paykel, Gaggenau, Norcool, Maytag and all other leading brands. Free local delivery.

THE GALLERIES

HIGH STREET, ALDERSHOT, HAMPSHIRE GU11 1PE, ☎ 01252 341111, FAX: 01252 329800, **e-mail:** thegalleries@web-hq.com, www.thegalleriesaldershot.co.uk, 9–6 MON–SAT, 10–4 SUN. **FACTORY SHOPPING VILLAGE**

This town centre shopping mall has 20 discount shops on two levels such as Bed & Bath Works for bedlinen and bathroom ware; Cotton Traders casual wear; Designer Room selling women's and men's designer fashion; Hush Puppies shoes; Kitchen Kiosk with branded kitchen and homeware ranges including barbecues and some electrical goods such as bread making machines; Leading Labels selling men's, women's and childrenswear; MX Active for men's, women's and children's branded denim and casual wear; Optisave, an optician selling designer branded glasses; Pilot selling young women's fashions; Pocket Phone selling mobile phones and accessories; Roman Originals womenswear; Room for furniture and household accessories; Suits You men's shirts, suits and casual separates as well as Autonomy womenswear; and Young's dress hire; Surf

Skate and Snow for branded casual and activity wear; Toyzone for children's toys; and XS Music selling CDs and videos. The centre also has a café, wheelchair access, a lottery kiosk and baby changing facilities.

HEREFORDSHIRE

APPLIANCE SOLUTIONS

ELECTRIC HOUSE, BYE STREET, LEDBURY, HEREFORDSHIRE HR8 2AG, ☎ 01531 636369, FAX: 01531 636797, 9–5 MON–FRI, 9–4 SAT. **PERMANENT DISCOUNT OUTLET**

New, graded white goods (washing machines, fridges etc) all with twelve months' guarantee from brands such as Zanussi, Hotpoint, Servis, Bosch, Creda, Delonghi, Electrolux, Whirlpool, AEG and Candy. Public car park in Bye Street or free parking at the nearby swimming pool just off Bye Street.

THE FACTORY SHOP

52 BROAD STREET, LEOMINSTER, HEREFORDSHIRE HR6 8BS, ☎ 01568 613944, 9–5.30 MON–SAT, 10–4 SUN. **FACTORY SHOP**

See page 579 (CHESH)

HERTFORDSHIRE

BhS FOR LESS

GALLERIA OUTLET CENTRE, COMET WAY, HATFIELD, HERTFORDSHIRE AL10 0XR, ☎ 01707 258351, 10–8 MON–FRI, 10–6 SAT, 11–5 SUN. **FACTORY SHOP IN A FACTORY SHOPPING VILLAGE**

BhS for Less sells the high street chain's men's, women's and childrenswear ranges, plus selections from its home and lighting ranges, at discounts of at least 30% and up to 75%.

KENT

B & A WHELAN

52 HIGH STREET, BLUE TOWN, NEXT TO SHEERNESS DOCKS, KENT ME12 1RW, ☎ 01795 663879, FAX: 01795 661934, 9–5 SEVEN DAYS A WEEK. **PERMANENT DISCOUNT OUTLET**

Manufacturers of concrete garden ornaments, they sell more than 2,500 different items including benches, gnomes, bird baths and sundials, all sold at prices which are about 50% less than those charged in most garden centres. Parking.

CATALOGUE BARGAIN SHOP

19A PRESTON STREET, FAVERSHAM, KENT ME13 8NZ, ☎ 01795 591203, www.bargaincrazy.com, 9–5.30 MON–SAT, 10–4 SUN. **PERMANENT DISCOUNT OUTLET**

See page 577 (CAMBS)

LITTLEWOODS CATALOGUE OUTLET STORE

MCARTHURGLEN DESIGNER OUTLET ASHFORD, KIMBERLEY WAY, ASHFORD, JUNCTION 10 OF M20, KENT TN24 0SD, ☎ 01233 625242, 10–6 MON–FRI, 8 ON THUR, 9–6 SAT, 11–5 SUN. **FACTORY SHOP IN A FACTORY SHOPPING VILLAGE**

Littlewoods clearance shops offer up to 70% off the catalogue price for clothing and offer big discounts off electrical goods. Stock changes constantly and varies from day to day but can include well-known brand names such as Berlei and Gossard lingerie, Vivienne Westwood, Pamplemousse leisurewear, Nike and Adidas sports shoes, and Timberland and Caterpillar footwear. Stock depends on the size and location of the shop: larger shops get the longer discontinued runs, while smaller shops get overruns with only a small amount of colour and size variations left. Littlewoods also runs a mobile shop which operates in cities which don't have a sale shop. For details of venues for the sales, which usually take place once a month, write to Melanie Lamb, c/o Crosby DC Kershaw Avenue, Endbutt Lane, Crosby, Merseyside L70 1AH.

MCARTHURGLEN DESIGNER OUTLET CENTRE

KIMBERLEY WAY, ASHFORD, JUNCTION 10 OF M20, KENT TN24 0SD, ☎ 01233 895900, www.mcarthurglen.com/ashford, 10–6 MON–FRI, 8 ON THUR, 9–6 SAT, 11–5 SUN. **FACTORY SHOPPING VILLAGE**

Voted 'Retail Destination of the Year' 2001 in the Retail Week awards, the McArthurGlen Designer Outlet Ashford in Kent is one of Europe's most spectacular shopping destinations. The outlet offers over 70 top brands and designer labels at up to 50% off typical retail prices. there is a food court, cafés, a children's play area, and parking for over 1,500 cars. A shuttle bus runs between the town centre, station and the outlet every eight minutes. Shops include: Ben Sherman, Cotton Traders, Designer Room/Classic Room, Daks, Fire Trap, Gap, Lee Cooper, Levi's Littlewoods Catalogue Outlet, Marks and Spencer, Mexx, Miss Sixty, Mountain Warehouse, Pilot, Polo Jeans Co. Factory Store, Proudfoot, Roman Originals, Thomas Pink, Tog 24, Tommy Hilfiger, Warehouse, Warner's, Windsmoor, Baron Jon, Ben Sherman, Cotton Traders, Daks, Fire Trap, Fred Perry, Gap, Lee Cooper, Levi's, Petroleum, Proudfoot, Suits You, The Suit Company, Thomas Pink, Van Heusen, Woodhouse, Donnay, Fila, Gap, JoKids, Mexx, Nike, Reebok, Toyzone, Clarks, Ecco, Jane Shilton Kiplings, Lilley & Skinner, Soled Out, Antler, Kipling, Samsonite Company Stores. Arran Aromatics, Body Shop, Chapelle Jewellery, Claire's Outlet, Gizmo, One 2 One, Picture Port, Revlon, Sekonda, Sunglass Hut International, Watch Station, Walker and Hall, Woods of Windsor, Bed and Bath Works, Bookends, Bose, China Place, Cloverleaf, Design House, Edinburgh Crystal, Le Creuset, Mountain Warehouse, Price's Candles, Professional Cookware Company, Spiegelau, Waterford Wedgwood, Whittard of Chelsea, XS Music and Video.

T J HUGHES

THE CHEQUERS SHOPPING CENTRE, PADS HILL, MAIDSTONE, KENT ME15 6AT, ☎ 01622 771600, FAX: 01622 753374, **e-mail:** info@tjhughes.co.uk, www.tjhughes.co.uk, 9–5.30 MON–SAT, 10–4 SUN. **PERMANENT DISCOUNT OUTLET**

See page 579 (CHESH)

THE FACTORY SHOP LTD

THE FOREMAN CENTRE, HIGH STREET, HEADCORN, KENT TN27 9NE, ☎ 01622 891651, 9–5.30 MON–SAT, 10–4 SUN. **FACTORY SHOP**

See page 579 (CHESH)

LANCASHIRE

BOTTOMS MILL CO LTD

ROCHDALE ROAD, WALSDEN, LANCASHIRE OL14 7UB, ☎ 01706 812691, FAX: 01706 815389, **e-mail:** enquiries@bottomsmill.co.uk, 9.30–5 MON–SAT, 10.30–4.30 SUN. **FACTORY SHOP**

Cotton textile manufacturers, the factory shop sells a wide range of household textiles, pottery, tea towels, sheets, cloths, lighting and fabrics. Opposite the Gordon Rigg's Garden Centre.

BUILT-IN KITCHEN APPLIANCES

33–35 BELMONT ROAD, LIVERPOOL, LANCASHIRE L6 5BG, ☎ 0151 263 8966, FAX: 0151 263 8966, www.builtinkitchenappliances.com, 9–5 MON–FRI, 9–4.30 SAT, 10–4 SUN. **PERMANENT DISCOUNT OUTLET**

Hobs, ovens, dishwashers, fridges, freezers, sinks and taps from top brand names such as AEG, Neff, Bosch, Canon, Franke, Blanco, Artriflo and Astracast, all at prices which can be up to 30% off top department store prices. If you know the make and model number of the item you want, phone and find out their best price. Nationwide delivery.

CATALOGUE BARGAIN SHOP

UNIT 1, EASTGATE RETAIL PARK, ACCRINGTON, LANCASHIRE BB5 6PW, ☎ 01254 879195, www.bargaincrazy.com, 9–8 MON–FRI, 9–6 SAT, 10.30–4.30 SUN.

KINGSWAY, BURNLEY, LANCASHIRE BB11 1AB, ☎ 01282 420202, www.bargaincrazy.com, 9–5 MON–SAT, 7 ON THUR, 10.30–4.30 SUN.

40–42 MARKET STREET, CHORLEY, LANCASHIRE PR7 2SE, ☎ 012572 68325, www.bargaincrazy.com, 9–5.30 MON–SAT, 10.30–4.30 SUN.

HALL BANK, WORSLEY RD, PATRICROFT, ECCLES, MANCHESTER, M30 8NR, ☎ 0161 787 7726, www.bargaincrazy.com, 10–5.30 MON–FRI, 8 ON THUR, 9–5 SAT, 10.30–4.30 SUN.

UNITS 1–2, HIGH STREET, HULME, MANCHESTER M15 5AF, ☎ 0161 226 5379, www.bargaincrazy.com, 9–8 MON–SAT, 9 ON THUR, FRI, 11–5 SUN.

UNIT 3, THE PARSONAGE RETAIL PARK, LEIGH, LANCASHIRE WN7 5SJ, ☎ 01942 671911, www.bargaincrazy.com, 9–8 MON–FRI, 9–6 SAT, 11–5 SUN.

UNIT 4, QUEENS RETAIL PARK, QUEENS STREET, PRESTON, LANCASHIRE PR1 4HZ, ☎ 01772 884104, www.bargaincrazy.com, 9–8 MON–FRI, 9–6 SAT, 10.30–4.30 SUN.

82–83 EGARTON WALK, ELLESMERE CENTRE, WALKDEN, MANCHESTER M28 3ZD, ☎ 0161 703 9311, www.bargaincrazy.com, 9–5.30 MON–SAT. **PERMANENT DISCOUNT OUTLET**

See page 577 (CAMBS)

CATALOGUE DISCOUNT STORES

2 BURY OLD ROAD, CHEETHAM HILL, MANCHESTER M8 7JN, ☎ 0161 795 9312, FAX: 0161 7407 274, 9–5.30 MON–SAT. **PERMANENT DISCOUNT OUTLET**

See page 580 (CO DURH)

DALE MILL DISCOUNTS

DALE STREET, MILNROW, NEAR ROCHDALE, LANCASHIRE OL16 3NJ, ☎ 01706 359737, 9.30–6 MON–WED, FRI, 9.30–8 THUR, 9.30–5.30 SAT, 10–5.30 SUN. **PERMANENT DISCOUNT OUTLET**

A wide range of items from clothes and shoes for all the family to kitchenware, furniture, tablecloths, beds and bedding, televisions and general electrical goods, fridges, cookers, microwaves, kitchen and bedroom fittings and units, all on sale at discounted prices. On site there is also a designer clothes store and sportswear outlet, plus a new conservatory extension selling glassware, pottery, dried flowers, table lamps and other household goods.

GORSE MILL LIGHTING

GORDON STREET, OFF JARDINE WAY, BROADWAY, CHADDERTON, OLDHAM, LANCASHIRE OL9 9QW, ☎ 0161 628 4202, FAX: 0161 652 0947, 9.30–5 MON–FRI, 7 ON THUR, 10–5 SAT, 11–5 SUN. **PERMANENT DISCOUNT OUTLET**

240,000 square feet dedicated to lighting up your home. One of Britain's largest decorative light manufacturers, this shop claims to house the biggest display of lighting in the country. The range includes halogen, garden and security lights as well as crystal fittings at savings of between 30% – 75% off high street prices. Lampshades start at as little as 50p and also come in a variety of sizes, patterns and colours. Gorse Mill supplies major chainstores and has vast ranges of decorative lighting, outdoor lighting, crystal chandeliers and ceiling fans, as well as Chinese and Portuguese pottery. Coffee shop, parking for 300 cars, disabled facilities.

LITTLEWOODS CATALOGUE DISCOUNT STORE

185 STAMFORD STREET, ASHTON-UNDER-LYNE, LANCASHIRE OL6 7PY, ☎ 0161 339 0966, 9–5.30 MON–SAT.

UNIT 2, KINGS STREET, FARNWORTH, LANCASHIRE BL4 7AZ, ☎ 01204 861464, 9–5.30 MON–SAT, 10.30–4.30 SUN.

69–74 LORD STREET, FLEETWOOD, LANCASHIRE FY7 6DS, ☎ 01253 773418, 9–5.30 MON–SAT, 10.30–4.30 SUN.

UNIT 3, MONUMENT BUILDINGS, LONDON ROAD, LIVERPOOL LANCASHIRE L3 8JY, ☎ 0151 708 6118, 9–5 MON–SAT, 9.30–5.30 TUE, 11–5 SUN.

160 MARINE ROAD, CENTRAL MORECAMBE, LANCASHIRE LA4 4BU, ☎ 01524 412074, 9.30–5.30 MON, 9–5.30 TUE–SAT, 10.30–4.30 SUN. **PERMANENT DISCOUNT OUTLET**

See page 578 (CHESH)

NORTHERN REALISATIONS

ALBION MILL, ST MARKS STREET, BOLTON, LANCASHIRE BL3 6NR, ☎ 01204 365911, www.realnorth.co.uk, 9.30–5.30 MON–FRI. **SECONDHAND SHOP**

Second user computer and office equipment, though not furniture. Most of the stock is government clearance and it is sold by catalogue auction online only. There is a sister company, CFU Ltd, at this site which offers similar stock on an over-the-counter basis. Their telephone number is 01204 388600.

SALTON EUROPE

PRINCESS STREET, FAILSWORTH, ON THE A62 MANCHESTER TO OLDHAM ROAD, LANCASHIRE M35 0HS, ☎ 0161 947 3000, 9–5.30 MON, WED–FRI, CLOSED TUE, 9–1 SAT. **FACTORY SHOP**

Discontinued lines and factory seconds of Pifco, Carmen, Haden, Salton, Russell Hobbs, Westclox, Mountain Breeze and Tower, as well as some perfect lines. For example, kettles, irons, steamers, clocks, deep fat fryers, toasters, fans, haircare, saucepan sets, slow cookers, mini ovens, air cleaners, George Forman health grills, ionisers and aromatherapy products. Also Christmas tree lights in season in clear, white and coloured, and outdoor festive decorative lights.

T J HUGHES

59–63 CHURCH STREET, BLACKBURN, LANCASHIRE BB1 5AF, ☎ 01254 693333, FAX: 01254 693232, **e-mail:** info@tjhughes.co.uk, www.tjhughes.co.uk, 9–5.30 MON– SAT, 11–5 SUN.

MONS SQUARE, NEW STRAND, BOOTLE, LANCASHIRE L20 4SY, ☎ 0151 922 4397, FAX: 0151 933 1622, **e-mail:** info@tjhughes.co.uk, www.tjhughes.co.uk, 9–5.30 MON– SAT.

4 CURZON STREET, BURNLEY, LANCASHIRE BB11 1BB, ☎ 01282 838383, FAX: 01282 435400, **e-mail:** info@tjhughes.co.uk, www.tjhughes.co.uk, 9–5.30 MON–SAT, 11–4 SUN.

105 LONDON ROAD, LIVERPOOL, LANCASHIRE L3 8JA, ☎ 0151 207 2600, FAX: 0151 298 1339, **e-mail:** info@tjhughes.co.uk, www.tjhughes.co.uk, 9–5.30 MON– SAT, 11–5 SUN.

UNIT 32, TOWN SQUARE SHOPPING CENTRE, OLDHAM, LANCASHIRE OL1 1XF, ☎ 0161 628 3880, FAX: 0161 628 3886, **e-mail:** info@tjhughes.co.uk, www.tjhughes.co.uk, 9–5.30 MON– SAT.

FISHERGATE CENTRE, PRESTON, LANCASHIRE PR1 8HJ, ☎ 01772 887326, FAX: 01772 887328, **e-mail:** info@tjhughes.co.uk, www.tjhughes.co.uk, 9–5.30 MON–SAT, 8 ON WED, 11–5 SUN.

UNIT 6-7, THE WHEATSHEAF CENTRE, ROCHDALE, LANCASHIRE OL16 1NZ, ☎ 01706 750555, FAX: 01706 750666, **e-mail:** info@tjhughes.co.uk, www.tjhughes.co.uk, 9–5.30 MON– SAT, 10.30–4.30 SUN.

86 RAVENS WAY, SALFORD SHOPPING CITY, SALFORD, MANCHESTER, M6 5JA, ☎ 0161 736 1472, FAX: 0161 736 0656, **e-mail:** info@tjhughes.co.uk, www.tjhughes.co.uk, 9–5.30 MON– SAT.

UNIT 1, THE HARDSHAW CENTRE, ST HELENS, LANCASHIRE WA10 1EB, ☎ 01744 453221, FAX: 01744 453065, **e-mail:** info@tjhughes.co.uk, www.tjhughes.co.uk, 9–5.30 MON– SAT, 10.30–4.30 SUN.

31–36 ARNDALE CENTRE, CHESTER ROAD, STRETFORD, MANCHESTER, LANCASHIRE M32 9BB, ☎ 0161 866 9733, FAX: 0161 864 4627, **e-mail:** info@tjhughes.co.uk, www.tjhughes.co.uk, 9–5.30 MON– SAT, 10–4 SUN.

27–31 SANKEY STREET, WARRINGTON, LANCASHIRE WA1 1XG, ☎ 01925 634 4321, FAX: 01925 445966, **e-mail:** info@tjhughes.co.uk, www.tjhughes.co.uk, 9–5.30 MON– SAT, 10.30–4.30 SUN. **PERMANENT DISCOUNT OUTLET**

See page 579 (CHESH)

TERRY'S STORES URMSTON LTD

47 STATION ROAD, URMSTON, MANCHESTER M41 9JG, ☎ 0161 748 6011, 9.30–5 MON–SAT, CLOSED WED. **PERMANENT DISCOUNT OUTLET**

Described as 'the final resting-place for ex-catalogue stock', Terry's sells everything that is normally available by catalogue at half price. This includes leather jackets, jeans, shoes, trainers, dress and curtaining fabric, whatnot stands, nests of tables, dining tables and chairs, bedlinen, curtains, electrical goods, wedding and bridesmaids dresses. The company has been in operation for 46 years and is privately owned.

THE FACTORY SHOP

SHAWBRIDGE STREET, CLITHEROE, LANCASHIRE BB7 1NA, ☎ 01200 428784, 9–5.30 MON–SAT, 10.30–4.30 SUN.

LANCASTER LEISURE PARK, WYRESDALE ROAD, LANCASTER, LA1 3LA, ☎ 01524 846079, 10–5 MON–SAT, 11–5 SUN. **FACTORY SHOP**

See page 579 (CHESH)

WINFIELDS

HAZEL MILL, BLACKBURN ROAD, HASLINGDEN, ROSSENDALE, LANCASHIRE BB4 5DD, ☎ 01706 227916, FAX: 01706 831125, **e-mail:** info@winfields.co.uk, www.winfields.co.uk, 10–5.30 MON–FRI, 8 ON THUR, 9–5.30 SAT, 11–5 SUN. **PERMANENT DISCOUNT OUTLET**

Winfields is a big mill discount store with other outlets in Barrow-in-Furness, Middleton and Hull, offering tremendous savings on shoes. There is a wide variety of outdoor and indoor furniture, timber decking, garden tools, pet accessories, cookware, utensils, electrical goods, bath towels, mirrors, picture frames, and gifts such as watches, crystalware and beauty products, with new stock arriving weekly. Luggage can be found in the Winair holiday department. Dine or take a break at Cloggers, the restaurant. Free car parking. Wheelchair friendly.

LEICESTERSHIRE

APPLIANCE CENTRE

87 LOTHAIR ROAD, AYLESTONE PARK, LEICESTER, LEICESTERSHIRE LE2 7QE, ☎ 0116 244 0150, 7.45–5.45 MON–FRI. MAIL ORDER. **PERMANENT DISCOUNT OUTLET**

Small shop selling cookers, range cookers, ovens, hobs, hoods, washing machines, dishwashers, fridges, freezers, American refrigeration, sinks, etc, at competitive prices. As well as selling perfect goods, many products are offered as seconds or 'B' grade. These usually consist of slightly imperfect goods damaged in transit or ex-display or service/catalogue returns which have been in use for a very short period of time. All appliances carry a full 12 months guarantee and all prices include delivery (mainland GB only). A full range of literature is available from most leading manufacturers. These include AEG, Amana, Asko, Belling, Blanco, Bosch, Cannon, Creda, De Dietrich, Electrolux, Fisher & Paykel, Frnake, Leisure, Liebherr, Maytag, Neff, Siemens, Smeg, Stoves, Zanussi etc. Before ordering any new appliances/sinks for your fitted kitchen, it's worth talking to Appliance Centre who can save you a lot of money compared with kitchen showroom prices. Phone before travelling to ascertain the current stock availability of the appliances you require as there is a high turnaround of goods. They also supply granite worktops and stone and slate flooring. Installation is available in some areas – details available on request.

CATALOGUE BARGAIN SHOP

UNIT D, WHITWICK RETAIL PARK, COALVILLE, LEICESTERSHIRE LE67 3FA, ☎ 01530 830294, www.bargaincrazy.com, 9–8 MON–SAT, 9 ON THUR, FRI, 10–4 SUN. **PERMANENT DISCOUNT OUTLET**

See page 577 (CAMBS)

RUTLAND LIGHTING

THISTLETON ROAD INDUSTRIAL ESTATE, MARKET OVERTON, OAKHAM, RUTLAND LE15 7PP, ☎ 01572 767587, FAX: 01572 767420, 9–4 MON–SAT. **PERMANENT DISCOUNT OUTLET**

Sells a full range of lampshades, table and floor lamps, chandeliers, bulbs, outdoor and indoor lights, plus other manufacturers' ends of lines and chainstore seconds. Most lines have genuine reductions on normal retail prices. This shop is small and within the factory itself unlike the

Grantham, Lincolnshire, shop which is large and on the high street. Stock is mainly manufactured on site although some is bought in or imported.

LINCOLNSHIRE

CATALOGUE BARGAIN SHOP

12–14 SILVER STREET, GAINSBOROUGH, LINCOLNSHIRE DN21 2DP, ☎ 01427 810604, www.bargaincrazy.com, 9–5.30 MON, THUR, FRI, 8.30–5 TUE, 9–5 WED, 8.30–5.30 SAT, 10–4 SUN.

29–31 THE STRAIT, LINCOLN, LINCOLNSHIRE LN1 1JD, ☎ 01522 527276, www.bargaincrazy.com, 9–5.30 MON–SAT, 10.30–4.30 SUN. **PERMANENT DISCOUNT OUTLET**

See page 577 (CAMBS)

STAGE 2

TRITTON RETAIL PARK, TRITTON ROAD, LINCOLN, LINCOLNSHIRE LN6 7YA, ☎ 01522 560303, 10–8 MON–FRI, 9–6 SAT, 11–5 SUN AND BANK HOLIDAYS. **PERMANENT DISCOUNT OUTLET**

See page 577 (CAMBS)

THE FACTORY SHOP

MALT KILN ROAD, BARTON ON HUMBER, NORTH LINCOLNSHIRE DN18 5JT, ☎ 01652 636701, 9–7 MON, TUE, WED, 9–8 THUR, FRI, 8.30–7 SAT, 10–4 SUN.

43 HIGH STREET, MABLETHORPE, LINCOLNSHIRE LN12 1XA, ☎ 01507 473705, 9.30–6 MON–SAT, 10.30–4.30 SUN.

CARRE STREET, SLEAFORD, LINCOLNSHIRE NG34 7TW, ☎ 01529 410155, 9–5.30 MON–SAT, 10–4 SUN.

51 FLEET STREET, HOLBEACH, SPALDING, LINCOLNSHIRE PE12 7AU, ☎ 01406 422180, 9–5 MON–SAT, 10–4 SUN. **FACTORY SHOP**

See page 579 (CHESH)

LONDON

APPLIANCE DIRECT

6 HIGH STREET, HARLESDEN, LONDON NW10 4LX, ☎ 020 8838 3338, FAX: 020 8838 3364, WWW.APPLIANCEDIRECTUK.COM, 9.30–5.30 MON–FRI, 10–5.30 SAT. **PERMANENT DISCOUNT OUTLET**

Specialise in ex-display and graded white electrical goods. For example new, cosmetically damaged washing machines from £160. They also sell fridges, cookers, ranges, deep fat fryers, blenders, vacuum cleaners, toasters, irons, food processors, American fridges, dishwashers and extractor hoods and fans.

AUDIO GOLD

31 PARK ROAD, CROUCH END, LONDON N8 8TE, ☎ 020 8341 9007, **e-mail:** enquiries@audiogold.co.uk, www.audiogold.co.uk, 11–6 MON–SAT, CLOSED THUR. **SECONDHAND SHOP**

Small shop with friendly, unintimidating atmosphere where old, loved music machines can get a second life. Catering for the run-of-the-mill end of the secondhand hi-fi market as well as the esoteric and expensive end. Particular bargains can be found in the imposing speaker areas as most people trading in equipment tend to trade down, not up, in size. Most equipment is guaranteed for three months. One of the few places left in London where you can still get a good range of turntables.

BUYERS & SELLERS LTD

120–122 LADBROKE GROVE, LONDON W10 5NE, ☎ 0845 080 2202, FAX: 020 7221 4113, **e-mail:** lowestprices@buyers-sellers.co.uk, 9.30–5.30 MON–FRI, 6 ON THUR, 9.30–4.30 SAT, 10–5.30 WED. **PERMANENT DISCOUNT OUTLET**

Buyers & Sellers is one of the UK's largest independent retail outlets, selling a range of domestic appliances for kitchen and home from top brands such as Amana, Miele, Smeg and Bosch at bargain prices – usually the best to be found anywhere. Appliances on sale range from fridges, freezers, ovens, microwaves and hobs to vacuum cleaners, washing machines, dishwashers, tumble dryers and cookers, all complete with manufacturers' guarantees. Knowledgeable and friendly staff offer expert advice. Nationwide delivery service. Telephone orders taken. Credit cards accepted.

CATALOGUE BARGAIN SHOP

252 GREEN LANES, PALMERS GREEN, LONDON N13 5TU, ☎ 020 8886 9532, www.bargaincrazy.com, 9–5.30 MON–SAT, 10–4 SUN. **PERMANENT DISCOUNT OUTLET**

See page 577 (CAMBS)

DISCOUNT COOKERS

97 RUSHEY GREEN, CATFORD, LONDON SE6 4AF, ☎ 020 8461 5273, 9–6 MON–SAT. **PERMANENT DISCOUNT OUTLET**

New and reconditioned models from New World, Whirlpool and Canon with more than 2,000 new cookers in stock at any one time. Because they buy in bulk to supply their five south-east London shops, they can offer competitive prices – although they say that the more expensive the cooker you buy, the better the discount. They also stock between 400 to 500 reconditioned cookers at prices from £100 upwards – which works out at between 25% to 50% cheaper than when new – as well as some new ex-display models. All the cookers come with a six month guarantee and there is free delivery within the M25 area. Countrywide delivery is by courier. The shop is next door to Blockbuster Video.

DISPOSAL SERVICES AGENCY (DSA)

ROOM 727, MINISTRY OF DEFENCE, 6 HERCULES ROAD, LONDON SE1 7DJ, ☎ 020 7261 8968, www.disposalservices.agency.mod.uk. **PERMANENT DISCOUNT OUTLET**

The Disposal Services Agency is an agency of the Ministry of Defence set up to dispose of surplus equipment. It runs the largest disposal operation in the UK, organising the sale of both military equipment and commodities in use commercially, such as embassy furniture, government department office furniture, closed-down RAF-base vehicles and housing stock, ex-marine boats, ex-army tents, boots and ski equipment, medical and dental equipment, clothing, ship and aircraft spares, scrap metal and IT equipment. The DSA uses companies throughout the UK, each with their own specialist area, to dispose of stock. These companies also dispose of stock from a host of other, usually public sector, organisations varying from fire brigades and hospitals to health authorities and the police. Equipment from these companies varies from kitchen equipment and fax machines to mobile radios, cars, generators, jewellery and telecommunications equipment to food trolleys, X-ray equipment, telephones, uniforms, dinghies, fishing nets, photocopiers and chair lifts. Visit the website to find out which companies sell which products and how to contact them direct.

HITACHI FACTORY SHOP

LIGHT AND SOUND, 166 HIGH STREET NORTH, LONDON E6 2JA, ☎ 020 8472 1373, FAX: 020 8472 6667, **e-mail:** factoryshop@btclick.com, www.inter-discount.co.uk, 10–6.30 MON–FRI, 10–6 SAT. **FACTORY SHOP**

Hitachi's official factory outlet sells returned and former display items at discounts averaging 25%. This can include CD players, DVD players, televisions, videos, hi-fis, fridges, microwaves, vacuum cleaners, radio cassettes, Walkmans and accessories. Now stocking electronic accessories for the amateur electronics enthusiast, all at very competitive prices.

HOT & COLD INC

13–15 GOLBORNE ROAD, LONDON W10 5NY, ☎ 020 8960 1200 OR 1300, 10–5.30 MON–FRI, 10–5 SAT. **PERMANENT DISCOUNT OUTLET**

Supplies domestic appliances from nearly one hundred brands. Range now includes American fridge freezers and range cookers. A total of about 10,000 different items, at prices which they claim will beat any genuine competitor's. In fact, they are so sure of this that they promise to refund the difference if you find you could have bought the same product elsewhere at the same time for a lower price, provided you give them proof of that within two weeks of purchase. All goods are brand new, perfect and guaranteed. They specialise in built-in equipment, but they can also supply freestanding appliances. Also ends of lines, some at less than half the original price. Prices include VAT. Delivery can be arranged countrywide.

ICELAND CLEARANCE WAREHOUSE

120–132 CAMBERWELL ROAD, LONDON SE5 0EA, ☎ 020 7708 4347, www.iceland.co.uk, 9–5.30 MON–SAT, 10–4 SUN. **PERMANENT DISCOUNT OUTLET**

Iceland's showroom near Camberwell Green has a clearance section which sells a wide range of shop-soiled or damaged packaging kitchen equipment from large US-style fridges to microwaves, kettles, tumble dryers, washing machines, dishwashers and cookers, but no built-in ovens, at discounts of about 20%. The showroom also has brand new stock at full price. Items in the clearance section could be there as a result of being damaged on delivery, because it broke down within two weeks of being purchased and has been reconditioned, because it is part of a range or a manufacturer no longer being sold by Iceland's 600-plus branches or because of Iceland's policy of lending appliances to customers whose machines have broken down within one year of purchase. The loaned machine, which may only have been used for a few days, is then sold off at discount. The clearance section is at the back of the Iceland showroom.

MORRY'S

39–40 THE BROADWAY, EDMONTON, LONDON N9 0TJ, ☎ 020 8807 6747, 8.30–5 MON–SAT, CLOSED 1 ON THUR. **PERMANENT DISCOUNT OUTLET**

Liquidation stock which includes some famous makes and can comprise anything from gardening equipment (shovels, forks and hoses) and household items to electrical equipment (CDs, radios, televisions, radio alarms) and clothing for men, women and children. For example, BhS padded jacket £3.99, normal retail price £30; Etam dress £2, normal retail price £40. Everything is at least half the retail price. Specialises in Philips electrical equipment from CD players and videos, car stereos and radio cassettes to shavers and baby alarms, all with full repair and spares back-up. If you live nearby, drop in frequently as stock is constantly changing.

THE CASH EXCHANGE

352 HOLLOWAY ROAD, LONDON N7, FAX: 020 7609 2100, FAX: 020 7609 9070, www.cashexchangelondon.co.uk, 10–6 MON–SAT. **PERMANENT DISCOUNT OUTLET**

Permanent discount outlet which operates rather like a pawn brokers. It takes unwanted household and electrical items and gives you cash. Unredeemed items are sold off at very low prices. For example, laptop computers from £200, top of the range televisions, worth £1,500, for £700. International money transfer services are available, and a 24-hour electrical repair service, offering very competitive rates, is also on site.

APPLIANCE DIRECT

192 STATION ROAD, EDGWARE, MIDDLESEX HA8 7AR, ☎ 020 8952 2228, FAX: 020 8952 2228, WWW.APPLIANCEDIRECTUK.COM, 9.30–5.30 MON–FRI, 10–5.30 SAT. **PERMANENT DISCOUNT OUTLET**

See page 591 (LOND)

MIDDLESEX

STEWART & YOUNG

30 AND 105–107 HIGH STREET, HAMPTON HILL, MIDDLESEX TW12 1NJ, ☎ 020 8977 1193, FAX: 020 8296 9310, 9–5.30 MON–FRI, 9–4.30 SAT. **PERMANENT DISCOUNT OUTLET**

Sells and services domestic household goods. As they belong to the Euronics group, the biggest buying group in Europe, prices match those of big stores. Where Stewart & Young have the edge is that they include delivery, installation to existing fittings and removal of any old machine in their price, excluding refridgeration. The branch at 30 High Street specialises in cookers, refrigeration and built-in appliances. Washing machines, tumble dryers, vacuum cleaners, dishwashers etc can be found at 105 High Street.

THE SALVAGE SHOP

34–40 WATLING AVENUE, BURNT OAK, MIDDLESEX HA8 0LR, ☎ 020 8952 4353, **e-mail:** lss@salvage1.co.uk, www.salvage1.co.uk, 9–5.30 MON–SAT, 10–4 SUN. **PERMANENT DISCOUNT OUTLET**

An Aladdin's cave of salvaged stock for the avid bargain hunter, most of which has been the subject of insurance claims for fire or flood, salvage, bankruptcy or is simply clearance stock. Stock changes every two or three days and regular visitors have found anything from half price Kenwood Chefs, televisions and toys to furniture, kitchen items, linens and especially fantastic bargains in designer clothing. Yves Saint Laurent, Armani, Ungaro, Hugo Boss and Valentino, as well as all major high street names, are just some of the names to be found (though the labels are often cut out). Discounts range from 50% to 80%. Phone first to check stock.

NORFOLK

SECONDHAND LAND

113–117 MAGDALEN STREET, NORWICH, NORFOLK NR3 1LN, ☎ 01603 611922, www.secondhandland/norwich.com, 9–6 MON–THUR. **SECONDHAND SHOP**

Sells televisions, videos, computers, hi-fi systems, recording equipment – all of which are, as the name suggests, secondhand. Some are reconditioned, all come with a three or six month guarantee. A two-year-old 26-inch standard television set with remote control and Teletext costs between £75 to £125. They now also buy and sell mobile phones. Free local delivery.

THE FACTORY SHOP LTD

NORWICH STREET, EAST DEREHAM, NORFOLK NR19 1AD, ☎ 01362 691868, 9–5.30 MON–SAT, 10–4 SUN.

52 LONDON ROAD, HARLESTON, NORFOLK IP20 9BZ, ☎ 01379 854860, 9–5.30 MON–SAT, 10.30–4 SUN.

LYNN ROAD, SNETTISHAM, NORFOLK PE31 7QG, ☎ 01485 544441, 9–5.30 MON–SAT, 10–4 SUN. **FACTORY SHOP**

See page 579 (CHESH)

NORTHAMPTONSHIRE

SHOWHOME WAREHOUSE

11–17 FRANCIS COURT, WELLINGBOROUGH ROAD, RUSHDEN, NORTHAMPTONSHIRE NN10 6AY, ☎ 01933 411695, 10–5 TUE– SUN, 11–3 MON. **PERMANENT DISCOUNT OUTLET**

The contents of quality show homes are sold seven days a week at this 20,000 square foot warehouse. Savings normally range from 50% to 70% off store prices. About 50% of their stock is sold each week and different stock arrives daily. Choose from a range of kitchen appliances, lounge furniture, three-piece suites, dining tables and chairs, rugs, study and bedroom furniture, oil paintings, mirrors, ornaments, televisions and videos, patio and garden furniture and gym equipment. The range is eclectic: from suits of armour to lion's heads, Tiffany lampshades to leather zebras, handpainted furniture to mahogany classics, alien-shaped CD racks to antique carts made into bookcases or sets of oars turned into coat racks. Because a high percentage of their business comes from trade, prices exclude VAT but still represent very good value for money. For example, elaborate metal bed, £175, normally £750; dining room table and chairs, £350, normally £1,500; washer-dryer, £300, usually £500 to £600. Occasional auctions take place during the year: phone for details.

NORTHUMBERLAND

CATALOGUE BARGAIN SHOP

51 SHIELDS ROAD, BYKER, NEWCASTLE UPON TYNE, TYNE & WEAR NE6 1DJ, ☎ 0191 265 6033, www.bargaincrazy.com, 9–6 MON–SAT, 8 ON THUR, FRI, 10.30–4.30 SUN. **PERMANENT DISCOUNT OUTLET**

See page 577 (CAMBS)

CATALOGUE DISCOUNT STORE

15 THE PRECINCT, THE IN CENTRE, JARROW, TYNE & WEAR, ☎ 0191 483 4318, 9–5 MON–SAT.

8 THE FORUM SHOPPING CENTRE, WALLSEND, NORTHUMBERLAND NE28 8JR, ☎ 0191 236 9501, 9–5 MON–SAT. **PERMANENT DISCOUNT OUTLET**

See page 580 (CO DURH)

NO FRILLS DIY STORE

WHITLEY ROAD, LONGBENTON, NEWCASTLE UPON TYNE, TYNE & WEAR NE12 9SZ, ☎ 0191 270 0393, FAX: 0191 215 0823, 9–8 MON–SAT, 10–4 SUN. **PERMANENT DISCOUNT OUTLET**

See page 577 (BEDS)

REMINGTON

ROYAL QUAYS, NORTH SHIELDS, NEWCASTLE UPON TYNE, TYNE & WEAR, ☎ 0191 258 3622, 10–6 MON–SAT, 11–5 SUN. **FACTORY SHOP IN A FACTORY SHOPPING VILLAGE**

See page 579 (CHESH)

ROYAL QUAYS OUTLET CENTRE

COBLE DENE, NORTH SHIELDS, NEWCASTLE UPON TYNE, NEAR A19, TYNE & WEAR NE29 6DW, ☎ 0191 296 3743, **e-mail:** outletcentres@realm-ocm.com, www.royalquaysoutletcentre.co.uk, 10–6 MON–SAT, 11–5 SUN. **FACTORY SHOPPING VILLAGE**

Forty-two shops with leisure facilities nearby including a full-scale steam railway, working harbour, Roman ruins and the usual seaside attractions. Adjacent to the Wet and Wild water park which attracts 350,000 visitors a year and next door to an international ferry terminal, the centre has a nautical feel to it. There is a great range of shops, many new, stocking famous name brands, all with up to 50% discounts off normal retail prices. Phone for more details.

SCOOPS CATALOGUE DISCOUNT STORE

8 THE FORUM SHOPPING CENTRE, WALLSEND, TYNE & WEAR NE28 8JR, ☎ 0191 236 9501 9–5 MON–SAT. **PERMANENT DISCOUNT OUTLET**

See page 580 (CO DURH)

NOTTINGHAMSHIRE

BUNNY APPLIANCE WAREHOUSE

UNIT 1 AND 2, BUNNY TRADING ESTATE, GOTHAM LANE, BUNNY, NOTTINGHAM NG11 6QJ, ☎ 0115 984 4357, www.bunnyuk.com, 10–5 MON–FRI, 10–4 SAT, 11–3 SUN. **PERMANENT DISCOUNT OUTLET**

Large warehouse with 10,000 fitted kitchen appliances. They specialise in built-in kitchen appliances, stocking all leading brands from AEG to Zanussi at up to 60% discounts. There is a large showroom displaying 60 gas and electric single and double ovens, and 200 ceramic, halogen, gas and electric hobs are always in stock. Specialise in American fridges and fridge freezers with up to £500 off, and range cookers. They offer excellent advice and service.

CATALOGUE BARGAIN SHOP

24–29 LEEMING STREET, MANSFIELD, NOTTINGHAMSHIRE NG18 1NE, ☎ 01623 623353, www.bargaincrazy.com, 9–5.30 MON–SAT, 10–4 SUN.

50 MAIN STREET, BULWELL, NOTTINGHAM, NOTTINGHAMSHIRE NG6 8EY, ☎ 0115 927 8373, www.bargaincrazy.com, 9–5.30 MON–SAT, 10–4 SUN. **PERMANENT DISCOUNT OUTLET**

See page 577 (CAMBS)

DAYCLEAR LIGHTING LTD

85A CROMFORD ROAD, LANGLEY MILL, NOTTINGHAM, NOTTINGHAMSHIRE NG16 4EP, ☎ 01773 763787, 9–5 MON–SAT. **FACTORY SHOP**

Lampshades, table lamps, chandeliers and decorative lighting at manufacturers prices. There are usually at least 300 lines in stock at any one time. For example, 12in table lamps with pleated shades, £6.99; three-arm solid brass chandelier, £68; standard lamp, £27.95. There is parking at the rear of the building.

LIQUIDATION SUPPLIES

26 LONDON ROAD, RETFORD, NOTTINGHAMSHIRE DN22 6AY, ☎ 01777 711151, FAX: 01777 711151, 9–5.30 MON–FRI, 9–5 SAT. **PERMANENT DISCOUNT OUTLET**

Factory soiled, new dishwashers, cookers, fridges, washing machines and built-in ovens, all with a one-year guarantee, at discount prices. A wide range of makes are available. Brand new appliances are also stocked to order and sold at very competitive prices. Free delivery and connection on electrical appliances within a 30-mile radius. Interest free credit is available. Parking available.

THE FACTORY SHOP

DONCASTER ROAD, LANGOLD, WORKSOP, NOTTINGHAMSHIRE DN22 7HY, ☎ 01909 731115, 9 -5.30 MON–SAT, 10–4.30 SUN. **FACTORY SHOP**

See page 579 (CHESH)

SHROPSHIRE

T J HUGHES

RIVERSIDE AND PRIDEHILL SHOPPING CENTRE, SHREWSBURY, SHROPSHIRE SY1 1BU, ☎ 01743 358359, FAX: 01743 271222, **e-mail:** info@tjhughes.co.uk, www.tjhughes.co.uk, 9–5.30 MON– SAT, 10.30–4.30 SUN. **PERMANENT DISCOUNT OUTLET**

See page 579 (CHESH)

SOMERSET

CHAPLINS SUPERSTORES HOME & GARDEN

BINDON ROAD, TAUNTON, SOMERSET TA2 6AA, ☎ 01823 288017, FAX: 01823 336189, 9–8 MON–FRI, 9–6 SAT, 10.30–4.30 SUN. **PERMANENT DISCOUNT OUTLET**

A wide range of merchandise for the bargain hunter, including garden tools, plants, fertilisers and accessories; toys; adults clothing and shoes; stationery; household textiles; electrical equipment; DIY items; glass and china; bathroom accessories; partyware; candles; food accessories. Spades are available at £4.99, trowels at 99p, shears at £5.99 (while stocks last).

REMINGTON

CLARKS VILLAGE FACTORY SHOPPING CENTRE, FARM ROAD, STREET, JUNCTION 23 OF M5, SOMERSET BA16 0BB, ☎ 01458 840209, 9–6 MON–SAT, 11–5 SUN. **FACTORY SHOP IN A FACTORY SHOPPING VILLAGE**

See page 579 (CHESH)

T J HUGHES

FAIRFAX HOUSE, HIGH STREET, WESTON-SUPER-MARE, SOMERSET BS23 1HA, ☎ 01934 414466, FAX: 01934 419911, **e-mail:** info@tjhughes.co.uk, www.tjhughes.co.uk, 9–5.30 MON–SAT, 11–5 SUN. **PERMANENT DISCOUNT OUTLET**

See page 579 (CHESH)

THE FACTORY SHOP LTD

MART ROAD, MINEHEAD, SOMERSET TA24 5BJ, ☎ 01643 705911, 9.30–5.30 MON–SAT, 11–5 SUN. **FACTORY SHOP**

See page 579 (CHESH)

STAFFORDSHIRE

CATALOGUE BARGAIN SHOP

95 CHURCH STREET, BILSTON, STAFFORDSHIRE WV14 0BJ, ☎ 01902 353624, www.bargaincrazy.com, 9–5.30 MON–SAT, 9.30–3.30 SUN.

UNIT 2, CHASE CENTRE, CHURCH STREET, CANNOCK, STAFFORDSHIRE WS11 1AP, ☎ 01543 468614, www.bargaincrazy.com, 9–8 MON–FRI, 9–6 SAT, 10.30–4.30 SUN.

FREEPORT TALKE OUTLET MALL, PIT LANE, TALKE PITS, STOKE-ON-TRENT, STAFFORDSHIRE ST7 1XD, ☎ 01782 775740, www.bargaincrazy.com, 9.30–8 MON–FRI, 9.30–6 SAT, 11–5 SUN. **PERMANENT DISCOUNT OUTLET**

See page 577 (CAMBS)

CATALOGUE DISCOUNT STORE

63 HIGH STREET, BROWNHILLS, STAFFORDSHIRE WS8 6HH, ☎ 01543 372933, 9–5.30 MON–SAT. **PERMANENT DISCOUNT OUTLET**

See page 580 (CO DURH)

CATERING RESALES

MEADOW STREET, CHESTERTON, NEWCASTLE UNDER LYME, STAFFORDSHIRE ST5 7HU, ☎ 01782 564563, FAX: 01782 564850, **e-mail:** sales@cateringresales.co.uk, www.cateringresales.co.uk, 9–5 MON–FRI, 9–1 SAT. PHONE FIRST. **SECONDHAND SHOP**

Secondhand and reconditioned catering equipment. Stainless steel sinks and tables, six-burner cookers, fryers, griddles, both gas and electric, but no saucepans or pans.

CHROMAVISION

29 LONSDALE STREET, STOKE-ON-TRENT, STAFFORDSHIRE ST4 4DT, ☎ 01782 848153, FAX: 01782 744105, 9.30–6 MON–SAT. **PERMANENT DISCOUNT OUTLET**

Ex-rental former display models and manufacturers' returns in televisions, videos and satellites at bargain prices. Stocks all top brands. Also sells microwaves, cookers, vacuum cleaners, hi-fis, washing machines and fridge freezers.

DOMESTIC APPLIANCES

92 HIGH STREET, TUNSTALL, STOKE-ON-TRENT, STAFFORDSHIRE ST6 5TJ, ☎ 01782 833303, 9–5 MON–SAT. **PERMANENT DISCOUNT OUTLET**

Reconditioned Hotpoint washing machines as well as fridge freezers, tumble dryers and cookers from different manufacturers. Also new repro tables, beds and chairs imported from abroad and sold at low profit margins.

ELECTRIC LIGHT CO

135 NEWCASTLE STREET, BURSLEM, STOKE-ON-TRENT, STAFFORDSHIRE ST6 3QJ, ☎ 01782 812821, FAX: 01782 836888, **e-mail:** elclights@aol.com, 8–5.30 MON–FRI, 8.30–1 SAT. **PERMANENT DISCOUNT OUTLET**

A permanent discount outlet, the Electric Light Company don't keep stock in store, but allow customers to take away a catalogue, to browse at their leisure at home, before ringing them with a product number. As a general rule, discounts are 15% for the range of glass, ceramic, plaster, centre, wall, and outside lights, although gold and crystal lights, which can cost £1,000, will attract a higher discount. Halogen downlighters are on offer from £15, complete with transformer.

HYLANDS

WESTERN ROAD, MEIR, STOKE-ON-TRENT, STAFFORDSHIRE ST3 6AJ, ☎ 01782 319402, 9–5.30 MON–SAT. **PERMANENT DISCOUNT OUTLET**

Electrical goods from televisions, CD players and stereos to washing machines, dishwashers and ovens at very competitive prices. Brands sold include Panasonic, Toshiba, Samsung and Sony in brown goods and Creda, Hotpoint, Zanussi and Bosch in white goods.

L & M EUROTRADING

WOODLANDS, LEYCETT LANE, NEWCASTLE UNDER LYME, STOKE-ON-TRENT, STAFFORDSHIRE ST5 6AD, ☎ 01782 839555, FAX: 01782 839555, 9–6 MON–SAT **SECONDHAND SHOP**

Clearance company for businesses which relocate or shut down, specialising in the catering market, especially pubs, clubs, restaurants and supermarkets. When they go in, they take everything from bulbs to desks, chairs, computers, racking and shelving. You can find almost anything here, but if you're looking for anything to do with preparing food, there are fridges, freezers, cookers, microwaves, plates, saucepans, stainless steel sinks and tables. Cookers range from domestic size to commercial six-burner versions; freezers from domestic to 20ft by 18ft walk-in types, stainless steel sinks from 6ft to 14ft.

MARTIN DAWS

8 LAMB STREET, HANLEY, STOKE-ON-TRENT, STAFFORDSHIRE ST1 1PQ, ☎ 01782 205122, 9–5.30 MON–SAT. **PERMANENT DISCOUNT OUTLET**

They sell ex-rental and new, branded television sets, Sky Digital, satellite, hifis, widescreen televisions and video recorders, all with a guarantee of at least six months. They also offer very good deals on new contract and pay-as-you-go mobile phones.

SCOOPS CATALOGUE DISCOUNT STORES

UNIT 3, 567–569 BEARWOOD SHOPPING CENTRE, SMETHWICK, STAFFORDSHIRE B66 4BH, ☎ 0121 434 3086, FAX: 0121 429 8488, 9–5.30 MON–SAT, 11–3 SUN. **PERMANENT DISCOUNT OUTLET**

See page 580 (CO DURH)

SPECTRUM SERVICES

5–13 HIGH STREET, TUNSTALL, STOKE-ON-TRENT, STAFFORDSHIRE ST6 5TE, ☎ 01782 826162, FAX: 01782 811464, www.spectrum-services.com, 9–5.30 MON–FRI, 9–3.30 SAT. **PERMANENT DISCOUNT OUTLET**

Graded electrical items which have either been returned because of a slight cosmetic mark or because the packaging is damaged. Stock includes cookers, fridges, freezers, tumble dryers, microwaves, vacuum cleaners, and both gas and electric cookers from Zanussi, Electrolux, Hoover, Creda and Hotpoint.

TELETRONIX

21 HIGHERLAND, NEWCASTLE UNDER LYME, STAFFORDSHIRE ST5 2TF, ☎ 01782 661925, FAX: 01782 870328, **e-mail:** sales@teletronix.co.uk, www.tvdirect.co.uk, 9.15–5.30 MON–FRI, 9.15–5 SAT. **PERMANENT DISCOUNT OUTLET**

Ex-catalogue and A-grade television and video sets, the latter only used a few times while demonstrating, at good prices. All sets carry a 12-month guarantee. New sets cost from £89 for a 20-inch set from Alba or Bush with Fastext; ex-catalogue videos cost from £59 with remote control. Daewoo nicam videos for sale from £69. New grey imports (televisions and videos) also for sale, up to £500 off normal retail prices.

THE FACTORY SHOP

QUEEN STREET CAR PARK, QUEEN STREET, MARKET DRAYTON, STAFFORDSHIRE TF9 1EQ, ☎ 01630 655673, 9–5 MON–SAT, 10–4 SUN. **FACTORY SHOP**

See page 579 (CHESH)

TV WAREHOUSE

UNIT 49, IMEX BUSINESS PARK, ORMOND STREET, OFF DUKE STREET, FENTON, STAFFORDSHIRE ST4 3NP, ☎ 01782 593303, 10–5.30 MON–SAT. MAIL ORDER. **PERMANENT DISCOUNT OUTLET**

Sells both new, graded (manufacturers' returns) televisions, videos, hi-fis, washing machines, tumble dryers, fridges, freezers and built-in appliances at either reduced or very competitive prices. It is often well worth making a phone call to see how large a saving can be made on an item, especially on built-in appliances, because discounts can be up to 30% off the recommended retail price. Mail order is available. Major credit cards are accepted. Ample free parking is available.

SUFFOLK

THE CURTAIN AGENCY AND PERIOD HOUSE INTERIORS

73 HIGH STREET, NEEDHAM MARKET, IPSWICH, SUFFOLK IP6 8AN, ☎ 01449 722885, 10–5 MON–FRI, 10–1 SAT. **SECONDHAND SHOP**

An emporium of quality secondhand and new made-to-measure or ready-to-hang curtains. There is also a great range of permanently cut-price, quality fabrics available by the metre. These include designer names such as Gainsborough Silk Weaving Co for classic brocades; Linwood chenille, Archive printed linens, and Toile de Jouy from GP & J Baker; Parker Knoll fabrics for upholstery; and many others. Old and new Continental accessories, including tie-backs and trimmings, are also available. The shop also has a large stock of old French linen sheets, many hand woven and monogrammed, which are made into sumptuous curtains and Roman blinds as well as being used for luxurious bed linen and upholstery. Decorative, French garden and occasional furniture, period chandeliers, wall lights, old armchairs (for re-upholstering), traditional curtain poles and fittings, together with unusual gifts makes this an Aladdin's cave of inspiration for anyone wanting something special for their home.

THE FACTORY SHOP

BARTON BUSINESS CENTRE, BARTON ROAD, BURY ST EDMUNDS, SUFFOLK IP32 7BQ, ☎ 01284 701578, 9.30–5 MON–FRI, 10–6 SAT, 10–4 SUN.

LONDON ROAD, WRENTHAM, NR BECCLES, SUFFOLK NR34 7HJ, ☎ 01502 676100, 9–5.30 MON–SAT, 10.30–4.30 SUN. **FACTORY SHOP**

See page 579 (CHESH)

SURREY

RDO KITCHEN APPLIANCES (1)

BANCROFT ROAD, REIGATE, SURREY RH2 7RP, ☎ 01737 240403, FAX: 01737 224155, **e-mail:** info@rdo.co.uk, www.rdo.co.uk, 9–5.30 MON–FRI, 9–4.30 SAT. **PERMANENT DISCOUNT OUTLET**

Any kitchen appliance you can think of with up to 6,000 items to choose from. Specialises in British, French and German brand names – Maytag, Miele, Admiral, Belling, Dyson, Liebherr, Gaggenau, Zanussi, De Dietrich, Britannia, Neff, Bosch, AEG, Smeg, Falcon, Creda – at trade prices. There are continuous special offers – phone for details. Delivery nationwide. Range of more than 300 appliances constantly on show, including built-in and freestanding appliances. Visa and MasterCard phone orders accepted. Huge discounts available.

RDO KITCHEN APPLIANCES (2)

AMERICAN APPLICANCE CENTRE, REIGATE BUSINESS MEWS, ALBERT ROAD NORTH, REIGATE, SURREY RH2 9EG, ☎ 01737 229730, FAX: 01737 247763, **e-mail:** info@rdo.co.uk, www.rdo.co.uk, 9–5.30 MON–FRI, 9–4.30 SAT. **PERMANENT DISCOUNT OUTLET**

All makes of American applicances are sold here, including Whirlpool, Amana, Maytag, Admiral, Fisher & Paykell, LG, Samsung, Viking and many more. Vast new showroom displaying fridge-freezers with ice and water dispensers, large capacity washing machines and tumble driers, top loaders, range cookers and extractor chimney hoods. This is one of the largest American applicance showrooms in the south east. Delivery can be arranged nationwide. Special offers are constantly available: phone for details of the latest deals.

THE FACTORY SHOP LTD

THE ENGINE SHED, CONSORT WAY EAST, HORLEY, SURREY RH6 7AU, ☎ 01293 823883, 9–5.30 MON–SAT, 10–4 SUN. **FACTORY SHOP**

See page 579 (CHESH)

THE LIGHTING AGENCY & TRADING COMPANY

LION & LAMB YARD, FARNHAM, SURREY GU9 7LL, ☎ 01252 719192, FAX: 01252 719192, www.lightingagency.co.uk, 10–5.30 MON–SAT. **PERMANENT DISCOUNT OUTLET**

Lighting Agency and Trading Company in Farnham offers a wide variety of quality secondhand and antique chandeliers and wall lights, many of which have been rewired to a tested and certified UK standard. Others which have not been wired have the electrical or gas parts removed for easy rewiring. A wiring service can be provided. The Lighting Agency also offers a unique range of small chandeliers available in many colours and sizes. This Aladdin's Cave of shades, lamps and chandeliers is often the haunt of dealers and design decorators.

SUSSEX

T J HUGHES

14–26 THE BROADWAY, CRAWLEY, SUSSEX RH10 1DT, ☎ 01293 537373, FAX: 01293 611676, **e-mail:** info@tjhughes.co.uk, www.tjhughes.co.uk, 9–5.30 MON–FRI, 8 ON THUR, 9–6 SAT, 11–5 SUN.

177–178 TERMINUS ROAD, EASTBOURNE, SUSSEX BN21 3NX, ☎ 01323 732222, FAX: 01323 730110, **e-mail:** info@tjhughes.co.uk, www.tjhughes.co.uk, 9–5.30 MON–FRI, 9–6 SAT, 10.30–4.30 SUN. **PERMANENT DISCOUNT OUTLET**

See page 579 (CHESH)

THE FACTORY SHOP LTD

BRIGHTON MARINA, THE VILLAGE SQUARE, BRIGHTON, SUSSEX BN2 5WA, ☎ 01273 818590, 10–6 MON–FRI, 10–6 SAT, 10.30–4.30 SUN. **FACTORY SHOP IN A FACTORY SHOPPING VILLAGE**

See page 579 (CHESH)

WARWICKSHIRE AND WEST MIDLANDS

LITTLEWOODS CATALOGUE DISCOUNT STORE

14–16 NORTH STREET, RUGBY, WARWICKSHIRE CV21 2AF, ☎ 01788 565116, 9.30–5.45 MON–WED, 9–5.45 THUR–SAT. **PERMANENT DISCOUNT OUTLET**

See page 578 (CHESH)

STAGE 2

AUSTIN DRIVE, COURTHOUSE GREEN, COVENTRY, WARWICKSHIRE CV6 7NS, ☎ 024 76 681520, 10–8 MON–FRI, 10–5 SAT, 11–5 SUN. **PERMANENT DISCOUNT OUTLET**

See page 577 (CAMBS)

BORSHCH ELECTRIC

NEPTUNE HOUSE, UPPER TRINITY STREET, BORDESLEY, BIRMINGHAM, WEST MIDLANDS B9 4EG, ☎ 0121 773 6361, FAX: 0121 771 0453, 9–5.30 MON–SAT, 10–4 SUN AND BANK HOLIDAYS. **PERMANENT DISCOUNT OUTLET**

Sells gas and electric items including fridges, freezers, fridge/freezers, washing machines, microwaves, dishwashers, ovens, vacuum cleaners and a small selection of smaller electrical items for the kitchen such as toasters and kettles, which are manufacturers' new graded returns, from this 10,000 square foot showroom. These are not A grade and therefore cannot be sold in high street stores. All are guaranteed for parts and service. Examples of prices include fridges from £79; cookers from £119; microwaves from £69; washing machines from £150; fridge/freezers from £129; gas fires from £129; tumble dryers from £99; built-in ovens £109. Manufacturers on sale include Zanussi, Candy, Servis, Hotpoint, Bosch, Leisure, Canon, Creda, Baumatic and White Knight. A full delivery service is available.

CATALOGUE BARGAIN SHOP

ROCK BOTTOM CLEARANCE, 24–28 KING STREET, DUDLEY, WEST MIDLANDS DY2 8NY, ☎ 01384 458112, www.bargaincrazy.com, 9.30–5.30 MON–SAT, 10–4 SUN.

78 HIGH STREET, STOURBRIDGE, WEST MIDLANDS DY8 1DX, ☎ 01384 374544, www.bargaincrazy.com, 9–5.30 MON–SAT, 10–4 SUN.

17 BRADFORD STREET, WALSALL WEST MIDLANDS WS1 1PB, ☎ 01922 722286, www.bargaincrazy.com, 9–5.30 MON–SAT, 10.30–4.30 SUN. **PERMANENT DISCOUNT OUTLET**

See page 577 (CAMBS)

CATALOGUE DISCOUNT STORE

SWAN CENTRE, COVENTRY ROAD, YARDLEY, BIRMINGHAM, WEST MIDLANDS B26 1AJ, ☎ 0121 707 6585, 9–5.30 MON–SAT.

UNIT 67, THE MOOR CENTRE, BRIERLEY HILL, DUDLEY, WEST MIDLANDS DY5 3AH, ☎ 01384 262537, 9–5.30 MON–SAT. **PERMANENT DISCOUNT OUTLET**

See page 580 (CO DURH)

GORSE MILL LIGHTING FACTORY SUPERSTORE

35 SUTTON NEW ROAD, ERDINGTON, BIRMINGHAM, WEST MIDLANDS B23 6TD, ☎ 0121 373 3333, 9.30–5 MON–FRI, 7 ON THUR, 10–5 SAT, 11–5 SUN. **FACTORY SHOP**

See page 588 (LANCS)

INTERNATIONAL STOCK LTD

95–100 REA STREET, DIGBETH, BIRMINGHAM, WEST MIDLANDS B5 6HA, ☎ 0121 622 3232, **e-mail:** mail@international-stock.co.uk, www.international-stock.co.uk, 9–5 MON–SAT, 10–4 SUN, CLOSED 1 ON WED.

1–17 SILVER STREET, KING'S HEATH, BIRMINGHAM, WEST MIDLANDS B14 7QX, ☎ 0121 443 3232, FAX: 0121 444 1792, **e-mail:** mail@international-stock.co.uk, www.international-stock.co.uk, 9–6 MON–SAT, CLOSED 1 ON WED. **PERMANENT DISCOUNT OUTLET**

Bankrupt, fire and flood damaged articles from CDs and videos, household goods and clothes to DIY tools and television sets, carpets and cookers. The branch at King's Heath is a two-storey warehouse with ever-changing stock. The upper floor is devoted to electrical goods, some marked down to 30% of their normal retail cost. The Digbeth branch sells bigger items such as kitchens, flooring, tiles, dining room and lounge furniture, central heating radiators and a large clothing section for all the family, all of which is sold below wholesale price and in some cases below manufacturers' cost price. Top brand name kitchens, when in stock, are discounted by 75%.

LITTLEWOODS CATALOGUE DISCOUNT STORE

236 HAWTHORN ROAD, KINGSTANDING, BIRMINGHAM, WEST MIDLANDS B44 8PP, ☎ 0121 373 1276, 9.30–5.30 MON–FRI, 9–5 SAT.

299–303 COVENTRY ROAD, BIRMINGHAM, WEST MIDLANDS B10 0RA, ☎ 0121 772 1637, 9.30–5 MON–SAT, 10–5 WED, 11–4 SUN. **PERMANENT DISCOUNT OUTLET**

See page 578 (CHESH)

SALTON EUROPE

BRIDGNORTH ROAD, WOMBOURNE, WOLVERHAMPTON, WEST MIDLANDS WV5 8AQ, ☎ 01902 356510, 9–4.30 TUE–FRI, 9–12.30 SAT. **FACTORY SHOP**

See page 589 (LANCS)

SCOOPS CATALOGUE DISCOUNT STORE

63 HIGH STREET, BROWNHILLS, WEST MIDLANDS WS8 6HH, ☎ 01543 372933, 9–5.30 MON–SAT.

UNIT 6–7 MOOR CENTRE, BRIERLEY HILL, DUDLEY, WEST MIDLANDS DY5 3AH, ☎ 01384 262537, 9–5.30 MON–SAT.

SWAN MARKET CENTRE, YARDLEY, BIRMINGHAM, WEST MIDLANDS, ☎ 0121 707 6585, 9–5.30 MON–SAT. **PERMANENT DISCOUNT OUTLET**

See page 580 (CO DURH)

T J HUGHES

27 BELL STREET, MANDER CENTRE, WOLVERHAMPTON, WEST MIDLANDS WV1 3PT, ☎ 01902 428011, FAX: 01902 420248, **e-mail:** info@tjhughes.co.uk, www.tjhughes.co.uk, 9–5.30 MON– FRI, 8.30–5.30 SAT, 10.30–4.30 SUN. **PERMANENT DISCOUNT OUTLET**

See page 579 (CHESH)

WILTSHIRE

IN EXCESS

131 NETHERHAMPTON ROAD, SALISBURY, WILTSHIRE SP2 8NA, ☎ 01722 414444, 9–5.30 MON–SAT, 10–4 SUN. **PERMANENT DISCOUNT OUTLET**

See page 582 (CO DURH)

MCARTHURGLEN DESIGNER OUTLET GREAT WESTERN

KEMBLE DRIVE, SWINDON, JUNCTION 16 OF M4, WILTSHIRE SN2 2DY, ☎ 0800 316 4352 FREE INFORMATION LINE OR 01793 507600, www.mcarthurglen.com, 10–6 MON–FRI, 8 ON THUR, 9–6 SAT, 11–5 SUN. **FACTORY SHOPPING VILLAGE**

The McArthurGlen Designer Outlet Great Western offers over 100 stores selling top names and designer brands at up to 50% off typical retail prices. Housed in the restored Great Western Railway buildings, everything is conveniently located under one roof. A large open plan area dedicated to homewares has everything for the house and home. Facilities include a food court, children's play area, licensed creche and ample parking. Stores include: U Wear/I Wear, Warner UK Ltd, Antler, Ecco Shoes, Walker & Hall, Liz Claiborne, Viyella, Austin Reed, Suits You, Alexon, Jaeger, Windsmoor, Aquascutum, Olsen, Jacques Vert, Overland/Caterpillar, Episode, Long Tall Sally, Pilot, Triumph, Cotton Traders, Villeroy & Boch, Baron Jon, Clarks, HKA, Burberry, Remington, Regatta, Just Sweets, Easy Jeans, Ben Sherman, JoKids, Donnay, Le Creuset, Puma, Tog 24, XS, Gap, Big L, Soled Out, Ted Baker, Nike, Timberland, Quiksilver, Whittard, Marks and Spencer, Polo Jeans Company, Gant, Calp, The Design House, Dartington Crystal, Duvet and Pillow Shop, Henri Lloyd, Mexx, Ravel, The Luxury Beauty Store, Thomas Pink, Thorntons, Tie Rack, Julian Graves, Hanro, Jane Shilton, Birthday, Toy Zone, Bookends, Sofa Works, Designer Room, Petroleum, Next, Daks Simpson, Suit Company, Price's Candles, Claire's Accessories, Samsonite, Van Heusen, Cloverleaf, Poole Pottery, Spiegelau, Edinburgh Crystal, Woods of Windsor, Staffordshire Pottery, Waterford Wedgewood, Stuart Crystal, Gleneagles, The Garden Outlet, Ponden Mill, Jane Heath, Sheridan Australia, Tefal, Professional Cookware, and Oneida.

REMINGTON

MCARTHURGLEN DESIGNER OUTLET GREAT WESTERN, KEMBLE DRIVE, SWINDON, JUNCTION 16 OF M4, WILTSHIRE SN2 7AA, ☎ 01793 430515, 10–6 MON–FRI, 8 ON THUR, 9–6 SAT, 11–5 SUN. **FACTORY SHOP IN A FACTORY SHOPPING VILLAGE**

See page 579 (CHESH)

THE FACTORY SHOP LTD

23–25 NEW PLACE, CORSHAM, WILTSHIRE SN13 0HL, ☎ 01249 712160, 9–5.30 MON–SAT, 10–4 SUN.

36–37 ROUNDSTONE STREET, TROWBRIDGE, WILTSHIRE BA14 8DE, ☎ 01225 751399, 9–5 MON–SAT.

24 MARKET PLACE, WARMINSTER, WILTSHIRE BA12 9AN, ☎ 01985 217532, 9–5 MON–SAT. **FACTORY SHOP**

See page 579 (CHESH)

WORCESTERSHIRE

CATALOGUE BARGAIN SHOP

233 WORCESTER ROAD, MALVERN LINK, MALVERN, WORCESTERSHIRE WR14 1SY, ☎ 01684 893062, www.bargaincrazy.com, 9–5.30 MON–SAT, 10.30–4.30 SUN. **PERMANENT DISCOUNT OUTLET**

See page 577 (CAMBS)

T J HUGHES

1 HIGH STREET, KIDDERMINSTER, WORCESTERSHIRE DY10 2DS, ☎ 01562 745687, FAX: 01562 744025, **e-mail:** info@tjhughes.co.uk, www.tjhughes.co.uk, 9–5.30 MON– SAT, 10–4 SUN. **PERMANENT DISCOUNT OUTLET**

See page 579 (CHESH)

THE FACTORY SHOP LTD

NEW ROAD, PERSHORE, WORCESTERSHIRE WR10 1BY, ☎ 01386 556467, 9–5 MON–FRI, 9–5.30 SAT, 10.30–4.30 SUN. **FACTORY SHOP**

See page 579 (CHESH)

YORKSHIRE

BRANDMART

5 NORTH STREET, RIPON, NORTH YORKSHIRE HG4 1JY, ☎ 01765 601156, 9–5 MON–SAT. **FACTORY SHOP**

See page 584 (GLOS)

CATALOGUE BARGAIN SHOP

KAYS SHOP, HOLME LANE, OFF TONG STREET, BRADFORD, WEST YORKSHIRE BD4 6NA, ☎ 01274 681711, www.bargaincrazy.com, 9.30–5.30 MON–SAT, 7 ON THUR, 10.30–4.30 SUN.

FREEPORT DESIGNER OUTLET VILLAGE, CARRWOOD ROAD, GLASSHOUGHTON, CASTLEFORD, WEST YORKSHIRE WF10 4SB, ☎ 01977 519112, www.bargaincrazy.com, 10–8 MON–FRI, 10–6 SAT, 11–5 SUN.

UNITS 2–3, LEGER CENTRE, THORNE ROAD, DONCASTER, SOUTH YORKSHIRE DN2 4GB, ☎ 01302 341506, www.bargaincrazy.com, 9–8 MON–FRI, 10–6 SAT, 11–5 SUN.

57–59 MARKET PLACE, HECKMONDWIKE, WEST YORKSHIRE WF16 0EZ, ☎ 01924 402674, www.bargaincrazy.com, 9–5.30 MON–SAT, 10–4 SUN.

42 JOHN WILLIAM STREET, HUDDERSFIELD, WEST YORKSHIRE HD1 1ER, ☎ 01484 535112, www.bargaincrazy.com, 9–5.30 MON–SAT, 10.30–4.30 SUN.

28 NEW BRIGGATE, BRIGGATE, LEEDS, WEST YORKSHIRE LS1 6NU, ☎ 0113 243 6425, www.bargaincrazy.com, 9–5.30 MON–SAT, 11–5 SUN.

MARSHALL STREET, LEEDS, WEST YORKSHIRE LS1 1UL, ☎ 0113 254 2350, www.bargaincrazy.com, 10–5 MON–FRI, 7 ON THUR, 9–5.30 SAT, 10.30–4.30 SUN.

51 ACKLAM ROAD, MIDDLESBROUGH, NORTH YORKSHIRE TS5 5HA, ☎ 01642 825925, www.bargaincrazy.com, 9–5.30 MON–SAT, 10.30–4.30 SUN. **PERMANENT DISCOUNT OUTLET**

See page 577 (CAMBS)

CATALOGUE DISCOUNT STORES

UNIT 6, HILLSBOROUGH BARRACKS SHOPPING MALL, SHEFFIELD, SOUTH YORKSHIRE S6 2GY, ☎ 0114 234 5726, FAX: 0114 234 5006, 9–5.30 MON–SAT, 11–5 SUN. **PERMANENT DISCOUNT OUTLET**

See page 580 (CO DURH)

FREEPORT CASTLEFORD DESIGNER OUTLET VILLAGE

CARRWOOD ROAD, GLASSHOUGHTON, CASTLEFORD, JUNCTION 32 OF M52, WEST YORKSHIRE WF10 4SB, ☎ 01977 520153, www.freeportcastleford.com, 10–8 MON–FRI, 10–6 SAT, 11–5 SUN. **FACTORY SHOPPING VILLAGE**

Designer outlet village with over 75 shops, indoor and outdoor children's play areas and a wide range of restaurants with easy access from the M52 and 3,500 free car parking spaces. Shops include Amazing Jeans, Baron Jon, BhS For Less, Charles Clinkard, Clarks, Cromwells, Churchill, Ciro Citterio, Craghoppers, CBS, Claire's Accessories, Cotton Traders, Damart, Edinburgh Crystal, Donnay, Double Two, Event Jewellery, Easy Jeans, Edinburgh Woollen Mill, Elle, Fila, Giorgio, Gossard, XS Music, Jane Shilton, John Partridge, Kappa, Kitchen and Table, Kurt Muller, Leading Labels, Lee Cooper, Littlewoods, London Leathers, Mexx, Mobile Phone Store, Nike, Nickleby's, Next to Nothing, Outrage, Petroleum, Picture Port, Pilot, Ponden Mill, Proibito, Rio Jewellery, Roman Originals, Regatta, Room, Ice Jeans, Sergio Tacchini, Sportsmill, Spotlight, Startrite Shoes, Remainders Book Depot, Designer Room, Garden Outlet, Shoe Collection, Toy Factory, Time, X Catalogue Store, Thorntons, Trespass, Waterford Wedgwood, Windsmoor.

LIGHT FANTASTIC

PARKLAND BUSINESS CENTRE, ALBION ROAD, GREENGATE, BRADFORD, WEST YORKSHIRE BD10 9TQ, ☎ 01274 623450, 9.30–5 MON–SAT, 10.30–4 SUN. **FACTORY SHOP**

Lighting factory shop claiming to be the biggest selection of discounted quality lighting in Yorkshire from light bulbs to chandeliers. All lampshades are made in their own factory, so are all made in Britain. They also offer a lampshade re-covering service to your own specifications: you supply the frame and your own fabric. For those looking for outdoor and garden lighting, they hold lots of manufacturers' catalogues from which you can order. Delivery takes seven to 10 days and prices are still reduced by 15% to 20%. They also stock candles, oil burners, mirrors, giftware and pictures. There is a free car park and a children's play area on site.

LITTLEWOODS CATALOGUE DISCOUNT STORE

FREEPORT CASTLEFORD DESIGNER OUTLET VILLAGE, CARRWOOD ROAD, GLASSHOUGHTON, CASTLEFORD, JUNCTION 32 OF M52, WEST YORKSHIRE WF10 4SB, ☎ 01977 517899, 10–8 MON–FRI, 10–6 SAT, 11–5 SUN.

602–608 ATTERCLIFFE ROAD, SHEFFIELD, SOUTH YORKSHIRE S9 3QS, ☎ 0114 244 1611, 9.30–5 MON–WED, 9–5.30 THUR–SAT. **PERMANENT DISCOUNT OUTLET**

See page 578 (CHESH)

MCARTHURGLEN DESIGNER OUTLET

ST NICHOLAS AVENUE, FULFORD, JUNCTION OF A19 AND A64, YORK, NORTH YORKSHIRE YO19 4TA, ☎ 01904 682720, www.mcarthurglen.com/york, 10–6 MON–SAT, 8 ON THUR, 11–5 SUN. **FACTORY SHOPPING VILLAGE**

The McArthurGlen Designer Outlet York is one of Europe's largest covered designer outlets with over 120 stores offering top brands and designer labels with discounts of up to 50% off typical retail prices. Find everything from men's, women's and children's clothing to accessories, shoes, sportswear, luggage, homewares, toys, books, and gifts. Facilities include a food court, a children's play area and free parking. Stores include: Armani, Autonomy, Ben Sherman, Burberry, Calvin Klein Jeans, Cerruti 1881, Chilli Pepper, Cotton Traders, Daks Simpson, Episode, Escada Sport, Gap Outlet, Guess, Hugo Boss, Jacques Vert, Jaeger/Viyella, Jesire/Esensual, Kabuki, Klass, Levi's, Margaret Howell, Marks & Spencer Outlet, Mergler, Mountain Warehouse, Nitya, Olsen, Pilot, Polo Ralph Lauren, Pringle, Proibito, Proudfoot Leather, Roman Originals, Ronit Zilkha, Ted Baker, The Designer Room, Thomas Pink, Tog 24, Tommy Hilfiger, Windsmoor, Alfred Dunhill, Baronjon, Ben Sherman, Haggar, HKA, Marlboro Classics, Paul Smith, Petroleum, Pour Homme, Rockport, Suit Company, Suits You, Timberland, Adidas, Diadora, Donnay, Reebok, Toyworld, Birthdays, Bodum, The Body Shop Depot, Bookends, Franchetti Bond, Le Creuset, Oneida, Paper Mill, Price's Candles, Remington, Scent To You, Whittard Kitchen, Woods of Windsor, XS Music & Video, Bed & Bath Works, China China, Coloroll, Descamps, Garden Outlet, Jane Heath, La Casa del Christallo, Lights 4 Less, Pictureport, Room, Slipperbox, Spiegelau, Professional Cookware, Daniel Footwear, Famous Footwear, Pavers, Rockport, Shoe Studio, Soled Out, Julian Graves, Thorntons, Antler, Kangol, Liberty, Travel Accessory, Chapelle Jewellery, Claire's Accessories, Designer Shades, Monet, Tie Rack, and The Watch Store.

MR VALUE

KILLINGHALL ROAD, BRADFORD, WEST YORKSHIRE BD3 8DN, ☎ 01274 669674, 9–7 MON–FRI, 9–5.30 SAT, 10–4 SUN. **PERMANENT DISCOUNT OUTLET**

A discount store offering a wide selection of goods which are catalogue returns, factory rejects, seconds and ends of lines – everything from clothes with the labels cut out to tapes, kettles, televisions, microwaves, irons, toasters, bedlinen, towels, sweets, artificial flowers, batteries, toiletries, crockery, glass, stationery, pots and pans, toys and bins. Kitchen equipment brand names include Russell Hobbs and Morphy Richards. There is also a department for mobility, selling wheelchairs, scooters etc.

NO FRILLS DIY STORE

115–125 LEADMILL ROAD, SHEFFIELD, SOUTH YORSHIRE S2 4AZ, ☎ 0114 276 1454, FAX: 0114 272 5083, 9–8 MON–SAT, 10–4 SUN.

NAVIGATION YARD, WAKEFIELD, WEST YORKSHIRE, ☎ 01924 369660, FAX: 01924 364421 9–8 MON–SAT, 10–4 SUN. **PERMANENT DISCOUNT OUTLET**

See page 577 (BEDS)

QLM LTD

IDLE ROAD, IDLE, BRADFORD, WEST YORKSHIRE BD2 2AL, ☎ 01274 642222, 9.30–6 MON–SAT, 5.30 ON WED, 11–5 SUN. **PERMANENT DISCOUNT OUTLET**

Toys, household goods, clothes, food, electrical equipment, garden implements, kitchenware and furniture, all sold at discounted prices. For example, reject garden forks £6.99, spades £4.99, pruning tools £2.99 to £19.99.

REMINGTON

THE YORKSHIRE OUTLET, WHITE ROSE WAY, DONCASTER, SOUTH YORKSHIRE DN4 5JH, ☎ 01302 366434, 10–6 MON–SAT, 11–5 SUN.

MCARTHURGLEN DESIGNER OUTLET YORK, ST NICHOLAS AVENUE, FULFORD, JUNCTION OF A19 AND A64, YORK, NORTH YORKSHIRE YO19 4TA, ☎ 01904 677899, 10–6 MON–SAT, 8 ON THUR, 11–5 SUN. **FACTORY SHOP IN A FACTORY SHOPPING VILLAGE**

See page 579 (CHESH)

SCOOPS CATALOGUE DISCOUNT STORES

ENTERPRISE 5, 5 LANE ENDS, IDLE, BRADFORD, WEST YORKSHIRE BD10 8EG, ☎ 01274 622300, 9–8 MON–FRI, 9–6 SAT, 10–4 SUN.

SHIRETHORNE CENTRE, 34–43 PROSPECT STREET, HULL, EAST YORKSHIRE, HU2 8PX, ☎ 01482 224354, FAX: 01482 221729, 9–5.30 MON–SAT.

25 TOWN STREET, ARMLEY, LEEDS, WEST YORKSHIRE LS12 1UX, ☎ 0113 263 1825, FAX: 0113 231 9885, 9–5.30 MON–SAT.

41 BARNSLEY ROAD, SOUTH ELMSHALL, PONTEFRACT, WEST YORKSHIRE WF9 2RN, ☎ 01977 642256, FAX: 01977 650 629, 9–5.30 MON–SAT. **PERMANENT DISCOUNT OUTLET**

See page 580 (CO DURH)

SHADES & SHADOWS

186 TONG ROAD, ARMLEY, LEEDS, WEST YORKSHIRE LS12 1QW, ☎ 0113 279 4840, 8.30–5 MON–SAT, 6 ON THUR, 10–3 SUN. **FACTORY SHOP**

Factory seconds lighting shop with more than 3,000 lines in stock and new merchandise arriving daily. Prices from 50p up to £600, most of which are half the normal price. Houses the largest range of Tiffany lighting in the North, many at half price.

T J HUGHES

51-57 ST SEPULCHRE GATE, DONCASTER, SOUTH YORKSHIRE DN1 1UB, ☎ 01302 363119, FAX: 01302 363126, **e-mail:** info@tjhughes.co.uk, www.tjhughes.co.uk, 9–5.30 MON–SAT, 10–4 SUN.

121 FERENSWAY, HULL, EAST YORKSHIRE, HU1 3UW, ☎ 01482 326174, FAX: 01482 329767, **e-mail:** info@tjhughes.co.uk, www.tjhughes.co.uk, 9–5.30 MON– SAT, 10.30–4.30 SUN.

18-19 CAPTAIN COOK SQUARE, MIDDLESBROUGH, NORTH YORKSHIRE TS1 5UB, ☎ 01642 220902, FAX: 01642 220903, **e-mail:** info@tjhughes.co.uk, www.tjhughes.co.uk, 9–5.30 MON– SAT, 11–5 SUN.

50 HIGH STREET, SHEFFIELD, SOUTH YORKSHIRE S1 1QH, ☎ 0114 272 8121, FAX: 0114 272 3146, **e-mail:** info@tjhughes.co.uk, www.tjhughes.co.uk, 9–5.30 MON– SAT, 11–5 SUN. **PERMANENT DISCOUNT OUTLET**

See page 579 (CHESH)

THE FACTORY SHOP

PARK ROSE POTTERY, CARNABY COVERT LANE, CARNABY, BRIDLINGTON, EAST YORKSHIRE YO15 3QF, ☎ 01262 603518, 10–5 MON–SAT, 10.30–4.30 SUN.

WHEATLEY LANE, LEEDS ROAD, ILKLEY, WEST YORKSHIRELS29 8BS, ☎ 01943 604514, 9–5.30 MON–SAT, 10.30–4.30 SUN.

LIGHTWATER VALLEY SHOPPING VILLAGE, NORTH STAINLEY, RIPON, NORTH YORKSHIRE HG4 3HT, ☎ 01765 635438, 10–6 MON–SAT, 11–5 SUN. **FACTORY SHOP**

See page 579 (CHESH)

THE FACTORY VALUE SHOP

LAWKHOLME LANE, KEIGHLEY, WEST YORKSHIRE BD21 3JQ, ☎ 01535 611703, 9.30–5 MON–SAT, 10.30–4.30 SUN. **FACTORY SHOP**

Wide range on sale includes men's, women's and children's clothing and footwear; household textiles; toiletries; hardware; luggage; lighting, electrical goods and bedding, most of which are chainstore and high street brands at discounts of approximately 30% to 50%. There are kitchen and furniture displays. The Cape Country Furniture range is on sale with free-standing kitchens, as well as living, bedroom and dining furniture. There are weekly deliveries and brands include famous names such as Adidas, Nike, Joe Bloggs and Brabantia, among others. Lines are continually changing. Few factory shops offer such a variety under one roof. To round off your visit, there are excellent tea rooms offering homemade foods and home baking.

THE LIGHTING FACTORY SHOP

GELDERD ROAD, LEEDS, WEST YORKSHIRE LS12 6NB, ☎ 0113 276 7491, 9–5 MON–SAT, 10–4 SUN. **FACTORY SHOP**

First quality, seconds and end-of-line lighting for the house and garden at competitive prices. Large range includes wall lights, spots, fluorescents, table lamps, student and children's lamps, glass shades, party lights, security and garden lighting. Also light bulbs and fluorescent tubes.

THE MILL DISCOUNT DEPARTMENT STORE

BRADFORD ROAD, BATLEY, WEST YORKSHIRE WF17 5LZ, ☎ 01924 423172, FAX: 01924 446096, www.themillbatley.com, 9.30–5.30 MON–SAT, 10–4 SUN. **PERMANENT DISCOUNT OUTLET**

The Mill Discount Department Store is the largest Mill retail outlet in the UK, attracting more than one million visitors every year. Situated in a restored Victorian Mill in the heart of West Yorkshire, The Mill offers massive savings in a department-sotre format. This all-weather centre consists of four floors together with an external parade selling heavily discounted branded men's, women's and children's fashions, sportswear, homewares, accessories, music, vidoes, sunglasses, books, toys, perfumes, luggage, gifts, shoes, fabrics and lighting. Readmans, whose name is synonymous with unbeatable value, has opened there recently. This is the company's second major stores, offering good quality women's, men's and children's wear, lingerie, shoes, homewares and linens at remarkably low prices. Among over 300 brand names sold at The Mill are Puma, Pilot, HKA, Leeds United, Liz Claiborne, Elle, Jumper, Kasper, Amazing Jeans, Spicy, Urban Turban, Chilli Pepper, Tigi Wear, Ponden Mill, Woods of Windsor, Gleneagles Crystal, Dartington, Arthur Price, Skopos home furnishings, Jane Shilton, Book Depot, Toy Factory, Eye Zone, Famous Footwear, Hush Puppies, Lee Cooper, MX Active, Berghaus, Craghopper, Julian Graves, Fox's Biscuits, John Bull and Lion Confectionery. The complex can be reached by car, coach and train. Junction 40 of the M1 and junctions 27 and 28 of the M62 are within five and six miles of the site respectively. Batley Station on the Trans-Pennine railway is just five minutes walk from The Mill, providing easy access to Leeds and Manchester. There are more than 500 car parking spaces and coach parking is available. Amenities include children's creche, self-service licensed restaurant serving hot and cold food and drinks, Yorkshire Board Information Centre and disabled access.

THE YORKSHIRE OUTLET

WHITE ROSE WAY, JUNCTION 3 OF M18, DONCASTER LAKESIDE, SOUTH YORKSHIRE DN4 5JH, ☎ 01302 366444, **e-mail:** cprimrose@realm-ocm.com, www.theyorkshireoutletcentre.co.uk, 10–6 MON–SAT, 11–5 SUN. **FACTORY SHOPPING VILLAGE**

The Yorkshire Outlet, Doncaster, has a great range of stores offering up to 50% off recommended retail prices, with new products and bargains, some of which are electrical, arriving daily. The centre has a range of restaurants, a children's play area, wheelchair hire, and free parking.

YOU & YOURS

UNIT 9, CROWN POINT RETAIL PARK, HUNSLET ROAD, LEEDS, WEST YORKSHIRE LS10 1ET, ☎ 0113 234 1924, 10–5 MON, 10–7 TUE–FRI, 9.30–6 SAT, 11–5 SUN.

98–100 NEW STREET, HUDDERSFIELD, WEST YORKSHIRE HD1 2UD, ☎ 01484 543301, 9–5.30 MON–SAT.

WESTFIELD, INGLEBY ROAD (OPPOSITE GRATTAN), BRADFORD, WEST YORKSHIRE BD99 2XE, ☎ 01274 624611, 10–5.30 MON, 10–8 TUE–FRI, 9–5.30 SAT, 11–5 SUN. **PERMANENT DISCOUNT OUTLET**

See page 579 (CHESH)

SOUTH WALES

CATALOGUE BARGAIN SHOP

FFALDS ROAD SHOPPING CENTRE, PYLE CROSS, PYLE, BRIDGEND, SOUTH WALES CF33 6BH, ☎ 01656 746426, www.bargaincrazy.com, 9–8 MON–FRI, 9–6 SAT, 10.30–4.30 SUN.

PIONEER SUPERSTORE, BRYN-SERTH ROAD, RHD-Y-BLEW, EBBW VALE, GWENT, SOUTH WALES NP3 5YD, ☎ 01495 309297, www.bargaincrazy.com, 9–8 MON–THUR, 9–9 FRI, 9–6 SAT, 10–4 SUN.

61 HIGH STREET, MERTHYR TYDFIL, MID GLAMORGAN, SOUTH WALES CF47 8DE, ☎ 01685 385653, www.bargaincrazy.com, 9–5.30 MON–SAT.

MIDWAY RETAIL PARK, PONTYPRIDD, SOUTH WALES CF37 5NX, ☎ 01443 843718, www.bargaincrazy.com, 9–8 MON–FRI, 9–6 SAT, 11–5 SUN.

UNIT 1A, HAVENS HEAD RETAIL CENTRE, MILFORD HAVEN, PEMBROKESHIRE, SOUTH WALES SA73 3AU, ☎ 01646 697407, www.bargaincrazy.com, 9–8 MON–FRI, 9–6 SAT, 10.30–4.30 SUN.

31 STATION ROAD, PORT TALBOT, WEST GLAMORGAN, SOUTH WALES SA13 1NN, ☎ 01639 899419, www.bargaincrazy.com, 9–5.30 MON–SAT.

229–230 HIGH STREET, SWANSEA, WEST GLAMORGAN, SOUTH WALES SA1 1NY, ☎ 01792 456748, www.bargaincrazy.com, 9–5.30 MON–SAT, 10–4 SUN. **PERMANENT DISCOUNT OUTLET**

See page 577 (CAMBS)

CRAZY MAC'S

PONTARDULAIS ROAD, FFORESTFACH, SWANSEA, SOUTH WALES SA5 4BA, ☎ 01792 585828, FAX: 01792 585566, **e-mail:** lss@salvage1.co.uk, www.salvage1.co.uk, 9.30–6 MON–THUR, 9.30–8 FRI, 9–6 SAT, 11–5 SUN. **PERMANENT DISCOUNT OUTLET**

An Aladdin's cave of salvaged stock for the avid bargain hunter, most of which has been the subject of insurance claims for fire or flood, salvage, bankruptcy or is simply clearance stock. Stock changes every two or three days and regular visitors have found anything from half price Kenwood Chefs, televisions and toys to furniture, kitchen items, linens and especially fantastic bargains in designer clothing. Yves Saint Laurent, Armani, Ungaro, Hugo Boss and Valentino, as well as all major high street names, are just some of the names to be found (though the labels are often cut out). Discounts range from 50% to 80%. Phone first to check stock.

LITTLEWOODS CATALOGUE DISCOUNT STORE

MCARTHURGLEN DESIGNER OUTLET WALES, THE DERWEN, BRIDGEND, JUNCTION 36 OF M4, SOUTH WALES CF32 9SU, ☎ 01656 665700, 10–8 MON–FRI, 10–6 SAT, 11–5 SUN. **FACTORY SHOP IN A FACTORY SHOPPING VILLAGE**

See page 578 (CHESH)

MCARTHURGLEN DESIGNER OUTLET

THE DERWEN, BRIDGEND, JUNCTION 36 OF M4, SOUTH WALES CF32 9SU, ☎ 01656 665700, www.mcarthurglen.com/bridgend, 10–8 MON–FRI, 10–6 SAT, 11–5 SUN. **FACTORY SHOPPING VILLAGE**

The McArthurGlen Designer Outlet in Bridgend is Wales' premier designer outlet. Set out in a friendly village street style the outlet has over 80 stores with everything from men's, women's and children's clothing to accessories, shoes, sportswear, luggage, homewares, toys, books, and gifts. All stock is excess stock sold by the retailers themselves at 30% to 50% off typical retail prices. The outlet also has over 1,800 free parking spaces, a food court, two children's play areas and a nine-screen Odeon cinema. Stores include: Reebok, Calvin Klein, Tie Rack, Ciro Pearls, Monet, Picture Port, Ciro Citterio, Bookends, Bed & Bath, Clover House, Overland, Pepe, Famous Footwear, Nickelbys, The Suit Company, Birthdays, Toyzone, Vans, Red/Green, Whittards, Travel Accessories, Ecco, Jacques Vert, Warners, Next, Windsmoor, Pilot, Petroleum, Roman Originals, Antler, Julian Graves, The Watch Shop, Knickerbox, Wedgewood, The Garden Outlet, Claire's Accessories, Clarks, Donnay, JoKids, Ben Sherman, Smiths Signature, Spiegelau, Royal Worcester/Edinburgh Crystal, Littlewoods, Helly Hansen, Woodies, Lee Cooper, Van Heusen/Viyella/Jaeger, Ted Baker, Cotton Traders, Royal Doulton, Walker and Hall, Professional Cookware Co, Thorntons, Price's Candles, Mountain Warehouse, John Partridge, Remington, U Wear/I Wear, Nike, The Body Shop, Mexx, Suits You, Designer Rooms, Winning Line, Tog 24, Elle, Chilli Pepper/Watsons, HKA, XS, Soled Out, Timberland, Carphone Warehouse, Levi's, and The Craft Outlet.

REMINGTON

MCARTHURGLEN DESIGNER OUTLET WALES, THE DERWEN, BRIDGEND, JUNCTION 36 OF M4, SOUTH WALES CF32 9ST, ☎ 01656 766722, 10–8 MON–FRI, 10–6 SAT, 11–5 SUN. **FACTORY SHOP IN A FACTORY SHOPPING VILLAGE**

See page 579 (CHESH)

THE FACTORY SHOP

SNOWDROP LANE, HAVERFORDWEST, SOUTH WALES SA61 1ET, ☎ 01437 766000, 9–5.30 MON–SAT, 10.30–4.30 SUN. **FACTORY SHOP**

See page 579 (CHESH)

NORTH WALES

CATALOGUE BARGAIN SHOP

UNITS F1–F2, FLINTSHIRE RETAIL CENTRE, FLINT, NORTH WALES CH6 5RR, ☎ 01352 732460, www.bargaincrazy.com, 9–8 MON–FRI, 9–6 SAT, 10.30–4.30 SUN.

6–8 MADOC STREET, LLANDUDNO, GWYNEDD, NORTH WALES LL30 2TP, ☎ 01492 877561, www.bargaincrazy.com, 9–5 MON–SAT, 10.30–4.30 SUN.

OLD KERRY ROAD, NEWTOWN, POWYS, NORTH WALES SY16 1BJ, ☎ 01686 628283, www.bargaincrazy.com, 9–5.30 MON–SAT, 10–4 SUN. **PERMANENT DISCOUNT OUTLET**

See page 577 (CAMBS)

T J HUGHES

UNIT B, HENBLAS SQUARE, CHESTER STREET, WREXHAM, CLWYD, NORTH WALES LL13 8BA, ☎ 01978 359555, FAX: 01978 359500, **e-mail:** info@tjhughes.co.uk, www.tjhughes.co.uk, 9–5.30 MON– SAT, 11–5 SUN. **PERMANENT DISCOUNT OUTLET**

See page 579 (CHESH)

THE FACTORY SHOP LTD

BRUNSWICK ROAD, BUCKLEY, CLYWD, NORTH WALES CH7 2EF, ☎ 01555 759017, FAX: 01555 759018, 9.30–5.30 MON–SAT, 10.30–4.30 SUN. **FACTORY SHOP**

See page 579 (CHESH)

SCOTLAND

CATALOGUE BARGAIN SHOP

315–317 HIGH STREET, COWDENBEATH, FIFE, SCOTLAND KY4 9QJ, ☎ 01383 611054, www.bargaincrazy.com, 9–5.30 MON–SAT, 11–4 SUN.

12–16 CADZOW STREET, HAMILTON, LANARKSHIRE, SCOTLAND ML3 6DG, ☎ 01698 421112, www.bargaincrazy.com, 9–5.30 MON–SAT, 12–4 SUN.

THE FORGE SHOPPING CENTRE, PARKHEAD, GLASGOW, SCOTLAND G31 4EB, ☎ 0141 556 5352, www.bargaincrazy.com, 9–6 MON–SAT, 11–5 SUN. **PERMANENT DISCOUNT OUTLET**

See page 577 (CAMBS)

FREEPORT SCOTLAND OUTLET VILLAGE

FIVE SISTERS, WESTWOOD, WEST CALDER, NEAR JUNCTION 4 OF THE M8, WEST LOTHIAN, SCOTLAND EH55 8QB, ☎ 01501 763488, www.freeportscotland.com, 10–6 SEVEN DAYS A WEEK. **FACTORY SHOPPING VILLAGE**

Designer outlet village with more than 25 shops offering up to 50% off high street prices, as well as a café and free parking. Outlets for women include The Designer Room, Mexx, London Leathers, Versace, Klass, Select, Iceberg and Jean Scene. Menswear is available from Ciro Citterio, Versace, Double Two, Madhouse, Leading Labels, Iceberg, Mexx, Nickleby's and Proibito. Sweet-toothed visitors can savour the chocolates at Thorntons. Other shops include Tog 24, Bags Etc, Charles Clinkard, Outdoor Adventure, Book Depot, Churchill China and Ponden Mill.

T J HUGHES

127–135 TRONGATE, GLASGOW, SCOTLAND G1 5HG, ☎ 0141 548 8400, FAX: 0141 552 6297, **e-mail:** info@tjhughes.co.uk, www.tjhughes.co.uk, 9–5.30 MON– FRI, 8 ON THUR, 9–6 SAT, 11–5 SUN. **PERMANENT DISCOUNT OUTLET**

See page 579 (CHESH)

THE FACTORY SHOP LTD

56 CHAPEL STREET, CARLUKE, SOUTH LANARKSHIRE, SCOTLAND ML8 4BA, ☎ 01555 759017, FAX: 01555 759018, 9–5 MON–FRI, 9–5.30 SAT, 10–5 SUN.

BURNSIDE MILL, CUPAR, FIFE, SCOTLAND KY15 4DQ, ☎ 01334 650661, FAX: 01334 656772, 9.30–5.30 MON–SAT, 10–5 SUN.

DRAKEMYRE, DALRY, AYRSHIRE, SCOTLAND KA24 5JD, ☎ 01294 832791, 10–5 MON–SAT, 11–5 SUN.

54–60 HIGH STREET, ANNAN, DUMFRIES, SCOTLAND DG12 6AJ, ☎ 01461 207687, 9–5 MON–SAT, 10.30–4.30 SUN. **FACTORY SHOP**

See page 579 (CHESH)

Sportswear & Equipment

BEDFORDSHIRE

GOSSARD FACTORY SHOP

GROVEBURY ROAD, LEIGHTON BUZZARD, BEDFORDSHIRE LU7 4SN, ☎ 01525 859749, FAX: 01525 850038, 9.30–5.30 MON–SAT. **FACTORY SHOP**

Factory shop sells seconds and discontinued ranges of Gossard and Berlei underwear including bras, briefs, suspender belts and bodies at discounted prices (no nightwear or long-line slips). Most of the stock is last years trade catalogue styles at discounts of between 25% and 75%. large car park at rear of building; wheelchair ramp.

BUCKINGHAMSHIRE

ROHAN DESIGNS PLC

1–3 KNEBWORTH GATE, GIFFORD PARK, MILTON KEYNES, BUCKINGHAMSHIRE MK14 5QD, ☎ 01908 615407, FAX: 01908 616624, www.rohan.co.uk, 9.30–5.30 MON–SAT. **FACTORY SHOP**

High performance fabrics with unique design features ranging from waterproof jackets to the famous Rohan bags. Seconds and discontinued items available at discount prices. Also sells shirts, trousers, T-shirts and fleeces.

CHESHIRE

ADIDAS

MCARTHURGLEN DESIGNER OUTLET CHESHIRE OAKS, KINSEY ROAD, NEAR ELLESMERE PORT, JUNCTION 10 OF M53, CHESHIRE CH65 9JJ, ☎ 0151 355 6893, FAX: 0151 355 0816, 10–8 MON–FRI, 9–6 SAT, 11–5 SUN. **FACTORY SHOP IN A FACTORY SHOPPING VILLAGE**

Specialising in a wide range of sports apparel for men, women and children, this store sells end of season products at 30% to 70% off RRP. Footwear and accessories such as sports bags, shin-pads etc. Saloman outdoor wear and the Adidas golf range are also stocked. Regular promotions run throughout the year.

CALANGE AND BUSHBABY

PO BOX 61, STOCKPORT, CHESHIRE SK3 0AP, ☎ 0161 474 7097, FAX: 0161 476 2647, **e-mail:** sales@calange.co.uk, www.calange.com, www.bush-baby.com, 9–5 MON–FRI. **DESIGNER SALES**

Twice-yearly sales of adults and childrens performance leisure and outdoor gear such as technical legwear, waterproof jackets, warm hats, fleeces and child carriers from birth to three years, at incredibly cheap prices. On sale are ends of lines, imperfects and some design samples which they haven't pursued into full manufacturing. Phone or write to be put on the mailing list.

CLARKS FACTORY SHOP

CHESHIRE OAKS OUTLET, KINSEY ROAD, NEAR ELLESMERE PORT, JUNCTION 10 OF M53, CHESHIRE CH65 9JJ, ☎ 0151 356 7492, 10–8 MON–FRI, 9–6 SAT, 11–5 SUN. **FACTORY SHOP IN A FACTORY SHOPPING VILLAGE**

Clarks International operate a chain of factory shops nationally which specialise in selling discontinued lines and slight sub-standards for men, women and children from Clarks, K Shoes and other famous brands. These shops trade under the name of K Shoes Factory Shop or Clarks Factory Shop and while not all are physically attached to a shoe factory, they are treated as factory shops by the company. Customers can expect to find an extensive range of quality shoes, sandals, walking boots, slippers, trainers, handbags, accessories and gifts, while their major outlets also offer luggage, sports clothing, sports equipment and outdoor clothing. Brands stocked include Clarks, K Shoes, Springer, CICA, Hi-Tec, Caterpillar, Kickers, Timberland, Regatta, Craghoppers, Kangol, Kangaroo Poo, Diadora, Mercury, Antler, Eminent, Travelon, Hudson and Carlton, although not all are sold in every outlet. Phone first to find out what your particular store is offering. Discounts are from 30% to 60% off the normal high street price for perfect stock.

MCARTHURGLEN DESIGNER OUTLET

KINSEY ROAD, NEAR ELLESMERE PORT, JUNCTION 10 OF M53, CHESHIRE CH65 9JJ, ☎ 0800 316 4352 FREE INFORMATION LINE OR 0151 348 5600, FAX: 0151 357 3744, www.mcarthurglen.com/cheshireoaks, 10–8 MON–FRI, 9–6 SAT, 11–5 SUN. **FACTORY SHOPPING VILLAGE**

The McArthurGlen Designer Outlet Cheshire Oaks is Europes largest designer outlet with over 140 stores selling top brands and designer names at up to 50% off typical retail prices. Facilities include a food court, a children's play area and free parking. Stores include: Gap Outlet, Big L, Fruit of the Loom, Monsoon, Timberland, Tie Rack, Principles, Petroleum, James Barry, Donnay, Aquascutum, Burberrys, Viyella, Warehouse, Racing Green, Famous Footwear, Jeffrey Rogers, Liz Claiborne, Winning Line, Overland, Ciro Pearls, Diesel, Jokids, Fred Perry, Travel Accessory Outlet, Baron Jon, La Senza, Nike, Next to Nothing, Helly Hansen, Jane Shilton, Joe Bloggs, Birthdays, Thorntons, Toyworld, D2, Pilot, Jumper, Clarks, Villeroy & Boch, Episode, Windsmoor, Jaeger, Daks Simpson, Mexx, Bed & Bath Works, Woods of Windsor, The Suit Company, XS Music & Video, Suits You, Claires Accessories, Lee Cooper, Tog 24, Fila, Warners, Cecil Gee, Remington, Whittard of Chelsea, Kitchen Store, Denby, Edinburgh Crystal, Price's Candles, Reebok, Hobbs, Kurt Muller, Bookends, Pictureport, Kappa, Easy Jeans, Woodhouse, Designer Room, DKNY, Ponden Mill, U Wear/I Wear, Penn, Le Coq Sportif, Roman Originals, Revlon, Monet, Walker and Hall, Ben Sherman, Van Heusen, Austin Reed, Antler, Ecco, Blazer, Watson/Chillii Pepper, Red/Green, Soled Out, Carphone Warehouse, Cotton Traders, Royal Doulton, Royal Worcester, Oneida, Proibito, Vans, Reiss, Garden Outlet, Proudfoot Leather, Playtime Toys, Wedgwood, Prima Tessuti, Natural World, WHSmith, Littlewoods, Bose, The Body Shop, Samsonite, Adidas, Kangol, Dune, Marks & Spencer Outlet, Daniel Footwear, Polo Jeans Company, The North Face, Elle, Sergio Tacchini, Autonomy, Chapelle, Fiorelli, Julian Graves, Spiegelau, Bose, Kitch N Sync, Early Learning Centre, Tommy Hilfiger, Triumph and Professional Cookware.

NIKE FACTORY STORE

MCARTHURGLEN DESIGNER OUTLET CHESHIRE OAKS, KINSEY ROAD, NEAR ELLESMERE PORT, JUNCTION 10 OF M53, CHESHIRE CH65 9JJ, ☎ 0151 357 1252, FAX: 0151 355 6724, www.nike.com, 10–8 MON–FRI, 9–6 SAT, 11–5 SUN. **FACTORY SHOP IN A FACTORY SHOPPING VILLAGE**

Mens, women s and childrens footwear, clothing and equipment. Trainers, jackets, T-shirts, polo shirts, sweatshirts, shorts, pants, tracksuits, golf balls, footballs, golf bags, gloves, socks and caps. Nike has been making clothes for people who are inspired by sports since 1972. This factory store sells garments only one season behind the high street. The selection is from their European product line, and there are approximately 10,000 pairs of shoes and 20,000 items of clothing to choose from, all at a minimum of 30% off normal retail prices. You will also find slight seconds on sale (marked and signed in store as B grades). The store has four clearance sales throughout the year (phone for details). There are a further 10 factory stores throughout the UK and Ireland.

REDGREEN

MCARTHURGLEN DESIGNER OUTLET CHESHIRE OAKS, KINSEY ROAD, NEAR ELLESMERE PORT, JUNCTION 10 OF M53, CHESHIRE CH65 9JJ, ☎ 0151 356 3660, 10–8 MON–FRI, 9–6 SAT, 11–5 SUN. **FACTORY SHOP IN A FACTORY SHOPPING VILLAGE**

RedGreen is Scandinavian leisurewear for men and women. The high quality and classic design has a nautical heritage and a stylish look. The collection includes outerwear, sweaters, shirts, trousers, skirts, dresses, sweatshirts, T-shirts, tailored jackets, footwear and accessories at discount of between 25% and 70%.

THE FACTORY SHOP LTD

UNIT 1 EDDISBURY SQUARE, FRODSHAM, CHESHIRE WA6 6QS, ☎ 01928 734624, FAX: 01928 734906, 9–5.30 MON–SAT, 10.30–4 SUN. **FACTORY SHOP**

Wide range on sale includes men s, women's and childrens clothing and footwear; household textiles; toiletries; hardware; luggage; lighting; electrical goods; and bedding, most of which are chainstore and high street brands at discounts of approximately 30% to 50%. There are kitchen and furniture displays and on sale is the Cape Country Furniture range with free-standing kitchens, as well as living, bedroom and dining furniture. There are weekly deliveries and brands include famous names such as Adidas, Nike, Joe Bloggs and Brabantia, among others. Lines are continually changing and few factory shops offer such a variety under one roof. Parking is free.

THE FAMOUS BRUNSWICK WAREHOUSE LTD

UNIT 5B, THE ROACK, GREEN LANE, BIRKENHEAD, CHESHIRE CH41 9AG, ☎ 0151 650 1505, **e-mail:** northshoe@mcmail.com, 10–8 MON–FRI, 9–6 SAT, 11–5 SUN.

UNIT 3, ST DAVIDS RETAIL PARK, SALTNEY, CHESTER, CHESHIRE CH4 8SN, ☎ 01244 676431, **e-mail:** northshoe@mcmail.com, 9–6 MON–SAT, 10–4 SUN.

UNIT 1B, 2 GRAND JUNCTION RETAIL PARK, EARLE STREET, CREWE, CHESHIRE CW1 2RP, ☎ 01270 254156, **e-mail:** northshoe@mcmail.com, 10–8 MON–FRI, 9–6 SAT, 11–5 SUN.

UNIT 3, COCKHEDGE CENTRE, COCKHEADGE WAY, WARRINGTON, CHESHIRE WA1 2QQ, ☎ 01925 232306, **e-mail:** northshoe@mcmail.com, 9–6 MON–WED, SAT, 9–7 THUR, FRI, 10.30–4.30 SUN.

49 DEWHIRST ROAD, BIRCHWOOD, WARRINGTON, CHESHIRE WA3 7PG, ☎ 01925 822718, **e-mail:** northshoe@mcmail.com, 9–6 MON–WED, SAT, 9–8 THUR, FRI, 10.30–4.30 SUN. **PERMANENT DISCOUNT OUTLET**

Self-service discount store chain with 60 branches selling branded sportswear and sports footwear, such as Nike, Adidas and Reebok, as well as non-branded footwear at discounts of 50%. Also a reasonable selection of clothing and accessories. Phone the number above for details of your nearest branch.

TOG 24

MCARTHURGLEN DESIGNER OUTLET CHESHIRE OAKS, KINSEY ROAD, NEAR ELLESMERE PORT, JUNCTION 10 OF M53, CHESHIRE CH65 9JJ, ☎ 0151 356 7477, **e-mail:** mail-order@tog24.com, www.tog24.com, 10–8 MON–FRI, 9–6 SAT, 11–5 SUN. **FACTORY SHOP IN A FACTORY SHOPPING VILLAGE**

Tog 24 is the UK's fastest-growing brand name in outdoor clothing and leisurewear. The company utilises the world's finest performance fabrics, including GoreTex and Polartec, to produce merchandise which caters for all the family for all seasons. Their range includes fleeces and waterproofs for the winter, and trekking ranges, shorts and T-shirts for the summer. They also stock accessories, including sunglasses, toiletries and swimwear. All merchandise is available by mail order: phone 01924 236507 for a brochure or to order. All prices here are at least 30% below RRP.

TOMMY HILFIGER

MCARTHURGLEN DESIGNER OUTLET, CHESHIRE OAKS, KINSEY ROAD, ELLESMERE PORT, CHESHIRE CH65 9JJ, ☎ 0151 355 4501, FAX: 0151 355 2201, www.tommy.com, 10–8 MON–FRI, 9–6 SAT, 11–5 SUN. **FACTORY SHOP IN A FACTORY SHOPPING VILLAGE**

Sells mens and women s sportswear, sweatshirts, polo shirts, jeans, T-shirts, jackets, mens underwear and accessories.

CO DURHAM

CATALOGUE DISCOUNT STORES

UNIT 17, IN SHOP CENTRE, 12 WRIGHTON HOUSE, TRENCHARD AVENUE, THORNABY ON TEES, CO DURHAM TS17 9EP, ☎ 01642 751935, 9–5 MON–SAT. **PERMANENT DISCOUNT OUTLET**

Grattan catalogue store, selling a wide selection of items from those featured in the catalogue, including women's, men's, children's, home, sportswear, electrics and toys. All items are discounted by up to 50% with regular special promotions. All stores offer a 14-day refund policy, and a 12-month guarantee on electrical items. A wide range of brands are in stock on a regularly changing basis. Each store carries a slightly different range, so please phone to check that they have what you want in stock.

FACTORY SHOP

LINGFIELD WAY, YARM ROAD BUSINESS PARK, DARLINGTON, CO DURHAM DL1 4XX, ☎ 01325 469 181, FAX: 01325 381386, **e-mail:** tensorlimited@aol.com., www.tensormarketing.co.uk. 9–5 MON–FRI, 10–4.30 SAT. **FACTORY SHOP**

Part of Tensor Marketing Ltd, a marketing company specialising in innovative products with a huge range of goods covering home and garden, office, motoring, gifts, novelties, pets, pest control systems, security, health and fitness, sport and leisure. The garden section has a range of items including gutter flushes, hammer and edging fencing, mole chasers, foldaway wheelbarrows, garden lighting sets, weeders, garden thermometers, corner plant stands, garden hoses and obelisks. Order from the shop, the website or by mail order brochure.

THE FACTORY SHOP

24 COMMERCIAL STREET, CROOK, CO DURHAM DL15 9HP, ☎ 01388 763211, 9–5.30 MON–SAT, 10.30–4.30 SUN. **FACTORY SHOP**

See page 613 (CHESH)

THE FAMOUS BRUNSWICK WAREHOUSE LTD

1–2 WEST ROW, DARLINGTON, CO DURHAM DL1 5PL, ☎ 01325 488446, **e-mail:** northshoe@mcmail.com, 9–5 MON–SAT.

25 JACKSON STREET, GATESHEAD, TYNE & WEAR, ☎ 0191 477 2364, **e-mail:** northshoe@mcmail.com, 9–5 MON–SAT.

UNIT 2A, SANDS INDUSTRIAL ESTATE, SWALWELL, GATESHEAD, TYNE & WEAR NE16 3DG, ☎ 0191 488 1333, **e-mail:** northshoe@mcmail.com, 9–7 MON–FRI, 9–6 SAT, 10–4 SUN.

UNIT 3 ANCHOR RETAIL PARK, MARINA WAY, HARTLEPOOL, CO DURHAM TS24 0XB, ☎ 01429 264519, **e-mail:** northshoe@mcmail.com, 10–7 MON–FRI, 9–6 SAT, 11–5 SUN.

UNIT 2, PETERLEE RETAIL DEVELOPMENT, HOWLETCH LANE, OFF EASTINGTON ROAD, PETERLEE, CO DURHAM SR8 2BL, ☎ 0191 587 0709, **e-mail:** northshoe@mcmail.com, 9–6 MON–SAT, 10–4 SUN.

CHARLOTTE STREET, SOUTH SHIELDS, TYNE & WEAR NE33 1QQ, ☎ 0191 427 6545, **e-mail:** northshoe@mcmail.com, 9–5 MON–SAT, 9–6 THUR, 10–4 SUN.

UNIT 4, PALLION RETAIL PARK, WOODBINE TERRACE, SUNDERLAND, TYNE & WEAR SR4 6TY, ☎ 0191 565 7302, **e-mail:** northshoe@mcmail.com, 9.30–6 MON–WED, 9.30–7 THUR, FRI, 9–6 SAT, 10.30–4.30 SUN.

UNIT 4, OLD FULWELL ROAD, ROKER, SUNDERLAND, TYNE & WEAR SR6 0JD, ☎ 0191 565 0965, **e-mail:** northshoe@mcmail.com, 9–6 MON–SAT, 7 ON THUR, 10–4 SUN.

42 WHITES MARKET, SUNDERLAND, TYNE & WEAR SR1 3DG, ☎ 0191 514 2653, **e-mail:** northshoe@mcmail.com, 9–5 MON–SAT. **PERMANENT DISCOUNT OUTLET**

See page 613 (CHESH)

CORNWALL

THE FACTORY SHOP

OLD STATION YARD, BERRYCOMBE ROAD, BODMIN, CORNWALL PL31 2NF, ☎ 01208 78492, 9–5.30 MON–SAT, 10.30–4.30 SUN.

MOUNT AMBROSE, SCORRIER, REDRUTH, CORNWALL TR15 1QT, ☎ 01209 219116, 9.30–5.30 MON–SAT, 10–4 SUN. **FACTORY SHOP**

See page 613 (CHESH)

CUMBRIA

GAYNOR SPORTS

MARKET CROSS, AMBLESIDE, CUMBRIA LA22 9BT, ☎ 015394 33305, **e-mail:** sales@gaynors.co.uk, www.gaynors.co.uk, 9–6 MON–SAT, 10.30–4.30 SUN, SUMMER. 9–5.30 MON–FRI, 9–6 SAT, 10.30–4.30 SUN, WINTER. **FACTORY SHOP**

One of the largest equipment stores in the north-east. Brands offered at competitive prices include Berghaus, Sprayway, The North Face, Craghoppers, Regatta, Lowe Alpine and Karrimor. Gaynor Sports Factory Outlet guarantees a minimum of 30% savings on normal retail prices of the stock offered for sale. Join its email database for up-to-date information on the latest offers.

HI-PENNINE OUTDOOR SHOP

MARKET SQUARE, ALSTON, CUMBRIA CA9 3QN, ☎ 01434 381389, 10–4 MON–FRI, 10–5 SAT, 11–3 SUN. MAIL ORDER. **FACTORY SHOP**

Sells GoreTex and Polartec fleece clothing including jackets, windproof trousers, mitts, gaitors, scarves, headbands, travel bags, rucksacks and hats all manufactured under the Mountain Range label. The Outdoor Shop sells seconds and ends of lines at discounts of up to 25%. There is also a mail order service.

JOHN CHAPMAN LTD

GALLERY HOUSE, HARRABY GREEN BUSINESS PARK, CARLISLE, EXIT 42 OF M6, CUMBRIA CA1 2SS, ☎ 01228 514514, FAX: 01228 515758, **e-mail:** sales@chapman-bags.demon.co.uk, www.chapman-bags.co.uk, 8–5 MON–THUR, 8–2 FRI. MAIL ORDER. **FACTORY SHOP**

Classic, traditional leather and canvas luggage, weekend bags, travel bags, handbags, rucksacks, duffle bags, luggage shoulder bags, folio bags, grips, suitcases, garment carriers, suiters, washbags and briefcases. John Chapman manufacture for top department stores both in the UK and overseas and sell overmakes in their factory shop and by mail order at prices which are much cheaper than the retail prices charged by their retail clients. There are more than 100 styles in this collection of classic bags of extremely rugged construction made with strict quality control and great attention to detail. They are made from fine multi-layered cotton canvas bonded together with natural rubber and with real leather strappings and bindings, solid brass buckles, loops and studs and the heaviest zips available, sewn with two rows of heavy stitching. For mail order, add £4.75 postage and packing.

K VILLAGE OUTLET SHOPPING

LOUND ROAD, KENDAL, NEAR JUNCTION 36 OF M6, CUMBRIA LA9 7DA, ☎ 01539 732363, **e-mail:** mdixon@realm-ocm.com, www.kvillage.co.uk, 9.30–6 MON–FRI, 9–6 SAT, 11–5 SUN (9.30–5.30 MON–FRI NOVEMBER TO MARCH). **FACTORY SHOPPING VILLAGE**

Twelve outlets including Cotton Traders, Crabtree & Evelyn, Dartington Crystal selling Cloverleaf as well as glassware, Van Heusen, Denby Pottery, The Food Factory, Ponden Mill, Prices Candles, Tog 24, National Trust Gift Shop and a giant K Shoes factory shop selling a wide range of labels from K Shoes, Clarks, Cica, Delsey and Antler, as well as a full-price K Shop. There is also a heritage centre where you can discover the history of shoemaking, a 150-seater restaurant, a coffee shop, children's play area, baby changing facilities, a riverside picnic area, disabled facilities and free parking. Take the South Kendal exit and follow the signs for K Village.

THE FAMOUS BRUNSWICK WAREHOUSE LTD

UNIT 5, THE BRIDGES RETAIL PARK, FLAT WALKS, WHITEHAVEN, CUMBRIA CA28 7RQ, ☎ 01946 694706, **e-mail:** northshoe@mcmail.com, 9–6 MON–SAT, 7 ON THUR, 10.30–4.30 SUN. **PERMANENT DISCOUNT OUTLET**

See page 613 (CHESH)

TOG 24

UNIT 4, MARKET CROSS, AMBLESIDE, CUMBRIA LA22 9BT, ☎ 01539 433913, **e-mail:** mail-order@tog24.com, www.tog24.com, 9.30–6 MON–SAT, 10–5 SUN.

10 CRAG BROW, BOWNESS, CUMBRIA LA23 3BX, ☎ 01539 488656, **e-mail:** mail-order@tog24.com, www.tog24.com, 9.30–5.30 MON–THUR, 9.30–6 FRI, SAT, 10–5.30 SUN.

9 MARKET SQUARE, KESWICK, CUMBRIA CA12 5BJ, ☎ 01768 780876, **e-mail:** mail-order@tog24.com, www.tog24.com, 10–5 MON–FRI, 9.30–5.30 SAT, SUN. **FACTORY SHOP**

K VILLAGE, LOUND ROAD, KENDAL, CUMBRIA LA9 7DA, ☎ 01539 721555, **e-mail:** mail-order@tog24.com, www.tog24.com, 9.30–6 MON–FRI, 9–6 SAT, 11–5 SUN. **FACTORY SHOP IN A FACTORY SHOPPING VILLAGE**

See page 613 (CHESH)

DERBYSHIRE

ADIDAS

MCARTHURGLEN DESIGNER OUTLET MANSFIELD, MANSFIELD ROAD, SOUTH NORMANTON, ALFRETON, JUNCTION 28 OF M1, DERBYSHIRE DE55 2ER, ☎ 01773 545135, FAX: 01773 524720, 10–6 MON–SAT, 8 ON THUR, 11–5 SUN. **FACTORY SHOP IN A FACTORY SHOPPING VILLAGE**

See page 611 (CHESH)

HAWK FACTORY CYCLE STORES

960 LONDON ROAD, ALVASTON, DERBY, DERBYSHIRE DE24 8PY, ☎ 01332 756666, 9–6 MON–SAT, 9–4.30 SUN. **FACTORY SHOP**

Sells all types of adult s and childrens bikes direct to the public at factory prices. Children's trikes start at £26.99, adults' mountain bikes £79.99 for women, £89.99 for men, normally 149.99. There are also clearance shops in South Yardley, Birmingham (0121 742 3332), Nottingham (0115 958 5900), Coventry (0247 622 2783), Shrewsbury (01743 344554), Cannock (01543 361656) and Cradley Heath (01384 636535).

KARRIMOR

THE PEAK STORE, THE RUTLANDS SQUARE, BAKEWELL, DERBY, DERBYSHIRE DE45 1BJ, ☎ 01629 815115, www.karrimor.com, 10–5 MON–SAT, 11–5 SUN. **FACTORY SHOP**

Best known for their comprehensive range of rucksacks, Karrimor also make an outstanding range of outdoor equipment for walkers, climbers and campers. The factory shop sells seconds, former display items, samples and clearance stock at discounts of between 15% and 25% and always stocks the current season's range.

MASSON MILLS SHOPPING VILLAGE

DERBY ROAD, MATLOCK BATH, NEAR MATLOCK, DERBYSHIRE DE4 3PY, ☎ 01629 760208, FAX: 01629 761525, 10–5.30 MON–SAT, 11–5 SUN. **FACTORY SHOPPING VILLAGE**

Anchored by Edinburgh Woollen Mills and set on four floors, this shopping village is set in regenerated 18th century mill building with a working textile museum and conference facilities. There are shops selling fashion, golfwear and equipment, gifts, speciality foods and country goods and include Julian Graves food items, Woods of Windsor, and Ponden Mill selling bedlinen and towels. The top floor is a designer clothing store stocking labels such as DKNY, Kangol, Ben Sherman, Miss Sixty, Tommy Hilfiger and many others, all with up to 50% off normal retail prices. There is a riverside restaurant on site.

MCARTHURGLEN DESIGNER OUTLET

MANSFIELD ROAD, SOUTH NORMANTON, ALFRETON, JUNCTION 28 OF M1, DERBYSHIRE DE55 2ER, ☎ 01773 545000, www.mcarthurglen.com/mansfield, 10–6 MON–FRI, 8 ON THUR, 9–6 SAT, 11–5 SUN. **FACTORY SHOPPING VILLAGE**

The McArthurGlen Designer Outlet Mansfield has recently undergone a year-long development programme, transforming it from an open-plan department store layout to individual shops. The new look outlet is now bigger and better. Find all your favourite brands at discounts of up to 50% off typical retail prices. Facilities include a childrens play area, a food court and plenty of free parking. Stores include: Antler, Banana Books, Bed & Bath Works, Big L, Camille Lingerie, Chapelle, Claire s Accessories, Coloroll, Cotton Traders, Donnay, Edinburgh Crystal, Harbi, Jaeger, Jane Shilton, Julian Graves, Kitch N Sync, Leading Labels, Lee Cooper, Mountain Warehouse, Pavers Shoes, Petroleum, Pilot, Price's Candles, Professional Cookware, Remington, Roman Originals, Sky, Soled Out, Speedo, Sportsmill, Suits You, Thorntons, Tog 24, Toyworld, Revlon, Marks & Spencer Outlet, Windsmoor, Sportz, Reebok, Jumper, HKA, Proudfoot Leather, Garden Outlet, Lilley & Skinner, Adidas, Viyella, Whittards, XS Records and many more.

PEAK VILLAGE

CHATSWORTH ROAD, ROWSLEY, (ON THE A6 BETWEEN BAKEWELL AND MATLOCK) DERBYSHIRE DE4 2JE, ☎ 01629 735326, www.peakvillage.co.uk, 9.30–5.30 MON–SAT, 10–5 SUN, EXCEPT CHRISTMAS DAY. **FACTORY SHOPPING VILLAGE**

More than 20 factory outlets including Leading Labels, Cotton Traders, Luggage & Bags, The Book Depot, Pavers Shoes, Sports & Mountain Warehouse, Yeoman Outdoors outdoor wear and equipment, Ponden Mill, Mansworld, New Beginnings and Woodlands Fitness Centre, all just 30 minutes from the M1 at the entrance to the Peak District National Park. On-site catering includes Massarella's Restaurant, which offers everything from an ice cream sundae to a traditional Sunday roast. The Wind in the Willows Attraction is a magical journey through the world of Ratty, Badger, Mole and of course the irrepressible Mr Toad. The latest sound and lighting effects bring Kenneth Grahame's classic tale to life in an enchanting recreation that's not just for kids! Free parking for up to 400 cars. Recently opened the Woodlands Fitness Centre.

R S DESIGNER LEISUREWEAR LTD

192194 NORMAN STREET, COTMANHAY, ILKESTON, DERBYSHIRE DE7 8NR, ☎ 0115 932 3865, FAX: 0115 877 9915, **e-mail:** roger@sweatshirtsdirect.co.uk, www.sweatshirtsdirect.co.uk, 9.30–3.30 MON–FRI. SAT: PHONE FIRST. **PERMANENT DISCOUNT OUTLET**

Sports, leisurewear, sweatshirts and cardigans for schoolwear in sizes from 1 year to XXXXL (60in waist) at discounts of up to 50%. Women's cardigans, sweatshirts and ski pants plus a variety of clothes, but no shoes, ranging from 1 to 12. All the merchandise is made up of overmakes, slight imperfects and end of season lines. There is a permanent sale rail. There is also a made-to-measure service which caters for all shapes and sizes, as well as an embroidery service.

THE FAMOUS BRUNSWICK WAREHOUSE LTD

UNIT 4, SOUTHGATE RETAIL PARK, NORMANTON ROAD, DERBY, DERBYSHIRE DE23 6UX, ☎ 01332 204532, **e-mail:** northshoe@mcmail.com9–6 MON–WED, SAT, 9–8 THUR, FRI, 11–5 SUN. **PERMANENT DISCOUNT OUTLET**

See page 613 (CHESH)

TOG 24

DERBYSHIRE DESIGNER OUTLET VILLAGE, MANSFIELD ROAD, SOUTH NORMANTON, DERBYSHIRE DE55 2JW, ☎ 01773 545206, **e-mail:** mail-order@tog24.com, www.tog24.com, 10–6 MON–FRI, 8 ON THUR, 9–6 SAT, 11–5 SUN. **FACTORY SHOP IN A FACTORY SHOPPING VILLAGE**

See page 613 (CHESH)

TOYWORLD STORE FACTORY OUTLET

MCARTHURGLEN DESIGNER OUTLET MANSFIELD, MANSFIELD ROAD, SOUTH NORMANTON, ALFRETON, JUNCTION 28 OF M1, DERBYSHIRE DE55 2JH, ☎ 01773 545 333, www.toyworldstore.com, 10–6 MON–FRI, 8 ON THUR, 9–6 SAT, 11–5 SUN. **FACTORY SHOP IN A FACTORY SHOPPING VILLAGE**

See page 613 (CHESH)

DEVON

ATLANTIC VILLAGE OUTLET CENTRE

CLOVELLY ROAD, OFF A39, WEST OF BIDEFORD, NORTH DEVON, ☎ 01237 422544, **e-mail:** rmorris@realm-ocm.com, www.atlanticvillage.co.uk, JULY–MID SEPT, 9.30–7 MON–SAT, 11–5 SUN; MID SEPT–MID OCT AND EASTER TO JULY 9.30–6.30 MON–SAT, 11–5 SUN; MID OCT–EASTER 9.30–5 MON–SAT, 11–5 SUN. **FACTORY SHOPPING VILLAGE**

More than 30 shops with famous names and Devon's largest interactive maze make this village a good family day out. Shops include Banana Books; Claires Accessories; Colony Candles; Cotton Traders, Designer Room, Ecco; Edinburgh Woollen Mill; Event Jewellery; Jane Shilton; Jean Scene; Julian Graves; Nickelby s; Pavers Shoes; Pilot; Ponden Mill; Puma; Roman Originals; Room, selling home accessories, fabrics and soft furnishings; Sportsmill; Suits You; Tog 24; Toyzone; Triumph; Warners; Windsmoor; XS Sound & Media. Free car parking, disabled and baby changing facilities. Atlantic Village also features an attractive piazza, cafs, a food court, visitor garden, arts and crafts market, open-air amphitheatre, and an adventure park set in an additional three-acre site linked to the shopping area by the piazza and amphitheatre. The Adventure Park features a mystery maze, adventure golf, wreckers cove and adventure play boat.

BOB LOVELL SPORTS

36 FORE STREET, BRIXHAM, DEVON TQ5 8DZ, ☎ 01803 859115, FAX: 01803 859845, **e-mail:** Sales@Lovell-Rugby.co.uk, www.Lovell-Rugby.co.uk, MAIL ORDER. **PERMANENT DISCOUNT OUTLET**

Discounted rugby gear among other full-price stock.

EXETER SURPLUS

BAKERS YARD, ALPHINBROOK ROAD, MARSH BARTON INDUSTRIAL ESTATE, EXETER, DEVON EX2 8SS, ☎ 01392 427508, 8.30–5 MON–SAT. **PERMANENT DISCOUNT OUTLET**

Operates from a 4,000 square foot retail unit and a 10,000 square foot trade site half a mile away on Christow Road, the latter specialising in quality, nearly-new office furniture and shelving. Retail goods include engineering equipment, hand tools, clothing, a large range of outdoor goods, chandlery, a range of tents, bedding and domestic furniture, kayaks, rope and chain, canvas sheets, rucksacks, boots and shoes, overalls, ceremonial clothing and an enormous amount of miscellaneous one-off items, all very competitively priced. The outdoor leisure market is their new specialisation.

STEWARTS

58 60 FORE STREET, BRIXHAM, DEVON TQ5 8DZ, ☎ 01803 852000, FAX: 01803 852000, 9–5 MON–SAT, 10–4 SUN.

RICHMOND COURT, DAWLISH, DEVON EX7 9PL, ☎ 01626 895022, FAX: 01626 895022, 9–5 MON–SAT, 10.30–4.30 SUN.

24–26 QUEEN STREET, NEWTON ABBOT, DEVON TQ12 2EF, ☎ 01626 362721, FAX: 01626 362721, 9–5.30 MON–SAT.

9–15 STATION ROAD, TEIGNMOUTH, DEVON TQ14 8PE, ☎ 01626 775616, FAX: 01626 775616, 9–5.30 MON–SAT, 10.30–4.30 SUN.

37 FORE STREET, TOTNES, DEVON TG9 5HN, ☎ 01803 865093, FAX: 01803 865093, 9–5 MON–SAT, 10–4 SUN. **FACTORY SHOP**

Branded merchandise from most of the major UK chainstores, all well-known high street department store names, offered at a discount of 40% to 70% off normal high street prices. The garments are selected with great care by experienced buyers direct from factories worldwide to bring customers top quality merchandise at highly competitive prices.

TOG 24

ATLANTIC VILLAGE, CLOVELLY ROAD, BIDEFORD, NORTH DEVON EX39 3QU, ☎ 01237 473799, **e-mail:** mail-order@tog24.com, www.tog24.com, 10–6 MON–SAT, 8 ON THUR, 10.30–4.30 SUN. **FACTORY SHOP IN A FACTORY SHOPPING VILLAGE**

See page 613 (CHESH)

DORSET

BAILIE HOUSE WAREHOUSE

STURMINSTER MARSHALL, DORSET BH21 4AE, ☎ 01258 857112, www.middleditchsalvage.com, OPEN 10–6 FRI, 10–5 SAT, 10–2 SUN. **PERMANENT DISCOUNT OUTLET**

Wide range of goods which are the result of insurance claims due to fire, flood, burglary or other insurance problems. A salvage warehouse which has been in operation for 38 years, stock includes sports clothing from names such as Nike, Adidas and Reebox; cricket, tennis and keep fit outfits; men's casual clothing including Fred Perry, underwear and socks; women's fashion including jeans, jackets, tops, many from top London boutiqes; records, CDs, books, pine furniture, curtain and upholstery fabrics.

THE CATALOGUE SHOP

401 LYMINGTON ROAD, HIGHCLIFFE, DORSET BH23 5HE, ☎ 01425 271202, FAX: 01425 278478, **e-mail:** thecatalogueshop@virgin.net, www.the catalogueshop.virgin.com, 9–5 MON–SAT, 10–5 SUN. **PERMANENT DISCOUNT OUTLET**

Returns, damaged and worn goods as well as clearance lines and ends of lines of branded merchandise from mail order catalogues. This includes mens, women s and childrens wear, footwear, bedding, curtains, furniture, exercise equipment and leather coats. These items are always in stock but the shop also has an ever-changing range of items as well. Turnover is very fast with new deliveries every day. All items are sold at less than 50% of the catalogue price starting at 99p, with branded trainers from £14.99.

ESSEX

CLACTON FACTORY SHOPPING VILLAGE

STEPHENSON ROAD WEST, CLACTON-ON-SEA, ESSEX CO15 4TL, ☎ 01255 479595, FAX: 01255 430777 INFORMATION LINE, 10–6 MON–SAT, 11–5 SUN. **FACTORY SHOPPING VILLAGE**

Forty eight units centred around a Victorian winter garden comprising the following: Banana Bookshop selling books, games and stationery; Because Its There (BIT) for sports and camping equipment; Bed & Bath Works, a homeware outlet with discounted branded linens and housewares from Janet Reger, Sheridan, Christy and Kingsley; Birthdays, stocking mainstream cards and gifts from manufacturers such as Andrew Brownsword, Disney, Parker, Galt and Warner Brothers; Camille for lingerie; Caterpillar selling foorwear from the Cat range; Choice, which sells family clothing from Next; Claire s Accessories; Clinkards family footwear from Churchs, Gabor, Bally and Loake; Cook N Dine kitchenware, glass and ceramics; Cotton Traders casual wear; Dannimac outdoor wear; Designer Room selling designer fashion for men and women; Event fashion costume jewellery and watches from Accurist, Timberland, Seiko and Timex; Garden Store selling garden furniture, barbecues and equipment and, in season, Christmas decorations; Jacques Vert selling womenswear; JD Sports selling branded sports merchandise from Adidas, Nike, Reebok, Ellesse and Le Coq Sportif; Joanna Hall selling handbags from the Jane

Shilton range; Julian Graves foods and nut mixes; Kids Play Factory with toys from ranges such as Fisher-Price and Lego; Leading Labels, with mens and women s fashions; Mobile Phone Shop; MX Active selling branded denim and casual wear for men, women and children; Nickelbys fashion wear for men and women; Olli Moda selling branded jeans and casual wear; Pilot, a young womens fashion outlet; Ponden Mill with a range of bedlinen and bathroom ware; Price's Candles; Roman Originals womenswear; Sasperilla for young womens fashions; Spotlight, a young women s fashion outlet; Suits You mens shirts, suits, and casual separates as well as wedding hire and Autonomy womenswear; Thorntons chocolates; Tog 24 outdoor activity wear; Windsmoor women's fashions; Travel Accessory Shop with travel goods from Delsey and Samsonite; Woods of Windsor toiletries and gift items; XS Music CDs and videos. There are also two restaurants, a tourist information centre, parking for 1,000 cars and a bus service link to Clacton-On-Sea town centre and railway station.

FREEPORT BRAINTREE DESIGNER OUTLET VILLAGE

FREEPORT ESSEX VILLAGE, CHARTER WAY, CHAPEL HILL, BRAINTREE, JUNCTION 8 OF M11, THEN A120, ESSEX CM77 8YH, ☎ 01376 348168, www.freeportbraintree.com, 10–6 MON–SAT, 8 ON THUR, 11–5 SUN. **FACTORY SHOPPING VILLAGE**

Freeport Braintree is a designer outlet village with over 80 shops. Situated in the heart of Essex with easy access from the A120, Freeport Braintree has its own dedicated railyway station and is only a one-hour journey from central London. Womenswear includes Aquascutum, Amazing Jeans, Antonio d'Errico, Box Fresh, Burberry, Christian Lacroix, Cotton Traders, Elle, Gossard, Karen Millen, Ted Baker, Tommy Hilfiger and Versace and The Designer Room with a host of designer labels. Menswear includes Aquascutum, Cecil Gee, Ciro Citterio, Cotton Traders, Kurt Muller, Nickleby's, Proibito, Ted Baker, Tommy Hilfiger, Van Heusen and Versace. For children there's Base 2 Base, Mexx and Toy Dome; there is also plenty to keep children entertained, such as the Cheeky Chimps indoor play area. Sportwear outlets include Brand Fusion, Donnay, Fila, Mountain Warehouse, Nike, Reebok, Regatta and Trespass. Footwear is covered by Ecco Shoes, Franchetti Bond, Hush Puppies, Jane Shilton, Lilley & Skinner, Soled Out and Vans Shoes. Shops selling household goods from kitchenware to pot pourri include Churchills, Denby, Edinburgh Crystal, Glen Eagles, Le Creuset, Professional Cookware, The Design House, Waterford Wedgwood and Villeroy & Boch. Other retail outlets, selling everything from luggage to music, include Body Shop, Carlton, Claire s Accessories, Designer Shades, Mobile Phone Store, Watch Store and XS Music, and there are no less than six cafs and restaurants on site.

NIKE FACTORY STORE

FREEPORT ESSEX VILLAGE, CHARTER WAY, CHAPEL HILL, BRAINTREE, ESSEX CM7 8YH, ☎ 01376 320674, FAX: 01376 327469, www.nike.com, 10–6 MON–SAT, 8 ON THUR, 11–5 SUN. **FACTORY SHOP IN A FACTORY SHOPPING VILLAGE**

See page 612 (CHESH)

REGATTA

FREEPORT ESSEX VILLAGE, CHARTER WAY, CHAPEL HILL, BRAINTREE, ESSEX CM7 4YH, ☎ 01376 349755, FAX: 01376 349755, www.regatta.com, 10–6 MON–SAT, 8 ON THUR, 11–5 SUN. **FACTORY SHOP IN A FACTORY SHOPPING VILLAGE**

Regatta is the UKs biggest supplier of outdoor clothing and equipment for the whole family. The ranges comprise wovens, waterproofs, fleece, rucksacks and accessories for men, women and children, and are suitable for a whole range of outdoor activities. Regatta prides itself on offering excellent quality products at very reasonable prices. Craghoppers, the innovator in travel and outdoor wear, is a technical brand that leads with innovation. Its offering of waterproofs, fleece, wovens and rucksacks are intended for travel at home or abroad and suitable for a wide range of climates. All stock is sold here at discounted prices of at least 30%.

THE FACTORY SHOP LTD

THE CROSS ROADS, KELVEDON ROAD, TIPTREE, ESSEX CO5 0LJ, ☎ 01621 817662, 9–5.30 MON–SAT, 10–4 SUN. **FACTORY SHOP**

See page 613 (CHESH)

TOG 24

CLACTON FACTORY OUTLET VILLAGE, STEPHENSON ROAD WEST, CLACTON-ON-SEA, ESSEX CO15 4TL, ☎ 01255 435035, **e-mail:** mail-order@tog24.com, www.tog24.com, 10–6 MON–SAT, 8 ON THUR DURING SUMMER AND AT CHRISTMAS, 11–5 SUN. **FACTORY SHOP IN A FACTORY SHOPPING VILLAGE**

See page 613 (CHESH)

TOMMY HILFIGER

UNIT G6, FEEPORT DESIGNER VILLAGE, CHAPEL HILL, BRAINTREE, ESSEX CM7 8YH, ☎ 01376 342985, FAX: 01376 349482, www.tommy.com, 10–6 MON–SAT, 8 ON THUR, 11–5 SUN. **FACTORY SHOP IN A FACTORY SHOPPING VILLAGE**

See page 613 (CHESH)

GLOUCESTERSHIRE

BRANDMART

WESTWARD ROAD, CAINSCROSS, STROUD, GLOUCESTERSHIRE GL5 4JE, ☎ 01453 756655, 9–5 MON–SAT, 10–4 SUN. **FACTORY SHOP**

The original factory shop in Cainscross, Stroud, has recently relocated next door into a 12,000 square foot premises and is now trading under the name of Brandmart, offering even more savings on branded household and family goods. The range includes men's, women's and children's clothing and footwear, household textiles, toiletries, hardware, luggage, lighting, electrical goods and bedding, most of which are chainstore and high street brands at discounts of between 30% and 50%. There are weekly deliveries and brands include famous names such as Calvin Klein, Adidas, Nike, Fcuk, Cat, Reebok, Ben Sherman, Kangol, Timberland and many more. There are kitchen and furniture displays and a new line in Cape Country furniture on sale. Ranges are continually changing and few factory shops offer such a variety under one roof. The shop has its own car park.

MASH

INNSWORTH TECHNOLOGY PARK, INNSWORTH LANE, GLOUCESTER, GLOUCESTERSHIRE GL3 1DL, ☎ 01452 730577, FAX: 01452 731999, **e-mail:** tim@dowco.co.uk, www.mashcamping.com, 8.30–5.30 MON–FRI, 8.30–5 SAT, 10–4 SUN, BANK HOLIDAYS. **SECONDHAND SHOP**

Warehouse/shop carrying an extensive range of backpacking and camping equipment, outdoor clothing, tools, Gelert tents, Sunngas cookers, Victorinox knives, Maglite torches and government surplus stock at discount prices.

HAMPSHIRE

ADIDAS

GUNWHARF QUAYS, PORTSMOUTH, HAMPSHIRE PO1 3TA, ☎ 02392 779974, FAX: 02392 779975, 10–6 MON, WED, 10–8 TUE, THUR, 10–8 FRI, SAT, 11–5 SUN. **FACTORY SHOP IN A FACTORY SHOPPING VILLAGE**

See page 611 (CHESH)

CAMEO SPORT AND LEISURE

92 HIGH STREET, COWES, ISLE OF WIGHT PO31 7AW, ☎ 01983 297219, www.lostproperty4sale.com, 10–5 SEVEN DAYS A WEEK. **SECONDHAND SHOPS**

Run by the son of the owner of Cameo of Cowes, this shop also specialises in buying and selling unclaimed lost property and bankrupt stock but with the emphasis on sportswear: tennis rackets, wet suits, surf boards and anything to do with sports generally.

GUNWHARF QUAYS

PORTSMOUTH HARBOUR, HAMPSHIRE PO1 3TZ, ☎ 023 9283 6700, FAX: 023 9283 6701 **e-mail:** info@gunwharf-quays.com, www.gunwharf-quays.com, SUMMER: 10–6 MON–WED, 10–8 THUR–SAT, 11–5 SUN . WINTER: 10–6 MON–SAT, 11–5 SUN. **FACTORY SHOPPING VILLAGE**

Designer outlet shopping centre comprising 65 stores on a site next to Portsmouth Harbour station and Portsmouth Historic Dockyard, home to HMS Victory and the Mary Rose. As well as the designer outlets, which include Adidas, Benetton, Ben Sherman, Burberry, cK Calvin Klein, Crabtree & Evelyn, Ecco, Episode, Fenn Wright & Manson, Gap, Gieves & Hawkes, Marks & Spencer, Nicole Farhi, Nike, Tommy Hilfiger, Villeroy & Boch, Waterford Wedgwood and Whittard of Chelsea, there are 20 restaurants, bars and coffee shops, an 11-screen cinema, 26-lane bowling complex, comedy club and a year-round events programme.

NIKE FACTORY STORE

UNITS 46, GUNWHARF QUAYS, PORTSMOUTH, HAMPSHIRE PO1 1AA, ☎ 023 9275 2822, FAX: 023 9275 2903, www.nike.com, 10–6 MON–WED, 10–8 THUR–SAT, 11–5 SUN. **FACTORY SHOP IN A FACTORY SHOPPING VILLAGE**

See page 612 (CHESH)

PRET A PORTER

SHOP ONE, 18 20 HIGH STREET, RINGWOOD, HAMPSHIRE BH24 1AF, ☎ 01425 476090, 10–5 MON–SAT. **DRESS AGENCIES**

Dress agency selling top designer fashions which offers a range of skiwear, accessories and aprés skiwear is available from October to February. Stock is seasonal and around 200 new items are added to the range every week to ensure a continuous flow of new and exciting items.

THE GALLERIES

HIGH STREET, ALDERSHOT, HAMPSHIRE GU11 1PE, ☎ 01252 341111, FAX: 01252 329800, **e-mail:** thegalleries@web-hq.com, www.thegalleriesaldershot.co.uk, 9–6 MON–SAT, 10–4 SUN. **FACTORY SHOPPING VILLAGE**

This town centre shopping mall has 20 discount shops on two levels such as Bed & Bath Works for bedlinen and bathroom ware; Cotton Traders casual wear; Designer Room selling women's and mens designer fashion; Hush Puppies shoes; Kitchen Kiosk with branded kitchen and homeware ranges including barbecues and some electrical goods such as bread making machines; Leading Labels selling men's, women's and childrenswear; MX Active for mens, women s and childrens branded denim and casual wear; Optisave, an optician selling designer branded glasses; Pilot selling young women's fashions; Pocket Phone selling mobile phones and accessories; Roman Originals womenswear; Room for furniture and household accessories; Suits You men s shirts, suits and casual separates as well as Autonomy womenswear; and Youngs dress hire; Surf Skate and Snow for branded casual and activity wear; Toyzone for children s toys; and XS Music selling CDs and videos. The centre also has a caf, wheelchair access, a lottery kiosk and baby changing facilities.

TOG 24

GUNWHARF QUAYS, PORTSMOUTH, HAMPSHIRE PO1 3TU, ☎ 0239 283 3717, **e-mail:** mail-order@tog24.com, www.tog24.com, 10–6 MON–WED, 10–8 THUR–SAT, 11–5 SUN. **FACTORY SHOP**

See page 613 (CHESH)

TOMMY HILFIGER

UNIT 7, GROUND FLOOR, GUNWHARF QUAYS, PORTSMOUTH, HAMPSHIRE PO1 3TA, ☎ 01233 646622, FAX: 01233 645375, www.tommy.com, 10–6 SEVEN DAYS A WEEK. **FACTORY SHOP IN A FACTORY SHOPPING VILLAGE**

See page 613 (CHESH)

UNITED FOOTWEAR

117 125 FRATTON ROAD, PORTSMOUTH, HAMPSHIRE 0239 282 6799, 9–5.30 MON–SAT, 10–4 SUN. **PERMANENT DISCOUNT OUTLET**

This shoe retailer, established for over 135 years, sells shoes for all the family as well as clothes, handbags, sports shoes, boots, giftware and household goods, all at discounted prices. Famous brands include Clarks, K Shoes, Elmdale, Grenson, Loakes, Caterpillar and Adidas. Part of a national chain.

WHITELEY VILLAGE OUTLET SHOPPING

OFF THE M27 BETWEEN SOUTHAMPTON AND PORTSMOUTH, JUNCTION 9 OF M27, HAMPSHIRE PO15 7LJ, ☎ 01489 886886, FAX: 01489 886887, www.whiteleyvillage.com, 10–6 MON–SAT, 11–5 SUN. **FACTORY SHOPPING VILLAGE**

Whiteley Village has more than 50 outlets, all offering shoppers up to 50% savings on high street prices. Top designer names fashion names are here – including Antonio DErrico, Banana Bookshop, Camille Lingerie, Lilley & Skinner, Roman Originals, Surf, Skate & Snow, Top Table, High & Mighty, Chilli Pepper, Claire s Accessories, Helter Skelter, Cloverleaf, Marzotto, Cotton Traders, D2 Jeans, Elle, Emma Sommerset, Ethos, The Baggage Factory, Ghost, HKA, Jane Shilton, Jasper Conran Jeans, Jigsaw, John Jenkins, John Partridge, Joseph, Julian Graves, Mobile Phone Store, Outdoor Direct, Photo Optix, Pilot, Ponden Mill, Pringle, Proibito, Puma, Rio Jeweller and The Designer Room with a host of designer labels. Refreshments are available from Starbucks Coffee and Boswells Restaurant. There is free parking on site for 1, 400 cars, as well as an area for coaches.

HEREFORDSHIRE

M & M SPORTS FACTORY SHOP

LEOMINSTER INDUSTRIAL ESTATE, SOUTHERN AVENUE, LEOMINSTER, HEREFORDSHIRE HR6 0SP, ☎ 01568 616161, FAX: 01568 619555, **e-mail:** sales@mandmsports.com, www.mandmsports.com, 10–8 THUR, 10–5 FRI, SAT, 10–4 SUN. **FACTORY SHOP**

M & M Sports is the UKs largest sports and leisurewear mail order company, offering brand names for all the family at huge discounts including Nike, Adidas, Reebok, Fila, Ellesse, Berghaus and Rockport. Five catalogues a year are packed with all types of sports clothing, footwear and watches. M&M buys up huge quantities of end-of-line ranges direct from the manufacturers and passes on the massive savings to its customers. The M&M Factory Shop sells discontinued catalogue items. A football kit catalogue is available, while the Equipment Catalogue offers products for golf, tennis, cricket, cycling, fishing, snooker, fitness equipment plus a lot more. To order a catalogue, phone or fax the above telephone numbers or visit their website where orders can be placed and there are many internet-only sale offers. Just click on the Exclusive Internet Offers logo.

STEWARTS

33 HIGH STREET, ROSS-ON-WYE, HEREFORDSHIRE HR9 5HD, ☎ 01989 762403, FAX: 01989 762403, 9.30–5.30 MON–SAT, 10–5.30 SUN. **FACTORY SHOP**

See page 618 (DEV)

THE FACTORY SHOP

52 BROAD STREET, LEOMINSTER, HEREFORDSHIRE HR6 8BS, ☎ 01568 613944, 9–5.30 MON–SAT, 10–4 SUN. **FACTORY SHOP**

See page 613 (CHESH)

HERTFORDSHIRE

GALLERIA OUTLET CENTRE

COMET WAY, HATFIELD, HERTFORDSHIRE AL10 0XR, ☎ 01707 278301, www.factory-outlets.co.uk, 10–8 MON–FRI, 10–6 SAT, 11–5 SUN. **FACTORY SHOPPING VILLAGE**

The Galleria Outlet Centre, often referred to as the bargain hunters best-kept secret, based in north London, houses more than 80 retail outlets. It offers a wide choice of shops for the discerning customer, providing up to 60% off designer labels and quality brands. The Designer Room is a must for branded men s and womens fashions at huge discounts, stocking DKNY, Jasper Conran, Ghost and Tommy Hilfiger clothing. Looking for a designer evening dress or smart-casual wear? Then visit Discount Dressing. For the latest in fashionable menswear, pay a visit to any of the leading menswear shops. City Menswear offers new season, discounted Yves Saint Laurent and Ben Sherman clothing; Choice sells ranges from Next; B52 Jeans stocks Levi s, Lee and Wrangler ranges; and Baron Jon sells a selection of international names from Versace to Valentino. Going on holiday or looking for a new set of luggage? Then visit the Baggage Factory which sells top quality brands including Carlton and Samsonite. For all your bathroom and bedroom needs pop in to Ponden Mill or the Bed and Bath Works, selling a selection of bed-linen, towels from Christy, soaps and duvets. BhS For Less sells a range of end-of-season mens women s and childrens fashions, as well as homewares and lighting. For all your footwear fancies, take a stroll to Charles Clinkard, Ecco, Soled Out and Pavers, selling great brand names including Timberland, Loake, Grenson, Nike, Reebok and Kickers. For women, D Kaye Cosmetics stocks a host of leading beauty and skincare ranges including Revlon, Max Factor, Lancome and Yardley, all at up to 75% off normal retail prices. Walker & Hall represent the finest in jewellery, stocking Tag, Gucci and Raymond Weil watches all at affordable prices. It also sells gold by weight and guarantees savings of at least 30% per gram. While, for the home, Chinacraft specialises in glass, china and giftware, from Wedgwood to Royal Doulton. If interior soft furnishings are on the agenda, then the Furniture Zone is the largest of its type, selling Oriental, middle eastern and Continental rugs, plus great ranges of sofas and sofa-beds, teak, cherry and oak furniture from Wall Nuts and the Khokhar Collection. To complement any room, the Big Picture and Big Poster sell modern and classical pictures ranging from 5 to 20,000. Visit the Garden Outlet Store for all your outdoor gardening and furniture requirements. Music Surplus, the home entertainment store, is a recent addition to the centre, selling a wide range of imported jazz, pop, chart and classical CDs, as well as the latest DVDs. For the PC enthusiast, UK Software sells CD-Roms at up to 70% off the normal retail price. Tool Ware House sells DeWalt, considered by many to be the Armani of the tool worlds, as well as offering fantastic savings on Black & Decker. The centre also offers three cafs, six restaurants and an abundance of childrens activities including Toddler World, a futuristic crazy golf course and bouncing slides as well as a mini go-karting track during weekends and holidays. With over 1, 800 free car parking spaces and a nine-screen UCI cinema, the centre offers a complete family day out. The Galleria Outlet Centre is a 20-minute drive from north London, and is signposted from junction 3 and 4 of the A1M.

OUTDOOR TRADING POST

GALLERIA OUTLET CENTRE, COMET WAY, HATFIELD, HERTFORDSHIRE AL10 0XR, ☎ 0800 413650, 10–8 MON–FRI, 10–6 SAT, 11–5 SUN. **FACTORY SHOP IN A FACTORY SHOPPING VILLAGE**

Specialist outdoor sports factory shop for skiers and urban hikers selling top quality brands such as Patagonia, Salamon, SOS, Lowe Alpine and North Face at reductions which average 30% to 40%. In the summer, they stock mostly outdoor and trekking gear and equipment with some lines in skiwear and equipment at final clearance prices. In the winter, from September to March, they carry the full range of premium brands in skiwear at the sort of prices you would pay for lower quality brands.

OUTDOOR WEAR

10–14 POTTER STREET, BISHOPS STORTFORD, HERTFORDSHIRE CM23 3UL, ☎ 01279 653694, 9–5.30 TUE–SAT. **PERMANENT DISCOUNT OUTLET**

Ends of lines from Karrimor, Berghaus, Tenson, Barbour, Levi's, Rohan and Drizabone in shirts, jeans, hats, and skiwear, all sold at approximately 20% discount.

TOG 24

GALLERIA OUTLET CENTRE, COMET WAY, HATFIELD, HERTFORDSHIRE AL10 0XS, ☎ 01707 258088, **e-mail:** mail-order@tog24.com, www.tog24.com, 10–8 MON–FRI, 10–6 SAT, 11–5 SUN. **FACTORY SHOP IN A FACTORY SHOPPING VILLAGE**

See page 613 (CHESH)

KENT

MCARTHURGLEN DESIGNER OUTLET CENTRE

KIMBERLEY WAY, ASHFORD, JUNCTION 10 OF M20, KENT TN24 0SD, ☎ 01233 895900, www.mcarthurglen.com/ashford, 10–6 MON–FRI, 8 ON THUR, 9–6 SAT, 11–5 SUN. **FACTORY SHOPPING VILLAGE**

Voted Retail Destination of the Year 2001 in the Retail Week awards, the McArthurGlen Designer Outlet Ashford in Kent is one of Europe's most spectacular shopping destinations. The outlet offers over 70 top brands and designer labels at up to 50% off typical retail prices. there is a food court, cafs, a children's play area, and parking for over 1,500 cars. A shuttle bus runs between the town centre, station and the outlet every eight minutes. Shops include: Ben Sherman, Cotton Traders, Designer Room/Classic Room, Daks, Fire Trap, Gap, Lee Cooper, Levi's Littlewoods Catalogue Outlet, Marks and Spencer, Mexx, Miss Sixty, Mountain Warehouse, Pilot, Polo Jeans Co. Factory Store, Proudfoot, Roman Originals, Thomas Pink, Tog 24, Tommy Hilfiger, Warehouse, Warner's, Windsmoor, Baron Jon, Ben Sherman, Cotton Traders, Daks, Fire Trap, Fred Perry, Gap, Lee Cooper, Levi's, Petroleum, Proudfoot, Suits You, The Suit Company, Thomas Pink, Van Heusen, Woodhouse, Donnay, Fila, Gap, JoKids, Mexx, Nike, Reebok, Toyzone, Clarks, Ecco, Jane Shilton Kiplings, Lilley & Skinner, Soled Out, Antler, Kipling, Samsonite Company Stores. Arran Aromatics, Body Shop, Chapelle Jewellery, Claire's Outlet, Gizmo, One 2 One, Picture Port, Revlon, Sekonda, Sunglass Hut International, Watch Station, Walker and Hall, Woods of Windsor, Bed and Bath Works, Bookends, Bose, China Place, Cloverleaf, Design House, Edinburgh Crystal, Le Creuset, Mountain Warehouse, Price's Candles, Professional Cookware Company, Spiegelau, Waterford Wedgwood, Whittard of Chelsea, XS Music and Video.

THE FACTORY SHOP LTD

THE FOREMAN CENTRE, HIGH STREET, HEADCORN, KENT TN27 9NE, ☎ 01622 891651, 9–5.30 MON–SAT, 10–4 SUN. **FACTORY SHOP**

See page 613 (CHESH)

TOG 24

MCARTHURGLEN DESIGNER OUTLET ASHFORD, KIMBERLEY WAY, ASHFORD, JUNCTION 10 OF M20, KENT TN24 0SD, ☎ 01233 647357, **e-mail:** mail-order@tog24.com, www.tog24.com, 10–6 MON–FRI, 8 ON THUR, 9–6 SAT, 11–5 SUN.

DE BRADLEI WHARF, CAMBRIDGE ROAD, DOVER, KENT CT17 9BY, ☎ 01304 216126, **e-mail:** mail-order@tog24.com, www.tog24.com, 9.30–5.30 MON–FRI, 9.30–6 SAT, 11–5 SUN. **FACTORY SHOP IN A FACTORY SHOPPING VILLAGE**

See page 613 (CHESH)

TOMMY HILFIGER

UNIT 5 MCARTHUR GLEN DESIGNER OUTLET, KIMBERLEY WAY, ASHFORD, KENT TN24 0SD, ☎ 01233 646622, FAX: 01233 645375, www.tommy.com, 10–6 MON–SAT, 8 ON THUR, 11–5 SUN. **FACTORY SHOP IN A FACTORY SHOPPING VILLAGE**

See page 613 (CHESH)

LANCASHIRE

ALLSPORTS

99 ALBANY WAY, SALFORD 6, LANCASHIRE M6 5JA, ☎ 0161 736 8582, www.allsports.co.uk, 9–5.30 MON–SAT. **PERMANENT DISCOUNT OUTLET**

Allsports is a standard shop with a dedicated area of marked-down goods at the rear. These are all damaged or end of season and there are great bargains to be had. Goods can be one-offs to particular items in various sizes. Stock varies from day to day so you could be delighted one day and disappointed the next. Typical bargains are British and foreign football shirts at between one quarter and one half of the normal perfect price. There are also trainers, sports goods, clothing, football boots, including some Manchester United merchandise. There are deliveries every day.

BOUNDARY MILL STORES

BURNLEY ROAD, COLNE, LANCASHIRE BB8 8LS, ☎ 01282 865229, www.boundarymill.co.uk, 10–6 MON–FRI, 9 ON THUR, 9–6 SAT, 11–5 SUN, 10–6 BANK HOLIDAYS, OPENS AT 10 ON SUNDAYS FOR BREAKFAST AND BROWSING, PURCHASES CAN BE MADE FROM 11.

PERMANENT DISCOUNT OUTLET

One of the largest clearance stores in Britain, it covers more than 100,000 square feet with over 300 quality brands, all now under one roof. Many of the top end of the high street designer labels are on sale here for both women and men. Womens labels include: Alexon, Windsmoor, Austin Reed, Eastex, Planet, Jaeger, Jacques Vert, Liz Claiborne and Viyella. Men s labels include: Austin Reed, Centaur, Dannimac, Farah, Pierre Cardin, Lyle & Scott and Yves St Laurent. The women's and men's departments are very extensive – not to mention impressive – and cover the whole range from casual to evening wear with reductions of between 30% and 70%. There are also large leisurewear departments for women and men including Polo Ralph Lauren, Timberland, Wrangler and Tog 24, and a whole floor dedicated to womens lingerie. The new extension building, which links the fashion and home stores, contains a massive shoe department stocking Bally, Nine West and Hush Puppies, among others. On the ground floor, there is a huge new cookshop stocking up-to-the-minute ranges and a greatly extended luggage department including Globetrotter, Antler and Jane Shilton. The home store sells brand-name home furnishings, glass and china including Dorma, Sanderson, Denby, Edinburgh Crystal, Dartington Crystal, Portmeirion, Royal Worcester, Villeroy & Boch and Wedgwood. Four times a year, there are special sales at which prices are discounted further. Most of the stock is end of lines with the occasional marked seconds. There is a choice of food outlets: a large coffee shop, a restaurant and a pub, and there is extensive free parking.

CATALOGUE DISCOUNT STORES

2 BURY OLD ROAD, CHEETHAM HILL, MANCHESTER, LANCASHIRE M8 7JN, ☎ 0161 795 9312, FAX: 0161 7407 274, 9–5.30 MON–SAT. **PERMANENT DISCOUNT OUTLET**

See page 614 (CO DURH)

CRAGHOPPERS

FREEPORT SHOPPING VILLAGE, ANCHORAGE ROAD, FLEETWOOD, LANCASHIRE FY7 6AE, ☎ 01253 778372, FAX: 01253 778372, www.regatta.com, 10–6 MON–WED, 10–8 THUR, FRI, 10–6 SAT, SUN. **FACTORY SHOP IN A FACTORY SHOPPING VILLAGE**

Craghoppers, the innovator in travel and outdoor wear, is a technical brand that leads with innovation. Its offering of waterproofs, fleece, wovens and rucksacks are intended for travel at home or abroad and suitable for a wide range of climates. All stock is sold here at discounted prices of at least 30%.

FREEPORT FLEETWOOD OUTLET VILLAGE

ANCHORAGE ROAD, FLEETWOOD, 12 MILES FROM JUNCTION 3 OF M55, LANCASHIRE FY7 6AE, ☎ 01253 877377, www.freeportfleetwood.com, 10–6 SEVEN DAYS A WEEK, 8 ON THUR, FRI. **FACTORY SHOPPING VILLAGE**

Large, brightly-coloured New-England-style seaside shopping village. There are more than 40 shops selling at up to 50% off high street prices, as well as restaurants, family attractions and free parking. Womens fashions include Next to Nothing, Spotlight, Easy Jeans, VF Corp, Double Two, Warner s, Edinburgh Woollen Mill, The Designer Room, Giorgio, BhS for Less, Madhouse and Roman Originals. For men, there is Petroleum, Ciro Citterio, Double Two, Giorgio, VF Corp, Madhouse, Easy Jeans and BhS for Less. Sportswear and outdoor wear shops include Sports Mill, Craghoppers, Regatta and VF Corp. Footwear outlets comprise Lilley & Skinner, Jane Shilton, Shoe Sellers, BhS For Less, Next to Nothing and Petroleum.

Sweet-toothed visitors can indulge at Thorntons or The Sweet Shop, and there is Julian Graves for nuts and dried fruits. Household outlets include Ponden Mill, Dartington Crystal, Home Zone, Picture Port and China Traders. Childrenswear stockists include Next to Nothing, BhS for Less, Vecopri, VF Corp and Giorgio. Other stores include Woods of Windsor, Hallmark Cards and Gifts, XS Music & Video, Claire's Accessories, Watch Store and Book Depot.

KARRIMOR

PETRE ROAD, CLAYTON-LE-MOORS, ACCRINGTON, LANCASHIRE BB5 5JZ, ☎ 01254 893134, www.karrimor.com, 10–5 MON–FRI, 7.30 ON THUR, 10–4 SAT.

THE DESIGNER OUTLET AT THE LOWRY, QUAYS ROAD, SALFORD QUAYS, MANCHESTER M5 2SQ, ☎ 0161 848 8429, www.karrimor.com, 10–8 MON–FRI, 9–7 SAT, 11 0 5 SUN. **FACTORY SHOP**

See page 616 (DERBY)

PRO IMAGE LTD

20 BRIDDON STREET, STRANGEWAYS, MANCHESTER M3 1LS, ☎ 0161 839 2845, FAX: 0161 839 5830, 10–6 MON–WED, 10–8 THUR, FRI, 10–5 SAT, SUN. **PERMANENT DISCOUNT OUTLET**

Waterproof golf suits, waterproof trousers and tops for men and women.

REGATTA

FREEPORT SHOPPING VILLAGE, ANCHORAGE ROAD, FLEETWOOD, LANCASHIRE FY7 6AE, ☎ 01253 777705, FAX: 01253 777705, www.regatta.com, 10–6 MON, TUE, WED, SAT, SUN, 10–8 THUR, FRI. **FACTORY SHOP IN A FACTORY SHOPPING VILLAGE**

See page 620 (ESSEX)

THE FACTORY SHOP

SHAWBRIDGE STREET, CLITHEROE, LANCASHIRE BB7 1NA, ☎ 01200 428784, 9–5.30 MON–SAT, 10.30–4.30 SUN.

LANCASTER LEISURE PARK, WYRESDALE ROAD, LANCASTER, LANCASHIRE LA1 3LA, ☎ 01524 846079, 10–5 MON–SAT, 11–5 SUN. **FACTORY SHOP**

See page 613 (CHESH)

THE FAMOUS BRUNSWICK WAREHOUSE LTD

UNIT 6, ASHTON RETAIL PARK, 102 WELLINGTON ROAD, ASHTON UNDER LYNE, LANCASHIRE OL6 6DJ, ☎ 0161 330 7400, **e-mail:** northshoe@mcmail.com9–5 MON–FRI, 6 ON THUR, SAT, 10.30–4.30 SUN.

UNIT C, 454 BROOKWAY RETAIL PARK, ALTRINCHAM ROAD, BAGULEY, MANCHESTER, LANCASHIRE M23 9BL, ☎ 0161 945 1441, **e-mail:** northshoe@mcmail.com10–6 MON–WED, 10–8 THUR, FRI, 9–6 SAT, 11–5 SUN.

UNIT B2, TOWNSMOOR RETAIL PARK, BLACKBURN, LANCASHIRE BB2 3DY, ☎ 01254 278772, **e-mail:** northshoe@mcmail.com9.30–6 MON–WED, 9.30–7 THUR, FRI, 9–6 SAT, 11–5 SUN.

CHURCHILL WAY, LEYLAND, LANCASHIRE PR25 2LZ, ☎ 01772 455053, **e-mail:** northshoe@mcmail.com9–6 MON–WED, SAT, 9–7 THUR, FRI, 10.30–4.30 SUN.

24 MIDDLETON GARDENS, MIDDLETON, LANCASHIRE M24 4DF, ☎ 0161 653 9905, **e-mail:** northshoe@mcmail.com9–6 MON–SAT.

UNIT 4B, CABLES RETAIL PARK, STELEY WAY, RAINHILL, PRESCOT, MERSEYSIDE, LANCASHIRE L34 5NO, ☎ 0151 426 8262, **e-mail:** northshoe@mcmail.com9–6 MON–WED, SAT, 9–7 THUR, FRI, 10–4 SUN.

UNIT 2C, QUEENS RETAIL PARK, PRESTON, LANCASHIRE PR1 4HZ, ☎ 01772 253003, **e-mail:** northshoe@mcmail.com9–6 MON, TUE, FRI, SAT, 9–7 WED, THUR, 10.30–4.30 SUN.

UNIT E1, REGENTS PARK, ORDSALL LANE, SALFORD, MANCHESTER, LANCASHIRE M5 3TP, ☎ 0161 833 2173, **e-mail:** northshoe@mcmail.com10–6 MON–WED, 10–7 THUR, FRI, 9–6 SAT, 11–5 SUN.

UNIT D, WARRINGTON NEW ROAD, ST HELENS RETAIL PARK, ST HELENS, LANCASHIRE WA9 1JJ, ☎ 01744 754410, **e-mail:** northshoe@mcmail.com9–6 MON–WED, SAT, 9–7 THUR, FRI, 10–4 SUN.

UNIT 19, ELLESMERE RETAIL PARK, WALKDEN, WORSLEY, LANCASHIRE M28 3ZD, ☎ 0161 790 330, **e-mail:** northshoe@mcmail.com9–6 MON–WED, SAT, 9–7 THUR, FRI, 10.30–4.30 SUN.

25 LOIRE DRIVE, ROBIN PARK, WIGAN, LANCASHIRE WN5 0UH, ☎ 01942 211901, **e-mail:** northshoe@mcmail.com10–6 MON, TUE, 10–7 WED, FRI, 10–8 THUR, 9–6 SAT, 11–5 SUN. **PERMANENT DISCOUNT OUTLET**

See page 613 (CHESH)

TOG 24

7 THE LINKWAY, HORWICH, BOLTON, LANCASHIRE BL6 6JA, ☎ 01204 469899, **e-mail:** mail-order@tog24.com, www.tog24.com, 10–6 MON–FRI, SAT, 8 ON WED, THUR, 11–5 SUN.

BOUNDARY MILLS STORE, BURNLEY ROAD, COLNE, LANCASHIRE BB8 8JN, ☎ 01282 870042, **e-mail:** mail-order@tog24.com, www.tog24.com, 10–6 MON–FRI, 9 ON THUR, 9–6 SAT, 10–5 SUN. **FACTORY SHOP, FACTORY SHOP IN A FACTORY SHOPPING VILLAGE**

See page 613 (CHESH)

TOMMY BALLS

HART STREET MILL, BLACKBURN, LANCASHIRE BB11HW, ☎ 01254 261910, 10–5 MON–SAT, 11–5 SUN. **PERMANENT DISCOUNT OUTLET**

A large discount shoe warehouse selling quality shoes from leading British manufacturers for the whole family. Some are seconds, all are brand new. There is also a store at Eanam, which sells reconditioned footwear: phone 01254 261910.

UNITED FOOTWEAR

12 LORD STREET, LEIGH, LANCASHIRE, ☎ 01942 604440, 9–5.30 MON–WED, 9–8 THUR, 9–6 FRI, 9–5.30 SAT.

68–70 OLDHAM STREET, MANCHESTER, LANCASHIRE, ☎ 0161 228 1706, 9–5.30 MON–SAT.

126 FRIARGATE BROW, PRESTON, LANCASHIRE, ☎ 01772 204410, 9–5.30 MON–SAT, 11–4.30 SUN.

CARRMILL ROAD, OFF EAST LANCS ROAD, ST HELENS, LANCASHIRE, ☎ 01744 737777, 9–6 MON–WED, 9–8 THUR, FRI, 9–5.30 SAT, 10–4 SUN. **PERMANENT DISCOUNT OUTLET**

See page 623 (HAMPS)

WINFIELDS

HAZEL MILL, BLACKBURN ROAD, HASLINGDEN, ROSSENDALE, LANCASHIRE BB4 5DD, ☎ 01706 227916, FAX: 01706 831125, **e-mail:** info@winfields.co.uk, www.winfields.co.uk, 10–5.30 MON–FRI, 8 ON THUR, 9–5.30 SAT, 11–5 SUN. **PERMANENT DISCOUNT OUTLET**

Winfields is a big mill discount store with other outlets in Barrow-in-Furness, Middleton and Hull, offering tremendous savings on shoes. In addition, Winfields has a massive selction of outdoor wear, fleeces, waterproofs, wellingtons, hiking boots, socks, hats, scarves and gloves for all the family. Dine or take a break at Cloggers, the restaurant. Free car parking. Wheelchair friendly.

LEICESTERSHIRE

CHARTERHOUSE RETAIL OUTLET

173 CHARNWOOD ROAD, SHEPSHED, LOUGHBOROUGH, LEICESTERSHIRE LE12 9NN, ☎ 01509 505050, FAX: 01509 507373, **e-mail:** factoryshop@charterhouse-holdings.co.uk, www.charterhouseholdings.co.uk, 9.30–6 MON–SAT, 11–4 SUN. **FACTORY SHOP**

The Charterhouse Retail Outlet was established 30 years ago and now enjoys its reputation as probably the largest factory shop of its kind in the UK. With over 2 million worth of stock always available, Charterhouse offers family clothing, fashion, footwear, kitchenware, homeware and more all ex-chain and branded products at a fraction of high street prices. Womenswear includes casual, evening, swimwear, nightwear and lingerie all styles and sizes. Childrenswear ranges from babies upwards with a special department for early teen fashions. Men will also find an excellent selection of branded sportswear, smart and casual clothing as well as footwear. The expanded kitchenware and household department stocks a huge selection of home and gift ideas, including luggage and toiletries. There is free parking, a children's play area, parent and baby room, wheelchair access and café area. The outlet is only one mile from Junction 23 of the M1.

UNITED FOOTWEAR

114 MAIN STREET, NEWBOLD VERDON, LEICESTERSHIRE, ☎ 01455 822407, 9–8 MON–FRI, 9–5.30 SAT, 10–4 SUN. **PERMANENT DISCOUNT OUTLET**

See page 623 (HAMPS)

LINCOLNSHIRE

BOUNDARY MILL STORES

AT DOWNTOWN SUPERSTORE, GONERBY MOOR, A1, GRANTHAM, LINCOLNSHIRE NG32 2AB, ☎ 01476 591001, 9.30–5.30 MON–SAT, 11–5 SUN. **PERMANENT DISCOUNT OUTLET**

See page 626 (LANCS)

GYMPHLEX SPORTSWEAR

BOSTON ROAD, HORNCASTLE, LINCOLNSHIRE LN9 6HU, ☎ 01507 523243, **e-mail:** sales@gymphlex.co.uk, **DESIGNER SALES**

Holds a one day factory shop sale just once a year: phone 01507 523243 for details. Your chance to buy a huge range of sportswear for all the family: jogging pants, tracksuits, rugby and football shirts, rugby shorts, T-shirts, polo shirts, Lycra swimwear, leotards, tights, socks. Some of the stock is seconds, some overmakes. The rest is freshly-made stock which is specially reduced for the sale.

THE FACTORY SHOP

MALT KILN ROAD, BARTON ON HUMBER, NORTH LINCOLNSHIRE DN18 5JT, ☎ 01652 636701, 9–7 MON, TUE, WED, 9–8 THUR, FRI, 8.30–7 SAT, 10–4 SUN.

43 HIGH STREET, MABLETHORPE, LINCOLNSHIRE LN12 1XA, ☎ 01507 473705, 9.30–6 MON–SAT, 10.30–4.30 SUN.

CARRE STREET, SLEAFORD, LINCOLNSHIRE NG34 7TW, ☎ 01529 410155, 9–5.30 MON–SAT, 10–4 SUN.

51 FLEET STREET, HOLBEACH, SPALDING, LINCOLNSHIRE PE12 7AU, ☎ 01406 422180, 9–5 MON–SAT, 10–4 SUN. **FACTORY SHOP**

See page 613 (CHESH)

THE FAMOUS BRUNSWICK WAREHOUSE LTD

UNIT A, VICTORIA RETAIL PARK, VICTORIA STREET NORTH, GRIMSBY, LINCOLNSHIRE DN31 1NX, ☎ 01472 250622, **e-mail:** northshoe@mcmail.com9–6 MON–WED, SAT, 9–7 THUR, FRI, 10.30–4.30 SUN.

THE CARLTON CENTRE, OUTER CIRCLE ROAD, LINCOLN, LINCOLNSHIRE LN2 4WA, ☎ 01522 520037, **e-mail:** northshoe@mcmail.com9–6 MON–WED, SAT, 9–7 THUR, FRI, 10–4 SUN.

UNIT 2, CARLTON STREET, OFF STATION ROAD, SCUNTHORPE, LINCOLNSHIRE DN15 6TZ, ☎ 01724 857307, **e-mail:** northshoe@mcmail.com9–6 MON–WED, SAT, 9–7 THUR, FRI, 10–4 SUN. **PERMANENT DISCOUNT OUTLET**

See page 613 (CHESH)

TOG 24

BOUNDARY MILL STORES, GONERBY MOOR, ON THE A1, GRANTHAM, LINCOLNSHIRE NG32 2AB, ☎ 01476 591001, **e-mail:** mail-order@tog24.com, www.tog24.com, 9.30–5.30 MON–SAT, 11–5 SUN. **FACTORY SHOP IN A FACTORY SHOPPING VILLAGE**

See page 613 (CHESH)

VOGUE CLOTHING AGENCY

94 EASTGATE, LOUTH, LINCOLNSHIRE LN11 9AA, ☎ 01507 604233, 10–5 MON–FRI, 9.30–5.30 SAT. **DRESS AGENCY, HIRE SHOP**

Trading for 27 years, this shop stocks a wide range of middle to high quality designer womens clothing. Consisting of two floors situated next to Curry's on the main street, the shop has recently introduced a department carrying a range of skiwear and motorcycle clothing, including one piece and two piece suits and boots.

LONDON

CATALOGUE BARGAIN SHOP

252 GREEN LANES, PALMERS GREEN, LONDON N13 5TU, ☎ 020 8886 9532, www.bargaincrazy.com, 9–5.30 MON–SAT, 10–4 SUN. **PERMANENT DISCOUNT OUTLET**

Catalogue Bargain Shop is a growing national chain of stores which obtains the majority of its goods from mail order giants Great Universal and Kays, and offers a range of clothing for all the family, a wide selection of shoes, bed linen, household goods, electrical equipment and hundreds of other catalogue items at very competitive prices. The merchandise consists of ends of ranges and previous season s stock for which there is no longer space when the catalogues change.

DISPOSAL SERVICES AGENCY (DSA)

ROOM 727, MINISTRY OF DEFENCE, 6 HERCULES ROAD, LONDON SE1 7DJ, ☎ 020 7261 8968, www.disposalservices.agency.mod.uk. **PERMANENT DISCOUNT OUTLET**

The Disposal Services Agency is an agency of the Ministry of Defence set up to dispose of surplus equipment. It runs the largest disposal operation in the UK, organising the sale of both military equipment and commodities in use commercially, such as embassy furniture, government department office furniture, closed-down RAF-base vehicles and housing stock, ex-marine boats, ex-army tents, boots and ski equipment, medical and dental equipment, clothing, ship and aircraft spares, scrap metal and IT equipment. The DSA uses companies throughout the UK, each with their own specialist area, to dispose of stock. These companies also dispose of stock from a host of other, usually public sector, organisations varying from fire brigades and hospitals to health authorities and the police. Equipment from these companies varies from kitchen equipment and fax machines to mobile radios, cars, generators, jewellery and telecommunications equipment to food trolleys, X-ray equipment, telephones, uniforms, dinghies, fishing nets, photocopiers and chair lifts. Visit the website to find out which companies sell which products and how to contact them direct.

SWIMGEAR

11 STATION ROAD, FINCHLEY, LONDON N3 2SB, ☎ 020 8346 6106, FAX: 020 8346 7211, www.swimgear.co.uk, 9.30–5 MON–FRI. MAIL ORDER. **PERMANENT DISCOUNT OUTLET**

A mail order company which also operates via a retail outlet opposite Finchley Central station. As well as selling their swimwear at less than the normal retail price by not putting the full markup on their products, they also sell discontinued and ends of line ranges of swimwear for men, women and children at between 20% to 30% less than normal retail prices. They also stock swimming hats, bubble hats, kickboards, goggles and flippers in adult and childrens sizes. Flippers normally cost about £18.50, but can be bought here for about 8 in black rubber; Lycra trunks, plain £7.35 up to £10 for patterned ones. Bikinis are on sale all year round, with womens swimwear ranging up to size 50 with Swimgear's own brand, full colour Mark One brochure or leaflet. Prices are lower than would be offered at swim meets and retail shops. As part of their service, they do not cash your cheque until your full order has been completed. Postage and packaging extra. Orders over £20 are post free, excluding heavy items such as flippers and shampoo on which p&p is charged.

TOG 24

PUTNEY EXCHANGE SHOPPING CENTRE, PUTNEY HIGH STREET, LONDON SW15 1TW, ☎ 020 8785 3565, **e-mail:** mail-order@tog24.com, www.tog24.com, 9–6 MON–SAT, 11–5 SUN. **FACTORY SHOP IN A FACTORY SHOPPING VILLAGE**

See page 613 (CHESH)

MIDDLESEX

THE SALVAGE SHOP

3440 WATLING AVENUE, BURNT OAK, MIDDLESEX HA8 OLR, ☎ 020 8952 4353, **e-mail:** lss@salvage1.co.uk, www.salvage1.co.uk, 9–5.30 MON–SAT, 10–4 SUN. **PERMANENT DISCOUNT OUTLET**

An Aladdin's cave of salvaged stock for the avid bargain hunter, most of which has been the subject of insurance claims for fire or flood, salvage, bankruptcy or is simply clearance stock. Stock changes every two or three days and regular visitors have found anything from half price Kenwood Chefs, televisions and sports equipment to furniture, kitchen items, linens and especially fantastic bargains in designer clothing. Yves Saint Laurent, Armani, Ungaro, Hugo Boss and Valentino, as well as all major high street names, are just some of the names to be found (though the labels are often cut out). Discounts range from 50% to 80%. Phone first to check stock.

NORFOLK

LATHAMS

BRIDGE STREET, POTTER HEIGHAM, GREAT YARMOUTH, NORFOLK NR29 5JE, ☎ 01692 670080, 9–5.30 MON–SAT, 10–4 SUN. **FACTORY SHOP**

Sell a wide range of fashions, hardware, china, fishing tackle, books, gardening equipment, linen, groceries and Christmas gifts at very reasonable prices. Most of the makes are high street labels and consist of discontinued lines and seconds. Also jewellery concessions, shoes, computer games kiosk, coffee shop and garden centre.

NORWICH CAMPING SPORTS AND LEISURE

52 56 MAGDALEN STREET, NORWICH, NORFOLK NR3 1JE, ☎ 01603 615525, FAX: 01603 623150, 9–5.45 MON–SAT. **PERMANENT DISCOUNT OUTLET**

Reductions of up to 50% on skiing jackets, one-pieces and salopettes all year round. This includes brand names such as Berghaus, ONeill and Quiksilver, in childrens sizes too. Also many ends of lines and last year's colours in fleeces, cagoules and waterproofs, as well as some reductions on ski boots and tents. Now stock an extensive range of climbing equipment at competitive prices.

THE FACTORY SHOP LTD

NORWICH STREET, EAST DEREHAM, NORFOLK NR19 1AD, ☎ 01362 691868, 9–5.30 MON–SAT, 10–4 SUN.

52 LONDON ROAD, HARLESTON, NORFOLK IP20 9BZ, ☎ 01379 854860, 9–5.30 MON–SAT, 10.30–4 SUN.

LYNN ROAD, SNETTISHAM, NORFOLK PE31 7QG, ☎ 01485 544441, 9–5.30 MON–SAT, 10–4 SUN. **FACTORY SHOP**

See page 613 (CHESH)

NORTHAMPTONSHIRE

UNITED FOOTWEAR

75–79 STAMFORD ROAD, KETTERING, NORTHAMPTONSHIRE 01536 481855, 9–5.30 MON–SAT, 10–4 SUN. **PERMANENT DISCOUNT OUTLET**

See page 623 (HAMPS)

NORTHUMBERLAND

CATALOGUE DISCOUNT STORES

15 THE PRECINCT, THE IN CENTRE, JARROW, TYNE & WEAR, ☎ 0191 483 4318, 9–5 MON–SAT.

8 THE FORUM SHOPPING CENTRE, WALLSEND, NORTHUMBERLAND NE28 8JR, ☎ 0191 236 9501, 9–5 MON–SAT. **PERMANENT DISCOUNT OUTLET**

See page 614 (CO DURH)

KARRIMOR

GROUND FLOOR, 810 FENKLE STREET, ALNWICK, NORTHUMBERLAND NE66 1HR, ☎ 01665 510753, www.karrimor.com, 9.30–5.30 MON–FRI, 9.30–5 SAT, 11–4 SUN. **FACTORY SHOP**

See page 616 (DERBY)

NIKE FACTORY STORE

UNIT 7, ROYAL QUAYS FACTORY OUTLET CENTRE, COBLE DENE, MAYHOLE ROAD, NORTH SHIELDS, NEWCASTLE UPON TYNE, NEAR A19, TYNE & WEAR, NE29 6DW, ☎ 0191 270 8796, www.nike.com, 10–6 MON–SAT, 8 ON THUR, 11–5 SUN. **FACTORY SHOP IN A FACTORY SHOPPING VILLAGE**

See page 612 (CHESH)

OMEGA OUTDOOR FACTORY SHOP

COQUET ENTERPRISE PARK, AMBLE, NORTHUMBERLAND NE65 0PE, ☎ 01665 710080, FAX: 01665 710081, **e-mail:** enquiries@omegaoutdoor.co.uk, www.omegaoutdoor.co.uk, 10–5 MON–FRI, 11–4 SAT. **FACTORY SHOP**

High-performance outdoor clothing, including samples and ends of runs, as well as ski wear and lightweight tents, at value-for-money factory prices. Omega was the manufacturer of clothing for the officials of the 1999–2000 Tour de France and also produced garments for the James Bond film, The World is Not Enough. They also supplied uniforms for the British winter Olympics teams.

ROYAL QUAYS OUTLET CENTRE

COBLE DENE, NORTH SHIELDS, NEWCASTLE UPON TYNE, NEAR A19, TYNE & WEAR NE29 6DW, ☎ 0191 296 3743, **e-mail:** outletcentres@realm-ocm.com, www.royalquaysoutletcentre.co.uk, 10–6 MON–SAT, 11–5 SUN. **FACTORY SHOPPING VILLAGE**

Forty-two shops with leisure facilities nearby including a full-scale steam railway, working harbour, Roman ruins and the usual seaside attractions. Adjacent to the wet and wild water park which attracts 350,000 visitors a year and next door to an international ferry terminal, the centre has a nautical feel to it. There is a great range of shops, many new, stocking famous name brands, all with up to 50% discounts off normal retail prices. Phone for more details.

SHARK GROUP

NORDSTROM HOUSE, NORTH BROOMHILL, NEAR AMBLE, MORPETH, NORTHUMBERLAND NE65 9UJ, ☎ 01670 760365, FAX: 01670 761343, **e-mail:** sales@sharkgroup.co.uk, www.sharkgroup.co.uk, 2–4 MON–FRI (ALL YEAR ROUND), 10–12 SAT (APRIL–MID-DEC).
FACTORY SHOP

Manufactures and sells in the factory shop Shark wetsuits, cag tops, sailing suits, boots, gloves and accessories for men, women and children at factory prices. Childrens one-piece wetsuits from £45, adults' two-piece wetsuits from £89, adults' one-piece wetsuits from £69. Also sell the Shark Country range of jackets, over trousers, fleeces and accessories in Real Tree camo and loden green. Special sales are held from time to time. The shop closes for the factory holidays in late May/early June and late July/early August and late October as well as bank holiday weekends.

THE FAMOUS BRUNSWICK WAREHOUSE LTD

UNIT 1A, ALBION RETAIL PARK, COWPEN ROAD, BLYTH, NORTHUMBERLAND NE24 5BS, ☎ 01670 367951, **e-mail:** northshoe@mcmail.com9–5.30 MON–SAT, 6 ON THUR, FRI, 9.- 530 SAT, 10–4.30 SUN.

2–3 GREEN MARKET, ELDON SQUARE, NEWCASTLE UPON TYNE, TYNE & WEAR NE1 6EP, ☎ 0191 261 2976, **e-mail:** northshoe@mcmail.com9–5 MON–SAT.

120–122 GRAINGER MARKET, NEWCASTLE UPON TYNE, TYNE & WEAR NE1 5QN, ☎ 0191 261 2903, **e-mail:** northshoe@mcmail.com9–5 MON–SAT.

UNIT 3, COAST ROAD RETAIL PARK, NORTHAM ROAD, NORTH SHIELDS, TYNE & WEAR, NE29 7PQ, ☎ 0191 257 2557, **e-mail:** northshoe@mcmail.com9–6 MON–WED, SAT, 9–7 THUR, FRI, 10–4.30 SUN.

UNIT 2B, GALLERIES RETAIL PARK, TOWN CENTRE, WASHINGTON, TYNE & WEAR NE38 7RW, ☎ 0191 417 7447, **e-mail:** northshoe@mcmail.com9–6 MON–WED, SAT, 9–7 THUR, FRI, 10–4 SUN. **PERMANENT DISCOUNT OUTLET**

See page 613 (CHESH)

TOG 24

32 HIGH FRIARS, ELDON SQUARE, NEWCASTLE UPON TYNE, TYNE & WEAR NE1 7XG, ☎ 0191 260 2810, **e-mail:** mail-order@tog24.com, www.tog24.com, 9–5.30 MON–FRI, 8 ON THUR, 9–6 SAT, 11–5 SUN.

ROYAL QUAYS FACTORY OUTLET CENTRE, COBLE DENE, NORTH SHIELDS, NEWCASTLE UPON TYNE, NEAR A19, TYNE & WEAR NE29 6DW, ☎ 0191 258 3754, **e-mail:** mail-order@tog24.com, www.tog24.com, 9.30–6 MON–SAT, 9.30–8 THUR, 11–5 SUN. **FACTORY SHOP IN A FACTORY SHOPPING VILLAGE**

See page 613 (CHESH)

TOYWORLD STORE FACTORY OUTLET

ROYAL QUAYS FACTORY SHOPPING OUTLET, COBLE DENE, NORTH SHIELDS, NEWCASTLE UPON TYNE, NEAR A19, TYNE & WEAR NE29 6DW, ☎ 0191 257 3333, www.toyworldstore.com, 10–6 MON–SAT, 11–5 SUN. **FACTORY SHOP IN A FACTORY SHOPPING VILLAGE**

See page 613 (CHESH)

NOTTINGHAMSHIRE

HAWK FACTORY CYCLE STORES

CRAVEN ARMS SITE, WOODBURGH ROAD, NOTTINGHAM, NOTTINGHAMSHIRE NG3 1AA, ☎ 0115 958 5900, 9–6 MON–SAT, 9–4.30 SUN. **FACTORY SHOP**

See page 616 (DERBY)

SPEEDO FACTORY SHOP

ASCOT ROAD, NOTTINGHAM, NOTTINGHAMSHIRE NG8 5AT, ☎ 0115 910 5142, 9–5 WED–SAT, 10–4 SUN. **FACTORY SHOP**

Speedo own-brand swimwear, goggles, sports bags, leisure tops and shorts at about half the normal retail price. Also Berghaus jackets, fleeces, trousers, walking boots, trainers and rucksacks. There is another Speedo outlet at the McArthurGlen Designer Outlet Centre in Mansfield, Derbyshire.

THE FACTORY SHOP

DONCASTER ROAD, LANGOLD, WORKSOP, NOTTINGHAMSHIRE DN22 7HY, ☎ 01909 731115, 9 -5.30 MON–SAT, 10–4.30 SUN. **FACTORY SHOP**

See page 613 (CHESH)

THE FAMOUS BRUNSWICK WAREHOUSE LTD

SPRINGFIELD RETAIL PARK, BULWELL, NOTTINGHAM, NOTTINGHAMSHIRE NG6 8AJ, ☎ 0115 951 9286, **e-mail:** northshoe@mcmail.com10–6 MON–WED, 10–7 THUR, FRI, 9–6 SAT, 10–4 SUN. **PERMANENT DISCOUNT OUTLET**

See page 613 (CHESH)

UNITED FOOTWEAR

BEECH AVENUE, OFF SHERWOOD RISE, OFF A60, NOTTINGHAM, NOTTINGHAMSHIRE, ☎ 0115 979 2799, 9–6.30 MON–FRI, 9–5.30 SAT, 10–4 SUN.

See page 623 (HAMPS)

WRANGLER LEE

PEPPER ROAD, CALVERTON, NOTTINGHAMSHIRE NG14 6LJ, ☎ 0115 965 4043, 9.30–5.30 MON–SAT. **FACTORY SHOP**

Previous season's stock as well as overmakes and seconds. Mens, women s and youths jeans and casual wear, plus Jansport backpacks, at 30% to 70% below high street prices.

OXFORDSHIRE

BICESTER OUTLET SHOPPING VILLAGE

PINGLE DRIVE, BICESTER, JUNCTION 9 OF M40, OXFORDSHIRE OX6 7WD, ☎ 01869 323200, 10–6 SEVEN DAYS A WEEK. **FACTORY SHOPPING VILLAGE**

Described as Bond Street comes to Bicester, Bicester Village has established itself as the UK s leading outlet shopping destination in terms of offering the largest selection of international brand names to choose from. Currently there are 90 outlet shops offering quality merchandise at discounts of up to 60%, sometimes even more. The choice of famous brands at Bicester Village is second to none. International names include a Polo Ralph Lauren store, which now stocks more goods from their women's sport and home collections, Donna Karan, Versace, Christian Lacroix, Escada, Cerruti 1881 and TSE Cashmere. New arrivals from the international fashion scene are La Perla, Nautica, Gieves & Hawkes, Tommy Hilfiger, Tods, MaxMara, Salvatore Ferragamo, Zegna, Calvin Klein, Charles Tyrwhitt, Sand, Links, Nautica, Musto and Holland & Holland. Both of Britain's leading designers, Nicole Farhi and Paul Smith, have shops with goods from their men's and women' s collections. Karen Millen and Whistles both cater for the younger set with much more womens fashion to be found in The Designer Room, Episode, Hobbs, Jigsaw and Inwear Matinique. Top high street names are also well represented by Benetton, Principles, French Connection, Monsoon and Racing Green. The more classic customer also has an unequalled choice with Burberry, Aquascutum, Jaeger, Mulberry and the Scandinavian company RedGreen, whose nautical style of casual wear is very popular. Rugged outdoor wear can be found at Helly Hansen, Tog 24, the climbing and walking specialist. Active sportswear, represented by Fred Perry and Reebok, has now been joined by one of America's most famous sports shoe brands, Vans. A comprehensive collection of shoes, including many ranges for children, can be found in Clarks, with elegant high fashion styles in Charles Jourdan from Paris. Also, for women's shoes, handbags and accessories, there is Jane Shilton; for luggage, there is the Samsonite shop, plus the exciting addition of the first TAG-Heuer outlet, which stocks end-of-line designer watches, all fully guaranteed, at very attractive prices. Lingerie and underwear is to be found at Warners and Triumph, with HOM, the French brand, for the men; and the finest French childrenswear at Petit Bateau; English fragrances at Penhaligon's; make-up, bath and body therapies at Molton Brown, and soaps and gifts at Woods of Windsor. For the home, there are Prices candles and towels and duvets from another leading French brand, Descamps; cutlery from Oneida; china and crystal from Villeroy & Boch and Waterford Wedgwood and fine linens and accessories for the home from The White Company. The Cosmetic Company stocks well-known skincare products, cosmetics and fragrances for men and women. Bicester Village is something akin to a one-floor department store and menswear, which can often be found in the designer shops, is also well represented in its own right with Dunhill, Blazer, Sand, Savoy Taylors Guild, Oscar Jacobson and Dockers, plus another international touch being provided by Cerruti Menswear, all offering good size ranges in a wide choice from very casual through to traditional business clothes. To complete the day out at Bicester Village, take home some popular titles from Books etc, get to know more about the location for a return visit from the Tourist Information Centre, and regain strength with top quality refreshment at Pret-A-Manger or Starbucks. There are cash machines, a children's play area, free parking and a shuttle bus (which is free from Thursday to Sunday) and taxi connection to Bicester North Station, which is on the Chiltern Railways line, and runs between Marylebone and Birmingham. Bicester Village is one hours drive from London, two miles from Junction 9 on the M40. Take the A41 and follow signs for Village Retail Park.

CLARKS FACTORY SHOP

BICESTER OUTLET SHOPPING VILLAGE, 27 PINGLE DRIVE, BICESTER, JUNCTION 9 OF M40, OXFORDSHIRE OX26 6WD, ☎ 01869 325646, 10–6 SEVEN DAYS A WEEK. **FACTORY SHOP IN A FACTORY SHOPPING VILLAGE**

See page 611 (CHESH)

NAUTICA

BICESTER OUTLET SHOPPING VILLAGE, PINGLE DRIVE, BICESTER, JUNCTION 9 OF M40, OXFORDSHIRE OX6 7WD, ☎ 01869 248770, www.nautica.co.uk, 10–6 SEVEN DAYS A WEEK. **FACTORY SHOP IN A FACTORY SHOPPING VILLAGE**

Nautica, the sports and casual wear brand, is now operating from its first factory shop at Bicester Village. It stocks men's sportswear and seasonal denim products.

REDGREEN

BICESTER OUTLET SHOPPING VILLAGE, PINGLE DRIVE, BICESTER, JUNCTION 9 OF M40, OXFORDSHIRE OX6 7WD, ☎ 01869 323324, 10–6 SEVEN DAYS A WEEK. **FACTORY SHOP IN A FACTORY SHOPPING VILLAGE**

See page 612 (CHESH)

THE FAMOUS BRUNSWICK WAREHOUSE LTD

THE CALTHORPE CENTRE, BANBURY, OXFORDSHIRE DX16 5HS, ☎ 01295 266519, **e-mail: e-mail:** northshoe@mcmail.com9–6 MON–SAT, 11–5 SUN. **PERMANENT DISCOUNT OUTLET**

See page 613 (CHESH)

TOG 24

BICESTER OUTLET SHOPPING VILLAGE, PINGLE DRIVE, BICESTER, JUNCTION 9 OF M40, OXFORDSHIRE OX6 7WD, ☎ 01869 323278, **e-mail:** mail-order@tog24.com, www.tog24.com, 10–6 SEVEN DAYS A WEEK. **FACTORY SHOP IN A FACTORY SHOPPING VILLAGE**

See page 613 (CHESH)

TOMMY HILFIGER

80–81 BICESTER VILLAGE, PINGLE DRIVE, BICESTER, OXFORDSHIRE, OX6 7WD, ☎ 01869 247699, FAX: 01869 247355, www.tommy.com, 10–6 MON–SAT, 11–5 SUN. **FACTORY SHOP IN A FACTORY SHOPPING VILLAGE**

See page 613 (CHESH)

SHROPSHIRE

HAWK FACTORY CYCLE STORES

15 CASTLE STREET, SHREWSBURY, SHROPSHIRE SY1 1QQ, ☎ 01743 344554, 9–6 MON–SAT, 9–4.30 SUN. **FACTORY SHOP**

See page 616 (DERBY)

STEWARTS

19–21 CROSS STREET, ELLESMERE, SHROPSHIRE SY12 0AW, ☎ 01691 624478, FAX: 01691 624478, 9.30–5.30 MON–FRI, 9–5.30 SAT, 10–4 SUN. **FACTORY SHOP**

See page 618 (DEV)

THE FAMOUS BRUNSWICK WAREHOUSE LTD

UNIT K, WREKIN RETAIL PARK, TELFORD, SHROPSHIRE TF1 2DE, ☎ 01952 222802, **e-mail:** **e-mail:** northshoe@mcmail.com10–6 MON–WED, 10–7 THUR, FRI, 9–6 SAT, 10–4 SUN. **PERMANENT DISCOUNT OUTLET**

See page 613 (CHESH)

SOMERSET

CLARKS FACTORY SHOP

CLARKS VILLAGE FACTORY SHOPPING CENTRE, FARM ROAD, STREET, JUNCTION 23 OF M5, SOMERSET BA16 0BB, ☎ 01458 843163, 9–6 MON–SAT, 11–5 SUN. **FACTORY SHOP IN A FACTORY SHOPPING VILLAGE**

See page 611 (CHESH)

CLARKS VILLAGE OUTLET SHOPPING

FARM ROAD, STREET, JUNCTION 23 OF M5, THEN A39, SOMERSET BA16 0BB, ☎ 01458 840064, **e-mail:** bgodwin@realm-ocm.com, www.clarksvillage.co.uk, APRIL–OCTOBER 9–5.30 MON–SAT, 11–5 SUN, NOVEMBER–MARCH 10–6, MON–SAT, 11–5 SUN. **FACTORY SHOPPING VILLAGE**

Purpose-built village of brick-built shops with extensive car parking facilities. Restaurant, fast food stands, carousel, indoor and outdoor play areas, and working village pottery and artists studio. Here, there are 57 shops with more planned. Shops include: Body Shop, Reebok selling the Reebok brand, Rockport and the Greg Norman Collection; Monsoon/Accessorize, Benetton, Wrangler, The Designer Room, Jaeger, Viyella, Alexon, Triumph/Hom, Gossard, Clarks Factory Shop, Rohan, Windsmoor, Liz Claiborne, Calvin Klein, Van Heusen, Next, Warehouse, Tom Sayers men's sweaters and trousers, Warners lingerie, Tog 24 outerwear, Jane Shilton handbags, luggage and shoes, The Suit Company and Blazer and Event jewellery. There is also a purpose-built china and glass pavilion and many other stores, all with up to

50% off famous name brands.

THE FACTORY SHOP LTD

MART ROAD, MINEHEAD, SOMERSET TA24 5BJ, ☎ 01643 705911, 9.30–5.30 MON–SAT, 11–5 SUN. **FACTORY SHOP**

See page 613 (CHESH)

THE SPORTS FACTORY

CLARKS VILLAGE FACTORY SHOPPING CENTRE, FARM ROAD, STREET, JUNCTION 23 OF M5, SOMERSET BA16 0BB, ☎ 01458 843156, 9–6 MON–SAT, 11–5 SUN. **FACTORY SHOP IN A FACTORY SHOPPING VILLAGE**

Wide range of sports clothes and accessories, some of which are only stocked in season (for example, cricket bats and tennis rackets in summer only). There is also cricket gear and leisure clothing (Timberland and Regatta). All are discontinued lines and are between 10% and 40% cheaper than in the high street.

TOG 24

CLARKS VILLAGE FACTORY SHOPPING CENTRE, FARM ROAD, STREET, JUNCTION 23 OF M5 SOMERSET BA16 0ND, ☎ 01458 840468, **e-mail:** mail-order@tog24.com, www.tog24.com, 9–6 MON–SAT, 10–5 SUN. **FACTORY SHOP IN A FACTORY SHOPPING VILLAGE**

See page 613 (CHESH)

STAFFORDSHIRE

ALLSORTS FURNITURE

23 HAMILL ROAD, BURSLEM, STOKE-ON-TRENT, STAFFORDSHIRE ST6 1AJ, ☎ 01782 833006, FAX: 01782 833006, 10–5 MON–SAT. **PERMANENT DISCOUNT OUTLET**

Household goods, furniture and exercise equipment at discounts of up to 60%. Furniture includes new three-piece suites, pine tables and chairs, television cabinets, nests of tables and kitchen furniture, as well as pine furniture imported from Denmark. Household goods include pots and pans, ovenware, casserole dishes, kettles etc. There are also suitcases, exercise bikes, step striders, walking and running machines, but no clothes, fabrics or curtains.

AMERICAN DISCOUNT GOLF

7581 NEWCASTLE ROAD, TRENT VALE, STOKE-ON-TRENT, STAFFORDSHIRE ST4 6QE, ☎ 01782 747787, FAX: 01782 844142, **e-mail:** stoke@americangolf.co.uk, 9.30–6.30 MON–FRI, 9–6 SAT, 10–4 SUN. **PERMANENT DISCOUNT OUTLET**

A wide selection of discounted golf equipment and apparel: sweaters, rainsuits, gloves, clubs, balls everything you need for a golf game. Stocks all the top names including Wilson, MacGregor, Callaway, Lynx and Mizuno. This is just one of 53 stores around the UK: dial 0845 050 5115 to be connected to your nearest branch.

BDF NEWLIFE

MARTINDALE, HAWKS GREEN, CANNOCK, STAFFORDSHIRE WS11 2XN, ☎ 01543 468888, FAX: 01543 505989, **e-mail:** info@bdfnewlife.co.uk, 9.30–10 MON–SAT, 10–4 SUN, 10–5 BANK HOLIDAYS. **PERMANENT DISCOUNT OUTLET**

8,000 square foot charity superstore which sells both new merchandise donated by most of the top high street stores and nearly-new. This is the sort of shop where you can find anything from a girls party dress to a two-seater rowing boat, men's shoes to a cooler bag, in between towels, jewellery, family clothes, furniture, mattresses (new with damaged packaging), beds, clocks, golf bags, umbrellas, wallpaper and designer dresses. Stock changes every 45 minutes. All the profits go to charity. Membership is by donation averaging £2. The shop is on one floor so is very accessible and has disabled toilet facilities. As the store also takes counterfeit goods from national Trading Standards departments seizures, stress is put on not believing any labelling or assuring authenticity. There are also branches in Kirkby-in-Ashfield, Nottinghamshire and Stoke Aldermoor, Coventry.

CYCLIST DISCOUNT CENTRE

DAVENPORT STREET, LONGPORT, STOKE-ON-TRENT, STAFFORDSHIRE ST6 4HS, ☎ 01782 822988, FAX: 01782 822988, 9.30–6 MON–SAT, 11–4 SUN. **PERMANENT DISCOUNT OUTLET**

Sells every type of bike from mountain and road bikes to hybrid bicycles from leading brands such as BMX, Cord Butler, Raleigh and B1 and K2, the latter two being imported continental makes as well as cheaper ranges from Concept, Universal and Baracuda.

FREEPORT TALKE OUTLET MALL

FREEPORT TALKE OUTLET MALL, PIT LANE, TALKE PITS, STOKE-ON-TRENT, OFF JUNCTION 16 OF M6 THEN TAKE THE A500 AND THE A34, FOLLOWING SIGNS TO TALKE, STAFFORDSHIRE ST7 1XD, ☎ 01782 774113, www.freeporttalke.com, 9.30–8 MON–FRI, 9.30–6 SAT, 11–5 SUN. **FACTORY SHOPPING VILLAGE**

Fully covered indoor outlet mall with a range of restaurants, including Burger King and Café Ritazza, and an indoor soft play area for children. Womenswear includes The Designer Room, Edinburgh Woollen Mill, Nickelby's, Pilot, Spotlight, Roman Originals and Leading Labels. Menswear includes The Suit Company, Double Two, Petroleum, Nickelby's, Madhouse and Tog 24. Childrenswear can be found at Used Co Kids. Other shops on site include: Claires Accessories, Charles Clinkard, Jane Shilton, Bags Etc, Trespass, Streetwise Sports, The Golf Company, Catalogue Bargain Shop, Julian Graves, Kitchen and Table, Toy World, Thorntons, Birthdays, Room, Mobile Phone Store, Book Depot, Picture Port, Ponden Mill and XS Music.

HAWK FACTORY CYCLE STORES

UNIT 1, WATLING STREET BUSINESS PARK, WATLING STREET, CANNOCK, STAFFORDSHIRE WS11 3NB, ☎ 01543 361656, 9–6 MON–SAT, 9–4.30 SUN.

FORGE LANE, CRADLEY HEATH, STAFFORDSHIRE B64 5AL, ☎ 01384 636535, 9–6 MON–SAT, 9–4.30 SUN. **FACTORY SHOP**

See page 616 (DERBY)

PARTRIDGE ENGLAND LTD

POWER STATION ROAD, TRENT MEADOWS, RUGELEY, STAFFORDSHIRE WS15 2HS, ☎ 01889 584438, 9–5 MON–FRI, 9–4 SAT. **FACTORY SHOP**

Partridge specialises in fashionable outdoor clothes and accessories. Ranges include waxed jackets, GoreTex jackets, waterproof jackets, tweeds, quilts, fleece jackets and waistcoats, knitwear, shirts, chinos, hats and caps. Discontinued lines are on sale at discounted prices with a minimum of 30% and up to 70% off during promotions.

TOG 24

FREEPORT TALKE OUTLET MALL, PIT LANE, TALKE PITS, STOKE-ON-TRENT, STAFFORDSHIRE ST7 1QE, ☎ 01782 787558, **e-mail:** mail-order@tog24.com, www.tog24.com, 9.30–8 MON–FRI, 9.30–6 SAT, 11–5 SUN. **FACTORY SHOP IN A FACTORY SHOPPING VILLAGE**

See page 613 (CHESH)

TOYWORLD STORE FACTORY OUTLET

FREEPORT TALKE OUTLET MALL, PIT LANE, TALKE PITS, STOKE-ON-TRENT, STAFFORDSHIRE ST7 1QE, ☎ 01782 777744, www.toyworldstore.com, 10–8 MON–FRI, 10–6 SAT, 11–5 SUN. **FACTORY SHOP IN A FACTORY SHOPPING VILLAGE**

See page 613 (CHESH)

SURREY

TOG 24

WHITGIFT CENTRE, CROYDON, SURREY CR0 1LP, ☎ 020 8680 7902, **e-mail:** mail-order@tog24.com, www.tog24.com, 10–6 MON–FRI, 8 ON THUR, 9–6 SAT, 10–5 SUN. **FACTORY SHOP IN A FACTORY SHOPPING VILLAGE**

See page 613 (CHESH)

SUSSEX

BRIGHTON MARINA

CITY OF BRIGHTON AND HOVE, EAST SUSSEX BN2 5WB, ☎ 01273 818504, FAX: 01273 818701, 10–LATE SEVEN DAYS A WEEK. **FACTORY SHOPPING VILLAGE**

The UK and Europe's largest marina. Boasts an exciting range of outlet shops combined with excellent bars, restaurants and leisure facilities. Currently hosts 11 outlet stores, such as PULSE skating solutions, The Factory Shop, Leading Labels and many more. The marina is currently investing millions into additional facilities, planned to open at the end of 2002, which will include a further 16 outlet stores including some household names.

RICARA

1 OLD MARKET AVENUE, CHICHESTER, SUSSEX PO19 1DR, ☎ 01243 778850, FAX: 01243 778850, www.ricara.co.uk, 9–5 MON–SAT. **FACTORY SHOP**

12 SURREY STREET, LITTLEHAMPTON, SUSSEX BN17 5BG, ☎ 01903 723843, FAX: 01903 718401, www.ricara.co.uk, 9–5 MON–SAT, 10–4 SUN.

22 HIGH STREET, LITTLEHAMPTON, SUSSEX BN17, FAX: 01903 723843, FAX: 01903 718401, www.ricara.co.uk, 9–5 MON–SAT. **FACTORY SHOP**

Sells mainly schoolwear and mens casual wear, and branded sportswear such as unisex cycling shorts, track suits and leggings at very reasonable prices discounts can be up to 50%. Brands include Nike and Adidas and specialised outfits for karate, kickboxing, boxing, tae kwon do, judo etc are also available.

STOCKLEY TRADING

UNIT N1011, BRIDGE ROAD, RIVERSIDE INDUSTRIAL ESTATE, LITTLEHAMPTON, SUSSEX BN17 5DF, ☎ 01903 732392, FAX: 01903 732754, **e-mail:** sales@stockleytrading.co.uk, www.stockleytrading.co.uk, 9–6 MON–FRI, 9.30–5 SAT, 10–4 SUN. **PERMANENT DISCOUNT OUTLET**

Warehouse shop which sells a range of outdoor wear and sportswear at wholesale prices. There is a good selection of branded leisurewear from Adidas, Umbro, Nike, Reebok, Fila, CAT, Fred Perry, Ben Sherman and Timberland among others. Stock varies, so phone to check stock before visiting if you are after something in particular. The outdoor wear department sells everything from underwear to hats and coats from names such as Regatta, Champion and Opentrack, and the equestrian department offers value for money on leading brands such as Weatherbeeta, Dublin, Stylo and Harry Hall.

THE FACTORY SHOP LTD

BRIGHTON MARINA, THE VILLAGE SQUARE, BRIGHTON SUSSEX BN2 5WA, ☎ 01273 818590, 10–6 MON–FRI, 10–6 SAT, 10.30–4.30 SUN. **FACTORY SHOP IN A FACTORY SHOPPING VILLAGE**

See page 613 (CHESH)

TOG 24

THE VILLAGE SQUARE SHOPS, BRIGHTON MARINA VILLAGE, BRIGHTON, SUSSEX BN2 5WA, ☎ 01273 818759, **e-mail:** mail-order@tog24.com, www.tog24.com, 10–6 MON–SAT, 10–5 SUN. **FACTORY SHOP IN A FACTORY SHOPPING VILLAGE**

See page 613 (CHESH)

WARWICKSHIRE AND WEST MIDLANDS

HAROLD BIRD & SON

NORTHGATE, ALDRIDGE, WALSALL, WEST MIDLANDS WS9 8UB, ☎ 01922 451444, 8–5 MON–THUR, 8–3.45 FRI, 9–2 SAT. **FACTORY SHOP**

Golf club manufacturers for some of the mail order catalogues such as Kays and Littlewoods, the brands sold in the factory shop here aren t well known but the prices are very keen indeed. Free parking.

HAWK FACTORY CYCLE STORES COVENTRY

82–92 FOLESHILL, FOLESHILL, COVENTRY, WARWICKSHIRE CV1 4JJ, ☎ 0247 622 2783, 9–6 MON–SAT, 9–4.30 SUN.

1781–1793 COVENTRY ROAD, SOUTH YARDLEY, BIRMINGHAM, WEST MIDLANDS B26 1DS, ☎ 0121 742 3332, 9–6 MON–SAT, 9–4.30 SUN. **FACTORY SHOP**

See page 616 (DERBY)

JAMES GILBERT FACTORY OUTLET

56 ST MATTHEWS STREET, RUGBY, WARWICKSHIRE CV21 3BY, ☎ 01788 333889, FAX: 01788 540795, **e-mail:** sales@james-gilbert.com, www.james-gilbert.com, 9–5 MON–SAT. **FACTORY SHOP**

Attached to the James Gilbert Rugby Football Museum selling rugby goods, outdoor wear and souvenirs and gifts. This rugby football specialist outlet has a constant throughput of discontinued lines at discounted prices from playing gear to leisure wear.

THE FAMOUS BRUNSWICK WAREHOUSE LTD

UNIT 12, ONE STOP SHOPPING CENTRE, 2 WALSALL ROAD, PERRY BARR, BIRMINGHAM, WEST MIDLANDS BA2 1AA, ☎ 0121 356 4107, **e-mail:** northshoe@mcmail.com9–6 MON–WED, SAT, 9–7.30 THUR, FRI, 11–5 SUN.

UNIT 2, TOWN WHARF, SHAW STREET, WALSALL, WEST MIDLANDS WA2 8PQ, ☎ 0192 616361, **e-mail:** northshoe@mcmail.com10–6 MON–WED, 10–8 THUR, FRI, 9–6 SAT, 11–5 SUN. **PERMANENT DISCOUNT OUTLET**

See page 613 (CHESH)

UNITED FOOTWEAR

926–928 STRATFORD ROAD, BIRMINGHAM, WEST MIDLANDS, ☎ 0121 778 1978, 9–5.30 MON–SAT, 10–4 SUN.

74 BRADFORD STREET, WALSALL, WEST MIDLANDS, ☎ 01922 641577, 9–5.30 MON–SAT, 10–4 SUN. **PERMANENT DISCOUNT OUTLET**

See page 623 (HAMPS)

WILTSHIRE

ADIDAS

MCARTHURGLEN DESIGNER OUTLET GREAT WESTERN, KEMBLE DRIVE, SWINDON, JUNCTION 16 OF M4, WILTSHIRE SN2 2DY, ☎ 01793 651854, FAX: 01793 651856, 10–6 MON–FRI, 8 ON THUR, 9–6 SAT, 11–5 SUN. **FACTORY SHOP IN A FACTORY SHOPPING VILLAGE**

See page 611 (CHESH)

MCARTHURGLEN DESIGNER OUTLET GREAT WESTERN

KEMBLE DRIVE, SWINDON, JUNCTION 16 OF M4, WILTSHIRE SN2 2DY, ☎ 0800 316 4352 FREE INFORMATION LINE OR 01793 507600, www.mcarthurglen.com, 10–6 MON–FRI, 8 ON THUR, 9–6 SAT, 11–5 SUN. **FACTORY SHOPPING VILLAGE**

The McArthurGlen Designer Outlet Great Western offers over 100 stores selling top names and designer brands at up to 50% off typical retail prices. Housed in the restored Great Western Railway buildings, everything is conveniently located under one roof. A large open plan area dedicated to homewares has everything for the house and home. Facilities include a food court, childrens play area, licensed creche and ample parking. Stores include: U Wear/I Wear, Warner UK Ltd, Antler, Ecco Shoes, Walker & Hall, Liz Claiborne, Viyella, Austin Reed, Suits You, Alexon, Jaeger, Windsmoor, Aquascutum, Olsen, Jacques Vert, Overland/Caterpillar, Episode, Long Tall Sally, Pilot, Triumph, Cotton Traders, Villeroy & Boch, Baron Jon, Clarks, HKA, Burberry, Remington, Regatta, Just Sweets, Easy Jeans, Ben Sherman, JoKids, Donnay, Le Creuset, Puma, Tog 24, XS, Gap, Big L, Soled Out, Ted Baker, Nike, Timberland, Quiksilver, Whittard, Marks and Spencer, Polo Jeans Company, Gant, Calp, The Design House, Dartington Crystal, Duvet and Pillow Shop, Henri Lloyd, Mexx, Ravel, The Luxury Beauty Store, Thomas Pink, Thorntons, Tie Rack, Julian Graves, Hanro, Jane Shilton, Birthday, Toy Zone, Bookends, Sofa Works, Designer Room, Petroleum, Next, Daks Simpson, Suit Company, Price's Candles, Claire's Accessories, Samsonite, Van Heusen, Cloverleaf, Poole Pottery, Spiegelau, Edinburgh Crystal, Woods of Windsor, Staffordshire Pottery, Waterford Wedgewood, Stuart Crystal, Gleneagles, The Garden Outlet, Ponden Mill, Jane Heath, Sheridan Australia, Tefal, Professional Cookware, and Oneida.

NIKE FACTORY STORE

MCARTHURGLEN DESIGNER OUTLET GREAT WESTERN, KEMBLE DRIVE, SWINDON, JUNCTION 16 OF M4, WILTSHIRE SN2 2DY, ☎ 01793 484440, FAX: 01793 430092, 10–6 MON–FRI, 8 ON THUR, 9–6 SAT, 11–5 SUN. **FACTORY SHOP IN A FACTORY SHOPPING VILLAGE**

See page 612 (CHESH)

OLD DAIRY SADDLERY LTD

GREENWAY FARM, TOCKENHAM, SWINDON, WILTSHIRE SN4 7PP, ☎ 01793 849284, **e-mail:** odsaddlery@talk21.com, www.olddairysaddlery.co.uk, 10–5 MON–FRI, 9.30–5 SAT, 10–1 SUN. **PERMANENT DISCOUNT OUTLET**

A large shop on a farm, selling outdoor wear, a wide range of horse rugs, saddlery, equipment and country clothing etc at competitive prices. Also stocks Cliff Barnsby, Maintain Horse and Kyra K saddlewear.

REGATTA

MCARTHURGLEN DESIGNER OUTLET GREAT WESTERN, KEMBLE DRIVE, SWINDON, JUNCTION 16 OF M4, WILTSHIRE SN2 2DY, ☎ 01793 520900, FAX: 01793 520900, www.regatta.com, 10–6 MON–FRI, 8 ON THUR, 9–6 SAT, 11–5 SUN. **FACTORY SHOP IN A FACTORY SHOPPING VILLAGE**

See page 620 (ESSEX)

THE FACTORY SHOP LTD

23 25 NEW PLACE, CORSHAM, WILTSHIRE SN13 0HL, ☎ 01249 712160, 9–5.30 MON–SAT, 10–4 SUN.

36–37 ROUNDSTONE STREET, TROWBRIDGE, WILTSHIRE BA14 8DE, ☎ 01225 751399, 9–5 MON–SAT.

24 MARKET PLACE, WARMINSTER, WILTSHIRE BA12 9AN, ☎ 01985 217532, 9–5 MON–SAT. **FACTORY SHOP**

See page 613 (CHESH)

TOG 24

MCARTHURGLEN DESIGNER OUTLET GREAT WESTERN, KEMBLE DRIVE, SWINDON, JUNCTION 16 OF M4, WILTSHIRE SN2 2DY, ☎ 01793 695966, **e-mail:** mail-order@tog24.com, www.tog24.com, 10–6 MON–FRI, 8 ON THUR, 9–6 SAT, 11–5 SUN. **FACTORY SHOP IN A FACTORY SHOPPING VILLAGE**

See page 613 (CHESH)

WORCESTERSHIRE

BLUNTS SHOE MARKET

51 UPPER TYTHING, WORCESTER, WORCESTERSHIRE WR1 1DT, ☎ 01905 27738, 9–5.30 MON–SAT. **PERMANENT DISCOUNT OUTLET**

This shoe retailer, established for over 135 years, sells shoes for all the family as well as clothes, handbags, sports shoes, boots, giftware and household goods, all at discounted prices. Famous brands include Clarks, K Shoes, Elmdale, Grenson, Loakes, Caterpillar and Adidas. Part of a national chain.

EVESHAM COUNTRY PARK SHOPPING AND GARDENING CENTRE

COUNTRY PARK MANAGEMENT, EVESHAM, AT THE NORTHERN END OF THE EVESHAM BYPASS, AT ITS JUNCTION WITH THE STRATFORD ROAD, WORCESTERSHIRE WR11 4TP ENQUIRIES: 01386 41661; GARDEN CENTRE: 01386 761888; APPLE BARN RESTAURANT: 01386 761333; VALE WILDLIFE VISITOR CENTRE: 01386 443348; COARSE FISHING/GOTTFRIED: 07973 147323, 9–6 MON–SAT (WINTER 5.30), 10.30–4.30 SUN. **FACTORY SHOPPING VILLAGE**

Courtyard shops and garden centre providing a wide variety of goods at bargain prices. Designer and brand name mens and women s fashions from Leading Labels, leisurewear from Cotton Traders, coordinated soft furnishings, bedlinen and duvets from Ponden Mill, household goods from Lifestyles, dried fuits, nuts and packaged herbs from Julian Graves, an extensive range of books from The Book Depot, plus quality plants, colourful pots and garden equipment. Luggage & Bags sells a range of quality branded luggage and travel goods at great prices. There is also restaurant, wildlife centre, coarse fishing on the River Avon, and a miniature railway for a real country day out.

UNITED FOOTWEAR

80–81 HIGH STREET, DUDLEY, WORCESTERSHIRE, ☎ 01384 238492, 9–5.30 MON–SAT, 10–4 SUN.

NEW ROAD, KIDDERMINSTER, WORCESTERSHIRE, ☎ 01562 744022, 9–6 MON–SAT, 8 ON THUR, 9–1 SUN. **PERMANENT DISCOUNT OUTLET**

See page 623 (HAMPS)

YORKSHIRE

ADIDAS

MCARTHURGLEN DESIGNER OUTLET YORK, ST NICHOLAS AVENUE, FULFORD, JUNCTION OF A19 AND A64, YORK, NORTH YORKSHIRE YO19 4TA, ☎ 01904 655 811, FAX: 01904 628509, 10–6 MON–SAT, 8 ON THUR, 11–5 SUN. **FACTORY SHOP IN A FACTORY SHOPPING VILLAGE**

See page 611 (CHESH)

ALT-BERG BOOTMAKERS

GALLOWFIELDS INDUSTRIAL ESTATE, RACECOURSE ROAD, RICHMOND, NORTH YORKSHIRE DL10 4XB, ☎ 01748 850615, **e-mail:** sales@altberg.co.uk, www.altberg.co.uk, **FACTORY SHOP**

Top quality, British craftsmen made walking, hiking, motor bike and military boots for men and women in a wide range of sizes. Nearby shop in Finkle Street, Richmond, sells outdoor clothes, some of which are at reduced prices.

BRANDMART

5 NORTH STREET, RIPON, NORTH YORKSHIRE HG4 1JY, ☎ 01765 601156, 9–5 MON–SAT. **FACTORY SHOP**

See page 621 (GLOS)

BRETT HARRIS LTD

WATERLOO MILLS, HOWDEN ROAD, SILSDEN, WEST YORKSHIRE BD20 0HA, ☎ 01535 654479, FAX: 01535 652503, **e-mail:** info@snugpack.com, www.snugpak.com, HOLDS OCCASIONAL FACTORY SALES. **FACTORY SHOP**

Manufacturers of sleeping bags, cold weather clothing, and compression sacks, most of which are exported, they sell discontinued lines, demo models and slight seconds at occasional sales. These sales, which are usually held on Saturday mornings, offer stock discounted by up to 50%. Phone for the date of their next sale.

BROOKS FACTORY OUTLET STORES

SOUTH LANE, ELLAND, NEAR HALIFAX, WEST YORKSHIRE HX5 0HQ, ☎ 01422 377337, 9.30–5.30 MON–SAT, 8 ON THUR, 11–5 SUN.

BUYWELL RETAIL PARK, THORP ARCH, WETHERBY, NORTH YORKSHIRE LS23 7BJ, ☎ 01937 541895, 9.30–5.30 MON–SAT, 11–5 SUN. **PERMANENT DISCOUNT OUTLET**

Walk through the store and you can't fail to find a bargain. New stock arrives daily from well-known names such as Nike, French Connection, Gabicci, Klass, Camille and Ben Sherman. Apart from mens and women's clothes, they sell sportswear, linens, lingerie, shoes, accessories, luggage, towels, coordinated bed linen, household textiles, duvets, pillows and lots more from names such as Monogram and Ponden Mill. Everything under one roof at up to 50% off high street prices. The Elland store has a coffee shop.

CATALOGUE DISCOUNT STORES

UNIT 6, HILLSBOROUGH BARRACKS SHOPPING MALL, SHEFFIELD, SOUTH YORKSHIRE S6 2GY, ☎ 0114 234 5726, FAX: 0114 234 5006, 9–5.30 MON–SAT, 11–5 SUN. **PERMANENT DISCOUNT OUTLET**

See page 614 (CO DURH)

CLARKS FACTORY SHOP

THE YORKSHIRE OUTLET, WHITE ROSE WAY, DONCASTER, SOUTH YORKSHIRE DN4 5JH, ☎ 01302 322663, 10–6 MON–SAT, 11–5 SUN. **FACTORY SHOP IN A FACTORY SHOPPING VILLAGE**

See page 611 (CHESH)

CRAGHOPPERS

FREEPORT CASTLEFORD DESIGNER OUTLET VILLAGE, CARRWOOD ROAD, GLASSHOUGHTON, CASTLEFORD, JUNCTION 32 OF M52, WEST YORKSHIRE Wf10 4SB, ☎ 01977 667111, FAX: 01977 557771, www.craghoppers.com, 10–8 MON–FRI, 10–6 SAT, 11–5 SUN. **FACTORY SHOP IN A FACTORY SHOPPING VILLAGE**

See page 626 (LANCS)

FREEPORT CASTLEFORD DESIGNER OUTLET VILLAGE

CARRWOOD ROAD, GLASSHOUGHTON, CASTLEFORD, JUNCTION 32 OF M52, WEST YORKSHIRE WF10 4SB, ☎ 01977 520153, www.freeportcastleford.com, 10–8 MON–FRI, 10–6 SAT, 11–5 SUN. **FACTORY SHOPPING VILLAGE**

Designer outlet village with over 75 shops, indoor and outdoor children's play areas and a wide range of restaurants with easy access from the M52 and 3,500 free car parking spaces. Shops include Amazing Jeans, Baron Jon, BhS For Less, Charles Clinkard, Clarks, Cromwells, Churchill, Ciro Citterio, Craghoppers, CBS, Claire's Accessories, Cotton Traders, Damart, Edinburgh Crystal, Donnay, Double Two, Event Jewellery, Easy Jeans, Edinburgh Woollen Mill, Elle, Fila, Giorgio, Gossard, XS Music, Jane Shilton, John Partridge, Kappa, Kitchen and Table, Kurt Muller, Leading Labels, Lee Cooper, Littlewoods, London Leathers, Mexx, Mobile Phone Store, Nike, Nickleby's, Next to Nothing, Outrage, Petroleum, Picture Port, Pilot, Ponden Mill, Proibito, Rio Jewellery, Roman Originals, Regatta, Room, Ice Jeans, Sergio Tacchini, Sportsmill, Spotlight, Startrite Shoes, Remainders Book Depot, Designer Room, Garden Outlet, Shoe Collection, Toy Factory, Time, X Catalogue Store, Thorntons, Trespass, Waterford Wedgwood, Windsmoor.

FREEPORT HORNSEA OUTLET VILLAGE

ROLSTON ROAD, HORNSEA, JUNCTION 38 OFF THE M62, EAST YORKSHIRE HU18 1UT, ☎ 01964 534211, www.freeporthornsea.com, 9.30–6 SEVEN DAYS A WEEK. **FACTORY SHOPPING VILLAGE**

The original British factory shopping village with over 40 shops offering discounts of up to 50% off high street prices. The village also boasts leisure attractions for all ages, ranging from an adventure playground to a themed soft play area and exciting rides for children. Womenswear labels include Alexon, Designer Room, Roman Originals, Arkwright's Mill, Select, Damart, Edinburgh Woollen Mill, Double Two, Mexx and London Leathers. Sportwear and outdoor clothing are available from Tog 24, Regatta and Sports Mill. Footwear is sold by Famous Footwear, Lilley & Skinner and Charles Clinkard. Menswear stores include The Suit Company, Double Two, Nickleby's, London Leathers and Giorgio. Other shops include Woods of Windsor, Thorntons, Masters Jewellery, Edinburgh Crystal, Waterford Wedgewood, Hallmark, Laura Ashley, The Book Depot, Claire's Accessories, Churchill China and Ponden Mill.

KARRIMOR

31 WINDSOR TERRACE, WHITBY, NORTH YORKSHIRE YO21 1ET, ☎ 01947 820945, www.karrimor.com, 9.30–5.30 MON–FRI, 9–5 SAT, 10–4 SUN. **FACTORY SHOP**

See page 616 (DERBY)

MCARTHURGLEN DESIGNER OUTLET

ST NICHOLAS AVENUE, FULFORD, JUNCTION OF A19 AND A64, YORK, NORTH YORKSHIRE YO19 4TA, ☎ 01904 682720, www.mcarthurglen.com/york, 10–6 MON–SAT, 8 ON THUR, 11–5 SUN. **FACTORY SHOPPING VILLAGE**

The McArthurGlen Designer Outlet York is one of Europe's largest covered designer outlets with over 120 stores offering top brands and designer labels with discounts of up to 50% off typical retail prices. Find everything from men's, women's and children's clothing to accessories, shoes, sportswear, luggage, homewares, toys, books, and gifts. Facilities include a food court, a children's play area and free parking. Stores include: Armani, Autonomy, Ben Sherman, Burberry, Calvin Klein Jeans, Cerruti 1881, Chilli Pepper, Cotton Traders, Daks Simpson, Episode, Escada Sport, Gap Outlet, Guess, Hugo Boss, Jacques Vert, Jaeger/Viyella, Jesire/Esensual, Kabuki, Klass, Levi's, Margaret Howell, Marks & Spencer Outlet, Mergler, Mountain Warehouse, Nitya, Olsen, Pilot, Polo Ralph Lauren, Pringle, Proibito, Proudfoot Leather, Roman Originals, Ronit Zilkha, Ted Baker, The Designer Room, Thomas Pink, Tog 24, Tommy Hilfiger, Windsmoor, Alfred Dunhill, Baronjon, Ben Sherman, Haggar, HKA, Marlboro Classics, Paul Smith, Petroleum, Pour Homme, Rockport, Suit Company, Suits You, Timberland, Adidas, Diadora, Donnay, Reebok, Toyworld, Birthdays, Bodum, The Body Shop Depot, Bookends, Franchetti Bond, Le Creuset, Oneida, Paper Mill, Price's Candles, Remington, Scent To You, Whittard Kitchen, Woods of Windsor, XS Music & Video, Bed & Bath Works, China China, Coloroll, Descamps, Garden Outlet, Jane Heath, La Casa del Christallo, Lights 4 Less, Pictureport, Room, Slipperbox, Spiegelau, Professional Cookware, Daniel Footwear, Famous Footwear, Pavers, Rockport, Shoe Studio, Soled Out, Julian Graves, Thorntons, Antler, Kangol, Liberty, Travel Accessory, Chapelle Jewellery, Claire's Accessories, Designer Shades, Monet, Tie Rack, and The Watch Store.

NIKE FACTORY STORE

MCARTHURGLEN DESIGNER OUTLET ASHFORD, KIMBERLEY WAY, ASHFORD, JUNCTION 10 OF M20, WEST YORKSHIRE WF10 4PS, ☎ 01233 661894, FAX: 01233 640535, www.nike.com, 10–6 MON–SAT, 8 ON THUR, 11–5.30 SUN.

FREEPORT CASTLEFORD DESIGNER OUTLET VILLAGE, CARRWOOD ROAD, GLASSHOUGHTON, CASTLEFORD, JUNCTION 32 OF M52, WEST YORKSHIRE WF10 4PS, ☎ 01977 517605, FAX: 01977 517704, www.nike.com, 10–8 MON–FRI, 10–6 SAT, 11–5 SUN. **FACTORY SHOP IN A FACTORY SHOPPING VILLAGE**

See page 612 (CHESH)

REGATTA

FREEPORT CASTLEFORD DESIGNER OUTLET VILLAGE, CARRWOOD ROAD, GLASSHOUGHTON, CASTLEFORD, JUNCTION 32 OF M52, WEST YORKSHIRE WS10 4SB, ☎ 01977 557771, FAX: 01977 557771, www.regatta.com, 10–8 MON–FRI, 10–6 SAT, 11–5 SUN.

FREEPORT SHOPPING VILLAGE, ROLSTON ROAD, HORNSEA, EAST YORKSHIRE HU18 1UT, ☎ 01964 536610, FAX: 01964 536610, www.regatta.com, 9.30–6 SEVEN DAYS A WEEK. **FACTORY SHOP IN A FACTORY SHOPPING VILLAGE**

See page 620 (ESSEX)

THE FACTORY SHOP

PARK ROSE POTTERY, CARNABY COVERT LANE, CARNABY, BRIDLINGTON, NORTH YORKSHIRE YO15 3QF, ☎ 01262 603518, 10–5 MON–SAT, 10.30–4.30 SUN.

WHEATLEY LANE, LEEDS ROAD, ILKLEY, WEST YORKSHIRE LS29 8BS, ☎ 01943 604514, 9–5.30 MON–SAT, 10.30–4.30 SUN.

LIGHTWATER VALLEY SHOPPING VILLAGE, NORTH STAINLEY, RIPON, NORTH YORKSHIRE HG4 3HT, ☎ 01765 635438, 10–6 MON–SAT, 11–5 SUN. **FACTORY SHOP**

See page 613 (CHESH)

THE FACTORY VALUE SHOP

LAWKHOLME LANE, KEIGHLEY, WEST YORKSHIRE BD21 3JQ, ☎ 01535 611703, 9.30–5 MON–SAT, 10.30–4.30 SUN. **FACTORY SHOP**

Wide range on sale includes men's, women's and children's clothing and footwear; household textiles; toiletries; hardware; luggage; lighting, electrical goods and bedding, most of which are chainstore and high street brands at discounts of approximately 30% to 50%. There are kitchen and furniture displays. The Cape Country Furniture range is on sale with free-standing kitchens, as well as living, bedroom and dining furniture. There are weekly deliveries and brands include famous names such as Adidas, Nike, Joe Bloggs and Brabantia, among others. Lines are continually changing. Few factory shops offer such a variety under one roof. To round off your visit, there are excellent tea rooms offering homemade foods and home baking.

THE FAMOUS BRUNSWICK WAREHOUSE LTD

UNIT 16, PHASE 2, FORSTER SQUARE RETAIL PARK, BRADFORD, WEST YORKSHIRE BD1 4BA, ☎ 01274 394699, **e-mail:** northshoe@mcmail.com, 9.30–6 MON, 9.30–8 TUE–FRI, 9–6 SAT, 11–5 SUN.

UNIT 2, THE WHEATLEY CENTRE, WHEATLEY HALL ROAD, DONCASTER, SOUTH YORKSHIRE DN2 4PE, ☎ 01302 343866, **e-mail:** northshoe@mcmail.com10–8 MON–FRI, 9–6 SAT, 10.30–4.30 SUN.

UNIT 1B, WESLEY SQUARE, GOOLE, SOUTH YORKSHIRE DN14 5EZ, ☎ 01405 768358, **e-mail:** northshoe@mcmail.com9–6 MON–SAT, 10–4 SUN.

UNIT 3, WESTSIDE RETAIL PARK, GUISELEY, LEEDS, WEST YORKSHIRE LS20 9NE, ☎ 01943 870565, **e-mail:** northshoe@mcmail.com10–6 MON–WED, SAT, 10–7 THUR, FRI, 10.30–4.30 SUN.

NORTHGATE RETAIL PARK, ALBION STREET, HECKMONDWIKE, WEST YORKSHIRE WF16 9LQ, ☎ 01924 408942, **e-mail:** northshoe@mcmail.com9–6 MON–WED, SAT, 9–7 THUR, FRI, 10–4 SUN.

UNIT 7, KINGSTON SHOPPING CENTRE, HOLDERNESS ROAD, HULL, EAST YORKSHIRE, HU9 2AA, ☎ 01482 211157, **e-mail:** northshoe@mcmail.com9–5.30 MON–WED, THUR, FRI, 9–6 SAT, 10–4 SUN.

UNIT 5A, HESSLE ROAD, HULL, HUMBERSIDE HU3 2AA, ☎ 01482 620519, **e-mail:** northshoe@mcmail.com9–5.30 MON–WED, 9–6 THUR–SAT, 10–4 SUN.

UNIT 16, KEIGHLEY RETAIL PARK, HARDINGS ROAD, KEIGHLEY, WEST YORKSHIRE BD21 3NJ, ☎ 01535 600793, **e-mail:** northshoe@mcmail.com10–6 MON–WED, SAT, 10–8 THUR, FRI, 11–5 SUN.

SEACROFT GREEN LEEDS, WEST YORKSHIRE LS14 6JD, ☎ 0113 265 1071, **e-mail:** northshoe@mcmail.com9–6 MON–SAT, 7 ON THUR, FRI, 11–5 SUN.

UNIT 2A, HEELEY RETAIL PARK, CHESTERFIELD ROAD, SHEFFIELD, SOUTH YORKSHIRE S8 0RG, ☎ 0114 258 3100, **e-mail:** northshoe@mcmail.com10–8 MON–FRI, 9–6 SAT, 11–5 SUN.

UNIT 20B, TEESIDE RETAIL PARK, TEESIDE, NORTH YORKSHIRE TS17 7BW, ☎ 01642 634163, **e-mail:** northshoe@mcmail.com10–8 MON–FRI, 9–6 SAT, 11–5 SUN.

UNIT 6, CLIFTON MOOR RETAIL PARK, CLIFTON MOOR, YORK, NORTH YORKSHIRE YO3 4WZ, ☎ 01904 690399, **e-mail:** northshoe@mcmail.com9–6 MON–WED, SAT, 9–7 THUR, FRI, 10.30–4.30 SUN. **PERMANENT DISCOUNT OUTLET**

See page 613 (CHESH)

THE MILL DISCOUNT DEPARTMENT STORE

BRADFORD ROAD, BATLEY, WEST YORKSHIRE WF17 5LZ, ☎ 01924 423172, FAX: 01924 446096, www.themillbatley.com, 9.30–5.30 MON–SAT, 10–4 SUN. **PERMANENT DISCOUNT OUTLET**

The Mill Discount Department Store is the largest Mill retail outlet in the UK, attracting more than one million visitors every year. Situated in a restored Victorian Mill in the heart of West Yorkshire, The Mill offers massive savings in a department-store format. This all-weather centre consists of four floors together with an external parade selling heavily discounted branded men's, women's and children's fashions, sportswear, homewares, accessories, music, vidoes, sunglasses, books, toys, perfumes, luggage, gifts, shoes, fabrics and lighting. Readmans, whose name is synonymous with unbeatable value, has opened there recently. This is the company's second major stores, offering good quality women's, men's and children's wear, lingerie, shoes, homewares and linens at remarkably low prices. Among over 300 brand names sold at The Mill are Puma, Pilot, HKA, Leeds United, Liz Claiborne, Elle, Jumper, Kasper, Amazing Jeans, Spicy, Urban Turban, Chilli Pepper, Tigi Wear, Ponden Mill, Woods of Windsor, Gleneagles Crystal, Dartington, Arthur Price, Skopos home furnishings, Jane Shilton, Book Depot, Toy Factory, Eye Zone, Famous Footwear, Hush Puppies, Lee Cooper, MX Active, Berghaus, Craghopper, Julian Graves, Fox's Biscuits, John Bull and Lion Confectionery. The complex can be reached by car, coach and train. Junction 40 of the M1 and junctions 27 and 28 of the M62 are within five and six miles of the site respectively. Batley Station on the Trans-Pennine railway is just five minutes walk from The Mill, providing easy access to Leeds and Manchester. There are more than 500 car parking spaces and coach parking is available. Amenities include children's creche, self-service licensed restaurant serving hot and cold food and drinks, Yorkshire Board Information Centre and access for the disabled.

THE SPORTS FACTORY

THE YORKSHIRE OUTLET, WHITE ROSE WAY, DONCASTER, SOUTH YORKSHIRE DN4 5JH, ☎ 01302 322 663, 10–6 MON–SAT, 11–5 SUN. **FACTORY SHOP IN A FACTORY SHOPPING VILLAGE**

See page 637 (SOM)

THE YORKSHIRE OUTLET

WHITE ROSE WAY, JUNCTION 3 OF M18, DONCASTER LAKESIDE, SOUTH YORKSHIRE DN4 5JH, ☎ 01302 366444, **e-mail:** cprimrose@realm-ocm.com, www.theyorkshireoutletcentre.co.uk, 10–6 MON–SAT, 11–5 SUN. **FACTORY SHOPPING VILLAGE**

The Yorkshire Outlet, Doncaster, has a great range of stores offering up to 50% off recommended retail prices, with new products and bargains arriving daily. The centre has a range of restaurants, a children's play area, wheelchair hire, and free parking.

TOG 24

THE YORKSHIRE OUTLET, WHITE ROSE WAY, DONCASTER, SOUTH YORKSHIRE DN4 5PH, ☎ 01302 364123, **e-mail:** mail-order@tog24.com, www.tog24.com, 10–6 MON–SAT, 11–5 SUN.

SPEN VALE MILLS, STATION LANE, HECKMONDWIKE, WEST YORKSHIRE WF16 0NQ, ☎ 01924 409314, **e-mail:** mail-order@tog24.com, www.tog24.com, 10–5 MON–SAT, 11–5 SUN.

FREEPORT HORNSEA OUTLET VILLAGE, ROLSTON ROAD, HORNSEA, EAST YORKSHIRE HU18 1UT, ☎ 01964 535308, **e-mail:** mail-order@tog24.com, www.tog24.com, 9.30–6 SEVEN DAYS A WEEK.

UNIT 23, BRUNSWICK PAVILION, SCARBOROUGH, NORTH YORKSHIRE YO11 2PA, ☎ 01723 377760, **e-mail:** mail-order@tog24.com, www.tog24.com, 9.30–5 MON–SAT, 11–5 SUN.

93–94 CHURCH STREET, WHITBY, NORTH YORKSHIRE YO22 4BH, ☎ 01947 820456, **e-mail:** mail-order@tog24.com, www.tog24.com, 10–5 EVERY DAY.

MCARTHURGLEN DESIGNER OUTLET YORK, ST NICHOLAS AVENUE, FULFORD, JUNCTION OF A19 AND A64, YORK, NORTH YORKSHIRE YO19 4TA, ☎ 01904 677814, **e-mail:** mail-order@tog24.com, www.tog24.com, 10–6 MON–SAT, 8 ON THUR, 11–5 SUN. **FACTORY SHOP IN A FACTORY SHOPPING VILLAGE**

See page 613 (CHESH)

TOMMY HILFIGER

MCARTHURGLEN DESIGNER OUTLET YORK, ST NICHOLAS AVENUE, FULFORD, JUNCTION OF A19 AND A64, YORK, NORTH YORKSHIRE YO1 4RE, ☎ 01904 627247, FAX: 01904 679268, www.tommy.com, 10–6 MON–SAT, 8 ON THUR, 11–5 SUN. **FACTORY SHOP IN A FACTORY SHOPPING VILLAGE**

See page 613 (CHESH)

UNITED FOOTWEAR

ROOLEY LANE, DUDLEY HILL, (A6036 RING ROAD), BRADFORD, WEST YORKSHIRE, ☎ 01274 680322, 9–8 MON–FRI, 9–5.30 SAT, 10–4 SUN.

178 EASTERLY ROAD, LEEDS, WEST YORKSHIRE, ☎ 0113 249 3244, 9–5.30 MON–SAT, 10–4 SUN. **PERMANENT DISCOUNT OUTLET**

See page 623 (HAMPS)

YOU & YOURS

WESTFIELD, INGLEBY ROAD (OPPOSITE GRATTAN), BRADFORD WEST YORKSHIRE BD99 2XE, ☎ 01274 624611, 10–5.30 MON, 10–8 TUE–FRI, 9–5.30 SAT, 11–5 SUN.
PERMANENT DISCOUNT OUTLET
Sells surplus stock from both Grattan and Freemans catalogues. Womenswear, childrenswear, menswear and household items, at up to 50% off catalogue prices. Includes a wide range of brands from both designer and high street on a regularly changing basis. Electrical goods are sold at discounts of up to 30% off catalogue prices, and include many big-name brands. 14-day refund policy.

SOUTH WALES

CRAZY MAC'S

PONTARDULAIS ROAD, FFORESTFACH, SWANSEA, SOUTH WALES SA5 4BA, ☎ 01792 585828, FAX: 01792 585566, **e-mail:** lss@salvage1.co.uk, www.salvage1.co.uk, 9.30–6 MON–THUR, 9.30–8 FRI, 9–6 SAT, 11–5 SUN. **PERMANENT DISCOUNT OUTLET**
An Aladdin's cave of salvaged stock for the avid bargain hunter, most of which has been the subject of insurance claims for fire or flood, salvage, bankruptcy or is simply clearance stock. Stock changes every two or three days and regular visitors have found anything from half price Kenwood Chefs, televisions and toys to furniture, kitchen items, linens and especially fantastic bargains in designer clothing. Yves Saint Laurent, Armani, Ungaro, Hugo Boss and Valentino, as

well as all major high street names, are just some of the names to be found (though the labels are often cut out). Discounts range from 50% to 80%. Phone first to check stock.

FESTIVAL PARK FACTORY SHOPPING VILLAGE

FESTIVAL PARK, VICTORIA, EBBW VALE, GWENT, SOUTH WALES NP23 8FP, ☎ 01495 350010, FAX: 01495 307363, 9.30–5.30 MON–SAT, 7 ON THUR, 11–5 SUN. **FACTORY SHOPPING VILLAGE**

Factory shopping village with over 40 shops offering a wide range of top brand goods and designer labels, many at half the recommended retail price. Factory shops include: fashion from Windsmoor, Designer Room, Leading Labels, Double Two, Pilot and Roman Originals; shoes from Pavers; china and crystal from Wedgwood and Stuart Crystal; golfing and sports equipment from Edinburgh Woollen Mill and Sportz; chocolates from Thorntons; leisurewear from Cotton Traders; luggage and bags from Antler; accessories from Claire's and lots more. Built on the former site of the National Garden Festival of Wales, there are over 70 acres of woodland and parkland to explore either on foot or on the land train which operates from Easter to September on weekends and during school holidays, weather permitting. Within the park you can visit the woodland craft centre, owl sanctuary and lakes. There is a 200-seat restaurant, with panoramic views over the valley, serving both snacks and cooked meals. The car park has dedicated spaces for both the disabled and parent and toddler. There is free wheelchair hire and baby changing facilities.

MCARTHURGLEN DESIGNER OUTLET

THE DERWEN, BRIDGEND, JUNCTION 36 OF M4, SOUTH WALES CF32 9SU, ☎ 01656 665700, www.mcarthurglen.com/bridgend, 10–8 MON–FRI, 10–6 SAT, 11–5 SUN. **FACTORY SHOPPING VILLAGE**

The McArthurGlen Designer Outlet in Bridgend is Wales' premier designer outlet. Set out in a friendly village street style the outlet has over 80 stores with everything from men's, women's and children's clothing to accessories, shoes, sportswear, luggage, homewares, toys, books, and gifts. All stock is excess stock sold by the retailers themselves at 30% to 50% off typical retail prices. The outlet also has over 1, 800 free parking spaces, a food court, two children's play areas and a nine-screen Odeon cinema. Stores include: Reebok, Calvin Klein, Tie Rack, Ciro Pearls, Monet, Picture Port, Ciro Citterio, Bookends, Bed & Bath, Clover House, Overland, Pepe, Famous Footwear, Nickelbys, The Suit Company, Birthdays, Toyzone, Vans, Red/Green, Whittards, Travel Accessories, Ecco, Jacques Vert, Warners, Next, Windsmoor, Pilot, Petroleum, Roman Originals, Antler, Julian Graves, The Watch Shop, Knickerbox, Wedgewood, The Garden Outlet, Claire's Accessories, Clarks, Donnay, JoKids, Ben Sherman, Smiths Signature, Spiegelau, Royal Worcester/Edinburgh Crystal, Littlewoods, Helly Hansen, Woodies, Lee Cooper, Van Heusen/Viyella/Jaeger, Ted Baker, Cotton Traders, Royal Doulton, Walker and Hall, Professional Cookware Co, Thorntons, Price's Candles, Mountain Warehouse, John Partridge, Remington, U Wear/I Wear, Nike, The Body Shop, Mexx, Suits You, Designer Rooms, Winning Line, Tog 24, Elle, Chilli Pepper/Watsons, HKA, XS, Soled Out, Timberland, Carphone Warehouse, Levi's, and The Craft Outlet.

NIKE FACTORY STORE

MCARTHURGLEN DESIGNER OUTLET WALES, THE DERWEN, BRIDGEND, JUNCTION 36 OF M4, SOUTH WALES CF32 9SU, ☎ 01656 655588, FAX: 01656 655056, www.nike.com, 10–8 MON–FRI, 9–6 SAT, 11–5 SUN. **FACTORY SHOP IN A FACTORY SHOPPING VILLAGE**

See page 612 (CHESH)

REDGREEN

MCARTHURGLEN DESIGNER OUTLET WALES, THE DERWEN, BRIDGEND, JUNCTION 36 OF M4, SOUTH WALES CF32 9SU, ☎ 01656 645464, 10–8 MON–FRI, 10–6 SAT, 11–5 SUN. **FACTORY SHOP IN A FACTORY SHOPPING VILLAGE**

See page 612 (CHESH)

STEWART'S

12 PIER STREET, ABERSTWYTH, CEREDIGION, SOUTH WALES SY23 2LJ, ☎ 01970 611437, FAX: 01970 611437, 9–5. MON–SAT.

UNIT 4, BETHEL SQUARE SHOPPING CENTRE, BRECON, POWYS, SOUTH WALES LD3 7HU, ☎ 01874 610260, FAX: 01874 610260, 9–5.30 MON–SAT, 11–4 SUN.

MARLAS ROAD, PYLE CROSS, NR BRIDGEND, MID GLAMORGAN, SOUTH WALES CF33 6AY, ☎ 01656 744988, FAX: 01656 744988, 9.30–5.30 MON–SAT, 12–4 SUN.

2–4 CARDIFF ROAD, Y TWYN, CAERPHILLY, MID GLAMORGAN SOUTH WALES CF83 1JN, ☎ 02920 888054, FAX: 02920 888054, 9–5.30 MON–SAT.

21–22 GREYFRIARS, CARMARTHEN, CARMARTHENSHIRE, SOUTH WALES SA31 3NB, ☎ 01267 232208, FAX: 01267 232021, 9–5.30 MON–SAT, 11–4 SUN.

LONDON HOUSE, HARFORD SQUARE, LAMPETER, CEREDIGION, SOUTH WALES SA48 7HD, ☎ 01570 422205, 9.30–5.30 MON–SAT, 5 ON WED.

52 STEPNEY STREET, LLANELLI, CARMARTHENSHIRE, SOUTH WALES SA15 3TR, ☎ 01554 776957, FAX: 01554 776957, 9–5 MON–SAT.

7–11 MONNOW STREET, MONMOUTH, MONMOUTHSHIRE, SOUTH WALES NP5 3EF, ☎ 01600 716926, FAX: 01600 716926, 9.30–5.30 MON–SAT.

GLAMORE TERRACE, NEW QUAY, CEREDIGION, SOUTH WALES SA45 9PL, ☎ 01545 560740, FAX: 01545 560740, 9.30–5.30 MON–SAT, 11–5 SUN.

144 HIGH STREET, PORTHMADOG, GWYNEDD, SOUTH WALES LL49 9NU, ☎ 01766 514166, FAX: 01766 514166, 9–5.30 MON–SAT, 12–4 SUN.

THE STRAND, SAUNDERSFOOT, PEMBROKESHIRE SOUTH WALES SA69 9GE, ☎ 01834 812579, FAX: 01834 812579, 9–5.30 MON–SAT, 10–5.30 SUN.

BREWERY TERRACE, SAUNDERSFOOT, PEMBROKESHIRE SOUTH WALES SA69 9HG, ☎ 01834 813169, FAX: 01834 813169, 9.30–5.30 MON–SAT, 10–5.30 SUN.

HIGH STREET, TENBY, PEMBROKESHIRE, SOUTH WALES SA70 7EW, ☎ 01834 844621, FAX: 01834 844621, 9.30–5.30 MON–SAT, 10–5.30 SUN. **FACTORY SHOP**

See page 618 (DEV)

THE FACTORY SHOP

SNOWDROP LANE, HAVERFORDWEST, SOUTH WALES SA61 1ET, ☎ 01437 766000, 9–5.30 MON–SAT, 10.30–4.30 SUN. **FACTORY SHOP**

See page 613 (CHESH)

TOG 24

MCARTHURGLEN DESIGNER OUTLET WALES, THE DERWEN, BRIDGEND, JUNCTION 36 OF M4, SOUTH WALES CF32 9SU, ☎ 01656 767033, **e-mail:** mail-order@tog24.com, www.tog24.com, 10–8 MON–FRI, 10–6 SAT, 11–5 SUN.

FESTIVAL PARK OUTLET CENTRE, VICTORIA, EBBW VALE, GWENT SOUTH WALES NP23 8FP, ☎ 01495 301902, **e-mail:** mail-order@tog24.com, www.tog24.com, 9.30–5.30 MON–SAT, 7 ON THUR, 11–5 SUN. **FACTORY SHOP IN A FACTORY SHOPPING VILLAGE**

See page 613 (CHESH)

NORTH WALES

COTSWOLD ROCK BOTTOM

HOLYHEAD ROAD, BETWS-Y-COED, CONWY, NORTH WALES LL24 0AP, ☎ 01690 710234, FAX: 01690 710304, **e-mail:** rockbottom@cotswold-outdoor.co.uk, 9–6 MON, TUE, THUR, SUN, 10–6 WED, 9–7 FRI, SAT. **PERMANENT DISCOUNT OUTLET**

Last season's colours and styles in outdoor clothing, fleeces, waterproofs, shorts, trousers, T-shirts, walking boots, camping gear, canoe and camping equipment. Top brands are sold including Lowe Alpine, Berghaus, Helly Hansen, North Face, Mountain Hardware and Columbia, some with markdowns of 50%. Excellent, if small, selection of canoe equipment with good discounts on spray decks, buoyancy aids and waterproofs. Climbing equipment includes shoes, harnesses, clips etc. All original prices displayed.

STEWART'S

23 MOSTYN STREET, LLANDUDNO, GWYNEDD NORTH WALES LL30 2NL, ☎ 01492 870733, FAX: 01492 870733, 9–5.30 MON–SAT, 10 – 4 SUN.

Y MAES, PWLLHELI, GWYNEDD NORTH WALES LL53 5HG, ☎ 01758 701130, FAX: 01758 701130, 9.30–5 MON–SAT. **FACTORY SHOP**

See page 618 (DEV)

THE FACTORY SHOP LTD

BRUNSWICK ROAD, BUCKLEY, CLYWD, NORTH WALES CH7 2EF, ☎ 01555 759017, FAX: 01555 759018, 9.30–5.30 MON–SAT, 10.30–4.30 SUN. **FACTORY SHOP**

See page 613 (CHESH)

THE FAMOUS BRUNSWICK WAREHOUSE LTD

UNIT H, FLINTSHIRE RETAIL PARK, HOLYWELL ROAD, FLINTSHIRE, NORTH WALES CH6 5GB, ☎ 01352 731942, **e-mail:** northshoe@mcmail.com, 9–6 MON–WED, SAT, 9–7 THUR, FRI, 10–4 SUN.

UNIT 4, ISLAND GREEN RETAIL PARK, WREXHAM, CLWYD, NORTH WALES LL13 7NB, ☎ 01978 310999, **e-mail:** northshoe@mcmail.com, 9–6 MON–SAT, 11–5 SUN. **PERMANENT DISCOUNT OUTLET**

See page 613 (CHESH)

SOUTHERN SCOTLAND

BALMORAL MILL SHOP

16 CHURCH LANE, GALSTON, AYRSHIRE, SCOTLAND KA4 8HF, ☎ 01563 820213, FAX: 01563 821740, **e-mail:** millshop@balmoralknitwear.co.uk, www.balmoralmill.com, 9–5 MON–SAT, 12–5 SUN, ALSO BANK HOLIDAYS. **FACTORY SHOP**

Sells cashmere and lambswool knitwear, embroidered knitwear, sweatshirts, polo shirts, bowling and golf attire and schoolwear, some of which is brand name and some own label, but all sold at factory direct prices. Women's, men's, children's and babywear are all stocked. Popular ranges are Alice Collins, Emreco, Lyle and Scott, Gabicci, Farah, Hodgsons and Poppy. Examples of prices include embroidered sweatshirts £14.95, polo shirts from £4.95, lambswool jumpers £22.95, seconds from £1.95. Telephone, mail and e-mail orders welcome.

GRETNA GATEWAY OUTLET VILLAGE

GLASGOW ROAD, GRETNA, SCOTLAND DG16 6GG, ☎ 01461 339028, FAX: 01461 339100 INFORMATION LINE, **e-mail:** info@gretnagateway.com, www.gretnagateway.com, 10–6 SEVEN DAYS A WEEK. **FACTORY SHOPPING VILLAGE**

Thirty trading outlets with a planned second phase of 20 shops. Includes Episode, Bags Etc, Designer Room, Directions Design Studio, Design House, DKNY, Edinburgh Woollen Mill, Jane Shilton, John Partridge, Price's Candles, Polo Ralph Lauren (stocking clothes for men, women and children as well as homewares), Reebok, Rockport, Tag Heuer, The Golf Company, Tog 24, Tommy Hilfiger, La Casa del Cristallo, Book Depot, Mexx, Claire's Accessories, Pavers Shoes, Chapelle Jewellery, Thorntons, Van Heusen and Whittards. There is a children's play area, disabled access, free parking and restaurants.

THE FACTORY SHOP LTD

DRAKEMYRE, DALRY, AYRSHIRE, SCOTLAND KA24 5JD, ☎ 01294 832791, 10–5 MON–SAT, 11–5 SUN.

54–60 HIGH STREET, ANNAN, DUMFRIES SCOTLAND DG12 6AJ, ☎ 01461 207687, 9–5 MON–SAT, 10.30–4.30 SUN. **FACTORY SHOP**

See page 613 (CHESH)

THE FAMOUS BRUNSWICK WAREHOUSE LTD

UNIT 14, THE LOREBURN CENTRE, HIGH STREET, DUMFRIES, SCOTLAND DG1 2BD,

☎ 01387 268758, **e-mail:** northshoe@mcmail.com9–5.30 MON–SAT, 12–4 SUN. **PERMANENT DISCOUNT OUTLET**

See page 613 (CHESH)

TOG 24

GRETNA GATEWAY OUTLET VILLAGE, GLASGOW ROAD, GRETNA, AYRSHIRE SCOTLAND DG16 5GG, ☎ 01461 339080, **e-mail:** mail-order@tog24.com, www.tog24.com, 10–6 SEVEN DAYS A WEEK. **FACTORY SHOP IN A FACTORY SHOPPING VILLAGE**

See page 613 (CHESH)

TOMMY HILFIGER

UNIT 36–37, GRETNA GATEWAY OUTLET VILLAGE, GRETNA, SCOTLAND DG16 5GG, ☎ 01461 339162, FAX: 01461 339017, www.tommy.com, 10–6 MON– SUN. **FACTORY SHOP IN A FACTORY SHOPPING VILLAGE**

See page 613 (CHESH)

CENTRAL SCOTLAND

ANTARTEX VILLAGE VISITOR CENTRE

LOMOND INDUSTRIAL ESTATE, ALEXANDRIA, DUMBARTONSHIRE G83 0TP, ☎ 01389 752393, FAX: 01389 750656, 10–6 SEVEN DAYS A WEEK. **FACTORY SHOP**

Large, rambling building with a coffee shop, well signposted off the A82, which has a vast retail area and additional manufacturing workshops where you can watch sheepskin jackets being made, or enjoy whisky tasting. It's difficult to tell how good the prices are as most are not double ticketed to show the original and sale price, but there are bargain sections. Edinburgh Woollen Mill has a large area, and other labels on sale include Pitlochry, Country Rose and Regatta. As well as clothes and shoes for men (new One Valley range of waterproof jackets, Hippo and PG Fields) and women and children, there are tea towels, toys, books, food, gifts, blankets, mugs, candles, CDs and tapes, table mats, sports equipment and countrywear. There is a big golf department selling Wilson, Spalding and Arnold Palmer equipment at discounts of 20% to 30% and lots of different workshops. Close to the Loch Lomond outlet village.

CASHMERE AT LOCHLEVEN

LOCHLEVEN MILLS, KINROSS, SCOTLAND KY13 8DH, ☎ 01577 861999, 9–5.30 MON–SAT. **FACTORY SHOP**

For over 100 years Todd and Duncan have been spinning finest cashmere yarn by the side of picturesque Loch Leven in Kinross. Their adjacent factory shop acts as an ideal focal point for those eager to purchase sophisticated cashmere lines at affordable prices. Visitors will be captivated by The Cashmere Story, a visually stimulating pictorial history of the journey taken by cashmere from the barren plains of Mongolia, through the traditional Scottish yarn spinning processes, and on to its final destination – the catwalks of the world's leading fashion designers. The shop provides a terrific selection of clothing of perfect quality, with no damaged goods or seconds. Labels stocked include their own popular Kinross Cashmere label, as well as complementary classics from famed collections such as Daks, Henri White, and Barrie, and the full Pringle range of both men's and women's fashion sportswear. The shop and visitors' centre are located about half an hour's drive from Edinburgh and just five minutes from the M90 motorway.

CORSTON SINCLAIR LTD

INDUSTRIAL PROTECTIVE CLOTHING, 36 GLENBURN ROAD, COLLEGE MILTON NORTH, EAST KILBRIDE, SCOTLAND G74 5BA, ☎ 01355 238161, FAX: 01355 263682, **e-mail:** sales@corstonsinclair.com, www.corstonsinclair.com, 8.30–4.30 MON–THUR, 8.30–4 FRI. **PERMANENT DISCOUNT OUTLET**

Designer trainers from Reebok, Nike, Dunlop and Inter trainers as well as protective clothing (safety helmets, safety footwear, overalls), sports and leisure items: jeans, shorts, sweatshirts, socks and underwear at discounts of between 20% and 30% off normal retail prices.

FREEPORT SCOTLAND OUTLET VILLAGE

FIVE SISTERS, WESTWOOD, WEST CALDER, NEAR JUNCTION 4 OF THE M8, WEST LOTHIAN, SCOTLAND EH55 8QB, ☎ 01501 763488, www.freeportscotland.com, 10–6 SEVEN DAYS A WEEK. **FACTORY SHOPPING VILLAGE**

Designer outlet village with more than 25 shops offering up to 50% off high street prices, as well as a café and free parking. Outlets for women include The Designer Room, Mexx, London Leathers,Versace, Klass, Select, Iceberg and Jean Scene. Menswear is available from Ciro Citterio, Versace, Double Two, Madhouse, Leading Labels, Iceberg, Mexx, Nickleby's and Proibito. Sweet-toothed visitors can savour the chocolates at Thorntons. Other shops include Tog 24, Bags Etc, Charles Clinkard, Outdoor Adventure, Book Depot, Churchill China and Ponden Mill.

LOCH LOMOND FACTORY OUTLETS

MAIN STREET, ALEXANDRIA, JUNCTION 17 OF M8 THEN A82, LOCH LOMOND, SCOTLAND G83 0UG, ☎ 01389 710077 , FAX: 01389 605500 INFORMATION LINE., ☎ 01389 607259, **e-mail:** info@lochlomondoutlets.co.uk, www.lochlomondoutletcentre.co.uk, 9.30–5.30 SEVEN DAYS A WEEK. **FACTORY SHOPPING VILLAGE**

Just off the A82, the main route between Glasgow and the West Highlands and Islands, and only one mile from Loch Lomond, this factory outlet centre combines history, heritage, adventure and shopping under one roof. Shops include Bags Etc selling luggage items; Book Depot, Designer Room (Klass, DKNY, Elle), Global Emporium for gifts, Jean Scene for branded denim wear; Julian Graves foods and nut mixes; Leading Labels, Nickleby's, Pavers Shoes, Ponden Mill for bed-linen and bathroom ware; Ramseys womenswear; Room offering homes accessories and furniture; Stuart Crystal; Sportz selling sportswear from Adidas, Nike, etc; Tog 24 for outdoor wear; Trespass; Card & Party Place (greetings cards and posters). There is also Ceramic Experience (a unique opportunity to decorate your own ceramics and pottery merchandise plus a children's soft play area), a Motoring Heritage Centre telling the history of the Scottish motor car industry with a collection of vintage cars, and The Gallery Cafe selling meals, snacks and sandwiches.

MACKINNON MILLS

KIRKSHAW ROAD, COATBRIDGE, SCOTLAND ML5 4SL, ☎ 01236 440702, 10–5.30 MON–FRI, 10–6 SAT–SUN. **FACTORY SHOP**

Working woollen mill that sells some seconds and perfect woollens with labels such as Lyle & Scott, Antartex and Edinburgh Woollen Mill. They also sell golf equipment, Scottish music tapes, dress jewellery, books, shoes, bags and bedding. Meals are served in the coffee shop.

MCARTHURGLEN DESIGNER OUTLET

ALMONDVALE AVENUE, LIVINGSTON, WEST LOTHIAN, JUNCTION 3 OFF THE M8, BETWEEN EDINBURGH AND GLASGOW, SCOTLAND EH54 6QX, ☎ 01506 423600, FAX: 01506 423602, www.mcarthurglen.com/livingston, 10–6 SEVEN DAYS A WEEK, 8 ON THUR. **FACTORY SHOPPING VILLAGE**

The McArthurGlen Designer Outlet Livingston offers over 80 stores full of top brands and designer labels at up to 50% off typical retail prices. There is a food court, cafés and restaurants as well as an eight-screen licensed cinema, health and fitness club and free parking for 1, 800 cars. Stores include: Gap Outlet, XS, Designer Shades, Marks & Spencer Outlet, The Body Shop Outlet, Van Heusen/Jaeger/Viyella, One to One, Antler, Clarks, Suits You, Chappelle, Banana Books, Toyworld, Donnay, Whittard, Price's Candles, Aquascutum, Revlon, The Paper Mill Shop, Regatta, Jane Shilton, Brand Fushion, Early Learning Centre, CK Jeans, Jockey, Autonomy, Cotton Traders, Black and Decker, Room, Surf, Skate and Snow, Ronit Zilkha, Ted Baker, Proudfoot, Thornton's, Arran Aromatics, Bon Bleu, Jokids, Soled Out, Windsmoor, Suit Co, Easy Jeans, Roman Originals, Julian Graves, Directions, Sportz, Lilley & Skinner, Armani, Ben Sherman, Petroleum, Samsonite, Tog 24, Outdoor Scene, Trespass, Logo, Levi's, Professional Cookware, Coloroll, Jane Heath, Bed & Bath, Denby, Pictureport, Waterford/Wedgewood, Poole Pottery, Lights 4 Less, Cloverhouse, Gleneagles, Edinburgh Crystal and Speigelau.

NIKE FACTORY STORE

UNIT 28, STERLING MILLS DESIGNER OUTLET VILLAGE, TILLICOULTRY, CLACKMANNANSHIRE, SCOTLAND FK13 6HN, ☎ 01259 750148, FAX: 01259 753867, www.nike.com, 10–6 SEVEN DAYS A WEEK. **FACTORY SHOP IN A FACTORY SHOPPING VILLAGE**

See page 612 (CHESH)

NORTH CAPE (SCOTLAND) LTD

ROYAL SCOT LTD, BANDEATH ESTATE, THROSK, NEAR STIRLING, SCOTLAND FK7 7NP, ☎ 01786 819700, FAX: 01786 819701, **e-mail:** info@north-cape.com, www.north-cape.com, 1–4 MON–FRI, 12–4 SAT. **FACTORY SHOP**

North Cape manufactures a leading range of outdoor clothing, including Rhovyl thermal underwear, Coolmax underwear, Polartec fleece ranges and waterproofs. The factory shop sells seconds, surplus stock and discontinued lines at large discounts.

REGATTA

MCARTHURGLEN DESIGNER OUTLET VILLAGE, ALMONDALE AVENUE, LIVINGSTON, SCOTLAND EH54 6QX, ☎ 01506 429813, FAX: 01506 429813, www.regatta.com, 10–6 SEVEN DAYS A WEEK, 8 ON THUR. **FACTORY SHOP IN A FACTORY SHOPPING VILLAGE**

See page 620 (ESSEX)

SNOW SENSE

2 HOWE STREET, EDINBURGH, SCOTLAND EH3 6TD, ☎ 0131 662 4487 **e-mail:** sue@snowsense.co.uk, www.snowsense.co.uk, 5.30–7.30 TUE AND THUR (MID OCT–END MAR), 12.30–5 FRI, 10.30–5.30 SAT, SUN DURING HIGH SEASON ONLY. **DRESS AGENCY**

Open only during the ski season, there is everything here that the enthusiastic skier could want, from new and nearly-new salopettes and ski jackets to gloves, goggles and other accessories as well as the hardware: blades, boards, boots, skis and poles. Also have a selection of ex-display clothing and equipment from top brand names including Lange, Saloman, Nordica and SOS. Children's gear a speciality.

STERLING MILLS DESIGNER OUTLET VILLAGE

TILLICOULTRY, NEAR STIRLING, CLACKMANANSHIRE, MIDWAY BETWEEN M9 AND M90, SCOTLAND FK13 6HQ, ☎ 01259 752100, www.sterlingmills.com, 10–6 SEVEN DAYS A WEEK. **FACTORY SHOPPING VILLAGE**

This factory shopping centre guarantees prices of at least 30% off typical high street prices and sometimes as much as 70%. Outlets so far include Mountain Warehouse, Adidas, Penny Plain, Enigma Candles, Jacques Vert, The Officers' Club, Bed & Bath Works, Book Depot, Claire's Accessories, Cotton Traders, Denby Pottery, Designer Room, Double Two, Julian Graves, Nike, Nickelby's, Pavers Shoes, Proibito, Roman Originals, Thorntons, Tog 24, Bags Etc, USA Golf Wear House, VF Corporation Factory Store, Winning Line, XS Music, Charles Clinkard, Naf Naf Chevignon, The Toy Factory, Pilot, Real Jewellery, The Sweet Factory, The Design House, Watson Chilli Pepper, Regatta, Blue Ridge, Playtex and more. There's a restaurant on site, and the very large Sterling Furniture Centre is situated opposite.

THE FACTORY SHOP LTD

56 CHAPEL STREET, CARLUKE, SOUTH LANARKSHIRE, SCOTLAND ML8 4BA, ☎ 01555 759017, FAX: 01555 759018, 9–5 MON–FRI, 9–5.30 SAT, 10–5 SUN.

BURNSIDE MILL, CUPAR, FIFE, SCOTLAND KY15 4DQ, ☎ 01334 650661, FAX: 01334 656772, 9.30–5.30 MON–SAT, 10–5 SUN. **FACTORY SHOP**

See page 613 (CHESH)

THE FAMOUS BRUNSWICK WAREHOUSE LTD

UNIT 1, KILBOWIE RETAIL PARK, CLYDEBANK, SCOTLAND G81 4QH, ☎ 0141 952 4914, **e-mail:** northshoe@mcmail.com, 10–6 MON–SAT, 7 ON THUR, 10–5 SUN.

UNIT 3, FARADAY RETAIL PARK, COATBRIDGE, SCOTLAND ML5 3SQ, ☎ 01236 449095, **e-mail:** northshoe@mcmail.com, 10–6 MON–WED, 10–8 THUR, FRI, 9–6 SAT, 10–6 SUN.

ST JAMES RETAIL PARK, DUMBARTON, SCOTLAND G82 1RB, ☎ 01389 762897, **e-mail:** northshoe@mcmail.com10–6 MON–WED, SAT, SUN, 10–7 THUR, 9–6 FRI.

UNIT 8, MEADOWBANK RETAIL PARK, MARIONVILLE ROAD, EDINBURGH SCOTLAND EH7, FAX: 0131 652 2885, **e-mail:** northshoe@mcmail.com, 10–6 MON–WED, 10–8 THUR, 10–7 FRI, 9–6 SAT, 11–5 SUN.

11 GRAHAMS ROAD, CENTRAL RETAIL PARK, FALKIRK, SCOTLAND FK1 1LD, ☎ 01324 671177, **e-mail:** northshoe@mcmail.com, 10–6 MON–WED, 10–7 THUR, FRI, 9–6 SAT, 10–5 SUN.

UNIT 9, HAMILTON RETAIL PARK, DOUGLAS STREET, HAMILTON, SCOTLAND ML3 0DF, ☎ 01698 286120, **e-mail:** northshoe@mcmail.com, 10–7 MON–FRI, 8 ON THUR, 9–6 SAT, 10–6 SUN.

UNIT 4, PHASE 2, RIVERWAY RETAIL PARK, IRVINE, SCOTLAND KA12 8AG, ☎ 01294 204042, **e-mail:** northshoe@mcmail.com, 9–6 MON–WED, SAT, 9–7 THUR, FRI, 10–6 SUN.

PORTLAND GATE, KILMARNOCK, SCOTLAND KA1 1HZ, ☎ 01563 537145, **e-mail:** northshoe@mcmail.com, 9–5.30 MON–WED, 9–6 THUR–SAT, 11–5 SUN.

8–20 HIGH STREET, KIRKCALDY, SCOTLAND KY1 1LU, ☎ 01592 205257, **e-mail:** northshoe@mcmail.com, 9–6 MON–SAT, 11–5 SUN.

UNITS 55A AND 25, THE PLAZA SHOPPING CENTRE, PAISLEY, SCOTLAND PA1 1EL, ☎ 0141 848 9127, **e-mail:** northshoe@mcmail.com, 9–6 MON–SAT, 11–5 SUN.

UNIT 3A, WEST END RETAIL PARK, CROW ROAD, PARTICK, GLASGOW, SCOTLAND G11 7SA, ☎ 0141 337 3822, **e-mail:** northshoe@mcmail.com, 10–6 MON–WED, 10–8 THUR, 10–7 FRI, 9–6 SAT, 10–6 SUN.

181 NETHERAULD HOUSE ROAD, POLLOCKSHAWS, GLASGOW, SCOTLAND G43 2YP, ☎ 0141 632 5841, **e-mail:** northshoe@mcmail.com10–6 MON–WED, 10–7 THUR, FRI, 9–6 SAT, 10–5.30 SUN.

UNIT 10, THE CALEDONIAN CENTRE, NEW ASHTREE STREET, WISHAW, SCOTLAND ML2 7UR, ☎ 01698 350055, **e-mail:** northshoe@mcmail.com10–6 MON–WED, 10–8 THUR, FRI, 9–6 SAT, 10–6 SUN. **PERMANENT DISCOUNT OUTLET**

See page 613 (CHESH)

TOG 24

LOCH LOMOND FACTORY OUTLETS, MAIN STREET, ALEXANDRIA, STRATHCLYDE, SCOTLAND G83 0UG, ☎ 01389 607175, **e-mail:** mail-order@tog24.com, www.tog24.com, 9.30–5.30 SEVEN DAYS A WEEK.

MCARTHURGLEN DESIGNER OUTLET LIVINGSTON, ALMONDVALE AVENUE, LIVINGSTON, SCOTLAND EH54 6QX, ☎ 01506 413630, **e-mail:** mail-order@tog24.com, www.tog24.com, 10–6 SEVEN DAYS A WEEK, 8 ON THUR.

STERLING MILLS DESIGNER OUTLET VILLAGE, TILLICOULTRY, CLACKMANNANSHIRE SCOTLAND FK13 6HN, ☎ 01259 753911, **e-mail:** mail-order@tog24.com, www.tog24.com, 10–6 SEVEN DAYS A WEEK.

FREEPORT VILLAGE FIVE SISTERS, WEST CALDER, JUNCTION 4 OF M8, WEST LOTHIAN SCOTLAND EH55 8QB, ☎ 01501 762823, **e-mail:** mail-order@tog24.com, www.tog24.com, 10–6 SEVEN DAYS A WEEK. **FACTORY SHOP IN A FACTORY SHOPPING VILLAGE**

See page 613 (CHESH)

SCOTTISH HIGHLANDS AND ISLANDS

TOG 24

CITY QUAY, CAMPERDOWN STREET, DUNDEE, SCOTLAND DD1 3ND, ☎ 01382 223883, **e-mail:** mail-order@tog24.com, www.tog24.com, 9.30–5.30 MON–SAT, 11–5 SUN. **FACTORY SHOP**

See page 613 (CHESH)

NORTHERN IRELAND

GILFORD MILL

45 MINUTES SOUTH OF BELFAST, NEAR BANBRIDGE, NORTHERN IRELAND. **FACTORY SHOPPING VILLAGE**

Due to open in autumn 2003; these were the only details we had as we went to press.

OCTOPUS SPORTSWEAR MFG LTD

UNIT 1, DUBLIN ROAD INDUSTRIAL ESTATE, STRABANE, COUNTY TRYONE, NORTHERN IRELAND BT82 9EA, ☎ 028 7188 2320, 9–5.30 MON–THUR, 10–4 FRI–SAT. **FACTORY SHOP**

Manufactures own-brand sportswear: shorts, jerseys, socks, pants, hooded tops, sweatshirts and sell seconds and clearance lines at discounts of between 50% and 75%.

Food & Leisure

BRISTOL

BOOKENDS

UNIT 23, EASTWALK, YATE SHOPPING CENTRE, BRISTOL BS17 0AS, ☎ 01454 312359, FAX: 01497 847889, **e-mail:** bookends@madasafish.com, www.bookspostfree.com, 9–5.30 MON–SAT. **SECONDHAND SHOP**

Publishers' returns, as well as new and review copies, including recently published books, usually at half price or below.

BUCKINGHAMSHIRE

BOOKENDS

22 HIGH STREET, MARLOW, BUCKINGHAMSHIRE SL7 1AW, ☎ 01628 890 007, FAX: 01497 847889, **e-mail:** bookends@madasafish.com, www.bookspostfree.com, 9.30–6 MON–SAT, 11–5 SUN. **SECONDHAND SHOP**

See above.

THE CHILTERN BREWERY

NASH LEE ROAD, TERRICK, AYLESBURY, BUCKINGHAMSHIRE HP17 0TQ, ☎ 01296 613647, www.chilternbrewery.co.uk, 9–5 MON–SAT. **FOOD AND DRINK DISCOUNTER**

Four beers are now produced here: three draught and four bottled. Take your own pint container and fill with beer from £1.50 per pint. Also stocks mustards and chutney with beer, marmalade with malt, pickled onions with hops, and fruit cake with barley wine. Also three new beer sausages and beer shampoo. Their latest development includes personalised beer labels for as little as £26.95 for 12 bottles. There is free parking and a museum with conducted tours on Saturdays: phone first for details.

WILKINSON STORES

UNIT 1–2, BRITANNIA WALK, AYLESBURY, BUCKINGHAMSHIRE HP20 1QR, ☎ 01296 399940, www.wilko.co.uk, 9–5.30 MON–SAT, 10.30–4.30 SUN. **PERMANENT DISCOUNT OUTLET**

Family-owned business offering value on the high street through its 205 stores, selling 25,000 high quality, low-priced essential everyday products for all the family including kitchenware, household disposables, clothing, DIY decoration, stationery, homewares, bedlinen, picture frames, china, cutlery, toys, pet foot, curtains, mirrors, gardening equipment including outdoor furniture, Christmas decorations, confectionery and seasonal goods. It also caters for the ardent gardener with fertiliser, grass seed – loose or boxed – plants, insecticides, composts – both multi-purpose or tub and basket – garden tools, strimmers, hoses and attachments, watering cans, water butts, wheelbarrows, and reels on wheels. In season, they sell bedding plants, garden lights, coolboxes, paint, paint brushes and rollers, and climbing plants such as honeysuckle, but as the summer progresses these are replaced by barbecues and picnic ranges. Phone 01909 505505 for details of your local outlet or visit their website.

CAMBRIDGESHIRE

GALLOWAY & PORTER LTD

THE PADDOCKS, CHERRYHINTON ROAD, CAMBRIDGE, CAMBRIDGESHIRE, ☎ 01223 367876, PHONE FOR SALE DATES.

30 SIDNEY STREET, CAMBRIDGE, CAMBRIDGESHIRE CB2 3HS, ☎ 01223 367876, **e-mail:** galporl@aol.com, 8.45–5 MON–FRI, 9–5.15 SAT. **PERMANENT DISCOUNT OUTLET**

Regular book warehouse sales are held at this outlet about once a month on a Saturday from 9am to 5pm at which most books cost £1, regardless of the original price. There are new hardback copies in the huge variety of tomes, covering many subjects including children's. Free parking. The branch at Sidney Street stocks secondhand as well as new discounted books.

THE WORKS

BRIDGE STREET, PETERBOROUGH, CAMBRIDGESHIRE PE1 1DW, ☎ 01733 358496, 9–5.30 MON–FRI, 7 ON THUR, 8–6 SAT, 10–4 SUN. **PERMANENT DISCOUNT OUTLET**

One of 163 branches of this remainders company for books, particularly travel guides and glossy hardbacks, cards, gifts, toys, ornaments, gift wrap, stationery, videos and CDs, all at discounted prices. Phone 0121 313 6000 for your local branch.

CHESHIRE

BOOKTHRIFT

71–73 CHESTERGATE, MACCLESFIELD, CHESHIRE SK11 6DY, ☎ 01625 615046, 9.30–5.30 MON–SAT.

19 PILLORY STREET, NANTWICH, CHESHIRE CW5 5BZ, ☎ 01270 611664, 9.30–5 MON–SAT. **PERMANENT DISCOUNT OUTLET**

One of many outlets supplied by a central warehouse with remaindered books, all first hand, sold at around half price. Most are the result of over buying on the part of bookshops and overprints by publishers and they include hard and soft backs, fiction, fact, reference and academic. They sell some stationery and local ordnance survey maps at full price. Also stock a wide range of current bestselling titles at discounted prices of up to 25%, sometimes more. A 10% discount is given on all customer orders. Phone 01728 604604 for details of your nearest outlet.

MCARTHURGLEN DESIGNER OUTLET

KINSEY ROAD, NEAR ELLESMERE PORT, JUNCTION 10 OF M53, CHESHIRE CH65 9JJ, ☎ 0800 316 4352 FREE INFORMATION LINE OR 0151 348 5600, FAX: 0151 357 3744, www.mcarthurglen.com/cheshireoaks, 10–8 MON–FRI, 9–6 SAT, 11–5 SUN. **FACTORY SHOPPING VILLAGE**

The McArthurGlen Designer Outlet Cheshire Oaks is Europe's largest designer outlet with over 140 stores selling top brands and designer names at up to 50% off typical retail prices. Facilities include a food court, a children's play area and free parking. Stores include: Gap Outlet, Big L, Fruit of the Loom, Monsoon, Timberland, Tie Rack, Principles, Petroleum, James Barry, Donnay, Aquascutum, Burberrys, Viyella, Warehouse, Racing Green, Famous Footwear, Jeffrey Rogers, Liz Claiborne, Winning Line, Overland, Ciro Pearls, Diesel, Jokids, Fred Perry, Travel Accessory Outlet, Baron Jon, La Senza, Nike, Next to Nothing, Helly Hansen, Jane Shilton, Joe Bloggs, Birthdays, Thorntons, Toyworld, D2, Pilot, Jumper, Clarks, Villeroy & Boch, Episode, Windsmoor, Jaeger, Daks Simpson, Mexx, Bed & Bath Works, Woods of Windsor, The Suit Company, XS Music & Video, Suits You, Claire's Accessories, Lee Cooper, Tog 24, Fila, Warners, Cecil Gee, Remington, Whittard of Chelsea, Kitchen Store, Denby, Edinburgh Crystal, Price's Candles, Reebok, Hobbs, Kurt Muller, Bookends, Pictureport, Kappa, Easy Jeans, Woodhouse, Designer Room, DKNY, Ponden Mill, U Wear/I Wear, Penn, Le Coq Sportif, Roman Originals, Revlon, Monet, Walker and Hall, Ben Sherman, Van Heusen, Austin Reed, Antler, Ecco, Blazer, Watson/Chillii Pepper, Red/Green, Soled Out, Carphone Warehouse, Cotton Traders, Royal Doulton, Royal Worcester, Oneida, Proibito, Vans, Reiss, Garden Outlet, Proudfoot Leather, Playtime Toys, Wedgwood, Prima Tessuti, Natural World, WHSmith, Littlewoods, Bose, The Body Shop, Samsonite, Adidas, Kangol, Dune, Marks & Spencer Outlet, Daniel Footwear, Polo Jeans Company, The North Face, Elle, Sergio Tacchini, Autonomy, Chapelle, Fiorelli, Julian Graves, Spiegelau, Bose, Kitch N Sync, Early Learning Centre, Tommy Hilfiger, Triumph and Professional Cookware.

POYNTON FROZEN VALUE

PARK LANE, POYNTON, CHESHIRE SK12 1RE, ☎ 01625 871322, 9–5.30 MON–FRI, 9–5 SAT.
FOOD AND DRINK DISCOUNTER

Sell a range of brand name and low calorie ready-made meals at discounts of, on average, one third off the normal retail price. The meals have usually been created for famous high street stores and include Marks & Spencer oven chips, individual chicken or steak pies, wholemeal quiches and pizzas. Also Romantica ice cream and Sainsbury and Tesco ready-meals, and hundreds of other lines as and when available.

RENAHALL LTD

UNIT 343, SILK HOUSE, PARK GREEN, MACCLESFIELD, CHESHIRE SK11 7QJ, ☎ 07901 815521, FAX: 01625 429888, **e-mail:** info@renahall.co.uk, www.renahall.co.uk, MAIL ORDER ONLY. **PERMANENT DISCOUNT OUTLET**

Sells vitamins, minerals and dietary supplements at low prices. Postage and packing cost £1, no matter how big your order. Vitamin C is sold in powder form, avoiding the cost of tabletting (pure ascorbic acid, 240g for £9.25; calcium ascorbate 240g £12.50). Vitamin E is sold in both powder (100g for £18.50) and capsule (100 capsules 500iu for £10) form. Multi-vitamin and mineral tablets cost just £3.50 for 150 tablets, and 400mg folic acid tablets cost £6 for 300. E-mail or phone for a price list.

THE BODY SHOP DEPOT

UNIT 141, CHESHIRE OAKS, KINGSLEY ROAD, ELLESMERE PORT, SOUTH WIRRAL CH65 9JJ, ☎ 0151 356 3632, FAX: 0151 356 3629, www.the-body-shop.com, 10–8 MON–FRI, 9–6 SAT, 11–5 SUN. **FACTORY SHOP IN A FACTORY SHOPPING VILLAGE**

Popular ends of lines from a range of toiletries, The Body Shop Colourings make-up, gifts and accessories, bath, sun and skincare products, all of which are priced from 20% to 70% less than in its high street sites.

THORNTONS

MCARTHURGLEN DESIGNER OUTLET CHESHIRE OAKS, KINSEY ROAD, NEAR ELLESMERE PORT, JUNCTION 10 OF M53, CHESHIRE CH65 9JJ, ☎ 0151 355 5637, www.thorntons.co.uk, 10–8 MON–FRI, 9–6 SAT, 11–5 SUN. **FACTORY SHOP IN A FACTORY SHOPPING VILLAGE**

The UK's leading specialist confectionery retailer has more than 400 shops and franchises nationwide selling a wide range of boxed and loose chocolate and sugar confectionery. The factory outlets sell three different categories: misshapes, discounted lines and standard lines. Misshapes are loose chocolates which are the result of new product development, product trials or end of production runs which cannot be packed as Thorntons standard lines. They are packed into assorted bags and offer a saving of 35% to 55% off the recommended retail price of standard 'loose line' products. Discounted lines are excess to Thorntons' normal retail requirements and can be as a result of excess seasonal or export stock, discontinued lines or packaging changes. These products, when available, are offered at a discount of 25% to 50% off the standard retail price. Standard lines from the full Thorntons range are also on sale at normal prices.

TOYWORLD STORE FACTORY OUTLET

MCARTHURGLEN DESIGNER OUTLET CHESHIRE OAKS, KINSEY ROAD, NEAR ELLESMERE PORT, JUNCTION 10 OF M53, CHESHIRE CH65 9JJ, ☎ 0151 355 9998, www.toyworldstore.com, 10–8 MON–FRI, 9–6 SAT, 11–5 SUN. **FACTORY SHOP IN A FACTORY SHOPPING VILLAGE**

Toyworld Store Factory Outlets are Europe's largest toy factory outlet retailer. They offer an enormous range of branded products which may be surplus stocks, end of ranges or cancelled orders, and are therefore able to sell their products at up to 70% off normal high street prices. Their range includes famous names such as: Action Man, Barbie, Bandai, Crayola, Corgi, Fisher-Price, Hasbro, Hornby, Lego, Little Tikes, Meccano, Tomy, V-Tech and many more, all at unbelievably low prices.

TRAVEL ACCESSORY

MCARTHURGLEN DESIGNER OUTLET CHESHIRE OAKS, KINSEY ROAD, NEAR ELLESMERE PORT, JUNCTION 10 OF M53, CHESHIRE CH65 9JJ, ☎ 0151 357 3248, 10–8 MON–FRI, 9–6 SAT, 11–5 SUN. **FACTORY SHOP IN A FACTORY SHOPPING VILLAGE**

Luggage and travel-related products and executive cases, handbags from leading brands such as Tripsport, Delsey, Head, Taurus and Globetrotter. Each product is offered at a substantially reduced price compared to those found on the high street due to being production overruns, discontinued ranges or colours and last season's products. Discounts range from 30% to 75% off high street prices.

WILKINSONS HOME & GARDEN STORES

THE MARKET CENTRE, CREWE, CHESHIRE CW1 2NG, ☎ 01270 250754, www.wilko.co.uk, 8.30–5.30 MON–WED, 8.30–6.30 THUR–SAT, 10–4 SUN. **PERMANENT DISCOUNT OUTLET**

See page 656 (BUCKS)

CORNWALL

CORNISH MARKET WORLD

STADIUM RETAIL PARK, PAR, ST AUSTELL, CORNWALL PL25 3RP, ☎ 01726 812544, FAX: 01726 812346, **e-mail:** info@cornishmarketworld.co.uk, www.cornishmarketworld.co.uk, 9–5 SAT, SUN AND BANK HOLIDAYS, AND WED JUNE-SEPT. **PERMANENT DISCOUNT OUTLET**

Huge indoor market that sells an enormous range of goods and food at very competitive prices: for example, a good quality breadmaker, £45. Sells clothes, fabrics, phones, bags, tools, electric equipment, motability equipment, jewellery and furniture. There is a good butchers, fish, and fruit and veg stands.

REDRUTH BREWERY (1742) LTD

THE BREWERY, FOUNDRY ROW, REDRUTH, CORNWALL TR15 1RB, ☎ 01209 313250, 12–6 MON–FRI, 10–4 SAT. **FACTORY SHOP**

Factory shop selling beers and lagers with damaged labels, as well as trial brews and those which are close to sell-by date at reduced prices. Also sell regular stock at slightly below retail prices.

TRAGO MILLS

ARWENACK STREET, FALMOUTH, CORNWALL TR11 3LF, ☎ 01326 315738, www.trago.co.uk, 9–5.30 MON–SAT, 10.45–4.45 SUN.

TWOWATERSFOOT, LISKEARD, CORNWALL PL14 6HY, ☎ 01579 348877, www.trago.co.uk, 9–5.30 MON–SAT, 10.45- 4.45 SUN. **PERMANENT DISCOUNT OUTLET**

The historic Trago's original Cornish site is in the Glynn Valley on the A38 between Liskeard and Bodmin. You can bargain hunt here for brand name art materials, bathrooms and bedrooms and ceramics, carpets and rugs, clothing, DIY and home improvement, furniture, garden accessories, gifts, textiles, lighting, pet care, saddlery, stationery, tools, motoring products, toys and sport equipment and much more. There's a restaurant and picnic area by the beautiful Fowey river bank, free parking and disabled access. The Falmouth store is smaller, with only limited free car parking outside, but there is a public car park adjacent.

COUNTY DURHAM

BAKEBEST TRADING AS NORTHUMBRIAN FINE FOODS

DUKESWAY, TEAM VALLEY INDUSTRIAL ESTATE, GATESHEAD, CO DURHAM NE11 0QP, ☎ 0191 442 4400, FAX: 0191 442 4455, 9.30–3 MON–FRI. **FOOD AND DRINK DISCOUNTER**

Value-for-money cakes, biscuits and snack foods from this north-east-based company which manufactures biscuits and cakes under its own brand names, including Cake Break, Sunwheel, Knightsbridge and Bronte. They also produce a selection of private label goods for many of the high street supermarkets. The factory shop sells overruns of its entire range at very reasonable prices. Availability varies but typically includes plain and chocolate biscuits, flapjacks, cookies, confectionery and cakes.

GATEAUX DIRECT

19–20 DOUGLAS COURT, 11TH AVENUE, TEAM VALLEY TRADING ESTATE, GATESHEAD, COUNTY DURHAM NE11 0JY, ☎ 0191 491 4139, FAX: 0191 491 4139, 9–5 MON–SAT
FACTORY SHOP

Not just delicious frozen desserts – but also frozen meals such as curries and Italian-style meals such as lasagne at very low prices.

TOYMASTER FACTORY OUTLET

50–51 THE CORNMILL SHOPPING CENTRE, DARLINGTON, COUNTY DURHAM DL1 1LT, ☎ 01325 363222, www.toyworldstore.com, 9–5.30 MON–SAT. **FACTORY SHOP IN A FACTORY SHOPPING VILLAGE**

Toymaster Factory Outlets are part of Europe's largest toy factory outlet retailer. They stock the very latest toys at amazing prices as well as TP outdoor products. They also offer an enormous range of branded products, which may be surplus stocks, end of ranges or cancelled orders, and are therefore able to sell those products at up to 70% off normal high street prices. Their range includes famous names such as: Action Man, Barbie, Bandai, Crayola, Corgi, Fisher-Price, Hasbro, Hornby, Lego, Little Tikes, Meccano, Tomy, V-Tech and many more, all at unbelievably low prices.

CUMBRIA

K VILLAGE OUTLET SHOPPING

LOUND ROAD, KENDAL, NEAR JUNCTION 36 OF M6, CUMBRIA LA9 7DA, ☎ 01539 732363, **e-mail:** mdixon@realm-ocm.com, www.kvillage.co.uk, 9.30–6 MON–FRI, 9–6 SAT, 11–5 SUN (9.30–5.30 MON–FRI NOVEMBER TO MARCH). **FACTORY SHOPPING VILLAGE**

Twelve outlets including Cotton Traders, Crabtree & Evelyn, Dartington Crystal selling Cloverleaf as well as glassware, Van Heusen, Denby Pottery, The Food Factory, Ponden Mill, Prices Candles, Tog 24, National Trust Gift Shop and a giant K Shoes factory shop selling a wide range of labels from K Shoes, Clarks, Cica, Delsey and Antler, as well as a full-price K Shop. There is also a heritage centre where you can discover the history of shoemaking, a 150-seater restaurant, a coffee shop, children's play area, baby changing facilities, a riverside picnic area, disabled facilities and free parking. Take the South Kendal exit and follow the signs for K Village.

DERBYSHIRE

BOOKTHRIFT

5A ST JOHNS STREET, ASHBOURNE, DERBYSHIRE DE6 1GP, ☎ 01335 300299, 9.30–5.30 MON–SAT, 11.30–5 SUN.

PRIORY NURSERIES, HALL FARM, MAIN STREET, BREEDON ON THE HILL, NEAR DERBY, DERBYSHIRE DE73 1AT, ☎ 01332 290912, 9.30–5.30 MON–SAT.

44 SADDLEGATE, DERBY, DE1 3NQ, ☎ 01332 290912, 9.30–5.30 MON–SAT.

ILKESTON CO-OP, 12 SOUTH STREET, ILKESTON, DERBYSHIRE DE7 5SG, ☎ 0115 930 2021, 9–5.30 MON–SAT. **PERMANENT DISCOUNT OUTLET**

See page 657 (CHESH)

DE BRADELEI MILL SHOPS LTD

DE BRADELEI HOUSE, CHAPEL STREET, BELPER, DERBYSHIRE DE56 1AR, ☎ 01773 882442, FAX: 01773 829830, 9.30–5.30 MON–FRI, 9.30–6 SAT, 10.30–4.30 SUN. **PERMANENT DISCOUNT OUTLET**

A delightful Mill centre with individual shops based round a central courtyard, each one selling top brand names in fashions and footwear for men and women, along with Liberty giftware. The womenswear includes such names as Paul Costelloe, Windsmoor, Planet, Precis Petite, Alexon, Kaliko, Eastex, Minuet Petite, Liz Claiborne, Jaeger Knitwear Shop, French Connection, Elle, Country Casuals, Elvi, top American and German designer labels, plus many more. The menswear range includes underwear, socks, sweaters, trousers, jackets, coats and suits from labels such as Wolsey, French Connection, Jaeger Knitwear Shop and Glenmuir. Robert Leonard's Menswear provides Pierre Cardin, Gabicci, Gurteen, Oakman and many more. There is a large shoe department with an excellent range of shoes and accessories for men and women. A Tenson department sells outerwear for men and women. The giftware department offers a superb collection of Liberty giftware with scented candles, Arran Aromatic toiletires, photo frames, baskets, toilet bags and chocolates from Italo Suisse. Chevin Coffee Shop serves delicious home-cooked food throughout the day. De Bradelei Mill Shop has its own car park with alternative parking nearby; coach parties are always welcome though booking is preferred.

DENBY POTTERY VISITOR CENTRE

DERBY ROAD, DENBY, NR RIPLEY, DERBYSHIRE DE5 8NX, ☎ 01773 740799, www.denbyvisitorcentre.co.uk, 9.30–5 MON–SAT, 10–5 SUN (CENTRE), 11–5 SUN (FACTORY SHOP). **FACTORY SHOP**

Denby has been welcoming visitors to its pottery for many years. The largest of the Denby Factory Shops is located in the Visitor Centre. It sells both seconds and first quality pieces. Discounts on the large range of seconds start at 20% off the first quality RRP, with regular bargains offering much greater savings all the year round (see Factory Shops on their web site for dates and details). At the Visitor Centre you can go on a fascinating tour of the factory to see how Denby is made, then browse around the shops, which include an award-winning Cookshop (with free cookery demonstrations daily), Garden Centre, Dartington Crystal Factory Shop, Gift Shop, Artists Gallery area and Restaurant. Entry to the centre and parking are free and there are picnic and children's play areas. You can also watch traditional skills on a visit to the new Glass Studio at Denby.

LUGGAGE & BAGS

THE PEAK VILLAGE, CHATSWORTH ROAD, ROWSLEY, DERBYSHIRE DE4 2JE, ☎ 01629 732 883, 9.30–5.30 MON–SAT, 10–5 SUN. **FACTORY SHOP IN A FACTORY SHOPPING VILLAGE**

Luggage and travel-related products, plus executive cases, handbags and umbrellas from leading brands such as Samsonite, Delsey, Head, Taurus and Globetrotter. Each product is offered at a substantially reduced price compared to those found on the high street due to being production overruns, discontinued ranges or colours and last season's products. Discounts range from 30% to 75% off high street prices.

MCARTHURGLEN DESIGNER OUTLET

MANSFIELD ROAD, SOUTH NORMANTON, ALFRETON, JUNCTION 28 OF M1, DERBYSHIRE DE55 2ER, ☎ 01773 545000, www.mcarthurglen.com/mansfield, 10–6 MON–FRI, 8 ON THUR, 9–6 SAT, 11–5 SUN. **FACTORY SHOPPING VILLAGE**

The McArthurGlen Designer Outlet Mansfield has recently undergone a year-long development programme, transforming it from an open-plan department store layout to individual shops. The new look outlet is now bigger and better. Find all your favourite brands at discounts of up to 50% off typical retail prices. Facilities include a children's play area, a food court and plenty of free parking. Stores include: Antler, Banana Books, Bed & Bath Works, Big L, Camille Lingerie, Chapelle, Claire's Accessories, Coloroll, Cotton Traders, Donnay, Edinburgh Crystal, Harbi, Jaeger, Jane Shilton, Julian Graves, Kitch N Sync, Leading Labels, Lee Cooper, Mountain Warehouse, Pavers Shoes, Petroleum, Pilot, Price's Candles, Professional Cookware, Remington, Roman Originals, Sky, Soled Out, Speedo, Sportsmill, Suits You, Thorntons, Tog

24, Toyworld, Revlon, Marks & Spencer Outlet, Windsmoor, Sportz, Reebok, Jumper, HKA, Proudfoot Leather, Garden Outlet, Lilley & Skinner, Adidas, Viyella, Whittards, XS Records and many more.

PEAK VILLAGE

CHATSWORTH ROAD, ROWSLEY, (ON THE A6 BETWEEN BAKEWELL AND MATLOCK), DERBYSHIRE DE4 2JE, ☎ 01629 735326, www.peakvillage.co.uk, 9.30–5.30 MON–SAT, 10–5 SUN, EXCEPT CHRISTMAS DAY. **FACTORY SHOPPING VILLAGE**

More than 20 factory outlets including Leading Labels, Cotton Traders, Luggage & Bags, The Book Depot, Pavers Shoes, Sports & Mountain Warehouse, Yeoman Outdoors outdoor wear and equipment, Ponden Mill, Mansworld, New Beginnings and Woodlands Fitness Centre, all just 30 minutes from the M1 at the entrance to the Peak District National Park. On-site catering includes Massarella's Restaurant, which offers everything from an ice cream sundae to a traditional Sunday roast. The Wind in the Willows Attraction is a magical journey through the world of Ratty, Badger, Mole and of course the irrepressible Mr Toad. The latest sound and lighting effects bring Kenneth Grahame's classic tale to life in an enchanting recreation that's not just for kids! Free parking for up to 400 cars. Recently opened the Woodlands Fitness Centre.

THORNTONS

MCARTHURGLEN DESIGNER OUTLET MANSFIELD, MANSFIELD ROAD, SOUTH NORMANTON, ALFRETON, JUNCTION 28 OF M1, DERBYSHIRE DE55 2JW, ☎ 01773 545289, www.thorntons.co.uk, 10–6 MON–FRI, 8 ON THUR, 9–6 SAT, 11–5 SUN. **FACTORY SHOP IN A FACTORY SHOPPING VILLAGE**

See page 658 (CHESH)

TOYWORLD STORE FACTORY OUTLET

MCARTHURGLEN DESIGNER OUTLET MANSFIELD, MANSFIELD ROAD, SOUTH NORMANTON, ALFRETON, JUNCTION 28 OF M1, DERBYSHIRE DE55 2JH, ☎ 01773 545 333, www.toyworldstore.com, 10–6 MON–FRI, 8 ON THUR, 9–6 SAT, 11–5 SUN. **FACTORY SHOP IN A FACTORY SHOPPING VILLAGE**

See page 658 (CHESH)

WILKINSON STORES

13 INSTITUTE LANE, ALFRETON, DERBYSHIRE DE55 7BQ, ☎ 01773 836845, www.wilko.co.uk, 9–5.30 MON–THUR, SAT, 9–6 FRI, 10–2 SUN. MAIL ORDER. **PERMANENT DISCOUNT OUTLET**

See page 656 (BUCKS)

DEVON

ATLANTIC VILLAGE OUTLET CENTRE

CLOVELLY ROAD, OFF A39, WEST OF BIDEFORD, NORTH DEVON, ☎ 01237 422544, **e-mail:** rmorris@realm-ocm.com, www.atlanticvillage.co.uk, JULY–MID SEPT, 9.30–7 MON–SAT, 11–5 SUN; MID SEPT–MID OCT AND EASTER TO JULY 9.30–6.30 MON–SAT, 11–5 SUN; MID OCT–EASTER 9.30–5 MON–SAT, 11–5 SUN. **FACTORY SHOPPING VILLAGE**

More than 30 shops with famous names and Devon's largest interactive maze make this village a good family day out. Shops include Banana Books; Claire's Accessories; Colony Candles; Cotton Traders, Designer Room, Ecco; Edinburgh Woollen Mill; Event Jewellery; Jane Shilton; Jean Scene; Julian Graves; Nickelby's; Pavers Shoes; Pilot; Ponden Mill; Puma; Roman Originals; Room, selling home accessories, fabrics and soft furnishings; Sportsmill; Suits You; Tog 24; Toyzone; Triumph; Warners; Windsmoor; XS Sound & Media. Free car parking, disabled and baby changing facilities. Atlantic Village also features an attractive piazza, cafés, a food court, visitor garden, arts and crafts market, open-air amphitheatre, and an adventure park set in an additional three-acre site linked to the shopping area by the piazza and amphitheatre. The Adventure Park features a mystery maze, adventure golf, wrecker's cove and adventure play boat.

DAVID & CHARLES

BRUNEL ROAD, NEWTON ABBOT, DEVON TQ12 4PU, ☎ 01626 323219, OPEN 8.30–5 MON–THUR, 8.30–4.30 FRI. **PERMANENT DISCOUNT OUTLET**

Craft and cookery books, cross stitch packs, jigsaws and some craft basics such as paint and glitter glue. The books are either rejects, damaged or overstock at reduced prices.

EXETER SURPLUS

BAKERS YARD, ALPHINBROOK ROAD, MARSH BARTON INDUSTRIAL ESTATE, EXETER, DEVON EX2 8SS, ☎ 01392 427508, 8.30–5 MON–SAT. **PERMANENT DISCOUNT OUTLET**

Operates from a 4,000 square foot retail unit and a 10,000 square foot trade site half a mile away on Christow Road, the latter specialising in quality, nearly-new office furniture and shelving. Retail goods include engineering equipment, hand tools, clothing, a large range of outdoor goods, chandlery, a range of tents, bedding and domestic furniture, kayaks, rope and chain, canvas sheets, rucksacks, boots and shoes, overalls, ceremonial clothing and an enormous amount of miscellaneous one-off items, all very competitively priced. The outdoor leisure market is their new specialisation.

TRAGO MILLS SHOPPING AND LEISURE PARKS

LIVERTON, NEWTON ABBOT, DEVON TQ12 6JD, ☎ 01626 821111, www.trago.co.uk, 9–5.30 MON–SAT, 10.45–4.45 SUN. **PERMANENT DISCOUNT OUTLET**

The biggest range of discounted goods in the West Country, with a whole range of activities to keep the family amused on the 100 acre site. Sells virtually everything from men's, women's and childrenswear, gardening equipment and cookware to wallpaper, carpets and fitted kitchens. Most are branded goods and there is a café, pizza bar and petrol station. A reasonable amount of the women's fashion comes from high street multiples. The menswear offers a wide range of clothes, as well as all-leather classic brogues and Oxford shoes, and Doc Martens in the Shoes Yard. For the home, there are Black & Decker Dustbusters, Hotpoint dryers and washing machines with cosmetic blemishes; curtain fabrics from Monkwell, Sekers, Filigree, Laura Ashley as well as Janet Reger for Vantona double quilt covers, with matching sheets, pillow cases and valances. There is a vast range of tiles including Pilkington seconds. A huge gardening section with everything from hose pipes and garden machinery to ikported trees and shrubs. An excellent leisure section offers bicycles and accessories, golf gear, keep-fit systems, fishing rods and flies. Comparison prices are not given here, although staff say most items are discounted by up to 50%, so if you're looking for a bargain, make sure you've done your homework on the high street first. The best deals are in fabrics, carpets, tiles and DIY. There is a leisure park with a giant free fall slide, supakart and family go-kart circuit, bumper boats, trawler rides, swan pedalos, pirate ship, aquablasters, orbiters, shooting gallery, remote control cars and cruisers, forklifts and mini-diggers, fun dungeon, animal park, model railway, narrow gauge steam railway, nature reserve, coarse fishing, Edwardian penny arcade and plenty of space to picnic and to park.

DORSET

CD & BOOK & VIDEO SELECTIONS

DORCHESTER DORSET DT2 7YG, ☎ 01305 848725, **e-mail:** sales@cdselections.com, www.cdselections.com, MAIL ORDER ONLY. **PERMANENT DISCOUNT OUTLET**

CD, Book & Video Selections publishes its bargain selection of CDs, tapes, books and videos five times a year. Two editions are 56 or more pages; three editions are sale supplements. These full-colour guides offer a remarkable range of classical, opera, jazz, easy listening and popular CDs with prices starting at 99p. Overstocks, deletions and ongoing titles are selected for value for money. All sales are backed by a full refund guarantee. CD, Book & Video Selections also sells popular and general interest videos, and bargain books. The company also publishes specialist catalogues for opera and jazz. All stock is now available on the company's website at www.cdselections.com.

IN EXCESS

354–358 ASHLEY ROAD, PARKSTONE, POOLE, DORSET BH14 9DF, ☎ 01202 740188, 9–5.30 MON–SAT, 10–4 SUN.

80–83 DOLPHIN CENTRE, POOLE, DORSET, ☎ 01202 673534, 9–5.30 MON–SAT, 10–4 SUN.

SOMERFORD ROAD, CHRISTCHURCH, DORSET BH23 3PH, ☎ 01202 481438, 9–5.30 MON–SAT, 10–4 SUN. **PERMANENT DISCOUNT OUTLET**

In Excess is stacked full of bankrupt stock from stationery and paint to DIY tools and cleaning materials, plumbing materials, screws, bolts, nuts, and telephone accessories. It also houses, in season, garden furniture and pots aimed at the starter garden lover and decking. Plastic tables and chairs start at £2.95 for a chair and from £5.95 to £12.95 for a table; terracotta pots start from 50p and there are also 'antiqued' stone pots.

OLIVES ET AL LTD

UNIT 1, NORTH DORSET BUSINESS PARK, ROLLSMILL, STURMINSTER NEWTON, DORSET DT10 2HP, ☎ 01258 474300, **e-mail:** enquiries@olivesetal.co.uk, www.olivesetal.co.uk, 8–5 MON–FRI. **FOOD AND DRINK DISCOUNTER**

Factory shop selling marinated olives, extra virgin olive oils, sauces and snacks. All products are free from any artificial additives and totally authentic. Olives Et Al prepare olives exactly as they would be in a Mediterranean home. Their olive oils are all single variety and great value. Their sauces are all homemade using classic recipes and the best ingredients. Their snack range includes roasted broad beans (habas) and chilli puffs. They also trade online at www.olivesetal.co.uk.

S MOORES

THE BISCUIT BAKERY, MORCOMBELAKE, NEAR BRIDPORT, DORSET DT6 6ES, ☎ 01297 489253, 9–5 MON–FRI, 9–1 SAT (MAY TO DECEMBER). **FOOD AND DRINK DISCOUNTER**

Ten different brands of broken biscuits including shortbreads, walnut crunch, chocolate chip and ginger biscuits sold in 800 gram bags at 30% saving. Tend to sell out very early in the day, so don't leave your visit until late in the afternoon. There is also a small gallery of West Country paintings and bakery bygones and a new viewing gallery for visitors to look around the factory.

THE HOUSE OF SARUNDS LTD

UNIT 1, HOLLAND WAY BUSINESS CENTRE, HOLLAND WAY, BLANDFORD FORUM, DORSET DT11 7RU, ☎ 01258 450200, FAX: 01258 450606, 9–5 MON–FRI. **FACTORY SHOP**

Confectionery factory shop in particular fine Belgian and English chocolates including Guylian, as well as coffee beans, Turkish delight and marshmallow.

THE POOLE POTTERY FACTORY SHOP

THE QUAY, POOLE, DORSET BH15 1RF, ☎ 01202 668681, FAX: 01202 649082, 9–5.30 MON–SAT, 10.30–4.30 SUN. PHONE FOR SEASONAL OPENING TIMES. **FACTORY SHOP**

The Poole Factory Shop is still the cheapest place to buy the widest selection of Poole Pottery. All the old favourite ranges such as Dorset Fruit, Vincent and Vineyard are joined by new exciting ranges like Fresco. The critically acclaimed new 'Living Glaze' gift range which uses a glazing method pioneered at Poole nearly 40 years ago is now also available. The shop has long ceased to be just an outlet for Poole Pottery. It now boasts some of the top brands in giftware such as Dartington, Colony Candles and, more recently, Julian Graves. All these plus the new cook shop makes it the perfect place for the first-time housebuyer to buy practically all their home essentials – it is fast becoming the biggest gift shop in the south. Poole Pottery has recently undertaken an extensive site redevelopment responding to their own research which suggested that both parents and children prefer a separate area to paint plates, throw pots and learn the ancient skills of the potter. The activity area can now be found on a floor of its own offering more freedom and security. This can now be found on the ground floor at the rear of the building. Glass blowing demonstrations are regularly held. In addition you can enjoy an a la carte, table d'hote meal with fine wines and unique harbour views at Carters restaurant, or opt for a light snack in the tea room or self-service area. A new, exciting fashion floor is now also here, with labels available including Excel, Reflection, Morgan and many others. Top quality suits, lingerie, shoes etc are all on sale at factory shop prices.

ESSEX

BAGGAGE DEPOT BARKING

VICARAGE FIELDS SHOPPING CENTRE, BARKING, ESSEX IG11 OLZ, ☎ 020 8591 1961, 9–5.30 MON–SAT. **PERMANENT DISCOUNT OUTLET**

Luggage and travel-related products and executive cases, handbags, umbrellas from leading brands such as Samsonite, Delsey, Head, Taurus and Globetrotter. Each product is offered at a substantially reduced price compared to those found on the high street due to being production overruns, discontinued ranges or colours and last season's products. Discounts range from 30% to 75% off high street prices.

BRANDLER GALLERIES

1 COPTFOLD ROAD, BRENTWOOD, ESSEX CM14 4BN, ☎ 01277 222269, **e-mail:** john@brandler-galleries.com, www.brandler-galleries.com/www.thomas-art.com/www.noddy-art.com, 10–5.30 TUE–SAT. PHONE FIRST IF LOOKING FOR A PARTICULAR ITEM. **PERMANENT DISCOUNT OUTLET**

Prints, sculptures and paintings of a high standard at prices which reflect the low overheads outside London. Works by Diana Armfield, Bill Bowyer, Fred Cuming, Bernard Dunstan, Mary Fedden, David Tindle, Carel Weight, Andy Warhol, David Hockney, Picasso and others of a similar calibre. Prices range from £45 to £20,000. for example, they sold a Turner watercolour for £18,500 which would have cost as much as £75,000 in Bond Street. There are original book illustrations for Noddy, Postman Pat, Captain Pugwash, Rupert etc. Also offer a framing service and free car park. Artwork for children's books including Noddy, Postman Pat, Thomas the Tank Engine, etc.

CLACTON FACTORY SHOPPING VILLAGE

STEPHENSON ROAD WEST, CLACTON-ON-SEA, ESSEX CO15 4TL, ☎ 01255 479595, FAX: 01255 430777 INFORMATION LINE, 10–6 MON–SAT, 11–5 SUN. **FACTORY SHOPPING VILLAGE**

Forty eight units centred around a Victorian winter garden comprising the following: Banana Bookshop selling books, games and stationery; Because It's There (BIT) for sports and camping equipment; Bed & Bath Works, a homeware outlet with discounted branded linens and housewares from Janet Reger, Sheridan, Christy and Kingsley; Birthdays, stocking mainstream cards and gifts from manufacturers such as Andrew Brownsword, Disney, Parker, Galt and Warner Brothers; Camille for lingerie; Caterpillar selling foorwear from the Cat range; Choice, which sells family clothing from Next; Claire's Accessories; Clinkards family footwear from Church's, Gabor, Bally and Loake; Cook 'N Dine kitchenware, glass and ceramics; Cotton Traders casual wear; Dannimac outdoor wear; Designer Room selling designer fashion for men and women; Event fashion costume jewellery and watches from Accurist, Timberland, Seiko and Timex; Garden Store selling garden furniture, barbecues and equipment and, in season, Christmas decorations; Jacques Vert selling womenswear; JD Sports selling branded sports merchandise from Adidas, Nike, Reebok, Ellesse and Le Coq Sportif; Joanna Hall selling handbags from the Jane Shilton range; Julian Graves foods and nut mixes; Kids Play Factory with toys from ranges such as Fisher-Price and Lego; Leading Labels, with men's and women's fashions; Mobile Phone Shop; MX Active selling branded denim and casual wear for men, women and children; Nickelbys fashion wear for men and women; Olli Moda selling branded jeans and casual wear; Pilot, a young women's fashion outlet; Ponden Mill with a range of bedlinen and bathroom ware; Price's Candles; Roman Originals womenswear; Sasperilla for young women's fashions; Spotlight, a young women's fashion outlet; Suits You men's shirts, suits, and casual separates as well as wedding hire and Autonomy womenswear; Thorntons chocolates; Tog 24 outdoor activity wear; Windsmoor women's fashions; Travel Accessory Shop with travel goods from Delsey and Samsonite; Woods of Windsor toiletries and gift items; XS Music CDs and videos. There are also two restaurants, a tourist information centre, parking for 1,000 cars and a bus service link to Clacton-On-Sea town centre and railway station.

FREEPORT BRAINTREE DESIGNER OUTLET VILLAGE

FREEPORT ESSEX VILLAGE, CHARTER WAY, CHAPEL HILL, BRAINTREE, JUNCTION 8 OF M11, THEN A120, ESSEX CM77 8YH, ☎ 01376 348168, www.freeportbraintree.com, 10–6 MON–SAT, 8 ON THUR, 11–5 SUN. **FACTORY SHOPPING VILLAGE**

Freeport Braintree is a designer outlet village with over 80 shops. Situated in the heart of Essex with easy access from the A120, Freeport Braintree has its own dedicated railyway station and is only a one-hour journey from central London. Womenswear includes Aquascutum, Amazing Jeans, Antonio d'Errico, Box Fresh, Burberry, Christian Lacroix, Cotton Traders, Elle, Gossard, Karen Millen, Ted Baker, Tommy Hilfiger and Versace and The Designer Room with a host of designer labels. Menswear includes Aquascutum, Cecil Gee, Ciro Citterio, Cotton Traders, Kurt Muller, Nickleby's, Proibito, Ted Baker, Tommy Hilfiger, Van Heusen and Versace. For children there's Base 2 Base, Mexx and Toy Dome; there is also plenty to keep children entertained, such as the Cheeky Chimps indoor play area. Sportwear outlets include Brand Fusion, Donnay, Fila,

Mountain Warehouse, Nike, Reebok, Regatta and Trespass. Footwear is covered by Ecco Shoes, Franchetti Bond, Hush Puppies, Jane Shilton, Lilley & Skinner, Soled Out and Vans Shoes. Shops selling household goods from kitchenware to pot pourri include Churchills, Denby, Edinburgh Crystal, Glen Eagles, Le Creuset, Professional Cookware, The Design House, Waterford Wedgwood and Villeroy & Boch. Other retail outlets, selling everything from luggage to music, include Body Shop, Carlton, Claire's Accessories, Designer Shades, Mobile Phone Store, Watch Store and XS Music, and there are no less than six cafés and restaurants on site.

NEW HALL VINEYARDS

CHELMSFORD ROAD, PURLEIGH, CHELMSFORD, ESSEX CM3 6PN, ☎ 01621 828343, FAX: 01621 828343, **e-mail:** newhall.wines@virgin.net, www.newhallvineyard.fsbusiness.co.uk, 10–5 MON–FRI, 10–1.30 SAT, SUN. **FOOD AND DRINK DISCOUNTER**

Specialises in white wine – Muller, Bacchus, Huxelrebe and Chardonnay – on which it offers discounts of up to 10% depending on the quantities you buy. There is an annual English wine festival during the first weekend in September and guided tours are available from May to September. Book in advance – phone for details.

SWAINEY ADENEY BRIGG, PAPWORTH LEATHER GOODS

NURSERY ROAD, OFF LONDON ROAD, GREAT CHESTERFORD, ESSEX CB10 1QW, ☎ 01799 531521, 10–5.30 TUE–SAT. **PERMANENT DISCOUNT OUTLET**

Handmade business cases and luggage in leather and leather trim, all manufactured in their own factory. Goods offered for sale here are discontinued lines or seconds in briefcases, executive cases, folios, document cases, attache cases, suitcases, suit carriers, travel bags, holdalls, umbrellas, and small leather goods.

THE BODY SHOP DEPOT

UNIT D10, BLOCK D, DESIGNER OUTLET VILLAGE, CHARTER WAY, CHAPEL HILL, BRAINTREE, ESSEX CM7 8YH, ☎ 01376 528149, www.the-body-shop.com, 10–6 MON–SAT, 8 ON THUR, 11–5 SUN. **FACTORY SHOP IN A FACTORY SHOPPING VILLAGE**

See page 658 (CHESH)

THE WAREHOUSE (BOOKSALE) COMPANY

69 HIGH STREET, MALDON, ESSEX CM9 5EP, ☎ 01621 841292, www.ukbooks.org.uk, 9–5 MON–SAT. **PERMANENT DISCOUNT OUTLET**

Booksale now boasts more than 100 shops throughout the UK: phone 0121 313 6000 for details of your nearest store. It sells books, stationery, pictures, paints and artist's materials, all at enormously discounted prices. Paperbacks and hardbacks cost from £2; children's books 50p. Also open on some Sundays during the summer: phone first to check.

THORNTONS

FREEPORT ESSEX VILLAGE, CHARTER WAY, CHAPEL HILL, BRAINTREE, ESSEX CM7 8YH, ☎ 01376 347242, www.thorntons.co.uk, 10–6 MON–SAT, 8 ON THUR, 11–5 SUN. **FACTORY SHOP IN A FACTORY SHOPPING VILLAGE**

CLACTON FACTORY OUTLET VILLAGE, STEPHENSON ROAD WEST, CLACTON-ON-SEA ESSEX CO15 4TL, ☎ 01255 220527, www.thorntons.co.uk, 10–6 MON–SAT, 8 ON THUR, 11–5 SUN. **FACTORY SHOP IN A FACTORY SHOPPING VILLAGE**

See page 658 (CHESH)

VILLEROY & BOCH (UK) LIMITED

FREEPORT ESSEX VILLAGE, CHARTER WAY, CHAPEL HILL, BRAINTREE, ESSEX CM7 8YH, ☎ 01376 348168, 10–6 MON–SAT, 8 ON THUR, 11–5 SUN. **FACTORY SHOP IN A FACTORY SHOPPING VILLAGE**

One of six factory outlets for Villeroy & Boch, this shop carries an exclusive range of tableware, crystal and cutlery from Europe's largest tableware manufacturer. A varied and constantly changing stock, including seconds, hotelware and discontinued lines, on sale at excellent reductions, always makes for a worthwhile visit.

WILKINSON STORES

UNIT 11, WESTGATE PARK CENTRE, FODDERWICK, BASILDON, ESSEX SS14 1WP, ☎ 01268 526534, www.wilko.co.uk, 9–5.30 MON–FRI, 9–6 SAT, 10–4 SUN. **PERMANENT DISCOUNT OUTLET**

See page 656 (BUCKS)

GLOUCESTERSHIRE

BOOKENDS

26 WESTGATE STREET, GLOUCESTER, GLOUCESTERSHIRE GL1 2NW, ☎ 01452 331011, FAX: 01452 331011, **e-mail:** bookends@madasafish.com, www.bookspostfree.com, 9–5.30 MON–SAT. **SECONDHAND SHOP**

See page 656 (BRIS)

INFLATAMANIA

UNIT 8, MEAD PARK, MEAD ROAD, CHELTENHAM, GLOUCESTERSHIRE GL53 7EF, ☎ 01242 231231, FAX: 01242 231919, **e-mail:** info@inflatamania.co.uk, www.inflatamania.co.uk, 9–6 MON–FRI (WEEKENDS BY APPOINTMENT). **HIRE SHOPS**

Exciting adventure play inflatables and bouncy castles including the popular balloon typhoon, bugsy caterpillar, games zone and play centre: ultra-light, ultra-bright, and ultra-safe. Available for hire and for sale. New for 2002 are fun wooden toys: traditional favourites for children and the young at heart. Puzzles, learning games and hand-puppets. Ideal for gifts and stocking fillers.

SPRING GRAND SALE

SUDELEY CASTLE, WINCHCOMBE, NEAR CHELTENHAM, GLOUCESTERSHIRE, ☎ 01367 860017, FAX: 01367 860177, **e-mail:** nheslam@aol.com, 10–6 THUR, FRI, SAT. **DESIGNER SALES**

There are now three annual Grand Sales taking place countrywide. The Christmas Grand Sale in London, with over 120 different small companies selling their merchandise to the public, is the largest. This takes place in mid-late November each year. Quality is high and covers everything from dried flowers to bath accessories, Amish quilts to silverware, wooden toys to hand-painted kitchenware, antiques to handmade furniture, luxurious bedlinen to faux fur throws, pewter cutlery to glass vases, garden furniture to deck chairs, often at discount because they are ends of lines. There is a Spring Grand Sale at Sudeley Castle, Winchcombe, near Cheltenham, Gloucestershire, usually at the end of April/beginning of May, and a Summer Grand Sale at Ripley Castle, near Harrogate, North Yorkshire, in June. Both feature food, toys, games, travel bags, garden furniture and equipment as well as decorative home accessories. Phone the above number for more details. A proportion of the ticket revenue goes to charity.

HAMPSHIRE

BAGGAGE FACTORY

52 WHITELEY VILLAGE, WHITELEY WAY, FAREHAM, HAMPSHIRE PO14 7LJ, ☎ 01489 573333, www.baggagefactory.co.uk, 10–6 MON–SAT, 11–5 SUN. **FACTORY SHOP IN A FACTORY SHOPPING VILLAGE**

This outlet sells bags, cases and wallets, some well-known brand names such as Antler, Carlton, Skyway and Samsonite, at prices from 10% to 40% lower than the high street.

GUNWHARF QUAYS

PORTSMOUTH HARBOUR, HAMPSHIRE PO1 3TZ, ☎ 023 9283 6700, FAX: 023 9283 6701 **e-mail:** info@gunwharf-quays.com, www.gunwharf-quays.com, SUMMER: 10–6 MON–WED, 10–8 THUR–SAT, 11–5 SUN. WINTER: 10–6 MON–SAT, 11–5 SUN. **FACTORY SHOPPING VILLAGE**

Designer outlet shopping centre comprising 65 stores on a site next to Portsmouth Harbour station and Portsmouth Historic Dockyard, home to HMS Victory and the Mary Rose. As well as the designer outlets, which include Adidas, Benetton, Ben Sherman, Burberry, cK Calvin Klein, Crabtree & Evelyn, Ecco, Episode, Fenn Wright & Manson, Gap, Gieves & Hawkes, Marks & Spencer, Nicole Farhi, Nike, Tommy Hilfiger, Villeroy & Boch, Waterford Wedgwood and Whittard of Chelsea, there are 20 restaurants, bars and coffee shops, an 11-screen cinema, 26-lane bowling complex, comedy club and a year-round events programme.

IN EXCESS

43–45 HIGH STREET, WEST END, SOUTHAMPTON, HAMPSHIRE SO30 3LU, ☎ 0238 046 4545, 9–5.30 MON–SAT, 10–4 SUN.

64–66 SHIRLEY HIGH STREET, SHIRLEY, SOUTHAMPTON, HAMPSHIRE SO15 3TE, ☎ 02380 771657, 9–5.30 MON–SAT. **PERMANENT DISCOUNT OUTLET**

See page 663 (DORS)

THORNTONS

UNIT 66, GUNWHARF QUAYS, PORTSMOUTH, HAMPSHIRE PP01 3TX, ☎ 023 9287 7036, www.thorntons.co.uk, 10–8 SUN–WED, 10–9 THUR–SAT IN SUMMER. 10–6 SEVEN DAYS A WEEK IN WINTER. **FACTORY SHOP IN A FACTORY SHOPPING VILLAGE**

See page 658 (CHESH)

WILKINSON STORES

22–30 BRIDGE STREET, ANDOVER, HAMPSHIRE SP10 1BN, ☎ 01332 551241, www.wilko.co.uk, 9–5.30 MON–SAT, 10–4 SUN. MAIL ORDER.

THE MALLS SHOPPING CENTRE, 4 LODDON MALL, BASINGSTOKE, HAMPSHIRE RG21 7HY, ☎ 01538 386669, www.wilko.co.uk, 9–5.30 MON–FRI, 8.30 -5.30 SAT, 10–4 SUN. **PERMANENT DISCOUNT OUTLET**

See page 656 (BUCKS)

HEREFORDSHIRE

BOOKENDS CASTLE

9 CASTLE STREET, HAY-ON-WYE, HEREFORDSHIRE HR3 5BU, ☎ 01497 821572, FAX: 01497 821572, **e-mail:** bookends@madasafish.com, www.bookspostfree.com, 9–5.30 SEVEN DAYS A WEEK.

THE PAVEMENT, HAY-ON-WYE, HEREFORDSHIRE HR3 5BU, ☎ 01497 821341, FAX: 01497 847889, **e-mail:** bookends@madasafish.com, www.bookspostfree.com, 9–8 MON–SAT, 11–5 SUN. **SECONDHAND SHOP**

See page 656 (BRIS)

HERTFORDSHIRE

BAGGAGE FACTORY

GALLERIA OUTLET CENTRE, COMET WAY, HATFIELD, HERTFORDSHIRE AL10 OXR, ☎ 01707 257779, www.baggagefactory.co.uk, 10–8 MON–FRI, 10–6 SAT, 11–5 SUN. **FACTORY SHOP IN A FACTORY SHOPPING VILLAGE**

See page 667 (HAMPS)

CD WAREHOUSE UK

3 THE PARADE, HIGH STREET, WATFORD, HERTFORDSHIRE, ☎ 01923 252300, 10–6.30 MON–FRI, 7.30 ON THUR, 9–7 SAT, 11–6 SUN. **COMPACT DISCS**

Buy and sell secondhand CDs and DVDs at discounted prices. Branches also in Watford (01923 252300), Wimbledon (020 8543 2355) and Brighton (01273 731310).

GALLERIA OUTLET CENTRE

COMET WAY, HATFIELD, HERTFORDSHIRE AL10 0XR, ☎ 01707 278301, www.factory-outlets.co.uk, 10–8 MON–FRI, 10–6 SAT, 11–5 SUN. **FACTORY SHOPPING VILLAGE**

The Galleria Outlet Centre, often referred to as the bargain hunter's best-kept secret, based in north London, houses more than 80 retail outlets. It offers a wide choice of shops for the discerning customer, providing up to 60% off designer labels and quality brands. The Designer Room is a must for branded men's and women's fashions at huge discounts, stocking DKNY, Jasper Conran, Ghost and Tommy Hilfiger clothing. Looking for a designer evening dress or smart-casual wear? Then visit Discount Dressing. For the latest in fashionable menswear, pay a visit to any of the leading menswear shops. City Menswear offers new season, discounted Yves Saint Laurent and Ben Sherman clothing; Choice sells ranges from Next; B52 Jeans stocks Levi's, Lee and Wrangler ranges; and Baron Jon sells a selection of international names from Versace to Valentino. Going on holiday or looking for a new set of luggage? Then visit the Baggage Factory which sells top quality brands including Carlton and Samsonite. For all your bathroom and bedroom needs pop in to Ponden Mill or the Bed and Bath Works, selling a selection of bedlinen, towels from Christy, soaps and duvets. BhS For Less sells a range of end-of-season men's women's and children's fashions, as well as homewares and lighting. For all your footwear fancies, take a stroll to Charles Clinkard, Ecco, Soled Out and Pavers, selling great brand names including Timberland, Loake, Grenson, Nike, Reebok and Kickers. For women, D Kaye Cosmetics stocks a host of leading beauty and skincare ranges including Revlon, Max Factor, Lancome and Yardley, all at up to 75% off normal retail prices. Walker & Hall represent the finest in jewellery, stocking Tag, Gucci and Raymond Weil watches all at affordable prices. It also sells gold by weight and guarantees savings of at least 30% per gram. While, for the home, Chinacraft specialises in glass, china and giftware, from Wedgwood to Royal Doulton. If interior soft furnishings are on the agenda, then the Furniture Zone is the largest of its type, selling Oriental, middle eastern and Continental rugs, plus great ranges of sofas and sofa-beds, teak, cherry and oak furniture from Wall Nuts and the Khokhar Collection. To complement any room, the Big Picture and Big Poster sell modern and classical pictures ranging from £5 to £20,000. Visit the Garden Outlet Store for all your outdoor gardening and furniture requirements. Music Surplus, the home entertainment store, is a recent addition to the centre, selling a wide range of imported jazz, pop, chart and classical CDs, as well as the latest DVDs. For the PC enthusiast, UK Software sells CD-Roms at up to 70% off the normal retail price. Tool Ware House sells DeWalt, considered by many to be the Armani of the tool worlds, as well as offering fantastic savings on Black & Decker. The centre also offers three cafés, six restaurants and an abundance of children's activities including Toddler World, a futuristic crazy golf course and bouncing slides as well as a mini go-karting track during weekends and holidays. With over 1, 800 free car parking spaces and a nine-screen UCI cinema, the centre offers a complete family day out. The Galleria Outlet Centre is a 20-minute drive from north London, and is signposted from junction 3 and 4 of the A1M.

THE BODY SHOP DEPOT

UNIT 36, A1 GALLERIAS, HATFIELD, HERTFORDSHIRE AL10 9TF, ☎ 01707 267376, FAX: 01707 251920, www.the-body-shop.com, 10–8 MON–FRI, 10–6 SAT, 11–5 SUN. **FACTORY SHOP IN A FACTORY SHOPPING VILLAGE**

See page 658 (CHESH)

WHITTARD

GALLERIA OUTLET CENTRE, COMET WAY, HATFIELD, HERTFORDSHIRE AL10 0XR, ☎ 01707 273930, 10–8 MON–FRI, 10–6 SAT, 11–5 SUN. **FACTORY SHOP IN A FACTORY SHOPPING VILLAGE**

Sells tea, coffee, coffee-making equipment (cafetieres and stove-top espressos) and a wide range of china at discount prices.

KENT

BAGGINS BOOK BAZAAR

19 HIGH STREET, ROCHESTER, KENT ME1 1PY, ☎ 01634 811651, FAX: 01634 840591, www.bagginsbooks.co.uk, 10–5.50 SEVEN DAYS A WEEK. **SECONDHAND SHOP**

Largest secondhand bookshop in England with prices from 50p to £500. Deals in rare and secondhand books, but also sells some brand new review copies at substantial discounts. Prices of the older books depend on their condition. Book search service also offered. Can obtain any book in or out of print, subject to availability.

DE BRADELEI WHARF

DE BRADELEI WHARF (DOVER) LTD, CAMBRIDGE ROAD, DOVER, KENT CT17 9BY, ☎ 01304 226616, FAX: 01304 226636, 9.30–5.30 MON–FRI, 9.30–6 SAT, 11–5 SUN. **PERMANENT DISCOUNT OUTLET**

Large outlet in superb maritime setting just off the Dover Seafront, selling top brand names for all the family, including shoes. The womenswear includes such names as Paul Costelloe, Dannimac, Windsmoor, Planet, Precis Petite, Alexon, Kaliko, Eastex, Minuet Petite, Country Casuals, Elle, French Connection, Tigi Wear, plus top American and German designer labels, handbags and much more including a new accessory department. The menswear range includes underwear, socks, coats, sweaters, jackets, suits and trousers from labels such as Wolsey, Countrywear, French Connection, Virgin and Tog 24. Robert Leonard's Menswear provide Greiff, Pierre Cardin, Gabicci, Gurteen, Oakman, Saville Row, John Slim and many more. For children, there are brands such as OshKosh B'Gosh, Lily by Lily, Smarties, Vitamins, Rebble Pebble, Zip-Zap, O'Neill, MCA and Hickory as well as fluffy toys and melamine tableware with Pokemon and Toy Story 2 designs as well as a new department selling clothing, shoes, books and scientific toys. There is a large shoe department featuring international shoes for all the family and a wonderful Home Furnishings Department. The Interior Design shops sell bedding, towels, top-name furnishing fabric, cushions, throws, furniture and curtains. The Glass and China Department has an amazing selection from Waterford/Wedgwood, Stuart Crystal, Royal Doulton, Arthur Price of England Silverware, Staffordshire Tableware, Churchill, Cloverleaf, Hornsea Pottery, Cristal d'Arques and much more. There is superb Liberty shop in the giftware department and a Cromwell and Morgan Cook Shop. Parking is easy with a large car park behind the store. The Waves Coffee Shop is open all day, serving delicious home-cooked food.

MCARTHURGLEN DESIGNER OUTLET CENTRE

KIMBERLEY WAY, ASHFORD, JUNCTION 10 OF M20, KENT TN24 0SD, ☎ 01233 895900, www.mcarthurglen.com/ashford, 10–6 MON–FRI, 8 ON THUR, 9–6 SAT, 11–5 SUN. **FACTORY SHOPPING VILLAGE**

Voted 'Retail Destination of the Year' 2001 in the Retail Week awards, the McArthurGlen Designer Outlet Ashford in Kent is one of Europe's most spectacular shopping destinations. The outlet offers over 70 top brands and designer labels at up to 50% off typical retail prices. there is a food court, cafés, a children's play area, and parking for over 1,500 cars. A shuttle bus runs between the town centre, station and the outlet every eight minutes. Shops include: Ben Sherman, Cotton Traders, Designer Room/Classic Room, Daks, Fire Trap, Gap, Lee Cooper, Levi's Littlewoods Catalogue Outlet, Marks and Spencer, Mexx, Miss Sixty, Mountain Warehouse, Pilot, Polo Jeans Co. Factory Store, Proudfoot, Roman Originals, Thomas Pink, Tog 24, Tommy Hilfiger, Warehouse, Warner's, Windsmoor, Baron Jon, Ben Sherman, Cotton Traders, Daks, Fire Trap, Fred Perry, Gap, Lee Cooper, Levi's, Petroleum, Proudfoot, Suits You, The Suit Company, Thomas Pink, Van Heusen, Woodhouse, Donnay, Fila, Gap, JoKids, Mexx, Nike, Reebok, Toyzone, Clarks, Ecco, Jane Shilton Kiplings, Lilley & Skinner, Soled Out, Antler, Kipling, Samsonite Company Stores. Arran Aromatics, Body Shop, Chapelle Jewellery, Claire's Outlet, Gizmo, One 2 One, Picture Port, Revlon, Sekonda, Sunglass Hut International, Watch Station, Walker and Hall, Woods of Windsor, Bed and Bath Works, Bookends, Bose, China Place, Cloverleaf, Design House, Edinburgh Crystal, Le Creuset, Mountain Warehouse, Price's Candles,

Professional Cookware Company, Spiegelau, Waterford Wedgwood, Whittard of Chelsea, XS Music and Video.

THE BODY SHOP DEPOT

UNIT 18, ASHFORD DESIGNER OUTLET VILLAGE, C/O GALLIFORD NORTHERN, OFF ROMNEY MARSH ROAD, ASHFORD, KENT TN23 1EX, ☎ 01233 612312, www.the-body-shop.com, 10–6 MON–FRI, 8 ON THUR, 9–6 SAT, 11–5 SUN. **FACTORY SHOP IN A FACTORY SHOPPING VILLAGE**

See page 658 (CHESH)

LANCASHIRE

ABAKHAN FABRICS

34–44 STAFFORD STREET, LIVERPOOL, LANCASHIRE L3 8LX, ☎ 0151 207 4029, FAX: 0151 298 1809, 9.30–5 MON–SAT, 10–4 SUN.

111–115 OLDHAM STREET, MANCHESTER, LANCASHIRE M4 1LN, ☎ 0161 839 3229, FAX: 0161 839 3339, 9.30–5.15 MON–SAT, 7 ON THUR.

20–22 MANCHESTER ROAD, PRESTON, LANCASHIRE PR1 3YH, ☎ 01772 202677, 9.30–5.15 MON–SAT, 7 ON THUR. **FACTORY SHOP**

See page 657 (CHESH)

ANTLER LTD

ALFRED STREET, BURY, LANCASHIRE BL9 9EF, ☎ 0161 764 5241, 10–4 SEVEN DAYS A WEEK. **FACTORY SHOP**

Factory shop selling leather goods: handbags, business cases, bags, trolley covers as well as travel aids and suitcases. All the products are quality seconds and ends of lines. Free parking.

BCP AIRPORT PARKING AND TRAVEL SERVICES

MANCHESTER AIRPORT LANCASHIRE, ☎ 0870 013 4586 (RESERVATIONS) PLEASE QUOTE BP744, **e-mail:** reservations@bcponline.co.uk, www.bcponline.co.uk, 8–9, SEVEN DAYS A WEEK. **PERMANENT DISCOUNT OUTLET**

BCP provides secure, value-for-money car parking at Belfast, Birmingham, Bristol, Cardiff, East Midlands, Edinburgh, Gatwick, Glasgow, Humberside, Leeds Bradford, Liverpool, London City, Luton, Manchester, Newcastle, Prestwick, Southampton, Stansted, with prices from just £2.65 per day. From an extra £24.95 you can save time by being met at the airport terminal on your departure and return as part of BCP's Meet and Greet Parking service. Your car is then taken to the BCP secure car park nearby. Or you can pre-book a chauffeur-driven airport car to and from the airport. This service is ideal if you live within 30 miles of your departure airport: prices start from about £60 return. To book and save pounds on airport parking and 10% on lounges and chauffeur-driven cars, either phone the BCP reservations line, or book online and quote reference BP744. BCP will confirm your booking by post with directions to your car park or details of the pick-up or meeting arrangements if using the Meet and Greet Parking service.

FARMHOUSE BISCUITS

SOUTHFIELD STREET, NELSON, LANCASHIRE BB9 9PX, ☎ 01282 613520, 8.30–4.30 THUR, 8.30–3.30 FRI. **FACTORY SHOP**

Factory shop selling homemade biscuits, some packaged, some in plastic bags which are bought by the pound (not all of which are broken), some in tins which are slightly damaged returns from shops such as Harrods, Fortnum & Mason and Jenners. Some of the biscuits are dairy-free. Also sells some sweets and chocolates.

FREEPORT FLEETWOOD OUTLET VILLAGE

ANCHORAGE ROAD, FLEETWOOD, 12 MILES FROM JUNCTION 3 OF M55, LANCASHIRE FY7 6AE, ☎ 01253 877377, www.freeportfleetwood.com, 10–6 SEVEN DAYS A WEEK, 8 ON THUR, FRI. **FACTORY SHOPPING VILLAGE**

Large, brightly-coloured New-England-style seaside shopping village. There are more than 40 shops selling at up to 50% off high street prices, as well as restaurants, family attractions and free parking. Women's fashions include Next to Nothing, Spotlight, Easy Jeans, VF Corp, Double Two, Warner's, Edinburgh Woollen Mill, The Designer Room, Giorgio, BhS for Less, Madhouse and Roman Originals. For men, there is Petroleum, Ciro Citterio, Double Two, Giorgio, VF Corp, Madhouse, Easy Jeans and BhS for Less. Sportswear and outdoor wear shops include Sports Mill, Craghoppers, Regatta and VF Corp. Footwear outlets comprise Lilley & Skinner, Jane Shilton, Shoe Sellers, BhS For Less, Next to Nothing and Petroleum. Sweet-toothed visitors can indulge at Thorntons or The Sweet Shop, and there is Julian Graves for nuts and dried fruits. Household outlets include Ponden Mill, Dartington Crystal, Home Zone, Picture Port and China Traders. Childrenswear stockists include Next to Nothing, BhS for Less, Vecopri, VF Corp and Giorgio. Other stores include Woods of Windsor, Hallmark Cards and Gifts, XS Music & Video, Claire's Accessories, Watch Store and Book Depot.

GARDENERS CHOICE MILL SHOP

STANDROYD MILL, COTTONTREE, COLNE, LANCASHIRE BB8 7BW, ☎ 01282 873341, www.LBSGroup.co.uk, 9–5 MON–FRI, 9–4 SAT, 10–4 SUN. **FACTORY SHOP**

Horticultural and garden sundries specialists catering for the smaller garden. You can visit the small factory shop or go next door to LBS Horticulture, and buy in bulk (prices at LBS are trade plus VAT). Items on sale include spades, gloves, bulbs, seeds, benches, cloches, hanging baskets, cane trellis, secateurs, wheelbarrows, pergolas, garden furniture, fertiliser, weedkiller, insecticide, hosepipes, poly tunnels. They don't sell electrical gardening instruments or plants.

GERARDS ICE CREAMS CO LTD

WILLIAM STREET, ARDWICK, MANCHESTER, LANCASHIRE M12 5FX, ☎ 0161 274 3622, 9–4 MON–SUN. **FOOD AND DRINK DISCOUNTER**

Sells all types of ice cream at very competitive prices.

GIFTTREE

CHURCHBRIDGE WORKS, HENRY STREET, ACCRINGTON, LANCASHIRE BB5 4EU, ☎ 01254 237324, 9–5 MON–SAT

REEDYFORD MILL, WESTFIELD ROAD, NELSON, LANCASHIRE BB9 7YM, ☎ 01282 619540, FAX: 01282 696639, 9–5 MON–SAT. **PERMANENT DISCOUNT OUTLET**

Items from the Express Gifts mail order catalogues at reduced prices including cards, giftwrap, gifts, stationery, kitchenware, household products, clothes and toys, including Galt products. Discounts in most departments range from at least 50% off original catalogue selling prices.

HALLMARK

FREEPORT SHOPPING VILLAGE, ANCHORAGE ROAD, FLEETWOOD, LANCASHIRE FY7 6AE, ☎ 01253 773854, 10–6 SEVEN DAYS A WEEK, 8 ON THUR, FRI. **FACTORY SHOP**

A wide range of cards to suit every occasion, as well as soft toys, wrapping paper, bows, gift cards from names such as Forever Friends, Gordon Fraser and, of course, Hallmark. Almost all the stock here is ends of lines as the card business demands constant change and therefore some unsold lines. Most of the items are half price. Cafés, children's play areas and free parking.

HI-LIFE DINERS CLUB

THE EPICENTRE, 5 HARDHORN ROAD, POULTON, NEAR BLACKPOOL, LANCASHIRE FY6 7SR, ☎ 01253 884477, **e-mail:** info@Hi-Life.uk.com, www.Hi-Life.uk.com, 24-HOUR MEMBERSHIP LINE. **PERMANENT DISCOUNT OUTLET**

The Hi-Life Club has been operating for more than 18 years in the north-west of England and is the biggest diners' club of its type, with more than 60,000 members. Members can choose from among 800 north-west restaurants, most of which now give two meals for the price of one. Restaurants included vary and include Le Petit Blanc, Hard Rock Cafe, Rhodes & Co, Café Rouge, Henry's table, Beefeaters, Brewers' Fayre, Millers' Kitchen, Pizza Express, TGI Fridays etc. Every cuisine is covered from French to Indian, English or Mexican. The club literature says that most people save £100s or even £1,000s per year and there's a no-quibbble money back guarantee if you're not delighted with your membership. Membership costs £39.95 per annum.

KIPPAX BISCUITS

FACTORY SHOP, KING STREET, COLNE, LANCASHIRE BB8 9HU, ☎ 01282 864198, FAX: 01282 868891, 10–3.45 MON, WED, FRI, SAT, CLOSED 1–1.15. **FOOD AND DRINK DISCOUNTER**

More than 100 different types of biscuits from ginger wafers and shortbread to plain assorted and chocolate sold in packets, tins or loose. Broken biscuits also sold very cheaply. Coach parties welcome by prior appointment only.

THE TOY FACTORY

UNIT F3, THE DESIGNER OUTLET AT THE LOWRY, SALFORD QUAYS, MANCHESTER, LANCASHIRE M5 2WZ, ☎ 0161 877 7745, www.thetoyfactory.co.uk, 10–8 MON–FRI, 9–7 SAT, 11–5 SUN. **FACTORY SHOP IN A FACTORY SHOPPING VILLAGE**

The Toy Factory Outlets are part of Europe's largest toy factory outlet retailer. They offer an enormous range of branded products which may be surplus stocks, end of ranges or cancelled orders, and are therefore able to sell their products at up to 70% off normal high street prices. Their range includes famous names such as: Action Man, Barbie, Bandai, Crayola, Corgi, Fisher-Price, Hasbro, Hornby, Lego, Little Tikes, Meccano, Tomy, V-Tech and many more, all at unbelievably low prices.

THORNTONS

FREEPORT VILLAGE, ANCHORAGE ROAD, FLEETWOOD, LANCASHIRE FY7 6AE, ☎ 01253 770710, www.thorntons.co.uk, 10–6 SEVEN DAYS A WEEK, 8 ON THUR, FRI. **FACTORY SHOP IN A FACTORY SHOPPING VILLAGE**

See page 658 (CHESH)

TOYWORLD STORE FACTORY OUTLET

FREEPORT SHOPPING VILLAGE, ANCHORAGE ROAD, FLEETWOOD, FYLDE LANCASHIRE FY7 6AE, ☎ 01253 773776, www.toyworldstore.com, 10–8 MON–FRI, 9–6 SAT, 11–5 SUN. **FACTORY SHOP IN A FACTORY SHOPPING VILLAGE**

See page 658 (CHESH)

LEICESTERSHIRE

PIC A CHIC

FACTORY SHOP, NOTTINGHAM ROAD INDUSTRIAL ESTATE, ASHBY DE LA ZOUCH, LEICESTERSHIRE LE6 51DR, ☎ 01530 413077, 9–4 MON–FRI, 9–12 SAT. **FOOD AND DRINK DISCOUNTER**

Full range of frozen foods sold at discounted prices, open to wholesale or the general public. These include barbeque and party foods, ready meals, Pukka Pies, gateaux and cheesecakes. They also sell a specialist line of chicken portions and southern fried chicken portions.

LINCOLNSHIRE

WILKINSON STORES

2 THE BROADWAY, ASHBY, SCUNTHORPE, LINCOLNSHIRE NG5 7EL, ☎ 01724 867767, www.wilko.co.uk, 9–5.30 MON–FRI, 8.30–5.30 SAT, 10–4 SUN. MAIL ORDER.

2 THE BROADWAY, ASHBY, SCUNTHORPE, LINCOLNSHIRE DN16 2SN, ☎ 01724 867767, www.wilko.co.uk, 9–5.30 MON–SAT, 8.30–5.30 ON THUR, 10–4 SUN. **PERMANENT DISCOUNT OUTLET**

See page 656 (BUCKS)

LONDON

BIBLIOPHILE BOOKS

5 THOMAS ROAD, LONDON E14 7BN, ☎ 020 7515 9222, FAX: 020 7538 4115, **e-mail:** orders:biblipphilebooks.com, www.bibliophilebooks.com, OPERATES 8.30–5 MON–FRI. MAIL ORDER. **PERMANENT DISCOUNT OUTLET**

Mail order books from biographies and art, to literature and general tomes at half price or less. Stock is brand new remainders, plus reprints, rare and sometimes signed editions. Send for free catalogue or shop online.

BOOKENDS

108 CHARING CROSS ROAD, LONDON WC2H OSN, ☎ 020 7836 3457, FAX: 01497 847889, **e-mail:** bookends@madasafish.com, www.bookspostfree.com, 9–8 MON–SAT, 12–6 SUN. **SECONDHAND SHOP**

See page 656 (BRIS)

BOOKS FOR AMNESTY

139 KING STREET, HAMMERSMITH, LONDON W6, FAX: 020 8746 3172, 10–6 MON–FRI, 10–4 SAT.

26 CAMDEN HIGH STREET, LONDON NW1 0JH, ☎ 020 7388 0070, 10–6 MON–SAT. **SECONDHAND SHOP**

New books hot off the presses, many of which are critics' copies, at reductions of 25% to 30%. Also remainders, secondhand and some antiquarian books, secondhand CDs, records and videos.

BOOKTHRIFT

22 THURLOE STREET, LONDON SW7 2LT, ☎ 020 7589 2916, FAX: 020 7589 0522, 10–8 MON–FRI, 10–7 SAT, 12–7 SUN. **PERMANENT DISCOUNT OUTLET**

See page 657 (CHESH)

CD WAREHOUSE UK

51A NEW BROADWAY, EALING, LONDON W5 5AH, ☎ 020 8567 2122, 10–7 SEVEN DAYS A WEEK.

46 THE BROADWAY, WIMBLEDON, LONDON SW19, FAX: 020 8543 2355, 10–7 SEVEN DAYS A WEEK. **COMPACT DISCS**

See page 668 (HERTS)

CHAMBERLAIN

75 KENTISH TOWN ROAD, LONDON NW1 8NY, ☎ 020 7485 4488, www.chamberlaincycles.co.uk, 8.30–6 MON–SAT. **PERMANENT DISCOUNT OUTLET**

Sells Giant, Dawes, Raleigh, Gary Fisher and Scott bikes for adults and children, as well as helmets, baskets and tyres. Stock changes constantly and the owner says that their prices will not be beaten.

GLOUCESTER ROAD BOOKSHOP

123 GLOUCESTER ROAD, LONDON SW7 4TE, ☎ 020 7370 3503, FAX: 020 7373 0610, 9.30–10.30 MON–FRI, 10.30–6.30 SAT, SUN AND BANK HOLIDAYS. **SECONDHAND SHOP**

Secondhand books, also catalogues in modern first editions and rare antiquarian books. A reader who recommended this shop said they are strong on all areas: literature, arts, history etc, all in good condition, well displayed and categorised. Book prices range from 20p to £200.

HALF-PRICE POTS

340 FULHAM ROAD, LONDON SW10 9UH, ☎ 020 7376 4808, 10–5.30 SEVEN DAYS A WEEK. **PERMANENT DISCOUNT OUTLET**

Terracotta pots from around the world at extremely competitive prices. The pots come in all shapes and sizes from China, Spain, Morocco, Mexico and Tunisia, Egypt, Turkey and India. Prices range from 20p to £1,000 and include antique pots and storage jars reclaimed from the desert. Stock changes constantly.

HALF-PRICE TICKET BOOTH

THE BOOKING HALL, LEICESTER SQUARE STATION, LONDON WC2, FAX: 020 8427 6566, THE CRITERION THEATRE, PICCADILLY CIRCUS, LONDON W1, FAX: 020 8427 6566, www.uktickets.co.uk, **e-mail:** minaxi@uktickets.co.uk, **PERMANENT DISCOUNT OUTLET**

Here's where you can pick up official half-price and discounted theatre tickets for many of the popular West End musicals and plays, usually for that day's performance. Also tickets for sold out musicals and plays. Turn up in person at the two outlets, or phone 020 8427 6566.

LONDON FOR LESS

222 KENSAL ROAD, LONDON W10 5BN, ☎ 020 8964 4242, FAX: 020 8964 4141 **e-mail:** admin@metropolis.co.uk, www.smartsave.com, **PERMANENT DISCOUNT OUTLET**

Anyone who likes visiting London may like to take advantage of London for Less. Usually promoted to American visitors, it has recently been launched to the domestic British market. For just £12.95, you get a package which includes a discount card providing discounts at over 250 places in central London, plus a 288-page full colour guidebook and a fold-out map. Discounts are applicable for up to four people for up to eight days. Example of discounts include: 20% off 45 attractions and museums such as Madame Tussaud's; 20% off ticket prices at shows, concerts, operas and ballets, such as The London Philharmonic; 20% off rack rates at 42 hotels such as The Rochester Hotel; 20% off the total bill at 90 restaurants; and 20% off all goods at 50 shops. Shops included range from Piccadilly Souvenirs, situated right next to Piccadilly Circus to House of Cashmere on Oxford Street selling famous brand-name clothes. Books are also available at £5.95 for European cities: Amsterdam, Athens, Barcelona, Berlin, Bruges, Brussels, Budapest, Copenhagen, Dublin, Florence, Hamburg, Iceland, Istanbul, Lisbon, Madrid, Milan, Munich, Paris, Prague, Rome, Salzburg, Venice, Verona, Vienna and, for the USA, guides on: New York, California, Florida, Hawaii, Las Vegas, Los Angeles, Orlando, San Francisco and western USA; and Malaysia, Singapore and Thailand. All For Less titles can be purchased at book shops, at the Britain Visitor Centre on Lower Regent Street or via the above telephone number.

ONESWOOP LTD

COMMONWEALTH HOUSE, MEZZANINE FLOOR, 2 CHALKHILL ROAD, LONDON W6 8DW, ☎ 0845 330 8535, www.carbusters.com, **PERMANENT DISCOUNT OUTLET**

Permanent discount website whereby you can receive overseas quotes on car prices via the internet. Select the make, model and specification and you will receive an exact quote from an overseas dealer, which will include delivery charges, legal costs and VAT registration. It takes an average of three months for cars to be delivered. Oneswoop is a Which? Web Trader approved site. You can contact the sales department through the website (above) or by phoning 0845 330 8535.

OXFAM SUPER SAVING SHOP

570 KINGSLAND ROAD, LONDON E8 4AH, ☎ 020 7923 1532, 9.15–5.15 MON–SAT. **SECONDHAND SHOP**

Vast secondhand shop selling loads of cheap bric a brac, records and clothes. Stock is made up of unsold items from Oxfam's other shops in London so it's very cheap indeed. For example, bric-a-brac items from 9p; items of clothing from £2.29; electrical items (which have all been tested), such as lamps, from £2.99. Other end-of-line Oxfam shops include Kilburn, Burnt Oak, Tooting and Walthamstow.

POSTSCRIPT

DEPT GDD00, 24 LANGROYD ROAD, LONDON SW17 7PL, ☎ 020 8767 7421, FAX: 020 8682 0280, **e-mail:** enquiries@postscriptbooks.co.uk, www.psbooks.co.uk, 9–5.30 MON–FRI. MAIL ORDER ONLY. **PERMANENT DISCOUNT OUTLET**

Specialises in high quality books by mail at greatly reduced prices. Unlike the big book clubs, you are under no obligation to buy at any time. The selection covers a huge range of interests from art, gardening, cookery, biography, travel and reference to history, philosophy, psychology and literature – from classic works to the frankly esoteric – many of which cannot be found in bookshops and all priced at a fraction of publishers' latest prices. Phone for their free catalogue.

RAINBOW

249 AND 253 ARCHWAY ROAD, HIGHGATE, LONDON N6 5BS, ☎ 020 8340 8003, FAX: 0208 372 5484, 10.30–5.30 MON–SAT. **DRESS AGENCY**

Number 249 sells mainly secondhand items, while no. 253 is new merchandise and toys. At 249, the shop is divided into six selling areas which are rented out on a day-to-day basis. Examples of goods on sale are adults and children's clothing, baby equipment, toys, books, bric-a-brac, arts and crafts. The shop is in Highgate so there is a big variety of good quality designer clothes and other interesting goods. As there is no middle man, there are loads of bargains to be had. The shop at 253 has a large and fascinating selection of new toys at reasonable prices. They stock traditional wooden toys such as rocking horses, fots, trains, garages and dolls' houses from, among others, Brio, Galt, Escor and Plan Toys. They also sell Lego, Playmobil, TY Beanies, dressing up, books, creative kits, nostalgic pocket money toys and lots more. Ends of lines are discounted throughout the year. Highgate tube and buses are near by and there's free parking in the side streets and right outside to load and unload.

MIDDLESEX

BCP AIRPORT PARKING AND TRANSFER SERVICE

HEATHROW, MIDDLESEX, ☎ 0870 013 4586 (RESERVATIONS) PLEASE QUOTE BP744, **e-mail:** reservations@bcponline.co.uk, www.bcponline.co.uk, 8–9 SEVEN DAYS A WEEK. **PERMANENT DISCOUNT OUTLET**

See page 671 (LANCS)

THE SALVAGE SHOP

34–40 WATLING AVENUE, BURNT OAK, MIDDLESEX HA8 0LR, ☎ 020 8952 4353, **e-mail:** lss@salvage1.co.uk, www.salvage1.co.uk, 9–5.30 MON–SAT, 10–4 SUN. **PERMANENT DISCOUNT OUTLET**

An Aladdin's cave of salvaged stock for the avid bargain hunter, most of which has been the subject of insurance claims for fire or flood, salvage, bankruptcy or is simply clearance stock. Stock changes every two or three days and regular visitors have found anything from half price foot spas, televisions and toys to grooming equipment, kitchen items, linens and especially fantastic bargains in designer clothing. Yves Saint Laurent, Armani, Ungaro, Hugo Boss and Valentino, as well as all major high street names, are just some of the names to be found (though the labels are often cut out). Discounts range from 50% to 80%. Phone first to check stock.

NORFOLK

GILCHRIST CONFECTIONERY LTD

UNITS 1 AND 2, OXBOROUGH LANE, FAKENHAM, NORFOLK NR21 8AF, ☎ 01328 862632, 8.30–4 MON– FRI, 9–12 SOME SATS. **FOOD AND DRINK DISCOUNTER**

Factory shop underneath the offices sells all sorts of chocolate items – walnut whips, petit fours, mints, Thomas the Tank Engine chocolates, Christmas chocolate tree decorations – to well-known department stores. Seconds and misshapes are sold in bags for £1; overmakes at half price. Stock varies from week to week.

MONEY £ACTS

MONEY FACTS HOUSE, 66–70 THORPE ROAD, NORWICH NR1 1BJ, ☎ 01603 476476, www.moneyfacts.co.uk, **PERMANENT DISCOUNT OUTLET**

Very little in this life comes free and often saving money involves spending some first. This is true in the case of Money £acts, the guide to savings, investment and mortgage rates, national savings and annuities, which operates an update by fax. Whether you want to find out what the interest rates are on mortgages or where to open your savings account to get the best rates, you simply dial the relevant fax number and wait for the information to appear at your end. Commercial and residential mortgage information is updated daily, as is savings information. Cost is not more than 75p per minute.

REAL FACTORY SHOP (CARTWRIGHT & BUTLER)

HEMPSTEAD ROAD INDUSTRIAL ESTATE, HOLT, NORFOLK NR25 6ES, ☎ 01263 711447, FAX: 01263 711595, www.realfactoryshop.co.uk, 9–5 MON–SAT, 10–4 SUN. **FOOD AND DRINK DISCOUNTER**

Sells overstocks of the full range of famous Cartwright & Butler foods: preserves, pickles, chutneys, marmalades, biscuits, seasonings and spices, as well as overruns of own-label product. There's a wide range of non-foods including candles, fragrant products, toys and baskets, and they specialise in unique gift boxes, baskets and hampers containing a combination of goodies.

THE WORKS

31 GENTLEMANS WALK, NORWICH, NORFOLK NR2 1NB, ☎ 01603 667209, 9–6 MON–SAT, 8 ON THUR, 10.30–4.30 SUN. **PERMANENT DISCOUNT OUTLET**

See page 657 (CAMBS)

NORTHAMPTONSHIRE

TANDEE NURSERIES

BARNWELL ROAD, THURNING, NEAR OUNDLE, NORTHAMPTONSHIRE PE8 5RJ, ☎ 01832 293755, www.tandee.co.uk, 9–5 SEVEN DAYS A WEEK. **FACTORY SHOP**

This grower of quality nursery stock sells direct to the public at trade prices. You can buy shrubs, conifers, trees, perennials, bedding plants, climbers, hedging and fruit trees at this large centre. Climbers which normally cost £7 are £3.95 here; trees which cost £35 are £15.95 while conifers are four for £10 and shrubs cost from £2.95.

NORTHUMBERLAND

BARGAIN BAGGAGE FACTORY SHOP

BUGATTI HOUSE, NORHAM ROAD, NORTH SHIELDS, NE29 7HA, ☎ 0191 258 4451, FAX: 0191 258 2983, **e-mail:** modrec.int@modrec.co.uk, www.modrecinternational.com, 10–2 TUE, 10–3 WED, THUR, FRI. **FACTORY SHOP**

Leather goods from Pierre Cardin, Gina Ferrari, Cardin Weekender and Executive Essentials at discounts of up to 50%. Suitcases, weekend bags, handbags, wallets, purses, briefcases, attache cases and small leather gifts. Situated next door to Welch's sweet factory.

BARTER BOOKS

ALNWICK STATION, ALNWICK, NORTHUMBERLAND NE66 2NP, ☎ 01665 604888, FAX: 01605 604444, **e-mail:** webquery@barterbooks.co.uk, www.barterbooks.co.uk, OPEN 9–7 SEVEN DAYS A WEEK. **SECONDHAND SHOP**

One of the second largest secondhand book shop in the UK has, as you would imagine, an enormous range of books in a wide variety of subjects.

THE BODY SHOP DEPOT

ROYAL QUAYS FACTORY OUTLET CENTRE, COBLE DENE ROAD, NORTH SHIELDS, TYNE & WEAR NE29 6DW, ☎ 0191 259 6145, www.the-body-shop.com, 10–6 MON–SAT, 8 ON THUR, 11–5 SUN. **FACTORY SHOP IN A FACTORY SHOPPING VILLAGE**

See page 658 (CHESH)

THORNTONS

SOUTH PARADE, ROYAL QUAYS SHOPPING CENTRE, COBLE DENE, NORTH SHIELDS NE29 6DN, ☎ 0191 258 0623, www.thorntons.co.uk, 10–6 MON–SAT, 11–5 SUN. **FACTORY SHOP IN A FACTORY SHOPPING VILLAGE**

See page 658 (CHESH)

TOYWORLD STORE FACTORY OUTLET

ROYAL QUAYS FACTORY SHOPPING OUTLET, COBLE DENE, NORTH SHIELDS, NEWCASTLE UPON TYNE, NEAR A19, TYNE & WEAR NE29 6DW, ☎ 0191 257 3333, www.toyworldstore.com, 10–6 MON–SAT, 11–5 SUN. **FACTORY SHOP IN A FACTORY SHOPPING VILLAGE**

See page 658 (CHESH)

TYNEDALE RETAIL PARK

HEXHAM, NORTHUMBERLAND NE46 3PJ, ☎ 01434 607788, 10–6 MON–FRI, 9.30–6 SAT, 11–5 SUN. **PERMANENT DISCOUNT OUTLET**

With 15,000 square feet of retail selling across a 10 acre site, all at ground level except the restaurant which has access via a lift, the Tynedale Retail Park is accessible to all. Here you will find overstocks and clearance lines at up to 50% off normal retail prices. Quality names such as Windsmoor, Jaegar, French Connection, Timberland, Elle and Edinburgh Woollen Mill are just a few of the brands available. The clothing is just for adults, but there are shoes for adults and children. There is also furniture, linen, electrical items, bath accessories, toys, gifts and DIY equipment. The main section is a garden centre which also has pets, golf, sporting and outdoor wear departments. The child-friendly restaurant has a kids zone, parking is free and there are disabled facilities on site.

NOTTINGHAMSHIRE

EDWARDIAN CONFECTIONERY LTD

HUTHWAITE, BARKER STREET, NOTTINGHAMSHIRE NG17 2LJ, ☎ 01623 554712, 8–6 MON–FRI, 9–1 SAT. **FOOD AND DRINK DISCOUNTER**

Sweets and rock sold at two-thirds of the shop price. Range includes peanut brittle, treacle slab, caramel slab and chocolate, all of which can be bought either whole or broken up. Approximately 70 types of boiled sweets made on the premises.

WESTON MILL POTTERY

EGG PACKERS WORKSHOP, NAVIGATION YARD, MILLGATE, NEWARK, NOTTINGHAMSHIRE NG24 4TY, ☎ 01636 676835, www.wmpot.co.uk, 9.30–4.30 MON–SAT, 11–4.30 SUN, BANK HOLIDAYS. SOMETIMES CLOSED SUN IN JAN AND FEB SO PHONE FIRST. **FACTORY SHOP**

Manufacturer of terracotta wares, which they supply to many high street retailers. Garden pots in a variety of shapes and sizes are handthrown on the premises. Quality clay and high-firing make these frost resistant. A range of imported troughs, urns and large pots are also available at discounted prices. Weston Mill also produces items for the kitchen and home, including chicken roasters, tandori pots, garlic cellars and egg racks. Seconds and discounted items are always on sale at bargain prices. A large range of bird care products is also available.

WILKINSON STORES

2–6 FRONT STREET, ARNOLD, NOTTINGHAM, NOTTINGHAMSHIRE NG5 7EL, ☎ 0115 926 0805, www.wilko.co.uk, 9–5.30 MON–FRI, 8.30–6 SAT, 10–4 SUN. **PERMANENT DISCOUNT OUTLET**

See page 656 (BUCKS)

OXFORDSHIRE

BICESTER OUTLET SHOPPING VILLAGE

PINGLE DRIVE, BICESTER, JUNCTION 9 OF M40, OXFORDSHIRE OX6 7WD, ☎ 01869 323200, 10–6 SEVEN DAYS A WEEK. **FACTORY SHOPPING VILLAGE**

Described as 'Bond Street comes to Bicester', Bicester Village has established itself as the UK's leading outlet shopping destination in terms of offering the largest selection of international brand names to choose from. Currently there are 90 outlet shops offering quality merchandise at discounts of up to 60%, sometimes even more. The choice of famous brands at Bicester Village is second to none. International names include a Polo Ralph Lauren store, which now stocks more goods from their women's sport and home collections, Donna Karan, Versace, Christian Lacroix, Escada, Cerruti 1881 and TSE Cashmere. New arrivals from the international fashion scene are La Perla, Nautica, Gieves & Hawkes, Tommy Hilfiger, Tod's, MaxMara, Salvatore Ferragamo, Zegna, Calvin Klein, Charles Tyrwhitt, Sand, Links, Nautica, Musto and Holland & Holland. Both of Britain's leading designers, Nicole Farhi and Paul Smith, have shops with goods from their men's and women's collections. Karen Millen and Whistles both cater for the younger set with much more women's fashion to be found in The Designer Room, Episode, Hobbs, Jigsaw and Inwear Matinique. Top high street names are also well represented by Benetton, Principles, French Connection, Monsoon and Racing Green. The more classic customer also has an unequalled choice with Burberry, Aquascutum, Jaeger, Mulberry and the Scandinavian company RedGreen, whose nautical style of casual wear is very popular. Rugged outdoor wear can be found at Helly Hansen, Tog 24, the climbing and walking specialist. Active sportswear, represented by Fred Perry and Reebok, has now been joined by one of America's most famous sports shoe brands, Vans. A comprehensive collection of shoes, including many ranges for children, can be found in Clarks, with elegant high fashion styles in Charles Jourdan from Paris. Also, for women's shoes, handbags and accessories, there is Jane Shilton; for luggage, there is the Samsonite shop, plus the exciting addition of the first TAG-Heuer outlet, which stocks end-of-line designer watches, all fully guaranteed, at very attractive prices. Lingerie and underwear is to be found at Warners and Triumph, with HOM, the French brand, for the men; and the finest French childrenswear at Petit Bateau; English fragrances at Penhaligon's; make-up, bath and body therapies at Molton Brown, and soaps and gifts at Woods of Windsor. For the home, there are Price's candles and towels and duvets from another leading French brand, Descamps; cutlery from Oneida; china and crystal from Villeroy & Boch and Waterford Wedgwood and fine linens and accessories for the home from The White Company. The Cosmetic Company stocks well-known skincare products, cosmetics and fragrances for men and women. Bicester Village is something akin to a 'one-floor department store' and menswear, which can often be found in the designer shops, is also well represented in its own right with Dunhill, Blazer, Sand, Savoy Taylors Guild, Oscar Jacobson and Dockers, plus another international touch being provided by Cerruti Menswear, all offering good size ranges in a wide choice from very casual through to traditional business clothes. To complete the day out at Bicester Village, take home some popular titles from Books etc, get to know more about the location for a return visit from the Tourist Information Centre, and regain strength with top quality refreshment at Pret-A-Manger or Starbucks. There are cash machines, a children's play area, free parking and a shuttle bus (which is free from Thursday to Sunday) and taxi connection to Bicester North Station, which is on the Chiltern Railways line, and runs between Marylebone and Birmingham. Bicester Village is about one hour's drive from London, two miles from Junction 9 on the M40. Take the A41 and follow signs for Village Retail Park.

BOOKS ETC

BICESTER OUTLET SHOPPING VILLAGE, PINGLE DRIVE, BICESTER, JUNCTION 9 OF M40, OXFORDSHIRE OX26 6WD, ☎ 01869 325417, www.booksetc.co.uk, 10–6 SEVEN DAYS A WEEK. **FACTORY SHOP IN A FACTORY SHOPPING VILLAGE**

This shop sells a wide range of books, including popular paperback and hardback fiction, classics, cookery titles, children's books and reference tomes, as well as wrapping paper and greetings cards. All books are sold at a discount of at least 30% off the reccommended retail price and many are available at even greater savings. The village also has a restaurant, a children's play area and free parking.

THE RED HOUSE

WINDRUSH PARK, WITNEY, OXFORDSHIRE OX29 0YD, ☎ 01993 893456, FAX: 01993 776813, www.redhouse.co.uk, MAIL ORDER. **PERMANENT DISCOUNT OUTLET**

A no-commitment book club with an excellent catalogue of children's books, The Red House covers both educational matters, from reading skills to history, and practical activity books as well as fiction. The books are a mixture of hardback and paperback from a variety of different publishers, and good savings are to be made. Occasionally some CD-Roms are available. You can see the comprehensive range of books by visiting the website where you can also buy online. Here, they have introduced Bookends, books for children and adults at very low prices.

SHROPSHIRE

BARN BOOKS

PEAR TREE FARM, NORBURY, WHITCHURCH, SHROPSHIRE SY13 4HZ, ☎ 01948 663742, FAX: 01948 663742, **e-mail:** barnbooks@barnbooks.co.uk, www.barnbooks.co.uk, 10–5 FRI, SAT, SUN, BANK HOLIDAYS AND BY APPOINTMENT. **PERMANENT DISCOUNT OUTLET**

Remainders, publishers' returns and secondhand books of an excellent quality and range. Comprehensive gardening, architecture and countryside selection as well as children's books. The bookshop is set in beautiful countryside with ample parking, visit the website for more information and a map.

CLASSICAL PASSIONS

PO BOX 7, OSWESTRY, SHROPSHIRE SY10 9WF, ☎ 01691 670 750, FAX: 01691 670 747. **e-mail:** classical-passions@yahoo.co.uk, 9.30–6.30 MON–FRI, 10–4 SAT. **PERMANENT DISCOUNT OUTLET**

Mail order company which claims to better most prices for CDs, cassettes, DVDs and videos. Rather than operating by catalogue, you simply phone up – having checked prices locally – and find out what their best price is. As their name suggests they are classical specialists, but they deal in any type of music and any video on general release. Postage is free on orders of £20 or more, 90p up to £20. Worldwide mail order is also available.

HARRY TUFFINS SUPERMARKET AND PETROL STATION

CRAVEN ARMS, SHROPSHIRE SY7 9PU, ☎ 01588 672202, 8–6 MON–WED, SAT, 8–8 THUR, FRI, 10–4 SUN. **PERMANENT DISCOUNT OUTLET**

Supermarket selling foodstuffs, garden furniture and household goods at incredibly competitive prices. The store offers a vast range of tinned food, pickles, sauces, dried foods, soups, cereals, wine, household cleaning products, kitchen equipment, stationery and DIY. Instore fruit and vegetables. Harry Tuffins bottled mineral water is available at Churchstoke.

THE ART BOOKSHOP

3 QUALITY SQUARE, LUDLOW, SHROPSHIRE SY8 1AR, ☎ 01584 872758, 10–5 FRI, SAT. **PERMANENT DISCOUNT OUTLET**

Superb range of specialist stock of new art, design and architecture books as well as secondhand books. Some books are reduced by 25% to 50%, while there is a bargain box of books at £2 each.

SOMERSET

CHAPLINS SUPERSTORES HOME & GARDEN

BINDON ROAD, TAUNTON, SOMERSET TA2 6AA, ☎ 01823 288017, FAX: 01823 336189, 9–8 MON–FRI, 9–6 SAT, 10.30–4.30 SUN. **PERMANENT DISCOUNT OUTLET**

A wide range of merchandise for the bargain hunter, including garden tools, plants, fertilisers and accessories; toys; adults clothing and shoes; stationery; household textiles; electrical equipment; DIY items; glass and china; bathroom accessories; partyware; candles; food accessories. Spades are available at £4.99, trowels at 99p, shears at £5.99 (while stocks last).

CLARKS VILLAGE OUTLET SHOPPING

FARM ROAD, STREET, JUNCTION 23 OF M5, THEN A39, SOMERSET BA16 0BB, ☎ 01458 840064, **e-mail:** bgodwin@realm-ocm.com, www.clarksvillage.co.uk, APRIL–OCTOBER 9–5.30 MON–SAT, 11–5 SUN, NOVEMBER–MARCH 10–6, MON–SAT, 11–5 SUN. **FACTORY SHOPPING VILLAGE**

Purpose-built village of brick-built shops with extensive car parking facilities. Restaurant, fast food stands, carousel, indoor and outdoor play areas, and working village pottery and artists' studio. Here, there are 57 shops with more planned. Shops include: Body Shop, Reebok selling the Reebok brand, Rockport and the Greg Norman Collection; Monsoon/Accessorize, Benetton, Wrangler, The Designer Room, Jaeger, Viyella, Alexon, Triumph/Hom, Gossard, Clarks Factory Shop, Rohan, Windsmoor, Liz Claiborne, Calvin Klein, Van Heusen, Next, Warehouse, Tom Sayers men's sweaters and trousers, Warner's lingerie, Tog 24 outerwear, Jane Shilton handbags, luggage and shoes, The Suit Company and Blazer and Event jewellery. There is also a purpose-built china and glass pavilion and many other stores, all with up to 50% off famous name brands.

THE BODY SHOP DEPOT

UNIT 36, CLARKS VILLAGE, STREET, SOMERSET BA16 0BB, ☎ 01458 441952, FAX: 01458 441562, www.the-body-shop.com, 9–6 MON–SAT, 11–5 SUN. **FACTORY SHOP IN A FACTORY SHOPPING VILLAGE**

See page 658 (CHESH)

THE BOOK BARN

17–18 MARKET PLACE, GLASTONBURY, SOMERSET BA6 9HL, ☎ 01749 689040, **e-mail:** bookbarn@netcomuk.co.uk, 9–6 MON–SAT, 12–5 SUN.

WEST STREET, WELLS, SOMERSET BA5 2HJ, ☎ 01749 689040, **e-mail:** bookbarn@netcomuk.co.uk, 9.30–5.30 MON–SAT, 12–5 SUN. **SECONDHAND SHOP**

Vast quantity of used books are sold in this huge shop. You can phone, fax or email for a book for which you are searching – there is no charge for searches. There is another branch in Wells.

THE POT PEOPLE

CLARKS VILLAGE FACTORY SHOPPING CENTRE, FARM ROAD, STREET, JUNCTION 23 OF M5, SOMERSET BA16 0BB, ☎ 01458 840652, 9–6 MON–SAT, 10–5 SUN. **FACTORY SHOP IN A FACTORY SHOPPING VILLAGE**

A family-run business, the Pot People have years of experience producing a wide variety of pots and ornaments for garden centres and retails all round the country. In 1993, they started selling their garden stoneware directly to the public at wholesale prices, about half what you might expect to pay for similar stoneware products. When shopping at Clarks Village, they will happily deliver your purchase directly to your car, wrapped in sacking to help prevent damage en route. Ornaments include cherub bird baths, £20, normal price, £36; swag pots, £12, usually £25; plumed tubs, £11, usually £20.95; lion's head troughs, £18, usually £36; sundials, £35, usually £77.75. They also sell bedding plants, shrubs and cut flowers, all at wholesale prices.

THORNTONS

CLARKS VILLAGE FACTORY SHOPPING CENTRE, FARM ROAD, STREET, JUNCTION 23 OF M5, SOMERSET BA16 0BB, ☎ 01458 841553, www.thorntons.co.uk, 9–6 MON–SAT, 11–5 SUN. **FACTORY SHOP IN A FACTORY SHOPPING VILLAGE**

See page 658 (CHESH)

STAFFORDSHIRE

CANNOCK GATES LTD

MARTINDALE, HAWKS GREEN INDUSTRIAL ESTATE, CANNOCK, STAFFORDSHIRE WS11 2XT, ☎ 01543 462500 (MAIL ORDER FOR CANNOCK GATES AND THE GARDEN FACTORY), ☎ 08703 308160 (MAIL ORDER FOR CANNOCK BEDS), ☎ 08703 308158, **e-mail:** sales@cannockgates.co.uk, www.cannockgates.co.uk, 9–6 MON–SAT, 10–4 SUN (SUMMER), 9–5 MON–SAT (WINTER). **PERMANENT DISCOUNT OUTLET**

Three mail order companies under the umbrella of Cannock Gates Ltd: Cannock Gates, Cannock Beds and The Garden Factory. All offer a mail order catalogue and customers are sent regular updates and special offers. There are special deals in a wide range of wrought iron and wooden gates, as well as an ever-growing selection of garden loungers, wrought iron beds, gazebos, parasols, garden arches, wooden planters, cast-iron garden furniture, gifts and accessories. Cannock Beds has a factory shop at Unit 6, The Cedars Business Centre, Avon Road, Cannock, Staffordshire WS11 1LJ.

FREEPORT TALKE OUTLET MALL

FREEPORT TALKE OUTLET MALL, PIT LANE, TALKE PITS, STOKE-ON-TRENT, OFF JUNCTION 16 OF M6 THEN TAKE THE A500 AND THE A34, FOLLOWING SIGNS TO TALKE, STAFFORDSHIRE ST7 1XD, ☎ 01782 774113, www.freeporttalke.com, 9.30–8 MON–FRI, 9.30–6 SAT, 11–5 SUN. **FACTORY SHOPPING VILLAGE**

Fully covered indoor outlet mall with a range of restaurants, including Burger King and Café Ritazza, and an indoor soft play area for children. Womenswear includes The Designer Room, Edinburgh Woollen Mill, Nickelby's, Pilot, Spotlight, Roman Originals and Leading Labels. Menswear includes The Suit Company, Double Two, Petroleum, Nickelby's, Madhouse and Tog 24. Childrenswear can be found at Used Co Kids. Other shops on site include: Claire's Accessories, Charles Clinkard, Jane Shilton, Bags Etc, Trespass, Streetwise Sports, The Golf Company, Catalogue Bargain Shop, Julian Graves, Kitchen and Table, Toy World, Thorntons, Birthdays, Room, Mobile Phone Store, Book Depot, Picture Port, Ponden Mill and XS Music.

THORNTONS

FREEPORT TALKE OUTLET MALL, PIT LANE, TALKE PITS, STOKE-ON-TRENT, STAFFORDSHIRE ST7 1XD, ☎ 01782 787793, www.thorntons.co.uk, 10–8 MON–SAT, 11–5 SUN. **FACTORY SHOP IN A FACTORY SHOPPING VILLAGE**

See page 658 (CHESH)

TOYWORLD STORE FACTORY OUTLET

FREEPORT TALKE OUTLET MALL, PIT LANE, TALKE PITS, STOKE-ON-TRENT, STAFFORDSHIRE ST7 1QE, ☎ 01782 777744, www.toyworldstore.com, 10–8 MON–FRI, 10–6 SAT, 11–5 SUN. **FACTORY SHOP IN A FACTORY SHOPPING VILLAGE**

See page 658 (CHESH)

WILKINSON STORES

OLD HALL STREET, HANLEY, STOKE-ON-TRENT, STAFFORDSHIRE, ☎ 01782 279225, www.wilko.co.uk, 8.30–6 MON–FRI, 8 ON THUR, 11–5 SUN. MAIL ORDER.

BROOKS STREET, LEEK, STAFFORDSHIRE ST13 5JE, ☎ 01538 386669, www.wilko.co.uk, 9–5.30 MON, TUE, THUR, 8.30–5.30 WED, FRI, SAT.

CASTLE HOUSE, 47–48 IRONMARKET, NEWCASTLE UNDER LYME, STAFFORDSHIRE ST5 1PD., ☎ 01782 714334, www.wilko.co.uk, 8.30–5.30 MON–SAT. **PERMANENT DISCOUNT OUTLET**

See page 656 (BUCKS)

SUFFOLK

BOOKTHRIFT

10 MARKET PLACE, SOUTHWOLD, SUFFOLK IP18 6EE, ☎ 01502 724999, 9.30–5.30 MON–SAT, 11–5 SUN. **PERMANENT DISCOUNT OUTLET**

See page 657 (CHESH)

SURREY

BEANOS

MIDDLE STREET, CROYDON, SURREY CR0 1RE, ☎ 020 8680 1202, FAX: 020 8680 1203, **e-mail:** enquiries@beanos.co.uk, www.beanos.co.uk, 10–6 MON–FRI, 9–6 SAT. ALSO MAIL ORDER. **SECONDHAND SHOP**

The largest secondhand record store in Europe with more than two and a quarter million items on display in this three-storey shop. The three floors of nostalgia cover all formats and styles of music, a Sixties-style café and mini-cine on the top floor and a small stage on the middle floor with live bands performing every Saturday. They also run a mail order service which endeavours to search out and provide all musical requirements. A GDD reader says they have a wide choice of CDs at an average price of £7.

HOMELINK INTERNATIONAL

LINFIELD HOUSE, GORSE HILL ROAD, VIRGINIA WATER, SURREY GU25 4AS, , ☎ 01344 842642, FAX: 01344 842642, **e-mail:** exchange@homelink.org.uk www.homelink.org.uk 9–6 SEVEN DAYS A WEEK. **PERMANENT DISCOUNT OUTLET**

Home exchange is a great way to see the world, have a holiday and save money. You pay for travel, food and holiday spending only and you get to taste someone else's lifestyle! Homelink, in business since 1953, publishes a worldwide directory listing members interested in exchanging homes for holidays. An annual subscription of £95 brings three directories a year. Phone them for more details or visit their website.

RICHMOND BOOK SHOP

20 RED LION STREET, RICHMOND, SURREY TW9 1RW, ☎ 020 8940 5512, 9.30–6 FRI AND SAT. **PERMANENT DISCOUNT OUTLET**

A wide selection of secondhand books including many recent publications. Subject areas include, Art, Architecture, Aviation, Biography, Cookery, English Literature, Fiction, Film, History, Military, Nautical, Poetry, Plays, Travel and many more. Occasionally they will be open for longer periods on different days: phone for more details.

THE BOOK PEOPLE LTD

CATTESHALL MANOR, CATTESHALL LANE, GODALMING, SURREY GU7 1UU
ORDER LINE 0870 607 7740, FAX: 0870 607 7720., www.thebookpeople.co.uk, **PERMANENT DISCOUNT OUTLET**

The catalogue promises no membership, no contract to sign, no further obligation, savings of up to 75% off high street prices, phone, fax or post ordering, guaranteed delivery within seven working days, and reduced price postage and packing for pensioners. There are 13 pages of children's books, a variety of romantic novels; gardening and cookery titles; some sports books and many contemporary autobiographies. Package and posting costs £2.95 regardless of the size of order. Orders are taken by friendly and helpful staff. Phone the number above for a catalogue, or visit the website.

SUSSEX

BAGGAGE FACTORY

8 THE VILLAGE SQUARE, BRIGHTON MARINA, BRIGHTON, WEST SUSSEX BN2 5WA, ☎ 01273 699996, www.baggagefactory.co.uk, 10–6 MON–SUN. **FACTORY SHOP IN A FACTORY SHOPPING VILLAGE**

See page 667 (CORN)

BRIGHTON MARINA

CITY OF BRIGHTON AND HOVE, EAST SUSSEX BN2 5WB, ☎ 01273 818504, FAX: 01273 818701, 10–LATE SEVEN DAYS A WEEK. **FACTORY SHOPPING VILLAGE**

The UK and Europe's largest marina. Boasts an exciting range of outlet shops combined with excellent bars, restaurants and leisure facilities. Currently hosts 11 outlet stores, such as PULSE skating solutions, The Factory Shop, Leading Labels and many more. The marina is currently investing millions into additional facilities, planned to open at the end of 2002, which will include a further 16 outlet stores including some household names.

BCP AIRPORT PARKING AND TRANSFER SERVICE

GATWICK, SUSSEX, ☎ 0870 013 4586 (RESERVATIONS) PLEASE QUOTE BP744, **e-mail:** reservations@bcponline.co.uk, www.bcponline.co.uk, 8–9 SEVEN DAYS A WEEK. **PERMANENT DISCOUNT OUTLET**

See page 671 (LANCS)

CD WAREHOUSE UK

163 WESTON ROAD, BRIGHTON, EAST SUSSEX, ☎ 01273 731310, 9–6 MON–WED, 9–8 THUR, 9–7 FRI, SAT, 10–6 SUN. **COMPACT DISCS**

See page 668 (HERTS)

EDGCUMBE TEA AND COFFEE

WICKS HOUSE, FORD LANE, FORD, ARUNDEL, SUSSEX BN18 0DF, ☎ 01243 555775, FAX: 01243 555997, **e-mail:** sales@edgcumbes.co.uk, www.edgcumbes.co.uk, 9–6 MONDAY TO FRIDAY. MAIL ORDER. **FOOD AND DRINK DISCOUNTER**

Primarily trade suppliers, Edgcumbe sell direct to personal shoppers and have some very good bargains in ends of lines. They offer top quality tea blends in tea bag or loose form and a 'roast and post' coffee service by mail order – within 24 hours of ordering, you will find fresh coffee on your doorstep. They roast and blend their own coffee on site to order, and you can enjoy a range of flavoured coffee from amaretto to choc-mint. Because of their low overheads, the prices are very competitive. For example, £25 for 3,000 tea bags of English Breakfast blend. Van delivery service to local areas.

WARWICKSHIRE AND WEST MIDLANDS

THE CRAFT COMPANY

23 COTEN END, WARWICK, WARWICKSHIRE CV34 4NT, ☎ 01926 492505, FAX: 01926 492535, **e-mail:** heather@craftcompany.co.uk, 9–5.30 MON–SAT. MAIL ORDER ALSO. **PERMANENT DISCOUNT OUTLET**

Needlecraft warehouse which also operates a mail order leaflet. Due to bulk buying, savings are between 5% and 10%. There is every type of thread, tapestry wool, stranded cotton, shade cards, metallic threads, crochet cotton, flexi-hoops, needles, tapestry frames, scissors, beads, anchor accessories such as organiser boxes, as well as fabrics (Aida, Evenweave and Zweigart linens). They also sell sugar craft equipment, marzipan, fondant, cutters, drums, boards, boxes, pillars, sugar craft colours, wires, stamens, ribbons, nozzles, sugarcraft tools, crimpers, candles, mottoes, special occasion cakes and veiners by retail and mail order.

THE OUTLET

HATTON COUNTRY WORLD, DARK LANE, HATTON, NEAR WARWICK, WARWICKSHIRE CV35 8XA, ☎ 01926 842761, **e-mail:** hatton@hattonworld.com, www.hattonworld.com, 10–5 SEVEN DAYS A WEEK. **PERMANENT DISCOUNT OUTLET**

Hatton Country World consists of a Shopping Village with 25 craft and specialist shops and an antiques centre and, for bargain hunters, The Outlet, a department-style store selling discounted brand names in women's and men's clothes, kitchenware and gifts. All are housed in a charming cluster of converted Victorial farm buildings. There is a farm park and outdoor activity centre.

WILTSHIRE

IN EXCESS

131 NETHERHAMPTON ROAD, SALISBURY, WILTSHIRE SP2 8NA, ☎ 01722 414444, 9–5.30 MON–SAT, 10–4 SUN. **PERMANENT DISCOUNT OUTLET**

See page 663 (CORN)

INTERVAC INTERNATIONAL HOME EXCHANGE

COXES HILL BARN, NORTH WRAXALL, WILTSHIRE SN14 7AD, ☎ 01225 892011, FAX: 01225 892011, **e-mail:** holiday@intervac.co.uk, www.intervac.co.uk, **PERMANENT DISCOUNT OUTLET**

With a comprehensive guide available on the internet, home exchange is a great way to see the world, have a holiday and save money. You pay for travel, food and holiday spending only and make hotel bills a thing of the past! You also take on a home that has all the facilities and comforts you take for granted and sample another lifestyle and region from a better perspective: not as a tourist, but as part of the community. Subscribe at £99 per annum for full website and internet access and listing, and to receive an up-to-date listing of 12,500 homes in 50 countries, including your own personal listing. Cost includes a photo of your property which is published in both the brochure and the website. Internet listings are regularly updated. You can subscribe either online or by post. The directory is updated three times a year. Please phone for more details.

MCARTHURGLEN DESIGNER OUTLET GREAT WESTERN

KEMBLE DRIVE, SWINDON, JUNCTION 16 OF M4, WILTSHIRE SN2 2DY, ☎ 0800 316 4352 FREE INFORMATION LINE OR 01793 507600, www.mcarthurglen.com, 10–6 MON–FRI, 8 ON THUR, 9–6 SAT, 11–5 SUN. **FACTORY SHOPPING VILLAGE**

The McArthurGlen Designer Outlet Great Western offers over 100 stores selling top names and designer brands at up to 50% off typical retail prices. Housed in the restored Great Western Railway buildings, everything is conveniently located under one roof. A large open plan area dedicated to homewares has everything for the house and home. Facilities include a food court, children's play area, licensed creche and ample parking. Stores include: U Wear/I Wear, Warner UK Ltd, Antler, Ecco Shoes, Walker & Hall, Liz Claiborne, Viyella, Austin Reed, Suits You, Alexon, Jaeger, Windsmoor, Aquascutum, Olsen, Jacques Vert, Overland/Caterpillar, Episode, Long Tall Sally, Pilot, Triumph, Cotton Traders, Villeroy & Boch, Baron Jon, Clarks, HKA, Burberry, Remington, Regatta, Just Sweets, Easy Jeans, Ben Sherman, JoKids, Donnay, Le Creuset, Puma, Tog 24, XS, Gap, Big L, Soled Out, Ted Baker, Nike, Timberland, Quiksilver, Whittard, Marks and Spencer, Polo Jeans Company, Gant, Calp, The Design House, Dartington Crystal, Duvet and Pillow Shop, Henri Lloyd, Mexx, Ravel, The Luxury Beauty Store, Thomas Pink, Thorntons, Tie Rack, Julian Graves, Hanro, Jane Shilton, Birthday, Toy Zone, Bookends, Sofa Works, Designer Room, Petroleum, Next, Daks Simpson, Suit Company, Price's Candles, Claire's Accessories, Samsonite, Van Heusen, Cloverleaf, Poole Pottery, Spiegelau, Edinburgh Crystal, Woods of Windsor, Staffordshire Pottery, Waterford Wedgewood, Stuart Crystal, Gleneagles, The Garden Outlet, Ponden Mill, Jane Heath, Sheridan Australia, Tefal, Professional Cookware, and Oneida.

THORNTONS

MCARTHURGLEN DESIGNER OUTLET GREAT WESTERN, KEMBLE DRIVE, SWINDON, JUNCTION 16 OF M4, WILTSHIRE SN2 2DY, ☎ 01793 692438, www.thorntons.co.uk, 10–6 MON–FRI, 8 ON THUR, 9–6 SAT, 11–5 SUN. **FACTORY SHOP IN A FACTORY SHOPPING VILLAGE**

See page 658 (CHESH)

WILTON SHOPPING VILLAGE

MINSTER STREET, WILTON, SALISBURY, WILTSHIRE SP2 0RS, ☎ 01722 741 211, www.thewsv@eagleone.co.uk, 9.30–5.30 MON–SAT, 11–5 SUN. **FACTORY SHOPPING VILLAGE**

On the former site of the Royal Wilton Carpet Factory, this village uses the refurbished original factory dye houses and 300-year-old, listed, historic courtyard buildings to house factory shops selling fashion and homewares at discounted prices. It includes shops such as Cotton Traders, Double Two, Edinburgh Woollen Mill, Julian Graves, Old Traditions, Ponden Mill, Remainders Books, Roman Originals, Scotts of Stow and the Wilton Carpet Factory Shop. Free parking, coffee shop, children's play area and disabled facilities. A riverside café is also open during the summer, serving homemade food and refreshments.

WORCESTERSHIRE

EDINBURGH CRYSTAL

ROYAL WORCESTER VISITOR CENTRE, SEVERN STREET, WORCESTER, WORCESTERSHIRE WR1 2NE, ☎ 01905 746000 (CENTRE TEL NO), ☎ 01905 619503, **e-mail:** general@royal-worcester.co.uk, www.royal-worcester.co.uk, 9–5.30 MON–SAT, 11–5 SUN. MAIL ORDER.
FACTORY SHOP

The Victorian buildings of Royal Worcester's visitor centre lead into the heart of a world famous porcelain industry that was founded in 1751. Wide range of Edinburgh Crystal crystalware, among others, from glasses and vases to tumblers and bowls at discounts of between 33% and 50%. The shop sells firsts and seconds of crystal from one third off the normal price. There are also special promotional lines at discount prices up to 70% off seconds. Visitors can also shop in Wigornia Court where a myriad of home accessories and factory outlets selling cutlery, crystal, candles, linen, kitchen utensils, rugs and giftware can be found. Parking and disabled facilities available.

EVESHAM COUNTRY PARK SHOPPING AND GARDENING CENTRE

COUNTRY PARK MANAGEMENT, EVESHAM, AT THE NORTHERN END OF THE EVESHAM BYPASS, AT ITS JUNCTION WITH THE STRATFORD ROAD, WORCESTERSHIRE WR11 4TP ENQUIRIES: 01386 41661; GARDEN CENTRE: 01386 761888; APPLE BARN RESTAURANT: 01386 761333; VALE WILDLIFE VISITOR CENTRE: 01386 443348; COARSE FISHING/GOTTFRIED: 07973 147323, 9–6 MON–SAT (WINTER 5.30), 10.30–4.30 SUN.
FACTORY SHOPPING VILLAGE

Courtyard shops and garden centre providing a wide variety of goods at bargain prices. Designer and brand name men's and women's fashions from Leading Labels, leisurewear from Cotton Traders, coordinated soft furnishings, bedlinen and duvets from Ponden Mill, household goods from Lifestyles, dried fuits, nuts and packaged herbs from Julian Graves, an extensive range of books from The Book Depot, plus quality plants, colourful pots and garden equipment. Luggage & Bags sells a range of quality branded luggage and travel goods at great prices. There is also restaurant, wildlife centre, coarse fishing on the River Avon, and a miniature railway for a real country day out.

ROYAL WORCESTER VISITOR CENTRE

SEVERN STREET, WORCESTER, WORCESTERSHIRE WR1 2NE, ☎ 01905 746000, FAX: 01905 619503, **e-mail:** general@royal-worcester.co.uk, www.royal-worcester.co.uk, 9–5.30 MON–SAT, 11–5 SUN. MAIL ORDER. **FACTORY SHOP**

The Victorian buildings of Royal Worcester's visitor centre lead into the heart of a world famous porcelain industry that was founded in 1751. Royal Worcester's factory shops carry an extensive range of quality bone china tableware, porcelain oven-to-tableware, giftware and figurines. The factory seconds shop offers quality seconds at greatly reduced prices. Visitors can also shop in Wigornia

Court where a myriad of home accessories and factory outlets selling cutlery, crystal, candles, linen, kitchen utensils, rugs and giftware can be found. Parking and disabled facilities available.

YORKSHIRE

BOOKTHRIFT

34 BRIDGEGATE, HEBDEN BRIDGE, WEST YORKSHIRE HX7 8EX, ☎ 01422 845526, 9.30–5.30 MON–SAT, 11–5 SUN. **PERMANENT DISCOUNT OUTLET**

See page 657 (CHESH)

BROOKS FACTORY OUTLET STORES

SOUTH LANE, ELLAND, NEAR HALIFAX, WEST YORKSHIRE HX5 0HQ, ☎ 01422 377337, 9.30–5.30 MON–SAT, 8 ON THUR, 11–5 SUN.

BUYWELL RETAIL PARK, THORP ARCH, WETHERBY, NORTH YORKSHIRE LS23 7BJ, ☎ 01937 541895, 9.30–5.30 MON–SAT, 11–5 SUN. **PERMANENT DISCOUNT OUTLET**

Walk through the store and you can't fail to find a bargain. New stock arrives daily from well-known names such as Nike, French Connection, Gabicci, Klass, Camille and Ben Sherman. Apart from mens and women's clothes, they sell sportswear, linens, lingerie, shoes, accessories, luggage, towels, coordinated bed linen, household textiles, duvets, pillows and lots more from names such as Monogram and Ponden Mill. Everything under one roof at up to 50% off high street prices. The Elland store has a coffee shop.

FREEPORT CASTLEFORD DESIGNER OUTLET VILLAGE

CARRWOOD ROAD, GLASSHOUGHTON, CASTLEFORD, JUNCTION 32 OF M52, WEST YORKSHIRE WF10 4SB, ☎ 01977 520153, www.freeportcastleford.com, 10–8 MON–FRI, 10–6 SAT, 11–5 SUN. **FACTORY SHOPPING VILLAGE**

Designer outlet village with over 75 shops, indoor and outdoor children's play areas and a wide range of restaurants with easy access from the M52 and 3,500 free car parking spaces. Shops include Amazing Jeans, Baron Jon, BhS For Less, Charles Clinkard, Clarks, Cromwells, Churchill, Ciro Citterio, Craghoppers, CBS, Claire's Accessories, Cotton Traders, Damart, Edinburgh Crystal, Donnay, Double Two, Event Jewellery, Easy Jeans, Edinburgh Woollen Mill, Elle, Fila, Giorgio, Gossard, XS Music, Jane Shilton, John Partridge, Kappa, Kitchen and Table, Kurt Muller, Leading Labels, Lee Cooper, Littlewoods, London Leathers, Mexx, Mobile Phone Store, Nike, Nickleby's, Next to Nothing, Outrage, Petroleum, Picture Port, Pilot, Ponden Mill, Proibito, Rio Jewellery, Roman Originals, Regatta, Room, Ice Jeans, Sergio Tacchini, Sportsmill, Spotlight, Startrite Shoes, Remainders Book Depot, Designer Room, Garden Outlet, Shoe Collection, Toy Factory, Time, X Catalogue Store, Thorntons, Trespass, Waterford Wedgwood, Windsmoor,

HALLMARK FACTORY SHOP

DAWSONS LANE, BRADFORD, WEST YORKSHIRE BD4 6HW, ☎ 01274 689399, 10–5.30 MON–FRI, 10–2 SAT.

FREEPORT HORNSEA OUTLET VILLAGE, ROLSTON ROAD, HORNSEA, EAST YORKSHIRE HU18 1UT, ☎ 01964 533080, 9.30–6 SEVEN DAYS A WEEK. **FACTORY SHOP**

See page 672 (LANCS)

LIGHTWATER VILLAGE AND FACTORY SHOPPING

NORTH STAINLEY, RIPON, NORTH YORKSHIRE HG4 3HT, ☎ 01765 634508, FAX: 01765 635359, www.lightwatervalley.co.uk, 10–5.30 MON–SUN. **FACTORY SHOPPING VILLAGE**

Large complex of retail and factory outlets with a wide range of branded womenswear including blouses, skirts, suits, dresses, lingerie, outerwear, shoes and accessories as well as menswear from jeans and outdoor wear to formal wear. Shoes, jewellery, home furnishings, crystal and glass, a large range of pottery, garden products, toys, cheese and confectionery. There is a restaurant and coffee shop serving snacks and refreshments, free parking and disabled facilities. A family theme park on site boasts the Ultimate Rollercoaster, the longest in Europe.

MCARTHURGLEN DESIGNER OUTLET

ST NICHOLAS AVENUE, FULFORD, JUNCTION OF A19 AND A64, YORK, NORTH YORKSHIRE YO19 4TA, ☎ 01904 682720, www.mcarthurglen.com/york, 10–6 MON–SAT, 8 ON THUR, 11–5 SUN. **FACTORY SHOP**

The McArthurGlen Designer OutletYork is one of Europe's largest covered designer outlets with over 120 stores offering top brands and designer labels with discounts of up to 50% off typical retail prices. Find everything from men's, women's and children's clothing to accessories, shoes, sportswear, luggage, homewares, toys, books, and gifts. Facilities include a food court, a children's play area and free parking. Stores include: Armani, Autonomy, Ben Sherman, Burberry, Calvin Klein Jeans, Cerruti 1881, Chilli Pepper, Cotton Traders, Daks Simpson, Episode, Escada Sport, Gap Outlet, Guess, Hugo Boss, Jacques Vert, Jaeger/Viyella, Jesire/Esensual, Kabuki, Klass, Levi's, Margaret Howell, Marks & Spencer Outlet, Mergler, Mountain Warehouse, Nitya, Olsen, Pilot, Polo Ralph Lauren, Pringle, Proibito, Proudfoot Leather, Roman Originals, Ronit Zilkha, Ted Baker, The Designer Room, Thomas Pink, Tog 24, Tommy Hilfiger, Windsmoor, Alfred Dunhill, Baronjon, Ben Sherman, Haggar, HKA, Marlboro Classics, Paul Smith, Petroleum, Pour Homme, Rockport, Suit Company, Suits You, Timberland, Adidas, Diadora, Donnay, Reebok, Toyworld, Birthdays, Bodum, The Body Shop Depot, Bookends, Franchetti Bond, Le Creuset, Oneida, Paper Mill, Price's Candles, Remington, Scent To You, Whittard Kitchen, Woods of Windsor, XS Music & Video, Bed & Bath Works, China China, Coloroll, Descamps, Garden Outlet, Jane Heath, La Casa del Christallo, Lights 4 Less, Pictureport, Room, Slipperbox, Spiegelau, Professional Cookware, Daniel Footwear, Famous Footwear, Pavers, Rockport, Shoe Studio, Soled Out, Julian Graves, Thorntons, Antler, Kangol, Liberty, Travel Accessory, Chapelle Jewellery, Claire's Accessories, Designer Shades, Monet, Tie Rack, and The Watch Store.

MR VALUE

KILLINGHALL ROAD, BRADFORD, WEST YORKSHIRE BD3 8DN, ☎ 01274 669674, 9–7 MON–FRI, 9–5.30 SAT, 10–4 SUN. **PERMANENT DISCOUNT OUTLET**

A discount store offering a wide selection of goods which are catalogue returns, factory rejects, seconds and ends of lines – everything from clothes with the labels cut out to tapes, kettles, televisions, microwaves, irons, toasters, bedlinen, towels, sweets, artificial flowers, batteries, toiletries, crockery, glass, stationery, pots and pans, toys and bins. Kitchen equipment brand names include Russell Hobbs and Morphy Richards. There is also a department for mobility, selling wheelchairs, scooters etc.

QLM LTD

IDLE ROAD, IDLE, BRADFORD, WEST YORKSHIRE BD2 2AL, ☎ 01274 642222, 9.30–6 MON–SAT, 5.30 ON WED, 11–5 SUN. **PERMANENT DISCOUNT OUTLET**

Toys, household goods, clothes, food, electrical equipment, garden implements, kitchenware and furniture, all sold at discounted prices. For example, reject garden forks £6.99, spades £4.99, pruning tools £2.99 to £19.99.

SUMMER GRAND SALE

RIPLEY CASTLE, RIPLEY, NEAR HARROGATE, NORTH YORKSHIRE, ENQUIRIES: 01367 860017, FAX: 01367 860177, **e-mail:** nheslam@aol.com, 9.30–5.30 MON–FRI. **DESIGNER SALES**

There are now three annual Grand Sales taking place countrywide. The Christmas Grand Sale in London, with over 120 different small companies selling their merchandise to the public, is the largest. This takes place in mid-late November each year. Quality is high and covers everything from French lavender sachets, hand-painted furniture, made-to-measure blinds, 19th century wall clocks, unusual watercolours, cinammon-scented apple wreaths, traditional American tinware, children's pyjama cases, candle sconces; handmade Indian pickles, bamboo placemats, embossed copper sketchbooks, Art Deco mirrors, silk embroidered cushions, herbal tinctures, English garden trugs, African shopping baskets, handmade wrapping paper, elegant kitchen woodware, beaded handbags, bespoke Ottomans, fine champagne, baby sleeping bags, nautical mirrors, painted dog and cat beds, ties and matching cufflinks, antique Bergeres suites, Egyptian cotton bedlinen, often at discount because they are ends of lines. There is a three-day Spring Grand Sale at Sudeley Castle, Winchcombe, near Cheltenham in Gloucestershire, usually at the end of April/beginning of May, and a four-day Summer Grand Sale at Ripley Castle, near Harrogate, North Yorkshire, in June. Both feature food, travel bags, toys, games, garden furniture and equipment as well as decorative home accessories. Phone the above number to put your name on the mailing list. A proportion of the ticket revenue goes to charity.

THE BODY SHOP DEPOT

MCARTHURGLEN DESIGNER OUTLET YORK, ST NICHOLAS AVENUE, FULFORD, JUNCTION OF A19 AND A64, YORK, NORTH YORKSHIRE YO19 4TA, ☎ 01904 613873, www.the-body-shop.com, 10–6 MON–SAT, 8 ON THUR, 11–5 SUN. **FACTORY SHOP IN A FACTORY SHOPPING VILLAGE**

See page 658 (CHESH)

THE DARLEY MILL CENTRE

DARLEY, NEAR HARROGATE, NORTH YORKSHIRE HG3 2QQ, ☎ 01423 780857, 9.30–5.30 MON–SAT, 11–5 SUN. **PERMANENT DISCOUNT OUTLET**

The centre offers a great day out for the whole family, combining great bargains in clothing, crockery, linens, crafts and exclusive gifts, with lots for children to see and do. This fine 17th-century corn mill has one of the largest water wheels in Yorkshire and there's a licensed restaurant with an outdoor dining terrace.

THE MILL DISCOUNT DEPARTMENT STORE

BRADFORD ROAD, BATLEY, WEST YORKSHIRE WF17 5LZ, ☎ 01924 423172, FAX: 01924 446096, www.themillbatley.com, 9.30–5.30 MON–SAT, 10–4 SUN. **PERMANENT DISCOUNT OUTLET**

The Mill Discount Department Store is the largest Mill retail outlet in the UK, attracting more than one million visitors every year. Situated in a restored Victorian Mill in the heart of West Yorkshire, The Mill offers massive savings in a department-sotre format. This all-weather centre consists of four floors together with an external parade selling heavily discounted branded men's, women's and children's fashions, sportswear, homewares, accessories, music, vidoes, sunglasses, books, toys, perfumes, luggage, gifts, shoes, fabrics and lighting. Readmans, whose name is synonymous with unbeatable value, has opened there recently. This is the company's second major stores, offering good quality women's, men's and children's wear, lingerie, shoes, homewares and linens at remarkably low prices. Among over 300 brand names sold at The Mill are Puma, Pilot, HKA, Leeds United, Liz Claiborne, Elle, Jumper, Kasper, Amazing Jeans, Spicy, Urban Turban, Chilli Pepper, Tigi Wear, Ponden Mill, Woods of Windsor, Gleneagles Crystal, Dartington, Arthur Price, Skopos home furnishings, Jane Shilton, Book Depot, Toy Factory, Eye Zone, Famous Footwear, Hush Puppies, Lee Cooper, MX Active, Berghaus, Craghopper, Julian Graves, Fox's Biscuits, John Bull and Lion Confectionery. The complex can be reached by car, coach and train. Junction 40 of the M1 and junctions 27 and 28 of the M62 are within five and six miles of the site respectively. Batley Station on the Trans-Pennine railway is just five minutes walk from The Mill, providing easy access to Leeds and Manchester. There are more than 500 car parking spaces and coach parking is available. Amenities include children's creche, self-service licensed restaurant serving hot and cold food and drinks, Yorkshire Board Information Centre and access for the disabled.

THE TOY FACTORY

FREEPORT CASTLEFORD DESIGNER OUTLET VILLAGE, CARRWOOD ROAD, GLASSHOUGHTON, WEST YORKSHIRE WF10 4SB, ☎ 01977 551900, www.thetoyfactory.co.uk, 10–8 MON–FRI, 10–6 SAT, 11–5 SUN. **FACTORY SHOP IN A FACTORY SHOPPING VILLAGE**

See page 673 (LANCS)

THE YORKSHIRE BOOK CLEARANCE OUTLET

94 NEW STREET, HUDDERSFIELD, WEST YORKSHIRE HD1 2UP, ☎ 01484 544855, OPEN 9.30–5.30 MON–SAT. **PERMANENT DISCOUNT OUTLET**

Current books, some of which may be slightly damaged (a creased cover, for example). Large selection including fiction, cookery, health, history, travel and children's books. Also sells videos and computer disks. There is another branch in York.

THE YORKSHIRE OUTLET

WHITE ROSE WAY, JUNCTION 3 OF M18, DONCASTER LAKESIDE, SOUTH YORKSHIRE DN4 5JH, ☎ 01302 366444, **e-mail:** cprimrose@realm-ocm.com, www.theyorkshireoutletcentre.co.uk, 10–6 MON–SAT, 11–5 SUN. **FACTORY SHOPPING VILLAGE**

The Yorkshire Outlet, Doncaster, has a great range of stores offering up to 50% off recommended retail prices, with new products and bargains arriving daily. The centre has a range of restaurants, a children's play area, wheelchair hire, and free parking.

THORNTONS

FREEPORT CASTLEFORD DESIGNER OUTLET VILLAGE, CARRWOOD ROAD, GLASSHOUGHTON, CASTLEFORD, JUNCTION 32 OF M52, WEST YORKSHIRE WF10 4SB, ☎ 01977 519746, www.thorntons.co.uk, 10–8 MON–FRI, 10–6 SAT, 11–5 SUN.

THE YORKSHIRE OUTLET, WHITE ROSE WAY, DONCASTER, SOUTH YORKSHIRE DN4 5JH, ☎ 01302 320206, www.thorntons.co.uk, 10–6 MON–SAT, 11–5 SUN.

FREEPORT HORNSEA OUTLET VILLAGE, ROLSTON ROAD, HORNSEA, EAST YORKSHIRE HU18 1UT, ☎ 01964 536724, www.thorntons.co.uk, 9.30–6 SEVEN DAYS A WEEK.

MCARTHURGLEN DESIGNER OUTLET YORK, ST NICHOLAS AVENUE, FULFORD, JUNCTION OF A19 AND A64, YORK, NORTH YORKSHIRE YO19 4TA, ☎ 01904 679227, www.thorntons.co.uk, 10–6 MON–SAT, 8 ON THUR, 11–5 SUN. **FACTORY SHOP IN A FACTORY SHOPPING VILLAGE**

See page 658 (CHESH)

THE TOY FACTORY

UNIT H2–H3, THE YORKSHIRE MILL VILLAGE, BRADFORD ROAD, BATLEY, WEST YORKSHIRE WF17 5LZ, ☎ 01924 444477, www.thetoyfactory.co.uk, 9.30–5.30 MON–SAT, 11–5 SUN. **FACTORY SHOP IN A FACTORY SHOPPING VILLAGE**

See page 673 (LANCS)

TOYWORLD STORE FACTORY OUTLET

UNIT 28, NORTH POINT SHOPPING CENTRE, BRANSHOLME, HULL, EAST YORKSHIRE HU7 4EE, ☎ 01482 833540, www.toyworldstore.com, 9–5.30 MON–SAT.

BUTTERLEY STREET, HUNSLET, LEEDS, WEST YORKSHIRE LS10 1ES, ☎ 0113 234 2221, www.toyworldstore.com, 10–5 FRI–SAT, 11–5 SUN.

MCARTHURGLEN DESIGNER OUTLET, NABURN, YORK, ST NICHOLAS AVENUE, FULFORD, JUNCTION OF A19 AND A64, YORK, NORTH YORKSHIRE YO19 4TA, ☎ 01904 639 333, www.toyworldstore.com, 10–6 MON–SAT, 8 ON THUR, 11–5 SUN.

THE YORKSHIRE OUTLET, WHITE ROSE WAY, DONCASTER, SOUTH YORKSHIRE DN4 5JH, ☎ 01302 365511, www.toyworldstore.com, 10–6 MON–SAT, 11–5 SUN. **FACTORY SHOP IN A FACTORY SHOPPING VILLAGE, FACTORY SHOP**

See page 658 (CHESH)

SOUTH WALES

BOOKENDS

DOCK STREET, NEWPORT, MONMOUTHSHIRE, SOUTH WALES NP9 1FU, ☎ 01633 222086, FAX: 01497 847889, **e-mail:** bookends@madasafish.com, www.bookspostfree.com, 9–5.30 MON–SAT. **SECONDHAND SHOP**

See page 656 (BRIS)

CRAZY MAC'S

PONTARDULAIS ROAD, FFORESTFACH, SWANSEA, SOUTH WALES SA5 4BA, ☎ 01792 585828, FAX: 01792 585566, **e-mail:** lss@salvage1.co.uk, www.salvage1.co.uk, 9.30–6 MON–THUR, 9.30–8 FRI, 9–6 SAT, 11–5 SUN. **PERMANENT DISCOUNT OUTLET**

An Aladdin's cave of salvaged stock for the avid bargain hunter, most of which has been the subject of insurance claims for fire or flood, salvage, bankruptcy or is simply clearance stock. Stock changes every two or three days and regular visitors have found anything from half price Kenwood Chefs, televisions and toys to furniture, kitchen items, linens and especially fantastic bargains in designer clothing. Yves Saint Laurent, Armani, Ungaro, Hugo Boss and Valentino, as well as all major high street names, are just some of the names to be found (though the labels are often cut out). Discounts range from 50% to 80%. Phone first to check stock.

HARRY TUFFINS SUPERMARKET AND PETROL STATION

KNIGHTON SHELL GARAGE, POWYS, SOUTH WALES LD17 1DA, ☎ 01547 528645, 8–6 MON–WED, SAT, 8–8 THUR, FRI, 10–4 SUN. **PERMANENT DISCOUNT OUTLET**

See page 680 (SHROP)

MCARTHURGLEN DESIGNER OUTLET

THE DERWEN, BRIDGEND, JUNCTION 36 OF M4, SOUTH WALES CF32 9SU, ☎ 01656 665700, www.mcarthurglen.com/bridgend, 10–8 MON–FRI, 10–6 SAT, 11–5 SUN. **FACTORY SHOPPING VILLAGE**

The McArthurGlen Designer Outlet in Bridgend is Wales' premier designer outlet. Set out in a friendly village street style the outlet has over 80 stores with everything from men's, women's and children's clothing to accessories, shoes, sportswear, luggage, homewares, toys, books, and gifts. All stock is excess stock sold by the retailers themselves at 30% to 50% off typical retail prices. The outlet also has over 1, 800 free parking spaces, a food court, two children's play areas and a nine-screen Odeon cinema. Stores include: Reebok, Calvin Klein, Tie Rack, Ciro Pearls, Monet, Picture Port, Ciro Citterio, Bookends, Bed & Bath, Clover House, Overland, Pepe, Famous Footwear, Nickelbys, The Suit Company, Birthdays, Toyzone, Vans, Red/Green, Whittards, Travel Accessories, Ecco, Jacques Vert, Warners, Next, Windsmoor, Pilot, Petroleum, Roman Originals, Antler, Julian Graves, The Watch Shop, Knickerbox, Wedgewood, The Garden Outlet, Claire's Accessories, Clarks, Donnay, JoKids, Ben Sherman, Smiths Signature, Spiegelau, Royal Worcester/Edinburgh Crystal, Littlewoods, Helly Hansen, Woodies, Lee Cooper, Van Heusen/Viyella/Jaeger, Ted Baker, Cotton Traders, Royal Doulton, Walker and Hall, Professional Cookware Co, Thorntons, Price's Candles, Mountain Warehouse, John Partridge, Remington, U Wear/I Wear, Nike, The Body Shop, Mexx, Suits You, Designer Rooms, Winning Line, Tog 24, Elle, Chilli Pepper/Watsons, HKA, XS, Soled Out, Timberland, Carphone Warehouse, Levi's, and The Craft Outlet.

THE BODY SHOP DEPOT

UNIT 81, DESIGNER OUTLET VILLAGE, THE DERWEN, BRIDGEND, SOUTH WALES CF32 9SU, ☎ 01262 673502, www.the-body-shop.com, 10–8 MON–FRI, 10–6 SAT, 11–5 SUN. **FACTORY SHOP IN A FACTORY SHOPPING VILLAGE**

See page 658 (CHESH)

THORNTONS

MCARTHURGLEN DESIGNER OUTLET WALES, THE DERWEN, BRIDGEND, JUNCTION 36 OF M4, SOUTH WALES CF32 9SU, ☎ 01656 657104, www.thorntons.co.uk, 10–8 MON–FRI, 10–6 SAT, 11–5 SUN. **FACTORY SHOP IN A FACTORY SHOPPING VILLAGE**

FESTIVAL PARK FACTORY SHOPPING CENTRE, VICTORIA, EBBW VALE, GWENT SOUTH WALES NP3 6FP, ☎ 01495 305099, www.thorntons.co.uk, 10–6 MON–SAT, 11–5 SUN. **FACTORY SHOP IN A FACTORY SHOPPING VILLAGE**

See page 658 (CHESH)

WILKINSON STORES

10–13 CARDIFF STREET, ABERDARE, MID-GLAMORGAN, SOUTH WALES CF44 7DP, ☎ 01685 870393, www.wilko.co.uk, 9–5.30 MON–THUR, 9–6 FRI, SAT, 10–4 SUN. MAIL ORDER.

CIBI WALK SHOPPING CENTRE, FOGMORE STREET, ABERGAVENNY SOUTH WALES NP7 5AJ, ☎ 01685 870393, www.wilko.co.uk, 8.30–5.30 MON–THUR, 8.30–6 FRI, SAT, 10–4 SUN. MAIL ORDER. **PERMANENT DISCOUNT OUTLET**

See page 656 (BUCKS)

HARRY TUFFINS SUPERMARKET AND PETROL STATION

CHURCHSTOKE, MONTGOMERYSHIRE, POWYS, NORTH WALES, ☎ 0588 620226, 8–6 MON–WED, SAT, 8–8 THUR, FRI, 10–4 SUN. **PERMANENT DISCOUNT OUTLET**

See page 680 (SHROP)

SOUTHERN SCOTLAND

GRETNA GATEWAY OUTLET VILLAGE

GLASGOW ROAD, GRETNA, SCOTLAND DG16 6GG, ☎ 01461 339028, FAX: 01461 339100 INFORMATION LINE, **e-mail:** info@gretnagateway.com, www.gretnagateway.com, 10–6 SEVEN DAYS A WEEK. **FACTORY SHOPPING VILLAGE**

Thirty trading outlets with a planned second phase of 20 shops. Includes Episode, Bags Etc, Designer Room, Directions Design Studio, Design House, DKNY, Edinburgh Woollen Mill, Jane Shilton, John Partridge, Price's Candles, Polo Ralph Lauren (stocking clothes for men, women and children as well as homewares), Reebok, Rockport, Tag Heuer, The Golf Company, Tog 24, Tommy Hilfiger, La Casa del Cristallo, Book Depot, Mexx, Claire's Accessories, Pavers Shoes, Chapelle Jewellery, Thorntons, Van Heusen and Whittards. There is a children's play area, disabled access, free parking and restaurants.

THORNTONS

GRETNA GREEN GATEWAY OUTLET VILLAGE, GLASGOW ROAD, GRETNA GREEN, SCOTLAND DG16 5GG, ☎ 01461 339189, www.thorntons.co.uk, 10–6 MON–SAT, 8 ON THUR, 11–5 SUN. **FACTORY SHOP IN A FACTORY SHOPPING VILLAGE**

See page 658 (CHESH)

CENTRAL SCOTLAND

ANTARTEX VILLAGE VISITOR CENTRE

LOMOND INDUSTRIAL ESTATE, ALEXANDRIA, DUMBARTONSHIRE G83 0TP, ☎ 01389 752393, FAX: 01389 750656, 10–6 SEVEN DAYS A WEEK. **FACTORY SHOP**

Large, rambling building with a coffee shop, well signposted off the A82, which has a vast retail area and additional manufacturing workshops where you can watch sheepskin jackets being made, or enjoy whisky tasting. It's difficult to tell how good the prices are as most are not double ticketed to show the original and sale price, but there are bargain sections. Edinburgh Woollen Mill has a large area, and other labels on sale include Pitlochry, Country Rose and Regatta. As well as clothes and shoes for men (new One Valley range of waterproof jackets, Hippo and PG Fields) and women and children, there are tea towels, toys, books, food, gifts, blankets, mugs, candles, CDs and tapes, table mats, sports equipment and countrywear. There is a big golf department selling Wilson, Spalding and Arnold Palmer equipment at discounts of 20% to 30% and lots of different workshops. Close to the Loch Lomond outlet village.

BCP AIRPORT PARKING AND TRANSFER SERVICE

GLASGOW, SCOTLAND, ☎ 0870 013 4586 (RESERVATIONS) PLEASE QUOTE BP744, **e-mail:** reservations@bcponline.co.uk, www.bcponline.co.uk, 8–9, SEVEN DAYS A WEEK. **PERMANENT DISCOUNT OUTLET**

See page 671 (LANCS)

STERLING MILLS DESIGNER OUTLET VILLAGE

TILLICOULTRY, NEAR STIRLING, CLACKMANANSHIRE, MIDWAY BETWEEN M9 AND M90, SCOTLAND FK13 6HQ, ☎ 01259 752100, www.sterlingmills.com, 10–6 SEVEN DAYS A WEEK. **FACTORY SHOPPING VILLAGE**

This factory shopping centre guarantees prices of at least 30% off typical high street prices and sometimes as much as 70%. Outlets so far include Mountain Warehouse, Adidas, Penny Plain, Enigma Candles, Jacques Vert, The Officers' Club, Bed & Bath Works, Book Depot, Claire's

Accessories, Cotton Traders, Denby Pottery, Designer Room, Double Two, Julian Graves, Nike, Nickelby's, Pavers Shoes, Proibito, Roman Originals, Thorntons, Tog 24, Bags Etc, USA Golf Wear House, VF Corporation Factory Store, Winning Line, XS Music, Charles Clinkard, Naf Naf Chevignon, The Toy Factory, Pilot, Real Jewellery, The Sweet Factory, The Design House, Watson Chilli Pepper, Regatta, Blue Ridge, Playtex and more. There's a restaurant on site, and the very large Sterling Furniture Centre is situated opposite.

THE BODY SHOP DEPOT

UNIT 16, DESIGNER OUTLET CENTRE, ALMONDVALE AVENUE, LIVINGSTON, SCOTLAND EH54 6QX, ☎ 01506 410483, FAX: 01506 460410, www.the-body-shop.com, 10–6 MON–WED, 10–8 THUR, 10–6 FRI–SUN. **FACTORY SHOP IN A FACTORY SHOPPING VILLAGE**

See page 658 (CHESH)

THE TOY FACTORY

UNIT 12, STERLING MILLS DESIGNER OUTLET VILLAGE, DEVONDALE, TILLICOULTRY, CLACKMANNANSHIRE, SCOTLAND FK13 6HQ, ☎ 01259 751951, www.thetoyfactory.co.uk, 10–6 SEVEN DAYS A WEEK. **FACTORY SHOP IN A FACTORY SHOPPING VILLAGE**

See page 673 (LANCS)

THORNTONS

LOCH LOMOND FACTORY OUTLET CENTRE, MAIN STREET, ALEXANDRIA, STRATHCLYDE, SCOTLAND G83 0UG, ☎ 01389 729994, www.thorntons.co.uk, 10–6 SEVEN DAYS A WEEK.

MCARTHURGLEN DESIGNER OUTLET LIVINGSTON, ALMONDVALE AVENUE, LIVINGSTON, WEST LOTHIAN, JUNCTION 3 OFF THE M8, BETWEEN EDINBURGH AND GLASGOW, SCOTLAND EH45 6QP, ☎ 01506 420100, www.thorntons.co.uk, 10–6 MON–SAT, 8 ON THUR, 11–5 SUN.

STERLING MILLS FACTORY OUTLET, TILLICOULTRY, SCOTLAND FK13 6NS, ☎ 01259 753875, www.thorntons.co.uk, 10–6 MON–SAT, 8 ON THUR, 11–5 SUN. **FACTORY SHOP IN A FACTORY SHOPPING VILLAGE**

See page 658 (CHESH)

TOYWORLD STORE FACTORY OUTLET

MCARTHURGLEN DESIGNER OUTLET, ALMONDVALE AVENUE, LIVINGSTON, WEST LOTHIAN, SCOTLAND EH54 6QX, ☎ 01506 462 221, www.thetoyfactory.co.uk, 10–6 SEVEN DAYS, 8 ON THUR. **FACTORY SHOP IN A FACTORY SHOPPING VILLAGE**

See page 658 (CHESH)

SCOTTISH HIGHLANDS & ISLANDS

EDINBURGH CRYSTAL

CAITHNESS GLASS VISITOR CENTRE, INVERALMOND INUSTRIAL ESTATE, PERTH, SCOTLAND PH1 3TZ, ☎ 01738 492320 (CENTRE TEL NO), ☎ 01738 492300, **e-mail:** visitor@caithnessglass.co.uk, www.caithnessglass.co.uk, 9–5 MON–SAT, 10–5 SUN MAR–NOV, 12–5 DEC–FEB. **FACTORY SHOP**

Wide range of Edinburgh Crystal crystalware, among others, from glasses and vases to tumblers and bowls at discounts of between 33% and 50%. The shop sells firsts and seconds of crystal from one third off the normal price. There are also special promotional lines at discount prices up to 70% off seconds.

SHAW'S DUNDEE SWEET FACTORY

THE KEILLERS BUILDING, 34 MAINS LOAN, DUNDEE, SCOTLAND DD4 7BT, ☎ 01382 461435, www.shawsdundee.co.uk, JAN AND FEB CLOSED. MARCH, APRIL, MAY, WED ONLY 1.30–4. OPEN EASTER MONDAY WEEK, MON–FRI 1.30–4. JUNE AND JULY, MON–FRI 11–4. CLOSED LAST WEEK OF JULY, FIRST WEEK OF AUGUST. SEPTEMBER, OCTOBER, NOVEMBER,

DECEMBER, WED ONLY 1.30–4. OPEN SCOTTISH BANK HOLIDAYS 1.30–4. CLOSED CHRISTMAS AND NEW YEAR. **FOOD AND DRINK DISCOUNTER**

Large self-service shop with a wall of 100 jars of sweets to pick and mix from. Specialises in fudge, toffees and boiled sweets, and Scottish Tablet. You can taste the sweets while they are still hot and freshly made. Special offers always available. Free car and coach park (large parties please phone first), disabled facilities.

TOYWORLD STORE FACTORY OUTLET

CITY QUAY FACTORY OUTLET VILLAGE, VICTORIA DOCK, CAMPERDOWN STREET, DUNDEE, SCOTLAND DD1 3ND, ☎ 01382 206333, www.thetoyfactory.co.uk, 9.30–5.30 MON–SAT, 11–5 SUN. **FACTORY SHOP IN A FACTORY SHOPPING VILLAGE**

See page 658 (CHESH)

WALKER'S SHORTBREAD FACTORY SHOP

ABERLOUR-ON-SPEY, OFF A95, MORAY, SCOTLAND AB38 9PD, ☎ 01340 871555, **e-mail:** enquiries@walkers-shortbread.co.uk, www.walkersshortbread.com, 8.30–5 MON–FRI, 9–2 SAT. **FACTORY SHOP**

Misshapes and ends of lines of these famous shortbread biscuits and Scotch oatcakes, plus a wide variety of other tasty cakes and biscuits. Many of the products are in presentation boxes and packs and make excellent gifts. The factory shop is on the banks of the River Spey and on the well publicised Malt Whisky trail. Joseph Walker's original bakery shop is further along the high street in Aberlour and this, along with other bakery shops in Elgin and Grantown-on-Spey, also carry a reduced range of factory shop products.

Regional Index

Index of Mail Order Discounters

REPORT FORM
EARN £10

Write and tell us about a Good Deal shop you have visited and, if we publish details based on your information, we'll send you a cheque for £10.

TO: **The Good Deal Directory**
PO Box 4, Lechlade, Glos GL7 3YB
or fax to: 01367 860177

Name of Outlet . . . .

. . . .

Address . . . .

. . . .

. . . .

Telephone number . . . .

Type of Merchandise . . . .

. . . .

. . . .

Comments

Please write as much as possible, explaining in detail the type of goods sold, quality, any brand names, whether labels are cut out, discounts, car parking facilities, etc.

Please continue overleaf …

Signed . . . .

Name (capitals please) . . . .

Address . . . .

. . . .

. . . .

. . . .

Telephone no. . . . .

e-mail . . . .

Date . . . .

REPORT FORM
EARN £10

Write and tell us about a Good Deal shop you have visited and, if we publish details based on your information, we'll send you a cheque for £10.

TO: **The Good Deal Directory**
PO Box 4, Lechlade, Glos GL7 3YB
or fax to: 01367 860177

Name of Outlet ....

....

Address ....

....

....

Telephone number ....

Type of Merchandise ....

....

....

Comments
Please write as much as possible, explaining in detail the type of goods sold, quality, any brand names, whether labels are cut out, discounts, car parking facilities, etc.

Please continue overleaf ...

Signed ....

Name (capitals please) ....

Address ....

....

....

....

Telephone no. ....

e-mail ....

Date ....